CW00952030

THE CAMBRIDGE HISTORY OF

ENGLISH LITERATURE, 1660–1780

*

The Cambridge History of English Literature, 1660–1780 offers
readers discussions of the entire range of literary expression from
the Restoration to the end of the eighteenth century. In essays by
thirty distinguished scholars, recent historical perspectives and new
critical approaches and methods are brought to bear on the classic authors and texts of the period. Forgotten or neglected authors
and themes as well as new and emerging genres within the expanding marketplace for printed matter during the eighteenth century
receive special attention and emphasis. The volume's guiding purpose is to examine the social and historical circumstances within
which literary production and imaginative writing take place in the
period and to evaluate the enduring verbal complexity and cultural
insights they articulate so powerfully.

JOHN RICHETTI is A. M. Rosenthal Professor of English at
the University of Pennsylvania. He has held Fellowships from
the Guggenheim Foundation, the American Council of Learned
Societies and the National Endowment for the Humanities and
has taught at Rutgers University and Columbia University. His
publications include *Popular Fiction before Richardson, 1700–1739*
(1969), *Defoe's Narratives: Situations and Structures* (1975), *Philosophical Writing: Locke, Berkeley, Hume (1983)* and *The English Novel in
History, 1700–1780* (1999). He is editor of *The Cambridge Companion
to the Eighteenth-Century English Novel* (Cambridge, 1996).

THE NEW CAMBRIDGE HISTORY OF
ENGLISH LITERATURE

The New Cambridge History of English Literature is a programme
of reference works designed to offer a broad synthesis and contextual survey of the history of English literature through the
major periods of its development. The organisation of each volume
reflects the particular characteristics of the period covered, within
a general commitment to providing an accessible narrative history
through a linked sequence of essays by internationally renowned
scholars. The History is designed to accommodate the range of
insights and fresh perspectives brought by new approaches to the
subject, without losing sight of the need for essential exposition and
information. The volumes include valuable reference features, in
the form of a chronology of literary and political events, extensive
primary and secondary bibliographies and a full index.

The Cambridge History of Medieval English Literature
EDITED BY DAVID WALLACE

The Cambridge History of Early Modern English Literature
EDITED BY DAVID LOEWENSTEIN AND JANEL MUELLER

The Cambridge History of English Literature 1660–1780
EDITED BY JOHN RICHETTI

IN PREPARATION

The Cambridge History of English Romantic Literature
EDITED BY JAMES CHANDLER

The Cambridge History of Twentieth-Century English Literature
EDITED BY LAURA MARCUS AND PETER NICHOLLS

THE CAMBRIDGE
HISTORY OF
ENGLISH LITERATURE,
1660–1780

*

Edited by

JOHN RICHETTI

CAMBRIDGE
UNIVERSITY PRESS

PUBLISHED BY THE PRESS SYNDICATE OF THE UNIVERSITY OF CAMBRIDGE
The Pitt Building, Trumpington Street, Cambridge, United Kingdom

CAMBRIDGE UNIVERSITY PRESS
The Edinburgh Building, Cambridge, CB2 2RU, UK
40 West 20th Street, New York, NY 10011–4211, USA
477 Williamstown Road, Port Melbourne, VIC 3207, Australia
Ruiz de Alarcón 13, 28014 Madrid, Spain
Dock House, The Waterfront, Cape Town 8001, South Africa

http://www.cambridge.org

© Cambridge University Press 2005

This book is in copyright. Subject to statutory exception
and to the provisions of relevant collective licensing agreements,
no reproduction of any part may take place without
the written permission of Cambridge University Press.

First published 2005

Printed in the United Kingdom at the University Press, Cambridge

Typeface Dante 10.5/13 pt.   *System* LaTeX2ε [TB]

A catalogue record for this book is available from the British Library

ISBN 0 521 78144 2 hardback

The publisher has used its best endeavours to ensure that the URLs for external websites referred to
in this book are correct and active at the time of going to press. However, the publisher has no
responsibility for the websites and can make no guarantee that a site will remain live or that the
content is or will remain appropriate.

Contents

Contents

PART III
LITERATURE AND INTELLECTUAL LIFE: THE
PRODUCTION AND TRANSMISSION OF CULTURE

Contents

ix

Contents

Illustrations

Acknowledgements

This project was begun years ago with the encouragement of Josie Dixon at the Cambridge University Press. Over the last few years, Linda Bree at the Press has provided expert advice and sustaining patience and faith in the enterprise. I owe both of them a deep debt of gratitude for their steady and sure guidance over this long haul. I want, also, to thank Saul Steinberg, whose sponsorship of my A. M. Rosenthal Chair at the University of Pennsylvania provided crucial financial support for my work through the last several years. Friends too numerous to mention have also given generously of their support, and I am especially grateful to my colleague at Penn and the editor of the medieval volume of the New Cambridge History, David Wallace, for his encouragement and example. And of course my greatest debt is to my collaborators in this enterprise, the thirty colleagues whose essays make up this volume. Among them, I especially want to thank for their smart advice on my own introduction to the book, Dustin Griffin, Isabel Rivers, Clifford Siskin and Steven Zwicker. John Sitter gave me invaluable help with the chronology.

Notes on contributors

PAULA BACKSCHEIDER is Philpott-Stevens Eminent Scholar in English at Auburn University, Alabama. Among her books is *Daniel Defoe: His Life* (1990), which won the British Council Prize in 1990 and was selected by *Choice* as one of the ten Outstanding Academic Books for 1990. She is also the author of *A Being More Intense* (1984), *Daniel Defoe: Ambition and Innovation* (1986), *Spectacular Politics: Theatrical Power and Mass Culture in Early Modern England* (1993) and *Reflections on Biography* (also a *Choice* Outstanding Academic Book, 1999). She has edited *Selected Fiction and Drama by Eliza Haywood* (1999), and, with John Richetti, the anthology, *Popular Fiction by Women, 1680–1730* (1998). She has recently completed *Inventing Agency, Inventing Genre: Eighteenth-Century Women Poets and Their Poetry*.

JEFFREY BARNOUW is Professor of English and Comparative Literature at the University of Texas at Austin. He has published essays on Bacon, on Hobbes, on Leibniz, on Vico, on Johnson, on Schiller and on Charles Sanders Peirce. His most recent books are *Propositional Perception. Phantasia, Predication and Sign in Plato, Aristotle and the Stoics* (2002) and *Visceral Deliberation and Signs. Mental Activity and Practical Intelligence in Homer's Odyssey* (2003).

LANCE BERTELSEN is Professor of English at the University of Texas at Austin. He is the author of *The Nonsense Club: Literature and Popular Culture, 1749–1764* (1986) and *Henry Fielding at Work: Magistrate, Businessman, Writer* (2000).

TERRY CASTLE is Walter A. Haas Professor of the Humanities at Stanford University. She is the author of a number of books, including *Clarissa's Ciphers: Meaning & Disruption in Richardson's 'Clarissa'* (1982), *Masquerade and Civilization: The Carnivalesque in Eighteenth-Century English Culture and Fiction* (1986), *The Apparitional Lesbian: Female Homosexuality and Modern Culture* (1993), *The Female Thermometer: Eighteenth-Century Culture and the Invention of the Uncanny* (1995) and *Boss Ladies, Watch Out! Essays on Women, Sex, and Writing* (2002). She is the editor of *The Literature of Lesbianism: A Historical Anthology from Ariosto to Stonewall* (2003) and writes frequently for journals and periodicals such as *The London Review* and the *Times Literary Supplement*.

FRANS DE BRUYN is Professor of English Literature at the University of Ottawa in Canada. He is the author of *The Literary Genres of Edmund Burke: The Political Uses of Literary*

Form (1996). He is currently writing a book on the relation between Georgic poetry and scientific writing in the eighteenth century.

ROBERT DeMARIA, JR is the Henry Noble MacCracken Professor of English at Vassar College. His books include *Johnson's Dictionary and the Language of Learning* (1986), *Samuel Johnson: A Critical Biography* (1994) and *Samuel Johnson and the Life of Reading* (1997). He is the editor of *British Literature 1640–1789: An Anthology*, 2nd edn (2001), *Gulliver's Travels* (2001) and, with Gwin J. Kolb, the forthcoming volume in the *Yale Edition of the Works of Samuel Johnson, Johnson on the English Language*.

J. A. DOWNIE is Professor of English at Goldsmiths College, University of London. His books include: *Robert Harley and the Press: Propaganda and Public Opinion in the Age of Swift and Defoe* (1979) and *Jonathan Swift, Political Writer* (1984). He is the editor of the 'Party Politics' volume of *The Political and Economic Writings of Daniel Defoe* (2000), one of the first eight volumes of the *Complete Works of Daniel Defoe*. He is working on a book called *The Making of the English Novel*.

WILLIAM C. DOWLING is Distinguished Professor of English at Rutgers University. He is the author, most recently, of *The Epistolary Moment: the Poetics of the 18th-Century Verse Epistle* (1991), *Literary Federalism in the Age of Jefferson* (1999) and *The Senses of the Text: Intensional Semantics and Literary Theory* (1999). Among his other books are *Language and Logos in Boswell's Life of Johnson* (1981), *Jameson, Althusser, Marx: an Introduction to The Political Unconscious* (1984) and *Poetry and Ideology in Revolutionary Connecticut* (1990).

CAROLE FABRICANT teaches in the English Department at the University of California, Riverside. The author of *Swift's Landscape* (1982; reissued 1995), she has published widely on eighteenth-century, Irish and postcolonial topics. She is currently editing *Jonathan Swift's Miscellaneous Prose* and collaborating on an edition of *Swift's Irish Writings*. She received a Guggenheim Fellowship in 1999 for her book-length study exploring the problems of colonial representation in eighteenth-century Ireland.

DAVID FAIRER is Professor of Eighteenth-Century English Literature at the University of Leeds. His most recent book is *English Poetry of the Eighteenth Century, 1700–1789* (2003). He is also the author of *Pope's Imagination* (1984), *The Poetry of Alexander Pope* (1989) and many essays on eighteenth-century and Romantic poetry. He has edited *The Correspondence of Thomas Warton* (1995), and (with Christine Gerrard) *Eighteenth-Century Poetry: An Annotated Anthology*, 2nd edn (2003).

ROBERT FOLKENFLIK is Professor of English at the University of California, Irvine. He has published *Samuel Johnson, Biographer* (1978), *The Culture of Autobiography: Constructions of Self-Representation* (1993), an edition of *Sir Launcelot Greaves* for the standard edition of Tobias Smollett (2002) and the Modern Library edition of Laurence Sterne's *Tristram Shandy* (2004).

DUSTIN GRIFFIN is Professor of English at New York University and the author of *Patriotism and Poetry in Eighteenth-Century Britain* (2002), *Literary Patronage in England,*

1650–1800 (1996), *Satire: A Critical Reintroduction* (1994), *Regaining Paradise: Milton and the Eighteenth Century* (1986), *Alexander Pope: The Poet in the Poems* (1978) and *Satires Against Man: The Poems of Rochester* (1974).

ROBERT D. HUME is Evan Pugh Professor of English Literature at Penn State University. He is author and co-author of numerous books and articles, mostly on drama, theatre and opera in the period 1660–1800. His books include *The Development of English Drama in the Late Seventeenth Century* (1976), and most recently *Reconstructing Contexts: The Aims and Principles of Archaeo-Historicism* (1999) and – with Judith Milhous and Gabriella Dideriksen – *Italian Opera in Late Eighteenth-Century London, Volume 2: The Pantheon Opera and Its Aftermath, 1789–1795* (2001).

J. PAUL HUNTER is the Barbara E. and Richard J. Franke Professor Emeritus at the University of Chicago and now teaches spring semesters at the University of Virginia. His scholarly and critical work has mostly involved prose fiction (*Before Novels*, 1990, won the Gottschalk Prize of the American Society for Eighteenth-Century Studies in 1991), but he is now at work on a cultural history of the couplet, tentatively entitled *Sound Argument*, and is preparing the 9th edition of the *Norton Introduction to Poetry*.

THOMAS KEYMER is currently Leverhulme Major Research Fellow at St Anne's College, Oxford. His books include *Richardson's Clarissa and the Eighteenth-Century Reader* (1992), *Sterne, The Moderns, and the Novel* (2002) and *The Cambridge Companion to English Literature from 1740 to 1830* (ed., with Jon Mee, 2004). He has edited a wide range of fiction, journalism and travel writing from the period, and is general editor (with Peter Sabor) of *The Cambridge Edition of the Works and Correspondence of Samuel Richardson* (in progress).

LAWRENCE LIPKING is Chester D. Tripp Professor of Humanities at Northwestern University. His books include *The Ordering of the Arts in Eighteenth-Century England* (1970), *The Life of the Poet: Beginning and Ending Poetic Careers* (1981, which won the Christian Gauss Award), *Abandoned Women and Poetic Tradition* (1988) and *Samuel Johnson: The Life of an Author* (1998).

HAROLD LOVE is Emeritus Professor in the School of Literary, Visual and Performance Studies at Monash University, Australia. He has edited the works of Southerne (1988, with R. J. Jordan) and Rochester (1999) for Oxford University Press. His books include *Scribal Publication in Seventeenth-century England* (1993) and *Attributing Authorship: an Introduction* (2002).

FELICITY A. NUSSBAUM is Professor of English at the University of California Los Angeles, and the author most recently of *The Limits of the Human: Fictions of Anomaly, Race, and Gender in the Long Eighteenth Century* (2003) and editor of *The Global Eighteenth Century* (2003). An earlier book, *The Autobiographical Subject: Gender and Ideology in Eighteenth-Century Britain*, was co-winner of the Louis Gottschalk Prize awarded by the American Society for Eighteenth-Century Studies in 1989. Her other publications include *Torrid Zones: Maternity, Sexuality, and Empire in Eighteenth-Century Narrative* (1995) and *The Brink of All We Hate: Satires on Women, 1660–1750* (1984), as well as a co-edited collection (with Laura Brown) entitled *The New Eighteenth Century: Theory, Politics, English Literature* (1987).

KAREN O'BRIEN is Reader in English Literature at the University of Warwick. She is the author of *Narratives of Enlightenment: Cosmopolitan History from Voltaire to Gibbon* (1997), winner of the British Academy's Rose Mary Crawshay Prize, and of *Feminist Debate in Eighteenth-Century Britain* (forthcoming). She is currently writing a study of British literature and the British Empire, 1660–1800, the subject of her 2001 British Academy Warton Lecture.

MICHAEL B. PRINCE is Associate Professor of English at Boston University and Assistant Dean of the College of Arts and Sciences, where he is the founding director of the College of Arts and Sciences Writing Program. His recent work includes *Philosophical Dialogue in the British Enlightenment* (1996), 'The Eighteenth-Century Beauty Contest', in *Eighteenth-Century Literary History: An MLQ Reader* (1999), 'Heidegger's Turn to Poetry and the Paradox of Overcoming', *Fulcrum* 2, June 2003, 'Mauvais Genres', *New Literary History*, Fall 2003 and 'Editing Shaftesbury's *Characteristicks*', *Essays in Criticism*, January 2004.

JAMES RAVEN is Professor of Modern British History at the University of Essex and Director of the Cambridge Project for the Book Trust. He has written widely on the history of printing, publishing and reading practices in eighteenth-century Britain, Europe and the colonies. His books include *British Fiction 1750–1769* (1987), *Judging New Wealth* 1992), (co-authored) *The English Novel 1770–1829* (2000), *London Booksellers and American Customers* (2002) and *Commercialization of the Book: Booksellers and the Commodification of Literature in England 1450–1900* (2004) and he continues to direct the Arts and Humanities Research Board–Oxford project 'Mapping the Print Culture of Eighteenth-Century London'.

JOHN RICHETTI is A. M. Rosenthal Professor of English at the University of Pennsylvania. His most recent book is *The English Novel in History 1700–1780* (1999). Among his other books are *Popular Fiction Before Richardson: 1700–1739* (1969; rpt. 1992), *Defoe's Narratives: Situations and Structures* (1975), *Philosophical Writing: Locke, Berkeley, Hume* (1983). He has also edited *The Columbia History of the British Novel* (1994), *The Cambridge Companion to the Eighteenth-Century English Novel* (1996) and (with Paula Backscheider) *Popular Fiction by Women: 1660–1740* (1997) and the Penguin *Robinson Crusoe* (2000).

ISABEL RIVERS is Professor of Eighteenth-century English Literature and Culture at Queen Mary, University of London, and Co-Director of Dr. Williams's Centre for Dissenting Studies. Her books include *The Poetry of Conservatism* (1973) and *Reason, Grace, and Sentiment: A Study of the Language of Religion and Ethics in England, 1660–1780*, 2 vols. (1991–2000); she has also edited *Books and their Readers in Eighteenth-Century England* (1982) and *Books and their Readers in Eighteenth-Century England: New Essays* (2001), and written a number of articles of an interdisciplinary nature on seventeenth- and eighteenth-century literature and religion. She has contributed articles on Tillotson, Watts and Doddridge among others to the *Oxford Dictionary of National Biography* (2004) She is working on a new book entitled *Vanity Fair and the Celestial City: Dissenting, Methodist, and Evangelical Literary Culture in England, 1720–1800*.

MICHAEL SEIDEL is Jesse and George Siegel Professor in the Humanities at Columbia University. He has written widely on eighteenth-century literature, especially on satire and on the novel. His books include *Epic Geography: James Joyce's Ulysses* (1976), *Satiric Inheritance: Rabelais to Sterne* (1979), *Exile and the Narrative Imagination* (1986), *Robinson Crusoe: Island Myths and the Novel* (1991) and *James Joyce: A Short Introduction* (2002). He is an associate editor of the *Columbia History of the British Novel* (1994) and co-editor of the first two volumes in the Stoke Newington *Works of Daniel Defoe*.

STUART SHERMAN, Associate professor of English at Fordham University, is editor of the section on the Restoration and eighteenth century in the *Longman Anthology of British Literature*. He received the Gottschalk Prize from the American Society for Eighteenth-Century Studies for his *Telling Time: Clocks, Diaries, and English Diurnal Form, 1660–1795* (1996). He is also the recipient of the Quantrell Award for Undergraduate Teaching, as well as fellowships from the American Council of Learned Societies and the Chicago Humanities Institute.

CLIFFORD SISKIN is the William B. Ransford Professor of Literary History at Columbia University. The author of *The Historicity of Romantic Discourse* and *The Work of Writing: Literature and Social Change in Britain 1700–1830*, Siskin is also co-editor, with Anne Mellor, of the Palgrave-Macmillan series in Enlightenment, Romanticism and the Cultures of Print. His new book is on the eighteenth-century genre that became the thing that we love to blame: The System.

JOHN SITTER is Notre Dame Professor of English at the University of Notre Dame. He has written and edited several works concerning Restoration and eighteenth-century English literature, including *Literary Loneliness in Mid-Eighteenth-Century England* (1982), *Arguments of Augustan Wit* (1991), two volumes on eighteenth-century poets in the *Dictionary of Literary Biography* series (1990, 1991) and *The Cambridge Companion to Eighteenth-Century Poetry* (2001). His interests include satire and poetry from the Renaissance to the present. He is working on a book entitled 'The Knowledge of Eighteenth-Century Poetry,' a primarily cognitive study of writers from Pope to Blake.

PATRICIA MEYER SPACKS is Edgar Shannon Professor of English at the University of Virginia, and is the author, most recently, of *Privacy: Concealing the Eighteenth-Century Self* (2003). Among her other books are *The Insistence of Horror: Aspects of the Supernatural in Eighteenth-Century Poetry* (1962), *The Poetry of Vision: Five Eighteenth-Century Poets* (1967), *An Argument of Images: the Poetry of Alexander Pope* (1971), *The Female Imagination* (1975), *Imagining a Self: Autobiography and Novel in Eighteenth-Century England* (1976), *Gossip* (1985), *Desire and Truth: Functions of Plot in Eighteenth-Century English Novels* (1990) and *Boredom: the Literary History of a State of Mind* (1995).

FIONA STAFFORD is Reader in English at the University of Oxford and Fellow and Tutor of Somerville College. Her books include *The Sublime Savage: James Macpherson and the Poems of Ossian* (1988), *The Last of the Race: the Growth of a Myth from Milton to Darwin* (1994) and *Starting Lines in Scottish, Irish and English Poetry: from Burns to Heaney* (2000). She has also edited novels by Jane Austen and Mary Shelley, and published essays on Scottish, Irish and English literature in the eighteenth and nineteenth centuries.

WILLIAM B. WARNER is Professor of English at the University of California at Santa Barbara. His primary publications have explored the history and origins of the English novel: *Reading Clarissa: the Struggles of Interpretation* (1979) and *Licensing Entertainment: the Elevation of Novel Reading in Britain, 1684–1750* (1998). He has also published on theory and media culture. He is currently pursuing research on eighteenth-century transatlantic communication within the British empire in the period before the American Revolution. He serves as Director of the University of California Digital Cultures Project.

STEVEN N. ZWICKER is Stanley Elkin Professor of Humanities at Washington University, St Louis. He has written on Dryden in *Dryden's Political Poetry* (1972), *Politics and Language in Dryden's Poetry: Arts of Disguise* (1984), *Lines of Authority: Politics and English Literary Culture, 1649–1689* (1993); and he has edited *John Dryden: A Tercentenary Miscellany* (2000) and the *Cambridge Companion to John Dryden* (2004); and with David Bywaters *John Dryden: Selected Poems* (2001). With Kevin Sharpe he has edited *Politics of Discourse: The Literature and History of Seventeenth-Century England* (1987), *Refiguring Revolutions: Aesthetics and Politics from the English Revolution to the Romantic Revolution* (1998) and *Reading, Society, and Politics* (2003).

Introduction

JOHN RICHETTI

In these early years of the new century, there is an urgent need to rewrite the literary histories of Britain that are now nearly a hundred years old and showing their age for contemporary students and scholars. The last Cambridge Literary History of the period – volumes VIII to X of a twenty-volume set, *The Cambridge History of English Literature* – appeared between 1906 and 1917, at its end right in the thick of the Great War. Devoted mainly to essays on the great male writers of the period – for example, volume IX is subtitled 'From Steele and Addison to Pope and Swift' and volume X is called 'The Age of Johnson' – these volumes remain an impressive achievement, full of essential information and deep as well as gracefully worn learning that modern scholars might well envy and seek to emulate. The old *Cambridge History of English Literature* is still very useful and well worth reading. But there is a serenity in its essays by predominantly male Oxbridge dons that at the beginning of another new century we no longer possess; there is in those volumes an untroubled confidence in their enterprise and in the value of literary history that has been eroded if not destroyed by nearly a century of intellectual upheaval as well as by profound social and moral transformations in Anglo-American culture and in the world at large. Since that first Cambridge history appeared, literary studies have changed as radically as the political and social world we live in, and in the last forty years or so, since the early 1960s, there has been a disorienting succession of intellectual revolutions (the word is not too strong) whereby the notion that literature is a privileged artistic and cultural institution has been challenged by many critics. In their traditional effort to find moral value and aesthetic structure and coherence in the great works from the past, literary studies are for many contemporary observers in crisis. For the most part, the academic study of literature has sought to develop other methods and perspectives that respond to what some critics and scholars feel has been overlooked or at least not appreciated fully – the inescapable involvement of literary works in the historical and cultural world of which they are a part. The history of literature is now inseparable from the history of just about everything else, and all students of literature now possess a heightened and even obsessive awareness of the deep, inescapable interpenetration of the literary and the socio-cultural.

But perhaps more than in other chronologically considered 'fields' of English literature, criticism and scholarship on the Restoration and the eighteenth century have tended to resist new approaches, as scholars often enough in the past have sympathised with the (apparent but not always simple or straightforward) socially conservative attitudes of some of the most powerful writers such as Dryden, Pope, Swift, Johnson and Burke of this century and a half we call for a traditional but quite arbitrary convenience the 'long eighteenth century'. And yet in spite of such lingering nostalgia in some quarters, scholarly and literary-historical understanding of this long eighteenth century has, I think, clearly altered in various significant and even dramatic ways. Thanks in large measure to a series of intellectual revisions or one might even say reconceptions in the larger field of literary study and in related fields such as social and political history and, most recently, the newly invigorated history of publishing and printing or the 'history of the book', the literary canon for the long eighteenth century, from 1660 to about 1780, has been expanded substantially and the number of authors and works that a new history of this period will need to consider is much larger and more diverse than it was forty years ago. (Or, in the most radical formulation of new approaches, the notion of a canon of great works and writers serving a cultural and moral elite has been vigorously challenged and in some cases effectively abandoned in favour of a comprehensive ambition to understand all writing as part of the larger field of ideological production.) In addition to contention about which authors and works need to be considered by literary history, attention and emphasis in literary study of the Restoration and eighteenth century have shifted decidedly away from those formal genres encompassing poetry and drama, moral essays and prose satire to more demotic and journalistic writing, to the emerging popular novel and under the impetus of feminist criticism to women writers, both novelists and poets.

Now sharing the stage with the almost exclusively male intellectual elite, whose writings in the past constituted our idea of eighteenth-century British literary culture, is a varied cast of writers, including some (male and female) from the working classes, and a motley supporting crew of hack writers, journalists and pamphleteers, as well as enterprising or often enough unscrupulous printers and booksellers (publishers) who provided the entrepreneurial energy and capital behind much of this writing. Scholars in the field now appreciate as never before the unprecedented growth, especially in London, of a new market for printed matter in these years, and the solemn idea of literature has been traded in by many commentators for the more inclusive and disorderly notion of literary or textual production for this new and expanding market. In recent years, literary history in general has altered its methods and approaches in response to this newly heightened awareness of the complex process of literary production. Many critics and scholars have strenuously attempted to widen literary history's perspective and to complicate its self-understanding, reminding itself always of the sometimes neglected truism that literature is a part of culture at its largest and most enveloping, not just a reflection or expression of cultural activity but also an active participant in creating and propagating the ideas, feelings and programmes that constitute culture (which is always, we need to keep reminding ourselves, an arena of struggle and contestation for dominance as rival versions of what is important strive with each other). The object of historical study for most scholars in the field is now, in short, literary and cultural production in a wider arena than that defined by the traditional canon and by the expressive acts of individual authors, and the notion of literature as a stately succession of masterpieces produced by author-heroes who manage somehow to speak across the centuries to a universalised audience has been largely replaced by a far less exalted and elitist understanding of literature (a concept that has itself been interrogated and demystified, replaced for many by the neutral term, 'writing') and by a deeper and broader sense of the cultural and the ideological functions that literature serves within its particular socio-historical situations.

For example, the five male novelists of the mid-century that posterity seems to have decided were the best – Defoe, Richardson, Fielding, Smollett and Sterne – have been surrounded in new and interesting ways by their predecessors and contemporaries, mostly women, as well as by an intensified emphasis on the insistent needs of the marketplace as it generated a historically unprecedented kind of audience eager to read a new species of popular and even sensational fiction. The new novel of the eighteenth century has been to some extent reconceived by current scholarship and criticism as a response to these unprecedented market conditions and publishing opportunities, an anticipation of modern mass entertainment media, and as a field of competing formats and discourses at various levels (a reaction to deep cultural and social changes) rather than a unified triumph of individual artistic vision and literary and moral authority that founds a new species of narrative. Like other literary forms, moreover, the new novel has been implicated in the suspicion (encouraged by the work of the French intellectual historian Michel Foucault and by the American critical school that calls itself 'New Historicism' as well) that high culture is in some important sense related to the exercise of power, which is seen as essentially a means for the ruling minority not only to imagine itself as an entity but also to regulate or police marginal and unruly sectors of society, specifically women and the labouring majority of the population. So for many critics the moral and social realism of Richardson and Fielding is now profitably (if partially) understood from this perspective as one option among several, as a cultural position rather than as a universalist discovery or neutral extension of a newly developed and more sensitive set of representational narrative techniques.

For another example of revisionist perspectives, the work of the Scriblerians or Tory satirists as they have been called – Pope, Swift, Gay, Arbuthnot and their circle – has been enriched and complicated by giving equal time, as it were, and sympathetic attention to the hard-pressed professional writers ('Dunces' is Pope's term in *The Dunciad*) they satirised, and the group's often antagonistic and contemptuous relationship to popular and demotic writing and entertainment has been explored as the secret source of their comic vigour and subversive humour. Without these colourful opponents, it can be argued, the Scriblerians are merely nostalgic reactionaries, but facing the forces of modern 'Dulness', as they called it, they come into sharp focus as vigorously and memorably oppositional. Indeed, popular writing, entertainment and instruction for an emerging mass-market audience, now appears clearly to be in the ascendant during the early decades of the eighteenth century, and the high literary culture of those years can be seen as in many ways an attempt to control or contain (or appropriate) these new social and cultural phenomena, which some critics contend anticipate later developments in mass and popular culture.

At the same time, late twentieth-century 'literary theory' – with its persistent attention to what it sees as the disabling instability and potential incoherence of the text and the limitations of language as a means of representing or reproducing reality – has created a critical climate that has eroded the monumental status of those authors traditionally considered central to the period. Much recent scholarship has turned profitably from a curatorial or antiquarian emphasis on preserving and reverently annotating the masterpieces of the age and from the tracing of literary-historical genealogies to a historical contextual approach that is sensitive, especially, to the economic pressures of the evolving marketplace for print in which they were produced. As our own literary culture at the beginning of the twenty-first century moves slowly away from the dominance of print media, scholars have become aware of the origins of that dominance in the early eighteenth century (especially in England, with its uniquely liberal bourgeois culture and in the larger European context its relatively free and uncensored press), and eighteenth-century British writing has been located within those shifting social and economic circumstances that created in London a new and indeed unprecedented secular marketplace for books and ideas in which those writers who have traditionally been thought of as the period's major authors (Dryden, Addison, Steele, Defoe, Pope, Swift, Gay, Fielding, Richardson, Johnson, Boswell and others) played their role and indeed defined themselves within these new conditions for literary and cultural production. To some extent, literary historians have always been aware, to take a few obvious examples, that Dryden wrote his plays to support himself and to please aristocratic patrons, that Defoe worked feverishly to make his living in the print market as a journalist and political operative, that Pope's career depended upon his skilful marketing of his Homer translations, that Swift hoped to prosper and gain ecclesiastical preferment by writing for his political masters, that Gay and Fielding made a great deal of money from their plays, that Johnson was essentially a very talented hack, a writer who produced his work to order for money, that all eighteenth-century writing, in short, had particular and practical purposes, material origins and effects. But current scholarship always seeks to highlight these questions, to place such circumstances in the foreground of their discussions, to reinsert literary activity at the dead centre of the practical and actual world that generated it, in a word, to historicise it.

In addition, thanks largely to the influential work of revisionist historians of various and indeed opposing persuasions such as J. G. A. Pocock, J. C. D. Clark, John Brewer, W. A. Speck, E. P. Thompson, Linda Colley and others, this new contextualist approach to the literature of the period has been accompanied and stimulated by a thorough re-examination of the politics and history of the emerging fiscal and military nation state (Brewer's terms) that Britain became in the course of the eighteenth century. These historians and others have banished some old simplifications, and misleadingly absolute oppositions, between Whig and Tory, court and country, aristocrats and bourgeoisie, have been complicated. In Clark's strongly argued revisionist view, the liberal and Whiggish picture of an essentially secular, progressive and enlightened eighteenth-century Britain has given way to an understanding which is attentive to the strong persistence of traditional forms of moral authority and religious belief. This historical revisionism stresses the difficult birth pangs of early modernity in the eighteenth century and the slow shift from traditional landed forms of wealth and hierarchal social organisation to a credit and consumer economy and a relatively fluid (compared to other European nations) social order. From quite another perspective on the period, leftist social historians associated with the pioneering work of E. P. Thompson have stressed just how efficiently the British ruling classes, their power and status derived from traditional landed wealth and new money made in commerce and in overseas adventures as well as in systematic state corruption, imposed their dominance by a combination of increasingly brutal repression and persuasive political theatre that employed the rituals of monarchy and aristocracy to maintain social stability. Recent historical study also pays special attention to the unresolved dynastic tensions in Britain whereby Jacobitism was more than a fringe belief and loyalty to the exiled Stuarts lingered dangerously and powerfully until the middle of the century as a challenge to the Hanoverian establishment. These redefined political and moral ideologies and conflicts are both reflected and refracted in literary discourse, and the new *Cambridge History of English Literature, 1660–1780* seeks to trace relationships between the shifts in ideology and various transforming literary genres such as the periodical moral and political essay, the Georgic poem, the travel account and the novel, which promote and reflect political, economic and imperial alterations in British identity. The new *Cambridge History of English Literature, 1660–1780* takes into account Britain's emergence by the middle and later years of the eighteenth century as the single most powerful European imperial nation and explores colonial themes and transatlantic affiliations in literary expression, as Britain comes to surpass France and Spain as the dominant power in North America and in India. Indeed, a number of the chapters dwell on the key project of much eighteenth-century imaginative writing: to construct a national literary tradition and in the process to participate in the invention of the modern *British* nation. (It is worth noting, by the way, that in spite of our calling it the 'Cambridge History of English Literature' this volume takes in the literary history of Britain, of writing in the English language from the political entity we now call the United Kingdom.)

The chapters in the new *Cambridge History of English Literature, 1660–1780* seek to articulate and to exemplify, but also in some cases to evaluate critically (and even at times sceptically), these new emphases and approaches. Part of the guiding purpose of this collaborative volume is the traditional and in fact essential responsibility of literary history: to provide for the student new to the period an introduction to the varieties, sources and purposes of imaginative writing or literary expression from the Restoration to the 1780s. The volume moves steadily and comprehensively if not always directly or chronologically through the history of literary activity, tracing its shifting standards of aesthetic worth and purpose, its reception and its conditions of production, in the long eighteenth century in Britain. Some chapters feature a fullness of information on particular topics and offer readers the recovery (for example, the chapter on drama in the mid and late century or the chapter on the sentimental novel) of works and authors no longer widely read or studied. In some cases, the treatment in the chapters strives to be recuperative, with the effort being to repair a long-standing neglect of material (such as poetry and novels written by women) or to describe a subject, uncongenial to contemporary readers but vital to the majority of an eighteenth-century audience, such as religious writing, or to recover a perspective and purpose (for example, the political density and specificity of the political and polemical essay) that we need to take in order to understand the period more completely or fully than we have in the past. In some cases, our contributors have sought to restore the actualities of literary practice, to describe what the theatre, for example, was really like in the Restoration and in the middle of the century, to evoke the climate in which poetry was produced and consumed by a fairly wide audience, in which the social, moral or political essay was a vehicle for a generally recognised and valued eloquence, in which the prose poems of the bard, 'Ossian', that James Macpherson said he had translated from the Scots Gaelic, caused a sensation. A couple of chapters treat philosophical and historical writing, which in the eighteenth century was part and parcel of the ensemble of texts that an educated person would have included in the category of literature.

Coverage of this sort of the textual field, to use an ugly but accurate contemporary term, is accompanied by the articulation in the chapters that follow of those debates and controversies that constitute the current state of knowledge and understanding of this body of writing, and I hope the book will thus serve as well the needs of a more experienced or knowledgeable group of readers. Various contributors explore the terrain of this expanded literary field and seek to provide a full account of the newly complicated and contexualised aesthetic value and cultural resonances of the authors and works in the traditional canon. Dryden, Rochester, Behn, Congreve, Pope, Swift, Addison, Steele, Lady Mary Wortley Montagu, Gay, Defoe, Thomson, Johnson, Boswell, Fielding, Richardson, Burney, Smollett and Sterne are significant presences in the volume, although only two chapters (on Dryden and Swift) deal specifically and exclusively with one author. Other chapters feature non-canonical authors and materials, paying attention especially to publishing history and literary production in a wider and neutral sense, to the interactions between 'popular' writing and elite culture. With some chronological overlapping, some chapters trace the transformations of modes and genres such as the periodical essay, the Georgic poem, prose fiction, the familiar letter, the political essay, the verse epistle, drama and satire under the pressure of changing social and historical circumstances. Other chapters focus on the achievements of particular writers in relation to both changing generic forms and historical circumstances. Several chapters take up the vexed and crucial question of gender, highlighting the recent recuperation of women writers and their new visibility as major forces and figures with a tradition of their own and indeed a dominant and even founding importance in the emergence of the new novel. The traditional topics and subjects of literary history, in other words, have been retained, more or less, in the new *Cambridge History of English Literature, 1660–1780*, but our effort has been to see them from new or fresh perspectives, within the wider contexts of early twenty-first-century revisionist historiography and literary scholarship.

The guiding purpose in the volume as a whole is to pursue two main projects that I hope the reader will understand as engaging in an implicit dialogue with each other, revealing in their distinct interests and emphases the presence in current understanding of rival if often enough complementary accounts of British eighteenth-century literary culture: first, to tell again from our own early twenty-first-century perspective the story of aesthetic and formal achievement and enduring literary, intellectual and cultural power in these authors and others, and second, to understand all literary production during this period in the widest and most comprehensive social, historical, political and cultural contexts. To be sure, for those who work on the British eighteenth century, what is now labelled cultural studies (in non-polemical and relatively unselfconscious and often merely positivistic rather than critical forms) has traditionally been a large part of literary-historical understanding of the period, and pure aesthetic/formalistic analysis or belles lettrestristic appreciation has never really been an option for understanding writing that was so clearly rooted in its socio-cultural moment. Indeed, the formal analysis of literature divorced from moral or political or social purpose is a latter-day notion, only slowly emerging in critical thinking of the late eighteenth century, and although we may well read eighteenth-century works in a formalist spirit, such a viewpoint was literally inconceivable to those who created and read them. In an obvious and important sense, British eighteenth-century writing was deeply embedded in and overtly addressed social, political and moral issues, and literary historians have always stressed the essentially occasional and often specifically political or didactic and pragmatic purposes of even the most classic texts such as *Absalom and Achitophel, Robinson Crusoe, Gulliver's Travels, The Dunciad, The Beggar's Opera, Rasselas, Clarissa* or *Reflections on the Revolution in France*. What we tend to call 'literature' had not yet been compartmentalised

8

into belles lettres, and what we now consider essentially imaginative writing included a large and comprehensive field of literary and intellectual activity that was in fact inseparable from other discourses or disciplines that have since the eighteenth century been compartmentalised, and that we would now label history, theology, philosophy, law, politics and so on. This emergence of literature in our sense is in fact the topic of the last chapter in the volume and an implicit theme in many of the preceding chapters. So this history, overall, seeks to chart various kinds of intersections and cross-fertilisations across this tremendously varied and vital body of writing, to include much more than the poems, plays and novels that we have been accustomed to think of as the boundaries of imaginative writing, to give the reader some sense of the capacious variety and diversity of what the greatest critic of the age, Samuel Johnson, always referred to with reverence as literature.

PART I

*

LITERARY PRODUCTION AND DISSEMINATION: CHANGING AUDIENCES AND EMERGING MEDIA

Publishing and bookselling 1660–1780

JAMES RAVEN

The Restoration introduced remarkable changes to a book trade erratically regulated by the state but now driven by vast commercial opportunity. Escalating consumer demand spurred renewed attempts by government and the Stationers' Company to control the location and number of printing presses and the subject of publication. As the money economy deepened and prices stabilised, foodstuffs became relatively cheaper. Increased disposable income boosted the demand for non-essential and luxury goods. Prominent among the luxuries were books and print. The transformation of the literary market that followed was distinguished by bitter struggles within the trade but also by an extraordinary range of products, producers, circulation methods and literary intermediaries. During the next century the changes notably advanced the publication of religious guidebooks, novels, periodical reviews, magazines, daily, weekly and country-town newspapers, dictionaries and etiquette books. The market supported unprecedentedly famous booksellers and authors, the first library societies and commercial circulating libraries, literary reviewers, and finer distinctions between popular, polite and elite forms of literature, their suppliers and consumers.

Parliamentary renewal of the Printing Acts (also known as the licensing laws) lasted, with interruptions, until 1695, while the creation of a Licenser (superseding the Stationers' Company as a de facto censor) did not effectively outlive the appointment of Roger L'Estrange (serving from 1663 until the Revolution of 1688).[1] Thereafter, existing legislation against libel and blasphemy offered ministers and judges last-resort controls that were also capable of extension during times of political crisis. Successive Printing Acts, restricting printing to London, Oxford, Cambridge and York, protected Stationers' Company rights

---

1 For L'Estrange see John Barnard and D. F. McKenzie (eds.), *The History of Book in Britain: Volume IV 1557–1695* (Cambridge: Cambridge University Press, 2002), pp. 3, 427, 543–4, 546, 546, 765–7.

and properties and thus served as a government quid quo pro for the assistance of the Company in identifying clandestine and potentially seditious printing. The first Act of 1662 limited London printing houses to twenty-four including the three King's Printers and one other special patentee. No print shop was allowed to house more than three presses or more than three apprentices, and importation of books printed overseas was banned. This first Act lapsed upon the proroguing of parliament in March 1679, was revived in June 1685 and then renewed twice more, until spring 1695. In February 1695 the Commons accepted a committee recommendation to reject renewal and establish better regulation of the press. A new committee drafted such a bill, but the Lords reversed it, determined to revive the original act. This was rejected by the Commons after a call for a conference, and no bill resulted.[2] According to Macaulay the lapse of the Printing Acts ('the day on which the emancipation of our liberties was accomplished') did 'more for liberty and for civilisation than the Great Charter or the Bill of Rights' but even he was forced to admit that commercial considerations played a part.[3]

Restoration government attempts to control printing and publishing were but one expression of the changing patronage and economics of the manufacture and circulation of books. The expanding marketplace eroded familiar systems of patronage and encouraged commercial innovation, from subscription publishing and part-issue to retail by auction and sale catalogue. Shored up by the Licensing Acts' attempts to recreate their extensive pre-Civil War powers, the Stationers' Company presided over the technical regulation of the trade for the next hundred years or more. The Company maintained its role as financial protector and disperser of dividends, as well as controlling official apprenticeship, entry to trade and its own office-holding (and dividend-rich) hierarchy. But the Company was rarely a force for innovation and seemed increasingly obdurate.[4] All its policing responsibilities, moreover, were effectively overshadowed by the efforts of new associations of booksellers to control publication and keep out trespassers. By the end of the seventeenth century the first formalised 'congers' or monopolistic associations of London booksellers

---

2 Raymond Astbury, 'The Renewal of the Licensing Act in 1693 and its Lapse in 1695', *The Library* 5th ser., 33 (1978), 296–322.

3 Thomas Babington Macaulay, *The History of England from the Accession of James the Second*, 2 vols. (London: Longman, 1848), vol. II, ch. 21.

4 Cyprian Blagden, *The Stationers' Company: A History 1603–1959* (London: Allen and Unwin, 1960); Robin Myers, *The Stationers' Company Archive, 1551–1984* (Winchester and Detroit: St Paul's Bibliographies, 1990); Robin Myers and Michael Harris (eds.), *The Stationers' Company and the Book Trade, 1550–1990* (Winchester and New Castle, DE: St Paul's Bibliographies and Oak Knoll Press, 1997).

appeared. They were dynamic and re-forming cartels that were to dominate the English book trade for much of the next century.

Much of the new protectionism relied on particular interpretations of parliamentary legislation, but also represented new economic imperatives in which literary properties were defended by a powerful oligopoly of leading bookseller-publishers. The private commerce in reprinting rights became the central contest in the regulation and expansion of the book trade, but it was effectively as much a dam against the rising tide of consumer interests as against the expansion in the number and type of publishing booksellers. Such a regulatory structure allowed controlling cartels to set prices at artificially high levels, irrespective of production costs. This protectionism was eventually breached by a new generation of literary entrepreneurs in the 1770s. All the while, writers largely remained pawns in the literary marketplace; a famous few gained fortunes from their books but none undermined the overall commercial structure of the book trade in which authors were routinely the very last to benefit financially from publication.

The other broad constraint to market advance was technological. Until the second decade of the nineteenth century no technical innovations undermined a publishing industry governed by the manual printing press. Even after the invention of the steam-driven printing press in the 1810s, its adoption was so slow and so circumscribed by high production costs that no real market advance was possible until the transport and distribution revolution of the 1830s. All expansion in the volume and circulation of literature in the 120 years after 1660 has to be explained in terms of the limitations of the hand printing press. Certain basics are clear: new entrants to both the London and provincial trade, the challenge to and relaxation of official and unofficial restrictive practices, the expansion of the country newspaper and book distribution network, a much increased individual and institutional demand, financial and organisational innovation and an improved productivity and flexibility advanced by finance from new sources and in unprecedented volume.

This enlargement of the book trade needs careful delineation. Estimates based on title counts of publications often ignore subsequent editions and never take account of the continuing trade in all books, including imported and second-hand books. Even where retrospective bibliography provides a general profile of the number of separately published titles, this offers no sure indication of the total volume of publication given the extreme variation in the size of print runs. Thus although title numbers might appear modest in the late seventeenth century with a steep take-off curve after about 1740 (about 1,700 different printed titles were issued in 1660, just over 2,000 in 1700, but almost 4,000 in 1780) the actual expansion in publication is much more complex. Surviving printed items are very disparate, ranging from locally printed ephemera, hand-bills, ballads, sale catalogues, petitions and odd miscellanies that defy classification. The gentle increase in titles in the decades following the Restoration also hides an apparently enormous growth in the quantity of print, notably in religious and instructional small books (a few pages long, inexpensive, in duodecimo format). Finally, in addition to increased reprinting rates of popular titles and steady sellers, trade in old and second-hand books flourished at renowned shops such as that of Christopher Bateman in Paternoster Row or at open-air stalls as in Moorfields, just outside the London city walls beyond Little Britain. The German traveller, Conrad von Uffenbach, thought Bateman's shop 'the best in England . . . the floors piled up with books'. As Henry Plomer wrote, 'probably no bookseller's shop in London was better known in the days of Swift and his contemporaries'.[5]

One other extraordinary, but often overlooked post-Restoration renewal concerned manuscript production and circulation. Print had eclipsed but never entirely supplanted scribal publication. Copyists remained indispensable to the publication of music, illicit tracts and verse, particular religious and secular 'separates', parliamentary speeches and diurnals and intelligence from home and abroad (designed to counter the policing efforts of the state).[6]

The future in the book trade, however, was with print. After vigorous growth from the late 1690s, printed publication rates mushroomed between the late 1740s and the end of the century. The annual rate of growth in publication as measured by number of titles (including different editions) averaged 1.5 per cent between 1740 and 1780. After the Restoration greater toleration also allowed a more open display of diversity – if temporarily subject to the violent political reversals of the 1680s. The term catalogues issued by booksellers between 1668 and 1709 provide a very general sense of market interests. Over these forty years divinity accounted for 30 per cent of all titles and 42 per cent of all new titles. Excluding the large catch-all group of 'miscellanies', history comprised the next largest category with some 8 per cent of all titles, followed by law, maths, classics and poetry. The increased publication of new

---

5 Henry Plomer, *A Dictionary of the Printers and Booksellers who were at Work in England, Scotland, and Ireland from 1668 to 1725* (London: Bibliographical Society, 1968), pp. 24, 25.
6 Harold Love, 'Oral and Scribal Texts in Early Modern England', in Barnard and McKenzie (eds.), *History of the Book in Britain*, pp. 97–121; Harold Love, *Scribal Publication in Seventeenth-Century England* (Oxford: Clarendon Press, 1993).

titles in divinity stands out, advancing from under a third of total publications in 1668–74, to an average of about 37 per cent in 1675–89, and over 45 per cent in 1690–1709. Between 1700 and 1705 more than half of all new titles were classified as divinity.[7]

Such profiles do not take account of edition numbers and sizes, but they expose the often ignored religious foundation of the developing book trade. The commodification of literature in the final third of the seventeenth century advanced from the production of steady sellers, mostly religious works, but most also adapted to new standards of presentation. Bibles, common prayer books, psalters, schoolbooks and blank books proved the most obvious subjects for commercial makeovers, with changes in shape and size and in the design of typefaces, page settings and bindings. Between 1663 and 1706 production of almanacs by the Stationers' Company ensured its highest dividends, but four other monopolies also protected the Company's (often delegated) manufacture of psalms, psalters, primers and ABCs (the latter also instilling moral precepts).[8] After the Restoration all were increasingly produced in duodecimo or smaller, while institutional demand ensured continuing bulk orders for larger formats. Between 1664 and 1666 alone, some 34,700 Psalms were issued in multiple formats constituting the mainstay of the expanded market for religious literature.[9] Still more radical repackaging of titles ensured the prolonged life of other titles. George Herbert's *Temple*, notably issued in seven editions between 1660 and 1709 and metamorphosed into a prayer book (complete with alphabetical tables), contrasts remarkably with the failure of Donne to be reprinted after a 1669 edition.[10] In the secular market, and in the decades before the novel became the leading fashionable book, play publication was the most notable target for repackaging. Seventeenth-century booksellers almost always published plays individually as quartos, with collected editions in folio. Very few octavo or smaller format plays were issued. The first such for Shakespeare was Nicolas Rowe's 1709 edition.[11] By the 1720s the appearance of plays in smaller format pointed to both the courting and the creation of different custom.

7 Barnard and McKenzie (eds.), *History of the Book in Britain*, tables 4 and 7.
8 John Barnard, 'Some Features of the Stationers' Company and its Stock in 1676/7', *Publishing History* 36 (1994), 5–38.
9 John Barnard, 'The Stationers' Stock 1553/4 to 1705/6: Psalms, Psalters, Primers and ABCs', *The Library* 6th ser., 21 (1999), table 2, p. 4.
10 T. A. Birrell, 'The Influence of Seventeenth-Century Publishers on the Presentation of English Literature', in M.-J. Arn and H. Wirtjes (eds.), *Historical and Editorial Studies in Mediaeval and Early Modern England for Johan Gerritsen* (Groningen: Wolters-Noordhoff, 1985), pp. 163–73.
11 Ibid., p. 166.

In many ways it was this engagement with commercial presentation that inspired many later publishing successes, the great majority concerned with non-religious literature. Essential also, however, were fundamental structural changes to the book trade in the early decades of the eighteenth century, led by the establishment of the powerful cartels and the development of new methods of sale. For many decades itinerant and fixed-sale retailing of books had grown increasingly distinct. At the close of the seventeenth century chapmen and pedlars continued as a mainstay of small book distribution, and the 2,500 pedlars, selling chapbooks and ballads registered in 1696–7, represented only a fraction of the total of petty sellers of print at this date. The chapmen remained a colourful feature of both city and country book trading throughout the eighteenth century, but now firmly relegated to the ranks of the vulgar and excluded from the polite world. Even by 1679 the Lord Mayor and Court of Aldermen published new restrictions, complaining that the streets 'are much pestered with a sort of loose and idle persons, called Hawkers, who do daily Publish and Sell Seditious Books, Scurrilous Pamphlets, and scandalous Printed Papers'. In total, ninety-six London booksellers petitioned against the chapmen and their sale of 'greater numbers of bound bookes as Bibles Common prayers &c. with Counterfitt bindings whereby the Buyer is cheated, and the shopkeepers prejudiced'.[12]

For the majority of metropolitan booksellers, the sales of open market publications available from permanent shops now became the basis for survival. Provincial sales outlets were extended and London booksellers launched new titles of both religious and 'entertaining and instructive' literature with no advanced assured custom. English printed auction catalogues date from at least 1676, the early auctioneers usually acting as agents who had usually not bought outright the libraries that they sold.[13] Boosting the second-hand market, the auctions (normally with established sale times) were often attended with other attractions to entice custom. In the 1690s, for example, William Cooper introduced artificial lighting to illuminate winter evening sales of his books, and the Thames ice fairs (when the river froze over) hosted numerous curiosity stalls complete with printed mementos for visitors. Booksellers promoted sales as entertainments, and outings to both bookshops and the

12 Cited in S. Hodgson, 'Papers and Documents Recently Found at Stationers' Hall', *The Library*, 4th ser., 25 (1944), 27.
13 Robin Myers, 'Sale by Auction: The Rise of Auctioneering Exemplified', in Robin Myers and Michael Harris (eds.), *Sale and Distribution of Books from 1700* (Oxford: Oxford Polytechnic Press, 1982), pp. 126–63; H. G. Pollard and A. Ehrman, *The Distribution of Books by Catalogue* (Cambridge: Roxburghe Club, 1965).

stalls of fairs and markets became frequent subjects for diarists and travel writers.[14]

The prominence given to the profession of bookselling points to real transformation, although contemporary terminology can often confuse. The conveniently broad job-description 'bookseller' referred throughout this period to both financing publisher and a retailer of books. The 'topping' bookseller undertook the financing, printing and distribution of books to other booksellers or directly to the public, while the term 'publisher' sometimes referred to those issuing rather than financing publications.[15] Alternatively, a retailing but (in modern terms) non-publishing bookseller (often a general merchant) might also run a press for local jobbing printing. 'Publication', as making a book public, might also be applied to its dissemination in the broadest (and often deliberately ambiguous) sense, including as a continuous process. This explains the frequent repetition over several days or weeks of the advertisement for books and pamphlets 'this day published', although some even then interpreted it as a canny commercial ploy. In Restoration England, then, variously defined makers and dealers of books moved in and out of bookselling, many with varying fortunes, and often in combination with other trade. Between 1660 and 1700 about 650 individuals feature more than twice in the 'printed for' imprint citations for those years. The same imprints suggest that anywhere between 150 and 250 publishing booksellers operated at some time in the same period, with the reach of the Stationers' Company by no means as extensive as it believed. A 1684 list of booktraders included members of fourteen different livery companies, including the haberdashers, fishmongers and girdlers.[16]

One of the fundamental changes evident even by 1700 was that many leading publishing booksellers often opted to contract out to printers rather than to operate multiple presses in their own shops. Save for a few leading and adaptable city pressmen like William Bowyer and William Strahan, London printers became the servants of leading publishing booksellers (an enslavement actually anticipated by L'Estrange). An attempt of 1660–1 and another as late as

---

14 A list is given in James Raven, *Judging New Wealth: Popular Publishing and Responses to Commerce in England, 1750–1800* (Oxford: Clarendon Press, 1992), pp. 274–6.

15 See Michael Treadwell, 'London Trade Publishers, 1675–1750', *The Library*, 6th ser., 4 (1982), 99–134.

16 Calculations from Giles Mandelbrote, 'From the Warehouse to the Counting-House: Booksellers and Bookshops in Late 17th-Century London', in Robin Myers and Michael Harris (eds.), *A Genius for Letters: Booksellers and Bookselling from the 16th to the 20th Century* (Winchester and New Castle, DE: St Paul's Bibliographies and Oak Knoll Press, 1995), pp. 49–84; Blagden, *The Stationers' Company*, pp. 169–70.

1763 by printers to establish their own livery company were ruthlessly defeated. At the same time, the non-renewal of the Printing Acts did effect a new freedom to print news, to have unlimited printing houses and to print anywhere in the country. Within a month of the lapse of the Printing Acts five additional newspapers appeared in London, two of which, *The Post Boy* and *The Flying Post*, proved long runners. Led by William Bonny, who established his printing press in Bristol in April 1695 (apparently in anticipation of the lapse of the licensing laws), country-town printers spearheaded an entirely different structural change – not in book publishing but in the establishment of local jobbing printing, advert-carrying newspapers and the creation of an agency network for the London booksellers to market their wares throughout the country.

Printers first moving out of London remained fearful of the reimposition of legal restrictions and expansion was relatively modest before the 1740s, but with both economic and demographic growth, and a confidence that press liberties were to continue, the selling of London books and newspaper publishing in the country towns increased sharply after mid century. Excluding London, nineteen towns boasted populations greater than 10,000 in 1750. Five of these, Bristol, Norwich, Liverpool, Newcastle and Birmingham, claimed more than 20,000 inhabitants. In market towns new customers were created by the proprietary subscription libraries, literary societies and, from the 1760s, London-style commercial circulating libraries that were all part of the 'urban renaissance' and emergent 'leisure town' identified with eighteenth-century Britain.[17] This provincial market, together with the equally striking advance of the country-house library, underpinned the publishing and business strategies of booksellers in London for the next century.

The most successful book merchants were twenty or more enterprising bookseller-publishers, many of whom had arrived in London from the country (or from Scotland) with (at least in comparison to earlier generations) little or no previous knowledge of the trade. Although several of the greatest booksellers did rise through the ranks of the Company, scant professional training was actually required to take part and to succeed in the increasingly diverse world of publishing and bookselling (and thereby also offering a sharp contrast with the printers, compositors and other apprenticed labourers

---

17 Peter Borsay and Angus McInnes, 'Debate: Leisure Town or Urban Renaissance?', *Past and Present* 126 (Feb. 1990), 189–202; Rosemary Sweet, *The English Town 1680–1840: Government, Society and Culture* (London: Longman, 1999).

of the print shop). There remained in the trades many family alliances and interconnections, and for many printers and booksellers these increasingly provided the requisite introductions and sometimes the capital. The success of the outsiders, therefore, in this transformative age, often extended to the founding of new trading dynasties. In the 1660s and 1670s only about 3 per cent of all apprentices bound to the Stationers' Company came from book trade families compared to 17 per cent between 1717 and 1727.[18] Failure rates were high as one might expect in this high-risk business. By contrast, the meteoric rises of a few self-made and founder-father booksellers became the stuff of legend: Robert Dodsley the footman, Thomas and James Harrison the sons of a Reading basketweaver, Thomas Wright the son of a Wolverhampton buck-lemaker, Ralph Griffiths the watchmaker and William Lane the poultryman's son. Many of the successful first-generation traders and their heirs, such as the Longmans, Murrays, Rivingtons, Strahans and Robinsons also attained civic and even parliamentary distinction.[19]

The most successful bookselling career realised spectacular wealth. Jacob Tonson I set new standards when he died in 1737 worth in excess of £40,000. In the mid 1760s Thomas Osborne claimed a similar fortune. For such men the purchase of an estate was an obvious attraction, and by the end of the century far fewer of the great booksellers lived over the shop. William Strahan, MP, left an estate in Norfolk at his death in 1785, in addition to £95,000 in moveable wealth. James Dodsley, heir and brother of Robert, left over £70,000 and a landed estate near Chislehurst.[20]

The wealthiest booksellers at the end of this period were also the beneficiaries of more than sixty years' domination by the powerful London congers. Even before the fabled success of the great Restoration bookseller Henry Herringman (d. 1704), the greatest profits in book publication in England (but less so in Scotland) derived from the ownership of copyrights

18 Christine Ferdinand, 'Towards a Demography of the Stationers' Company 1601–1700', *Journal of the Printing Historical Society* 21 (1992), 51–69; Mandelbrote, 'From the Warehouse to the Counting-House', p. 51.
19 Raven, 'The Book Trades', in Isabel Rivers (ed.), *Books and Their Readers in Eighteenth-Century England: New Essays* (London and New York: Continuous and Leicester University Press, 2001), pp. 1–34.
20 Kathleen M. Lynch, *Jacob Tonson: Kit-Cat Publisher* (Knoxville, TN: University of Tennessee Press, 1971), p. 174; John Nichols, *Literary Anecdotes of the Eighteenth Century*, 9 vols. (London: Nichols, Son and Bentley, 1812), vol. III, pp. 401, 649, vol. VI, p. 438; Thomas Rees and John Britton, *Reminiscences of Literary London from 1779 to 1853* (London, 1896; rpt. Detroit: Gale Research Co., 1969), p. 26; J. A. Cochrane, *Dr Johnson's Printer: The Life of William Strahan* (Cambridge, MA: Harvard University Press, 1964).

to successful titles. The fundamental division between different booksellers remained between those who invested and dealt in the ownership of the copyright to publication (whether by independent or collaborative financing of a new copyrighted work or by purchase of an existing copyright share), and those who either printed, sold or distributed books for existing copyright-owners or who traded entirely outside the bounds of copyright materials.

The information offered about the connections between booksellers in the imprint line on almost all title pages is difficult to interpret. Some booksellers (and some authors, wholly or partly) acted as the publisher, that is, as the entrepreneur accepting the risk of financing publication; others remained as manufacturers of the product, already assured of payment even if the book sold badly; still others (including many general traders) served in various distributive and retail capacities, also identified at the time as the 'publishers' or issuers of books to a wider audience. Single names of booksellers might appear to be the simplest indicators to publication, but it cannot be taken for granted that a book 'printed for' a particular bookseller was entirely paid for by that bookseller. Moreover, where a book was sold by a consortium of booksellers, some or all might contribute to the financing of its publication (in proportions usually unknown), and it was not always the case that all those listed had contributed directly to publication costs. Arrangements between booksellers listed as the principal financing publishers ('printed for' etc) and first-level associates ('also sold by' etc) usually, but not always, implied an agreement to share costs roughly in proportion to the number of copies to be taken by the participating shops. Newspaper advertisements for these titles extend the problem further, often including additional names of 'sold by' booksellers to those listed on the title page or advertisements at the end of the book.

Despite these perplexities, we can at least be certain that in most cases inclusion of a name in an imprint line indicates some sort of financial involvement. This is particularly the case when the author is mentioned – almost always as 'printed for the author'. Where a bookseller was unwilling to take the risk of publishing a book, he might nevertheless print or ensure the printing of the work on the understanding that the author advanced the costs. In some cases the provision of the actual paper, not merely its costs, was expected. Here, with the author as publisher, the bookseller often acted as little more than a vanity press, although in some cases authorial risk-taking did pay off. To most booksellers, the acceptance of such a commission must have seemed like simple jobbing printing. Many title pages hide known commission agreements 'on account of the author' where the publisher-writer assumed responsibility for any loss.

The right to reproduce a book throughout this period, however, was almost always bought outright by the bookseller-publisher or consortium of booksellers. Most copyrights were then divided into shares between several combining booksellers. Such division was made according to the booksellers' stake in the original financing of the publication, and part-shares formed the staple investments to be bought at the London trade auctions. The greatest accumulator of the second half of the eighteenth century was probably George Robinson, who was a keen rival to established literary investors by the early 1770s, and before 1780 had, according to John Nichols, 'the largest wholesale trade that was ever carried on by an individual'.[21]

Two further critical features stand out in this literary production history. First, with a few very notable exceptions, most books had little intrinsic value. Copyrights to most publications fetched relatively little at sale, and authors were paid paltry sums for their initial surrender of rights to works which booksellers knew were very unlikely to be reprinted or to return much profit in their own right. The second critical issue is that reprints of popular book titles were to feature significantly in literary market development and to be a key encouragement to new booksellers (as well as a key temptation to overreach). The assault on the publishing monopoly maintained by the leading booksellers' associations was finally successful only in 1774, but even then the framework for the protection of sale and investment in rights to *new* works remained intact in the final decades of the century. Clarified rather than undermined by the earlier legal battles, the copyright laws brought new riches to those with the skill to favour the right authors and publications.

The value of all copyright shares manifestly depended on their remaining exclusive rights to publish. A Copyright Act introduced in 1710 limited copyright to existing publications to twenty-one years for books already in print and fourteen years for new books. After expiration of the fourteen-year term, copyright remained with the author, if living, for a second fourteen-year term, even though the author's rights were more technical than actual, and ones, apparently, not seriously considered by those drafting the bill. Most authors implicitly surrendered all claims to subsequent entitlement. The licensing laws have been characterised as typical of the 'ill-drafted legislation in which

---

21 Collection of Literary Assignments of George Robinson, Manchester Central Library MS F 091.A2; John Nichols, *Literary Anecdotes of the Eighteenth-Century*, 9 vols. (London, 1812–15), vol. III, pp. 445–6.

royal order was restored',[22] but if so, then the 1710 Act created even more confusion. Confusion, however, can always be exploited by those with the greatest economic clout. Immediately following the mid-century technical expiration of rights to older works and works first protected under this statute, the booksellers' associations successfully argued that the Act's spirit sanctioned perpetual copyright under Common Law. A 1768–9 King's Bench decision and then injunction by the Court of Chancery prohibited Alexander Donaldson, the Scots challenger to the London trade now operating in the Strand, from continuing cut-price reissues of the works of Thomson and others. This ruling marked the summit of the efforts by closed associations of booksellers to control copyright, but their claims collapsed in 1774 when the House of Lords overturned the 1768 restraining injunction and confirmed the limitations of the 1710 Act. The ruling extinguished the booksellers' invocation of Common Law to sanction perpetual copyright. A bill to quash the Lords' verdict failed in the following year.[23]

The way was now open for those outside the charmed circle of major copy-holding booksellers to publish cheap reprint editions of classic works. From the mid 1770s, the reprinting of popular texts rejuvenated the market, and, most notably, advanced provincial and female custom. At first, these ventures were led by London booksellers taking advantage of the loss of control by the booksellers' associations, but soon, in what was a much more competitive market, a regrouping of copyright-owners re-established familiar methods of sharing the financing of publication.

The other challenge identified by leading London booksellers involved Irish piracies and Scottish reprints, particularly those of novels and miscellanies. Many Irish reprints were half the price of the London originals. Cheaper paper was used, as well as closer printing, and sometimes hidden abridgement enabled two- or three-volume works to be compressed into a single volume. Despite vociferous protests from the London trade at mid century, however, the threat from Ireland was either largely illusory or a trumped-up promotional gambit. As now seems clear, Dublin reprints were never imported in sufficient numbers nor aimed at the right targets to pose an effective direct challenge to the London booksellers, even if the effects on the Scottish trade, and

22 Michael Treadwell, '1695–1995: Some Tercentenary Thoughts on the Freedoms of the Press', *Harvard Library Bulletin* n.s. 7 (1996), 3–19.
23 Mark Rose, *Authors and Owners: The Invention of Copyright* (Cambridge MA and London: Harvard University Press, 1993); and Gwyn Walters, 'The Booksellers in 1759 and 1774: The Battle for Literary Property,' *The Library*, 5th ser., 29 (1974), 287–311.

Scots incursions in England, are more debatable. At least until the problems of the 1790s, Dublin publishers appear to have concentrated on an expanding and potentially valuable Irish market.[24] They had more to fear from London booksellers than London booksellers had to fear from them. Scottish competition was more complicated. It was possible to argue that many Scottish reprints were legally published within the limits of the 1710 Act, and the costs and likely ineffectiveness of prosecution deterred actions against the efforts of the Edinburgh and Glasgow presses. In the early 1780s Scots booksellers were themselves under threat by Irish piracies smuggled in and bearing false imprints. In all of this, title-page assertions of being printed in London cannot always be taken at face value.[25]

These battles over literary property transformed the market in popular publishing, if not always in obvious ways. Eventually – although this was far from evident by 1780 – all these considerations pointed towards the primacy of what John Murray called the 'simple publisher',[26] that is the bookseller, risking all (and often failing), and acting on his own in negotiations with the author and the rest of the trade. The further consequence was that many of the most successful operators had raised their start-up capital from diverse outside sources and entered the trade with practical if not financial expertise learned from a previous profession. Few new titles benefited from the opportunities to reprint old favourites. Rather, the efforts of many booksellers, based on novel promotional techniques, advertising and more adventurous retail and distribution, continued to erode the power of closed booksellers' associations, and all book publishing responded to the changed market and marketing activities.

Fundamental to these marketing advances were the changing distributive networks in which the dominance of London, the dynamic hub of the book trade, increased in several ways. London had already assumed new importance in the Restoration trade. In 1644 77 per cent of all British publications were London printed, rising to 84 per cent in 1676 and 85 per cent in 1688.[27] In 1700 the population of the capital had reached about 675,000, and throughout the

24 M. Pollard, *Dublin's Trade in Books 1550–1800* (Oxford: Clarendon Press, 1989).
25 Warren MacDougall, 'Smugglers, Reprinters and Hot Pursuers: The Irish–Scottish Book Trade and Copyright Prosecution in the Late Eighteenth Century,' in Myers and Harris (eds.), *Stationers' Company*, pp. 151–83.
26 Cited in William Zachs, *The First John Murray and the Late Eighteenth-Century Book Trade* (London: British Academy and Oxford University Press, 1998), p. 61.
27 D. F. McKenzie, 'Printing and Publishing 1557–1700: Constraints on the London Book Trades', in Barnard and McKenzie (eds.), *History of the Book in Britain*, pp. 553–67, and table 8 (p. 792).

eighteenth century something over a tenth of the population lived in London. By 1750 London's population matched that of all country towns put together, and by 1780 its population exceeded 700,000, almost a third larger than Paris and indeed all other European cities. London, the site of hundreds of trades and industries, was the centre of a vast consumer's market which dominated the British economy. The book trade, always based in London, responded to demand led by the metropolitan population and institutions, and swollen by the fast advancing country custom. In striking contrast to many other developing industries of the period, moreover, relocational factors, namely the pursuit of raw materials and new sources of power, did not directly affect this production of books, magazines and newspapers.

Within the eighteenth-century metropolis different districts also came to host different bookselling specialisms. John Macky's 1714 guidebook identified 'divinity and classicks' on the north side of St Paul's Churchyard, 'law, history and plays' near to Temple Bar, 'French-booksellers' in the Strand and in Little Britain and Paternoster Row, and 'booksellers of antient books in all languages' sited in and around Westminster Hall.[28] These were very general associations and to them we might add law books, newspapers and political pamphlets in the Exchange, financial news and guidebooks in Cornhill, and novels, magazines and fashionable titles in Covent Garden, Fleet Street and the Row. At least in the early eighteenth century Little Britain, the area between Smithfield and Aldersgate Street, hosted mixed trades with small shops of booksellers and printers all on a very intimate scale. Paramount, by at least 1740, was Paternoster Row and the neighbouring traditional booktrading site of St Paul's Churchyard. This precinct was home to the majority of the leading booksellers of the second half of the eighteenth century.[29]

The commercial topography of the trade was especially conspicuous in the case of the publication of novels. After mid-century many of the leading publishers of fashionable literature, like the firm of George Robinson (and family) and John Bew, operated from the Row. Other novel specialists, like Thomas Hookham (with his partner James Carpenter) and John and Francis Noble, set up shop in the newly built and fashionable squares and lanes of the West End.[30]

---

28 John Macky, *A Journey Through England*, 2 vols. (London, 1714), vol. 1, p. 205, cited in Mandelbrote, 'From the Warehouse to the Counting House,' p. 50.
29 James Raven, 'Location, Size and Succession: The Bookshops of Paternoster Row before 1800,' in Robin Myers, Michael Harris and Giles Mandelbrote (eds.), *The London Book Trade: Topographies of Print in the Metropolis from the Sixteenth Century* (London: British Library, 2003), pp. 89–126.
30 James Raven, 'The Noble Brothers and Popular Publishing,' *The Library*, 6th ser., 12 (1990), 293–345.

Still others, like William Lane and his Minerva Press in Leadenhall Street, made an address famous despite an unusual site. The distribution is telling. Some of the leading publishers of novels worked within the established network and even as prominent members of their guild, the Stationers' Company; others seemed to relish the challenge to the book-trade establishment and made the popular novel a weapon in their battle for commercial and public success. Self-publicists like the Nobles, Lane, and Hookham and Carpenter can be credited with pioneering efforts in the establishment of commercial circulating libraries and in the publication of fashionable, almost production-line novels.[31]

In fact no other literary genre better confirmed the advance of specialist booksellers than the novel. Novels, together with playbooks, verse and other fictional miscellanies, also featured prominently in booksellers' derivative ventures, notably commercial circulating libraries, as well as in fresh advertising and promotional ploys. Most commentators immediately identified the novel as a distinctive class of book, and, in this age of Linnaeus, many described novels as a fashionable and commercial 'order', 'species', 'kind', 'race', or 'tribe'. As the publication of novels advanced, the number of new novels issued each year also fluctuated markedly, however, often because of their especial sensitivity to commercial vicissitude. Not only was a fashionable publishing 'season' given greater precision, generally extending from November to May (and thus spanning the division of the calendar year), but imprint post-dating was common, designed to extend the currency of the novel and other modish titles. Particular vogues (such as the novel-in-letters, a very distinctive undertaking from mid century) contributed to the distinction of the fashionable booksellers. Over 40 per cent of all novel titles first published in the 1770s and 1780s were epistolary, a variety soon eclipsed in the 1790s by historical and Gothic narratives that were ill-suited to relation by letters.[32]

The more adventurous bookseller-publishers further experimented in book presentation, exploiting the advances in paper manufacture and type founding and design (that constituted, indeed, the extent of technological development in the book trades). After reliance on imported quality paper, pioneering Scottish production of paper increased some tenfold between 1750 and 1780, and English home production of paper increased from some 2,000 tons in 1700

31 James Raven, *British Fiction 1750–1770: A Chronological Check-List of Prose Fiction Printed in Britain and Ireland* (London and Cranbury, NJ: Associated University Press, 1987).
32 James Raven, 'The Novel Comes of Age', in Peter Garside, James Raven and Rainer Schöwerling (eds.), *The English Novel 1770–1829: A Bibliographical Survey of Prose Fiction Published in the British Isles*, 2 vols. (Oxford University Press, 2000), vol. I, pp. 15–121.

to about 15,000 tons per annum in 1800.[33] Until at least the 1720s most of the type used in Britain was imported and of a poor standard. In 1674 Thomas Grover set up his London type foundry in Aldersgate Street, and from the 1730s substantial printers, and especially those engaged in book work, experimented with new type.[34] Most prized was that made by William Caslon and his successors, while in Birmingham in the 1750s John Baskerville set new standards in the manufacture of both type and paper, certainly influencing Alexander Wilson's important new type produced in Edinburgh from 1772.[35] Although the basic design of the printing press remained almost unchanged, improved rolling presses, used for the printing of metal engravings, became an important adjunct to the arts of the pressman. Specialist craftsmen introduced improvements to engraving and copper-plate techniques, particularly from mid-century when the artist-engraver George Vertue listed fifty-five London engravers.[36] Both printers and some notable booksellers, including John and Paul Knapton, worked closely with picture, print and map makers.[37] As demand for prints and book illustrations escalated, the reworking of heavily used plates became more common, and although still rare, a few more coloured prints and illustrations were attempted. By mid century many booksellers adopted prints created by stipple, a combination of engraved dots and etching (where acid was used to create the ink-holding grooves) and, a decade or so later, aquatint (based on the application of resin to craze the copper-plate surface. The mezzotint – a method of engraving copper or steel plates for printing, in which the surface of the plate is first roughened uniformly, the 'nap' thus produced being afterwards completely or partially scraped away in order to produce the lights and half-lights of the picture, while the untouched parts of the plate give the deepest

33 Alistair G. Thomson, *The Paper Industry in Scotland, 1590–1861* (Edinburgh and London: Scottish Academic Press, 1974), p. 74; D. C. Coleman, *The British Paper Industry, 1495–1860* (Oxford: Clarendon Press, 1958); Alfred H. Shorter, *Water Paper Mills in England* (London: Society for the Protection of Ancient Buildings, 1966).

34 Daniel Berkeley Updike, *Printing Types: Their History, Forms and Use: A Study in Survivals*, 2 vols. (Cambridge, MA: Belknap Press, 1962), vol. II, pp. 101–24; Talbot Baines Reed, rev. edn by A. F. Johnson, *A History of the Development of Old English Letter Foundries* (London: Faber and Faber, 1952).

35 F. E. Pardoe, *John Baskerville of Birmingham: Letter-Founder and Printer* (London: F. Muller, 1975); Johnson Ball, *William Caslon, 1693–1766: The Ancestry, Life and Connections of England's Foremost Letter-Engraver and Type-Founder* (Kineton: Roundwood Press, 1973).

36 Michael Harris, 'Scratching the Surface: Engravers, Printsellers and the London Book Trade in the Mid-Eighteenth Century,' in Arnold Hunt, Giles Mandelbrote and Alison Shell (eds.), *Book Trade and its Customers, 1450–1900* (Winchester and New Castle, DE: St Paul's Bibliographies and Oak Knoll Press, 1997), pp. 95–114.

37 Louise Lippincott, *Selling Art in Georgian London: The Rise of Arthur Pond* (New Haven, CT and London: Yale University Press, 1983).

shadows – demanding more updating and a relatively expensive procedure, also increased in popularity as a consequence of the rising status of English painting (a popular subject for mezzotint reproductions).[38]

In many of the same fashionable streets of London that housed these artists, the first-generation commercial circulating libraries opened in the 1740s.[39] Developed from the ad hoc lending services of London retailing booksellers, few of these pioneer libraries survived for more than a few years. Their publishing, stocking and lending arrangements, however, became the framework for the establishments of Thomas Lowndes, the Nobles, Lane, Hookham, John Bell and many others. Publisher-booksellers operating circulating libraries sent up to two-fifths of their own editions to supply their libraries and those of counterparts.[40] For both commercial libraries and the grander proprietary and society libraries, regional variation was marked, and although interest in the expanding country market was important, the London market again proved pivotal. Here was a market close to the centres of production, with fewer distribution problems and with affluent and fashionable custom, particularly in the parliamentary and social season. In support, choice products of the London booksellers offered very particular (and almost always highly exaggerated) textual and visual representations of their shops, reading-rooms and customers.

Such developments – from the illustrated or fashionably printed book to the high-profile lending library – depended upon a shrewd evaluation of the changing market, and one that was also essential in terms of the simple economics of the publishing house. The publisher-bookseller remained notably handicapped by the requirement to have so much capital tied up in a particular item of production (an edition) before any part of this could be sold to realise returns. Pricing decisions depended largely on changes in the potential for onward selling. With transport costs consistently high in the first centuries of print, the transformation in the economics of distribution over this period very obviously affected marketing strategies and calculations for text and edition production. In particular, improvements in transport routes and distance-times encouraged the development of discount systems to promote greater retail distribution in the country. Distribution costs had always been a

---

38 Timothy Clayton, *The English Print 1688–1802* (New Haven, CT and London: Yale University Press, 1997); Sven H. A. Bruntjen, *John Boydell, 1719–1804: A Study of Art Patronage and Publishing in Georgian London* (New York and London: Garland Press, 1985).
39 Notably St Martin's Lane and its environs, Raven, 'Noble Brothers', pp. 94–9.
40 Raven, 'English Novel Comes of Age', p. 93 (and further references, pp. 71–103, 110–13).

significant add-on, and with booksellers' margins so tight, allowing very little scope for the major tie-up of capital in printed and warehoused stock, the efficiency of transportation remained critical. All these factors underpinned the urgency of selling editions in which so much was usually invested. Nor was cheap print excluded from this assessment. Where carriage costs were paid for by the bookseller-publishers, these contributed significantly to production costings. Questions about delivery expenses feature persistently in the new studies of some of the most important (and diverse) booksellers of the period, including John Murray, the Nobles, John Stockdale and Robert Dodsley, with his reliance on the Coopers and other trade publishers to provide a marketing network.[41]

Newspaper publication provided the crucial support given to the extended selling of books and print, while increased newspaper production and circulation was itself supported by a combination of road improvement and the activity of postmasters. Across the country the maintenance of newspaper circuits secured the solvency of main book distributors for the London publishers. Among the most active of the regional stationer-printers and newspaper publishers were William and Cluer Dicey of Northampton, John Binns of Leeds, Thomas Saint of Newcastle and in the south, the Farleys of Exeter and Bristol, Samuel Hazard of Bath, Benjamin Collins of Salisbury and Robert Goadby of Sherborne.[42] In many of the rapidly enlarging towns of the final third of the century there was a further major increase in the number of book trades firms. In Newcastle, for example, where two firms operated in 1700 and about fifteen throughout the period between 1730 and 1770, twenty-six were working in 1776 and thirty in 1782. It was, however, the increasingly efficient despatch of the London newspapers to the country customers that offered the surest advertising vehicle for the leading booksellers. In 1760 London boasted four daily newspapers and five or six tri-weeklies, and by 1783 nine dailies and ten bi- or tri-weeklies. By 1780 the Post Office annually despatched some 3 million London newspapers to the country. Total sales of newspapers in

---

41 Zachs, *First John Murray*, ch. 2; Raven, 'Noble Brothers'; *The Correspondence of Robert Dodsley 1733–1764*, ed. James E. Tierney (Cambridge: Cambridge University Press, 1988); Harry M. Solomon, *The Rise of Robert Dodsley: Creating the New Age of Print* (Carbondale, IL and Edwardsville: Southern Illinois University Press, 1996); James Raven, *London Booksellers and American Customers: Transatlantic Literary Community and the Charleston Library Society, 1748–1811* (Columbia, SC: University of South Carolina Press, 2002).

42 C. Y. Ferdinand, *Benjamin Collins and the Provincial Newspaper Trade in the Eighteenth Century* (Oxford: Clarendon Press, 1997); Ian Jackson, 'Print in Provincial England: Reading and Northampton, 1720–1800', unpublished Ph.D. diss. Oxford University, 2003.

England amounted to some 7.3 million in 1750, 9.4 million in 1760, 12.6 million in 1775 and over 16 million in 1790.[43]

Such commercial advertising remained crucial,[44] reinforced by booksellers' catalogues increased in number and sophistication. In addition to the auction sale catalogues and the defunct term catalogues, many booksellers routinely printed stock catalogues and even selected title listings inserted in the back of their publications. From mid century, literary periodicals and then the emulative monthly magazines offered listings of new publications. Boosted by newspaper advertising, the greatly expanded volume of print resulted in broadened distribution and, evidently, a wider readership. Yet given the doubts about the extent to which increased book production in this period indicates a greatly increased number of book readers (given that demand from institutions and from those already in the habit of acquiring books was more obvious than that from working men and women), the extension of print by means of newspaper circulation represents the most pointed evidence for expanded literacy and for a greater audience for new literature.[45] In the remoter extremities and depths of the country 'this day published' notices inserted in local newspapers by the London booksellers provided additional means of learning not just of new titles but of how to acquire them. Local booksellers served as intermediaries, but many rural customers (like those overseas) also sent their orders directly to the publisher.

One basic publishing characteristic endured, however. High capital overheads and continued commercial risks ensured the printing of a relatively small number of copies to most editions. Labour costs of composition and presswork usually made very small print-runs unviable, while the risks of high capital expenditure and storage cautioned against large editions. For much of the century the greatest production expense resulted from composition and presswork, although the proportion of both to total production costs varied greatly and further depended upon advertising, copyright and incidental costs. Ledger entries in the surviving Longman accounts suggest that paper amounted to between a quarter and a half of total production costs. Printing

43 'Report on Reform and Improvement of the Post Office', *Parliamentary Papers* 1807, 2: 219; PRO, A.o.3/950 ff; Michael Harris, *London Newspapers in the Age of Walpole: A Study of the Origins of the Modern English Press* (London and Toronto: Associated University Press, 1987), pp. 28, 200 n. 60.

44 R. B. Walker, 'Advertising in London Newspapers, 1650–1750', *Business History*, 15 (1973), 112–30; revenue tables are provided in A. Aspinall, 'Statistical Accounts of the London Newspapers in the Eighteenth Century,' *English Historical Review*, 63 (1948), 201–32.

45 See James Raven, 'New Reading Histories, Print Culture, and the Identification of Change: The Case of Eighteenth-Century England', *Social History* 23 (1998), 268–87.

expenses ranged between a fifth and a third of total costs. Bills for printing sent to Longman were calculated at rates per sheet, with additional labour charges for the corrections made to the presswork before the sheets left the printing house.[46]

Most book editions therefore remained at about 750 copies, although booksellers of novels and library editions more confidently ventured the publication of small-run books in two or more volumes. The clear exception to such prudence were the monster editions of popular titles reprinted over and over again, such as schoolbooks, hymn books, and the like. Some playbooks in their modern smaller formats reached editions of 2,000 copies or more, and in some cases even octavo histories, where proven sellers, were issued in 4,000-copy editions; but these pall before the huge printings commissioned by Longmans (our best surviving evidence) for staple titles such as Watts's *Hymns*, Johnson's *Dictionary* and numerous schoolbooks, including an 18,000-copy edition of Fenning's spelling manual. Even so, the question of risk had to be measured carefully. Trade histories sorrowfully rehearsed the saga of Andrew Millar's first 1751–2 edition of Fielding's *Amelia* of 8,000 copies in two impressions. Millar had hoped to emulate the runaway success of *Tom Jones* (10,000 copies printed between 1749 and 1750), but was left embarrassed, with copies still for sale ten years later.

Surviving production costings offer critical comparisons between cost and retail prices. Tantalisingly high profit potentials are obvious, but risks remained high in a market where even an edition of 500 copies might prove a slow earner. In almost all cases, however, allowance has to be made for discount to the retailing booksellers buying within the trade and for the vagaries of payment and credit arrangements to both individual and trade customers. The trade discount offered to other booksellers, some of whom were library managers, was especially important for provincial retailers developing local markets for new literature. A large proportion of trade offers in the final quarter of the century were advertised as bound; earlier discounts often specified sheets. By far the most common advertised price remained that of the volume sewed in paper or boards, leaving the buyer with the option of having a book bound according to his or her choice, and the binding either undertaken by the retailing bookseller or independently. The novel and *belles lettres* specialist, Hookham, allowed his trade customers a free copy for every twenty-five bought.[47] From their

46 Reading University Library, Longman Impression Book H4 (1794–1801), reproduced in *The House of Longman*, 1794–1914 microfilm edn (Cambridge: Chadwyck Healey, 1978), reel 37.
47 PRO Chancery Masters' List, Ledgers of Hookham and Carpenter, 1791–98.

opening years in the 1740s, the even more populist Noble brothers offered a trade discount of 14 per cent on twenty-five volumes of the same title. If country booksellers were able to sell their volumes for, say, the metropolitan price of three shillings, the potential for profit appears large. In practice, however, the largest profits were taken by the London wholesalers.

The one outstanding complication in all this remained the continuing problem of securing payments. Reliance on credit and the uncertainty of many credit notes added to the overheads carried by all types of booksellers and to the niceties of calculations in pricing and sizing an edition. Credit terms allowed by booksellers to both trade and direct customers were, by modern standards, extraordinarily generous. An allowance of six months seems to have been quite normal, and some overseas customers expected eighteen months or even two years' grace between order and the payment of an invoice. This blighted relations within a colonial market in which all major London booksellers participated despite its extreme frustration for all parties.[48]

What seems to have allowed greater diversification in trading practices from about the 1740s, despite the structural handicaps, was a deepening of money markets and the financial infrastructure. Many booksellers drew capital from external sources, and, even more significantly, readier circulation and more flexible use of assets were ensured by new means of accessing capital and limiting risk. Nevertheless, in a society in which individual trust so determined credit and debt relations, banking provisions remained based primarily on the credit reputation of the customers. As a result the book merchants benefiting most from new financial mechanisms and opportunities were those such as Strahan, Cadell, Robinson, and the Rivingtons, all able to demonstrate the respect and trust of a far-flung commercial elite. By contrast, the humblest operators struggled to cope with credit and risk conveyance, while the grandest booksellers diversified investments into property, annuities and a broader range of commercial and banking activity. None, however, could avoid the continuing sensitivity of credit broking, insurance services and economic confidence to external commercial pressures. The crisis years of American war in the 1770s, for example, can be clearly identified in charts of book trades' output and bankruptcies.

It is for good reason that the final participant discussed in this account of bookselling and publishing is the writer. Ultimately it was the author who had to choose the best option for having a work published. He or she faced great risk if they rejected the usually meagre outright sale of the manuscript. Before

---

48 See Raven, *London Booksellers and American Customers*, pp. 84–165.

the early nineteenth century few writers – and certainly very few first-time writers – could avoid such sales. The sale of a manuscript to a bookseller and the usual surrender of all subsequent rights doomed most writers to a paltry income. A very few distinguished scholars, clerics and essayists did exchange their manuscripts for substantial sums, but such deals were rare. Swift accepted £200 for *Gulliver's Travels* in 1726, *Night Thoughts* was sold by Young between 1742 and 1745 for 220 guineas, and Fielding made £700 from *Tom Jones* in 1749. Far more typical were Milton's total income of £10 for *Paradise Lost* in 1667, and Burney's sale of *Evelina* for £30 in 1778. Most of those claiming any title to being a 'professional' writer were largely unrecognised scribblers and translators. In the early eighteenth century the average sale by an author to a bookseller for a novel manuscript was reckoned at half a guinea.[49]

An author's only alternatives were subscription schemes or self-financed publication. Commission agreements whereby the bookseller put up the capital for printing an edition, on the understanding that the author would bear any loss, seem to have been very rare. Nevertheless, it seems that a bookseller rarely turned down a book if financing were available, even though it is simply not known how many manuscripts of authors looking for booksellers' support were refused. Negotiations over publication where the bookseller acted wholly or even in part as financing publisher are obscure. Few letters survive between first-time or even popular writers and booksellers, and refusals are rarely glimpsed. One, admittedly self-interested commentator, the popular publisher John Trusler, even suggested that the more underhand booksellers might agree to print a book at the author's expense and then print half as many again, selling, moreover, the booksellers' portion first and then claiming unsold copies as entirely from the number paid for by the author.[50]

The other possible alternatives were subscription schemes where booksellers also often acted as collecting agents. Subscription publishing enabled authors and booksellers to publicise large and expensive quality books, but they offered no simple transition to a market-based literature. Most early subscriptions agreements consigned all future returns to the financing bookseller-publisher rather than to the author or the person paid for the copy. For particularly risky projects the authors, their friends or patrons organised subscription themselves, but the cautious involvement of booksellers also increased after a few turn-of-the-century successes. Dryden's *Virgil* in 1697 – the first major literary subscription undertaken (if as a translation) by a living writer – offered

---

49 Raven, *British Fiction*, pp. 23–4; see also Raven, 'Novel Comes of Age', pp. 50–6.
50 John Trusler, *Modern Times: Or the Adventures of Gabriel Outcast*, 3 vols. (London: Printed for the Author, 1785), vol. III, p. 39.

both decent returns to its bookseller, Jacob Tonson, and a small fortune of £1,200 for the author. By the third edition in folio of 1709, Tonson cleared a profit of at least £95 (or over 16 per cent of his initial outlay) for the first edition, but Dryden gained in total between £900 and £1,000.[51]

The most spectacular triumph was that of Pope, who claimed more than £10,000 from his translations of the *Iliad*, 1715–20, and the *Odyssey*, 1725–6, but the scheme (and the bidding war he engineered between booksellers) was uniquely profitable (if mischievously alluring to successors).[52] Even those writers capable of pursuing innovative publishing schemes also rarely escaped arguments with the booksellers. Contracts often contained ambiguous references to edition numbers and definitions and the timing of printing and costs of extras.[53]

Throughout this period all participants in the book trades depended upon demand, distributive services, trade regulation and material supplies (largely of paper, type, and increasingly, binding papers and leathers). Copyrights, the currency of the wealthiest most successful publishing booksellers, proved both relatively cheap and investable, despite the high-profile and successful challenges to the conger system. Most authors – and the increasingly 'mechanick' printers – retained very weak bargaining positions, despite the fabled profits of a few literary lions and even fewer printing houses. Advancing consumer demand, served first by popular religious publishing, burgeoned with the establishment of provincial printer-newspaper publishers and the expansion of the broader distribution system. Certain closed systems endured for most of the period (like the copyright sales) or were created (as with the publication of so many novels to stock circulating libraries). The oligopoly of the leading London publishers ensured various other market constraints, and notably the high price mark-ups that sustained an expanding retail operation with discounting to provincial agents.

For booksellers taking on the full financial risk of publishing, the costs of paper, type and labour were not the sole determinants of profits, given that price structures, encompassing considerations of design and market profile, were based on more than the factor costs of manufacture. The idea that a title

---

51 John Barnard, 'The Large- and Small-Paper Copies of Dryden's *The Works of Virgil* (1697): Jacob Tonson's Investment and Profits and the Example of Paradise Lost (1688)', *Papers of the Bibliographical Society of America* (1998), 259–71.

52 David Foxon (rev. and ed. by James McLaverty), *Pope and the Early Eighteenth-Century Book Trade* (Oxford: Clarendon Press, 1991).

53 John Barnard, 'Dryden, Tonson, and the Patrons of *The Works of Virgil* (1697)', in Paul Hammond and David Hopkins (eds.), *John Dryden: Tercentenary Essays* (Oxford: Clarendon Press, 2000), pp. 174–238; Dustin Griffin, *Literary Patronage in England, 1650–1800* (Cambridge: Cambridge University Press, 1996).

might yet prove a surprise success must have encouraged some booksellers, and was certainly a spur to new marketing and promotional enterprise. Those publishers supporting wholesale back-lists for a decade or more, however, required a particular balance between printing sufficient copies of an edition to maximise the unit costs of the press work, but limited enough to avoid tying up capital in unsold stock and the burden of long-term storage space. The dozen or so most successful London bookseller-publishers accumulated spectacular wealth, often entering the trade without formal training but with the acumen to manage new sources of finance. After all, sea-captain John (Mac)Murray set up as bookseller in 1768 because, in his words, 'many blockheads in the trade are making a fortune'.[54]

Literary production and patronage flourished according to the regulatory and economic structure of the book trade but also as a result of the broader resources of the state, its population and its leading consumers. The profile of book publication changed as booksellers reacted more speedily and effectively to market demands, publishing specialist works in response to new professional interests as well as to new fashions in entertainment and instruction. The commodification of literature did not, however, necessarily result in cheaper new books. Prices far higher than production costs could be imposed by cartels of leading booksellers at least until the legal battles over copyright in the late 1760s, but in many respects also continuing thereafter. In presenting new books as the 'necessaries' and 'decencies' of middle-class life while they clearly remained expensive luxuries, booksellers had to develop ever more sophisticated marketing and distributional techniques. New supporting agencies ranged from commercial libraries and subscription book-clubs to private debating societies and the solemn recommendations of the periodical reviews. Publication rates soared, and by the final decades of the eighteenth century a highly commercial organization increasingly determined a socially diverse and divisive literature. Yet the most remarkable thing was that all was achieved within the technological constraints of the hand press.

54 Henry Curwen, *A History of Booksellers, the Old and the New* (London: Chatto and Windus, 1874), pp. 161–2.

2

The social world of authorship 1660–1714

DUSTIN GRIFFIN

The period from 1660 to 1714 witnessed what might be called the birth of the modern English author. For it is during these years that there began to appear many of the features by which we define modern authorship: copyright legislation, widespread identification of the author on the title page, the 'author by profession', bookselling as a commercial enterprise, a literary 'marketplace', the periodical essay and political journalism. But it is important not to assume that the practice of authorship *c.* 1700 closely resembled the practice of authorship today, or even in 1800. Far from being an 'independent' man of letters, reflecting a highly individual sensibility, the typical author in the late seventeenth and early eighteenth centuries was enmeshed in an intricate web of social and political connections that not only defined a writer's working life but defined literary production itself. Most writing of the period was 'occasional' – prompted by some public event or controversy in the politics of church or state or the world of letters. Many writers in the early part of the period were aligned with a powerful courtier or minister – the Duke of Buckingham, the Duke of York, the Earl of Shaftesbury, the Duke of Monmouth, the Earl of Rochester – or hoped to be, so that they could attract the attention and encouragement of a patron. Even at the end of the period many writers attached themselves to Whig and Tory ministers, Lord Somers, Robert Harley, or the Earl of Halifax. Even those who did not take part in high politics were enmeshed in dense private networks. To understand the writing of this period fully, we need to understand its political and social dimensions.

We also need to understand what changes took place in the social and political world of authorship from *c.* 1660 to *c.* 1714, a half-century during which England's political world underwent considerable change. This chapter lays out the main lines of the socio-political world of Restoration and early eighteenth-century authorship, assesses the literary importance of the various associations that connected writers to each other and to the larger world and surveys the changes in the world of authorship that took place between 1660, when Charles II returned from exile in France, and 1714, when the death of his niece Queen Anne brought her distant cousin, the Elector of Hanover, to the throne of England.

The social dimension of writing

It is a commonplace of literary history that Restoration literary life was for the most part organized around the court. Even those writers, like Andrew Marvell, who criticised the measures of the king's ministers were careful to preserve at least the appearance of loyalty to the crown and took their bearings from what was happening at Whitehall and Westminster. Some writers of course kept their distance. But even John Milton was visited by literary friends and admirers from the court world, including Marvell and John Dryden. John Bunyan, who spent time in Bedford gaol, is perhaps the exception. For the rest, writing in this period was an essentially social practice, at every stage of literary production, from inspiration or invention, through composition, to the presentation on the page, to its consumption by readers or listeners. Much of the lighter verse of the day took its origin in witty conversation among friends. Some of what eventually reached print as John Wilmot, the Earl of Rochester's epigrams probably began as impromptu witticisms uttered in company. More generally, conversation primed the writer's pump. Dryden wrote to a fellow poet reminding him of 'our Genial Nights; where our discourse is neither too serious, nor too light; but alwayes pleasant, and for the most part instructive: the raillery neither too sharp upon the present, nor too censorious on the absent; and the Cups only such as will raise the Conversation of the Night, without disturbing the business of the Morrow.'[1] It was on such witty conversation that Dryden and the other dramatists of the day said they modelled the dialogue of their stage comedies. In a dedication to Rochester, Dryden avowed that 'the best Comick writers of our Age, will joyn with me to acknowledge, that they have copy'd the Gallantries of Courts, the Delicacy of Expression, and the Decencies of Behaviour, from your Lordship, with more success, then if they had taken their Models from the Court of *France*'.[2] Social gatherings provided writers not only models of conversation, but also news from court that might occasion a poem or a pamphlet, or gossip upon which satirical squibs might be written. Such witty conversation served also to stimulate a

---

1 John Dryden, *Works*, 20 vols., ed. H.T. Swendenberg *et al.* (Berkeley: University of California Press, 1956–90), vol. XI, pp. 320–1.
2 *Ibid.*, vol. XI, p. 221.

kind of literary competition. Dryden writes of the power of 'emulation' to serve as the 'Spur of Wit': 'Great Contemporaries whet and cultivate each other: And mutual Borrowing, and Commerce, makes the Common Riches of Learning, as it does of the Civil Government.'[3]

When conversation took literary form it was often cast in essentially social genres. One such genre is the familiar epistle from a writer to his 'dear' or 'honoured' friend, sometimes from one writer to another. Dryden wrote at least a dozen such poems, including epistles to the painter Sir Godfrey Kneller, the dramatists William Congreve and Thomas Southerne, and his 'Honour'd Kinsman, John Driden, of Chesterton'. In his early years Pope published a number of familiar epistles and, in his later career, a set of imitations of the verse epistles of Horace. Not every 'friend' so addressed was in fact a close acquaintance. Dryden's editors suggest that his poem 'To My Friend Mr J. Northleigh' was meant primarily to flatter the recipient, whom Dryden did not in fact know well, and that his bantering epistle to Sir George Etherege was designed less as an expression of friendship than as a witty model of gentlemanly exchange. Aphra Behn wrote an epistolary poem to the poet-translator Thomas Creech as a way of declaring a literary affiliation she wished to claim. Many familiar epistles served to commend another writer's work, to seal a literary alliance or to advertise a writer's political affiliations, as with Dryden's 1660 poem to his 'Honored Friend' Sir Robert Howard, which, by praising a noted royalist, enabled a poet who had recently published a poem 'to the Glorious Memory of [Oliver] Cromwell' to reassure the court of his new-found royalist principles.

A related form is the 'letter from the town to a friend in the country'. Examples include Rochester's 'Letter from Artemiza in the Town to Chloe in the Countrey' and Anne Finch's 'Ardelia's Answer to Ephelia who had invited her to come to her in town', which reverses the typical pattern. Modelled on an actual exchange of letters, the 'letter from the town', like the familiar epistle, implies that writing is a form of social interaction, and that writers are linked with each other in social networks. Poems cast as letters between real or fictitious people – such as Rochester's 'Epistolary Essay from M. G. to O. B.' – are also common.

Another social form is the prologue and epilogue delivered from the stage by an actor in the main theatrical piece. Communicating directly with an audience addressed as 'you', the prologue and epilogue comment, typically

3 *Ibid.*, vol. IV, p. 12. Cf. *ibid.*, vol. XIII, p. 10; vol. XVII, pp. 44, 377.

in bantering style, on the action of the play and on the reception that the actor hopes to prompt. The audience is intended to recognise the speaker not only as a character in the play but as a well-known actor or actress. Thus Nell Gwyn appears at the end of Dryden's *Tyrannic Love* (1669), where in the part of St Catherine she has been murdered and fallen to the floor. As a bearer prepares to carry her off, she suddenly sits up: 'Hold, are you mad, you damn'd confounded Dog, / I am to rise, and speak the Epilogue', whereupon she addresses the audience in the character of 'the Ghost of poor departed *Nelly*'.

Yet another form that advertises the social character of writing is the dialogue, in which parts are written for two or more voices. The most notable example in the period is Dryden's *Essay of Dramatic Poesy* (1668), cast as a conversation among four young men during an outing on the Thames. Rochester has two 'Pastoral Dialogues' and several other poems for several voices. Add to them the many satiric poems, typically based on Horatian models, written in a conversational tone and addressed to an imaginary interlocutor, such as Rochester's 'Allusion to Horace' ('Well Sir, 'tis granted, I said Dryden's Rhimes, / Were stoln, unequal, nay dull many times . . .'), and others in which the interlocutor responds or interrupts (Rochester's 'Satyr Against Mankind' and Pope's 'Epistle from Mr. Pope to Dr Arbuthnot' are familiar examples). Related to the dialogue is the answer poem, in which one poem is 'answered' by another, as with Rochester's 'Song' ('Give me leave to raile at you') and 'The Answer', probably written by Lady Rochester.

Nor was it uncommon for the process of composition itself to be social. One of the best-known plays of the period, *The Rehearsal*, is usually attributed to the Duke of Buckingham and his circle. Collaboration was in fact a widespread practice, even with the most successful authors (six Dryden plays have co-authors), and it extended well into the eighteenth century. Collaboration took many different forms: a professional poet working with an amateur (Dryden with Sir Robert Howard); a senior writer with a novice (Dryden correcting the poems of William Walsh); a pair of friends working as equals (Pope and Swift in their *Miscellanies*); a pair of professionals working together as a contractual business arrangement (Dryden and Nathaniel Lee); a senior poet with assistants or 'auxiliaries' (Pope's translation of Homer's *Odyssey*). It is not always possible to separate out the contributions made by the several authors. Critics of Pope's *Dunciad Variorum* (1729) are not taken in when Pope attributes parts of the work to William Cleland, Richard Bentley, or the invented Ricardus Aristarchus and Martinus Scriblerus. But they still debate the degree of Pope's supervision of many of the footnotes to the *Variorum* apparently composed by his friend and literary executor, William Warburton.

Other collaborations were responsible for major literary productions of the period, from such periodicals as *The Tatler, The Spectator* and *The Guardian*, to the great translations of *Juvenal and Persius* (1696), in which Dryden appears alongside ten other translators. It was common for translations of the classics to be produced by a team, one of them serving as the lead writer, and the project to be coordinated by a bookseller. Examples include the translation of *Ovid's Epistles* (1680), produced for the bookseller Jacob Tonson by Dryden and others, and *Plutarchs Lives* (1683), translated by 'Several Hands' (including Dryden). The bookseller was also the key figure, both originator and manager, in the publication of most of the original poetry of the period, much of which appeared not in volumes with a single author but in poetic miscellanies. Tonson was himself responsible for a series of such miscellanies, from *Miscellany Poems* in 1684 (to which Dryden contributed fifteen poems) to *Sylvae* in 1685 (Dryden contributed the 'Preface' and another fourteen poems), to *Examen Poeticum* in 1693 (Dryden contributed the 'Dedication' and six poems). For most other poets, women especially, publication in a miscellany was the only way in which their work might reach the public. Many other ephemeral satirical poems, circulating as broadsheets or in manuscript, were gathered in the successive editions of *Poems on Affairs of State* (1689–1705), perhaps the most popular poetical miscellany of the age. Some of the major satires of the period, including Marvell's 'Last Instructions to a Painter', were first published in these volumes.

The next stage in the production of literary work – the presentation on the page and in a sewn volume – often had the effect of underscoring the social dimension of authorship. A literary work in this period was commonly dedicated to a patron, equipped with an 'epistle dedicatory' honouring the patron's lineage, accomplishment, and taste, and alluding gratefully and gracefully to the poet's association with him. It was often escorted into print by a commendatory poem or two. The printed version of a stage play was typically accompanied by a prologue and epilogue from the author's 'dear friends' and admirers, as well as (especially in the case of Dryden) a critical 'preface' addressed to the reader.

Finally, literature in this era was often read socially. In 1691 Dryden read his new play *Cleomenes* aloud to the family of Lawrence Hyde, Earl of Rochester, to whom it was dedicated. Pope read the revised *Rape of the Lock* to his friends before its publication in March 1714. Beyond such private circles were the larger public forums of the day, the coffee houses where Londoners gathered to read the latest satiric broadsheets or *Spectators*; the circles that formed around Restoration courtiers to read and remark on the latest manuscript satires; and the public theatres, well-lit playhouses in which viewers could see and feel themselves part of a large audience and feel free to comment aloud on the action on stage.

To emphasise the social dimension of authorship is not to reduce the author to the voice of the community, a Foucauldian 'author-function', some necessary instrument through which writing is presented to a reading public. The circumstances in which writers were enmeshed limited authorial freedom and exerted pressures but also afforded opportunities. The pressures – to produce a polemical argument to suit a particular occasion or the political desires of a patron or paymaster, to adopt a coterie or conventional style – were sufficiently strong to make it difficult for scholars, faced with an anonymous text from this period, to determine authorship. The canons of even such major figures as Rochester and Daniel Defoe are still being actively debated. Those same circumstances, however, also presented opportunities that an author might seize in order not only to find a receptive audience or to advance a career but to impress the text with a distinctive stamp. The writers whose work we still read are generally those who discovered how to turn literary occasions to their own advantage.

The changing world of authorship

But were the social circumstances of authorship unchanged from *c.* 1660 to *c.* 1714? The traditional answer is that the changes were substantial: that a culture in which an author typically sought to please the court gave way to a culture in which an author typically addressed a broader 'reading public'; that the typical social gathering in which literature was discussed and even produced shifted from the aristocrat's coterie to the public coffee house or the meetings of the famous Kit-Cat and Scriblerus Clubs, where social rank counted for less than wit; that the cultural authority of the gentleman amateur gave way to that of the 'professed author'; that the limited circulation of writing in manuscript within narrow circles gave way to the wider dissemination of written texts in 'print culture'; that the writer emerged from dependence on various forms of patronage into increasing financial independence; and that, added together, these several changes pointed towards the gradual liberation and professionalisation of the writer.

This was the standard account in literary histories from the middle of the nineteenth century to the last decades of the twentieth. It reflects a view of English history found most prominently in Macaulay's *History of England* (1849), where the court of Charles II is seen as depraved, frivolous and morally callous,

Restoration comedy a scene of immorality and debauchery, and patronage a degrading 'traffic in praise' which left the writer somewhere 'between a pandar and a beggar'. If the cultural villain was Charles II, his brother James II (1685–8) was the political villain: rigid, absolutist about the royal prerogative and determined to foist an alien Roman Catholicism on sturdily Protestant England. But after the Glorious Revolution, in Macaulay's view, all changed. The new (safely Protestant) king, William III, is the country's liberator and the author's champion. Men of merit are rewarded with salaried positions in the civil service and with new-found dignity.[4]

Macaulay's 'Whig' version of English history, in which the Stuart dynasty represents the bad old past and the Revolution of 1688 the beginning of the glorious English present, underlay Alexandre Beljame's *Men of Letters and the English Public in the 18th Century* (which appeared in French in 1883), and A. S. Collins' *Authorship in the Days of Johnson* (1927). Both Beljame and Collins tell stories of cultural and political 'progress' and the 'emancipation' of the writer from the shackles of patronage and government licensing. Beljame, whose work had renewed influence in England when finally translated in 1948, saw the Restoration as a time when there was as yet no 'reading public' and authors were compelled to seek the favour of courtiers. But, in his view, after 1688 the writer's status rose. Private patronage largely ceased, and in Addison's day a reading public was well established. Pope, whose contract with a bookseller to produce a translation of Homer made his fortune, dedicated the book not to a patron but to William Congreve, a fellow writer. Maintaining his detachment from both Whigs and Tories, Pope was the first real independent 'man of letters'.

This inspiring account of the rise of the writer as hero received support from James Saunders' *The Profession of English Letters* (1964), from the popularisation in the 1990s of Jürgen Habermas' discussion of the 'bourgeois public sphere' in early eighteenth-century England,[5] and from studies of the rise of 'print culture' in the eighteenth century. But other recent work on the circumstances of authorship in the late seventeenth and early eighteenth centuries prompts a reconsideration of the story of liberation and professionalisation, and shows that the old manuscript culture did not simply give way to print culture about 1700: the two cultures coexisted for decades, print very vigorous

---

4 In this paragraph and the next I draw on my 'Fictions of Eighteenth-Century Authorship', *Essays in Criticism*, 43 (1993), 181–94.
5 First presented in his *Strukturwandel der Öffentlichkeit* in 1962 but not widely discussed until it was translated into English in 1989 as *The Structural Transformation of the Public Sphere* (Cambridge, MA: M.I.T. Press).

in the Restoration, and manuscript culture persisting well into the eighteenth century.

Literary circles

Literary circles are a prominent feature of the Restoration cultural landscape. To some extent they descend from coteries of the Caroline period, including the 'Sons of Ben' (poets who gathered around Ben Jonson in the 1630s) and the group of musicians and writers assembled in the 1650s by Henry Lawes. While the former group celebrated Cavalier culture in its ascendancy, the latter served to preserve that culture through the years of the Interregnum. Lawes, who presented concerts at his London house, published the works of the Cavalier poet, William Cartwright (with fifty-four commendatory poems by his royalist friends), and two collections of Cavalier *Aires and Dialogues* (1653, 1655). The most prominent of the literary circles after the Restoration was probably the one gathered around the Duke of Buckingham. Although the court was the symbolic centre of culture – and Charles II himself the nominal judge of literary merit as well as the dispenser of patronage – his court, like courts in most ages, was riven by factions – groups of courtiers vying for influence over the king or resisting the influence of a favourite. In the early years one polarising figure was the Earl of Clarendon (1609–74), Lord Chancellor and, as father-in-law of James, Duke of York, the king's brother, suspected as would-be kingmaker. When Clarendon fell, after a bout of political infighting, James himself served to divide the court into groups that favoured and opposed his policy of increasing the power of the crown and (after James' conversion to Roman Catholicism in 1673, and Charles' continuing failure to produce a legal heir) into those who looked forward to his accession to the throne and those who feared it. George Villiers, 2nd Duke of Buckingham (1628–87), was an early favourite of the king (his father had been the favourite of the king's father), and an opponent of both Clarendon and James. At Cambridge in the 1640s he made friends with Abraham Cowley and Martin Clifford, who would join the informal circle that gathered around him after the Restoration. Both Clifford and, later, Samuel Butler (author of the famous *Hudibras*) served as his secretary. Thomas Sprat, who later became a bishop, served as his chaplain. Clifford, Butler and Sprat were all commoners, dependent on Buckingham's largesse. Others, including Rochester, Sir Charles Sedley and Charles Sackville, Lord Buckhurst (later Earl of Dorset) were less clients than cronies, fellow aristocrats, though of lower rank. Buckingham, a member of the ministry as well as a talented wit, was the acknowledged leader. One of his earliest literary

efforts was a stage comedy, *The Country Gentleman*, written in collaboration
with Sir Robert Howard but suppressed before it could be performed in 1669
because it ridiculed two political allies of the Duke of York. About the same
time Buckingham and his friends (though not Howard this time) produced a
linked series of satires on a heroic poem, *The British Princes* (1669), by Howard's
brother, Sir Edward Howard, probably by the 'time-honoured method of circulating the growing file from writer to writer'.[6] The most famous literary
production of this group was *The Rehearsal*, another satire on high heroic
rhetoric, cast in the form of a play-within-a-play, probably composed in the
early 1660s but not performed until 1671. Buckingham's collaborators included
Clifford, Butler and Sprat.

The Buckingham circle illustrates the close link between literature and
politics in the Restoration. The members shared a pleasure in wit and satire, a
sceptical debunking attitude towards received truths and (presumably) some
delight in debauchery, but, as Harold Love suggests, the group's 'ultimate
rationale was political'[7] – opposition to the Yorkist party. Another well-known
literary circle in the 1670s was probably more devoted to debauchery than
to politics. The group that gathered around Rochester at his Ranger's Lodge
at Woodstock included many court wits earlier associated with Buckingham,
including Sedley, Buckhurst and Sir Fleetwood Shepherd. A 1677 letter from
Rochester to a friend refers to an 'assembly' of wits gathered at Woodstock,
where they are engaged in composing a 'libell'.[8] Cynical about politics, and
disengaged from court infighting, Rochester's group was more interested in
literary quarrels with members of a faction gathered around John Sheffield,
Earl of Mulgrave, linked politically with the Yorkists. Rochester's 'merry gang'
is in effect named in 'An Allusion to Horace' (*c.* 1676), an attack on Dryden
that closes by appealing to the only judges Rochester hopes to please:

> I loathe the Rabble, 'tis enough for me,
> If Sidley, Shadwell, Shepherd, Wycherley,
> Godolphin, Buttler, Buckhurst, Buckingham,
> And some few more, whom I omit to name
> Approve my Sense, I count their Censure Fame.[9]

6 Harold Love, *Scribal Publication in Seventeenth-Century England* (Oxford: Oxford University
  Press, 1993), p. 245.
7 *Ibid.*, p. 253.
8 John Wilmot, Earl of Rochester, *Letters*, ed. Jeremy Treglown (Chicago: University of
  Chicago Press, 1980), pp. 163–4.
9 Rochester, *Poems*, ed. Keith Walker (Oxford: Oxford University Press, 1984), p. 102.
  Shadwell and Wycherley are the comic dramatists Thomas Shadwell and William
  Wycherley; Godolphin is Sidney Godolphin (1645–1712), a witty young Tory MP who
  later rose to eminence as Lord Treasurer under King William and Queen Anne.

Dryden, the butt of the poem's satire, had once dedicated a play to Rochester, but by 1676 had fallen out with his patron and had aligned himself with Mulgrave, joining with him to write 'An Essay upon Satyr' (1679), which satirises Rochester, Sedley and Buckhurst (now Earl of Dorset). In the late 1670s Rochester exchanged lampoons with Mulgrave and with another member of the Mulgrave circle, Sir Carr Scroope. The violence and virulence of the language suggests an attempt to invoke the archaic idea that satire can kill, or at least can destroy the enemy's reputation – as wit, as lover, as courtier-poet. But the poems so echo each other as to suggest a ritualised exchange of witty insults, an insider's game between men of the same social rank, displaying their ability to work in a conventional, stylised literary form before an appreciative audience of courtiers. Rochester and Mulgrave also challenged each other's authority as literary judge. By commending Shadwell and deprecating Dryden, Rochester in the 'Allusion to Horace' had explicitly questioned Dryden's wit, and implicitly impugned Mulgrave's taste. In the most famous of Restoration lampoons, 'MacFlecknoe' (c. 1676), Dryden not only explicitly attacks Shadwell but implicitly attacks Shadwell's champion, Rochester, subtly appropriating and redeploying Rochester's insults, and in effect claiming that he knows better than Rochester how to display a gentleman's witty superiority.

The poems produced in the Buckingham and Rochester circles were designed not for wide readership but for an elite audience in and around the court. Their purpose was broadly political – to advance an agenda in parliament, or at least to enhance the group in the swirling world of personal court politics, where reputation was everything, and a rapier-like wit a means to social power. Membership within coteries was itself unstable – a writer might gravitate from one group to another – and within a literary circle satires and songs served also to attempt to consolidate social ties between men. Some evidence suggests that in Rochester's circle, where drinking was said to 'engender' wit, where a woman might have to yield to the attractions of the 'rival bottle' and a rake might choose a 'sweet soft page' who 'does the trick worth forty wenches', the pleasures of the literary coterie went beyond homosocial male bonding. For courtier poets such as Rochester, Dorset and Mulgrave coterie writing was also a means of confirming their shared conviction of the superiority of witty gentlemen over the working writers of the day. For the latter – Dryden, Shadwell and others – association with a coterie was primarily a means to patronage, whether it took the form of gifts, hospitality (Dryden was 'kept . . . generously' at the house of Sir Robert Howard), or introductions to more powerful patrons, perhaps the king himself. Both Dryden and Shadwell rose to become Poet Laureate not only because of their talents but also because of their connections.

In recent years scholars have begun to uncover evidence of other literary circles, including several to which women writers had access. Among Katherine Philips' poems is one addressed 'To the excellent Mrs A. O. upon her receiving the name of Lucasia, and adoption into our society. 29 Decemb 1651'.[10] Probably originating in the 1640s, when she was still in a lady's boarding school, Philips' 'Society' preserved some of the cultural habits of the Caroline court, including the taking of pastoral *noms de plume* – Philips' own was 'Orinda' – and the celebration of 'Friendship' of a Platonic cast. The Society included both men and women, though the friendship between Orinda and Lucasia, which occasioned the largest number of Philips' poems, has been seen as the defining centre. Addressed to friends, celebrating both friendship and (at a time when they were in eclipse) royalist political ideals, the poems by Philips and her friends were apparently intended for private circulation.

In the 1680s another group may have gathered around Mary of Modena, Duchess of York and later (in 1685) Queen of England.[11] Her establishment at court included, among her Maids of Honour, the poets Anne Killigrew and Anne Finch (Anne Kingsmill before her marriage). Sharing loyalty to the Stuart family, and encouraged by the queen to perform plays and translate Italian romances, Mary of Modena's circle of female attendants may have found in their small community both a focus and an audience for their writings. But this coterie was more private than Buckingham's: Finch took care not to be known as a 'versifying Maid of Honour'.[12] Very little evidence survives to suggest that members of other literary circles or coteries actually met as a group: they might better be called loose epistolary 'networks' in which writers (both male and female) adopted pseudonyms, exchanged or answered poems, and sometimes appeared jointly in manuscript collections or even in printed works. Mary Lee, Lady Chudleigh, who wrote some thirty-five familiar epistles, exchanged compliments with Elizabeth Thomas and Mary Astell, and had links to both Dryden and the poet John Norris of Bemerton. Anne Wharton (Rochester's niece, and younger sister of Dryden's 'Eleonora') corresponded with Gilbert

10 Katherine Philips, *Collected Works*, 3 vols., ed. Patrick Thomas (Stump Cross, Essex: Stump Cross Books, 1990), vol. I, pp. 101–2.

11 Carol Barash, *English Women's Poetry, 1649–1714: Politics, Community, and Linguistic Authority* (Oxford: Oxford University Press, 1996), pp. 149–72.

12 Barbara McGovern, *Anne Finch and Her Poetry: A Critical Biography* (Athens, GA: University of Georgia Press, 1998), p. 25.

Burnet (future Bishop of Salisbury), exchanged verses with Aphra Behn, and contributed to Tonson's *Miscellany Poems* (1684). Her commendatory poem on her uncle was itself commended in poems by Waller and others.[13] Mary Astell had a wide circle of correspondents, both male and female, including Norris of Bemerton. Jane Barker, who addressed occasional poems to a wide range of family and friends (mostly men), appeared in print together with 'several Gentlemen of the Universities'.[14] Anne Finch exchanged poems with several obscure friends as well as with Pope.[15]

Coteries continued to be a feature of the literary world after the Glorious Revolution and were not limited to 'manuscript culture'. In the 1690s the best known of them was probably the so-called 'Christ Church wits', led by Henry Aldrich, Dean of Christ Church College, Oxford, and including several tutors at the college, Francis Atterbury (later Bishop of Rochester), Robert Freind (later head of Westminster School) and his brother John Freind, and several Christ Church students, including William King (later a respected neoLatin poet). Sharing a traditional view that humane learning, based on the classics, was the province of men of the world, they became embroiled in one of the most contentious episodes in the 'Battle of the Ancients and the Moderns' in England. When Sir William Temple's championing of the ancients in his *Ancient and Modern Learning* (1690) drew an attack in 1694 from William Wotton, Aldrich, aligned with Temple, asked young Charles Boyle, a Christ Church student and future Earl of Orrery, to prepare an edition of the epistles of late-classical writer, Phalaris, whose merits Temple had praised. Boyle's edition (1695), produced with the assistance of the Christ Church group, drew fire from another classical scholar, Richard Bentley. A further exchange between Boyle and Bentley followed, the 'Boyle' contribution again compiled with the assistance of other Christ Church wits.

In this instance members of a literary circle joined in order to engage in a public controversy, fought out in print, suggesting that coteries were taking new forms as print spread further into the culture. But a slightly later group of Christ Church writers demonstrates that the older model of coterie, a manuscript-based circle linked by family, class and political sympathies, continued to shape literary relations. A manuscript collection in the Bodleian Library

---

13 See *Rochester: The Critical Heritage*, ed. David Farley-Hills (London: Routledge & Kegan Paul, 1972), pp. 104–11.

14 For details, see Kathryn King, 'Jane Barker, *Poetical Recreations*, and the Sociable Text', *ELH* 61 (1994), 551–70.

15 McGovern, *Anne Finch*, pp. 121–2; *The Anne Finch Wellesley Manuscript Poems*, ed. Barbara McGovern and Charles H. Hinnant (Athens, GA: University of Georgia Press, 1998), pp. 10–22, 68–70.

at Oxford (Top. Oxon. e. 169, fol. 75) contains Latin verse, some prose epitaphs and an epitaph on the poet John Philips, author of 'The Splendid Shilling' and *Cyder*. Most of the epitaphs are by Christ Church men, and Philips himself was at Christ Church. A linked series of manuscripts in the Nottingham University Library (Pw V 334–5, 388–9, 441) contains a set of epitaphs on Philips, apparently much beloved by his contemporaries, including fellow poet Edmund Smith, also a Christ Church man. Although his poems were well known, Philips, who published anonymously, seems not to have aimed at literary fame or fortune, but to have written 'for his own diversion'.[16] ('The Splendid Shilling', written while he was at Christ Church, and dedicated to a fellow student, was published without authorization in 1701.) *Cyder*, dedicated to two Christ Church contemporaries, has a pro-Stuart political programme: it compliments Civil War royalists and their descendants, Nonjuring clergymen and Tory statesmen. Philips presented two leather-bound copies to the dedicatees and one hundred large-paper copies to his friends.

Clubs

During the years in which private literary circles gathered at Christ Church, more public gatherings were taking place at Christopher Cat's coffee house in London, where the bookseller Jacob Tonson convened the meetings of the Kit-Cat Club. Its members included most of the leading men of letters of the 1690s (Addison, Steele, Congreve, Samuel Garth, Sir John Vanbrugh), a few gentleman amateurs (the Earl of Dorset, who twenty years earlier had been Rochester's fellow court wit, and William Walsh, who befriended the young Alexander Pope), the painter Sir Godfrey Kneller, several members of the governing 'Whig Junto' (including the Lord Chancellor, John Lord Somers and the Earl of Halifax), and some twenty young aristocrats and junior ministers aligned with Somers. What bound the members together were Whig (and later Hanoverian) politics, a taste for letters and male gallantry that took the form of formally 'toasting' the young female 'beauties' of the day in verse.[17]

The literary significance of the Kit-Cat Club, which met from c.1697 to c.1717, is difficult to assess. While large claims have been made – 'not just a set of

---

16 Samuel Johnson, *Lives of the Poets*, 3 vols., ed. G. B. Hill (Oxford: Oxford University Press, 1905), vol. 1, p. 324.

17 Despite their Whig orientation, the Kit-Cats paid the expenses of the funeral of Dryden, not only a Tory but a Jacobite, in 1700, probably because of close links between Dryden and several Kit-Cats, Tonson (his publisher), Dorset (a key patron) and Congreve (his 'dear friend' and later his editor).

wits but in reality the patriots that saved Britain', 'the Whig party in its social sphere', 'a Club that gave direction to the State', a means whereby Tonson might match writers with patrons for his own benefit as their bookseller[18] – the Kit-Cats may have been little more than a social club and 'informal political forum'. Men of letters were always a minority of the membership. Johnson mentions the club only twice in his *Lives of the Poets*. Contemporaries – particular Tories – often commented satirically on the alleged power and influence of the Kit-Cats, but their observations can be discounted as partisan rhetoric. No literary works, apart from a few epigrams and verses for toasting, are known to have originated in the Club.

By contrast, the contemporary Scriblerus Club has long been associated with some of the greatest works of the period – *Gulliver's Travels*, *The Beggar's Opera*, *The Dunciad*. Its literary members – Swift, Gay, Pope, Arbuthnot – were more distinguished than the Kit-Cat writers, and their literary interests dominated Club meetings. It is often assumed that the Scriblerians were the Tory reply to the Whig Kit-Cats, but apart from Harley, who served as the Club's 'patron' (but perhaps not a 'member'), and Swift, then employed by Harley, the members did not at that time have exclusive connections with Tory politicians. The Club in effect grew out of two groups – the Saturday Club (1710–11) and the Brothers Club (1711–13) – in which promoting a Tory political agenda was the main business.[19] But the Scriblerians, who began to meet in the spring of 1714, were more interested in mocking the unlearned than in routing the Whigs. Their invention of 'Martinus Scriblerus', whose life they proposed to write and whose works they proposed to edit and publish, constituted their primary literary activity.

The Club only met for a few months, breaking up in part because of the fall from power of their patron in the summer of 1714 and Swift's departure for Ireland, even though the friendships nourished during those months endured for as long as the writers lived. Literary projects that can be traced directly to Club meetings are relatively minor: two stage plays, *The What D'Ye Call It* (1715) and *Three Hours After Marriage* (1717), in which Pope, Gay and Arbuthnot probably each had a hand, and the *Memoirs of Martinus Scriblerus*, which

---

18 Kathleen Lynch, *Jacob Tonson, Kit-Cat Publisher* (Knoxville: University of Tennessee Press, 1971), pp. 37, 41; Harry Geduld, *Prince of Publishers: A Study of the Work and Career of Jacob Tonson* (Bloomington: University of Indiana Press, 1969), pp. 151, 152.

19 The best accounts of the Scriblerus Club are found in Robert Allen, *The Clubs of Augustan London* (Cambridge, MA: Harvard University Press, 1933) and in Charles Kerby-Miller's edition of *The Memoirs of Martinus Scriblerus* (New Haven, CT: Yale University Press, 1950).

occupied Pope and Swift from time to time and finally appeared in 'the first book of a work, projected in concert by Pope, Swift, and Arbuthnot . . . [of which] the design was never completed'. Some scholars hold that even the greatest works of Swift, Pope and Gay ought to be regarded as 'fragments of their great design'.[20] Such claims can be traced to Pope, who told Joseph Spence about 1730 that Swift 'took his first hints for *Gulliver*' from the *Memoirs*.[21] But it is doubtful that chapter 16 of the *Memoirs*, dealing with Scriblerus' 'Travels', was the real seed for *Gulliver's Travels*. Pope, who got some of the details wrong, was not a disinterested witness, and the author of *A Tale of a Tub* did not need 'the works of the unlearned' to write about the abuses of learning in the third voyage of his *Travels*. Pope's own *Peri Bathous* (1728) might appropriately be called Scriblerian, but the *Dunciad Variorum* (1729), in which Martinus Scriblerus appears as a commentator, astonishingly transcends any Scriblerian origins. The seed that led to *The Beggar's Opera* may be Swift's 1716 letter to Pope suggesting a 'Newgate pastoral',[22] but Pope, Swift and Gay would have been friends and correspondents, interested in each other's work, even if the Scriblerus Club had never met.

What distinguished the Kit-Cat Club and the Scriblerians from the literary coteries of the Restoration and later? The 'Christ Church wits', it should be noted, were sometimes called a 'club' by later eighteenth-century observers.[23] And membership overlapped: some – Orrery, the two Freinds, Simon Harcourt – who took part in the Christ Church circles were later associated with the Tory Brothers Club.[24] Both coteries and clubs combined interests in party (or factional) politics and in letters; both served to link writers and prospective patrons. Like coteries, clubs remained closed societies: prospective members were occasionally proposed and rejected. But clubs were more organised groups, with regular meetings and sometimes officers and rules; distinctions of rank counted for less; and no single figure served as the dominating

20 Patricia Bruckmann, *A Manner of Correspondence: A Study of the Scriblerus Club* (Montreal: McGill-Queen's University Press, 1997), p. 8.
21 Joseph Spence, *Observations, Anecdotes, and Characters of Books and Men*, 2 vols., ed. James Osborne (Oxford: Oxford University Press, 1966), vol. I, p. 56.
22 Jonathan Swift, *Correspondence*, 5 vols., ed. Harold Williams (Oxford: Oxford University Press, 1963–5), vol. II, p. 215.
23 Eustace Budgell's *Memoirs of the Lives and Characters of the Illustrious Family of the Boyles; particularly of the late eminently learned Charles Earl of Orrery* (London, 1732), refers to the 'Club of Wits at *Christ-Church*' (p. 134). Lady Mary Wortley Montague knew of 'Atterbury and his club' (*Complete Letters*, 3 vols., ed. Robert Halsband (Oxford: Oxford University Press, 1965–7), vol. III, p. 58.
24 Kerby-Miller, in *The Memoirs of Martinus Scriblerus*, p. 267, notes that they were also 'friends and associates of most of the Scriblerus group'.

centre. Perhaps the clubs could be said to mark the rising social status of the writer, but not (by 1714 anyway) the shift from an aristocratic to a middle-class (or meritocratic) culture.

The coffee house and the 'public sphere'

Clubs sometimes met in private quarters, sometimes in a back room in public taverns and coffee houses. In part because of its prominence – and its idealisation – in the pages of contemporary periodicals, the coffee house early acquired and has long retained a reputation in literary history as the key site for cultural conversation and literary production in early eighteenth-century London. It was in coffee houses, so it is said, that *The Spectator* was read and poems written, critical judgements debated and reputations made. The first number of *The Tatler* in 1709 informed readers that its accounts of poetry would be reported from 'Will's Coffee-house', famous since the days of Dryden as the meeting place of wits. By 1713, according to *The Guardian*, Button's Coffee House was the preferred forum, made fashionable by Addison. Johnson passed on stories about Will's and Button's, and Macaulay gave a famous account of the coffee houses in his *History*, as places where people of all kinds gathered not only to drink coffee and to smoke but to discuss the news and the latest productions in polite letters. Beljame discussed them in similar terms, as did G. M. Trevelyan and Leslie Stephen in their widely read social histories of England. It was on Stephen and Trevelyan that Habermas, trained as a sociologist, relied in his influential argument about the coffee house and the 'public sphere' in his *Structural Transformation of the Public Sphere*. In his view it was in the first decades of the eighteenth century that a 'bourgeois public sphere' opened up in England, between the 'private realm' and the court-dominated 'sphere of public authority'. In the 'public sphere', a space not controlled by the state, took place critical debate, at first 'ignited by works of literature and art' but 'soon extended to include economic and political disputes'. The physical site of the public sphere, he claimed, was the coffee house, in which 'aristocratic society' and 'bourgeois intellectuals' could meet on equal terms. Social rank and status were disregarded: 'the authority of the better argument could assert itself against that of the social hierarchy and in the end could carry the day'.[25]

Since its translation into English in 1989 this argument has been widely cited, and its broad claims about the democratisation of the literary world in the early eighteenth century widely (although not universally) accepted. But a more careful reading of Habermas and more critical reading of contemporary

25 Habermas, *Structural Transformation of the Public Sphere*, pp. 32–6.

sources (which tend either to demonise or to idealise the coffee house)[26] suggests that his argument should be treated sceptically. To a large extent the 'public sphere', as he himself conceded, was less a social reality than an 'idea'. The world of the coffee house was in practice not a public site for rational debate. It was not open to women or servants. By the first decade of the eighteenth century it was less likely that a coffee house would be a meeting place for all kinds and ranks than a clubby place where one might meet one's own kind and hear only opinions that reassuringly echoed one's own. Some contemporary observers suggest, furthermore, that the typical coffee house club discussion was not free and open, but dominated by one figure who 'presided', settling any dispute, as Dryden was said to do at Will's. Pope's veiled account of Addison at Button's coffee house, where like Cato he 'gave his little Senate law'," and sat 'attentive to his own applause' ('Epistle to Dr Arbuthnot', lines 209–10), is echoed by Swift's account of 'Battus' (perhaps a caricature of Dryden), who in his elbow chair at the head of the table at Will's

> Gives judgement with decisive air
> To him the tribe of circling wits,
> As to an oracle submits.
> He gives directions to the town,
> To cry it up, or run it down.[27]

Such reports should be discounted as satiric exaggeration but are probably not fundamentally inaccurate. In the same poem Swift suggests that those wits who gathered at coffee houses collected scraps of literary rules and clichés, repeating what they read, and judging by rote. A 1714 play, anticipating Swift's sneer, laughed at 'the young scribblers of the times' who 'pay their attendance nightly' at Button's, 'to keep up their pretensions to sense and understanding'.[28]

Habermas argues that the new bourgeois public sphere appears after the Revolution of 1688 – after the lapse of the Licensing Act in 1695, after the aristocratic patron was replaced by the bookseller, after the theatre began to attract not simply courtiers but a broad audience, after the appearance of a 'reading public'. But, as Habermas knew, the coffee house was by 1714 a well-established social institution, first appearing in London in the 1650s. In

---

26 For information on coffee houses, see Bryant Lillywhite, *London Coffee Houses* (London: Allen & Unwin, 1963), and Henry B. Wheatley, *London, Past and Present*, 3 vols. (London: J. Murray, 1891).

27 'On Poetry: A Rhapsody', lines 282–6, in Jonathan Swift, *Complete Poems*, ed. Pat Rogers (London: Penguin, 1983), p. 529. Cf. the 'Authority' of Eubulus, in *Spectator* 49, in 'his little Diurnal Audience'.

28 Charles Gildon, *A New Rehearsal*, quoted in Wheatley, *London, Past and Present*, vol. 1, p. 316.

their early years, furthermore, coffee houses were controversial, giving rise to printed complaints – such as the *Maidens Complaint against Coffee, or The Coffee House Discovered* (1663), and the *Character of a Coffee House* (1673) – of unruly behaviour and licentious speech. The king's ministers were sufficiently concerned about the contentious if not actually seditious debate that coffee houses were ordered closed in 1675. (The order was quickly withdrawn, not because coffee houses were in fact orderly places but because it was clear that they could not be easily controlled.) When we recall the heated polemical atmosphere of the years from 1660 to 1685, in which the central matters of church and state – the succession to the throne, the relative claims of the Anglican, Roman and Dissenting churches – were angrily argued in print, in 'Remarks', 'Animadversions' and 'Answers', we should perhaps conclude the 'public sphere' of free, animated and adversarial debate was at its height in the Restoration years, and that it was superseded by a 'polite sphere' of cultural consensus-building, an invention of the early eighteenth century.

To be sure, the decade and a half after 1688 experienced the 'rage of party', as Whigs and Tories contested eleven general elections in fourteen years, and such writers as Defoe, Swift and Steele were engaged by the party leaders to advance their political agendas in the new partisan periodicals of the day, the Tory *Review* and *Examiner*, the Whig *Freeholder* and *Whig Examiner*, and others. Habermas, downplaying the role of the openly political periodicals, claims that literary debate in the coffee houses and in the pages of *The Spectator* was in effect a dry run for the free and open debate on political matters that soon became possible as the 'public sphere' gained strength. But some contemporary evidence suggests that rather than serving as a voice for opposition to the political authority of the crown and the aristocracy, *The Spectator* was designed in effect to defuse political tension. Johnson observes that the first of the *Spectator* papers 'shewed the [Whiggish] political tenets of its authors' (*Lives*, vol. II, p. 92), but adds that Addison soon announced he would avoid 'the outrages of a party' (No. 16) so as not to lose half of his potential readers. What is more, Addison seems to have regarded the essays as a way of diverting public attention not only from an eagerness for political 'news' but from political divisions altogether: 'Among those Advantages which the Publick may reap from this Paper, it . . . draws Mens Minds off from the Bitterness of Party, and furnishes them with Subjects of Discourse that may be treated without Warmth or Passion' (No. 262).[29] The evasion of party politics in Addison's

---

29 Cf. Johnson: the 'tendency' of *The Tatler* and *The Spectator* was to 'divert the attention of the people from publick discontent': 'to minds heated with political contest they supplied cooler and more inoffensive reflections' (*Lives*, vol. II, p. 94).

extraordinarily successful essays might mark them as subtly political after all in a broader sense – suppressing public debate in order to silence disruptive voices and buttress the status quo.[30]

Manuscript culture and print culture

By the time of *The Spectator* it is commonly assumed that Addison and other writers had become fully engaged in 'print culture' – that they reached a broad, diverse, and largely anonymous audience through the medium of print, legal copyright to their works passing into the hands of booksellers whose interests were increasingly commercial. A piece of writing, which once existed in a single copy in the hand of the author, now was reproduced as thousands of copies set in uniform print. In this view the writer, who could once count on an intimate relationship with a small circle of listeners and readers, was now gradually detached from a 'present and familiar audience'.[31] But early eighteenth-century writing shows that many authors cultivated a distinctive voice, and, whether or not they addressed a particular real reader (as Pope addresses Dr Arbuthnot), seemed to retain a strong sense of the presence of the imagined reader (as Gulliver addresses his 'gentle reader') who is rallied, instructed, rebuked or merely diverted. And further study has begun to show that the standard pictures of the author's social relationships in 'manuscript culture' and in 'print culture' need to be redrawn to fit historical circumstances.

The 'advent of print' (putatively located about 1700) did not suddenly transform the world of writing. During the Restoration a thriving print culture – of sermons, controversial prose and broadside ballads, of plays and poems, of the works of older authors such as Spenser and contemporaries such as Milton – coexisted with a culture in which poems – particularly satires and occasional verse – were distributed in manuscript. Copies of manuscripts, made by authors, collectors or professional scribes, circulated widely, often in linked groups, often acquiring annotation along the way. Sometimes sold, sometimes passed from friend to friend, many eventually made their way into print in unauthorised editions and were in the modern sense 'published'. But the copying of manuscripts, especially by professional scribes, was itself

30 Cf. Paula McDowell, *The Women of Grub Street* (Oxford: Oxford University Press, 1998), on Addisonian politeness as a means to 'delimit democracy' (p. 285), and Lawrence Klein, 'Coffeehouse Civility, 1660–1714', *Huntington Library Quarterly* 59 (1997), 31–51, on Addison's recasting of the coffee house as model of politeness.

31 Bertrand Bronson, 'Strange Relations: The Author and his Audience', in *Facets of the Enlightenment* (Berkeley: University of California Press, 1968), p. 299.

a kind of 'publication'. Scribes might produce multiple copies of transcribed texts, and sell them through booksellers whose stock-in-trade also included printed books. In such 'scribal communities', authors were joined not only with other authors but with readers and annotators, bound to each other by a steady exchange of manuscripts and the transmission of privileged information. Such literary exchange, Love suggests, was 'a mode of social bonding whose aim was to nourish and articulate a corporate ideology' that joined both allies and rival factions as members of a single Restoration elite and confirmed their authority to control affairs of state.[32] To exchange lampoons with an enemy is at the same time to recognise him as an equal. (A gentleman does not issue a challenge to an underling.) The stylised exchange of insults reflected a shared language that embodied a deeply cynical view of the fictions of monarchical legitimacy and aristocratic honour. Even if Robert Julian, who collected and sold manuscripts, was regarded (like the bookseller Edmund Curll a generation later) as an unscrupulous disseminator of scandal, he was a kind of coordinator of an aristocratic scribal community, 'Secretary to the Muses'.[33]

In the case of satirical poems the authors themselves typically made little effort to distribute their work or to see it into print. But in other cases authors working in manuscript culture sought access to a wide audience, or even to print. As Margaret Ezell notes, one typical pattern in the late seventeenth century was to write 'first for a select coterie audience and later for a commercial public'.[34] This was the case with several aristocratic women writers: the Duchess of Newcastle, Mary Lady Chudleigh and Anne Finch. Even Katherine Philips appeared in print in her lifetime. While she professed distress at the unauthorised publication of her *Poems* in 1664, she seems to have sought wider exposure by sending her poems to a noblewoman whom she did not know but hoped to draw into her 'Society'.[35]

Some enterprising promoters made the move from manuscript to print seem effortless. The *Gentleman's Journal* (1692–5), soliciting contributions from its polite readers, and deploying 'interactive genres' that invited readers to answer questions and solve poetic 'enigmas', in effect recreated in print a

---

32 Love, *Scribal Publication*, 180.
33 For Julian, see Brice Harris, 'Captain Robert Julian Secretary to the Muses', *ELH* 10 (1943), 294–309, and Love, *Scribal Publication*, pp. 249–67.
34 *The Poems and Prose of Mary, Lady Chudleigh*, ed. Margaret Ezell (Oxford: Oxford University Press, 1993), p. xxvi.
35 Peter Beal, *In Praise of Scribes* (Oxford: Oxford University Press, 1998), pp. 148–9.

private (though not elite) literary circle.[36] But the practice of circulating manuscripts continued, even on the part of authors who had already appeared in print.[37] As Pope was beginning his career, he circulated many of his poems in manuscript before he allowed them to be printed, perhaps reflecting youthful diffidence and Horatian patience ('Keep your piece nine years') as well as older ideas about the author as gentleman amateur who writes for himself and his friends: these appear prominently in the 'Preface' to his *Works* (1717). His *Pastorals*, written as early as 1704, were not printed until 1709. But a fair copy, in Pope's own hand, circulated among his friends. A satiric portrait of Addison written in 1716 and circulated in manuscript was not printed until 1735. Pope exchanged manuscript poems with a number of writers, typically enclosing them in letters, to William Walsh, for example, himself a late-Restoration gentleman author, or to Lady Mary Wortley Montagu, when she was sending back reports from her travels in Turkey. Pope's practice, which Ezell calls 'social authorship',[38] does not simply replicate that of Rochester, for Pope, though he liked to think of himself as a gentleman writer, was also a master of the new world of print. He published his poetic exchange with Anne Finch in his *Miscellany Poems on Several Occasions*, and his *Pastorals* were always destined for print. Even the holograph manuscript was carefully inscribed 'in common printing character', and 'beautifully formed, so as in all to imitate a printed book'.[39]

Once Pope's works were printed, he did not treat them as mere commodities, identical replicas that bore no marks of authorial presence. Although he generally avoided Dryden's practice of writing a formal 'epistle dedicatory', Pope inscribed many of his poems – the *Pastorals*, *Windsor-Forest*, *Rape of the Lock*, the translation of the *Iliad* – to distinguished friends. And like Dryden before him he deployed the subscription system so as to exchange compliments with his noble subscribers, supplying them with fine paper copies and printing their names as a sign of their distinction as well as his own.

Pope was one of the first fully successful 'professional' writers, but even after he made his writing the 'business' of his life, he remained a very skilled

---

36 See Margaret Ezell, 'The *Gentleman's Journal* and the Commercialization of Restoration Coterie Literary Practices', *Modern Philology* 89 (1991–2), 323–40.

37 Jane Barker, who appeared in print in 1688, later assembled a manuscript collection for private circulation.

38 Margaret Ezell, *Social Authorship and the Advent of Print* (Baltimore, MD: Johns Hopkins University Press, 1999), pp. 61–83.

39 Jonathan Richardson, quoted in Alexander Pope, *Works*, ed. Whitwell Elwin and J. W. Courthope, 10 vols. (London: J. Murray, 1871–9), vol. I, p. 239.

manipulator and beneficiary of the system of literary patronage that had largely funded writing throughout the Restoration. Although many literary histori-ans followed Beljame in declaring that by Pope's day private patronage by 'the great' had largely ceased, more careful study of the circumstances of literary production, of the complete texts of eighteenth-century printed works, which commonly include a dedication and/or an address to the reader, and of the language of dedications themselves, demonstrates that the patronage system remained in place until the end of the eighteenth century, binding many if not most authors to patrons in a complex cultural economy, through which certain clearly understood benefits were exchanged.[40] From the patron came not only cash payments, but 'encouragement', 'protection', 'favour' and the stamp of cultural 'authority'. Valuable invitations might in turn lead to 'intro-ductions' to people of influence, and to other invitations by potential patrons, perhaps to an annual pension, or a place as his lordship's private secretary, chaplain or rector of the local parish church. In exchange the author-client offers a kind of symbolic 'property' in the dedicated work, and an array of services, from mere entertainment to editorial tasks and the composition of commissioned works, to the drafting of political pamphlets. Less material, but no less important, a poet in Pope's day might help secure for a patron (as Pope did for Lord Burlington) a reputation for 'magnificence', might confirm a patron's cultural authority and might succeed in making the patron's name live on long after his death. In such a literary system authors and patrons are closely and symbiotically bound.

But authors in Pope's day – and in Dryden's day, for that matter – need not be regarded as mere flatterers, panders or (as Pope called Horace), 'court slaves'. Not only did they receive clearly understood benefits, they also found means to resist the cultural authority of patrons and to assert their own counter-claims. Close reading of Dryden's dedications to Rochester, Mulgrave, and Dorset typically reveals a proud man of letters who carefully circumscribes the patron's role and lays claims to his own 'rights' and his own share of praise: ''Tis my praise', Dryden says to his honoured kinsman, 'to make thy Praises last.' A generation later Pope remained a beneficiary of the patronage system. Though he preferred to promote an image of himself as an independent man of letters ('No Man's Heir, or Slave'), Pope, as Johnson noted, 'seems to have wanted neither diligence nor success in attracting the notice of the great'.[41] Like Dryden he contrived ways to resist the authority of the very patrons whose favour he

40 For an elaboration of this argument, see Dustin Griffin, *Literary Patronage in England, 1650–1800* (Cambridge: Cambridge University Press, 1996).
41 Johnson, *Lives*, vol. III, p. 90.

successfully sought, typically converting great men into his 'friends'. But Pope's example did not establish the freedom of the 'independent' man of letters. No other self-made writer in the century enjoyed Pope's financial success. His extraordinary achievement depended upon his genius, indefatigable industry and unique ability to manipulate traditional patrons, the subscription system, and the emerging literary marketplace.

Pope may serve as an appropriate figure with whom to conclude a survey of the writer's social world. Deeply enmeshed in extensive social and political networks which gave shape to his career and inspired most of his poems, Pope managed to extricate himself from those social circumstances in a process that might be described, in words borrowed from Johnson, as the 'predominance of genius'.[42] *Windsor-Forest*, for example, promotes the interests of Pope's political friends, and was indeed, as he says, virtually demanded of him: '*Granville* commands . . . / What Muse for *Granville* can refuse to sing?' (lines 5–6). But for all his poem's celebration of the Tory Peace of Utrecht Pope distances himself – quite literally – from the world of the court and the nascent emporium of 'Albion's Golden Day', repeatedly retiring or retreating into 'sylvan shades'; conveys misgivings about the expense of blood (whether in sylvan war or in imperial combat); and hints that his own poetic future will lie in some direction other than that prescribed by his powerful friends. Pope converts the ostensible occasion for the poem – the imminent signing of the Peace – into an occasion for announcing his own literary programme, closing with lines that signal the Virgilian career – from pastoral to Georgic to yet higher modes – to which he aspires. By the same token, *The Rape of the Lock*, commonly regarded as a quintessentially social poem, contains within it something quite different. The poem's occasion, we usually say, is the dispute between two families in Pope's largely Roman Catholic social circle near Binfield, and its purpose, so Pope himself said, was to heal that breach: 'A common acquaintance and well-wisher to both [John Caryll], desired me to write a poem to make a jest of it, and laugh them together again.'[43] But in fact Pope himself knew the families only slightly, and readers of the poem have long noticed the satire that shades whatever good-humoured effort at reconciliation the poem contains. Pope's poem is famously ambiguous, prompting debate even about the function of Clarissa (the poem's apparent mouthpiece). The conclusion – in which Belinda's lock

---

42 *Ibid.*, vol. III, p. 243.
43 Spence, *Observations, Anecdotes, and Characters of Books and Men*, vol. I, p. 44. Pope's account of the poem is given prominence by the Twickenham editors, who print it in the first paragraph of the editorial introduction (*Poems of Alexander Pope*, 11 vols., ed. John Butt *et al.* (New Haven, CT: Yale University Press, 1938–68), vol. II, p. 81).

is lost to all but 'quick poetic eyes', and in which what shall be 'consecrate[d] to Fame' is *'This Lock'* – not only Belinda's curl but also the poem itself, this very *Lock* – suggests that Pope's primary interest is to launch himself into a public career of delicate satire and mock-heroic. Many critics now read the poem for its sexual politics but we can also read it for what it has to say about Alexander Pope and the power of poetry.

Popular entertainment and instruction, literary and dramatic: chapbooks, advice books, almanacs, ballads, farces, pantomimes, prints and shows

LANCE BERTELSEN

At the chaotic intersection of English popular and print cultures stands Hogarth's magnificent female hawker, anchoring *The Idle 'Prentice Executed at Tyburn* (1747), the eleventh plate of a didactic moral history engraved in a consciously unpolished style and priced to appeal to an apprentice class at the crossroads of virtue and pleasure:

> The Effects of Industry & Idleness Exemplified in the Conduct of two fellow prentices in twelve points Where calculated for the use & instruction of those young people wherein every thing nescessary to be convey'd to them is fully described in words as well as figure . . . [E]very thing necessary to be known was to be made as inteligible as possible and as fine engraving was not necessary to the main design provided that which is infinitely more material viz the characters and Expressions were well preservend, the purchase of them became within the reach of those for whom they [were] cheifly intended.[1]

In this description, written in 1763, Hogarth fairly sums up the complex of instruction, entertainment, ostensible simplicity and affordable prices that had characterised the production and marketing of popular literature and drama for the previous hundred years. Of course, simplicity of intention in no way guaranteed simplicity of result, and in the hawker and her surroundings we find the abundant paradoxes linking official or commercial productions and popular responses to them: a legal demonstration of terror and control results in a chaotic festival fuelled by irreverence and gin; a printed 'Last Dying Speech' makes a marketable celebrity of a condemned man who has yet to

---

1 William Hogarth, 'Autobiographical Notes', *The Analysis of Beauty*, ed. Joseph Burke (Oxford: Clarendon Press, 1955), p. 225.

The IDLE 'PRENTICE Executed at Tyburn.

Proverbs Chap. 1. Ver. 27, 28.
When fear cometh as desolation, and their
destruction cometh as a Whirlwind; when
distress cometh upon them, then they shall
call upon God, but he will not answer.

Plate 11

Fig. 3.1 The Idle 'Prentice Executed at Tyburn by William Hogarth (1747)

speak; a ragged, dirty female carrying a child at the periphery of the crowd becomes a central symbol for popular print culture as she cries a minatory publication she probably cannot read to a socially mixed audience who will buy it more for entertainment than instruction. And the engraving in which all these phenomena occur exudes an energy and edginess that nearly obliterates its intended moral suasion.

Such are the paradoxes of popular art in a society whose popular culture was so deeply intermeshed with an emergent middle class and an expropriating elite as to make drawing of distinct lines of aesthetic or material demarcation virtually impossible. Hogarth's *Industry and Idleness* was 'cheifly' intended for apprentices, but everybody bought it; chapbooks designed for the poor were routinely read to or by well-to-do children; 'traditional' ballads were made new with topical lyrics and hummed in the streets by all classes; original plays from licensed theatres quickly found their way in modified form to theatrical booths at the fairs; popular literature provided the basis and subject matter for the greatest of elite literary satires.

Because of such crossing patterns of influence and usage, eighteenth-century English 'popular culture' itself remains a concept without precise definition. One view has set the 'little tradition' of popular culture against the 'great tradition' of elite learning and art, and while acknowledging significant interaction between the two traditions nevertheless argues for something close to the complete disengagement of popular and polite by 1800. More complex models have stressed lines of continuity and interaction between the two traditions in particular activities and beliefs (denominational religious customs, for example), but complete separation in other venues and practices. A 'pluralist' approach has called the entire category of 'popular culture' into question, arguing that there are many popular cultures in shifting and ambiguous relationship to each other and to a variegated elite culture. This kind of non-categorical approach becomes even more compelling in addressing the cultures of eighteenth-century England, when commerce was transforming the traditional relationship of 'high' and 'low' and producing a commercialised 'popular culture' that was particularly strong in London. As the eighteenth century progressed, hybrid commercialised culture spread its influence over an extraordinary efflorescence of new roads into the smallest rural hamlets; and on these roads travelled, as they had for centuries, chapmen carrying goods and news to the hinterlands. From the late seventeenth century, they also carried one of the more truly 'popular' commercial print items: small books written, printed and priced to appeal specifically to poor, uneducated people.

Together with cloth, ribbon, thread, needles and other small household items carried by chapmen, chapbooks – as they would come to be called in the nineteenth century – provided isolated villages and farm communities throughout England with one of their strongest material and textual links to the manufactures, practices and ideas of the larger world. Reviving a tradition of jestbooks, ballads and popular entertainments that had been partially suppressed during the Commonwealth, eight-, twelve- or twenty four-page chapbooks, usually sold uncut and unstitched for a penny, flooded the popular market for literature during the Restoration and eighteenth century. By 1700, it is estimated that there were 10,000 chapmen in England, carrying something like half a dozen chapbooks, along with a few larger books at three and nine pence, among the various manufactured articles in their packs.[2] Chapmen themselves had long been part of the popular entertainment industry, adept at telling stories, spreading gossip and news, regaling potential customers with tales of life on the road. In the chapbook this oral tradition became a kind of 'printed folklore', textualised in the form of small, illustrated books, whose subject matter included songs, fairy tales, chivalric romances, crime, executions, prophecies, bawdy jokes, supernatural events, travel, adventure, religion and advice. Although exact figures for chapbooks do not exist for the late seventeenth century, another popular form, almanacs, were printed at the rate of 400,000 annually throughout the 1660s and sales continued at one third of a million copies per year throughout the eighteenth century.[3] The chief printers of chapbooks in the eighteenth century, William Dicey and his son Cluer, produced over 150 chapbook titles by themselves and it is estimated that in the eighteenth and nineteenth centuries there were over 250 printers of chapbooks in London and another 140 in the provinces.[4]

Chapbook literature resists easy summary. Perhaps the largest percentage of titles were prose and metrical chivalric romances, folk tales and fairy stories filled with adventure, travel and heroic deeds. Many were shorter versions of the sixpenny and shilling romances bought by more prosperous readers. The story of Guy of Warwick, the archetype of chapbook heroes, appears in

2 Margaret Spufford, *Small Books and Pleasant Histories* (London: Methuen & Co, 1981), pp. 115–19; Susan Pedersen, 'Hannah More Meets Simple Simon: Tracts, Chapbooks, and Popular Culture in Late Eighteenth-Century England', *Journal of British Studies* 25 (1986), 98.

3 Bernard Capp, *English Almanacs 1500–1800: Astrology and the Popular Press* (Ithaca, NY: Cornell University Press, 1979), pp. 281–83; Leslie Shepard, *The History of Street Literature* (Newton Abbot: David & Charles, 1973), pp. 26–8.

4 Victor E. Neuburg, *The Penny Histories* (London: Oxford University Press, 1968), p. 27.

both prose and verse chapbooks skilfully abridged from longer works that form a rich narrative tradition stretching back to the first half of the thirteenth century. A quintessential English hero, Guy demonstrates that the disadvantage of birth can be overcome by merit as he wins fair Phillis and rises to an earldom despite being 'meanly born'.[5] His adventures on the Continent and in the Holy Land provide a model of how English virtue will triumph over the chicanery of foreigners and perhaps exemplifies the role of chapbooks in disseminating to the poor the growing sense of nationhood as a shared set of cultural and political values that characterises higher political discourse of the period. Other English favourites such as 'Jack the Giant Killer', 'Robin Hood' and 'Dick Whittington and his Cat' also featured witty and cunning heroes, sometimes of humble origin, who were sympathetic to the poor, irreverent to the powerful and quick to take advantage of opportunities to thrive. Modern anti-establishment types from current novels found their way into chapbooks as well: both *Moll Flanders* and *Robinson Crusoe* were crudely adapted to the abbreviated format.[6]

Songbooks probably formed the second largest category of chapbooks. Dance, drink, sex and general enjoyment of life were their primary subjects, without explicit political content except occasional anti-French sentiment. Here again irreverence and merriment take on implicit socio-political overtones as the poor eschew the hard work advocated by the great for a life of ease and irresponsibility. In *The Author's Farce* (1730), Henry Fielding would summarise this tendency in a song written about the 'Jolly Nobody', a traditional representation of the underclasses and a potentially subversive nonconformist, who 'does nothing at all / But eat and snore / And drink and roar, / From whore to the tavern / From tavern to whore'.[7] The roaring intensifies in chapbooks containing jokes, riddles and humorous tales – exemplified by *Joe Miller's Jests* (1739), a work which appeared in both chapbook and larger formats. Descending from the earliest English jestbooks, the *Hundred Merrie Tales* (1526) and *Tales and Quicke Answers* (c. 1535), and more immediately from *Pinkethman's Jests* (1720) and *Polly Peachum's Jests* (1728), *Joe Miller's Jests* went through dozens of editions, adding or updating jokes in accordance with what James Osborn

---

5 John Simons (ed.), *Guy of Warwick and Other Chapbook Romances* (Exeter: University of Exeter Press, 1998), pp. 19–21, 55.
6 Pat Rogers, *Literature and Popular Culture in Eighteenth-Century England* (Brighton, Sussex: The Harvester Press, 1986), pp. 168–97.
7 Henry Fielding, *The Author's Farce*, ed. Charles B. Woods (Lincoln, NE: University of Nebraska Press, 1966), pp. 52–3.

formulated as 'Joe Miller's Law': 'that a good name (of a well-known person-ality, living or dead) tends to replace a less known one'.[8] Combining topicality, irreverence and merriment, jestbooks throughout the century tailored their titles and contents to the latest cause célèbre. Thus the witty, rebellious John Wilkes became the folk hero of *Wilkes' Jest Book; or the Merry Patriot* (1770); and, much to the delight of tavern-keepers, provided an excuse to get drunk as often as possible: 'for whenever any prosperous event happened to him, their customers got merry for *Joy*; – and when ever it happened otherwise, they have got drunk thro' *Vexation*'.[9] Wilkes' well-known cheekiness and trickery must have seemed a political manifestation of the craftiness of the maidservants, apprentices and other disenfranchised folk who used their wits against the great in chapbook after chapbook; simultaneously, however, the propensity to attribute proverbial wit and tricks to famous people may have affected the development of modern biography as a kind of 'wit and wisdom' repository. Filled with jests, bons mots and devastating rejoinders, Boswell's *Life of Johnson* (1791) has been called by Ronald Paulson, 'the ultimate jestbook'.[10]

A motley combination of history, biography, crime stories, supernatural events, religious tales and moral advice rounds out the subjects of chapbook literature. History and biography encompassed various eras and venues, with speeches by Wilkes jostling lives of Elizabeth and tales of famous shipwrecks abutting descriptions of feral children. Crime stories tended to the sensational and morbid, sharing these characteristics, interestingly, with religious books: both included deathbed conversions, remarkable visions and morbid descrip-tions of everlasting torment. But very few early religious accounts feature the kinds of prosaic Christian lives that characterised the morally responsible, if dull, innovations of the 'Cheap Repository of Moral and Religious Tracts' (1795), a collection specifically designed to counteract the subversive implica-tions of traditional chapbooks. Conceptualised by Hannah More (who also wrote most of the tracts), promoted by Horace Walpole and supported by prominent Evangelicals, the 'Cheap Repository' distributed its publications gratis to the rural poor, hawkers, Sunday schools and charity children. The idea was to reform both the morals and the politics of the poor by offering an alternative to 'indecent' popular literature in the form of tales and poems in which the bad or rebellious are inevitably punished, traditional penny literature

8 Joseph Spence, *Observations, Anecdotes, and Characters of Books and Men, Collected from Conversation*, ed. James M. Osborn, 2 vols. (Oxford: Clarendon Press, 1966), vol. I, p. xxxii.
9 *Wilkes' Jest Book; or the Merry Patriot* (London, 1770), pp. 6–7.
10 Ronald Paulson, *Popular and Polite Art in the Age of Hogarth and Fielding* (Notre Dame, IN: University of Notre Dame Press, 1979), pp. 64–84.

shunned and Christian family life extolled. As in More's verse tale of 'Patient Joe,' cheerful contentment with one's economic and social lot was the primary virtue:

> In trouble he bow'd him to God's holy will;
> How contented was Joseph when matters went ill!
> When rich and when poor he alike understood
> That all things together were working for good.[11]

Such insistent complacency helps contextualise William Blake's imaginative flights and acid parodies in *Songs of Innocence and of Experience* (1789), which in part represent responses to earlier 'improving' literature for children and the poor. Isaac Watts' *Divine Songs Attempted in easy Language, for the Use of Children* (1715) – expanded and reprinted throughout the eighteenth century – was perhaps the most influential of these works.[12] In a representative example, Watts preached 'Against Lying' in easy-to-read rhymes about universal surveillance and eternal punishment:

> Then let me always watch my Lips,
> Lest I be struck to Death and Hell,
> Since God a Book of Reckoning keeps
> For ev'ry Lye that Children tell.[13]

But children's books, a genre redefined by the writer, printer and bookseller, John Newbery, were not always so frighteningly moralistic. Newbery's first children's publication, *A Little Pretty Pocketbook* (1744), was 'intended for the Instruction and Amusement of little Master Tommy and pretty Miss Polly; with an agreeable Letter to each from *Jack the Giant Killer*; as also a Ball and Pincushion, the Use of which will infallibly make Tommy a good Boy and Polly a good Girl'.[14] The playful, almost ironic tone ('infallibly') is typical of Newbery, a marketing genius who included a ball and pincushion with the book for an extra two pence. By the time of his death in 1767, Newbery had recreated children's literature and produced at least one classic, the *History of Little Goody Two-Shoes* (1765). His books, however, typify the problem of defining 'popular

---

11 [Hannah More], 'Patient Joe: Or, the Newcastle Collier', *Cheap Repository Shorter Tracts* (London, 1798), p. 387.

12 M. F. Thwaite, *From Primer to Pleasure* (London: The Library Association, 1963), pp. 52–4; Heather Glen, *Vision and Disenchantment: Blake's 'Songs' and Wordsworth's 'Lyrical Ballads'* (Cambridge: Cambridge University Press, 1983), pp. 8–32.

13 Isaac Watts, *Divine Songs Attempted in easy Language, for the Use of Children*, 13th edn (London, 1735), pp. 22–3; my thanks to Andrew Cooper for this reference.

14 John Newbery, *A Little Pretty PocketBook*, ed. M. F. Thwaite (New York: Harcourt, Brace & World, 1967), pp. 2–4, 53.

literature', since they were beautifully produced and comparatively expensive at 6d. Nevertheless, as the century progressed, children's books became less expensive, and by 1800 they were widely available in one penny and half-penny versions – prices affordable to all but the poorest labourer.[15]

At the same time, many presumably 'adult' chapbooks seem to have been considered (at least in non-Evangelical quarters) appropriate reading for well-to-do children. James Boswell summarised this interesting intersection during a visit to 'the old printing-office in Bow Churchyard kept by Dicey' in 1763:

> There are ushered into the world of literature *Jack and the Giants*, *The Seven Wise Men of Gotham*, and other story-books which in my dawning years amused me as much as *Rasselas* does now. I saw the whole scheme with a kind of pleasing romantic feeling to find myself really where all my old darlings were printed. I bought two dozen of the story-books and had them bound up with this title, *Curious Productions*.

Boswell's inscription in *Curious Productions* further conflates 'story-books' (for children) and the adult popular culture from which they derive:

> I shall certainly some time or other write a little story-book in the style of these. It will not be a very easy task for me; it will require much nature and simplicity and a great acquaintance with the humours and traditions of the English common people. I shall be happy to succeed, for he who pleases children will be remembered with pleasure by men.[16]

The imbrication of popular adult and children's literature in eighteenth-century England seems unconsciously memorialised by a popular culture that in the succeeding two hundred years has made bastardised versions of *Gulliver's Travels* and *Robinson Crusoe* by far the most well-known works of the period – works considered by the general public primarily as children's tales.[17] In the eighteenth century, then, significant literary figures who contributed to the development of children's literature might include Daniel Defoe and Jonathan Swift, as well as Newbery's son-in-law Christopher Smart, who in 1768 published *Parables of Our Lord and Saviour Jesus Christ. Done into familiar verse, with occasional applications, for the use and improvement of younger minds* and William Blake, who in 1793 produced *For Children: The Gates of Paradise*.

15 J. H. Plumb, 'The Commercialization of Leisure in Eighteenth-Century England', in Neil McKendrick, John Brewer, J. H. Plumb (eds.), *The Birth of a Consumer Society* (Bloomington, IN: Indiana University Press, 1982), pp. 272–3, 301–6.

16 James Boswell, *Boswell's London Journal 1762–1763*, ed. Frederick Pottle (New York: McGraw-Hill, 1950), p. 299.

17 F. J. Harvey Darton, *Children's Books in England* (Cambridge: Cambridge University Press, 1932), pp. 106–7.

Children were also addressed in the ubiquitous advice and conduct books that since the early seventeenth century had attempted to teach readers of all classes their relative duties to each other, as well as more specific skills. In the late seventeenth century, for example, the prolific Hannah Wolley produced *The Gentlewoman's Companion: or, A Guide to the Female Sex Containing Directions of Behaviour, in All Places, Companies, relations and Conditions, from their Childhood Down to Old Age* (1675), a multi-subject volume which offered not only guidance in social behaviour, but also medical advice (bad breath, sore breasts) and recipes from 'Artichoaks Stewed' to 'Warden-Tarts'. Somewhat down the social scale, Wolley's *The Compleat Servant-Maid; or The Young Maiden's Tutor* taught women how to qualify for the positions of 'Waiting-Woman; Nursery-Maid; House-Keeper; Dairy-Maid; Chamber-Maid; Laundry-Maid; Cook-Maid; House-maid; Under-Cook-Maid; Scullery-Maid' in a complete hierarchy of domestic service. The most widely read domestic conduct book was *The Whole Duty of Man, laid down in a Plain and Familiar Way for the Use of All, but especially the Meanest Reader*, with over twenty-five editions between 1653 and 1797. Intended to provide guidance in the moral and social relations for the entire family, *The Whole Duty of Man* spawned numerous imitations and variations, including Daniel Defoe's religiously oriented *Family Instructor* (1715).

Advice books teaching specific skills ranged from cookbooks to 'letter-writers'. John Hill's highly successful *The Young Secretary's Guide* (1687), like most other letter-writers, included information about forms of salutation, superscription, spelling and other technical matters. But the period's most famous collection of model letters, Samuel Richardson's *Letters Written to and for Particular Friends, on the Most Important Occasions* (1741) – commonly known as *Familiar Letters* – ignored technical advice altogether, focusing instead on moral issues in model letters that addressed subjects more typical of domestic conduct books: duties of wife to husband, duties of parent to children, duties of children to parents, duties of masters and mistresses to servants, duties of servants.[18] Richardson's first novel, *Pamela* (1740), elaborated these issues in integrated fictional form and in particular seemed to offer a dramatic response to one of the central questions of eighteenth-century class and gender relations: 'How is an innocent servant girl to act when her wicked master decides it is his right to seduce her?'[19] This and other questions dealing with proper

---

18 Katherine Hornbeck, 'Richardson's *Familiar Letters* and the Domestic Conduct Books', *Smith College Studies in Modern Languages* 19. 2 (January 1938), 1–29.

19 J. Paul Hunter, *Before Novels: The Cultural Contexts of Eighteenth-Century Fiction* (New York: W. W. Norton, 1990), p. 94.

female responses to various social and emotional circumstances were to have a determining effect on the development of both the domestic conduct book and the novel.

From the turn of the century onward, women's conduct books outnumbered conduct books for men, and the changing subject matter and ideology of such books – abstract virtue on the ascendant; cookery and livestock management dwindling – contributed to establishing the norms of middle-class female behaviour dramatised in 'domestic fiction'.[20] As domestic ideology designated women the 'natural' managers of family life, it also expanded their role in managing and reforming servants, creating new class-based tensions within the household. Simultaneously exploitative and exploitable, the touchy dynamic of domestic service was addressed in many conduct books, ambiguously considered by Swift in 'Directions to Servants', and given material form in the simultaneously regulatory and voyeuristic practice of the Fieldings' Universal Register Office, a combination of labour exchange, travel agency and information office.[21] On the men's side, advice books for apprentices were common, and included Richardson's earliest publication, *The Apprentice's 'Vade Mecum': or, Young Man's Pocket-Companion* (1734). The genre of apprentice's guide achieved a remarkable graphic manifestation in Hogarth's *Industry and Idleness*, an engraved series that not only served 'for the use & instruction of those young people' but offered a visual record of a range of popular materials and entertainments: broadsides titled *Whittington Ld Mayor* and *The London Prentice*, a ballad based on *Moll Flanders*, two copies of *The Prentices Guide*, a *London Almanack*, signboards, drummers, fiddlers, butchers playing marrow bones and cleavers, a legless hawker crying *Jesse or the Happy Pair. A New Song*, a Tyburn hanging, the Lord Mayor's procession, and the female hawker crying *The last dying Speech & Confession of Tho Idle*.

In terms of number alone, two of the above products, almanacs and broadsides, dominated Restoration and eighteenth-century popular literature. Almanacs were purchased in extraordinary numbers (400,000 annually in the late seventeenth century) by all levels of society, and a remarkable number survive in the libraries of the gentry and professional classes, sometimes embellished with the handwritten annotations of their owners.[22] Broadsides,

---

20 Nancy Armstrong, *Desire and Domestic Fiction: A Political History of the Novel* (Oxford: Oxford University Press, 1987), pp. 59–95.
21 On the Universal Register Office, see Lance Bertelsen, *Henry Fielding at Work: Magistrate, Businessman, Writer* (New York: Palgrave, 2000), pp. 35–59.
22 Capp, *English Almanacs*, p. 60.

whether in prose or ballad form, were the earliest 'newspapers': print vehicles for political proclamations, current sensations, up-to-date advertisements, newest songs and latest protests, as well as more traditional humorous, religious and romantic subjects.

Although almanacs were first of all practical documents providing readers with a monthly calendar and important anniversaries for the coming year, more idiosyncratic and 'literary' qualities could be found in the 'Observations' for a given month, which could include pointed commentary of a political, astrological or meteorological nature printed alongside the calendar itself. For almanacs with a strongly astrological emphasis, such as Francis Moore's *Vox Stellarum* or John Partridge's *Merlinus Liberatus*, prognostication (and thus entertainment) became a primary feature, and elaborate planetary bunkum served to underwrite rather generalised predictions concerning the rise and fall of nations and great men. Predictably, occult excesses produced attacks by anti-astrological almanacs, some of which substituted instruction for star-gazing. Yet, as Linda Colley has suggested, astrological almanacs could provide their own form of instruction, particularly in matters of national history and identity. Although emphasising the future, their 'Observations' constantly referred to the past, listing historical events on specific dates, offering retrospective analysis of the effect of the stars on recent history, and perhaps constituting 'the only history lesson the majority of Britons received'.[23] All of these practices are invoked in the most celebrated episode of literary history involving almanacs: Jonathan Swift's premature burial of John Partridge in *The Bickerstaff Papers* (1708–9). Swift's parody not only assumes that readers of all social levels will recognise the conventions of the almanac writing, but points up the strict control exercised over the lucrative almanac trade by the Stationers' Company. Since 1603, the Company had possessed exclusive rights to license almanacs and to eliminate almanac-makers of whom it disapproved: Partridge's fictional 'death' happened to coincide with the discontinuation of Partridge's almanac from 1710 to 1713 because of a dispute with the Stationers' Company. Thus was born the legend that Swift had killed off the astrologer not only fictionally but professionally. In fact, Partridge was back in business by 1713 and continued to publish almanacs until his irrefutable death in 1715.

If almanacs dealt most insistently with the future and the past, the broadside was the literary vehicle of choice for engaging the present. The typical

---

23 Linda Colley, *Britons: Forging the Nation 1707–1837* (New Haven, CT: Yale University Press, 1992), p. 22.

broadside of the Restoration and eighteenth century was a folio sheet of heavy paper printed on one side with verse, prose, illustrations or a mixture of the three.[24] In their earliest form, broadsides carried official proclamations and were posted in public places to inform the populace of new acts, battles, peace treaties and other political phenomena. They also were used to advertise lotteries, goods (including printed goods) and services. But by far the most popular form of broadsides were half-penny and penny broadside ballads. These too were often stuck up on walls, both indoors and outdoors. Joseph Addison, describing country public houses in *The Spectator* No. 85 (7 June 1711), found them rich in printed matter:

> when I enter any House in the Country . . . I cannot for my Heart leave a Room before I have thoroughly studied the Walls of it, and examined the several printed Papers which are usually pasted upon them. The last Piece that I met with upon his Occasion, gave me the most exquisite Pleasure . . . [It] was the old Ballad of the *Two Children in the Wood*, which is one of the Darling Songs of the Common People, and has been the Delight of most *Englishmen* in some Part of their Age.[25]

Such 'printed Papers' provided pleasure not only textually but visually, since they were usually adorned with generalised woodcuts (ships, trees, Britannia) appropriate to their subject.

Yet to think of broadside ballads as conveying primarily traditional content would be to neglect their highly topical nature. For old tunes were incessantly being re-fitted with new words and pictures to form what Leslie Shepard calls 'a kind of musical journalism, the forerunner of popular prose newspapers, and a continuation of the folk tradition of minstrelsy'.[26] This evocative mixture of the familiar and the new is adumbrated in the phrase 'sung to the tune of . . .' which served in lieu of expensive musical notation. Within this interactive complex, new material (and updated versions of old material), like the predictions and historical observations of the almanacs, looked simultaneously forwards and backwards, promising novelty, but novelty made understandable and acceptable through familiar forms and cultural references.

The significant role of women in producing, disseminating and performing broadsides and ballads underwrites the period's tendency metaphorically to identify popular literary forms with marginal cultural figures. Although in the latter seventeenth century the ballad market was dominated by male producers

24 Dianne Dugaw, *Warrior Women and Popular Balladry, 1650–1850* (Cambridge: Cambridge University Press, 1989), p. 16.
25 *The Spectator*, ed. Donald Bond, 5 vols. (Oxford: Clarendon Press, 1965), vol. 1, pp. 361–2.
26 Shepard, *Street Literature*, p. 21.

such as Francis Coles, Thomas Vere, John Wright, William Thackeray – and in
the eighteenth century by William Dicey and John Marshall (both prodigious
publishers of chapbooks as well) – the female ballad monger and broadside
hawker was (materially and symbolically) central to the trade, a phenomenon
brilliantly imaged by William Hogarth in the hawker and child at the centre of
the Tyburn scene from *Industry and Idleness*. The hawker's squalor, maternity
and open-mouthed bawl encapsulate the view of popular literature as a matrix
of filth, procreation and noise most remarkably textualised by Alexander Pope
in *The Dunciad*. But it also points towards the reality of life for hawkers and
ballad singers, who were often illiterate, homeless women (in 1701 Esther
Haggart listed her address as 'the gravel pitts in old So-hoe'), raising children
alone.[27] In these women and their male counterparts, oral performance and
textual production intersected in the socio-cultural environment of the street:
popular broadsides, like printed ballads, inscribed showmanship into the literary medium – a medium that was then, paradoxically, once again cried by
poor men and women in the open air. Not surprisingly, the authors of street
literature often attempted to convey in their work the textures of oral transmission and memory. The polemicist and print worker Elinor James, for example,
tailored her radical, prayer-laden broadsides to an audience accustomed to
political commentary and story-telling characterised by repetition, digression
and personal subjective intrusions. Nor was James averse to advertising herself
by name as the author of distinctly underclass religious and political opinions
on major national events including the Exclusion Crisis, the 1688 Revolution
and the Accession of George I. In the postscript to *Elinor James's Advice to the
King and Parliament* (1715), for example, she managed both a nod to the new
king and a rather deeper bow to her more usual audience: 'and so the Lord
guide and direct King George that came from *Hanover*. My Heart is in great
Heaviness for the helpless Poor for fear they should want, and their Cries come
up to Heaven for Justice, which the Lord prevent'.

The majority of broadsides and ballads were, of course, not as personal or
polemical as Elinor James'. They covered everything from the latest London
freaks to political demonstrations to upcoming hangings, and they, in common
with much pamphlet literature, were often directly, even physically, linked
to the various 'shows' of London. In a typical example, Hogarth's hawker
cries *The last dying Speech & Confession of Tho Idle* in the middle of a crowd
generated by a hanging 'match' at Tyburn – a particularly fruitful arena for the

---

27 Paula McDowell, *The Women of Grub Street: Press, Politics, and Gender in the London Literary
Marketplace 1678–1730* (Oxford: Clarendon Press, 1998), pp. 26, 58–62.

cross-fertilisation of text and performance. What Peter Linebaugh calls 'the classic and most massive presence of the eighteenth-century working class, the Tyburn hanging' generated preliminary publicity in the form of criminal speeches, confessions, biographies and ballads which in turn assured large turn-outs for the events and a ready assembled market for further literary selling. Having read or heard a fictional last dying speech or ballad or short biography of the condemned, the London populace could then experience the real thing in what must have been an excruciatingly tense moment of public theatre. The condemned themselves rode through the streets with much fanfare and were allowed to speak from the gallows – although the publication of their actual words in the Ordinary of Newgate's *Account* was sometimes prevented, especially if they dealt with such touchy subjects as the Hanoverian Succession, the sanctity of private property, the sovereignty of money or acceptable norms of sexual conduct.[28] All of these events were grist for the popular press and, given an extraordinary criminal subject like Jack Sheppard or Jonathan Wild, could generate an extended and various body of work encompassing almost all popular genres and extending to more sophisticated spin-offs in the form of novels (*Moll Flanders*, *Jonathan Wild*) and plays (*The Beggar's Opera*).

One such spin-off, John Gay's *The Beggar's Opera* (1728), offers a dazzling parodic anatomy of the subjects, genres and practices of eighteenth-century popular literature and performance. The play itself is embedded in the world of the poor and a ballad industry that both supports and caters to it. Intro-duced by a 'Beggar' who has 'a small yearly salary for [his] catches', it was, we are told, 'originally writ for the celebrating the marriage of James Chanter and Moll Lay, two most excellent ballad-singers'.[29] In writing new lyrics to the melodies of traditional folk and street ballads, Gay followed (though with spectacular wit and invention) the ballad writer's practice of creating topical lyrics 'to be sung to the tune of . . .' In making his hero the gallant highway-man Macheath, Gay engaged one of the favourite topics of street ballads, the extraordinary criminal. His tongue-in-cheek heroicising of Macheath's exploits in crime and love re-enacts the popular mythologising, in broadsides and pam-phlets, inspired by the escapes and romances of actual criminals. The most inspirational criminal of all in the 1720s was the protean Jack Sheppard, whose exploits as an escape artist (often with the help of women) had spawned a large public following and whose literary fate constitutes an exemplary history of the

28 Peter Linebaugh, *The London Hanged: Crime and Civil Society in the Eighteenth Century* (Cambridge: Cambridge University Press, 1992), pp. 38, 88–91.
29 John Gay, *The Beggar's Opera*, ed. Edgar V. Roberts (Lincoln: University of Nebraska Press, 1969), p. 5.

ways in which crime narratives, street ballads, topical lyrics and popular theatre could cross-pollinate. In the weeks immediately following Sheppard's hanging before an enormous crowd on 16 November 1724, a spate of narratives appeared, including A *Narrative of All the Robberies, Escapes, &c of John Sheppard* – published only a day after Sheppard's death by John Applebee and possibly written by Daniel Defoe. By 28 November 1724, Sheppard's story had been turned to account as popular theatre: John Thurmond's *Harlequin Shepard* introduced a dancing Sheppard in pantomime at Drury Lane and included the ballad 'Newgate's Garland' penned by none other than John Gay.[30] And Gay's 'Newgate's Garland', it turns out, was set to the tune of 'The Cut Purse' or 'Packington's Pound', a song from the sixteenth century which Ben Jonson had used in *Bartholomew Fair* and which Gay would use again in in Act III of *The Beggar's Opera* for Lockit's reflection on 'friendship'.[31] But before Gay would translate the insights suggested by *Harlequin Shepard* into *The Beggar's Opera*, another play called *The Prison-Breaker; or, the Adventures of John Sheppard* (1725) would recast the story as a farce. And *The Prison-Breaker*, though never staged, would eventually be adapted by Thomas Walker (with the addition of numerous songs) as *The Quaker's Opera; or, The Escapes of Jack Sheppard* to be performed in August 1728 at the Lee–Harper–Spiller booth, Bartholomew Fair, in direct competition with Gay's *Beggar's Opera*, then in summer performance at both Yeates' booth and the Fielding–Reynolds booth, Bartholomew Fair, after a monumental run since January 1728 on the somewhat more exalted stage of John Rich's Lincoln's Inn Fields.[32]

The phenomenon of theatrical booths 'borrowing' *The Beggar's Opera* and attempting to exploit its success with spin-offs like *The Quaker's Opera* leads us to the fairs, those sites of multiple popular amusements existing in direct or tangential relationship both to the ephemeral productions of traditional country 'strollers' and to the more permanent theatrical venues in town. By 1680, Bartholomew and Southwark Fairs had added theatrical performances to their ubiquitous rope-walking and puppet shows, the most popular being the 'droll', a combination of rant, sentiment, patriotism, and farcical slapstick that appealed particularly to underclass spectators. By 1700, more spectacular plays joined the drolls, in a development that made the 'noble fair', according to Tom Brown,

---

30 Linebaugh, *The London Hanged*, pp. 7–41; Emmet L. Avery, ed., *The London Stage 1660–1800, Part 2: 1700–1729* (Carbondale, IL: Southern Illinois University Press, 1960), p. 797.

31 Calhoun Winton, *John Gay and the London Theatre* (Lexington, KY: University Press of Kentucky, 1993), pp. 75–80.

32 Leo Hughes, *A Century of English Farce* (Princeton, NJ: Princeton University Press, 1956), pp. 218–19; Avery, ed., *The London Stage*, p. 985.

quite another thing than what it was in the last age. It not only deals in the humble stories of Crispin and Crispianus, Whittington's cat, Bateman's ghost . . . but it produces operas of its own growth, and is become a formidable rival to both the theatres . . . [I]t traffics in heroes; it raises ghosts and apparitions; it has represented the Trojan-horse, the workmanship of the divine Epeus; it has seen St George encounter the dragon, and overcome him.[33]

The subjects of Brown's catalogue suggest that theatricals at the fairs could be something like dramatised versions of chapbook literature. In the work of Elkanah Settle – who authored both *St George for England* (and, according to Pope, acted the dragon in a suit of green leather) and the perennial favorite, *The Siege of Troy* – this connection was made explicit: the 1703 edition of the *Siege* contained a long chapbook-style account of the legendary events portrayed in the play. Settle had a reputation as the best contriver of machinery in England; and Mrs Mynns, the chief promoter of spectacular shows in Settle's era, was said to have spent ten months preparing the Smithfield fair production of Settle's opus.[34] The chaotic energy of the theatrical booths was caught brilliantly by Hogarth in *Southwark Fair* (1733) – a print called in his advertisements simply 'The Fair' and 'the Humours of a Fair'. Dominating the center of this print is 'Lee and Harpers Great Booth' displaying a large signboard of the Trojan horse announcing: 'The Siege of Troy is here.' Below the signboard, costumed actors stand on a balcony playing to the crowd below. In the left foreground, the balcony of the 'Ciber and Bullock' theatrical booth collapses, ironically illustrating the play, *The Fall of Bajaset*. The print contains a panoply of popular entertainers and entertainments – a female drummer, hurdygurdy-woman, bagpiper, black bugler, chien savant, juggler, rope-dancer, contortionist, fire-eater, professional fighter, peepshows, waxworks, puppets – exemplifying the London sights, sounds and shows that Swift and Pope found so fascinating and frightening. Indeed, Swift – in an image conflating curiosity and duress – described himself as being 'fasten'd by the Eyes' to the monster shows at Charing Cross.[35] The chaotic, disorienting energy of the fair, the street and popular entertainment – like the spirit of *carnival* these sites embody – at once called into question official or normative categories and definitions (including the definition of what it is to be properly human) and provided Augustan satire

33 Tom Brown, *Amusements Serious and Comical*, ed. Arthur L. Hayward (London: Routledge & Sons, Ltd., 1927), p. 143.
34 Rogers, *Literature and Popular Culture*, pp. 13, 87–99.
35 Jonathan Swift, 'Part of the Seventh Epistle of the First Book of Horace', in *The Poems of Jonathan Swift*, ed. Harold Williams, 3 vols. 2nd edn (Oxford: Clarendon Press, 1958), vol. I, p. 172.

with multiply allusive settings and motifs. The radically altered perspectives and activities that characterise Swift's *Gulliver's Travels* (diminutive landscapes, giants, pygmies, intelligent animals, rope-dancers, freaks of nature, etc.) would have been found throughout the metropolis at popular shows, spectacles and exhibitions, as well as advertised and illustrated in broadsides and ballads.[36] Pope's 'Smithfield Muses' (the aesthetics and politics of the fair and the street), along with their potent Grub Street sister, Dulness, embody a negative literary appropriation of popular forms and symbols that paradoxically draws its very life and power from the matrix of eighteenth-century popular culture – a culture Pope immortalises while presuming to despise.[37] *The Dunciad*'s brilliant catalogues of transgressive generation – 'How Tragedy and Comedy embrace; / How Farce and Epic get a jumbled race; / How Time itself stands still at her command, / Realms shift their place, and oceans turn to land'(I, lines 67–70) – would have been impossible but for Pope's close acquaintance with the mixed genres, the spectacles, the monsters, the upside-down worlds of the fair, the show and the literature of the street.[38]

The symbolic politics implicit in the elite literary appropriation of transgressive sites was sometimes manifested concretely in the physical suppression of fairs and shows. At the same time, versions of popular spectacle and drama could be employed to reinforce an overt politics of authority. The rituals of execution and physical desecration – as in the dismembering of Cromwell's exhumed body on 30 January 1661 – were popular forms of political theatre used to great effect by Charles II, who also excelled in crafting less brutal royal spectacles that comprised the range of popular entertainments and practices (processions, pageants, bonfires, maypoles, dancers, tumblers, drolls). In the hands of such master showmen as John Tatham, Restoration pageants could be adjusted to suggest symbolically not only support and adulation but active negotiation and inquiry by a populace intent on understanding the source and range of authority.[39] The dialogue between popular and elite, and resistance and authority, implicit in such productions was dramatically enacted in less choreographed versions of street theatre – demonstrations, riots,

---

36 Dennis Todd, *Imagining Monsters: Miscreations of the Self in Eighteenth-Century England* (Chicago: University of Chicago Press, 1995).

37 Peter Stallybrass and Allon White, *The Politics and Poetics of Transgression* (London: Methuen, 1986), pp. 80–124.

38 Alexander Pope, *The Poems of Alexander Pope*, ed. John Butt (New Haven, CT: Yale University Press, 1963), p. 355.

39 Paula Backscheider, *Spectacular Politics: Theatrical Power and Mass Culture in Early Modern England* (Baltimore, MD: Johns Hopkins University Press, 1993), pp. 3–66.

Fig. 3.2 *Southwark Fair* by William Hogarth (1733)

festivals – throughout the eighteenth century, peaking at various moments of political crisis: the Revolution of 1688–9, the Stuart invasions of 1715 and 1745, the Wilkes affair, the Gordon Riots. But within the theatres themselves – in the presentation of texts and scenarios intended chiefly to entertain – there also existed a struggle for hegemony, in this case between the so-called 'irrational', but vastly popular, entertainments epitomised by farce and pantomime and an elite theatrical tradition that stressed the priority of language.

Although since the Renaissance farcical elements had energised both comedies and tragedies and pervaded numerous seventeenth-century drolls, farce as a significant theatrical genre rose to prominence in fits and starts during the period 1695–1715, its development sparked mainly by competition between Lincoln's Inn Fields, Drury Lane and Haymarket Theatres. Characterised by extravagant situations, bizarre props, exaggerated acting, disguise, concealment and often violent physical action, the farce afterpiece became one of the most popular elements of the eighteenth-century theatre's 'whole show' and consequently the target of critics who viewed it – along with pantomime – as evidence of the degradation of English drama and public taste. As early as 1710, when the regular use of a farce afterpiece was still in its infancy, the economic and structural necessity of catering to 'popular' tastes was already being lamented:

> When we see no Audience now can bear the Fatigue of the two Hours good Sense tho' Shakspear or Oatway endeavor to keep 'em awake, without the promis'd Relief of the Stage-Coach, or some such solid Afterlude, a few Lines indeed are now and then forced down their Throats by the help of this Gewgaw, 'tis tack'd to the Tragedy or rather the Tragedy to it, for 'tis the Money Bill.[40]

The 'Relief' offered by 'the Stage-Coach' alludes to one of the more important early contributions to the 'Money Bill', George Farquhar's *The Stage-Coach* (1704) – a farce that held the stage for decades. Based on LaChapelle's *Carrosses d'Orleans*, *The Stage-Coach* brought together a stock set of characters – young suitor, young girl, rival booby squire, dictatorial father, rough coachman – at a country inn where night-time mayhem ensued, including the usual pursuits, escapes, comic violence and an episode in which a servant groping for a keyhole in the dark sticks his finger in the coachman's mouth – with predictable results. If this scenario seems to look forward to Fielding's the inn at Upton in *Tom Jones*, it also reminds us how similar situation-based farces were to the sit-coms of today.

---

40 Charles Johnson, preface to *The Force of Friendship* (1710), quoted by Hughes, *English Farce*, pp. 86–7.

Henry Fielding himself contributed markedly to the development and diversification of the farce. His *The Mock Doctor* (1732) – a truncated adaptation of Molière's *Medicin malgré lui* – included the usual farce elements but also featured nine songs, making the work a kind of miniature ballad opera. Even before *The Mock Doctor*, Fielding had been experimenting with mixed genres: infusing farces with burlesque elements and writing main pieces attacking farces in farce form. In the tradition of John Gay's *The What D'ye Call It* (1715) – a 'tragi-comi-pastoral farce' that included a burlesque tragedy in the play-within-the play tradition of *The Rehearsal* – Fielding's three-act play, *The Author's Farce* (1730), included a puppet play-within-the-play that ridiculed the 'low' taste of the town and its promulgators, Monsieur Pantomime (John Rich), Dr Orator (Orator Henley) and Sir Farcical Comick (Colley Cibber), among others. But in what seems almost an homage to the power of 'low' taste, the play ends with the hero Luckless, transformed to the King of Bantam, pardoning and employing (in human form) the same purported enemies of culture.[41] As was the case with many productions debunking the popular entertainments of the town, *The Author's Farce* drew much of its energy from the popular forms and culture it ostensibly disparaged; and despite persistent attacks from critics, the farce afterpiece continued to please a paying audience. By mid-century farce had achieved something like a normative two-act form in the hands of David Garrick, and for the rest of the century it held its place in the repertory against the encroachments of another beloved and reviled form of popular theatrical entertainment, pantomime.

Tracing its ancestry from Renaissance *commedia dell'arte* and 'Italian night scenes' through the farces, burlesques, dances, masques and acrobatics that served as 'entertainments' in late seventeenth- and early eighteenth-century theatrical bills, English pantomime emerged as a dominant theatrical form during the 1723–4 season with the competing production of two pantomimes based on the Faust legend at Drury Lane and Lincoln's Inn Fields. For the next thirty years, pantomimes were the most consistently profitable product of the licensed London theatres and flourished as well at unlicensed venues: Goodman's Field's, Sadler's Wells, the Little Theatre at the Haymarket, the theatrical booths of the London fairs and provincial theatres. In their subject matter, pantomimes were both elite and popular, alternating a 'serious' plot, often drawn from classical mythology, with a 'comic' or 'grotesque'

41 Robert D. Hume, *Henry Fielding and the London Theatre 1728–1737* (Oxford: Clarendon Press, 1988), pp. 63–8.

plot focusing on the escapades of Harlequin. It was this second element –
combining radical physicality (tumbling, dance, frenetic motion) with rapidly
transforming costumes, scenery and situations – that recalled the traditions
of the fairground and carnivalesque performance.

Harlequin's antics delighted the majority of the audience, but disturbed elite
critics who execrated pantomimes as vulgar spectacles signalling the decline
of the English stage. The most famous Harlequin of the period was John Rich,
who under the stage name 'Lun' created, produced and acted in pantomimes
that remained in the repertory for most of the century: *Apollo and Daphne:
or, Harlequin Mercury* (1725), *Harlequin a Sorcerer: With the Loves of Pluto and
Proserpine* (1725), *Perseus and Andromeda* (1730), *Orpheus and Eurydice* (1740) and
many others. During his time as manager of Lincoln's Inns Fields and Covent
Garden Theatres, Rich in particular and pantomimes in general were routinely
attacked by critics ranging from Pope (who made pantomime librettist Lewis
Theobald the mock-hero of the 1728 *Dunciad*) to Hogarth (who in 1724 attacked
pantomimes, farces and the managers of both Lincoln's Inn Fields and Drury
Lane theatres in *A Just View of the British Stage*, in which plays by Shakespeare and
Congreve are used for toilet paper while sheets inscribed *Harlequin Faustus* and
Harlequin Sheperd cover the faces of Tragedy and Comedy). But the hybridising
and transformative vitality of pantomime, yoking a 'Thousand jarring Things
together,' prevailed with an irreverent cultural smirk emblematised in the most
notorious comic turn from *Perseus and Andromeda*, when Rich as Harlequin
transformed himself into a (English?) dog and pissed on the leg of the foppish
petit-maître who was his rival.[42]

The hyper-kineticism associated with pantomime, besides delighting audiences, had a profound effect on the acting style of David Garrick, who was
accused of importing 'pantomime gesture . . . miserable expedients fit only for
a booth in a fair' into the performance of elite drama.[43] In practice, Garrick
combined the popular physicality of pantomime with a keen appreciation of
great dramatic texts, particularly Shakespeare's. In so doing, he fused 'classically' valorised dramatic speech and the expressive energy of pantomimic
movement into his famous 'natural' acting style. He also wrote and produced
highly profitable pantomimes, one of which, *Harlequin's Invasion* (1759), not
only exemplifies the use of topical reference (a rumoured French invasion

---

42 John O'Brien, 'Eighteenth-Century Pantomime and the Cultural Location of Entertain-
ment(s)', *Theatre Journal* 50.4 (1998), 489–510.
43 Robert Morris, cited in Leigh Woods, *Garrick Claims the Stage: Acting as Social Emblem in
Eighteenth-Century England* (Westport, CT: Greenwood Press, 1984), p. 19.

during the Seven Years' War) to update old scenarios (the Harlequin versus Shakespeare motif had been used in the 1741 *Harlequin Student*) but scenically and physically enacts the contradictions in Garrick's dramatic practice. The comic plot involves the invasion of Parnassus by the 'Powers of Pantomime'. An innovative *speaking* Harlequin gambols through the usual stage business (dances, decapitations, transformations) only to see in the end (projected in a huge transparency) his invading fleet destroyed by a storm. Then: '*Trap Bell Shakespeare Rises: Harlequin Sinks.*' The disjunctions between the two theatrical forms are performed by the material bodies onstage: Harlequin's fluid, grotesque body is physically displaced by the statuesque, classical body of Shakespeare. But all of this business occurs within the scenic frame and energetic medium of pantomime: *Harlequin's Invasion* explicitly attempts to elevate the elite body of drama represented by Shakespeare, while implicitly threatening to pull down the pedestal 'by situating the elitist tableau as a single still point in a whirling, transformative, transgressive world created by Harlequin's body'.[44]

The growing emphasis on the physical and the spectacular in the English theatre was not confined to pantomimes. As licensed theatres grew larger, scenery and special effects grew more elaborate. In unlicensed venues, various 'entertainments' that minimised spoken dialogue and maximised spectacle (pantomimes, farces, musicals, burlettas) proliferated as theatrical entrepreneurs scrambled to find ways to evade the Licensing Act. The special effects techniques of magic lantern and Chinese shadows (both of which used strong light to illuminate painted transparencies as entertainments in themselves or as backgrounds for shadow figures) were crucial to these developments.[45] Transparencies were first introduced to a popular audience at Bartholomew Fair in Settle's *The Siege of Troy* and became increasingly a production element in licensed theatres: the final scene of Garrick's *Harlequin's Invasion* includes not only the transparency of the pantomime fleet but an appearing and disappearing prison that combined trapdoor gimmickry with transparencies. Entertainments without actors began to be exhibited. In the late 1770s, the impresario Philip Astley produced a series of brief comic scenes played out in silhouette as part of a show that included the more traditional popular entertainments of a conjuring horse and a man who played a concert on a stringless violin and imitated bird songs. During the same period, Philippe de Loutherbourg

44 Denise S. Sechelski, 'Garrick's Body and the Labor of Art in Eighteenth-Century Theater', *Eighteenth-Century Studies* 29 (1996), 377–8.
45 Richard D. Altick, *The Shows of London* (Cambridge, MA: Harvard University Press, 1978), pp. 117–27.

was revolutionising special effects at Drury Lane, employing a combination of transparencies, lighting and mechanical figures. In 1781, he brought together all these elements, minus actors, at the Eidophusikon, advertised as 'Various imitations of Natural Phenomena, represented by Moving Pictures', and later expanded his production to include a scene of the building of Pandemonium from *Paradise Lost*. But despite its obvious appeal to a populace hungry for spectacle, Loutherbourg's show at five shillings per person was far beyond the reach of most Londoners.

The economic and aesthetic disjunctions between popular culture and popular entertainment, between taste and accessibility, between the traditional and the commercialised, are particularly evident in expensive theatrical spectacles, but affect the discussion of even more minor subgenres of 'popular' literary and dramatic entertainment. In 1726, for example, John Henley opened an Oratory in Newport Market – soon removed to its more famous location in Clare Market – where he delivered for the next thirty years remarkable rambling orations to an audience made up of 'lower- and middle-class tradesmen, often liberally sprinkled with the butchers of Newport and Clare Markets, enlivened now and again by visitors from Oxford and Cambridge or by rowdy gangs of young lawyers from the Temple, and graced by more illustrious visitors who came to see and hear for themselves this much talked-of celebrity'.[46] Orator Henley's audience and practice embody the contradictions inherent in the concept of 'popular entertainment and instruction, literary and dramatic', for as 'instruction' his orations had genuine popular appeal to tradesmen and butchers hungry for knowledge, while for smirking law students, wits and elites they seem to have functioned primarily as entertaining objects of ridicule. Henley himself worked both sides of the aisle, providing religious orations on Sundays and topical, burlesque orations on Friday, at the same time promoting his performances in brilliantly chaotic advertisements that canvass the range of popular preoccupations:

> Is the Queen of Spain dead? Room for Cuckolds
> At the ORATORY
> The Corner of Lincoln's Inn Fields, near Clare-Market, Tomorrow, in the Evening, at half an Hour after Six, after the Exhortation and Prayers, the Lecture will be on the Adventures of Peter and his man Paul, celebrated this Week; a German Court; the Intrigues of Count Polton and Baron Compellum to bite the Country; an Italian Count; Cardinal Gibbi risen from the Dead, and his Singing-Bird promoted to the Cage at Windsor; a Cock's Challenge

---

46 Graham Midgley, *The Life of Orator Henley* (Oxford: Clarendon Press, 1973), pp. 73–90.

to a Cock-pit Lady; the Irish and English Register, a Match; Ladies invited to a Sale of precious Stones; the King of P. in second Mourning; the Report of a Pop-gun in White-powder . . . the State a Tumbler; Westminster People good, good; the grand Prior of Fulham, &c . . .[47]

Henley also inspired imitators and parodists, the most famous of whom, Christopher Smart, opened on 30 December 1751 at the Castle-Tavern in Pater-Noster Row *The Old Woman's Oratory*, starring Smart in petticoats as 'Mrs Mary Midnight' – herself a stage incarnation of Smart's journalistic persona in *The Midwife; or the Old Woman's Magazine* (1751–53).

Ostensibly a take-off on Henley's establishment, Smart's *Old Woman's Oratory* was in practice a madcap vaudeville show featuring precisely the kinds of popular entertainments one would have found in the fairs and shows of London: smart animals, a dancer who performed without touching 'the Ground either with . . . hands or feet,' marrow-bones and cleavers, an 'admired dulcimer, a favourite saltbox, and a really curious Jew's harp,' a fellow who 'imitates farting and curtseying to French horn' and Smart in drag cavorting on stage and reciting poetry from the back of an ass. Seemingly a parodic version of popular entertainment offered by a prize-winning poet and wit from Cambridge, the show could as easily be classified as a genuine popular entertainment presented by a impecunious hack turned impresario. As a journalistic persona, Smart's Mary Midnight reiterates the paradox. Recalling the folk and print tradition of wise or cunning women (most famously, Mother Shipton), an 'Old Woman' and 'Midwife' named Mary Midnight authors a journal that is politically radical, proto-feminist and highly irreverent; but to a knowing coterie, 'Mary Midnight' is Kit Smart, Cambridge scholar and poet turned hack author turned tavern performer, trying to make a little money by making coffee-house wits laugh.[48] In this light, Henley himself could be considered a consciously commercialised, theatrical version of the stereotypical belching, bawling Puritan preachers caricatured by Swift. And this is precisely the point made by Pope's phrasing in *The Dunciad Variorum*, when he calls Henley 'Oh great Restorer of the good old Stage, / Preacher at once, and Zany of thy Age!'(III, 201–2).[49] The intermingling of popular literary forms and entertainments with commercialised literary, dramatic and parodic reincarnations of them is perhaps the chief phenomenon complicating the sifting

---

47 Advertisement for 26 June 1742, in Daniel Lysons, *Collectanea*, B. M. 1889, e. 6; quoted in Midgley, *Orator Henley*, p. 88. *Collectanea* is a unique scrapbook of press cuttings made by Daniel Lysons, now in the British Museum, containing many Henley advertisements from newspapers which have not been preserved.

48 Lance Bertelsen, 'Journalism, Carnival, and *Jubilate Agno*', *ELH* 59 (1992), 357–84.

49 Pope, *The Poems of Alexander Pope*, p. 415.

of genuinely popular productions and the productions of the marketing phenomenon called 'Grub Street'. In their attacks, the Augustans seem to have
made no such distinctions; and in a society inventing commercialised popular
culture perhaps no such distinctions are possible.

Henley's promotional flair not only reminds us that this was the age of
a new breed of entrepreneurs and impresarios (Jonathan Tyers, John James
Heidegger, Colley Cibber, Richard Nash, John Rich, *et al.*), but suggests that
advertising itself might be considered a new form of popular entertainment and
instruction.[50] In *The Idler* No. 40 (20 January 1759) Samuel Johnson wrote that
'Advertisements are now so numerous that they are very negligently perused,
and it is therefore become necessary to gain attention by magnificence of
promises, and by eloquence sometimes sublime and sometimes pathetic.'[51]
And Richard Brinsley Sheridan's Mr Puff in *The Critic* (1779) seems a prototype
of the modern shill: 'a Practitioner in Panegyric, or to speak more plainly
a Professor in the art of Puffing'.[52] Essayists from Addison through Bonnell
Thornton had recognised signboards as a popular commercial art form; and
in 1763 Thornton with the help of William Hogarth brought the concept to
life in the 'Sign Painters Exhibition' – simultaneously a satire on the elite
art exhibitions and a slightly tongue-in-cheek homage to signboards as art.[53]
Hogarth himself was a master advertiser and marketer whose subscription
tickets were often miniature works of art. But more importantly Hogarth was
the inventor of a serial graphic form that encompassed elements of graphic
satire, popular theatre, chapbooks, advice books and the novel, while recording
with unprecedented accuracy and detail the popular culture of his time.

Although the seventeenth century had seen a sporadic output of social and
political prints along with woodcut headings to broadside ballads, English
graphic satire really begins with Hogarth's *Emblematical Print of the South
Sea Scheme* (1721), one the few indigenous entries in a spate of Dutch reissues or adaptations provoked by the bursting stock bubble. For the rest of
the eighteenth century, graphic satire flourished in the hands of such artists
and engravers as Matthew and Mary Darly, Robert Dighton, James Gillray,
Thomas Rowlandson and a host of anonymous contributors. Displayed in
print-shop windows, hung up like washing on stalls and fence railings, etched

50 Rogers, *Literature and Popular Culture*, pp. 10–28.
51 Samuel Johnson, *The Idler and The Adventurer*, eds. W. J. Bate, John M. Bullitt, L. F. Powell
(New Haven, CT: Yale University Press, 1963), p. 125.
52 Richard Brinsley Sheridan, *The Critic*, ed. Cecil Price, 2 vols. (Oxford: Clarendon Press,
1973), vol. II, p. 511.
53 Ronald Paulson, *Hogarth*, 3 vols. (New Brunswick, NJ: Rutgers University Press, 1993),
vol. III, pp. 336–61.

and engraved prints provided literate and illiterate Londoners visual commentaries on everything from Walpole's rear end to the Macaroni fad.

But it was Hogarth who invented the print series and in so doing forged connections with a range of popular literary and dramatic forms. His first original series, *A Harlot's Progress* (1732), was inspired by crime fiction and employed theatrical conventions he had absorbed while painting scenes from *The Beggar's Opera*. A steep one-guinea subscription price limited the availability of the first edition, but the prints themselves were on display and according to George Vertue 'captivated the Minds of most People persons of all ranks & conditions from the greatest Quality to the meanest'.[54] Hogarth quickly authorised copies to be made and sold for five shillings to a more genuinely popular audience. The theatrical connection was immediately realised (in reverse) with the publication of several plays based on the series, then the production of 'a new Pantomime Entertainment' at Sadler's Wells called *The Harlot's Progress* and, moving up the theatrical hierarchy, the great success of *The Harlot's Progress, or The Ridotto-Al-Fresco* (1733) at Drury Lane. This was the beginning. Through the course of his career, Hogarth would continue to push the boundaries of popular and polite entertainment: conjoining genres, instructing as well as scandalising – and adjusting prices in an attempt to reach an audience comprising all Englishmen and women. His work is the alpha and omega of any consideration of popular entertainment and instruction during his lifetime, and perhaps the greatest example of the range and power of popular art in eighteenth-century England.

54 *Ibid.*, vol. I, pp. 237–314; George Vertue, *Notebooks*, 6 vols. (Oxford: Oxford University Press, 1934–55), vol. III, p. 58.

4

Novels on the market

WILLIAM B. WARNER

A new form of entertainment on the market: the novels of amorous intrigue

In the seventeenth century, first on the Continent and then in England, a modest new form of print entertainment appeared, but it seems to have taken its readers by storm. It was called 'the novel', and was viewed by contemporaries like Aphra Behn, William Congreve and Gottfried Wilhelm von Leibnitz as a symptom of a 'novel' turn in modern taste. This novel was short (compared to romance), written in prose rather than poetry, usually took sex and/or love as its topic and was usually set in the present rather than in some earlier ancient or legendary era. The most successful English writers of novels between 1683 and 1740 were Aphra Behn, Delariviere Manley and Eliza Haywood. Their success came from their development of a specific type of novel, the novel of amorous intrigue, designed to appeal to readers in the burgeoning English market in printed books. But these novels of the late seventeenth and early eighteenth century have been an embarrassment to most of the English literary history of the novel written since the late eighteenth century. Intent upon legitimatising the novel as a form of literature, literary histories of the novel written in the many years between Clara Reeve's *Progress of Romance* (1785) and Ian Watt's *The Rise of the Novel* (1957) have laboured to efface the centrality of the enormously popular novels of amorous intrigue. By doing so, most literary history has obscured the productive symbiosis between this early type of English fiction, and those narratives written by the three canonical authors usually installed in the position of the fathers of the English novel: Daniel Defoe, Samuel Richardson and Henry Fielding.

By looking at how Aphra Behn became the first successful writer of these novels, we will be in a position to grasp the centrality of the novel of amorous intrigue for the emergence of the elevated and morally improving novels of the eighteenth century. Several factors led Aphra Behn to turn from writing plays to writing novels. With the intensification of the political turbulence around the issue of Protestant succession to the throne after 1683, Behn, as a dedicated party writer, found the theatre closed to her. The recent success of the short Continental novel (of Madame de Lafayette and others) had demonstrated its potential as a form of print entertainment. Finally, the elopement of Henrietta Berkeley, a member of a prominent Tory family, with her brother-in-law, Ford, Lord Grey of Werke, a leading supporter of the Duke of Monmouth, offered Behn a way to contribute, during the height of the Succession Crisis, to the propaganda campaign on behalf of Charles II. What resulted in the aftermath of these events was Behn's most ambitious novel, *Love Letters Between a Nobleman and His Sister*, published in three successive installments in 1684, 1685 and 1687.

A brief look at one episode in *Love Letters* will reveal the signal traits of the novels of amorous intrigue. Near the end of Behn's *Love Letters*, the heroine Silvia carries on an intrigue with a young nobleman named Don Alonzo. Within the context of the novel's account of Silvia's movement from impassioned lover to jaded libertine, this intrigue suggests her gradual moral debasement. Silvia's character becomes flattened and simplified, as character is subordinated to the artifice of intrigue, coolly and cunningly performed. This episode offers a prototype of the novels of amorous intrigue, the narrative formula that Behn uses in her short novels published after *Love Letters* (for example, *The Fair Jilt*, *The Unlucky Chance* and others), that Manley would modify and incorporate in the anthology of adventures and scandals that compose the *New Atalantis*, (1711–12) and that Haywood perfects into the numerous novels she published after the success of her best-selling first novel, *Love in Excess* (1719). By describing Silvia's affair with Don Alonzo as if it were an autonomous novel, and suggesting what makes it typical of many novels published by Behn, Manley and Haywood through the 1730s, I can develop a general profile of the novels of amorous intrigue, and clarify the moral scandal of their popularity.

Here is a brief sketch of the Don Alonzo adventure. Silvia dresses as a young man, Bellumere, and sets out on the road. At a small tavern she is struck by the appearance of a young Don Alonzo, whom the master of the hotel reports is of quality but is now 'Incognito, being on an Intrigue'.[1] At supper Don Alonzo and the disguised Silvia drink wine and share stories of erotic conquest. Don Alonzo tells Bellumere/Silvia of the wager he entered into at court to seduce a countess and the success of his enterprise. Silvia, fired with passion, meditates

---

1 *Love Letters Between a Nobleman and His Sister*, vol. II of *The Works of Aphra Behn*, ed. Janet Todd (Oxford: Oxford University Press, 1993), p. 386. All further references in the text are to this edition.

exposing her true sex but conceals herself for fear of his proven 'inconstancy'. Don Alonzo denies having ever been subject to love, but reports his passion at the sight of a woman he had seen passing in the street in Brussels, the 'whore' of one who had recently taken orders, who turns out of course to be Silvia herself. Forced to share a bed with Don Alonzo in the crowded inn, Silvia delays going to bed, stays dressed and awake to avoid discovery. After exchanging rings as a token of friendship, each goes by separate roads to Brussels. The second part of the episode begins with Silvia's appearance in lavish equipage and apparel on the 'Toure' (p. 416). Don Alonzo falls in love with this anonymous beauty. Silvia then assumes a masquer's garb to follow Don Alonzo into the park. She contrives that he sees upon her ungloved hand the ring which Don Alonzo has given Bellumere. After an artful duel of wits, Silvia refers the aroused and ardent Don Alonzo to Bellumere's apartment. Silvia believes 'her Conquest was certain: He having seen her three times, and all those times for a several Person, and yet was still in Love with her: And she doubted not when all three were joyn'd in one, he would be much more in Love than yet he had been' (p. 420). At her apartment, Silvia greets Don Alonzo as Bellumere, leaving him ravished and confused to hear the same voice in this man which he has just heard in the fair unknown beauty in the park. Silvia/Bellumere offers to introduce his/her 'sister' to Don Alonzo, retires to get the 'sister'/the anonymous court beauty/the incognito, and returns in 'a rich nightgown' to be recognized as three in one and as Silvia (p. 421). After eight days and nights of erotic pleasure, Silvia contrives a temporary return to her affair with Philander, and pays off with sex Philander's retainer Briljard, who is an invaluable assistant throughout the intrigue. The novel's last page offers a final postscript on the affair: Silvia and Briljard take such good advantage of Don Alonzo that 'they ruin'd the Fortune of that young Nobleman' (p. 439).

In the Don Alonzo episode of *Love Letters* narrative action comes under the sway of the intriguer's intrigue. Alonzo's arousing narrative embeds a brag of absolute erotic mastery. Finding her ambition piqued, Silvia is called to the seduction of Don Alonzo. Although contingencies of setting and situation are fraught with erotic potential, sexual resolution is blocked. The libertine's aim is not a merely physical possession, but a psychic mastery won through the other's confused erotic surrender. This requires an organised imbroglio or entanglement of the action, achieved through an intrigue, allowing the intriguer to prevail over the dupe/adversary, and turning that victory into a communication to a third position, sometimes a general public, sometimes a select intimate, who can register and applaud the intriguer's skill. To develop such an action, part two of the Don Alonzo episode shows the intriguing protagonist developing a scheme – pivoting on a succession of cross-gendered masquerades – that takes control of the action. This follows a general pattern whereby the intriguer develops probabilistic calculations of his or her opponent's behaviour out of a Machiavellian anthropology that as Walter Benjamin says in another context assumes 'the uniformity of human nature, the power of the animal instinct and emotions, especially emotions of love and fear'.[2] The mastery of the schemer depends on a general knowledge of psychology and physiology. Over the shoulder of the intriguer, the reader watches the social exchange, illuminated by the harsh irony of the scheme.

The intriguer's machinations, consolidated into a scheme, become the plot's engine. The scheme entails a sadistic flattening of the social field and its agents which, in its turn, assures the cynical superiority of the intriguer. While embedded in intrigue, the protagonist cannot have the luxury of a 'deep' identity; a shifting set of social masks allows him or her to manipulate the social, as if from the outside, as a fixed and limited set of codes, conventions, types. The intriguer is essentially alone and self-interested in his/her intriguing; alliances of purpose are provisional and open to disruption; the scheme is shaped to divide all others into solitary agents. By becoming an artist of manipulation, the intriguer turns plot into plotting, the theatre of history into a spectacle of theatricality. Issues of point of view, epistemology or narrative framing so important in other types of novels are here subordinated to a direct narrative of the headlong rush of the action. The very simplicity of character and motive – characters come freighted with almost no history, each agent automatically seeks to expand his/her power vis-à-vis others – gives these novels the ludic immediacy of a game. At the same time, the plotting of rival egos produces an accelerating complication of the action, which none can fully control. The plot hooks the reader. Whether the scheme succeeds (as here) or misfires, brings sex (as here) or death (as in other novels), an unveiling of identities closes the action. The fiction often ends with a movement out of the magic circle of intrigue to the banality of the ordinary, here marked by Don Alonzo's financial ruin. To adapt Clausewitz's famous adage, the novel of amorous intrigue suggests that sex is politics pursued by other means.

Behn composed the first novels of amorous intrigue in Britain by splicing together several distinct elements: the stingingly abusive satiric discourse of

2 Walter Benjamin, *The Origins of German Tragic Drama*, introduction by George Steiner, trans. George Osborne (London: Verso New Left Books, 1985), pp. 95–6. Benjamin is quoting Wilhelm Dilthy.

early English party politics; the French secret histories of Lafayette and Gabriel de Bremond, with their disguised reference to public figures; and the Spanish dramas and novellas of court intrigue, with their scheming protagonists. In their crossing of love and politics, the machinations of the schemer are at first articulated by means of the ground rules of political strife, but end up transforming the love plot into a kind of political discourse. Critics have suggested how Behn's *Love Letters*, as well as her most famous novel, *Oroonoko* (1688), lend themselves to reading as a political allegory of the betrayal of a monarch by his people. But even Behn's novels of amorous intrigue, which have no overt political reference (*The Fair Jilt*, *Agnes de Castro*, *The History of the Nun: or, the Fair Vow-Breaker*, all 1688) involve an ethos of power, rivalry and cunning consonant with the diplomatic and military manoeuvring of the early modern state.

The enormous popularity of the novels of amorous intrigue may derive from their bold validation, within the space of fictional entertainment, of the attractions of erotic freedom. In *Civilisation and Its Discontents* (1930), Freud argues that the most basic forms of culture demand a massive instinctual renunciation. That repression is the condition of the possibility of culture accounts for the effect of deflection most characteristic of entertainment. In order to please, entertainment diverts its consumers away from the ordinary. Through their free assent to the rule-bound space of entertainment, the entertained win, for the duration of the entertainment, a reprieve from the inhibitions of culture. But entertainment never constitutes an utterly different world; instead, it sustains an oblique relation to the culture it entertains.

While Delariviere Manley exploits the novel of amorous intrigue for her scandalous chronicles of her Whig opponents, most successfully in the *New Atalantis* (1709–10), it is Eliza Haywood who develops the novels of amorous intrigue into a distinctive type of formula fiction. After the success of her first novel, *Love in Excess* (1719), published like *Love Letters* in three instalments, Haywood wrote thirty-six novels over the next decade. The traits of these short erotic novels make them the prototype of the formula fiction of our own day: they subordinate complexity of character to intricacy of plot; keep their reader guessing 'what will happen' next; indulge in banal didacticism; follow pre-established formulas; and allow incompleteness and last-minute revision. Formula fiction restructures reading according to the central imperative of the print market: to encourage the seriality of books read, pleasures indulged and purchases made. The octavo and duodecimo formats are favoured for novels because those formats decrease costs and increase portability, especially when compared with the giant folio editions typical of seventeenth-century French romances. The market puts a distinct pressure on the content of printed books, promoting the contradictory logic of all fashion: a sanctification of the proven formula along with a valorisation of novelty. This double impulse – towards the proven hit and a new product – helps explain the proliferation in this period of the publication of sequels: the serial meets the market's demand to be recurrently new.

This account of the role played by the novels of amorous intrigue in the development of formula fiction within early modern print-media culture offers an alternative to the twentieth-century feminist literary history that helped to recover Behn, Manley and Haywood for modern readers. One strand of feminist criticism has considered these three novelists as early instances of 'women's writing', where a female author writes as a woman for other women, so as to reflect upon, and sometimes contest, life within patriarchy. Even when the feminism of these early women writers is open to sustained questioning, the goal of feminist literary history remains to isolate a more or less autonomous current of women's writing for inclusion in the canon of valued literary works. A second way of reading the novels of amorous intrigue reads backwards from the contemporary romance novel, so as to situate them as an early instance of women's popular culture. Developed out of Marxist understanding of the various ways narrative can express the legitimate utopian longings of subordinate groups, and following modern cultural studies of women's romance, this mode of reading enables critics to put aside questions of literary genre or aesthetic value, and focus upon the fantasy life of early modern women. That is to say, perhaps too often modern feminist critics find the same implicit rage at patriarchal oppression behind all women's fiction. One critic, Ros Ballaster, finds an alternative way to chart the compositional strategies of Behn, Manley and Haywood. Lacking British models for this fiction, these authors looked to seventeenth-century France, where they found a broad band of 'feminocentric' narratives which they could popularise. Ballaster undertakes an 'analysis of the specific address that Behn, Manley, and Haywood make to female readers and the interpretive conflict between the genders that is the structuring feature of their amatory plots'.[3] However, it is the modern critic rather than Behn, Manley or Haywood who seems to 'address' these texts to women readers; it is she, not they, who insert the possessive ('women's') adjective into the generic designation, 'women's amatory fiction'. The French romances, secret histories, scandalous chronicles and novels that offered models for Behn, Manley

---

3 Ros Ballaster, *Seductive Forms: Women's Amatory Fiction from 1684 to 1740* (Oxford: Oxford University Press, 1992), pp. 66, 29.

and Haywood were written and read by both men and women.[4] If one looks more closely at the French texts Ballaster invokes, the term 'feminocentric' becomes problematic in other ways. In those novels and romances that render the woman the object of desire, narrative often focuses upon the affect of those male characters who aspire to relatively remote women. Are these texts centred on the women they monumentalise, or the men who love them? Secondly, Behn's dedications are usually to men; her novels, like those of Manley, are intended to intervene in political culture and must 'address' men to do so; in the beginning of the second part of *Love in Excess*, a poem by Richard Savage celebrates Haywood as a mistress of the passions for both sexes. Finally, there is evidence that men as well as women read and enjoyed the novels of amorous intrigue during the first half of the eighteenth century. Only much later in Haywood's career, with the *Female Spectator* (1744), does Haywood's writing appear to be directed at female as opposed to male readers. Scholars have not yet demonstrated for the early eighteenth century the sort of market segmentation reviewers describe later in the century, and which has been an important part of print media ever since.

By seeking to gender the origin, content and destination of these novels (as from women, about women, to women), feminist critics align their readings with the project that motivates virtually all post-Enlightenment feminist and Marxist interpretations of popular culture: how does the subject who would be free (here woman) resist or negotiate some compromise with the power of an oppressive system (here patriarchy) in order to win authority in view of (some possible future) liberation? The use of this leading question to guide reading underestimates something we will find repeatedly in the novels of amorous intrigue: the fact that their inventive complications of the ordinary courtship plot, through the use of masquerade, incite a desire which is polymorphous, and exploits the pleasures of cross-gender identification. Precisely because they blur the identity of subject positions, these fictions can hail a general reader.

I would like to suggest another, albeit more circuitous, way to articulate the novels of amorous intrigue with feminism. Although they cannot be assimilated to a consistent feminist politics, Behn, Manley and Haywood develop forms of entertainment crucial to modern forms of subjectivity, including post-Enlightenment feminism. Like their precursors on the Continent, Behn,

---

4 For the heroic romance, Madeleine de Scudéry is central, but so are Honoré d'Urfé and Gautier de la Calprenède. While Marie d'Aulnoy and Lafayette are influences for Manley and Behn, so too are novels written by men, like the *Lettres Portugaises*. On the practices of collaboration that blur the gender boundaries of authorship in seventeenth-century French salon writing, see Joan DeJean, *Tender Geographies: Women and the Origins of the Novel in France* (New York: Columbia University Press, 1991), pp. 1–16.

Manley and Haywood mix new comedy situations with a cynical, modern libertine ethos so as to intensify the erotic tension, gender strife and sexual explicitness of the conventional love story. The discourse of liberation propounded in their novels is woven out of particular Restoration and eighteenth-century contexts – the realist political discourse developed out of Hobbes, Machiavelli and Mandeville; the Tory individualism and libertinism epitomised by such Restoration rakes as the Earl of Rochester; and a baroque aesthetics of excess. Behn, Manley and Haywood weave these elements into tightly wrought narratives which represent sexualised bodies and amoral egos plotting to secure their own pleasures at the expense of others. The formal traits of these novels (their brevity, their subordination of all narrative interest to intricate plotting and the shell-like emptiness of their protagonists) support their ideological content: a licentious ethical nihilism and a sustained preoccupation with sex explicitly rendered.

By developing the first formula fiction on the market, Behn, Manley and Haywood invent a form of private entertainment that incites desire, and promotes the liberation of the reader as subject of pleasure. It is the novels of amorous intrigue that Richardson and Fielding set out to reform and replace in the 1740s. All these early novels – from Behn to Fielding – play a crucial role in the formation of the bourgeois public sphere, the Enlightenment critique of the self's self-imposed tutelage, the late-century revolutions, and modern feminism, which begins in England with Mary Wollstonecraft in the 1780s and 1790s. This, I will argue, is the actual if circuitous sense in which Behn, Manley and Haywood contribute to the formation of modern feminism. Rather than anticipating modern feminism, as does the centuries-long European 'querelles des femmes' or Mary Astell's proto-feminist tract, *A Serious Proposal to the Ladies for the Advancement of their True and Greatest Interest* (1695), the novels of amorous intrigue do something more general and global: as a form of media culture they teach readers, men as well as women, to articulate their desires and put the self first, through reading novels where characters do so.

Thus, the new formula fiction of Delariviere Manley and Eliza Haywood achieves its distinctive popularity and scandal by appealing not to any particular type of reader but to the general reader. Haywood's reader is 'general' in the sense of 'not limited in scope' or narrowly restricted in its range of address. Joined only by their engagement with the novel, a diverse group of readers can enjoy the same novel, so its reading can become 'general' in the second sense of 'widespread', 'common' or 'prevailing'. It is useful to specify what the general reader is not. The general reader does not have a clearly delimited ideological position within the cultural field; nor is the general reader a subject with a defining difference of class, race, gender or sexual preference; nor does the general reader have a specifiable identity, such that a novelist would know in advance how to move her or him. Instead, formula fiction requires thinking the reader – whether as a group or as a single individual – as plural in interests, with a perversely polymorphous readiness to be hooked by many types of readerly enjoyment. The general address of these novels is borne out by evidence that men as well as women were avid consumers of the novels of amorous intrigue. For the writer and bookseller working the early modern print market, this indeterminate but alluring 'general reader' becomes the target audience. It has been so for publishers ever since.

The debate about reading

The novels of amorous intrigue support the pleasure-seeking reader sequestered in a more or less private act of reading. These novels also trigger a public sphere debate joined by writers like Shaftesbury, Leibnitz, Samuel Johnson, and novelists like Manley, Haywood, Defoe, Penelope Aubin, Richardson, Fielding and many others. The issue might be put this way: how is culture to license – that is sanction but also control – the powerful new reading pleasures these novels produce? What made this question especially vexed is the nature of the institution that brought novels to readers. As a powerful, inchoate and ambient system, the market in printed books seems to have a will of its own: no one (person or institution) controls the market. The disrepute and illegitimacy that clings to novels throughout this period results from its close entanglement with the market. Many of the vices attributed to these novels are also traits ascribed to the market: both breed imitation, incite desire, are oblivious to their moral effects and reach into every corner of the kingdom. As part of the new culture of the market, novels appear to induce an uncanny automatism in authors and readers. In an introductory chapter to *Tom Jones*, Fielding relegates novel writers to the lowest rank of authors, because 'to the composition of novels and romances, nothing is necessary but paper, pens and ink, with the manual capacity of using them'.[5] Once they had become 'the thing', nothing could stop novels on the market. Producers appear as mere

5 Henry Fielding, *The History of Tom Jones, A Foundling*, introduction and commentary by Martin C. Battestin, text ed. Fredson Bowers (Oxford: Oxford University Press), Book IX, chapter 1, p. 489.

agents of the market. Writing later in the eighteenth century, Clara Reeve uses the by now clichéd terms to describe the accelerating production of novels. Rampant production allows bad imitations to proliferate, and the market develops new institutions to deliver novels indiscriminately into the hands of every reader:

> The press groaned under the weight of Novels, which sprung up like mushrooms every year . . . [Novels] did but now begin to increase upon us, but ten years more multiplied them tenfold. Every work of merit produced a swarm of imitators, till they became a public evil, and the institution of Circulating libraries, conveyed them in the cheapest manner to every bodies hand.[6]

An uncontrolled multiplicity of novels threatens culture with metastasis.

The popularity of these novels incites the anti-novel discourse of the early eighteenth century. Many moralists and cultural critics of the early modern period deplored the way the market pandered to readers who eschewed morally improving books in favour of novels that entertained. As both novelists and their critics conflate the dangerous pleasures of reading novels with those associated with the sexualised body, the debate about the novel of amorous intrigue becomes lodged within the novels of Manley and Haywood. For example, Manley and Haywood find an ingenious way to counter the suspicion of their novels: they incorporate a figure of the novel reader, almost always gendered female, within their plot. Thus, in Manley's *New Atalantis* (1709–1710), the Duke seduces his ward Charlot by giving her free run of his library of erotic literature. In Haywood's *Love in Excess* (1719) the hero and heroine come to recognise their love for each other over the course of their debate about the dangers of novel reading. In this way Manley and Haywood embed the central warning of the anti-novel discourse – erotic reading leads to sexual danger – within their own erotic novels.

But what, one might ask, is so pernicious about reading novels? Writing near the end of the century in *The Progress of Romance* (1785), Clara Reeve stages a debate between the book's protagonist, the woman scholar Euphrasia, and a high cultural snob named Hortensius. Hortensius develops a wide-ranging indictment of novel reading, one that reflects the orthodox position Reeve is challenging throughout her literary history. First, novels turn the reader's taste against serious reading: a person used to this kind of reading will be disgusted

---

6 Clara Reeve, *The Progress of Romance*, 2 vols. (Colchester, 1785), vol. II, p. 7. Further references in the text are to this edition.

with every thing serious or solid, as a weakened and depraved stomach rejects plain and wholesome food.' Second, novels incite the heart with false emotions:

> The seeds of vice and folly are sown in the heart, – the passions are awakened, – false expectations are raised. – A young woman is taught to expect adventures and intrigues . . . If a plain man addresses her in rational terms and pays her the greatest of compliments, – that of desiring to spend his life with her – that is not sufficient, her vanity is disappointed, she expects to meet a Hero in Romance. (vol. ii, p. 78)

Finally, novels induce a dangerous autonomy from parents and guardians: 'From this kind of reading, young people fancy themselves capable of judging of men and manners, and . . . believe themselves wiser than their parents and guardians, whom they treat with contempt and ridicule' (vol. ii, p. 79). Hortensius indicts novels for transforming the cultural function of reading from solid nourishment to exotic tastes; from preparing a woman for the ordinary rational address of a plain good man to romance fantasies of a 'hero'; from reliance upon parents and guardians to belief in the young reader's autonomy. Taken together, novels have disfigured their reader's body: the taste, passions and judgement of stomach, heart and mind. Here, as so often in the polemics around novels, the novel reader is characterised as a susceptible female, whose moral life is at risk. By strong implication, the woman reader is most liable to catch and is most responsible for transmitting the media virus of novel reading.

Given the novel's address to and success with a broad spectrum of general readers, why, during the British eighteenth century, do writers so often circulate this stereotype of the novel reader as female? No doubt, as with contemporaneous moral critics of vanity and luxury, these writers mobilise a powerful vein of misogyny to locate the responsibility for the commodification of reading in women. Repeating certain themes of eighteenth-century misogyny can help consolidate the femininity of the novel reader. If we understand the eighteenth-century topos of the woman novel reader not as a representation of what was, but as a discursive formation, what function does this figure serve? First, this figure allows for a simplification of reading. Through the assumption that women are easy to understand, or as Pope in his 'Epistle to a Lady' writes, 'women have no character at all', it is supposed that the female reader will easily receive the impressions to which she is exposed, and will therefore imitate novels most automatically. But secondly, attributing novel reading to the female sex mystifies reading: the woman reader becomes a fascinating enigma. Finally, the figure of the woman reader eroticises reading through the presumption of an automatic relay: if a reader reads erotic novels, then she will act out by having sex. This figure of the woman reader can function as an admonitory figure for men as well as women: because novels render readers sensitive and erotic, they menace men with feminisation. By gendering the argument against novel reading, the anti-novel discourse deploys commonsense notions of gender difference to promote a containment of novel reading.

The abject figure of the woman reader, as a mindless and robotic consumer of print on the market, allows those who circulate this figure to sort reading into the good and the bad, that which is to be encouraged and that which is to be suppressed. In other words, the cultural struggle around novel reading is the secondary effect of a more global effort to institutionalise book reading. The spectre of the novel-reading automaton is an inverse after-image of the Enlightenment project of rationally motivated reading; the latter produces the former as its own particular nightmarish phantasm. Michel de Certeau has suggested that the project of Enlightenment is structured around a certain concept of education as mimicry, with a 'scriptural system' that assumes that 'although the public is more or less resistant, it is molded by (verbal or iconic) writing, that it becomes similar to what it receives, and that it is imprinted by and like the text which is imposed on it'.[7] By de Certeau's account, the expansion since the eighteenth century of the powers that inform (from standardised teaching to the media) has reinforced the presumption that only producers initiate and invent. Correlatively, this model assumes the idea of the consumer as a passive receptacle.[8] The early eighteenth-century anti-novel discourse promotes the fear that the novel reader will become absorbed in unconscious mimicry. But both novel reading's dangers and its teaching opportunity, its currency as a debased market culture and its potential for elevation, arise from the same idea: that a reader/consumer can be made to conform to the object.

Elevating the novel

The scandal of novel reading for entertainment incited various responses. While the conservative critics advocated simple abstention from novel reading, writers like Daniel Defoe and Penelope Aubin adopted a different strategy. Aubin and Defoe enter the market not only to sell books but also to change

---

7 Michel de Certeau, *Practice of Everyday Life*, trans. Steven F. Rendall (Berkeley and Los Angeles: University of California Press, 1984), p. 167.
8 *Ibid.*

reading by developing novelistic entertainments that have an ethically improving design. In seven novels published between 1721 and 1728, Penelope Aubin turns away from the brisk modernity and explicit sexuality of the novels of amorous intrigue, and returns to the style and content of the heroic romances of La Calprenède and Scudéry. This return to romance lifts her characters out of the ego-centred plots of media culture, and gives a nostalgic 'retro' feel to her novels. Aubin's first novel, *The Life of Madame de Beaumount, a French Lady* (1721), is replete with patiently endured trials and miraculous escapes told through a complex narrative scheme, which features an anthology of embedded narratives. Belinda, the central heroine, has a magically radiant virtue that the hero, Mr Luelling, need only see and hear in order to love. In spite of their indebtedness to aristocratic French models, Aubin's novels have a distinctly English, bourgeois, Protestant cast: her narratives are guided by a particularly insistent doctrine of providential rewards, whereby 'strange' and wonderful 'accidents' guarantee final happiness to the virtuous. Aubin's novels make the heroine's physical virginity the indispensable criterion of virtue. In 1739, the same year Richardson was writing the *Familiar Letters* and *Pamela*, Richardson printed and wrote the anonymous preface to a posthumous collection of Aubin's seven novels, *A Collection of Entertaining Histories and Novels*.

In his last novel, *Roxana* (1724) Daniel Defoe develops a very different strategy for rewriting the reading experience provided by the novels of amorous intrigue. Critics have noted the affiliations between Defoe's text of 1724 and the secret histories made popular by Behn, Manley and Haywood. The third-person narratives of Behn, Manley and Haywood take the reader into an affect-laden, supercharged sympathy with the thoughts and sensibilities of the characters. Their narratives reach an extreme of sympathetic identification in the big sex scenes, where purple prose encourages absorption in the rhythms of the action. Defoe's first-person narrative allows him to make Roxana one who not only lives, but, after living, recollects and interprets. This double-voiced narrative projects Roxana as a character who is as absorbed by her experience as an absorbed reader; but, at the same time, Roxana is a narrator who subjects that character to analytical control through an act of writing. If one considers *Roxana* as a single novel, it offers a somewhat haphazard sequence of episodes, with cross-references and a progress of sorts, woven together by the secondary retrospective narrative. But, as with *Love Letters*, the *New Atalantis* and *Love in Excess*, there are fundamental problems with treating *Roxana* as a single novel: is the novel consistent with itself? Is the central character self-identical? The novel is a collection of Roxana's erotic adventures, with her jeweller, with the French prince, with the Dutch merchant, etc. Instead of writing *Roxana* as a unity, Defoe fashions a 'serial' named 'Roxana' that effects a parodic repetition of the novels of amorous intrigue. In *Roxana* Defoe performs an experiment: he applies the modus vivendi of the novels of amorous intrigue to a world organised according to different principles. What results at its most prosaic level is a practical critique of these novels as actual models for social behaviour: beauty can't last for ever; men throw off their mistresses when they lose their charms; sex leads to pregnancy; and so on. None of these mundane realities prevents Roxana, as the 'series' lead, from achieving spectacular success. By editing her narrative, Defoe subjects the naive absorbed reader to critique and reformation. The violence of this cultural project is evidenced by the problematic ending of *Roxana*. *Roxana*'s sudden ending offers less a conclusion than a collapse of the narrative, one intended to disrupt a naive reader's thoughtless absorption.

The *Pamela* media event

The publication of *Pamela* in 1740, and the responses to it, did much to change the cultural location and meaning of novel reading. At the centre of Richardson's project is a simple compositional move: *Pamela* overwrites the novels of amorous intrigue. This entails an intimate but antagonistic relation between Richardson's elevated novel and the novels he would replace. *Pamela* recounts how a young girl imbued with prudential paternal warnings and innocent of novel reading nonetheless finds herself within a novel. When her young master indulges in novelistic assumptions about their common situation, and pressures her to yield to his desires, she refuses to play the novelistic role of seduced victim. Pamela takes the 'lead' in Mr B's novel, but then rewrites his plot as a story of virtue in distress. The heroine only escapes her captivity within the novel by deflecting the action through a new kind of writing – the letter journal with which the heroine records her trials. When Mr B accepts her journal's narrative of their common situation as truthful, she has won a husband by reforming his reading practices. Mr B's reform models the reform Richardson wants for all novel readers.

Pamela's intertexts – the conduct book tradition and the novel of amorous intrigue – lead to two utterly unacceptable directions for the action. The novels of amorous intrigue suggest the first bad result – Pamela seduced into an affair with Mr B. At the same time, the conduct book Richardson interrupts writing in order to compose *Pamela* – the *Familiar Letters* – suggests a result that is no less unacceptable to successful narrative development: Pamela sees the threat of Mr B's schemes and returns to her father's house. Such a result would obey the literal injunction of letter 2 of *Pamela*, as well as the advice tendered by a father in letter 138 of the *Familiar Letters*, and immediately followed in letter 139 with his dutiful daughter's announcement that she is returning home as instructed. In order to achieve a rewriting of both the novels of amorous intrigue and the conduct discourse, Richardson must steer narrative action between the Scylla of virtuous withdrawal and the Charybdis of compliant seduction.

What takes Pamela and Mr B past the danger of an early short circuit of their story? Nothing within the text appears more crucial than the disguise scene, where Pamela, the woman who claims not to have read novels, acts like a heroine from one by appearing incognito in her country dress. Here is the first episode of the novel in which Pamela becomes ambiguously complicit with the codes of love, disguise and manipulation fundamental to the novels of amorous intrigue. Up to that scene, Pamela's story could have ended in virtuous withdrawal, but after that scene, where Mr B wins a kiss from Pamela, Mr B's desire is triggered and he develops his plot to remove Pamela to his Lincolnshire estate, and expose her virtue to erotic attack. But beyond its effect upon Mr B, the scene offers a performance in excess of Pamela's intended meaning. This helps explain the liability to misreading built into the anti-novel named *Pamela*.

The print market where *Pamela* appears may best be described as an 'open' system. By this I do not mean that it is random or chaotic, nor that it is free of constraints. But neither is it a self-regulating totality that sustains some essential character through the sort of homeostasis proper, for example, to many biological systems. The print market is a system of production and consumption where no one can control or guarantee the meanings that sweep through its texts. It is open to seismic shifts and dislocations. Lacking centralised censorship or certification, the market is influenced by any who can get their writing printed. Here there are no commonly recognised standards, and remarkably few limits as to what can be said or written. The non-hierarchical character of this system means that it is difficult to get any semantic effects to have staying power – what is published is always open to revision and cooptation by someone else's writing. The openness of a system that enables Richardson to rewrite earlier novels also exposes *Pamela* to rewriting. To publish on the early modern print market is to be thrown into involuntary collaboration. In order to discipline the market *Pamela* appeared within, and in order to counteract *Pamela*'s dangerous proximity to the novel of amorous intrigue, Richardson launched a carefully orchestrated promotional campaign for the text. The promotional campaign is striking for two reasons: its success in anticipating the future misreadings of *Pamela* and its failure to protect the novel from these misreadings. With *Pamela*, Richardson hoped to transcend the debased and compromised terrain of media culture entertainments.

Richardson hoped, one might venture to say, that *Pamela* would so reform its reader that it would replace all novels, and be the last and only fiction its reader would want to read. Of course it did not turn out that way. Instead, *Pamela* provoked a torrent of critique, defence, sequels and rip-offs in the print culture of 1741–2. The reforming ambition behind *Pamela* and its extraordinary popularity combined to incite the anti-Pamelist reaction. Three anonymous responses to *Pamela* were published between April and June 1741: Fielding's *Shamela*, the anonymous *Pamela Censured* and Haywood's *Anti-Pamela*.[9] All three of these texts situate *Pamela* by using the terms of the debate about novel reading, and all three betray anxiety about the effects of absorption in novel reading. Haywood, Fielding and the author of *Pamela Censured* felt that Richardson's cure for novel reading was worse than the disease. Each condemns *Pamela* for the way it invites its readers to see too much. For Fielding, Richardson's *Pamela* does not solve the problem posed by a surrender to absorptive reading, or the danger of a naive acting out of novelistic scenarios. Instead, the very loftiness of Richardson's moral aims, and his putting Pamela forward as an example of virtue to its reader, threatens to produce a 'hyper'-absorption of the reader.

As a rejoinder to *Pamela*, Fielding writes a novel that displays many forms of naive reading, tests them by experience and finds them wanting. The textual education provided by *Joseph Andrews* is finally ironic: it turns out there is no book that can teach virtue by modelling it. Building upon the general address and entertainment potential of media culture, Fielding's performative novel puts a middle term – the author/narrator – between the reader and the story told. By incorporating a critical reflection upon reading into his text, Fielding locates his novel in the new discursive space opened by the *Pamela* media event: a public-sphere debate about what reading is and should be. Instead of offering any prescriptive example of reading, *Joseph Andrews* weaves an open matrix of variable reading practices: reading as pleasurable consumption, as dialogic conversation, as a performative entertainment. Fielding does

---

9 See Thomas Keymer and Peter Sabor, eds. *The Pamela Controversy: Criticisms and Adaptations of Samuel Richardson's Pamela, 1740–1750*, 6 vols. (London: Pickering & Chatto, 2001).

not function as an all-knowing God, but as a leader of the revels. By developing a distinct new form of English comic novel, explicitly modelled upon Cervantes, Fielding promotes his own mode of elevated, critically self-aware novel reading.

How does the *Pamela* media event affect the cultural location of novels, and, after this media event, what sorts of critical practices can proliferate around them? The very ambition of Richardson's project to reshape novel reading raises the stakes around novel reading, and this, as we have seen, becomes a provocation to those who refuse his 'scheme' for reforming novel reading. The success of *Pamela* as a 'new species' of elevated novel reading, and the intensity of the counter-offensive of the anti-Pamelists, not only precipitated a debate about what reading for pleasure should be. This debate also meant that the contending readers of the *Pamela* media event, in order to support or deflate *Pamela*'s pretensions, start reading *Pamela* in ways that are important to the long-term institutionalisation of novel reading. To state the case most schematically, now readers start engaging in the sort of sympathetic identification with and critical judgement of fictional character that will lie at the centre of novel reading from Richardson, Fielding and Burney through Jane Austen, George Eliot and Henry James. *Pamela*'s readers 'read through' the words and ideas of the novel's eponymous heroine in order to assess her character with the view of discovering whether 'Pamela' is what the text's subtitle declares – a personification of virtue – or its reverse, a mere sham. By conferring on a character in a novel some of the free-standing qualities of a real person, and insisting that judgements of literary character reflect as much on those who judge as on the judged, both sides in the *Pamela* wars confer an unprecedented moral seriousness upon the evaluation of fictional characters. The strife around *Pamela* draws readers into particular practices of detailed reading: selecting what to read so as to emphasise one thing instead of another; being provoked by incomplete descriptions; filling out the picture to one's own taste; using one's imagination to read between the lines; discerning the supposedly 'real' intention of the author; and, finally, distinguishing 'the proper' from the 'improper' in a text, in order to judge whether a text is 'readable' or 'unreadable.' All these practices of reading may produce a more or less 'qualified' reading, which in turn becomes an index of a reader's position in the social hierarchy. By identifying the lives of characters with their own lives and by indulging a sympathetic confusion of the imaginary and the real, readers relocate the distinction fiction/reality from an opposition between novel and the world to one within different kinds of novels. Habermas suggests that this new way of reading letter novels was integral to the constitution of a critical public sphere of private subjects.[10]

This chapter's account of the complex antagonism of the novels of amorous intrigue and the elevated novel suggests a revision of the standard account of the rise of the novel in the eighteenth century. Before the emergence of the novel into literary studies and literary pedagogy, novels played a role in several crucial cultural episodes: first, the debate over the course of the eighteenth century about the pleasures and moral dangers of novel reading; second, novels are said to articulate distinct national cultures; and finally, novels are touted as offering the most realistic representation of modern life. It is through these three articulations that the novel secures its place as a type of literature. While the traditional rise of the novel thesis draws upon the Enlightenment's own account of its surpassing of an earlier benighted belief in myth and superstition, that thesis contributes to the formation of literary studies, where *the* novel coalesces as an object of study. Thus, I would claim that the English novel at mid eighteenth century is not a type of literature. Only retroactively, after the broad acceptance – by the nineteenth century – of novels as a literary type – can developments around the mid eighteenth century and after be seen, retroactively, as contributions to that project. Early contributions to the idea that the novel could be a literary form include Fielding's formal experiments in *Tom Jones*, the critical claims made for the new novels in Johnson's *Rambler* essay no. 4 and the emergence of systematic criticism in England with the *Monthly Review* (1749 onwards) and the *Critical Review* (1756 onwards). Add to these key critical developments the following subsequent events: the writing of a capacious and complex literary history (in Clara Reeve and John Dunlop); the inclusion of novel reading in various pedagogical projects (Scottish lecturers like Hugh Blair); the multi-volume editions of the eighteenth-century novel by Laetitia Barbauld and Walter Scott; and the interpretation by Scott, Hazlitt and others of novels as a crucial expression of the morals, manners and spirit of the nation. Only after this work done in the seventy years after 1750 does *the* novel emerge as a literary type as well as a form of entertainment.

My readings of Behn, Manley and Haywood also suggest the liabilities of the literary paradigm for interpreting the novels of amorous intrigue. Any effort to place these novels under the rubric of literature ends finding them lacking and falling short. Where one kind of reading is thrown up (the novel as literature), another is thrown down (the novel as entertainment); where one

---

10 Jürgen Habermas, *The Structural Transformation of the Public Sphere*, trans. Thomas Burger (Cambridge, MA: M.I.T. Press, 1989), p. 50.

kind of pleasure is licensed, another is discredited. This turbulent vortex of reciprocal appearance and disappearance is mis-seen as the origin of the novel. But in order for the elevated novel to appear, the novel of amorous intrigue must be made to disappear. This is a secret interdependency of 'high cultural object' (dubbed 'the novel') and its effaced precursors. It is often thought that popular fiction develops as a middle- or low-brow reaction to a pre-existent high culture. I think the history of the early novel in Britain suggests the reverse. The very concept of the novel as a high literary form results from unease with the absorptive reading of the 'low' amorous novel developed within early print-media culture. The novel, as a literary form with claims to modern cultural capital, was produced as a stay against early modern novel reading practices that, by their atavistic power, threatened to short-circuit the Enlightenment educational project.

PART II

*

LITERARY GENRES: ADAPTATION AND REFORMATION

5

Restoration and early eighteenth-century drama

HAROLD LOVE

The Restoration theatre, while in many ways a new creation, maintained important continuities with pre-1642 practice. The indoor playhouse lit by candlelight and charging high prices had existed since Shakespeare's time. Perspective scenery had been used in Caroline court masques and in D'Avenant's interregnum entertainments. Although the Elizabethan thrust stage (out into the audience space) was abandoned, acting took place in front of the proscenium arch, not behind it as in present-day scenic theatres. Actors still had to be the 'servants' of some powerful person: the King's Company, who were regarded as legal successors to the earlier King's Men, belonged to the royal household and the Duke's Company to that of the king's brother, James, Duke of York. Caroline models of censorship were restored, with the Master of the Revels required to approve scripts for performance and the Surveyor of the Press those for printing. Elements of the old actor–sharer system were in evidence as late as 1695 with the brilliant Lincoln's Inn Fields troupe. What then had changed? The most momentous innovation was the restriction of trade to no more than two companies at any one time, which was undertaken to protect the large investments in buildings and scenery and the steep rise in manpower necessary to meet raised audience expectations. The King's Company patentee, Thomas Killigrew, boasted to Pepys that the stage was 'now by his pains a thousand times better and more glorious then ever heretofore'.[1] The new roofed theatres were handsome, brick constructions, employing the continental technology of illusionism based on wing-and-shutter scenery (that is, painted canvas backgrounds and borders run on from the sides) and the use of machines. The radical rewriting of pre-1642 plays, often deplored today, was a necessary adjustment to this

---

1 *The Diary of Samuel Pepys*, ed. Robert Latham and William Matthews, 11 vols. (London: G. Bell & Sons, 1970–), vol. VIII, p. 55 (12 February 1667).

technology. The second important change was that women's parts could at last be played by women: an irresistible tide of heterosexuality transformed what had earlier been an ambiguous spectacle of females portrayed by males. The pre-1642 doubling of parts was also abandoned, meaning that a player could earn a salary by a few minutes' appearance in a performance instead of having to manage several changes of role and costume. New, more individualistic conceptions of both personal and artistic identity were responsible for this, and also for collaboration between dramatists becoming much less frequent.

The pace of playing had certainly changed. Rewritings of older plays always cut severely, as there was no longer time for so many words. Dryden's heroic plays and Wycherley's comedies are fast-moving conceptually, with each ingenious simile or paradoxical couplet immediately capped by another, but visually were designed to put the performers on stage for long periods, relatively motionless, in order to be stared at and listened to. Lighting limitations were one reason for this, but deference contributed too. It was considered ill-mannered, and when royalty was present close to treasonable, to turn one's back on persons of superior rank. Discussions of acting technique, which now begin to appear, emphasise gesture rather than mobility and lay their main stress on a physiological accuracy in the delineation of 'the passions' in their mechanistic, Cartesian formulation. 'Alas! what Machines are we!' comments Bevil junior in 4.1 of Steele's *The Conscious Lovers*, observing Myrtle's sudden change of affect on reading the letter.[2]

The Restoration theatre, then, was an illusion factory whose particular way of manufacturing illusion predetermined many aspects of the verbal texts of plays. We mistake their nature when we read them without understanding this; yet, when we read them as literature we need not be doing them a disservice. During the Interregnum the reading of plays had increasingly been done for its own sake rather than as a way of imagining or reimagining a performance; moreover, it was a dramatist, Fletcher, who was held up as the supreme model of wit, elegance and courtliness in writing, values which for royalist readers carried a strong political charge. The restored drama was determined not to surrender this newly acquired prestige. Dryden's contempt for Chapman's Jacobean *Bussy D'Ambois* arose from his conviction that once the charms of action and presence were removed the play was valueless as a

---

2 *The Plays of Sir Richard Steele*, ed. Shirley Strum Kenny (Oxford: Clarendon Press, 1971), p. 357. Descartes' theory is expounded in *Traité des passions de l'âme* (1649).

text for reading.[3] Mr Bayes in his manic direction of the play-within-a-play in Buckingham's burlesque, *The Rehearsal* (1671), is as concerned as any director with visual effect ('Gentlemen, I must desire you to remove a little, for I must fill the Stage') but his main preoccupation as an author is with the utterance of words ('your Heroic Verse never sounds well, but when the Stage is full') and his highest moments of self-congratulation are produced by striking lines ('Is not this good language now? is not that elevate? 'Tis my *non ultra*, I gad').[4] There was also a seductive affinity, originally argued in D'Avenant's preface to his epic *Gondibert* (1651), between the heroic poem and heroic drama, which could now be envisaged as an attempt to realise Virgilian or Ariostan values in the more instructive medium of presented action.[5] Prologues and epilogues ceased to be texts for the theatre alone and became valued as poems in their own right: much of the best satire of the period has come down in this form, as well as some of its most incisive criticism.[6] With the novel still in embryo and much poetry confined to manuscript, drama was acknowledged not simply as a form of literature worthy to be read with attention, but as the pre-eminent form of vernacular literature.[7] Dryden's *Of Dramatic Poesie* (1668) placed current English achievement ahead of that of the ancients, the French and the Elizabethans. Even the humblest play publication now appeared with a dedication and often a preface, which might, as in the Dryden–Shadwell exchanges over the nature of true comedy, be part of an extended controversy. When Congreve came to edit his writings for the *Works* of 1710, he did so in the confidence that he was the leading literary figure of his day, not simply the best dramatist – Pope's dedication to him of the *Homer* was an acknowledgement of this status. In their franker moments the playwrights might concede that Shakespeare and Jonson had excelled them in genius but never wavered in their belief that theirs was the more 'correct' creativity.[8] Shakespeare, by this assessment, had lived too early to refine his understanding of nature through a

---

3 *The Works of John Dryden*, gen. eds. Edward Niles Hooker, H. T. Swedenberg, Jr and Alan Roper, 20 vols. (Berkeley and Los Angeles: University of California Press, 1956–89), vol. XIV, p. 100.
4 4.1. 267–8, 270–1, 85–6 in George Villiers, 2nd Duke of Buckingham, *The Rehearsal*, ed. D. E. L. Crane (Durham, NC: University of Durham Press, 1976).
5 *Sir William Davenant's Gondibert*, ed. David F. Gladish (Oxford: Oxford University Press, 1971), pp. 15–16; see also p. xi.
6 Pierre Danchin's monumental edition, *The Prologues and Epilogues of the Restoration 1660–1700*, 7 vols. (Publications de l'Université de Nancy II, 1981–8) makes it possible to explore the riches of this previously scattered corpus.
7 Paulina Kewes, *Authorship and Appropriation: Writing for the Stage in England, 1660–1710* (Oxford: Oxford University Press, 1998), pp. 27–31 and throughout.
8 See on this point Dryden, *Works*, vol. XI, pp. 203–18.

knowledge of art, and, consequently, had to be purged of his many barbarisms. Jonson had art but lacked urbanity.

It was with this double confidence – theatrical and literary – that the play-wrights of the Restoration set off to make a new beginning in English drama. Everything was to be reformed in the light of up-to-date values, which may be summed up as politeness, ease and irreverence in comedy and grandeur, fine language and amazement in the graver forms. They could count, moreover, on widespread public enthusiasm for their project. The professionals were proud of the support given to their work by the court, and often boasted of having used leading courtiers as models of heroism in tragedy and conversational brilliance in comedy. It is true that the king's own tastes were as innocent of the 'seraphic part' as his love-life: delighted with Thomas Durfey's bustling sex farce, *A Fond Husband* (1677), he insisted that his poet laureate, Dryden, compose a similar piece, the outrageous *The Kind Keeper; or Mr Limberham* (1678). Yet, audiences were never, except at the court's own well-appointed theatre at Whitehall, the coterie of legend; instead, the public theatres saw a confluence of court, city and 'town' elements in which it was the last-named (discussed below) which was to prove dominant. The mercantile city, despite the rough handling its inhabi-tants received in the comedies, always contributed considerably to audiences, with the most ambitious theatre of the time, the Duke's at Dorset Garden (1671), constructed well within its boundaries. When Killigrew complained to Pepys about the loss of the city audience it was because they had deserted his own performances for the other company's visually spectacular offerings.[9]

The heroic play and baroque tragedy

The most original creation of the Restoration period was not its comedy but the so-called heroic play.[10] The best-known examples were conceived for a performing style developed by the King's Company which employed a stylised

---

9 *Diary of Samuel Pepys*, vol. VIII, p. 56.
10 Restoration drama has been well served by detailed narrative histories, beginning with Allardyce Nicoll's 1923 account, later reissued as the first volume of his six-volume *A History of English Drama 1660–1900*, 6 vols. (Cambridge: Cambridge University Press 1959), with its still valuable listing of the entire repertoire, and continued in Robert D. Hume's lucid and magisterial *English Drama in the Later Seventeenth-century* (Oxford: Oxford University Press, 1976) and Derek Hughes' interpretively inventive *English Drama 1660–1700* (Oxford: Oxford University Press, 1996). For this reason I will concentrate in this chapter on those works and dramatists of greatest interest to modern readers and directors. Dates are those of production, when known, and will sometimes be earlier than those of first publication.

vocal delivery known as 'speaking to a tone', and were written in rhymed, pentameter couplets, though there are also blank-verse plays which belong to the genre in all but that respect. Plots are historical or mythical. The plays are famous for verbal rants, frequent appearances by ghosts, and characters who might be mistaken on first encounter for walking inventories of the Cartesian passions. While rich in representations of religious ritual, Christian as well as pagan, they tend to be strongly anti-clerical and often, either situationally or by introducing 'atheistical' speeches, anti-Christian. With Puritanism discredited as seditious and hypocritical, Romanism as an agent of secular tyranny and Anglicanism for its reliance on state coercion, art turned to the magnification of human capacities as a way of filling the spiritual void. James G. Turner identifies a 'displacement of religious sensibilities in the hastily assembled secular-hedonist culture of Restoration England'.[11] The plays are also marked by a sensationalism so outrageous as to verge on the surreal. Nathaniel Lee's *Nero* (1675), having used up matricide, incest and self-deification in its opening act, becomes so desperate for further horrors as to introduce two different ghosts in successive scenes.

Despite their excesses these remarkable dramas were also a potent mythical expression of ideological conflict, one that had to remain mythical because the real message – a Hobbesean one in Dryden's case and a Calvinist one in Lee's – could not be uttered openly. In Britain the birth-throes of the modern were intensified by uncertainty whether the path forward was to be that of a revived Caesarism on the model of France or that of a consensual oligarchy within which medieval notions of distributed power would be preserved through the parliament and the common law. There was also the third way of an untrammelled individualism, which found its theatrical personification in Dryden's Almanzor from *The Conquest of Granada*. Derek Hughes diagnoses an 'absence of a larger order to contain and harmonise the atomistic conflict of individual wills' and 'a general failure of the systems that traditionally express and sustain man's social character'.[12] Dryden's and Lee's heroic plays are radiographs of a schizoid political subjectivity. The genre's preoccupation with the nature and transformations of power means that it is richly open to Foucaultian readings; but the more pressing challenge is to find an aesthetic appropriate to these remarkable works, for we are not going to understand them until we have learned how to enjoy them. This must involve an unembarrassed acceptance

11 James E. Turner, 'The Libertine Sublime: Love and Death in Restoration England', *Studies in Eighteenth-century Culture* 19 (1989), 112.
12 Hughes, *English Drama 1660–1700*, pp. 306, 104.

of their un-British obsession with the extreme and that the extreme is never more than a hair's breadth away from the absurd. Dr Johnson recognised that Dryden loved living dangerously on exactly this boundary, and it is equally true of the other proponents of the genre. The figurative language of the plays brings vitalistic and mechanistic constructions of reality into daring collisions that annihilate both.[13]

The genre took shape in the hands of its first master, Roger Boyle, Earl of Orrery, as an attempt to create an English equivalent of the French rhymed tragedy and prose romance. Orrery wrote as a former associate of Cromwell, *The General* (1664) being an exculpatory resumé of this now embarrassing episode. The 'usurpation play' was to remain a favourite genre of the Restoration stage, finding its burlesque reflection in *The Rehearsal* when the two kings of Brentford are temporarily supplanted by the Physician and the Gentleman Usher. The closely related 'siege' play also had a long history. In Henry Nevile Payne's *The Siege of Constantinople* (1674) and John Crowne's *The Destruction of Jerusalem by Titus Vespasian* (1677), the threat to the doomed city is a double one from an imperial foe without and rebels within, the first group figuring the threat of France and the second that of Geneva. Payne was a Catholic: in Protestant versions the rebels within became cannibalistic Jesuits. Both genres make extensive play with a character-type we might call 'the ambitious statesman', whose origins lie in Jacobean satires on William Cecil, Earl of Salisbury but which attached itself in the 1670s to to the Whig leader Shaftesbury.

Orrery was soon overtaken by more innovative masters in Dryden and Lee. Although French models continued to be invoked and sometimes quarried, Gallic restraint was now abandoned. Dryden's heroic plays and tragedies are conventionally seen as an anomalous and fundamentally frivolous departure from the main tradition of British drama. Literary treatments of his serious plays have largely concentrated on the unrhymed work from the latter part of his stage career, especially *All for Love* (1678) and *Don Sebastian* (1689), while the great succession of rhymed plays comprising *The Indian Queen* (1664), *The Indian Emperor* (1665), *Tyrannic Love* (1669), *The Conquest of Granada by the Spaniards* I and II (1670–1), *The State of Innocence* (1674 but unacted) and *Aureng Zebe* (1675), with which should be numbered the 'serious' scenes of *Secret*

---

13 See Johnson's remarks on 'unideal vacancy' in *The Lives of the English Poets*, ed. George Birkbeck Hill, 3 vols. (Oxford: Clarendon Press, 1905), vol. I, p. 460. Dryden's figurative language is considered in Harold Love, 'Constructing Classicism: Dryden and Purcell' in Paul Hammond and David Hopkins (eds.), *John Dryden: Tercentenary Essays* (Oxford: Oxford University Press, 2000), pp. 92–112; 'Dryden's "unideal vacancy" ', *Eighteenth-Century Studies* 12 (1978), 74–89; and 'Dryden's Rationale of Paradox', *ELH* 51 (1984), 297–313.

Love (1667) and *Marriage à-la-Mode* (1671), are left to genealogists of the grand narratives of colonialism, imperialism and orientalism. As just suggested, the problem is primarily one of finding an enabling aesthetic. We need to accept that these are by any standards beautifully crafted works, and that a good part of this craftsmanship was devoted to virtuoso ratiocination, as signally in *The State of Innocence*, 4.1. 11–120, where Adam and Raphael suspend the action in order to debate the nature of free will. Not having been educated to regard the Scholastic practice of academic disputation as the highest form of intellectual endeavour, we are unequipped today to recognise the extent to which, both as adaptation and as parody, it is central to Dryden's conception of dialogue.

In any case, worries over unseriousness cease to be an issue when we turn from Dryden to the other master of the heroic play, Nathaniel Lee, for Lee, once past the excesses of *Nero*, is serious even to a fault. His central concern is with the pursuit of what Turner has called the 'libertine sublime', defined as a 'heroisation of sexuality' in 'an England lurching out of control, where political authority has become entangled with sexual extremism'.[14] But in his case this pursuit is conducted in the shadow of vast and obscure historical processes that occasionally fulfil but more often frustrate the intoxicating promise of all-transcending passion. The informing vision is the Augustinian or proto-Marxist one of history as the relentless working of a machine. The outcome of *Lucius Junius Brutus* is a 'vast turn' woven by fate on its 'eternal Loom'; in *The Massacre of Paris* the plot to murder the Protestants is both a 'Mighty Engine' with a 'main Beam' and a 'New Ruin' that runs on wheels.[15] World history is read backwards in Puritan, providentialist terms from the trauma of the English revolution and forward to dreams of universal empire. In the classical plays the agent of history is Rome in its rise to world domination. *Sophonisba* (1675) asks our sympathy for the victims of this success; but haunting Lee throughout his career was a sense that the same imperative was active in the events of his own day.

Lee's dialogue, while most famous for its show-stopping rants, has a turbulent music quite different from the syllogistic patterning of Dryden's couplets. The most successful of his rhymed dramas was *The Rival Queens* (1677), a brilliant baroque divertissement in which his transcendental imaginings were accommodated to the polished art of Charles Hart and Michael Mohun as Alexander the Great and the honest general, Clytus. Both had been boy actors

14 Turner, 'The Libertine Sublime', pp. 106, 112.
15 4.1. 160–3; 1.1. 109; 1.2. 1–2, cited from *The Works of Nathaniel Lee*, ed. Thomas B. Stroup and Arthur L. Cooke, 2 vols. (New Brunswick, NJ: Scarecrow Press, 1954–5).

before 1642. Hart was the more elegant of the pair while Mohun generally took the more vigorous parts. The two queens of the title were played by Rebecca Marshall and Elizabeth Boutell, the first representatives of the pairing of a strong dramatic actress with an ingénue which was to be perfected in the partnership of Elizabeth Barry and Anne Bracegirdle in the United and Lincoln's Inn Fields companies. Along with *Theodosius* (1680) it was still a repertoire piece in the 1830s. Through allusion and quotation Lee is also an informing presence of eighteenth-century fiction.[16]

Yet Lee's most powerful drama was written after he had abandoned Hart and rhyme for Betterton and blank verse. *Lucius Junius Brutus Father of His Country* (1680), dealing with the overthrow of the Tarquin kings in Rome, was a barely disguised re-enactment of the events of 1641 and what the Whigs were hoping would be the events of 1681: Machiavelli's *Discorsi* was Lee's manual for the arts of revolution. The title character is the most monstrous of all Lee's monsters, a father who, in order to confirm the people of Rome in their rejection of royalism, presides unflinchingly over the execution of his two sons and the humiliation of the women of his family. At the conclusion of the play the question of how sense is to be made of this terrible history is projected straight back to the audience. Are we in Brutus' last-act orations (filched from Bacon and Seneca respectively) confronted with an agonisingly won moment of resolution or with the demented ravings of a madman, or of a mad author? And what of the gods who supposedly direct this whole process? Brutus is profuse throughout the play in his public addresses to them but in speaking privately seems to doubt their very existence: 'If there be Gods, they will reserve a room, / A Throne for thee in Heav'n' (4.1. 574). The same concession had been made earlier in the play by Lucrece at the moment when her suicide was about to precipitate the initial revolt: 'If there be Gods, O, will they not revenge me?' (1.1. 352). Since gods are necessary to sustain empire they must be willed into existence by the actions of godlike humans: deification, treated semi-comically in *Nero* and as unconscionable hubris in *The Rival Queens*, is now given a portentous seriousness. But if the gods may not exist, fate certainly does in the form of a superhuman power working towards an obscure but preordained outcome. Lee's other great political play, *The Massacre of Paris*, was written in response to the events of the Popish Plot (in 1678, Titus Oates, a fanatical anti-Catholic, claimed – falsely but convincingly for a while – that there was a Catholic and French plot to murder the king and his Protestant supporters and place a Catholic government in their place). The play proceeds

---

16 For examples see Turner, 'The Libertine Sublime', p. 99.

in compressed, fragmentary scenes, recalling Shakespeare's method in *Antony and Cleopatra*, in which the human agents, seen in their moments of crisis almost as if by flashes of lightning, are shown to be driven by the same mighty providential force, now identified with Calvinist determinism.

Whereas Lee and Dryden had achieved their best effects through a full-blooded embracing of the artificial, there is a refreshing immediacy to Thomas Otway's tragedies, which began with the rhymed *Alcibiades* (1675) and *Don Carlos* (1676). Otway turned to blank verse in 1680 with *The History and Fall of Caius Marius* (1680), in which a Tory political fable was bulked out with a subplot plagiarised from *Romeo and Juliet*, before advancing to the lasting achievement of *The Orphan* (1680) and *Venice Preserv'd* (1682). That both were written for Betterton's company with its less hieratic style, and that this company possessed the greatest actress of the time in Elizabeth Barry, is one reason for their freshness of approach; but it must also be conceded that Otway lacks the intellectual engagement with his material that we find in Dryden and Lee – the politics and history even of *Venice Preserv'd* are perfunctory and cartoonish. His gift lay in the depiction of intense, destructive interpersonal relationships.

John Crowne's *The Destruction of Jerusalem by Titus Vespasian* (1677), an immense ten-act drama for performance over two nights, written for the King's Company in a bid to win over the Dorset Garden audience, invokes the endemic Restoration nightmare of a divided people unable to resist the attack of a unified and disciplined enemy. Jerusalem is recognisably the England of the early 1640s in which fanatical Pharisees agitate against a virtuous, Laud-like high priest; then, with the arrival in Part two of the besieging Romans, the model changes to that of the present-day nation confronting the power of Louis XIV's France. Scenes narrating a thwarted love affair between the Jewish queen, Berenice, and the Roman emperor, Titus, draw on Racine's *Berenice*, a play whose importance for Restoration England is shown by its being translated by Otway for the rival house. Titus is a modernising ruler wholly subordinated to the imperatives of secular empire and his personal fame, being in this respect the aesthetic as well as the ideological foe of the priests of the temple, which is portrayed by Crowne as a realm of unearthly beauty evoked through religious ritual and orientalist exoticism. Through the doomed sacramental world of the city strides the hyperactive Almanzor-like figure of the warrior prince, Phraartes, representing the other modernism of atheism and the pursuit of the erotic sublime. The death of Clarona, the high priest's daughter, drives him to madness in which, in a Dryden-like collision of vitalism and mechanism, he vows to destroy the sun, the symbol of lust and empire, by cutting it into democratic stars.[17] The play concludes with the burning of the temple and the actual or imminent deaths of all the Jewish characters with the exception of the now discarded Berenice. To turn from the excesses of this colossal work to Crowne's blank-verse *The Ambitious Statesman* (1679) is to enter a claustrophobic world in which honesty is helpless to resist evil. The most reflective of the dramatic commentaries on the Exclusion crisis, it recalls Webster's *The Duchess of Malfi* in its anatomisation of the morbidities of power. Crowne's career was a long one, also embracing Shakespeare adaptations and some excellent satirical comedies. He was the first Harvard alumnus to make a name for himself in literature.

Elkanah Settle, by contrast, was a crowd-pleaser who wandered into a league too big for him. The success of his extravagant usurpation play *The Empress of Morocco* (1673), whose quarto contains invaluable woodcut illustrations of the Dorset Garden facade and scenery, immediately brought forth the splenetic *Notes and Observations on the Empress of Morocco*, mostly by Crowne but with contributions by Dryden and Shadwell, which is notable for being the first extended close reading of a dramatic text in the language. Unfortunately, he was unable to rival the achievement of the *Empress*. *The Female Prelate* (1680), a politically charged retelling of the medieval Pope Joan myth, never quite makes up its mind whether it wants to be melodrama or burlesque. His career took him from Dorset Garden to Bartholomew Fair and then to an old age as a professional writer of funeral elegies.

The rhymed heroic play had a longer afterlife than is usually realised – Charles Hopkins' *Boadicea, Queen of Britain* appeared as late as 1697 – but had ceased to interest the leading dramatists even before the absorption of the King's Company into the Duke's in May 1682. Henceforth, the tone in tragedy was set by Betterton and Barry with their preference for a less stylised emotionality. Barry had been sacked from the King's Company because of her inability to master its arcane arts of vocalisation but in her new environment inspired a genre of innovative 'she-tragedies'. Otway began the trend, being succeeded after his death by John Banks, whose *The Unhappy Favourite* (1681) was the earliest dramatic treatment of the story of Elizabeth I and Essex. Southerne's *The*

---

17   Aloft! – I see her mounting to the Sun! –
     The flaming Satyr towards her does roul,
     His scorching Lust makes Summer at the Pole.
     Let the hot Planet touch her if he dares! –
     Touch her, and I will cut him into Stars,
     And the bright chips into the Ocean throw! –
     (*The Destruction of Jerusalem by Titus Vespasian.*
     The second part (London, 1677), pp. 54–5.)

Fatal Marriage (1694), very loosely based on a story by Aphra Behn, gave Barry her finest leading role, though the play was weakened by the need to insert a comic subplot for the company's rising star, Anne Bracegirdle. Its successor, *Oroonoko* (1695), again derived from Behn but performed by Christopher Rich's younger Drury Lane company, is more effective in its blending of satirical and heroic plots and has generated considerable interpretive comment for its treatment of race and slavery. Hughes finds its thematic unity in the notion that 'the universal principle of human intercourse is the sale of the body, whether in the marriage-market or the slave-market'.[18] Congreve in *The Mourning Bride* (1697) was more successful than Southerne had been in combining the talents of Barry and Bracegirdle, besides providing a splendid part for the aging Betterton. Constructed around a series of by now thoroughly familiar stage effects, the play is of interest for its perfection of a particular kind of Augustan tragic diction that trembles continually on the edge of banality, and in lesser hands would not escape it, but here achieves a classical luminosity which mirrors the superbly sculpted prose of his comedies. Congreve the miniaturist is evident in every speech. Barry's immediate successors reproduced her parts without possessing her genius; however, thanks to her, for more than a century English theatre possessed a repertoire of leading roles for women stars who in Shakespeare were condemned to second- and third-best. Notable among these were Nicholas Rowe's *The Fair Penitent* (1703), distantly reliant on Massinger's *The Fatal Dowry*, and *Jane Shore* (1714), two long-popular anticipations of the nineteenth-century 'fallen-woman' play. The theatrical frisson of *Jane Shore* was seeing actors playing the same parts as they did in *Richard III* in a fuller exploration of what was only a passing episode of Shakespeare's tragedy.[19]

The serious drama of the Restoration and early eighteenth century was always strongly drawn to Greek and Roman topics. The turbulent years of the Exclusion Crisis (1678–82), in which the Whigs led by the Earl of Shaftesbury attempted to pass a bill whereby Charles' Catholic brother, James, would be excluded from the royal succession in favour of the king's illegitimate and Protestant son, the Duke of Monmouth, and the six years of Tory triumphalism that followed, confirmed a fashion for plays in which specific ancient parallels were found for modern predicaments. As baroque exuberance gave way to a more restrained manner, a kind of drama emerged in which a political theme was developed with a show of learning around a plot from Livy or Plutarch. In the more adroit examples the political theme is kept ambiguous enough to

---

18 Hughes, *English Drama 1660–1700*, p. 425.
19 For Rowe see J. Douglas Canfield, *Nicholas Rowe and Christian Tragedy* (Gainsville, FL: University of Florida Press, 1977).

admit of more than one interpretation. In Southerne's *The Fate of Capua* (1700) the situation of a city allied to Rome going over to Hannibal and then paying the price in extirpation and enslavement would seem a warning to Scotland or Ireland against admitting the Pretender; but our knowledge that the dramatist was a crypto-Jacobite suggests the possibility of a more radical reading in which it is Britain as a whole that must pay the price for its disobedience to its rightful king. His *The Spartan Dame* (1719 after thirty years on the banned list) presents its central character, Cleombrotus, as a monstrous parody of William III. Addison's *Cato* (1713) performed the political balancing act so well that, while the work of a partisan Whig, it was appropriated by both revolutionary Americans (George Washington had it performed for his troops) and British Tories. The domestic tradition in tragedy, inspired by Otway's *The Orphan*, produced a further masterpiece in George Lillo's prose tragedy *The London Merchant; or, The History of George Barnwell* (1731), a reworking of an Elizabethan ballad narrative about a virtuous apprentice driven to theft and murder by his infatuation for a vengeful female libertine.

The Restoration musical

Looking into history for the ancestors of the works of Lloyd-Webber and Sondheim, which hold such a powerful dominance over contemporary live theatre, as good a starting point as any is the creation in 1611 of Shakespeare's *The Tempest*. Anyone who has seen a production that faithfully included all of the scripted requirements for music, including the masque and the interludes between the acts, will have realised that it is already halfway to being a musical; it also made what for its time was an adventurous use of spectacle. In 1667, when D'Avenant and Dryden rewrote it as a machine play (that is to say, employing a lot of stage machinery – trapdoors, spectacular transformations etc.) using women actors, while simultaneously giving its Neoplatonic worldview a Hobbesean revamp, they further expanded the musical element. In 1674 it was revived at Dorset Garden as a full 'semi-opera', with music by Matthew Locke, inaugurating a long series of similar productions by the Duke's Company. Shadwell drew upon French comédie-ballet for *Psyche* (1675), with music by Locke and Giovanni Battista Draghi; then followed Dryden's *Albion and Albanius* (1685), set by Louis Grabu, and three Purcell settings: a revision of Fletcher's *The Prophetess* (1690), Dryden's *King Arthur* (1691), and *The Fairy-Queen* (1692), a free adaptation of *A Midsummer Night's Dream*. By this period few plays were without interpolated songs, while others, such as Rochester's adaptation of Fletcher's *Valentinian* (1684) with music by Grabu, contained substantial ballets or masques. The masque as an independent form was perpetuated in Crowne's *Calisto*, performed in the court theatre in 1675 by royal and noble amateurs with professional assistance and a huge orchestra. Established repertoire pieces such as *The Rival Queens* were converted into semi-operas to meet the new demand. The term 'musical' is not normally used for these pieces but their theatrical function was precisely that of the modern blockbuster stage musical and their popularity strongly influenced the work of a number of dramatists, not all of whom contributed to the genre directly. One of their by-products was a superb harvest of theatre songs, which may be sampled in the six volumes of Thomas Durfey's *Wit and Mirth: or Pills to Purge Melancholy* (1719–20).

Comedy

'Restoration comedy' indicated until quite recently a small body of plays by Etherege, Wycherley and Congreve, Vanbrugh and Farquhar, and a high-camp performing style in which the man and woman of sense were likely to be as gaudily overdressed as the fools.[20] Critics of the earlier part of the last century classified the plays as 'comedies of manners', drawing attention to their artificiality and elegance, and stressing their indebtedness to court culture. However, the major critical preoccupation prior to the 1960s was with the comedies' morality, which, having been castigated by Jeremy Collier in his *Short View of the Immorality and Profaneness of the English Stage* (1698), was further impugned by Macaulay in a famous *Edinburgh Review* essay of 1841 and, from a perspective based on the moral and cultural requirements for serious art as defined by the influential English critic, F. R. Leavis, by L. C. Knights in a *Scrutiny* article of 1937.[21] The stock defence, following Charles Lamb's 'On the artificial comedy of the last century' (1821), was one that denied them any serious engagement with real life by classifying them as 'Idle gallantry . . . a dream, the passing pageant of an evening'.[22] The extent to which the plays

---

20 The assumptions behind this tradition are still latent in J. L. Styan, *Restoration Comedy in Performance* (Cambridge: Cambridge University Press, 1986). A more historically aware perspective is given by Jocelyn Powell, *Restoration Theatre Production* (London: Routledge, 1984). Peter Holland, *The Ornament of Action* (Cambridge: Cambridge University Press, 1979) uses the styles of the original performers of roles as an aid to critical interpretation. Judith Milhous and Robert D. Hume, *Producible Interpretations: Eight English Plays, 1675–1707* (Carbondale, IL: Southern Illinois University Press, 1985) consider various possibilities for selected plays in modern performance.
21 L. C. Knights, 'Restoration Comedy: the Reality and the Myth', reprinted in his *Explorations* (London: Chatto and Windus, 1946), pp. 131–49.
22 Charles Lamb, *Essays of Elia* (London: Oxford University Press, 1946), p. 205.

had been marginalised in literary discussion is shown by the fact that their most industrious early twentieth-century editor was the somewhat scandalous cleric, Montague Summers, whose other main interest lay in demonology and the occult. That cultural change has made the terms of this prolonged debate largely irrelevant should not be allowed to blind us to its former centrality to critical discussions. The concentration on style was one way of evading any engagement with content. Dryden could be accommodated to the 'manners' model on the strength of *An Evening's Love* (1668), *The Assignation* (1672) and the comic scenes of *Secret Love* (1667) and *Marriage à-la-Mode* (1671).

From the 1950s onward there was a stronger recognition of the libertine, philosophically questioning aspect of the comedies.[23] This new emphasis encouraged John Harrington Smith to identify the till-then-neglected come-dies of Thomas Southerne as among the finest of their age.[24] Otway's three mature comedies, *Friendship in Fashion* (1678), *The Souldier's Fortune* (1680) and *The Atheist* (c. 1683) could claim a place in this reformulated tradition on the grounds of their irreverence towards the laws of God and man, as could those of Shadwell, who in his long career as house dramatist for Dorset Garden stood for good sense and a regulated hedonism without matching the elegance of his Drury Lane contemporaries. While his *Epsom-Wells* (1672) and *The Virtuoso* (1676), a satire on ignorant pretenders to science, are little more than exuberant romps, *A True Widow* (1678) is a thoughtful, formally inventive piece, whose penultimate act ingeniously places its characters in the theatre as spectators of the performance of a knockabout sex-farce in the style of Thomas Durfey. The character Carlos in that comedy appears to be based on the real-life Epicurean wit, Sir Charles Sedley, who had also sat for Medley in Etherege's *The Man of Mode*.[25]

Of course, to narrow Restoration comedy to a small canon of comedies of manners or of wit was to omit much of the total production of comic dramas written for the Restoration stage. Allardyce Nicoll in his *History* was the first scholar to survey the whole body of surviving comedies, farces and burlesques and to attempt a division into types and traditions. A line of densely contrived

---

23 Two influential contributions to this reconceptualisation were Thomas H. Fujimura, *The Restoration Comedy of Wit* (Princeton, NJ: Princeton University Press, 1952) and Dale Underwood, *Etherege and the Seventeenth-century Comedy of Manners* (New Haven, CT: Yale University Press, 1957).

24 John Harrington Smith, *The Gay Couple in Restoration Comedy* (Cambridge, MA: Harvard University Press, 1948), p. 144.

25 Sedley helped in the polishing of Shadwell's play, and was himself the author of two accomplished comedies, *The Mulberry-Garden* (1668) and *Bellamira* (1687), recently re-edited by Holger Hanowell (Frankfurt, 2001). For a collective appraisal of Shadwell, see Judith Slagle, ed., *Thomas Shadwell Reconsider'd*, published as *Restoration* 20 (1996).

'Spanish plot' plays was inaugurated by Sir Samuel Tuke's *The Adventures of Five Hours* (1663). John Harrington Smith isolated a genre of 'gay couple' comedies (in the old-fashioned sense of the word), drawing heavily on Fletcherian models, especially those of *The Chances* and *The Wild Goose Chase*, but giving greater autonomy to the female protagonist.[26] Francis Fane's *Love in the Dark, or The Man of Bus'ness* (1675) and the two parts of Behn's *The Rover* (1677 and 1681) are the most accomplished representatives of a line of comedies inspired by the Continental pre-Lenten carnival. Shadwell's strident insistence on being a disciple of Ben Jonson is sustained only in his first comedy, the libellous, perfunctorily plotted *The Sullen Lovers* (1668). Durfey and Edward Ravenscroft specialised in five-act farcical comedies, the longest lived of which was Ravenscroft's *The London Cuckolds* (1681), in which three city husbands are forced to accept the agreed destiny of their kind. Robert D. Hume in *English Drama in the Later Seventeenth Century* further distinguishes the various subgenres of comedy, farce and burlesque, while arguing that they should not be judged either in achievement or intention by the standards of the comedies of wit, but by the ways they individually set out to entertain.

While the notion of Restoration comedy as the creation of the court and of the audience as dominated by courtiers is now thankfully behind us, it is necessary to consider its varying degrees of concern, felt across the whole range of genres, with the court, the city and the new urban entity of the town. During the later years of the Interregnum and the first years of the Restoration, there was a large migration of gentry families from the country to London. In earlier times the men may have come for legal business or to sit in parliament but the women and children were generally left behind. This unsatisfactory situation was succeeded by a pattern in which whole families became householders in the newly built streets of what is now the West End, returning to their estates only for the summer. In Dryden's *Marriage à-la-Mode* Melantha is 'a Town-Lady, without any relation to the Court' who nonetheless is ludicrously fixated on the place. Doralice, a true woman of the court, outlines a pecking order which runs from people like herself through the 'little Courtiers wife', the 'Town-Lady' and the 'Merchants Wife' to 'the Countrey Gentlewoman that never comes up'.[27] But the pull of the court was fading. New to urban living, the country-dwellers developed their own mode of sociability known as 'the visit' to replace the court-oriented levee: many scenes of the comedies are depictions of visits in this technical sense. The Restoration decades saw

26 Smith, *Gay Couple*.
27 1.1. 182; 3.1. 154, 155, 159, 162–2 (Dryden, *Works*, vol. XI, pp. 233, 161–2).

the evolution of a new town-centred style of living based on the pursuit of pleasure through public and private entertainment, including that provided by the theatres.

We can study the effects of this social experiment on one representative family through Susan E. Whyman's study of the Verney letters, which includes an invaluable chapter on the decorum and practice of visits.[28] But family letters are guarded in their treatment of the pressures that this new exposure to pleasure and perpetual company placed on the institutions of marriage and courtship, which were also the foundation of class integrity and oligarchic hegemony. Comedy, along with the extraordinarily informative prologues and epilogues, supplied all-important lessons in how to maximise the opportunities of a life of urban hedonism without falling into the many traps, of which the most damaging was a perpetual invitation to behavioural excess. Two recurring themes are that of the country innocent newly arrived in the town and either succeeding or failing at learning its lessons, and that of an inappropriate commitment to country virtues of frankness, honesty and fidelity in a milieu whose operating premise was distrust of others and perpetual self-disguise.

Insofar as the town had a centre or senate to which questions of identity and rules of behaviour were referred it was the theatre auditoria, especially that of Drury Lane. In Wycherley's *The Country Wife* (1675), shortly before the beginning of the action, Horner, having resigned the social identity of predatory rake for that of despised eunuch, visits the theatre in order to see exactly what rights and privileges the town is going to assign him, and in 1.1. 174–89 receives the reports of his spies on what that judgement had been. Otherwise, the play makes use of each of the themes just identified, with Margery Pinchwife as the country innocent and Alithea as the apparent sophisticate who is still of the country in her self-destructive fidelity to the unworthy Sparkish (not only a fool but one who, like Melantha, keeps rushing off to the court where he has no business). The play covers the full range of town life-styles from that of the accomplished hypocrites of the Fidget and Squeamish families to the imperceptive, self-centred Sparkish, the worldly-wise but unscrupulous Harcourt, and Horner, who through his assumption of an invented identity becomes able to see through the masks worn by others. Wycherley's 'court' play, by contrast, is *The Plain Dealer* (1676), in which the town is castigated for its institutionalised hypocrisy, its commodification of emblems of rank and the

28 Susan E. Whyman, *Sociability and Power in Late-Stuart England: the Cultural Worlds of the Verneys 1660–1700* (Oxford: Oxford University Press, 1999), esp. pp. 87–109.

autonomy it has offered to women. Although this criticism is not uttered by a courtier, a race outwardly mocked in the character of Lord Plausible, but by a misanthrope sea-captain, the anxieties that produce the extraordinary Olivia–Manley–Fidelia plot are court anxieties not town ones.[29] The theatre, in addition to its other roles, had become a publicity outlet for a commercial pleasure industry concerned with the sale of fashionable clothes, luxuries of all kinds, and the bodies of expensively clad prostitutes. These things had once had a hierarchical function, identifying their possessors with the court, but were now indiscriminately vendible, making frugality just another irrelevant country value. The subplot concerning the litigious widow Blackacre empha-sises that the life of town pleasure could only be lived if one possessed ample supplies of money. Wycherley's rakes, like Congreve's Valentine in *Love for Love* and Wycherley himself in real life, lived it on credit, relying on piratical marriages to preserve them from debtors' prison.[30] Their function was not to create wealth but to dissipate it in conspicuous consumption.

The concern with the invention of the town and the teaching of its essential lessons unifies a group of dramas that have never held together satisfactorily as comedies of wit or of manners. Once the nature of this new urban entity and the urgency of its need to define its relationship with both the city and the court is recognised, it becomes possible to speak of town comedy in the same sense as one speaks of city comedy and the more restricted genre of court comedy, of which Dryden can now be seen as the principal exponent.[31] As we would expect, these issues are treated with more subtlety in comedies written for Drury Lane, in the heart of the 'geographical' town, than those meant for Dorset Garden; however, Crowne's *The Country Wit* and Durfey's *Madame Fickle* (both 1676), from the latter house, can be enrolled as downmarket dramatic treatments of the theme of the innocent newly arrived from the country, while Etherege's *The Man of Mode* (1676), the most brilliant of the early 'wit comedies', was also a Dorset Garden play. In the last case it should be noted that though

---

29 It should be noted that Buckingham, Rochester, Dorset, Mulgrave and others of the historical 'court wits' who were Wycherley's friends had served at sea during the Dutch wars and had pretensions to be considered naval heroes.

30 B. Eugene McCarthy, *William Wycherley: a Biography* (Athens, OH: Ohio University Press, 1980) gives a fascinating account of the accumulation and squandering of the Wycherley family fortunes and of the appalling consequences of this for the dramatist. J. Douglas Canfield, *Tricksters and Estates: On the Ideology of Restoration Comedy* (Lexington, KY: University Press of Kentucky, 1997) explores the wider social antagonisms that fuelled the contentions over property.

31 Restoration city comedy is represented by plays such as Ravenscroft's hilarious *The London Cuckolds* (1681), Crowne's *The City Politiques* (1683), Behn's *The Luckey Chance* (1686), briefly discussed below, and the city farces of Thomas D'Urfey.

Wycherley and Etherege were involved in their private lives with the court, the wider courtly circle that sponsored their comedy, headed by Buckingham, Rochester, Dorset and Sedley, with Shadwell as its chief professional, was by the crucial year 1675 in political opposition to the court and increasingly estranged from its ceremonies. While Dorimant, loosely modelled on Rochester, is the ostensible hero of Etherege's comedy, it is Medley, the perpetual town visitor and scandalmonger, who is the play's true authority figure because he possesses the power to assign identities and explode reputations. Dorimant in 5.1. 215–17 demands that Loveit withdraw her former public favour to Sir Fopling because ''t will be a common place for all the Town to laugh at me, and *Medley*, when he is Rhetorically drunk, will ever be declaiming on it in my ears'.[32] Status in the court was determined by rank and power; in the town it rested on a public judgement that was easily swayed by ridicule.

The mature comedies of Etherege, Wycherley, Otway, Shadwell, Southerne, Congreve and Vanbrugh are all town comedies in the sense of being concerned with how identity and hierarchies are to be established within this new social formation and with providing guidance about what is to be expected on a day-to-day basis from its inhabitants. They also present models of how one might, on one hand, make use of the town's greatest gift of an enlightened and tolerant hedonism, and, on the other, sink into dependence and contempt. The 1690s brought comedy of a darker tone focused on the problems of modifying country notions of marriage to meet the circumstances of town freedom. Southerne explored this theme in his two finest comedies, *The Wives' Excuse* (1691) and *The Maid's Last Prayer* (1693). Hughes draws attention to the depiction in the first of these of 'the subtle, inventively particularised humiliations and temptations' of the abused wife, Mrs Friendall.[33] It is the town, portrayed through the set scenes of a music meeting, a perambulation in the Mall and a grand assembly, which is the source of these temptations; but, because the town is still in the process of being invented, it will be modified by this particular wife's undemonstrative triumph in rejecting the predatory seducer, Lovemore. *The Maid's Last Prayer* presents a grimmer picture in which, as in city comedy, all relationships have become subordinate to the economic one and adulterous intrigues are just another currency of the basset table. Vanbrugh turned the marriage question into uproarious farce in *The Relapse* (1696), a sequel to Colley Cibber's moralistic *Love's Last Shift* of the same year, and treated it with unsettling domestic realism in *The Provok'd Wife* (1697).

32 Sir George Etherege, *The Man of Mode*, ed. John Conaghan (Edinburgh: Oliver & Boyd, 1973), p. 99.
33 Hughes, *English Drama 1660–1700*, p. 457.

The Provok'd Husband (1728) combined a dissonant marriage plot by Cibber with a 'country family in town' subplot by Vanbrugh, separately published as A Journey to London. Dryden's late Amphytrion (1690) offers a mythologised, libertine perspective on the marriage issue.

Two of the four comedies of William Congreve, The Double Dealer (1693) and The Way of the World (1700), have the state of marriage as a central issue. In both cases the examination takes place within a plot concerned with the attempt of an interloper to invade and seize control of an upper-class family, which at the last moment is able to reconstitute itself so as to defeat him, the threat being thus to a class, not simply to a particular element within it. In the first play, it is the malevolent characters, played in the original by Betterton and Barry, who dominate. In the second, control is not actually surrendered, since, thanks to legal trickery, the interloper, Fainall, never had the power to do genuine harm; but the stratagem brings with it a sense of pathos that the lives of likeable people should depend on such trickery and on the ambiguous talents of the wit-hero, Mirabell. That The Way of the World is the most brilliant stage comedy in the Restoration tradition is a judgement that I have no wish to challenge; however, long-standing complaints about its heartlessness are harder to dismiss, not for the normally advanced reason that the characters behave heartlessly (which is perfectly acceptable in comedy) but because its moments of burgeoning seriousness are so easily subverted by our awareness of Congreve's supreme technical mastery. Whether in watching or in reading, it is hard to avoid being distracted by the skill with which effects are produced. In this respect Love for Love (1695), while no less virtuosic and enjoyable for its virtuosity, creates a stronger dramatic effect through its redemptive fable of a prodigal town wit's discovery both of his own long-repressed spontaneity and the vacuousness of his commodified view of women. To return to Congreve's first comedy, The Old Batchelour (1693), in which the mechanistic pursuit of other people's bodies and cash is presented as a wholly natural way of town living, is to realise how far he had travelled in a short career.

Restoration comedy as defined by politeness, irreverence and ease is usually held to have come to an end with the work of George Farquhar, who died in 1707. Two of his plays, The Recruiting Officer (1706) and The Beaux' Stratagem (1707) continue to have regular revivals, the former especially in Australia, where the first recorded performance of European drama was of this play by a troupe of convicts wearing uniforms borrowed from their gaolers.[34] One way

34 There is a fictional recreation of this bizarre event in Thomas Kenneally's novel The Playmaker (1987) and Timberlake Wertenbaker's dramatic adaptation, Their Country's Good.

forward was found through what is called sentimental or exemplary comedy, a genre whose early milestones were Cibber's *Love's Last Shift* and Steele's *The Conscious Lovers* (1722), loosely based on Terence's *Andria*. The most striking innovation of the second play was its questioning of the ethics of duelling: in early comedies a woman's social standing had rested on the readiness of a male to risk his life in order to protect her from insult, a situation which in *The Wives' Excuse* had prompted a cold-hearted piece of blackmail in which a predatory lover exposes a husband as a coward in an attempt to gain an ascendancy over his wife. It was not Steele's or Cibber's fault that the arrival of a higher moral tone in comedy coincided with an overall decline in the quality of offerings: this resulted from the energy of the best writers being increasingly diverted to the better rewarded and less stringently supervised fields of translated verse, polemic and prose fiction. The prolific dramatists of the first half of the eighteenth century were hard-working theatre professionals such as Cibber himself, Susanna Centlivre, Henry Fielding and Charles Johnson. Cibber in his *Apology* (1740) has also left us by far the best theatrical memoir of the age.

The period from the 1690s onward created a valuable space for women dramatists, especially Centlivre, Charlotte Clarke, Elizabeth Cooper, Eliza Haywood, Delariviere Manley, Mary Pix and Catherine Trotter. Their success rested on the earlier achievement of Aphra Behn, whose work subversively reshapes the reigning conventions to express a female apprehension of the politics of gender. Her makeover of Thomas Killigrew's *Thomaso* into the two parts of *The Rover* is a critique as well as an adaptation. Behn's emergence as a dramatist coincided with a recognition that the drawing power of actresses was at least as great as that of the male stars and the accession of Lady Davenant between 1668 and 1673 as titular patentee of the Duke's Company. Actresses wanted parts that they felt at home in: male dramatists such as Banks and Southerne were able to do this to an extent (Southerne turning to Behn's fiction as a source of plots) but Behn and her successors were obviously privileged in this respect. Women theatregoers were also making a considerable contribution to the economics of the playhouses, whether it was the wealthy ladies in the boxes, or the theatre prostitutes paying their half-crown for the pit or their one-and-sixpence for the middle gallery night after night. The extent of female influence on repertoire becomes clear once regular newspaper advertisements begin and we find plays revived 'at the request of several ladies'. Behn had every encouragement to build a career in the theatre and made the most of it: to be dogged by poverty was a fate she shared with most of her male compeers.

It is generally agreed that Behn's main talent lay in comedy rather than tragedy. *The Rover* has proved itself on the modern stage, while *The Luckey Chance* (1686) has joined the classical reading comedies of the period. If *The False Count* (1681) is read alongside Shadwell's *Bury Fair* (1689) as adaptations of *Les Précieuses ridicules*, Behn's play is unmistakably the more engaging. Her preferred mode was the Restoration version of Jacobean city comedy, also practised by Durfey and Ravenscroft, in which resourceful wives and daughters undermine the schemes of males by whom they are treated as commodities to be acquired and disposed of in the way of trade. In *The Luckey Chance* one such city husband gambles away his wife's honour and then agrees to connive at her unwitting rape in order to satisfy the debt. Behn's most talented successor was Susanna Centlivre, whose *The Busy Body* (1709) contains a similar episode in which Sir George Airy pays Sir Francis Gripe for the right to woo Gripe's intended wife, Miranda, while Gripe listens. Like Molière, Centlivre learned her craft as a member of a company of strollers, where one of her parts was Lee's Alexander in *The Rival Queens*. Her mastery of stage effect and inventiveness in the construction of *lazzi* (comic routines derived from the Italian *commedia dell'arte*) ensured that her three best comedies, *The Busy Body*, *The Wonder: a Woman keeps a Secret* (1714) and *A Bold Stroke for a Wife* (1718) would remain in the acting repertoire until well into the nineteenth century. Mary Pix's *The Beau Defeated* (1700) revives Wycherley's theme in *The Plain Dealer* of the levelling tendencies of the town. When in Act 5 the bogus knight, Sir John Roverhead, is charged with not being a gentleman by birth he coolly retorts 'Thou unpolish'd thing, I answer thy Affront, with my Mien, my Dress, my Air, all shew the Gentleman, and give the lye to thy ill mannered Malice.'[35] His anti-type, the social-climbing cit, Mrs Rich, is punished for her blind infatuation with the court by being tricked into marriage to a country clod with hardly a thought beyond fox-hunting.

That the drama of the early eighteenth century is generally of less literary interest than that of the Restoration follows from several causes, of which the often cited bourgeoisification of the audience need not be the most important. (Despite the pull of Italian opera, members of upper-class and professional families continued to support spoken theatre throughout the century and to exercise direct influence on repertoire.) A more pressing reason was the removal of two great incentives to the writing of new plays, one theatrical and the other ideological. The principal cause of the remarkable outpouring of new works for the theatre following the Restoration had been that the

---

35 Mary Pix, *The Beau Defeated: or, The Lucky Younger Brother* (London, 1700), p. 39.

existing repertoire was no longer suited to the new technology of illusion. The period after 1700 saw no corresponding revolution in scenery, lighting or stage design to demand the creation of new kinds of theatre, except in the fields of grand opera and of wordless pantomime, where the difference lay in a more intensive use of already existing scenes and machines. It was likewise the case that the great ideological questions addressed in the heroic plays and baroque tragedies had largely been resolved by the national choice made in 1688 and confirmed in 1714. In comedy the experiment in new forms of urban living represented by the invention of the town was by 1710 an achieved success with its hierarchies and conventions stable and fully internalised. While certain basic lessons still required to be preached, they were not of the kind to inspire works of genius. In any case, the patent theatres now had at their disposal such a rich repertoire of older works in both genres that there was no urgent call for new ones. As had been the case since the Restoration, stock plays were regularly rewritten for revival, often being cut back from a whole-show entertainment to the first element in a multi-item programme. The versions found in late eighteenth-century acting editions are of these reduced forms.

At the popular level, where we do find considerable creativity, the most successful new form was the ballad opera, which made a sensational debut with Gay's *The Beggars' Opera* in 1726. A movement towards increasingly varied nightly programmes encouraged the writing of a lively body of farcical after-pieces. The period also saw an interest in works that played with the illusion of theatricality in a self-reflexive way. Foreshadowed by Beaumont and Fletcher's Jacobean *The Knight of the Burning Pestle*, this tradition can be traced back to D'Avenant's *The Playhouse to be Let* (1663) and produced its first masterpiece in 1671 with Buckingham's *The Rehearsal*. The considerable corpus of later plays which made use of this device is examined in Dane Smith's *Plays about the Theatre in England*.[36] Those which use the rehearsal device, or in which, as in the last act of *A Midsummer Night's Dream*, characters in the play become the audience at a performance, were always constructed round a burlesque of some kind, a genre which had an independent existence from the time of Thomas Duffet's *The Empress of Morocco* (1673), *The Mock-Tempest* (1674) and *Psyche Debauch'd* (1675), Drury Lane send-ups of Dorset Garden spectaculars.

The dramatic work of Henry Fielding draws on all these traditions of self-reflexive and popular theatre. Farce is represented by *The Intriguing Chambermaid* (1734); ballad opera gets a turn in *The Welsh Opera* (1731), *The Lottery* (1731), *An Old Man Taught Wisdom, or the Virgin Unmasked* (1732) and *The Mock*

36 Dane Smith, *Plays about the Theatre in England* (London: Oxford University Press, 1936).

Doctor (1732); straight burlesque is brought to a triumphant pitch of absurdity in *The Life and Death of Tom Thumb the Great* (1730); cultural commentary is represented by *The Author's Farce* (1730), in which the low state of comedy, tragedy and opera is the subject of an interpolated puppet show; the onstage audience convention is used in a number of plays, of which the most developed are *Pasquin* (1736) and *The Historical Register for 1736* (1737). These pieces have a vitality that is curiously absent from Fielding's five- and three-act comedies, perhaps because he was freed in them from the need to equal the standards of a strong inherited tradition. Unfortunately his double role as theatrical satirist and active manager able to bring his own pieces to the boards at will proved too much for the government of the day, who responded with the Licensing Act of 1737. This codified earlier forms of censorship into a rigid discipline exercised through the Lord Chamberlain's office and institutionalised kinds of moral and political censorship in the theatre from which other forms of writing were by now comparatively free. While finely crafted works for the stage did continue to appear, any incentive to experiment with form or to offer radical challenges to the status quo was severely lessened and Restoration irreverence was to survive into the next half-century only in the work of such resourceful marginal figures as Samuel Foote. While Fielding's transfer from drama to the novel is usually presented as an unalloyed good, it is possible that it robbed the English theatre of a dramatist who only needed the advent of Garrick to propel him to greatness.

The collective achievement of the period 1660–1750 had nonetheless been considerable. We return to the comedy for its tough-minded questioning of social and familial pieties, for the wit and vivacity of its language, and for its unashamed fun. We should also revisit its heroic plays and tragedies, learning their conventions, resensitising ourselves to their baroque aesthetic and acknowledging the seriousness of their engagement with a fundamental revolution in Western understandings of the self and the world. In exploring both the comic and the 'serious' plays of the period we are admitted directly to the design shop of the Enlightenment and allowed to inspect not only those ideological fabrications that were to endure but some fascinating prototypes that were never taken further.

6

Dryden and the poetic career

STEVEN N. ZWICKER

Three hundred years after Dryden's death nothing could be more obvious than the breadth and authority of his career. He is the most important poet of the late seventeenth century. He perfected the heroic couplet and deployed the idioms of literary mockery with unprecedented skill and originality; he wrote masterful Pindarics (metrically varied odes, so called after the Greek poet, Pindar) and beautiful commemorative verse; he wrote the greatest political satire of the language; and he absorbed and translated the idioms of Latin poetry over an entire lifetime, creating an English Virgil that for some, even now, has no rival. If we add Dryden's work as playwright and literary theorist to his accomplishments as poet and translator, we might wonder if there is, in the early modern period, another career so various and fecund. Dryden invented, perhaps not quite from whole cloth, the heroic drama; together with Purcell he fashioned an English opera; after Sidney's *Defence* (1595), Dryden's *Essay of Dramatic Poesy* (1668) is the defining text of the early modern literary imagination. And no one – not Milton or Marvell, not Browne or Burton, not even Clarendon – could touch the subtlety, the mastery and the ironies of Dryden's prose.

Yet the retrospective view – from the beginning of the twenty-first century, or indeed from the late 1690s, back over four decades of tremendous literary industry – gives a kind of logic to this literary life that would have been difficult to see as it was under construction, a coherence that belies how little was or could have been planned, how much was opportune and adventitious. Dryden's greatest satire originated in a hint dropped at court, his most sublime tragedy was the result of a political reversal that forced him back to the public theatre; even the idea of a literary career gives a false stability to the haphazardness of Dryden's literary production, and not his alone. How much of a steady literary career might be imagined amidst the hazards and instabilities of late seventeenth-century public life or within a system of aristocratic

Fig. 6.1 *John Dryden* by Sir Godfrey Kneller (1693)

patronage that must have seemed, to those practising under its care, the very emblem of that blind goddess Fortuna?

Not that Dryden lacked the training – the schoolboy diet of translation, the immersion in the texts of classical antiquity, the knowledge of modern vernaculars and their literatures – or, apparently, the ambition for some kind of a career in letters, but rather that until he was about thirty-five years old there is little evidence of either the breadth of literary culture or the capacity for sustained invention out of which we might imagine the classic literary career emerging. Nor do the beginnings of this career give any sense that Dryden cared about the classic scheme of literary development: pastoral through Georgic to epic. From the beginning we feel rather the pressure of opportunity: poetry on the death of a young aristocrat, on the death of Oliver Cromwell, on the restoration of Charles Stuart and then on his coronation, a New Year's Day poem to the Lord Chancellor, and commendatory verse for a book on Stonehenge by Walter Charleton, the man who then nominated him for membership in the Royal Society. These poems evidence the call of opportunity and a certain kind of public ambition, but they are hardly classic stepping-stones in the career of a Renaissance man of letters. Indeed, to publish verse in 1659 on the death of the Lord Protector and a year later on the restoration of Charles Stuart suggests not only that Dryden failed to plan a career on the model of Virgil or Spenser, but that he did not seem to be planning in any particularly fastidious way at all. Nor is the proximity of *Heroic Stanzas* (1659) to *Astraea Redux* (1660) the only evidence of a lack of planning in this literary life, nor would Dryden be allowed to forget the mistake when he had later made himself a real literary life.[1]

There is of course nothing unusual about a career crafted from patronage and public occasion. What is surprising about Dryden's version of such a career is how little of it, at first, seems aimed at announcing literary arrival or putting pressure on occasion and its forms, that is, how little literary ego seems to be involved in these transactions with occasion. Think, by contrast, of Milton dwelling upon himself as emerging artist in *Lycidas*; or Marvell, aged thirty, bursting the seams of country-house poetry and thinking deeply and mysteriously upon his own person and art at Lord Fairfax's Yorkshire estate; or Spenser elaborating a youthful Virgilian humility in *The Shepherd's Calendar*. By comparison, Dryden seems not merely unreflective in a literary way – unconcerned with poetry as vocation, with his own emergence on the literary scene – but nearly invisible in his early poems. The first acts of self-reflection can be observed, not in the early poetry, but in the accomplished and sophisticated prose of the *Essay of Dramatic Poesy* (1665–6/8). Here Dryden announces his profession as a man of letters and, rather obliquely, begins to observe himself in the act, to intimate that he is a writer looking not simply

---

1 *Heroic Stanzas* was issued again in 1681 as *An Elegy on the Usurper O. C. By the Author of Absalom and Achitophel, published to shew the Loyalty and Integrity of the Poet*; again, with the same title, in 1682; and, in 1687, as *A Poem Upon the Death of the Late Usurper . . . By the Author of 'The H – – – d and the P – – – – – r'*.

at occasion but at himself making occasion. And how characteristic that he should do so, initially, as comedy, that he should begin to inhabit his own art through powers of ironic self-observation. Is there a moment more brilliant in the whole of the *Essay* than its closing scene where Dryden portrays himself as Neander, the young man on the make, passionately defending the new drama and so eagerly pursuing the thread of his own discourse he fails to notice that the fiction of his own making is about to be terminated? Here Dryden creates and inhabits his own art: he is simultaneously a character within the drama of the *Essay*, the master of its voices, and the victim, by an ever so slight embarrassment, of its ironies. Such reflexivity announces the beginning of a career that involved not only the making of great poetry but also the theorising and marketing of literary culture and the fashioning of new idioms of art, and at every point negotiating the art and life of a writer in the midst of public passions and occasions.

The making of great poetry

Every one of Dryden's great poems was written to occasion. Perhaps *MacFlecknoe* (1678/82) or *The Hind and the Panther* (1687) affect a slight elevation above mere occasion, but soon enough they yield their programme and circumstance, nor should we be wholly surprised that even the most intimate, the most touching of Dryden's verse, the elegies on Oldham and Purcell, were commissioned for print publication. They are no less powerful as acts of self-expression or commemoration for their origins in the commerce of print, but to insist on these origins is to identify something important about Dryden's circumstance and temperament as poet: that he understood the exchange value of art; that he wrote almost exclusively for print at a time when manuscript and print were rival modes of literary publication;[2] and that however verbally hesitant or socially awkward he may have been, he understood and he used his art in the most public of ways and circumstances.

In the late seventeenth century, poetry was an instrument for self-assertion, for fashioning cultural authority, and for celebrating, and savaging, the great. Whatever the verdict of history on the moral and tactical values enshrined by late Stuart political culture, that culture was the very circumstance of Dryden's art, and out of its mixed virtues came not only Dryden's poetry but also political philosophy, history writing, science and architecture of an extraordinary

---

2 Harold Love documents the relations between print and manuscript in *Scribal Publication in Seventeenth-Century England* (Oxford: Oxford University Press, 1993).

range and quality. Politics and occasion endowed that art with an unsettled energy and a capacity for irony that everywhere mark and distinguish its great texts. It may be merely a romantic or modernist prejudice to think that partisanship and commercial exchange compromise literature, but it is a powerful prejudice and one that has long ordered not only the romantic and post-romantic canon but elevated the literature of the vaguely unemployed over that of the commissioned and occasioned poet. Think of the stylish John Donne, so underemployed before taking orders; or the idle Earl of Rochester; or the idling Andrew Marvell; or, after 1660, the unemployable John Milton. It is in part, I suggest, a nineteenth-century bourgeois prejudice nurtured by Romantic myths of poetic isolation and estrangement that would insist on the alliance between imagination and unemployment, but beyond an aristocratic disdain for profession altogether, nothing like that prejudice inhibited the vigorous relations between the practice of literature and patronage, commission, and occasion in the whole of the early modern world.

Of course mere patronage and partisanship hardly guaranteed either energy or irony, as the many volumes of occasioned art issued throughout this age amply testify.[3] But the forces of patronage, partisanship and print culture could release powerful energies and ambitions, and no career illustrates their combined potency more than Dryden's. We can see the beginnings of that career in the quite conventional, but clearly ambitious, poems Dryden wrote on public deaths and political occasions. Where he seems finally to reach beyond himself and first explicitly to imagine himself in the act of writing poetry is *Annus Mirabilis* (1666/7), Dryden's verse on the Anglo-Dutch commercial wars of 1665–6, the Great Fire, and the plague that decimated London, events that he and a number of others tried to fashion as a 'year of wonders'. That 1666 was also unfolding as a year of disasters is in part what makes Dryden's engagement with publicity and public occasion something worth beholding; for even in this relatively naive text, it is Dryden's ability to put into tension the energies of celebration and the knowledge of disaster that turns *Annus Mirabilis* into a key text for understanding the formation of both his genius and his career. Long stretches of Dryden's verse in *Annus Mirabilis* seem merely official work: just so many ships and sea battles, so many portraits of English heroism and Dutch cowardice. Even the cool and slightly mechanical optimism of its closing prophecies seems like literary business as usual. But the disaster of the Great Fire imposed its own demands on *Annus Mirabilis*, and Dryden's

3 These volumes are described by Arthur E. Case, *A Bibliography of English Poetical Miscellanies, 1521–1750* (Oxford: Printed for the Bibliographical Society at the University Press, 1935).

willingness to admit disaster into the interpretive net of his poem, to spin and
to reimagine the fire first as sexual predation (lines 881–8) then as a Witches'
Sabbath (lines 889–92), and his decision to situate Stuart monarchy amidst the
fire's ashes and ruins (lines 949–76, 1036–80) – these decisions forced from him a
newly strategic intelligence, an ability to rescue, to refashion and reinterpret,
to discover within misalliance and misadventure new ways of performing
familiar work:

> Such was the rise of this prodigious fire,
>> Which in mean buildings first obscurely bred,
> From thence did soon to open streets aspire,
>> And straight to palaces and temples spread.
>> . . .
> The winds, like crafty courtesans, withheld
>> His flames from burning but to blow them more,
> And every fresh attempt, he is repelled
>> With faint denials, weaker than before.
>
> And now, no longer letted of his prey,
>> He leaps up at it with enraged desire,
> O'relooks the neighbours with a wide survey,
>> And nods at every house his threat'ning fire.
>
> The ghosts of traitors from the bridge descend
>> With bold fanatic spectres to rejoice:
> About the fire into a dance they bend
>> And sing their Sabbath notes with feeble voice.[4]
>> (vol. I, p. 95, lines 857–92)

So it was with disaster in 1666, and so, in vastly more interesting ways, it would
become in the crises over the Popish associations and procreative failures that
stained the court in the late 1670s and early 1680s.

But the work of strategic intelligence that begins to appear in *Annus Mirabilis*
is only part of the poem's importance. The other half of the story is the emergence of literary self-consciousness: Dryden's willingness to situate himself as
author within the precincts of the text. Such work often takes place within
the paratextual prose of dedication and preface, but in Dryden's hands these
business locations of literature come to exhibit, no less than poem or play, the
signs of his genius. They are important sites of his literary art both for the
ways that he reveals and explains himself and for the subtlety and craft with

---

4 All citations to Dryden's poetry and prose, unless otherwise indicated, are to the texts
in James Kinsley, ed., *The Poems of John Dryden*, 4 vols. (Oxford: Oxford University Press,
1958), and indicated in the text by volume, page and line numbers.

which he performs that work. *Annus Mirabilis* is prefaced first by a delicately ironic dedication of this poem of royalist apologetics to that hotbed of civil war discontent and Restoration radicalism, the City of London – 'that City, which has set a pattern to all others of true Loyalty, invincible Courage and unshaken Constancy' (vol. 1, p. 42, lines 4–5) – and then by a letter to Sir Robert Howard in which Dryden sets out the important precedents for his work as poet and historian. His models are, Dryden tells us, Ovid and Virgil: Ovid first and foremost, Ovid for his delicate touches, Ovid for his power to move and sway our feelings, Ovid for the example of his style and for the delicacy of his imagination. But *Annus Mirabilis* has almost nothing to do with Ovidian forms and imagination, with generic subversions and transformations, with Ovid's fascination for the psyche and feelings for heterogeneity. It is Virgil who provides the inspiration and the idioms for this poem's work as epic and history, and Dryden's strategic covering of one influential poet by another is virtually a map to his later work with models and precedents, with the poetry of classical antiquity and with the theatrical exemplars of England and France. Not that Dryden aims wholly to hide his debts either in the Preface to *Annus Mirabilis* or elsewhere, but rather that he would display them in sufficiently complex and variegated a manner as both to suggest the complicity of his work with other literatures and literary models and to obscure the exact patterns of indebtedness, partially to cover, as it were, the tracks that he has elsewhere laid down. So it is with the obscuring of Virgil's importance by Ovid in the Preface to *Annus Mirabilis*; so it would be with Shakespeare and Jonson, with Corneille and Molière, and with so many others on so many other occasions. What the texts of *Annus Mirabilis* amply illustrate is the force and the resourcefulness of a first-rate literary intelligence even if they do not yet convey the genius of the poet; but that will not be so very long in coming.

Almost exactly a decade later, and after a hugely busy time making up one play after another, Dryden began to write the poetry which made his contemporary and his lasting fame. *MacFlecknoe* was written and put into manuscript circulation by 1676, *Absalom and Achitophel* came in 1681, *The Medall* and *Religio Laici* in 1682, the great classical translations – Horace, Lucretius, Juvenal and Virgil – began to be published in 1685, *The Hind and the Panther* early in 1687, and from these same years came a series of elegies and odes – for John Oldham (1684), for Anne Killigrew (1686), for Eleonora, Countess of Abingdon (1692), and for St Cecilia's Day celebrations (1687 and 1697) – that evidence Dryden's remarkable lyric gift, a talent we less associate with him than the measures of insult and anger.

And, of course, satire there was in plentiful supply: 'They say my Talent is Satyre; if it be so, 'tis a Fruitful Age; and there is an extraordinary Crop to gather. But a single hand is insufficient for such a Harvest: They have sown the Dragons Teeth themselves; and 'tis but just they shou'd reap each other in Lampoons' (Dedication to *Eleonora* [1692], vol. II, p. 584). So Dryden wrote in 1692. He had begun the harvest some years earlier in verse with *MacFlecknoe* and *Absalom and Achitophel*, and in the theatre, in collaboration with Nathaniel Lee with whom he wrote *Oedipus* (1679) and that powerful intervention in the politics of Exclusion, *The Duke of Guise* (1683), with its satiric address to the Whigs, the City of London, the Dissenters and their clergy, and those principals of exclusionary plotting, the Earl of Shaftesbury and the Duke of Monmouth. But there were occasions and targets enough for many satiric hands to help in gathering an extraordinary crop in satires and lampoons on venality, corruption and folly. Dryden had a number of gifted, though not necessarily like-minded, contemporaries to help him in this job: Marvell in the early decades of the Restoration; Rochester, Oldham, Dorset in the decades of his own great satires; later Swift and Defoe would lend a hand; and Pope would inherit the rich and tangled skeins of satire in the early decades of the eighteenth century. But no one mingled the tones of indignation and irony in quite the way that Dryden managed, and especially in his masterpieces of political and literary satire, *Absalom and Achitophel* and *MacFlecknoe*.

Who were Thomas Shadwell and Richard Flecknoe that Dryden should have made such hay from their poems and plays, that he should, in *MacFlecknoe*, have written them forever into the history of dunces and fools? Here we return to the force of occasion. For us, the distance between Dryden's achievements and those of Shadwell or Flecknoe is enormous. Shadwell and Flecknoe are mere gnats and fleas, and certainly part of *MacFlecknoe's* pleasure lies in the way that Dryden crushes the opposition while cultivating tones of dignity and outrage; it is just such pleasure that we get from watching Pope twist and torture poor Sporus, though Pope had, in Lord Hervey – in Hervey's access to the great, in Hervey's erudition and style, in the brilliance of Hervey's malice – a target worthy his envy and venom. This could hardly be said for the authors of *The Virtuoso* or *Love's Dominion*. But the distance between the laureate and his literary peers was not, for Dryden's contemporaries, and perhaps not for Dryden himself, quite so obvious. Richard Flecknoe had published some thirty books, and Dryden's tiresome rival, Thomas Shadwell, had the temerity not only to challenge Dryden for public favour – he was a hugely popular commercial playwright – and for aristocratic patronage but also to criticise his dramatic idioms and theories and to ridicule Dryden on stage and in print.[5] With *MacFlecknoe* Dryden struck back; the poem is the decisive battle in a series of skirmishes and encounters, but it is only one text in a web of manuscript, performance and print. We read it as a freestanding event, but it was prompted by, and it was woven out of, an elaborate set of texts and gestures. Fully to appreciate the poem is to hear its resonance with a world of print and performance. The poem's drama of succession – who will rule 'Through all the Realms of Non-sense, absolute', who will wage 'immortal War with Wit' (vol. 1, p. 265, lines 6, 12) – reflects not only on literary politics but also on affairs of state.

By the late 1670s Londoners were aware both of theatrical warfare and of the growing crisis of a real succession that was about to be played out well beyond the confines of theatre and coffee house. Two indomitable forces brought about that crisis: sex and religion. Sex was the person of Charles II who had plenty of appetite and productivity, but no legitimate heir; religion was the fear of Popery. The political drama of succession began in the late 1670s with a plot supposedly concocted by the king's wife, Catherine of Braganza, and his Roman Catholic brother and heir apparent, James, Duke of York. Together, it was whispered, they would murder the king, crown the Duke of York and betray the country to Louis XIV. Rumour and false witness were woven into a conspiracy, a Popish Plot, which just about brought down the government and returned the country to civil war. The fear of Popery, slavery and subjugation to France and Rome were of course nothing new in a century that had begun with the Gunpowder Plot (1605) and in a country where memories of the rule of bloody Mary and the sacrifice of the Protestant martyrs were ritually stirred. But in the Restoration such fears and conspiracies were compounded by the open conversion of the king's brother to Rome, by Charles II's repeated and suspicious moves for a religious toleration that would embrace both Dissenters and Papists, and by rumours of the king's secret alliance with and financial dependence on Louis XIV. Had the marriage of Charles II and Catherine of Braganza produced an heir, rumour and conspiracy would have come to nothing; but appetite and incapacity had produced only bastards. Now one of them, the Duke of Monmouth, seemed to offer an alternative to Roman Catholic rule. Opposition to Roman Catholic rule emerged in the form of a parliamentary bill that sought the exclusion of the Duke of York from succession.[6] The Earl of Shaftesbury, leader of that opposition, also

---

5 On their relations, see Richard L. Oden, ed., *Dryden and Shadwell: The Literary Controversy and 'MacFlecknoe'* (Delmar, NY: Scholars' Facsimiles and Reprints, 1977).

6 See J. P. Kenyon, ed., *The Stuart Constitution 1603–1688, Documents and Commentary* (Cambridge: Cambridge University Press, 1986), pp. 376–7, 387–9.

urged legitimising the Duke of Monmouth. The efforts at Exclusion eventually collapsed, but they produced political skirmishing and trials, executions and exiles, and an enormous amount of print in every imaginable form, including two texts that had a very great impact on literature and politics: Dryden's *Absalom and Achitophel* and Locke's *Two Treatises of Government*.

Absalom and Achitophel resembles a number of political pamphlets and poems – it is a biblical allegory, and it is a satire; it is by turns heroic and comic; it is a gallery of cartoons and dignified portraits as well as drama and dialogue. But in its audacity and complexity and in a comic daring that orchestrates simultaneously so many themes and tones, it is also unlike anything that had come before. Even when we have scanned all the sources and models to which Dryden surely turned – not least among them a recent epic by that outcast and near-regicide, John Milton – we will not have exhausted this brilliant performance. Dryden takes conventional schemes of biblical allegory and familiar satiric turns and he renders them at once known and difficult exactly to recognise. Charles II is David; the Earl of Shaftesbury is Achitophel; the Duke of Monmouth, Absalom; Anne Buccleuch, the charming Annabel his bride; and soon we are absorbed in all the particularity and indeterminacy of the poem. *Absalom and Achitophel* is a caustic narrative, it offers a set of exacting parallels, it highlights and heightens all the sordid particulars of sexual indiscretion and personal exhaustion, of rumour, plot and innuendo – the poem is on very intimate terms with all the dirt and buzz of late seventeenth-century politics. Yet it is a poem, a fiction, an invention, and of the first order, and not because its congruence with the facts of the Exclusion Crisis is difficult to map, but because its energies are subtler, more delicate and more powerful than those even of Whitehall and Westminster. Its art everywhere mixes the comic and the grand; every corner, even its most wicked moment, is transformed by an incomparable style and by a perfect sense of timing, by rhythms and rhymes handled with a most telling exactness, and by an irony that suffuses the whole:

> In pious times, e'r Priest-craft did begin,
> Before Polygamy was made a sin;
> When man, on many, multiply'd his kind,
> E'r one to one was, cursedly, confined:
> When Nature prompted, and no law deny'd
> Promiscuous use of Concubine and Bride;
> Then, Israel's Monarch, after Heaven's own heart,
> His vigorous warmth did, variously, impart
> To Wives and Slaves: And, wide as his Command,

Scatter'd his Maker's Image through the Land.
Michal, of Royal blood, the Crown did wear,
A Soyl ungratefull to the Tiller's care:
Not so the rest; for several Mothers bore
To Godlike David, several Sons before.
But since like slaves his bed they did ascend,
No True Succession could their seed attend.

(vol. 1, p. 217, lines 1–16)

Of the political analysis that the poem does provide, that, unlike its poetry, is conventional and familiar. The cornerstone of Tory patriarchalism had been published a year before in Sir Robert Filmer's *Patriarcha* (1680), a storehouse of royalist argument and imagery; but Dryden is wary of the archness and absolutism of its arguments, and his engagement with patriarchal authority is sentimental rather than analytic. He would convince us of the warmth and wisdom of fatherly rule; he conjures paternity as sentiment and sacrifice. The image of David is not only bathed in an aura of sexual indulgence at the poem's opening but in paternal solicitude at its close: 'Oh that my Power to Saving were confin'd' (vol. 1, p. 242, line 999). And while Dryden puts a bit of backbone into the language of patriarchal authority in David's closing speech, he himself, in the address on government, shies away from the authority and authoritarianism of absolute rule. He is for mixed constitutions, for patchwork and partial solutions, perhaps even for a recognition that politics is transient and miscellaneous. Dryden would eventually come to such a view of the structures not only of governance but even of poetry – especially in *Fables* (1700), that superb miscellany with which his own career closes – but in the early 1680s Dryden had plenty of authority left for his own art, and there is nothing in the least patchwork or compromised about the structures he would make in the coming few years. Poems like *The Medall*, *Religio Laici* and even the more complex and baroque forms of *The Hind and the Panther* are superb examples of literary architectonics.

By the early 1680s Dryden had gotten to a place of tremendous self-assurance in his writing. He had sought the approval and done the bidding of the Stuart court for twenty years, and he knew his way around its foibles and urgencies, its programmes and personalities. He was a brilliant laureate and the energy of his writing everywhere suggests the pleasures of engagement with public life. Now, all of a sudden, Dryden seems to have discovered religion. How else do we account for the appearance of *Religio Laici* in 1682 and of *The Hind and the Panther* in 1687? Even if we understand that *The Hind and the Panther* was written in part to claim purity of motive in changing religions – and Dryden's contemporaries could not help noting the suspicious timing of the conversion to Roman Catholicism, a year or so into the reign of James II – what could have promoted Dryden's declaration of Anglican piety in the fall of 1682? Or rather we might ask what, other than religion, could have prompted *Religio Laici*? And why look for other motives?

To the second question there seems an obvious enough answer. There is nothing in the writing up to 1682 to suggest that Dryden had the slightest interest in a literature of confession or in the conduct of the spiritual life, and there is a good deal that points if not to a corrosive scepticism about spirituality then certainly to a worldly disdain for priestcraft in all of its forms. Are there moments in *Absalom and Achitophel* that Dryden relishes more than the gratuitous attack on Roman Catholic spirituality in a mocking send-up of the Mass (lines 118–25), or the smearing of all religions with accusations of self-interest and venality (lines 98–107)? If this is an unusual preparation for spiritual confession, then we should not be surprised at exactly how indifferent the spirituality of *Religio Laici* seems to be in both a technical and an impressionist sense. What *Religio Laici* urges is not the singularity of the Anglican confession but the possibility of achieving salvation by just about any and every form of spiritual discipline. In the Preface to *Religio Laici* Dryden wrote, 'It has always been my thought, that Heathens, who never did, nor without Miracle cou'd hear of the name of Christ were yet in a possibility of Salvation' (vol. 1, p. 303, lines 38–40). And that breadth of toleration is extended into the poem, which while it reviews the intellectual fallacies of heathens and pagans would not exclude them from the bliss of Christian salvation. Not for nothing did one contemporary write the word 'Atheisticall' on the title page of his copy of *Religio Laici*.[7]

No one knows exactly when or why Dryden began to prepare his conversion to Rome, but it could not have been long after the accession of James II in 1685. Dryden's contemporaries made malicious glosses on his conversion, and, running to the other extreme, twentieth-century scholars have offered elaborate schemes to explain how the spiritual programme of *Religio Laici* leads directly down the path to Rome. It is tempting to follow Dryden's own directive in *Religio Laici*, to 'wave aside each extreme' in charting this pilgrim's progress. But in the matter of Dryden's religions, it is difficult to feel that the middle path is anything more than a rhetorical convenience. Simply to assume

---

7 That contemporary was the collector, antiquary and parliamentarian Narcissus Luttrell; Luttrell's copy is now part of the Percy J. Dobell collection at the Folger Shakespeare Library, and is reproduced in *John Dryden, Selected Poems*, eds. Steven N. Zwicker and David Bywaters (Harmondsworth: Penguin, 2001), p. 163.

the integrity of both of Dryden's spiritual confessions obscures, first, how very unusual religious confession was, altogether, for this poet and polemicist (and for most elite males in the later seventeenth century), and, second, how striking are the contradictions between *Religio Laici* and *The Hind and the Panther*.

We often know almost exactly when Dryden wrote his poems, and from the clues that he drops in the Preface to *The Hind and the Panther* we can tell that its composition took place over a few months in the late fall of 1686 and early spring of 1687. It was in these months that James II concocted a new political strategy, one aimed not at persuading the Anglicans to take off the Penal Laws, but at winning the cooperation of Protestant sectaries for his programme of religious toleration. In nearly two years of trying, James failed to persuade the Anglicans to repeal the Penal Laws and Test Act (the first referring to a series of laws designed since Elizabethan times to penalise Catholics for practising their religion, the latter to a statute first passed in 1673 that required office holders to take communion in the Anglican church) – a programme that Dryden claims that he himself was participating in through the composition of *The Hind and the Panther*. Now, in the early spring of 1687, James grew more desperate and prepared to issue, in both Edinburgh and London, a Declaration of Indulgence that would nullify the Penal Laws and Test Act by the simple fiat of royal writ. The aims of James II with regard to his co-religionists were transparent enough, even if the policies to achieve those aims shifted according to opportunity; the king would, one way or another, by parliamentary or extra-parliamentary means, staff the army, the government and the universities with fellow Catholics. In that cause James applied whatever pressure he could, and recruited what forces he might avail himself of. Not the least distinguished spokesman for the religion of kings, and for his own political strategies, was the poet laureate, historiographer royal and now fellow Roman Catholic, John Dryden.

James knew of the long history of Dryden's efforts on behalf of royal persons and programmes; indeed, he had been allied with the poet laureate since the early days of the Restoration. Now he would call upon the laureate to assist him in securing relief from the Penal Laws and Test Act. So much Dryden seems to admit in the Preface – 'I was alwayes in some hope, that the Church of England might have been perswaded to have taken off the Penal Lawes and the Test, which was one Design of the Poem when I propos'd to my self the writing of it' (vol. II, p. 468, lines 62–5). Though at the same time, and sensitive to charges of religious compliance and political complicity, Dryden insists that such an official aim as parliamentary persuasion was utterly his own, the wholly private inclination of a private man: 'As for the Poem in general, I will only thus far satisfie the Reader: That it was neither impos'd on me, nor so much as the Subject given me by any man' (lines 56–7). There is something peculiar and characteristic about Dryden's manner here: first he anticipates (indeed stirs) curiosity about the origins and motives of the poem by announcing it as a subject of public interest; next he teases and entices – 'I will only thus far satisfie' (though he could satisfy further); finally he denies that the writing of the poem was laid on him or that its 'Subject' given him 'by any man'. But the coyness of this denial arouses more interest than it lays to rest. What, after all, is the 'Subject' of *The Hind and the Panther*? Surely that subject, however we are inclined to parse it, may well have been of Dryden's invention – and there is a flood of invention and allegorising in this poem's fables and dramas – but the poem also has a set of public programmes which could not have been simply the business of the laureate as private man. Nor, once we have begun to unfold these programmes, is it altogether clear whose business is conducted in *The Hind and the Panther*. Contemporaries found the poem baffling and upsetting; one of them wrote sarcastically of 'Mr Bayes' (the nickname by which this laureate was often satirised), 'Sir, The Present you have made me of the *Hind and Panther*, is variously talked of here in the Country. Some wonder what kind of Champion the Roman Catholics have now gotten: for they have had divers ways of representing themselves; but this of Rhiming us to death, is altogether new and unheard of, before Mr Bayes set about it.'[8] And it has few modern defenders. But with its allegories and mysteries, its intricate fabling mode and daring mixture of genres, it is among the most interesting documents of late seventeenth-century rhetoric and psychology.

And allegory, fable and mystery were to become dominant themes in the rest of Dryden's career. *The Hind and the Panther* was published in the spring of 1687, and the third part of this poem is dark with foreboding. It did not take a genius to see, in the increasingly desperate moves of James II, political disaster for English Roman Catholics. The disaster came soon enough in the form of a Glorious Revolution, 'glorious' because the revolution of 1688 secured,

---

8 Martin Clifford, 'Reflections on The Hind & Panther. In a Letter to a Friend.' *Notes upon Mr Dryden's poems: in four letters . . . ; to which are annexed some Reflections upon the Hind and panther, by another Hand* (London: 1687), p. 17. On Dryden's anticipation of this response, see Ann Cotterill, 'Parenthesis at the Center: The Complex Embrace of "The Hind and the Panther"', *Eighteenth-Century Studies* 30. 2 (1996–7), 139–58.

through a bloodless coup, the safety of the Protestant religion and of such Protestant properties as the crown of the three kingdoms. But to those who were Roman Catholics or who had converted to Roman Catholicism or who took their oaths of allegiance and non-resistance seriously, the revolution that brought William of Orange and Princess Mary to James' throne could not have appeared particularly glorious. For the remaining years of his life Dryden was loyal to his new religion and his old politics. Like fellow Jacobites, Dryden protested the illegality and immorality of the revolution, and his writing in the 1690s is coded, transparently and not so transparently, with Jacobite gestures and themes. This is true of *Don Sebastian* (1690), the tragedy Dryden wrote on his return to the commercial theatre in 1689 and it is also true of the English Virgil that occupied him in the middle years of the 1690s, and of the collection of translations and original verse gathered and published as *Fables* shortly before Dryden died in 1700.

But the poetry of Dryden's last decade was not simply a rewriting of the same personal and political story. There is in Dryden's work of the 1690s a profusion of invention, a richly figurative harvest, and not simply of the lampoons and satires that Dryden described in his Preface to *Eleonora*. In the late poetry there is also a Lucretian embrace of flux and change, a willingness to abandon the incisive partisan drama of *Absalom and Achitophel* or *The Medall* for a cooler, more diffuse poetic tempered by a meditative impulse. The 1690s were also a decade for celebrating younger writers, for imagining the continuity of literary inheritance and for commemorating virtuous lives, indeed for constructing 'a Memorial of [his] own Principles to all Posterity'.[9] The poetry of the 1690s displays the full breadth of Dryden's meters and measures, a great figurative richness and a touching and occasional abandon to lyric melancholy. When Dryden wrote, in 1700, "Tis well an Old Age is out, / And time to begin a New' (vol. IV, p. 1765, lines 96–7), it was only in part the hopeful greeting of a new century; it was also farewell to his own age.

But so to write of the last decade is perhaps to cast too much regret over years that were, for Dryden, remarkably productive. He composed more verse in these years than in any comparable earlier period of his life, and at its centre stood the great monument of the 1690s, a complete English Virgil. In 1693 he signed a contract with his publisher Jacob Tonson to produce this translation,

---

9 In a letter to Charles Montague written *c.* October of 1699, Dryden so refers to his verse epistle, 'To My Honor'd Kinsman, John Driden of Chesterton'; *The Letters of John Dryden*, ed. Charles E. Ward (Durham, NC: University of North Carolina Press, 1942), p. 120 and notes.

and there promised to write nothing else until the Virgil was complete.[10] The elaborate folio containing the Virgil was published in the summer of 1697, and in the middle years of this decade Dryden laboured over the difficulties of translating Virgil's art. But he had been preparing for this translation his whole life: it was the culmination of a relation with the great poet of Augustan Rome that had begun in his days as a schoolboy at Westminster. Virgil was the most important poet in Dryden's literary life and he more often borrows from and alludes to Virgil than to any other literary figure. If in such texts as the Preface to *Annus Mirabilis* or to *Sylvae* (1685) or even in the Dedication to the *Works of Virgil* (1697), Dryden evinces a nervous awareness of how deeply he is indebted to Virgil – for his own most characteristic gestures, for his efforts at epic gravity, for his notions of the literary sublime, for his diction and imagery, for the very idea of what public poetry might aspire to be – then we should not be surprised that Dryden tries to cover his tracks a bit. He would, early on, tell us that Ovid was more important to him than Virgil; late in his life, he would decide that Homer more exactly suited his temperament than the moody Virgil (Preface to *Fables*, vol. IV, p. 1448), but he could say those things only because early and late he knew exactly how deep his debts to and kinship with Virgil were, and the culmination in repaying those debts was the translation of all of Virgil's poetry.

The fabric of the translation expresses all the complexity of Dryden's poetry itself. Here we find Dryden's elegiac and epic measures, the gravity and sublimity that he learned from Virgil and of course the hidden and not so hidden strokes of political argument, aggression and innuendo. Without suggesting that contemporary politics were a constant presence in his mind as he laboured, Dryden lets us see, on occasion, just how deeply those politics went in the work of translation. He wrote in the Dedication of the secret understanding that one poet had of another, and he cites his reading of the funeral games in book 5 of the *Aeneid* as one of the places where he, never mind the learned commentators, knew exactly how Virgil wrote: commending friends, rewarding allies, punishing those who had 'disoblig'd the Poet, or were in disgrace with Augustus, or Enemies to Maecenas' (vol. III, p. 1016, lines 509–51). And whether or not we think that such a model of epic poetry informs Virgil's

---

10 'The said John Dryden doth hereby further Covenant promise grant and agree in manner aforesaid to and with the Said Jacob Tonson that he the Said John Dryden will not write translate or publish or assist in the writing translating or publishing of any other book or thing to be printed (Except as herein is after Excepted) until he Shall have finished & prepared for the Presse the Translation of Virgill aforesaid.' See *The Works of John Dryden*, gen. eds. E. N. Hooker and H. T. Swedenberg, Jr, *et al.*, 20 vols. (Berkeley and Los Angeles: University of California Press, 1956–2002), vol. VI (1987) ed. William Frost, p. 1179.

composition of the *Aeneid*, it surely informs, and repeatedly, the work of his late seventeenth-century translator, and not only in the translation itself, but in the elaborate paratextual apparatus of the folio with its subscription lists, its plates taken from an earlier translation but re-engraved to allow the careful fitting of Dryden's patrons to Virgil's poetry and, emphatically, in the long and elaborate essay that prefaces this translation.[11] Dryden's work with Virgil, over four decades, in all its forms, in preface and essay, in allusion and adaptation, in secret borrowing and proud translation, is crucial to any estimate of his poetry or of the ways in which he made possible, however complex and compromised its idioms, an English Augustan age.

Theorising, marketing and defending literary culture

Dryden is the most important poet of the late seventeenth century, but he is not without company, and we need name only Milton, Marvell and Rochester to suggest how distinguished that company was. But who can rival Dryden as theorist of and apologist for contemporary literature? To name Sir Robert Howard, Luke Milbourne, Thomas Rymer, John Dennis and Jeremy Collier is simply to underscore this point. In creating Restoration literary theory, Dryden towered above his contemporaries, perhaps in this mode of writing more than in any other. Had he written nothing other than the *Essay of Dramatic Poesy*, it would assure his position in the history of literary criticism. It is an urbane, deeply informed exercise in comparative literature and literary history, a vindication of the English theatre and English literary temperament and an argument on behalf of modernity; its learning is considerable, but lightly worn; and it is a comic masterpiece: a critique of intellectual rigidity, and a brilliant send-up of Sir Robert Howard, a minor poet and literary polemicist and Dryden's brother-in-law and sometime collaborator, who emerges from its pages as an epitome of intellectual vanity, aggression and self-importance (not, coincidentally, traits of which Dryden himself was found to be wholly innocent). The portraits of Lord Buckhurst (Eugenius) and Sir Charles Sedley (Lisideus) are more deferential, softer, perhaps more generalised in the interests of the literary dialectics of the essay – the definition of wit, the debate over rhyme, the merits of the ancients and the moderns, the relations between

---

11 See John Barnard, 'Dryden, Tonson, and the Patrons of the Works of Virgil (1697)', in Paul Hammond and David Hopkins (eds.), *John Dryden: Tercentenary Essays* (Oxford: Oxford University Press, 2000), pp. 174–239; and S. Zwicker, *Politics and Language in Dryden's Poetry: The Arts of Disguise* (Princeton, NJ: Princeton University Press, 1984), pp. 177–205.

literary generations, the inquiry into the unities, the imitation of nature, the rivalry of French and English drama – but Dryden's self-portrait is full of characteristic touches, at once bold and shy. Neander is the 'new man', apologist for the contemporary literary temper and for the genius of its new theatre, an epic drama of rhyming couplets, of exalted scenes and sentiments of love and of heroic idioms of courtesy and conduct.

In its own day (and that day was short, from the mid-1660s to the mid-1670s), this heroic drama was immensely popular. Pepys was insatiable in all his theatrical appetites and so we might be suspicious of his enthusiasm for heroic drama, but the sober Mary Evelyn was dazzled by the purity and valor of a play like *The Conquest of Granada*: 'one would imagine it designed for an Utopia rather then our Stage'.[12] We may not share Mary Evelyn's taste for utopian theatre, but Dryden's theorising, practice and celebration of the heroic drama is striking evidence of his powers of literary invention, polemics and marketing. In the *Essay* and then repeatedly in prefaces, epilogues, defences and dedications Dryden unfolded the rules, explicated the form and urged the genius of 'Heroique Plays': their 'just and lively Image of humane nature, in Actions, Passions, and traverses of Fortune,' their 'Ideas of Greatness and Virtue,' their heightened characters and poetic recitatives, their florid idioms, diversity of plot and 'profusion of incident.' Dryden postulated and defended the theory of the heroic play episodically and over a long period of time, and the relations between theory and performance are more tangled in this genre than in any other, but the capacity to work simultaneously as theorist and practitioner, and to do so near the beginning of his career, is a notable achievement.[13] Nor should we ignore the ways in which the development of the heroic drama also allowed Dryden to publicise, even to polemicise, his own importance as a writer.

Dryden's theatrical rivals answered with their own polemics; his self-publicising caught the attention, and provoked the contempt, of literary courtiers and aristocrats like the Duke of Buckingham, and the Earl of Rochester. In his mocking play, *The Rehearsal* (1671/2), Buckingham aimed to deflate the pretensions of the heroic drama and to undermine the ideological programme of personal grandeur and political absolutism sponsored by that drama. Though Buckingham's assault did not much diminish the commercial appeal of heroic drama, *The Rehearsal*, with its mimicry of Dryden's mannerisms, surely tarnished his personal reputation. But Dryden did not

---

12 *The Works*, vol. XI (1978), ed. John Loftis and David Rodes, p. 411.
13 On the tangled skein of theory and practice of the heroic drama, see Michael Gelber, *The Just and the Lively* (Manchester: Manchester University Press, 1999), pp. 118–44.

suffer ridicule in silence, and he gave as good as he got. Like Buckingham, Dryden insisted on the compounding of civics and aesthetics; in a series of brilliant and humiliating couplets in *Absalom and Achitophel* (lines 544–68), Dryden argued that Buckingham's vanity and volatility were, at every point, implicated in his wilful and rebellious politics.

To Rochester's charge, in the *Allusion to Horace*, of critical arrogance and opportunism, Dryden replied, in the Preface to *All for Love*, with a superb personal retort and a telling defence of literary poise and professionalism: 'We who write, if we want the Talent, yet have the excuse that we do it for a poor subsistence; but what can be urg'd in their defence, who not having the Vocation of Poverty to scribble, out of meer wantonness take pains to make themselves ridiculous?'[14] Dryden's self-defence is a statement of vocation no less than a claim to literary authority, but for Dryden such authority was profession, not priestly calling. Milton had once urged an ideal of the poet as priest and prophet; Dryden now argued that letters were a way of getting a living. The exigencies of the market were a crucial condition for Dryden, even (or perhaps especially) as he formulated his response to Rochester in the Preface to *All for Love*, and as he wrote his dedication of the play to Thomas Osborne, first Earl of Danby, who as Lord Treasurer held a powerful position in Charles II's government and one on which Dryden was directly dependent for his income as laureate. In the prefatory texts to *All for Love* Dryden sought to strike at Rochester, to caress and compliment Danby, to praise the moderation, poise and balance of the king's government, and to fend off rivals for the patronage of the great; he also aimed to conjure with Shakespeare and lay claim to the dignity of blank verse, to steer the middle course between the formality and fussy precision of the French and the folly, illiteracy and slovenliness of his critics, and, of course, to achieve success in the commercial theatre with a play that superbly condenses the rich, nearly anarchic structures of *Antony and Cleopatra*. In *All for Love* Dryden abandons rhyme, martial heroism, bombast and histrionics; and he chastens heroic endeavour with late-blooming desire in a complex endorsement of eastern mysteries.[15]

In terms of sophisticated literary and critical address, in self-defence and mocking adversarial engagement, in delicate political positioning and manoeuvring for patronage, the preface and dedication of *All for Love* form the very paradigm of Dryden's critical practices. When Swift wished to mock Dryden as literary entrepreneur, he ridiculed his dedications and prefaces, but they

---

14 *The Works*, vol. XIII (1984), ed. Maximillian E. Novak, p. 14.
15 See Anne Huse, 'Cleopatra, Queen of the Seine: The Politics of Eroticism in Dryden's "All for Love"', *Huntington Library Quarterly* 63 (2000), 23–46.

exemplify, more than the work of any of his contemporaries – and both Swift and Pope learned eagerly from Dryden in this regard – how a writer might at once participate in theorising and practising his own art and simultaneously prepare for and shape its reception. In these practices, Dryden had no peer. And ambidexterity is true, early and late, of Dryden's career as a literary theorist. We see can see these accomplishments fully developed as early as the prefatory texts to *Annus Mirabilis*, where Dryden coyly engages with the Lord Mayor, court of aldermen, sheriffs and common council of London, and more straightforwardly with Sir Robert Howard, then with the Duchess of York, and finally, through flattering cameos and portraits, with the king, the Duke of York, Prince Rupert and the Duke of Albermarle. Quite a complex system of engagement and flattery, nor was Dryden misguided in his calculation for favour; it was surely a performance like that elaborated in the texts of *Annus Mirabilis* that won Dryden the attention and admiration he needed for appointment as poet laureate And the complexity of this engagement with patrons, politicians and readers is repeatedly matched in Dryden's critical career, and nowhere more so than in the elaborate and ambitious critical essays that Dryden wrote prefatory to his translations of Latin poetry.

Dryden's earliest publication on the theory of translation came in the prefaces to *Ovid's Epistles* (1680) and *Sylvae* (1685), two collections in which Dryden joined forces with Jacob Tonson to produce commercial literary anthologies. And how like Dryden to begin thinking about the foundations of an art just when he began professionally to publish that art. He had practised the craft of translation from the time he was a schoolboy, but he began to theorise what would be the sustaining literary work of his last years only with his participation in the many-handed Ovid of 1680. Here he announced his classic typology of translation: metaphrase, paraphrase and imitation. He practised all three, but what now interests us most is his art of imitation, a mode of translation that he perfected on the grounds of his own insights into and intimacy with the ancients, an art dependent both on his own literary development and on his kinship with the poets of Latin antiquity, especially with Ovid and Virgil.

When Dryden first addressed his relations to Ovid and Virgil in the Preface to *Annus Mirabilis* his sense of debt to Virgil was so powerful that he felt the need to shield the force of Virgil behind an elaborate claim of kinship with Ovid. By 1685 (Preface to *Sylvae*), Dryden's self-confidence allowed him both to broaden his earlier, defensive appreciation of Virgil and to remark, as he announces the beginning of his formal career as translator of Virgil, the extraordinary difficulty of translating a poet who weigh'd not only every thought, but every Word and Syllable. Who was still aiming to crowd his sense into as narrow a compass as possibly he cou'd; for which reason he is so very Figurative, that he requires, (I may almost say) a Grammar apart to construe him . . . [Virgil] can never be translated as he ought, in any modern Tongue: To make him Copious is to alter his Character; and to Translate him Line for Line, is impossible . . . In short, they, who have called him the torture of grammarians, might also have called him the plague of translators; for he seems to have studied not to be translated.

(vol. 1, pp. 392–3, lines 91–143)

Yet out of this paradox, this prefacing translations of Virgil with a confession of their near impossibility, came a new assertion of intimacy with Virgil and the trope of literary privilege and understanding,

I encourag'd my self to renew my old acquaintance with Lucretius and Virgil; and immediately fix'd upon some parts of them which had most affected me in the reading . . . . I have both added and omitted, and even sometimes very boldly made such expositions of my Authors, as no Dutch Commentator will forgive me. Perhaps, in such particular passages, I have thought that I discover'd some beauty yet undiscover'd by those Pedants, which none but a Poet cou'd have found . . . I desire the false Criticks wou'd not always think that the thoughts are wholly mine, but that either they are secretly in the Poet, or may be fairly deduc'd from him: or at least, if both those considerations should fail, that my own is of a piece with his, and that if [Virgil] were living, and an Englishman, they are such, as he wou'd probably have written.

(vol. 1, pp. 390–1, lines 8–32)

The passage foreshadows Dryden's disquisition on kinship with Virgil spun out in the Dedication of the *Aeneid*. In the middle of this passage, however, just after he thrusts together the Dutch commentators, false critics and pedants (the fools against whom he and Virgil are arrayed), Dryden touches on that secret kinship that so marks his work on Virgil in the 1690s when he possesses an understanding of Virgil that allows him to bend and shade his translations – first to express particular topical and political urgencies and then to shape the whole of Virgil in ways that suggest his own broad ideological concerns.

As in his earlier critical work in fashioning the heroic drama, Dryden as translator is running his theoretical shop, his business of literary criticism, out of his needs as a writer – and always with Dryden the professional and the commercial have intimate contact with the theoretical and the creative. No matter how disinterested the appreciation or formulation of literary otherness – the particular and native genius of Ovid or Virgil or Chaucer – it is in the interests of fashioning his own full literary personality that Dryden writes literary theory and literary criticism. Early on it is epic theatre, then it is translation; in the 1690s, after a brilliant career as literary and political satirist, Dryden addressed the history and practice of satire in Latin antiquity. *A Discourse Concerning the Original and Progress of Satire* (1693) not only displays a mastery of the tropes and commonplaces of literary history, it also claims for Dryden a position within that history and the inheritance of the twinned strands of Juvenalian and Horatian satire. In the Dedication of Virgil's *Aeneid* (1697) Dryden similarly fashions a history of literary form, a model of Virgilian writing and a defence of the genius of his own work in fashioning an English Virgil. Here as elsewhere Dryden is at once apologist and self-promoter, European man of letters and English patriot, shrewd commercial tactician and weary Jacobite idealist. Mixed motives distinguish all of Dryden's efforts in the workshop of literary theory; and indeed mixture and miscellany come to be crucial markers of Dryden's work as literary editor, translator and entrepreneur for the last twenty years of his life. From the time of the many-handed translation of Ovid's *Epistles* (1680) through *Miscellany Poems* (1684), *Examen Poeticum* (1693), *The Annual Miscellany: for the Year 1694* and *Fables* (1700) Dryden worked together with his long-time publisher Jacob Tonson in fashioning a taste and a market for literary miscellany and translation. Not that either translation or the publication of miscellanies were wholly new projects, but rather that Dryden brought to both a distinction of taste and an understanding of the literary market unparalleled in his time. Indeed, there is no writer before (or after) Dryden whose literary energy and enterprise – whose capacity for inventing, theorising and marketing literature – allowed such a varied application of talent in the commercial theatre, in literary criticism, in bruising literary polemics and dangerous political exchange, in translation, adaptation and collaboration, in lyric poise and in elegy and epithet.

Fashioning new idioms of art

Without Dryden the literary forms of Augustan England would have been difficult to practise. He put his stamp on the crucial genres of Restoration literature, but as important as formal experimentation and innovation was Dryden's fashioning of the tones and idioms of literary irony. Dryden created Restoration literature by creating a literary voice that was not known before him. Of course irony itself was hardly unknown. No one had demonstrated the capacity of irony to negotiate the contradictory claims of political allegiance more beautifully than Andrew Marvell, and yet Marvell's contribution to Restoration literature looks, next to Dryden's, hectic and narrow. After the

Horatian Ode and *Upon Appleton House* Marvell used irony devastatingly, but only for local effect. After the early 1650s irony was no longer a way of literary life for Marvell as it became for Dryden in the mid-1660s and as it was to remain for Dryden through the creation of his greatest poems and prose, even to the last effect in the verse that Dryden wrote for the restaging of Fletcher's *The Pilgrim* in 1700.

No one before Dryden had quite managed to combine the intelligence of weary indifference, indignity and anger with an enthusiasm for political service and celebration. It was clearly that combination that angered and unnerved Swift, who must have seen in Dryden at once the model for his own satiric anger and elevation and that moral and literary lifeblood casually mixed with and compromised by programmes of service, indeed servility. Yet for Dryden service and irony were hardly an inhibiting combination; in fact their intimacy (and perhaps their friction) seems the very condition of his most interesting work. Before Dryden there had been nothing, for example, quite like *Absalom and Achitophel*. The dressing up of political crisis as scriptural drama had a notable tradition in seventeenth-century England, but the complexity of Dryden's engagement with scriptural politics was not merely unusual, it was unprecedented. Who before Dryden had managed to use Scripture at once to celebrate and to debunk, to excuse, palliate and extenuate on the one hand and to ridicule and debase on the other, and to do all this through a medium that the poet was busy simultaneously deploying and subverting (even, at moments, ridiculing, as if he had no fear of damaging his own instrument of praise), and subverting because he was eager to tie the tradition and the idioms of scriptural politics both to a rebellious past and to contemporary outbursts of spiritual enthusiasm and political irregularity? If Dryden was not fashioning an altogether new idiom of political art with *Absalom and Achitophel*, he was certainly handling traditional tropes and schemes with remarkable dexterity and daring, creating a work which through irony allowed all the idioms of praise and blame to operate simultaneously at a kind of maximum efficiency. Even that most mysterious of Dryden's creations, *The Hind and the Panther*, manages through a kind of contradictory motion to acknowledge the dullness and slowness, the insufferable simplicity, of James II and yet to strike against the enemies of that king, his religion and his converts.[16] Dryden came to the work of literary satire with a thorough knowledge of classical models and vernacular traditions; what he added was something absolutely his own, his own sense of timing and his own ability to float the contradictory motions of

16 See S. Zwicker, 'Paradoxes of Tender Conscience', *ELH* 63 (1996), 851–69.

praise and blame within a linguistic force field that is at once the most elusive and the most distinctive condition of his writing.

We have long understood the contribution that poems like *Absalom and Achitophel*, *MacFlecknoe* and *The Medall* made to the practice of English satire; Dryden's prose represents as significant a contribution to the idioms of literary expressiveness as his verse, though perhaps to our ears Dryden's prose seems so familiar, so easy and fluent, so natural in idiom and expression, that it is difficult to think of it as innovative. Yet if we look before Dryden, at Jonson's *Timber*, at Chapman's Preface to his translation of Homer, at Davenant's Preface to *Gondibert*, we are struck more by the distance and antiquity of his predecessors than by the familiarity and flexibility of their critical idiom or of their prose. What in Dryden is most striking, most original, most innovative – and yet most difficult to describe – is the voice of his critical prose, and it is voice that points to the distinctiveness of Dryden's art:

> 'Tis with a Poet, as with a Man who designs to build, and is very exact, as he supposes, in casting up the Cost beforehand: But, generally speaking, he is mistaken in his Account, and reckons short of the Expence he first intended: He alters his Mind as the Work proceeds, and will have this or that Convenience more, of which he had not thought when he began. So has it hapned to me; I have built a House, where I intended but a Lodge: Yet with better Success than a certain Nobleman, who beginning with a Dog-kennil, never liv'd to finish the Palace he had contrv'd. (vol. IV, p. 1444, lines 1–9)

So begins the Preface to *Fables Ancient and Modern* (1700), Dryden's last anthology of poems and translations. Nothing in the Preface or in the translations seems immediately or obviously innovative – perhaps Dryden's modernising of Chaucer and the slightly aggressive tone taken in its defence might catch our eye – but what I want to urge as most worthy our attention, as we study the innovations of Dryden's art, is the voice that emerges from the prose above, at once wholly idiomatic and utterly Dryden's own in its half apologetic tone, its assurance near to self-satisfaction, its touch of shyness, its sly topicality, the inevitability of its wandering syntax and above all its ironies.

Indeed, we might think that Dryden's greatest gift to English prose – above the direct suppleness of his style, above its clarity and uncluttered facility – is his ability to live within and outside his own writing. How characteristic of Dryden that the paragraph should begin so offhandedly, so deferentially, even apologetically, and with a characteristic touch of self-deflation, and that it should close with such wicked self-assurance. Dryden is his own initial subject: the poet who designed to build and, naively, supposed himself 'exact' beforehand, only to be caught off guard by his own inexactness and by his gifts and ambitions. How modest and winning this all seems as the sentences manage self-admiration amidst self-deprecation, and wander innocently towards their conclusion – Dryden has built a house of poetry and translation where he had intended a mere outpost of verse as he shuffled among his favourite writers.

But Dryden is not quite finished with his work on ambition and architectonics; in the final gesture of the sentence he trains his sights outwards. The ironies that are first warmed at his own expense are set fully in motion as Dryden contrasts his modesty, taste and, by implication, the eternity of his own 'contrivance' against the ambitions and devices of 'a certain Nobleman, who beginning with a Dog-kennel, never liv'd to finish the Palace he had contriv'd'. The target is Dryden's old enemy, the Duke of Buckingham, who had mocked him in that witty contrivance, *The Rehearsal*. The juxtaposition of dog kennel and palace manages to debase grandiosity, ridicule failed ambition and suggest that the proper measure of Buckingham's talents might be taken not only by contrasting his finished work, the dog kennel at Cliveden (and I think Dryden would also have us apply that image to *The Rehearsal*), with the palace of which Buckingham dreamed, but as well with the home, and the eternity, that Dryden realised through the poetry that Buckingham had once debased. What makes Dryden's prose shine is the tremendous efficiency of its ironies, its ability to work simultaneously as personal memoir, literary history and caustic satiric engagement. For his translation of Virgil, Dryden had developed a model of the way Virgil worked – simultaneously with an eye on eternity and on business at hand; Virgil wrote Augustus Caesar and the Roman empire into the eternity of verse, and yet he was not so busy with eternity as to forget that there were debts to pay and scores to settle in the present. Dryden wrote exactly in this manner, indeed it would have been difficult for him to conceive one part of his writing life without the other. He had little interest in mere lampoon; and no matter how distant and elevated the idioms and landscapes in which he allowed his imagination to work, Dryden invariably anchored his writing in the spaces and relations of late seventeenth-century London.

It may not be surprising that Dryden's mastery and efficiency as an ironist would be available at the end of a long career in a political culture that thrived on irony and innuendo; what is surprising is how early and how keenly Dryden developed his technique of self-deprecation and attack, of irony and innuendo. The first poems seem altogether innocent of irony, though perhaps we should not discount the presence of a certain kind of irony in the cool and baffling *Heroic Stanzas*, an experiment in the construction of a public figure and in the management of tone that Dryden did not repeat. But in prose Dryden came early and fully into his own. The twinning of self-confidence and self-deprecation everywhere brightens the *Essay of Dramatic Poesy*, and the dedication of *Annus Mirabilis* is a little masterpiece of irony. And after the 1660s, no doubt thanks to Dryden's steady work in the theatre, his technique of projecting his voice simultaneously into contradictory spaces enabled him to cultivate techniques of irony as a poet that he had already developed in his prose. It may seem that the poet as ironist so amply on display in *MacFlecknoe* sprang suddenly and fully formed out of the theatrical controversies and rivalries of the 1670s, but Dryden's development as an ironist is fully in motion a decade before the circulation of *MacFlecknoe*. Nor of course did 1688 and the end of his career as apologist for the Stuart court mean that Dryden had quite retired into the innocence and simplicity he claimed as his own as he stepped aside from the offices of poet laureate and historiographer royal. If anything, Dryden's mastery of irony and innuendo reached new heights in his last years when their cultivation must have seemed both a necessity and a familiar pleasure. It is difficult exactly to calculate how much of the mode of Dryden's work as poet, translator and critic in the 1690s was determined by the self-regulation to which he had accustomed himself and how much of irony's wariness was imposed by the changing temper of the 1690s, the surge of moral regularity and regulation, but what we can say is that there is a kind of brilliant collaboration between Dryden's misfortunes, his necessities and his gifts. He returned to the theatre and turned to translation, to writing for an income, because he had to; and he turned to these modes with the capacity of writing both into and against his circumstances as Catholic convert, as Jacobite and as satirist who had by the 1690s a long history of both servicing clients and savaging enemies, and of performing a superb high-wire act by balancing these offices against one another.

Dryden's long career of fashioning literary irony made possible not only new measures and heights of mockery and invective – nothing could be clearer than the ways in which Pope's *Dunciad* drew on the example of *MacFlecknoe* – but even more importantly, Dryden made possible a range of tones that suffuse the writings of Swift, Hervey and Pope. They could have gotten the mock-heroic elsewhere, but they could not have gotten a career floated on irony before Dryden. Critics have long wondered at Swift's animosity toward Dryden; for lack of a better answer they have sometimes supposed that Dryden's early dismissal of the poetic ambitions of 'cousin Swift' generated the long career of abuse that characterises Swift's relations with Dryden. But perhaps the abuse came less from a wounded ego than from Swift's sense of overwhelming indebtedness to Dryden for what is the central idiom of his own writing. And how interesting that Swift lashes Dryden's prose more than his poetry – there the shoe pinched too tightly; and while Swift ridicules the length and pretension and slavishness of Dryden's art of preface and dedication, it is exactly from that subtle, complex and variegated prose that Swift learned the possibilities of an irony of infinite regress.

At one moment Dryden seems to prize himself too much, at another he is too covered in apology, and yet both these stances, carefully manufactured and displayed (and yet perhaps too exactly reflective of a psyche that must in varying degrees and at different moments have been both precarious and assertive), are held in suspension by a sense of irony that constitutes the medium of his best writing, an irony that leavens the erudition of the *Essay of Dramatic Poesy*, that mocks a bit the author's own sophistication, that proclaims detachment and elevation above literary rivals and political enemies, above the humiliation of political and religious conversion and yet that somehow allows all the busy work of partisanship that centrally occupies Dryden's career. The self-awareness that irony produces and displays is, in Dryden's case, derived from a profound self-doubt coupled with the thrill of invention and self-display.

The great literary formation that we might think of as Dryden's legacy is less formal invention and generic innovation than the fashioning of a voice through which he might conduct all the varied business that came his way as a man of letters, in part protégé of the great and in part literary entrepreneur. Irony is the most elusive and the most distinctive of Dryden's gifts, it is an art of aggression and restraint and it is on display throughout his career, not perhaps at the very beginning, but certainly by the time he wrote the *Essay of Dramatic Poesy*, and then everywhere in the great poetry of the mid-career, in the brilliant odes and moving elegies, in the veiled writing that followed the Glorious Revolution, what we might think of as Dryden's years of 'inner exile', and surely and subtly everywhere in the translations of the last decade when rummaging among other poets' verse, and pausing over favourite lines, Dryden turned Ovid's Latin and Boccaccio's Italian into an English unmistakably his own.

And yet we still might wonder, what exactly constituted Dryden's voice, or, indeed, his person? The printed record is voluminous; yet for all the words we have only a shadowy sense of the person. Dryden did not hide from public view – he is quite visible in the literature of personal abuse and in the professional writing of his contemporaries – and yet he eludes us.[17] Aubrey was to have included an account in *Brief Lives*, but the pages were left blank. Perhaps Dryden was no less a mystery to his contemporaries than to us:

> John Dryden, Esq.; A person whose Writings have made him remarkable to all sorts of Men, as being for a long time much read and in great Vogue. It is no wonder that the Characters given of him, by such as are or would be thought Wits, are various; since even those who are generally allow'd to be Such, are not yet agreed in their Verdicts. And as their Judgments are different, as to his Writings; so are their Censures no less repugnant to the Managery of his Life, some excusing what these condemn, and some exploding what those commend: So that we can scarce find them agreed in any One thing, save this, That he was Poet Laureat and Historiographer to His late Majesty.[18]

Remarkable and various, much read and in great vogue, yet we can scarce find his contemporaries 'agreed in any one thing, save this,' That he was Poet Laureat and Historiographer to His late Majesty' – so Gerard Langbaine wrote of Dryden in the 1690s.

There is something deeply suggestive about Langbaine's casual sentences; they allow us to see, for a moment, Dryden disappearing into his art. He had spent his last years cultivating the alchemy of translation – an art of disappearing. But Dryden's disappearances had begun long before these translations. He had formed a literary career in an extraordinarily difficult political culture, one not merely premised on acts of oblivion but on the relentless cultivation of irony and deceit. Irony allowed Dryden to develop a sense of that complexity and contingency; perhaps too it allowed him to fashion a life that was continuous, and complicit, with his art. Is that why Langbaine's 'wits' remarked the paradox of a laureate at once omnipresent and elusive? Irony allowed Dryden to perfect a way of writing and a way of being in the world; it was his great gift. But it was not exercised without some cost. For Dryden, that cost must have been the danger (and temptation) of disappearing into his art; for us, as we try to feel our way back toward his art and his circumstance, it is the sense there will always be something about his person in danger of a kind of infinite regress – even as we approach closer to the passions and occasions of his art, the poet himself remains just beyond our reach.

---

17 See Hugh Macdonald's *John Dryden: A Bibliography of Early Editions and of Drydeniana* (Oxford: Oxford University Press, 1939), 'Drydeniana', pp. 187–315; Macdonald's collection has been supplemented by Paul Hammond, 'Appendix: Some Contemporary References to Dryden', In Hammond and Hopkins (eds.), *John Dryden: Tercentenary Essays*, p. 359–400.
18 Gerard Langbaine, *An Account of The English Dramatick Poets* (Oxford, 1692), p. 130.

7

Political, satirical, didactic and lyric poetry (1): from the Restoration to the death of Pope

J. PAUL HUNTER

Literary history has not been kind to British poetry of the late seventeenth and eighteenth century, far preferring poems of the periods just before and after. The reasons are many, having at least as much to do with subsequent patterns of taste as with the poetry itself.[1] But the poetry does have features that make it seem especially difficult or odd to readers of later times, especially those with post-romantic ideas of what poetry is or should be. Despite Romantic claims to have reformed poetry along democratic lines (claims that did open up important new topics and directions, but that also ultimately narrowed what was considered 'poetic'), poetry before the Romantics was open to wider uses and was more varied in topic and tone. Poetry then was more inclusive in several ways: treated a greater variety of subjects, used a larger range of voices and styles, aspired to more cultural uses and aimed at more diverse, less self-chosen audiences. As Joseph Trapp (Professor of Poetry at Oxford University) observed in a series of early eighteenth-century lectures, poetry's scope properly involved *'every Being in Nature, and every object of the Imagination'*.[2]

Poetry regularly invaded all forms of discourse and performed many kinds of services later restricted to prose: philosophical argument, for example, and didactic and utilitarian guides for ordinary life and activity. No subject was considered truly unpoetic; the range was from panegyric to invective and from

I am grateful to A. R. Braunmuller, Joseph Levine, John Richetti, David Vander Meulen and Cynthia Wall for their comments on earlier drafts of this chapter and I thank Elise Pugh for valuable bibliographical information about Edmund Waller.

1 The hardest single problem for modern readers involves unfamiliarity with, or hostility to, the kind of intense and incessant rhyme that the couplet depends on. The couplet dominated the history of English poetry for more than two centuries, but once a resistance to it developed, the reaction among both poets and readers was strong; readers ever since the mid nineteenth century have had a lot of trouble seeing much difference, except in extreme instances, between good and bad couplets.

2 Joseph Trapp, *Lectures on Poetry* (London, 1742), p. 13.

delicacy and admiration to horror and gross disgust, from raucous and bawdy comedy to solemn high-mindedness. Poets felt free to write about God or 'upon Nothing', to create poems out of myth, science, philosophy, religion or everyday life; to focus poems on estates, schooldays, clothes, gardens, pets, maggots, battles, sex, paintings or excrement; to address their poems to lovers, enemies, kings, duchesses, other poets, actresses or servants. But public events and issues were the privileged topics and most popular subjects of poems. A large proportion of poems addressed the prevailing topics of conversation and debate and attended to major national events and public occasions more generally, arguing social, political, religious, moral and practical quotidian issues. Every poet who aspired to major cultural recognition consciously celebrated those happenings regularly and lengthily, and 'public', 'occasional' poems were popular and, often, among the most carefully crafted and best poems of the period. But the marking of 'occasions' often extended to private and personal, as well as public and social, human occasions in poems that took a variety of forms, lengths and modes, and that used tones from panegyric to satiric.

Poetry was written, and marketed, to appeal to readers with all kinds of tastes, previous reading experiences and social backgrounds. 'Mainstream' or 'official' poetry could be formal, allusively demanding and very expensive to buy; it often derived from extensive learning and study and drew heavily on classical, especially Latin, sources, frequently in fact translating or imitating well-known passages, episodes and tropes. But there was also much verse of easier access and lesser intellectual pretence, part of the substantial literature of 'popular culture' that had been brought about by increased literacy and the proliferation of print a century earlier. Poems were addressed to the everyday concerns of farmers, tradesmen and housemaids as well as to those concerned with larger issues of state or public welfare or the recreations of the leisure classes; Joseph Addison, for example, wrote elaborate poems, in Latin, on bowling and skating, and there are hundreds of 'advice' poems on daily activities. By the late seventeenth century, booksellers had learned to market widely and well a host of traditional kinds of verse with folk roots and long histories of oral transmission: ballads, lampoons, songs from plays and other performances, lyrics of love, friendship and other human relationships, and (especially later in the period) hymns and songs of devotional praise. Not everyone thought of such productions – especially if they were anonymous, earthy, based in pagan folklore or obviously oral in origins – as 'poetry'. But the borders of *belles lettres* (or 'literature') were then only beginning to be patrolled carefully, so that distinctions between approved and disapproved texts were less rigid and class tastes less fully predetermined. In the structure, titling and packaging of print texts, one can see conscious appeals to readers with particular 'high' or 'low' tastes, but categories were notoriously loose, and sophisticated readers included the simplest wares among their purchase while new readers could be very ambitious and ranging in their poetic tastes.

Only about half the total populace was literate by the Restoration – with the highest rates in Scotland and in urban areas, especially London – and readership did not increase substantially by the middle of the eighteenth century. But literacy rates had, earlier in the seventeenth century, risen sharply so that perhaps two-thirds of English-speaking men and about one-third of women were, during this whole period, potentially in the market for reading materials of some kind.[3] And of those who *could* read, most regularly included poetry among their reading choices: they virtually *had* to, if they wished to be thought well informed, for poetry drove, as well as responded to, most public conversations. Poetry was especially prominent for readers in London where booksellers vied to offer the most modish and relevant wares and where poetry regularly constituted a substantial percentage of their fare, probably higher than in any previous age, certainly higher than in any subsequent one.[4] Some later historical commentators – misled perhaps by the elegant and expensive dress of folio offerings, by the complex classical allusiveness of some of the most famous poems of the period, or by snooty and dismissive comments by would-be guardians of taste – have emphasised inaccessibility by implying that poetry then was written by and for the few.[5] And *some* poetry, to be sure, did select its audience by education and reading experience (and thus by class and to some extent gender), but most of the poetry of the period was just as accessible, at least on the surface, as prose. Even the most ambitious and demanding poets regularly took care to make their work available to new readers who might lack formal or extended education and who had learned to read for utilitarian – including religious – reasons. Alexander Pope, for example, who was regarded by nearly everyone (including his many enemies) as the most gifted, influential and challenging poet of the period, took pains to make his most ambitious work widely accessible, insisting that his publisher issue cheap as well as luxury editions of his work and adding explanatory footnotes

3 Reliable numbers are notoriously hard to come by; I have summarised the most reliable information in *Before Novels* (New York: W. W. Norton, 1990).
4 About one in seven printed texts was primarily in verse, based on counts of Foxon numbers and the *English Short Title Catalogue* titles, a far higher percentage than in later times; present figures for Anglophone poetry are well under 1 percent.
5 David Daiches, for example, speaks of poetry's audience as 'a civilized urban group whose education [poets] could take for granted', and is 'struck by the limitation of audience and subject matter' (*A Critical History of English Literature* (London: Secker and Warburg, 1960), p. 591).

that were superfluous for his most sophisticated readers but that admitted ordinary readers into his 'in' group even while seeming to brand them, along with the rival poets he attacked, as 'out.'

Both the poetic itch and the poetic habit were widespread, blurring across classes and economic groups. Poetry was near the centre of conversation in a variety of public places and among a range of social groups, and many people – not necessarily poets in the public definition or even in their own eyes – wrote poetry regularly and sometimes very well. In the ages just past, writing poetry had been associated with genteel leisure and the birthrights of aristocracy; it extended to others largely through professional writing in the marketplaces of theatre or court. But by the late seventeenth century, and then much more dramatically by the mid eighteenth century, the desire (and ability) to write poetry, either rhetorically or expressively, broadened considerably. Poetry, then, was neither a badge of the elite nor a code that outsiders had to crack; it was a standard option for all kinds of topics and levels, and it invaded all kinds of printed texts. And quite a variety of people – across classes, genders, locations and experiences – helped create it.

And the sheer number of practising poets was large. When readership expanded radically in the early to mid seventeenth century, writership had begun to enlarge then as well, and between the earlier years of this period and the later ones (especially between 1720 and 1750) there is a notable explosion of poems from the middling and lower classes, especially among women. Encouraged by a context in which the insistent, intense rhyme of couplets established an expectation of concentrated, concise and tight lines, amateur as well as 'professional' poets quickly developed a knack for pointed, smooth, echoic verse, responding to a kind of cultural ear that had been developing since the early seventeenth century. The fact that the vast majority of poetry of the period used the couplet as its basic unit meant not only that readers knew what to expect and how to expect it, but that even inexperienced writers were ready from the start to read, think and write in terms of a dominant verse form that readers could already hear in their heads. The result was that even beginning poets knew quickly what the expected sounds and patterns of verse were like, and that the most tentative of novices learned fairly fast how to turn a couplet and how to write paragraphs of verse that were, if not strikingly original in sentiment or structurally groundbreaking in form, yet competent, smooth, coherent and readable.

Most of the poetry is firmly anchored in current events and manners – it is present-centred – and its topicality means that not all of it reads easily now to those without specialised historical knowledge. One result is that the canon of the period has narrowed misleadingly, partly to divert attention away from slippery topicalities and partly to conform to later, more sedate notions of what the eighteenth century was about. Rhetorical poems ask for knowledge of issues as well as strategies; topical poetry demands a lot of historical information; long poems require leisure time and a friendly, patient sensibility. One of the inherent dangers of literary histories, anthologies, classrooms, scholarly traditions and other canon-promoting devices is that the selection process is inevitably biased along some particular set of criteria beyond aesthetic quality – ideological, moral, social or habitual – often unconsciously. It is of course important to make distinctions, about quality as well as about directions that insist and prevail, and in this chapter I will stress artistic high points and the most influential and lasting trends. But I also want to suggest, as nearly as possible, the range of what was available to readers and popular with them then. I want to indicate the variety of topics and tones that offered themselves to contemporary readers and point to the many forms, garbs and packagings that poetry came in. And, too, I mean to be fair to the barriers that stand between the poetry and our own reading habits and assumptions, noting the historical prejudices that may make modern readers resistant, as well as describing features in the poetry itself which obscure it for readers distant in time or space.

Access to poetry

Print was the most common vehicle for poetry of the time, but it was not the only one. One might 'hear' poetry, at least brief snatches of it, in a variety of places. The theatre was one potential venue; among the frequent dramatic revivals (and adaptations) were many blank-verse plays by Shakespeare, his contemporaries and successors, and at certain moments there were many new plays in verse.[6] Prologues and epilogues were regularly written (and spoken) in pentameter couplets, and it may well be that for Londoners (and playgoers) these introductory and concluding set-pieces of a theatrical evening represented the most frequently heard vocal renderings of rhymed verse. Plays also often featured 'songs', new or revived; theatrical evenings included occasional verse interludes; and in public places and at some public events (such as

6 Tragedies especially. Besides the run of heroic plays in the 1660s and 1670s, quite a few new blank verse plays were staged around the turn of the century; see, for example, Charles Hopkins, *Friendship Improv'd; or the Female Warriour* (1700); Thomas Southerne, *The Fate of Capua* (1700); John Dennis, *Iphigenia* (1700) and *Liberty Asserted* (1704); Joseph Trapp, *Abra-Mule: or, Love and Empire* (1704); and Samuel Tuke, *Adventures of Five Hours: A Tragicomedy* (1704). But some comedies were also in verse.

hangings at Tyburn) one could hear urban ballads sung even while they were hawked about in cheap printed broadsides celebrating the moment. And, no doubt (though there are astonishingly few records of such events), poetry must have sometimes been recited, or read or at least briefly quoted (certainly, it was discussed often) in social gathering places such as coffee houses, alehouses, inns and drawing rooms.

Not all access to poetry was necessarily, therefore, written and costly. But the most important vehicle for poetry beyond print was still the manuscript, often circulated from hand to hand in ways that guaranteed knowledge of poems within certain circles (usually quite elite circles) before they were formally published – or even in lieu of print publication.[7] A number of Restoration poets – John Wilmot, Earl of Rochester, and Katherine Philips are the most obvious examples – established their reputations almost wholly through private circulation of their poems. And the private-circulation paradigm (though fading) continued into the eighteenth century: the young Pope, barely twenty-one when his first poems were published, was already regarded as a major poet because everyone whose critical opinion mattered in London had read and admired his poetry *before* it saw print. Publication sometimes followed from fame, rather than creating it.

What counted as poetry? To most contemporary minds, poetry meant verse. Usually – dominantly – that meant both metrical rhythm and rhyme – concentrated rhyme, with consecutive rhyming lines ('couplets') far and away the most popular variety. Blank verse also had adherents, in just about every decade, though unrhymed verse was never a majority taste despite the popularity of Milton and his sustained power as a model throughout the eighteenth century. When poetry was read aloud, rhythm and rhyme could of course be heard, and silent readers heard it in their mind's ear, but the defining signs of poetry were actually visual rather than oral. Despite the powerful and predictable consciousness of repeated sound that rhyme represented, the baldest indicator was the generous blank space on the page, the conspicuous consumption of paper that manifested itself in large margins, both horizontal and vertical. Poems in stanzas typically were printed with spaces between stanza breaks; and couplet poetry, as well as blank verse, was usually divided into stanza-like paragraphs, normally with indentations and often with a line or more of blank space marking the divisions. Lineation guided the voice (or

7 See Margaret Ezell, *Social Authorship and the Advent of Print* (Baltimore: Johns Hopkins University Press, 1999), Harold Love, *Scribal Publication in Seventeenth-Century England* (Oxford: Clarendon Press, 1993) and Arthur F. Marotti, *Manuscript, Print, and the English Renaissance Lyric* (Ithaca, NY: Cornell University Press, 1995).

imagined voice), of course, but the generous spacing on the page also signalled a certain luxury of time and expense of effort, real in the case of readers from the leisure classes, aspiring and envious in the case of rising readers among merchants, labourers and others just beginning to depend on reading for pleasure or profit.

The couplet, especially the 'heroic' (pentameter or decasyllabic – ten syllable) couplet, dominated poetry throughout the period, as it had since the early seventeenth century and largely continued to late into the century. It was virtually obligatory to use couplets in writing 'heroic' poems (or epics) and other long, ambitious poems in narrative or philosophical modes, so that nearly anyone employing another strategy (usually blank verse, but occasionally some rarer form such as the nine-line Spenserian stanzas (James Thomson's *Castle of Indolence*, for example)) was making a conscious statement of dissent. The 'heroic' couplet was so called because of a prevailing sense of its steady dignity and supposed close analogy to the metres of the ancients, especially celebrated Latin poets like Virgil, Horace and Ovid, and so was de rigueur for most long and ambitious poems. But the power of the form became so nearly hegemonic for serious poetry that shorter poems were also regularly drawn into its power of expectation. Most poems labelled 'epistles', for example – whether they were really public orations or meandering arguments on the one hand, or informal personal notes or memos on the other – were written in pentameter couplets, as were nearly all satires and most elegies, pastorals and Georgics, as well as the short, pithy epigrams which retained, in a light-hearted and playful way, some of their witty and pointed utility from an earlier age.

Tetrameter (or octosyllabic, eight-syllable) couplets had their adherents, too, and in the hands of especially skilled employers like Andrew Marvell (whose artful use of long vowels and delaying consonantal disjunction gave them slowed pacing and artificial magnitude) could be used in much the same way. More often, though, 'shortened' couplets (usually tetrameter, but also sometimes trimeter and even dimeter – four, three, and two foot lines) were used for comic or mock-serious purposes as in Pope's Lilliputian poems about *Gulliver's Travels*. Four-stress couplets seemed to many ears then (as to many still) to have a quick, jog-trot quality friendly to comedy and burlesque: the most famous employers of them were Samuel Butler, the early Restoration Puritan-baiter whose *Hudibras* (1663–78) was probably the most-read single poem in the second half of the seventeenth century,[8] and Jonathan Swift,

---

8 'Hudibrastic' became a standard name for octosyllabic verse with consciously doggerel meter and forced comic rhymes.

who later turned their comic force more towards self-mockery and other issues of pretence, unmasking and psychosexual discovery. Cross-rhyme such as abab or abcabc (that is, rhyme that links lines across intervening ones) found its way into a variety of stanza forms, especially quatrains patterned on the ballad stanza[9] that became very popular both for short personal poems about love, friendship or family and for pert social observations or behavioural examinations (the English version of *vers de société*). But if you add up all the surviving lines written in cross-rhyme and blank verse between 1660 and 1750, they will not altogether constitute a close quantitative competitor to the number of consecutively rhymed lines. And pentameter couplets are about four times as frequent as all other couplets (shorter and longer, from monometer to tetrameter and hexameter to fourteener) put together. The pentameter couplet, then, was not just dominant as a model, but so expected and habitual as to seem obligatory: not to write heroic couplets was to make an explicit minority statement, and not many made it, though some did it repeatedly, forcefully and notably – Thomson very successfully in *The Seasons* (1730), for example, and many others, like the briefly celebrated John Philips and the stubborn, against-the-grain critic and poet John Dennis, whose temperamental antipathy to rhyme was almost pathological.

Still, readers found poems – just as poems found readers – in many varieties and forms: if rhyme, even a specific pattern of rhyme, was predictable, other matters of presentation were not. Not only were topics and levels of formality greatly varied, but so were the shapes and packages in which poems were produced and marketed. Short topical poems that could be printed on a single sheet (such as ballads) were often hawked at public events or sold through stalls such as those that for much of the period crowded St Paul's Churchyard and London Bridge, as well as being available through the usual booksellers in or near the Strand, Fleet Street and the Poultry. More ambitious poems, especially 'occasional' poems commemorating some public event (a battle, a coronation, the death of a public figure), often were published separately as well but in much more impressive dress and with noticeably more elegant typography. Usually such poems were printed in folio or large quarto and quite carefully typeset; their generous paging and spacing – usually with large spaces between verse paragraphs and exaggerated margins, printed on good quality paper – bespoke a firm sense of luxury in a paper-expensive economy. Such a poem of, say, twelve to sixteen pages (that is, a poem of 200–400 lines

---

9 Half a century later, the hymn nearly replicates the ballad stanza; both are, of course, typographical variations on the fourteener.

SEVERAL OCCASIONS. 105

To Mr. POPE.

TO praife, yet ftill with due Refpect to praife,
    A *Bard* triumphant in immortal Bays,
The *Learn'd* to fhow, the *Senfible* commend,
Yet ftill preferve the Province of the *Friend,*
What Life, what Vigour, muft the Lines require?
What Mufick tune them? what Affection fire?

O might thy Genius in my Bofom fhine!
Thou fhouldft not fail of Numbers worthy thine,
The brighteft Antients might at once agree
To fing within my Lays, and fing of thee.

Horace

Fig. 7.1 First page of 'To Mr Pope' by Parnell from *Poems on Several Occasions Written by Dr Thomas Parnell, Late Arch-Deacon of Clogher and Published by Mr Pope* (London: Bernard Lintot, 1722)

in length), was often sold for 6d or a shilling, radically (six to twelve times) more than the penny that single-page ballads fetched, for these texts were meant to be kept and perhaps collected sooner or later into a binding with other similarly printed poems or pieces of prose. Books that collected large numbers of poems, either of a single poet or some sort of other grouping, were proportionately more expensive; a typical volume of 200–300 pages might cost 5s. or so, though elegance, demand or greed could raise the price considerably. Individual poems, even brand-new ones, often were included too in longer works and (increasingly) were part of the contents of periodicals. Some of Swift's best short verse ('Description of the Morning' and 'Description of a City Shower') made its first appearance in *The Tatler*, and Elizabeth Singer (later Rowe) was regularly featured in *The Athenian Mercury*; a generation later *The Gentleman's Magazine* included poems among its regular features.

Printed collections (usually called 'miscellanies', a term that suggests their assorted character) had, since the sixteenth century,[10] been popular as ways of bringing together poems that had topics or forms or some other feature in common, and they had the great virtue of being able to introduce new work and quietly situate it among familiar favourites. The alert reader could thus come into possession of a fair body of recognised work and also venture on to new ground, getting a large number of texts for a fraction of the price of separate ones. But the late seventeenth century, especially after the expiration of the Licensing Act in 1695, elevated the miscellany to new levels of frequency, popularity and sophistication. Poems not easily available could thus become more widely known or re-engaged, raising their cultural stock; and poems that did not make an immediate impact quite often got another chance in a regulated and specified context. Too, miscellanies provided a sampling and eclectic mixture of poetic possibilities that individual purchase did not necessarily approximate. Miscellanies represent a kind of commercial triumph that also widened the horizons of typical readers who, whatever their interest in poetry, could become bewildered and overwhelmed by a bookseller's range of available texts.

Miscellanies were of many kinds and qualities. Many were motivated by partisan or ideological concerns and gathered work of like-mindedness. Others were opportunistic ventures launched by booksellers who had a convenient group of copyrights on hand and thus could cheaply advertise and provide samples of writers they featured. Sometimes, too, booksellers gathered together

10 A few such collections, such as *Songs & Sonnets* (often called *Totell's Miscellany* (1557)), or *England's Helicon* (1600) were well known, but the numbers of such collections were, relative to the late seventeenth century, very small.

separate poems that were not selling well, printed a collective title page and thus got rid of slow stock at a bargain group rate. A two-volume 'collection' of 1717, for example, offered (for ten shillings) nearly a thousand pages of familiar works from recent years, all paginated individually in lengths from sixteen to forty pages each; it brought together poems by, among others, Dryden, Daniel Defoe, Sir John Denham, Nahum Tate, Sir Richard Blackmore, William Shippen, Samuel Cobb, Ned Ward and John Philips, most with separate title pages indicating printings between 1708 and 1710.[11] And there were, following conversational trends, many thematic, topical and occasional collections celebrating public events. Such volumes tended to gather well-known texts already published separately but might also become the vehicle for new poems. The death of Dryden in 1700, for example, led to two volumes of memorials: *Luctus Brittannici: or the Tears of the British Muses: for the Death of John Dryden* (London, 1700) included more than twenty poems in English (some by famous poets, others by unknowns) and a supplement added still others in Latin; and *The Nine Muses. Or, Poems Written by Nine several Ladies upon the Death of the late Famous John Dryden* (1700) collected the tributes of women poets. There were also specialty volumes of other kinds, for example competitive poems on a particular enduring issue (*The London Medley: Containing the Exercises Spoken by Several Young Noblemen and Gentlemen at the Annual Meeting of the Westminster Scholars . . . on a Parallel between the Ancients and Moderns* (1731), topical collections on contemporary issues like the controversy surrounding what was called 'occasional conformity', whereby Nonconforming Protestant Dissenters took Anglican communion to qualify technically for public office (*A Collection of Poems, For and Against Dr Sacheverel* (in four parts, 1710–11)), poems associated with a particular place (*The Tunbridge-Miscellany: Consisting of Poems, &c. Written at Tunbridge-Wells this Summer. By Several Hands* [1712]) or poems united by a comic or satirical attitude such as the *Poems on Affairs of State* volumes which collected, beginning in 1695, a wide range of political poems (many by major figures like Marvell and Waller) that had been, for safety's sake, circulated only privately; most of the age's plentiful anti-Catholic poetry, for example, only became public then. Some of these poems were incendiary and sexually as well as politically risqué; some were also among the now most famous (and best) satirical poems of the time, Andrew Marvell's *Last Instructions to a Painter*, for example.

Many of the miscellanies set out to introduce (or harvest) the best of current writing whatever its focus or to enhance the reputation of a poet or group

---

11 *A Collection of the Best English Poetry, by Several Hands . . . In Two Volumes* (London: T. Warner, 1717).

of poets who were regarded as culturally important or influential. The six Tonson Miscellanies (produced by the bookseller Jacob Tonson between 1684 and 1709, but sometimes called the 'Dryden Miscellanies' because the earlier volumes were heavily devoted to his work and were thought to have been edited by him) gathered poems of exceptionally high quality; the intention of reclaiming, especially in the third and fourth volumes, Dryden's tainted reputation after his political fall quietly became a project in showcasing the best work of emerging contemporaries. The final volume represents a landmark: it both introduces Pope as a poet and celebrates his entry into print with poetic tributes from William Wycherley and 'Another Hand', probably William Walsh. Pope's work remained at the centre of attention in miscellanies for nearly forty years, until (just after Pope's death) a youthful footman-turned-poet, Robert Dodsley, began to collect (in the so-called *Dodsley Miscellanies*) poems that announced a much changed literary milieu featuring a direction and taste that was clearly post-Pope. In the meanwhile Pope's own work as editor and arbiter (not to mention as the dominant poet of his time) powerfully influenced the direction of miscellanies and of his contemporaries' taste more generally. The five editions of Bernard Lintot's *Miscellany* between 1712 and 1727 may have been edited by Pope himself; certainly they bear strong traces of his guidance, and they remain a record of his dominance of poetic craft (and the commercial success of poetry) during the period.

Collections of an individual poet (or of a more or less coherent small group of poets, such as the Roscommon, Mulgrave and Richard Duke *Poems* of 1717) were also common. Such collections frequently were of 'classic' poets – that is, mostly those from earlier ages – and the frequency of editions of certain poets (Spenser, Jonson, Milton, Cowley or Waller, e.g.) indicates both popularity and directions of taste at particular moments. Waller, for example, who lived long and late into the seventeenth century (he died at age eighty-one in 1687, but his best work was largely pre-Restoration), was wildly popular and much imitated for more than a half century after his death: 'Easy Waller' he was called in honour of his metrical skills and smooth and mellow effects, and at least sixteen editions or printings were offered for sale between 1682 and 1732. Another extremely popular figure, though his popularity waxed and waned depending on the reputation of odes at a particular moment, was Abraham Cowley (1618–67). Milton remained throughout the period a powerful influence in spite of (and in part because of) the fact that his dominant blank-verse choices went against the grain of prevailing couplet practice. In every decade, there were significant imitations, often prominently labelled ones, of his style, some (to be sure) indifferent to his poetic intentions but nevertheless sincere in their homage and determined in their direction. The stature of Milton (especially after his death in 1674) is, in fact, almost impossible to exaggerate. The common apprenticeship or coming-of-age practice throughout the period usually involved youthful imitation of past masters, and Milton was a standard figure to imitate or practise on – at least as important as Spenser (or, later, Dryden) in the English tradition and almost equal to the model that Latin poets such as Virgil or Horace provided. But 'lesser' poets of the past also retained substantial popularity; there were repeated editions, for example, of Carew, Quarles and Herbert. Collected volumes of individual contemporary poets tended to appear in middle or late life or just after death; in booksellers' stalls the old and the new, the living and the dead, jostled amiably for sales. By the early eighteenth century, the book trade had begun to challenge the traditional patronage system, but the effect was less to interrupt the poetry / politics nexus than to stimulate even more competition among poets and to intensify public consciousness of what poetry had to offer.

And there were many other kinds of collections, some aspiring and some merely opportunistic, that similarly purported to present important poems for pleasure or emulation. Often texts were pirated by unscrupulous booksellers (and there was no guarantee of authenticity, textual integrity, attribution or care in printing), and title pages might use familiar names to lure readers while the book itself was crowded with the work of other – often lesser, often unnamed – writers. Title pages were, after all, advertising strategies, and their facts were widely understood to be sometimes more accurate than others. The net result of all this gathering and commissioning and warehousing and reprinting was that bookstalls teemed with poems, and readers had rich and varied choices.

Poetic identities and poetic careers

The commercial marketing of poetry increasingly depended on name recognition, and the power of authorial identity grew substantially between the 1660s and the 1740s: whatever the long-term fortunes of 'the author' and authority, the currency of poets' names and public recognition of reputations increasingly in the period became crucial to the book trade. Booksellers tended to rely heavily on familiar texts and stable reputations even while trying to give the impression that they were receptive and attentive to new voices. But reputations, even for accomplished poets, could be slow to develop, and few, no matter how successful, gained through poetry more than a bare subsistence from either patrons or booksellers. Pope's meteoric rise to prominence and financial comfort was the exception rather than the rule, and aspiring poets – especially those outside London or without connections to booksellers or the world of letters – could find it hard to get their work noticed: they usually remained inglorious even if they were not mute. And the recognition itself was sometimes uncertain, ambiguous or fleeting. Advertising and public relations strategies seem rather low-key or even puzzling by modern standards, though contemporary readers probably understood the codes and shorthand and silences better than we do. Beyond word of mouth and the gossip of coffee houses, the main book device for trading on reputation involved title pages where, in the case of a dedicated volume, the author's name or title or position or social status ('John Dryden,' 'the D– of W–n.', 'Dean S–,' 'a Lady of Quality,' 'William Broome, Chaplain to the Right Honourable Charles Lord Cornwallis, Baron of Eyre, Warden, Chief Justice, and Justice in Eyre, of all His Majesty's Parks, &c. on the South Side of Trent') usually appeared prominently, though sometimes indirectly by reference to previous work ('By the Author of the True-Born Englishman'). But often there is also a certain coyness or mysterious silence about attribution, with print refusing to say what many readers seem already to have known, the author of a text published 'anonymously'. Even in collections issued by subscription when patrons (and virtually all buyers) would obviously know whose poems they were supporting, sometimes neither the title page nor the text names the author.[12] Often, too, miscellanies involving several authors provide a list of some of them on the title page but then omit others equally represented inside but who presumably are less likely to command attention. Just as often a mere handful of the included poems are directly attributed to authors, leaving readers to scramble to discover or recall the right matching of text to poet in the body of the book. Anonymity, then, was a slippery concept; anonymity, attribution and authorship were all, in fact, highly problematic terms and concepts at the time for those who made or sold books. And texts were often falsely attributed as well, either on title pages or in tables of contents; poets sometimes report themselves bewildered or enraged to be associated with texts that were not theirs or that they did not wish to claim as theirs. Because volumes devoted to one author often included a few poems by others ('by another hand'), keeping attributions straight could be very challenging. It is no wonder that authors who wished to duck responsibility for a particular lampoon or political observation used the contexts of uncertainty to issue plausible (though often false) denials. Some

---

12 See, for example, *Poems on Several Occasions. Published by Subscription* (Manchester, 1733); there is an 'Address to all My Subscribers' (300 of them are listed), but it is unsigned. See also *Poems on Several Occasions*, Shrewsbury, Tho. Durston, for the Author, 1727.

poets genuinely tried to keep their work from seeing print – truly writing only for friends or their own pleasure – and others, though willing to have their work made public, genuinely sought to avoid attribution or credit, sometimes out of modesty and sometimes out of legal apprehension or physical fear.[13]

Still, poetic reputations developed, canons were posited and booksellers counted on public expectation. Fame and poetic recognition took many forms and degrees. We can distinguish four more or less distinct categories of career intention and productivity. The first consists of those whose primary life or career commitment was to poetry – poets by *profession* whether or not they were professional poets in the commercial, made-their-living-by-that-means sense. Those in this group thought of themselves as poets and were considered so by their contemporaries, however they made their livings: some were, for example, playwrights, clergymen, physicians, diplomats, civil servants or lived on inheritances. But in their goals they identified primarily with becoming known for poetry of quality and cultural ambition, regarding poetry as their chief means of expression. This group includes highly visible figures like Dryden, Pope, Blackmore and Edward Young, but also others as varied as Katherine Philips, Matthew Prior, Mary Lady Chudleigh and Stephen Duck, who accepted recognition and celebrity more reluctantly or uncertainly but took poetry and their own poetic role very seriously indeed.[14]

A second, more comprehensive group also put primary emphasis on their writings but had a different sense of identity – with letters and learning and human reflection more generally rather than specifically with poetry: they were writers by self-definition but only secondarily poets. These men (and not a few women) of letters and learning wrote history, theology, philosophy, social analysis and sometimes memoirs and argumentative accounts of public affairs, and for them poetry was a subset of knowledge and writing more generally, a contributory part to a larger vocation of historical, philosophical and cultural understanding. Some in this group (Swift, for example, or John Norris, or Joseph Trapp) were gifted and skilled poets, though in most cases their excellence in one or more other modes has tended historically to obscure their poetic merits. This group has its roots in Renaissance humanism, and its traditions are mainly classical and genteel, but its impetus, energy and variety come from the modern proliferation and enlarged functions of print. Many in the group by the late seventeenth century – when the vernacular had taken

---

13 There is a substantial historical record of writers and booksellers being physically assaulted.
14 Some drifters from the aim: Wycherley, Etherege, Congreve.

over many traditional Latin functions and when the book trade needed a whole new range of skills, perspectives and reaches – look to present-day eyes a lot more like journalists, hacks and 'professional' writers and compilers than scholars and literati, for its members include not only self-appointed cultural custodians such as Sir William Temple, Sir Robert Boyle, Lady Mary Wortley Montagu, Bishop Berkeley, John Dennis and Joseph Addison, but also Aphra Behn, Charles Gildon, Ned Ward, Eliza Haywood, Daniel Defoe and John Oldmixon. The kinds of intellectual and cultural work that such writers did vary widely, of course, and qualitative distinctions have to be made among them, but they have in common a commitment to analysis of the past and present and to the importance of the written word – a commitment that sometimes meant writing in verse.

Those in the third group wrote poetry more offhandedly, occasionally and inconsistently, but many of them still accumulated a reasonable body of work – usually about a volume's worth – some of it ambitious and some merely playful or informal or even trifling. The typical volume for these poets was entitled *Poems on Several Occasions* (or with variations such as *Poems on Various Subjects* or *Poems on Particular Occasions* or *Miscellany Poems on Several Subjects*), and it usually included a modest collection of work written over a lifetime of fitful activity. Many, but not all, of these poets were formally educated, learned and interested in classical texts, and often their work included translations of passages from standard works, especially Virgil, Horace, Ovid and Statius. Sometimes one or two longer, fairly ambitious original poems were part of the collection (and one suspects that many of these poets were also quietly at work on a 'big' poem that they probably did not expect to publish), but most of the poems in these volumes were short and written on private and personal occasions rather than public ones of national magnitude. A lot of the poems were, one way or another, addressed to friends, some labelled as 'epistles', others merely titled in a to-someone format ('To the Ladies', 'To a Child of Quality of Five Years Old', 'To Miss Charlotte Pulteney in her Mother's Arms', 'To Mr Gay . . . On the Finishing his House', 'To a Young Lady with Some Lampreys', 'To the Earl of Warwick. On the Death of Mr Addison'). Often a veneer of conscious fiction covers situation and personnel; many poets celebrated friends or lovers under fictional 'poetic' names (Clarissa, Sylvia, Sacharissa, Mira, Stella, Myrtello, etc.) or otherwise engaged an open artificiality, formalisation and generalisation of sentiment and expression.

Poetic virtue for these poets usually consisted in wit, canny observation, formal control, genial good humour and graceful compliment, although often there were satirical and sobering moments. The historical model for them – no matter their own social background – involved the habits of court and genteel expectations of leisurely, unlaboured play. The qualities of the Cavalier poets were not so much invoked as coyly (and distantly) imitated, and it was not just the court poets of the Restoration (such as Sedley, Rochester, Dorset and Mulgrave) and aristocratic ladies (such as Margaret Cavendish (Duchess of Newcastle), Lady Chudleigh, and Anne Finch (Countess of Winchilsea)) who wrote in this way, but those of the middling sort and even from labouring classes, especially later in the period. Among the best of these modest and modestly productive poets before 1750 are Katherine Philips, John Pomfret, William Congreve, Sarah Fyge Egerton, William Diaper, Thomas Tickell, Isaac Watts, Thomas Parnell, Elizabeth Thomas, Mary Barber, Sarah Dixon and Mary Leapor. But many others were readable and engaging versifiers; among those who had at least a modest following among readers in the late seventeenth century were Benjamin Keach and John Bunyan (both of whom wrote very popular devotional poetry), Elizabeth Singer Rowe ('Philomela' or 'the Pindaric Lady' whose pious poems had an enthusiastic readership), and Samuel Wesley the elder (who when young produced a facetious sophomoric collection called *Maggots*, and, older, produced an epic-like life of Christ, verse versions of both the Old and New Testaments, and three sons and a daughter who, in addition to their historical influence on religion, wrote substantive poetry).[15] And there was, of course, an army of satirists and political versifiers who helped set the conversational agenda in coffee houses: John Oldham, Robert Wild, Robert Gould, Edward Howard, William King, Thomas Ken and John Tutchin. A generation later, there were many more near-masters of the social modes: Edmund Smith, Aaron Hill, Mary Masters, John Hughes, Thomas Cooke, James Delacour and Paul Whitehead, for example, and some who aspired semi-successfully towards grander verse: John Dyer, Hildebrand Jacob, Walter Harte and Richard Glover. The fact that many of these names have faded or fallen into complete obscurity testifies both to the success of dominant poets, especially Dryden and Pope, in creating a historical sense that only a few poets mattered, and to the power of the great books syndrome that has dominated literary history since the early twentieth century and dominates still, despite challenges to the received canon.

A fourth group wrote or published poetry even more occasionally, usually only under some particular provocation or inspiration. Most of these poets

15 John and Charles were mainly known for hymns; Samuel (the younger) and Hetty Wright wrote more variously.

published just a few poems, usually for some special public occasion. David Foxon's convenient catalogue of separately published poems lists literally thousands of examples of poets now known to have written, between 1701 and 1750, only a poem or two, some of them famous in other pursuits – Robert Harley, Bishop Berkeley and Luke Milbourne, for example – and others now totally otherwise unknown. Some few of these poems suggest talent, if not necessarily formal execution, just as impressive as that of the more famous. Constantia Grierson, for example, who apparently wrote rarely and died young, shows immense learning, tough-minded formal discipline and verbal resonance that might have, in a longer life or better circumstances, produced major work. But almost all the poets in this group were not widely known in their own time and are forgotten in ours; their significance in history consists in their demonstration of just how deep was the cultural urge to versify on virtually any subject that generated personal or national energy. Older literary history tended to deal only with the first two of these four categories, though noting an occasional example of the third, but it is hard to understand the full force of poetry's wide appeal in the age without noting the great number and variety of people who were poets at least sometimes and without seeing that some occasions, public and private, could make poets of (nearly) all readers.

Directions: the power of poetic kinds or genres

Individual authorial sensibility and ideological affiliation were arguably **not** the most important determinants in the topic, tone or direction of a poem, or at least so it seems. In the rhetorical world of the time, expectation counted for a lot, and beyond situation and circumstance there were crucial factors of tradition, both ancient and modern, both local and Roman. The neoclassical idea of genre had an especially powerful influence, in part because particular subject matter was expected to trigger certain conventions and invoke specific poetic traditions, habits and procedures. The idea of genre or poetic kind – the notion that a certain tone, style and set of conventions unites poems of demonstrable similarity across times, places and cultures – was powerfully expressed throughout the period, but it is sometimes hard to know just how literally to take the often-rigid statements of critics (and sometimes of poets) because practice does not always follow theory. There is, in fact, a notorious departure in practice from much of the best-known and most articulate genre theory, complicated by the rampant envy (and accompanying distrust) of French tradition which by the late seventeenth century had become the main modern conduit into the English tradition for classical ideas of genre.

One significant context for the ambivalence towards genre and towards French neoclassicism involves the national agenda to create a distinct native poetic voice and tradition. The powerful post-Restoration desire to create a British tradition is easy for literary history to underrate, for (from our perspective on canon) the Elizabethans already had mounted such a programme quite successfully: no one would seem to need to apologise, in 1660, for a tradition that already could look back to Chaucer, Spenser, Marlowe, Sidney, Jonson, Herbert and Shakespeare. But Chaucer seemed remote and inaccessible, and the Elizabethans and Jacobeans seemed, despite vast accomplishments, still rough and crude and not yet characteristic of a firm language tradition or of British culture as it wished to conceive itself. Even though they admired the poetry of their immediate predecessors enormously, Restoration critics had larger doubts about its power as a distinct and continuing body of work, and there was a strong tendency to think of it as providing a kind of workshop or pre-tradition on which to build: certainly early poetry needed to be polished, 'refined' and 'improved'. The Civil Wars seemed to divide a present age of experience from a former, now lost, world of innocence; 'before the Flood' seemed a transcendent metaphor for early modern writing to more than just Dryden. What the 'previous age' had done was too little, too tentative, too unself-conscious, too rugged and perhaps still too European to fully create, in a modern spirit, a literature fully appropriate to the English language, British temperament and modern 'refinement'. The desire to establish a polished, fresh, mature and distinctly national tradition was very strong, but it was channelled through a powerful sense of past and present models, largely Rome from the past and France from the present. Steering a new course that was in part indebted to both these cultures but that preserved British independence and originality was no easy task.[16]

The leading recent and contemporary French critics of the neoclassical persuasion – Boileau, Rapin, Bossu – were much admired and quoted by British critics and poets anxious to develop a strong, somewhat parallel, native tradition of letters. But they were also distrusted and resisted, if often silently and unconsciously. In part this was just because they were French and therefore suspect on political, religious, moral, climatic and temperamental grounds. But the distrust also went beyond xenophobia and nationalism and involved a larger sceptical habit of mind, a native distrust of systems and general resistance to neat categories, literary or otherwise – a sense of English exceptionalism that

---

16 The fullest account of the nationalist agenda in poetry is in Howard Weinbrot, *Britannia's Issue* (Cambridge: Cambridge University Press, 1995).

could grudgingly be extended to the rest of 'Britain' but that was certainly not European. Still, many critical accounts of poetic kinds pay homage, sometimes quite slavishly, to the standard French neoclassical categories and hierarchy of kinds, and many praise the sense of order that taxonomy had given to a chaotic landscape of letters.

The idea of genres, or poetic kinds, expressed the directional aim with force if not precision. French neoclassicism took its cues from both the theory and practice of the ancients, and it seemed to regard as universal the paradigms of Greece and Rome, often combining Aristotelian rigour of definition with a near-Platonic sense of forms. To the neatness of kinds that distinguished a consistency of subject matter, tone and scope, modern neoclassicism (from the Italian Renaissance forward) had added stricter rules, heightened the sense of hierarchy and implied a categorisation founded in nature. Boileau's authoritative discussion implies that the orders are distinct, natural and central, representing both degrees of challenge and orders of difficulty. And British critics and theoreticians, if not always poets, tended to follow him. The critical treatises of Joseph Trapp (*Lectures on Poetry*, 1742) and Charles Gildon (*The Complete Art of Poetry*, 2 vols., 1718) lay out distinctions between genres quite elaborately, and their discussions basically follow the French way of moving through the traditional genres one by one – with individual sections on epic, tragedy, elegy, epigram, pastoral, etc. Trapp's treatise, which originated in lectures he gave, in Latin, three decades earlier at Oxford, devotes eighteen of his twenty-nine chapters to elaborating genre.

But the poetry itself presents, in its quietly rebellious freedom, a quite different picture of the genre issue. Often poems pay titular homage to kinds, labels and conventions; Pope and Ambrose Philips (and many others) unapologetically wrote *Pastorals*, John Gay wrote *The Birth of the Squire. An Eclogue*, Blackmore regularly labelled his long poems as epics or heroic poems, Georgics sometimes identified themselves on title pages, early on, in method and Virgilian loyalty, and nearly every poet wrote several elaborate-stanzaed poems with 'ode' or 'pindarique' in the title or subtitle. But the poetry follows the generic definitions and rules at some distance and tolerates extraordinary latitude. Inversions and mock versions abound, especially prominently in transferring country conventions into urban settings (Gay's *Trivia, or the Art of Walking the Streets of London*, for example, or Montagu's *Town Eclogues*). Labelling itself takes on a quietly revised sense of genre and classical precedent; more poems categorise themselves in new or newly renovated terms – essay, epistle, letter, tale, imitation, dialogue – than apply the traditional ones associated with French classification. And, in fact, most poems of the period are ultimately very difficult to classify accurately within either the traditional or new categories. For most poets, fewer than one in five poems are identified by any kind of generic label, and among those plainly labelled, a very large percentage mock, tease or play fast and loose with the conventions and expectations. Pope is perhaps more confident and liberated than the typical aspiring poet (and certainly more so than the prose critics), but his allowance of a grace beyond the reach of art, and especially of genre-bending, represents poetic practice more accurately than the rules-conscious insistences of critics such as Gildon and Trapp or Dennis. Dryden's famous 1668 formulation of his own subjective preferences ('I admire [Jonson], but I love Shakspeare'), in spite of clear critical principles that point the other way, stands for much of the poetic practice of the period. Poems are critically expected to follow classical and generic precedent, but there is no penalty for not doing so, and in practice most poems are anti-generic, non-generic or consciously mixed. One can readily identify *Absalom and Achitophel* (which was published simply as *Absalom and Achitophel: A Poem*) as a satire, an allegory, a political poem, a narrative poem, a parable, a biblical parallel, a set of character sketches and host of other appropriate labels, but none of these, except sometimes 'satire', is among the classical or neoclassical kinds. What are we to call, in standard genre terms, *Religio Laici, A Letter from Italy, The Spleen, Alma, The Rape of the Lock, Verses on the Death of Dr Swift, The Seasons,* or *An Essay on Man*? In each case, a series of possible labels suggests itself, but these are seldom the classic genre terms, and the fact that several labels are better than any one should tell us that genre designation is a starting rather than a defining point, a convenience towards expectation rather than final statement.

Here, for example, is a poem about an ordinary couple that Prior simple titled 'An Epitaph':

> Interr'd beneath this Marble Stone,
> Lie Saunt'ring Jack, and Idle Joan.
> While rolling Threescore Years and One
> Did round this Globe their Courses run;
> If Human Things went Ill or Well;
> If changing Empires rose or fell;
> The Morning past, the Evening came,
> And found this Couple still the same.
> They Walk'd and Eat, good Folks: What then?
> Why then They Walk'd and Eat again:
> They soundly slept the Night away:
> They did just Nothing all the Day:

And having bury'd Children Four,
Wou'd not take Pains to try for more.
Nor Sister either had, nor Brother:
They seem'd just Tally'd for each other.

    Their Moral and Oeconomy
Most perfectly They made agree:
Each Virtue kept it's proper Bound,
Nor Trespass'd on the other's Ground.
Nor Fame, nor Censure They regarded:
They neither Punish'd, nor Rewarded.
He car'd not what the Footmen did:
Her Maids She neither prais'd, nor chid:
So ev'ry Servant took his Course;
And bad at First, They all grew worse.
Slothful Disorder fill'd His Stable;
And sluttish Plenty deck'd Her Table.
Their Beer was strong; Their Wine was *Port*;
Their Meal was large; Their Grace was short.
They gave the Poor the Remnant-meat,
Just when it grew not fit to eat.

    They paid the Church and Parish-Rate;
And took, but read not the Receit:
 For which They claim'd their *Sunday*'s Due,
Of slumb'ring in an upper Pew.

    No Man's Defects sought They to know;
So never made Themselves a Foe.
No Man's good Deeds did They commend;
So never rais'd Themselves a Friend.
Nor cherish'd They Relations poor:
That might decrease Their present Store:
Nor Barn nor House did they repair:
That might oblige Their future Heir.

    They neither Added, nor Confounded:
They neither Wanted, nor Abounded.
Each *Christmas* They Accompts did clear;
And wound their Bottom round the Year.
Nor Tear, nor Smile did They imploy
At News of Public Grief, or Joy.
When Bells were Rung, and Bonfires made;
If ask'd, They ne'er deny'd their Aid:
Their Jugg was to the Ringers carry'd;
Who ever either Dy'd, or Marry'd.

Their Billet at the Fire was found;
  Who ever was Depos'd, or Crown'd.

  Nor Good, nor Bad, nor Fools, nor Wise;
They wou'd not learn, nor cou'd advise:
Without Love, Hatred, Joy, or Fear,
They led – a kind of – as it were:
Nor Wish'd, nor Car'd, nor Laugh'd, nor Cry'd:
And so They liv'd; and so They dy'd.[17]

Now this poem is a lot of different things – a character, a retirement poem, a golden mean poem, a fable, an inverted elegy, even a version of estate poem – but clearly it is not, except in its setting up of expectations, an epitaph: no one would engrave sixty-two lines for this pair, and the poem follows none of the standard conventions of pointedness, concision or even wit. Like the couple, it too is a kind of 'as it were', and the balance and symmetry that rule throughout their boring but almost canonical lives ('threescore years and one') turn out to be disvalues, inversions or absences of virtue – a kind of leaden mean. Prior draws upon truistic assumptions and terms, including those of genre, to demonstrate (over and over) that abstract values can be reduced, in living instances, to behaviour that has no value at all. It is astonishing how often in the poetry of the time labels turn out this way – starters for a crucial process of readerly understanding about the relationship between names, concepts and things, but woefully unsatisfactory for classification.

But if they privileged echo over copying, emulation over rule, temperament and circumstance over definition, the poets of the age also had older, especially classical, predecessors constantly in mind, and their apprenticeship normally consisted of long exercises in translation or paraphrase of episodes from classical epics (as well as incidents retold from the Bible and other older texts or mythologies). They thus strove for some of the systematic distinctions of the French and aspired to their discipline and sense of order, but they continued to distrust dependence and rules, which most Britons still, even after a much Europeanised court in the Restoration, thought of as southern, legalistic, authoritarian and Popish. They did subscribe generally to the approximate sense of hierarchy that made long and complex poems – epics – superior to short and simple ones such as pastorals or lyrics. And they labelled poems by kind on title pages whenever they could usefully suggest a claim, but also gave

17 *Poems on Several Occasions*, ed. R. A. Waller (Cambridge: Cambridge University Press, 1905), pp. 184–5.

themselves a lot of native latitude born of nationalistic resistance and distrust of authority.

If the hierarchy of traditional genres – with epic at the top – meant anything at all to English poetic practice, it involved implied distinctions between simple and complex, long and short, ambitious and playful, more than any precise descriptions of subject, scope or tone. The 'Virgilian progression' model, sometimes said to have governed the shape of classic literary careers such as Dryden's and Pope's, may have prompted poets to write early pastorals, later Georgics or Georgic-like didactic poems, and ultimately long poems (though seldom real epics); but the paradigm mainly marks developing ambition, maturity and confidence rather than genre-based imitation per se. If there was a loyalty to precedent, it was to the conceptual advance from simple to complex rather than to slavish career-modelling or to a belief in clear genre distinctions. The less exclusive modal terms in the title of this chapter and the next – political, didactic, satirical and lyrical – offer a more historically accurate description of actual forms and trends.

Public and political poetry: praise and blame

Writing about public affairs and events seemed obligatory to poets ambitious of reputation or dependent on writing for their livelihood, in part because the complexities of public life were always in need of thoughtful interpretation and in part for more mundane, practical and self-serving reasons. Politics in post-Civil War England were especially partisan, controversial and nasty, and poets typically were just as opinionated as anyone, and (if anything) more openly aligned with parties and causes. Most were publicly identified with either Whig or Tory alliances and often with a specific patron or group of patrons; usually their opinions about public developments were known and their support for causes widely sought. They were, after all, wordsmiths in an age that relished argument, respected rhetorical ability and admired verbal persuasion. The patronage system that most poets literally lived by – in which writers were given support money by wealthy and prominent patrons, usually in response to texts dedicated or indebted to them – often meant that poets wrote to please not just a general public but a very specific reader, usually someone with strong interests in public policy and events of political or economic significance. Poetry then sometimes took the form of propaganda (though usually quite sophisticated propaganda), and poets were significant participants in public debate and discussion, often from a position near the seats of power. Few shunned the public stage or avoided topical issues; the time had not yet come when distance from public affairs was prized, rewarded and considered virtuous.[18]

Theoretically, poetic 'occasions' were to be moments of praise and exaltation: effusions of loyalty to cultural leaders or those who triumphed over circumstance and anchored national or cultural values of some demonstrable sort. The most common public occasions for poetry – those which provoked the most important poets to call upon their most inspired talents – were events that seemed both politically and nationally decisive. The Duke of Marlborough's victory at Blenheim was one such event – Foxon lists twenty-four surviving individual poems about it, including celebrated and often reprinted ones by John Philips, *Bleinheim* (*sic*) (1704) and Addison, *The Campaign*.[19] And so was the ensuing Peace of Utrecht which pacified (temporarily) age-old wars with France; poets as ranging as Marshall Smith, Henry Crispe, Bevil Higgons and Trapp (and at least six anonymous poets) addressed that event, and Pope's *Windsor-Forest* was, among many other things, a celebration of its moment and implications ('And Peace and Plenty tell, a STUART reigns' (line 42)). Royal birthdays, deaths of the famous and anniversaries of coronations or other major events called, too, for panegyric.[20] But panegyric in a world of conflict and dispute implicitly promised opposition or disagreement with some other person or view, and in truth the inevitable other side of panegyric was satire: opposition, attack, derogation, lampoon, undermining – persuasion *against*, which was simply the opposite of celebration or argument in favour. Implying that their temperaments and values were more positive than their reputations, Dryden said that satirists would in another age write poems of praise. But in fact poets in his own satiric age (including himself) alternately wrote paeans to their heroes and satires on their villains. Satire and panegyric are two sides

---

18 One popular minor poetic form, the retirement poem which took its impetus from Latin models, celebrated distance from power and urban or court strife. John Pomfret's poem, *The Choice* (1700), is the *locus classicus* of the type and it was one of the most popular and often reprinted poems in the eighteenth century. But even this form, dependent as it is on values of the country, solitude, rest and indolence, testifies to an assumed norm of activity near the seats of power.

19 And others followed. See, for example, Elijah Fenton's 'An Ode to the Sun for the New-Year, 1707' which also dwells on the leadership and exploits of Anne and Marlborough, and Nicholas Rowe's *A Poem upon the Late Glorious Successes of Her Majesty's Arms* (also 1707).

20 Only those poets officially committed to a particular position or course – the poet laureate, for example, whose direct loyalties were to the crown – were openly obliged to write on such occasions. The laureate legally had to write only two poems a year – on the occasion of the monarch's declared birthday and on New Year's Day – but most understood that their duty encompassed support of crucial decisions and moments; and even those whose relationship to a patron was less contractual (if no less obligatory) got out their pens when the occasion summoned.

of the same coin; their currency equally depends on a poetic economy of public interest, engagement and discussion – what has come to be known as 'the public sphere' where more or less enlightened citizens of many stripes involve themselves in public discourse about ethos, directions and policy – and praise and blame are equally a part of both oral and written evaluation and argument.

Not all public poetry was ideological, and not all ideological poetry was directly political. But the tendency to regard public occasions as poetically obligatory (and the related habit of associating major occasions with the practices of patronage and patrons' loyalties) reinforced the sense that poetry was essentially a rhetorical, persuasive and practical art. There was a lot more to poetry than public issues, but public and political loyalties tended to trump private feelings, and in any case they generated more – and more ambitious – poems to be culturally reckoned with. Poems about private life and relationships – less obligatory, shorter, usually not published separately and generally intended for fewer eyes – are often, however, just as rhetorical and sometimes almost as 'political'. Not all poets fully draw out the larger implications – political, philosophical, social, economic or moral – of the many issues they represent or investigate: love across social lines, emotional imbalances and tensions, gender roles and inequalities, family governance, role expectations and compensations in the workplace, emotional imbalances, country/city contrasts, sexual frustrations and failures, the stubborn resistances of nature and habit. But the age was more willing than most to open and explore sources of disagreement and friction and to view small, private matters in larger shared terms. Its spirit was rumbustious and fractious rather than serene, and the veneer of polite respect and deference that characterises the poetry of panegyric and social compliment masks deep anxieties and divisions. Poetry in an important sense led the way in exposing the fissures between surface acceptance of things as they are and a baring of deep human divisions. Pope's assertion that 'Whatever is, is RIGHT' (An Essay on Man, 1, 294) represents a philosophical willingness to take the world on its own terms, not satisfaction with things in their present conditions. Most of Pope's career, and that of most other public poets and satirists, involved advocacy for radical change in both manners and morals, and when he described the life of a poet as 'a warfare upon Earth' he was describing not only his own beleaguered experience as an activist rhetorician, but also the unsettling crossfire felt by many an author whose pen took up the burden of the present.

Many other situations and circumstances, not necessarily triggered by a particular event, also qualified as obligatory to individual poets at particular moments. In the 1690s, repeated attacks on the foreign birth of William III and on his non-English values, for example, led Daniel Defoe to write one of the most immediately effective political poems ever written, *The True-Born Englishman* (1700), which defended William's patriotism by pointing out that all Englishmen had foreign lineage of some kind. Defoe had many self-serving reasons for defending his king, but loyalty and principle were also among his motives, and the poem in any case succeeded not because of motives or sincerity but because Defoe was a master rhetorician who gauged his audience well and touched a responsive cultural chord. Practical consequences were not, obviously, the only criteria for determining a poem's power, but they were one measurable way of deciding the immediate effectiveness of argument. Those who view poetry as somehow above the exigencies of human quotidian circumstance or who regard poetry as by nature subversive and so unable to intervene in public argument on the side of authority and power – that is, those who buy post-Romantic principles of distance, disengagement and derogation – will find such uses of poetry inappropriate, objectionable and puzzling, but poets then found themselves in, or wedged themselves into, positions of relative power and public influence, and they used, without flinching, their pens as weapons on behalf of friends, causes, values and their own welfare.

The hazards of such central participation and powerful influence in the public sphere were many and great. Often poets were suspected of being less, or differently, committed than they publicly seemed, capable of choosing sides on the basis of personal interest or the prospect of gain and thus not the moral guides and cultural guardians they claimed to be. And if contemporary poetry enjoyed its central place in public attention, it also risked seeming too topical, transitory, quarrelsome and self-important. Poetry's own disputes sometimes overshadowed larger political and social issues, and increasingly, especially after the vitriolic exchanges between Pope and his detractors between 1717 and the early 1740s, the public responded with disaffection or even disgust to what often seemed petty self-absorption. Poetry, and the world of letters and learning more generally, later in the century paid a price for its high profile, and much of poetry's later withdrawal to the margins of public affairs can be traced to public disillusionment with both the failures and successes of poetry's high profile in the later Stuart and early Georgian years.

Then, too, a poetry of ideological commitment and pugnacity risked wearing out its rhetorical machinery and dulling both its edge and the responses of its readers. The rigours – and sometimes downright nastiness – of satire and lampoon offended many sensibilities, and reputations for strength, directness, honesty, principled analysis and clarity could quickly turn into judgements of bias, exaggeration and personal meanness. Even in ages most friendly to its values and uses, satire creates nervous appreciation and often nagging doubts about motives. And the perils of panegyric are, in a different way, just as great. Writing persuasive compliment is hard, and writing it repeatedly in a context of rhetorical inflation is harder. The main issue is finally not sincerity or authenticity (though plenty of commendatory poems were generated in need or greed and conceived more in a spirit of sycophancy than genuine admiration), but an ability to be cleverly persuasive about virtues and values. But in an age of fulsome dedications and a national need to praise public accomplishments, panegyric can quickly go thin; Swift's parodic version of the difficulties of hack writing, in which the 'author'-narrator of *A Tale of a Tub* discovers that 'the materials of Panegyric being very few in number, have been long since exhausted'[21] has very real and painful equivalents in the actual writing of serious as well as journeyman poets.

Poetry's status in the world ultimately suffered for its willingness to engage the deepest passions of opinion and unrest, but readers willing to search the particulars behind glib textual reference in the poetry of the period can get at, more easily than in most times, the complexities within. Most often, the rough pugnacity was close to the surface, one reason why Dryden accurately described his times as requiring satire. Satire was in fact both the attitude and form characteristic of the whole age. Disappointment, anger and even vitriol brought out the best in some poets, including many of the most famous ones of the period.

Didactic and satirical poetry

The terms and tones of didactic poetry on the one hand (with its voice of caring, sweet reasonableness and soft persuasion) and of satiric verse on the other (with its characteristic mode of declamation, denunciation, disappointed disgust and damnation) could hardly be more opposite, but the two kinds are methodologically, like the attitudes of praise and blame, closely related. Both are born of a deep sense of commitment to public issues and social and moral choice, and a stated primacy of instruction over delight is central to both. Both have deeply committed and reformist aims of turning public sentiment persuasively in a particular direction, one by advocating what to do and creating

---

21 *The Prose Works of Jonathan Swift*, ed. Herbert Davis, 14 vols. (Oxford: Basil Blackwell, 1957), vol. 1, p. 30.

a climate of virtuous emulation, the other by cautiously urging evitation, resistance and avoidance by providing warnings of imminent dangers: one says go, and the other pause, denounce, resist and correct. Despite persistent doubt and depression about the present state of the world, belief in the viability of some moral or cultural ideal sponsors the instructive aim in each case. In that sense poetry of the time was insistently hopeful, if not genuinely optimistic, about human perfectibility or at least amelioration, even if preoccupied with insistent human failings and wrong directions.

Poets often describe themselves as driven to satire – by circumstance, commitment or temperament – and creative energies for many flowed most freely and effectively in that mode. Over the years satire has proved the most durable poetic legacy of the time, and many of the best-known poems from the period, then and now, are satires: Butler's *Hudibras*; Dryden's *MacFlecknoe* and *Absalom and Achitophel*; Rochester's *Satyr against Reason and Mankind*; Garth's *Dispensary*; Defoe's *Reformation of Manners*; Blackmore's *Satyr against Wit*; Pope's *Rape of the Lock, Dunciad, Moral Essays* and *Imitations of Horace*; Swift's 'lady poems' such as 'A Beautiful Young Nymph going to Bed' and 'The Progress of Beauty'; and Edward Young's *Love of Fame*. Many of these poems are direct, outspoken, uncompromising, angry and scathing, even crude – bordering on lampoon or libel in their naming of names and specificity of iniquity and blame. Others – more gentle, subtle, teasing and seemingly under tighter control – are often equally devastating in their implication. The job of satire, as these poets defined it, was to go after vice and corruption wherever they found it and whatever its benign form, and to be unsparing in assigning social and ethical responsibility as well as in describing the simple lapses or utter depravity of behaviour itself. And although the authorial stance is typically one of righteous outrage, satirists often self-consciously find themselves confessing their own humanity and imperfection, duly and deliberately taking on judgemental and scourging tasks they know will leave them open to criticism of their own human limits and fallibilities. The most convincing satiric representations are usually those that make deliberate use of irony in trying to uphold tough, almost superhuman standards in a conscious context of human limitations that include satirists themselves. There is within satire a powerful sub-tradition of the satirist satirised, with writers feeling very much caught up in the corruption their satire describes, though the rhetorical stance of total innocence and noble objectivity is also widely at work in the period.

Women poets are usually said to be less ferocious and vituperative in their satires, and it is true that they generally wrote fewer and less sweeping satires than did the most prominent male satirists, just as they tended to address public subjects less often and with less pretension to inside or superior knowledge and authority. But many women wrote powerful individual satires on both broadly social and more personal topics; Montagu, for example, had nearly as biting a wit as did her frequent antagonist Pope, and when they went head to head she was just as direct and often as clever (in, for example, 'Verses Address'd to the Imitator of . . . Horace . . . By a Lady'), and she can be scathing and ruthless when she goes after the double standard in sex and gender issues (as in 'Epistle from Mrs Yonge to Her Husband'). Much in fact, but by no means all, of women's satire is directed at gender roles. Any reader who doubts female power and range in satire needs to take a hard look at Chudleigh's work, even in her short, informal poems ('Wife and servant are the same, / But only differ in the name'),[22] and at attitudes, tones and generic shifts constantly at work in Mary Leapor's youthful poems, even when she is formally committed to a different poetic kind (as, for example, the way she slides into the satiric mode from the safe confines of a house- or estate-poem in *Crumble-Hall*).[23] And the earlier, tough poems of Aphra Behn – though not necessarily motivated or characterised by the same moral stances (or postures) that characterise some other satirists – had both the temperament and wit to produce withering criticisms of the manners and habits of her contemporaries. Her famous poetic dialogue with Rochester ('The Imperfect Enjoyment' versus 'The Disappointment') demonstrates not only her fertile and powerful competitive streak but a creative ability to translate conventional role expectations into strategies that privilege female perspective and values.

The strength and resonance of the major satires usually derive from their projected sense of how contemporary habits and manners violate some larger, lasting tradition of values, and there is often a clear and powerful moral vision that, however exaggerated, seems almost mythic in its good/evil insistences. Dryden's *MacFlecknoe*, for example, draws on readers' traditional expectations of rational intelligence, orderly procedures, mentorship, monarchical succession, Judeo-Christian body–spirit dichotomies and England's (and London's) superiority over 'northern,' Irish and 'barbarian' cultures to create a sense of displaced and perverted social and political order in contemporary literary taste and the reward system. Pope, in the several redactions of *The Dunciad*, picks up most of Dryden's inverted machinery (in which Nonsense and Stupidity

22 Lines 1 and 2 of 'To the Ladies' (1703).
23 Not published until 1751, but written much earlier (she died in 1746, at the age of twenty-four).

replace meaning and wit) and translates it into a universe where Dulness, disorder and darkness triumph over light, clarity and order to extend more cosmically the sense that vice and ignorance are rewarded and the just, meritorious and creative punished ('Art after Art goes out, and all is Night', as Pope puts it at the end of the fourth book of *The Dunciad*). Similarly in *The Rape of the Lock*, Pope works from traditional expectations of epic behaviour, social hierarchies, gender-role relationships, love-and-war analogies and battle-of-the-sexes metaphors, and human dependence on fate and a framework of botched supernatural controls in order to present a society in which irrational and erring humans discover the superficial gods they deserve and live out their glittering but meaningless lives in an inverted world where everyone has lost an understanding of values, obligations and even ordinary sexual rituals. In practice, the analogies and inversions are never quite as neat as a summary of them would suggest, but the assumptions and inversions of value set up much of the poetic structure, and much of the fun of the satire – and satire *is* about fun and readerly pleasure at least as much as it is about moral certainties – involves imperfect negotiations between principle and quotidian imperfection of whatever kind. Objects of satire range from powerful national policies, professions and cultural forces to passing fads and tastes, from Dryden's *The Medal. A Satyr against Sedition* (1682) and the anonymous *A Satyr against the French* (1691) to Gould's *A Satyr against Wooing* (1698), Richard Ames' *The Female Fire-Ships. A Satyr against Whoring* (1691), Ned Ward's *More Priestcraft* (1705), Mehetabel Wright's 'Wedlock. A Satyr' (*c.* 1725), Paul Whitehead's *Manners: A Satyr* (1739), and John Freke's *The History of Insipids*.

One of the most powerful and influential satires of the 1680s – Dryden's *Absalom and Achitophel*, which had scores of sequels and imitators over the next full generation – made its essential point through the very complication of focus and uncertainty. It is unwavering in its support of Charles II's sovereign claims (and the absurdity and corruption of the rebellion of Monmouth, his illegitimate son), and it uses the expectational force of biblical allegory to assert a parallel with ancient Israel and King David, but the opening lines suggest both the firm allegiance to monarchical principle and the bemused acceptance of human fallibility, even in a king.

> In pious times, e'r priestcraft did begin,
> Before *Polygamy* was made a Sin;
> When Man on many multipli'd his kind,
> E'r one to one was cursedly confin'd;
> When Nature prompted, and no Law deni'd,

Promiscuous Use of Concubine and Bride;
Then *Israel's* Monarch after Heavens own heart,
His vigorous warmth did, variously, impart
To Wives and Slaves; And, wide as his Command,
Scatter'd his Maker's Image through the Land.

(lines 1–10)

Charles's irrepressible and irresponsible sexuality (and its results) are funny here but also serious; the occasion of the poem underscores the implications, but at the same time the regal amorality of Charles is acknowledged, admitted and tolerated if not approved. The tone, only partly satiric, is everything; nothing vindicates Charles's behaviour, but his Davidic position (David's precedent in part gives Charles licence) makes him seem understandable, human, comically immune – even a bit generous and appealing, an image of free-market circulated coinage more than failed kingship. The Civil Wars are not far in the background here, and these Caroline peccadilloes in the context of shared government seem far less threatening than past behaviour: the argument of allegory and precedent works both ways, and Charles/David seems much less an evil than the manipulative alternatives of Achitophel's untrustworthy men and worse principles. There is finally nothing simple about the ethical and political alternatives, but there is also nothing ambiguous about why the present monarchy needs to be preserved; subtle and complex art has been brought to bear in a pressing, volatile and defining political moment.

Satire was in the period essentially political, rather than social or economic or moral – and thus about stability and preservation of balance rather than any kind of redistribution or shading of property or values. But early in the period (up through the 'glorious' revolution of James II's 'abdication') the political thrust was more pointed, unambiguous, direct and aimed at royal prerogatives and royalty itself; later the focus (though the royal family may have been even less popular and more distrusted, and the ministry was regarded as utterly corrupt) came to be more on literary politics, with the larger political issues being, at least somewhat, subordinated to cultural issues with political alliances. Still, plenty of criticism, some of it unrelievedly vituperative, was directed at powerful political figures, George I and II and Robert Walpole in particular; Pope's famously ironic *Epistle to Augustus* (1737) is one example (though as in most poems of its time, criticism of the king was subordinated to larger observations about the time), and the several anonymous poems about Walpole's domestic life and his wife and mistress (see, for example, *The Rival Wives. Or, the Greeting of Clarissa to Skirra in the Elysian Shades* and *The Rival Wives Answer'd; or, Skirra to Clarissa*, both 1738, each 400 lines long) are lesser but equally indicative instances. The 1730s were rich in such poems, and there were always eligible public figures to single out for the focus of blame. But increasingly satire turned inward upon itself, and its energies were directed at other writers, wars among the poets and the process of satire itself.

A lot of the satiric poems in the last third of the period – roughly from about 1717, the time that Pope took control of the literary scene – were in fact aggressive defences of satire or explanations of why poetic careers were organised in terms of its methods and aims. Pope's *Epistle to Dr Arbuthnot* (1735) is, in effect, his apologia for his life of writing, and the two poems that constitute the 'Epilogue to the Satires' are equally explanations of satire's necessity; knaves, he insists here, are 'sham'd by *Ridicule* alone' and satire is a 'sacred Weapon . . . Sole Dread of Folly, Vice, and Insolence' (lines 211–13, Dialogue II). Most individual satires throughout the whole period, in fact, offer a self-conscious explanation of why satire in general, and this satire in particular, is morally and practically required. Winners tend to write the histories of battle, and literary history has traditionally privileged the views and vision of Pope and his friends, who often had a tenable ethical position and who usually were more articulate and rhetorically effective. But on both sides, the claims of implication are, from the point of view of history, patently exaggerated, and claims of self-innocence or excessive humanity are part of the standard repertoire of representation, as are the claims of cosmic repercussions of the evils being exposed. But this does not mean that satirists were not sincere in regarding their causes as righteous. Most, as in many ideological or cultural frays, were firmly convinced of the merits of their position, and their power derives from the zeal and coherence of their effort and their commitment to poetry as a public, rhetorical force.

There was also lighter, earthier, less insistent and more limited-in-scope satire. If the grand satires, with their cultural, national and sometimes global claims, have dominated posterity's view of the period, less-charged critical poems – sometimes called social satires – were even more prevalent and may have reached more readers with their attention to manners more than morals, to peccadilloes more than crimes or sins, to everyday and ordinary behaviour rather than the influence of the prominent and mighty, or to some particular cultural annoyance rather than larger patterns of responsibility. The tone here is often one of bemused tolerance or gentle twitting more than righteous outrage. Poets such as Prior, Addison, Chudleigh, Gay, Hill, Leapor, Mary Barber and Paul Whitehead were quite good at catching poignant behavioural moments or habits and seeing their absurdity or social inappropriateness. Quite a bit of the poetry of family and friendship involves gentle satire (though some of that poetry is also distinctly lyrical), and women poets often found it especially attractive because it offered the opportunity to make meaningful cultural comment without appearing to venture too high or too deep into political or philosophical pretence – though both then and later this modest posture has sometimes meant that their satiric intentions were under-read or undervalued. There were, alternatively, poets (almost always male, Cavendish is the only major counter-example) who pretended to the high seriousness of scourges and moral warriors but who actually were more like cartoonists and adjusters: they announce their quarry with flailing bluster and claim huge consequence, but usually end up at best with superficial observation on insignificant matters. Robert Gould in the later Restoration and Ned Ward at the turn of the century are prominent, typical examples; their charges are often trivial, and the satire is bland, toothless and pretty insignificant.[24] Still other satirists, more artful perhaps but also severely limited, chose to focus their attacks on a single issue or a limited social group; such for example now seems Sir Samuel Garth's attack on physicians and apothecaries, *The Dispensary* (1699), though it was extremely popular and highly regarded in its time, going through at least ten editions by 1741. The reason that satire developed so powerfully during the period and that classic examples still retain their power now has more to do with ambition, clarity of vision and clever argument than with the fingering of specific targets; good satirists are not always right about cultural or moral matters, but they are persuasive spokespeople for a definable larger perspective, and they are careful, if not always accurate, sorters and arguers of examples. It is usually the quality of observation, cogency of perspective and appeal of imaginative wit, rather than sincerity, honesty or factuality, that gives satire its bite.

Didactic poems similarly range over varieties and sizes of issues; Trapp said that 'any Thing in the World may be the Subject of this Kind of Poem: The Business or Recreations of the City, or the Country; even the Conduct of common Life and civil Converse'.[25] Often they offer positive advice that complements satiric denunciation, suggesting models and precepts, sometimes quite directly and unapologetically: there is advice about everything

---

24 Ward's best known poems are about London sights and habits at the turn of the century, and his most famous single work is perhaps *Hudibras Redivivus; or, a Burlesque Poem on the Times* (1705–7) But a later publication suggests in its title the way that Ward worked. It is titled *Truth in Rhyme, To suit the Time, or, The Parish Guttlers. A Merry Poem. As it is Acting every Day with great Applause Near the Poors House, Gray's Inn lane, With the Comical Adventures of Simon Knicky Knocky, Undertaker, Church Warden and Coffin-maker* (1732); a 'guttler' is a glutton.
25 *Lectures on Poetry*, p. 200.

from cooking, gardening, smoking, directing servants, and making or drinking wine to moral uprightness and governing the nation. Later readers have often responded badly to a sense of being preached to or lectured at, and poems of strong religious conviction or constrictive ethical vision – and there are plenty of both – seldom find willing readers now. But the desire to instruct on a wide variety of large and small issues (and the willingness to be instructed) was very powerful in the period, a joint product of a traditional Judeo-Christian sense of community and shared ethic (on the one hand) and (on the other) a developing sense of public-sphere responsibilities and effective influence. And some of didacticism's manifestations were very attractive, especially in gentle and caring accounts of the domestic sphere and in loose, often comical adaptations of Virgil's Georgic instructions for daily labour.

The Georgic was not the only alternative for would-be didactic poets, but it was the most common allusive mode for instructive poems about work. Virgil had provided, for his time, a very practical set of directions for agricultural progress and their basis and implications in seasonal rhythms and a well-ordered state. Addison's standard 'Essay on Virgil's Georgics' (1692) describes a 'poetry which consists in giving plain and direct instructions to the reader, whether they be moral duties . . . or philosophical speculations . . . or rules of practice' and makes it sound culturally decisive.[26] Virgil was, as in epic, an inspiring if slightly intimidating master and model, and most followers found it easier to invoke and chase him rather than try to do, in modern times, what he did for Augustan Rome: model an integrated order of politics, economy and labour. The result was mostly evident in instructive poems about everyday activities without obvious political implication – walking, brewing, making wine, baking or playing sports – and often they were light-hearted in spirit and tone and had an air of holiday and play similar to many lyrics, though some also aspired to larger effects.

Surprisingly few poems actually call themselves Georgics: John Gay subtitled the final version (1720) of *Rural Sports* 'A Georgic' (the first was simply called 'A Poem'), and John Philips' lengthy *Cyder* (1600 lines long), is also simply subtitled 'A Poem in Two Books', though it too plainly invites Virgilian comparison.[27] Gay's *Wine* (1708) and *Trivia: Or the Art of Walking the Streets of London* (1716) also imply, in procedures if not titles, generic allusion and imitative fealty.

---

26 Published in *The Works of Virgil . . . Translated in to English Verse by Mr Dryden* (London: Jacob Tonson, 1697).

27 Georgic continues to be important into the next age: see, e.g. Dyer's *The Fleece*, Smart's *The Hop-Garden*, James Grainger's *The Sugar-Cane*, Richard Jago's *Edge-Hill*.

In spite of the fact that most poets were, throughout the period, urban in both location and temperament, they frequently envisioned, somewhat nostalgically, a world which cultivated the soil and made cider, wine, tea, chocolate, tobacco and other pleasure- or luxury-producing natural products seem somehow, at least tangentially, related to larger concepts of order. And many other poems, often modelled on John Denham's *Cooper's Hill* more directly than on Virgil, have strong Georgic features and aims. *Windsor Forest*, for example, envisions the landscape rising up and collaborating in a global commerce growing out of the recent pact with France. Near the end of the poem, old Father Thames in a climactic declamation envisions the land in effect 'growing' a navy for both defence and trade:

> Thy Trees, fair *Windsor!* Now shall leave their Woods,
> And half thy Forests rush into my Floods,
> Bear *Britain's* Thunder, and her Cross display
> To the bright Regions of the rising Day. (lines 385–8)

And there are many other descriptive or 'place' poems – famous ones like Thomson's *Seasons* and Dyer's *Grongar Hill* and little-known ones like *Leighton-Stone-Air* (by Joseph Harris, 1701), *Woodstock Park* (by William Harison, 1706) *The Bason* (by Charles Coffey, 1717), *The Beauties of Enfield* (by Henry Baker, 1725), *The Description of Bath* (by Mary Chandler, 1733) or *Stowe, The Gardens* (by Gilbert West, 1732) – that are, in a broad sense, Georgics. Works that we tend to label descriptive-didactic, topographical, loco-descriptive, landscape, prospect, house or estate poems often are in fact nearly indistinguishable in intent and method from those labelled Georgics: the memory or even air of tradition is characteristically more important than labels and rules.[28]

Nearly everyone, in fact, who aspired to instruct the times on any subject followed or invoked Virgil in some sense. The notion that poets could assist ordinary readers in their experience of everyday life and work was more fundamental than any pursuit of a particular poem's agenda or, in fact, any definition of genre. Edward Baynard's *Health, a Poem. Shewing How to Procure, Preserve, and Restore It* (1716), for example, though hardly a distinguished poem as poem, was reprinted at least twelve times by 1720, and many other writers gave equally practical verse advice, though in many tones and degrees of seriousness: Matthew Concannen offered *The Match at Football* (1722), Thomas Mathison *The Goff* (golf) (1743), James Dance *Cricket* (1744), Nicholas James *Wrestling* (1742) and William Shenstone *Colemira: A Culinary Eclogue* (1737).

---

28 And philosophical poems are closely related too.

And, too, there were scores of more ambitious and longer didactic poems about larger, more ruminative matters. The argument in such philosophical, theological and historical poems is often complex and sometimes couched in highly technical terms, and the very magnitude of these poems is intimidating; though they lack the conventional machinery and usually the narrative thread of epic, they often have at least as much intellectual ambition, and sometimes as distinct a national and cultural focus. The best known today is Pope's extremely ambitious *Essay on Man* in four long books; it aims to 'vindicate the ways of God to Man', and the Milton echo underscores what is in effect a claim of direct didacticism on a heroic scale. Philosophers historically have tended to find verse a distraction and to reject or dismiss any argument delivered poetically, but writers in the early eighteenth century who believed they had something worth teaching often did it poetically and lengthily. Some poets presented themselves, as did Pope, in a more or less tentative 'essay' mode, and the dialectical give-and-take of careful argument in the age is often underappreciated. These poems are full of present participles – everything seems quivering and suspended in equipoise – and seldom is action completed. But many poems consciously and prominently modelled their teaching project, whatever its subject, in a more seemingly finalised and certain way on Horace's *Ars Poetica* (which was repeatedly translated as *The Art of Poetry*); there were, for example, *The Art of Cookery* (by William King, 1708), *The Art of Dress* (by J. D. Breval, 1717), *The Art of Dancing* (by Soame Jenyns, 1727), *The Art of Politicks* (by James Bramston, 1729), *The Art of Preaching* (by Robert Dodsley, 1735), *The Art of Life* (by James Miller, 1739), *The Art of Preserving Health* (by John Armstrong, 1744) and *The Art of Printing* (by Constantia Grierson, published in 1764 but written by 1733). But whatever their tone and immediate reader relationship, almost all philosophical, devotional and meditative poems, however argumentative or contemplative in mode, are finally didactic poems with some kind of design on the reader, and many are long, demanding and ambitious both intellectually and rhetorically: for example, W. C.'s *The Death of Knowledge* (1684), William Dawes' *An Anatomy of Atheism* (1694), John Pomfret's *Reason* (1700), Giles Jacob's *Human Happiness. A Poem. Adapted to the Present Times* (1721), Joseph Thurston's *The Fall* (1732), Trapp's *Thoughts upon the Four Last Things: Death; Heaven; Judgment; Hell* (four parts, 1734–5), Walter Harte's *An Essay on Reason* (1735), Henry Brooke's *Universal Beauty* (1735), Robert Nugent's *An Essay on Happiness* (1738), Leonard Welsted's *The Summum Bonum; or Wisest Philosophy* (1741), Thomson's *Liberty* (1738), or the anonymous *Religion the Only Happiness* (1694) and *Political Justice* (1736).

Lyric

It is usually said that Restoration and early eighteenth-century poets have little interest in celebratory verse, explore private matters seldom and shallowly and that they are not good at lyric and very little concerned to explore it. Sometimes it is even said that the age is anti-lyrical. The charge of incompetence and lack of interest in lyric is both true and untrue: very few short, celebratory, romantic and musical poems for the period have come down to us in insistent and omnipresent ways, in the way for example that Jonson, Herrick, Blake and Wordsworth – or even Francis Quarles or John Clare – can be said to be lastingly lyrical. And few poets set about as, say, Herbert and Donne or Keats and Coleridge did, to create strings of short, subjective celebratory verses that might, or might not, add up to sequences or signals of a longer group or title. Short poems in the period generally do not have the energy, ambition or demand of longer works; the distinction between serious intention and holiday play tended to be more rigid than in earlier or later times, and less formal, more personal poems did not command the attention that public poetry did. And there is less genuinely cheerful and festive, as opposed to publicly celebratory, verse in the period than in some other times: poets of these generations were more likely to be troubled by temperamental, situational and interruptive difficulties in love and friendship than blinded or besotted by overwhelming passion.

But our sense of lyric then is also skewed by expectation, and modern readers are less likely to search for – or even to read when found – magical, fantasy, or fable poems like Tickell's *Kensington Gardens* or the child-friendly poems of Ambrose Philips. Except for a few poems by, say, Prior and a handful of poets resurrected by recent anthologists such as Roger Lonsdale,[29] the modern reader is not likely to have sampled much of the personal or informal poetry of the period and thus may not have actually confronted the variety the age has to offer. Certainly the standard anthologies offer little of it, and literary histories say nothing about it. What is quite astonishing when one reads broadly across the period is how many short, topical, intimate and accessible poems there are that define themselves generically simply by a titular 'on': 'On a Romantic Lady' (Mary Monck), 'On the Prospect of Planting Arts and Learning in America' (George Berkeley), 'On My Late Dear Wife' (Jonathan Richardson), 'On a Miscellany of Poems' (Gay). Such poems – informal, unpretentious, conversational, and often witty, amusing and poignant – offer a variety of winning

---

29 See the *New Oxford Book of Eighteenth-Century Verse* (Oxford: Oxford University Press, 1984) and *Eighteenth-Century Women* Poets (Oxford: Oxford University Press, 1989).

and unusual perspectives on ordinary private life and circumstances, and in spite of a certain calculated distance – they often involve a clichéd situation and use stock poetic names – there are some wonderful representations and observations on everyday life. Why then the scanty or negative reputation for lyric?

The answer, I think, is that there are few poems that offer a clear, uncluttered, direct, untroubled and simple view of human interrelationships. Certainly the poems are not devoid of engagement and passion, but the mind of the period treasures – or perhaps only trusts – complication, circumstantiality, interruption, uncertainty and even disappointment above conventional satisfactions.[30] Lyric in the period is more likely to be qualifying and exception-making than purely celebratory; gather ye rosebuds while ye may is, for this period, more likely to be concerned with the particulars of 'while' or the uncertainties of 'may'. The best lyrics, then, are likely to feature the unusual, peculiar, qualifying and subjective rather than the expected, whereas what audiences liked most to 'share' involved experiences that lots of people had in common. There was, then, a disjunction between the modal understanding of how knowledge of experience was sharable and poetic consciousness of subjective insecurity, something that later poets like Wordsworth never quite 'got'. It is no wonder that the age 'found' itself in lyric most fully when an interest in hymns offered a sense of shared or communal praise, admiration, reverence and worship. Many of the best lyrics, especially in the latter part of the period, were (though historically underappreciated because of later cultural directions) devotional poems intended for communal performance or repetition in unison: the hymns of Addison, Watts, John and Charles Wesley, and (later) John Newton, William Cowper and Augustus Montague Toplady.[31]

Still. There were in the period wonderful, effective, accomplished and polished secular lyrics celebrating both personal triumph and emotional human complications, if usually with a conscious sense of artifice and let's pretend, or careful qualification about human reality and limit. Both Swift and Prior, for example, are wonderful at finding the poignant and touching in highly unlikely or incongruous relationships (the Stella poems, 'To a Child of Quality'). The other arts – music, painting, sculpture – often provided a metaphor for emotional release and exposure: in the many poems addressed to composers or

30 See David Morris, 'A Poetry of Absence', in *The Cambridge Companion to Eighteenth-Century Poetry*, ed. John Sitter, Cambridge: Cambridge University Press, 2001, pp. 225–48.
31 See J. R. Watson, *The English Hymn: A Critical and Historical* Study (Oxford, Clarendon Press, 1997).

musicians and in poems advising painters how to paint or in describing their galleries of accomplishments. The ubiquitous poems about birthdays, marriages and deaths also release much sharable feeling of dependence, intimacy and caring. Poems addressed to individuals are often in fact both personal reminders of unique circumstance and sharings of communal values. 'To' poems, often as conversational as epistolary, license an unusual combination of the private and the social. If there are few outpourings of unchannelled, uncensored and unexamined feeling, it is because the age had enormous respect for things unsaid or beyond saying.

The story of the ode (or 'pindaric' and 'anacreontic'), which was generally viewed as the poetic home of unbridled emotion, is especially complex. Very popular in the last years of the Commonwealth and early years of the Restoration, odes then took their impetus primarily from the reputation of Abraham Cowley who, hard as it is to imagine now, was widely considered to be the best mid seventeenth-century poet. How actually Pindaric these poems were (that is, how closely they did – or should – follow the example of Pindar (c. 500 BC)) became a subject of extensive critical debate[32]), but huge numbers of poems in the early Restoration, then again in the Williamite and early Queen Anne years, and yet again in the 1730s identified themselves as odes with a heritage in ancient Greek celebratory verse. Cowley's 'Ode to the Royal Society', a solemn tribute to the intellectual ambitions of the age, became the sober model for many poems (including early Swift poems very different from the ones remembered now) celebrating public accomplishments, but Cowley also provided models for more personal tributes. The ode was the vehicle for many a celebratory poem – celebratory about anything – but seemed to the age especially apt for dealing with, or expressing, extravagant emotions or for describing the effects of other arts (especially music) that featured non-verbal or extra-rational means, as in Dryden's 'Ode on the Death of Henry Purcell' or the frequent St Cecilia's Day odes (such as Dryden's *Alexander's Feast*). The ode was also disproportionately used to celebrate the beauties and arts of women, as in Dryden's 'To the Pious Memory of the Accomplished Young Lady Mrs Anne Killigrew . . . An Ode'.

---

32 William Congreve, in his 'Discourse on the Pindarick Ode' prefixed to his *Pindarique Ode . . . on . . . The Duke of Marlborough* (1706), says:

> There is nothing more frequent among us, than a sort of Poems intituled Pindarique Odes; pretending to be written in Imitation of the Manner and Stile of Pindar, and yet I do not know that there is to this Day extant in our Language, one Ode contriv'd after his Model. What Idea can an English Reader have of Pindar . . . when he shall see such rumbling and grating Papers of Verses, pretending to be Copies of his Works?　　　　(fol. A1)

One small generic complication involves loyalty to specific models; some poets identified Anacreon, a follower and near contemporary of Pindar, as their inspiration, and others identified with the more regular stanzas of Horatian odes and wrote more symmetrical, orderly and rational poems with fine distinctions and subtle emphases. But in practice most ode-poets were more interested in finding elaborate, varied and free-seeming stanzas that would accommodate the lyric impulse than they were in any precise pindaric or anacreontic form. Long and complex stanzas, with some very short lines and others very long and with extremely varied rhyme schemes, were the rule; often stanzas had twenty or more lines, and there could be many stanzas of different lengths and kinds of rhyme. The typical ode was much longer than we usually think of a lyric as being, almost always extending to four or more text pages, and sometimes two or three times that long. Few, however, exceeded 200 lines in length; their special breathless and rhapsodic existence was sponsored by the notion that longer poems needed more dependable and predictable rhythms (that is, heroic couplets), whereas odes were emotional effusions that purposely distanced themselves from a discourse of reasoned argument. The ode, then, was seen in sharp contrast to – and a temporary relief from the discipline of – the reigning couplet. Lower in the hierarchy of forms than those kinds that needed couplets, odes nevertheless were regarded by many as filling out the tonal ranges of poetic possibility, and by the middle of the eighteenth century began to take on greater responsibilities, and larger ambitions, in the changing aesthetic. But, earlier, odes were thought to be effective in celebrating major political and cultural occasions – and many were highly regarded as successful celebratory moments – but not many of them have endured well; James Sutherland defined the 'unhappy legacy of Abraham Cowley to his fellow countrymen, the Pindaric Ode' very articulately: 'fatally easy to write, almost impossible to write well'.[33]

The epic impulse and the shape of poetic careers

Every critic talked about the epic extensively, usually proclaiming or assuming it to represent the highest and most ambitious form of poetry; Dryden said that 'A heroic poem . . . is undoubtedly the greatest work of which the soul

---

33 James Sutherland, *English Literature of the Late Seventeenth Century* (New York: Oxford University Press, 1969), p. 154. On lyrics in the period generally, and especially on the ode, see Joshua Scodel, 'Lyric Forms', in Steven N. Zwicker (ed.), *The Cambridge Companion to English Literature 1650–1740* (Cambridge: Cambridge University Press, 1998), pp. 120–42.

of man is capable to perform.'[34] But poets generally found the epic standard rather steep, and the impulse to write epic was, for most poets who were realistic about their talents, a lot more common than actual epic ascents. For one thing, Milton provided an intimidating standard against which to compete and judge themselves; his two great successes seemed to have satisfied at once the desire to Christianise epic and to provide a national, Protestant example of epic transformation to modern learning and values. For another, despite its ambitions and hopes for an emerging national tradition, the age was painfully aware of its unheroic character and recent history. It was all very well to celebrate military victories and constitutional successes, but a nation with fresh memories of civil war – and vivid awareness that its governance had changed radically in every generation from 1648 to 1714 – was not ultimately very confident of either its lasting accomplishments or its practical plans for ways of proceeding.

Many poets who were ambitious in their own right settled for classical translations instead. Dryden, famously, did a full translation of *The Aeneid* in his late years (1696), a work that can be regarded as the epic culmination of his career. And less than two decades later when he was still a very young man, Pope undertook to 'English' Homer's *Iliad* and then (with substantial help from collaborators) *The Odyssey*. There were in fact many Englished Homers and Vergils for contemporary readers to choose from – some perhaps representing personal epic ambitions on the part of translators, others springing from more commercial motives. But although nearly every poet who had even faint access to Latin or Greek undertook to translate famous passages from the classical epics (as well as from many other less ambitious or famous ancient works), few of the recognised major poets actually courted the epic muse in a sustained way. Prior wrote an ambitious epic/philosophical poem (more or less on the model of Cowley's *Davideis*) called *Solomon on the Vanity of the World*, but his contemporaries (and posterity) continued to regard him more highly for shorter, lighter verse. And some lesser poets also tried, far more miserably. Edward Howard ambitiously celebrated recent national history in *Carolaides* in 1689, for example; Elizabeth Singer Rowe tried an eight-book (later expanded to ten-) *History of Joseph* in 1736; Richard Glover wrote a nine-book (later expanded to twelve-) extravaganza called *Leonidas* the next year; and Thomas Elwood reworked Cowley's materials into his own *Davideis* (from

---

34 As quoted by Dustin Griffin in *Regaining Paradise* (Cambridge: Cambridge University Press 1986), p. 46 (from preface to *Aeneid*, 1697).

a Quaker viewpoint) in 1712. And a couple of middling talents that history has treated unkindly, Richard Blackmore and Samuel Wesley the elder, made lengthy, repeated tries to harness epic in high-minded religious and nationalistic ways. I mentioned earlier (p. 176) Wesley's biblical versifications; and the prolific Blackmore, who published no fewer than eight epics, worked more variously with both religious and national myth (*Prince Arthur*, 1695, *Eliza*, 1705, *Job*, 1712, *Alfred* 1723). Both poets are marginally better than history has claimed – though each has classic patches of bathos – but neither did much for the ambition to epic, and perhaps both contributed inadvertently to the growing notion that epic was impossible to write in such an unheroic time.[35]

Changes and trends: periods within periods

Throughout this chapter I have proceeded, with few exceptions, synchronically, as if there was a certain constancy of aim and effect from 1660 to the middle of the eighteenth century. And there are a great many conceptions, commitments and habits that are continuous throughout the period, but there are also many changes of mind, emphasis and direction that constantly challenge the continuities. The following ten shifts within the period are especially worth noting:

1. The demographics of poets broadened considerably. At the time of the Restoration, many of the most prominent poets were members of the aristocracy and upper gentry or socially prominent at court: Dorset, Roscommon, Mulgrave, Buckingham, Rochester, Sedley, the Duchess of Newcastle, Lady Chudleigh, the Countess of Winchelsea. By the 1730s only the ageing Lord Lansdowne and Lady Mary Wortley Montagu from that social level had real literary reputations, while among the new voices many were from the labouring, as well as the middling, classes: Stephen Duck (thresher), Mary Collier (farmer), Robert Tatersal (bricklayer), John Bancks (weaver), Robert Dodsley (footman) and Mary Leapor (working class, perhaps a cook). And many, many women poets had published volumes, quite a few involving substantial subscription lists.
2. Booksellers, though still concentrated in London, had expanded considerably into provincial cities, and quite a few volumes of poetry were published

---

35 Quite a few other epic efforts centred on Judeo-Christian history, most often on the stories of Joseph, Job, Jonah, David or Solomon.

in smaller towns and cities like Bristol, Canterbury, Manchester, Norwich, Oxford and York.

3. Though patronage remained a significant sponsoring force throughout the period, commercial publishing ventures controlled, by the second decade of the eighteenth century, an increasing market share; and patronage itself involved a much larger and more varied group of people, mainly because the developing subscription system drew upon the financial resources of people from more varied social and economic backgrounds.

4. Poems about the sister arts early in the period were likelier to concentrate on music (St Cecilia odes, etc) and those later in the period on painting. In part this shift involved the temperament of individual poets – Dryden liked and wrote operas; Pope took formal lessons in painting – but the shift also marks a changed sense of where poetry's sense of itself lies, in either sound or sight.

5. Early in the period an extraordinary number of poems were written to be set to music, and poems called song, madrigal, cantata and lyric were quite common – so much so that both miscellanies and collections of individual poets often had titles such as *Songs and other Poems* (by Alexander Brome, 1661), or *Poems and Songs* (by Thomas Flatman, 1674). Later such titles were unusual except for poets who went very much against the grain; Isaac Watts, for example entitled his 1706 collection *Horae Lyricae, Poems Chiefly of the Lyric Kind.*

6. Discomfort with panegyric grew increasingly intense as dedicatory rhetoric and praise of public occasions expanded and inflated. And praise came to seem to readers more and more strained and artificial.

7. The prestige of poets at court and in government began to show a notable decline. The Restoration court may not always have respected the literary community as much as it said it did – Dryden's intermittently paid laureateship is one indicator of ambivalence – but poets were near the centres of power under both Charles II and James II and again, with some slippage perhaps, under Anne. But soon after the Hanoverians took the throne, nearly all pretence of respect for poetry, or for letters generally, disappeared. Poets in just about all ages complain that they have no influence or recognition, but that claim gained increasing credibility during the period.

8. Emphasis on the need for improved oral conversation, metrical smoothness in verse and refinement in both thought and verbal expression seems to have borne both formal and cultural fruit. Pope, one of whose aims was to become the first 'correct' poet in English, became a kind of poster child for higher standards in rhythm and rhyme.

9. The urban 'triumph' in letters, as well as in cultural aims and values more generally, peaked and began a descent. While urban themes and preoccupations dominated most poetry in the period, adverse reaction noticeably began to set in by the third decade of the eighteenth century, and a kind of rural nostalgia became important in poetry. The movement peaked later in the century, but already early in the careers of Thomson, Shenstone and Dyer, one can see a rising weariness with politics and urbanity and the stirrings of a cult of simplicity and unsophisticated and unsorted feeling. Concomitant with this movement was a developing distrust of a nationalism that was perceived to be cosmopolitan and urban-centred, along with a rise of localism and regionalism.

10. Satire lost some of its cultural force as it became increasingly omnipresent, aggressive and shrill; and disillusion with its methods and tones grew towards satiety by the end of the period.

The changes are marked by shifts in the domination of central figures. The period covered here was once subdivided conveniently into the 'Age of Dryden' and the 'Age of Pope,' and if that distinction is a little too neat – not allowing for an almost rudderless period in between – it is accurate in implying that a single figure tended to dominate, indeed virtually rule, the world of writing during this time (as did Samuel Johnson, despite his own limited poetic talents, after Pope's death). In spite of the constant battles among themselves (and continuous vyings for power), the poets mostly acknowledged (even when they resented or made fun of) the dominant leadership of Dryden from the early 1660s until he lost his official positions of poet laureate and historiographer royal when James II was deposed in 1688.[36] Similarly (and even more fully) Pope from his youth set the tone for virtually everything that happened in poetry; by 1717 when at the age of twenty-nine his *Works* were published, until his death, almost no development in poetry writing or publishing occurred without his involvement, leadership or provocation. The grounds of the domination of the two were somewhat different: Dryden owed his power early to his dramatic talents and connections, later to his dominant satirical and critical reputation, while Pope's early-recognised superior talent for technical accomplishment and his involvement in the public sphere gave him virtual control over what

36 A rather mean-spirited spoof, quite possibly by his successor Shadwell, appeared in 1689: *The Address of John Dryden, Laureat to his Highness the Prince of Orange.* In it, 'Dryden' promises the new king that he is capable of changing his religion yet again (and can bend before any other wind) so that he can retain the laurel.

had become a quite sophisticated publishing world. But the effect was much the same, involving alternations of sycophancy and mindless attack. In between these two sub-ages (the final decade of the seventeenth century and most of the first two decades of the eighteenth), poets were not exactly leaderless, but functions divided in curious ways. Addison, presiding over what Pope called his 'little senate', probably has the best continuing claim to personal poetic influence, but he was not himself very productive as a poet and, despite his reputation, only a few of his poems were well known. Quantitatively, the hands-down winner was Blackmore, and he had a much higher reputation among his contemporaries than now seems plausible. But qualitatively, the dominant poet was, increasingly, Prior who published a variety of middle-length poems of many kinds (*Henry and Emma*, for example, and *Alma, or the Progress of the Mind*) and whose short poems were widely included in miscellanies and widely cited, quoted and read.

John Dryden continued to have strong contemporary admirers right up until his death, at age sixty-nine, at the turn of the century, but his last years were something of an anti-climax for the man who dominated the Anglophone literary world of his time as no figure had done before and as only Pope and Samuel Johnson have done since. Not everyone loved Dryden, and some (for a variety of reasons) did not respect his literary directions or judgement, but from even before he was appointed poet laureate in 1668 until his dismissal from that position there was little question about who was in charge of literary production and taste. His full career is detailed in chapter 6, but here I want to underscore how importantly he figured the age's conception of what poetry was about.

Other poets – arguably, Marvell, Rochester, Behn and Katherine Philips, and even Mulgrave and Anne Killigrew, as well as Milton – may have had more eloquent and triumphant poetic moments than did Dryden, but over a period of three decades he rose to occasion after occasion in writing the key works and pointing others in the age's dominant direction. Those who did not take Dryden fully seriously paid for their mistake, for his penchant for dividing the worthy and the unworthy – as in *MacFlecknoe* – achieved wide cultural acceptance. The fact that he was often, at the same time, a comic and even despised figure in no way diminishes the reality of his literary power as leader and stimulus, as a compromiser between classical ideals and modern needs, and as himself a shrewd and sensitive observer of the current scene. He often captured in a few terse lines, or even a phrase, a striking characterisation of a person, situation, issue or moment, and his quick summaries are often memorable, as in his 1700 character of the times:

'Tis well an Old Age is out,
And time to begin a New
(final lines of
The Secular Masque)

or his allegorical characterisation of contemporary Englishmen in *Absalom and Achitophel*:

. . . a Headstrong, Moody, Murmuring race,
As ever try'd th' extent, and stretch of grace;
God's pamper'd people, whom, debauch'd with ease,
No king could govern, nor no God could please.
(I, 45–8)

And no one has ever been as striking and arresting as Dryden is in his beginnings:

Our Author by experience finds it true,
'Tis much more hard to please himself than you . . .
(Prologue to *Aureng Zebe*)

All humane things are subject to decay . . .
(*MacFlecknoe*)

Dim, as the borrow'd beams of Moon and Stars
To *lonely, weary, wandring* Travellers,
Is *Reason* to the *Soul*. (*Religio Laici*)

Well then, the promis'd Hour is come at last;
The present Age of Wit obscures the past . . .
('To Congreve')

Why should a foolish Marriage Vow,
Which long ago was made,
Oblige us to each other now
When Passion is decay'd?
(Song from *Marriage-à-la-Mode*)

The poets who flourished at the turn of the century or just after – Pomfret, Garth, Diaper, Hughes, Parnell, Hill, Finch, Egerton, Chudleigh, Tickell, John and Ambrose Philips, Monck – have never gotten much attention since then, eclipsed almost totally by Dryden's twilight and afterglow and the brilliant rising star of Pope's reputation,[37] but they were all more than competent poets who even now still read quite well. Many were good translators, others were proficient at either the moral reform verse that characterised, in the wake of royal crackdown schemes, the Williamite years, or the light-hearted, playful, nearly Cavalier verse of Queen Anne's reign (though satire began to be very powerful again once the glow of Blenheim (and Marlborough) began to fade). I have already spoken of Prior's special skills and effects, largely underestimated by literary historians. Finch's reputation, too, is also narrower than it should be (as a *female* poet fond of reverie and light romantic notions) whereas she can rise to complex analysis and incredibly skilled verse music, as in 'Ardelia's Answer to Ephelia'. Tickell, too (caught early on in small rivalry with Pope), deserves more than a peripheral and eccentric reputation, and Sarah Egerton, just now beginning to get her due, sometimes wrote brilliantly and always well.

No one, before or since, has thoroughly dominated the British realm of letters as did Pope for nearly three decades. The age for a third of a century was his in virtually every sense – his was the power, glory, talent, watermark and market canniness – and even though many despised, attacked and belittled him, hardly anyone doubted that he was the most gifted and accomplished poet of his time, whatever one thought of his ideas, politics, character and personality. Pope had the booksellers of his time eating out of his hands; and (quite literally) he invented the modern idea of what a poet was. He was the first figure to make a living wholly from writing poetry in the English language (and living more than comfortably on his income from poetry, especially his translations, and, in fact, becoming modestly rich). He made a life of verse-writing plausible as a vocation as well as calling. And he parlayed his fame into acquaintance (and often friendship) with nearly everyone of note in his time. He did not have the intellectual range, sophistication or grace of a Voltaire, for example, but he was *the* British writer of the time that everyone from the Continent wanted to meet, and the English aristocracy almost fought to make his acquaintance and entertain him. For better and worse, the world of poetry revolved around his talent, his work, his opinions and his divisive partisanship.

The irony of his commanding cultural position was not lost on observers. His parents were middling sorts of modest means, his father a merchant,

---

37 And Pat Rogers is probably right that in their own time they were underappreciated because of the lingering reputation of Dryden: 'it was the looming shadow of Dryden which inhibited ambition and weakened nerve' (*The Augustan Vision* (London: Weidenfeld and Nicolson, 1974), p. 109).

neither parent formally educated; worse, they were Roman Catholics and thus could not own property, legally live within twelve miles of London or send their child to university. He grew up sickly and alone, living mainly in a world of books and older adults; his parents were forty-six and forty-eight when he was born. And a pre-teen accident and subsequent illness left him badly crippled and in permanent ill health; as an adult he rose up only to four foot six in height and was so painfully hunchbacked he had to be strapped into a harness before he could rise, though observers often commented on his fine and delicate facial features. That this underprivileged outsider could succeed in, let alone reign over, literary London and Britain is a testimony not only to his ability and incessant work ethic, but also to the changing circumstances and expectations for a life of writing.

The Pope–Swift 'circle' (in various forms: as the 'Scriblerians' during the reign of Anne and later as a looser Opposition group during the Walpole years) included at one time or another Gay, Harley, Bolingbroke, Parnell, Hill and (in a sense) Fenton and Brome. Those not in the group often fared badly because in the Manichaean battles of wit, Pope and his friends had better weapons. Some few 'dunces' as defined by Pope survived or revived in spite of his portrayal – Theobald, Cibber, Addison, Dennis, Cavendish, Defoe, Haywood, Montagu – but quite a number of those whom he regarded as despicable or, worse, unspeakable are in fact worthy enough to be still readable: Settle, Pomfret, Thomson, Welsted, Harte, Brooke, Cooke, Dyer and Concannen, for example.

Usual historical estimates of the period's poetry speak (or spit) the name of Pope but seldom look deeper, except for a poem here and there. Pope's coin was then the shiniest and has also proved the most enduring, but there is much more to the poetic accomplishment of the period: other satirists, notably Dryden (who is now in unfortunate neglect), Rochester, Butler, Chudleigh, Montagu and Young are nearly as good; and the very different verse of Katherine Philips, Behn, Prior, Finch, Egerton, Tickell, Swift, Savage, Shenstone and Leapor offer us a period that exfoliates well beyond the usually asserted definitions and limits.

Eighteenth-century women poets

PAULA R. BACKSCHEIDER

If every eighteenth-century writer came to London carrying a play in his or her hand-baggage, every writer seems to have had pounds of poetry dating back to childhood stashed in bureau drawers. The earliest publications of most eighteenth-century writers are individual poems, and it is often forgotten that the first substantial, even book-length, publication of many writers known today as novelists or playwrights was a volume of poetry. Statistical studies of women writers by Judith Stanton reveal that poetry was women's most popular literary form, and she calculates that 263 women published poetry between 1660 and 1800 (in comparison, she tallies 201 women who published novels). Until 1760, however, the average number of women publishing poetry in a decade was 7; the figures Stanton gives for the next decades are 1760s: 19; 1770s: 36; 1780s: 55; and 1790s: 64.[1] Roger Lonsdale asserts that in the first decade of the eighteenth century only two women published collections of their poetry, while in the 1790s more than thirty did.[2] These figures do not really indicate just how much poetry women were writing or how many women were writing poetry. For instance, we are lucky to know about Jane Brereton, who as 'Melissa' carried on a verse correspondence in *The Gentleman's Magazine* in the mid 1730s, and only eight of Judith Cowper Madan's surviving poems have been published. In the eighteenth century, one was in a periodical, four in fashionable collections and one in her son Martin's

---

I would like to thank my research assistants Jessica Ellis, Melissa Roth and Kimberly Snyder for their dedicated and excellent work on this project.

1 Judith P. Stanton, 'Statistical Profile of Women Writing in English from 1660 to 1800', in Frederick Keener and Susan Lorsch (eds.), *Eighteenth-Century Women and the Arts* (New York: Greenwood Press, 1988), pp. 247–54; table on p. 251. These numbers are probably low; the English Short-Title Catalogue project has continued to reveal books of poetry, both anthologies and of individuals' works.

2 Roger Lonsdale, 'Introduction' to *Eighteenth-Century Women Poets* (Oxford: Oxford University Press, 1989), pp. xxi.

Hymn Book (1763).[3] The poetry of Susanna Blamire, among others, was published posthumously, and, because she published so often in periodicals, we will probably never know all the poems Mary Robinson wrote. Although earlier periodicals had published poetry, *The Gentleman's Magazine* and the host of magazines that sprung up in the 1730s and thereafter made publication for every would-be and serious poet relatively easy and, more important, commonplace. Edward Cave's *Gentleman's Magazine*, for example, provided eight pages with two columns of poetry in selected issues by 1733 and in all issues beginning in January 1735. In these years, some issues had nine or ten pages of poetry, and the issues announcing the winners of the poetry contests, such as the issue published in July 1735, had an additional 'extraordinary' section entirely devoted to poetry that was forty-four pages long. Both men and women could publish anonymously or under a pseudonym.

Collections of poems became increasingly popular and fashionable, and, again, some poems by women have come down to us only because of them. Anonymous publication was common in collections, too – sometimes because it was assumed that the readers would not need names attached to the poems. The importance of the collections is indicated by the fact that Anne Finch's *The Spleen* first appeared in Charles Gildon's *New Collection of Poems on Several Occasions* in 1701 and that Madan's and Constantia Grierson's poetry survives because it was included in collections. The popularity and notoriety of individual poets as well as the reigning taste of the town can be mapped by analysing these collections, especially those by Robert Dodsley and George Colman. In the periodicals and collections, beside a good deal of very indifferent verse, are some of the most important poems written in the century.

With a few exceptions, women poets of the century have not attracted the amount of attention of the female novelists or even the dramatists. Who, then, are the important women poets of this century? From Judith Stanton's 258 eighteenth-century poets, I have selected those who deserve mention here and close study. In the first generation: Elizabeth Singer Rowe, Mary Chudleigh, Sarah Fyge Egerton and Anne Finch.[4] Rowe's first volume of poetry was published in 1696, Chudleigh's and Egerton's in 1703 and Finch's in 1713. They

---

3 Seven of these poems can be found in Falconer Madan, *The Madan Family and Maddens in Ireland and England* (Oxford: printed for subscribers . . . by John Johnson, 1933), pp. 98–103; the eighth poem is published in Frederic Rowton, *The Female Poets of Great Britain*, ed. Marilyn L. Williamson (1853; Detroit: Wayne State University Press, 1981), p. 141.

4 In order to reduce confusion in this essay, I shall refer to the women poets by their surnames at the time of their deaths.

were joined by Mary Wortley Montagu, who was of their generation but with a few exceptions published later,[5] Jane Brereton, Mary Barber, Laetitia Pilkington, Catherine Trotter Cockburn, Elizabeth Tollet, Mary Chandler, Mary Masters and Mary Jones. Judith Madan and Constantia Grierson published poems that gained widespread admiration. The publisher and periodical editor Ralph Griffiths called Mary Jones the best woman writer since Katherine Philips,[6] and seventeen of her poems appeared in *Poems by Eminent Ladies*.[7] Then, joining them to publish collections or notable poems between 1735 and 1755, were Elizabeth Carter, Hester Chapone, Charlotte Lennox, Mary Leapor and Sarah Dixon. In the 1740s a number of successful women poets were born, including five important ones: Laetitia Barbauld, Hannah More, Susanna Blamire, Anna Seward and Charlotte Smith.

It is not surprising that women poets flourished by 1735. By 1720, women had more useful models for a career as a poet than men did, and, as they and their works became better known over the next sixty years, their influence spread.[8] Besides Aphra Behn and Katherine Philips, aspiring women poets now had Finch, Montagu, Chudleigh and Rowe as models, all different in their orientation to writing and in the verse they wrote. Evidence of the enabling power of these models abounds, in, for instance, dedications, letters and poems of tribute, such as Elizabeth Tollet's to Finch and Montagu and Clara Reeve's to Carter. Barber included poems by Rowe and Grierson in her collection, and Seward could recite Finch's *Life's Progress*. Mary Scott compliments Mary Chudleigh, Mary Barber, Constantia Grierson, Elizabeth Tollet, Mary Darwall, Mary Chandler, Charlotte Lennox and Laetitia Barbauld in *The Female Advocate; A Poem* (1774).[9] Childless, widowed young, separated from their husbands or living largely in retirement, these women were all comfortably affluent or even wealthy. They knew how to articulate an enabling role, which, in Egerton's words, was 'to know much, and speak little'. They often referred to their writing as 'the innocent Amusement of a solitary life'.[10] Sarah Dixon's preface to *Poems on Several Occasions* captures most of the common themes in the

---

5 Three of her town eclogues were published in 1716 by Edmund Curll, a few more poems in the 1730s and a collected edition in 1747. After that, she became the most anthologised woman of the century.
6 Lonsdale, *Eighteenth-Century Women Poets*, p. 156.
7 George Colman, *Poems by Eminent Ladies*, 2 vols. (London, 1755), vol. I, pp. 255–312.
8 That manuscript circulation as well as print contributed to reputations must be remembered.
9 Mary Scott, *The Female Advocate; A Poem. Occasioned by Reading Mr Duncombe's Feminead*, Gae Holladay (intro.), The Augustan Reprint Society, publication number 224 (Los Angeles: University of California Press, 1984).
10 Mary Chudleigh, 'Preface' to *Poems on Several Occasions* (London, 1703).

representations of their lives and positioning of themselves as poets: 'As to the following Pieces the Reader is to know they were the Employment (an innocent, and, she thinks, no improper Employment) of a Youth of much Leisure. Some little Taste of Poetry, improved by some Reading, tempted our Author to try her Talents, for her own Amusement, and the Diversion of her Friends, in a Country Solitude.'[11]

Preparing for a new definition and space for women poets, they wrote like other poets in the forms popular in their time, a time when poets self-consciously wrote in poetic 'genres', many classical, but also in others such as ballads, hymns, fables, and biblical narratives and paraphrases. They contributed to the development of distinctively British verse forms and techniques and, as we can recognise retrospectively, claimed some kinds of poetry for women. A serious, experimental poet writing in Metaphysical and Augustan forms, tones and language and developing her artistry within each, Finch often created elegant and original poems, and her 'Nocturnal Reverie' is justly appreciated for its achievement and its contributions to literary history. Wordsworth singled it and Pope's *Windsor Forest* out as the only poems composed between *Paradise Lost* and *The Seasons* to 'contain a single new image of external nature'.[12] He brought it to the attention of Alexander Dyce, the editor of *Specimens of British Poetesses* (1825), and the poem has been continuously anthologised since. Now recognised as both a precursor of Romanticism and an example of Augustan grace, it has line after line of specific, original images, some reflected in water rather than seen, and concludes with the famous lines that anticipate the great Romantics: 'But silent Musings urge the Mind to seek / Something too high for Syllables to speak . . . In such a *Night* let Me abroad remain, / Till Morning breaks . . .'[13]

Montagu was a topical, sometimes biting poet who wrote in fashionable forms as well as classical ones and made both more fashionable. Her satirical town eclogues are still admired, and 'Verses Written in the Chiosk of the British Palace' is a justly famous nature poem in smooth heroic couplets. It was Rowe, however, whose poetry fascinated women and whose life was an intriguing, even seductive model. She, too, was a serious, lifelong poet. Her poetry was among the most accessible, for it was regularly reprinted until

11 Sarah Dixon's 'Preface' to *Poems on Several Occasions* (Canterbury, 1740).
12 William Wordsworth, 'Essay, Supplementary to the Preface to the Second Edition of the *Lyrical Ballads*,' *The Prose Works of William Wordsworth*, ed. W. J. B. Owen and Jane W. Smyser (Oxford: Clarendon Press, 1974), vol. III, p. 73.
13 Anne Finch, *The Poems of Anne Countess of Winchilsea from the Original Edition of 1713 and from Unpublished Manuscripts*, ed. Myra Reynolds (Chicago: University of Chicago Press, 1903), pp. 269–70.

1855, and women's praise for it – not her piety – survives in numerous letters, dedications and poems. In 1739, Brereton wrote to Carter that Rowe 'had a fine Genius; and no Attachments in this World, to prevent her indulging, and improving it. Her Stile is flowing, and perfectly Poetical; her Descriptions are exceeding lively.'[14] Years after her death, Anna Laetitia Barbauld's 'Verses on Mrs Rowe' pays tribute to her harmony of sound and image and poetic 'fire' and asks that Rowe be her muse.[15] Rowe's first poems, as was common in the century, had been published in periodicals, and two numbers of the *Athenian Mercury* were devoted to them; her *Poems on Several Occasions, Written by Philomela* (1696) included the usual love, friendship, political, religious and social comment poems. All of these women wrote in a wide variety of forms, published in various venues and demonstrated their dedication to excellence and to continued experimentation and mastery.

Thus, women had a variety of life and literary styles on which to model a poetic career. They could turn from the retiring examples of Finch, Chudleigh and Rowe to the tumultuous, socially engaged lives of Montagu and Egerton. They could set the musical, sometimes metaphysical religious ecstasy of Rowe beside the clever, biting wit of Montagu. Rowe typically composes beautiful, interwoven lines, such as these from her translation of the beginning of the fourth book of Tasso's *Jerusalem*: 'Propitious god of love, my breast inspire / With all thy charms, with all thy pleasing fire: / Propitious god of love, thy succour bring.' Montagu's language is precise and spare, and her poems often include shockingly cynical observations, as the town eclogue 'Wednesday: The Tete à Tete' and 'Epistle from Mrs Y[onge]' do. Even within a single theme, however, readers had rich comparisons available. Montagu, for instance, expresses in 'An Answer to a Lady Advising me to Retirement' verse sentiments more associated with Rowe: 'You little know the Heart that you advise, / I view this various Scene with equal Eyes, / In crouded Court I find my selfe alone, / And pay my Worship to a nobler Throne.'

In the second half of the century, volumes of poetry and respected individual poems published in periodicals or fashionable collections made the names of more than a dozen women familiar. In the 1760s, Mary Darwall, Mary Collier and Clara Reeve published well reviewed volumes of poetry. Between then and the great flowering of women's poetry in the 1790s, Charlotte Smith, Laetitia Barbauld, Susannah Harrison, Hannah More, Helen Maria Williams,

---

14 Jane Brereton, *Poems on Several Occasions: By Mrs Jane Brereton. With Letters to her Friends, and an Account of her Life* (London, 1774), pp. xxix–xxx.
15 'Verses on Mrs Rowe', in William McCarthy and Elizabeth Kraft (eds.), *The Poems of Anna Letitia Barbauld* (Athens: University of Georgia Press, 1994), pp. 79–80.

Elizabeth Hands, Mary Robinson and Ann Yearsley were all recognised as important poets, and lesser-known poets such as Mary Savage and Ann Murry produced excellent poems. Joanna Baillie, Anne Bannerman and Anna Seward came to prominence in the 1790s. Poems written in social causes, especially abolition, increased the notoriety of some women poets and made the fame of, for example, Harriet and Maria Falconar and, perhaps, Amelia Opie. Charlotte Smith and Anna Seward are now being recognised as major contributors to the sonnet revival, and Barbauld, Seward, More and Baillie became fixtures and arbiters in the most influential literary circles.

Much has been made of the barriers to women writing poetry, and it has been popular to sort these poets by handicap. Sixteen of the forty poets named above had children; counting stepchildren when known, the average number they had was four. Yearsley had six, Madan nine, Darwall married a man with six children and had six more and Smith had twelve. Surprisingly few of the married women were childless (six); several of them were widowed early, as Rowe and Chapone were, and some married relatively late, as Amelia Opie did. Letitia Barbauld and her husband adopted a nephew, and Helen Maria Williams cared for her sisters' two sons after their parents' deaths. Perhaps notably, from the first generation of women poets Finch, Egerton and Rowe were all childless. Lists of unmarried women are impressively long, and among them were Elizabeth Carter, Mary Collier, Mary Jones, Mary Leapor, Clara Reeve, Joanna Baillie and Anna Seward. Women in these categories, however, often had considerable responsibility at some point in their lives for the care of ailing, aged parents or other relatives. Carter was responsible for much of the care of her siblings and managed her father's household until his death; Barbauld's husband went mad, and Anna Seward took care of her father, who for the last ten years of his life suffered from paralytic and apoplectic strokes. Hands, Jones, Leapor and Chandler also cared for elderly parents. Although unmarried, Chandler kept a millinery shop, Harrison and Hands were domestic servants and Collier worked as a washerwoman and brewer until she was an old woman. Pilkington, Robinson, and Smith spent time in debtors' prison and Williams in the Bastille.

A considerable amount of evidence survives that domestic situations encouraged poets' writing and that families often took pride in a daughter's, wife's or mother's poetry. Volumes of poetry were carefully collected by relatives and published with some difficulty. Heneage Finch, Anne's husband, copied out almost every poem in the manuscripts of her poetry and compiled the important folio manuscript of her work; throughout her life he encouraged her writing and took an active interest in it.[16] Some women were frequently in dialogue with family members in their poetry, and family events were constant inspirations. Barber often writes to and about her son, as she does in 'To Mrs Strangeways Horner, with a letter from my Son', which rejoices in the pleasure she finds in having a friend to share the news that her son has won a prize at the University of Dublin.[17] Mary Whateley Darwall was actively encouraged to write and her poems praised and appreciated by her family. Her husband John once wrote her a short poem that begins 'Enchanting Songstress', reminding her to write again after the birth of a baby.[18] One of her poems captures another side of the way family and poetry interact. Her 'On the Author's Husband Desiring her to Write Some Verses' preserves her willingness to put poetry aside for the pleasure she is finding in her children. She takes as her subject, 'Connubial Love! enchanting theme!' and writes several verses of a delightful ode on the subject and then breaks off, ' – But hark! – my darling infant cries, / And each poetic fancy flies', Poetry is flight and imagination, the 'darling infant' is solid and pleasing reality.[19] Charlotte Smith reared her twelve children almost entirely alone, and her literary output is formidable. Her scattered comments about being a mother and an 'Authoress' express a comfortable integration of these identities, and some of her most powerful poetry turns her private experiences into expressions of the human condition. A number of her sonnets and two of her odes are animated by her grief over the death of her daughter Anna Augusta de Foville; one of her sons lost a leg at Dunkirk in 1793, and both 'The Forest Boy' and an anecdote in *Beachy Head* relate stories of young men not quite aware of the price they might pay going to war. Smith's 'Reflections on some drawings of plants' transforms the Petrarchan sonnet into a woman's form. Written about her daughter, the poem is from the perspective of a mother, and, like Petrarch's, is about the absence of a loved one. Beginning 'I can in groups these mimic flowers compose,' it enjambs the octave and sestet, an innovation in the sonnet form that she made popular: 'But, save the portrait on my bleeding breast, / I have no semblance of that form adored.'[20]

16 Barbara McGovern, *Anne Finch and Her Poetry: A Critical Biography* (Athens, GA: University of Georgia Press, 1992), pp. 68–70.
17 Mary Barber, *Poems on Several Occasions* (London, 1734), pp. 189–93.
18 Ann Messenger, *Woman and Poet in the Eighteenth Century: The Life of Mary Whateley Darwall (1738–1825)* (New York: AMS Press, 1999).
19 Lonsdale, *Eighteenth-Century Women Poets*, pp. 261–2.
20 Charlotte Smith, 'Reflections on Some Drawings of Plants', from *The Poems of Charlotte Smith*, ed. Stuart Curran (New York: Oxford University Press, 1993), pp. 77–8.

For some women, domestic responsibilities competed painfully with the desire to write, but for others – perhaps an equal number – the desire to write poetry faded or could be exercised in occasional poems, some directed to the children or about them, or in work that progressed slowly or came in creative flashes. The stability of a home surely created a more conducive situation for writing than, for instance, Mary Darwall's wanderings in old age or Mary Chandler's work establishing a millinery shop, which she ran for thirty-five years.[21] Despite their reputation for being maudlin and trivial, excellent poems with considerable musicality and power about children survive, as lines such as these by Judith's daughter Maria Madan Cowper demonstrate: 'Who, to view thy peaceful form, / Heeds the winter-blowing storm? / Thy smiles the calm of heaven bestow . . .'[22] Ben Jonson is well known for his moving poem on his son, but Mehetabel Wright's 'To an Infant Expiring the Second Day of its Birth' is forgotten in spite of its tactile richness and powerful emotion: 'Tender softness, infant mild, / Perfect, purest, brightest child; / . . . Blooming, withering in an hour . . .'[23]

In focusing on the handicap that domestic life can be, all but a few critics and readers have missed the unbroken strain of delightful, gritty, often comic poems that are also 'domestic'. A few, like Barbauld's 'Washing Day', are often anthologised, but there are numerous, astonishingly varied, very high-quality poems in this category that remain unrecognised, except for rare attention to some as examples of Jonathan Swift's influence. Swift did know a number of women poets well and encouraged several of them, perhaps especially Mary Barber and Laetitia Pilkington. The appeal of some of Swift's poetry to women is not hard to see. He had a keen eye for the way character was revealed in domestic settings and for telling details. Often in unpretentious tetrameter couplets and colloquial language, his poems and theirs – and not all of them knew Swift – at their best can be acerbic, pointed, accepting and brave. Their poetry sounds realistic and resilient at the same time it describes gritty reality and resilient people. Mary Jones, an Oxford poet, for instance, in tetrameter lines quite different from her Popeian poetry, writes, 'Come, lest the dinner should be spoil'd, / The beef's already too much boil'd.'[24] A number of Sarah Dixon's poems, including 'The Slattern', combine homely detail with a satiric

---

21 Lonsdale describes Chandler as an 'industrious and courageous woman', *Eighteenth-Century Women Poets*, pp. 151–2.
22 'On Viewing her Sleeping Infant', Lonsdale, *Eighteenth-Century Women Poets*, pp. 270–1.
23 Mehetabel Wright's 'To an Infant Expiring the Second Day of its Birth' (1733), Lonsdale, *Eighteenth-Century Women Poets*, p. 115.
24 Mary Jones, 'Written at Fern-Hill, While Dinner was Waiting for Her', *Miscellanies in Prose and Verse* (Oxford, 1750), p. 68.

awareness of human pretentiousness (the would-be poet quits her writing to mend her broken petticoat string), and in 'Crumble Hall' Mary Leapor tours the greasy kitchen and, over and over, the dark, dusty passageway and stairs reveal the inconvenient design of the great house. Late in the century Elizabeth Hands captures the special delight many women found in Swift's poetry in her 'Critical Fragments, on some of the English Poets', which had stanzas imitating the form and content of several major poets, 'But SWIFT delights as much to rout / I'th' dirt, and then to throw't about.'[25] Crumble Hall, like most eighteenth-century structures *were* dirty, and these poets, Swift included, revelled in 'throwing it about' – setting up a hierarchy of nastiness, smearing the high and mighty with dirt and delighting in turning into wry poetry all the kinds of dirt from spider webs to gossip.

Quite apart from Swift, women were developing distinctive types of domestic poetry. For example, Jones, Dixon, Leapor and Hands were not writing under Swift's direct influence. The subjects and metrics become increasingly varied, and the adaptation of such forms as the friendship poem and the Horatian epistle alter tone and purpose. The great form of ethical poetry in the century, the Horatian verse letter, expressed a social or communal perspective. Usually addressed to a friend, such poems were a favourite site for commentary on society, politics, the arts and the state of the nation vis-à-vis its European competitors. Boileau's and Pope's are the finest examples and recognised for their 'graceful precision and dignified familiarity'.[26] Although women responded to, imitated and adapted them and produced poems on these conventional public and satiric subjects, the greatest number of their Horatian epistles are imagined in domestic settings. Many of them, like the poems by men, are about the writing of poetry and its usefulness and reception. A significant number are about the private sphere. Jane Brereton's 'Epistle to Mrs Anne Griffiths. Written from London, in 1718' joins many of the conventions of the Horatian epistle to those of the friendship poem. It begins, 'My best lov'd Friend! since ravish'd from thy Sight, / I've known no Joy, no Comfort, nor Delight', and goes on to describe how much the speaker misses her friend. In a long central section, however, she takes up one of the traditional subjects of the Horatian epistle, the conditions under which the best poetry is written. Brereton makes the two forms, one highly feminine and private

25 Elizabeth Hands, *The Death of Amnon. A Poem. With An Appendix: Containing Pastorals, and other Poetical Pieces* (Coventry, 1789. Reprint, London: Routledge/Thoemmes Press, 1996), p. 126.
26 *New Princeton Encyclopedia of Poetry and Poetics*, Alex Preminger and T. V. F. Brogan (eds.) (Princeton, NJ: Princeton University Press, 1993), s.v. 'verse epistle.'

and the other public and masculine, complementary and reinforcing: 'For me, who never durst to more pretend / Than to amuse myself, and please my Friend; / If she approves my unskilful Lays; / I dread no Critic, and desire no Praise.'[27]

Domestic poetry becomes increasingly complicated as women from the labouring classes began to be published. Mary Collier's *The Woman's Labour* is in our time one of the most anthologised poems, and still resonant is its picture of the woman going back and forth from her home ('Bacon and dumpling in the pot we boil, / Our beds we make') to her employer's ('We scarce can count what falls unto our share; / Pots, kettles, sauce-pans, skillets').[28] Hands' 'A Poem on the Supposition of an Advertisement . . . of the Publication of a Volume of Poems, by a Servant Maid' is one of the best satires of a gossipy, pseudo-literary gathering written in the century, and the anapestic tetrameter couplets she chooses make it a sprightly narrative.

That women were likely to be less educated and differently educated from men is often considered their second most serious handicap. An analysis of the women poets reveals their parents' striking dedication to their daughters' educations. It appears that only Chapone and Masters were actively discouraged, and the impoverished, uneducated parents of Grierson, Blamire, Darwall and Collier struggled to educate their children. For diverse reasons, ten of the poets can be classified as very well educated, and another ten as well educated. Eleven knew Latin and the classics well and several published translations of, for instance, Epictetus and Terence. The children of Dissenters were especially likely to be carefully educated, as Rowe and Barbauld were. Either as children or after marriage, most of them had access to well-stocked libraries. At least nine were daughters of clergymen, and four more married churchmen; the books and educations of their fathers and husbands provided lifelong advantages. Perhaps the most serious problems with women's educations and the culture's attitudes towards women were captured in 1737 by Catherine Trotter Cockburn, one of the most intelligent, educated and well-read poets:

> Than those restraints which have our sex confin'd,
> While partial custom checks the soaring mind.
> Learning deny'd us, we at random tread
> Unbeaten paths, that late to knowledge lead;
> By secret steps break thro' th' obstructed way,

---

27 Brereton, 'To Mrs Anne Griffiths,' *Poems on Several Occasions*, pp. 30 and 35.
28 Joyce Fullard (ed.), *British Women Poets 1660–1800: An Anthology* (Troy, NY: Whitson Publishing Company, 1990), pp. 308, 311.

Nor dare acquirements gain'd by stealth display.
If some advent'rous genius rare arise,
Who on exalted themes here talents tries,
She fears to give the work (tho' prais'd) a name,
And flies not more from infamy, than fame.[29]

These lines list almost all of the barriers women themselves felt, and most of them were conventional complaints before and after Cockburn wrote them. Two complaints on her list are commonplaces today, and, although she was married and had four children, she does not mention domestic responsibilities.

By this time, Cockburn had been a successful playwright, author of a popular epistolary fiction, the correspondent of John Locke and Gottfried Leibnitz and the publisher of philosophical tracts, which were read and praised by these men and others. The first woman since Aphra Behn to have a tragedy produced at a royal theatre, she was befriended by William Congreve and Charles, Earl of Dorset. Women playwrights largely gained access to production and publication through friends such as these and strong networks of actors and managers. Cockburn had absorbed this lesson, as Aphra Behn, Susanna Centlivre, Elizabeth Inchbald, Hannah More and other women poets did. The theatre was something of a rough and tumble world where such categories as 'feminine' and 'respectable' were quite different from those in daily life and in the milieu for poets, but some conventions were usefully transferred. As both a plea for fair play and chivalry, this poem reflects the dramatic prologues and epilogues that Cockburn knew so well. As we have seen, for most of the women 'Learning deny'd us' was not strictly accurate. Few men in the century were as well educated as Elizabeth Carter, Hannah More, Elizabeth Tollet and Anna Seward. The key phrase is 'we at random tread,' and, of course, any kind of equality ended early because women were barred from university study. We read of women who struggled to learn the classical languages and literature or of others who were deeply grateful to fathers, brothers or tutors who taught them, and it could be demonstrated that most women poets who use classical forms learned them from English poets, not the Latin and Greek originals. This circumstance might, however, explain women's significant contributions to the development of distinctively English forms of poetic kinds.

29 Catherine Trotter Cockburn, 'Verses, occasion'd by the Busts in the Queen's Hermitage, and Mr Duck being appointed Keeper of the Library in Merlin's Cave. By the Authoress of a Treatise (not yet publish'd) in Vindication of Mr Lock, against the injurious Charge of Dr Holdsworth', *The Gentleman's Magazine* 7 (May 1737), 308. An earlier version of this poem was published in her 1732 monograph, *The Busts set up in the Queen's Hermitage*.

Not surprisingly, the more privileged women are the most aware of the unevenness of their educations. Reflective, gently poignant lines on this topic often creep into poems on a variety of subjects. A number of poems convey a feeling of looking through an impenetrable glass and achieve a beauty of form to match the pleasure they are briefly experiencing or imagining. Laetitia Pilkington's 'Verses Wrote in a Library' begins, 'Seat for Contemplation fit, / Sacred Nursery of Wit! / Let me here enwrap'd in Pleasure, / Taste the Sweets of learned Leisure.'[30] Elizabeth Teft's lovely 'On Learning' shows an understanding of some of the greatest values of learning: 'I the first founders of great Rome would know / . . . Search out the nature of all things below, / From what great causes dire effects do flow; / In conference with deathless Homer be . . .'[31]

What becomes clear, however, is that the best of the poets studied poetry seriously, modern and ancient (when they could get it). Their imitations, adaptations and experimentations as well as references in their letters, introductions and other writings demonstrate their close and careful study of their craft. Even the most poverty-stricken mention precious volumes of poetry and re-work favourite poems. Perhaps the most adapted poem of the century for women was Alexander Pope's *Epistle to Arbuthnot*, and it has one section they obviously found exceptionally empowering. Over and over, women alluded to passages in this poem that made writing 'natural' and right for them. Reeve, for instance, described herself, 'What tho' while yet an infant young, / The numbers trembled on my tongue; / As youth advanc'd, I dar'd aspire, / And trembling struck the heavenly lyre.'[32] One of the best of these poems, Darwall's 'The Power of Destiny,' begins, 'Sure some malignant star diffused its ray, / When first my eyes beheld the beams of day; / Whose baleful influence made me dip in ink, / And write in rhyme before I knew to think.' In this poem, which maintains its smooth heroic couplets throughout, she imagines what would have happened had she been a man. 'Had I been bred at Gray's or Lincoln's Inn, / 'Mid lawsuits, empty quibbles, doubts and din', she writes, but concludes joyfully that no matter what profession she were in she would have 'fled in raptures' to 'Swift, Hill, Congreve, Cowley, Garth and Gay,' to 'serene delights and rural joys', where "stead of drafts, composed – an elegy.'[33]

30 Laetitia Pilkington's 'Verses Wrote in a Library' (1748), from *The Poetry of Laetitia Pilkington (1712–1750) and Constantia Grierson (1706–1733)*, ed. Bernard Tucker (Lewiston, ME: Edwin Mellen Press, 1996), p. 52.
31 Lonsdale, *Eighteenth-Century Women Poets*, p. 218.
32 Clara Reeve, 'To My Friend Mrs–', *Original Poems on Several Occasions* (London, 1769), pp. 10–11.
33 Lonsdale, *Eighteenth-Century Women Poets*, pp. 258–9.

Crucial to the female poetic career is permission to write, to make writing one of the most important things in life. Whether from an inherited sense of entitlement, a hard-won sense of self-worth and calling, or an unexpected success followed by sustained encouragement, permission turned into the Life of a Poet, a career as a poet.

The 'disadvantage' of women always comes down to the intangible that women never forget that they are *women* poets. Regardless of how strongly they understand 'poet' as a major, essential part of their identity, no matter their achievement as poet, they are always aware that they are *women* poets. It is hard to deny, however, that the greatest poets of the long eighteenth century had some adjective attached to 'poet' that competed in strength to marginalise and disempower. For instance, Milton was blind and a loser in the great cause of his life. The truth is that reception of women not only differed from decade to decade, from one woman to another, but in an individual's experience from one moment to another. Many women are very sturdy personalities, and adversity and injustice have always inspired poets. Cockburn speaks of 'partial custom', and that phrase had become a code for 'prejudice' even before the 1760s when women poets expressed the attitude that Darwall conveyed in her dedication, that she would 'look down with a just contempt on the invidious Reflections of . . . Prejudice'.[34] 'Prejudice' became the word that women writers habitually used to strike back at those who condemned them for writing or who took for granted that women's work was inferior, and it had been a code for some time for the terms in which many women and sympathetic men were discussing women's treatment in the literary marketplace. Cockburn's phrase 'partial custom' means the same thing and was the more common term in her generation; Sarah Egerton, for instance, begins 'The Emulation': 'Say, tyrant Custom, why must we obey / The impositions of thy haughty sway? / From the first days of life unto the grave, / Poor womankind's in every state a slave.'[35] A reviewer of Darwall's book began with the opposing term:

> It never can be a dispute with the liberal, whether the fine arts are the proper province for the exercise of female genius? – Nothing but the jealousy of our sex, and the envy of their own, would urge the least pretense for excluding the Ladies from any of those elegant and happy amusements which the arts of Imitation may afford them.[36]

34 Mary Whateley Darwall, 'Dedication' to *Original Poems on Several Occasions by Miss Whateley* (London, 1764), p. 8.
35 Lonsdale, *Eighteenth-Century Women Poets*, p. 31.
36 John Langhorne, '*Review of Original Poems, on Several Occasions*, By Mary Darwall', *Monthly Review* 30 (June 1764), 445. Biographical information about Darwall is from Messenger, *Woman and Poet in the Eighteenth Century*.

Although Darwall was an unusually independent and resolute woman, the unblushing terms in which she remarks on prejudice suggest that by then it was not acceptable to condemn women for writing. At long last, many women had come to feel that it was perfectly proper for them to write and that excuses were unnecessary. Clara Reeve's is a landmark statement on the subject:

> I formerly believed, that I ought not to let myself be known for a scribbler, that my sex was an insuperable objection, that mankind in general were prejudiced against its pretensions to literary merit; but I am now convinced of the mistake, by daily examples to the contrary. I see many female writers favourably received, admitted into the rank of authors, and amply rewarded by the public; I have been encouraged by their success, to offer myself as a candidate for the same advantages. I hope thus much [sic] may serve as a general apology for this undertaking.[37]

And no apologies were made by the generation that included Smith, Seward, Robinson and Baillie. In fact, some of them aggressively and even combatively claimed what Seward called, 'the Poet's triumph . . . his consciousness of powers / That lift his memory from oblivion's gloom.'[38]

What did women poets write? The answer is 'everything', and there are many misconceptions about the range of their subjects, the diversity of the forms in which they worked and the quality of their verse. And, although seldom remarked upon, possessors of special talents usually produce bi-polar art – pieces that show the highest ambition and polish and pieces that are whipped off to express a transitory emotion or amuse others or themselves. Roger Lonsdale has speculated that the use of 'styles that were being replaced by new fashions' worked against the popularity and contemporary reputations of women poets.[39] He gives as examples Anne Finch, Mary Jones and Mary Leapor, but it is important to remember that some male poets did the same without adverse effects. Alexander Pope is a notable example as he clung to the heroic couplet in a time when his contemporaries were writing quatrains and irregular odes, and today a case might be made that those who clung to Spenser, Milton, Waller and Pope have suffered less erasure than those seduced by D'Urfey, Prior, Young and Shenstone. In fact, almost no one has

37 Reeve, 'To the Reader,' *Original Poems*, p. xi.
38 Anna Seward, 'Sonnet xx', in *The Poetical Works of Anna Seward*, ed. Walter Scott (1810), 3 vols. (New York: AMS, 1974), vol. III, p. 141; and see also sonnets LIII and LXIV.
39 Lonsdale, *Eighteenth-Century Women Poets*, p. xxv.

taken serious notice of the lingering influences of these poets, especially the latter group, on women, and we can never forget that every age has innovators as well as poets who continue and carry forward existing forms.

The poetry of eighteenth-century women and men reveals a consistent longing for and appreciation of classical writers and a willingness to attempt the most respected traditional verse forms. It also testifies to their understanding and mastery of adapted, new and fashionable *English* forms. Sometimes women were leaders in popularising a form – as Anne Finch and Charlotte Smith were with, respectively, the fable and the sonnet. Sometimes a woman's poem in a well-established form rises magisterially out of a mountain of similar but wretched work, as Mary Jones' Horatian 'An Epistle to Lady Bowyer' and Susanna Blamire's ode 'O why should mortals suffer care' do. Jones self-consciously feminises Pope's *Epistle to Arbuthnot*, reworking and personalising both individual lines and the familiar sections of the classical apologia. Her perspective as petitioner is the opposite of Pope's; when she seeks a patron, his servant says, 'Verses! – alas! his lordship seldom reads . . . Reads not even tradesmen's bills, and scorns to spell. / But trust your lays with me – some things I've read, / Was born a poet, tho' no poet bred: / And if I find they'll bear my nicer view, / I'll recommend your poetry – and you.'[40] In contrast to Jones' acerbic lines and witty dramatisation, Blamire composes a *carpe diem* ode of considerable beauty that begins:

> O why should mortals suffer care
>> To rob them of their present joy?
> The moments that frail life can spare
>> Why should we not in mirth employ?
> Then come, my friends, this very hour
>> Let us devote to social glee;
> Tomorrow is a day unseen
>> That may destroy the fairest flower,
> And bring dull care to you and me,
>> Though so gay as we have been.[41]

In too many cases wherever we find a commonplace, such as that women did not write much political poetry, extensive reading in women's poetry proves it in error.[42] Wherever we find an important literary movement or fad, we

---

40 Fullard, *British Women Poets*, p. 47.
41 *Ibid.*, p. 453.
42 There is, however, relatively little work on women's political poetry. Recent studies of the political aspects of women's writing are Carol Barash, *English Women's Poetry, 1649–1714:*

find women. We also find major achievements, especially as the century progresses, such as Charlotte Smith's *Elegiac Sonnets*, which should never be omitted from literary histories. Finally, both men and women are often adversely affected by current fashions. Lonsdale writes of his *Eighteenth-Century Women Poets*:

> It may perhaps be a boast of the present anthology that it underrepresents the insipidity of the fashionable poetry of this period, the many eastern pastorals, legendary tales . . . imitations of Ossian, laments for dead birds and small animals, and all the odes to Fancy, Sensibility, Pity, and other personifications which proliferated and which teenagers were finding it all too easy to mimic . . .[43]

As Lonsdale implies, whatever women were doing, more men were doing just as badly. If women seldom wrote to and about children as well as Matthew Prior, neither did men – as Ambrose Philips illustrates.

In order to give some sense of the terrain that is women's poetry, I will use the work of Anne Finch as touchstone. Contemporaneous with Dryden, Behn, Congreve, Garth, Prior, Addison, Parnell, Pope and Gay, Anne Kingsmill Finch, Countess of Winchilsea, was a poet of astonishing range and versatility. She has long been reputed to be the best woman poet of the eighteenth century. Best known for the poems Wordsworth singled out (and cut freely in his *Poems and Extracts*), Finch is often the only woman included in overviews of the century's poetry. Nevertheless, only a few of her poems in an extremely limited number of styles are recognised, and her career is seldom contextualised. She can be, however, a guide to the poetry of her period and an introduction to what *women* poets throughout the century were doing.

Finch will always be known for her beautiful nature and retirement odes and Horatian poems. 'A Nocturnal Reverie', 'Petition for an Absolute Retreat', 'To the Nightingale', and 'The Spleen. A Pindaric Poem' have been consistently anthologised since the eighteenth century. 'Life's Progress,' a poem in quintains admired equally for its message and its poetic skill, begins, 'How gayly is at first begun, / Our *Life's* uncertain Race!' It exhibits many of Finch's justly admired techniques:

Politics, Community, and Linguistic Authority (Oxford: Clarendon Press, 1996) and Moira Ferguson, *Subject to Others: British Women Writers and Colonial Slavery, 1670–1834* (New York: Routledge, 1992).

43 Lonsdale, *Eighteenth-Century Women Poets*, p. xxxvi.

> How soft the first Ideas prove,
>   Which wander through our Minds!
> How full the Joys, how free the Love,
>   Which do's that early Season move;
>   As Flow'rs the Western Winds![44]

The precision of word choice and metre, the harmony and grace, the effective use of alliteration and the unexpected final image evoking a common, pleasant, rich sensory experience from nature are all typical of her work.

Far from anomalous, 'Life's Progress' is simply one of the best of many lyrics, many of which are quite short and, as would be expected of a poet with her social position and experiences, fashionable. Eighteen of eighty-one poems in Finch's *Miscellany Poems* are in this category and include 'A Song upon a Punch Bowl' and the Petrarchan 'Love, thou art best of Human Joys'. Related to this group is her theatre verse, a category which is almost unnoticed although written by most of the women poets of the century. Prologues, epilogues, songs and even short poetical speeches for specific characters, they are richly varied and ready-made spaces for social comment, a fact women poets did not miss. Left untitled in the Wellesley manuscript is a poem on William Wycherley's Sir Plausible in *The Plain Dealer* that Finch uses to condemn a kind of person that must have irritated her extremely: 'Fast as Camelions change their dye / Has still some applicable story / To gratify or Whig or Tory [*sic*] / And with a Jacobite in tatters / If met alone he smoothly flatters.'[45] Another example is Finch's 'An Epilogue to the Tragedy of Jane Shore to be spoken by Mrs Oldfield'.[46] It is a fine review of Shore's contrasting states of being with a running commentary on the culture's responses to the ageing of women and the prevailing double standard, not just in sexual matters but in general moral conduct. Theatre verse is an integral part of some women's œuvre.

---

44 *The Poems of Anne Countess of Winchilsea*, pp. 136–8; quotations from pp. 136 and 137.
45 *The Anne Finch Wellesley Manuscript Poems*, eds. Barbara McGovern and Charles H. Hinnant (Athens, GA: University of Georgia Press, 1998), p. 53. Supporters of James II, the Finches were displaced by his removal from the throne. They lived with friends until invited to live with a nephew, see McGovern, *Anne Finch and Her Poetry*, pp. 58–65. The Wellesley manuscript includes fifty-three poems, only one published by Reynolds. The editors speculate that it was transcribed to preserve her poems, not to prepare them for publication. Several poems are untitled.
46 Barbara McGovern has argued that Finch wrote this poem in dialogue with Pope, who had ended his epilogue for Rowe's benefit night by asking women to vote for their pleasure in the play by coming to 'stare the strumpet down', 'Finch, Pope, and Swift: The Bond of Displacement', in Donald C. Mell (ed.), *Pope, Swift, and Women Writers* (Newark, DE: University of Delaware Press, 1996), pp. 114–19.

Barber wrote 'Epilogue to a Comedy acted at Bath, where the Dutchess of Ormond was present' and printed her friend Constantia Grierson's 'Prologue to *Theodosius*: Spoken by Athenais at the Theatre in Dublin' in her *Poems on Several Occasions*. Pilkington and Reeve wrote prologues. Another kind of theatrical poetry was tributes to dramatists, and they vary from being addressed to predictable men (Tollet and Montagu on Congreve) to the surprising (Pilkington's 'To Samuel Foote'). Dodsley collected a number of theatre pieces in his 1737 *Collection*, but later anthologies increasingly exclude them.

Of Finch as well as Pope it might be said, 'If she be not a poet, where is poetry to be found?' She lived out what it means to be a serious writer by studying poetry, by writing frequently, by experimenting, polishing and revising her work, establishing herself as the kind of poet she wanted to be. In a dozen forms of poetry, she writes about poetic identity and calling, and many of her poems are simultaneously expressions of her approach to problems she faced as a writer and expressions of her life experiences, of a gendered sensibility. A familiar one is 'Circuit of Apollo'. Everyone wrote 'sessions of the poets' poems, and hers is as good as the best.[47] Aware that Aphra Behn, like herself, was from Kent, she begins the poem with a tribute to her and has Apollo visit the region. He discovers 'that poets were not very common / But most that pretended to verse were the women.' Finch presents herself as writing for her pleasure, 'Not seeking for Fame, which so little does last, / That e're we can taste itt [*sic*], the Pleasure is Past'.[48] These lines, like the myth of the reluctant-to-publish Katherine Philips, have often been quoted, sometimes as the proper attitude for a woman and sometimes as the mind-set that prevents women from achieving the heights of Milton and Pope. This poem's context is complicated, however, and its statement subtle. Finch had seen how fleeting fame was, indeed how it could bring troubles down on a family. She does say clearly that the bays 'wou'd be highly esteem'd'. Margaret Ezell has convincingly demonstrated how men and women of Finch's generation lived in a culture of manuscript circulation and circles of trusted (either because of their expertise or their friendship) readers.[49] Writers feared loss of control of the content of their manuscripts; the number of writers who complained about 'imperfect' copies and unauthorised

---

47 Many, like Prior's 'A Session of the Poets', record both changing literary tastes and the part politics played in a poet's popularity. It is notable that Aphra Behn is unfailingly included and often given high honours; Prior, however, finds her poetry too long and her day past.

48 *The Poems of Anne Countess of Winchilsea*, p. 94.

49 Margaret Ezell, *The Patriarch's Wife* (Chapel Hill: University of North Carolina Press, 1987), pp. 62–100.

publication is very high. Moreover, writers learned that their reputations were burnished or tarnished by the reputations of those who published them, as Elizabeth Singer Rowe learned from nearly life-long embarrassments visited on her by John Dunton, who pirated her work, surprised her at home and even published accounts of his lasting infatuation with her. Finch did not publish 'The Circuit of Apollo' in her lifetime. A comparison of whom women allowed to publish their novels, plays and poems shows the tightest and narrowest control over their poetry.

Today it is more common to print Finch's 'The Introduction', a poem in both surviving manuscripts but not published until Myra Reynolds' 1903 edition of her poetry. This poem includes the much-quoted lines, 'Alas! a woman that attempts the pen, / Such an intruder on the rights of men, / Such a presumptuous Creature, is esteem'd, / The fault, can by no vertue be redeem'd. / They tell us, we mistake our sex and way.'[50] This poem names famous women who 'excell'd of old' and laments the lowered status and education of women in her time; it is perhaps more interesting for its sociological content than for its poetic merit. A dozen of her other poems make more important statements about poetry and the poetic identity. And in writing almost obsessively on this subject, Finch is, again, representative.[51] Thus, in a similar vein, Charlotte Lennox has a fine pastoral, 'Aminta and Delia', which includes adept sections on poetry and on the writing of it. These poems are by no means timid; Lennox, for instance, asks, 'Thee, gentle Maid, may ev'ry Muse inspire, / And *Phoebus* bless thee with poetic Fire.'[52] In her novel *Julia*, Helen Maria Williams uses 'An Address to Poetry' to characterise the heroine and as part of a defence of writing poetry.[53] Joanna Baillie's *Address to the Muses* is a superb 'progress of poetry' poem filled with witty observations on herself as a poet. Women even felt free to insult the poets laureate, as did Anna Seward in Sonnet 53 and Harriet Falconar, who begins one poem, 'You might hear of Parnassus, but never did know it.'[54]

Finch is also a good guide to women poets' work because she was adapting existing forms, actually rejuvenating them, and she was extending some kinds of poetry already recognised as women's contributions to the genre. Fables

50 *The Poems of Anne Countess of Winchilsea*, pp. 4–5.
51 Joyce Fullard has a good selection of such poems in her *British Women Poets*.
52 Charlotte Lennox, *Poems on Several Occasions. Written by a Young Lady* (London, 1747), p. 15.
53 Helen Maria Williams, *Julia: A Novel*, 2 vols. (London, 1790), vol. I, pp. 15–24.
54 Harriet Falconar, 'Stanzas, Respectfully addressed to the Poet Laureate', *Poetic Laurels for Characters of Distinguished Merit . . . by Maria and Harriet Falconar* (London, 1791), p. 11.

make up about one-third of Finch's poetry,[55] and Myra Reynolds, speaking perhaps of original or 'imitated' fables written in English, says that they 'show her first in the field with a poetic form destined to great popularity'. Behn, Dryden, Swift, Prior and others wrote and translated fables, but Finch surpasses them in number, creativity, poetic skill and overall quality. Above all, she extends the range of subjects and social uses for them and is in no way imitating Dryden, Prior or Gay. Finch, therefore, was writing hers at the same time, not imitating them. Some of Finch's are translations of La Fontaine, like the best-known 'The Atheist and the Acorn'. Many of them punish or laugh at a man who believes he can run the universe better than God; they have didactic titles, like 'Man's Injustice towards Providence'. 'Jupiter and the Farmer' is a funny fable about a farmer who accepts Jupiter's high rent for a farm with the agreement that he can control the weather. Most of Finch's fables are original creations, featuring some daring and indeed quite astonishing statements about the experience of being a woman poet. 'The Critick and the Writer of Fables' lists the pressures to write various kinds of poetry and explains the appeal of the fable: 'Weary, at last, of the *Pindarick* way . . . To *Fable* I descend with soft Delight.' She explains how they 'Teach, as Poets shou'd, whilst they Divert.'[56]

As women poets embraced the form, they added much to the traditional imperative to teach and divert. Charlotte Smith found the fable a useful way to make pointed comments about such things as unfaithful husbands, and her reworkings of fables by Aesop, Pilpay (the eighth-century Arabic 'wise man') and La Fontaine often switch the perspective from male to female. Mary Leapor's exhibit her sharp powers of observations, her tart tongue and her unsparing themes, as do her 'The Fox and the Hen' and 'The Libyan Hunter'. Women increasingly used fables to punish class pretensions and to comment on gendered customs. In Mary Masters' 'The Rose and other Flowers, a Tale; inscribed to a young Lady', for example, a rose haughtily names herself queen of flowers but is put down by a cowslip.[57] Often written in hexameter couplets, the fables tell their stories efficiently and crisply. As Finch demonstrated, they were acceptable ways for women to write satire.

The only significant form of poetry that Finch inherited from women was the friendship poem in the tradition of Katherine Philips, and just as a book

---

55 The count is by Jamie Stanesa, 'Anne Finch (1661–1720)', in John Sitter (ed.), *Dictionary of Literary Biography*, vol. xcv (Detroit: Gale Research, Inc., 1990), p. 67.

56 *The Poems of Anne Countess of Winchilsea*, p. 153.

57 Mary Masters, 'The Rose and other Flowers', *Familiar Letters and Poems on Several Occasions*, 2 vols. (London, 1755), vol. II, pp. 159–62.

could be written on women's use of the fable, one needs to be written on the permutations of this type. Finch's range from the clichés of the genre to the truly original, many with surprising turns. Some of the best are about writing letters or exchanging poetry and are in the Wellesley manuscript poems. 'To a Friend In Praise of the Invention of Writing Letters' describes letters as 'baffling absence', and ends unexpectedly and imaginatively with what she unreservedly describes as a wish that would be very much at home in our own information age: 'Oh! might I live to see an Art arise . . . / That the dark Pow'rs of distance cou'd subdue, / And make me *See*, as well as *Talk* to You.'[58] 'To the Honorable the Lady Worsley at Longleate, Who had most obligingly desired my corresponding with her by Letters' and 'To Flavia, By whose perswasion, I undertook the following Paraphrase' suggest how integrated writing and female friendships were. Some of these poems, such as the one to Mrs Randolph, are Horatian epistles, others are dialogues, and a few are among her most experimental, as is 'To the Hon. Mrs H–n,' which is written in single-rhymed octosyllable tercets.[59]

Using Katherine Philips' forms and themes but also departing dramatically from the earlier poet's voices and conclusions, Finch increased the possibilities of the type significantly and is original in her use of such poems to write about writing. Among the fine poems in this tradition are Chudleigh's 'To Eugenia. On her Pastoral', Mary Jones's 'Of Desire. An Epistle to the Honourable Miss Lovelace' and Jane Brereton's 'On seeing Mrs Eliz. Owen, now Lady Longueville, in an embroider'd Suit, all her own Work'. These poems increasingly took a variety of sophisticated forms. Mary Leapor wrote a series of philosophic essays in heroic couplets, including one on friendship. Elizabeth Carter's poems are full of lines addressing women companions, such as 'Come dear *Emilia*, and enjoy / Reflexion's fav'rite Hour' from the lovely, musical, 'To–'

> The Midnight Moon serenely smiles,
>   O'er Nature's soft Repose;
> No low'ring Cloud obscures the Sky,
>   Nor ruffling Tempest blows.
> Now ev'ry Passion sinks to Rest,
>   The throbbing Heart lies still:
> And varying Schemes of Life no more
>   Distract the lab'ring Will.[60]

58 *The Poems of Anne Countess of Winchilsea*, p. III.
59 Respectively *ibid.*, pp. 52–5 and *The Anne Finch Wellesley Manuscript Poems*, pp. 13–14, 63–5.
60 Elizabeth Carter, *Poems on Several Occasions*, 2nd edn (London, 1766), pp. 65–7; quotations from pp. 66 and 65 respectively.

About the time this poem was written, Darwall wrote, 'I never studiously ranged thro' the Regions of Imagination to seek for Paths unexplored by former Writers; but sat down content to employ my humble Abilities on such Themes – as Friendship, Gratitude, and native Freedom of Fancy', all accepted topics for women poets. Her 'Epistle to a Friend' is a defence of female friendship in a time when husbands often restricted it and satirists doubted its sincerity and constancy. She invokes the authority of Shakespeare in her cause by using the story of Celia giving up everything to go with Rosalind.[61] Grierson's description of what women poets were doing is more accurate than Darwall's: 'Far different themes we in thy verses view; / Themes in themselves sublime and new'.[62]

Friendship poems increasingly came to compare female friendship and heterosexual love, as Darwall's did, and by doing so provided a place for important statements about normative pressures and female aspirations. For instance, Mary Masters' Marinda poems follow a common path in women's lives with the sequence 'To Marinda, at Parting', 'A Question to Marinda' and 'On Marinda's Marriage', and then another sequence beginning 'To Marinda, on the New-year, being the first Year of her Marriage'.[63] These poems, like the fables, became sites for social protest and complaint. Brereton's friendship poems are part of the century's critique of marriage. In 'Verses on the Loss of a Friend', with its story of a friend 'beguiled' by love, she writes, 'Yet soon she mourn'd the fatal Step she made, / I left to share a Grief I could not aid! / Grown thus forlorn by her unguarded Choice, / Her hapless Fortune damp'd my former Joys.'[64] Showing the other side of the coin, 'To a Lady. On her Marriage' praises her friend for her choice by calling the man a 'humane Philosopher' and a 'Man of Truth'. She invokes Pope's authority as the final compliment: 'An honest Man's the noblest Work of God.'[65] Finch, who makes it clear that she is writing within a happy marriage, did much to establish this line of poetry, and some poems addressed to husbands by a variety of women poets might be placed in this category.

Like Finch's, many of the loveliest friendship poems are also retirement poems. They open the solitary space where women have found liberty and beauty to a special presence, and they celebrate a different pleasure, as did

---

61 Darwall, *Original Poems on Several Occasions* (London, 1764), p. 5, and *Poems on Several Occasions* (Walsall, 1794), vol. 1, pp. 19–25 respectively.

62 She is describing Mary Barber's poetry, 'To Mrs Mary Barber, Under the Name of Sapphira', printed in Colman, *Poems by Eminent Ladies*, vol. 1, pp. 244–6.

63 Mary Masters, *Poems on Several Occasions* (London, 1733).

64 Brereton, *Poems on Several Occasions*, pp. 12–13.

65 *Ibid.*, p. 109.

Carter's 'Come dear *Emilia*'. Brereton's 'Verses on the Loss of a Friend' describes her retreat eloquently and adds, 'To crown all this, and make my Joys compleat, / A Friend I had near this belov'd Retreat / So well we lov'd, so faithful and so true.'[66] Barbauld's 'The Invitation: To Miss B*****' is a long retirement poem that draws upon Pope: 'Health to my friend, and long unbroken years, / By storms unruffled and unstain'd by tears.' The poem has unusual fervour and energy: 'Ye generous youth who love this studious shade, / How rich a field is to your hopes display'd!'[67] Women adapted the long tradition of male retirement poetry and passed it along greatly enriched.

Almost every poet named in this chapter can be treated as Finch has been here. There are a few poems, often arbitrarily or ideologically chosen, that are anthologised; there are little-known poems in the popular forms of the day and there are major poems written as part of the endeavour that all true poets undertake: to create original forms and important new uses for poetry. Notably, after Finch and her generation, women poets made significant contributions to almost every classical and English form and were major participants in the development and popularising of four genres of great importance to literary history. The ode, elegy, sonnet and metrical tale all attracted rich, disciplined experimentation and distinctive achievement. As a concluding illustration of the significance of women poets, I will briefly discuss the sonnet.

Women's contribution to the sonnet revival has received the most attention but is still far from being understood in any refined or detailed way. In 1784, Smith published *Elegaic Sonnets and Other Essays*, and that mood and the form seem especially congenial for her. Smith may have derived her title from the label given Thomas Gray's 'On the Death of Mr Richard West', which was published posthumously in 1775. His 'elegaic sonnet' with its affinities to the poetry of sensibility and melancholy was endlessly reprinted in collections. Today, among the slim output and mediocrity of the other revivalists (Thomas Edwards, Thomas Warton), Smith seems a giant. She let sensibility, the picturesque ode and sombre tones flow into her sonnets and impressively compressed them, thereby reinventing the sonnet and extending its purposes. Her 'Written at Penshurst, in autumn 1788' is illustrative of her transformative work. It is a fine meditation on the great house's past political and literary significance, and she gives the poem heightened significance by turning it into a statement asserting that the private *and* political are the poet's sacred domains.

---

66 *Ibid.*, p. 12.
67 Anna Laetitia Barbauld, *Poems of Anna Letitia Barbauld*, eds. William McCarthy and Elizabeth Kraft, pp. 9–15, quotation from p. 9.

Placing herself in the line of poets who have taken Penshurst, the ancestral home of the Sidneys, as a subject,[68] she invokes Waller, by then frequently chosen to represent refinement, melody and 'sweetness', and concludes with an affirmation of the poet's power to preserve the memory of heroes such as Algernon Sidney and poetic lovers such as Waller and Lady Dorothea Sidney. The poem begins with a prospect, and the poet's perspective is significant: the 'musing wanderer' seems to look down on the estate, comprehending it all, rather than looking at it from the same level or from within. The movement is backwards and forwards through history and around the estate and into the portrait gallery. In 1788, the British were reflecting on their history, for it was the anniversary of the Glorious Revolution, and, in the face of the event that seemed to be the symbol of British reason and liberty, William Dolben made his report on the conditions on slave ships and George III suffered his first bout of 'madness'. In a strikingly bold move for a poet, and especially a woman poet, she asserts the power of poetry and her status as bard. Comparing poetry to 'the fading canvas' in the time when the 'sister arts' were much celebrated, she claims that poetry is more permanent and affirms the nation's need for it. Hanging tangibly in the air is the unspoken question, 'How will England's future compare to its past?'

In working on the sonnets over years (and many editions), Smith expanded the snapshots of the moods of melancholy but also expanded the uses of the sonnet form. Instead of reading the sonnets as the record of her unstinting depression and complaints about her hard life (and that her life was hard no one will deny), we should read the sonnets on their own terms and as a sonnet cycle. Taking as the perspective the lonely wanderer, the bard who can travel and *see*, she derives power from this solitary, traditional moral judge. Just as the earlier writers of sonnet cycles delighted in creating precisely and in a variety of highly creative ways each mood of love, so she does with melancholy. Melancholy can be gentle or despairing, familiar or desperate, and its metaphors and voices are strikingly varied. For example, a number of her sonnets are clearly in the voices of literary characters, an innovation in sonnet writing that many women adapted from her.[69] Several of Smith's are drawn from the moods she imagines in the characters in *Macbeth*; another group are keyed to passages in *Werter*; and yet others, such as the fine 'To Night', were

68 Ben Jonson's 'To Penshurst' is one of his best known poems, and Edmund Waller wrote two, 'At Penshurst' ('Had Sacharissa lived when mortals made . . .') and 'At Penshurst' ('While in the park I sing, the listening deer . . .'). Smith's sonnet is in *The Poems of Charlotte Smith*, pp. 43–4.

69 Among the great Romantics, only Shelley's 'Ozymandias' seems related to this innovation.

written to reveal and deepen the minds of characters in her novels. Written at the time Sarah Siddons was drastically reinterpreting Lady Macbeth and giving unprecedented psychological depth to her character, the sonnets, such as 'To Oblivion' with its allusion to Macduff, take their melodramatic cast from the tragic moods of the play rather than from Smith's autobiography. Many poets of the period, including Anna Seward and Anne Bannerman, dramatised passages or moods in *Werter*, and including poetry in prose fiction was common and an unbroken strategy at least as early as the *New Arcadia*. Smith's 'To Night', for example, is 'spoken' by Godolphin, the despairing lover in *Emmeline* as he crosses the Channel. Again, in a setting bathed in history and contemporary tension, the sonnet goes beyond mood poetry. Another variant on the Spenserian sonnet, its ending combines a traditional eighteenth-century conclusion, the hope of reaching 'the ear of Heaven', with the Romantic conception of the mystical relationship between nature and the soul. As Daniel Robinson says, 'the association of landscape and soul is largely an innovation of Smith's'.[70]

Smith's greatest contributions to the sonnet revival are her experimentation with imagery, rhyme and form (which included renewed interest in sonnet cycles) and her ability to bring traditional women's kinds of poetry into the cycle. These things were continued by women poets of hers and the next generation. Anna Seward used the sonnet for friendship poems, as in 'To Honora Sneyd, Whose Health was always Best in Winter'. In 1796, Mary Robinson published *Sappho and Phaon*. This sonnet cycle was on the subject of Behn's contribution to Dryden's translation of the *Heroides* and one of the many examples of the importance of Sappho to English women poets, the best of whom were always called 'our British Sappho'. Anna Seward published exactly 100 sonnets in her 1799 collection, and she thought of herself as a poet, even more, perhaps, than did Finch and Smith. It is remarkable the number of times Seward invokes the poet in the first line of her sestets. In 'To Mr Henry Cary: On the Publication of his Sonnets', 'On Reading a Description of Pope's Garden' and 'Written . . . on the Death of the Poet Laureate' the volta (or turn between the octet and sestet) is the place where she turns specifically to how each poet embodies and has achieved the heights of poetry. Seward claimed that the sonnet, 'Severest of the order', was the supreme test of poetic membership, and Helen Maria Williams chose the form to stake women's claim to the sublime.

70 Daniel Robinson, 'Reviving the Sonnet: Women Romantic Writers and the Sonnet Claim', *European Romantic Review* 6 (1995), 115.

Women continued to experiment with poetics. Amelia Opie, for example, writes a number of sonnets that experiment with overlapping and interlocked rhyme schemes. 'Sonnet to Winter', in her 1802 *Poems*, rhymes ababcbcd-edefdf, thereby moving more by conjoined tercets than quatrains. Far better is Williams' 'Sonnet to the Moon' in her novel *Julia*. A Shakespearian sonnet found by the characters near the sad ending to the novel, its smooth and lovely opening compares well to other sonnets on the moon and achieves a statement on the sonnet form and its highest purposes: 'Thy light can visionary thoughts impart, / And lead the Muse to sooth a suff'ring heart.'[71] As she moves from a specific scene to the congenial feeling between humankind and nature and then to the possibility of the leap to some visionary comfort or understanding, Williams is replicating the movement of many of Smith's sonnets and modestly prefiguring the visionary, revelatory moment in many of the sonnets of Wordsworth and Keats.

The question is always asked, 'How good are the women poets, as individuals and collectively? What is their importance in literary history and to us today? Why are they important?' But these questions suggest an ignorance of literary history. We know that literary movements are not made by single great poets; they are collective efforts that express a number of things – the taste of a time, the longings and aspirations of a people, the creative genius of a poet and the feelings of an individual writer. If nothing else, criticism of the last ten years has taught us the inadequacies and dangers of creating a literary history out of great men. No one would today represent the history of the eighteenth-century novel as the parade of the dream team (Defoe, Richardson, Fielding, Sterne, Smollett). The 'minor' novelists have been discovered to be contributors in their own right and enablers to other writers, and additional ways of assessing excellence have emerged. The concentrated work of a generation of critics accomplished this reassessment, this remapping. The same work remains for critics of Restoration and eighteenth-century poetry, and the day is fast approaching when a segregated, abbreviated chapter such as this one will seem a lamentable period piece.

71 Williams, *Julia*, vol. II, p. 173.

Systems satire: Swift.com

MICHAEL SEIDEL

Swift's satiric vision

It is one of those wonderful quirks of language and history that 'Yahoo' is now the name of an Internet search engine, whereas Jonathan Swift invented the word as the degenerate moniker for the most irredeemable creatures on earth ever to sling excrement. Swift approached the early eighteenth century as Luddites today approach the early twenty-first: the new is a source of deep anxiety.[1] Not only did Swift resist experimental science, speculative philosophy, expanded credit-based trade economy, weapons technology and colonisation, but also modern ways of dispensing information – newspapers and journals, self-help literature, mass-culture entertainments, schemes for social improvement and memoir-based narratives. The more modern, progressive, immediate something was, the more Swift's satiric inner voice was suspiciously attuned to it and infuriated by it.

Swift's satire is abundant and various, but several themes and propositions dominate his work, some of which appear in his sermons, essays, and letters as well. One recurrent Swiftian notion holds that the human race is on a degenerative path. Things get worse for Swift; they do not get better: 'But men degenerate every day, merely by the folly, the perverseness, the avarice, the tyranny, the pride, the treachery, or inhumanity of their own kind.'[2] Another notion holds that even bad things are made worse by a spirit of opposition that factionalises all institutions, ideas, loyalties. Swift writes to his friend and

---

1 Given the kind of things Swift imagined in *Gulliver's Travels* at the cutting edge of his own age's science – virtuosi trying to extract sunbeams from cucumbers or to convert human waste back to the foodstuffs from which it originated – he might have savoured the following item in the *New York Times* of 19 July 1999 under the subhead, 'Chip Designers Search for Life After Silicon': 'Researchers at the Massachusetts Institute of Technology's Laboratory of Computer Science are trying to meld the digital with the biological by hacking the common E. coli bacterium so that it would be able to function as an electronic circuit.'
2 'Further Thoughts on Religion', in *Irish Tracts and Sermons, Prose Works*, ed. Herbert Davis (Oxford: Blackwell, 1963), p. 264.

Fig. 9.1 *Jonathan Swift* by Charles Jervas (*c.* 1718)

fellow satirist, Alexander Pope, on 10 January 1721, 'the spirit of Faction hath so universally possessed the minds of men, that they are not at leisure to attend to any thing else'.[3] A similar theme launches and explains one of Swift's first

3 Faction for Swift insures a kind of gracelessness in all things. He writes to a young acquaintance, the 'universal Depravity of *Manners*, is owing to the perpetual bandying of *Factions* among us for Thirty years past' ('A Letter to a Young Gentleman, Lately enter'd into Holy Orders', in *Irish Tracts and Sermons*, p. 79).

extended satiric offerings, *The Battle of the Books*, where contention has less to do with one faction being in the right about the achievements of learning through the ages and the other in the wrong, than with the sheer nastiness attendant upon perceived intellectual, psychological and physical aggrandisement – the desire to possess all of that which would be better shared by many. Taking sides is almost by definition an immoderate act, a need to obliterate rivals. It did not take Swift the writer long to figure out that satire best represents faction because it is most like it.

Swift is an unsettling writer (and a remarkably protean one), and it is not always a simple matter to isolate his own views amidst the exacerbations of personal and cultural contentions characteristic of his work. But perhaps viewing his more famous works through the lenses of his lesser-known ones better focuses his satiric vision. Swift's 'Thoughts on Various Subjects', a series of maxims on human behaviour, on politics, on religion, on ethics is a good place to begin. Swift here appears to write in a direct, relaxed mode, though his opinions can still be savage. He recognises that the model for literary prominence he sketches in one maxim is the same model of rivalry and paranoia that suits his own deeply felt sense of failed aspirations in English political life: 'When a true Genius appears in the World, you may know him by this infallible Sign; that the Dunces are all in Confederacy against him.'[4] In another maxim, Swift explains the need for revenge in a world he feels to be censorious. 'There are but three Ways for a man to revenge himself of a censorious World: To despise it; to return the like; or to endeavour to live so as to avoid it. The first of these is usually pretended; the last is almost impossible; the universal Practice is for the second' (p. 243).

Swift's maxim gets to the core of his satire. He regards misanthropy as a pretence, even though many of his contemporaries and almost all posterity deem him one. As for stoic acceptance, Swift dismisses that reaction to a censorious world as 'almost impossible'. The practice that comes closest to what Swift achieves in his satires is a kind of mimetic revenge. 'To return the like' is not merely the talion 'tit for tat' but the satiric 'tat for tat'. Swift's satire overwhelms its objects by becoming them. So many of Swift's great works, from the complicated parody of modern writing in *A Tale of A Tub*, to the riotous astrological predictions of *The Bickerstaff Papers*, to the seafaring double talk of *Gulliver's Travels*, to the cold-hearted calculations of 'A Modest Proposal', count on a strategy of annihilation by duplication.

4 'Thoughts on Various Subjects', in *A Tale of A Tub, With Other Early Works, 1696–1707, Prose Works*, ed. Herbert Davis (Oxford: Blackwell, 1965), p. 242. Subsequent references to 'Thoughts' are from this volume.

'Thoughts on Various Subjects' also marks central thematic concerns in Swift's satire. One maxim associates the urge for self-expression with a type of hypnosis: 'Positiveness is a good Quality for Preachers and Orators; because whoever would obtrude his Thoughts and Reasons upon a Multitude, will convince others the more, as he appears convinced himself' (p. 241). The key-word for Swift is 'obtrude', and the maxim is very close to the passage in *A Tale of A Tub* where Swift's narrator describes the struggle for ascendancy in a crowd. A 'fat unwieldy Fellow' complains of getting pressed at a mounte-bank's performance in Leicester-Fields. A weaver standing next to him finally explodes:

> A Plague confound you (*said he*) for an over-grown Sloven; and who (in the Devil's name) I wonder, helps to make up the Crowd half so much as your self? Don't you consider (with a Pox) that you take up more room with that Carkass than any five here? Is not the Place as free for us as for you? Bring your own guts to a reasonable Compass (and be d–n'd) and then I'll engage we shall have room enough for us all.[5]

'Reasonable Compass' is not the rule that measures the bulk of Swift's satiric world. As the *Tale*'s narrator soon enough points out, 'Whoever hath an Ambition to be heard in a Crowd, must press, and squeeze, and thrust, and climb with indefatigable Pains, till he has exalted himself to a certain Degree of Altitude above them' (p. 55).

Swift's satiric work encourages a kind of incursion and jostling. The high mingles with the low, ancient with modern, eloquence with slang, reason with fanaticism, fastidiousness with the most grotesque tics of body and mind. Swift's satire is crowded and substantive – it mobs the reader, sweeps him or her along with the sewer muck of a rainy day in London, reveals the things that people stuff in their pockets, the quack medicines that line apothecary's counters, the dull books that fill library shelves, the endless lists that comprise catalogues. His satire conjures a cluttered space, mental or actual. When Swift defines prose style as 'Proper words in Proper places',[6] he fails to mention just how many of those words he has in mind and just how confined those places. The physical look of a passage of Swift's in print will bear this out – nouns abounding. (For confirmation, glance at the passages from the last book of *Gulliver's Travels*, cited later in this essay on pages 255–6.)

5 *A Tale of A Tub*, ed. A. C. Guthklech and D. Nicol Smith (Oxford: Clarendon Press, 1958, reprinted 1973), p. 46. Subsequent references to *A Tale* are to this edition.
6 'A Letter to a Young Gentleman', in *Irish Tracts and Sermons*, p. 65.

Moreover, Swift understands that any claim for removing one's self from the immediacies of substantive experience is rendered moot by the immediate itself, the impress of sights, sounds, smells, pains, embarrassments, discomforts, equivocations, pontifications, obtrusions. These are trivial things, but they are not trivial the moment an individual experiences them, and life itself is a collection of present intensities for Swift and for his satires, making him one of the world's great realists. The following maxim from his 'Thoughts' bears again on his satiric works. 'Reflect on Things past, as Wars, Negotiations, Factions and the like; we enter so little into those Interests, that we wonder how Men could possibly be so busy, and concerned for Things so transitory: Look on the present Times, we find the same humour, yet wonder not at all' (p. 241).

For most of his mature life Swift held a prestigious position in the Anglican Church, the Dean of St Patrick's in Ireland, but his literary concerns were always of an immediate and material nature. He rarely let his religion – which in its private way was genuine – get in the way of his satire. Indeed, when religious affairs go public, there is a sceptical imp in Swift that takes over. He writes in 'Thoughts': 'Religion seems to have grown an infant with Age, and requires Miracles to nurse it, as it had in its Infancy' (p. 242). In the world of institutions and politics, Swift sees belief systems as a weapon in a war of factional interest: 'We have just Religion enough to make us *hate*, but not enough to make us *love* one another' (p. 241). Swift does not often speak of love, and when he does its absence absolves him from accounting for it.

For Swift, religious performance and controversy usually cover over baser interests. Even the opposite of belief – infidelity – is only the focal point of a greater material corruption, the mechanism that allows entrepreneurial forces within a culture to profit by the introduction of luxury at the expense of morality. Swift writes to a young man about to take orders in the church, and the cleverness of his phrasing connects unbelief to commerce: 'I therefore again conclude, that the Trade of *Infidelity* hath been taken up only for an Expedient to keep in Countenance that universal Corruption of *Morals*, which many other Causes first contributed to introduce and cultivate.'[7] From here it is but a short path to Swift's openly satiric remarks in his pseudo-free-thinking tract 'Argument Against the Abolishing of Christianity' that divides the core of religious doctrine from the public institution of the church: 'Nor do I think

---

7 *Ibid.*, p. 80.

it wholly groundless, or my Fears altogether imaginary; that the Abolishing of Christianity may perhaps bring the Church in Danger.[8]

When Swift deals with belief or the supernatural he converts what is unknowable into what is sociable or soothing or admonitory. There are instances in his writing on religious systems – ones not comfortably cited by Swift's more conservative critics – that sound his scepticism and bear on each and every one of his satiric creations. Like many of the early eighteenth-century freethinkers and atheists he attacks in his satires or commentaries,[9] Swift sees a disturbing relation between religion and hypocrisy: 'The want of belief is a defect that ought to be concealed when it cannot be overcome.'[10] Or: 'Although the number of pretended Christians be great, yet that of true believers, in proportion to the other, was never so small.'[11] Swift at his most radical distrusts the inexplicable insofar as individuals try to explain it. Those who too fervently claim to see non-verifiable things are in essence mad. In a maxim from 'Thoughts on Various Subjects,' Swift writes of mystics and second sightings, but his words serve for any visionary system. 'One Argument to prove that the common Relations of *Ghosts* and *Spectres* are generally false; may be drawn from the Opinion held that Spirits are never seen by more than one Person at a Time; That is to say it seldom happens that above one person in a Company is possest with any high Degree of Spleen or Melancholy' (p. 242).

What Swift makes clear here is not only his reluctance to base contra-demonstrative convictions on the testimony of believers, but a hint that such things are the product of a kind of lunacy. What begins with individual expression – in religion, in philosophy, in politics – soon enough approximates mass hysteria. *A Tale of A Tub*'s 'Digression on Madness' explains what happens, and it is no accident that Swift's phrasing is religious. 'When a Man's Fancy gets *astride* on his Reason, when Imagination is at cuffs with the Senses, and common Understanding, as well as common Sense, is Kickt out of Doors; the first Proselyte he makes, is Himself, and when that is once compass'd, the Difficulty is not so great in bringing over others' (p. 171). It may be that Swift's satires, in one way or another, are all digressions on madness. Even the

---

8 'Argument Against the Abolishing of Christianity', in *Bickerstaff Papers, and Pamphlets on the Church, Prose Works*, ed. Herbert Davis (Oxford: Blackwell, 1966), p. 36.

9 See, for example, 'Mr Collins's [Anthony Collins] Discourse of Free-Thinking' and 'Some Thoughts on Free-Thinking', in 'A Proposal for Correcting the English Tongue'; 'Polite Conversation', etc., *Prose Works* ed., Herbert Davis (Oxford: Blackwell, 1964), pp. 23–48; 49–50.

10 'Thoughts on Religion', in *Irish Tracts and Sermons*, p. 261.

11 'A Sermon upon the Excellency of Christianity', in *Irish Tracts and Sermons*, p. 249.

supposed fictional witnessing of personally presented events, say, in *Gulliver's Travels* – the entire series of incidents we are to take on the faith of the fictional contract: little people, giants, flying islands, talking horses – is more likely a projection of Gulliver's own crazed convictions upon multitudes.

Satiric practitioner

Paying close attention to Swift in action is the best way to get a sense of the force of his satire. Near the beginning of a familiar work, 'A Modest Proposal', a document purporting to solve Ireland's overpopulation problem in consort with the spirit of economic expediency and national projecting characteristic of the time, readers encounter the following passage.

> I think it is agreed by all Parties, that this prodigious Number of Children in the Arms, or on the Backs, or at the *Heels* of their *Mothers*, and frequently of their *Fathers*, is *in the present deplorable State of the Kingdom*, a very great additional Grievance; and therefore, whoever could find out a fair, cheap, and easy Method of making these Children sound and useful members of the Commonwealth, would deserve so well of the Publick, as to have his Statue set up for a Preserver of the Nation.[12]

The passage seems so inconsequential in comparison to the immodesty of the proposal itself that a reader might miss Swift's point, one that controls the satiric direction of the whole: the tract is immodest before it even issues its most outrageously modest proposal. Readers usually pay so much attention to the outlandish solution for Ireland – cannibalism – that they miss or underestimate the real driving force of the essay – the pushy, self-infatuated, jostling, insistent nature of a projector, whose calculated rhetoric obscures what is always primary in a modern projector's mind, the need for validation in a world of competing interests and deep professional rivalries. The fictional apparatus behind Swift's famous tract is less the metaphor of cannibalism, which is transparent in its absurdity, than the vainglory of the projector.

The alluring 'Statue' in the last sentence of the cited passage hovers over the entire tract. Does the writer think he will get one? What kind of projector would want one? What has happened to the modesty trope in writing, one so essential to generate readerly esteem? How do readers react to the proposal if it is confused with the underlying ambitions of the proposer? Swift's satire almost always resides uncomfortably inside a zone where the

---

12 Swift, 'A Modest Proposal', in *Irish Tracts, 1728–1733, Prose Works*, ed. Herbert Davis (Oxford: Blackwell, 1964), p. 109. Subsequent references are to this edition.

writing voice at once makes his satiric points and *is* his satiric point. A passage near the end of 'A Modest Proposal' complicates matters to an even greater extent.

> I PROFESS, in the Sincerity of my heart, that I have not the least personal interest, in endeavouring to promote this necessary Work; having no other Motive than the *publick Good of my Country, by advancing our Trade, providing for Infants, relieving the Poor, and giving some Pleasure to the Rich.* I have no children, by which I can propose to get a single Penny; the youngest being nine Years old, and my Wife past Child-bearing.
> (p. 118)

What happened to the statue? Unawareness and forgetting are modern characteristics in Swift's satire, and the immodesty trope does not go away merely because the projector articulates the integrity trope. Of course, he bases that integrity not on the premise that eating his nine-year-old daughter would be wrong, but that eating her would be sinewy and tasteless in the literal sense. Moreover, are we to presume it would be a benefit to have a child young enough to be killed, butchered, fricasseed, and eaten? What kind of a human soul would defend his integrity by arguing that it would be dishonest rather than cruel if he had an edible child at his disposal? This much, I suppose, we can grasp. But who controls the irony of cannibalism's '*giving some Pleasure to the Rich*'? Swift or the projector?

Whenever Swift's personal voice melds with his narrator's voice there is discomfort in his satire.[13] With a decade to go in his life (though Swift could hardly be sure of that) he wrote an apologia for his career in tetrameters, a conventionally satiric meter, 'Verses on the Death of Dr Swift'. The poem does as much as any in Swift's satiric canon to elaborate his thinking about his own place in the world of eighteenth-century life and literature, and about the propensities of his satiric nature. Swift begins his 'Verses' with a tortuous Rochefoucault maxim. Neither the French nor the English can quite say it straight. Here is the French: 'Dans l'adversité de nos meilleurs amis nous trouvons quelque chose, qui ne nous deplaist pas.' Here is Swift's translation:

---

13 One of the vexed issues in Swift criticism over many years involves the degree to which Swift's voice is ironically layered over, saturated through or distanced from the host of his narrative impersonations. It seems to me that the best response is different degrees in different ways at different times. Claude Rawson records the views of many when he describes 'the closeness of Swift's relation to the rhetorical postures he assumed through his fictional *personae*, a relation that oscillates between direct congruence and the kind of intimate mirror-opposition where self and anti-self complete one another' ('The Character of Swift's Satire: Reflections on Swift, Johnson, and Human Restlessness', in Rawson (ed.), *The Character of Swift's Satire: A Revised Focus* (Newark, DE: University of Delaware Press, 1983), p. 49).

'In the Adversity of our best Friends, we find something that doth not displease us.'[14] The double negative ('not dis . . .') makes the point with deference and distance. 'Something that displeases us' would be too normal; 'something that pleases us' too direct.

A similar maxim in Swift's own 'Thoughts on Various Subjects' hints that there is a kind of pleasure in what ought to be our own pain of loss: 'If a man will observe as he walks the Streets, I believe he will find the merriest Countenances in Mourning-Coaches' (p. 245). The death of a relative or friend may be unsettling, but the grammar of mourning creates a grace period of sorts for the human ego. I am not dead yet.

Swift's 'Verses' allow him to extend the implications of the maxim that begins it. There is something even in the projection of our own death the does not displease us, providing we can remain alive to record the aftermath. Swift begins his own poem by satirising its author's voice as dead before it speaks: '*Verses on the Death of Doctor Swift. Written by Himself.*' Nominally, 'Verses' is about the hypocrisy of Swift's friends. They worry over his age and infirmity, but truly wish that his ills innoculate them against their own: 'In such a Case they talk in Tropes, / And, by their Fears express their Hopes' (lines 117–18). In another sense, Swift's imagined death gives him one more chance to impose himself. Swift in this poem wants it both ways. He wants to be dead so he can reveal the truth about those who knew him; but he also wants to be dead so he might sketch yet one more time the intense rivalry that defines his sense of things in a contentious world.

> Give others Riches, Power, and Station,
> 'Tis all on me an Usurpation.
>
> (lines 43–4)

In a series of self-assessments – all in a document that holds hypocrisy to be the mark of individual expression – Swift claims that he represents values almost completely uncharacteristic of his time. The only problem is that many of these claims are designedly and immediately recognisable as partial truths or outright lies. Swift's friends would have probably known both the inaccuracies and the pleasure Swift took in them. More important, Swift as poet would recognise the lie – even manipulate it – whereas Swift as character in the poem may not. If the pretext of 'Verses' is self-love, the subtext is self-delusion. Indeed, Swift makes a point in the poem that surfaces in most all

14 *Swift's Poems*, ed. Harold Williams, 3 vols. (Oxford: Clarendon Press, 1937; second edition, 1958), vol. II, p. 551. Subsequent references are to this edition.

his satire: no one's vision of himself is ever valid when the context confuses or contaminates the motives of self-representation. The refusal to see one's own face in the mirror of satire is a kind of guaranteed delusion: 'Satyr is a sort of *Glass*, where Beholders do generally discover every body's Face but their Own.'[15] It is difficult to look in a glass and not see one's reflection. Even Gulliver in his miserable days at the end of his *Travels* sees his reflection when he looks, though he does not like the image: 'When I happened to behold the Reflection of my own Form in a lake or Fountain I turned away my Face in Horror and detestation of my self; and could better endure the Sight of a common *Yahoo*, than of my own Person.'[16] To look at a reflection and see nothing one has to sneak up on the mirror, or tilt it. Of course, if hypocrisy is the image represented, a reader can look it full in the face and act as if the image seen is someone or something else unseen. In 'Verses' Swift consciously resists seeing himself as he is, and deliberately creates a vision of himself recollected by another, a supposedly objective friend. But there are no objective friends. The ground or territory upon which accurate judgements exist in the poem is treacherous. Plausible and intelligent things said about Swift merge with the most grandiose of misstatements and distortions.

Early in the poem, Swift records his pride of place in relation to irony: 'Who dares to Irony pretend; / Which I was born to introduce, / Refin'd it first, and shew'd its Use' (lines 56–8). The pride is merited, but the irony that Swift uses most effectively is directed against the very tone of voice that here claims credit for it. Swift next plays out the 'woe is me' trope, the noble being in a degenerate era, neither fit nor ready for the changes that time exacts on those of advancing age. Swift's ear is a magnificent one. When the day of Swift's death arrives in his own imagination, he renders it, as he always does, by sounding the idioms of the moment: 'What has he left? And who's his Heir?' (line 154). Or, if the news arrives in the middle of a card game, 'The Dean is dead, (*and what is Trumps?*)' (line 228).

Swift's own voice (silenced) can no longer defend his life, but he can supply a 'what if?' What if an observer steps forward, 'One quite indifferent in the cause, / My Character impartial draws' (lines 305–6). The maxim of the poem would deny the possibility of the premise, and we already know by Swift's admission that the poem is written 'By Himself'. The briefest of looks at this impartial tribute belies the writer's self as he would have others see it. In the

15 'The Preface' to *The Battle of the Books*, in *A Tale of A Tub*, eds. Guthkelch and Smith, p. 215.
16 *Gulliver's Travels*, ed. Herbert Davis (Oxford: Blackwell, 1965), p. 278. Subsequent references are to this edition.

following lines very little is true about Swift's ambitions, attitudes or practices. Readers might credit his book sales and his originality, even his irony (though not its gravity). Readers might accept subsequent remarks on the effect of his *Drapier's Letters* in changing state policy,[17] and, later yet, the observation that too much satire flowed in his veins, but the bulk of his self-portrait is recognisable only as distortion. Almost every line here is problematic for those who knew the course of Swift's stifled (but expressed) ambitions and the bitterness of his career in regard to his early professional and political desires.[18] A proper commentary on the following lines would require something like a counter-biography.

> The Dean, if we believe Report,
> Was never ill receiv'd at Court:
> As for his Works in Verse and Prose,
> I own my self no Judge of those:
> Nor, can I tell what Critics thought 'em;
> But this I know, all People bought 'em;
> As with a moral View design'd
> To cure the Vices of Mankind:
> His Vein, ironically grave,
> Expos'd the Fool and lash'd the Knave:
> To steal a Hint was never known,
> But what he writ was all his own.
> He never thought an Honour done him,
> Because a Duke was proud to own him:
> Would rather slip aside, and chuse
> To talk with Wits in dirty Shoes:
> Despis'd the Fools with Stars and Garters,
> So often seen caressing *Chartres*:
> He never courted Men in Station,

17 *The Drapier's Letters* is perhaps the only work of Swift's that actually accomplished something politically concrete by encouraging the Irish to resist a planned English debasement of their coinage. But in those tracts Swift abjures almost all satire in order to get the Irish to take specific tactical action in regard to the debasing of coin: 'What I intend now to say to you, is, next to your duty to God, and the Care of your Salvation, of the greatest Concern to your selves, and your Children; your *Bread* and your *Cloathing*, and every common necessary of Life entirely depend upon it' (*The Drapier's Letters*, ed. Herbert Davis (Oxford: Blackwell, 1966), p. 3).

18 For example, Swift writes to Pope on 10 January 1721: 'I have conversed in some freedom with more Ministers of State of all Parties than usually happens to men of my level, and I confess, in their capacity as ministers, I look upon them as a race of people whose acquaintance no man would court, otherwise than upon the score of Vanity or Ambition.' *Correspondence*, ed. Harold Williams, 5 vols. (Oxford: Clarendon Press, 1963–5).

> *Nor persons had in Admiration;*
> Of no Man's greatness was afraid,
> Because he sought for no Man's Aid.
> Though trusted long in great Affairs,
> He gave himself no haughty Airs:
> Without regarding private Ends,
> Spent all his Credit for his Friends:
>   (lines 307–32)

One almost does not know where to begin. To say Swift was well received at court is to substitute hope for experience. All but one of his books were anonymously published. His aim was to vex, not cure.[19] Swift lashed more fools than he could count. Originality is unclear in a parodist. He took pride in his well-placed acquaintances and thought very little of dirty shoes, no matter who wore them. He courted men in station and sought aid for years on end, and envied peers aplenty. He gave himself airs when he felt like it, and he squirrelled considerable funds away for his own uses.

Swift cannot resist the urge to employ the elegiac form and then lie. But who exactly is supposed to be fooled? Is the joke a product of his own self-deprecating wit? Or is he emptying out another form again – the elegy – with obvious lies? Or has he written so often of values that belong to another time and another place that he believes he truly represents them by virtue of some mythical rewriting of the past? Could it be that Swift's true measure as a satirist is the realisation that the present always rewrites the past and that experience, really, is one long extended collection of moments in which humankind acts the same way – that is, badly, blindly and blissfully ignorant? The 'Verses' end with Swift in Irish exile, one last lie ('Was chearful to his dying Day'), and one last point about satire itself, that it literally pays to erect the house whose inhabitants it attacks:

> He gave the little Wealth he had,
> To build a House for Fools and mad:
> And shew'd by one satyric touch,
> No Nation wanted it so much.
>   (lines 479–82)

---

19 Swift has his doubts about satire as ameliorative, prophetic, or didactic, though he might except his *Drapier's Letters*, a work that helped save Ireland from yet another of many economic disasters at the hands of the English. Here is what Swift thinks generally about writers effecting change in satire or in any work: 'How is it possible to expect that mankind will take *Advice*, when they will not so much as take *Warning*' ('Thoughts on Various Subjects', in *A Tale of A Tub, Etc.*, ed. Davis, p. 241).

Swift and company

Swift is far and away the dominant satirist of his age, but he shared certain perspectives with others. In 'Verses' he presents a sketch of the contemporary history of the mode in which he writes, setting out the violent rhetoric of affiliation that characterises his time. Swift attributes the contentiousness of his work and that of the rest of his friends to the death of Queen Anne in 1714 and the coming in of the Whig ministry under the new Hanoverian kings (the first two Georges). The accuracy of Swift's presentation is not so much at issue as its conspiratorial bent. England embarks upon a new course of ruin that begins for Swift with an echo of revolutionary phrases from the previous century ('*By solemn League and Cov'nant bound*') and ends with his own exile in Ireland. Queen Anne dies, and here is what Swift pictures.

> When up a dangerous Faction starts,
> With Wrath and Vengeance in their Hearts:
> *By solemn League and Cov'nant bound*,
> To ruin, slaughter, and confound;
> To turn Religion to a Fable,
> And make the government a *Babel*:
> Pervert the law, disgrace the Gown,
> Corrupt the Senate, rob the Crown;
> To sacrifice old *England*'s Glory,
> And make her infamous in Story.
> When such a Tempest shook the land,
> How could unguarded Virtue stand?
>   With Horror, Grief, Despair the Dean
> Beheld the dire destructive Scene:
> His Friends in Exile, or the Tower,
> Himself within the Frown of Power;
> Pursu'd by base envenom'd Pens,
> Far to the Land of Slaves and Fens;
> A servile Race in Folly nurs'd,
> Who truckle most, when treated worst.
>   (lines 379–98)

Such is Swift's version, and for decades most literary historians ascribed to something like the scene Swift sketches for the new age of governmental and cultural life in England with the coming of the Hanoverians. Interpreters tended to operate under assumptions that were at once comforting in their clarity and distancing in their simplicity. The hard lines of satiric opposition from the early eighteenth century through the last decade of the Robert Walpole regime in the 1740s form around conserving Tory sensibilities and expanding Whig ones. Conserving Tories detested progressivists Whigs; civilised ancients disdained tasteless moderns; aristocratic poets found the middle-class novelists unbearable; the landed gentry distrusted the new monied men; glory fought priggish conscience; fideistic religion resisted enlightened doubt; gold laughed at credit. For mid twentieth-century literary historians, as for Swift, the newer culture of parliamentary government, financial markets and popular culture took a considerable toll on values of honour, integrity, class, the nobler literary forms, the quality and purity of language, the aesthetic measures of art, the ideals of scholarship, connoisseurship and taste.

More recent literary historians take a different approach, less a sorting out of how extremes register than of how positions meander and oscillate. One of the primary shifts in the practice of literary history over the last half-century is the elimination of literary winners and losers. Critics used to look for certain qualities in the works and writers they admired, and then assume those qualities reflected the rightness of aesthetic, moral or historical principles. To read mid twentieth-century literary histories – many of them astute in defence of style and intelligence – is to come upon the same nostalgically generated values summarised by Gulliver among the utopian Houhynhnms in the last book of the *Travels*, values reflecting interests unencumbered by impertinences of real time: 'Their Subjects are generally on Friendship and Benevolence; on Order and Oeconomy; sometimes upon the visible Operations of Nature, or ancient Traditions; upon the Bounds and Limits of Virtue; upon the unerring Rules of Reason; or upon some Determinations, to be taken at the next great Assembly; and often upon the various Excellencies of *Poetry*' (pp. 277–8).

Such timeless and implicitly judgemental criticism has given way over the course of the last fifty years to more analytical literary history. Forces that determine systems of taste, systems of thought, systems of representation are subject to the very analysis that used to produce taste, thought and representation. Therefore, the stability of traditional oppositions, though plausible in some nominal sense, has blurred over the years. Swift and Pope may have railed against the civil list and new money men of Walpole's government and the entire set of cultural assumptions connected to material values, but both of them were investors and lived in the world of financial dealings initiated by those they purportedly derided. Moreover, Swift's own political views, expressed explicitly in a letter to Pope, sound very like the same Whig dispensation against which he came to be so firmly rooted.[20]

One way to understand early eighteenth-century satire – especially that produced by those most critical of the newer Walpolian and Hanoverian orders – is to grasp that the game is over almost before it begins. By the time satirists pretend to recognise what they consider degenerate features of human or cultural experience, there is little hope of restoring those features to a previous condition, primarily because they probably never existed that way in the first place. Satire venerates a past to abuse and two-time the present.[21] When the Hanoverians came to power and when Swift and a group of his friends and fellow poets – Alexander Pope, John Gay, John Arbuthnot, Thomas Parnell, Robert Harley – broke off from what had been intellectual and cultural alliances with another group of wits led by Joseph Addison and his Kit-Kat Club, satiric animosity crystallised around the new Whig-oriented ruling order in England. Swift and others felt that the cultural productions of the age followed suit with what they deemed a modern barbarism in politics.

To the extent that the group forming Swift's circle share a focus – the satirists who mockingly named themselves the Scriblerians after the club they formed to create a composite satiric project in which they would represent under the rubric of a modern scribbling pedant's memoirs all they viewed in the age as corrupt, banal, stupid and tasteless – their work takes shape as attacks on systems in contemporary life that exist in large measure as the products of their own exaggerated invention. That is why the best Scriblerian satire is often more contemporary than the contemporary objects under attack. The

---

20 In his letter of 10 January 1721, Swift writes to Pope of his 'old' Whiggism, his positive stance on the 1688 Williamite succession, his anti-Jacobite position against divine right without law and 'opinions of the people'. He is against standing armies in peace time (later satirised by Gulliver in Lilliput); he is for annual parliaments because longer terms let in corruption; he favours cooperation between landed and monied interests, but prefers the former as more stable; he favours laws securing personal liberties of people, and is against any suspension of those laws, which he sees as tyranny. He restates these principles in an odd piece, 'Of Publick Absurdityes in England' (in *Miscellaneous and Autobiographical Pieces, Fragments, and Marginalia*, ed. Herbert Davis (Oxford: Blackwell, 1962), pp. 79–82).

21 Swift points to the past as a simpler, purer time, and, indeed, in a general way he connects simplicity to perfection: 'In short, that Simplicity, without which no human Performance can arrive to any great Perfection' ('A Letter to a Young Gentleman', in *Irish Tracts and Sermons*, p. 68). For many satirists, and no less so for Swift, simplicity is but a saving device to project estimable values far enough into the past so that even history is not really responsible for them. Swift's fascination with primitive Christianity is a similar case in point. The values he associates with the purer form of earlier Christianity are merely conveniences for abusing the present.

Scriblerians organised for the sole purpose of out-modernising the moderns. Theirs was a joint-venture company of abusive parody directed at popular public culture, government spoils and the expanded world of hack writers and periodical publishing. Alexander Pope's response to what he presented as the material aestheticism of his age was a massive send-up of contemporary clap-trap and popular taste, *The Dunciad*. John Gay's operatic vision of high-waymen, public servants and (by implication) politicians in the *Beggar's Opera* is a farcically comic representation of the contamination of the public sphere by the private. John Arbuthnot contributed the saga of the entrepreneurial John Bull, who much later in the eighteenth century became the cartoon representative of British imperial 'interests', a pot-bellied bourgeois with bad taste in plaids. Swift's reaction to what he saw as the loss of an ethical or religious core in modern England is a series of literary works that display as endemic the supposedly vacuous systems of government, new science and modern economy his satire was so adept at portraying.

'Systems satire' – to give it a name – is not satire against specific individuals, though there was a great deal of that, but against individuals who seem to stand for some sort of systemically distorted pattern in the culture. Systems satire assumes the part and whole are in cahoots; it represents a connection among seemingly disparate things – political life, familial life, professional life, cultural life, aesthetic life.[22] Swift makes the connection for his own age in a letter to Pope on 10 January 1721: 'I have been much concerned for several years past, upon account of the publick as well as of myself, to see how ill a taste for wit and sense prevails in the world, which politicks and South-Sea, and Party, and Operas and Masquerades have introduced.' In a note to a contemporary journal, *The Craftsman*, Swift writes about the head of the system, Robert Walpole, treasurer and then prime minister under the first Hanoverians, and nurturer of the 'Spoils System' of national government.

> His personal qualities are all derived into the most minute parts of his admin-istration. If this be just, prudent, regular, impartial, intent upon the public good, prepared for present exigencies, and provident of the future; such is the director himself in his private capacity: If it be rapacious, insolent, partial, palliating long and deep diseases of the public with empirical remedies, false, disguised, impudent, malicious, revengeful; you shall infallibly find the private life of the conductor to answer in every point; nay, what is more, every twinge of the gout or gravel will be felt in their consequences by the community.[23]

22 Modern-day examples of systems satire appear in such encyclopedic narratives as Joseph Heller's *Catch 22*, or Thomas Pynchon's *Crying of Lot 49* and *Gravity's Rainbow*.
23 'A Letter to the Writer of an Occasional Paper', in *Irish Tracts and Sermons*, p. 97.

The root idea in systems satire of the early eighteenth century is that the lure of the new expansionist money economy separates literary and social practices from every value but material ones. In his *Examiner* periodical, Swift comments on the formation of a credit economy to finance the long War of Spanish Succession. What began as necessary ends as universally abusive.

> By this means the Wealth of the Nation, that used to be reckoned by the Value of Land, is now computed by the Rise and Fall of Stocks: And although the Foundation of Credit be still the same, and upon a Bottom that can never be shaken; and although all interest be duly paid by the Public, yet through the Contrivance and Cunning of *Stock-Jobbers*, there hath been brought in such a Complication of Knavery and Couzenage, such a Mystery of Iniquity, and such an unintelligible *Jargon* of Terms to involve it in, as were never known in any other Age or Country of the World.[24]

A key principle in systems satire is conspiratorial conversion. Finance turns to fraud and affects all actions and activities, from trade to language transmission. For the Scriblerian satirist, the symbols of the Hanoverian system extend everywhere: failed families, ruined libraries, rabble-dominated theatres, immoral public places, tasteless buildings, corrupt deals, inflated, fraudulent and dull books, and a seeming inability to communicate in readable or speakable language. Swift in his satires and other works blames the debasement of language squarely on the pseudo professionalism of the modern age: 'Professors in most Arts and Sciences are generally the worst qualified to explain their Meanings to those who are not of their Tribe.'[25] It is the mixture of contemporary language systems – specialised vocabularies and nomenclatures – and the newer forms of memoir writing in which even the most middling merchant or professional or low life felt the impulse to record experience in printed form that served as the basis for most of Swift's systems satire and for the Scriblerian project in general.

Those writers who commit pen to paper in professional or, worse yet, low-life memoirs, are those Swift's own Gulliver (who is one of them) ironically condemns: 'I know very well, how little Reputation is to be got by Writings which require neither Genius nor Learning, nor indeed any other Talent, except a good Memory, or an exact *Journal*' (*Gulliver's Travels*, p. 292).[26] Who

---

24 *Examiner* for 2 November 1710 in *The Examiner, 1710–1711*, ed. Herbert Davis (Oxford: Blackwell, 1966), pp. 6–7.
25 'A Letter to a Young Gentleman', in *Irish Tracts and Sermons*, p. 66.
26 In *A Tale of A Tub*, Swift mocks the practice of publishing the last words of condemned criminals: 'I am informed, that worthy Citizen and bookseller, Mr *John Dunton*, hath made a faithful and a painful Collection, which he shortly designs to publish in Twelve Volumes in Folio, illustrated with Copper-Plates' (p. 59).

are these figures (some of them derelicts) who make up the backbone of the new voluminous vogue in journalistic narrative and memoir? The new secular modernists – government experts, academic virtuosi, cultural dilettantes – compose one group, and Swift's Gulliver hints at another when he describes for his Master Houyhnhnm in the last book of the *Travels* the scum with whom he has been sharing shipboard company for the latter part of his voyaging life, the adventurers who become the symbol of the John Dunton or Daniel Defoe-like fictional egos, those

> Fellows of desperate Fortunes, forced to fly from the Places of their Birth on Account of their Poverty or their Crimes. Some were undone by Law-suits; others spent all they had in Drinking, Whoring and Gaming; others fled for Treason; many for Murder, Theft, Poysoning, Robbery, Perjury, Forgery, Coining false Money; for committing Rapes or Sodomy; for flying from their Colours, or deserting to the Enemy; and most of them had broken Prison. None of these durst return to their native Countries for fear of being hanged, or of starving in a Jail; and therefore were under a Necessity of seeking a Livelihood in other Places. (pp. 243–4)

Swift carefully tracked the careers of those he considered down-class liter-ary entrepreneurs of the early eighteenth century. His *A Tale of A Tub* is, among other things, a compilation of hack-work parodies by an on-the-make literary adventurer not unlike the gadabout John Dunton, whose autobiography, *The Life and Errors of John Dunton Late Citizen of London* (1705), detailed the long trail of hack productions that made him the premier literary street sweeper of his time. Swift also enjoyed a career-long haunting of Daniel Defoe, a kind of par-odic séance in which Swift would find a way of mocking every pseudo-serious invented biography or autobiography that Defoe produced, culminating in *Gulliver's Travels*, which so painstakingly plays off and undermines *Robinson Crusoe*. It is no coincidence that Gulliver's wife lives off Newgate street, where Defoe spent so many uncomfortable months in prison; nor is it an accident that Gulliver in the third book ships out with a Captain Robinson, who is almost, as he puts it, a brother to him.

The paradox of systems satire – Swift's in particular – is that it feeds off the very energy of the forms it attacks. In *A Tale of A Tub*, the narrator writes of the 'superficial Vein among many Readers of the present Age' (p. 66), yet the whole of *A Tale* is a brilliant counterfeit of disposable literary forms and exercises. That is why most of its chapters are labelled 'digressions'. Modern writers require a wider domain of expression – more forms of writing. So Swift proposes the digression as a model for expansion of writerly terrain, a kind of perpetual inbetweenness. The same tactic appears again in Swift's designedly incoherent, *Tritical Essay upon the Faculties of the Mind*, where the essayist can barely finish a fragmented thought before seeking or grasping for another. Swift is at his best here as he revs the engine of superficiality to incredibly high speeds with almost no torque. The parody consists of a series of what he locates in others as 'thread-bare Quotations' loosely strung together. He begins by attacking the epicurean notion that 'the Universe was formed by a fortuitous Concourse of Atoms',[27] but the shape and design of the entire parody is exactly as the supposedly unlikely epicurean paradigm would have it. The essay is a prescription for coherence, but altogether randomly shaped.

Swift's satiric attacks are based not only on his ideological dislikes but also on the language in which ideas displeasing to him are conveyed. Writing reveals writers for who they are. It is never merely the assumptions, biases, prejudices, wrong-headedness of a position or an idea that irritates Swift, but the way those assumptions, biases, prejudices and wrong-headedness emerge in writing. His satire is ideographical. Language in the service of trash is at the heart of modernism for Swift, and even in his private marginalia (reading notes) he cannot give the subject up. He scribbles derisively of Gilbert Burnet's *History of My Own Times* that the author seems to write in a language that only barely resembles English. So that when Burnet praises Milton's *Paradise Lost* as the best poem that 'ever was writ, at least in our language', Swift slyly comments, 'A mistake for it is *in English*'.[28] In a letter to Pope on 20 April 1731, Swift calls life 'a ridiculous tragedy, which is the worst kind of composition'. For Swift, neither his human subjects nor his readers can escape bad 'composition'.

Model Scriblerians

Two fictional characters by the Scriblerians best attest to the power of systems satire in the earlier eighteenth century: Martinus Scriblerus and Lemuel Gulliver. The *Memoirs of the Extraordinary Life, Works, and Discoveries of Martinus Scriblerus* (1741), for which contributions were solicited by all the Scriblerians, was intended as a kind of mock-compendium of living, learning, travelling, loving, writing. Though some of the assignments were completed, much of the material compiled ended up elsewhere. For example, all of *Gulliver's Travels* derived from Pope's instructions to Swift for a Martinus chapter on travelling

---

27 *Tritical Essay*, in *A Tale of A Tub, Etc.*, ed. Davis, pp. 246–7.
28 'Marginalia', in *Miscellaneous and Autobiographical Pieces*, p. 270.

to a land of midgets, giants, virtuosi and melancholics. Other material ended up in transmuted form in works influenced by the Scriblerian venture. Some of the idiocies of the chapters on education reappear in the Tristra-paedia of Sterne's *Tristram Shandy*. But there is probably nothing so overtly ridiculous as the chapter on Martin in love with the Siamese twins from a London freak show, Lindamira and Indamora, a piece of nonsense that sends up every romance novelist from Aphra Behn to Eliza Haywood.

The *summa* of systems satire is the expansive and vituperative last book of *Gulliver's Travels* (1726) where Gulliver discourses to the Master Houyhnhnm on subjects reflecting the full Scriblerian agenda 'of Trade and Manufactures, of Arts and Sciences' (p. 245). As usual for Swift, the focus is on post-1688 English and European history, culminating in the War of Spanish Succession and the last years of Queen Anne, the subjects of two of Swift's serious books, *Conduct of the Allies* and *The History of the Four Last Years of Queen Anne*. It is no coincidence that Gulliver's last voyage corresponds to these same years, 1710 to 1714 (adding on, for good measure, 1715, the year in which Swift's patrons, ministers of state and fellow Scriblerians, Robert Harley and Henry St John Bolingbroke, faced charges for crimes against the state). Gulliver in the last book spares no thing, person or institution. 'In the Tryal of Persons accused for Crimes against the State the Method is much more short and commendable: The Judge first sends to sound the Disposition of those in Power, after which he can easily hang or save the Criminal, strictly preserving all due Forms of Law' (p. 250).

The ironic 'commendable' in reference to the state trials of Oxford and Bolingbroke is much more a reflex of Swift the satirist than Gulliver the modern adventurer. Indeed, at this point in the narrative Gulliver begins to sound most like Swift and his Scriblerian friends. The more Gulliver rants at all the modern professions, from statesman to lawyer to physician, the more difficult it is to separate his former progressivist and patriotic voice from the sneer of the systems satirist. Swift tries to finesse the matter by hinting that the mere strain of trying to describe modern England and Europe to a horse in the last book of the *Travels* forces Gulliver to change his perspective, but this makes little sense. It is much easier to imagine Gulliver isolated in his own country in the first place for harbouring views so inimical to the progress of modern culture and then inventing the *Travels* as a way of giving shape and vent to his discontent. Gulliver offers the standard Scriblerian argument that money and trade lead to luxury, the root of oppression, greed and virtually everything else that allows the focus on one subject to produce an indictment of all modern cultural activities.

Therefore since *Money* alone was able to perform all these Feats, our *Yahoos* thought they could never have enough of it to spend or to save, as they found themselves inclined from their natural Bent either to Profusion or Avarice. That the rich Man enjoyed the Fruit of the poor Man's Labour, and the latter were a Thousand to One in Proportion to the former. That the Bulk of our People were forced to live miserably, by labouring every Day for small Wages to make a few live plentifully.   (p. 251)

Gulliver continues: 'Hence it follows of Necessity that the vast Numbers of our People are compelled to seek their Livelihood by Begging, Robbing, Stealing, Cheating, Pimping, Forswearing, Flattering, Suborning, Forging, Gaming, Lying, Fawning, Hectoring, Voting, Scribling, Stargazing, Poysoning, Whoring, Canting, Libelling, Free-thinking, and the like Occupations' (p. 252).

One might wonder in the array of vices attributed to trade why Gulliver adds such Swiftian satiric subjects as stargazing (*Bickerstaff Papers*) or 'free-thinking' ('Argument Against the Abolishing of Christianity') to the list. But that misses the point. The list expands to include anything and everything. By the time Gulliver gets to his generic description of the statesman who runs the vast machinery of corruption and spoils in the modern nation he has absorbed the common anti-Walpolian rhetoric of the age. Gulliver uses the word that finally epitomises the system, 'Spoils'. 'That these *Ministers* having all Employments at their Disposal, preserve themselves in Power by bribing the Majority of a Senate or great Council; and at last by an Expedient called an *Act of Indemnity* (whereof I described the nature to him) they secure themselves from After-reckonings, and retire from the Publick, laden with the Spoils of the Nation' (p. 255).

A long paragraph sums up Gulliver's newly conceived view of his experiences in Houyhnhnmland (where at least some of the residents would like to execute him) in contrast to his experiences at home, which he seems not to have noticed for most of the years of his life or his voyages. The result is the most sustained piece of Scriblerian systems satire in all of Swift, one that turns its back, finally, on the milieu that Swift might have imagined for himself had he entered public life in any serious way back in England. Gulliver boasts of his condition as exile in horseland.

> I enjoyed perfect health of Body, and Tranquility of Mind; I did not feel the Treachery or Inconstancy of a Friend, nor the Injuries of a secret or open Enemy. I had no Occasion of bribing, flattering or pimping, to procure the Favour of any Great Man, or his Minions. I wanted no Fence against Fraud or Oppression: Here was neither Physician to destroy my Body, nor Lawyer to ruin my Fortune: Nor Informer to watch my Words and Actions,

or forge Accusations against me for Hire: Here were no Gibers, Censurers, Backbiters, Pickpockets, Highwaymen, House-breakers, Attorneys, Bawds, Buffoons, Gamesters, Politicians, Wits, Spleneticks, tedious Talkers, Controversists, Ravishers, Murderers, Robbers, Virtuosi; no Leaders or Followers of Party and Faction; no Encouragers to Vice, by Seducement or Examples: No Dungeon, Axes, Gibbets, Whipping-posts, or Pillories; No cheating Shopkeepers or Mechanics: No Pride, Vanity or Affectation: No Fops, Bullies, Drunkards, strolling Whores, or Poxes: No ranting, lewd, expensive Wives: No stupid, proud Pedants: Nor importunate, over-bearing, quarrelsome, noisy, roaring, empty, conceited, swearing Companions: No Scoundrels raised from the Dust upon the Merit of their Vices; or Nobility thrown into it on account of their Virtues: No Lords, Fidlers, Judges or Dancing-masters.   (pp. 276–7)

Satiric complications

It is easy enough to say Swift lambastes the usual Scriblerian retinue in the last book of *Gulliver's Travels*, but what distinguishes Swiftian satire is the instability of the voice inside his works. Casual sentences sometimes get to the heart of the matter. In the *Travels*, a seemingly thrown away line by Gulliver about one obscure ship's captain named Pockock touches on almost every middling, individualist narrator Swift has ever concocted, including Gulliver. The captain, who neglected to follow Gulliver's advice about cutting logwood in the bay of Campechy, 'was an honest man, and a good sailor, but a little too positive in his own opinions which was the cause of his destruction, as it has been several others' (p. 221). The sentence is a simple one, but it is also symptomatic. Confidence in the wrong thing produces the narrative worlds that Swift's characters inhabit. At this point in the *Travels*, Gulliver, having rested at home for five months, might have remained 'in a very happy Condition, if I could have learned the Lesson of knowing when I was well' (p. 221). Every subject would like to learn this lesson, but few of Swift's subjects ever do. The raw nerve of Swift's satire is the expressive but deluded subject, all those self-centred egomaniacs, the modern hack-for-hire in *A Tale of Tub*; the vainglorious political arithmetician in 'A Modest Proposal'; Lemuel Gulliver; even the dead Dean in 'Verses on the Death of Dr Swift.'

Gulliver never does get things absolutely straight about himself or his experience in the *Travels*. In Houyhnhnmland he is described by his horse master as a 'perfect *Yahoo*' (p. 237) after we have learned that the word for perfection in putative horse language is *houyhnhnm*. So Gulliver is a *houyhnhnm yahoo*, until we learn that *yahoo* means the antithesis of all things perfect. The text turns

Gulliver into an oxymoron. Gulliver ends up pontificating as a Scriblerian, but his shattered brain as traveller reveals another satiric possibility. He knows of places that are literally jumbled in his head, one of which he mentions earlier in his third voyage to Laputa, a place named *'Tribnia* by the natives called *Langden'* (p. 191). The anagram is 'Britain by the natives called England' which is not at all surprising in that Gulliver may have been driven mad by his own obsessive experiences even before he left England (of which we get hints throughout) – and surely before he writes up his memoirs. After all, he is always travelling to jumbled-up alphabetical places. When in Lilliput, for example, Gulliver finds himself in the capital city, *Mildendo*, he is in an alphabetic version of mid-Lond[e]n, or a city of *dildo-men*, little people. Later in Brobdingnag, the little Gulliver becomes something of a dildo man himself, at least in the presence of the Maids of Honour at court, one of whom performs a 'Trick' with him 'wherein', says Gulliver, 'the Reader will excuse me for not being over particular' (p. 119). Gulliver thinks he enjoys the highest honours – he is even a Nardac in Lilliput, though when unscrambled his order becomes, as is much else for Swift's cock-sure narrators, a 'Canard'.

Gulliver's dementia seems rooted in one of Swift's continual satiric obsessions, language. I do not think it an accident that when the text finally presents Gulliver as unbalanced it is precisely the linguistic apparatus that goes awry. The reading contract that honours Gulliver's veracity would have it that horses talk, but something else is going on in the satiric bowels of book four. Gulliver's capacity for language breaks down. He bases all that he experiences and thinks he experiences on the natural sounds of horses. Gulliver loses his mind when he loses the ability to distinguish language from sounds. Gulliver sees a horse in a field who 'neighed three or four times, but in so different a Cadence, that I almost began to think he was speaking to himself in some Language of his own' (p. 225). It is easy enough to maintain that Gulliver hears no more in the entire voyage than the neighing of horses, and he imposes upon that sound system a language that he thinks he speaks and continues to speak when he finally returns home. The text only points out words that in their orthography sound like versions of horse sounds, sounds that Gulliver begins to mimic, and sounds that even Gulliver describes in terms that signal distrust, the horse 'neighing several times by Turns, and varying the Sound, which seemed to be almost articulate' (p. 225).

'Which seemed to be almost' does not exactly inspire confidence, and the satiric action of the *Travels* has rendered seeming into fictional lunacy. Back home in England (if, indeed, he ever left), Gulliver has lost his bearings and assumed horse attributes: 'I fell to imitate their Gait and Gesture, which is now grown into a Habit; and my Friends often tell me in a blunt Way that *I trot like a Horse*' (p. 279). Does he have any friends? It seems he allows only his wife even proximate contact and walks around with tobacco or lavender up his nose to avoid the smell of his own species. He speaks comfortably only with horses in his stable: 'My Horses understand me tolerably well; I converse with them at least four Hours every Day' (p. 290). How does Gulliver know the language of English horses? Houyhnhnmland, by any account, is thousands upon thousands of miles from England. Does the reader – including readers operating under the contract that the *Travels* actually occurred – ever consider that language (even horse language) does not travel so easily from place to place with no migrational contact unless, of course, horses make the only sounds the vocal disposition of their species allow, a kind of Adamic horse language? Could it be that Gulliver (an *ur* Dr Doolittle) simply began talking to his horses in his own stable on his own volition without ever leaving his native country? Swift's satire is so unsettling that such a reading is neither unlikely nor undesirable.

In a letter to Pope on 27 November 1726 shortly after the publication of the *Travels*, Swift relays the story of an Irish bishop who concluded that the book 'was full of improbable lies, and for his part he hardly believed a word of it'. It is not the fatuousness of the bishop in even considering so obviously contrived material as improbable that amuses Swift, but the inclusion of the word 'hardly', as if some of it is believable. And by choosing to single out such a reaction to his work, Swift recognises that part of the joke of the *Travels* is at the expense of a reading audience increasingly trained to judge narrative by dubious (in his estimation) standards of reliability and accuracy. Potentially satiric subjects stimulate Swift as much as actual ones. Perhaps that *is* the final word on his satire: those who think they remain outside its reach are much more deeply inside than they could ever imagine or admit.

Persistence, adaptations and transformations in pastoral and Georgic poetry

DAVID FAIRER

Thomas Parnell's lines about the pastoral world take us to the heart of an age-old problem. 'Oft have I read', he begins, 'that Innocence retreats / Where cooling streams salute the summer Seats; / Singing at ease she roves the field of flowers / Or safe with shepherds lies among the bowers . . .' Having passed through a country fair, however, he had found 'No Strephon nor Dorinda', but a motley crew of randy, idle and drunken rustics:

> Are these the Virtues which adorn the plain?
> Ye bards forsake your old Arcadian Vein,
> To sheep, those tender Innocents, resign
> The place where swains and nymphs are said to shine;
> Swains twice as wicked, Nymphs but half as sage.
> Tis sheep alone retrieve the golden age.[1]

Where is pastoral innocence to be found? And how can any modern writer not view Arcadia ironically? By a shift of focus typical of early eighteenth-century satire, the sheep move centre-stage: the incidentals of pastoral become the guardians of its soul. The poet is self-consciously listening to his own bland rhetoric ('the Virtues which adorn the plain', etc.) before the final rueful comment emerges – conclusive, yet almost in parenthesis, as if he is turning away from the scene. After two thousand years of pastoral poetry Parnell (d. 1718) can find only one unsullied image remaining, and there seems no more to be said.

Yet Parnell died at the end of a decade in which the nature of pastoral had become a topic for debate among the most prominent writers of the

---

1 Parnell's untitled poem, from a loose undateable manuscript (here modernised), was first published in *Collected Poems of Thomas Parnell* eds. Claude Rawson and F. P. Lock (Newark, DE: University of Delaware Press; London and Toronto: Associated University Presses, 1989), pp. 421–2.

time. As a literary mode it was far from exhausted, and would soon receive a new lease of life from the next generation of poets. Why did it persist? One reason may be that pastoral had become a kind of punch-bag for hundreds of poets-in-training to test their powers on, in the hope of embarking on the *rota Virgiliana*, that 'canonical progress through the genres'[2] made by Virgil from pastoral (the *Eclogues*), through the 'middle style' (the *Georgics*), to the eventual epic achievement of the *Aeneid*. But long after its ideals had been deflated and its conventions mocked, pastoral survived to be beaten into new shapes. Its malleability, as a mode rather than a genre, offered opportunities for poetic experiment, and the widespread familiarity of its codes allowed for considerable ingenuity and playfulness.

The first decade of the century, however, also saw the establishment of the Georgic poem as a more dynamic genre that could engage productively with the contemporary British landscape.[3] After the Act of Union (1707) that united England and Scotland, people seemed to become interested in poetry about the organising and development of the young nation's resources, and Georgic's linking of time-hallowed tradition to new skills and opportunities provided a subtle way of confronting wider problems of continuity and innovation. Georgic also gave room for greater variety of tone and topic, and it drew economics and politics more directly into the picture. Work, trade, human ingenuity, social structures, national concerns – all these became features of a poetry that found inspiration in the idea of organic change. But after 1760, as poets looked for new forms of expression, the classical outlines of Pastoral and Georgic appeared increasingly constraining. The traditional duality of Nature and Art, which in different ways had underpinned each of them, was breaking down or being reconfigured in more subtle ways, and some of their character- istic features were variously absorbed into the wider embrace of topographical poetry and verse of a meditative and didactic character. By bringing Pastoral and Georgic together, this chapter will stress their differences,[4] and argue

2 John D. Bernard, *Ceremonies of Innocence: Pastoralism in the Poetry of Edmund Spenser* (Cam- bridge: Cambridge University Press, 1989), p. 6.
3 Anthony Low, in *The Georgic Revolution* (Princeton, NJ: Princeton University Press, 1985), traces a fascinating earlier history of the English Georgic mode from the Middle Ages to the seventeenth century.
4 There has been a deliberate tendency in some criticism to conflate the distinct char- acters of Pastoral and Georgic. See, for example, Richard Feingold, *Nature and Society: Later Eighteenth-Century Uses of the Pastoral and Georgic* (Hassocks: The Harvester Press, 1978), p. 16; and Michael McKeon, 'Surveying the Frontier of Culture: Pastoralism in Eighteenth-Century England', *Studies in Eighteenth-Century Culture* 26 (1998), 7–28. McKeon sees eclogue and Georgic as both operating within an 'oppositional structure' (p. 9). See note 27 below.

that they represent a crucial distinction in eighteenth-century poetry between ironic and organic form. As a stereotype, pastoral could be inverted, turned round, parodied and played with; but in order for all this to work it had to remain a stereotype. Georgic, on the other hand, was at home with notions of growth, development, variety, digression and mixture, and had a natural tendency to absorb the old into the new, and find fresh directions. Pastoral's limitations and Georgic's capaciousness were, in other words, equally fruitful; but they marked out different kinds of poetry.

Since the inauguration of the pastoral poem, or 'bucolic', in the third century BC by Theocritus, and its development in the *Eclogues* of Virgil, pastoral writing had been extended during the Renaissance into drama, prose narrative, satire, allegory and masque. Although its scope had in this sense widened, its conventions and subject matter remained limited. In the hands of court poets like Sannazaro and Tasso in Italy, or Sidney and Spenser in England, its commitment to the simple lives and language of shepherds and shepherdesses (or in Sannazaro's controversial development, fishermen and fisherwomen) came under strain; but this could give it a *faux-naif* quality that was useful when engaging with controversial contemporary issues. Spenser's militantly Protestant shepherds vigorously attack Romish 'pastors', and complain about being neglected by the great. Shakespeare the dramatist knew that an actual wanderer through English fields and woods would find, not Silvius and Phebe, but William and Audrey. During the 1630s, those uneasy years of parliament-free innocence under Charles I, the adequacy of Pastoral for dealing with urgent human questions was fully tested by Milton, whose rebellious spirit enjoyed pushing its conventions to breaking-point in his *Ludlow Masque* (1634) and his pastoral elegy, *Lycidas* (1637). In the Eden scenes of *Paradise Lost* (Milton's version of history's original pastoral episode) Adam and Eve are intelligent and dignified, and not yet encumbered with sheep.

The eighteenth century therefore inherited, as Parnell's verses confirm, a pastoral mode that was strained and stretched, and which already had self-conscious parodic elements embedded in it. The question of its relationship to 'real' life was by then an old one, but it was this very issue that brought it to the heart of current debate about the nature of poetry. Until the 1650s, ignored by classical literary theory, pastoral had been refreshingly free of rules. It was left to two French critics, Rapin and Fontenelle, to remedy this by constructing a set of principles within which to contain and judge this form of writing. Rapin's *Dissertatio de Carmine Pastorali* (1659) and Fontenelle's *Discour sur la nature de l'églogue* (1688) were translated into English in 1684 and

1695 respectively,[5] and their contrasting approaches (which reflected the two sides of the 'ancients versus moderns' controversy) had considerable influence on pastoral-writing in Britain. The Aristotelian Rapin declared the *Idylls* of Theocritus and the *Eclogues* of Virgil to be his absolute models, yet his ideas were filtered through the neoclassical critical tradition, and he repeatedly cited authorities among the *scholia* and the classical grammarians to support his 'rules' – to the extent of criticising Theocritus for not following them. Fontenelle, a disciple of Descartes, placed his faith in reason and experience, and quoted no authorities whatsoever. For Rapin, the pastoral was the most ancient form of poetry, and imitated the lives of shepherds in the Golden Age; for Fontenelle it showed eternal human nature and gave pleasure by picturing a leisured rural life without its toils and coarseness, and with love at its centre. But the neoclassicist and the rationalist did agree on several points – that pastoral must be simple and dignified, avoiding courtly wit on one side, and rustic clownishness on the other; and that hard work of any kind was banned.

These critical views raised questions that any aspiring writer of pastorals was forced to consider: was Pastoral, like drama and epic, subject to neoclassical rules? How directly should a poet engage with contemporary experience? Should Pastoral locate itself in eighteenth-century Britain, or in a timeless Golden Age? The terms of the British debate were set by French theory. Dryden's English translation of the *Eclogues* (1697), for example, was prefaced by Knightley Chetwood's defence of Virgil, based entirely on Rapin, 'Against some of the Reflections of Monsieur Fontanelle'. Dryden's critical dedication dismissed Fontenelle briskly, but was nevertheless uneasy about moments when Virgil himself seemed to have lost pastoral 'decorum' and slipped into the rustic or the pompous.[6]

An early eighteenth-century poet writing pastorals could not help but be entangled in issues such as these. Ironically, French theory was imposing critical sophistication on a poetic mode that privileged simplicity. The problem was to gauge which kind of simplicity was the right one.[7] At his best, Dryden had

5 René Rapin, *Dissertatio de Carmine Pastorali*, prefixed to his *Eclogae Sacrae* (1659), translated as 'A Treatise de Carmine Pastorali' in *Idylliums of Theocritus*, trans. Thomas Creech (Oxford, 1684); Bernard le Bovier de Fontenelle, 'Discours sur la nature de l'églogue' (1688), trans. Peter Motteux, 'Of Pastorals', published with Bossu's *Treatise of the Epick Poem* (London, 1695). For a full study, see J. E. Congleton, *Theories of Pastoral in England, 1684–1798* (Gainesville, FL: University of Florida Press, 1952).
6 John Dryden, 'To the Right Honourable Hugh, Lord Clifford', prefixed to the *Pastorals* in his *Works of Virgil, Translated into English Verse* (1697).
7 See the chapter on 'Simplicity' in Thomas G. Rosenmeyer, *The Green Cabinet: Theocritus and the European Pastoral Lyric* (Berkeley and Los Angeles: University of California Press, 1969), pp. 45–64.

shown what could be achieved by combining simple vocabulary and phrasing with a dignified manner, as when Moeris in the ninth eclogue sadly confronts his failing memory:

> The rest I have forgot, for Cares and Time
> Change all things, and untune my Soul to Rhyme:
> I cou'd have once sung down a Summer's Sun,
> But now the Chime of Poetry is done.
>
> (*Ecl.* IX, lines 70–3)

A lofty idea is made to come from the heart rather than the head. The Virgilian *umbra*, that eternal note of sadness, is always convincingly struck by Dryden, but other more light-hearted elements, like the binding of Silenus in Eclogue Six, also come vividly across. Where a masterly translator like Dryden had stylistic choices to make, a poet attempting original pastorals faced many more, and would invite the judgement of any knowledgeable reader. So when the sixth volume of Tonson's *Miscellanies* appeared in 1709 containing two sets of 'Pastorals', by Ambrose Philips and the twenty-one-year-old Pope,[8] the literary world was bound to compare them and assess their critical allegiances. They seemed to offer a contrast between the principles of Rapin and Fontenelle that made this inevitable. Where Philips's poems were firmly located in the English countryside, Pope's (in spite of references to Thames and Windsor) belonged in the timeless landscape of neoclassical Pastoral. The result was something of a *cause célèbre*, in which Pope is usually seen to have had the upper hand.

Pope's *Pastorals* were written with critics in mind, and at his shoulder. The four poems circulated round his patrons with an accompanying 'Essay on Pastoral', picking up corrections here and a little burnish there, and were worked at and thoroughly revised to give them simplicity, propriety, and correctness. The young man, it seems, was determined to please everyone. In a fascinating act of critical diplomacy he followed Rapin and Fontenelle, Chetwood and Dryden, and praised Theocritus, Virgil, Tasso and Spenser. In his first published work Pope was taking no risks. He presents his enterprise as an act of purification, distilling the essence of Pastoral by filtering it through the best theories and the best models, and ensuring that 'Nature' is appropriately trimmed and ordered so as not to compromise his Art.

---

8 *Poetical Miscellanies: The Sixth Part* (London, 1709). Philips' six pastorals (four of which had been printed in 1708) opened the volume, and Pope's four pastorals closed it. See *The Poems of Ambrose Philips*, ed. M. G. Segar (Oxford: Basil Blackwell, 1937).

The poetic result is beautifully shaped. Pope uses the heroic couplet elegantly: phrases repeatedly echo each other in pleasing varied patterns, and images are satisfyingly mirrored. The shepherd-voices are always conscious of allusion, symmetry and paradox, and a harmonising lyric strain is never absent for long:

> How all things listen, while thy Muse complains!
> Such silence waits on *Philomela*'s Strains,
> In some still Ev'ning, when the whisp'ring Breeze
> Pants on the Leaves, and dies upon the Trees.
>
> ('Winter', lines 77–80)

This is not a song, however, but Lycidas' response to Thyrsis' lament for the dead Daphne. Rather than bring the lyrical moment back to the here and now, as Theocritus and Virgil tend to do, Pope suspends it magically as though the two shepherds are both caught up in something greater. But the nightingale (*Philomela*) is part of a simile, not a presence in the scene. We can gauge the different world of Ambrose Philips by comparing the close of his first pastoral:

> Now, to the waining Moon, the Nightingale
> In doleful Ditties told her piteous Tale.
> The Love-sick Shepherd list'ning found Relief,
> Pleas'd with so sweet a Partner in his Grief:
> 'Till by degrees her Notes and silent Night
> To Slumbers soft his heavy Heart invite.
>
> (lines 95–100)

Lobbin has likewise just ended his lament; but the word 'Now' brings a real bird into the scene. Her 'piteous Tale' alludes to the classical story of Philomela, but without the awkward assumption that the English shepherd knows this (as Pope's does). Lobbin can be comforted just by the music. The idea that Nature gives him a 'Partner' is a simple but effective one, as is the sympathetic partnering of 'soft' and 'heavy' in the last line (where his burden is laid down). Philips allows the phrase 'doleful Ditties' (line 96) to add an appropriately rustic Spenserian touch. It reminds us that this pastoral is not aspiring to be something else, but feels at home among country people.

It is tempting to see Ambrose Philips as taking risks (not always success-fully) with the homely 'Doric' elements of Theocritus and Spenser, while Pope aims for a more 'Virgilian' smoothness; but this would be to oversimplify both Philips and Virgil. A reader of Virgil's *Eclogues* comes to appreciate how the poet's language is responsive to moments of tension and conflict. He does not smooth out differences, but allows them to register – though without shifting linguistic gear as Theocritus does. In this respect Philips is sometimes more Virgilian than Pope. Also, the *Eclogues* are partly dramatic, a series of human engagements in which emotions encounter each other, and this is also truer of Philips' pastorals. His second pastoral is a dialogue between alienated adolescence (the lovesick Colinet) and cheerful old age (the philosophic Thenot), in which natural images register their different thoughts. The scene parallels Virgil's first eclogue, where Meliboeus and old Tityrus meet on the road. The former is heading for exile from his confiscated farm, while the other is returning to the home that has been restored to him; their talk contrasts alienation with joyful expectancy in a passionately evoked local landscape. The situation is full of irony, yet by the poem's close it is held in suspension, when Tityrus in simple and moving terms offers his friend rest for the night. It is with a sense of its absolute appropriateness that Philips ends his own pastoral with a translation of that final speech, as Thenot makes his young friend Colinet a similar offer:

> This Night thy Cares with me forget; and fold
> Thy Flock with mine, to ward th'injurious Cold.
> Sweet Milk and clouted Cream, soft Cheese and Curd,
> With some remaining Fruit of last Year's Hoard,
> Shall be our Ev'ning Fare: And for the Night,
> Sweet Herbs and Moss, that gentle Sleep invite.
>
> (lines 124–9)

With the folding of their flocks (the single detail Philips adds to his source) Colinet's pastoral 'Cares' find a homely perspective, and the mental and physical are drawn sympathetically together. Philips has clearly absorbed the Virgilian idea. With such examples in mind it becomes easier to appreciate why he was hailed as Britain's successor to Theocritus, Virgil and Spenser.[9] Though clearly a 'modern', he could be seen as representing the spirit of the two classical poets (who wrote before Pastoral was given neoclassical rules).

The critical acclaim came to a head with a series of five anonymous papers on pastoral poetry in *The Guardian* (1713) written by Thomas Tickell, who like Philips was a member of Addison's literary circle. These favoured the naturalised modern Pastoral advocated by Fontenelle, and most of the illustrations

---

9 The critical acclaim of Philips' pastorals is detailed by George Sherburn, *The Early Career of Alexander Pope* (Oxford: Clarendon Press, 1934), pp. 117–19.

were taken from Philips. Pope's more neoclassical poems were completely ignored. Tickell concluded that Philips's pastorals had more 'pretty Rusticity' than Virgil's, and were, with Spenser's, the most successful English writing in that mode.[10] This was just too much for Pope, who wrote a spoof essay of his own and managed to trick *The Guardian*'s editor, Richard Steele, into printing it. *The Guardian* 40 (27 April) pays ironic homage to Philips' 'pretty Rusticity', and choice examples are embarrassingly placed alongside Pope at his most elegant. The effect is like seating a thresher beside a countess (but who is the more embarrassed?). Pope finds the whole idea of an English 'Doric' hilarious, and as a climax he prints part of a ballad in the Somersetshire dialect 'which I chanced to find among some old Manuscripts':

> *Rager* go vetch tha *Kee*, or else tha Zun,
> Will quite be go, be vore c'have half a don . . .

Pope's editorial note (parodying E. K.'s glosses to Spenser's *Shepheardes Calender*[11]) explains that *Kee* is 'the *Kine* or *Cows*'. Like the best parody, this is very unfair and very amusing, and has its own energy and logic. Pope shapes Roger the cowherd's instructions into an impeccable heroic couplet whose caesuras are perfectly placed, and in doing so he draws attention to pastoral's uneasy collaboration between nature and art, naivety and sophistication, reality and fiction. At the core of Pastoral, this seems to suggest, is a potential gap for ironic play – one that Pope in his *Pastorals* had been determined to close. In the guise of mocking Philips, therefore, Pope's Somersetshire fragment is actually a nightmare inversion of his own *Pastorals*, evoking an all-too-real country world where it is poetic art that is unnatural, and elegance is indecorum.

By being a heavily coded form, the traditional 'Golden Age' Pastoral was particularly vulnerable to having its inner logic exposed. What we tend to think of as 'mock-' or 'anti-Pastoral' is often more truly the opening out for display of its ironic potential as a mode that is defined by what it excludes. All the things pastoral holds at bay – heroism, politics, money, war, time and death – are there to haunt it from an echo's distance. In *Englands Helicon* (1600) Marlowe's lyric, 'The Passionate Shepherd to his Love', was famously paired with Sir Walter Ralegh's 'The Nymph's Reply to the Shepherd':

---

10 *The Guardian* 30 (15 April). See *The Guardian*, ed. John Calhoun Stephens (Lexington, KY: University Press of Kentucky, 1982), p. 130.

11 Edmund Spenser's *The Shepheardes Calender* (1579) consists of twelve eclogues named for the twelve months. The poem includes introductory matter and glosses, written by one E. K., whose identity remains uncertain.

> . . . But could youth last, and love still breede,
>   Had joyes no date, nor age no neede,
>   Then these delights my minde might move,
>   To live with thee, and be thy love.

Ralegh intrudes an idea that is always hovering at the edge of pastoral, waiting to invade it. Classical Pastoral (as Keats understood in his 'Ode on a Grecian Urn') acknowledges 'realities', but holds itself off from them (Virgil's Tityrus and Meliboeus remain forever seated on the grass, eating their cheese and fruit). Hence the importance in Theocritus and Virgil of notes that echo from elsewhere. This is what gives their pastorals, for all the narrowness of representation, such a richness of implication. In a similar way the poems resist being subsumed into either the Golden Age or the world of *negotium* (everyday affairs). Theocritus and Virgil tend to explore moments of suspension between timeless myth and physical reality, when both are there *in potentia*. This is the irony inherent in classical Pastoral. Seen in these terms, Ralegh's reply is not strictly 'anti-Pastoral', but rather the intrusion of its usually unspoken conscience.

It is helpful to bear these points in mind when dealing with the supposed 'anti-' or 'mock-Pastorals' of the eighteenth century. It was Pope's ally, John Gay, who most successfully engaged with Pastoral as ironic form. His *Shepherd's Week* (1714) found its stimulus in the dispute between Pope and the Addison circle, and these six rural eclogues (one for each day of the labourer's week) are offered to the public in the voice of a Spenserian throwback who seems untouched by modern French elegance ('My Shepherd . . . sleepeth not under Myrtle shades, but under a Hedge').[12] With characters like Cuddy and Lobbin Clout, these pastorals seem at first to be taking Pope's line by ridiculing the Doric rusticity of the Spenser–Philips 'naturalising' school. The country ingredients pile up, and the lines sometimes creak like a market-stall:

> *Leek* to the *Welch*, to *Dutchmen Butter*'s dear,
> Of *Irish* Swains *Potatoe* is the Chear;
> *Oats* for their Feasts the *Scottish* Shepherds grind,
> Sweet *Turnips* are the Food of *Blouzelind*.
> While she loves *Turnips*, *Butter* I'll despise,
> Nor *Leeks* nor *Oatmeal* nor *Potatoe* prize.
>   ('Monday; or, The Squabble', lines 83–8)

The ironic 'joke' is that these homely items are assembled in a rhetorical *Collectio* (a gathering of terms at the end) beloved of Renaissance sonneteers.

12 John Gay, 'The Proeme', *The Shepherd's Week* (London, 1714), sig. A4[r].

Such effects can be expressively textured, as when in the same singing-contest Cuddy boasts about the soft and frisky Buxoma: 'Clean as young Lambkins or the Goose's Down, / And like the Goldfinch in her *Sunday* Gown' (lines 51–2). In Pope's equivalent pastoral, Strephon's celebration of Delia cannot permit any gap between art and life where irony might gather – and it is the life which is sacrificed. The rhetorical patterning is similar, but here there is no physical reality to compromise it:

> In Spring the Fields, in Autumn Hills I love,
> At Morn the Plains, at Noon the shady Grove;
> But *Delia* always; absent from her Sight,
> Nor Plains at Morn, nor Groves at Noon delight.
> ('Spring', lines 77–80)

Suddenly Pope's neatly arranged ingredients (Spring, Autumn, Morn, Noon, Plains, Groves) seem lifeless and predictable. It is Buxoma, pranked out like a goldfinch, whom we remember.

Gay has not accidentally discovered poetry through burlesque, but has creatively tapped into the living sources of classical pastoral, in which shepherds make poetry from the things around them – a currency (linguistic also) that they value and use. The original of both Pope and Gay is the singing-contest in Theocritus' Idyll Five (imitated in Virgil's third eclogue), where the two singers refer to items like goat-skins, olives, locusts, crickets, pine-cones, lamb's wool, honey, milk, heather, baskets of cheese, a wooden pail and so on. Gay delights in accumulating such materials ('joking Talk / Of Ashes, Leather, Oatmeal, Bran and Chalk', 'Tuesday', lines 43–4), and he collects them at the end of his volume in a four-page 'Alphabetical Catalogue of . . . material Things mentioned by this Author'. Gay turns much to laughter, but in doing so he works with the pastoral grain, not against it. The lament of Bumkinet and Grubbinol for the dead Blouzelinda ('Friday') remains moving because it bridges the gap between the conventions of pastoral elegy and the unpromising ingredients of Blouzelinda's life. Gay does not attempt to 'raise' her by suppressing indecorous material. The most famous lines in Pope's *Pastorals* work precisely in the opposite direction, with poetic art creating an amenable subject, not seeking to represent a recalcitrant one. In 'Summer' Pope is exquisitely celebrating the charms of an immaterial presence combining Diana and Flora: 'Where-e'er you walk, cool Gales shall fan the Glade, / Trees, where you sit, shall crowd into a Shade, / Where-e'er you tread, the blushing Flow'rs shall rise, / And all things flourish where you turn your Eyes' ('Summer', lines 73–6). After this,

Gay's lines about Blouzelinda seem to be written with one (winking) eye on Pope:

> Where-e'er I gad, I *Blouzelind* shall view,
> Woods, Dairy, Barn and Mows our Passion knew.
> When I direct my Eyes to yonder Wood,
> Fresh rising Sorrow curdles in my Blood.
>
> ('Friday; or, The Dirge', lines 41–4)

As Bumkinet passes their old haunts, his emotional arousal ('Fresh rising Sorrow') can only parody his former sexual passion, and the language of the dairy ('curdles') has its own decorum. At the end of the poem, he and his friend Grubbinol catch sight of 'bonny *Susan*', and their loss begins to be repaired as they carry her off for 'Ale and Kisses'. This ironic turn at the end of a love-complaint is not a sophisticated modern twist, but a characteristic feature of classical Pastoral.[13] Whatever was the original stimulus for Gay's *Shepherd's Week*, the result was, as Goldsmith recognised, in 'the true spirit of pastoral poetry. In fact, he more resembles Theocritus than any other English pastoral writer whatsoever.'[14]

Goldsmith's emphasis on the 'spirit' is significant. A key idea behind pastoral is limitation – of place, time and action. The pastoral space has no unique landmarks, and the history of the form is one of revisitings, repeatings and superimpositions. The love-complaint, the singing competition, the elegy and the wooing mark out its generic range, and from the Renaissance onwards these were endlessly reworked. Pastoral transmigrated through different bodies, each a temporary dwelling for its spirit. It is helpful to have such an image in mind when considering some of the many ingenious adaptations of pastoral poetry during the eighteenth century.

Lady Mary Wortley Montagu's *Town Eclogues* (1716) play intriguing variations on the traditional pastoral situations. The shepherd lads and lasses are here the beaux and belles of St James's, but these exotic creatures are trapped in the same endless round of wooing, competing and complaining. Instead of the glades, streams and rocks, their limited terrain is marked out by the drawing-room, card-table and boudoir, and a few select places of aristocratic resort round which they move ('Strait then I'll dress and take my wonted

---

13 See Theocritus, *Idylls*, VII.122–7; and Virgil, *Eclogues*, II.73.
14 From *The Beauties of English Poetry* (1767). See *Collected Works of Oliver Goldsmith*, ed. Arthur Friedman, 5 vols. (Oxford: Clarendon Press, 1966), V.322.

Range, / Through India shops, to Motteux's, or the Change').[15] Flavia, lying on a couch with her looking-glass turned from her, laments her lost beauty ravaged by smallpox; the ageing Lydia rails against the fashionable world she used to command; and two practised 'players', Smilinda and Cardelia, compete in voicing their passion – for men and cards respectively. A lost lover might be foreseen, but a lost queen of clubs is a disaster. Instead of a lamb or a carved cup they pledge a snuff-box and a trinket-case, and their friend Loveit is the judge between them. As the traditional scenario is acted out, their complaints echo one another until the language of love and the language of the card-table chime wittily together – two songs creating a single lament whose terms are interchangeable. Enclosed in their leisured routines, Lady Mary's characters explore the neurotic potential of pastoral romance, in whose rhetoric they are trapped. Mirrors and echoes begin playing tricks, and lines of escape are cut off. These swains and nymphs, she satirically suggests, have turned Arcadia into Hell.

Jonathan Swift also finds the Pastoral code fascinating, but rather than explore its spirit, he tends to dwell on the material body that it might wish to discard. In this respect he is a poet of anti-Pastoral – ironic play becomes burlesque inversion. He reverses Lady Mary's world of aristocratic minds at leisure, to focus on the labourer's body at work. His miniature 'Description of the Morning' (1709) is filled with busy workers transforming the city street into a parody of a pastoral landscape. Instead of birdsong there are clashing street-cries; the delicate breezes and showers are provided courtesy of Moll's whirling mop and the apprentice sprinkling the floor; Phoebus' chariot emerges as a hackney-coach and the only shepherd in sight is the prison turn-key waiting to pen his 'Flock' after their nocturnal thieving. In the process the pastoral vision is turned inside out to become an early exercise in urban documentary. Swift's later verse satire offers further travesties of Pastoral, but imbued with a new element of physical disgust. In his 'Pastoral Dialogue' (1732) the labourers are given a voice in Dermot and Sheelah, two Irish peasants who are weeding a baronet's courtyard while exchanging the most uncourtly of 'endearments'. In Swift's burlesque scene, 'Ditch' rhymes with 'Bitch', and 'Sluts' with 'Guts', and the lovers' immediate thoughts are on lice, sweat and bruised bums. But this world too has room for the exotic, represented not by an exquisite snuff-box, but its equally rare equivalent:

15 'Friday', lines 27–8.

> At an old stubborn Root I chanc'd to tug,
> When the Dean threw me this Tobacco-plug:
> A longer half-p'orth never did I see;
> This, dearest *Sheelah*, thou shalt share with me.
> (lines 25–8)

Swift also delights in the voyeuristic implications of the enclosed world where nymphs and swains act out their pastoral fantasy-games, and he enjoys taking revenge on those who live in its fictions. In 'The Lady's Dressing Room' (1732) Strephon's sexual passion for the absent Celia is brilliantly inverted: although she is gone, he finds so many physical remnants and excreta left behind that her body takes on a horrifying nearness and nastiness, and he becomes trapped in an imaginative world that had once charmed him.

By the time Swift wrote these poems the erotic potential of Pastoral had long been recognised. Its intimate encounters free of the constraints of the social world could naturalise sexual feeling by returning it to a prelapsarian innocence. This was the mission of Thomas Purney, for whom the ideal pastoral was a combination of innocence, tenderness and softness. Aided by his own theory of poetic enervation,[16] Purney produced a set of *Pastorals* (1717) in which pubescent girls and boys indulge their sexual curiosity and play love-games together. There is much soft simpering and patting of paps, and in the first pastoral ('Love and Innocence') the two girls, Soflin and Paplet, watched by Cubbin from a nearby bush, entwine like putti in an erotic fresco:

> So as she said (and who so sweet can sain)
> Her little Leg would in her *Fellow's* twine,
> Then dainty'd droppen Hand in *Soflie* Breast:
> Ah dainty Hand! how *Cubbin* yearn'd to kiss't![17]

Spenserian diction fuses with baby-talk to produce a unique poetic dialect, and in the process Pastoral is returned, along with language, nature and sex, to a primal infantile state. Rather than the innocent Cubbin, it is the modern reader who is made to play the role of voyeur.

Remote in a different way are William Diaper's fascinating *Nereides: or, Sea-Eclogues* (1712), which solve problems of prurience by taking us out into a free

---

16 'In order to compose a Pastoral Dialect entirely perfect; the first thing, I think, a Writer has to do, is . . . to enervate it and deprive it of all strength' (Thomas Purney, *A Full Enquiry into the True Nature of Pastoral* (1717); Augustan Reprint Society, no. 11 (1948), p. 60).

17 *The Works of Thomas Purney*, ed. H. O. White (Oxford: Basil Blackwell, 1933), p. 16. See Carson Bergstrom, 'Purney, Pastoral, and the Polymorphous Perverse', *British Journal for Eighteenth-Century Studies* 17 (1994), 149–63.

aquatic realm in which sea-nymphs and Tritons enact a variety of pastoral episodes modelled closely on Theocritus and Virgil.[18] Diaper's ocean with its varied moods has a range of sensuous possibilities that he fully exploits—'the vast unseen Mansions of the Deep, / Where secret Groves with liquid Amber weep' (Dedication 'To Mr Congreve, lines 21–2). In Eclogue XI, the nymph Eune and the Triton Melvin make love near the shore where land and sea meet; but when Eune wakes she finds herself alone on the dry sand, and weeps to see the 'distant Billows rowl' out of her reach. The ensuing climax is both erotic and natural: as she falls back into sleep, the tide begins to turn, and the languorous strength of the water reasserts itself:

> And now returning Waves by slow degrees
> Move on the Beach, and stretch the widen'd Seas.
> *Melvin* approaches with the rising Tide,
> And in his Arms enfolds his sleeping Bride.
>
> (lines 52–5)

Diaper celebrates the fluid variety of his medium, to the extent that in 'Eclogue IV' two ocean-dwellers gaze at a distant pastoral landscape and pity its limitations ('But ah! how wretched are those earth-born Slaves, / Compar'd with us, who cut thro' shining Waves!' (lines 5–6)). The irony is that in their seascape they re-enact all the scenes of classical Pastoral.

Diaper reinvigorated the old conventions by finding a new set of imagery. Later poets too, without having recourse to the satiric twists and inversions of Lady Mary and Swift, opened up other expressive possibilities and brought fresh life to the eclogue. Its stereotypical nature allowed for ingenious reworkings and witty substitutions. During the 1740s the mode was resuscitated by the poetic equivalent of blood-transfusion and electric shock. Two young poets towards mid-century used their apprentice-pastorals to announce their originality and ambition – a new language would come from the oldest of forms. In his *Persian Eclogues* (1742) William Collins turned to the Middle East to refresh English verse with what his preface calls the 'rich and figurative' language of Arabian and Persian poetry; but in 'Eclogue the Second' Hassan the camel-driver, fearful and hungry in the empty desert, is forced to recall the familiar 'green delights' that both he and Collins have left behind:

---

18 See the details given by Dorothy Broughton in *William Diaper: The Complete Works*, ed. Broughton (London: Routledge and Kegan Paul, 1952), pp. xxiv–xl.

> Here, where no Springs, in Murmurs break away,
> Or Moss-crown'd Fountains mitigate the Day:
> In vain ye hope the green Delights to know,
> Which Plains more blest, or verdant Vales bestow.
>
> (lines 23–6)

Once again, here in the desert the pastoral scene is ironically present as an imagined oasis, and the contrast allows Collins' exotic eclogues to be fully savoured. His Oxford friend, the seventeen-year-old Thomas Warton, declared his adventurousness in his title: *Five Pastoral Eclogues, The Scenes of which are Suppos'd to lie among the Shepherds, oppress'd by the War in Germany* (1745). Exploiting the latest news-reports of marauding troops, and interweaving them with evocations of the shepherds' innocent, timeless hiding-places (caves, grottoes and shady groves), Warton makes the most of atmospheric sound-effects and ruinous descriptions. In his blank-verse dialogues, the lost shepherdess has been abducted by a soldier, and the favourite lamb trampled by a troop of horse.[19]

This reaching out for the exotic and sensational suggests that the formal 'eclogue' with its conversing shepherds was having a final fling. By mid-century it is clear that without such stimuli some readers had become jaded, as William Shenstone wrote:

> So rude and tuneless are thy lays,
> The weary audience vow,
> 'Tis not th'Arcadian swain that sings,
> But 'tis his herds that low.[20]

The singing shepherd was being replaced by the lowing herd. The pastoral setting remained popular and was easily integrated into other poetic forms. Glimpses of Edenic innocence formed part of many descriptive poems, and the moods and imagery of pastoral elegy were infused into contemplative writing. The shepherd in Joseph Warton's *The Enthusiast: Or the Lover of Nature* (1744) is a solitary contemplater of nature, not a conversationalist, and the 'hoary-headed swain' of Thomas Gray's *Elegy Written in a Country Church Yard* (1751) nostalgically recalls a pastoral landscape that is now empty ('One morn

---

19 Later 'exotic' reworkings of Pastoral include Thomas Chatterton's 'African Eclogues' (1770), Edward Rushton's *West-Indian Eclogues* (Liverpool, 1787), and Robert Southey's 'Botany Bay Eclogues' (1794).
20 'On certain Pastorals', *The Works in Verse and Prose, of William Shenstone, Esq.*, 2 vols. (London, 1764), vol. 1, p. 210.

I miss'd him on the custom'd hill', line 109). New poetic genres offered fresh possibilities. An increasing interest in the lyrical voice retuned 'pastoral' in sophisticated ways: as early as 1731, Isaac Thompson was fusing pastoral lament and Ovidian heroic epistle to give his lovelorn shepherd the emotional range of Pope's Eloisa; and Shenstone himself in his 'Pastoral Ballad' transformed the garden into an expression of a neurotic self, registering his emotions in a palpitating lyric rhythm that anticipates Tennyson.[21]

An interest in specific landscapes and the real life of the countryside inevitably had its effect on Pastoral. Once Stephen Duck, the Wiltshire thresher, had produced *The Thresher's Labour* (1730) it became increasingly difficult to show pastoral figures 'simply chatting in a rustic row'[22] without rolling up their sleeves and getting to work. Christopher Smart's extraordinary 'Noon-Piece; or, The Mowers at Dinner' (1748) explodes the pastoral scene into assorted fragments: dancing cupids share the picture with English farmworkers; allegorical figures play while Tray the dog guards the workers' lunch; and 'Colin Clout and Yorkshire Will / From the leathern bottle swill' (the Spenserian shepherd sharing a drink with the modern labourer). The implements of work now form an integral part of Smart's scene:

> Their scythes upon the adverse bank
> Glitter 'mongst th'entangled trees,
> Where the hazles form a rank,
> And court'sy to the courting breeze.
>
> (lines 22–5)

This is the point where Pastoral meets the Georgic.

Rapin's view that Pastoral represented the earliest of all poetry was widely accepted in the early eighteenth century. Whether or not one agreed with his 'Golden Age' theory, Pastoral had become associated with a simplicity of language and manners, and an essential freedom from a specified place and time. Collins and Warton challenged both of these; but in shedding them the Pastoral mode somehow lost its centre of gravity, its defining limitation. While this was happening, the Georgic poem was becoming popular as a genre that naturally embraced the new and the specific. The paradoxical fact is that Georgic was by far the older genre. Its founding text, Hesiod's *Works and Days*, is dateable to the eighth century BC,[23] seven hundred years before its

---

21 'Pastoral VI. The Letter', in Isaac Thompson, *A Collection of Poems Occasionally Writ On Several Subjects* (Newcastle, 1731), pp. 30–4; 'A Pastoral Ballad', *Works of Shenstone*, vol. I, pp. 189–98.
22 Milton, 'On the Morning of Christ's Nativity', line 87.
23 *Hesiod: Works and Days*, ed. M. L. West (Oxford: Clarendon Press, 1978), p. 31.

defining text, Virgil's *Georgics*. But Virgil's poem was 'defining' in a different sense from his *Eclogues*. As a form that was characterised not by limitation but by its capaciousness, the Georgic opened itself to freer reworkings and extension to different topics. Welcoming variety of scenes, details of place and time and an appropriately specific, even technical, language, Georgic flourished by seeking new subjects for attention. If Pastoral had found its ironies in repeated scenic superimpositions and revisitings, Georgic represented the spirit of 'fresh woods, and pastures new' (Milton's words on leaving Pastoral behind).[24] It was therefore an appropriate mode for expressing the energies of trade and colonisation. Georgic's images tend to be dynamic ones that incorporate growth and change and reflect the harnessing of human ingenuity. This said, however, Georgic also has one foot in the known and familiar. It remembers the names of things, exploits local knowledge, passes on expertise, recalls histories, recommends the tried and tested. It is interested in reliable tools and techniques. But this doubleness at the heart of Georgic should not be seen as a disjunction. What appears at first to be a contradiction between stability and change is really a recognition of the relationship between conserving and extending.

In place of the Pastoral's ironic juxtapositions, the Georgic poem is keenly aware of mixture and variety. It tends to look for ways of improving existing materials by combining or adding to them. In *The Sugar-Cane: A Poem* (1764) James Grainger goes so far as to make this a general rule for all life on earth: 'In plants, in beasts, in man's imperial race, / An alien mixture meliorates the breed' (*The Sugar-Cane*, 1. 458–9).[25] New energy comes from drawing varied elements together or recycling what has decayed. There is a link to be made, therefore, between the significance of compost for the Georgic tradition, and its celebration of English as a 'mixed' language. In *The Hop-Garden* (1752), on hop-cultivation and beer-making, Christopher Smart praises the loamy soil of Kent in these terms:

> this the hop
> Loves above others, this is rich, is deep,
> Is viscous, and tenacious of the pole.
> Yet maugre all its native worth, it may
> Be meliorated with warm compost. . .
>
> (1:83–7)

---

24 Milton, *Lycidas*, line 193.
25 See John Gilmore, *The Poetics of Empire: A Study of James Grainger's The Sugar-Cane* (London and New Brunswick: The Athlone Press, 2000), p. 103.

As if to make his point that the 'native' can always be improved, Smart offers us the full mixture of English vocabulary, with its rich absorption of Latin ('viscous', 'tenacious', 'meliorated') and Norman French ('maugre'). Like other Georgic writers he is aware that the fertility of his 'native' English has been increased by a long history of linguistic assimilation. For all its celebration of tradition, the Georgic also comes to terms with change.

If Pastoral evoked the temperate poise and innocence of the Golden Age, or its Christian equivalent the Garden of Eden, the Georgic is located in the fallen world of corruption and death, the changing seasons and the necessity of human labour. In Genesis 3:23 an angry God insists that mankind has now become an integral part of an organic cycle of growth and decay: 'Therefore the Lord God sent him forth from the garden of Eden, to till the ground *from whence he was taken*' (my italics). Providentially, the curse was to become an opportunity. Hesiod had his own version of this fall, and in *Works and Days* (an alternative title might be 'Labour and Time') he announced that his was the Age of Iron, in which mankind 'will never cease from toil and misery by day or night'.[26] Hesiod's Greek poem is the original of the myth that toil is the modern condition in a world where Nature no longer offers its plenty freely, but demands endless labour from us, at a time when all social cohesion has been lost. The idea lies behind the passage about 'these iron Times' in James Thomson's 'Spring' (from *The Seasons*, 1730), where 'all / Is off the Poise within' (lines 274, 277–8) and nothing is stable or predictable any more. Work in this Hesiodic context offers some way of bringing order and connectedness to what Thomson calls our 'broken World' (line 318). Throughout *The Seasons* this lack of 'poise', and the need for repeated human effort to accommodate, or even understand, the forces of nature, check the poem's Newtonian optimism so as to create a more complex dynamic. Although finally for Thomson the earth is held in the providential embrace of 'The great eternal Scheme / Involving All, and in a perfect Whole / Uniting' (*Winter*, lines 1046–8), at the level of human activity those natural forces both forward and frustrate human toil, a double theme that Virgil's *Georgics* had developed.

Critics who see a complacent and leisured agenda behind the English Georgic never seem to mention Hesiod. For Rachel Crawford, for example, the concept of the 'happy swain' is 'central to the georgic vision', which celebrates

---

26 Hesiod, *Theogony and Works and Days*, trans. M. L. West (Oxford: Oxford University Press, 1988), p. 42. On the pain and discipline of the 'Hesiodic code', see Rosenmeyer, *The Green Cabinet*, pp. 20–3.

'a traditionalist scheme that equates happy labor with the soil'.[27] But the 'Nature' with which the Georgic poet works is the same ambiguous power the workers have to confront, a changeable force which nurtures and tortures while it tracks the cycle of the seasons. In *The Thresher's Labour* (1730) Stephen Duck expresses frustration at his repeated annual routine:

> . . . the same Toils we must again repeat:
> To the same Barns again must back return,
> To labour there for room for next Year's Corn.
>   Thus, as the Year's revolving Course goes round,
> No respite from our Labour can be found:
> Like *Sisyphus*, our Work is never done,
> Continually rolls back the restless Stone . . .
>
> (lines 275–81)

The undoing of his work, the continual rolling back, seems to owe something to the Hesiodic passage in *Georgic* I, where Virgil's farmer is seen as resisting the depredations of pests and the general tendency in Nature towards degeneration and reversal: 'So it is: for everything by nature's law / Tends to the worse, slips ever backward, backward.'[28]

Set against this principle is the possibility of reconstruction and development – the *en-ergy* that counters the *en-tropy*. Virgil's four-book *Georgics* were being written in momentous years (36–29 BC) when Rome was struggling from a period of civil war to one of peace and unity. After the final defeat of Mark Antony and Cleopatra (31 BC), Octavius Caesar was seen to be uniting the empire, reintroducing the old observances and traditions, founding colonies and restoring the republican constitution. It was a balance of conservation and innovation, a uniting of the *civis* and the *cultus*, the state and 'culture' in all senses, an ideal time for a poem on the arts of cultivation.[29] Understanding the new project, in 29 BC Virgil read his completed work to Octavius, ending Book I by recalling 'a world in ruins' – 'everywhere / So many wars, so many shapes of crime / Confront us; no due honour attends the plough, / The fields, bereft of tillers, are all unkempt' (1.505–7); then in the following book on the

---

27 Rachel Crawford, 'English Georgic and British Nationhood', *ELH* 65 (1998), 123–58 (p. 135). For Crawford the Georgic mode resisted the progressive and commercial, and presented Britain as a 'georgic Eden' (pp. 129, 135–6).

28 *Georgics*, 1.199–200; Virgil, *The Georgics*, trans. by L. P. Wilkinson (Harmondsworth: Penguin Books, 1982), p. 63. All further quotations are from this translation.

29 On the readership and social context of the *Georgics*, see Gary B. Miles, *Virgil's Georgics: A New Interpretation* (Berkeley, Los Angeles and London: University of California Press, 1980), pp. 1–63 ('The Roman Context').

cultivation of trees and vines he considers how to encourage new growth by sowing and propagating, but also engrafting: 'often we observe how one tree's branches / Can turn, with no harm done, into another's' (II.32–3). Unless this is carried out, says Virgil, the fruit will deteriorate, 'forgetting its old flavour' (II.59). There is a natural power in the Italian soil, but 'every tree needs labour, all must be / Forced into furrows, tamed at any cost' (II.61–2). Wounds need to be made by slits and wedges, but they will heal and produce a new growth that flourishes as never before.

This Georgic narrative was ready-made for a period in British history when two nations had recently been engrafted together. In 1707 the Act of Union united the parliaments of England and Scotland and superimposed their national flags. Civil war in the 1640s had been followed by decades of religious upheaval and constitutional uncertainty, and the newly constituted 'Great Britain' faced particular problems of continuity and change, both religious and political. This forms the subject of John Philips' two-book poem *Cyder* (1708), the first authentic English Georgic, which extends the concerns of Virgil to the soil and climate of Britain. For Philips it is a land of mixed soils: some are 'deceitful', 'penurious', 'stubborn' or 'devoid of spirit', others 'kinder'; but each has a 'Force and Genius' that by experience can be made adaptable. What should be avoided is the importation of a 'Rich Foreign Mold' (I.120) – such an 'alien Compost' (there are suggestions of the Hanoverian monarch-in-waiting here)[30] can have only a deceptive and temporary effect. In a long Virgilian passage on engrafting, Philips describes how the orchard-keeper needs to experiment with new relationships,

> and search how far
> Two different Natures may concur to mix
> In close Embraces, and strange Off-spring bear?
> Thoul't find that Plants will frequent Changes try,
> Undamag'd, and their marriageable Arms
> Conjoin with others. (I.301–6)

The resulting hybrid will flourish, and 'Ee'r-long their differing Veins / Unite, and kindly Nourishment convey' (I.282–3). In tune with Virgil's constitutional concerns, Philips' poem seeks to reconcile a continuous tradition of old skills and observances with the cultivation of fresh varieties. Ideally, experience and wisdom should combine with energy and inventiveness, and the new be

---

30 On the politics of the poem, see J. C. Pellicer, 'The Politics of *Cyder*', in *Cyder. A Poem in Two Books* eds. John Goodridge and J. C. Pellicer (Cheltenham: The Cyder Press, 2001), pp. i–xvi.

allowed to develop from the old. The poem's evolutionary politics emerges near the end in a Virgilian picture of the horrors of England's civil war when pruning-hooks became weapons ('Too oft alas! has mutual Hatred drench'd / Our Swords in Native Blood', ii.486–7). Philips celebrates the fact that 'Cyder-Land' remained loyal to the executed King Charles ('O Best of Kings!'), and that after years of tyranny the nation's liberties had recently been restored by another Stuart monarch, Queen Anne.

In ending his poem with a narrative of British constitutional history, Philips exploits the organic character of the Georgic by engrafting it on to its native siblings, the English 'country-house' poem (the tradition of Jonson's *To Penshurst* and Marvell's *Upon Appleton House*) and the prospect poem (Sir John Denham's *Cooper's Hill*), landscape economies that explore geo-historical continuities and disruptions. Denham's royalist survey of Windsor and the River Thames, with its moralised landscape marked by religious conflict, is especially close in mood to Philips, and *Cooper's Hill* remained a potent influence on the naturalised English Georgic. Pope's *Windsor-Forest* (1713) specifically reworks Denham to celebrate the Tory Peace of Utrecht ('And Peace and Plenty tell, a STUART reigns', line 42). In all these poems the small individual landscape tests out at local level the state's capacity to harness into an effective economy those potentially competing forces: freedom and obedience, change and continuity, individual and social good, the arts of war and the arts of peace.[31] In the *Georgics* Virgil had used his native Mantuan scene to signify the keeping of faith, a spot of ground where true values will remain, and where he will dedicate a shrine to Caesar ('where the Mincius, / Embroidering his banks with tender rushes, / In sweeping loops meanders. / In the middle of the shrine, as patron god, / I will have Caesar placed', iii.14–16). In Virgil's imagination the Empire is given a local habitation. Georgic geography in this way opens out a pastoral retreat to patriotic and political themes, reaching from the provincial riverbank to the national picture, and then through time and space to distant lands (on the doors of Virgil's shrine will be carved 'the hordes of Ganges / In battle and our Romulus' victory, / And here great Nile in flood', iii.26–9). Pope's *Windsor-Forest* has a similarly confident centrifugal movement that carries patriotic good faith outwards from his own native stream in the forest (the Loddon) via the national river (the Thames) to colonise the world. The resulting free

---

31 See the classic discussion of *concordia discors* in *Cooper's Hill* and *Windsor-Forest*, in Earl R. Wasserman, *The Subtler Language: Critical Readings of Neoclassic and Romantic Poems* (Baltimore, MD: Johns Hopkins University Press, 1959), pp. 35–168. On Denham, Pope and the 'paysage moralisé', see John Chalker, *The English Georgic: A Study in the Development of a Form* (London: Routledge & Kegan Paul, 1969), pp. 66–89.

trade will be of enormous gain to Britain ('Earth's distant Ends our Glory shall behold, / And the new World launch forth to seek the Old', lines 399–400). The opening up of foreign markets to British shipping was one of the benefits of the Utrecht treaty, and in Pope's poem the 'economy' of forces within a national and global system is here taking on its modern financial sense.

In Walpole's Britain of the 1730s, the Georgic had obvious appeal for the mercantile interest. Its language of beneficent growth and exploitation of resources could be used to naturalise the claims of commercial development. The economic writer John Bennet recommended improvements in trading conditions in language that sounds uncannily like a prose summary of a Georgic poem:

> the Colonies and Trade of *Great-Britain* may be likened to a most excellent Orchard[32] laid out and planted by Queen *Elizabeth*, suffered to grow by King *James*, unfenced and over-run in the next Reign, supported and taken Care of in the *Interregnum*, put into better Order on the Restoration; and having supplied us plentifully with all Sorts of Fruit ever since, both for our own and foreign Use, at length the Ground wants manuring, the old Walks repairing, the Trees pruning and nailing, and some to be removed, and others new planted; and the Whole, from the Goodness of the Soil, and Benefits of its Situation, capable of receiving prodigious Additions and Improvements.

This extract (p. 128) from Bennet's *The National Merchant: Or, Discourses on Commerce and Colonies; Being an Essay for Regulating and Improving the Trade and Plantations of Great Britain, By Uniting the National and Mercatorial Interests* (1736) shows how naturally the geo-historical economy of the Georgic could be made to serve the Whig interest. Its language of manuring, pruning, repairing and planting is less concerned with constitutional theory than with getting the system to function properly. For the royalist histories of Denham, Philips and Pope, Bennet substitutes a severely practical test of effective state organisation, and a concern with managing the nation's resources. Oliver Cromwell and the two Charleses are assessed on this basis only.

The improving of British industry and trade was one of the purposes of Georgic as a patriotic mode. Addressing his three-canto poem, *Agriculture* (1753), to the future George III (as part of an ambitious project entitled *Public Virtue*), Robert Dodsley aimed 'to delineate such objects of public virtue, as best may deserve the attention of a British Prince'.[33] These included a

32 Bennet's economic allegory compares interestingly with seventeenth-century images of the nation-as-orchard. See the royalist and Puritan versions discussed by Anthony Low, *Georgic Revolution*, pp. 225–6, 236–7.
33 Robert Dodsley, *Public Virtue. A Poem in Three Books. I. Agriculture. II. Commerce. III. Arts* (1753), dedication. Only Book I was published.

national oak-planting scheme. Works like John Dyer's *The Fleece* (1757) and Grainger's *Sugar-Cane* can be regarded as up-to-date reports on the state of the nation's cloth industry and its West Indian sugar plantations. Such poems, with their well informed documentation (often supplemented by footnotes) are full of practical advice,[34] and can incorporate quite naturally a specific recommendation (like Dyer's plans for linking the Rivers Trent, Severn and Thames, III.604–6) or a hymn to trade (Grainger's 'Mighty commerce, hail!', IV.322). Both Dyer and Grainger have direct knowledge of what they discuss, and their observations and advice are based on first-hand experience. In his Preface, Dr Grainger notes: 'Medicines of such amazing efficacy, as I have had occasion to make trials of in these islands, deserve to be universally known. And wherever, in the following poem, I recommend any such, I beg leave to be understood as a physician, and not as a poet.'[35] He expects to be judged by practical as well as poetic criteria.

For Virgil, the farmer-poet, the ideal of practical organisation is represented by the beehive, which forms the subject of his final book. This analysis of a state-in-miniature brings to a climax the *Georgics'* concern with how civic order should reflect the natural interdependence of all life. The worker-bees are practical and cooperative in maintaining their hive, but they may also have a spiritual dimension: 'Some have affirmed that bees possess a share / Of the divine mind and drink ethereal draughts; / For God, they say, pervades the whole creation, / Lands and the sea's expanse and the depths of sky' (IV.219–22). To see the earth as an animated system came naturally to the English Georgic, with its organic modes of thought, and its capacity to engage with the latest scientific discoveries. The mathematics of Newton, Shaftesbury's System of Nature, the worlds of microscope and telescope, combined to give a Georgic poem like Thomson's *Seasons* an extra philosophical/theological dimension. Both Hesiod and Virgil had reached from the plough to the stars, but Thomson delights in the new confidence with which an eighteenth-century British poet can contemplate everything from the minute sap vessels in a leaf to the intelligibility of the universe. Thomson's natural world owes much directly to Virgil. He has fully absorbed the *Georgics* both thematically and in detail, and many of its memorable passages have their direct equivalent in his poem: the

---

34 In *The Hop-Garden* Smart 'showed himself keen to keep up to date by . . . recommending the use of ventilating fans in hop kilns. Stephen Hales invented these in 1742, the first year of composition' (Chris Mounsey, 'Christopher Smart's *The Hop-Garden* and John Philips's *Cyder*: a Battle of the Georgics? Mid-Eighteenth-Century Poetic Discussions of Authority, Science and Experience', *British Journal for Eighteenth-Century Studies*, 22 (1999), 67–84 (p. 77).

35 In Gilmore, *The Poetics of Empire*, p. 90.

bees' society, the sexual passion in animals, storm, pestilence, the labours of the agricultural year, exotic excursions to the desert and the frozen steppes, the signs of changing weather – and so on. But Virgil's tentative suggestion of a universal life-force becomes in *The Seasons* the sustaining impetus of all creation. For Thomson, Earth is a living organism whose materials are forever in motion or waiting to have their energies released. In 'Spring' he prays ecstatically to the 'SOURCE OF BEINGS! UNIVERSAL SOUL / Of Heaven and Earth! ESSENTIAL PRESENCE . . .!' (lines 556–7). These are big concepts; but as he goes down on his knees, it is not to pray but to scrutinise the minute mechanisms of plant-life:

> By THEE the various vegetative Tribes,
> Wrapt in a filmy Net, and clad with Leaves,
> Draw the live Ether, and imbibe the Dew.
> By THEE dispos'd into congenial Soils,
> Stands each attractive Plant, and sucks, and swells
> The juicy Tide; a twining Mass of Tubes.
>
> (lines 561–6)

The world in miniature with its air ('live Ether') and ocean ('juicy Tide') bursts into activity, and the reader's imagination is pulled away from the abstract divine spirit to the rising sap of springtime, the true 'essential' element. The tiny fibres of vegetation become the tangible form of life's organic interconnectedness, its 'soul'. Indeed we have just seen a Virgilian bee 'Cling to the Bud, and, with inserted Tube, / Suck its pure Essence, its ethereal Soul' (lines 511–12).

Georgic is supremely adaptable and could take as its subject not only the natural world, but the organisation of the human body. For the physician-poet John Armstrong this too was a complex living economy with its equivalent of soil and climate, ripening and decay, energies and diseases. In *The Oeconomy of Love* (1736) the animating principle is the sexual appetite 'from whose quick Impulse Life / Subsists' (lines 286–7), and the human task is to turn this force of nature to best advantage ('we strive not to repress / . . . Her lawful Growth; ours be the Task alone / To check her rude Excrescences, to prune / Her wanton Overgrowth' (lines 278–82). Proper husbandry is therefore vital ('Husband your Vigour well', line 544), and variety of cultivation advisable ('Other Pursuits, their equal Share demand / Of Cultivation', lines 504–5). Armstrong's unembarrassed vocabulary of growth and fruition extends to the topic of puberty ('the parting Breasts / Wanton exuberant and tempt the touch, / Plump'd with rich Moisture from the finish'd Growth', lines 50–2), and even to a youth's nocturnal emissions ('mid the rage / Of the soft Tumult, every turgid Cell / Spontaneous disembogues its lucid store', lines 42–4). But this is a fallen Georgic world, not a pastoral Eden, and Armstrong is concerned with offering practical advice (and warnings) on everything from aphrodisiacs to impotence.

For him, the body is something to be cultivated with as much care as Virgil's grapes, and just as crops and livestock respond to a routine based on knowledge and experience, so the human body will flourish under a regimen of regular habits. This is the message of Armstrong's best known Georgic poem, *The Art of Preserving Health* (1744). Here the necessity of labour becomes a virtue: 'Toil, and be strong', he advises, 'By toil the flaccid nerves / Grow firm, and gain a more compacted tone' (Book III, lines 39–40). He recommends sustained 'Exercise' – not sudden bursts of energy, but a habitual routine, an awareness of the regular ticking of the body's clock. This placing of human labour within the greater scheme of things, finding a bodily pulse within the broader rhythm of Nature, takes us to the heart of the Georgic mode:

> . . . pliant nature more or less demands,
> As custom forms her; and all sudden change
> She hates of habit, even from bad to good . . .
> Slow may the change arrive, and stage by stage;
> Slow as the shadow o'er the dial moves,
> Slow as the stealing progress of the year.
>
> (Book III, lines 464–71)

Armstrong attunes himself to the organic implications of Georgic: the body should be synchronised with Nature's measured pace. Time is implacable, and 'change' must be accommodated. The less it disrupts, the more surely it will transform.

The Georgic was therefore well equipped for engaging with the momentous developments of the Industrial Evolution (as it should perhaps be called), in which the natural energies in soil, rock and water were harnessed to increasingly sophisticated processes. As we have seen, the Georgic's variety and adaptability, its interest in how things are organised, its geographical and historical dynamics and its openness to specialised vocabularies, allowed it to explore economies of many different kinds. It combined a respect for custom and experience with a practical interest in how things work and develop. In Dyer's *The Fleece*, we see the old and new worlds encountering each other, but in a context of continuity. This poem offers a survey of Britain's sheep-farming regions mapped out by the nation's rivers, and a historical account of how the wool trade developed over many centuries. We learn about the various breeds suited to different local conditions; and the individual types of cloth produced.[36] Dyer celebrates practised skills of many kinds, whether the efficiency of the Leeds wholesale cloth-market, or the village-woman's deftness at her spinning-wheel. But in the middle of these tributes to traditional techniques appears an alien invader, Lewis Paul's roller spinning-machine (the very latest 1750s technology):

> We next are shown
> A circular machine, of new design,
> In conic shape: it draws and spins a thread
> Without the tedious toil of needless hands.
> A wheel, invisible, beneath the floor,
> To ev'ry member of th'harmonious frame
> Gives necessary motion. One, intent,
> O'erlooks the work: the carded wool, he says,
> Is smoothly lapp'd around those cylinders,
> Which, gently turning, yield it to yon cirque
> Of upright spindles, which, with rapid whirl,
> Spin out, in long extent, an even twine.
> (Book III, lines 291–302)

The 'tedious toil' of humanity has been replaced by the spindles' 'rapid whirl'. The circles move continuously, their different speeds perfectly synchronised. A solitary worker indicates 'yon cirque' as if pointing to the heavens, and we notice how this new system of 'necessary motion' has been naturalised in Georgic fashion, unproblematically fitted into James Thomson's vocabulary of Newtonian providence – only here the 'harmonious frame' is made of wood and metal. Revolutionary technology is presented as part of a naturally evolving scheme.

When a poet wants to register change as a sudden, disruptive break with the past, the adaptable Georgic is no longer suitable. Here the ironies of Pastoral come into their own. Pastoral's use of juxtaposition and contrast replaces Georgic's concern with intermixture and development. Georgic's growth of experience gives way to Pastoral's lost innocence. Part of the power of Oliver Goldsmith's *The Deserted Village* (1770) is its rejection of the Georgic mode in favour of a return to Pastoral – or rather a frustrated longing to return.

36 See John Goodridge, *Rural Life in Eighteenth-Century Poetry* (Cambridge: Cambridge University Press, 1995), pp. 91–180.

The poem moves from the opening description of an Arcadian social circle ('Dear lovely bowers of innocence and ease', line 5) to distressing scenes of estrangement and dispersal ('yon widowed, solitary thing', line 131), but it refuses to connect up the two visions into an organic whole. Here Time is discontinuous, with the past set against the present; and the only signs of continuity are the lingering bits of vegetation which mark each of the three lost buildings that once gave the village its heart. The 'torn shrubs' (line 141), 'blossomed furze' (line 196), and 'yonder thorn' (line 221) are isolated landmarks that parody a Georgic concern with husbandry. In Auburn there is nothing to cultivate. It is part of Goldsmith's indictment of his age that at the centre of his poem is an aching void where Georgic might be. The poem finds no space for productive activity, but only its deleterious effects. We are presented not with an economy, but with unreconciled extremes of luxury and want. The poem also has a stylistic gap between its sentimental and satiric modes – circling repetitions for the lost pastoral society ('These round thy bowers their chearful influence shed, / These were thy charms – But all these charms are fled', lines 33–4) moving to ironic contrasts and inversions for the present scene ('Where wealth accumulates, and men decay'). The text of *The Deserted Village* exemplifies a lost coherence, a lack of common ground and continuous life. In place of this is an isolated pastoral idyll to which the poet cannot return. Instead, he suddenly reaches out to an exotic land of scorpions, tigers and tornadoes, as the place to start a new life – an episode the Georgic mode could accommodate, but which here has a suitably disruptive and ironic effect.

If Pastoral was able to develop its radical potential for signifying alienation and social division, or for imaging the inauguration of a pristine world (and thus become an appropriate mode of revolutionary discourse in the 1790s),[37] Georgic was easily assimilated into the mixed topographical or loco-descriptive poem.[38] In *The Task* (1785) William Cowper can integrate the art of cucumber-growing, the evil of cruelty to animals and the history of living-room furniture into a single poem, whose motto (*Fit surculus arbor* – 'The shoot becomes the tree') expresses a concern for how things grow and sustain themselves. His

37 See, for example, the Goldsmithian picture of French peasants celebrating the vintage in Helen Maria Williams, 'Epistle to Dr Moore' (1792), lines 11–42. In *Rights of Man* (1791–2) Thomas Paine attacks a 'mixed' and 'engrafted' (i.e. Georgic?) government, and sees natural rights as grounded in the Edenic primal scene. See *Rights of Man*, ed. Henry Collins (Harmondsworth: Penguin Books, 1969), pp. 88, 114, 162–3 and 191. On the influence of Georgic and topographical poetry on Burke's *Reflections* (1790), see David Fairer, 'Organizing Verse: Burke's *Reflections* and Eighteenth-Century Poetry', *Romanticism* 3 (1997), 1–19 (pp. 7–12).
38 Topographical poems with a persisting Georgic element include Richard Jago's *Edge-Hill* (1767), Henry James Pye's *Faringdon Hill* (1774) and Anne Wilson's *Teisa* (1778).

Yardley Oak (1792) offers us an ancient tree whose organic Burkean constitution has resisted the axe of revolution. Hollow and deformed, it is nonetheless a living system that has experienced the full rigours of the Georgic – time, disease, the weather, predators and decay – yet still manages to renew itself. Remarkably, both Pastoral and Georgic persisted throughout the eighteenth century, and by transforming and adapting in various ways, were able to offer their contributions to the political debates of the 1790s.

Political, satirical, didactic and lyric poetry (11): after Pope

JOHN SITTER

Poetry of the later eighteenth century is 'after Pope' creatively as well as chronologically. Much of it imitates, alludes to or reacts against the great poet of the first half of the century. Given how controversial Pope was in his own age, from the early *Essay on Criticism* (1711) to the final *Dunciad* (1743), it is remarkable that his name occurs nearly as frequently in poetry of the second half of the century.[1] Pope's influence extends nearly everywhere in the decades following his death, from the work of younger contemporaries such as Mary Leapor, Joseph Warton, Thomas Warton, Mary Jones, Mark Akenside and Thomas Gray, who published mainly in the 1740s and 1750s, to later poets publishing major works in the 1780s, such as William Cowper and George Crabbe. Writers of such strength as Samuel Johnson and Christopher Smart, who both wrote early verse indebted to Pope, may seem to have outgrown his influence. But it seems likely that the mature Johnson would have written more than two major verse satires had Pope not written so many, and that the oracular eccentricity of Smart's later style flows in part from a need to distance himself from the conversational urbanity Pope had perfected.

Characterising the period in other respects has proven more difficult, and arguably the study of its poetry has suffered as a result. Assumptions that the period is 'burdened' by 'anxiety', that it is the 'Age of Sensibility', or that its most important features are 'pre-Romantic' all present problems that go beyond terminology. They lead to selective readings of the period that exaggerate discontinuities with the past and anticipations of the future, as if satire and exposition disappeared from poetry with the deaths of Pope and Swift (1744, 1745) and lengthening shadows of lyric and autobiography soon

---

1 Occurrences of the word 'Pope' are a crude but useful comparative measure. *English Poetry (600–1900)*, an electronic database (ProQuest Information and Learning Company, 1996–2001) based on works listed in the *New Cambridge Bibliography of English Literature*, turns up 524 instances of 'Pope' for 1700 to 1750 and 443 for 1750 to 1800. Random sampling suggests that a slightly higher percentage of the occurrences in the second half of the century refer to the poet rather than the leader of the Roman Catholic Church.

Fig. 11.1 *Alexander Pope* by Jonathan Richardson (*c.* 1737)

covered all. Perhaps this selectivity has a more distorting effect on the readings of individual poems, predisposing one to decide in advance what should be present and obscuring distinctive achievement.

Tendentious readings begin almost immediately, and the most influential of all has been Wordsworth's, exemplified in his account of Gray's 'Sonnet on the Death of Richard West' (1742, published 1775) in the 1800 Preface to *Lyrical Ballads*. Reacting against what he regarded as artificial 'poetic diction', Wordsworth quoted the poem in full to argue that only five lines, which he put in italics, are of 'any value', precisely because they use the direct language of prose:

> In vain to me the smiling mornings shine,
> And reddening Phoebus lifts his golden fire:
> The birds in vain their amorous descant join,
> Or cheerful fields resume their green attire:
> These ears, alas! for other notes repine,
> *A different object do these eyes require.*
> *My lonely anguish melts no heart but mine;*
> *And in my breast the imperfect joys expire.*
> Yet morning smiles the busy race to cheer,
> And new-born pleasure brings to happier men:
> The fields to all their wonted tribute bear;
> To warm their little loves the birds complain.
> *I fruitless mourn to him that cannot hear,*
> *And weep the more because I weep in vain.*

Wordsworth seems to assume what countless critics since have assumed about Gray's poem, that direct personal statement is struggling to emerge from encumbering artificiality. The real difference runs deeper than the overt disagreement over diction.[2] Wordsworth keeps the autobiographical baldness that is the poem's most 'Wordsworthian' feature, while he disregards Gray's melancholy wit and self-mockery. Gray expresses this complex consciousness by beginning both the sonnet's octet and sestet with the conventional language of pastoral poetry and then shifting abruptly to direct statement; the *contrast* between natural fruition and human frustration, not merely the latter, is the poem's subject. Few poems of the later eighteenth century are so richly dialogic as Gray's, but his peculiar poise suggests the sort of alertness to tone that the period's poetry may demand.

2 The various editions of the Preface, including its Appendix on 'poetic diction', are available in R. L. Brett and A. R. Jones (eds.), *Lyrical Ballads* (London: Methuen, 1963, rev. 1965); see pp. 252–3.

Although political poetry continues to be written in the later eighteenth century, the poems that succeeding generations have usually found most interesting are not, as in the Restoration and early eighteenth century, intensely partisan or decisively ideological. Ministers, administrations and policies continue to be foolish, venal and dangerous, in verse as well as life, but most of the lampoons and satires have died with them. Why political myth and satirical mythopoesis should have grown less compatible in the second half of the century is difficult to say, but poets often appear less convinced that civic oppositions embody ultimate values. Two couplets that Samuel Johnson contributed to Oliver Goldsmith's *The Traveller* (1764) suggest a gulf between political events and ethical poetry:

> How small, of all that human hearts endure,
> That part which laws or kings can cause or cure.
> Still to ourselves in every place consigned,
> Our own felicity we make or find . . .[3]

Pope or Swift or Dryden agreed with these sentiments in some moods, but their great satires on public affairs flow from a conviction that laws, kings and private happiness belong to the same poetic order of things.

Satiric poetry

Johnson's two important satires, *London* (1738) and *The Vanity of Human Wishes* (1749), loose imitations of Juvenal's third and tenth satires, suggest the difference between the politically charged verse satire of the earlier period and a more diffuse mode that one of Johnson's modern biographers refers to as 'satire *manqué*' (frustrated or failed satire).[4] In *London* Johnson's speaker has no doubt that he is unhappy in London for political reasons. The capital of a 'groaning', 'cheated' and 'sinking' nation, London is now best suited for corrupt courtiers, French flatterers and assorted beneficiaries of 'publick crimes,' for anyone, that is, but the honest, poor, outspoken satirist. The poem's specifications of place and time ('now' as opposed to ancient England or even an England older than the age of Walpole) are as notable as its indignation. The poem has all three of the elements of traditional satire: 'an attack by means of a manifest fiction upon discernible historic particulars'.[5] *The Vanity*

---

3 Lines 429–32. Quotations from Goldsmith, Collins and Gray are from *The Poems of Gray, Collins, and Goldsmith*, ed. Roger Lonsdale (London: Longmans, 1969).
4 W. J. Bate, 'Johnson and Satire *Manqué?*', in W. H. Bond (ed.), *Eighteenth Century Studies Presented in Memory of Donald F. Hyde* (New York: Grolier Club, 1970), pp. 145–60.
5 Edward Rosenheim, *Swift and the Satirist's Art* (Chicago: University of Chicago Press), 31.

of Human Wishes, on the other hand, repeatedly goes beyond its Juvenalian source in elevating the general over the topical, locating unhappiness in the human condition rather than in historical conditions. Johnson immediately generalises the poem geographically and temporally, as its 'extensive view' stretches not only from China to Peru but from ancient history to the present, finding all eras pretty much alike. The poem generalises linguistically and fig-uratively as well. Even the definite article is pressed into service to create a sense of indefinite iteration: 'the gen'ral Massacre of Gold' has been occurring throughout human history, 'the gaping Heir' has been impatient for genera-tions, 'the baffled Prince' has been heading towards 'the fatal Doom' of defeat time after time. These generic agents and events merge readily into the host of personifications who haunt the poem, from 'Observation' in the opening lines, through 'Misfortune' and 'hissing Infamy,' to 'celestial Wisdom' at the close.

The element of 'attack' not surprisingly broadens into exposition and even-tually consolation in a poetic satire that uses historical particulars ultimately to merge them into abstraction ('Let Hist'ry tell . . .'). Johnson departs much more from Juvenal's tone than he had in *London*. Although Satire x is Juvenal's most philosophical, it has less of the pensive melancholy that distinguishes Johnson's poem throughout and especially in its conclusion. The religious scepticism and scorn of Juvenal become fideism and sympathy in Johnson. Juvenal mocks prayer in general: the last lines say roughly, 'if you still cannot outgrow the need to pray, at least ask for something harmless, like a sound mind in a sound body'. By contrast, Johnson raises a 'supplicating Voice' for the Christian virtues of faith, hope and charity, gifts with which 'celestial Wisdom calms the Mind, / And makes the Happiness she does not find.' Whether Johnson's studied withdrawal from the political realm makes *The Vanity of Human Wishes* a 'failed' satire, a 'tragic' satire or something else entirely, the poem embodies the tentative brooding, other-worldly personi-fication and uneasy resignation that become conspicuous in many kinds of non-satiric poetry during the middle and later eighteenth century.

But this trend should not obscure the fact that much satire in the Popean, epistolary, this-worldly mode continues to be written, some of it quite good. Mary Jones' *Miscellanies* of 1750 contains two particularly agile examples, 'An Epistle to Lady Bowyer' and 'Of Desire. An Epistle to the Honorable Miss Lovelace'. Both borrow openly from Pope (and perhaps obliquely from Edward Young); the first is in fact a sort of female *Epistle to Dr Arbuthnot*, and the second courts comparison with *An Epistle to a Lady*. So, too, does the first poem in Mary Leapor's 1748 *Poems upon Several Occasions*, 'Dorinda at her Glass', which, following its wittily insightful gallery of women preoccupied with appearance, also invokes Pope's *First Epistle of the First Book of Horace Imitated*:

> Hear this, ye fair Ones, that survive your Charms,
> Nor reach at Folly with your aged Arms;
> Thus *Pope* has sung, thus let *Dorinda* sing;
> 'Virtue, brave Boys, – 'tis Virtue makes a King':
> Why not a Queen? fair Virtue is the same
> In the rough Hero, and the smiling Dame . . .[6]

Leapor's death at the age of twenty-four, in 1746, seems a real loss to poetry. The posthumous *Poems upon Several Occasions* and her *Poems*, 1751, contain several works in an accomplished epistolary style, deft, witty and gracefully ruminative. While many of these do indeed depend heavily on Pope's example, they breathe on their own and show great promise. Leapor's reading was considerable, but the education of a kitchen maid had to be hard-won and intermittent. When we recall that at the same age Swift had probably completed but a single unsuccessful ode and that even the unusually precocious Pope had published only his *Pastorals*, *An Essay on Criticism* and the 1712 (sylphless) version of *The Rape of the Lock*, Leapor's accomplishment, especially in a mode requiring urbane sophistication, looks truly significant. Writing of death shortly before she herself became fatally ill, Leapor's 'Mira' pledges that when her time comes she will not

> wish to stretch the Line of Fate,
> That the dull Years may bear a longer Date,
> To share the Follies of succeeding Times
> With more Vexations and with deeper Crimes.
> ('An Epistle to a Lady', lines 55–8)

But the poems Leapor completed suggest that the follies of succeeding decades might have found a good satiric home had she lived into Horatian middle age. 'An Epistle to Artemisia. On Fame' brings Pope's autobiographical *Epistle to Dr Arbuthnot* to a female world. Unlike the famous Pope who is interrupted in his work by aspiring writers, Leapor is chided by a housekeeper for neglecting her domestic tasks and by other women for minding her muse more than her shoes. Her most sustained satire, 'Crumble-Hall', responds to Pope's account of Timon's Villa in the *Epistle to Burlington* and draws on Leapor's first-hand

6 The poems by Jones and Leapor are most readily accessible in *Eighteenth-Century Poetry: An Annotated Edition*, eds. David Fairer and Christine Gerrard (Oxford: Blackwell Publishers, 1999).

experience below stairs and in kitchens, where 'fires blaze; the greasy Pave-
ments fry; / And steaming Odours from the Kettles fly' (lines 58–9). Leapor
achieves a remarkable combination of playfulness and plangency, ridiculing
bad husbandry and mourning the trees about to be felled:

> But, hark! what Scream the wond'ring Eye invades!
> The *Dryads* howling for their threaten'd Shades:
> Round the dear Grove each Nymph distracted flies
> (Tho' not discover'd but with Poet's Eyes) . . .
>
> (lines 165–8)

Many late eighteenth-century poets known for their non-satiric works wrote
some satires. Thomas Gray wrote two brief works in the 1760s, 'The Candidate'
and 'On Lord Holland's Seat Near Margate', not intended for publication.
Goldsmith's 'Retaliation' (1774) is still anthologised. Some of Cowper's and
Crabbe's work is satiric, although as we shall see their most interesting poems
tend to move towards didactic musing rather than sustained ridicule or attack.
The only poet in the second half of the century to make his reputation wholly
as a satirist was Charles Churchill.

Like an earlier satiric poet and libertine, the Earl of Rochester, Churchill
died at the age of thirty-three, his death probably hastened by venereal disease.
Churchill wrote much more than Rochester and polished much less. In a
poetic career of less than four years, from 1761 to 1764, he wrote over 14,000
lines of verse and published nearly all of it. The poems are of course very
uneven, sometimes brilliantly comic, sometimes almost unreadable, nearly
always vigorous and vehement. His fame has suffered from the topicality of
much of his work as well as from haste. The raciness that made his poems
best-sellers in the 1760s has not worn well, and by 1816, Byron, an admirer who
seems to have learned much from him, could describe him, in 'Churchill's
Grave', as the 'comet of a season'. A carefully edited volume of Churchill's
selected poetry, containing perhaps a quarter of his verse, could today make
him more accessible, but the task would not be simple. While *The Prophecy
of Famine*, attacking Bute, and *The Times*, largely an assault on homosexuality,
are hopelessly mired in historical partisanship and anxieties, parts of nearly all
of Churchill's other poems should be included – and excluded.

The Rosciad, an attack on popular actors, launched Churchill's career in
March of 1761, and *The Apology* confirmed his popularity a month later. *The
Rosciad* mocked nearly every actor of note save David Garrick, an omission
Churchill corrected in passing in *The Apology*, which aims most of its personal

satire at Tobias Smollett. But the poem interests later readers more for its statement of general satiric principles, including his professed preference for Dryden over Pope. Although *The Apology* is more reminiscent of several of Pope's Horatian poems than of any single work of Dryden's, Churchill prefers Dryden's 'strong invention', 'noblest vigour' and 'varied force' to Pope's 'polished numbers and majestic sound'. Churchill vows not to refine away the 'gene'rous roughness of a nervous line' (The Apology, line 355), a promise he had little trouble keeping, equating overly smooth versification with decadent modernity and operatic eunuchs. His opposition of 'vigour' to 'sound' actually harks back to satire before Dryden, to the angry young satirists of the 1590s such as John Marston and John Donne, who made the harshness of the 'satyr' a mark of alienated sincerity.

Night, published in January of 1762, announces another kind of alienation. Here Churchill sets himself and his friend Robert Lloyd against the tamely conformist values of the 'prudent' majority:

> Let slaves to business, bodies without soul,
> Important blanks in Nature's mighty roll,
> Solemnize nonsense in the day's broad glare:
> We NIGHT prefer, which heals or hides our care.
>
> (lines 7–10)

The poem is an odd mixture of social criticism, bohemian bravado and earnest individualism. The honest partisans of night will continue to pay court to 'wine's gay god' and to women (Churchill and the wife he had married at eighteen would soon separate) 'tho' in our teeth are hurl'd / Those *Hackney Strumpets*, PRUDENCE and the WORLD' (lines 294–5). He then goes on to anatomise both terms. 'Prudence', its 'sense perverted', is now merely another name for 'hypocrisy'; as for the 'World', at present 'no more it means, we find, / Than many fools in the same opinion join'd' (lines 302–3, 357–8). Satirists have often declared themselves in the minority, trumpeting their independence; but Churchill's individualistic relativism and self-referentiality are extreme. Both qualities make his work uniquely interesting but also render much of his satire ethically and formally incoherent.

His next and longest work, *The Ghost*, shows the fascination and frustration of his eccentricity. Ostensibly about the supposed Cock-Lane Ghost (which aroused the curiosity of Horace Walpole, Samuel Johnson and others), the poem of over 4,500 tetrameter lines becomes as it progresses both more political and more a poem about whatever Churchill can think of next. The first two books, published in March of 1762, run to 526 and 808 lines and focus reasonably well on the incident and the surrounding question of superstition. But in book three (1,266 lines, October) Churchill has begun to advertise the work's 'bold contempt of every rule' and to make, or seek to make, a virtue of its 'rambling, wild, digressive wit' (lines 60, 84). Book four (1,934 lines, November, 1763) carries the game even further, beginning three paragraphs in a row, for example, with the phrase 'But, to return'. The poem appeared in instalments simultaneously with the first several books of Laurence Sterne's *Tristram Shandy*, and Churchill praises Sterne's method,

> Where each *Digression*, seeming vain,
> And only fit to entertain,
> Is found, on better recollection,
> To have a just and nice Connection . . .
>
> (III.971–4)

Churchill identifies Sterne's manner more closely than he catches it. Unlike Churchill's roaring 'I', Sterne's Tristram is comically differentiated from the author; moreover, Sterne does not attempt to combine, as Churchill does, whimsicality with Juvenalian indignation. Still, Churchill's emulation of Sterne forms an important part of his 'aesthetic of spontaneity'.[7] The aesthetic blurs into an ethic as Churchill seems increasingly to value impulsiveness and emotion, a bias he shares with not only Sterne but other 'sentimental' fiction writers of the second half of the century. But again, the sentimental, relativistic ethos often sorts ill with satire. By book four of *The Ghost*, Churchill proclaims full individualism: 'Let every man enjoy his whim; / What's he to me, or I to him?' (lines 215–16). He then launches into a long celebration of credulity and private imagination:

> Some few in *knowledge* find relief;
> I place my comfort in *belief.*
> Some for *Reality* may call;
> FANCY to me is All in All . . .
>
> (IV.289–92)

Despite traces of mock-encomium, Churchill's irony is only partly under control, and the satirist is thus left closer to solipsism than to clear social norms, a problem Churchill sometimes seeks to counter with volume rather than argument.

7 The phrase is used by Lance Bertelsen in his account of Churchill in *The Dictionary of Literary Biography, Volume 109: Eighteenth-Century British Poets, Second Series*, ed. John Sitter (Detroit: Gale Research Inc., 1991), 88. See also T. E. Blom, 'Eighteenth-Century Reflexive Process Poetry', *Eighteenth Century Studies* 10 (1976), 52–72.

But it would be a mistake to see Churchill's satires only as failures. The defence of Churchill by a poet so different and so judicious as Cowper must be given weight. Conceding Churchill's carelessness, Cowper praises his 'daring strokes of fancy' and the 'bold masculine character' that is his 'great peculiarity'.[8] The same conflicts that diffuse many of his satiric attacks also frequently energise his poems. Part of Churchill's 'peculiarity' is his readiness to put uncertainty and ambivalence at centre-stage, projecting internal argument into staged debate. Since the debates are themselves likely to be contradictory and unresolved, the effect is a striking, unstable compound of self-disclosure and exposé, a sort of confessional satire.

One example must stand for many. *An Epistle to William Hogarth* was published in July of 1763, shortly after Hogarth had satirised Churchill and his friend John Wilkes in *The Times* and just before he would caricature Churchill so memorably in *The Bruiser*. Hogarth was in failing health by this point (he would die a year later), and Churchill without mercy emphasises Hogarth's physical and mental frailty ('Hence, Dotard'). But then Churchill decides – *after* several hundred lines of attack – that in view of Hogarth's condition it now 'seems rank cowardice to give the stroke' (line 628). We might take this remark simply as further ridicule but for the fact that the poem immediately ends with a poignant paragraph on the senility of Swift, Steele and other instances of 'humbled Genius'–including Hogarth. This odd conclusion matches the eccentricity of the rest of the poem, an epistle in which it has taken Churchill over 300 lines to get to Hogarth. Much of the first half of the work is a debate between the satirist and 'Candour', a personification (representing good will), who urges the poet to write in other modes. Her arguments allow the author to insist that he is too honest *not* to write satire, that the age demands it, and so on. But Candour's charge that Churchill, 'dup'd by thy vanity', purveys a brand of 'guilty rage' that actually discourages virtue because it 'Sicklies our hopes with the pale hue of Fear' is never really refuted (lines 244, 275, 285). The phrasing suggests an incongruous Hamlet of the streets and night-cellars. The final effect is one of strong conviction (satire must continue and Hogarth deserves it) built on a keen sense of the arbitrary, improvisational nature of all such convictions.

The internal debate that surfaces repeatedly in Churchill's work crystallises in a passage in *Gotham* (March to August of 1764), his most sustained flight of

---

8 Cowper's praise of Churchill is quoted by James Laver in his edition of *Poems of Charles Churchill* (New York: Barnes and Noble, 1970), p. xlix. The passages from the poems follow *The Poetical Works of Charles Churchill*, ed. Douglas Grant (Oxford: Clarendon Press, 1956). Byron remembers Churchill in 'Churchill's Grave'.

fancy, a 'noble and beautiful poem' in Cowper's estimate. Churchill creates an imaginary kingdom and imagines himself as its king. This utopian conceit allows him to comment on the less than utopian aspects of actual, English monarchy and to expound on the qualities of the ideal 'patriot king'. Asking himself whether he is ready to assume the role, Churchill writes,

> have I explored my heart,
> That labyrinth of fraud, that deep, dark cell,
> Where, unsuspected, e'en by me, may dwell
> Ten thousand follies? Have I found out there
> What I am fit to do, and what to bear?
> Have I trac'd ev'ry passion to its rise,
> Nor spar'd one lurking seed of treach'rous vice?
> Have I familiar with my nature grown?
> And am I fairly to myself made known?
>
> (III.55–63)

The questions seem more than rhetorical. At its best, Churchill's satire conveys the nervous energy of self-examination, self-implication and a vigorous mind rarely at rest.

Both Cowper and Crabbe are poets of real satiric ability whose longer works tend, however, towards a more didactic mode, more presentational and essayistic than ridiculing. Cowper might first appear to be the major satirist of the later decades of the century. He had imitated two of Horace's satires early (1759) and adroitly, and his most sustained work before *The Task* is a group of eight long poems in couplets published in his *Poems* of 1782 and later referred to collectively as the 'Moral Satires'. But the label was not Cowper's own, and for good reason. While two of the poems, 'Table-Talk' and 'Hope', may be read primarily as satires, the others contain only scattered satiric passages. Cowper's stronger satires are to be found among his protest poems against slavery, some of which are bitterly comic and ironic. Satirists need not have been on the side of history to remain accessible, but the reader's task is easier when they were. The anti-slavery poems require less suspension of disbelief today than do satiric poems like 'The Modern Patriot' in which the supporters of American independence are anarchists or than some of his evangelical poems in which keeping the Sabbath with insufficient strictness appears to threaten national welfare.

Cowper's powerful series of poems against the slave trade that were published in newspapers and magazines in 1788 include 'The Negro's Complaint', 'The Morning Dream' and 'Pity for Poor Africans'. The first relies primarily on pathos but ends by satirically challenging the English 'slaves of gold' to 'Prove

that you have human feelings, / Ere you proudly question ours' (lines 45–8).
The utopian vision of the second poem gains ironic force from its allusion to
James Thomson's familiar 'Rule, Britannia' (1740), with its refrain that 'Britons
never will be slaves'; Cowper dreams

> That Britannia, renown'd o'er the waves
> For the hatred she ever has shown
> To the black-sceptred rulers of Slaves –
> Resolves to have *none of her own*.[9]

In 'Pity for Poor Africans' a comfortable speaker laments the slaves' lot but
'must be mum, / For how could we do without Sugar and Rum?' (lines 5–6).
Even more sardonic are 'Sweet Meat has Sour Sauce', published posthumously,
and 'Epigram' (1792), which compares the addition of lamb's blood to clarify
wine with the use of '*negro*'s blood' in sugar production, arguing that the
efficacy is 'in the blood of innocence alone – / Good cause why planters never
try *their own*' (lines 7–8).

'Table-Talk' was placed at the beginning of the collection of the eight long
poems of 1782, and it is modelled substantially on Pope's 'prologue' to his
satires, the *Epistle to Dr Arbuthnot*. The poem mentions Pope directly (lines
646–61), commending not only his 'harmony' but also his ability to give
'virtue and morality a grace'. This is high praise from Cowper, in view of
his frequently quoted observation that Pope's accomplishment 'Made poetry
a mere mechanic art; / And ev'ry warbler has his tune by heart' (lines 654–5);
Cowper seems to mean that Pope's ethical achievement ('In verse well dis-
ciplin'd, complete, compact' (lines 647)), has since devolved to mere facility
in most writers: a 'servile trick and imitative knack' (line 666). But while
Cowper admires Pope and the 'serious mirth' of Pope's fellow Scriblerians
John Arbuthnot and Jonathan Swift, 'Table-Talk' hints at the distrust of satire
that will surface more completely in other poems: 'Satire has long since done
his best', and now Religion must take over (lines 728–39). The fifth poem
of this group, 'Hope', contains satiric character sketches that match most of
Pope's in the *Epistles to Several Persons*, but the next poem, 'Charity,' questions
the usefulness of satire and the motives of both satirists and their readers
(lines 491–556). Three years later in *The Task* Cowper asks rhetorically, 'what

---

9 *The Poems of William Cowper*, eds. John D. Baird and Charles Ryskamp, 3 vols. (Oxford:
Clarendon Press, 1980–95) (vol. III, p. 17, lines 45–8); on these and other anti-slavery poems
see Suvir Kaul, *Poems of Nation, Anthems of Empire: English Verse in the Long Eighteenth
Century* (Charlottesville: University Press of Virginia, 2000), pp. 230–68.

can satire, whether grave or gay? / . . . What vice has it subdued? whose heart reclaim'd / By rigour, or whom laugh'd into reform? (II.315–21). Most of his longer poems may thus be approached more profitably as didactic works designed, as he put it too modestly in 'A Poetical Epistle to Lady Austen' (1781), 'To catch the triflers of the time, / And tell them truths divine and clear, / Which, couch'd in prose, they will not hear' (lines 20–2).

Didactic / discursive poetry

The term 'didactic' often is more evaluative than descriptive. When Shelley declared that 'didactic poetry is my abhorrence' (Preface to *Prometheus Unbound* (1820), penultimate paragraph) he was introducing a work that many of the eighteenth-century writers whom he was reacting against might have considered highly didactic. Shelley appears to have in mind poetry which does only what might be done as well in prose, such as delivering precepts. But the proper boundaries of poetry and prose are of course historically variable rather than natural. In Wordsworth's elegant formulation in the Preface to *Lyrical Ballads*, the 'exponent or symbol held forth by metrical language must in different eras of literature have excited very different expectations'.[10] Through much of the seventeenth and eighteenth centuries those expectations included conversational tuition, realised in the pedagogical mode of many verse 'essays' of the Restoration and, most successfully, in Pope's *Essay on Criticism*, *Essay on Man* and epistles. While not easy to define, the 'didactic' poem might be distinguished, negatively and roughly, with the help of Sir William Temple's 1690 essay 'Of Poetry'. Temple differentiates six recurrent motives for poetry: 'praise, instruction, story, love, grief, and reproach'.[11] The following section will concentrate on poems in which the second of these poetic impulses is not overwhelmed by one of the others.

Taking later eighteenth-century didactic poetry to begin with several blank verse poems of the 1740s – Edward Young's *Night-Thoughts*, Joseph Warton's *The Enthusiast*, Thomas Warton's *The Pleasures of Melancholy*, Mark Akenside's *The Pleasures of Imagination* – one sees how discursive poems become more subjective and expressive, less essayistic and more mixed with personal narrative. Abandoning the couplet was itself a way of marking distance from Pope, moving away from the 'Essays on moral Subjects' to which, Joseph Warton

10 Wordsworth, *Lyrical Ballads* (see note 2), p. 243.
11 'Of Poetry', 1690, in *Five Miscellaneous Essays by Sir William Temple*, ed. Samuel Holt Monk (Ann Arbor, MI: University of Michigan Press, 1963), p. 186.

would complain in 1746, the 'Public has been so much accustom'd of late'.[12] It could also be a way of announcing expansiveness. Pope himself did not attach ideological values to the couplet, merely suggesting pragmatically that it could provide a linguistic elevation that would lessen the need for other heightening devices:

> I have nothing to say for rhyme, but that I doubt whether a poem can support itself without it in our language, unless it be stiffened with such strange words as are like to destroy our language itself. The high style that is affected so much in blank verse would not have been borne even in Milton, had not his subject turned so much on strange out-of-the-world things as it does.[13]

Several of the practitioners of blank verse declare at once their Miltonic rather than Popean allegiance and their concern with 'out-of-the-world' themes. Referring to Pope and *An Essay on Man*, Young writes, 'Man too he sung: *immortal* man I sing', and at the close of *Night-Thoughts* takes pride in having 'outwing'd' the 'flaming Limits of the World' (1.452, IX.2414–16). Akenside's poem does not begin empirically from Pope's 'scene of Man' but transcendentally 'from heaven' (1.57).[14] Thomas Warton immediately ascends Mount Tenerife to find Contemplation, 'Remote from man, conversing with the spheres' ('The Pleasures of Melancholy', line 16), so that she might lead him in turn to the solitude-loving Melancholy, and his brother Joseph transcends the daylight world to glimpse Virtue herself in her (and his own) 'midnight-walks' ('The Enthusiast', line 188). These very different poems of the 1740s have in common the aim of leading the reader into new paths and perspectives, which are also presented as returns to something loftier, the restoration of a kind of poetic truth function that had been lost. Beyond that shared mission, there are significant generational differences separating Young, born five years before Pope, from Akenside and the Wartons, born in the 1720s. For Young, 'Born in an Age more Curious, than devout' (IX.1832), the return is to Christian orthodoxy; for Akenside and the Wartons, whose poetic commitments are

12 Joseph Warton makes this statement in the prefatory Advertisement (quoted below on p. 309) to his *Odes on Various Subjects*, 1746. Two modern facsimiles of this volume are available, one introduced by Joan Pittock (Delmar, NY: Scholars' Facsimiles & Reprints, 1977), and one by Richard Wendorf (Los Angeles: William Andrews Clark Memorial Library, University of California, Los Angeles, 1979).

13 Joseph Spence, *Observations, Anecdotes, and Characters of Books and Men*, ed. James M. Osborn (Oxford: Clarendon Press, 1966), vol. I, p. 173 (June 1739, number 365).

14 Quotations from Young and Akenside are from *Night Thoughts*, ed. Stephen Cornford (Cambridge: Cambridge University Press, 1989) and *The Poetical Works of Mark Akenside*, ed. Robin Dix (Cranbury, NJ, and London: Associated University Presses, 1996).

Neoplatonic and vaguely deistic, poetry sponsors aesthetic rather than religious instruction.

Partly because it was in the religious mainstream and partly because of its apparent autobiographical melodrama, *Night-Thoughts* was immediately more popular than the work of the Wartons and Akenside and long remained so. Isaac Watts could speak of Dryden, Pope and Young as a triumvirate even before *Night-Thoughts* appeared; afterwards, it is not unusual to hear Young mentioned with Milton. *The Complaint: or, Night-Thoughts on Life, Death, and Immortality*, to use its full title, appeared in nine 'nights' from 1742 to 1746, sprawling to nearly 10,000 lines. It might be better known today had Young ended it, as he contemplated, after the fourth book. This portion of the poem, about a quarter of the whole, is more autobiographical, though loosely so, and less tendentious than some of the later sections. Young tells a recognisable story of grieving and meditation on mortality, from 'The Complaint' of Night I to 'The Christian Triumph' over the fear of death in Night IV. Thus far, *Night-Thoughts* is a 'recovery' narrative of some immediacy: it traces the speaker's return to equanimity following a series of losses and his rediscovery of religious conviction after ruminations on 'Time, Death, Friendship' (Night II) and the harrowing death of a blameless young woman, 'Narcissa' (Night III), modelled on Young's daughter-in-law. Night V stages a 'Relapse', however, and much of the rest of the poem is devoted to a more polemical recovery, converting the young infidel and 'man of the world', Lorenzo. Young had trouble either resigning or resolving his theme; Night IX, 'The Consolation', is nearly as long as the first four together.

Modern readers find *Night-Thoughts* difficult to read in part for what many of Young's contemporaries found attractive, its mixture of emotional display and disputation. The poem does not lend itself to anthologising; as Samuel Johnson observed: its 'excellence . . . is not exactness, but copiousness; particular lines are not to be regarded; the power is in the whole'.[15] Until 1989 it had been out of print for over a century. Young's exclamatory mode and his epigrammatic wit are sometimes memorable ('Procrastination is the thief of time'), but they also strain against the expansiveness of blank verse, lapsing into unrhymed couplets ('*Gold* glitters most, where *Virtue* shines no more; / As Stars from absent Suns have leave to shine' (v.666–7)) and setting up conflicting expectations.

A larger problem is modern impatience with leisurely rumination in verse. When T. S. Eliot observed (in 'The Metaphysical Poets' [1921]) that Tennyson

15 Samuel Johnson, 'Young', in *Lives of the Poets*, 2 vols., (London: J. M. Dent, 1925), vol. II, p. 362.

and Browning 'ruminated', he was lodging a complaint and urging the Imagist programme for poetry – eliminating explanation and narrative – that came to dominate much twentieth-century verse. Despite many interesting long discursive poems, we still tend to expect poems to be oblique, lyric and short. Young's readiness to magnify feelings and to ramify arguments remains uncongenial today, but this resistance is worth overcoming. The success of *Night-Thoughts* and its influence on Romanticism, especially in Germany, cannot simply be attributed to piety. Young taught generations of readers to find 'enthusiasm' acceptable in poetry and to expect autobiography in the philosophical poem.

Less conspicuously confessional than *Night-Thoughts*, Mark Akenside's *The Pleasures of Imagination* (1744) shows as clearly the movement toward expressive didacticism. While Pope's *An Essay on Man* (first published anonymously) gives little clue to the poet's age or personal situation, Akenside's reader knows at once that the poet is youthful and unattached, just as surely as the poet of *Night-Thoughts* is an ageing mourner. *The Pleasures of Imagination* is part essay on aesthetics and part portrait of the young artist. In general, the second version of the poem, which Akenside revised and expanded in maturer years, tones down some of the youthful daring of the original, but the expressive emphasis hardly disappears. In fact, the unfinished revision (published as *The Pleasures of the Imagination* in 1772, two years after Akenside's death) contains a decisively 'Wordsworthian' apostrophe to the hills and rivers of his youth

> and that delightful time
> When all alone, for many a summer's day,
> I wandered through your calm recesses, led
> In silence by some powerful hand unseen.
> (IV.42–5)

The Pleasures of Imagination is an ambitious poem in scope and manner, an astonishing achievement for a poet of twenty-one. Drawing on Plato, Shaftesbury, Addison, Francis Hutcheson and others, Akenside undertakes the project of restoring the lost unity of imagination, understanding and will:

> Thus was beauty sent from heav'n,
> The lovely ministress of truth and good
> In this dark world: for truth and good are one,
> And beauty dwells in them, and they in her,
> With like participation. Wherefore then,
> O sons of earth! would ye dissolve the tye?
> (I.372–7)

The vital tie dissolves in Akenside's view when pleasure is pursued without regard to cognition or conduct. In the poem's most extended narrative, which comprises most of book two, the youthful poet's crisis of belief finds expression and cure through the allegorised mirror vision of a youth who temporarily follows the smiling Euphrosyne and forgets the more matronly Virtue. He is then set upon by the avenging 'son of Nemesis' – a secularised version of Milton's Sin – until he remembers the voice of Virtue, recovers his faith in providence, and learns to accept worldly suffering – 'all that edge of pain' – as part of the world's beauty.

Akenside's vision now seems more willed than imagined, and his poetry has suffered a fate similar to Young's: more than a century of frequent reprintings, then a full century of neglect, followed recently by the tentative resurrection of a scholarly edition. The once broad popularity and influence of *The Pleasures of Imagination* (it is echoed in poems by Gray, Coleridge, Wordsworth and Keats) make it worth reconsideration, and Akenside's capaciousness, daring and fluent mastery of blank verse repay sympathetic reading.[16] The narrative of the youth's dissociation and reintegration points to not only autobiography but also metapoetic reflection. The allegorical vision embodies both the poet's crisis and the poem's mission, which for Akenside is nothing less than the reconciliation of poetry and philosophy, estranged since the end of the previous century, 'when Locke stood at the head of one party, and Dryden at the other'.[17]

The projection of the self into the statement of ideas finds its most memorable expression, of course, in Gray's *Elegy Written in a Country Church-Yard* (1751). Readers who know nothing else of eighteenth-century poetry often know the *Elegy*, and almost everyone has heard something about paths of glory leading but to the grave and flowers wasting their sweetness on the desert air. Many virtues contribute to the poem's perennial power, including Gray's exquisite phrasing, layered allusions and the hypnotic pacing of his quatrains; but the feature most representative of its historical moment is its creation of an exemplary didactic self. The role of the self as exemplar grew significantly while Gray worked on the poem. The Eton College manuscript version lacks the poem's 'Epitaph', in which the speaker (now ventriloquising) leaves a version of himself as instance of the imagination's hunger for immortality. Whether self-effacing ('to Fame unknown') or self-aggrandising

---

16 Fairer and Gerrard (Eighteenth-Century Poetry, p. 490) note that Ann Yearsley responds to Akenside in 'To Mr ****, an Unlettered Poet, on Genius Unimproved', and numerous echoes of Akenside in Collins and Gray are noted by Lonsdale. Abbie Findlay Potts gives more credit to Akenside than most Wordsworthians in his *Wordsworth's Prelude: A Study of its Literary Form* (Ithaca, NY: Cornell University Press, 1953).

17 Akenside's note to *The Pleasures of Imagination*, II. 30; see *The Poetical Works*, 162.

('Melancholy mark'd him for her own'), the epitaph exemplifies the compulsion to leave 'Some frail memorial' that 'Implores the passing tribute of a sigh'.

When Johnson, often impatient with Gray's other poetry, said of the *Elegy* that if Gray had 'written often thus, it had been vain to blame, and useless to praise him', he evidently had in view the poem's nice balance of public precept and private feeling: 'The *Church-Yard* abounds with images which find a mirror in every mind, and with sentiments to which every bosom returns an echo.'[18] The double meaning of 'sentiments' helps illustrate the particular way in which much mid eighteenth-century writing is 'sentimental'. As today, the word can refer equally to feelings, often inarticulate, or to opinions, often memorably stated. Gray's *Elegy* is never inarticulate (its speaker is *not* the 'mute' Milton who might be buried nearby), but it ranges from atmospheric emotionalism grounded in the personal, contingent moment ('leaves the world to darkness and to me' line 4) to unconditioned generalisations. The latter may be expressed as statements ('The paths of glory' line 36), commands ('Let not Ambition mock their useful toil' line 29) or rhetorical questions ('Can storied urn or animated bust / Back to its mansion call the fleeting breath?' lines 41–2). In this respect, the *Elegy* is the 'Sonnet on the Death of Richard West' writ large, exploiting with more scope and control the poignant tension between fleeting subjectivity and abiding propositions.

James Beattie's *The Minstrel; or, The Progress of Genius* (1771–4) illustrates what for the contemporaneous rhetorician Hugh Blair is a borderline case of didactic poetry. Granting that all poetry makes or should make 'some useful impression', Blair distinguishes among the poetic means of instruction: 'This impression is most commonly made in poetry, by indirect methods; as by fable, by narration, by representation of characters; but didactic poetry openly professes its intention of conveying knowledge and instruction.'[19] Beattie's narrative of Edwin, a shepherd's son who becomes a poet, affords many opportunities for 'indirect' exposition. The poem focuses on 'primitive' imagination (Edwin lives in a pre-literate society, and Beattie tells his 'Gothic' tale in Spenserian verse), on the poetic personality (a 'lone enthusiast' given to talking to himself, Edwin seems mad to some of the villagers), and especially on the role of the rural environment in the early development of the 'visionary boy'. Although less ambitious than Wordsworth's *The*

18 Johnson, 'Gray', *Lives*, vol. II, p. 392.
19 Hugh Blair, lecture XL in *Lectures on Rhetoric and Belles Lettres* (New York: D. Huntingdon, 1814), 447.

Prelude, or The Growth of the Poet's Mind, Beattie's *Minstrel* is nonetheless the first English poem to teach that childhood and poetry may be parts of the same subject.

The didactic self put forward in Oliver Goldsmith's two major poems, *The Traveller* (1764) and *The Deserted Village* (1770), and in George Crabbe's *The Village* (1783) is a man dependent paradoxically for his poetic insight on early familiarity with rural life and adult estrangement from it. Like Gray's *Elegy*, *The Traveller* seems to have grown in subjectivity as it developed over several years. What appears to be its earliest version, lacking about a quarter of the whole, proceeds directly to the survey of social life in Italy, Switzerland, France, Holland and England. A lengthy introductory section in the published poem praises Goldsmith's brother, a country clergyman, and frames the subject in more personal terms. The new section calls attention so dramatically to the distance between the benign rootedness of the brother's life ('Blest be that spot, where cheerful guests retire' (line 1)) and the 'remote, unfriended, melancholy' lot of the poet ('But me, not destined such delights to share' (line 23)) as to redefine the subject. The poem's comparative sociology now becomes part of the wandering speaker's quest for happiness, a journey ending in the insistence that the differences so keenly observed in the bulk of the poem make little difference: 'Why have I strayed from pleasure and repose, / To seek a good each government bestows?' (lines 425–6). This tension between sameness and difference surfaces in the comparative survey as well. On the one hand, hierarchy exists everywhere, 'For just experience tells, in every soil, / That those who think must govern those that toil' (lines 371–2). Yet some hierarchies seem especially repellent; an oligarchy of the sort England shows signs of becoming – 'one sink of level avarice' – is a place where 'Laws grind the poor and rich men rule the law' (lines 359, 386).

The Traveller blames the replacement of natural 'social' ties by the merely 'fictitious bonds' of 'wealth and law' largely on 'stern depopulation', the subject that Goldsmith would make his own with *The Deserted Village*. Demographic change would seem an unpromising subject for poetry, but Goldsmith combines real affection for rural life, nostalgia for what has been lost, political indignation and melancholy alienation into a uniquely beautiful poetic tutorial. The speaker's presence is less melodramatic than in *The Traveller* but more functional and more affecting in its understatement. The speaker is no longer of his (putatively) native Auburn but had fondly hoped to retire there, before seeing its changes. With gentle irony, he admits to imagining his distinction as well as the village's tranquillity:

I still had hopes, for pride attends us still,
Amid the swains to show my book-learned skill,
Around my fire an evening group to draw,
And tell of all I felt and all I saw . . .

(lines 89–92)

The speaker appears only a few times after this section, just enough to keep the supposed autobiographical connection alive and, at the close, to enliven the parade of personifications with first-person intimacy: 'Even now, methinks, as pondering here I stand, / I see the rural virtues leave the land' (lines 397–8). Many of Goldsmith's contemporaries, including Johnson, and many later readers have been sceptical of the attack on 'luxury' as socially pernicious, arguing instead that new money brought more good than dislocation. That the argument may be unresolvable and perennial – replayed in later debates over 'progress', 'development', 'free trade' or 'globalisation' – helps explain the poem's continuing appeal.

The Village (1783) answers the idealisation of rural life that Crabbe disliked in the Pastoral generally – 'themes so easy' (1.32) – and probably in recent semi-pastoral poems like The Deserted Village. The didactic self Crabbe constructs is a gruff speaker impatient with convention, who promises to draw the 'real picture of the poor' and 'paint the cot, / As truth will paint it, and as bards will not' (1.5, 53–4).[20] This sympathetic but hard-headed anti-bard takes on the role of documentary correspondent, giving deluded urban readers a report on conditions in the country. While he suggests that rural conditions have always been grim and nostalgia always a delusion, he also projects a nostalgia of his own which depicts the past as a period of relative innocence, if not ease. The 'swain' who used to plough fields is now 'intoxicated' with hopes of becoming rich through piracy; the youths who formerly turned to 'rural games' and 'merry mischief' after labour are now lurking at all hours by the seacoast to receive smuggled goods or hoping for shipwrecks (1.89–118). The contrast between Then and Now is of course a common feature of satire, but Crabbe's speaker seems more concerned with teaching complacent readers – 'gentle souls who dream of rural ease, / Whom the smooth stream and smoother sonnet please' (1.174–5) – than with judging the rural poor. Closest to satire are his depictions of figures of ill-used authority, such as the physician who 'first insults the victim whom he kills' or the clergyman too busy to preside over a poor man's funeral (1.285, 345–8). For all his anti-poetic realism, Crabbe's

---

20 Quotations from Crabbe are from The Complete Poetical Works, eds. Norma Dalrymple-Champneys and Arthur Pollard, 3 vols. (Oxford: Clarendon Press, 1988).

speaker shares some of the features of the sentimental hero. Keenly alert to the 'life of pain' that surrounds him and eager to gain broader sympathy for it, he puts an improbably eloquent soliloquy in the mouth of an ageing shepherd, some twenty lines of metaphoric and rhetorical balance (1.208–27). This daring reappropriation (rather than rejection) of pastoral convention helps create the image of a new urbanity, embodied in a poetic guide who knows more than his metropolitan readers about real country life and more than his villagers about the real causes of their suffering. His is a sophistication that allows analysis but not indifference; he is estranged, not detached.

The most complex created self in English poetry between Pope and Wordsworth is the subject of Cowper's *The Task* (1785). Cowper shares more in religious viewpoint with Young than any of the other poets under discussion, but his poem constructs a more realistically autobiographical and engaging speaker than the theatrical 'I' of *Night-Thoughts*. That he does so despite much that is doctrinally rigid, and in about half as many lines as Young, indicates Cowper's range of feeling, precision and subtly modulated blank verse. Although he occasionally displays Young's fondness for epigram ('God made the country, and man made the town', 'Variety's the very spice of life' (1.749, II.606)), he never seems to be writing loose couplets. When a sentiment happens to fall neatly within two lines, such as 'They love the country, and none else, who seek / For their own sake its silence and its shade' (III.320–1), no exclamation point, real or imagined, closes it. Cowper's unparalleled ability to keep his blank verse quiet – free from Young's declamation – is central in a poem that so deeply celebrates the quiet life. Country tranquillity is congenial for Cowper ('My very dreams were rural'), but it is more broadly essential for poetry and truth. 'The poet's treasure, silence' is requisite for wisdom, 'a pearl with most success / Sought in still water' and most of all for hearing the 'STILL SMALL VOICE' of God (1.235, III.381–2, IV.700, V.685).

Voice is the underlying subject of *The Task*, which is not only a didactic poem but a poem about didacticism, a meditation on the available means of instruction. Cowper seeks a poetic counterpart to the 'teaching voice' of Christianity, a discourse he believes superior to all others because 'whom it teaches it makes prompt to learn' (V.858–9). Its power to move the passions while instructing the intellect had long been seen as differentiating poetry from mere exposition, but Cowper quietly associates the act of poetic creation – described memorably in the passage in book II beginning 'There is a pleasure only poets know' (lines 284–304) – with the creative speech act of God, 'Whose word leaps forth at once to its [the soul's] effect, / Who calls for things that are not, and they come' (V.686–7). Remembering Cowper as the oblique and 'unambitious' (IV.798) poet of gardens and pleasant walks, we may forget how directly *The Task* confronts the question of the poet's pedagogical mission. That mission seems to be especially urgent in bad times, and the times are bad, Cowper insists, largely because of bad teaching. The clergy should be reaching where satire no longer can, but pulpits are now likelier occupied by fops than by serious instructors. Most culpable are the universities. Cowper traces the origin of various national vices to 'Profusion', a sort of advanced 'Luxury', and finds the root cause of Profusion in the near disappearance of instruction and 'Discipline' from Cambridge and Oxford (II.667–779). In such a climate, even a poet wishing to lay down the 'satyric thong' (III.26) may be required to pick up the 'harp of prophecy', and in fact large parts of *The Task*, particularly in books II and IV, tend toward the jeremiad.[21] Even book III, 'The Garden', devotes 150 lines explicitly to miseducation and false learning (lines 139–289) before turning to cucumbers, geraniums and rural virtues.

Cowper's poetry impressed younger contemporaries as different as William Blake and Jane Austen in part because he made integrity his theme. Cowper famously portrayed himself in *The Task* as a 'stricken deer that left the herd / Long since' (III.108–9), but Cowper as Man of Sensibility in Retirement is unlike the wounded weepers in the sentimental novels of the 1770s and after. His range of feeling is greater, including indignation as well as sympathy, and *The Task* presents a self who seems to be looking at the world rather than in a mirror. Self-revelation and social vision cooperate as Cowper builds up a portrait of a poet removed from society who eagerly reads the newspapers (the subject of much of book IV), intent upon preserving an identity uninfected by the national fever but incapable of indifference. 'What's the world to you?' asks an imagined interlocutor, eliciting this elaboration of Terence's *nil a me alienum puto*:

> Much. I was born of woman, and drew milk
> As sweet as charity from human breasts.
> I think, articulate, I laugh and weep
> And exercise all functions of a man.
> How then should I and any man that lives
> Be strangers to each other?   (III.196–201)

Such a declaration gains force because one sees these 'functions' of humanity continually working in the poem, as Cowper observes, reflects and voices

---

21 See, for example, *The Task*, VI.747–58 ('Sweet is the harp of prophecy') and *Table Talk*, lines 478–99 ('A terrible sagacity informs / The poet's heart').

authentic ambivalence. Looking towards London at the close of book III, the poet sees 'Much that I love, and more that I admire, / And all that I abhor'. Accordingly he concludes, 'I can laugh / And I can weep, can hope, and can despond, / Feel wrath and pity, when I think on thee!' (lines 840–2). Cowper's sympathies are impressively manifold and intellectually coherent. He moves, for example, from tenderness for worms to an exploration of the inborn responsiveness to natural environments that in our time has been called 'biophilia', or from pity for an individual prisoner in the Bastille to an endorsement of universal human rights (VI.563, IV.689–779, V.379–537). And his sympathy is often most impressive when leisurely rumination distils into laconic realisation. Thus, a long description of a frugal couple's chilling failure to find enough heat or food in their bare cottage comes down suddenly to the barest fact: 'With all this thrift they thrive not' (IV.399). At this level, the doctrinal precepts scattered throughout *The Task* bear less of the poem's didactic weight than does the example of an observant speaker engaged, for all his fragility, in ideal conversation with the world.

Lyric poetry

The story of lyric poetry from the 1740s into the 1780s resembles one of the mid-century's own odes. It begins abruptly, proceeds irregularly, exhibits flashes of brilliance and passages of obscurity and concludes with a mixture of daring and diffidence. The lyric marks the sharpest break with the Age of Pope, not because appreciably more lyric poems were published in the later decades but because many practitioners of lyric poetry chose it in no small part for its distance from Pope. In the 1740s Mark Akenside, Joseph Warton and William Collins published volumes of odes, and for many readers and writers lyric poetry would become identified with 'pure' or essential poetry. Warton's prefatory note to his *Odes on Various Subjects* (1746) argued that a change of taste was required:

> The Public has been so much accustom'd of late to didactic Poetry alone, and Essays on moral Subjects, that any work where the imagination is much indulged, will perhaps not be relished or regarded. The author therefore of these pieces is in some pain least certain austere critics should think them too fanciful and descriptive. But as he is convinced that the fashion of moralizing in verse has been carried too far, and as he looks upon Invention and Imagination to be the chief faculties of a Poet, so he will be happy if the following Odes may be look'd upon as an attempt to bring back Poetry into its right channel.

One should take sceptically Warton's claims of restoration ('bring back') and correction ('right channel') since nearly every succeeding generation has declared the need to return to the genuine current of national poetry. But that such a claim should centre on lyric poetry marks a conceptual and qualitative change. Odes poured steadily upon the land from the late seventeenth century on, but, apart from Dryden's, we read those from the Restoration to the 1740s historically, symptomatically, but not poetically. Swift's Pindaric failures interest solely as Swift's, those of lesser writers as curious tombs of dead ideologies and misplaced sublimities. But at mid-century the ode suddenly focuses the creative energy of a new generation, with the publication in 1745 of Akenside's *Odes on Several Subjects*, in 1746 of Warton's *Odes on Various Subjects* and, especially, of Collins' *Odes on Several Descriptive and Allegoric Subjects*, and in 1747 of Gray's 'Ode on a Distant Prospect of Eton College'. A few years later Gray would begin the genuinely Pindaric 'The Progress of Poesy', publishing it in 1757 with the genuinely sublime 'The Bard'.

Although Gray found too much of 'the frigid' in Akenside's odes and even joked about one of his own being a 'high Pindarick upon stilts',[22] the achievement of the generation of poets coming of age in the 1740s was to associate the ode with personal urgency rather than civic declamation. Not that patriotic themes disappear. Warton and Collins both write odes to Liberty, for example. Akenside voiced nationalistic pride in his odes 'On Leaving Holland' and 'On Lyric Poetry' (1745) as well as in later odes such as 'To the Country Gentlemen of England' (1758). Gray's odes in the 1750s clearly address civic as well as private concerns. Even the turn of the century would find the Romantic poet Helen Maria Williams composing an 'Ode to Peace'. But many of the best mid-century lyric poems succeed by enacting private visionary experience, in contrast to the choral projections of the period's countless anthems.[23]

The three odes that Gray completed in 1742 were published after those of Warton and Collins (the Eton ode in 1747, 'Ode on the Spring' in 1748 and 'Ode to Adversity' in 1753) but anticipate some of their emphases. The lines teem with personifications – 'making persons of abstracted things', Thomas Warton would say – which are sometimes barely realised, as in the catalogue of 'ills' awaiting the boys once they leave Eton, but which sometimes can preside singly over an entire poem, as does the figure of Adversity.[24] This ode,

22 Roger Lonsdale (ed.), *The Poems of Gray, Collins, and Goldsmith*, p. 156.
23 Suvir Kaul uses the term 'anthem' for the period's 'lyrics or songs that enunciate a confident collectivity and project it into the future'; see *Poems of Nation*, p. 9.
24 Thomas Warton wrote of personifying 'abstracted things' in an unpublished essay on a 'Romantic Kind of Poetry'. The essay is quoted and discussed by David Fairer in 'The

which Gray alternately referred to as a 'Hymn', follows the pattern of most of Collins' odes (the pattern Keats would adapt for his odes to Melancholy and Indolence): the poet as votary describes a goddess and his own regard for her, then requests or prophesies her beneficence toward him or the country. Gray asks Adversity 'To soften, not to wound my heart' ('Ode to Adversity', line 44) and thus bring the gifts of sympathy and self-knowledge. The pattern partly derives, like much else in the poetry of this generation, from the early poetry of Milton; but the odes tend to go beyond the witty celebration and affiliation of 'L'Allegro' and 'Il Penseroso' to emphasise the poet's personal vision and vulnerability.

The sense of prophetic vision granted to the speaker, fleetingly and perhaps dangerously, distinguishes the very best of the mid-century odes: Collins's 'Ode to Evening' and 'Ode on the Poetical Character' and Gray's 'The Progress of Poesy' and 'The Bard'. Collins' apostrophe to Evening as his 'Maid compos'd' is doubly apt, since she is not only self-possessed but a composition of the landscape's many sensuous particulars. The combination of solicitude and erotic ardour with which the poet addresses this insistently female personification is unmatched until Keats' ode 'To Autumn'. In the 'Ode on the Poetical Character' the personification of Fancy is at once modest and highly sexual, 'retiring' with God in order to conceive triplets: 'visions wild', Apollo, and 'All the shadowy tribes of Mind' that are the new subject of poetry (lines 22, 39, 47). Despite the confidence of this vision, with its privileged glimpse of divine creation and Milton's imagined Eden, the conclusion insists that the 'inspiring bowers' are now closed to 'every future view'. This ending may be a near-tragic declaration of inadequacy or belatedness, but it might also assert prophetic power, a determination to have the last word.

Such are the endings of Gray's odes, which also combine imagined strength and impotence. The prophetic poet of 'The Bard' can bring history, as represented by King Edward I (who in the late thirteenth century ruthlessly conquered Wales and made it a part of his kingdom) to a halt and speak truth to power – briefly. The poet sees what the mighty cannot, and he compels them to listen. But the poem will end, of course, with his suicide, and the death of the last of the Welsh bards at least suggests the precarious height and marginality of the modern poet. The speaker of 'The Progress of Poesy' assumes the high ground less literally than does the bard, but he too uses it to forestall reply. The modern poet of this poem sees, as surely as the bard, images

Poems of Thomas Warton the Elder?' *Review of English Studies*, n.s., 26 (1975), 287–300, 395–406.

invisible to prosaic eyes, in this case the flow of poetry itself, in the evocative if elusive form of a 'rich stream of music'. What a modern reader might take as a conventional abstraction – the literary 'current' or 'mainstream' – is for Gray both a concept and poetic embodiment, a stream to be seen and heard at once: 'Now rolling down the steep amain, / Headlong, impetuous, see it pour: / The rocks and nodding groves rebellow to the roar' (lines 10–12). His vision of the great force of poetry (the poem was originally called 'The Power of Poetry') and its 'progress' down to the present moment marks his prophetic power but also his debilitating lateness, in a time when the 'Thoughts that breathe and words that burn' in great lyric poetry are 'heard no more' (lines 109–10). Gray nonetheless ends the poem by declaring his achievement 'Beyond the limits of a vulgar fate' and himself 'Beneath the Good' but 'far above the Great'. Virtue and power are clearly distinct; the poet looks up to one and down, far down, upon the other.

The fantasy of compelling attention and belief is just that. None of the volumes of odes enjoyed great popularity, and the self-conscious use of personification and prophecy shows the strain of fusing intellectual sophistication and mythic belief. Collins' great unfinished 'An Ode on the Popular Superstitions of the Highlands of Scotland, Considered as the Subject of Poetry' (1749–50; published 1784) addresses this problem directly. Collins envies his Scottish friend John Home the folk beliefs that he might write about upon returning to his native land, where 'rural faith' still prevails over 'sober Truth' (lines 32, 189). The present-day Highlands are, in Collins' imagining, as propitious for poetry as the sixteenth century was for Tasso, who 'Believed the magic wonders which he sung'. Collins's generous encouragement to his friend is also wistful: 'Unbounded is thy range' (lines 32, 138, 189, 199). The Enlightenment's progressive elimination of 'magic wonders' was better for everyday life, many thinkers realised, than for poetry, especially poetry so closely tied to the irrational as lyric poetry. Ambivalence regarding the lessening of credulity contributes to the marginal status of so many lyric personifications that are not mythological figures but also not merely capitalised abstractions. The desire to have it both ways – scientifically and religiously, loosely speaking – crystallises in Christopher Smart's touching description, in 'A Morning Piece, or an Hymn for the Hay-makers' (1748), of 'dawn's ambiguous light' in which 'Back to their graves the fear-begotten phantoms run'.[25] The graves seem to be real, the phantoms phenomenal.

---

25 *The Poetical Works of Christopher Smart*, eds. Karina Williamson and Marcus Walsh, 4 vols. (Oxford: Clarendon Press, 1980–7), vol. IV, p. 140. (lines 4–5).

In *A Song to David* (1763) Smart overcame ambivalence through sustained religious ecstasy. In Smart's vision, all creation strives toward divine 'adoration', an energy personified through some twenty-one of the poem's eighty-six stanzas. Smart's personification is not iconic in the manner of Collins and others, for 'she' is assigned gender only once and then rather obscurely. Still, the figure allowed Smart to fuse nature into one collective or monolithic force and still delight in sensuous particularity:

> Now labour his reward receives,
> For ADORATION counts his sheaves
> To peace, her bounteous prince;
> The nectarine his strong tint imbibes
> And apples of ten thousand tribes,
> And quick peculiar quince.
>
> (lines 349–54)

But Smart's idiosyncratic achievement had little influence. The *Song* was for many of his contemporaries further evidence of his madness. One reviewer called it a 'fine piece of ruins', which 'must at once please and affect a sensible mind'.[26]

Three works published shortly after Smart's death (1771) indicate the growing importance of lyric poetry and its independence from Pindar and prophecy. The full title of the first, by the young and pioneering Sanskritist Sir William Jones, suggests its practical and theoretical significance: *Poems Consisting Chiefly of Translations from the Asiatick Languages. To which are added Two Essays, 1. On the Poetry of the Eastern Nations. 11. On the Arts, commonly called Imitative* (1772). In the second essay especially, Jones severs any remaining ties between the lyric and Aristotelian 'imitation'. (Based on drama, Aristotle's *Poetics* had never been well suited to the discussion of non-dramatic poetry, though regularly invoked.) Jones uses Indian poetry to argue that expression of passions, not mimesis, is the fundamental lyric motive and subject. Even in 'countries, where no kind of *imitation* seems to be much admired', he asserts, the arts '*of expressing the passions in verse, and of enforcing that expression by melody*, are cultivated to a degree of enthusiasm'. Furthermore, it 'seems probable the that *poetry* was originally no more than a strong, and animated expression of the human passions, of *joy* and *grief*, *love* and *hate*, *admiration* and *anger*, sometime pure and unmixed, sometimes variously modified and combined'.[27] Jones' list of

---

26 See *ibid.*, vol. II, pp. 100–1 for the poem's reception.
27 Sir William Jones, *Poems Consisting Chiefly of Translations from the Asiatick Languages* (1772), pp. 202–3.

six passions might not seem far from Temple's delineation, quoted earlier, of the six recurrent subjects of poetry: 'praise, instruction, story, love, grief, and reproach'. But the disappearances of 'instruction' and 'story' from Jones' account emphasise that poetry is now coming to be defined as non-didactic, non-narrative and short.

Two other works significant for the development of the lyric poetry in this decade are the *Poems* (1773) by the young Anna Laetitia Aikin (later Barbauld), and a new edition of *Poems* (1777) by the established Thomas Warton. Barbauld's volume includes hymns, graceful love songs and several odes that evoke Collins, if not in ardour and density of imagery, in persuasive apostrophe and atmospheric subtlety. Her 'Ode to Spring' follows Collins' unrhymed 'Ode to Evening' without disappearing in its wake, while it also anticipates something of the quiet, organic concentration of Keats' 'To Autumn' in its attention to the season's processes:

> Unlock thy copious stores; those tender showers
> That drop their sweetness on the infant buds,
> And silent dews that swell
> The milky ear's green stem . . .
> Now let me sit beneath the whitening thorn,
> And mark thy spreading tints steal o'er the dale;
> And watch with patient eye
> Thy fair unfolding charms.[28]

Thomas Warton's *Poems* is important because 'with additions' in 1777 it came to contain as many sonnets as odes. The sonnet had nearly disappeared between the late seventeenth century and the middle of the eighteenth century. Gray wrote the now well-known 'Sonnet on the Death of Richard West', quoted at the beginning of this chapter, in 1742, but it was not published until 1775. Thomas Edwards published a number of accomplished sonnets in the 1740s and 1750s, but most of them are in an epistolary manner that makes the form seem an arbitrary choice. (Sonnet v: 'On a Family-Picture' and Sonnet XLIII: 'My gracious God, whose kind conducting hand' are poignant exceptions.) Samuel Johnson was able to generalise in his *Dictionary* of 1755 that the sonnet 'is not very suitable to the English language, and has not been used by any man of eminence since Milton'. But the publication of a group of nine sonnets by the noted scholar and poet Thomas Warton (who would be named laureate in 1785) helped give the form a hint of the prestige it had in an earlier era. His example

---

28 *The Poems of Anna Laetitia Barbauld*, eds. William McCarthy and Elizabeth Kraft (Athens, GA: University of Georgia Press, 1994), pp. 78–9, lines 25–8, 33–6.

influenced William Lisle Bowles directly and Charlotte Smith indirectly in the next decade. The importance of Smith's *Elegiac Sonnets* (1784) and Bowles' *Sonnets, Written Chiefly on Picturesque Spots* (1789) for Wordsworth and Coleridge is well known. After reading Bowles, an enthusiastic Coleridge concluded that the sonnet is most properly a 'small poem, in which some lonely feeling is developed'. While not only Wordsworth and Shelley but Coleridge himself would write some sonnets on civic themes, Coleridge's formula describes the mainstream uses of the form in the nineteenth and twentieth centuries quite well. More significantly, 'the development of some lonely feeling' becomes, after the eighteenth century, the dominant ideal for lyric poetry generally, and increasingly that means poetry at large.[29] This specialisation of 'poetic' experience – epitomised in Wordsworth's reduction of Gray's sonnet to a plain statement of 'lonely anguish' – would have puzzled most of the poets discussed in this chapter.

29 The phrases come from the prefatory note to 'A Sheet of Sonnets' that Coleridge had printed in 1796. For the preface see *The Complete Poetical Works*, ed. E. H. Coleridge, 2 vols. (Oxford: Clarendon Press, 1912), vol. II, p. 1139.

Drama and theatre in the mid and later eighteenth century

ROBERT D. HUME

Almost all 'histories' of eighteenth-century English drama have focussed on the new plays. This is a natural and in some ways defensible way to proceed, but 'new plays' are a product of the theatre system in which they are produced, and any attempt to treat them in glorious isolation must inevitably produce fallacious and misleading results. New plays did not beget one another, and neither were they necessarily a major influence on their immediate successors. Between 1730 and 1790 something like 85 per cent of the mainpiece performances in London were of old plays – many of them several decades old or more. New plays tended to be written as vehicles for the principal performers, and consequently the parts those performers took in stock plays had a major influence on the new works written for them. Innovation was rarely a desideratum; neither was literary merit a prime concern. Whatever critics of the time had to say, plays served primarily as popular entertainment.

To comprehend eighteenth-century drama as it was written and experienced in its own day, one must start by realising three things. First, only a few of the plays have ever received attention from twentieth-century critics, and most of those plays are atypical. Second, a performance did not consist of one comedy or tragedy viewed in decorous silence. People came, wandered about and left; those who stayed bought refreshments and talked. Many of the mainpieces were not comedy or tragedy but musical. Most nights included an afterpiece as well as a mainpiece, and a great many nights featured interpolated entertainments of various sorts – song, dance, spectacle. Third, a lot of audience members evidently avoided new plays. In the course of a season Drury Lane and Covent Garden generally mounted 50 or 60 different mainpieces (mostly warhorses) over about 200 nights. New mainpieces rarely survived more than nine nights (which gave the author three benefits) and plenty died after three nights (or even a single night) with empty houses. Revival after the first season was fairly uncommon.

No analytical history of English drama from *circa* 1730 to *circa* 1790 has ever been written. In his *A History of English Drama, 1660–1900*, Allardyce Nicoll provides useful lists of plays in the appendices to Volumes II and III, but only crude descriptions in the text, imposing broad and reductive categories. Nicoll's accounts of plays are almost wholly untheatrical and give only a limited sense of evolution in taste or genre.[1] How to conceptualise the period is a legitimate question, and some common views need scrutiny. The cliché that long dominated scholarship says that *circa* 1700 a flood of horrible 'sentimental' comedy displaced tough 'Restoration' satire, with the result that comedy 'turned, like a penitent prodigal, to the comedy of tears'.[2] Eventually, according to this narrative, 'sentimental comedy' was heroically challenged by the noble and admirable Goldsmith and Sheridan, who triumphantly reasserted the dominance of 'laughing' comedy. This is a wonderful story, but unfortunately quite untrue. It derives from Goldsmith's brilliant but self-serving 'Essay on the Theatre' (1773), and even casual scrutiny of performance statistics completely explodes it.[3] A very different way of seeing this era is as 'The Age of Garrick', duly followed by 'The Age of Kemble'. This perspective has the virtue of acknowledging the degree to which the theatre of Georgian London was an actors' theatre, but it is at best a radically incomplete picture that valorises atypical performers and eliminates some major parts of the repertory from our attention. A third approach treats censorship imposed by the Licensing Act of 1737 as a calamity that blights English drama until the time of Shaw. There is considerable truth in this view, as in the corollary claim that the explosive rise of the novel in the 1740s follows from the redirection of authorial energy into the new genre. But derogation is not analysis, and this perspective is of little help in understanding and appreciating what was happening in English drama. To write a meaningful narrative history of new plays is not feasible. We can, however, try to see how the dominant genres changed and how they were affected by theatrical circumstances.

1 Allardyce Nicoll, *A History of English Drama, 1660–1900*, 6 vols. (Cambridge: Cambridge University Press, 1952–9) (originally written in the 1920s).
2 John Harold Wilson, *A Preface to Restoration Drama* (1965; rpt. Cambridge, MA: Harvard University Press, 1968), p. 129.
3 Serviceable statistics have been available since the publication of John Genest's ten-volume *Some Account of the English Stage* in 1832.

A false start: the 1730s

English drama was decidedly stodgy in the two decades prior to the explosive success of *The Beggar's Opera* in 1728. The theatrical union of 1708 (which combined the acting company at the Queen's Theatre, Haymarket, with the one at Drury Lane) reduced London to a condition of virtual non-competition in spoken drama. Following the accession of George I in 1714, a second licensed company was allowed to open, and thereafter two theatres competed in a desultory way, staging few new plays and avoiding direct competition by formal agreement.[4] When Gay's oddity enjoyed a startling sixty-two nights in barely more than half a season, its success revealed the existence of a much larger potential audience than had been coming to the theatre. In short order, pick-up troupes were occupying the Little Haymarket, and in 1729 Goodman's Fields was built to attract audiences closer to the City. For the first time since 1642 more than two companies were competing actively in London.

The 1730s was a period of exciting experimentation.[5] The plays have received little critical attention beyond those of Gay, Fielding and Lillo. Like the plays of the 1660s, they mostly represented a learning process for a new generation of playwrights, and the results, if interesting, were rarely very satisfactory. The one major generic innovation and success of the 1720s had been John Rich's pantomimes at Lincoln's Inn Fields. Such works as *The Necromancer, or Harlequin Dr Faustus* (1723), *Apollo and Daphne* (1726), *The Rape of Proserpine* (1727) and *Perseus and Andromeda* (1730) ran up enormous numbers of performances right through the 1760s. Drury Lane was quick to mount imitations, and such works remained omnipresent and conspicuous in both companies' offerings for the next half-century, though most twentieth-century critics have either condemned them or pretended that pantomime did not exist. In a sense, they represent a popular-culture version of the Jacobean masque. They were afterpieces stressing music, dance and spectacular technical effects; text was the least important feature. They attracted big audiences for long periods, holding greater appeal than any plays in 'legitimate' genres – as surviving account books clearly show.

The unprecedented success of *The Beggar's Opera* naturally generated a flurry of ballad operas. Some sixty were produced in the following decade,

---

4 See Judith Milhous and Robert D. Hume, 'The London Theatre Cartel of the 1720s: British Library Additional Charters 9306 and 9308', *Theatre Survey* 26 (1985), 21–37.

5 For a detailed analysis of theatrical circumstances and repertory, see Robert D. Hume, 'The London Theatre from *The Beggar's Opera* to the Licensing Act', *The Rakish Stage* (Carbondale, IL: Southern Illinois University Press, 1983), pp. 270–311.

but save for a few lightweight afterpieces (e.g. the Coffey–Mottley *The Devil to Pay*, 1731, Fielding's *The Intriguing Chambermaid*, 1734, and *The Virgin Unmasked*, 1735), none flourished and stayed in the repertory. Quite a few tragedies were produced, most of them exercises in the very tired heroic-intrigue mode (Walker's *The Fate of Villainy*, 1730) or conscientious pseudo-classical bores such as Mallett's *Eurydice* (1731). 'Patriot drama' with thematic anti-Walpole implications tended to be the most successful variety of 'Roman' play, exemplified in Madden's *Themistocles* (1729) and Martyn's *Timoleon* (1730). The best of the traditional tragedies was Thomson's *Sophonisba* (1730), which ran up ten nights in its first season, but was never professionally revived.[6] The one important innovator in tragedy was George Lillo, much of whose work was produced by summer companies and fringe groups. *The London Merchant* (1731) is a moralistic tear-jerker that was still getting staged in Dickens' day as a warning to apprentices who might succumb to wicked women and rob their masters. However bathetic, it possesses a vividness and a pertinence to its audience utterly lacking in the stilted – one might say ossified – accounts of Roman emperors that had long been the model for English tragedy. Back in 1703 Rowe had experimented with bourgeois tragedy in *The Fair Penitent*, but only with Lillo did the idea really start to catch hold. In *Fatal Curiosity* (1736), Lillo improved his concept in what is now regarded as the foundational European 'fate' tragedy: an impoverished old couple murder a wealthy visitor, only to discover that he is their long-lost son – returned incognito and about to reveal his identity. The roots of this form lie in pathetic drama; Southerne's *The Fatal Marriage* (1694) – which remained a repertory staple – is an obvious ancestor.

The majority of the mainpiece comedies of the thirties are uninspired. They do represent, at long last, a decisive move beyond the old 'Restoration' stereotypes that had continued to dominate the theatres' new offerings, albeit in diminished and sanitised form. The rakish norms disappear, but are not replaced very satisfactorily. Ostensibly, the new comedies are satire in the London Social Comedy mode. Fielding's sodden *The Modern Husband* (1732) and *The Universal Gallant* (1735) attempt harsh satire on serious moral matters; John Kelly's *The Married Philosopher* (1732) and James Miller's *The Man of Taste* (1735) are preachy but much less heated. Where the old comedy shows us rebellious individuals making reasonable accommodations to society, thirties comedy takes an essentially social viewpoint. Its ideal is the *honnête homme* in harmony with his society. These plays are neither exemplary in the fashion of

---

6 Five later performances in the *London Stage Index* are actually of Lee's play of 1675.

Steele's *The Conscious Lovers* (1722) nor 'sentimental' in the *comédie larmoyante* fashion of the 1760s.

The best comedies of the thirties are burlesques or political satires (or both). Fielding was the premier comic dramatist, and though his 'serious' efforts are far from first-rate, his irregular plays are brilliant. *The Author's Farce* (1730) mocks the world of Grub Street; *Tom Thumb* (1730) travesties heroic drama quite hilariously;[7] *Pasquin* (1735) and *The Historical Register* (1737) are chaotically funny smears on major political and literary figures from Colley Cibber to Sir Robert Walpole.

Had drama developed unimpeded by the effects of the Licensing Act, it would very likely have evolved quite differently than it actually did. The big patent theatres were never enthusiastic about satire or experimentation. When John Rich built Covent Garden to replace Lincoln's Inn Fields in 1732, he basically replicated his old theatre and continued his repertory policy unchanged. Even when Drury Lane hired the popular Fielding in the same year, management showed no inclination to have him write the sort of spoofs that had been so successful at the Little Haymarket in 1730, let alone a satire like *The Welsh Opera* (1731), in which the king and queen are represented as a country bumpkin squire and his termagant wife, with Walpole as their butler.[8] The logical policy for the patent companies was to stress their large repertory of classics – a bit of Shakespeare, a bit of Fletcher and a flock of post-1660 plays with heavy emphasis on Congreve, Vanbrugh, Farquhar, Cibber and Steele.[9] Both continued to invest heavily in pantomime. New plays were expensive, troublesome, risky – and, if successful, open to piracy. The patent theatres would probably have stuck to proven favourites even without the Licensing Act, and their offerings were headed back that way by 1733. What the Licensing Act made impossible was niche theatres. The Little Haymarket had enjoyed a string of major hits (most of them Fielding's), and Fielding was hoping to build a theatre of his own in 1737. Relatively small, cheap venues could mount political and social satires, burlesques and experimental work without much investment or risk. The legal extermination of all such potential competition

---

7 Fielding expanded it as *The Tragedy of Tragedies* in 1731, and added a lot of footnotes for the sake of readers.
8 How much this work contributed to the silencing of the Little Haymarket is not clear, but Fielding's expanded version, *The Grub-Street Opera*, was kept off the stage and published only in mysterious circumstances.
9 On the importance of these writers to the repertory past mid century, see Shirley Strum Kenny, 'Perennial Favorites: Congreve, Vanbrugh, Cibber, Farquhar, and Steele', *Modern Philology* 73 (1976), S4–S11.

helped reduce the vitality of English drama to the vanishing point in the two decades after the passage of Walpole's vindictive and destructive bill.

The importance of the Licensing Act

The regulatory act that became law in June 1737 is probably the single most important influence on the history of British theatre. It had two key provisions: that only two theatres (plus the King's Theatre, which housed Italian opera) would be permitted in London, and that everything performed on stage must receive a prior license from the Lord Chamberlain of the king's household. The restriction on the number of 'legitimate' theatres remained technically in force until 1843; censorship was not abolished until as late as 1968. The results were calamitous, though perhaps not for the obvious reasons. Both the origins of the Act and its effects have been poorly understood.

The forces that led to the passage of the Act were a combination of simple anti-theatricalism and government dislike of unregulated theatres that sometimes took potshots at the king's ministers and even his family. The Elizabethan system of censorship carried out by the Master of the Revels had fallen into desuetude by 1715, when Drury Lane used the patent granted to Sir Richard Steele as an excuse to refuse the licenser his fees.[10] Few moral outrages ensued, but the Earl of Chesterfield's famous denunciation of the Licensing Act notwithstanding, practically everyone at the time agreed that censorship was reasonable and even desirable. Contrary to still-current twentieth-century myth, there is little evidence that Walpole was unduly upset by Fielding's *Historical Register*, but he was definitely infuriated by harsher and more serious kinds of attacks.[11] The anonymous *The Fall of Mortimer* (1731) implied that Walpole was guilty of treason and should be executed (and got the theatre raided and closed without recourse to legal niceties). In the spring of 1737, Havard's *King Charles the First* implied that an evil minister could lead to the downfall of a king, and Dodsley's *The King and the Miller of Mansfield* attacked corruption at court in very blunt terms. Even Chesterfield admitted that Havard's diatribe should have been suppressed (though it was not).

10 Colley Cibber, *Apology*, ed. Robert W. Lowe, 2 vols. (London: Nimmo, 1889), vol. 1, pp. 276–9.
11 Chesterfield's ringing attack on partisan censorship was delivered in the House of Lords in June 1737, just before the passage of the bill. Differing versions appeared in print in *Fog's Journal* (2 July 1737), *The Gentleman's Magazine* (July), and *The London Magazine* (August).

The government wanted control of what was said and shown on stage, though probably it cared very little how many venues there were. Suppressing the non-patent houses was a sop to Covent Garden and Drury Lane, which raised no objection to censorship and steep licensing fees, probably feeling that they were a small price to pay for permanent establishment of an unchallenged joint monopoly. Fielding could have been just as thoroughly muzzled by censorship alone. In fact, censorship probably made relatively little difference to the course of English drama. All seventeenth-century plays had been licensed, but plenty of them were tough, opinionated and controversial. After 1737 the spectre of the licenser was enough to prevent much direct political satire, but most actual censorship concerned very minor matters of decorum. Only about twenty scripts were refused outright, and most of those wound up getting performed after revision.

The real impact of the Licensing Act results from the limitation of venues. Legally guaranteed freedom from pesky little competitors, Drury Lane and Covent Garden promptly reverted to an ultra-conservative repertory policy. Covent Garden mounted only three new mainpieces in the 1740s. Variety was achieved by staging neglected plays by Shakespeare: the abrupt revival of his comedies *circa* 1740 is no accident. Beyond that, farcical afterpieces could be had aplenty, and had cheap. London was, of course, a rapidly growing city. Without the Licensing Act, three or four or five 'legitimate' playhouses would probably have been in operation by the end of the century. As things turned out, the two patent theatres simply expanded their seating capacity from time to time in the hope of capitalising on an enormous potential gross. Capacity increased from *circa* 800–1,000 early in the century to about 1,400 at Covent Garden in 1732. By 1790 it was in the vicinity of 2,000–2,200. Covent Garden was rebuilt in 1792 with a capacity of 3,000; Drury Lane reopened after total reconstruction in 1794 with a capacity of 3,600.[12] Richard Leacroft's scale reconstructions make vivid to the eye just how cavernous these theatres had become.[13] Inevitably, these monster houses changed the kind of drama that could be staged in London. The disappearance of seventeenth-century comedy of wit was caused not only by changing morals but by acoustics. What worked in these vast, echoing barns was musicals, ranting melodrama and the sorts of naval spectacles that became popular during the Napoleonic era.

---

12 See Edward A. Langhans, 'The Theatres', chapter 2 of *The London Theatre World, 1660–1800*, ed. Robert D. Hume (Carbondale, IL: Southern Illinois University Press, 1980), esp. pp. 61–5.

13 Richard Leacroft, *The Development of the English Playhouse* (London: Eyre Methuen, 1973).

Comedy and tragedy

The key to understanding comedy as it was written in the eighteenth century lies in recognising that very different types of 'comedy' coexisted during all decades of this period and that there is no tidy evolution from 'satiric' to 'sentimental'.[14] Comedies of the Carolean period were not generically uniform, and by the first quarter of the new century a broad spectrum of work was regularly produced, running the gamut from farcical to exemplary. Farces, many of them afterpieces, aim to elicit benevolent indifference or amused contempt (Farquhar's *The Stage Coach*, 1701?). Satiric comedy invites a sense of superiority and disdain (Cibber, *The Non-Juror*, 1717). Humane comedy invites audience good will for its flawed but decent characters (Farquhar's *The Beaux Stratagem*, 1707). Reform comedy calls for strong approval and relief (Centlivre, *The Gamester*, 1705). Exemplary comedy (a rarity) invites outright admiration and emulation (Steele, *The Conscious Lovers*, 1722). Work continued to be written in all of these modes for more than half a century, but the overall character of the drama altered considerably in the course of that time. Many twentieth-century critics condemned virtually *all* eighteenth-century comedies as 'sentimental', but this is to ignore major differences of tone and outlook. Harsh satire in the fashion of Wycherley, Otway and Southerne does indeed disappear, but to confuse amiable humour and 'sentimentalism' is a serious error. Belief in human goodness was on the rise during the eighteenth century, and dominant concepts of humour changed quite drastically: the Hobbesian concept of laughter expressing superiority and contempt gave way to one of sympathetic laughter as a recognition of kinship.[15] Laughing at human failings or foibles is very different from demanding admiration for near-perfect characters (exemplary comedy) or inviting tears of sympathy for virtue in distress as in the *comédie larmoyante*.

If one makes these distinctions, then farce and humane comedy are always the dominant forms, both in terms of new titles produced and total number of performances. The notion of what is 'satiric' did change. Goldsmith and Johnson both looked to Vanbrugh and Cibber's *The Provok'd Husband* (1728) as a splendid model for laughing comedy, but it has been unhesitatingly classified as sentimental (and condemned) by virtually all twentieth-century scholars. If,

14 For a fuller analysis, see Hume, 'The Multifarious Forms of Eighteenth-Century Comedy' (1981), rpt. as chapter 7 of *The Rakish Stage*. For a broader concept of 'humane comedy', see Shirley Strum Kenny, 'Humane Comedy', *Modern Philology* 75 (1977), 29–43.

15 On which see Stuart M. Tave, *The Amiable Humorist: A Study in the Comic Theory and Criticism of the Eighteenth and Early Nineteenth Centuries* (Chicago: University of Chicago Press, 1960).

to be sure, one believes that 'reform' is impossible and ridiculous, then any play turning on reform becomes contemptible. Numerous critics contributed to the myth of sentimental dominance, but the most influential was Ernest Bernbaum.[16] If the presence of 'sensibility' condemns a play as sentimental, then all eighteenth-century comedy stands convicted. There is sensibility aplenty in Goldsmith's *She Stoops to Conquer* (1773) and in the resolution of the Teazles' marital problems in Sheridan's *The School for Scandal* (1777). The later eighteenth century valued sensibility in a way that the later seventeenth did not, and its virtual omnipresence is only to be expected. The revisionist movement has significantly altered critical perceptions, though mere fact and logic cannot easily obliterate the prejudices of many decades.[17] Back in 1962 George Winchester Stone, Jr, pointed out that between 1747 and 1776 no more than 10 per cent of mainpiece performances were of 'sentimental' comedy – and he was using a radically inclusive definition.[18]

A good index to mid eighteenth-century taste in comedy is Benjamin Hoadly's *The Suspicious Husband* (1747). It was a major triumph for Garrick as the rakish but temporarily frustrated Ranger, and it ran up more than 250 performances by the end of the century. It possesses many of the features of 'Restoration comedy', but preserves virtue and frustrates the rake's designs. The audience can enjoy the chase without feeling guilty about the outcome. None of the famous 'sentimental' comedies of the post-1737 period came even close to the popularity of Hoadly's rather sanitised pseudo sex-comedy.

The principal mid-century comic dramatists were Foote, Macklin, Garrick, Colman the elder and Murphy. All were of the 'laughing comedy' persuasion as it was understood in the third quarter of the century. We may note that Garrick, Macklin and Foote were star actors, and that Garrick, Colman and Foote were important managers. They made a lot of money from their plays,

---

16 Ernest Bernbaum, *The Drama of Sensibility* (Boston: Ginn, 1915). The most recent overview is Frank H. Ellis, *Sentimental Comedy: Theory and Practice* (Cambridge: Cambridge University Press, 1991).

17 See particularly Arthur Sherbo, *English Sentimental Drama* (East Lansing, MI: Michigan State University Press, 1957); Robert D. Hume, 'Goldsmith and Sheridan and the Supposed Revolution of "Laughing" against "Sentimental" Comedy' (1972), rpt. in *The Rakish Stage*, pp. 312–55; Richard W. Bevis, *The Laughing Tradition: Stage Comedy in Garrick's Day* (Athens, GA: University of Georgia Press, 1980). With very different agendas and methodologies, all three critics demonstrate conclusively that 'sentimental' comedy was never by any definition even remotely close to dominant in new plays or repertory performances in any decade, let alone throughout the eighteenth century.

18 *The London Stage, 1660–1800, Part 4, 1747–1776*, ed. George Winchester Stone, Jr, 3 vols. (Carbondale, IL: Southern Illinois University Press, 1962), vol. I, pp. clxii–clxv.

but they were creating vehicles for themselves and their companies, and with the arguable exception of Macklin these people were more dramatic carpenters than playwrights per se.

Samuel Foote is essentially a special case, an actor who specialised in personal satire, mostly staged under his own management in the summers at the Little Haymarket.[19] He was a brilliant mimic who picked his targets carefully to stay on the right side of the censor and avoid dangerous confrontations: Samuel Johnson claimed to be prepared to break his bones if 'taken off'. Foote mounted more than twenty such shows over thirty years. Among the best are *The Minor* (1760; a trashing of the Methodists) and *Piety in Pattens* (1773; a parody of the Pamela story). Most of these works were essentially farcical afterpieces with the added tang of abusive personal references. They have scant literary merit of any kind, but for a whole generation they attracted large audiences. Foote gloried in the title of 'the English Aristophanes', but he was more entertainer than reformer and refrained from biting the audience that patronised him.

The seven fat volumes of plays by Garrick in the standard edition are testimony to his industry, though five of them comprise adaptations of various sorts. Of the original plays, only *The Clandestine Marriage* (a 1766 collaboration with Colman) is more than an afterpiece or a *pièce d'occasion*. Garrick was a brilliant play doctor, and there is no way to tell how many plays he helped adapt for the stage. He had no great literary pretensions: he tried to make scripts work in the theatre, and in many cases he kept his name off the results. His commitment to laughing comedy has never been disputed, though he could write to Hoadly, 'I rejoice that you wept at ye West-Indian.'[20] Most of his own writing was farce or pastiche.

Charles Macklin, by contrast, attempted much more serious and probing treatment of character and tried to redirect satiric comedy towards a more positive kind of sympathetic satire.[21] He wrote only a few plays over a long life, some of which failed, but his ambition and originality were exceptional. *Love à la Mode* (1759) is a trivial farce, but a gem of its kind. Scottish, Irish, Jewish

---

19 Foote politicked to great effect, and received a special patent for summer theatre in 1766 after losing a leg as the result of a practical joke by the Duke of York.

20 *The Letters of David Garrick*, eds. David M. Little and George M. Kahrl, 3 vols. (London: Oxford University Press, 1963), vol. II, p. 739.

21 See Matthew J. Kinservik, *Disciplining Satire: The Censorship of Satiric Comedy on the Eighteenth-Century London Stage* (Lewisburg, PA: Bucknell University Press, 2002). Kinservik prints *The Spoiled Child*, a hitherto unknown incomplete MS play by Macklin that contains unique notes on how the playwright conceived his characters and how various scenes were to be performed in order to elicit the audience response he wanted.

and horsy suitors compete for the beauteous Charlotte, with Sir Callaghan O'Brallaghan the winner. Performance history suggests that the audience long delighted in Macklin's biting characterisations and keen ear for colloquial speech. *The Married Libertine* (1761) is a reform comedy, didactic but psychologically probing. *The Man of the World* (1781) reached the stage only after twelve years of struggle with the licenser and major revisions. Unlike Garrick, Macklin was prepared to write himself repellant parts, and Sir Pertinax Macsycophant is among the most vivid of eighteenth-century characters. In staged form, the comedy is a family melodrama, with forced marriage failing and the central character storming offstage leaving an ugly mess unresolved.

By the standards of Wycherley or Congreve, Goldsmith and Sheridan are rather soft-boiled. Goldsmith's *The Good-Natur'd Man* (1768) is a bustling city comedy and *She Stoops to Conquer* (1773) a country romp – the latter likeable enough that it still holds the stage. So does Sheridan's *The Rivals* (1775), famous for Mrs Malaprop. Sheridan deals in clichés: overbearing father pushing his choice of a wife on his son; the romance-mad girl; the amorous older woman; the coward shirking a duel – but they are presented with exuberance. Sheridan's masterpieces are *The School for Scandal* (1777) and *The Critic* (1779). The former contains genuine satire unrevoked at the end: Lady Sneerwell and her scandalmongering cronies are nasty pieces of work, and so is the polished hypocrite, Joseph Surface, unmasked in the famous 'screen scene'. But Sheridan is happy to forgive and reward the good-hearted wastrel, Charles Surface, and he supplies a reform solution to his marital discord subplot. The glory of the play lies in its energy and language. *The Critic* is in the tradition of *The Rehearsal* (1671). It exuberantly mocks the conventions of eighteenth-century tragedy, mostly with generalised targets, but devastatingly singling out Cumberland as Sir Fretful Plagiary.

Hugh Kelly and Richard Cumberland are the writers usually lambasted by modern opponents of sentimental comedy. Kelly's *False Delicacy* (1768) outdrew Goldsmith's first play, earning his enmity and condemnation. It is indeed a highly 'genteel' play, but Kelly both presents sensibility and criticises its excesses. As Richard W. Bevis observes, 'One needs only to compare Kelly's *False Delicacy*, whose very title criticizes a favorite sentimental trait, with Whitehead's *The School for Lovers*, a thoroughly sentimental comedy of the same general type, to see how impure and satirically undercut Kelly's "sentimentalism" is.'[22] Kelly was more a political journalist than a playwright,

---

22 Bevis, *The Laughing Tradition*, p. 56.

and reading his six plays again after twenty years away from them I am struck mostly by how stiff and contrived they seem. Cumberland wrote a much larger number of more professional plays. His most famous is *The West Indian* (1771), a tremendous and lasting success. Cumberland believed in goodness of heart, but he sought affectionate laughter and his work is rarely namby-pamby genteel. He was a genuine champion of victims of racial and religious prejudice, and most of his comedies are more devoted to didactic preachment than to sentiment.

'Comedy' has no clear and distinct meaning in the later eighteenth century, and Goldsmith's laughing/sentimental dichotomy bears little relationship to actual practice at the time. A much more revealing piece of criticism is Horace Walpole's 'Thoughts on Comedy' (said to be 'Written in 1775 and 1776' but clearly completed about 1786).[23] Walpole finds character more important than plot, approves 'gentility' and upper-class characters and expects a 'moral'. He expresses enthusiasm for radically different sorts of comedies: Jonson's *The Alchemist* (1610), Congreve's *The Double-Dealer* (1693), Cibber's *The Careless Husband* (1704). He disapproves of easy ethnic targets and gross fools. 'Comedy' for Walpole and his contemporaries comprises a jumble of disparate possibilities.

English comedy of the 1770s and 1780s finds farce, humane comedy and satiric comedy all flourishing.[24] If there is a clear trend, it is towards increasing emphasis on what Diderot in 1758 called 'serious comedy' as opposed to 'gay comedy'. The results of this shift are clearly evident in some of the major comedies of the 1790s. Inchbald's *Lover's Vows* (1798) is a drama of sensibility, exhibiting genteel feeling. Holcroft's *The Deserted Daughter* (1795) is pathetic, aiming to rouse suspense and empathy for virtue in distress. Holcroft's *The Road to Ruin* (1792) is a moral melodrama, exhibiting folly and error to make a didactic/satiric point. Cumberland's *The Jew* (1794) is a humanitarian drama that exhibits social problems to rouse didactic empathy. Nineties comedy moves into the realm of social issues, or as one critic has characterised it, 'sentimental satire'.[25]

---

23 *The Works of Horatio Walpole, Earl of Orford*, 5 vols. (London: G. G. and J. Robinson and J. Edwards, 1798), vol. II, pp. 315–22.
24 Some examples. Farce: Murphy, *Three Weeks After Marriage* (1776); humane: Burgoyne, *The Heiress* (1786); satiric: Macklin, *The Man of the World*, and in a very different key, Holcroft, *Duplicity*, both staged in 1781.
25 Dougald MacMillan, 'The Rise of Social Comedy in the Eighteenth Century', *Philological Quarterly* 41 (1962), 330–8. On the nineties milieu, see Chris Jones, *Radical Sensibility: Literature and Ideas in the 1790s* (London: Routledge, 1993).

What, meanwhile, of tragedy?[26] The *London Stage* performance calendar shows that a substantial proportion of new mainpieces were tragedies, and critics of the time loudly demanded yet more of them, written according to classical precepts. To modern sensibilities, most of them seem dismal or worse. Some failed outright and vanished; others enjoyed a *succès d'estime* and nine nights, but only a few entered the repertory. Although Addison's *Cato* was a staple for both theatres, somehow its innumerable imitators failed to bring the formula to life. William Whitehead's *The Roman Father* (1750) is an example. People cranked out a lot of attempts at the old heroic intrigue mode, most of them as stale and mechanical as Samuel Johnson's *Irene* (1749). A few tragedies did rise to a higher level and succeeded in the theatre. Edward Moore's *The Gamester* (1753) is glaringly melodramatic and its wretched protagonist actually commits suicide, but the play has genuine intensity. Lillo's example notwithstanding, bourgeois tragedy did not flourish. Some of the most successful tragedies were exercises in souped-up patheticism. Arthur Murphy's *The Orphan of China* (1759) and *The Grecian Daughter* (1772) indulge in gratuitous bathos and plot excess, romantic scenery and flashy staging. Their great and lasting popularity is evidence of a taste now hard to comprehend – and of pleasure in the talents of the favourite performers who brought these monstrosities to life. A more appealing piece is John Home's *Douglas* (1757), a pathetic and heroic representation of feuds among Scottish clans that oddly blends Lillo, Shakespeare and what we now think of as Romantic melodrama almost two generations before that form emerged.

Tragedy suffered more than comedy from a gap between critics' prescriptions and audience taste. Looking at playwriting as it was actually practised in the last third of the eighteenth century, one finds no dominant formula in either genre. Horace Walpole's views are once again worth taking seriously here. Defending *comédie larmoyante*, he observes that it might better be called *tragédie bourgeoise* (showing a melancholy story in private life, unconnected with kings and heroes) or *tragédie mitigée* (a serious story without catastrophe). This is precisely what we find happening in the next decade in the various sorts of 'serious comedy' I have defined: in defiance of critical precept, dramatists created a middle way that does not correspond to genre theory.[27]

26 Nicoll's remains the fullest account. See also Clarence C. Green, *The Neo-Classic Theory of Tragedy in England During the Eighteenth Century* (Cambridge, MA: Harvard University Press, 1934).
27 Fred O. Nolte, in *The Early Middle Class Drama (1696–1774)* (Lancaster, PA: privately published, 1935) has argued that pathetic comedy and domestic tragedy are part of

Ballad opera, burletta, comic opera and English opera

The sequence of new comedies and tragedies provides no tidy or interesting narrative as one proceeds through the eighteenth century. To see what was actually happening in the realm of new theatrical work one must reject the blinders of genre theory and see the repertory as it really was. Musicalisation was central to the development of English theatrical forms in this period, but other than *The Beggar's Opera* few of the successful and influential new works have enjoyed much critical attention or respect. Ignoring the commercial dominance of the musical in the eighteenth century is bad historical practice, since the Licensing Act made separation of forms by venue impossible. Covent Garden and Drury Lane had a joint monopoly, and if musical shows had enormous appeal for the audience, then musical shows would constitute a high proportion of the repertory – and did so. The attraction of music, of course, was not new. The 1674 'operatic' version of Shakespeare's *The Tempest* was probably the most popular show of the late seventeenth century. It retained its place in the repertory into the 1750s, and then, following Garrick's further adaptation of 1756, ran steadily to the end of the century in various musicalised guises that brought the show back towards its Shakespearean origins. Motteux's revamping of *The Island Princess* as a semi-opera in 1699 proved one of the most popular shows for the next thirty years, far outstripping the performance histories of Purcell's expensively mounted *King Arthur* and *The Fairy Queen* from the same decade. The fantastic and lasting popularity of *The Beggar's Opera* (performed more than any other work during the eighteenth century) derived at least in part from its musical appeal.

Twentieth-century critical prejudices proved profoundly inimical to any attempt to deal with the eighteenth-century repertory as it really was. One must admit that eighteenth-century criticism was equally hostile and made virtually no attempt to theorise the heavily musical forms that dominated the stage, or to analyse the results in any serious way. There is, indeed, a huge difficulty. Playwrights and composers were not working in clearly defined genres, so (not surprisingly) generic borderlines do not really exist. Classifications are *ex post facto*, and mostly unsatisfactory. Certain differentiations make sense, up to a point. Is the work all-sung with recitative, or does it intersperse songs with spoken dialogue? Is the music purpose-composed by a single person to a

---

the European *drame bourgeois* movement. His ideas about evolution seem too tidy, but Voltaire, Kotzebue and Lessing make better comparisons for Cumberland and Holcroft than most of their English contemporaries.

libretto, or are new words fitted to old music of many sorts, ballad-opera style? Mainpieces and afterpieces tend to have significantly different conventions. Some musicals were cheaply and simply staged; others were the eighteenth-century equivalent of blockbuster musicals of the late twentieth century such as *Miss Saigon* or *The Phantom of the Opera*, replete with super-fancy and incredibly costly staging and dazzling special effects. As Richard Bevis rightly says, 'It is difficult to separate the musicalization of comedy from its drift towards spectacle.'[28] The major productions of the 1790s were stunning, but required enormous and extremely risky investment.

Fully granting the smudginess of all borderlines, I will suggest that English musical drama of the eighteenth century can be fairly well understood in terms of four (or perhaps four and a half) types: ballad opera, burletta/burlesque, comic opera and English opera. Italian opera as performed throughout the period at the King's Theatre, Haymarket, is an (almost) separate matter. Pantomime is not quite so separate but does constitute an essentially distinct entity.

Ballad opera sets new words to a wide variety of old tunes, most of them popular and familiar. It also alternates dialogue and song. Of the sixty-nine songs in *The Beggar's Opera*, twenty-eight have been traced to English ballads and twenty-three to popular Irish, Scottish and French tunes. The remainder come from such composers as Handel (two), Purcell (three), Bononcini, Carey and Eccles. As Gay invented the genre, it was 'a complex vehicle for both harsh and subtle satire', but 'for most of his successors it quickly became little more than a way of padding out farces with popular music'.[29] The large number of ballad operas staged in the 1730s notwithstanding, the form never really took firm root. Virtually all of the mainpieces failed outright, and only a few favourite afterpieces entered the repertory. Love of musical shows did not diminish, and other kinds were tried even in the thirties. The Carey–Lampe *The Dragon of Wantley* (1737) is a hilarious low-burlesque spoof of Italian opera that played regularly for thirty years. The Dalton–Arne adaptation of Milton's *Comus* (1738) ran steadily into the seventies at both theatres, and revamped into afterpiece form it continued to do so through the end of the century.

Burletta, the second subgenre requiring attention, is a relatively small and specialised phenomenon, at least so far as the eighteenth-century patent

---

28 Bevis, *The Laughing Tradition*, p. 66.
29 Curtis Price and Robert D. Hume, 'Ballad Opera', in Stanley Sadie (ed.), *The New Grove Dictionary of Opera*, 4 vols. (London: Macmillan, 1992), vol. I, pp. 289–92. The standard survey remains Edmond McAdoo Gagey's *Ballad Opera* (New York: Columbia University Press, 1937), though he entirely ignores the music.

theatres go. It derives from Italian *opera buffa* of the intermezzo variety: the success of Pergolesi's *La serva padrona* in London in 1750 is generally regarded as an early inspiration. The first 'English' burletta was Kane O'Hara's *Midas*, performed in Dublin in 1762 and at Covent Garden in 1764 (a rare instance of a provincial show being brought to London with success – initially as a mainpiece, from 1766 as an afterpiece). Like other early exemplars, *Midas* was in verse and all-sung. It satirises the conventions of *opera seria*; the music was a *pasticcio*, taken from popular sources as well as Italian and English opera. As Nicholas Temperley observes, however, 'the music rarely participated in the joke'.[30] The connections to both ballad opera and a burlesque like *The Dragon of Wantley* are obvious. Several notable burlettas of this sort were mounted in the next fifteen years: Barthélémon's *The Judgment of Paris* (1768), Arnold's *The Portrait* (1770), O'Hara's *The Golden Pippin* (1773), and Dibdin's *Poor Vulcan* (1778). The first version of *The Golden Pippin* contained overt and nasty personal satire on members of the royal family and was refused point-blank by the licenser; it was successfully staged only after a radical declawing. The appeal of this satiric mini-opera form was capitalised on very early by Garrick, whose *A Peep Behind the Curtain* (1767) is a flippant, self-reflexive satire that incorporates a burletta version of the Orpheus story.

A major change of direction in the burletta form was signalled by Covent Garden's 1780 production of *Tom Thumb*, reworked in this style but employing spoken dialogue. Between 1780 and 1843 (when the patent duopoly was revoked) a large number of burlettas were staged at pleasure gardens, the Royal Circus and numerous non-patent theatres, cloaking what amounted to light comedies of many sorts with a semblance of legality that consisted of the claim to be 'all-sung'. Musical content diminished, and mere rhyme was considered sufficient to serve as recitative.

Burletta came into being at almost exactly the time that the patent theatres were experimenting successfully with comic opera in English – or, to be more precise, one might say operetta with spoken dialogue. No clear generic title or rules ever emerged, and the form cannot be precisely distinguished from predecessors or successors. The kingpin of the comic opera of the 1760s was Isaac Bickerstaffe, whose career was cut short in 1772 when he fled the country to avoid prosecution for sodomy.[31] *Love in a Village* (1762) is actually a revamping

---

30 Nicholas Temperley, 'Burletta', *New Grove Dictionary of Opera*, vol. 1, pp. 648–9. On the genre, see Phyllis T. Dircks, *The Eighteenth-Century English Burletta*, ELS Monograph Series (University of Victoria (Vancouver), 1999).

31 See Peter A. Tasch, *The Dramatic Cobbler: The Life and Works of Isaac Bickerstaff* (Lewisburg, PA: Bucknell University Press, 1971).

of Charles Johnson's failed ballad-opera *The Village Opera* (1729) with music composed and selected by Thomas Augustine Arne. Thirty-six of the forty-two musical numbers were fully composed; orchestra and orchestration were far more elaborate than in ballad opera, with major demands on horns, oboes and bassoons. Where ballad opera was musically rudimentary, comic opera in this form was immensely more ambitious. One might fairly say that – dialogue excepted – this was an English version of the *opera buffa* that was sweeping the Continent, and it was claiming a place at the patent theatres in direct competition with the Italian version on offer at the King's Theatre, Haymarket. Comic opera is, to be sure, more entertaining with witty dialogue in a language one understands. Bickerstaffe was to repeat his success with *The Maid of the Mill* (1765, employing the *Pamela* story; music by Arnold) and *Lionel and Clarissa* (1768; music by Dibdin). All of these shows were produced at Covent Garden.

Drury Lane responded not with pastiche opera but with what Fiske terms 'one-composer dialogue opera'. Garrick's *Cymon* (1767, with boring music by Michael Arne) is a thoroughly silly pseudo-Arthurian monstrosity, but it was a great success and remained (with increasingly fancy staging) popular into the nineties. Dibdin's afterpiece *The Padlock* (1768) was a major triumph. Its plot now reminds us of *The Barber of Seville*, but its special feature was the old man's negro servant, Mungo, played by Dibdin himself in blackface: slavery was just starting to become a major public issue in Britain. The piece ran up fifty-four nights its first season and more than a hundred its first three, remaining a repertory staple for decades. Dibdin musicalised Garrick's *The Jubilee* (1769), brought to Drury Lane after the Shakespeare festivities in Stratford as a flashily staged procession and miscellany show. It ran ninety-one nights its first season, flimsy concoction or no. Dibdin likewise supplied the music for Garrick's full-length *A Christmas Tale* (1773), Arne for his *May Day* (1775).

Special notice should be taken of two 'operas'. T. A. Arne's *Artaxerxes* (Covent Garden, 1762) is virtually unique in attempting to create *opera seria* in English, following a Metastasian libretto that had been set by Hasse and J. C. Bach in Italian. Arne went so far as to employ castratos. The piece is musically fine and manages some complexity of character despite its essentially melo-dramatic plot. It proved popular and was performed well into the nineteenth century. In many ways it is unique, but in others it looks ahead to the English opera melodramas of the nineties. Sheridan and Linley's *The Duenna* (Covent Garden, 1775) was an even greater success: with the exception of *The School for Scandal*, no other mainpiece was performed as often between 1775 and the end of the century. The work is a musical pastiche with a standard 'immured daughter' plot. What seems mawkish today clearly touched Sheridan's audience, and Linley's sensitive, imaginative arrangement of the music no doubt contributed to the work's lasting success.

The musical developments of the eighties and nineties both continued and extended those of the seventies. O'Keeffe's *The Castle of Andalusia* (1782; music by Arnold), *The Poor Soldier* (1783; music by Shield), and *The Farmer* (1787; music by Shield) were all major hits. The first is a step towards the Gothic shows of the nineties; the third is essentially farcical. All were expensive, flashy productions, and Roger Fiske is correct in observing that such operas 'became the most profitable items in the repertoire'.[32] The major shows of the nineties were composed by Stephen Storace, a friend of Mozart who had done creditable Italian operas. With Cobb he wrote *The Haunted Tower* (1789) and *The Siege of Belgrade* (1791), both loudly advertised as 'English opera' though the latter drew heavily on Martín y Soler. Storace died in 1796, just as he was completing the music for Colman Jr's *The Iron Chest*, an exuberant exercise in popular Gothicism. The gigantic new theatres of the 1790s were ideally suited to music and theatrical pyrotechnics, and the managers naturally sought out and commissioned such shows.[33]

Acting style, changeable scenery and audience

The plays we have been surveying were mostly written for one of two common purposes: to display favourite actors and actresses to good effect or to employ the technical resources of theatres increasingly devoted to lavish scenery and machinery – or sometimes both. The third quarter of the eighteenth century is sometimes referred to as 'The Age of Garrick' but to do so severely distorts reality. Garrick was unquestionably important. He was the most dazzling and popular actor of his time, and his impact on Drury Lane's receipts can be documented from surviving account books. As co-manager of Drury Lane he was far from having unlimited power to do anything he pleased, but he exercised vast influence on the choice of both repertory and new plays. Playwrights disappointed by refusal tended to see

32 Roger Fiske, *English Theatre Music in the Eighteenth Century* (1973; 2nd edn, Oxford: Oxford University Press, 1986), p. 453.

33 Growing competition from concerts undoubtedly contributed to rapid increase in musical entertainment at the theatres late in the century. See Simon McVeigh, *Concert Life in London from Mozart to Haydn* (Cambridge: Cambridge University Press, 1993).

him as villain and dictator, but the large amount of surviving correspondence about playscripts conclusively demonstrates Garrick's acute sensitivity to his performers' 'lines' and to the preferences of the customers he needed to lure into the theatre. Garrick peddled 'serious' drama as best he could, but he mounted plenty of pantomime and lots of trash, and the proof of his wisdom lies in the fat profits his company made. No one knew better than Garrick the truth of Johnson's oft-quoted observation in his prologue for the opening of Drury Lane in September 1747 at the start of Garrick's twenty-nine years of management:

> The drama's laws, the drama's patrons give,
> For we that live to please, must please to live.[34]

If the audience wanted pantomime, farce, musicals and technical razzle-dazzle – and they did – Garrick would give it to them.

Garrick was the first 'star' in the eighteenth-century theatre in the modern sense of that concept. Some imported opera singers might be so described, particularly the castratos Nicolini and Farinelli, but no one until Garrick systematically exploited the press and cultivated support not only among the gentry but among the middle-class *littérateurs* who could help a publicity machine. Garrick bought stock in newspapers, cultivated reviewers, joined social clubs, dined out, entertained, corresponded, wrote prologues for all sorts of occasions, danced attendance on the great and famous, distributed tickets, put out press releases and created a minor industry in portrait distribution. The amount of press coverage Garrick enjoyed, decade in and decade out, was totally without precedent.

As a performer, Garrick was fabulously successful but not very influential. He thrilled audiences from 1741 to 1776, succeeding in a large majority of his ninety-six roles. Extensive testimony can be found expressing spectators' delight. What all the commentary finally tells us, however, is that Garrick was *sui generis*. His protégés could not do what he did and never amounted to much. John Philip Kemble, from 1783 his successor as principal performer (and later manager) at Drury Lane, was an utterly different sort of actor – large, stately, conventionally handsome and effective mostly in different roles in very different ways. Reviews are little assistance in recreating any sense of what Garrick did and why it worked, though ecstatic reviews there are aplenty. Newspapers and magazines began to cover the theatres much more seriously

---

34 'Prologue Spoken by Mr Garrick at the Opening of the Theatre in Drury-Lane, 1747', *Samuel Johnson: The Complete English Poems*, ed. J. D. Fleeman (New York: St Martin's Press, 1971), p. 82.

on a day-by-day basis in the 1760s, and by the 1790s one can find appreciative or critical commentary on virtually every show.[35]

Attempts to reconstruct the acting style of the eighteenth century have met with only limited success. Neither impressionistic rapture nor censure from spectators is much help, and until the time of Mrs Siddons there is far more commentary on male than female acting. Insofar as theorists wrote treatises about the theory and practice of acting, virtually all of them wrote about tragedy not comedy – and one cannot, in any case, be at all sure how well practice exemplified the theory. Most of the theory is Continental, or derived from Continental sources, which renders it even more suspect. What we can be more or less sure of is that many performers of tragedy and opera made extensive use of a codified system of gesture, body position and facial expression that helped convey emotion and story, even to an audience that did not understand Italian, for example.[36] Beyond the specifics of acting style and technique, we can look to the broader subject of character and the ways in which it can be conveyed in the theatre. In tragedy and serious comedy, late eighteenth-century dramatists were unquestionably much more conscious of repertory staples than of mostly very short-lived new plays, and consequently the ways in which major actors and actresses conceived and communicated character in the classic repertory (especially in Shakespeare) had a major impact on the construction of vehicles for those same performers. In our early twenty-first-century view the gap between 1780s and 1790s scripts and our conceptions of *Hamlet* or *Macbeth* is enormous, but eighteenth-century writers certainly thought that they were creating characters in a Shakespearean mould. If this was the way it seemed on stage, all one can say is that a lot is lost in the reduction from a performance seen then to its text read now.

Writing from a vantage point in which electric light and electric machinery can perform wonders on the stage, we inevitably have difficulty comprehending the thrill experienced by the eighteenth-century audience when exposed to the utmost that a changeable-scenery theatre lit by candles could produce.[37] Wing-and-shutter scenery now looks merely quaint, and even the improving oil-lamp lighting of the end of the eighteenth century (with gas shortly to

35 The only broad treatment is Charles Harold Gray's *Theatrical Criticism in London to 1795* (New York: Columbia University Press, 1931). Much remains to be learned in this realm.

36 For a lavishly illustrated guide, see Dene Barnett, *The Art of Gesture: The Practices and Principles of 18th Century Acting* (Heidelberg: Carl Winter Universitätsverlag, 1987).

37 The standard study, now badly dated, remains Richard Southern, *Changeable Scenery* (London: Faber and Faber, 1952). For a good short treatment, see Colin Visser, 'Scenery and Technical Design', in Hume (ed.), *The London Theatre World*, pp. 66–118. Ingmar Bergman's film of *The Magic Flute*, done in a reconstruction of the Drottningholm Theatre, conveys a vivid sense of the theatrical experience.

come) would now seem incredibly dim and underlit. To the original audience, the scenic effects were as dazzling as the most stunning special effects in films today, and advances in lighting made the scenery painted by Philippe de Loutherbourg seem astonishing in the 1770s.[38] The size and technical capacity of the nineties theatres were better suited to a Gothic thriller like M. G. Lewis' *The Castle Spectre* (1797) than to more subtle and thoughtful kinds of entertainment. If the literary depth of the underlying scripts often seems minimal, one can only admit that most of them were not primarily intended for reading. Most were, to be sure, published, and popular plays could run through ten editions and many thousands of copies in a year or two. Tragedies appear mostly to have been printed as performed (sometimes with omissions indicated). Comedies were at times padded with material designed to appeal to readers of novels. Bevis has pointed out that comparison of printed texts with the censor's manuscripts proves that at times a substantial amount of 'sentimental' matter was added for readers that was not performed in the theatre.[39]

The constitution of the theatre audience is much less clear than one might hope. Prior to the nineteenth century there is really no way to determine exactly what sorts of people came and in what proportions. The standard studies work from peripheral evidence (letters, diaries, newspapers, references within plays), and all of them focus on the mid-century period. How the audience changed is difficult to guess, but it unquestionably comprised very different social and economic groups. The basic price structure in the second half of the eighteenth century was boxes, 5s.; pit, 3s.; first gallery, 2s.; second gallery, 1s. Even the second gallery price was not negligible when a shilling was a day's wages for a labourer, but plenty of lower-middle-class people could afford at least the occasional ticket. At five times that price, a place in a box was no doubt occupied by a very different sort of customer. There is no evidence that the two patent theatres attracted significantly different audiences. What we can say is that they pulled in a very broad spectrum of people, and that dramatists were highly conscious of the need to appeal simultaneously to the different constituencies that populated pit, boxes and galleries.[40]

---

38 On de Loutherbourg's career and impact, see Philip H. Highfill, Jr, Kalman A. Burnim and Edward A. Langhans, *A Biographical Dictionary of Actors, Actresses, Musicians, Dancers, Managers, and Other Stage Personnel in London, 1660–1800*, 16 vols. (Carbondale, IL: Southern Illinois University Press, 1973–93), vol. IV, pp. 300–14.

39 Bevis, *Laughing Tradition*, chapter 2, esp. pp. 37–9.

40 A rich if tricky source is the huge number of prologues and epilogues collected in Pierre Danchin's immensely useful twelve-volume edition of *The Prologues and Epilogues of the Eighteenth Century* (vols. I–IV Presses Universitaires de Nancy, 1990–3; vols. V–XII Éditions Messene, 1997–). Eight volumes are in print as of 2001.

What the audience went to see was mostly favourite performers in roles that showed them to advantage. Kitty Clive, James Quin, Susannah Maria Cibber, Hannah Pritchard, David Garrick, Ned Shuter, Tom King, John Philip Kemble . . . the list could be extended indefinitely. Playwrights did not have the luxury of writing for little theatres that could attract niche audiences for elitist work. A novelist might write for the few, but in the world of the patent duopoly a dramatist had no choice but to write for the many.

Monopoly and commercialism

The preference of later critics for the harsh, sceptical comedy of the late seventeenth century over the more genial forms of the eighteenth is in no way surprising. The one is relatively elitist, the other essentially popular entertainment. The old charge of rampant sentimentalism was a distortion, though it had some foundation in fact: views of human nature and humour changed a lot, and there is a concomitant softening in dramatic satire. But the now-discredited cliché that the 'failure' of Congreve's *The Way of the World* in 1700 signalled the collapse of 'Restoration comedy' under the onslaught of 'sentimental comedy' is simply nonsense. Congreve's play enjoyed almost 300 performances in London after its alleged failure, and ran right into the 1790s. There are few valid dichotomies here, and the more closely one looks, the murkier the waters become. In 1759, for example, Garrick mounted *Harlequin's Invasion*, a work of his own devising. It dramatises the conflict between traditional and debased genres by showing the invasion of Parnassus by Harlequin, who is eventually suppressed by Mercury as the agent of Shakespeare. Garrick may have wished that pantomime could be banished from Drury Lane, but he certainly knew that the audience loved the things, and this long-popular work draws heavily on pantomime devices and was, in fact, Drury Lane's Christmas show for the year. Whatever his ideals, Garrick the manager was a supreme pragmatist whose motto was 'If you can't beat 'em, join 'em'. The Christmas panto tradition is a glaringly obvious feature of the eighteenth-century theatre, but one that later critics have almost unanimously preferred to ignore, even though it persists in post-Victorian form to the present day.

Garrick was an extremely gifted manager who worked hard at his job and supported 'good' plays up to the limit of the audience's taste and tolerance. At the opposite extreme is Richard Brinsley Sheridan, an astoundingly lazy, incompetent and dishonest manager who made a complete shambles of Drury Lane between 1776 and 1809. Here again we see the evil effects of the Licensing Act. No one could open a better shop in competition, but actors who wanted other employment had no option but to go to Dublin or the provinces if they could not get work at Covent Garden. Sheridan could not be forced to sell, and in any case the sums involved in owning and operating a patent theatre were becoming astronomical. When Sheridan and his partners bought into Drury Lane, the property (including its right to perform) was valued at £70,000; £150,000 had to be raised to pay debts and construct the new theatre of 1794. As the scale of the business went up, the feasibility of gambling on experimental plays went down. In 1728 'house charges' were £50 per night; during Garrick's regime they were £63 (£84 with afterpiece); by the early nineties they were up to £180. The scale of the theatres, the companies, and the costs made experimentation prohibitively risky. One of the great ironies of gigantism was that the huge new theatres were almost never even close to full. Sheridan's exceptionally successful *Pizarro* (1799), for instance, ran to only 55 per cent of capacity.

The playwrights who tried to peddle their work to the patent theatres in the eighteenth century were a wildly diverse group. Roughly 150 different people (12 of them women) had plays professionally produced in London in the first half of the century; somewhat more than 200 (20 women) in the second half. Many were amateurs and hobbyists, but even among those writers who were regularly produced few can have thought of themselves primarily as playwrights. Several managers profited enormously from their own works (Cibber, Garrick, Foote, Sheridan, the two Colmans) and some actors did as well (Macklin). Murphy, Morton and Kelly became lawyers. Cobb worked for the East India Company, and Hannah Cowley was married to a man in its service. Account books (spottily extant after 1714) suggest that hardly anyone earned a living purely from playwriting until the 1780s. Fielding did for several years in the thirties, and Bickerstaffe did in the sixties. Towards the end of the century the redoubtable Elizabeth Inchbald did so,[41] as did John O'Keeffe and a very few others. But even as prolific and well-paid a writer as Cumberland was a civil servant. A lucky hit could make a playwright several hundred pounds, but the average was a lot lower and even major writers sometimes had plays die on the first night, earning them *nothing* from the theatre.[42] In these circumstances playwrights quite naturally pandered to the managers' desire for safe scripts that looked like sure-fire money-makers.

---

41 On Inchbald, see *Women in British Romantic Theatre: Drama, Performance, and Society, 1790–1840*, ed. Catherine Burroughs (Cambridge: Cambridge University Press, 2000).
42 See Judith Milhous and Robert D. Hume, 'Playwrights' Remuneration in Eighteenth-Century London', *Harvard Library Bulletin*, n.s. 10 (1999), 3–90.

From a twenty-first century critical perspective, little can be said in favour of tragedy as it was produced in this period. The comedy is far better, and though most of it is good-humoured, relatively few works can legitimately be described as 'sentimental'. It is not, however, very literary, profound, or original. Given the monopoly, the lack of motive for the theatres to compete and their spiralling size and costs, one can hardly expect anything else. A century earlier, drama benefited from increasing stress on 'originality' in authorship – plays were becoming literature. In the course of the eighteenth century the trend reversed: by the eighties and nineties a startling number of 'new' plays in London were adaptations of old work or translations of Continental shows.[43] German drama (particularly the work of Kotzebue) became a major source for British dramatists. The most interesting development in comedy is the move towards the social satire of the nineties, though the benevolist basis of that satire is almost totally foreign to present-day sensibilities. What principally characterises developments in late eighteenth-century drama, however, is the increasing dominance of musical forms and growing reliance on staging and spectacle.[44]

43 See Paulina Kewes, '"[A] Play, which I presume to call *ORIGINAL*": Appropriation, Creative Genius, and Eighteenth-Century Playwriting', *Studies in the Literary Imagination* 34 (2001), 17–47.
44 On the gradual incursion of non-patent theatres and alternative entertainment, see Jane Moody, *Illegitimate Theatre in London, 1770–1840* (Cambridge: Cambridge University Press, 2000).

Scottish poetry and regional literary expression

FIONA STAFFORD

At a Shrove Tuesday party in 1785, Robert Burns first heard 'When I upon thy Bosom Lean', a song by the local, Ayrshire poet, John Lapraik. He wrote at once to congratulate the author, but his verse letter, subsequently published as 'Epistle to J. L*****K, An Old Scotch Bard' is far more than a friendly tribute to a fellow poet. As Burns recreates his response to Lapraik's song, he takes the opportunity to express a sense of pride in the larger, shared culture of his native Scotland, while at the same time registering his sharp sense of the dilemmas facing contemporary poets whose familiar language and forms were different from those regarded as standard and acceptable by the period's influential men of letters. The contradictions inherent in prevailing aesthetic attitudes meet in Burns' poem, which is at once a celebration of local tradition and a manifestation of the complicated relationship between Scottish and English culture.

At the heart of Burns' epistle is an assertion of the superiority of raw, natural ability to the kinds of poetic practices that are acquired through a formal education:

> Your Critic-folk may cock their nose,
> And say 'How can you e'er propose,
> 'You wha ken hardly *verse* frae *prose*,
>   'To mak a *sang?*'
> But by your leaves, my learned foes,
>   Ye're maybe wrang.
>
> What's a' your jargon o' your Schools,
> Your Latin names for horns an' stools;
> If honest Nature made you *fools*,
>   What sairs your Grammars?   [serves]
> Ye'd better taen up *spades* and *shools*,   [shovels]
>   Or *knappin-hammers*.   [stone-breaking hammers]
>
> A set of dull, conceited Hashes,   [fools]
> Confuse their brains in *Colledge-classes!*

> They *gang in* Stirks, and *come out* Asses,   [young bullocks]
>   Plain truth to speak;
> An' syne they think to climb Parnassus
>   By dint o' Greek!
>
> Gie me ae spark o' Nature's fire,   [one]
> That's a' the learning I desire;
> Then tho' I drudge thro' dub an' mire
>   At pleugh or cart,   [plough]
> My Muse, tho' hamely in attire,
>   May touch the heart.[1]

No amount of Greek or Latin, it seems, can make up for a fundamental lack of talent or inspiration. Whatever the 'Critic-folk' may pronounce, the creation of true poetry is something that cannot be taught, occurring as naturally in the fields of rural Scotland as in great centres of learning.

While Burns' choice of vocabulary appears to signal his allegiance to the ideal of natural composition, however, this very preference is influenced by his own knowledge of current aesthetic trends. For the celebration of innate ability as opposed to composition according to critical rules had been commonplace since the 1750s and 1760s, when writers such as William Sharpe, Edward Young, Alexander Gerard and William Duff had begun to identify 'original genius' as essential to the greatest poetry. In praising Lapraik, Burns is thus echoing the kind of critical opinion that praised Shakespeare or Homer for their wild originality and truth to nature.[2] Indeed, the epistle is careful to establish the writer's own familiarity with contemporary literature in stanza four, which apparently recaptures his immediate response to hearing the Scottish song:

> I've scarce heard ought describ'd sae weel,
> What gen'rous, manly bosoms feel;
> Thought I, 'Can this be *Pope*, or *Steele*,
>   Or *Beattie's* wark;'
> They told me 'twas an odd kind chiel   [person]
>   About *Muirkirk*.
> ('Epistle to J. L*****K', lines 19–24)

---

1 'Epistle to J. L*****K, An Old Scotch Bard', lines 55–78, *The Poems and Songs of Robert Burns*, ed. James Kinsley, 3 vols. (Oxford: Clarendon Press, 1968), vol. 1, p. 87.

2 William Sharpe, *A Dissertation on Genius* (London, 1755); Edward Young, *Conjectures on Original Composition* (1759), ed. E. Morley (Manchester and London: Manchester University Press and Longman, 1918); William Duff, *An Essay on Original Genius* (London, 1767); Alexander Gerard, *An Essay on Taste* (Edinburgh, 1759), *An Essay on Genius* (London, 1774). The new appreciation of Shakespeare's natural genius can also be seen in works such as Richard Farmer, *An Essay on the Learning of Shakespeare* (Cambridge, 1767).

If the speaker thought first of Pope and Steele, he is clearly a man of educated taste and possessed of a capacity to respond with appropriate feeling to good poetry. At the same time, the offhand reference to 'the odd kind chiel about *Muirkirk'* implies that rural Scotland is filled with writers who not only equal England's best, but also fulfil the new aesthetic demands for innate genius. With characteristic irony, Burns is at once demonstrating an authority based on knowledge of current literary trends and values, while celebrating his own intuitive bond with the very kind of poet who embodies the new ideal of natural power.

As he plays with the ironies of admiring the untaught, Burns is quietly challenging contemporary aesthetic attitudes and presenting an alternative perspective. Lapraik's songs, like Burns' apparently spontaneous verse epistle, flow naturally from his situation, but in doing so they reveal their affinity with a distinctive Scottish tradition that has developed rather differently from the poetry of England. There are, in other words, kinds of poetic education that differ entirely from the Latin composition exercises approved by eighteenth-century schoolmasters and private tutors. 'Nature's fire', too, may be derived not merely from an uninterrupted response to the natural world or internal inspiration, but also from a deep familiarity with the traditions native to the poet's home. What might strike outsiders as the work of an inspired (i.e. uneducated) genius often appears very differently from inside the community familiar with the local traditions that the poet has inherited. Burns's 'Epistle to J. L*****K', though presenting itself as an unpremeditated response to a particular experience, in fact partakes of a tradition established by Allan Ramsay, whose epistolary exchanges with William Hamilton of Gilbertfield had been published in 1719.

The series of 'Familiar Epistles' begins with Hamilton's praise of Ramsay and includes favourable comparisons between the Scottish poet and some of the most admired English writers of the previous century:

> Tho *Ben* and *Dryden* of renown
> Were yet alive in *London* Town,
> Like Kings contending for a Crown;
>   'Twad be a Pingle,   [contention]
> Whilk o' you three wad gar Words sound   [make]
>   And best to gingle.[3]   [rhyme]

---

3 'Familiar Epistles between Lieutenant William Hamilton and Allan Ramsay', 'Epistle 1', lines 19–24, *The Works of Allan Ramsay*, ed. Burns Martin, John W. Oliver, Alexander Kinghorn and Alexander Law, 6 vols. (Edinburgh and London: The Scottish Texts Society, 1951–74), vol. 1, p. 116.

When Burns wrote to Lapraik some seventy years later apparently prompted by a recent personal experience, he was thus contributing to a genre of verse that sought to bind Scottish writers in a poetic brotherhood capable of rivalling their English neighbours. Even his childhood recollections:

> Amaist as soon as I could spell,
> I to the *crambo-jingle* fell,   [rhyming]
> Tho' rude an' rough,
> ('Epistle to J. L*****K, lines 44–6)

carry an echo of Hamilton's invitation to Ramsay: 'At Crambo then we'll rack our Brain, / Drown ilk [each] dull Care and aiking Pain' ('Epistle 1', lines 49–50). The composition of 'crambo' or clever doggerel, which seems in the 'Epistle to J. L*****K' to be something that came naturally to Burns as a boy, is also fulfilling Hamilton's pledge of friendship to Ramsay and those future poets who follow his example.

The 'spark o' Nature's fire' desired by Burns in his 'Epistle' is not then a sign of innate ability alone, as the following stanza makes clear:

> O for a spunk o' ALLAN's glee,   [spark]
> Or FERGUSON's, the bauld an' slee,   [bold and sly]
> Or bright L*****K's, my friend to be,
> If I can hit it!
> That would be *lear* enough for me,   [learning]
> If I could get it.
> ('Epistle to J. L*****K', lines 79–84)

In place of Pope, Steele and Beattie, Burns seeks inspiration from Ramsay, Fergusson and Lapraik – poets whose particular brand of 'fire' seems more congenial than that of the foremost eighteenth-century writers of poetry in English. Here, Burns is not only naming, but also alluding to the Scottish poets, for in addition to the explicit reference to Ramsay is a further echo of his verse correspondence with Hamilton:

> On the lear'd Days of *Gawn Dunkell*,   [learn'd] [Gavin Douglas]
> Our Country then a Tale cou'd tell,
> *Europe* had nane mair snack and snell   [nimble and sharp]
> At Verse or Prose;
> Our Kings were Poets too themsell,
> Bauld and Jocose.[4]

---

4 'Familiar Epistles', 'Answer 1', 55–60, *ibid.*, vol. 1, p. 120.

Ramsay's evocation of the learned days of Gavin Douglas is a reminder of Scotland's illustrious literary past, when her kings wrote poems and, by implication, her poets reigned supreme. As well as recalling the older Scottish tradition, Burns' stanza also conjures up the memory of his immediate predecessor, Robert Fergusson, whose poem on the Edinburgh celebrations for George III's thirty-sixth birthday in 1772 includes the following:

> O *Muse*, be kind, and dinna fash us,   [vex]
> To flee awa' beyont Parnassus,
> Nor seek for *Helicon* to wash us,
>   That heath'nish spring;
> Wi' Highland whisky scour our hawses,   [throats]
>   And gar us sing.[5]   [make]

Fergusson's preference for whisky as a prompter of poetry over the classical metaphor of the Muses' sacred springs is typical of the growing tendency to associate native Scottish poetry with a kind of hard-drinking, down-to-earth, predominantly male sociability. It is thus a highly appropriate memory for Burns to evoke in his own verse letter to Lapraik.

While the 'Epistle to J. L*****K' announces its allegiance to the recent line of poets who composed their verse in Scots, however, it is at pains to demonstrate that the choice is deliberate. The Scots language may come 'naturally' to this speaker, but its employment here is not the result of provincial limitation or plain ignorance. It is rather a careful artistic choice of the medium most suited to the poet's purposes, and one which allows for associations to flow from north and south of the Border. For even as Burns calls for inspiration from Ramsay and Fergusson, the very form of his invocation is also echoing Shakespeare's well-known prologue to *Henry V*, 'O for a Muse of fire'.[6] His recollection of the early inclination to versifying, too, though indebted to Hamilton's 'crambo', carries resonances of Pope's semi-autobiographical 'Epistle to Dr Arbuthnot', 'I lisp'd in Numbers, for the Numbers came', while the very desire for 'ae spark o' Nature's fire' is, as James Kinsley has pointed out, a witty allusion to *Tristram Shandy*: 'Great Apollo! if thou art in a giving humour, – give me, – I ask no more, but one stroke of native humour, with a single spark of thy own

---

5 'The King's Birth-Day in Edinburgh', lines 13–18, *The Poems of Robert Fergusson*, ed. Matthew P. McDiarmid, 2 vols. (Edinburgh and London: The Scottish Texts Society, 1954–6), vol. II, p. 52.

6 *King Henry V*, Prologue, line 1. Burns' familiarity with Shakespeare's works is evident in the numerous allusions in his correspondence; for specific reference to Henry V see Burns to Cleghorn, 25 October 1793, *The Letters of Robert Burns*, ed. J. De Lancey Ferguson, rev. edn, ed. G. Ross Roy, 2 vols. (Oxford: Clarendon Press, 1985), vol. II, p. 255.

fire along with it, – and send Mercury, with the *rules and compasses,* if he can be spared, with my compliments to – no matter.'[7]

Through his multiple allusions, Burns is effectively exploring the common-place metaphor of 'Nature's fire' and developing the notion that new creations can be ignited by those already alight. A few months later, in the preface to the Kilmarnock edition he would explain his relationship with Ramsay and Fergusson in a similar way: 'These two justly admired Scotch Poets he has often had in his eye in the following pieces; but rather with a view to kindle at their flame, than for servile imitation.'[8] The choice of writing in a literary tradition could thus be reconciled with the new aesthetic imperative of originality, since the new poem might be sparked off by the work of an earlier master. This did not mean, however, that the ensuing blaze would be the same. Even here Burns may be alluding playfully to Ramsay's account of how Hamilton's 'Bonny Heck' had 'warm'd' his breast and provoked 'emulation', for Burns is effectively picking up Ramsay's metaphor but using it for new purposes; or in other words, kindling at the flame but avoiding servile imitation.[9] Rather than feeling compelled to disguise his debts, Burns preferred to celebrate Scottish genius, and to place himself according to lines already set down by Ramsay and Fergusson. At the same time, he freely acknowledged his admiration for recent English poets such as Pope or Shenstone – a tactic that seemed to convey the honesty and proper humility of a rural bard, while also serving less obvious rhetorical ends.

Burns' evident familiarity with the English literary tradition makes it clear that there is nothing accidental about his choice of Scottish vocabulary and forms. It is not ignorance of English literature that makes him celebrate Scots, as any reader of the Kilmarnock edition of his *Poems, Chiefly in the Scottish Dialect* immediately discovers, since several of the pieces are composed entirely in literary English, while most of the 'Dialect' pieces are a careful mixture of Scots and English vocabulary.[10] In his deft defence of his own poetic practice, however, Burns reveals his acute awareness of the kinds of difficulties faced by eighteenth-century writers who were somehow situated outside the cultural

---

7 'An Epistle to Dr Arbuthnot', line 128, *Imitations of Horace*, ed. John Butt, vol. IV of *The Twickenham Edition of the Works of Alexander Pope*, 2nd edn (London and New Haven, CT: Methuen and Yale University Press, 1953), p. 105; Laurence Sterne, *Tristram Shandy*, ed. Howard Anderson (New York and London: W. W. Norton, 1980), 133.

8 *Poems and Songs*, vol. III, p. 972.

9 'Familiar Epistles', 'Answer 1', lines 28–30.

10 On Burns' use of Scots and English, see Thomas Crawford, *Burns: A Study of the Poems and Songs* (Edinburgh and London: Oliver and Boyd, 1960); R. D. S. Jack, 'Burns as Sassenach Poet', in K. Simpson (ed.), *Burns Now* (Edinburgh: Canongate, 1994), pp. 150–66.

mainstream, and whose natural forms of expression were regarded in the dominant intellectual circles as uncouth or backwards, and to be tolerated only in very limited areas of literature. For while it was fashionable for the educated to muse upon the possible existence of some 'mute, inglorious Milton' living and dying in rural seclusion, the language used for such meditations generally reflected a contemporary emphasis on correct diction and polished vocabulary.[11] No one could mistake the speaker of Gray's 'Elegy Written in a Country Church-Yard' for one of the rude forefathers who are celebrated wistfully in his poem. The attitude towards the rural inhabitants is thus somewhat double-edged, for while the elegist praises those dwelling far from the madding crowd, he is also promoting an ideal quite remote from the objects of his admiration through his own careful linguistic choices. In a sense, the unknown Miltons had to be mute, for their own modes of expression would be unlikely to please an audience conditioned to admire the cadences of *Paradise Lost*.

The majority of people living in villages in the mid eighteenth century spoke in a manner very different from Gray's polished verses: a fact that began to register in discussions of both pastoral poetry and work by writers from the labouring classes. The reception of Stephen Duck, the Wiltshire farm labourer, is a prime example of the contradictions inherent in the new enthusiasm for untaught genius. Duck's poems attracted astonished praise and even royal patronage, but the origins that made him seem remarkable also remained a problem for his more elevated readers. Joseph Spence's brief account of Stephen Duck, written in 1730, reveals the growing consciousness of the gap between regional speech and literary language, as his admiration for Duck's ability is suffused with unease about the Wiltshire labourer's mode of speaking:

> He seems to be a pretty good Judge too of a musical Line; but I imagine that he does not hear Verses in his own Mind, as he repeats them. I don't know whether you understand me. I mean that his Ideas of the Notes in a Verse, and his Manner of repeating the same Verse, are often different: For he points out an harmonious Line well enough; and yet he generally spoils its Harmony by his way of speaking it.[12]

In Spence's eyes, Duck's accent and provincial dialect present a huge obstacle to his literary development; he even goes so far as to observe that 'it seems

---

11 'Elegy Written in a Country Churchyard', line 59, *The Poems of Gray, Collins and Goldsmith*, ed. R. Lonsdale (London and New York: Longman, 1969), p. 128.

12 Joseph Spence, 'An Account of the Author, In a Letter to a Friend, written in the year 1730', in Stephen Duck, *Poems on Several Occasions* (London, 1736), p. xiv.

plain to me, that he has got *English* just as we get *Latin*'. English poetry thus seems a foreign field, to be attained only through study and reading, just as the more educated worked to acquire classical literature. Duck gradually mastered the couplets required for *The Thresher's Labour*, but abandoned his attempts at blank verse for *The Shunamite* (based on Kings 2:4) because he felt that 'his Language was not sublime enough'. Ironically, the very works that encouraged Duck to write also seem to have instilled a deep sense of inadequacy. As he devoured the accessible literary essays in *The Spectator*, for example, he was learning not only to improve his style, but also to 'take particular care to guard himself against Idiomatick ways of speaking'.[13] Addison's pejorative 'idiomatick' is the first recorded use of the term in English, but it seems to have fed straight into the growing concerns about the kinds of language appropriate for the higher literary forms. In the same essay on Milton, Addison recommends that the language of an heroic poem be 'Perspicuous and Sublime' – an ideal that plainly proved debilitating to many capable poets.[14] That Duck should have been aiming high is not in itself surprising, for otherwise, it seems, he was doomed by his background to 'Pastoral, and the lower kinds of Poetry'.[15]

Contemporary admiration for the natural and the native, apparently embodied in the culture of rural Britain, was thus fraught with contradictions. The poets who might embody an ideal of unspoiled innocence or, later in the century, of original genius, were often unable to communicate in language deemed acceptable for poetry without a degree of hard work and intellectual effort that threatened the very virtues for which they were admired. As the more talented sought to improve themselves through their reading in order to compose poetry that would meet contemporary linguistic standards, they became less and less representative of the communities that had fostered their native strengths. In the eyes of Raymond Williams, Duck's career had a tragic dimension: 'Within a few years Duck was writing, with the worst of them, his imitations from the classics, elevated and hollowed to the shapes of that fashionable culture which was not only a literary stance – the "high" tradition – but,

---

13 *The Spectator* No. 285, 26 January 1712, in *The Spectator*, ed. Donald F. Bond, 5 vols. (Oxford: Clarendon Press, 1965), vol. III, p. 10.

14 *The Spectator* No. 285, *ibid.*, vol. III, p. 10. For Milton's influence on poetry of the period see W. J. Bate, *The Burden of the Past and the English Poet* (London: Chatto and Windus, 1971); Harold Bloom, *The Anxiety of Influence* (New York: Oxford University Press, 1973); Dustin Griffin, *Regaining Paradise: Milton and the Eighteenth Century* (Cambridge: Cambridge University Press, 1986); Lucy Newlyn, *Paradise Lost and the Romantic Reader* (Oxford: Oxford University Press, 1993).

15 *The Spectator* No. 417, 28 December 1712, *The Spectator*, ed. Bond, vol. III, p. 564.

as always, a social ratification.'[16] Although, from a late twentieth-century perspective, Duck has been praised for putting 'the labour "back" into pastoral
verse', his subsequent absorption into the dominant literary culture reveals
the difficulties faced by poets whose own language and experience was so
different from that of the educated urban society of their day.[17]

At the same time, writers such as Burns, familiar from birth with the language and manners of country people, could not represent their own communities adequately through the elegant language of Gray or Shenstone. In
'The Cotter's Saturday Night', for example, Burns begins with an epigraph
from 'An Elegy Written in a Country Church-Yard', apparently designed to
introduce his poem as a representation of the kind of rural idyll celebrated by
Gray. Within a few lines, however, he rapidly shifts to diction more appropriate
to those whose lives are depicted in his poem:

> November chill blaws loud wi' angry sugh;   [whistling wind]
>   The short'ning winter-day is near a close;
> The miry beasts retreating frae the pleugh;   [dirty] [plough]
>   The black'ning trains o' craws to their repose:
> The toil-worn COTTER frae his labor goes,
>   *This night* his weekly moil is at an end,   [toil]
> Collects his *spades*, his *mattocks* and his *hoes*,
> Hoping the *morn* in ease and rest to spend,
> And weary, o'er the muir, his course does hameward bend.[18]

Burns's mixing of the Scottish language, climate and way of life with echoes
from Gray's famous poem, reveals both his first-hand knowledge of the countryside and a skilful engagement with current literary trends. His choice of the
Spenserian stanza, for example, evokes the work of two recent Scottish poets
who had succeeded in English: James Thomson, who adopted the form for *The
Castle of Indolence*, and James Beattie, who used it for *The Minstrel*. Burns'
poem nevertheless reveals, too, the kinds of problems faced by those who sought
to represent rural life truly, and yet whose very choice of subject was largely
determined by those aesthetic attitudes that ultimately threatened them with
the silence of an internalised sense of inferiority. When Francis Jeffrey praised

16 Raymond Williams, *The Country and the City* (1973; London: Hogarth Press, 1993), p. 90.
   Duck's suicide in 1756 suggests that the tragic dimension of his life was not merely a
   question of literary style.
17 Donna Landry, *The Muses of Resistance: Laboring-class Women's Poetry in Britain, 1739–1796*
   (Cambridge: Cambridge University Press, 1990), p. 62.
18 'The Cotter's Saturday Night', lines 10–18, *Poems and Songs*, vol. I, p. 146.

'The Cotter's Saturday Night' for its 'admirable fidelity and completeness', he still qualified his admiration: 'even in spite of the obscurity of the language'.[19] Although he had argued that Scots was 'highly poetical', Jeffrey's insistent associations between the native language and 'childhood' or 'olden time' carried the implication that poets who used it could hardly be expected to cope with weighty contemporary subjects or higher literary kinds. Praise of the rustic was in many respects limiting to those capable of producing such poetry, because of the related assumption that any truthful representation of rural life was likely to come from the pen of someone low and unsophisticated. Burns' presentation of his own poem as a 'simple Scottish lay', with its echo of the epigraph, Gray's 'short and simple annals', has a certain ironic edge in this cultural context.

Burns' very ability to adapt to contemporary aesthetic demands has also meant that some of his poems have not always fared well in the critical currents of the subsequent centuries. Although 'The Cotter's Saturday Night' was highly acclaimed by early readers of Burns, in the twentieth century it came to be seen by many as a sentimentalised and, despite its debts to Fergusson's 'The Farmer's Ingle', an over-Anglicised representation of Scottish rural manners. For readers keen to see Burns primarily as a robust spokesman for Scottish poetry, his comic and satirical poems, such as 'Death and Dr Hornbook', 'To a Mouse', 'Holy Willie's Prayer', 'Address to the De'il' or 'Tam o'Shanter', which present an exuberant colloquialism, have seemed vastly superior to his more English moments. Don Paterson's recent verdict is typical of this critical trend: 'As eloquent as he was in English, it was never Burns's native tongue; he had to think first, and this was generally fatal to the results. All his best work was written in Scots.'[20] The problem with Burns' English poetry, according to Paterson and many other later readers, is that it was too far from his everyday mode of speech – his English had to be learned from books, just as Joseph Spence had seen Stephen Duck labouring over *The Spectator* half a century before Burns began to write. The modern objection to Burns' English verse is thus reminiscent of Williams' assessment of Duck, and reveals the shift in attitudes to literary language that took place between the mid eighteenth and late twentieth centuries.

For although there was nothing new about the disjunction between everyday speech and the language of published poetry, the eighteenth century saw

---

19 Francis Jeffrey, review of R. H. Cromek, *Reliques of Robert Burns, Edinburgh Review* 13 (January, 1809), 249–76.
20 Robert Burns, *Poems, Selected by Don Paterson* (London: Faber, 2001), p. viii.

a rapid rise in the awareness of socio-linguistic issues.[21] Samuel Johnson's dismay when faced with speech 'copious without order, and energetic without rules' is characteristic of the period in which lexicographers and grammarians laboured to bring various dialects of the country under control and to establish meanings and principles applicable throughout the United Kingdom.[22] In the late 1750s, the Irish elocutionist Thomas Sheridan toured the country, lecturing to houses packed with people apparently eager to be told that 'dialects, are sure marks, either of a provincial, rustic, pedantic, or mechanic education; and therefore have some degree of disgrace annexed to them'.[23] If dialect was increasingly seen in terms of 'disgrace', it was hardly likely to appeal as a medium for any aspiring poet who already felt under-confident about his or her unelevated background.

In Scotland, the anxiety over language became acute. In 1761 Sheridan was invited to lecture in Edinburgh by the Select Society, whose members included the foremost thinkers of the day – Adam Smith, David Hume, Hugh Blair, John Jardine. As David Craig pointed out in his influential study, *Scottish Literature and the Scottish People*, these leading intellectuals all 'spoke broad Scots', and suffered varying degrees of anxiety about their manner of speech.[24] All were concerned, too, with improving communication so that ideas could flow clearly and elegantly, which generally meant in the purest English.[25] In doing so, they were strengthening the already prevalent notion that nothing but 'pure' English could be a suitable medium for higher literary forms.

The Scottish preoccupation with language had inevitable consequences for contemporary society, and the remarkable shift in Scottish speech that occurred in this period is widely attested. When Robert Kerr wrote his biography of William Smellie, who lived in Edinburgh from 1740 to 1795, for example, he recalled the inability of English judges earlier in the century to comprehend the language of the Scots Bar, commenting

21 Lynda Mugglestone has suggested that the late eighteenth century 'emerges as a period in which issues of correctness and purism relating specifically to matters of accent attained a hitherto unprecedented significance', while the related creation of 'non-localized and supra-regional norms' led to the condemnation of non-standard forms as 'deviations'. Lynda Mugglestone, 'Talking Proper' (Oxford: Clarendon Press, 1995), pp. 5–6.

22 Samuel Johnson, Preface to *A Dictionary of the English Language* (1755), in *The Oxford Authors: Samuel Johnson*, ed. Donald Greene (Oxford: Oxford University Press, 1984), p. 307.

23 Thomas Sheridan, *A Course of Lectures on Elocution* (London, 1762), p. 30.

24 David Craig, *Scottish Literature and the Scottish People 1680–1830* (London: Chatto and Windus, 1961), p. 57.

25 Robert Crawford, *Devolving English Literature* (Oxford: Clarendon Press, 1992), chapters 1–2. See also, Robert Crawford (ed.), *The Scottish Invention of English Literature* (Cambridge: Cambridge University Press, 1998).

even within memory, some of the best educated Scots men, and gentlemen of most respectable rank, continued to use the unadulterated broad Scots dialect . . . In the present day, however, young gentlemen, who are studying for the pulpit and the bar, uniformly make English elocution a part of their education; and the language of Scots people of family and education is fast assimilating to that of England.[26]

For many creative writers, the growing self-consciousness about language proved inhibiting to composition. As James Beattie observed, 'We who live in Scotland are obliged to study English from books, like a dead language. Accordingly, when we write, we write it like a dead language, which we understand but cannot speak; avoiding, perhaps, all ungrammatical expressions, and even the barbarisms of our country.'[27] Addison's warnings against the use of colloquialisms in literature sounded even more stern to a writer deeply embarrassed by his native turns of phrase: 'We are slave to the language we write, and are continually afraid of committing *gross* blunders; and, when an easy, familiar, idiomatical phrase occurs, dare not adopt it, if we recollect no authority, for fear of Scotticisms.'[28] Beattie's own horror of the non-standard even drove him to publish a list of *Scoticisms, arranged in Alphabetical Order, designed to correct improprieties of speech and writing* to help his fellow countrymen avoid the inelegancies that came to them so naturally.[29] His best-selling poem, *The Minstrel*, too, though tracing the progress of genius in the Scottish Highlands, nevertheless features a hero with the Anglo-Saxon name of Edwin, and describes the local scenery in polished English verses:

> The shepherd swain of whom I mention made,
> On Scotia's mountains fed his little flock.[30]

Edwin himself speaks neither Gaelic nor Scots, but has his thoughts translated by the narrator:

26 Robert Kerr, *Memoirs of the Life, Writings, and Correspondence of William Smellie* (1811), ed. Richard B. Sher, 2 vols. (Bristol: Thoemmes, 1996), vol. i, pp. 23–4.
27 James Beattie to Sylvester Douglas, Lord Glenbervie, 5 January 1778, in William Forbes, *An Account of the Life and Writings of James Beattie*, 2 vols. (Edinburgh, 1806), vol. ii, p. 17.
28 *Ibid.*
29 James Beattie, *Scoticisms, arranged in Alphabetical Order, designed to correct improprieties of speech and writing* (Edinburgh and London, 1787). See also James Basker, 'Scotticisms and the Problem of Cultural Identity in Eighteenth-Century Britain', in John Dwyer and Richard B. Sher (eds.), *Sociability and Society in Eighteenth-Century Scotland* (Edinburgh: Edinburgh University Press, 1993), pp. 82–95.
30 James Beattie, 'The Minstrel; or the Progress of Genius', Book I, stanza xii, lines 1–2, *The Minstrel, In Two Books: With some other Poems. A New edition* (London, 1784). The first book of 'The Minstrel' appeared in 1771, the second in 1774.

'O ye wild groves, O where is now your bloom!'
(The Muse interprets thus his tender thought).
(*The Minstrel*, Book I, stanza xxiii, lines 1–2)

Beattie's solution to the difficulty of presenting a northern idyll in acceptable language is simply to adopt the kind of English fashionable for poetry in the mid century. Since the speech of his Highland hero could not easily be reported, and the entire poem adopts a quasi-Spenserian romantic tone, there is nothing odd or jarring about the narratorial devices. *The Minstrel* has nevertheless struck many modern readers as somewhat artificial and distant from authentic Scottish life.

The contemporary success of Beattie's poem, however, demonstrates that many eighteenth-century readers, already conditioned by Macpherson's staggeringly successful *Poems of Ossian* to thrill to a thoroughly Anglicised version of remote Highland culture, were quite content with his approach.[31] Burns' admiration for Beattie is evident in the 'Epistle to J. L*****K' and elsewhere, but his own emphatic celebrations of Scots dialect also show that whatever the critical and popular approval of poems such as *The Minstrel*, there were other ways of representing Scottish life and talent. Beattie may have chosen to follow Thomson's successful adoption of English diction, but Ramsay and Fergusson represented an alternative tradition, and one which confirmed the growing sense of the value of the local and immediate.

Throughout Britain, the question of dialect was bound up with issues of class, but for those in Scotland the social dimension was complicated by the further political issue of nationhood. While many Scots were happy to regard themselves as 'Britons' and strove, like Beattie and Hume, to eradicate 'Scotticisms' from their literature, the decline of native traditions remained a matter of deep concern. Many of the Enlightenment figures who promoted the use of correct English were also heavily involved with James Macpherson's project of rescuing the surviving remnants of ancient Gaelic poetry from the Highlands, and thus exhibited a somewhat contradictory desire to encourage English while preserving Scottish tradition, which can be traced among Scottish literary circles to the early years of the century.[32]

For although the Gaelic culture of the Highlands suffered the greatest blows in this period as a result of government efforts to integrate the region more

---

31 *Fragments of Ancient Poetry* (1760), *Fingal* (1762), *Temora* (1763), in James Macpherson, *The Poems of Ossian*, ed. Howard Gaskill (Edinburgh: Edinburgh University Press, 1996).

32 Richard B. Sher, *Church and University in the Scottish Enlightenment* (Edinburgh: Edinburgh University Press, 1985); Fiona Stafford, 'Primitivism and the 'Primitive' Poet', in Terence Brown (ed.), *Celticism* (Amsterdam and Atlanta, GA: Rodopi, 1996), pp. 79–96.

fully and thus prevent further Jacobite Risings, a sense of cultural anxiety seems to have been prevalent throughout Scotland.[33] Scottish poetry had suffered a considerable loss after the Union of Crowns in 1603, which removed the court – and its associated literature – from north of the Border. But it was only after the Parliamentary Union of 1707 that the importance of Scotland's various cultural traditions began to achieve renewed recognition. Although reactions to the Union varied, the debates surrounding the dissolution of the Scottish parliament undoubtedly raised awareness of relations between England and Scotland, their respective histories, their common ground and, crucially, their cultural differences.[34] And while the new sense of difference encouraged an eager importation of English periodicals, books and ideas, it also brought into relief the distinctive aspects of Scottish literature. In the very year that the Treaty was being debated, the first important anthology of Scottish verse was published in Edinburgh by the patriotic printer, James Watson.

James Watson's Choice Collection of Comic and Serious Scots Poems, published in three volumes between 1706 and 1711, has often been singled out as 'the beginning of the eighteenth-century Scottish literary revival'.[35] It contains a startling mixture of poems, from 'The Cherry and the Slae' or 'The Solsequium' by the sixteenth-century court poet, Alexander Montgomerie, to much more recent work such as William Hamilton's 'The Last Words of Bonny Heck, a famous Greyhound in the Shire of Fife'. The genres range from comic song, peasant-brawl and satire, to more formal panegyric and epithalamium, with the language spanning a huge variety of social registers and regional variations. It is not the presence of one particular poem or poet that makes Watson's miscellany so important, but rather the very fact of its being a collection, with the capacity to bring the great diversity of Scottish poetry, old and new, courtly and popular, to a contemporary readership. Through *Watson's Collection*, poems such as Robert Sempill's 'The Life and Death of the Piper of Kilbarchan: or the Epitaph of Habbie Simson', which drew on older folk tradition for its distinctive six-line stanza, was able to reach a wide audience and thus influence

---

33 Charles Withers, *Gaelic in Scotland, 1698–1981* (Edinburgh: John Donald, 1984).
34 For recent approaches to the varied and complicated cultural implications of the Union, see e.g. Kenneth Simpson, *The Protean Scot: The Crisis of Identity in Eighteenth-Century Scottish Literature* (Aberdeen: Aberdeen University Press, 1988); Colin Kidd, *Subverting Scotland's Past: Scottish Whig Historians and the Creation of an Anglo-British Identity, 1689–1830* (Cambridge: Cambridge University Press, 1993); Murray G. H. Pittock, *Poetry and Jacobite Politics in Eighteenth-Century Britain and Ireland* (Cambridge: Cambridge University Press, 1994); Leith Davis, *Acts of Union: Scotland and the Literary Negotiation of the British Nation 1707–1830* (Stanford, CA: Stanford University Press, 1999).
35 David Daiches, *The Paradox of Scottish Culture: The Eighteenth-Century Experience* (London: Oxford University Press, 1964), p. 16.

the shape of vernacular poetry for the next century. 'Standard Habbie' was the metre adopted by Hamilton for 'Bonny Heck', used and lauded by Ramsay in his first 'Answer' to Hamilton, developed by Fergusson in poems such as 'The King's Birth-Day' or 'Elegy, on the Death of Scots Music' and finally taken up by Burns, after whom it often became known as the 'Burns stanza'.[36] The form is not only distinctively Scottish in origin, but was to become, through accumulating associations, a symbol for the vernacular tradition of Scotland. When Burns chose 'Standard Habbie' for his 'Epistle to J. L*****K', quoted above, he signalled his allegiance to a tradition that was at once alive, vital, well-established and distinct from English and classical literary forms.

Watson's volumes are more than a mere repository of old poems. The *Choice Collection* is, above all, a statement of faith in the intrinsic power of Scots poetry, in the face of prevailing prejudices: 'this being the first of its Nature which has been publish'd in our own Native *Scots* Dialect, the Candid Reader may be the more easily induced, through the Consideration thereof, to give some Charitable Grains of Allowance, if the Performance come not up to such a Point of Exactness as may please an over nice Palate'.[37] Watson was aware that his *Collection* would not be to everyone's taste, but his very reference to those with an 'over nice Palate' suggests a desire for more robust readers, capable of enjoying stronger meat. It is just the kind of challenge which anticipates Fergusson's later recourse to 'Highland whisky' rather than the springs of Helicon.

Watson's Choice Collection was the first of a long and vital tradition of Scottish anthologies which reflect an impulse to preserve native tradition, to celebrate the variety of Scottish life and talent and to ensure that older traditions would continue to flourish. When Allan Ramsay published his first collection of Scottish poetry, *The Ever Green*, in 1724, he presented the work of the Old Bards as an 'Intertainment that can never be disagreeable to any SCOTS MAN, who despises the Fopery [sic] of admiring nothing but what is either new or foreign, and is a lover of his Country'.[38] The same patriotic pride continues in the preface, as he describes the old poetry as a 'Product of their own Country, not pilfered and spoiled in the Transportation from abroad: Their *Images* are native, and their *Landskips* domestick; copied from those Fields and Meadows we every

---

36 Standard Habbie is the six-line stanza, rhyming aaabab, lines four and six being shorter, two-beat lines. For discussion, see Douglas Dunn, '"A Very Scottish Kind of Dash": Burns's Native Metric', in Robert Crawford (ed.), *Robert Burns and Cultural Authority* (Edinburgh: Edinburgh University Press, 1997), pp. 58–85.

37 *James Watson's Choice Collection of Comic and Serious Scots Poems*, ed. Harriet Harvey Wood, 2 vols. (Edinburgh and Aberdeen: The Scottish Texts Society, 1977, 1991), vol. 1, p. xvii.

38 Dedication to *The Ever Green*, *Works*, vol. IV, p. 235.

Day behold'. The celebration of the native then develops into a more explicit defence of the Scots language, as Ramsay urges Scottish gentlemen 'who are generally Masters of the most useful and politest *Languages*' to 'take Pleasure (for a Change) to speak and read their own'.[39] If eighteenth-century Scotland saw an increasing obsession with English pronunciation and vocabulary, it also enjoyed a counter-movement which upheld the value of Scots and Scotland. Ramsay's praise of the kind of poetry that 'copied from those Fields and Meadows we every Day behold', accorded perfectly with the prevailing post-Lockean aesthetic popularised by Addison, which emphasised the importance of direct responses to the external world.[40] But it also encompassed respect for the old and inherited in its emphasis on the poetry of the bards whose works embodied these very aesthetic ideals. Burns' invocation of 'Nature's fire' is thus indebted not only to the poetry of Ramsay and Fergusson, but also to the efforts of those publishers and editors who had championed the dual influences of the native environment and tradition.

The desire to reprint older poetry suggests a continuing need in certain Scottish circles to sidestep the problem of English. In earlier periods Scots had been a literary language of high standing, as reflected in the medieval and Renaissance poetry revived by Watson, Ruddiman, Hamilton and Ramsay. Republishing the poems of Henryson, Dunbar or Montgomerie offered firm evidence of the distinguished literary heritage of Scotland, and recalled a time when there was no awkwardness surrounding the use of Scots. Although the subjects of the older poems might sometimes be unelevated by contemporary critical standards, the popular attribution of a poem such as 'Christ's Kirk on the Green' to James V gave it a certain standing nevertheless.[41] The old ballads published by Ramsay and later collectors were also rooted in a warlike age when the Border country between England and Scotland represented bloody conflict rather than Union. Unlike some of the more sophisticated poetry of Scotland, however, the ballads were part of an oral tradition and so their

---

39 Preface to *The Ever Green, ibid.*, pp. 236–7. Cf. Ramsay's attack on 'such Pedants as confine Learning to the critical Understanding of the dead Languages, while they are ignorant of the Beauties of their Mother Tongue', in the Preface to his own *Poems* (1721), *Works*, vol. I, p. xviii.

40 *The Spectator* No. 417, 28 June 1712, describes how the poet, in order to form his imagination, 'must gain a due relish of the Works of Nature, and be thoroughly Conversant in the various Scenery of a Country Life', *The Spectator*, ed. Bond, vol. III, p. 563. Copies of *The Spectator* were regularly discussed at meetings of Ramsay's Easy Club, 'Journal of the Easy Club', 8 August 1712, *Works*, vol. v, p. 27.

41 For the origins of 'Christ's Kirk on the Green', see *Watson's Choice Collection*, vol. II, pp. 1–15; Allan H. Maclaine (ed.), *The Christis Kirk Tradition: Scots Poems of Folk Festivity* (Glasgow: The Association for Scottish Literary Studies, 1996).

appeal was not exclusively antiquarian. The numerous versions of ballads such as 'The Battle of Otterburn', 'The Twa Sisters' or 'Johnie Armstrong' testify to a vigorous oral culture in which poems relied for their continuing existence on singers living in communities.[42] By collecting and publishing popular ballads, eighteenth-century editors were strengthening a living tradition to which new writers could contribute without self-consciousness, whatever their mode of speaking.

Songs, too, had the capacity to both bind together generations and classes within Scotland and to travel beyond, apparently uninhibited by linguistic obstacles. The popularity of Scottish songs can be seen throughout the century, not only in mixed anthologies such as *The Tea-Table Miscellany* (1724–37), but also in William Thomson's collection of airs, *Orpheus Caledonius* (1725), or the later volumes collected by David Herd and published in 1769 and 1776.[43] In the closing decades of the century, James Johnson commissioned the writing talents of Robert Burns to provide material for his ambitious six-volume *The Scots Musical Museum* (1787–1803), while George Thomson invited contributions from Burns and, after his untimely death, from Joanna Baillie, Walter Scott, Alexander Boswell and Anne Grant.[44]

From Ramsay's experiments at the beginning of the century to those of Burns and Scott at its close, it is clear that Scotland's most able poets were also collectors and composers of traditional songs and ballads. In the Gaelic-speaking Highlands too, the great poets of the eighteenth century, Alasdair MacMhaighstir Alasdair (Alexander MacDonald), Iain (John) MacCodrum, Rob Donn MacAoidh (Rob Donn), Uilleam Ros (William Ross) and Donnchadh Bàn Mac an t-Saoir (Duncan Ban MacIntyre), created songs of the highest quality, which drew on the traditions of their native, and threatened, culture.[45] Throughout Scotland, the transformation of traditional oral material into written texts is one of the great achievements of the period, and

42 Various texts of these and other ballads are included in Francis J. Child (ed.), *The English and Scottish Popular Ballads* (1882–1898), 5 vols., facsimile edn. (New York: The Folklore Press, 1956). See also David Buchan, *The Ballad and the Folk* (London: Routledge, 1972).

43 Allan Ramsay, *The Tea-Table Miscellany*, 4 vols. (Edinburgh, 1724–1737); William Thomson, *Orpheus Caledonius* (London, 1725); David Herd, *Ancient and Modern Scots Songs* (Edinburgh, 1769, 1776). For useful discussion, see T. Crawford, *Society and the Lyric: A Study of the Song Culture of Eighteenth-Century Scotland* (Edinburgh: Scottish Academic Press, 1979); Pittock, *Poetry and Jacobite Politics*.

44 *The Songs of Robert Burns*, ed. Donald A. Low (London: Routledge, 1993); Kirsteen McCue, 'Burns, Women, and Song', in Crawford (ed.) *Robert Burns and Cultural Authority*, pp. 40–57; Ian McIntyre, *Dirt and Deity: A Life of Robert Burns* (London: Harper Collins, 1995), 309–334; *The Selected Poems of Joanna Baillie 1762–1851*, ed. Jennifer Breen (Manchester: Manchester University Press, 1999), pp. 8–16.

45 Alexander MacDonald published the first collection of contemporary Gaelic verse, *Ais-Eiridh na Sean-Chanoin Albannaich* ('The Resurrection of the Ancient Scottish Language')

although there has often been debate over the nature of the various revisions and adaptations that accompanied the transition from mouth to page, the sheer volume, quality and diversity is astonishing. And it is in these kinds of texts, that inhabit the fluid borders between an oral and a print culture, that the creative energies of the community at large can be felt most strongly. For the poems of Ramsay, Fergusson, MacDonald, MacIntyre, Burns or Scott, are all part of the larger collective energies that flow through the century, invigorating individual pieces and connecting works by different poets to earlier and later texts. To see the individual poems independently of their cultural context is rather like reading their lyrics without the airs that should accompany them – a legitimate but somewhat impoverished experience. Nor should this be seen as a detraction from the reputations of the individual writers, all of whom wrote a variety of highly sophisticated poems which merit close study. But the development of the vernacular tradition in the eighteenth century, both in the Lowlands where Scots was the traditional language and in the Highlands where Gaelic had always been spoken, was the work of many hands, and so the poems benefit from an awareness of allusive and generic connection.

The existence of larger cultural currents also enabled less established, and less personally ambitious figures to contribute. Both songs and ballads have a tendency towards anonymity, as they are taken up and sung by those who are not necessarily conscious primarily of the author. For women poets, these forms had an obvious appeal and their works, including Jean Elliott's 'The Flowers of the Forest' or Lady Lindsay's 'Auld Robin Gray' are among the most successful in the period. As Patrick Maxwell observed in his 'Memoir of Miss Blamire', when attempting to account for Susanna Blamire's reluctance to publish songs under her own name, 'The lady-writers of that period – as confessed by Lady Anne Lindsay was the case with herself . . . had a horror at seeing their names published as authors.'[46] Maxwell's difficulty in proving Blamire's authorship of 'The Waefu' Heart' and 'The Siller Croun', which had both appeared in the third volume of *The Scots Musical Museum*, demonstrates that the anonymity of Scottish songs enabled women writers to reach an enthusiastic audience without compromising their own reputations.

(Edinburgh, 1751). See also *Songs and Poems in the Gaelic Language by Rob Donn* (Inverness, 1829); *The Poems of Alexander MacDonald*, eds. A. MacDonald and A. MacDonald (Inverness: Northern Counties Newspaper and Printing Company, 1924); *The Songs of Duncan Ban Macintyre*, ed. A. Macleod (Edinburgh: Scottish Texts Society, 1952). For helpful discussion see Derick S. Thomson, *An Introduction to Gaelic Poetry* (London: Gollancz, 1977).

46 'Memoir of Miss Blamire', *The Poetical Works of Miss Susanna Blamire*, ed. Henry Lonsdale (Edinburgh, Glasgow and Carlisle, 1842), p. xlii.

Susanna Blamire's authorship of fine Scottish songs is particularly interesting for this discussion, since she was not a Scot. Her family lived near Carlisle, just south of the Border, which gave her an early familiarity with the Cumbrian dialect and Scots. Indeed, she composed poems in both languages, apparently preferring Scots to Cumbrian.[47] Although well read, and a capable composer of verse in standard literary English, Blamire was strongly influenced by Ramsay and the oral Scottish culture she encountered when staying with her sister at Gartmore. The success of her songs and their inclusion in Johnson's *Scots Musical Museum* are tributes not only to her own literary talents, but also to the encouraging capaciousness of the Scots vernacular tradition, which seems to have inspired the well known and the unestablished to try their hands at songs.

Blamire's fellow Cumbrian, Robert Anderson, also recalls being launched into poetry by Scottish songs. In his *Memoir*, Anderson recounts his experience of moving to London from Cumberland in 1794. When he visited Vauxhall Gardens for the first time, he remembers being 'disgusted with many of the songs, written in a mock pastoral Scottish style' and, confident of his own knowledge of the genuine tradition, he decided to tackle the problem: 'on the following day, I wrote four'.[48] Anderson succeeded in having his songs set to music and later in the year, had the satisfaction of hearing them played at Vauxhall. These were his first attempt at poetry, but when he returned to Carlisle he published a collection of *Poems on Various Subjects*, and in 1805, a volume of *Cumberland Ballads*.[49]

Anderson's anecdote about Vauxhall Gardens makes a telling contrast to many earlier tales of provincial poets encountering metropolitan tastes. For his impulse to write seems to have derived from a desire to educate rather than emulate the tastes of the capital city. Unlike Stephen Duck, who laboured under a sense of inferiority regarding his social position, manner of speaking and way of life, Robert Anderson presents himself as listening in horror to the inferior productions of London. Whether this merely reflects contrasting personalities, or the inevitable difference between a first-person memoir and a third-person

---

47 *Ibid.*, Appendix, 256.
48 The songs were 'Lucy Gray of Allendale', 'I sigh for the Girl I adore', 'The lovely brown Maid', 'Ellen and I', *The Poetical Works of Robert Anderson, Author of Cumberland Ballads, &c. To which is prefixed the Life of the Author, written by Himself*, 2 vols. (Carlisle, 1820), p. xxiv.
49 *Poems on Various Subjects* (Carlisle, 1798), a collection of poems in English, Scots and Cumbrian, included 'Epistle to a Young Lady, with a Copy of Relph's Poems', pp. 104–6, a tribute to Josiah Relph, whose *A Miscellany of Poems* (Wigton, 1747) was the first volume of poetry to be published in the Cumbrian dialect. For details of the various editions of Anderson's works, see *Anderson's Cumberland Ballads*, ed. T. Ellwood (Ulverston: W. Holmes, 1904).

biographical sketch, is difficult to ascertain. What is clear, however, is that by the 1790s, songs composed by those hailing from beyond the capital's educated literary circles could be performed in the centre without apology.

Although essays by critics such as Jeffrey continued to display the lingering influences of neoclassical notions of literary value, by the closing years of the century the aesthetic assumptions surrounding generic hierarchies had been severely shaken. The revolutionary decade witnessed an explosion of writings suited to wider audiences – pamphlets, ballads, novels, prints and songs, while the choice of language by any writer had become fraught with political implications.[50] A sense of regional value also intensified during the years of war with France, as local communities came to be treasured as the heart of the larger, national community, fostering British strength against foreign menace. This seems to have given a particular boost to dialect writings, as songs dealing with fears of invasion appeared to rally British spirits.[51] Michael Baron has observed that the new emphasis on regional culture may also reflect a more radical tendency to resist the centralising policies of the government and London values associated with the court.[52] These were all factors that contributed to the late-century success of Robert Burns' poetry, which demonstrated that the poems of a farm worker could stand boldly beside those of the most advantaged.

The importance of Burns for writers living outside the wealthy urban centres is hard to overstate. Even in the 1990s, the Nobel Laureate, Seamus Heaney, was still paying tribute to Burns for 'dispossessing the rights of written standard English and offering asylum to all vernacular comers'.[53] For northern poets two hundred years earlier, the impact of Burns' example is hardly imaginable. In his *Memoir*, Anderson describes the pilgrimage he made to Dumfries to visit Burns' tomb and the poems written on this hard, pedestrian journey. But it is obvious from the moving 'Epistle to Burns' written in 1796 that his older contemporary was at once a crucial model and an inspiration to the northern poet. Written in Standard Habbie, Anderson's verse epistle revisits

50 For information about the various texts and radical writing circles of the period, see Iain McCalman (ed.) *An Oxford Companion to the Romantic Age: British Culture 1776–1832* (Oxford: Oxford University Press, 1999). On the language debate, see Olivia Smith, *The Politics of Language 1791–1819* (Oxford: Oxford University Press, 1984).
51 See e.g. 'The Invasion', *Anderson's Cumberland Ballads*, p. 61; 'The Invasion', *The Yorkshire Dialect, exemplified in Various Dialogues, Tales and Songs, applicable to the County* (London, nd. c. 1810), which includes the following 'nobbut Inglishmen'll stand By yan another o' ther own good land', p. 8.
52 Michael Baron, *Language and Relationship in Wordsworth's Writing* (London and New York: Longman, 1995), p. 24.
53 Seamus Heaney, 'Burns's Art Speech', in Crawford (ed.), *Robert Burns and Cultural Authority*, pp. 216–33, 218.

Burns' 'Epistle to J. L*****K', and hence combines respect for the vernacular tradition with the characteristic pledge of camaraderie:

> Now tint me, Rab, I'm thinkin soon   [heed]
> To gi'e a ca' in DUMFRIES town: [give a call]
> Aiblins some bonie afternoon   [perhaps]
>   We twa may meet;
> If sae, we'se spen' a white half-crown –
>   Wow, 'twill be sweet!
>
> Wi' ye I lang to ha'e a rout;
> We'se pass ne night in mirth nae doubt;
> Haith man, we'se clink the stoup about,   [An oath: 'Faith']
>   And sing and play,
> And keep auld Time, the blinker, out   [cheat]
>   Till peep o' day.[54]

Anderson's adaptation of the traditional drinking pledge inherited from Ramsay, via Burns, is particularly poignant, since the epistle is inspired by the news that 'Rab has thrown his pen awa'. Within a month of its composition, Burns lay dead, transforming Anderson's verse epistle into a proleptic elegy.

This fine but little-known 'Epistle to Robert Burns' reveals the paradoxical nature of the vernacular tradition, in that what may seem an intensely localised and even nationalistic medium also has the capacity to cross borders. If the celebration of the Scots language in the eighteenth century represents a form of resistance to standard English, it is perhaps as much the standardisation as the Englishness that provoked opposition. For Anderson's verse letter reveals a strong sense of kinship with the poetry of Burns and even borrows his Scottish Muse:

> In cam' the Muse – 'twas just in time –
>   To do the rest.
>
> In naming BURNS, I saw her smile;
> Says she, 'I've known him a lang while,
> 'And ane sae free frae artfu' guile
>   Sae guid and true,
> 'And sic a bard in a' this isle
>   'I ne'er yet knew.
>
>   (lines 11–18)

54 'Epistle I. To Robert Burns. Written and sent to that celebrated Scottish Bard a few weeks before his death', lines 109–120, *Poems on Various Subjects* pp. 75–6. Anderson's 'Wow' is probably indebted to Ramsay and Hamilton's 'Familiar Epistles': 'Wow, wow! But we's be wonder fain', 'Epistle I', line 53.

The affinity may still be essentially regional – Dumfries being, after all, nearer to Carlisle than to Edinburgh – but it is evident that Anderson's praise of Burns has nothing to do with the kind of exclusively Scottish patriotism and hostility to the Union so often perceived in the work of Ramsay and Fergusson. Instead, Burns seems to represent the finest contemporary poetry. The use of dialect to achieve this height is of paramount importance to a poet such as Anderson, irrespective of national boundaries.

The admiration of Burns outside Scotland is important to any discussion of vernacular poetry and the question of regional literary expression, because it reveals that the appeal of his work – and by implication, the appeal of dialect poetry – is not necessarily limited to a small local audience. Just as Seamus Heaney's poetry has carried the names and concerns of his childhood home in Derry across the world, so too Burns' compositions have travelled far from Kilmarnock where they were originally published. Indeed, Thomas Crawford has even argued that Burns' songs, 'the most international' of his compositions, are 'among the most universal works of art to have been created in the British Isles'.[55] The point is an important one because a principal difficulty attending poetry written in non-standard English has always been that of basic comprehension. For if much of the vocabulary is unfamiliar beyond a certain region, and the local references hard for outsiders to grasp, then the quality of the work may only be recognised by a limited audience. Robert Fergusson's relative obscurity outside Scotland is probably partly attributable to his use of undiluted Scots language and subject matter, while Robert Anderson, who published his work by subscription in Carlisle, has maintained little poetic fame outside Cumbria. In the light of such examples, Crawford's celebration of Burns' internationalism is understandable.

To judge poetry by the size of its audience, however, can often be a rather dubious procedure, whether the assessment is based on immediate contemporary responses or represents the verdict of generations. As literary canons have come to be seen as shifting and amorphous, critics have grown wary of making absolute pronouncements on the importance of earlier poets, while the assumption that a small, local audience is somehow less valuable than a mass readership seems decidedly unsafe. If a comparison were to be made between the careers of Stephen Duck, who strove to acquire a fashionable literary language, and Robert Anderson, who continued to write in Scots and Cumbrian as well in the polite English of his day, then the purpose would surely be to reveal interesting facts about the individual writers, their poems and the

55 T. Crawford, *Burns*, pp. 335–6.

contexts in which they worked, rather than to establish a hierarchy. And it is perhaps the Gaelic poets of the period who make this point most eloquently, through their very occlusion from standard accounts of British literary history. The poems of Alasdair Mac Mhaighstir Alasdair or Donnchadh Bàn, though revered by Gaelic speakers since the eighteenth century, and figuring large in any anthology or critical account of Gaelic poetry, are scarcely known to students of English literature, because of their language. Even though Mac Mhaighstir Alasdair and Donnchadh Bàn, together with a host of other able poets, were working in Scotland, developing their native traditions and also imbibing influences from further south, their work has tended to remain largely unknown in the non-Celtic world until very recently.[56] To suggest that it is therefore essentially limited or unworthy of serious attention, however, would be deeply mistaken. Instead, it stands as a distinct tradition within the diverse literature of these islands, enormously rewarding to those able to enjoy its riches.

56 Awareness of the Gaelic tradition has been helped by the inclusion of Gaelic poems in major anthologies such as Roderick Watson (ed.), *The Poetry of Scotland: Gaelic, Scots and English* (Edinburgh: Edinburgh University Press, 1995); Robert Crawford and Mick Imlah (eds.), *The New Penguin Book of Scottish Verse* (London: Penguin, 2000).

PART III

*

LITERATURE AND INTELLECTUAL LIFE: THE PRODUCTION AND TRANSMISSION OF CULTURE

14

History and literature 1660–1780

KAREN O'BRIEN

The histories published between 1660 and 1780 include some of the most com-pelling and dazzling narrative performances in British literature. Historical writing occupied a central place in British culture throughout this period, and its prestige was, if anything, enhanced rather than diminished by its unprecedented commercial success. By the later part of the century, the genre (or, it might more accurately be said, family of genres) of history was widely recommended to readers of all ages and both sexes as a source of political instruction, moral insight, social awareness and imaginative diversion. His-tory was regarded, without qualification, as a branch of literature. This is not to say that writers or readers of history were unaware of or indifferent to the boundary between fact and fiction; simply that they did not feel that the artistic crafting of narrative was fundamentally at odds with its presentation of historical truth. In respect of its self-assured literariness, its generic stability and its prestige, history stands out, in the late seventeenth and eighteenth centuries, as a peculiarly conservative genre in an era of radical literary exper-imentation and change. While novels and poems were steadily transformed and reinvented during this period, narrative history underwent a process of consolidation. Dynamic and innovative in its adoption of new subject mat-ters and methodologies, this kind of history remained broadly resistant to formal experimentation. The era of Clarendon, Hume, Robertson, Catharine Macaulay and Gibbon, can thus paradoxically be said to represent an extraor-dinary expansion of the possibilities of traditional historical genre which was nevertheless at odds with the 'novelisation' of many other aspects of British literary culture.[1]

1 See Clifford Siskin, *The Work of Writing: Literature and Social Change in Britain, 1700–1830* (Baltimore, MD: Johns Hopkins University Press, 1998). Also Brean S. Hammond, *Professional Imaginative Writing in England, 1670–1740: 'Hackney for Bread'* (Oxford: Oxford University Press, 1997).

Reader expectations played a large part in the shaping and success of historical writing. From the late seventeenth century onwards, there was a widespread public perception that Britain lacked good quality narrative histories, especially national histories, along the classical lines of Thucydides, Livy or Tacitus. In the early part of the seventeenth century, there had been annalistic works such as William Camden's *Annales Rerum Anglicarum* or Francis Bacon's *Historie of the Reign of Henry VII* (1629), period-specific histories such as Milton's *History of Britain*, and extensive works of antiquarian scholarship into Britain's Roman archaeology and legal heritage; but there was nothing to compete with, say, the comprehensive histories of France written during the reign of Louis XIV, or, later, the *Histoire d'Angleterre* (1723–7) by the French writer Paul de Rapin-Thoyras. Booksellers tried repeatedly to satisfy the demand for a great national history by commissioning, reissuing and recompiling multi-volume histories of Britain, but for many decades few of these exhibited the kinds of narrative unity and coherence to be found in classical histories. It was not until the mid eighteenth century, with the publication of David Hume's *History of England* (1754–62), Tobias Smollett's *Compleat History of England* (1757–8), Catharine Macaulay's *History of England* (1763–83) and William Robertson's *History of Scotland* (1759) that British readers really started to feel that they possessed national histories of substantial range and quality, though even then there were persistent concerns about the distortions of regional or party-political bias (the three male historians mentioned above were Scottish, and Macaulay was a political radical). Other high-quality histories followed of Greece, of the Roman republic and empire, of medieval and Renaissance Europe, and of the Americas and India. The best and most enthusiastically received of these were single-author histories, written from a distinctive, though rarely obtrusive, critical perspective, and deeply indebted to the classical idea of history as an extended rhetorical performance designed to give readers a persuasive and engaging account of a particular reign, empire or epoch.

The critical and commercial success of narrative history – an expensive, capital-intensive form of publication – resulted from a unique partnership between historians and booksellers. The commercialisation of history broadened its appeal without compromising the genre's elite image. The resulting self-confidence of historians may have limited their appetite for formal experimentation, and insulated their works from the generic cross-fertilisation which might otherwise have come from the newer forms of biography and the novel. This chapter will argue, somewhat against the grain of recent criticism, that historians positively and progressively redefined their genre against the prose narrative forms of romance, biography and the novel, even though they freely

Fig. 14.1 *The Nine Living Muses of Great Britain* by Richard Samuel: Portraits in the Characters of the Muses in the Temple of Apollo (1779). Catharine Macaulay is seated, second from the right, with a scroll in her right hand. The other Muses are, standing from left to right, Elizabeth Carter, Anna Laetitia Barbauld, Elizabeth Sheridan, Hannah More, Charlotte Lennox; sitting left to right, Angelica Kauffman, Elizabeth Montagu, Elizabeth Griffin.

borrowed a number of stylistic elements and literary strategies. Moreover, I will argue that this process of generic stabilisation actually facilitated an expansion of the range and type of subject matter tackled under the heading of 'history'. For the first time, political history was padded out, and even partly dissolved into economic and social narratives; and aspects of private and cultural life, such as the status of women, the culture of chivalry, sexual mores, the literature of past ages, found a place in serious and systematic historical enquiry. In the long run, the Enlightenment preoccupation with what we would now call 'cultural history' did lead to a partial disintegration of the extended narrative form; some of its fragments appeared in new kinds of theoretical essay, such as Adam Ferguson's *Essay on the History of Civil Society* (1767) or Robertson's *Historical Disquisition* on India (1791). Yet the enlargement of subject matter also revitalised the genre, and laid the foundations for those well-rounded, narrative histories which were so popular and influential in nineteenth-century Britain.

The formal stability, stylistic restraint and (by the mid-eighteenth century) scholarly meticulousness of narrative histories enabled them to balance out what seventeenth- and eighteenth-century readers would otherwise have seen as a lack of personal weightiness on the part of most historians. Traditionally, history was regarded as a genre written by men of substantial worldly achievement and authority, more often than not writing from personal experience of the events they described. The examples readers had before them included Thucydides, Julius Caesar and Tacitus, and, more recently in England, Thomas More, Walter Raleigh and Francis Bacon: all of them statesmen and historians, and some eyewitnesses to the events they described. The wisdom such men had gained in public life was felt to give depth of meaning and exemplary force to their historical reflections. There were, of course, in the period under discussion, many historians who conformed to this model of the statesman–historian: for instance, Clarendon and Gilbert Burnet, who will be examined below, and also the diplomat and patron of Swift, William Temple, who wrote of his own times and of Anglo-Saxon England, and the Tory politician Henry St John, Viscount Bolingbroke, who composed sketches of British history for the 1730s political journal *The Craftsman*, and as well as the highly speculative *Letters on the Study and Use of History* (published posthumously in 1752).[2] Most late seventeenth- and eighteenth-century historians, however, could not claim to derive their authority from public experience. Naturally, this created acute difficulties for female historians, of whom there were very few. Catharine Macaulay attempted to surmount the problem by presenting herself in Roman pictorial guises in portraits, sculptures and frontispieces to her works.

The rise of the specialist historian, and the separation of history from the experienced or autobiographical voice, inevitably altered the way in which the past itself was conceptualised and narrated. The sense of the past as lived experience conveyed so vividly in the works of Clarendon, Burnet and Lucy Hutchinson was gradually replaced by a more philosophical concern with the hidden, the unforeseen and the unintended aspects of the past. History – the real story of what happened and why – was increasingly located outside the acts and perspectives of its main protagonists, and historians became more

---

2 William Temple, *Memoirs of what Passed in Christendom for the war begun 1672* (London, 1692) and *An Introduction to the History of England* (London, 1695).

preoccupied with general patterns of causation. This amounted, effectively, to the disengagement of history from the biographical, both at the levels of authorial voice and of historical interpretation. This process continued until late in the eighteenth century, by which time new kinds of biography and memoir (Boswell's *Life of Johnson*, for instance, or William Mason's *Memoirs* of Thomas Gray) transformed contemporary understanding of the relationship between a life and its era. Thomas Carlyle, writing in the early nineteenth century, signalled the reintegration of history and biography when he famously defined history as 'the essence of innumerable biographies'. To an extent, British history had come full circle back to its seventeenth-century roots, since for Carlyle, as for late seventeenth-century historians such as Clarendon, Burnet and Lucy Hutchinson, it was the life, or collection of lives, which essentially constituted the era. Although all of them believed that God's providential purpose lay behind the deeds of the actors of history, they demonstrated in their writings that it was the actors themselves who gave each era its moral drama and meaning. Lucy Hutchinson was a fervent Calvinist, and this is a tension which she resolves in her *Memoirs of the Life of Colonel Hutchinson*. The work (written soon after her husband died in prison in 1664, but not published until 1806) sets out to vindicate the political career of John Hutchinson, a senior military figure on the parliamentary side of the Civil War, but, at the same time, to affirm her faith that history is progressing towards a final millennium in which elect personages like him will gain ultimate recognition. The deep Calvinist sense of congruence between the individual moral life and the providential bearings of history is reinforced by her choice of a third-person narrative voice.[3]

Clarendon's *History of the Rebellion and Civil Wars in England* is, of all the histories written during this period, the one which conforms most closely to the classical idea of the instructive and reflective history written, often from first-hand experience, by a man of state. It is also the historical work which most meaningfully presents the past as the essence, if not of innumerable, then certainly of selected biographies. Edward Hyde (as he was before he was created Earl of Clarendon in 1660) was an MP and adviser to Charles I and his family during the Civil Wars. He started writing his history in 1646, at the king's request, after royalist military defeats forced him into exile in the Scilly isles, Jersey and Paris. After the Restoration, Clarendon returned to office as Lord Chancellor, effectively ruling England until his political overthrow in

---

3 See Lucy Hutchinson, *Memoirs of the Life of Colonel Hutchinson*, ed. N. H. Keeble (London: J. M. Dent, 1995), and Royce McGillivrary, *Restoration Historians and the English Civil War* (The Hague: Martinus Nijhoff, 1974).

1667. During a second exile in France, he composed a long autobiography, partly in order to vindicate his conduct. He then resumed his history of the Civil Wars, incorporating portions of the autobiography, and completing the manuscript in 1673, shortly before his death. The work was not published until 1702–4, during the reign of his granddaughter Queen Anne. It was at that time received as a work of marked, and to many, unpalatable, Tory bias, though this did not greatly injure its phenomenal sales and critical reputation. Clarendon wrote as a witness to many of the events described, but in such a way that, throughout the history, the third-person historical narrator subsumes the autobiographical voice into a distanced, critical retrospect. Clarendon was a lawyer by training, and his rhetorical style is, in the classical sense, forensic; he writes as though making the case – in a manner impassioned yet tempered with judicious or strategic concessions to opposing points of view – for a reading of the parliamentary rebellion as an 'apostasy' from political and national duty. Clarendon's prose incarnates his intricate yet coherent grasp of history: the very fabric of his writing, with its masterfully marshalled one-sentence paragraphs, its endless digressions, its dense weave of precisely modulated adjectives, and its double, treble, even quadruple qualifications, conveys both the inexorable momentum of events, and the delicate balance of causality.

Clarendon's transformation of his own, personal perspective into an encompassing, judicious narrative voice was of a piece with his philosophy of history as the collective moral effect of individual actions. In one of his unpublished papers he remarked: 'I take it to be no less the true end of history, to derive the eminency and virtue of those persons, who lived and acted in the times of which he writes, faithfully to posterity, than the counsels which were taken, or the actions which were done.'[4] For Clarendon, the act of historical writing was a moral reckoning with the lives of oneself and others (he opened the History with the declaration that he is writing 'that posterity may not be deceived'), but this is possible only because the past itself is not an entity larger than or external to the acts, choices, loyalties and betrayals of its particular agents.[5] The only force outside the interactions of men is providence; and, in the History, it is providence which suddenly and summarily installs Charles II on the throne in 1660 and which brings the 'castigation of heaven' on the self-indulgent and complacent kingdom of Charles I. This commitment to the notion of providence as the ultimate cause, was not, for Clarendon, at

4 *State Papers*, vol. II, p. 328, quoted in Richard Ollard, *Clarendon and his Friends* (Oxford: Oxford University Press, 1988), p. 330.
5 Edward Hyde, Earl of Clarendon, *The History of the Rebellion and Civil Wars in England*, ed. W. Dunn Macray, 6 vols. (Oxford: Oxford University Press, 1888, repr. 1992), vol. I, p. I.

odds with his declaration on the opening page that he intended to produce a narrative of 'natural causes and means' brought about by wickedness on the part of the many and salvaged by eminency and virtue on the part of the few.[6]

Although Clarendon's *History* begins by characterising the Civil Wars as a 'universal apostasy in the whole nation from their religion and allegiance', it quickly evolves into an extraordinarily minute account of the characters and motives of the chief royalist and parliamentary players who, by their impotence, selfishness or stupidity, pushed the nation into civil war. Clarendon dismisses the notion of deep-seated economic or social causes for the events of the 1640s and 1650s, and focusses instead on 'the pride of this man, and the popularity of that; the levity of one, and the morosity of another ... like so many atoms contributing jointly to this mass of confusion now before us'.[7] The early part of the *History* is thus dominated by a series of pen-portraits (including one of 'Mr Hyde') bringing to life the men and manners of the Caroline court. Those of Clarendon's enemies (the Earls of Bristol and Arundel, and parliamentarians such as John Hampden) are the most glittering, but all of them are particles, each with its own particular charge, contributing to the mass of confusion. Clarendon is measured in his assessment of those whom he admires and supports. There is, for instance, his long portrait of the Archbishop of Canterbury, William Laud, a figure detested and ultimately executed by the Puritan party:

> He was a man of great parts, and very exemplar virtues, allayed and discredited by some unpopular natural infirmities; the greatest of which (besides a hasty, sharp way of expressing himself,) that he believed innocence of heart and integrity of manners was a guard strong enough to secure any man in his voyage through the world, in what company soever he travelled and through what ways soever he was to pass ... [8]

From this insight into Laud's innately inflexible temperament, Clarendon builds up a general explanation as to why his religious policies put him and the king on a disastrous collision course with the Scots and with English Puritans. The conflict between king and parliament soon intensifies the friction between men of incompatible temperaments and views, creating an atmosphere of personal, as well as party, hostility which enables Cromwell to emerge as a leader. Cromwell is, according to Clarendon, a man with a special gift for using the bent of his temperament to his own advantage, and for managing conflicting

6 *Ibid.*, vol. 1, p. 2.
7 *Ibid.*, vol. 1, p. 4.
8 *Ibid.*, vol. 1, p. 120.

personalities to his own ends. Clarendon analyses the reasons for Cromwell's rapid ascent to power within the army:

> his strict and unsociable humour in not keeping company with the other officers of the army in their jollities and excesses, to which most of the superior officers under the Earl of Essex were inclined, and by which he often made himself ridiculous or contemptible, drew all those of the like sour or reserved natures to his society and conversation, and gave him opportunity to form their understandings, inclinations, and resolutions, to his own model. And by this he grew to have a wonderful interest in the common soldiers, out of which, as his authority increased, he made all his officers, well instructed how to live in the same manner with their soldiers, that they might be able to apply them to their own purposes.[9]

Throughout the *History of the Rebellion*, Clarendon never wavers from his view of Cromwell as a dissembler and a hypocrite (the 'brave, bad man' of the famous, final epitome); but he tempers his loathing with admiration for a personality which was strong and shrewd enough to prevail when others were deadlocked by their private passions and animosities.

As an eyewitness historian, whose own life provided the unobtrusive unifying structure of his narrative, Clarendon was the inspiration for another, hugely successful work of history derived from personal experience, Gilbert Burnet's *History of his Own Time*. Although its sales were similarly spectacular, the critical reception of Burnet's work was far more mixed and cool, which is in itself informative about the kinds of generic and epistemological distinctions which contemporary readers were able to make between histories, memoirs and autobiographies. Burnet started writing his work as an autobiography in 1683 when he was a rising Scottish clergyman, and already the author of the first volume of a scholarly *History of the Reformation of the Church of England* (1679–1715). By the time the *History of the Rebellion* appeared in print, however, Burnet was also able to think of himself (somewhat boastfully) as a figure of public stature comparable to Clarendon: he had become a major Whig political player, one of the architects of the Glorious Revolution, a bishop and an ecclesiastical advisor to William III. Following Clarendon's lead, Burnet refashioned his autobiography as a narrative history which began with the Restoration (preceded by an overview of the Civil War), and which eventually covered the period right up to his death in 1715. Like the *History of the Rebellion*, Burnet's work is a minute study of men and motive, and includes some memorable pen portraits of leading historical players. Burnet had none

9 *Ibid.*, vol. IV, p. 306.

of Clarendon's sophisticated sense of the interdependence of private temperaments and public choices, but he had a novelist's finely psychologised approach
to men's interior lives. One of the best passages is his portrait of Charles II as a
man scarred and hardened by the trauma of his Civil War experiences: a man
outwardly exuberant and promiscuous but inwardly detached:

> He was affable and easy, and loved to be made so by all about him. The great
> art of keeping him long was, the being easy, and the making of every thing
> easy to him . . . He had a very ill opinion both of men and women . . . He
> thought no body did service him out of love: And so was quits with all the
> world, and loved others as he thought they loved him.[10]

Like Clarendon, Burnet bequeathed the manuscript of his history to his sons,
and they then published the work in two instalments in 1723 and 1734. Burnet's
work is livelier, more irreverent, gossipy and informal than Clarendon's. It is
no more, no less *parti pris* on the opposite, Whig side of the political fence,
and continues to be used as a valuable source by modern historians. Yet,
outside the hardline Whig pale, it was greeted with much greater hostility and
widely dismissed as irredeemably biased work. Swift complained of Burnet
that: 'his observations are mean and trite, and very often false. His Secret
History is generally made up of coffee-house scandals, or at best from reports
at the third, fourth, or fifth hand.'[11] Part of the reason for this hostility can
be divined from Swift's use of the term 'secret history'; by secret history, he
meant insider history dedicated to the private, often sexual, motivations behind
the public actions of the powerful, the aristocratic and the royal. Despite its
classical antecedents, it was a kind of history which had never become entirely
respectable, and it had close generic affiliations with scandal chronicles and
satirical romances (for example, Delariviere Manley's *Secret History of Queen
Zarah*, 1705).[12] This is not what Burnet had aimed to write, but, by constantly
referring to himself in his history in the first person (at times, with so self-
satisfied an exaggeration of his own role in important affairs), he laid himself
open to this charge.

Clarendon occluded, but Burnet exposed, the problem of the relationship
between autobiography and history as an authoritative narrative of public
events. The problem was not simply one of partial or unreliable evidence. From
the early eighteenth century, readers were increasingly resistant to histories

---

10 Gilbert Burnet, *The History of His Own Time*, 2 vols. (London, 1723, 1734), vol. I, pp. 54–5.
11 *The Prose Works of Jonathan Swift*, ed. Herbert Davis, vol. V (Oxford, Blackwell, 1962),
p. 183.
12 On 'secret history', see Robert Mayer, *History and the Early English Novel: Matters of Fact
from Bacon to Defoe* (Cambridge: Cambridge University Press, 1997), chapter 5.

which blurred the line between memoir and impersonal narrative; at the same time, historians became more theoretically committed to the notion that history is intelligible as a structure larger than the thoughts and deeds of its individual participants. Far from being inspired by the philosophical and narrative possibilities offered by the memoir-history, historians after Clarendon and Burnet disengaged history from biography, and espoused the more abstract notions of causation and change. This process of disengagement is visible in the novels of the period, as well as the histories: we need only think of *Tom Jones*, a novel in which public history (including the 1745 Rebellion) features, but only as a remote background for the stories of the characters, and without any sense that their subjective experience of life is shaped by their historical context. This process was eventually reversed, and the interface between history and individual stories greatly enriched, much later in the century as the result of the growing preoccupation, in both novels and histories, with the social dimensions of life. In a novel like Scott's *Old Mortality*, for instance, fictive, individual lives become an imaginatively compelling way into a fully realised public history (in this case violent religious strife in late seventeenth-century Scotland). Personalities are formed and moral choices are made at the intersection between private life and public history, and history itself becomes a mode of experience, not an external structure of events. By the time that Scott was writing in the early nineteenth century, history had, in some respects, returned to the idea of the past as lived experience. In other respects, however, the philosophical underpinnings and generic range of history had changed beyond recognition. In his searching study of the transformation of late eighteenth-century historical practice, Mark Phillips writes of the resurgence of memoir and biography in this period, and the expanded possibilities for history which this brought: 'biography offers something more than a complement to the public concerns of history: it also stands as a gateway to a deeper sense of social life . . . [while memoir represents an] effort to appropriate biography to wider historiographical purposes, ones for which history proper still possessed insufficient formal or technical resources'.[13]

History before Scott may have lacked, as Phillips suggests, the technical resources to convey the past as something simultaneously imaginatively retrievable yet distanced by the very process of interpretation. Yet eighteenth-century historians were acutely aware of the need to make the past imaginatively accessible, as well as intelligible, if only to strengthen the kinds of

13 Mark Phillips, *Society and Sentiment: Genres of Historical Writing in Britain, 1740–1820* (Princeton, NJ: Princeton University Press, 2000), pp. 140, 296.

political argument they wished to make. They were, moreover, frequently reminded by contemporary novelists and critics that general, historical material not directly engaged with particular lives had only limited imaginative purchase. Samuel Johnson commented that:

> It is not easy for the most artful writer to give us an interest in happiness or misery which we think ourselves never likely to feel, and with which we have never yet been made acquainted. Histories of the downfall of kingdoms, and revolutions of empires, are read with great tranquillity; the imperial tragedy pleases common auditors only by its pomp of ornament and grandeur of ideas . . .[14]

Most commentators would have agreed with Johnson on the importance and moral efficacy of reader identification with particular characters. There was, however, genuine debate among them as to whether real or fictitious human stories had equal power to attract identification and to move. For Johnson, the real or fictional status of lives was not directly relevant to their imaginative power. By contrast, Hume, in his *Treatise of Human Nature* (1739–40), argued that the imaginative impact of the stories of real, historical characters was necessarily greater than those of fictional ones:

> If one person sits down to read a book as a romance, and another as a true history, they plainly receive the same ideas, and in the same order . . . [But the reader of history] has a more lively conception of all these incidents. He enters deeper into the concerns of the persons: represents to himself their action, and characters, and friendships, and enmities: he even goes so far as to form a notion of their features, and air, and person.[15]

This debate goes to the heart of perennial philosophical questions about the nature and moral efficacy of empathy. It became urgent by the mid eighteenth century once historians themselves started to adopt novelistic strategies of character representation in order to promote reader identification. Hume himself led the way with his overtly sentimental presentations of selected characters in his *History of England* (1754–62). The most conspicuous of these were Charles I at the time of his trial and execution, events which he described in even more emotive terms than Clarendon, though he admired Charles I far less; and James II (a monarch of whom Hume disapproved even more) when

---

14 Samuel Johnson, *The Rambler*, eds. W. J. Bate and A. B. Strauss, 3 vols. (New Haven, CT: Yale University Press, 1969), vol. I, p. 320.
15 David Hume, *A Treatise of Human Nature*, ed. Ernest C. Mossner (Penguin: Harmondsworth, 1969), p. 147.

he learns, after his ousting from the throne, that his favourite daughter Anne has betrayed him:

> He burst into tears when the first intelligence was conveyed to him. Undoubtedly he foresaw in this incident the total expiration of his royal authority: But the nearer and more intimate concern of a parent laid hold of his heart; when he found himself abandoned in his uttermost distress by a child, and a virtuous child, whom he had ever regarded with the utmost tender affection.[16]

A still more celebrated example, also of a figure of whom the author does not entirely approve but with whom he wishes his readers to sympathise, is the intimate and heart-rending portrait of Mary, Queen of Scots in Robertson's *History of Scotland* (1759). A reviewer (probably Hume himself) observed of Robertson's work that 'Queen Mary is presented to us, neither as a divine nor an infernal, but a human object; a woman with female failings; a character mixed with virtues and vices, such as merits, on many accounts, our condemnation, whilst there is room left for our pity in deploring her misfortunes.'[17] Smollett and Goldsmith, both novelists, imitated and extended Hume's sentimental techniques in, respectively, *The Compleat History of England* (1757–8) and *The History of England* (1777). Smollett gave a particularly wrenching account of the fate of Scottish Jacobites defeated in the 1745 Rebellion, while Goldsmith provided a lachrymose rendition of Hume's death of Charles I. In all of these cases the integration of sentimental interludes or biographical vignettes into national histories had an ulterior purpose: to engage and maintain reader involvement in what were primarily political narratives, and so gain assent for a particular interpretation of British constitutional history. In Hume's case, his sympathetic presentation of the (usually demonised) Stuart kings was designed to win readers over to a more nuanced, less thoughtlessly Whiggish reading of English history than the one peddled by previous historians. Robertson softened the controversial story of Mary, Queen of Scots into a pathetic personal tragedy in order to promote reconciliation between Jacobite and Whig factions in Scotland (where Mary was a Jacobite icon). Nothing in Robertson's own Whig background would have given him cause to sympathise with Mary, but by casting her as the vulnerable, flawed female casualty of a sentimental

---

16 David Hume, *The History of England*, ed. William B. Todd, 7 vols. (Indianapolis, IN: The Liberty Press, 1983), vol. VI, p. 513.

17 See David Raynor, 'Hume and Robertson's *History of Scotland*', *British Journal for Eighteenth-Century Studies* 10 (1987), 61, for the review and attribution. On this aspect of Hume and Robertson's work, see Karen O'Brien, *Narratives of Enlightenment: Cosmopolitan History from Voltaire to Gibbon* (Cambridge: Cambridge University Press, 1997), pp. 60–9 and 114–22.

drama, he was attempting to show Scotland a way to forgiveness and political progress.

The great narrative histories of the mid eighteenth century were diversified and enlivened, but not fundamentally generically altered by their borrowings from the novel. Historians were primarily concerned to create encompassing narratives of the economic, political and social forces which transformed the ancient and medieval worlds into the modern, comparatively enlightened world in which they were living; novelistic elements were adventitious to this. There were examples of formal experimentation in the histories written before 1780, most notably the adoption of the epistolary mode in works such as Goldsmith's *History of England in a Series of Letters from a Nobleman to his Son* (1764) or Catharine Macaulay's *History of England from the Revolution to the Present Time, in a Series of Letters* (1778); but these proved to be only superficial, presentational variations on an otherwise unchanged narrative format. Novels and histories evolved along parallel, rather than overlapping, lines in the direction of greater authorial distance and narrative mastery, and away from the models of the author as the manager of an archive of letters or documents. They also moved towards more secular and materialistic notions of causation (although many continued to allude or give credence to providential final causes), and towards fuller representation of the world of social and cultural experience. Yet, at the deepest level, the epistemological challenge posed by the novel to narrative history went unanswered until well into the nineteenth century. Novels parodied and appropriated historical modes of discourse, and might have been seen as a threat to the very notion that the past could be shaped into a narrative order without imposing supplementary fictionality. Works such as *The History of Tom Jones, A Foundling* and *Clarissa, or the History of a Young Lady* were 'histories', in the sense of an 'account' of a life or set of events, and they performed many of the same mimetic and instructive functions. Many novels derived strategies of factual authentication from historians' footnotes and discussions of manuscript provenance, often in order to distance themselves from the more fanciful world of romance. Some novelists, most notably Defoe, went so far as to foster public belief in the genuine historicity of their fictional works. Robert Mayer has discussed the initial public reception of *Robinson Crusoe* and *A Journal of the Plague Year* as real histories, as well as Defoe's own 'belief that fiction was a legitimate means of historical representation'.[18] Coming from Defoe, the author of a history of the Union of England and Scotland, a *Life* of the Duke of Marlborough and numerous other historical works, such a

18 Mayer, *History and the Early English Novel*, p. 172.

cavalier attitude towards the difference between history and fiction appears to challenge the new scientific notions of the 'factual'. Yet in most other cases, readers were able to see through the over-protestations of historical authenticity which were prefaced to so many early novels, and to maintain a separation between historical and non-historical writings. As Barbara Foley has argued, early modern readers did not live 'in some sort of epistemological haze', nor did they tend to perceive as a profound theoretical problem the fact that, in history as in fiction, 'truth' is necessarily an effect of textual representation.[19]

Seventeenth- and eighteenth-century historians were deeply interested in philosophical questions of historical truth, but this took a form very different from the question of epistemological overlap between history and the novel explored by modern critics.[20] Issues of linguistic referentiality, and of the truth-value of figural or empirical modes of discourse, were generally addressed as part of debates within the novel itself, rather than across the novel–history boundary. Historians, meanwhile, were more greatly exercised by the problems of the knowability of the remote past, and of the nature and intelligibility of historical causation. In relation to the remote past, historians, such as Bolingbroke in his *Letters on the Study and Use of History*, became more openly sceptical about the kinds of evidence available (despite the advances made in contempoary archaeology): the reliability of the Bible as a historical source was debated in this context, as was, more generally, the scientific status of the historical 'fact'. Historians engaged less negatively with the question of causation, and the need for an explanatory historical vocabulary over and above the characters and deeds of individual agents. In the mid eighteenth century they pioneered social, economic and cultural forms of historical analysis; but they were, at the same time, worried about the potential distortions to the past inflicted by their analytical methods and narrative presentation. Such problems preoccupied Hume, both as an epistemologist and as a historian, and they were also searchingly explored by Gibbon in his early work, the *Essai sur l'étude de la littérature* (1761). All historians, Gibbon argued, must search for the inner 'springs' of history, those particular and general causes which have significant effects; yet in inferring and recording the operation of causes, they can never entirely avoid leaving the imprint of their critical perspective on the narrative they assemble. The key is, somehow, to acknowledge and render visible the literariness of the historical operation without losing sight of the

---

19 Barbara Foley, *Telling the Truth: The Theory and Practice of Documentary Fiction* (Ithaca, NY: Cornell University Press, 1986), p. 110.
20 For example, Everett Zimmerman's *The Boundaries of Fiction: History and the Eighteenth-Century Novel* (Ithaca, NY: Cornell University Press, 1996).

fact that the past is an entity independent of the historian's attempts to make sense of it.

Gibbon's *History of the Decline and Fall of the Roman Empire* (1776–88) is, on the grandest scale, a search for the hidden 'springs' of a long and infinitely complex historical process: namely the decline of the Roman and Byzantine Empires from the third to the fifteenth centuries. The work is sustained by a palpable, yet never obtrusive or unduly decisive, authorial presence which constantly reminds the reader of both the act and limits of historical reconstruction. The geographical and chronological terrains of the *Decline and Fall* are vast, yet Gibbon does not flinch from seeking to present them as part of a coherent authorial point of view.[21] Gibbon's imaginative power is such that he is able to generate what the theorist Hayden White has called, 'the illusion of a centred consciousness capable of looking out on the world, apprehending its structure and processes'.[22] At the same time, his wry evaluations of (often conflicting or partial) primary sources in the text and footnotes render the process of historical interpretation visible, and potentially refutable. Gibbon's temper of mind is pervasively ironic; his irony is to be found, not so much in momentary sallies or in slowly-released, Swiftian assaults (with the famous exception of chapters 15 and 16, discussed below), but in the distance he sustains between himself and the self-deceived, distorted or perverse versions of the truth which others have given of their own or of other peoples' histories. Like Hume's, Gibbon's commanding authorial presence is, in part, negatively generated by this ironic distance. Yet, like Hume also, Gibbon's irony is to be distinguished from the kind of scepticism which finds narrative form and empirical content necessarily at odds with one and other; for both historians, the past, with its tissue of causes and effects, is intrinsically sequential, and therefore capable of narrative representation.

There were historians in the eighteenth century who experimented with ways of rearranging or breaking up the narrative unity of history, most notably Robert Henry, who presented periods thematically rather than chronologically in his *History of Great Britain, Written on a New Plan* (1771–93).[23] Moreover,

---

21 W. B. Carnochan has very well described the unique quality of Gibbon's vision: his visual construction of narrative as if from a lonely summit, his almost spatial comprehension of time and his theatrical division of Roman imperial history into floodlit stages, with glimpses into the dark areas offstage where hoards of barbarians breed and muster (W. B. Carnochan, *Gibbon's Solitude: The Inward World of the Historian* (Stanford, CA: Stanford University Press, 1987).

22 Hayden White, *The Content of the Form: Narrative Discourse and Historical Representation* (Baltimore, MD: Johns Hopkins University Press, 1987), p. 36.

23 The implications of Henry's work are discussed by Phillips in *Society and Sentiment*, pp. 3–8.

the extended essay and sketch became increasingly important vehicles for historical rumination, as the new kinds of legal theory, moral philosophy and political economy developed in Scottish universities began to infiltrate the study of history. Among Scottish Enlightenment works, Hume's essays (published from the 1740s), Adam Smith's lectures on jurisprudence (delivered in the 1750s and 1760s), Adam Ferguson's *Essay on the History of Civil Society* (1767) and Lord Kames' *Sketches of the History of Man* (1774) pioneered analyses of social evolution, the origins of property, economic development and the differences between social and cultural formations in different epochs and countries. Such historical speculations were better suited to the thematic essay form than to extended narrative. Robertson himself prefaced his narrative *History of the Reign of the Emperor Charles V* (1769) with a ground-breaking essay on the 'Progress of Society in Europe' in which he reflected on the rise and decay of feudalism. In Scotland and in England, there followed large numbers of historical essays on the nature and development of civil society, most of them centrally preoccupied with the origins of the Enlightened, modern world in which their authors felt they were living. Narrative historians, too, tried to integrate these new insights into the economic and social causes of change into their political histories, with varying degrees of success. Even the most advanced histories, such as Hume's *History of England* or Robertson's *History of Charles V* or *History of America* (1777), had a tendency to concentrate on political narrative, and to relegate economic and social speculations to appendices or separate subsections.

In the longer term, however, the economic and social theory of the Scottish Enlightenment vastly expanded the horizons of narrative history, particularly in the area of what we would now call cultural history, or, as it was then known, the history of 'manners'. 'Manners', which comprehended the customs, technology, culture, and gender and family relations of a given people at a given time, became a dominant subject in later eighteenth-century history. By 1783, the Scottish critic and philosopher Hugh Blair was able to observe with satisfaction that: 'it is now understood to be the business of an able Historian to exhibit manners, as well as facts and events; and assuredly, whatever displays the state and life of mankind, in different periods, and illustrates the progress of the human mind, is more useful and interesting than the detail of sieges and battles'.[24]

Scottish Enlightenment historians such as Hume, Robertson and John Millar were able to give sophisticated accounts of manners – the conventions of

---

24 Hugh Blair, *Lectures on Rhetoric and Belles Lettres*, ed. H. F. Harding, 2 vols. (Carbondale, IL: University of Southern Illinois Press, 1965), vol. I, p. 288.

medieval chivalry, for instance, or attitudes towards women in particular societies – as effects of particular types of economic and social organisation. In the works of other, particularly English, historians, however, the study of manners often became a more disembodied, though no less rich form of cultural antiquarianism: works of literary history such as Thomas Warton's *History of English Poetry* (1774–81) or Clara Reeve's *The Progress of Romance* (1785) derived from the new 'manners' history, as did works of specifically social history, such as William Alexander's *History of Women from the Earliest Antiquity to the Present Time* (1779) or Joseph Strutt's *Complete View of the Manners, Customs, Arms, Habits etc. of the Inhabitants of England* (1774–5). The tension between 'manners' as social science and as cultural antiquarianism remained unresolved in the eighteenth century, though readers welcomed both kinds as a more inclusive, engaging kind of history. Women readers, in particular, actively contributed to the promotion of this kind of history through personal and printed recommendations (for example Hester Chapone's essay on 'The Manner of Reading History' in her *Letters on the Improvement of the Mind*, 1773), through translation and anthologising, and, by the end of the eighteenth century, as writers themselves.

The history of manners opened a gateway to a fuller understanding of the lived experience of a people, in ways similar to the contemporary novel of manners; yet, at the same time, by treating subjective, private experience as part of a collective entity, manners history risked lacking the human interest of more biographical kinds of writing. In his *Journal of a Tour to the Hebrides*, James Boswell reproduces a conversation between himself, Johnson and the Scottish philosophical historian Lord Monboddo which makes clear the conflict between the knowledge value and imaginative purchase of 'manners' history:

> Monboddo: 'The history of manners is the most valuable. I never set a high value on any other history.' Johnson. 'Nor I; and therefore I esteem biography, as giving us what comes near to ourselves, what we can turn to use.' Boswell. 'But in the course of general history, we find manners. In wars, we see the dispositions of people, their degrees of humanity, and other particulars.' Johnson. 'Yes; but then you must take all the facts to get this, and it is but little you get.' Monboddo. 'And it is that little which makes history valuable.'[25]

Neither Boswell nor Monboddo succeed in making a case against Johnson's implicit charge that the history of manners, for all its engagement with people's

---

25 Boswell's *Journal of a Tour to the Hebrides with Samuel Johnson* (London: Heineman, 1936), p. 55.

private lives and cultural dispositions, cannot offer 'what comes near to ourselves'. For them, the real purpose of the history of manners is to reveal the essence of national identity; 'general' (i.e. political) history becomes more meaningful when it is deepened by the history of manners, and illuminates the distinctive spirit of different peoples. Neither Boswell nor Monboddo would have articulated this in these terms (the phrase 'national identity' was not in use at this time), but both are more typical of their age than Johnson in endorsing a shift in historical writing away from both biographical and political narrative towards genuinely national history.

It was, indeed, in the area of national history that the eighteenth-century study of manners effected the greatest transformation. Commercial history publishing in this period was dominated by the quest for a best-selling national history, and then, after the success of works by Smollett, Hume and Catharine Macaulay, for localised works of particular aspects of British cultural life. The transformation of British national history followed, a few steps behind, the trajectory of British literary history in the eighteenth century which moved from theories of progressive literary refinement to the celebration of a living artistic tradition in which modern writers could participate. The idea of national history as 'progressive refinement' was pervasive until late in the eighteenth century when the emphasis began to shift towards the idea of a living cultural tradition shaping the identity and behaviour of the British people. Literary scholarship also stimulated historical interest in the medieval and pre-medieval aspects of British cultural history, and this, in turn, motivated further investigation into the ethnic and racial roots of Britishness in the country's Celtic and Germanic heritage. A number of late eighteenth-century histories of pre-medieval Britain attempted to deduce distinctive and separate English, Scottish and Welsh ethnic or racial identities from what was known about the 'manners' of their ancient peoples: a new and significant development. Such works, including James Macpherson's *Introduction to the History of Great Britain and Ireland* (1771), John Pinkerton's *Dissertation on the . . . Goths* (1787) and John Whitaker's *Genuine History of the Britons Asserted* (1772), were highly controversial, especially where they entailed comparing the relative merits of Celts and Goths. Their ethnographic concerns were not per se incompatible with Enlightenment history (Gibbon, for example, encouraged Pinkerton in his researches), but they heralded the beginnings of a shift from the global anthropology of the Enlightenment to the nationally orientated ethnography of the nineteenth century. More generally, histories of Britain from the later eighteenth century tilted the balance between cosmopolitan and national perspectives in the direction of the latter: the social science of the Scottish Enlightenment was deployed in the service of national self-understanding, and Enlightenment-style histories of 'society' in England gradually gave way to philosophically informed histories of 'English society'.

Enlightenment histories such as Hume's *History of England*, Robertson's *History of Charles V*, Catharine Macaulay's *History of England* and Gibbon's *Decline and Fall*, are not usually thought to have been in any profound way preoccupied with questions of national identity. Rather, they are treated as though they were written in an era before such questions arose: according to some a golden era of more universal concerns with 'liberty', 'progress', justice and modernity. Yet it is important to recognise that, for all of these writers, a cosmopolitan approach to the past did, in itself, constitute a form of national awareness, and one which was intended to be exemplary to readers. Hume, Robertson and Gibbon adopted, simultaneously, an attitude of detachment towards the prejudices, religious bigotries and unexamined traditions of their own country, and one of commitment to the idea of a common European civilisation of which Britain was a part. Macaulay herself, though she made no intellectual investment in the idea of a European civilisation, adopted a similar pose of detachment from the English past the better to write as a would-be patriotic saviour of her country's liberties. Hume's *History of England* and Robertson's *History of Scotland* cast a self-consciously civilised, European eye over the peculiarities, anomalies and brutalities of British history. Robertson's *History of Charles V* tells the story of the emergence of modern Europe from the disorder of feudalism and the tumoil of the Reformation. Gibbon's *Decline and Fall* is, in part, an unfinished history of the rise of Europe after the ruin of the Roman Empire, and it ends, where Robertson's history begins, on the eve of the Renaissance and Reformation. Robertson's last, and arguably his best, major work, *The History of America*, explores the colonial dimension of early modernity in Europe, and he also wrote about European involvement with India. Enlightenment historians' sense of living and writing as Europeans went beyond the grand tourism and aesthetic preferences for all things French which characterised most wealthy men of their generation (although Gibbon did go on a grand tour, and Hume greatly enjoyed being lionised in Paris). Their intellectual culture was steeped in the French Enlightenment and in European Protestant traditions of criticism, legal theory and scholarship. They thought that the very things which made Britain distinctive – its constitutional monarchy, its Protestantism, its history of civil war and, most recently, its imperial adventures – could only be understood in the context of the European history which had shaped them. National history, for all of these historians, including Macaulay, could only be written from a detached or cosmopolitan vantage point which kept the wider, comparative context in view.

Hume's *History of England* attracted a good deal of suspicion and hostility when it first appeared largely because his detachment from national myths and cherished beliefs was so widely misinterpreted as party-political bias. The first two volumes (1754 and 1756), covering seventeenth-century British history, were the most controversial, particularly on account of their sympathetic portrayal of the Stuart monarchs. Hume did, indeed, borrow heavily from Clarendon, but this was not because he wanted to produce a hardline Tory work, rather to redress the party-political balance in contemporary national history. After the initial reception of Clarendon's *History* as a great but ultra-Tory work, the historical landscape had been dominated by Whig histories such as John Oldmixon's *Critical History of England* (1724), written as a radical alternative to Clarendon, or Rapin's *History of England* (1721–31 in English translation). In addition, Bolingbroke's *Craftsman* essays had helped to create a new kind of patriotic Whig history with which opposition groups and radicals continued to identify. Hume had a horror of vulgar Whiggery in all its forms, and his irreverent treatment of Whig historical myths was motivated by his fear that this kind of teleological history would win out in the end (to some extent, his fears were justified). He endeavoured to write as a moral philosopher interested in such matters as human behaviour under different historical conditions, the role of belief in human motivation, and religious fanaticism. He had none of Clarendon's interest in intricate webs of personalities, but he had an ironist's eye for the unintended or misunderstood consequences of individual actions. Hume's narrative orchestrates a broad repertoire of styles: by turns sentimental, satirical, clinically detached, informally Senecan or gravely decorous. These key changes allow him to rouse his readers from their 'dogmatic slumber' (in Hume's phrase) whilst maintaining overall coherence of narrative perspective.

Hume wrote his history backwards, following the seventeenth-century volumes with two volumes on the Tudor period (in 1759), and a further two on the Middle Ages in 1762. As he retreated chronologically, Hume became less interested in royal personalities and dilemmas, and more concerned to detect underlying patterns of political and social evolution in England, often in comparison with other European states at similar evolutionary stages. In appendices to the medieval volumes, Hume gave a pioneering account of the rise and fall of feudalism as a European social and economic system. These insights were not completely integrated into the main body of the narrative in which he often characterised medieval England as static and chaotic. He was also a little behind his times in his refusal to take seriously chivalric manners and literature, but he was innovative (and unWhiggish) in his treatment of the Catholic church as a force for social justice and change. Hume was more fired as a historian by the sixteenth century when England, like other more major European powers, started to become a viable, centralised state. He praised Elizabeth I, not as the good 'Queen Bess' of contemporary Whig history, but as a ruthless, effective monarch who helped to fashion a powerful English state out of the crumbling feudal order. The possibility that Elizabeth was not unduly concerned with traditional English liberties mattered far less to Hume than the fact that, even at the price of some religious persecution, she managed to create a stable political order. This was an order which was then ruined, in the seventeenth century, by a disastrous combination of royal intransigence and Puritan religious enthusiasm, but which recovered, by the end that period, ultimately creating the conditions for new and more meaningful kinds of civil, religious and political liberty.

After initial controversy, Hume's *History of England* rapidly eclipsed the rival works by Rapin, Smollett and Goldsmith, and enjoyed canonical status well into the nineteenth century. The most serious eighteenth-century competition faced by the Stuart volumes of Hume's *History* came from Catharine Macaulay's *History of England* (1763–83). This, along with its sequel *The History of England from the Revolution to the Present Time*, offered a radical alternative to Hume, but nevertheless maintained a similar detachment from the pieties and myths of English popular history: 'the people of England always are,' Macaulay asserted, 'half stupid, half drunk, and half asleep'.[26] Macaulay (no relation of her nineteenth-century namesake Thomas Babington) was a leading radical Whig *salonnière* and pamphleteer, hugely famous in her own lifetime both in Britain and North America. Her histories were an expression of her commitment to political reform, including the extension of the male franchise, the constitutional limitation of royal power, the removal of venality and corruption from all areas of public life and greater religious toleration, particularly of Protestant dissenters. Since Macaulay set out to provide a republican alternative to Hume's version of the English past, her histories are generally regarded as being diametrically opposed to his sceptical, philosophically informed history; yet the similarities between these histories, and the kinds of national awareness they aimed to promote, are as interesting as the differences. Both Hume and Macaulay wrote, according to their own lights, histories

---

26 Catharine Macaulay, *The History of England from the Revolution to the Present Time* (Bath, 1778), p. 372. The fullest study of Macaulay is Bridget Hill, *The Republican Virago: The Life and Times of Catharine Macaulay* (Oxford: Oxford University Press, 1992).

of liberty in England, and, for them, the evolving meanings and contexts of 'liberty' were constitutive of Englishness. Englishness, as they understood it, consisted in the idea of an interpretative national community, and did not derive from ethnic or cultural roots in a distant past. Like Hume, Robertson and, later, Gibbon, Macaulay tried to quash the idea, rapidly becoming an unassailable Whig myth in the late eighteenth century, that liberty was a kind of racial heritage which began among the Gothic invaders of the Roman Empire, and made its way to Britain with the Anglo-Saxons.

Macaulay was a devout Anglican, and wrote out of a set of more firmly held political, religious and moral certainties than Hume. Yet she too had a sophisticated sense of history as a process of accident and unintended consequence; she acknowledged that the very ideas for which she claimed permanent value (liberty, natural rights, freedom of conscience) had been stumbled upon by chance during the course of time. At the heart of Macaulay's *History of England* lies the Civil War, unrecognisable as the same set of events described in Clarendon's *History*, except in its concurrence that Cromwell was a 'base, vain-glorious man'.[27] For Macaulay, this was a contest between liberty and tyranny: the liberty achieved by the English Commonwealth (1649–53), at the not-too-high price of the execution of Charles I, was betrayed by the tyranny of Cromwell, and destroyed by human selfishness and fallibility. Liberty is an abstract ideal in Macaulay's histories, but, in its mid seventeenth century form, it is also an idea with social contexts and economic origins. Where Clarendon refused to trace the origins of the Civil War further back than the reign of Charles I, Macaulay links the 'appetite for liberty' among the parliamentary party to long-term economic causes: it was the increasing wealth of the middling section of society, brought about by the growth of commerce in the early seventeenth century, which changed their political expectations, and, ultimately gave them the confidence to challenge Charles I.[28] Macaulay's authorial persona is brisk, dismissive and unwavoringly self-confident, despite the public criticism meted out to her over her justification of the execution of Charles I. Liberty and progress are hardly anywhere to be found in English history after the Commonwealth, and she does not flinch from saying so. She does not draw attention to her femininity either as a source of insight or of anxiety, but shows instead by her critical handling of prominent figures such as Queen Mary II and Queen Anne ('the foot-ball of all who had an opportunity

---

27 Macaulay, *The History of England from the Accession of James I*, 8 vols. (London, 1763–83), vol. v, p. 99.
28 *Ibid.*, vol. v, p. 383.

of taking advantage of her weakness') that women have a duty to political progress and liberty from which their sex does not excuse them.[29]

A key area of difference between Macaulay and other Enlightenment historians, apart from the very different cast of her political beliefs, is that she thought that progress and liberty were only possible in Protestant religious cultures. The Catholicism of European countries such as France and Spain was, she believed, essentially incompatible with the civil and political liberties she endorsed. It was an assumption shared by Smollett, but not by other Enlightenment historians such as Hume, Gibbon, Henry, Robertson or Millar; for them, the comparatively civilised and refined condition of modern European states was more significant than their religious differences. In the cases of Hume and Gibbon, this cosmopolitan outlook proceeded from religious scepticism, and pious contemporaries were rightly suspicious of it. But in the case of Robertson, a leading figure in the Church of Scotland and pillar of the Edinburgh University establishment, cosmopolitanism was not incompatible with commitment to a fundamentally Protestant and providential view of history. Robertson adopted a moderate, ecumenical approach to the religious history of Europe, and employed comparative historical perspectives as a means of encouraging his readers to see beyond their intolerance and partiality as Protestant subjects of a Protestant monarchy. His great subject was the formation of modern Europe as a system of states and imperial powers; the reason he devoted so much of his career to the fifteenth and sixteenth centuries was that: 'It was during [Charles V's] reign . . . that the different kingdoms of Europe acquired internal vigour, that they discerned the resources of which they were possessed, that they came both to feel their own strength, and to know how to render it formidable to others.'[30] Modern refinement, for Robertson as for most later eighteenth-century historians, was not the preserve of Protestant countries, but the historical effect of a long process of intra-European cultural exchange. Robertson was particularly influential in his discussion of chivalry (generally dismissed as a form of barbarism by most previous historians) as a civilising force in medieval Catholic Europe: 'The wild exploits of those romantic knights who sallied forth in quest of adventures, are well known, and have been treated with proper ridicule. The political and permanent effects of the spirit of chivalry have been less observed.'[31] After Robertson, it was widely accepted that chivalry had, in the

---

29 Macaulay, *The History of England from the Revolution to the Present Time*, p. 271.
30 William Robertson, *The History of the Reign of the Emperor Charles V*, 3 vols. (London, 1769), vol. III, p. 432.
31 *Ibid.*, vol. I, p. 71.

long run, contributed to the 'polishing' of European manners, including the polite and humane treatment of women. Macaulay was unusual, in her time, in her refusal to accept that chivalry, or anything else, had enabled modern Europe to become a refined place: but then, as a woman, she had no reason to connive at the fiction that modern refinement promoted the cause of her sex.

Gibbon was influenced by Scottish Enlightenment ideas about the progress of refinement in modern Europe, and, like Hume, he adopted a sceptical, cosmopolitan attitude towards his own national history: 'It is the duty of the patriot to prefer and promote the exclusive interest and glory of his native country: but a philosopher may be permitted to enlarge his views, and consider Europe as one great republic, whose various inhabitants have attained almost the same level of politeness and civilisation.'[32] Gibbon was acutely aware of the limits and complacency of modern 'politeness and civilisation', and, like Hume, thought that they were only attainable in cultures which had divested themselves of religious superstition and enthusiasm. Gibbon's irony, especially when it is directed at the fanaticism of early and medieval Christianity, makes apparent the relationship between religious scepticism, cosmopolitanism and 'politeness and civilisation'; indeed, it is offered as evidence of the very civilisation which most historical epochs, with the exception of the Roman Empire, had failed to attain. In a well-known essay, F. R. Leavis described the way in which Gibbon allied, through irony, the pagan Roman and modern, sceptical points of view at the expense of Christianity:

> The decorously insistent pattern of Gibbonian prose insinuates a solidarity with the reader . . . establishes an understanding and habituates to certain assumptions. The reader, it is implied, is an eighteenth-century gentleman ('rational', 'candid', 'polite', 'elegant', 'humane'); eighteen hundred years ago he would have been a pagan gentleman, living by those standards (those of absolute civilisation); by these standards . . . the Jews and Christians are seen to have been ignorant fanatics, uncouth and probably dirty.[33]

Leavis is referring to the notorious chapters 15 and 16 of *The Decline and Fall* in which Gibbon addresses the role of Christianity in the Roman Empire, having covered the period from AD 98–337 without discussing the subject in any detail. Gibbon suddenly and belatedly exposes Christianity, through a slow-paced crescendo of irony, as the major cause of the decline of the empire. Gibbon's

---

32 Edward Gibbon, *The History of the Decline and Fall of the Roman Empire*, ed. David Womersley 3 vols. (Harmondsworth: Allen Lane, 1994), vol. II, p. 511.
33 F. R. Leavis, 'The Irony of Swift', in *The Common Pursuit* (London: Chatto and Windus, 1958), p. 75.

ostensible subject is the apparently providential triumph of this new religion, but it soon becomes clear that he holds Christianity largely responsible for the decay of Rome's once tolerant and sociable religious and civic culture.

An additional target of Gibbon's irony is the hysteria and hyperbole of early Christian commentators. He gives a much cooler estimate of the numbers of Christians actually martyred than the first Christian historians: 'the whole might consequently amount to about fifteen hundred, a number which, if it is equally divided between the ten years of the persecution, will allow an annual consumption of one hundred and fifty martyrs'.[34] The unemphatic irony of 'consumption' here belies its callousness, and Gibbon, who is not habitually inhumane, does not, in the end, settle for his own devastating indictment of the early Christians. Despite the coruscating ironies of chapters 15 and 16, his account of the relationship between Christianity and the decline of Rome becomes far more complex during the rest of the history. Even in the early part of the *Decline and Fall*, Christianity, for all its fanaticism, is clearly the only dynamic element in a complacent and stagnant Roman culture; in an empire sinking into the 'languid indifference of private life', the Christians create their own public world.[35] Moreover, by insisting upon the discontinuity between Christian and pagan cultures, Gibbon implicitly acknowledges that the significance of this new religion lay in its radical restructuring of social and sexual values, and its capacity to generate new modes of consciousness at a time when, among the pagans, 'the minds of men were gradually reduced to the same level, the fire of genius was extinguished'.[36] In subsequent volumes, Gibbon reveals the paradoxical, long-term consequences of the Christian revolution. He shows how, in Western Europe, Christianity adapted and protracted the Roman imperial culture which it had originally helped to undermine. Gibbon's own classically informed modernity becomes part of the evidence for this, as is his intellectual identity as a European. Even though Gibbon's history closes on a melancholy note, in the city of Rome, shortly before the fall of Constantinople, it is significant that he has made his readers so fully aware of the European history which has yet to come. Gibbon was no crass believer in inexorable human progress, but he did believe that modern Europe had absorbed the lessons and culture of Rome in ways which would make it far less likely to succumb to a similar process of decay and decline. The Britain of his day was establishing a global empire, but, with the right amount of political wisdom, balance and liberty, he did

34 *The Decline and Fall*, vol. 1, p. 579.
35 *Ibid.*, vol. 1, p. 83.
36 *Ibid.*

not think that it was inevitable that it would go the way of previous, ancient empires. To be modern, was, in part, to feel that the end of history had been reached, at least in the sense that the endless cycles of barbarian invasions and religious wars, and of the rise and fall of empires were now over. The modern age was, certainly, less heroic, less spectacular and less replete with opportunities for moral courage than those which had gone before; but it was some compensation to the readers of Gibbon, Hume, Macaulay and Robertson to have been offered such a vivid sense of imaginative participation in the turbulent currents of history from the safety of their eighteenth-century shore.

A preliminary discourse on philosophy and literature

MICHAEL B. PRINCE

Fig. 15.1 Frontispiece to *A Dialogue on Beauty. In the Manner of Plato* by George Stubbes (1731)

Merchant.	And do not I Exist?
Pyrrho.	I know not.
Merchant.	Well but you Exist.
Pyrrho.	Nor do I know that, neither.
Merchant.	Good God! A Pleasant incertainty this! But what's the meaning of those Scales?
Pyrrho.	They are to weigh the reasons on Each side; and after having weigh'd well and Consider'd all, I find I know nothing.[1]

I am grateful to Dove Pedlosky for assistance with the research that went into this chapter. Her unerring eye for the best citations has helped provide a foundation for the course of the argument.

1 Lucian, 'The Sects of Philosophers Expos'd to Sale by way of Auction', in *Lucian's Works*, trans. Ferrand Spence, 2 vols. (London, 1684), vol. II, pp. 19–20.

Introduction

Any attempt to limit the topic of philosophy and literature to a subset of the material that might be considered under that heading immediately replicates the theoretical conundrum that brought philosophy and literature into close proximity from the late seventeenth through the eighteenth century: the existing data exceed the frame of the genre appropriate to the occasion, in much the same way that, at the time, a scientific standard of empirical precision and comprehensiveness threatened the bounds of existing forms of philosophical writing and received accounts of ultimate order and design. Eighteenth-century writers confronted a seemingly inevitable implication of the scientific outlook, namely, that the range of empirical data about natural and moral topics is so vast that any assembly of available information constitutes a selective interpretation, or, when the point was pressed, as it often was by the likes of Hume, a fiction.

Between 1660 and 1800, writers across a wide spectrum of philosophical and literary activity were keenly aware of this problem. 'In the prosecution of a design so extensive', writes George Campbell at the beginning of his *magnum opus The Philosophy of Rhetoric* (1776), 'there are two extremes to be shunned. One is too much abstraction in investigating causes; the other, too much minuteness in specifying effects. By the first, the perspicuity of a performance may be endangered; by the second, its dignity may be sacrificed.'[2] Although we tend to hear the bowing and scraping of a neoclassicist gesturing towards the *via media*, eighteenth-century philosophers after Locke could not avoid encountering the dialectic between perspicuity and dignity on the cognitive or theoretical level. To meet the requirement of perspicuity, the writer was committed to an increasingly detailed level of inquiry and presentation; to meet the requirement of dignity, the writer was also committed to representing a general picture of things, usually the theologically sanctioned one. The first standard of scientific accuracy drove the level of analysis to a more and more minute increment, triggering hostile reactions to what George Berkeley called the 'minute philosophy'.[3] The second mandate of mutual intelligibility between mind and nature posited a natural limit to division, the assurance that what the mind finds out there as a result of an inductive process of information-gathering, corresponds to consistent and continuous forms.

---

2 George Campbell, *The Philosophy of Rhetoric*, ed. Lloyd F. Bitzer (Carbondale and Edwardsville, IL: Southern Illinois University Press, 1963), Preface, p. lxvii.
3 See Berkeley's *Alciphron, or the Minute Philosopher* (1732).

While it is easy to view the expectation of 'dignity' as the relic of a fading humanism, the theoretical problem that motivates Campbell has little to do with nostalgia. According to the paradoxical logic of empiricism itself, some version of dignity will need to be constituted on the empirical side, if a potentially never-ending process of materialist differentiation is to be turned to some advantage, or even rendered intelligible. There is no difference without sameness, and that source of continuity must be rendered rhetorically even where it cannot be confirmed philosophically. The problem that philosophers faced *as writers* – and by 'philosophers' I refer to male and female authors – was bound up in the tension Campbell describes between a proliferation of empirically derived facts and the possibility of their containment within a cognitive frame or discursive genre.

If anything, writers at the time were freer than we are today to experiment with various genres of exposition that might allow them to acknowledge and deflect the sceptical bind they were getting themselves into when framing their inquiries in up-to-date empirical terms. They did not yet operate in accordance with disciplinary distinctions between 'philosophy' and 'literature'; literature as a special disciplinary category only came into existence late in the period.[4] Nor was the academic essay or treatise the coin of the realm in learned letters. The question Stanley Cavell feels he must ask, and then refrain from answering – 'Is the issue of communication between philosophy and literature itself a philosophical or a literary issue?'[5] – would not have occurred to the writers under discussion here. No strict separation between speculative and mimetic or representational genres had yet occurred. No cordoning off of philosophical and literary canons for purposes of professional study had taken place. The audience for intellectual prose and poetry was proportionately larger and more diverse than it is today; and writers, whether literary or philosophical, wrote to be read, adjusting their style to the demands of an expanding market for print, a market, moreover, whose anticipated character was sceptical, self-interested and increasingly secular. If a technical language existed in philosophy, it went under the heading of an exploded 'scholasticism' and was everywhere on the run (prior to Kant, that is). If a theoretical language existed in criticism, it

---

4 The sense of 'literature' as an acquaintance with books of polite or humane learning dates from 1375, remains in use through to the time of Johnson's *Dictionary*, but becomes increasingly obsolete, replaced at the start of the nineteenth century by the modern notion of literature as a special body of (often national) works that 'has claim to consideration on the ground of beauty of form or emotional effects', a definition that the *Oxford English Dictionary* notes is of 'very recent emergence in both England and France'.

5 Stanley Cavell, *Disowning Knowledge in Six Plays of Shakespeare* (Cambridge: Cambridge University Press, 1987), p. 3.

went under the heading of an outmoded inventory of rhetorical figures for argument, which Laurence Sterne's *Tristram Shandy* will eroticise and deflate by adding 'the *Argumentum Tripodium*, which is never used but by the woman against the man; – and the *Argumentum ad Rem*, which, contrariwise, is made use of by the man only against the woman'.[6] Nor had philosophy and literature come entirely unhinged from a more powerful third term, theology, and the expectation, shared by all and sundry, that serious works by learned authors would either hasten or forestall the decline of revealed religion. All of these conditions made the conjunction of philosophy and literature more the norm than the exception during the late seventeenth and throughout the eighteenth century.

Yet even these provisos need to be qualified. For the time-honoured quarrel between philosophy and rhetoric certainly had its eighteenth-century counterparts. Locke's version was to pit 'dry Truth and real Knowledge' against 'Wit and Fancy', leaving little doubt on which side of the divide true philosophy (science) fell: 'if we would speak of Things as they are, we must allow, that all the Art of Rhetorick, besides Order and Clearness, all the artificial and figurative application of Words Eloquence hath invented, are for nothing else but to insinuate wrong *Ideas*, move the Passions, and thereby mislead the Judgment; and so indeed are perfect cheat'.[7] The battle was waged also on the side of literature. Poets, dramatists, satirists and novelists stigmatised philosophy and philosophers in the most unflattering terms. The character of Aristotle in Fontenelle's popular *Dialogues of the Dead* (English translation by John Hughes, 1708) complains that Anacreon, a mere drunken 'Scribbler of Sonnets, would have dared to rank himself with a Philosopher of my great Reputation'; while Anacreon accuses Aristotle of sitting up whole nights 'beating your Brains, and winnowing dry Distinctions and crabbed Questions of Logick'.[8] Swift's Laputian philosopher is an airy-headed cuckold 'so rapt in Speculation, that the Mistress and Lover may proceed to the greatest Familiarities before his Face, if he be but provided with Paper and Implements, without his *Flapper* at his side'.[9] Richard Steele makes the villain of his play, *The Conscious Lovers*, one Cimberton, 'a formal, philosophical, pedantic coxcomb . . . with all these

---

6 Laurence Sterne, *The Florida Edition of the Works of Laurence Sterne*, eds. Melvyn New and Joan New, 5 vols. (Gainesville, FL: University Presses of Florida, 1978), vol. I, p. 79 (*The Life and Opinions of Tristram Shandy, Gentleman*, vol. I, ch. 21).
7 John Locke, *An Essay concerning Human Understanding*, ed. Peter H. Nidditch (Oxford: Clarendon Press, 1975), Book III, chapter 10, sect. 34, p. 508.
8 M. de Fontenelle, *Fontenelle's Dialogues of the Dead*, trans. John Hughes (London, 1708), pp. 13–14.
9 Jonathan Swift, *Gulliver's Travels*, eds. Peter Dixon and John Chalker (London: Penguin Books, 1985), pp. 207–8.

crude notions of divers things, under the direction of great vanity and very little judgment'.[10] Of the twenty-four textual citations Johnson uses to illustrate definitions of 'philosophy,' 'philosopher' and 'philosophise' in his *Dictionary of the English Language* (1755), almost all are drawn from literary sources, and none places philosophy in an unambiguously positive light. Johnson's *Rasselas, Prince of Abyssinia* (1759) provides the familiar portrait of the natural philosopher as mad astronomer who believes his ideas control the movement of the spheres. Examples such as these could be multiplied almost indefinitely. 'The very *Name* is a kind of Reproach,' opines the sceptic, Philocles, in Shaftesbury's dialogue, *The Moralists*. 'The word IDIOT stood formerly as the Opposite to *Philosopher*: but now-a-days it means nothing more commonly than *the* PHILOSOPHER *himself.*'[11]

Despite the complex, even muddled state of the question, I shall propose a means of recovering some of the early modern terms within which the boundary between philosophy and literature was constituted, debated and crossed. I begin by moving from the general problem of division outlined above to an account of the two dominant ways in which philosophy as a field was divided between roughly 1660 and 1800. These two systems of knowledge exist side-by-side and in competition: they help explain why the same span of time would be characterised by the period designations of neoclassicism and Enlightenment. Their collision animates the intellectual and literary history of the period and provides a philosophical context for understanding the simultaneous emergence of philosophical aesthetics and the novel as dominant literary forms. Although this method of proceeding takes into account familiar problems in the history of ideas and canonical writers in the history of philosophy and literature, my purpose is also to provide a context within which to view the interventions of female philosophers such as Astell, Behn, Haywood, Carter and Wollstonecraft.

Dividing philosophy

In many ways, the historical transformations that concern us here are bound up in changing definitions of philosophy current between about 1660 and 1800.

---

10 Richard Steele, *The Conscious Lovers*, ed. Shirley Strum Kenny (Lincoln, NE: University of Nebraska Press, 1968), Act II, scene i, lines 41–4, p. 34.
11 The third Earl of Shaftesbury, *Characteristicks of Men, Manners, Opinions, Times*, 3 vols. (Indianapolis, IN: Liberty Fund, 2001), vol. II, p. 244. The Liberty Fund edition is a near facsimile of the 6th corrected edition of 1737–8 and is preferable to other new editions because it retains the three-volume structure and the late essays on the fine arts that were added posthumously to *Characteristicks*.

Two competing divisions descend to the early modern period from the classical and humanist past. In the first, philosophy was understood as the love of wisdom directed towards three ends: knowledge of nature (natural philosophy), knowledge of man (moral philosophy) and knowledge of divinity (theology, metaphysics). Francis Bacon was restating the received view when he observed that 'the contemplations of man either penetrate unto God, or are circumferred to nature, or are reflected or reverted upon himself. Out of which several inquiries there do arise three knowledges; divine philosophy, natural philosophy, and human philosophy or humanity'.[12] Within this tripartite division, there exists – and when threatened there was strenuously maintained – a vast reciprocity between the pursuit of wisdom (moral philosophy) and knowledge of things in their causes (natural philosophy). These two would be combined and reconciled under the supervision of a presiding third, namely metaphysics, or what philosophers understood at the time as 'Divine Philosophy'.

Students of late seventeenth and eighteenth-century philosophy and literature will have encountered the three philosophies in the multitude of works bearing out the argument from design, physico-theology or natural religion. Post-Reformation Protestant Christianity frequently asserted its rational, philosophical credentials by invoking some version of the three philosophies. Through the empirical study of nature, the scientific Christian would reveal evidence of deep and abiding order in the creation. This natural order would in turn verify what moral philosophers liked to call the 'communicable' attributes of God, those characteristics of divinity beyond mere existence such as orderliness and benevolence that provided a model for individuals to emulate in private and public life. In *The Universal Grammar* (1735), Benjamin Martin expresses the conventional wisdom: 'The Knowledge of the wonderful Works of God in Nature, is of the most exalted and divine Sort, which human Understanding can pretend to; and the more we know of this, the more perfect will be our Nature, and the more nearly shall we approach to the Image and Likeness of God.'[13]

The design argument needs to be understood less as an 'argument' in the history of ideas and more as a system of thought that extends to all provinces of culture, taking in the technical points of an emerging epistemology at one

---

12 Francis Bacon, *The Advancement of Learning and the New Atlantis*, ed. Arthur Johnston (Oxford: Clarendon Press, 1974), Book II, Part V, sect. 2, p. 83.
13 Benjamin Martin, *The Universal Grammar; Being a View of the Present State of Experimental Physiology, or Natural Philosophy* (London, 1735), fo. A3.

extreme and lending itself to political, economic and racial appropriation at the other. The title of a minor work by Richard Barton indicates the vast scope typical of design-based inquiries: *The Analogy of Divine Wisdom: in the Material, Sensitive, Moral, Civil and Spiritual System of Things* (Dublin, 1750). Two other titles give a sense of design's longevity despite what is generally taken to be Hume's devastating critique of the conceptual underpinnings of design by the middle of the eighteenth century: John Ray's *The Wisdom of God Manifested in the Works of the Creation* (1691) and William Paley's *Natural Theology: or, Evidences of the Existence and Attributes of the Deity, Collected from the Appearances of Nature* (1802).

My visual inscription, the headpiece to George Stubbes' Platonic *Dialogue on Beauty* (1731), shows the three philosophies in beautiful equipoise (fig. 15.1). The philosopher reclines beneath the tree of knowledge. He looks out over the expanse of his estate and all that it contains, to a miraculous, impossible figure, an invisible hand suspending the scales of justice from a cloud. He discovers in nature a projection of the balance of reason in his own mind, each confirming the other. The invisible hand manifesting the visible standard is a representative philosophical figure. Versions of it appear throughout eighteenth-century art and letters. In Adam Smith's *The Wealth of Nations* (1776), for instance, the invisible hand is the principal philosophical figure legitimating laissez-faire capitalism. Every instance of design represented in concrete terms depended upon a more or less explicit figure of this sort, whose purpose was to mediate between the diversity of natural and historical phenomena and the unity of a rational, and finally theological order. This figure is the third term, and is alternately represented as right reason, the *criterium veritatis*, the scale of justice, the law of nature, the standard of taste, the moral sense, common sense, the order of things, beauty, sublimity, dialectic. An adequate historical account of the shifting boundary between philosophy and literature would entail a history of the third term in its various incarnations.

Design seeks to preserve the theory of the mutual intelligibility of nature and revelation under conditions that have grown hostile to what Earl Wasserman called 'the divine analogy'.[14] It had several advantages as a mode of theological argument. For one, people could understand it. Design relied upon everyday observations of order in nature, and the quite natural impulse to infer a cause from the effect. John Ray stresses the popular appeal of design:

---

14 Earl Wasserman, 'Nature Moralized: the Divine Analogy in the Eighteenth Century', *ELH* 20 (1953), 39–73.

Neither are they [arguments *a posteriori*] *only convictive of the greatest and subtlest Adversaries, but intelligible also to the meanest Capacities. For you may hear illiterate Persons of the lowest Rank of the Commonalty, affirming, That they need no Proof of the being of a God, for that every Pile of Grass, or Ear of Corn, sufficiently proves that.*[15]

A second advantage was that design was deeply enough grounded in the natural sciences, whose methods it appeared to borrow, to claim credibility in the sceptical and contentious climate of modern thought. Ray continues,

There are indeed supernatural Demonstrations of this fundamental Truth, but not common to all Persons or Times, and so liable to Cavil and Exception by Atheistical Persons, as inward Illuminations of Mind . . . But these Proofs taken from Effects, and Operations, exposed to every Man's View, not to be denied or questioned by any, are most effectual to convince all that deny or doubt of it.[16]

Moderately sceptical yet comprehensive in their account of natural and divine order, design-based inquiries knit together the perspicuity expected of scientific discourses with the dignity expected of edifying works. The position was fundamentally optimistic, even as it relied upon a risky wager: the more complete our scientific knowledge in all domains, including natural history, the more thankful we will be for the embrace of a fundamentally beautiful and rational order. Design was vulnerable all along to an extension and radicalisation of its own sceptical premises, a point to which I shall return in a moment.

This system of correspondences provided a theological justification for social, political and cultural 'progress'. It is central to what Herbert Butterfield called 'the Whig interpretation of history'.[17] 'The whole natural World and Government of it is a Scheme or System, not a fixt but a progressive one', writes Joseph Butler in *The Analogy of Religion* (1736). 'The Author of Nature appears deliberate throughout his Operations; accomplishing his natural Ends, by slow successive Steps. And there is a Plan of things beforehand laid out . . . Thus, in the daily Course of natural Providence, God operates in the very same Manner, as in the Dispensation of Christianity; making one thing subservient to another, This to somewhat further, and so on through a progressive Series of Means, which extend, both backward and forward, beyond our utmost

15 John Ray, *The Wisdom of God Manifested in the Works of the Creation* (London, 1692), 'Preface', A5 verso.
16 *Ibid.*
17 Herbert Butterfield, *The Whig Interpretation of History* (London G. Bell & Sons, 1931).

View.'[18] When deployed in support of a specific view of religion, nationhood or race, design could also provide a blueprint for virulent xenophobia and the dialectical *Aufhebung* of whole peoples from the final end of History, a tendency monumentalised in Hegel but much in evidence during the preceding century. Commenting on the anomaly of the survival of the Jewish people within the scheme of Christian providence, the benevolent and liberal Protestant divine, John Wilkins, first secretary of the Royal Society, asserted that the suffering of the Jews, their having been 'very frequently persecuted, impoverished, murthered in vast multitudes' over the previous 1,600 years, proved 'they were intended for a standing Memorial and example to the world of the divine power and vengeance'. And he continued: 'To me it seems, amongst rational Arguments, one of the plainest, not only for the proof of a Deity, and a just Providence in pursuing that Nation with such exemplary Vengeance; but likewise for the Authority of Scripture, and the Truth of the Christian Religion.'[19]

The relation of literary production to this period concept is complex and far-reaching. The student of the period would do well to consider the role of literature both as an illustration of this world picture and, in the form of modern aesthetics, as a substitute for an argument beset by philosophical and historical difficulties. Design already assumed, as Butler's remarks illustrate, a fundamentally narrative cast. Terms like 'successive' and 'progressive' stand for a system of thought in which actions occur as in an artful narrative, through a necessary unfolding of events over time. In this system, succession is to temporality what transcendence is to spirituality. As one might expect, advocates of design did not consider the admixture of philosophy and literature a fault. Here, for instance, is Thomas Burnet in *The Theory of the Earth* (1691) taking the sceptics to task for their failure to grasp the imaginative structure of rational order:

> I might mention also upon this occasion another Genius and disposition in Men, which often makes them improper for Philosophical Contemplations; not so much, it may be, from the narrowness of their Spirit and Understanding, as because they will not take time to extend them. I mean Men of Wit and Parts but of short Thoughts, and little meditation and that are apt to distrust every thing for a Fancy or Fiction that is not the dictate of Sense, or made out immediately to their Senses. Men of this Humour and Character call

18 Joseph Butler, *The Analogy of Religion, Natural and Revealed* (London, 1736), pp. 192–3.
19 John Wilkins, *Of the Principles and Duties of Natural Religion: Two Books*, 4th edn (London, 1699), pp. 89–90.

such Theories as these, Philosophick Romances, and think themselves witty in the expression; They allow them to be pretty amusements of the Mind, but without Truth or Reality. I am afraid if an Angel should write the Theory of the Earth, they would pass the same judgment upon it; Where there is variety of Parts in a due Contexture, with something of surprizing aptness in the harmony and correspondency of them, this they call Romance.[20]

When 'men of wit and parts' subject the argument from design to the closest possible scrutiny, rejecting any claim that does not meet the strictest 'dictate of Sense', they expose (whether because they are 'of short Thoughts and little Meditation' or because they see clear through to Hume's eventual critique of natural religion) the leap of faith necessary at the far side of inductive inference. Burnet's reply is instructive: he does not reject the criticism; rather, he embraces it! 'Such Romances must all Theories of Nature, and of Providence be, and must have every part of that Character with advantage, if they be well represented. There is in them, as I may so say, a *Plot* or *Mystery* pursued through the whole Work, and certain Grand Issues or Events upon which the rest depend, or to which they are subordinate; but these things we do not make or contrive our selves, but find and discover them, being made already by the Great Author and Governour of the Universe.'[21] Although admittedly dependent upon the support of fiction, design discovers and does not merely construct the true order of nature. Within this system, which Richard Rorty discussed under the heading 'philosophy and the mirror of nature', the romance of realism and the realism of romance exist in perfect reciprocity.[22]

Here was a formula for a grand aesthetic. Burnet himself names it in a single telling phrase: 'clearly discover'd, well digested, and well reason'd in every Part, there is, methinks, more of Beauty in such a Theory, at least a more masculine Beauty, than in any Poem or Romance'.[23] The masculine part of 'masculine Beauty' derives from the comprehensiveness of the original claim. The supreme design is gendered male. All lesser beauties are implicitly female and vulnerable until redeemed within the logic of a providential narrative. Any number of eighteenth-century works play out literary turns on this philosophical frame, and even forms that appear immune to the optimism of design, such as tragedy, bear its imprint, for better and for worse (e.g. 'sentimental'

20 Thomas Burnet, *The Theory of the Earth,* 2nd edn (London, 1691), 'Preface', A2 verso.
21 *Ibid.*
22 See Richard Rorty, *Philosophy and the Mirror of Nature* (Princeton, NJ: Princeton University Press, 1979).
23 Burnet, *The Theory of the Earth,* 'Preface', A2 verso.

or Christian tragedy). In perhaps the best-known and most popular example, Richardson's *Pamela, or, Virtue Rewarded* (1740), the female heroine herself relates the following heavy-handed summary of her progress from near-rape victim to moral emblem:

> 'But see the wonderful ways of Providence! The very things that I most dreaded his seeing and knowing, the Contents of my Papers, have, as I hope, satisfy'd all his Scruples, and been a means to promote my Happiness. Henceforth let not us poor short-sighted Mortals pretend to rely on our own Wisdom; or vainly think, that we are absolutely to direct for ourselves. I have abundant Reason, I am sure, to say, that when I was most disappointed, I was nearer my Happiness. For, had I made my Escape, which was so often my chief Point of View, and what I had placed my Heart upon, I had escaped the Blessings now before me, and fallen, perhaps, into the Miseries I would have avoided!'[24]

Such bland moralising is saved from banality by the fact that for the last two volumes Pamela has ignored her own conclusion and striven with all her energy to determine her fate through writing. Similarly, on the level of literary form, the eventual assertion of providential design carries potency here and elsewhere in eighteenth-century letters only to the degree that it has been combined with other elements – letters, dialogues, vivid description, erotic plots – that forestall and render uncertain any direct arrival at the pious destination.

The itinerary through chaos to order was irresistible to writers across the spectrum. George Berkeley described the plot of his *Three Dialogues between Hylas and Philonous* (1713) in terms that evoke intellectualised epic: 'methinks, this return to the simple dictates of Nature, after having run through the wild mazes of philosophy, is not unpleasant. It is like coming home from a long voyage: a man reflects with pleasure on the many difficulties and perplexities he has passed through, sets his heart at ease, and enjoys himself with more satisfaction for the future.'[25] And in case any reader mistook the invisible hand guiding a seemingly sceptical exchange to the safe harbour of truth, Berkeley supplies that philosophical figure at the conclusion of his work. How is it, the materialist, Hylas, asks the idealist, Philonous, that a dialogue that has moved randomly through sceptical give-and-take nevertheless has reached an edifying conclusion? Here is Philonous' answer, which ends the dialogue:

24 Samuel Richardson, *Pamela, or, Virtue Rewarded*, eds. T. C. Duncan Eaves and Ben D. Kimpel (Boston: Houghton Mifflin, 1971), p. 261.
25 George Berkeley, *The Works of George Berkeley, Bishop of Cloyne*, eds. A. A. Luce and T. E. Jessup, 9 vols. (London: Thomas Nelson and Sons Ltd., 1949), vol. II, p. 168.

You see, Hylas, the water of yonder fountain, how it is forced upwards, in a round column, to a certain height; at which it breaks, and falls back into the basin from whence it rose: its ascent as well as descent, proceeding from the same uniform law or principle of *gravitation*. Just so, the same Principles which, at first view, lead to scepticism, pursued to a certain point, bring men back to common sense.[26]

Another stand-in for the invisible hand, Berkeley's fountain is a philosophical figure that asserts complete reciprocity between natural law, moral philosophy and divinity. It signals a moment of most austere confidence in neoclassical philosophy; it also marks the point where philosophy must turn to literature to effect a containment of scepticism it cannot manage on its own.

In addition to providing an ordering structure for novels and philosophical works, design also held sway over accounts of law, politics and education. Edward Wynne's *Eunomous: or Dialogues concerning the Law and Constitution of England* (1774) is typical in its assertion of an ideal isomorphism between the plot of English legal history and the dialectical unfolding of a literary order. 'To see it [English political history] after so many shocks, advancing each century still nearer to perfection; by the concurrence of a thousand events which time alone could disclose. To see it, at length arrived to that just equality in the distribution and exercise of power, that for so many ages it was stranger to . . . All this would recommend the design of that dialogue, if the execution would but in any degree be answerable to the design.'[27] Once again, a literary genre carries philosophical weight, legitimating the Whig view of progress through its dialectical structure.

As I have already suggested, design was as influential in its eclipse as in its preservation. Design is a hypothesis about order. It assumes the creation of a set that includes or at least accounts for all things. But it is manifestly impossible to include all things in one set, since sets work through a dialectic of inclusion and exclusion. John Ray admits as much, in a passage that anticipates Campbell's bind:

> My Text warrants me to run over all the visible Works of God in particular, and to Trace the Footsteps of His Wisdom in the Composition, Order, Harmony, and Uses of every one of them, as well as of those that I have Selected. But First, This would be a Task far transcending . . . the joint Skill and Endeavours of all Men now living, or that shall live after a Thousand Ages, should the World last so long. For no Man can find out the Work that God maketh from the Beginning to the End, *Eccles.* 3. 11.[28]

---

26 *Ibid.*, vol. II, pp. 262–3.
27 Edward Wynne, *Eunomous: or Dialogues concerning the Law and Consitution of England*, 3rd edn corrected (London, 1809), pp. 44–5.
28 Ray, *The Wisdom of God Manifested in the Works of the Creation*, 'Preface', A5.

The reference to *Ecclesiastes* shields the reader from the real point of concern in this passage: the method of scientific investigation that divides the whole into its simplest parts, and then keeps on dividing them as techniques of analysis improve, also bars any simple return to the order with which investigation began. According to the fashionable critique of induction available either in its ancient Pyrrhonian or modern empirical form, anything short of a complete inventory raises suspicions that the *a posteriori* process has been led by the nose by an *a priori* conviction that serves the temporal interests of the agent who declares this or that order of things to be the will of Providence. The anticipatory logic of a narrative that brings us through the errors and deviations of the past to an already achieved order was convenient to Protestants of a Whiggish cast who sought to legitimate the potential oxymoron of a 'revolutionary settlement' after 1688. Tory satirists extended the moderate scepticism built into design-based inquiries in order to undermine the supposed inevitability of the progressive narrative.[29] The mock progressions to anoint new kings in Dryden's *MacFlecknoe* and Pope's *Dunciad* are satirical accounts of legitimate succession gone awry. What the satirists held, and flamboyantly represented through outraged and outrageous fictions, was that as soon as the legitimate (because traditional, received) authority is supplanted by revolutionary means, any subsequent attempt to stabilise succession violates its own principle of revolution and becomes a political farce. Satiric discontinuity in the service of tradition confronts the continuity of progressive narratives. Tory satirists depend no less upon an invisible hand, but by and large avoid the discourse of design. They invoke the philosophical figure *via negativa* with heavy admixtures of irony, as when Jupiter arbitrates the controversy between ancient and modern learning in Swift's *Battel of the Books* by consulting his golden book (but relays nothing of what it says), or when the Will of the Father becomes the calm (but inaccessible) eye at the centre of the raging storm of religious controversy in Swift's *Tale of the Tub*.

In response to these epistemological and political challenges, advocates of design moved in two initially complementary directions. The internal problem of a surplus of empirical data brought about a further delimitation of inquiry to a search for certain representative natural events that epitomised the subordination of parts to whole characteristic of 'masculine Beauty'. Order in

29 On the relation between Augustan satire and extreme scepticism, see Roger D. Lund, 'Strange Complicities: Atheism and Conspiracy in *A Tale of a Tub*', in Robert DeMaria, Jr (ed.), *British Literature 1640–1789: A Critical Reader* (Oxford: Blackwell, 1999), and James Noggle, *The Sceptical Sublime: Aesthetic Ideology in Pope and the Tory Satirists* (Oxford: Oxford University Press, 2001).

the part would prove order in the whole, a metaphysics resuscitated through synecdoche. As a result, beauty in the fine arts and the standard of taste necessary to judge the same became an obsessive point of concern for moral philosophers during the first two thirds of the eighteenth century. This development receives its impetus from the third Earl of Shaftesbury, two of whose late essays on the plastic arts, written in his dying days, were appended to the second (posthumous) edition of *Characteristicks* (1713/14) and to most eighteenth-century editions thereafter. Responding to a visual composition of his own design, the 'Judgment of Hercules', Shaftesbury provided all subsequent eighteenth-century thinkers with a theory of how temporal succession and material diversity might be captured and brought to a stand in the static moment of the painted or sculpted image:

> Again, by the same means which are employ'd to call to mind *the Past*, we may anticipate *the Future*: as wou'd be seen in the case of an able Painter, who shou'd undertake to paint this History of HERCULES according to the third Date or Period of Time proposed for our historical Tablature. For in this momentary Turn of Action, HERCULES remaining still in a situation expressive of Suspense and Doubt, wou'd discover that the Strength of this inner Conflict was over, and that Victory began to declare her-self in favour of *Virtue*.[30]

Anticipating Lessing's *Laocoön* (1766) by fifty-three years, Shaftesbury focuses philosophical attention on the frozen or 'pregnant' moment of the plastic arts in order to stress the mind's ability to apprehend the highest degree of temporal and emotional diversity as if it were a unified experience. The objectivity of the scientist would become the disinterested aesthetic contemplation of the man of taste. Design is therefore contracted into the image of beauty; and the God of all Nature becomes 'a *Poet* [who] is indeed a second *Maker*; a just PROMETHEUS, under JOVE. Like that Sovereign Artist or universal Plastick Nature, he forms *a Whole*.'[31]

If a philosophy of beauty solved the internal problem of the proliferation of data within the framework of design, a further development within aesthetic theory became necessary to account for that which perforce falls outside even the ultimate set of 'masculine Beauty'. Early appeals to the sublime within the new aesthetics complement and are subservient to the dominant category of the beautiful. The need for a philosophy of the sublime is readily apparent in the clumsy attempts of design-based inquiries to circumscribe apparent exceptions to the rule of order. As we have seen, Wilkins must acknowledge

---

30 Shaftesbury, *Characteristicks*, vol. III, p. 218.
31 *Ibid.*, vol. I, p. 129. From 'Advice to an Author'.

the historical fact that there have existed nations and individuals that have survived quite well alongside or in ignorance of Christianity. In a somewhat more philosophical vein than his response to the survival of Judaism, Wilkins recasts the question as a problem of genre: 'Is there any Equity or the least colour of Reason in this? For a Man to make an Essay of the nature of any *Species* of things from such particular instances, as in their kinds are monstrous? Because Beasts may sometimes be brought forth with five legs, and it may be two heads, is it reason therefore to conclude, that no other shape is natural to their kind? . . . The Essay of any kind is rather to be taken from the best and most usual, than from the worst and most depraved part of it.'[32] For the purposes of an inquiry into philosophy and literature, this response to the problem of the anomaly is instructive. Wilkins reaches, as if by cultural instinct, to the received neoclassical theory of generic decorum, now giving it a biological twist, in order to naturalise his own preferred categories and demonise the exception. Sensing that the exception remains a threat to the authority of his established categories, he further transforms the monstrous into its own category. This second gesture provides a key to the appeal of the tradition of the Longinian sublime within a fading neoclassicism. The failure of 'masculine Beauty' to contain the diversity of historical phenomena leads moral philosophers to reframe the exception as an aesthetic event. Sublimity transforms the ugly into the beautiful.[33]

In the *Spectator* essays on 'The Pleasures of the Imagination' (1712), Addison popularises newly fashionable ideas of taste, genius and the sublime. The genre of the periodical essay both conveyed and transformed philosophical ideas by allowing Addison to highlight issues that were of interest to readers of an incipient middle class, while avoiding any excessively abstruse or complex treatment. Thus, at one point Addison observes that 'it is impossible for a Man of the greatest Parts to consider anything in its whole Extent, and in all its variety of Lights'.[34] This polite rendition of the sceptical problem within empiricism soon leads to a discussion of the sublime. Addison offers no philosophical explanation for how one topic leads to the next. More precise philosophers from Hutcheson through Burke to Gerard, Alison and Kant will want to know what it is about the mind's apperception of beauty and sublimity that solves the cognitive dilemma of our supposed inability 'to consider

---

32 Wilkins, *Of the Principles and Duties of Natural Religion*, p. 46.
33 On the role of the ugly in a theory of the beautiful, see my 'Mauvais Genres', *New Literary History* 34 (2003), 452–79.
34 Joseph Addison, *The Spectator* (No. 409), ed. Donald F. Bond, 5 vols. (Oxford: Clarendon Press, 1965), vol. III, p. 529.

anything in its whole Extent, and in all its variety of Lights'. Addison and his readers will have none of this philosophical precision; yet there is an odd cultural wisdom in such avoidance. The explanation Addison does provide for the pleasure of the sublime makes up in literary and psychological interest what it lacks in philosophical sophistication: 'There may indeed, be something so terrible or offensive, that Horror or Loathsomness of an Object may over-bear the Pleasure which results from its *Greatness, Novelty* or *Beauty*; but still there will be such a Mixture of Delight in the very Disgust it gives us . . . It fills the Soul with an agreeable Surprise . . . serves us for a kind of Refreshment, and takes off from that Satiety we are apt to complain of in our usual and ordinary Entertainments. It is this that bestows Charms on a Monster, and makes even the Imperfections of Nature please us.'[35] Even at this early stage in the history of modern aesthetics, the sublime of deformity enters as a supplement to the dominant category of beauty. With this shift we are well on the way to Burke's re-gendering of the beautiful as effeminate and the sublime as masculine.[36]

With regard to an inquiry into the boundary between philosophy and literature, the important point to make is that the philosophical recourse to aesthetic categories of the beautiful and the sublime soon brings philosophy to the limits of its own exposition. Philosophers who turn to aesthetic experience as a means of solving the epistemological dilemmas raised by modern empiricism place themselves in the position of verifying certain highly subjective (yet universal) triggers to experiences of the sublime and the beautiful. Because these experiences are defined by their suddenness, power and intensity, the slow, methodical discourse of reason soon becomes inadequate to its own subject. Francis Hutcheson is especially poignant on this theme. He begins his *Inquiry into the Original of our Ideas of Beauty and Virtue* (2nd edn, 1726) in a mood of confidence, certain that '*the* AUTHOR *of Nature has much better furnish'd us for a virtuous Conduct, than our Moralists seem to imagine, by almost as quick and powerful Instructions, as we have for the preservation of our Bodys: He has made* Virtue *a lovely Form, to excite our pursuit of it; and has given us strong* Affections *to be the Springs of each virtuous Action.*'[37] Yet by the end of two volumes, Hutcheson as much as acknowledges that his attempt to explicate these 'Springs' has knocked the philosophical ground out from under his feet:

35 *Ibid.*, vol. III, pp. 540–1.
36 Edmund Burke, *A Philosophical Enquiry into the Origin of our Ideas of the Sublime and Beautiful* ed. James T. Boulton (Notre Dame, IN, and London: University of Notre Dame Press, 1958). The gendering of the sublime as male and the beautiful as female is constant throughout the text.
37 Francis Hutcheson, *An Inquiry into the Original of our Ideas of Beauty and Virtue; in Two Treatises*, 2nd edn (London, 1726; reprt., New York: Garland Press, 1971), p. xv.

Where we are studying to raise any *Desire*, or *Admiration* of an Object *really beautiful*, we are not content with a *bare Narration*, but endeavour, if we can, to present the *Object* it self, or the most *lively Image* of it. And hence the *Epic Poem*, or *Tragedy*, gives a vastly greater Pleasure than the Writings of *Philosophers*, tho both aim at recommending *Virtue*. The representing the Actions themselves, if the Representations be *judicious*, *natural*, and *lively*, will make us admire the *Good*, and detest the *Vitious*, the *Inhuman*, the *Treacherous* and *Cruel*, by means of our *moral Sense*, without any Reflections of the *Poet* to guide our Sentiments.[38]

When it comes to the aesthetics of beauty and sublimity, literary representations trump philosophical reflections. Of course, the frenetic pace of philosophical commentary on the beautiful, the sublime and, especially, the standard of taste, over the next seventy years suggests that moral philosophers did not really believe that the arts could speak (morally) for themselves!

The three philosophies were imperiled throughout the period, and the dominant historical tendency was for them to split apart, torn from within by the methodological imperialism exerted by Natural Philosophy (a term that itself has little currency beyond the first half of the nineteenth century). Writers at the time were alert to an instability in the received model. James Burnett, Lord Monboddo, warns that 'Upon the whole, it appears to me, that, ever since *experimenting philosophy* came so much into fashion, our philosophy has had a great tincture of materialism and mechanism, which even the religious among us have not escaped . . . When I read the works of our natural philosophers, I should imagine there was nothing but matter and motion in the universe.'[39] The complex processes of secularisation associated with the English, Scottish and European Enlightenments have the effect of reducing the three philosophies to two, with Divine Philosophy the principal casualty. A second competing division of philosophy, usually credited to Cicero but very much a creature of the Enlightenment, imagined all of knowledge as divided into 'speculative' and 'practical' domains. The metaphysical, or divine, would be swallowed up by the speculative (the philosophical confirmation of divinity being a speculative problem), and the practical would expand its territory, no longer under constraint to justify each of its findings in light of a theological narrative or myth. Although natural and moral philosophy would still be viewed as complementary, the methodological tension between them, no longer buffered through the intercession of a mediating third, would lead

---

38 *Ibid.*, p. 262.
39 James Burnett, Lord Monboddo, *Antient Metaphysics: or, the Science of Universals,* 6 vols. (Edinburgh, 1779–99) vol. II, pp. 553–4.

(among other places) to the disintegration of the speculative project in favour of the practical, and, as a counter, to the invention of philosophical aesthetics as a means of rescuing the speculative from within the sphere of the practical (i.e. bodily *aesthesis*). The former of these developments is clearest in Hume. The latter, as we have already seen, takes its rise in Shaftesbury and Hutcheson, and is codified in Kant's *Critique of Judgment* (1790), where Kant explicitly situates aesthetic judgement as the necessary bridge between pure reason (which he links to Natural Philosophy) and practical reason (which he links to Moral Philosophy).[40]

Hume begins *An Enquiry concerning Human Understanding* (1748) by distinguishing two kinds of philosophers: 'The one considers man chiefly as born for action; and as influenced in his measures by taste and sentiment . . . The other species of philosophers consider man in the light of a reasonable rather than an active being, and endeavour to form his understanding rather than cultivate his manners. They regard human nature as a subject of speculation.'[41] As is often the case in Hume, one is uncertain whether this division, delivered with the air of neutral observation, is not laced with combative irony. In part, the opposition between practice and speculation captures Hume's own experience in the marketplace for philosophical writing. He had keyed his earlier *Treatise on Human Nature* (1739–40) to the audience for speculative philosophy, but found as a result that his work failed in commercial terms. Thereafter, as Jerome Christensen has observed, 'Hume displayed no detectable paternal reverence for the remains of his first brain child, which he vended through different agents in different packages to different markets at different times, adapting to the fluctuations of public taste.'[42] An expanding audience for popular philosophy helped erode the demand for speculative treatises. It gave philosophical legitimacy to literary genres. Behind the seemingly neutral division of philosophy into two, in other words, may be a sociological analysis of market conditions that are beginning to tip the balance from speculative to practical philosophy.

40 Immanuel Kant, *Critique of Judgment*, trans. J. H. Bernard (New York: Hafner Press, 1951), Introduction, p. 7. The passage comes from a section called 'Of the Division of Philosophy': 'Philosophy is correctly divided into two parts, quite distinct in their principles: the theoretical part, or *Natural Philosophy*; and the practical part, or *Moral Philosophy* (for that is the name given to the practical legislation of reason in accordance with the concept of freedom).'
41 David Hume, *An Enquiry concerning Human Understanding*, in *Enquiries concerning Human Understanding and concerning the Principles of Morals*, 3rd edn, ed. L. A. Selby-Bigge (Oxford: Clarendon Press, 1975), pp. 5–6.
42 Jerome Christensen, *Practicing Enlightenment: Hume and the Formation of a Literary Career* (Madison, WI: University of Wisconsin Press, 1987), p. 122.

Nevertheless, Hume's critique of the speculative project may be all the more corrosive for being less immediately sociological. After all, Hume was a philosopher and could therefore pretend that his purpose was to rescue the speculative, or true metaphysics, from its decoy: 'But as the matter is often carried further, even to the absolute rejecting of all profound reasonings, or what is commonly called *metaphysics*, we shall now proceed to consider what can reasonably be pleaded in [its] behalf.'[43] As one follows out the argument of the *Enquiry*, however, what can reasonably be pleaded on behalf of metaphysics turns out to be that the standard or criterion for metaphysical speculation can only be found (ironically and impossibly) within the practical domain of more or less frequently repeating events (probability).[44] In other words, if one pursues the speculative implications of modern empiricism to the logical nth degree, as Hume made a hobby horse of doing, then the third term of mediation that had previously upheld the correspondence of natural, moral and divine philosophy disintegrates. Hume is rather relentless on this point:

> These two propositions are far from being the same: *I have found that such an object has always been attended with such an effect*, and *I foresee, that other objects, which are, in appearance, similar, will be attended with similar effects*. I shall allow, if you please, that the one proposition may justly be inferred from the other: I know, in fact, that it always is inferred. But if you insist that the inference is made by a chain of reasoning, I desire you to produce that reasoning. The connection between these propositions is not intuitive. There is required a medium, which may enable the mind to draw such an inference, if indeed it be drawn by reasoning and argument. What that medium is, I must confess, passes my comprehension; and it is incumbent upon those to produce it, who assert that it really exists, and is the origin of all our conclusions concerning matters of fact.[45]

Hume rules out the conceptual operation that underlies inferential reasoning. Inferential reason, in turn, is the basis of the sort of analogical correspondence that unites the three philosophies in design and gives philosophical Christianity its *telos*. Readers at the time understood the larger implications of Hume's seemingly technical point about 'the medium'. By 'medium' Hume does not signal the golden mean. He alludes instead to that being through whose constant intercession the things of fallen nature are made intelligible to Mind or

---

43 Hume, *An Enquiry*, p. 9.
44 For an illuminating discussion of the problem of making the second philosophy (practical) first (metaphysical), see Jacques Derrida, *The Archeology of the Frivolous*, trans. John P. Leavey, Jr (Lincoln, NE and London: University of Nebraska Press, 1980), especially chapter 1.
45 Hume, *An Enquiry*, p. 34.

Spirit, and thereby redeemed as visible incarnations of God. The code was made quite explicit in Joseph Butler's *Analogy of Religion*: 'The whole Analogy of Nature removes all imagined Presumption against the general notion of *a Mediator between God and Man.*'[46] Responding to Hume's critique of inferential reason in his *View of the Principal Deistical Writers that have appeared in England in the last and present Century* (1754–5), John Leland tries to flush Hume out of his philosophical covert:

> By endeavouring to destroy all reasoning, from causes to effects, or from effects to causes; and not allowing, that we can so much as probably infer the one from the other, by arguing either *a priori*, or from experience, he subverts, as far as in him lies, the very foundation of those reasonings, that are drawn from the effects which we hold in the frame of the universe, to the existence of one supreme, intelligent, all-powerful cause; and accordingly we shall find, that he himself afterwards applies this principle to this very purpose.[47]

The question of the philosophical medium brings us around again to the figure of the invisible hand holding the scales of justice. Hume's purpose is to materialise the medium; yet the illustrator of Stubbes' Platonic *Dialogue on Beauty* is quite clear about the requirement that the agent behind the invisible hand remain nebulous. If, as I have asserted, the system of the three philosophies gave conceptual structure to a variety of literary genres, what are the implications for the field of literary representation of Hume's reduction of the three philosophies to two and the reversal of the usual hierarchy placing speculation above practice? If the figure of mediation has lost the aura of divinity, what will replace it in works still claiming to entertain *and* instruct? One answer to this question would direct us to the collection of texts now grouped under the heading of 'the novel'. For Richardson, Fielding, Sterne, Johnson, Burney and Austen, the philosophically relevant category becomes 'character', and the novel blends genres so as to constantly foreground the question of how to 'read' social characters in the absence of any prior template of interpretation (though, admittedly, Fielding stands closer to his Augustan allies in tying character to the satiric concept of essentialised social types). While dead set against recent trends in prose fiction, Johnson's *Rambler* no. 4 'On Fiction' is philosophically astute in viewing the representation of character – and the threat of mixed characters – as the single most important criterion for testing the moral value of the novel. Yet, however important the novel

---

46 Butler, *Analogy of Religion*, p. 194.
47 John Leland, *A View of the Principal Deistical Writers that have appeared in England in the last and present Century*, 3 vols. (London, 1754–5), p. 262.

became as a cultural phenomenon, it was only one of a number of responses to the philosophical challenges identified above. The larger philosophical context I have outlined establishes a more general category under which 'the novel' might plausibly be classed, namely works of popular philosophy that transmit scientific and moral knowledge to a large, heterogeneous readership by means of familiar, conversational genres. An implicit theory of the rise of the novel exists, in other words, in works not explicitly concerned with the novel.[48]

The case is once again clearest in Hume. His *Enquiry* is remarkable for the frequency with which attacks on speculative philosophy are coupled with a defence of new modes of popular philosophical writing. Hume champions kinds of popular intellectual prose directed neither to 'the mere philosopher' ('a character . . . commonly but little acceptable in the world') nor to 'the mere ignorant', but instead to 'the most perfect character', who attains 'an equal ability and taste for books, company, and business; preserving in conversation that discernment and delicacy which arise from polite letters; and in business, that probity and accuracy which are the natural result of just philosophy'. And he continues, 'in order to diffuse and cultivate so accomplished a character, nothing can be more useful than compositions of the easy style and manner . . . which require no deep application or retreat to be comprehended, and send back the student among mankind full of noble sentiments and wise precepts, applicable to every exigence of human life'.[49] Implicit throughout Hume's defence of popular philosophical writing is a recognition that such works appeal to modes of cognitive processing that are no less philosophical for being bound up with systems of representation. He provides philosophical support for Martha Nussbaum's assertion that there may be 'certain plausible views about the nature of the relevant portions of human life that cannot be housed within that form [abstract theoretical exposition] without generating a peculiar implicit contradiction . . . for an interesting family of such views, a literary narrative of a certain sort is the only type of text that can state them fully and fittingly, without contradiction'.[50] Where else but in the realm of vivid mimetic representation, one might ask, could a philosophy of the practical take hold? Writers of compositions in the easy style and manner, explains Hume, 'select the most striking observations and instances from common

---

48 I make this case in greater detail in *Philosophical Dialogue in the British Enlightenment: Theology, Aesthetics, and the Novel* (Cambridge: Cambridge University Press, 1996).
49 Hume, *An Enquiry*, p. 8.
50 Martha C. Nussbaum, *Love's Knowledge: Essays on Philosophy and Literature* (New York and Oxford: Oxford University Press, 1990), p. 7.

life; place opposite characters in a proper contrast; and alluring us into the paths of virtue by the views of glory and happiness, direct our steps in these paths by the soundest precepts and most illustrious examples. They make us *feel* the difference between vice and virtue; they excite and regulate our sentiments.'[51] Hume announces an ideal of philosophical writing that was shared by female and male writers, by Tories and Whigs, landed and city interests, clergy and deists throughout the eighteenth century. Kant had the entire tradition of eighteenth-century English philosophical literature in mind when he berated the 'disgusting hotch-potch of second-hand observations and semi-rational principles on which the empty headed regale themselves, because this is something that can be used in the chit-chat of daily life'.[52] He chose not to consider that the novel's popularity might have had a philosophical basis, or, as Hume put it, that 'All the philosophy, therefore, in the world, and all the religion, which is nothing but a species of philosophy, will never carry us beyond the usual course, or give us measures of conduct and behaviour different from those which are furnished by reflections on common life.'[53]

The problem of popular philosophy

This highly selective account of the relation of philosophy and literature has moved from opening reflections on the problem of method to a summary of two competing ways in which philosophy as a field was divided during the eighteenth century. The first, associated broadly with the period designation 'neoclassicism', defines a total system of knowledge divided into divine, natural and moral, yet united through design. The second, associated broadly with the period designation 'Enlightenment', divides philosophy into speculative and practical domains, while tipping the balance from speculation to practice. I associated each of these systems of knowledge with certain characteristic forms of composition; indeed, by focusing closely upon philosophical arguments in transition, it is possible to note moments, such as Hutcheson's appeal to tragedy and Hume's appeal to popular philosophy, when philosophical problems entail literary solutions. My purpose in directing the discussion along these lines was not, however, to take sides. Rather, if we follow the decline of the three philosophies into two; and if, further, we reject Kant's exclusion of popular philosophy as philosophically insignificant; then a context opens

---

51 Hume, *An Enquiry,* pp. 5–6.
52 Immanuel Kant, *Groundwork of the Metaphysics of Morals,* trans. H. J. Patton (New York: Harper and Row, 1964), p. 77.
53 Hume, *An Enquiry,* p. 146.

Fig. 15.2 Headpiece to *The Young Gentleman and Lady's Philosophy* by Benjamin Martin
(London, 1759–63)

within which to understand and appreciate the contributions of female philosophers, not at the margins of literary activity but instead at the centre of the
most important trends in the history of eighteenth-century thought. Women
writers understood the implications of the decline of the three philosophies
into two, and the collapse of the speculative into the practical. For Aphra Behn,
Judith Drake, Mary Astell, Eliza Haywood, Elizabeth Carter and Mary Wollstonecraft, the epistemological crisis dragging high philosophical discourse
down was matched by a political and educational crisis in the condition of
women lifting representations of material conditions up to the level of philosophical seriousness. Throughout the eighteenth century female philosophers
lead their male counterparts in the recognition that for philosophy to remain
relevant, it must become 'post-metaphysical'. They do not lack the intelligence
to write 'first philosophy'; instead they lack the inclination. The amelioration
of women's secondary status required an analysis of material conditions, for it
was there, in the codes of law, mores of society, restricted access to education,
conventions of courtship and marriage and history of misogyny that the 'philosophy' of female subjugation was clearest. This point holds even for writers
who are deeply religious, such as Mary Astell. When Astell invokes the Bible,
for instance, she does so in much the same way that Mary Wollstonecraft will
invoke the tradition of eighteenth-century conduct manuals and educational
tracts for girls and women in *A Vindication of the Rights of Women* (1792): she
reads as a cultural critic. '*The Relation between the two Sexes is mutual*', writes
Astell, '*and the Dependence Reciprocal, both of them Depending intirely upon GOD,
and upon Him only; which one wou'd think, is no great Argument of the natural
Inferiority of either Sex.*'[54]

Throughout Europe and England, many of the greatest writers of popular
philosophy were women. Some, such as Judith Drake, wrote quite directly
about the condition of women, using the edge of the Lockean *tabula rasa*
to assert the philosophical maxim that inequality is an acquired condition,
correctable when social opportunities (education, legal rights) are equalised.[55]
Others, such as Elizabeth Carter, worked through the veil of translation, particularly the translation of European works that framed the new science in
popular forms such as the letter, dialogue and short essay. Still others wrote
novels, novels often so different from the line of realism (Defoe–Richardson)
or learned wit (Fielding–Sterne) that the rightful place of someone like Eliza

54 Mary Astell, *Reflections upon Marriage*, 3rd edn (London, 1706), Preface, A3. Astell added
   the Preface in response to criticisms the first editions had received.
55 See Judith Drake, *An Essay in Defence of the Female Sex* (London, 1696).

Haywood as a progenitor of the early novel is still being debated, even though it was an accomplished fact when Henry Fielding was still in grammar school. Indeed, from the philosophical standpoint opened here, Eliza Haywood is a principal theorist of the rise of the novel, a point to which I shall return in a moment.

Female philosophers experience Campbell's dialectic between 'perspicuity' and 'dignity' in their own characteristic ways. In *Reflections on Marriage*, Astell observes that *'Sense is a Portion that* GOD *Himself has been pleas'd to distribute to both Sexes with an Impartial Hand, but Learning is what Men have engross'd to themselves.'*[56] 'Sense' is what Campbell meant by perspicuity, the ability to acquire detailed knowledge of nature through assiduous study; 'learning' corresponds with what he meant by 'dignity', the framing of knowledge in an intelligible form. Because men have controlled the frameworks of interpretation – the structures of intelligibility – Astell is forced to gender learning male. She would have viewed the frontispiece to Benjamin Martin's *The Young Gentleman and Lady's Philosophy* (1759–63) with critical scrutiny (fig. 15.2). Whereas the promise of popular philosophy written for 'gentlemen and ladies' is asserted through the visual trajectory leading from the stars through the open window, to the man's mind and through his discourse to the female, a more sceptical view of the matter would focus upon the male's loins, which fairly straddle the globe in a highly suggestive posture, and the contrast between their hands, his pointing up, Plato-like, to a philosophical ideal, and hers pointed down, more than Aristotle-like, to the material base.

Whereas Campbell seeks a classical balance between perspicuity and dignity, Astell is willing to risk immersion in the labyrinth of information. Yet here the work of women writers and translators as popularisers of the new science came into direct conflict with their ambition to liberate female readers from the literary structures of 'Men of Letters'. Popularisation required simplification, and simplification required the repackaging of information in familiar, literary genres. Introducing her translation of Francesco Algarotti's *Newtonianismo per le dame* (1737), published in English as *Sir Isaac Newton's Philosophy Explain'd for the Use of the Ladies. In Six Dialogues on Light and Colours* (1739), Elizabeth Carter celebrates Algarotti's use of dialogue to 'set Truth, accompanied with all that is necessary to demonstrate it, in a pleasing Light, and to render it agreeable to that Sex, which had rather *perceive* than *understand*'.[57] She links this sort

---

56 Astell, *Reflections on Marriage*, Preface, A2–A2 verso.
57 Elizabeth Carter, *Sir Isaac Newton's Philosophy Explain'd for the Use of the Ladies. In Six Dialogues on Light and Colours* (London, 1739), p. v.

of popular philosophy back to Fontenelle, whom she praises in these terms: 'Your *Plurality of Worlds* first softened the savage Nature of Philosophy, and called it from the solitary Closets and Libraries of the Learned, to introduce it into the Circle and Toilets of the Ladies.'[58] By their very decorum, polite conversational genres would limit the 'savage' specificity of factual knowledge and thereby render science accessible to those new to natural philosophy. 'Lines and mathematical Figures are entirely excluded, as they would have given these Discourses too Scientific an Air, and appeared formidable to those, who to be instructed must be pleased.'[59] Some accommodation of knowledge to the capacities of those with little or no scientific training was necessary at an early stage of enlightenment; yet, at a certain point, the very same allowance that enabled a beginner to enter the field of learning also held her back from the sort of detailed, up-to-date knowledge being transmitted to privileged males in the universities and academies.[60] As Astell already saw, the literary structures deployed to seduce women into the paths of learning could become impediments to 'sense'.

In the introduction to her own translation of Fontenelle's *Entretiens sur la Pluralité des Mondes* (1686), titled *A Discovery of New Worlds* (1688), Aphra Behn takes the unusual and commercially self-defeating step of attacking the author she has just translated. The passage is worth citing in full, as it captures the ideological dilemma all popularisers of natural philosophy would face over the next hundred years:

> I know a Character of the Book will be expected of me, and I am obliged to give it to satisfie my self for being at the pains to translate it, but I wish with all my heart I could forbear it; for I have that value for the ingenious French Author, that I am sorry I must write what some may understand to be a Satyr against him. The Design of the Author is to treat of this part of Natural Philosophy in a more familiar Way than any other hath done, and to make every body understand him: For this End, he introduceth a Woman of Quality as one of the Speakers in these five Discourses, whom he feigns never to have heard of any such thing as Philosophy before . . . I must tell you freely, he hath failed in his Design; for endeavouring to render this part of

58 *Ibid.*, p. ii.
59 *Ibid.*, p. vii.
60 In prefacing his own attempt to render the history of law in popular form, Edward Wynne comments favourably on both Fontenelle and Algarotti, but adds: 'a great part of these sciences may be worked into very pleasing dialogues, though the sciences themselves can never be thoroughly understood on such easy terms' (Wynne, *Eunomous*, p. 24). For an excellent discussion of this dilemma, see Ann Shteir, 'Botanical Dialogues: Maria Jackson and Women's Popular Science Writing in England', *Eighteenth-Century Studies* 23 (1990), 301–17.

Natural Philosophy familiar, he hath turned it into Ridicule; he hath pushed his wild Notion of the Plurality of Worlds to that heighth of Extravagancy, that he most certainly will confound those Readers, who have not Judgment and Wit to distinguish between what is truly solid (or, at least, probable) and what is trifling and airy: and there is no less Skill and Understanding required in this, than in comprehending the whole Subject he treats of.[61]

With remarkable prescience, Behn predicts the dead-end popular philosophy would represent for female writers and readers. Certainly, Fontenelle is to be praised for composing with female readers in mind and for extending a portion of the new science to them. But his work fails. Because the author mixes real science with popular entertainment, it becomes impossible for readers to tell truth from falsehood. The usual excuse that women would be incapable of understanding a purer exposition of science does not hold water because the intelligence needed to acquire solid knowledge in the sciences is no greater than the intelligence necessary to distinguish truth from romance in popular philosophy.

This sort of ambivalence is clearly on the minds of the most important female philosophers during the eighteenth century. In *The Female Spectator* (1744–6), Haywood tried to do for female readers what Addison and Steele had done for a more typically male, merchant-class readership in *The Spectator*. In 1745 Haywood penned a letter from 'Philo-Naturae' to *The Female Spectator*. Her plea was that women extend their conception of pleasure to include the close study of what 'Nature herself teaches, and every one's Curiosity, if indulged, would excite a Desire to be instructed in'.[62] Haywood's overt defence of this course of study is the traditional religious one: 'The Study of *Nature* is the Study of *Divinity*. – None, versed in the *One*, I am confident, will act contrary to the Principles of the *Other*.'[63] Yet women require this discipline not primarily to appreciate the final ends of Providence, but to internalise a method of probing inquiry, taking in even the sex-life of plants: 'Methinks, I would not have them, when the uncommon Beauty of any Plant strikes the Eye, content themselves with admiring its superficial Perfections, but pass from thence to the Reflection with what wonderful Fertility it is endowed, and what Numbers in another Season will be produced from its prolific and Self-generating Seed: – even the most common, which springs beneath their

---

61 M. de Fontenelle, *A Discovery of New Worlds*, trans. Aphra Behn (London, 1688), 'The Translator's Preface', A7 verso – A8.
62 Eliza Haywood, *Selections from the Female Spectator*, ed. Patricia Meyer Spacks (Oxford: Oxford University Press, 1999), p. 189.
63 *Ibid.*, pp. 196–7.

Feet as they are walking, has in it some particular Vertue, which it would not be unbecoming them to be acquainted with.'[64]

Like most writers of popular philosophy in her time, however, Haywood places limits upon this activity. She appears to cushion knowledge in just the way that upset Aphra Behn: 'I would not be thought to recommend to the Ladies . . . that severe and abstruse Part [of natural philosophy] which would rob them of any Portion of their Gaiety.'[65] It is not the specialisation in one or another science that interests Haywood, but instead a practice that makes women better perceivers and interpreters of the world around them: 'There are *Microscopes* which will shew us such magnificent Apparel, and such delicate Trimming about the smallest Insects, as would disgrace the Splendour of a [King's] Birth-day . . . The Glasses which afford us so much Satisfaction are as portable as a Snuff-Box, and I am surprized the Ladies do not make more Use of them in the little Excursions they make in the Fields, Meadows, and Gardens.'[66]

Haywood's ambivalence towards popular philosophy is even more vividly represented in her first major work of prose fiction, the runaway best-seller *Love in Excess; or The Fatal Enquiry: a Novel* (1720). In that work the apparently irresistible (although already married) Count D'Elmont turns his erotic attention to the beautiful Melliora, whose late father had appointed him guardian over her. Early in the extended seduction, he chances upon Melliora while she is reading:

> Melliora was so intent on a book she had in her hand, that she saw not the Count 'till he was close enough to her to discern what was the subject of her entertainment, and finding it the works of Monsieur L'fontenelle, 'Phylosophy madam at your age,' said he to her with an air which exprest surprize, 'is as wondrous as your other excellencies, but I am confident, had this author ever seen Melliora, his sentiments had been otherwise than now they seem to be, and he would have been able to write of nothing else but love and her.' Melliora blushed extremely at his unexpected presence, and the complement [*sic*] he made her; but recollecting herself as soon as she could, 'I have a better opinion of Monsieur L'fontenelle,' answered she, 'but if I were really mistress of as many charms as you would make me believe, I should think myself little beholding to nature, for bestowing them on me, if by their means I were deprived of so choice an improvement as this book has given me.' 'Thank Heaven then madam,' resumed he, 'that you were born in an age

64 *Ibid.*, p. 189.
65 *Ibid.*, pp. 188–9.
66 *Ibid.*, p. 191.

successive to that which has produced so many fine treatises of this kind for your entertainment; since (I am very confident) this, and a long space of future time will have no other theme, but that which at present you seem so much averse to.'[67]

Haywood's message is complex. On the one hand Melliora is clearly admirable for concerning herself with 'Phylosophy' at such an early age, and Fontenelle's popular astronomy is useful to her. But popular philosophy does not protect her from the advances of her would-be ravisher. In fact, Fontenelle's gallant style becomes something of go-between, permitting the witty and winning rake to trivialise the scientific aspirations of his beautiful prey.

With the instinct of a painter mixing pigments, Haywood literally embeds popular philosophy in a work she calls a novel. The implication is clear: popular natural philosophy may be a mixed blessing for female readers, but popular moral philosophy in the form of the novel is an unadulterated good. Haywood did not abandon her aspiration to provide female readers with 'portable glasses' through which to read complex natural phenomena. Rather she follows out the logic of the collapse of three philosophies into two, and the bifurcation of natural philosophy from moral philosophy, by focusing her lessons in epistemology upon the facts of social life, especially those facts that determine the well-being of women. For Haywood, the novel becomes the genre within which a reconciliation between 'perspicuity' and 'dignity', empirical realism and literary romance, could be effected for the benefit of female readers. She is the great progenitor of the novel because she takes the loss of the third term of mediation, the invisible hand holding the scales, as an opportunity to depict the fate of characters struggling to achieve happiness in the absence of a transcendental reference point.

Haywood wrote novels of epistemological initiation, using desire (romance) as the hook into the representation of practical social situations that almost always work to the disadvantage of female characters. For her there is no barrier to the mixture of romance and realism, even though later critics who helped determine the canon of the eighteenth-century novel drew a strict line between these.[68] Haywood wants romance and realism side by side, the fantasy

---

67 Eliza Haywood, *Love in Excess; or The Fatal Enquiry*, 2nd edn, ed. David Oakleaf (Ontario, Canada: Broadview Literary Texts, 2000), pp. 100–1.

68 The still indispensable reference point is Ian Watt's *The Rise of the Novel* (Berkeley, CA: University of California Press, 1957); for a thoughtful survey of Watt's influence on subsequent accounts of the novel, see John Richetti, 'The Legacy of Ian Watt's *The Rise of the Novel*', in Leo Damrosch (ed.), *The Profession of Eighteenth-Century Literature: Reflections on an Institution* (Madison, WI: University of Wisconsin Press, 1992), pp. 95–112.

and its consequences. In this sense she was not less the moral philosopher in her 'scandal' novels, and her 'scandal' novels might better be described as epistemological initiations into the hermeneutics of everyday life, where everyday life is shot through with structures of romance that characters absorb through acculturation.

A brief summary of one of Haywood's minor works will have to stand for a more detailed exploration of this point. Haywood's *The Mercenary Lover* (1726) portrays a stark initiation of two sisters into the interpretation of social texts. The narrator is not long in announcing her theme. Miranda, the older of two heiresses (left without guardian) is courted by a 'mercenary lover'. Neither sister suspects the type. After he gains the older sister's consent of marriage, Haywood writes

> 'Tis certain, indeed, that on one Side the Felicity was sincere and Compleat, *Miranda* truly lov'd, and believ'd herself as well belov'd; but alas! Where is the Skill to trace, or Rules to reach the unfathomable Heart of artful Man, practis'd in Wiles, experienc'd in Deceit, amidst the many Turnings Search is lost; and the short sight of Femal Penetration strives but in vain to pierce the hidden Depth.[69]

This passage restates the philosophical predicament that has been of concern in this chapter. For immersion in a theoretically endless maze of information, read: 'amidst the many Turnings Search is lost'; for the true knowledge derived from experience, read: 'pierce the hidden Depth'. The novelist's way across the divide cannot be through design or beauty or the sublime or any appeal to an invisible hand holding the scales. Instead, fiction depicts the challenge of reading social circumstances and other people as if they were texts, and the consequences of failing to do so accurately.

'The short Sight of Female Penetration' is an epistemological deficit that leads inexorably to seduction, betrayal and death. Once the older sister has been secured, Clitander, for that is the mercenary lover's name, sets his 'incestuous' sights on the younger sister, Althea. Her he seduces in a scene that replaces the Miltonic apple with 'Books . . . neither Religion, Philosophy, nor Morality' but instead 'certain gay Treatises which insensibly melt down the Soul'.[70] Althea finds herself 'wholly incapable of defending the Cause of Virtue against those Arguments which his superior Wit and Genius brought' and falls to his base

69 Eliza Haywood, *The Mercenary Lover, or the Unfortunate Heiresses* (London, 1726), rprt., New York: Garland Press, 1973, p. 12. This text is also available in *Selected Fiction and Drama of Eliza Haywood*, ed. Paula Backscheider (New York: Oxford University Press, 1999).
70 Haywood, *Mercenary Lover*, p. 17.

design. 'The Knowledge that Althea was with Child' predictably follows, and fills the hero with a horror of discovery 'almost proportion'd to his Crime'. The growing foetus collapses the time frame of the novella. Clitander devises a plan to protect himself from the anticipated consequences of Althea's condition. He aims first to convince Althea of the likelihood she will die in childbirth and second to have her sign 'a *Testament* legally drawn and sign'd by Witnesses' cutting off her sister and making him sole trustee of her estate. However, he directs his attorney to draft not a will but 'a Deed of Gift to himself, of all the Estate she was at that Instant in Possession of'. He assumes she will not read and interpret the parchment she must sign. 'But here, Heaven was pleas'd to put a Stop to his Proceedings.' She asks to read the document. He refuses, offering instead to read it to her. She watches him carefully, 'and perceiving that his Tongue consult'd his own invention more than the Parchmnent, she was both convinc'd and shock'd at the Deceit with which he treated her; and nothing is to be more wonder'd at than, that she, so far from all Artifice herself, cou'd all at once have her Eyes unseal'd to behold such monstrous baseness and Hypocrisy in Man'.[71] She grabs the document and throws it in the fire.

Haywood does not permit solidarity between the sisters; the younger cannot divulge the truth to the older. Events accelerate through an epistolary reconciliation, to a party Clitander throws for his wife on her birthday, which Althea agrees to attend. Clitander takes the occasion to poison Althea, who staggers out of Clitander's house into the street, as far as an apothecary's shop. The description of her final agony rivals Flaubert's of Emma also dying of poison at the end of *Madame Bovary*. Althea refuses last rites and dies raving, calling out the name of her undoer. Haywood cannot be accused of exercising a light touch. But her concern is not the well-made story or the propriety of romance. Her concern is with the challenges women face reading phenomena in the absence of a standard or scale of judgement for processing experience. That is why she does not stop with Althea's death or the reports Miranda receives from doctor, priest and apothecary confirming the culpability of her husband. She adds an autopsy scene, also described in lurid detail, at the end of which the surgeon presents Miranda with 'an Embrio of at least six Months Growth'.[72] The message is painfully obvious: women must claim the method of critical inquiry intellectually or it will be turned against them physically: the autopsy reveals the truth, but far too late.

To be sure, Haywood's own purposes were not especially well served by her typing characters so obviously. The sisters may mistake Clitander, but

---

71 *Ibid.*, pp. 34–5.
72 *Ibid.*, p. 57.

the reader never could. Novelists after Haywood, especially Frances Burney and Jane Austen, continue Haywood's pedagogical programme of recasting moral philosophy in the form of the novel, but they part company with her by more fully immersing the reader in the same interpretative perplexities that characters in their books face, as they learn to read complex social signs in the absence of a dependable guide or invisible hand.

Students of eighteenth-century philosophy and literature are the inheritors of the disciplinary divisions that have been of concern in this chapter. Within the present structure of undergraduate education, which usually calls upon students to major in English *or* Philosophy, and graduate education, which fosters research in even more restricted areas of specialisation, it has become increasingly difficult to recover the fluid interconnection of thought and style that was taken for granted during the Restoration and eighteenth century. How we frame our own inquiries into a world of letters that has not yet ratified the divisions of knowledge we now take for granted (as between theory and criticism, intellectual and material history, ideology and literature, elite and popular culture) makes all the difference.

Britain and European literature
and thought

JEFFREY BARNOUW

Charles II's restoration to the Stuart monarchy and Louis XIV's almost simultaneous assumption of personal rule following the death in 1661 of Cardinal Mazarin, who had served as chief minister after the death of Louis XIII to his widow, Anne of Austria, mark the beginning of a long period – more than a century – in which cultural relations between Britain and the Continent were dominated by rivalry and interchange with France. French influence in Britain had superseded the predominance of Italy and Spain carrying over from the Renaissance, and as part of the still important relations with the Netherlands the contribution of francophone Huguenots became central. In the late eighteenth century intercourse with Germany gained significance, soon to flourish with Romanticism.

For Britain and France these latter years of the seventeenth century were an extended era in which cultural stability and dynamism were combined, in which 'good sense' was a central value, promoted by satire and criticism, which increasingly reflected the new power of an informed public. There is an energy common to the English Restoration and the first half of the reign of Louis XIV, only partially captured by the labels 'neoclassicism' and *classicisme*, which carries over into an Enlightenment that is as important in Britain as in France. The common misnomer 'Age of Reason' for the European Enlightenment obscures its anti-rationalist character, which emerges clearly once the British component is given due weight, and that means including not only Locke and Hume, but the Third Earl of Shaftesbury, Mandeville, Addison, Gibbon, Johnson and even Burke, the last two so often mistaken for opponents of the Enlightenment. In this perspective the long eighteenth century, from the Restoration on, exhibits a strong European cultural continuity.

Competing with French classicism

In December 1660 the newly restored Charles II intervened in a literary discussion to suggest that the Earl of Orrery write a play on the French model. The result, *The General*, is considered (apart from Davenant's *The Siege of Rhodes*, performed in 1656 as an opera) the first heroic play in English. Dryden, eventually the foremost author of heroic drama, in effect acknowledges this priority in the letter to the earl prefixed to *The Rival Ladies* (1664). Charles' intervention can serve to epitomise the overt cultural influence coming from France with the returning court in the Restoration, influence consciously taken as a challenge for emulation. At the same time, the production of an opera during Cromwell's time suggests that Britain had been in continuous contact with cultural developments on the Continent and did not need the Restoration to open it up. French influence had become predominant (over Spanish and Italian) already in the court of Charles I, and there are parallel reactions against *preciosité* and the Metaphysicals' conceits in Britain and France. The cultural impact of France was even encouraged by the Interregnum in the sense that some portion of English culture had been forced to emigrate. Two main documents of the rise of English classicism, Davenant's 'Preface to *Gondibert*' ('To his much honour'd friend Mr Hobs') and Hobbes' 'Answer' were written in Paris in 1650.

In heroic drama 'the French model' Charles had in mind was Pierre Corneille, whose importance to Dryden is evident. Dryden's preface of 1664, his first such effort, is itself the beginning of an even more important genre, since his practice as a critic focused in his prefaces, the *'examen'* he prefixed to many of his own plays; and his practice, as Johnson pointed out in 1777 in his *Lives of the Poets*, founded a tradition of criticism in England. Here too he followed the lead of Corneille, who in 1660 had published his collected plays in three volumes with a theoretical *discours* and a set of *examens* of the plays introducing each volume.

Corneille's third *discours* showed Dryden how the 'unities' of action, time and place, insisted upon by the French Academy, 'could be liberalised into practical aids to the popular dramatist; and, in the *examens*, he showed by example how any given play could be analysed according to these rules. Justification-by-analysis is Corneille's object – he is, of course analysing his own plays; and fifteen of Dryden's are furnished with such analyses in the form of prefaces.'[1]

---

1 George Watson, 'Introduction' to John Dryden, *Of Dramatic Poesy and Other Critical Essays*, ed. Watson, 2 vols. (London: Dent Everyman's Library, 1962), vol. 1, p. viii.

The 1664 Preface says of *The Rival Ladies* that it is 'like small wines, to be drunk out upon the place, and has not body enough to endure the seas'. In fact Dryden did not 'travel well', never voyaging abroad nor gaining much foreign attention, unlike successors such as Pope and Addison. He is not affecting modesty, however, but preparing the chauvinist point that he has written in an English distinguished 'from the tongue of pedants, and that of affected travellers'. This reflects the wish that the English would leave off borrowing words from other nations. Yet in *Of Dramatic Poesy: An Essay* (written 1665–6) he has Lisideius use 'a propos' and 'mal a propos', the first uses in English and first of some forty borrowings attributed to him.[2] He may be using French words in the *Essay* partly to characterise the francophile Lisideius, but tellingly, along with Wycherley, he was himself the first to use 'critique' in English.

Dryden indeed exhibits a cultural patriotism that is only partly disguised by his enlisting in his preface to *The Rival Ladies* 'the most polished and civilized nations of Europe' to justify his decision to write his play in rhymed verse. Citing a Latin tag from the Scottish poet, Alexander Barclay, he asks whether the English want to continue in their reputation of admiring themselves and their works, while showing no respect (*despectui*) for other nations. Defence of his heroic couplet also leads him to remarks on the development of English poetic style that reveal the historicist frame of his criticism. The virtues of the diction he finds in Waller, Denham and Davenant bring verse closer to the order and clarity of prose, in a manner parallel to the contemporary progress of what came to be called classicism in France. This stylistic rapprochement and the rise of the end-stopped rhymed couplet can be traced back to the 1630s, and the French influence which had already become predominant then.[3]

In the 1630s French classicism had been established, with rules officially sanctioned by Richelieu and the Academy he founded. The dramatic unities were 'enforced' against Corneille's *Le Cid* by public censure in 1636. But that was the last such act by the Academy, and the progress of classicism is rather to be seen in Corneille's flexible handling of the unities as a means of *vraisemblance* directed by *bon sens*. From the Restoration on it was the writings of Boileau and Molière, followed by those of Racine and La Fontaine, that provided the challenge to English emulation. Boileau the critic was at least as important for Dryden as Boileau the satirist (his mock epic *Le Lutrin* was a model for Dryden and Pope). Rhymer translated René Rapin's *Reflexions sur la poétique*

---

2 See E. A. Horsman, 'Dryden's French Borrowings', *Review of English Studies* n.s. 1 (1950).
3 C. V. Wedgewood, *Seventeenth-Century English Literature* (Oxford: Oxford University Press, 1950), p. 121.

d'Aristote in 1674, and it had a lasting impact. John Dennis's *The Impartial Critic* (1693), directed against Rhymer's *Short View of Tragedy*, also criticised ideas from André Dacier's translation of Aristotle's *Poetics* published a year earlier. René Le Bossu's *Traité du poème epique* (1675) was praised by Dryden and Shaftesbury and heavily used by Dennis and Addison. Abbé Jean Baptiste Dubos, *Réflexions critiques sur la poésie et la peinture* (1719), was important for Hume. Addison's appreciation of Dominique Bouhours (*The Spectator* no. 62) epitomises the informing attitude they shared.

> *Bouhours*, whom I look upon to be the most penetrating of the French Cricks, has taken pains to shew, that it is impossible for any Thought to be beautiful which is not just and has not its Foundation in the Nature of things; That the Basis of all Wit is Truth; and that no Thought can be valuable, of which good Sense is not the Ground-work. *Boileau* has endeavoured to inculcate the same notion.[4]

The general reinforcement of critical sensibility in this spirit goes beyond what can be pinned down through citations and specific debts.[5] Such an approach is a key element of what came to be called the Enlightenment, which in general does not set such great value on either the rules or on reason as an independent faculty. French classicism has been mistakenly associated with rationalism, first through an implausible pedigree from Descartes, and then in forced parallel to Cartesianism. Reason, certainly a primary value for Boileau, Rapin and Bouhours, is identified with *le bon sens, le sens commun*, and includes an essential element of *délicatesse* or *finesse*. Rules have a role, but judgement is continuous with taste, and taste, like *délicatesse* and the *je ne sais quoi*, works by perceptions that are far from 'clear and distinct' (the Cartesian criteria for 'ideas' that are part of reason). From this dimension of seventeenth-century 'theory', which has as much to do with social perception and conduct as with the *bienséances* of poetry, there emerges not only the Leibniz-inspired 'new science' concerned with 'sensuous or confused representations', namely aesthetics, but also Leibniz's psychology of '*petites perceptions*', the foremost source for which is Hobbes' psychological conception of *conatus* or 'endeavour'. The influence of Hobbes' idea of the mind can be discerned in many of Dryden's critical essays, and later, in part by way of Leibniz, in those of Diderot.

---

4 Joseph Addison and Richard Steele, *The Spectator*, ed. Donald F. Bond, 5 vols. (Oxford: Clarendon Press, 1965), vol. I, p. 268.
5 See Scott Elledge and Donald Schier (eds.), *The Continental Model. Selected French Critical Essays of the Seventeenth Century, in English Translation*, rev. edn (Ithaca, NY: Cornell University Press, 1970).

A complementary dimension of French critical theory, not at all at odds with Boileau's classicism (concerned with affect and the effect of a work), was the complex impulse derived from the classical treatise *On the Sublime*, attributed to Longinus (a Greek rhetorician, *c.*212–73 AD), which was loosely translated by Boileau in 1674, and enlarged upon and applied to contemporary literature by him in his 1694 *Réflexions critiques*. A key idea in this treatise is the dynamic interaction between thoughts that inspire or challenge and striking (often simple) expressions, the extremity and effect of which go unnoted in the immediate agitation. There is in this critical notion a mutual dependence in which sublime language conveys thoughts that would be missed in more pedestrian terms, as such thoughts make sublime language supportable and even natural, and that dependence can be seen as an extension of the classical insistence on a close correlation of thought and word. Other Longinian themes – the role of posterity in determining the value of a work and establishing a canon, and the corresponding importance of catching inspiration and judgement from earlier poets – also become central. The critical idea of the sublime becomes a recurring emphasis among British critics, in Dennis, Addison, Burke and others, to be taken up in 1764 by Kant, who in 1790 gives it a different valence as part of his philosophical 'architectonic'.

The controversy known as the Quarrel of the Ancients and the Moderns seems largely to run parallel in France and Britain, but William Temple was provoked to his *Essay upon ancient and modern learning* (written in 1689 and rekindling debate in England) by Bernard de Fontenelle's *Digression sur les anciens et les modernes* (1688, following from his 1686 *Sur la pluralité des mondes*). An effective populariser of philosophical ideas, Fontenelle later had great influence mediating between British and French science as the Perpetual Secretary (and historian) of the Académie des Sciences. William Wotton joined the fray in 1694, intending to correct not only Temple but Charles Perrault, who had continued the Moderns' attack with *Parallèles des anciens et des modernes* (1688 ff.).

In Dryden we see a comparatist frame of mind emerging in his negotiating cultural rivalry with France or in the confrontation of 'Ancients and Moderns'. Such an approach is further informed by an awareness of the difference history makes. Judgement requires comparison. Dryden measures Jonson against Shakespeare, the Sister Arts, poetry, painting and music in particular, against one another, and for due appreciation of native gifts he needs the foil of French letters. The acknowledged model for his essayistic prose style was French. 'The nature of a preface is rambling, never wholly out of the way, nor in it. This I have learned from the practice of honest Montaigne.'[6] Much in Dryden's critical writing, including his comparative thinking, essayistic presentation and appreciation of Montaigne, seems to owe something to his absorption of the influence of Charles de Marguetel de Saint-Denis, Seigneur de Saint-Evremond (1616–1703).[7] He will be the first of a series of mediating figures considered next.

Saint-Evremond and the Huguenot connection

Saint-Evremond, exiled for political criticism of Mazarin, lived in England from 1661 to 1665 and from 1670 until his death in 1703. He is a key figure linking French culture to England. In 1665 he went to Holland to avoid the plague and perhaps because impending war between the two nations (with France possibly taking the Dutch side) would block his return to France. In Holland he associated with the brothers De Witt and the young Prince of Orange (later William III of England), and he sought out the scholars Heinsius and Vossius, and Constantin Huygens and Spinoza. He was also involved with the francophone Protestant colony, which the sceptical philosopher Pierre Bayle joined in 1681 and which grew with the 1685 revocation of the Edict of Nantes whereby religious toleration in France was curtailed.

Saint-Evremond was a friend of the Duke of Buckingham (whom he compared to his much-admired Petronius), of Waller and Temple. He was regarded as a literary pundit, particularly after 1675 when the Duchess Mazarin settled in London and began holding her salon, of which he was the oracle. After the Glorious Revolution of 1688 he received even greater recognition from his friend William of Orange, now William III. In 1689 Louis XIV finally authorised his return to France, but Saint-Evremond was no longer interested.[8] Fontenelle said, 'his voice was perfectly free because he lived in England, deprived of his fatherland'.

6 Dryden, *Preface to Fables Ancient and Modern*, in *Of Dramatic Poesy and Other Critical Essays*, ed. Watson, vol. II, p. 278, cf. vol. II, p. 9, comparing him to Plutarch for excellence in wandering.
7 Dryden wrote a 'character' of Saint-Evremond prefixed to a 1692 collection of his essays in English translation. On his 'penetration', Dryden writes, 'he generally dives into the very bottom of his authors, searches into the inmost recesses of their souls, and brings up with him those hidden treasures which had escaped the diligence of others' (*Of Dramatic Poesy and Other Critical Essays*, vol. II, p. 59).
8 On Saint-Evremond, see Quentin M. Hope, *Saint-Evremond. The Honnête Homme as Critic* (Bloomington, IN: Indiana University Press, 1962), and *Saint-Evremond and his Friends* (Geneva: Droz, 1999), and Joseph M. Levine, *Between the Ancients and the Moderns. Baroque Culture in Restoration England* (New Haven, CT: Yale University Press, 1999).

Saint-Evremond was (in his free way) a follower of Pierre Gassendi (1592–1655), an empiricist Epicurean who opposed Cartesian dogmatism with a classically informed scepticism and was a principal supporter of Hobbes in France. Saint-Evremond considered Hobbes England's *'plus grand génie'* since Bacon.[9] His anti-pedantic *honnête homme* manner (not a pose or disguise) and worldly Epicureanism mask his links to systematic thinkers like Hobbes and Gassendi, but his essayistic nonchalance gets radical ideas across engagingly, exemplifying the typical Enlightenment assimilation of philosophy to literature.

Many of Saint-Evremond's insights into literature and philosophy are grounded in his idea of *'les divers génies'* of different eras of a nation (Rome was his prime example) or of different nations in the same era. In his use of this 'spirit of the age' conception he looks forward to the Neapolitan Giambattista Vico and the political philosopher Montesquieu (1689–1755). This made his take on the Ancients versus Moderns or the French versus the English far more fruitful than most, since it gave the ideas of imitation and emulation a relativist twist. Modern writers must express the 'genius' of their own time and nation, but classical and foreign models are nonetheless important.

His insistence on founding fiction in reality or truth seems to anticipate Johnson. His favourite authors included the Roman historians and Lucian and Petronius, Machiavelli, Bacon, Hobbes and Grotius, Rabelais and Cervantes, Montaigne and Corneille. With Buckingham's help he learned to understand Ben Jonson's plays and came to admire Jonson (whom he ranked with Molière as masters of comedy among modern writers) but not Shakespeare, and he was somewhat ignorant of the lively London theatre in his own time, yet his essay 'De la Comédie anglaise' (1677) long had a positive influence on English opinion, and he wrote a play, *Sir Politick Would-Be*, extending the character and conceits of Jonson's *Volpone*, though it is French in spirit as well as language.

Here the contrast with Voltaire is striking. Saint-Evremond never learned English; Voltaire learned it with great speed, in part by going regularly to the London theatre (in the 1720s) with a prompt book. Voltaire was scornful of his predecessor yet in many ways picked up where he left off, a defender of French theatre vis-à-vis English, of the moral value of competitive desire and luxury and of the critical use of reason that undermines, in a Swiftian vein, the pride of 'the rational animal'.

That Saint-Evremond's legacy belongs to the Enlightenment is made clear (and was made concrete) by the work of Pierre Des Maizeaux, a Protestant

---

9 In the 1662 essay, 'Jugement sur les sciences ou peut s'appliquer un honnête homme'. A 1676 essay associated Hobbes with Spinoza.

refugee to Switzerland and then Holland, where he was a follower of Bayle (later translating him into English). Des Maizeaux came to England in 1699 and became a follower, biographer and editor of Saint-Evremond, and a friend of the 3rd Earl of Shaftesbury, as well as of the controversial Deist, John Toland; he had a hand in publishing pieces by Locke and Toland. Another member of the Huguenot exile community was Pierre Coste, who came over in 1697, again via Switzerland and Holland, and translated Locke's *Essay concerning Human Understanding* into French in 1700, a catalyst for the spread of the Enlightenment.[10]

Holland had been an important rival and model for England in various ways through much of the seventeenth century – a trading nation, controlling the seas and colonies, Protestant and for a while republican. One English policy common to Cromwell and the Stuarts was war against the Dutch connected with competition for trade. When Sir William Temple wrote his *Observations upon the United Provinces of the Netherlands* in 1673, he underscored the basis of rivalry but also (without saying so) the indications and causes of Holland's oncoming decline, which brought with it a decline in its cultural impact on England. But Holland's importance as an intermediary in what Bayle called the Republic of Letters was established in the seventeenth century.

Samuel Sorbière was another French Protestant who followed the route through Switzerland to Holland, but he kept one foot in France, where he was a follower of Gassendi. In 1643 his French translation of More's *Utopia* was published in Amsterdam. He also arranged for the 1647 publication of Hobbes' Latin *De Cive* in Amsterdam and then published his French translation of it in 1649. A French translation of *De Corpore Politico, or the Elements of Law* followed in 1652. Hobbes' own Latin version of *Leviathan* was published in Holland in 1668. Hobbes' success on the Continent owed much to Gassendi and the mathematician, Marin Mersenne, but also a good deal to Dutch publishers. This role persisted into the eighteenth century. The Amsterdam publisher Marc-Michel Rey, for example, brought out many works of Rousseau, Diderot, Holbach and Voltaire.

Sorbière made a fateful visit to England in 1663–4, when he was made a member of the Royal Society together with Christiaan Huygens, who had endeared himself to the Society by criticising Hobbes' efforts to square the circle, thus supporting charter member John Wallis in his controversy with Hobbes. (The main text of Hobbes' parallel controversy with Boyle, *Dialogus physicus, sive de*

---

10 On Des Maizeaux, Coste and other Huguenot cultural mediators, see Anne Goldgar, *Impolite Learning. Conduct and Community in the Republic of Letters, 1680–1750* (New Haven, CT: Yale University Press, 1995).

natura aeris of 1661 was dedicated to Sorbière.) In 1664 Sorbière published an account of his stay that was considered insulting by the spokesman (later historian) of the Society, Thomas Sprat, who published a response in 1665, rejecting what Sorbière said about the Society but also about the irregularity of English drama. Royal damage control was applied: Sorbière was held under arrest in France from July to October, while Charles II forbade any further responses. This controversy was in part the occasion of Dryden's *Of Dramatic Poesy*, which can be read in parallel with Sprat's 1667 *History of the Royal Society* for its deft mingling of patriotic and Francophile elements, in which the latter are most often a sop or a foil for the former.[11] The model for Sprat's *History*, acknowledged with fulsome but partly ironic praise, was Paul Pellisson-Fontanier's *Histoire de l'Académie française* (1653, translated 1657). J. E. Spingarn writes that Sprat's *Account of the Life and Writings of Cowley* (prefixed to the 1668 *Works*) 'is virtually the first literary biography in English' and seems to be modelled on Pellisson's *Discours sur les Œuvres de M. Sarasin* (prefixed to a 1656 edition of those *Œuvres*).[12]

In the 1664 Preface Dryden says he is 'sorry that (speaking so noble a language as we do) we have not a more certain measure of it, as they have in France, where they have an Academy erected for that purpose, and endowed with large privileges by the present king' (*of Dramatic Poesy*, vol. 1, p. 5). Here Dryden reflects another instance of royal influence. In 1662 the two-year-old Royal Society received the royal patent and welcomed Dryden as a member. By 1664 he was, with Evelyn, Waller and Sprat, on its committee 'for improving the English language'. He was soon dropped from the committee as his interest waned, and that programme, at least officially, came to nothing when its main supporter, Waller, died. But the importance of the Royal Society in promoting foreign relations and correspondence grew steadily.

International relations were not always harmonious. The dispute between Newton and Leibniz over priority in the invention of the calculus was a cause célèbre that began with Newton's disciple John Keill accusing Leibniz of plagiarism in the *Philosophical Transactions* of the Royal Society. When a retraction was demanded by Leibniz, the Society published a report in 1713, written by Newton, which condemned Leibniz. But international pressure brought

---

11 See George Williamson, 'The Occasion of *An Essay of Dramatic Poesy*', *Seventeenth Century Contexts*, rev. edn (Chicago: University of Chicago Press, 1969), pp. 272–88. Cf. Thomas Sprat, *History of the Royal Society*, eds. Jackson I. Cope and Harold Whitmore Jones (St Louis, MO: Washington University Studies, 1958), pp. xv–xvii. Sprat expressed outrage that Sorbière saw Hobbes as inheriting the mantle of Bacon, the Society's hero.
12 *Critical Essays of the Seventeenth Century*, ed. J. E. Spingarn, 3 vols. (Bloomington, IN: Indiana University Press, 1957), vol. 1, p. xlvi.

Newton to write to Leibniz setting out his case and asking for a response. In 1715 Leibniz wrote about the dispute to Princess Caroline, a friend since she had known him at the Court of Berlin in her youth and even more after her marriage to the Electoral Prince of Hannover, later George II of England. Leibniz told her a French journalist writing in Holland characterised it as a quarrel between Germany and England rather than between individuals. The involvement of Princess Caroline, concerned both to reach a true understanding of things and to effect a reconciliation, led to the correspondence between Leibniz and Samuel Clarke, published in 1717 (after Leibniz's death in 1716 but with his approval), in French and English on facing pages. The correspondence ranges over topics from gravity, the vacuum, space and time, God's intervention in the universe, the principle of sufficient reason and natural religion, and constitutes a significant work generated by the 'foreign relations' of English science and culture.

The founding and chartering of the Society fused innovative imitation of French example and continuity with one main cultural achievement of the Interregnum. The scientific community that formed the nucleus of the Society was already established, with Cromwell's brother-in-law, John Wilkins, playing a key role, by 1660, yet royal patronage, taking a striking new direction, made a great difference. Though clearly a vehicle of national pride, the Society professed, in Sprat's words in the *History*, 'not to lay the Foundation of an English, Scotch, Irish, Popish or Protestant Philosophy, but a Philosophy of Mankind'.[13] This echoed Bacon's hope in sending his Latin *Advancement of Learning* to the future Charles I, 'It is a book I think will live, and be a citizen of the world, as English books are not.'[14]

The advances of science in England were a main reason why, from the 1670s on, some English books came to be world citizens. A number of foreigners contributed to these advances and to the culture and communication of science, including the Society's co-Secretary (along with Wilkins), Henry Oldenburg, originally from Bremen, who began to edit its *Philosophical Transactions* in March 1665, just two months after the start of its French counterpart, the *Journal des Sçavans*.

The English of the 1660s, celebrating the coming of their 'Augustan age', looked not only to their new Augustus, Charles II, but to a parallel inauguration across the Channel – the personal rule (from 1661) of the Sun King. By 1674 Daniel Huet and Abbé Paul Tallement had anticipated Voltaire in calling the

13 Margery Purver, *The Royal Society: Concept and Creation*, (Cambridge, MA: M.I.T. Press, 1967), p. 151.
14 *Ibid.*, p. 149.

age of Louis XIV one of the marvellous periods in history and comparing it to those of Pericles and Augustus. But note that in Charles Perrault's poem, 'le Siècle de Louis le Grand' of 1687,

> Et l'on peut comparer, sans crainte d'être injuste,
> Le siècle de Louis au beau siècle dAuguste.
>
> [We can compare, without fear of injustice,
> The age of Louis with the age of Augustus]

follows the line, 'Ils sont grands, il est vrai, mais hommes comme nous' (They are great, it is true, but still men like us).[15] Perrault thus undercuts as well as exalts the worship of classical antiquity. In his *Siècle de Louis XIV* (1756) Voltaire says that, with regard to science, it could as well be called the age of the English as the age of Louis XIV. Before we turn to Voltaire and the French Enlightenment in the strict sense, there is another topic important to the age that demands attention, one that provoked both Saint-Evremond and Dryden, namely opera.

Handel: from Italian opera in London to oratorio in English

Saint-Evremond was himself an amateur composer, and one evening at Mme Mazarin's he sang an idyll he had written. The ensuing discussion turned to opera, then the rage in France, and he offered an impromptu criticism which he wrote down as a letter to one of the participants, Buckingham, in 1677 or 1678. (Most of his writings were elicited in some such way.) Opera is a 'bizarre mixture of poetry and music where the writer and the composer [are] equally embarrassed by each other'. As for the audience, 'Where the mind has so little to say, the senses needs begin to languish.' Opera is in its very idea an affront to *bon sens* and *vraisemblance*, 'the whole piece is sung from beginning to end, as if the characters on stage had conspired to present musically the most trivial as well as the most important aspects of their lives'. Some things in drama can appropriately be sung, such as vows, sacrifices and all that concerns the cult of the gods, but all conversation and debate, deliberation and advice, 'belongs to the actors and sounds ridiculous in the mouths of singers'.[16]

---

15 Charles Perrault, *Œuvres Choisis* (Paris: Brissot-Thivers, 1826), p. 290.
16 *The Essence of Opera*, ed. Ulrich Weisstein (New York: W. W. Norton, 1969), pp. 32–4.

These sentiments were shared by Dryden, who collaborated with the greatest English composer of the age, Henry Purcell, on what Dryden called a 'dramatic' or 'semi-opera', *King Arthur*, in which the plot was carried only by speaking parts, with interludes where deities and allegorical figures sang. Music was a signal that verisimilitude was being suspended. Antipathy to opera is evident in Dryden's preface to his earlier collaboration with the composer Grabu, a fully sung opera called *Albion and Albanius* (1685).

> The same reasons which depress thought in an opera, have a stronger effect upon the words; especially in our language: for there is no maintaining the purity of English in short measures, where the rhyme returns so quick, and is so often female, or double rhyme, which is not natural to our tongue, because it consists too much of monosyllables, and those too, most commonly clogged with consonants; for which reason I am often forced to coin new words, revive some that are antiquated, and botch others: as if I had not served out my time in poetry, but was bound apprentice to some doggrel rhymer, who makes songs to tunes and sings them for a livelihood. It is true, I have not been often put to this drudgery; but where I have, the words will sufficiently show, that I was then a slave to the composition, which I will never be again. It is my part to invent, and the musicians' to humour that invention. I may be counselled, and will always follow my friend's advice, where I find it reasonable; but will never part with the power of the militia.
>
> (*Of Dramatic Poesy*, vol. II, pp. 40–1)

This prejudice against English as a language to be set to music, invidiously compared not to French but Italian ('invented for the sake of poetry and music'), was for a long time fatefully shared by the greatest composer in England, though never English: Handel. Opera brought England into closer cultural contact with the continent than any literary form, and for decades Handel oversaw the hiring of Italian singers (many of them castrati) who were 'stars' in London. After *Albion and Albanius*, John Blow's *Venus and Adonis* and Tate and Purcell's *Dido and Aeneas*, there was no English opera of the fully sung sort before the eighteenth century. In the early years of the century Italian opera began to establish itself in London even before Handel assumed leadership as a result of the success of his *Rinaldo* in 1711. Two English operas went unstaged early in the century, partly because of the success of Giovanni Battista Bononcini's *Camilla* in 1706, a *Venus and Adonis* by John Hughes with music by the German composer who worked in England, Johann Pepusch, and *Semele* by Congreve and Eccles. In 1707 Addison wrote the libretto for an English opera, *Rosamond*, and its failure contributed to his dislike of Italian opera, expressed in numerous satiric essays in *The Spectator*.

In fact the leading literary figures of that generation were all hostile to Italian opera, but many of them were at the same time well disposed to Handel and made efforts to have him set English texts. But Handel knew opera must be in Italian, and he wanted to compose operas. Already in 1711 Handel met Pepusch and Hughes and began to collaborate with Hughes on a new setting of his *Venus and Adonis* from which two arias survive. In a 1712 preface Hughes wrote,

> As Theatrical Musick expresses a Variety of Passions, it is not requisite, even for the Advantage of the Sound, that the Syllables shou'd every where Languish with the same loose and vowelly Softness. But what is certainly of much more Consequence in Dramatical Entertainments, is, that they shou'd be perform'd in a Language understood by the Audience. One wou'd think there shou'd be no need to prove this.

Hughes was a contributor to the *The Spectator*, *Tatler* and *Guardian*, and friend to Pope, Gay and Arbuthnot, all of whom Handel met at the latest around 1712 in Burlington House. The great year of Handel's early composing in English was the period in 1717–18 spent at Cannons, the estate of James Brydges, Earl of Carnarvon (and from 1719 Duke of Chandos). As Pepusch was there as director of music, Handel was invited as composer-in-residence. At Cannons Handel wrote not only the so-called Chandos Anthems but his pastoral masque, *Acis and Galatea*, with a libretto by John Gay with help from Pope and Hughes, and an oratorio or sacred masque in English, *Esther*, which Pope adapted from Racine, possibly with help from Arbuthnot and Gay. As Christopher Hogwood writes, 'To a modern listener, who can find the emotional conviction of Galatea or Esther as compelling as the dilemmas of Tamerlano or Medea, Handel's addiction to *opera seria* can seem inexplicable.'[17] Only when the popularity of Italian opera in London was running out – signalled and hastened by the great success of John Gay's *Beggar's Opera*, for which Pepusch did the musical arrangement and Arbuthnot chose for the most part traditional tunes, but including one from Handel's *Rinaldo*, and only when competitors revived Handel's own *Acis and Galatea* in a public performance, soon followed by a similar revival of his *Esther*, in 1731 and 1732 respectively – did Handel begin to realise the possibilities of his English compositions. Beyond the Cannons works, Handel's settings of Dryden's St Cecilia Odes, the second for Dryden but first for Handel being *Alexander's Feast* (1736), followed by *Ode for St Cecilia's Day* (1739), show clearly enough that Dryden underestimated how effectively English could be set to music. Collaborating with Charles Jennens, he then set an adaptation of Milton's *L'Allegro ed il Penseroso* (1740), pointing

17 Christopher Hogwood, *Handel* (London: Thames and Hudson, 1984), p. 74.

forward to both *Samson* and *Messiah*. Finally, in a nice twist on his oratorio phase, Handel retrieved Congreve's typically racy libretto for the opera *Semele* and set it. It was presented on stage with a chorus but no represented action, that is, 'after the manner of an oratorio', in 1743.

Handel was the chief importer of Italian opera to London but became an exporter with the works of his 'second career'. Baron Gottfried van Swieten, an important reformer in Joseph II's Austria, did more than anyone to revive the music of Bach and Handel, and he commissioned Mozart to re-orchestrate and present four works of Handel, *Acis and Galatea* (1788), *Messiah* (1789), *Alexander's Feast* (1790) and *Ode to St Cecilia* (1790). At the end of the century Haydn renewed the British connection not only with his London symphonies (his last twelve, following 'the Oxford symphony', no. 92, so called for its association with his honorary doctorate of 1791) but with *The Creation* (1798) and *The Seasons* (1801), setting English texts.

Voltaire in England, England in Voltaire and the Enlightenment

Voltaire's stay in England from May 1726 to October/November 1728 had a profound effect on him and through this on the course of the Enlightenment. The work that reflects his experience there most directly, *Letters concerning the English Nation* (first published in English translation, in London 1733; in 1734 in France as *Lettres philosophiques*), holds up English institutions and attitudes as models for French imitation in what amounts to a programme – his first effort in that direction – for Enlightenment. He had come to England in part to arrange publication (by subscription, following the lead of Pope with his *Iliad*) of his epic on Henri IV, *La Henriade*, which promotes the idea of religious toleration, a theme of 'sceptical' 'erudite libertinism' since Montaigne, through images of the social and political consequences of intolerance. He had considered Geneva and Amsterdam as alternatives for its publication. It is important to note that Voltaire had planned the trip to London already in 1725, before French royal pressure led to his exile. To the earlier version, published clandestinely in Rouen in 1723 as *La Ligue*, he added among other things an apocryphal visit of Henri to Elizabeth I seeking support for his siege of Paris. A poem which Voltaire claimed he wrote at his departure suggested that he saw his own trip as a parallel.[18] When he appealed to George I in 1725 for

18 In a letter to M. D'Aigueberre, *c.* 8 May 1726, Voltaire, *Correspondance*, ed. Theodore Besterman, 13 vols. (Paris: Gallimard, Bibliotheque de la Pléiade, 1963), vol. 1, p. 184. This

authorisation to come to England, he affirmed he had long regarded himself as the king's subject and that his poem spoke with that liberty of which the king was the protector.[19]

Freedom of thought is not the same as 'freethinking', but the latter often provides a test of whether the former is real. Freedom of thought, Voltaire saw, depended on its being exercised as freedom of speech, and he looked upon England as the land of freedom of thought, and of a people accustomed to frank and bold speaking. Liberty was ingrained in the language. In a notebook he kept in England, and for the most part in English, he wrote,

> In England everybody is publick-spirited – in France everybody is concerned in his own interest only. An English man is full of taughts, French all in miens, compliments, sweet words and curious of engaging outside, overflowing in words, obsequious with pride, and very much self concerned under the appearance of a pleasant modesty. The English is sparing of words, openly proud and unconcerned. He gives the most quick birth, as he can, to his taughts, for fear of loosing his time.[20]

Voltaire took to English forthrightness, though at times he may have confused frankness with *gaulloiserie*.[21] Boswell interviewed him at Ferney in 1764 and reported, 'When he talked our language he was animated with the soul of a Briton. He had bold flights . . . He swore bloodily, as was the fashion when he was in England.'[22] But Voltaire realised that it was intellectual boldness that counted, not only the courage to say what one thinks, but the courage to think for oneself. On 12 August 1726, as he was still trying to decide whether or not to establish himself in London, he wrote that the arts were all honoured and rewarded there and that the only difference between men, whatever the

---

alleged letter and poem fragment may have been written as late as 1776, allowing Voltaire to give retrospective emphasis to his understanding of the turning point.

19 6 October 1725, Voltaire, *Correspondance*, vol. 1, p. 168. He had courted the English court in 1719 with a copy of *Oedipe* dedicated to George I and a reading of *La Ligue* to Lord Stair at the Embassy, resulting in the gift of a watch and a gold medal from George I.

20 Voltaire, *Candide and other Writings*, ed. Haskell Block (New York: Random House Modern Library, 1956), p. 556.

21 Thomas Gray heard of one incident from Lord Bathurst and Warburton.

> As he [Voltaire] supped one night with mr Pope at Twickenham, he fell into a fit of swearing and of blasphemy about his constitution. Old mrs Pope asked him how his constitution came to be so bad at his age, 'Oh! (says he) those damned Jesuits, when I was a boy, buggered me to such a degree that I shall never get over it as long as I live.' This was said in English aloud before the servants.

> (André Michel Rousseau, *L'Angleterre et Voltaire*, 3 vols. (Oxford: Voltaire Foundation, 1976; SVEC 145–7), vol. 1, p. 113)

22 *Boswell On the Grand Tour. Germany and Switzerland, 1764*, ed. Frederick A. Pottle (New York: McGraw-Hill, 1953), p. 293.

difference in their social standing, was that of merit. 'It is a country where people think freely and nobly without being held back by any servile fear. If I followed my inclination it would be there that I would establish myself with the intention of simply learning to think.'[23] Theodore Besterman mistakes the meaning of '*penser*' here: 'When Voltaire said that he hoped to learn to think in England, this must not be taken literally: he had already reflected to good purpose, and had already arrived at the essential ideas characteristic of his philosophy.'[24] Voltaire rather means self-reliance that needs to be learned and communicated, in the same sense Kant invoked in 'What is Enlightenment?' with the motto '*sapere aude*', that is, dare or have the courage to use your own understanding.

Voltaire's article, 'Freedom of Thought', in his *Philosophical Dictionary*, takes the form of a dialogue in which the English milord Boldmind exhorts the Spanish count Medroso, 'It's solely up to you to learn to think . . . dare to think on your own [*osez penser par vous-même*]', and affirms, 'Only since everyone has freely enjoyed the right to speak his mind, have we been happy in England.'[25] Learning to think is tied up with a public sphere and a tolerant competitive society. This collective experience becomes a resource of the language itself. In the 'Essay upon the Epick Poetry of the European Nations from Homer down to Milton', which he wrote in English in 1728 to accompany *La Henriade*, he says, 'The force of that idiom [English] is wonderfully heightened by the nature of the government which allows the English to speak in public, and by the liberty of conscience.'[26]

In the *Letters concerning the English Nation* Voltaire similarly connects the English form of government with their respect for literature and their proclivity to 'think'.

> The *French* are of so flexible a Disposition, may be moulded into such a Variety of Shapes, that the Monarch needs but command and he is immediately obey'd. The *English* generally think [*communément on pense*], and Learning is had in greater Honour among them than in our Country; an Advantage that results naturally from the Form of their Government. There are about eight hundred Persons in *England* who have a Right to speak in publick, and to support the Interest of the Kingdom; and near five or six Thousand may in their Turns, aspire to the same Honour. The whole Nation set themselves up as Judges over

23 Voltaire, *Correspondance*, vol. I, pp. 184–5.
24 Theodore Besterman, *Voltaire* (Chicago: University of Chicago Press, 1976), pp. 123–4.
25 Voltaire, *Dictionnaire philosophique*, eds. Raymond Naves and Julien Benda (Paris: Editions Garnier, 1967), p. 280, my translation.
26 Quoted in Rousseau, *L'Angleterre et Voltaire*, vol. I, p. 42 n. 7, who notes the thought and expression are taken from Addison. See *The Spectator*, vol. II, pp. 514–15.

these, and every Man has the Liberty of publishing his Thoughts with regard to publick Affairs; which shews, that all the People in general are indispensably oblig'd to cultivate their Understandings.[27]

The implication is that English people perceive their own interest in such involvement, 'in the same Manner as a Merchant is oblig'd to be acquainted with his Traffick' (*Letters concerning the English Nation*, Letter xx, p. 144).

Voltaire was initiated in English philosophy before he left the Continent by the urging and guidance of Lord Bolingbroke, whom he had known in France since 1722. In a letter of 27 June 1724, Bolingbroke advised him to read Locke's *Essay concerning Human Understanding*, as the work best suited to convert him to serious philosophy, and argued that the work of the Dutch scientist and mathematician Christiaan Huygens and Newton had shown Descartes in physics and Nicholas Malebranche in metaphysics to be poets rather than philosophers. Owen Aldridge maintains that Bolingbroke's letter 'prefigures every important ideological position' of the *Letters concerning the English Nation*.[28] Moreover, with the exception of Letter xii on Bacon, the letters dealing with philosophers are not among those he worked on in England. His serious engagement with the work of Locke and Newton begins only after his return to France in 1729. With help from his mistress, the Marquise du Châtelet, Voltaire soon became one of the prime propagators of Newtonianism in Europe, starting with *Elemens de la philosophie de Newton* (1738). She meanwhile went over to Leibniz and in particular his idea of *vis viva*, and her *Institutions de physique* of 1740 popularised that in France.

In the 1728 preface to 'The Epick Poetry of the European Nations' Voltaire writes, 'I am ordered to give an Account of my Journey into England.' Since 'the true Aim of a Relation is to instruct Men', he says he would offer only

> faithful Accounts of all the useful Things and of the extraordinary Persons, whom to know, and to imitate, would be a Benefit to our Countrymen. A Traveller who writes in that spirit, is a Merchant of a noble Kind, who imports into his own Country the Arts and Virtues of other Nations.
>
> I will leave to others the Care of describing with Accuracy, Paul's Church, the Monument, Westminster, Stonehenge, &c. I consider England in another view; it strikes my eyes as it is the Land which hath produced a Newton, a Locke, a Tillotson, a Milton, a Boyle . . .[29]

27 Voltaire, *Letters concerning the English Nation*, ed. Nicholas Cronk (Oxford: Oxford University Press, 1994), Letter xx, p. 98.
28 A. Owen Aldridge, *Voltaire and the Century of Light* (Princeton, NJ: Princeton University Press, 1975), p. 44.
29 Quoted in Besterman, *Voltaire*, p. 125. Neither Tillotson nor Boyle is mentioned in *Lettres philosophiques*.

Voltaire practises this trade, following through the analogy of the workings of commerce and Enlightenment. Travel narratives constituted an important locus of international cultural contact and exchange, and a literary genre in their own right. In two places in *Letters concerning the English Nation* Voltaire echoes the tone of a tourist guide, the description (Letter XXIII) of the monuments to men of letters in Westminster Abbey, and the description (Letter VI) of the Exchange where 'the Jew, the Mahometan, and the Christian transact together as tho' they all profess'd the same religion, and give the name of Infidel to none but bankrupts' (Letter VI, p. 34). Voltaire's English notebook opens, 'England is meeting of all religions as the Royal exchange is the rendez vous of all foreigners. When I see Christians, cursing Jews, methings I see children beating their fathers.'[30]

These passages were indebted to Addison's *Spectator* no. 69. The English notebook has more excerpts from *The Spectator* than any other prose work. One entry reads simply, 'Read the Spectator'.[31] He read it aloud to improve his English. Partly through Voltaire's advertisement, Addison became very popular in France. Marivaux, who did not read English, was led by the French translation of the periodical essays to launch his own *Spectateur français*. Yet it is rare to see Addison considered as a figure of the Enlightenment. If this is because he is not seen as sufficiently philosophical, that is an impression alien to the age of *philosophes*. In fact Addison was actively interested in contemporary French philosophy. He had visited Malebranche and discussed his theory of colour with him, and results of this can be seen in *Spectator* no. 387. Continental imitations of *The Spectator* in French, German and other languages were important vehicles for the spread of Enlightenment.

Historians of the Enlightenment have focused it in France, taking the radical critique or rejection of religion as a crucial component, even a criterion of inclusion. Just what the infamous is in Voltaire's battle cry, 'Ecrasez l'infâme' is not evident, but much of what he crusaded against was not present in England, or if it was, it was opposed by good Christians like Johnson. The Protestant Reformation anticipated the Enlightenment in some ways and the

---

30 From *Notebooks* in *Candide and Other Writings*, p. 555. On Commerce and Enlightenment, see pp. 557–8,
> In the countries in which commerce is not well developed, there is always some one who is extremely rich because the rest are poor.
> The same is true in matters of the spirit, in science and philosophy. The more an age is enlightened, the fewer the number of dominant geniuses, every one is comfortable, but hardly anyone has an immense fortune.

31 *Ibid.*, p. 559.

anti-clericalism of a Hobbes was no longer as necessary in the England which Voltaire knew.

The Scottish Enlightenment established its identity early in the eighteenth century and was recognised throughout Europe. Hume is an exemplar of 'the Enlightenment', but not of a British Enlightenment. The Dutch emigré pamphleteer, Bernard Mandeville is sometimes mentioned, and the Earl of Shaftesbury, but the English seem generally to have been elided or placed firmly in an opposing camp. 'The Age of Johnson' was also that of Hume, yet the two rarely meet in modern accounts of the period. Analogously, Donald Greene has shown how inconsistent and mistaken scholars like A. O. Lovejoy and Peter Gay are to note shared tendencies of Johnson and Voltaire and then speak of 'a strange pair of companions in arms' or incongruous allies. Beyond the fact that each was 'the most prolific and best known publicist of his own country during the eighteenth century', Greene details an impressive array of consonances, including their attacks on oppression, slavery, colonialism and war.[32] When in 1757 the English Admiral Byng was court-martialled and executed for failing to capture Minorca the previous year from the French, Johnson and Voltaire reacted with indignation at what many at the time considered a politically expedient move by the government. Voltaire intervened in 1762 for Jean Calas (a Huguenot convicted without proof of murdering his son), and Johnson's efforts to save the clergyman William Dodd from hanging for forgery brought about a change in the law. Intellectually, they stand alone together in their penetrating rejection of the facile assumptions and assurances of philosophical Optimism. They strike the same tone on the war of their countries over the colonies, 'The American dispute between the French and us is only the quarrel of two robbers for the spoils of a passenger.' Johnson said Voltaire's *Life of Charles XII* of Sweden was 'one of the finest pieces of historical writing in any language'.[33]

Finally, the real coincidence of *Rasselas* and *Candide* (1759) is deeper than critics have yet recognised. Even Greene misses the point of the 'Conclusion in which nothing is concluded'. Rasselas and the other characters in Johnson's moral fable do not return to Abyssinia or anywhere; they 'deliberated'

---

32 Donald Greene, 'Voltaire and Johnson', in Alfred J. Bingham and Virgil W. Topazio (eds.), *Enlightenment Studies in honour of Lester G. Crocker* (Oxford: The Voltaire Foundation, 1979), pp. 111–31. Cited p. 123. Mark J. Temmer, *Samuel Johnson and Three Infidels: Rousseau, Voltaire, Diderot* (Athens, GA: University of Georgia Press, 1988) construes the lives of Johnson and Rousseau as parallel and never intersecting, compares *Rasselas* to *Candide* and the *Life of Savage* to *Le Neveu de Rameau*.

33 *Johnsonian Miscellanies*, ed. G. B. Hiu, 2 vols. (Oxford: Oxford University Press, 1897), vol. II, p. 306.

and 'resolved' to return, and Johnson has forcefully revealed the danger of confusing resolution with actual doing in chapter 4. In a close parallel to the early effect of Pangloss' teachings in *Candide*, Rasselas and his sister make considering and resolving into alternatives to engagement and action. They are unwilling to risk disappointment and take the 'hap' out of happiness. Johnson reveals an obstacle to earthly happiness in the mind-set of which his main characters all develop some variant. Johnson's philosopher guide to Rasselas, Imlac, is closer to Voltaire's Pangloss than has been recognised. Including Johnson in the Enlightenment, as an apt counterpart to Hume and Voltaire, is an important step towards establishing the idea of an English Enlightenment.[34]

Other writers preceded Voltaire, or seconded him in getting French Anglomania under way. (The term 'Anglomanie' dates from the 1750s; a book was written attacking the phenomenon under that name by Louis-Charles Fougeret de Montbron in 1757.) The Swiss Béat de Muralt praised the English, on balance, in his *Lettres sur les Anglais et sur les Français* (1725). The Abbé Prévost was in England from 1728–31 and again frequently from 1733 on. He promoted its culture in his journal *Le Pour et Contre* (1735–40) and in indirect ways in his novels, *Mémoires et aventures d'un homme de qualité* (1728–31) (see Book 5), and *Le Philosophe anglais ou Histoire de Monsieur Cleveland* (1731–9) and in his translation of *Clarissa* (*Lettres angloises*, 1751).[35]

Montesquieu was in England from November 1729 to May 1731, sponsored by Lord Chesterfield, who introduced him to Pope and Swift. Like Voltaire he too was most immediately influenced by Bolingbroke. That he already had an apt and favourable sense of British government is shown by nos. 104 and 136 of *Lettres persanes* (1721). He distilled his political observations of England in

34 Roy Porter repeatedly advocated the idea of an English Enlightenment, for which Johnson was clearly important, but he was never sure how to fit him in. See 'The Enlightenment in England', in Porter and Mikulas Teich (eds.), *The Enlightenment in National Context* (Cambridge: Cambridge University Press, 1981), pp. 1–18, pp. 13, 15. In *The Enlightenment* (Studies in European History) (Atlantic Highlands, NJ: Humanities Press, 1990), p. 5, Porter includes only 'the Britons, Hume and Gibbon' in the front line of Enlightenment figures. He mentions Johnson only to compare him to Voltaire apropos *Candide*, p. 64, 'Johnson hated Voltaire . . . His own moral tale was a warning of the futility of over-inflated expectations of worldly bliss, not a handbook on how to be happy. *Rasselas* closed with a "Conclusion in which Nothing is Concluded"'. In *Enlightenment: Britain and the Creation of the Modern World* (London: Penguin, 2000), p. xxiv, he refers to 'those two mighty adversaries', Johnson and Hume, and contrasts the Christian humanism of *Rasselas* to 'the enlightened [who] always wanted, nay, *expected* to have their cake and eat it' (p. 20). He associates Johnson with Augustinian gloom as opposed to 'enlightened glee' (p. 157).

35 Thomas O. Beebee, *'Clarissa' on the Continent* (University Park, PA: Pennsylvania State University Press, 1990) also discusses the German translation of Johann David Michaelis from 1749 to 1753.

his discussion of a 'commercial republic, disguised as a monarchy', in *l'Esprit des Lois* (1748). This has confused some scholars, as it differs from the classical republic which he identified by its ruling principle of virtue (correlated with honour as the principle of monarchy and fear as that of despotism). In his insight into this new sort of republic, constituted by a mentality in which commerce played a positive role, he is close to Voltaire and to Hume, with whom he corresponded.

The importance of Britain for Diderot is almost as great, even though he never travelled there. His literary beginnings, translating Temple Stanyan's *History of Greece*, then Robert James' considerable *Medical Dictionary*, recall the Grub Street apprenticeship of Samuel Johnson. The great French encyclopedia, which Diderot directed together with D'Alembert (and for which Bacon is so important), grew out of a projected French version of Ephraim Chambers' *Cyclopedia*. Diderot's own thinking was called forth decisively by his translating (more freely) Shaftesbury's *Inquiry Concerning Virtue* in 1745. What his psychology derived via Leibniz from Hobbes has already been noted. His 'Eloge de Richardson' and his own novel, *Jacques le Fataliste*, testify to the impact and his understanding of Richardson and Sterne.

Richardson is also important for Rousseau's *Julie ou la nouvelle Heloïse*, more so than Rousseau allows, but the importance of Defoe's *Robinson Crusoe* is made palpable in his *Confessions*. The debt of Rousseau's *Social Contract* to Hobbes (more than to Locke) is richer and deeper than his citations and comments suggest, but his version of the social contract does constitute a break with the past. Rousseau manifests two significant turns of mind that have been taken to signal a superseding of the Enlightenment. First is a new importance and cast of sensibility, sometimes considered 'pre-Romantic', that one can find as well in Diderot, although awareness and use of the role of feeling was part of the Enlightenment throughout, essential to its varieties of empiricism. In this new turn of sensibility British figures such as the poet Edward Young and James Macpherson's 'translations' of the Scottish bard, Ossian, but also Shakespeare and Milton, attain a great following on the Continent and contribute to a cultural shift in which Germany will become the more prominent beneficiary than France, as the culture of the latter strives to recover from the Revolution.

The other new turn of mind in Rousseau is toward a moral autonomy seeking independence from experience. This so-called positive freedom has an important source in Shaftesbury and receives divergent further development in Kantian moral philosophy and in the driving ideas of a latter stage of the French Revolution including the Terror. The close of the 'long eighteenth century' as (neo)classicism and Enlightenment is marked by this European political and moral watershed more than anything. In his *On the Esthetic Education of Mankind* Friedrich Schiller reacts at one and the same time against Kantian rigorism and the Jacobin impasse. Some scholars see in Schiller's reaction, as in the parallel reaction of Burke, the beginnings of Romanticism. But both Schiller and Burke are writing from foundations that are proper to the Enlightenment. Against his own intention Kant opened the way for German Idealism and Romanticism, which became potent influences in Britain. The historical continuum of an age of 'good sense' and sensibility was finally broken.

Religion and literature

ISABEL RIVERS

The religious spectrum

It is now more widely recognised than it was a hundred years ago that seventeenth- and eighteenth-century English society and culture was essentially religious in its institutions, practices and beliefs, and that writing on religious subjects dominated the publishing market.[1] Yet as literary readers in the early twenty-first century, we still confine our attention to a handful of explicitly religious works of the period, and we tend to downplay the religious aims and aspects of other works that we regard as predominantly literary or political or philosophical. Behind the major religious works that are still re-edited and reissued today – notably Milton's *Paradise Lost* and Bunyan's *Pilgrim's Progress* – stretches a vast hinterland of works that went through multiple editions in the eighteenth century and often into the nineteenth, but that are now largely neglected except by specialists. This chapter provides a map for exploring this hinterland. But in order to understand the significance of particular works it is necessary first to consider three broad topics: the range of religious denominations and groups and the main political events that affected their relations with each other; the principal theological and philosophical issues that religious writers of different persuasions addressed; and the preferred kinds of religious writing and their functions.

The Church of England, re-established together with the monarchy at the Restoration in 1660, was unofficially divided into two broad groups, latitudinarian (or low church) and high church, though the clear demarcation and the increasing hostility between these groups dates from the Revolution of 1688. The latitudinarians (the label as originally employed by nonconformists in the 1660s and 1670s and taken up by high churchmen in the 1690s was pejorative)

---

1 See Ian Green, *Print and Protestantism in Early Modern England* (Oxford: Oxford University Press, 2000); Isabel Rivers, 'Religious Publishing', in Michael Suarez and Michael Turner (eds.), *The Cambridge History of the Book in Britain*, vol. v, 1695–1830 (Cambridge: Cambridge University Press, forthcoming).

regarded ecclesiastical organisation and ceremonies as 'things indifferent', i.e. things not prescribed in Scripture that the state had the right to determine, and they were Whigs in politics; high churchmen, on the other hand, regarded the authority of the church and particularly its bishops as distinct from that of the state, and they tended, though not invariably, to be Tory or even Jacobite in politics.

The most important group outside the Church of England were the non-conformists or dissenters. Under the Act of Uniformity of 1662 the sixteenth-century Book of Common Prayer, abolished by the Long Parliament in 1645 and now revised, was restored to use, and about 2,000 ministers who refused to accept it in its entirety, and among other things refused ordination by bishops, lost their livings on Bartholomew Day, 24 August 1662. The non-conformists, i.e. those who would not conform to the Church of England, consisted of Presbyterians, who hoped in vain to be 'comprehended' in a redefined Church of England with an altered liturgy, and Independents (or Congregationalists), Baptists and Quakers, who had no interest in 'comprehension' but who wanted 'indulgence' or toleration for their churches and sects. In the reigns of Charles II and James II penal laws were enacted against the nonconformists and severely enforced in order to bully them into conforming, without success; these laws were suspended briefly on four occasions by royal Declarations of Indulgence that were for the benefit of Roman Catholics as much as nonconformists. After the Revolution of 1688 attempts by sympathetic latitudinarians to achieve the comprehension of nonconformists failed; instead the so-called Toleration Act of 1689 exempted Trinitarian Protestant dissenters from the penal laws and allowed them freedom of worship, provided their ministers subscribed to those of the Thirty-Nine Articles of the Church of England that were concerned with doctrine, took the oath of allegiance (Quakers were allowed to affirm, since they thought swearing was forbidden by Scripture and had their premises licensed.

After 1689 the Church of England had to coexist, whether sympathetically or reluctantly, with Protestant dissent; though the number of dissenters was small, about 6 per cent of the population,[2] the fact of their lawful existence had enormous implications for the future. At the other end of the spectrum a significant number of high churchmen who refused the oath of allegiance to William III and Mary II, including the Archbishop of Canterbury, William Sancroft, several bishops and about 400 clergy, were ejected from their livings,

---

2 Michael R. Watts, *The Dissenters: From the Reformation to the French Revolution* (Oxford: Clarendon Press, 1985; first published 1978), p. 270.

and some formed a separate nonjuring church.[3] William III made John Tillot-son, the most prominent of the latitudinarians, Archbishop of Canterbury in Sancroft's place, and in the 1690s they became the most powerful group in the church. High churchmen were consistently hostile to the dissenters (except for a brief period of rapprochement when they were united against Catholicism under James II), and at the summit of their influence late in Queen Anne's reign Tory legislation was passed (but repealed by the Whigs in the reign of George I) that would have made the survival of dissent very difficult. There was no legal toleration either for Roman Catholics or for anti-Trinitarian Protestants for over a hundred years: Roman Catholic worship was unlawful until the second Catholic Relief Act of 1791, as was unitarian worship until the Unitarian Relief Act of 1813, though in practice there was little persecution; full Catholic emancipation had to wait until 1829. Like the dissenters, Roman Catholics suffered from civil disabilities: they could not qualify for university degrees (which required subscription in full to the Thirty-Nine Articles of the Church of England) or hold public office (which required the sacramental test, the taking of communion in the Church of England). Some dissenters, unlike Catholics, made themselves eligible for office by occasionally taking commu-nion in the established church (a practice known as 'occasional conformity', detested by high churchmen and briefly made illegal). Many orthodox Chris-tians regarded the views of different kinds of anti-Trinitarians – Arians, who thought Jesus was not consubstantial with God, and Socinians or unitarians, who thought Jesus was man not God – as leading inevitably to atheism, and not surprisingly holders of these views were often cautious in expressing them. The Blasphemy Act of 1698 was aimed especially at unitarians. Because of this climate it was and still is very difficult to pin down those outside the Christian pale, deists, freethinkers and sceptics, who tended to backtrack and equivocate when challenged.[4] Atheist was the ultimate term of abuse; no one in the eighteenth century used it as a dispassionate description of his own position.

From the 1730s both the Church of England and dissent were increasingly affected by the diverse movement known as the Evangelical Revival. Though its beginnings were small, and it attracted hostility from churchmen and dis-senters alike, it increased in size and influence through the century. The revival had its origins within the established church, though it also had links with the

---

3 See George Every, *The High Church Party 1688–1718* (London: SPCK, 1956).
4 See Isabel Rivers, *Reason, Grace, and Sentiment: A Study of the Language of Religion and Ethics in England, 1660–1780*, vol. II, *Shaftesbury to Hume* (Cambridge: Cambridge University Press, 2000), ch. I.

Congregational wing of dissent. The label covers a number of groups who sometimes cooperated and sometimes clashed with each other over organisation and doctrine: Calvinist Methodists and Arminian Methodists, who used irregular practices such as open-air and itinerant preaching and religious conferences, and evangelical or gospel clergy, who disliked the practices of the Methodists as destructive of church order, but who shared with them a belief that the eighteenth-century Church of England had wrongly abandoned the Reformation doctrines set out in its Articles and Homilies. Step by step, both Calvinist and Wesleyan (Arminian) Methodists eventually separated from the established church. Most English Calvinist Methodists joined Congregationalist or Baptist churches in the later eighteenth century, whereas the Wesleyans set up the Methodist Church, which itself split into separate bodies in the nineteenth century. The Welsh Calvinists also formed their own church. This new Methodist and evangelical dissent differed markedly from pre-revival old dissent, in particular the Presbyterians, who were decreasing in number and by the end of the century had largely become unitarian. The Church of England Evangelicals, on the other hand, untempted by and disapproving of separation, were to become an increasingly important party within the nineteenth-century church.

From the mid seventeenth to the late eighteenth centuries certain key theological and philosophical issues informed religious argument and writing. These can be seen as resolving into two main questions, concerning religious knowledge, or the proper relation between faith and reason, and religious conduct, or the proper relation between faith and works. Under the first heading can be placed the following more specific questions: what is the relation between natural religion, the principles of which are deduced by reason, and revealed religion, which is based on Scripture and accepted by faith? What is the authority of Scripture, and how is it to be interpreted? What are the evidences for the truth of Christianity? Are they primarily external, the biblical prophecies and miracles, or internal, the promptings of grace, or conscience or the Spirit? How is inspiration by the Holy Spirit as attributed to the authors of the Bible, and, more controversially, claimed by a few modern Christians, to be weighed against human reason and the light of nature? Under the second heading can be placed the question of the problematic status in the eighteenth century of the crucial Reformation doctrine of justification by faith alone, which was the official teaching of the sixteenth-century Articles of the Church of England, to which the Anglican clergy subscribed, and of the seventeenth-century Westminster Confession of Faith and Catechism, to which many Trinitarian dissenters adhered. Do good works, though they are the necessary fruit of faith, contribute nothing to salvation (the orthodox Reformation view)? Or are repentance, obedience and works a necessary part of justifying faith (as most of the Anglican clergy had come to believe)? Is salvation entirely the gift of divine grace, or does human effort play a part in the process? This disagreement was often covered in the period by the respective labels Calvinism and Arminianism.

Alongside these large questions are two related concerns, which ultimately had their origin in responses to the revolution in church and state of the 1640s and 1650s: the danger of enthusiasm in conduct and expression, and the need to establish an appropriate language for religion. Enthusiasm, which meant different things to different groups, was regarded by almost everyone as the enemy; some who were themselves labelled as enthusiasts (as the Arminian Methodist leader John Wesley was in the 1740s) disowned the label and instead attached it to others. It usually implied putting private experience and appeals to the Spirit above reason, Scripture and external authority, and faith in opposition to works. The problem of enthusiasm was closely related to that of appropriate language. After the Restoration churchmen perceived the excesses of puritan language as having contributed to the overthrow of church and monarchy, and a concerted programme was mounted by the latitudinarians for a plain, easy, rational, language that eschewed mystery, metaphor and cant. Yet religious language had to be persuasive as well as informative and argumentative: the task of the preacher and religious writer was not only to convince the reason but to move the affections and transform the hearer's or reader's life. The nonconformist and dissenting heirs of the puritans, followed in this by the Methodists and evangelicals, sought to find a new religious language that would meet the requirements of reason and plainness and yet would draw on earlier affectionate models and thus prove an appropriate vehicle for the religion of the heart.

Religious writing habitually fell into three main categories, doctrinal, controversial and practical divinity, though individual works often crossed these boundaries. Works in the first two categories were concerned with establishing the truth of specific doctrines and the evidences, natural and revealed, for Christianity, and with demolishing the positions of opponents of other denominations or beyond the Christian fold. Works in the third category, generally regarded as the most important, were concerned with the nature and practice of the Christian life and the path to salvation. In the following account the first two categories are explored briefly under the heading of works concerned with the defence and definition of religion, but more attention is given to the third, practical literature, under the headings of guides to the Christian life (in the form of sermons and devotional handbooks), accounts of Christian experience (journals, autobiographies and biographies), and Christian song (poetry, psalms and hymns). Among these forms are to be found the most popular works of religious literature with a wide readership across denominational boundaries.

The defence and definition of religion

An impressive array of late seventeenth- and early eighteenth-century expository works was designed to persuade deists, freethinkers and sceptics of the principles of natural religion – belief in a perfect God and the obligation to fufil moral duties – and then, when these had been satisfactorily established, of the inadequacy of natural religion divorced from revealed, and of the truth of the Christian religion as based on Scripture. This was the strategy employed by John Tillotson, perhaps the most famous preacher of his day, in his collections of sermons published from the 1660s to the 1690s. Of the many works written on this subject by Tillotson's contemporaries and successors, those by four writers achieved a particular standing as repeatedly cited authorities and as educational textbooks: John Wilkins, *Of the Principles and Duties of Natural Religion* (1675); John Locke, *An Essay Concerning Human Understanding* (1690, fourth edition, 1700, with important additions) and *The Reasonableness of Christianity, as Delivered in the Scriptures* (1695); Samuel Clarke, *A Discourse Concerning the Unchangeable Obligations of Natural Religion, and the Truth and Certainty of the Christian Revelation* (1706); and Joseph Butler, *The Analogy of Religion Natural and Revealed to the Constitution and Course of Nature* (1736).

Wilkins, leader of the latitudinarians in the Church of England after the Restoration, Bishop of Chester, and close friend of Tillotson, left the unpublished manuscript of *Natural Religion* to his friend at his death in 1672; Tillotson edited and published it in 1675, and though it is little known now it was regularly republished until the 1730s and figured in many reading lists for undergraduates and clergy until the end of the century.[5] Wilkins wrote in opposition to the 'Humour of Scepticism and Infidelity' abounding in the Restoration world, assuming that his reader would be *'an honest and teachable man'*,[6] and he set out the doctrines of natural religion clearly and concisely in order to win that reader round. *Natural Religion* falls into two books, the first showing

5 See Isabel Rivers, ' "Galen's Muscles": Wilkins, Hume, and the Educational Use of the Argument from Design', *Historical Journal* 36 (1993), 577–97.
6 John Wilkins, *Of the Principles and Duties of Natural Religion* (6th edn, London, 1710), pp. 1, 30.

the reasonableness of natural religion, the second the wisdom of practising its duties. The early chapters of Book I are concerned with establishing the moral certainty of the principles of religion, and Wilkins then goes on to consider arguments for the existence of God and to describe his perfections and the human duties that relate to his particular attributes. His argument in chapter 6 for the existence of God 'From the admirable contrivance of Natural Things' was to be particularly influential. In the second book he alters his method from intellectual to prudential persuasion, arguing in a manner characteristic of the latitudinarians that religion conduces to our outward and inward happiness in this world and urging the reader to verify it through experience. The final chapter argues briefly for 'the Excellency of the Christian Religion', warning the rational man not to ask for impossible standards of evidence.

Wilkins' interest in establishing the moral certainty of religious principles was to be taken much further by the philosopher John Locke, ultimately in some surprising directions. Locke, a member of the Church of England with many friends among the latitudinarian clergy, though not himself a cleric, began work on *An Essay Concerning Human Understanding* in about 1670 with the object of finding the principles of morality and revealed religion. There is material germane to contemporary religious debate in all four books (1, 'Of Innate Notions', 2, 'Of Ideas', 3, 'Of Words', 4, 'Of Knowledge and Opinion'), but it is the last that is particularly relevant here. In chapter 17, 'Of Reason', he differentiates propositions that are according to reason, above reason, and contrary to reason, an account that has clear implications for religion. Faith can only be given on good reason, and so cannot be opposed to it.[7] He was here drawing on earlier latitudinarian arguments,[8] but his version was to become particularly influential. In the following chapter, 'Of Faith and Reason, and their distinct Provinces', he goes on to explain that faith is the assent to a proposition not from the deductions of reason but as the result of an extraordinary communication from God, or revelation.[9] But though faith and reason have their distinct provinces, they are mutually supporting. Faith functions in matters which are above reason, but it is reason which determines what those matters are; and faith cannot accept matters which are contrary to reason, or without recourse to reason. To set faith in opposition to reason in this way is enthusiasm, as Locke explains in a very important chapter, 'Of Enthusiasm',

7 John Locke, *An Essay Concerning Human Understanding*, ed. P. H. Nidditch (Oxford: Clarendon Press, 1975), p. 687, ¶ 23–4.
8 E.g. Joseph Glanvill, 'Anti-fanatical Religion, and Free Philosophy', essay 7 of *Essays on Several Important Subjects in Philosophy and Religion* (London, 1676).
9 Locke, *Essay*, p. 689, ¶ 2.

added as a new chapter 19 to the fourth edition of the *Essay* in 1700. The enthusiast who 'takes away *Reason*, to make way for *Revelation*, puts out the Light of both'; it is only reason that can judge whether a revelation is from God.[10] In *The Reasonableness of Christianity* Locke's focus was on Scripture, and he somewhat changed his tack in replying to the freethinkers' charge that revelation was redundant. We need a saviour because establishing the duties of natural religion is too difficult for philosophers. Christian philosophers have found this easier than the heathen ones did, but that is because their knowledge of morality is initially from revelation and subsequently confirmed by reason. The gospel teaches the principles of natural religion which reason should in theory be able to make out but in practice finds too difficult; the gospel further provides the crucial motives for obeying the natural law in the promises it offers believers.[11] Though Locke's *Essay* was perceived in many quarters on first publication to be dangerous to religion, after the early accusations had subsided he was widely relied on by both churchmen and dissenters throughout the eighteenth century as a supporter of Christianity and an opponent of freethinkers.

Samuel Clarke's *Discourse Concerning . . . Natural Religion and . . . Christian Revelation* was originally given as the Boyle lectures for 1705 (his lectures of the previous year were entitled *A Demonstration of the Being and Attributes of God*), and then published in expanded form in 1706. The lectures were set up in 1691 under the terms of the scientist Robert Boyle's will 'for proving the Christian Religion against notorious Infidels, *viz. Atheists, Deists, Pagans, Jews* and *Mahometans*',[12] and in their published versions proved extremely popular. Clarke, a prominent Church of England clergyman whose Arian views were later to prevent him from rising to a bishopric, provided in his *Discourse* one of the fullest accounts of the inadequacy of natural religion alone. He argues that there is no tenable position called deism midway between atheism and Christianity; natural religion supposes revealed. Eternal moral obligations are binding on all rational beings (Proposition 1), but men are now too corrupt to deduce these obligations for themselves (Proposition 5), and only revelation will recover them from their degeneracy (Proposition 7).[13] A particular feature

---

10 *Ibid.*, pp. 698, ¶ 4, 704, ¶ 14.

11 John Locke, *The Reasonableness of Christianity As delivered in the Scriptures*, ed. John C. Higgins-Biddle (Oxford: Clarendon Press, 1999), ch. 14, pp. 148 ff.

12 Quoted in Richard Bentley's dedication to the trustees of *A Confutation of Atheism* (London, 1692), reprinted in *A Defence of Natural and Revealed Religion: Being a Collection of the Sermons Preached at the Lecture Founded by the Honourable Robert Boyle, Esq.*, eds. S. Letsome and J. Nicholl, 3 vols. (London, 1739), vol. 1.

13 Samuel Clarke, *A Discourse Concerning the Unchangeable Obligations of Natural Religion, and the Truth and Certainty of the Christian Revelation* (London, 1706), pp. 42, 45, 193, 241.

of Clarke's argument was his attack on attempts by freethinkers to use classical philosophers, especially Cicero, to provide a benign portrait of human nature and reason.

A more empirical, psychological approach to the problems of natural religion was taken by Joseph Butler, who was an admirer of Clarke and corresponded with him anonymously when he was a student. After being educated as a dissenter, Butler conformed to the Church of England and eventually rose to become Bishop of Gloucester and then of Durham. In the *Analogy of Religion* he tries to show that from the course of nature we are able to deduce that the world is under the moral government of God, and that this moral system is analogous to what we are taught in Scripture. Whatever difficulties we may have with Scripture, therefore, are no more objectionable than those we have with the course of nature. Butler insists that his method is based not on abstract reasoning but on matter of fact (part 2, chapter 8).[14] The first part of the book deals with natural religion and the second with revealed. From the course of nature we deduce that human beings are endowed with a moral nature (part 1, chapter 3) and that we live in a state of probation in order to fit us for a future state (part 1, chapter 5). God's moral government of the world, as revealed by the course of nature, and the scheme of Christianity, as revealed by Scripture, are both imperfectly comprehended by us (part 1, chapter 7; part 2, chapter 4), but both lead us to accept that life is a process of testing and improvement in the hope of a future reward.[15]

All the works discussed so far were methodical and expository, and lent themselves despite their length to pedagogical purposes: they were recommended, for example, by Daniel Waterland, Fellow of Magdalene College, Cambridge, in *Advice to a Young Student* (1730), Edward Bentham, Fellow of Oriel College, Oxford, in *An Introduction to Moral Philosophy* (1745), and Philip Doddridge, tutor of the dissenting academy at Northampton, in *A Course of Lectures on the Principal Subjects in Pneumatology, Ethics, and Divinity* (1763). They represent a very important and characteristic strand of writing about religion in late seventeenth- and early eighteenth-century England, in which logical argument and rhetorical plainness were used to define the relationship between natural and revealed religion and to defend the truth of Scripture. It was not part of their purpose to warm the reader's heart and affections, move his will and lead him to the Christian life. This was the function of the much larger and more important category of practical literature.

14 *The Works of Bishop Butler*, ed. J. H. Bernard, 2 vols. (London: Macmillan, 1900), vol. II, p. 266.
15 *Ibid.*, vol. II, pp. 55, 77, 120, 177–8.

Guides to the Christian life

The most widely circulated kinds of practical literature were sermons, devotional works and handbooks. Puritan preachers from the late sixteenth century had emphasised the importance of the pulpit rather than the altar in worship, and the sermon became a particularly important medium in the 1640s and 1650s, with the abolition of the Book of Common Prayer and the growth of Independent churches and sects. After the Restoration a concerted attempt was made, largely by latitudinarian preachers, to define and promulgate a new preaching style that would avoid both the ornamented and witty preaching of early seventeenth-century high churchmen and what was perceived to be the enthusiastic and inflammatory preaching of puritans and nonconformists.[16] Key works defining this new rationally persuasive style were the revised version of Wilkins' handbook for preachers, *Ecclesiastes, or, A Discourse concerning the Gift of Preaching* (1669), Simon Patrick, *A Friendly Debate betwixt . . . a Conformist [and] a Non-Conformist* (Part 1, 1669), James Arderne, *Directions concerning the Matter and Stile of Sermons* (1671), and Glanvill, 'Anti-fanatical Religion, and Free Philosophy' in *Essays on Several Important Subjects in Philosophy and Religion* (1676) and *An Essay concerning Preaching* (1678). The principal practitioner of this new style was Tillotson, who was said to have brought great numbers of nonconformists into the established church by his preaching; he himself owed a considerable debt to Wilkins and Isaac Barrow, whose posthumous works he edited in the 1680s. Tillotson was to exercise an extraordinary influence on the content and manner of preaching through the regular republication of his works in the first half of the eighteenth century, up to the edition by Thomas Birch (1752). The mid-century sermons of Laurence Sterne and James Woodforde, for example, like those of so many of their colleagues, are full of Tillotsonian echoes and borrowings.[17] There was an inevitable backlash from Methodists: the charismatic evangelist George Whitefield claimed, because of Tillotson's repudiation of the doctrine of justification by faith alone, that he knew no more about Christianity than Mahomet.[18]

A helpful survey of different traditions of preaching and practical writing that illuminates the differences between the Church of England and dissent was provided in Doddridge's *Lectures on Preaching* for his ministerial students

16 Rivers, *Reason, Grace, and Sentiment*, vol. 1, *Whichcote to Wesley* (1991), pp. 49–57.
17 Laurence Sterne, *The Sermons of Laurence Sterne*, ed. Melvyn New, *The Florida Edition of the Works of Laurence Sterne*, vols. IV–V (Gainesville FL: University Press of Florida, 1996), vol. V, p. 24; Norman Sykes, *From Sheldon to Secker: Aspects of English Church History 1660–1768* (Cambridge: Cambridge University Press, 1959), p. 177.
18 *Three Letters from the Reverend Mr G. Whitefield* (Philadelphia, 1740), pp. 2–3.

(delivered in the period 1729–51 but not published until 1804). Doddridge compared puritans, including Robert Bolton and Richard Sibbes, nonconformists of the last age, including Richard Baxter, John Howe and John Flavel, dissenting writers of the present age, including Isaac Watts and David Jennings, and writers of the established church, a long list including Tillotson, Barrow, Wilkins, Robert Leighton, Francis Atterbury and Thomas Secker. Doddridge, who admired all these preachers for different reasons, himself advised his students to avoid among other subjects the doctrines of natural religion and legalistic emphasis on sins and duties (much stressed by Anglicans) in their sermons, and to concentrate instead on the love of Christ, the covenant of grace, the operations of the Spirit and the privileges of the children of God. The 'strains' of preaching he recommended were the pathetic, insinuating, evangelical, spiritual and experimental, and Scriptural.[19]

Devotional literature – the literature of private prayer and meditation – had a very long history. An important Protestant development in the early seventeenth century was the handbook that combined theological instruction and advice about prayer with directions for private and public duties, of which the most long-lived example was Lewis Bayly's *The Practice of Pietie* (c. 1612), still in print in the nineteenth century. By the middle of the eighteenth century religious readers (such as Richardson's Clarissa) had a wide range of such books to draw on, a good deal of it from the mid and late seventeenth century. John Wesley's many editions, notably *A Christian Library* (fifty volumes, 1749–55), a collection of works of practical divinity that he edited and abridged for the benefit of his preachers, give the modern reader a broad view of the literature of many denominations and countries that fed into eighteenth-century religious culture, from the influential fifteenth-century *Imitation of Christ* by Thomas à Kempis to the works of Wesley's contemporary William Law.[20]

Practical books were particularly valued when a church or denomination was under political attack and it was difficult for its members to gather for worship unimpeded, as was the case of adherents of the episcopal Church of England from 1645 to 1660 and nonconformists from 1660 to 1688. Two such works published by Church of England clergy in the Interregnum that were to prove enormously influential were Jeremy Taylor's *Holy Living* (1650) and the anonymous *Practice of Christian Graces* (1658), better known by its subtitle

19 Philip Doddridge, *Lectures on Preaching*, in *The Works of the Rev. Philip Doddridge, D. D.*, eds. E. Williams and E. Parsons, 10 vols. (Leeds, 1802–5), vol. v, lectures 2–6.
20 Isabel Rivers, 'Dissenting and Methodist Books of Practical Divinity', in Rivers (ed.), *Books and their Readers in Eighteenth-Century England* (Leicester: Leicester University Press, 1982), pp. 145–59.

The Whole Duty of Man and usually attributed to Richard Allestree. Although they were designed for readers who were offended by both the doctrine and the discipline of the puritans – Taylor, who was twice imprisoned during this period, made it clear that his book was meant for those without access to illegal Church of England services[21] – they long outlasted their original circumstances. *Holy Living* was popular until the mid eighteenth century, and a formative influence on Wesley's development at Oxford in 1725 (he abridged the work (not very effectively) in volume XVI of *A Christian Library* (1752)). *The Whole Duty* became a standard manual of instruction for 150 years; the Society for Promoting Christian Knowledge (SPCK) distributed it widely to clergy, schools, parochial libraries and prisoners, both at home and in the plantations. Taylor and the author of *The Whole Duty* ignore Calvinist emphasis on predestination, depravity, conversion, justification by faith and the recognition of marks of election, and emphasise instead repentance, obedience and human responsibility for fulfilling the duties that are the condition of salvation. *Holy Living* is divided into three main aspects, deriving from Titus 2:11–12: sobriety, or our duty to ourselves, justice, or our duty to others, and religion, meaning in a strict sense our duty to God. *The Whole Duty* takes its title from Ecclesiastes 12:13, but it also draws on Titus 2:11–12, leading the reader step by step through public and private duties, including the reciprocal duties of parents and children, husbands and wives, and masters and servants (Partitions 14 and 15). Eighteenth-century evangelicals criticised it for omitting justifying faith: Henry Venn's *The Complete Duty of Man* (1763) was meant to remedy this omission, but it failed to dislodge *The Whole Duty* from its dominant place.

In the 1660s and 1670s a number of books by nonconformist writers served a similar purpose in providing religious guidance and moral support at a time when both ministers and congregations were under severe legal constraints. These ranged from brief pamphlets to weighty folios, and included *A Call to the Unconverted* (1658), *A Christian Directory* (1673, written 1664–5) and *The Poor Man's Family Book* (1674) by Richard Baxter, the moderate nonconformist leader and ejected minister of Kidderminster, who was twice imprisoned but lived to see the effects of the Toleration Act; *An Alarme to Unconverted Sinners* (published posthumously with an introduction by Baxter in 1672) by Joseph Alleine, the ejected assistant minister of Taunton, who died young from the

---

21 Jeremy Taylor, *Holy Living and Holy Dying*, ed. P. G. Stanwood, 2 vols. (Oxford: Clarendon Press, 1989), vol. I, pp. 5–6. See Isabel Rivers, 'Prayer-Book Devotion: the Literature of the Proscribed Episcopal Church', in N. H. Keeble (ed.), *The Cambridge Companion to Writing of the English Revolution* (Cambridge: Cambridge University Press, 2001), pp. 198–214.

effects of overwork and imprisonment; and the most famous of all such books, *The Pilgrim's Progress* (two parts, 1678 and 1684) by John Bunyan, the Bedford preacher, imprisoned for twelve years from 1660.

Nonconformist and later dissenting practical works differed from those written by members of the established church in three main ways: they emphasised the Christian life as a possibly perilous but ultimately triumphant journey to salvation, rather than a daily round of rules and duties to be observed; they gave careful attention to the different stages of Christian experience and the needs of different readers; and with the aim of awakening, encouraging and transforming these readers they aimed at arousing the affections and piercing the heart. The brief works aimed at unconverted sinners, Baxter's *Call* and Alleine's *Alarm*, were enormously popular (both sold 20,000 copies in the first year of publication, and continued to be best-sellers).[22] The most ambitious and important works are those which lead the reader from the lowest to the highest spiritual rank, from unbeliever to godly professor. Baxter had a particular interest in addressing different classes of readers systematically, as he explained in the preface to *A Call*, and he was always conscious of the biblical distinction between babes who should be fed on milk and those of full age who should be given strong meat (1 Corinthians 3:2, Hebrews 5:12–14). *A Christian Directory* is divided into four parts: Christian ethics, economics (which has topics in common with *The Whole Duty*), ecclesiastics and politics. The object of Part 1 is first to teach the ungodly how to attain to a state of grace, and then to help those who have it how to grow in grace and persevere to the end.[23] The most important chapters here are 2 and 3, 'Directions to Young Christians, or Beginners in Religion, for their Establishment and Safe Proceeding' (which covers some of the same material as *Pilgrim's Progress*) and 'The General Grand Directions for Walking with God, in a Life of Faith and Holiness'. *A Christian Directory* was designed for young ministers, masters of families and private Christians, but Baxter realised that its size (a large folio) and scope diminished its usefulness. His *Poor Man's Family Book*, cast in the form of a dialogue between Paul, a pastor, and Saul, an ignorant sinner, was designed as a late seventeenth-century replacement for Arthur Dent's *The Plaine Mans Path-way to Heaven* (1601), as Bunyan's *The Life and Death of Mr Badman* (1680) may also have been. Baxter's Paul explains in simpler and more dramatic

22 On sales see C. John Sommerville, *Popular Religion in Restoration England* (Gainesville, FL: University Presses of Florida, 1977), chs. 2 and 3; N. H. Keeble, *The Literary Culture of Nonconformity in Later Seventeenth-Century England* (Leicester: Leicester University Press, 1987), pp. 127–35; Green, *Print and Protestantism*, ch. 6.
23 Richard Baxter, *A Christian Directory*, in *Practical Works of the Rev. Richard Baxter*, ed. W. Orme, 23 vols. (London: James Duncan, 1830), vol. II, pp. 3–4.

terms than the magisterial voice of *A Christian Directory* how to become a Christian and live and die as one, while managing to cover much of the same ground.

Bunyan's approach in *The Pilgrim's Progress* to the problem of different readers' needs was much more imaginative than Baxter's. Among other works he had already written a more conventional short family handbook, *Christian Behaviour* (1663), designed to show the new convert how a life of holiness and good works flows from faith.[24] In 'The Author's Apology for his Book' prefacing *The Pilgrim's Progress* Part 1 he explains how he must employ 'Snares, Lines, Angles, Hooks and Nets' to catch different readers, some of whom 'must be grop'd for, and be tickled too'.[25] At the same time as tracing Christian's progress from unbelief and conversion through the varieties of Christian experience to godly death, he interweaves different methods for different kinds of reader, the babes and the strong (Part 2 makes far more concessions to the former), repeating the same doctrinal points through allegory, emblem, narrative, dialogue, catechism, marginal glosses and argument. He provides a succession of guides and instructors, notably Evangelist, the Interpreter and Greatheart (in Part 2), to help both pilgrims and readers through the difficulties of doctrine (especially the relation of faith to works) and the demands of the holy life. In his later allegory, *The Holy War* (1682), he tells the reader in advance that the key to the riddle lies in the window, i.e. the marginal glosses.[26] The pleasures of reading are essential for drawing in certain kinds of reader, but they are subservient to the understanding of doctrine.

As with the popular Anglican books described above, nonconformist guides from the later seventeenth century continued to be republished and widely read in the eighteenth, although in some quarters they were considered to be old-fashioned and in need of updating. Benjamin Fawcett, one of Doddridge's students, and himself minister at Kidderminster, abridged some of Baxter's books from the 1750s to the 1770s, including *The Poor Man's Family Book* as *Dialogues on Personal and Family Religion* (1769). Wesley published abridgements of Baxter's *Call to the Unconverted* and Alleine's *Alarm* in 1782, as part of a collection of tracts to be given away to the poor, having previously included *A Call* in volume XXIV of *A Christian Library* (1753). Several of Wesley's preachers recorded in their autobiographies, published in his *Arminian Magazine* in the 1770s and

---

24 John Bunyan, *Christian Behaviour*, ed. J. Sears McGee, in *The Miscellaneous Works of John Bunyan*, gen. ed. Roger Sharrock, 13 vols. (Oxford: Clarendon Press, 1976–94), vol. III, p. 9.

25 John Bunyan, *The Pilgrim's Progress*, ed. J. B. Wharey, 2nd edn, rev. Roger Sharrock (Oxford: Clarendon Press, 1960), p. 3.

26 John Bunyan, *The Holy War*, eds. Roger Sharrock and J. F. Forrest (Oxford: Clarendon Press, 1980), p. 5.

1780s, the impact of reading Alleine's *Alarm*, *Pilgrim's Progress* and Bunyan's autobiography *Grace Abounding* in their youth.[27] Bunyan was regarded as an uneducated author writing for those like himself, and in the first half of the eighteenth century he was ignored (with occasional exceptions) by the politer Presbyterian and Congregational wings of dissent. His Calvinist theology also made him unpalatable to some; when Wesley abridged *Pilgrim's Progress* Part I (1743) and *The Holy War* (in volume XXXII of *A Christian Library*, 1753) he was careful to leave out what he regarded as Bunyan's doctrinal errors. The growing popularity of *Pilgrim's Progress* in the later eighteenth century can in part be attributed to the efforts of evangelical clergy of the Church of England who were fully in sympathy with Bunyan's theology: John Newton and Thomas Scott published annotated editions in 1789 and 1795 respectively.

It would be wrong to imply that eighteenth-century readers of religious books were dependent on seventeenth-century classics. Three devotional handbooks written in the first half of the eighteenth century by authors of different religious persuasions were to have a very wide influence, not least on the revival: William Law's *A Practical Treatise upon Christian Perfection* (1726) and *A Serious Call to a Devout and Holy Life* (1729), and Doddridge's *The Rise and Progress of Religion in the Soul* (1745). The nonjuror Law addressed both his works primarily to wealthy and cultivated readers, with the object of making them renounce the world, submit themselves to the demands of the gospel and devote themselves totally to God. This uncompromising message is conveyed in *A Serious Call* by means of characters who exemplify on the one hand the favourite sins of the leisured, such as Classicus, Negotius and Flatus, and on the other the holy and useful lives they ought to lead, such as Paternus the Christian educator, Ouranius the country priest and Miranda the charitable gentlewoman. In addition to clearly and wittily defining and illustrating the nature of the devout life and its opposite, Law shows his readers how to organise their lives according to rule by following the canonical hours of prayer. (In this emphasis on self-regulation he resembles Taylor.) Although some readers found Law's view of the Christian life too demanding and his emphasis on works rather than faith unProtestant, his books were very widely read, admired and cited. Wesley, who was much indebted to Law but also quarrelled with him for his neglect of the doctrine of justification by faith, published many editions of his abridged versions of *Christian Perfection* and *A*

27 *The Arminian Magazine*, 2 (1779), 88; 3 (1780), 211, 373, 375; 4 (1781), 370. See Isabel Rivers, '"Strangers and Pilgrims": Sources and Patterns of Methodist Narrative', in J. C. Hilson, M. M. B. Jones and J. R. Watson (eds.), *Augustan Worlds* (Leicester: Leicester University Press, 1978), p. 195.

Serious Call. In the 1730s Law became a follower of the seventeenth-century German Lutheran mystic Jakob Boehme, and his remarkable later devotional works, notably *The Spirit of Prayer* (2 parts, 1749–50) and *The Spirit of Love* (2 parts, 1752–4), generated their own circle of admirers. Though Wesley deplored Law's turn to mysticism, he also published abridgements of his later works.

Law's books came out of the high church tradition and through the originally high church Wesley left their mark on Methodism. Doddridge's *Rise and Progress* came out of the tradition of moderate Baxterian Calvinism and helped to give an evangelical cast to dissent. The idea for the book originated with Isaac Watts, who had intended to write it himself; he had in mind a small book for the poor, an updated version of Baxter's *Call to the Unconverted*. When Doddridge took the plan over at Watts' request it became much longer and more elaborate, though Watts did his best, after trying out the manuscript on his servants, to make Doddridge simplify the style.[28] The subtitle of *The Rise and Progress* indicates that it is 'a Course of Serious and Practical Addresses, suited to Persons of every Character and Circumstance: with a Devout Meditation or Prayer added to each Chapter'. Doddridge makes explicit the link between the minister's preaching voice, the devotional handbook, and the guide to the Christian life. Following the Baxterian graduated method, he addresses in turn readers at every stage of Christian experience and follows through the chronological path of the Christian life, from the awakening of the careless sinner to the established Christian rejoicing in the prospect of death. As a publication the *Rise and Progress* was extremely successful: it was widely read by dissenters and evangelicals, and translated into Dutch, French and German. Watts, despite his criticisms, thought it the best book on practical religion in English.[29]

Christian experience

A particular branch of practical literature which was increasingly important for nonconformists, dissenters and evangelicals, but much less prominent among mainstream members of the Church of England, was the relating of Christian experience in the form of autobiographical and biographical narratives. Such writing was often described as experimental, i.e. appertaining to the experience of God in the soul and verifiable by appeal to the evidence of experience. One reason for making such writing widely available was that the individual on his journey would be encouraged and even saved from despair by learning

28 G. F. Nuttall, *Calendar of the Correspondence of Philip Doddridge DD (1702–1751)* (London: Stationery Office, 1979), no. 963, 10 April 1744.
29 *Ibid.*, no. 1005, 13 September 1744.

that his position was not unique, as Bunyan's Christian was when he heard a voice ahead of him in the Valley of the Shadow of Death repeating Psalm 23.[30] In the enlarged third edition of his autobiography, *Grace Abounding to the Chief of Sinners* (first published 1666), Bunyan described the shock of recognition that reading the experience of others could induce. He wrote that after coming across Martin Luther's book on Galatians, 'I found my condition in his experience, so largely and profoundly handled, as if his Book had been written out of my heart.'[31]

Narratives that combined spiritual and physical suffering and triumph had a particular resonance in the period of nonconformist proscription. The conversion and sustaining of characters by stories of others' experiences is a recurrent motif in *Pilgrim's Progress*: thus the monuments of Christian's combats on his journey to the Celestial City guide Christiana and her family on theirs. *The Life and Death of . . . Joseph Alleine* (1672), co-written by his wife Theodosia and ministerial colleagues, was designed, as Baxter said in his introduction, to help weak, discouraged, troubled Christians 'see that a genuine Christian life, is a Life of the greatest joy on earth'.[32] Baxter's moving memoir of his wife, *A Breviate of the Life of Margaret Baxter* (1681), describes both her inner life – her melancholy, the workings of her soul and then her lasting confidence of her salvation – and her public role as a minister's wife in the period of persecution, including dealing with fines and going to prison with him. The work is a 'breviate' because Baxter's friends advised him to cut the more personal details of the love story he had written, and the published version is thus deliberately constrained by the puritan tradition of godly biography. Lucy Hutchinson's life of her husband Colonel John Hutchinson, republican and regicide, who died in prison in 1664, was written for her children between 1664 and 1671 and remained unpublished until 1806. She was not constrained like Baxter by the supposed expectations of a public readership, and she was free to turn her biography to many purposes, personal, historical, political and religious. What links her work most closely to that of contemporary ministers writing for publication is her presentation of Hutchinson as a Christian hero whom God chose to afflict and who 'lived and died a conqueror', 'victorious over the Lord's and his enemies'.[33]

30 Bunyan, *Pilgrim's Progress*, p. 64.
31 John Bunyan, *Grace Abounding to the Chief of Sinners*, ed. Roger Sharrock (Oxford: Clarendon Press, 1962), p. 40, ¶ 129.
32 Theodosia Alleine *et al.*, *The Life & Death Of that Excellent Minister of Christ Mr Joseph Alleine* (London, 1673), p. 16.
33 Lucy Hutchinson, *Memoirs of the Life of Colonel Hutchinson*, ed. N. H. Keeble (London: Everyman, 1995), pp. 29, 336.

Two nonconformist heroes died not long after the passing of the Toleration Act, George Fox, the leading figure in the Society of Friends (or Quakers), in 1690 and Baxter in 1691, and in each case their followers soon published their autobiographies. Fox's *Journal*, dictated in the 1670s, was edited by Thomas Ellwood with a preface by William Penn and appeared in 1694;[34] *Reliquiae Baxterianae* (Baxter's remains), a huge collection of papers with an autobiographical narrative written in three parts (parts 1 and 2, 1664–5, part 3, 1670–85) was edited by Matthew Sylvester with the help of Edmund Calamy and published in 1696. Fox's journal deals with his experiences from 1643 to 1675, from the early years of the Civil War to the persecution of nonconformists in the reign of Charles II, with details of his interpretation of the gospel, his missionary travels in England, Ireland and America, his contempt for Presbyterians and Congregationalists as much as for the episcopal Church of England, his repeated periods of imprisonment and the growing strength of the Friends. *Reliquiae Baxterianae* provides a narrative of Baxter's own life and a history of the times, both political and religious, from the 1620s to the 1680s, with a detailed analysis in part 2 of the divisions between churches and sects at the Restoration and the failure of attempts to accommodate the nonconformists. His long account of his own spiritual development at the end of part 1 deliberately frustrates the reader's expectation of 'Soul-Experiments' and 'Heart-Occurrences'; instead he describes with great insight the different attitudes of his younger and maturer selves to intellectual speculation, the evidences for religion, the relationship between knowledge and experience and the position of other churches.[35]

No other religious autobiographies from the end of the seventeenth century have the range and penetration of these works by Fox and Baxter, though Ellwood's own account, *The History of the Life of Thomas Ellwood* (published posthumously by Joseph Wyeth in 1714), gives a fascinating picture of the social difficulties of a member of the lesser gentry turned Quaker, together with precise details of persecution after the Restoration. Fox's *Journal* was reissued, as was Ellwood's *Life*, several times in the eighteenth century, but the unwieldiness of Baxter's *Reliquiae* made it very difficult to use and it has never been republished in its original form. However, Baxter was to have an enormous indirect impact on the tradition of godly lives. The Presbyterian minister

---

34 For a recent edition eliminating the alterations of Ellwood and modern editors, see George Fox, *The Journal*, ed. Nigel Smith (Harmondsworth: Penguin Books), 1998.

35 *Reliquiae Baxterianae* (London, 1696), Part 1, ¶ 213, pp. 124–38, at 124. The whole section is in *The Autobiography of Richard Baxter*, abridged J. M. Lloyd Thomas, ed. N. H. Keeble (London: Everyman, 1985), chs. 10–11.

Edmund Calamy, who was to become the most important spokesman for nonconformity in the early eighteenth century, published a third-person *Abridgment* (1702) of Baxter's first-person narrative containing a great deal of new information: half the book consisted of an account of the nonconformist ministers ejected in 1662, building on information in Baxter,[36] and Calamy went on to expand this information much further in two more editions (1713 and 1727). We find in the first half of the eighteenth century a fruitful competition between dissenters and Anglicans to publish accounts of the sufferings of their respective religious ancestors in the conflicts of the mid and late seventeenth century. Thus Calamy's account was in part a response to Anthony Wood's hostile treatment of nonconformists and latitudinarians and admiration for high churchmen and nonjurors, forcefully expressed in *Athenae Oxonienses* (two volumes, 1691–92). In turn, John Walker's *An Attempt towards Recovering an Account of the Numbers and Sufferings of the Clergy of the Church of England* (1714) was a defence of the episcopal church of the Interregnum occasioned by Calamy's work. Walker drew for some of his portraits on Izaak Walton's life of Robert Sanderson (1678): Sanderson, who became Bishop of Lincoln after the Restoration, had his Common Prayer Book forced from him and torn by Cromwellian soldiers when he attempted to use it to conduct a service.[37] Lives of many influential mid and late seventeenth-century Anglican divines appeared in mid eighteenth-century biographical dictionaries, for example Barrow, Burnet, Glanvill, Patrick, Taylor and Tillotson. Much the most important of biographies of this kind was Thomas Birch's *Life of the Most Reverend Dr John Tillotson, Lord Archbishop of Canterbury* (prefixed to his edition of Tillotson's *Works*, 1752, 2nd enlarged edition, 1753), containing a wealth of quotation from Tillotson's private papers and contemporary published sources. Birch was deeply sympathetic to the figure who was the bugbear of high churchmen and nonjurors but who remained a model to most eighteenth-century Anglicans. Lives of this kind, however, while paying close attention to the subject's views of doctrine, church discipline and relations with other churches, on the whole eschewed the analysis of Christian experience that was essential to the nonconformist and dissenting traditions and that was to play such an important part in the Evangelical Revival.

36 *Reliquiae Baxterianae*, Part 3, ¶¶ 202–8; Edmund Calamy, *An Abridgment of Mr Baxter's History of his Life and Times* (London, 1702), ch. 9.
37 Izaak Walton, 'The Life of Dr Robert Sanderson', in *The Lives of John Donne Sir Henry Wotton Richard Hooker George Herbert and Robert Sanderson*, intro. George Saintsbury (London: Oxford University Press, 1927; rpt 1966), pp. 382–3.

The communication of experience in the form of journals, autobiographies, biographies and letters was crucial to the spread of the revival. The most important figure in this respect was John Wesley, who in addition to editing and publishing works of practical divinity was particularly interested in making known the exemplary experience of individuals both dead and living, as described by themselves or by others, in order to encourage his readers (the traditional motive) and test the validity of his own doctrines. From 1740 to 1791, he published extracts from his *Journal* in twenty-one parts (the last part appeared posthumously), covering his travels in Georgia, England, Germany and Ireland, describing his encounters, reading and spiritual experiences, with examples of conversations he had and letters he exchanged, and testifying to the initially hostile and later much more welcoming response to his role as evangelist.[38] It is unique both as a personal record published over a fifty-year period and as the fullest contemporary history of the development of Arminian Methodist doctrine and organisation. George Whitefield's accounts of his early life (1740, 1747) and his journals relating his experiences in England and America (1738–41) drew far more hostile comments than Wesley's did from the pulpit and in fiction; critics wrongly assumed that he preached faith instead of works, and disliked what they regarded as his emphasis on feeling instead of practice. In *A Short Account of God's Dealings with the Reverend Mr George Whitefield* (1740) he naively gave several hostages to fortune (he said, for example, that the fact he was born in an inn helped make him a suitable follower of Jesus, and that God called him 'from drawing wine for drunkards, to draw water out of the wells of salvation'), and he cut many objectionable passages of this kind for the edition of 1756.[39] It is important to note the transatlantic dimension of this literature of the revival: editions of Whitefield's *Short Account* and journals were published in Philadelphia and Boston, and achieved much larger sales in America than in England. This was partly because theologically he had more in common with New England Congregationalists than with most of the English clergy.[40]

Wesley was as much concerned with the experience of others as with his own. He edited and published a number of short lives as models for his

38 *Journals and Diaries*, ed. W. Reginald Ward and Richard P. Heitzenrater, *The Works of John Wesley*, vols. 18–24 (Nashville, TN: Abingdon Press, 1988–2003).
39 *Whitefield's Journals, To which is Prefixed his 'Short Account' and 'Further Account'*, ed. William Wale, facsimile with introduction by William V. Davis (Gainesville, FL: Scholars' Facsimiles and Reprints, 1969), pp. 27, 31.
40 Hugh Amory, 'The New England Book Trade, 1713–1790', in *A History of the Book in America*, vol. 1, *The Colonial Book in the Atlantic World*, ed. Hugh Amory and David D. Hall (Cambridge: Cambridge University Press, 2000), pp. 328–30.

preachers, the most important being his abridgement of Jonathan Edwards' *An Account of the Life of the Late Reverend Mr David Brainerd* (Boston, 1749, enlarged Edinburgh, 1765) as *An Extract of the Life of the Late Rev. Mr David Brainerd* (1768, reprinted several times). This biography-cum-journal of a missionary to the Indians who died of tuberculosis in Edwards' house in Northampton, Massachusetts, was required reading for Wesley's preachers: he recommended that they should follow Brainerd in 'total deadness to the world, and in fervent love to God and man'.[41] Wesley also began a monthly publication in 1778, *The Arminian Magazine* (continued from 1798 as *The Methodist Magazine*), partly to counter the effects of evangelical Calvinism, but also to disseminate 'the experience of pious persons, the greatest part of whom are still alive'.[42] The most important of the lives and letters he included were the autobiographies he commissioned from his preachers, which were subject to his stringent stylistic demands for clarity and plainness.[43] Some of the lives have an impact similar to that of Bunyan's *Grace Abounding*, to which their authors acknowledged their debt. For example, John Haime, a soldier who fought at the battle of Dettingen in Germany against the French in 1743, described his struggles with Satan and the effects of God's displeasure in terms that were physical as well as mental: he wept and howled, blood gushed from his nose and mouth, he thought he was on fire.[44]

The naiveté and directness of accounts such as Whitefield's and Haime's clearly differentiate them from more sophisticated works written for politer audiences who were fearful of enthusiasm. Doddridge's *Some Remarkable Passages in the Life of the Honourable Col. James Gardiner* (1747) was a conversion narrative of the close friend Doddridge described as a Christian hero, a one-time rake who was killed fighting the Jacobites at the Battle of Prestonpans. Doddridge had the difficult dual aim of persuading the doubting reader that Gardiner's experiences were not the product of enthusiasm and the devout reader that religious rapture must have a rational basis, and his style reflects this difficulty. Despite this complication, and the embarrassed reaction of some of Doddridge's friends, it was to become one of the most popular biographies in the revival.[45] It influenced John Newton, a former slave trader, whose own

41 *Minutes of Several Conversations*, in *The Works of the Rev. John Wesley*, 3rd edn, ed. Thomas Jackson, 14 vols. (London: Wesleyan-Methodist Book-Room, 1831), vol. VIII, p. 328. See Rivers, 'Strangers and Pilgrims', pp. 195–6; Rivers, 'Dissenting and Methodist Books', pp. 148–9.
42 *Arminian Magazine*, 1 (1778), vi.
43 Edited (with revisions) by Thomas Jackson as *The Lives of Early Methodist Preachers*, 3rd edn, 6 vols. (London: Wesleyan Conference Office, 1865–6).
44 *Arminian Magazine*, 3 (1780), 266–7.
45 See Rivers, *Reason, Grace, and Sentiment*, vol. 1, pp. 197–203.

brief account of his life at sea and conversion, *An Authentic Narrative of Some Remarkable and Interesting Particulars in the Life of* ***** (1764), was written in epistolary form to his friend Thomas Haweis, thus bringing together the evangelical interest in letters and lives and emphasising the importance of communicating Christian experience. Newton is an important example of a mid eighteenth-century churchman of dissenting origins (he was ordained with some difficulty shortly before the publication of the *Narrative*) who, like Whitefield, maintained close links with dissenters and rediscovered the Calvinism of the pre-Civil War Church of England. In turn he helped shape the theological development of the clergyman Thomas Scott, who described in his autobiography, *The Force of Truth: An Authentic Narrative* (1779), how with great reluctance he step by step abandoned his Socinianism and through his reading rediscovered the doctrines of justification by faith and predestination. Though Scott introduces his narrative as the dramatic conflict between his heart and his conscience, it is an account of an intellectual and historical process in which he learns that the doctrines scorned by himself and others as Methodist enthusiasm were the traditional doctrines of the Church of England.

Christian song

A very wide range of poetry of different kinds in the late seventeenth and eighteenth centuries dealt directly or indirectly with the subject of religion, and poets assumed on the part of their readers a general knowledge of biblical narrative and the arguments for natural religion, even when particular religious beliefs or practices were treated as objects of satire or as metaphors for another subject. Poetry which was essentially religious in its subject matter, concerned with praising God and explicating his two books of nature and Scripture, might take the form of long narrative or discursive poetry, usually in blank verse, or shorter lyrics, hymns and adaptations of the psalms, some of these intended for use in divine service. The greatest and most influential of all religious poems in English, John Milton's *Paradise Lost* (1667, revised 1674), widely read and cited right through the eighteenth century by Anglicans as much as dissenters despite Milton's well-known hatred of episcopacy and defence of the execution of Charles I, was drawn on to support both natural and revealed religion. The morning hymn of Adam and Eve (*Paradise Lost* v.153–208), itself based on Psalms 19 and 148 and the Benedicite from the Book of Common Prayer, illustrates the fundamental physico-theological argument that God's attributes of power and goodness are known through his works, which circle the Creator in a continuous act of praise. Milton's embodiment of this idea underlies the Anglican Joseph Addison's ode in *The Spectator* no. 465 (23 August 1712), in which the heavenly bodies sing of their divine maker to the ear of reason, and the deist James Thomson's 'A Hymn on the Seasons' (1730), intended as a conclusion to his long meditative and descriptive poem *The Seasons*, where with less orthodoxy the seasons in their round 'Are but the *varied* God'.[46] In contrast, Milton's explanation in Book III of the doctrine of the atonement, the Son's sacrifice of himself on behalf of fallen man to meet the demands of God's justice, was repeatedly quoted by the evangelical clergyman James Hervey in his prose dialogue *Theron and Aspasio* (three volumes, 1755), in which the polite gentleman Theron is converted by his friend Aspasio to unfashionable and impolite Reformation theology. The other religious poem on which Hervey drew heavily here and in his earlier very popular prose *Meditations and Contemplations* (1746–47) was the clergyman Edward Young's *Night Thoughts* (nine *Nights*, 1742–6), which held its place as one of the three best-selling long poems of the eighteenth century well into the nineteenth, the others being Thomson's *Seasons* and the evangelical William Cowper's *The Task* (1785). The deist Lorenzo of *Night Thoughts* is converted through dialogue with the inspired Christian poet. In singing 'Immortal man', and thus supplying the deficiencies of Alexander Pope's *Essay on Man* (1733–4), Young hoped to reach Milton's 'Strain' (*Night the First*, lines 450, 452).[47]

It was the hope of several writers in the early eighteenth century that a new inspired Christian poetry, following the example of the biblical poets and prophets as Milton had, would emerge to replace the profane poetry that emulated the classics. Proponents of this view such as the critic John Dennis in *The Grounds of Criticism in Poetry* (1704) and Isaac Watts in the revised preface to the enlarged second edition of *Horae Lyricae* (1709) offered as models among other books of the Bible Job, the Psalms, Isaiah and the Revelation of St John. George Frideric Handel's oratorios of the 1730s and 1740s based on biblical texts, notably *Israel in Egypt* and *Messiah*, can be seen as contributions to this movement. Interest in the Old Testament as poetry was magnified in mid century by the lectures of Robert Lowth, Professor of Poetry at Oxford in the 1740s, whose Latin *Praelectiones de Sacra Poesi Hebraeorum* (1753), translated as *Lectures on the Sacred Poesy of the Hebrews* (1787), explained for the first time to English readers how Hebrew verse was patterned. Two main strands of non-narrative, non-discursive devotional poetry that was essentially biblical in emphasis emerged in the eighteenth century: lyrics and odes that were written

46 James Thomson, *The Seasons*, ed. James Sambrook (Oxford: Clarendon Press, 1981), p. 254.
47 Edward Young, *Night Thoughts*, ed. Stephen Cornford (Cambridge: Cambridge University Press, 1989), p. 48.

to be read, and hymns and psalms that formed part of divine service. There were sixteenth- and seventeenth-century antecedents for both the devotional lyric and the metrical psalm, but the congregational hymn was an extraordinarily important late seventeenth- and early eighteenth-century innovation in both worship and literature. Some writers moved between genres designed for reading or congregational singing, for example the dissenter Watts, the high churchman Christopher Smart, and the evangelical Cowper; some concentrated on the latter, for example the Methodists John and Charles Wesley and the evangelical Newton.

The most important figure in the development of eighteenth-century hymnody was Isaac Watts. His first publication in verse, *Horae Lyricae* (1706), was aimed at a polite audience and contained several devotional poems (he had already written 200 hymns, but decided to publish the more elevated poems first to test public reaction). He followed this with *Hymns and Spiritual Songs* (1707, enlarged 1709), designed for a more popular audience, and *The Psalms of David imitated in the Language of the New Testament* (1719): the prefaces to the 1709 edition of *Hymns* and to *Psalms* both constituted important manifestos. The two volumes, usually printed in one, were to become a publishing phenomenon of massive proportions. Watts divided his *Hymns* into three books: paraphrases of biblical texts, general divine subjects, and hymns for the Lord's Supper. His version of the Psalms was not intended as a translation: as the title made clear, they were 'imitated in the Language of the New Testament and applied to the Christian State and Worship'. One of his best-known hymns, 'Jesus shall reign where'er the sun', is an imitation of Psalm 72, part 2; another, 'Our God our help in ages past', is based on Psalm 90: 1–5. Watts was not the first to introduce hymn singing into dissenting services, but he made it customary, and he regarded this as his principal service to dissent.

Several of Watts' hymns appeared (with modifications) in John Wesley's first hymn book, *A Collection of Psalms and Hymns* (published at Charlestown, 1737, during his unhappy American mission); it also contained adaptations of poems from George Herbert's *The Temple* (1633) and translations of German hymns. In making hymn singing a central feature of worship Wesley owed a debt both to English dissent and to German Moravians and pietists; though he was to quarrel for theological reasons with the English Moravians, their passionate religious language gave a distinctive colour to early Methodist hymnody. Wesley edited and published several other collections under this title and that of *Hymns and Sacred Poems* (1739), the latter being the first collection to contain hymns by Charles Wesley. By far the most important was *A Collection of Hymns for the Use of the People called Methodists* (1780), containing 525 hymns, of which the majority were by Charles Wesley; as its title suggests, this was the standard hymn book for the Methodist societies. John Wesley described it as 'a little body of experimental and practical divinity'. It is arranged in five parts, 'according to the experience of real Christians', including hymns exhorting sinners in part 1 (beginning with 'O for a thousand tongues to sing'), and those for believers groaning for full redemption in part 4 ('Love divine, all loves excelling' is in this category).[48] The description and arrangement (though not some of the theology) are reminiscent of a dissenting handbook, but Charles Wesley drew in several of his hymns on Anglican sources, notably Young's *Night Thoughts* and the Book of Common Prayer. Worship by the Methodist societies was always meant by the Wesley brothers as an adjunct to, not a replacement for, worship in parish churches. In this their practice differed markedly from that of the dissenters, whose ancestors had repudiated the Church of England liturgy, and of more conservative Anglicans.

In the later sixteenth century the Book of Common Prayer was supplemented by the singing of metrical psalms from *The Whole Booke of Psalmes* (1562), known from two of its contributors as 'Sternhold and Hopkins'; at the end of the seventeenth century this 'old version' was officially replaced by *A New Version of the Psalms of David* (1696) by Nahum Tate and Nicholas Brady, though Sternhold and Hopkins continued in use. Hymns as distinct from metrical psalms had no place in traditional Anglican worship. An interesting but failed attempt both to replace the 'new version' and to provide a hymn book suitable for the Church of England was made by the layman Christopher Smart in *A Translation of the Psalms of David*, published together with *Hymns and Spiritual Songs for the Fasts and Festivals of the Church of England* (1765).[49] Smart had earlier made a mark with his five blank verse poems on the divine attributes, a standard topic of natural religion, each of which won the Seatonian Prize at Cambridge (1750–6), but his subsequent religious poems, including *A Song to David* (1763), had little impact. (*Jubilate Agno*, written *c.* 1758–63 during his incarceration in a madhouse, was first published in 1939.) His hymns unusually are arranged not according to the process of salvation, as in the collections by dissenters and Methodists, but to the calendar of the Christian year, from New Year's Day to the Holy Innocents (December 28).

---

48 John Wesley, *A Collection of Hymns for the Use of the People called Methodists*, ed. Franz Hildebrandt and Oliver A. Beckerlegge, *The Works of John Wesley*, vol. VII (Nashville: Abingdon Press, first pub. Oxford: Oxford University Press, 1983), p. 74.

49 See the introductions to Christopher Smart, *Religious Poetry 1763–1771*, in *The Poetical Works of Christopher Smart*, ed. Karina Williamson and Marcus Walsh, 6 vols. (Oxford: Clarendon Press, 1980–96), vol. II, and *A Translation of the Psalms of David*, in Smart, *Poetical Works*, vol. III.

Smart's inability to find an audience differentiates his hymns sharply from those produced in collaboration by Newton and Cowper, *Olney Hymns* (1779). The great majority were written by the curate Newton, not as part of the church liturgy but for prayer meetings he held in a special room in Olney; sixty-seven were by the layman Cowper. This evangelical collection is more closely related to dissenting and Methodist hymnody than to the structure and emphases of the Book of Common Prayer. Newton divided the hymns into three books, 'On select Passages of Scripture', 'On Occasional Subjects', and 'On the Rise, Progress, Changes, and Comforts of the Spiritual Life'. His famous hymn 'Amazing grace', entitled 'Faith's review and expectation', is based on 1 Chronicles 17:16–17 and appears in book 1; Cowper's 'GOD moves in a mysterious way', entitled 'Light shining out of darkness', appears in book 3. Cowper's two important later volumes, *Poems* (1782) and *The Task* (1785), employed Popean couplets and Miltonic blank verse respectively to argue for a new evangelical voice in poetry; the success of these books suggests the extent to which by the end of the eighteenth century the Evangelical Revival had infiltrated not just popular religion but polite literature.

Literary criticism and the rise of national literary history

LAWRENCE LIPKING

One story that eighteenth-century critics liked to tell about themselves was the triumph of criticism itself, its rise and progress from modest beginnings before the Restoration to a respected place in English literature. 'Dryden may be properly considered as the father of English criticism, as the writer who first taught us to determine upon principles the merit of composition', Samuel Johnson wrote in his *Prefaces, Biographical and Critical, to the Works of the English Poets* (1779–81).[1] Earlier poets like Shakespeare 'wrote without rules', and a few hints had been given by Jonson and Cowley, 'but Dryden's *Essay on Dramatick Poetry* [1668] was the first regular and valuable treatise on the art of writing'.[2] Since that time, Johnson continues, sound critical principles had become 'universally practised'; even the common reader was now a good critic.

The success story of criticism is exemplified by Johnson's own *Prefaces*. Commissioned to enhance a massive collection of English poetry from Cowley to Gray, they were soon printed separately as Johnson's *Lives of the English Poets*, which went through many editions. Readers valued the critical effort to sort and judge the poets who represented the nation, and the pleasures of poetry seemed incomplete without the pleasures of talking about it. Johnson's stature as a leading authority on language and literature as well as the conduct of life contributed to the keen public interest in his opinions. But the habit of supplying works with critical prefaces had been ingrained in English since the time of Dryden, who constantly formulated principles to justify what he published. Without such a preface, a new text might look naked. Each time an eighteenth-century writer ventures another kind of prose fiction, for instance, the reader must first be instructed on the rules of the genre. Thus Delariviere

---

1 Samuel Johnson, *Lives of the English Poets*, ed. G. B. Hill (3 vols., Oxford: Clarendon Press, 1905), vol. I, p. 410.
2 *Ibid.*, vol. I, p. 411.

Manley introduced *The Secret History of Queen Zarah and the Zarazians* (1705) by translating a French essay that justified the psychological truth of her own sort of 'History', and Henry Fielding went still further, in *Joseph Andrews* (1742) and *Tom Jones* (1749), by explaining his critical principles not only in prefaces but also in chapters within each 'comic Epic-Poem in Prose'. Evidently the task of a writer was not only to provide entertaining reading but also to teach the audience how to read.

A growing reading public stands behind this surge of criticism. As the population of literate men and women increased and more and more books were printed, a new set of experts took charge of sifting the good from the bad and moulding the tastes of readers. Addison's critical essays in *The Spectator* (1711–12) were often said to have refined the intellectual and literary life of the nation. 'By the blandishments of gentleness and facility', Johnson wrote, 'he has made Milton an universal favourite, with whom readers of every class think it necessary to be pleased.'[3] Beginning in the 1680s, periodicals set out to describe and evaluate 'the works of the learned', and later the founding of *The Gentleman's Magazine* (1731), *The London Magazine* (1732), *The Monthly Review* (1749), and in 1756 both Johnson's short-lived *Literary Magazine* and Smollett's ambitious *Critical Review*, institutionalised the process of superintending the world of letters. Such journals traded on a public desire for widely accepted critical standards.

The attention to readers also changed the orientation of criticism. Previous English critics had written guides for fledgling poets, as in George Puttenham's *Arte of English Poesie* (1589), or defences of the poet's trade, as in Sir Philip Sidney's *Apology for Poetrie* (1598). Books that spelled out rules for poets to follow continued to be popular in the eighteenth century; Edward Bysshe's *Art of English Poetry* (1702) went through nine editions, and Joseph Trapp's prescriptive series of Oxford lectures, *Praelectiones Poeticae* (1711–19), was translated as *Lectures on Poetry* in 1742. But most influential Restoration and eighteenth-century criticism addressed art from the reader's point of view. The Horatian formula of 'instruction and delight', originally offered as advice to the craftsman, eventually served as the universal principle or final cause of poetry. 'The only end of writing', according to Johnson, 'is to enable the readers better to enjoy life, or better to endure it.'[4] Hence the central issues of criticism were defined or adjudicated in terms of effects on readers.

---

3 *Ibid.*, vol. II, p. 147.
4 'Review of [Soame Jenyns] *A Free Inquiry into the Nature and Origin of Evil*', in *Samuel Johnson*, ed. Donald Greene (Oxford: Oxford University Press, 1984), p. 536.

This readjustment of critical priorities stands out clearly in the long debate about the unities of time, place and action in drama. Historically, insistence on the unities might be understood as a formal requirement derived from the ancients, as a test of the skill of the playwright, or as a demand that faithful imitations of life should cleave to one chain of events in a single place and time. By these criteria some purists concluded that Shakespeare lacked art. In British criticism, however, the issue eventually contracted to whether or not an audience could accept rapid shifts in time, place and action, and the example of Shakespeare proved that violating the unities need not interfere with the power to instruct and delight. A similar logic grounds the discussion of many other traditional concerns – for instance, the nature of beauty, the use of rhyme, or the presence of pagan gods in Christian art. In each case, eighteenth-century British arguments reach conclusions by referring to effects on the mind, not to formal or metaphysical absolutes. The influence of Locke accelerated this critical shift towards readers' responses. New, empirical investigations set out to explore the psychological bases of art. Tragedy, for example, posed a difficult question: why did events that would be unbearably painful if witnessed in the real world give pleasure on the stage? Whatever the answer might be, it had to be sought in laws of human nature.

Not all readers respond in the same way, however. Despite widespread agreement that critical principles must be rooted in human nature, critics often disagreed about what was essentially human. As early as the mid seventeenth century, such philosophers and divines as Henry More and Isaac Barrow suggested that people are naturally disposed to be good, and this belief gradually prevailed until it reached a peak with the vogue of 'the man of feeling' in the 1770s. Yet doctrines of original sin or Hobbesian self-interest also had many adherents. These irreconcilable views of human nature led to opposing critical schools – for instance, some critics might favour sentiment, and others satire. Similarly, philosophers persistently sought a touchstone for universal standards of taste. Most eighteenth-century critics depended on the assumption that perceptions of art, like perceptions of wholesome and rotten food, were commonly shared, so that everyone could learn to distinguish good art from bad. So long as *prejudice* was controlled by *good sense*, David Hume argued in 1757, the principles of taste would be 'nearly, if not entirely the same in all men'.[5] But even Hume conceded that in practice tastes differed, if only because of 'the different humours of particular men' and 'the particular manners and

---

5 David Hume, 'Of the Standard of Taste', in *Essays, Moral, Political, and Literary* (1777), ed. Eugene F. Miller (Indianapolis, IN: Liberty Classics, 1987), p. 241.

opinions of our age and country'.[6] The laws of human nature could not assure any consensus on whether Racine or Shakespeare wrote better plays.

Nor did readers all embrace the same interests, allegiances and parties. From a dissenter's point of view, an appeal to the reader or common reader was likely to mask the genuine diversity of readers beneath a specious veil of uniformity. *The* reader would always be a mental construct, designed not only to take in a large public but also to leave out the wrong sorts of people, those who belonged to an outcast religion, gender or class. Sceptical English critics often compared this ideal constructed audience with the actual persons who came to see a play. Thus Aphra Behn addresses the lively preface of her comedy *The Dutch Lover* (1673) to 'Good, Sweet, Honey, Sugar-candied READER', thereby mocking potential critics as well as writers who fawn on them, and she goes on to describe 'the most assiduous Disciples of the Stage' as 'the fondest and lewdest crew about this Town', completely indifferent to 'musty rules of Unity' or anything but a good time.[7] The rise of criticism in the Restoration is constantly ruffled by gibes at every attempt to set rules or legislate the unanimity of readers. In a nation whose deep wounds were far from healed, any definition of binding critical principles evoked the Act of Uniformity (1662), which required clergymen to subscribe to the Thirty-Nine Articles of the Anglican church. Nonconformist and Catholic writers would not subscribe to such rules.

Yet constructing an ideal set of well-informed readers might also be viewed as crucial to building a nation. Insofar as *An Essay of Dramatick Poesie* inaugurates a new age of criticism, it does so by deliberately fashioning a model of what an English critical school might be in a revived, triumphant and civil kingdom. Dryden sets his dialogue on the day of a naval battle, when three persons of 'witt and Quality' and one up-and-coming parvenu poet ('Neander', or Dryden himself) coast on the Thames and listen to distant cannons. As the Dutch vessels retreat the sound gradually fades, and the four friends celebrate victory by debating how well modern English drama compares with the best of the ancients, the French, and the age of Jonson, Fletcher and Shakespeare. The *Essay* strives for balance; each participant is allowed to make valid points. Indeed, the dialogical method itself ensures a happy medium of ideas. The initial definition of a play as 'A just and lively Image of Humane Nature, representing its Passions and Humours, and the Changes of Fortune to which

6 *Ibid.*, p. 243.
7 *The Works of Aphra Behn*, ed. Janet Todd, 7 vols. (London: Pickering & Chatto, 1992–6), vol. v, pp. 160–1.

it is subject; for the Delight and Instruction of Mankind',[8] makes room for each turn in the debate that follows. If ancient and French plays present images that are more regular and therefore more just, the images of English plays are more lively; if the French excel in representing passions, the English excel at humours and changes of fortune; if the ancients are more instructive, the moderns are more delightful; if the blank verse of Shakespeare's generation was closer to nature, the rhyme of current playwrights raises nature to a higher pitch. This exchange of ideas results in clearer critical principles but no winners and losers; and when the friends finally part, their conversation has not been exhausted and might well be resumed another day.

The illusion of an urbane and elegant symposium, intensely concerned with the state of the nation yet also floating free from particular, narrow interests, accounts for much of the charm of the *Essay*. By focussing on drama, Dryden can proceed as if the Civil Wars never happened. No one needs to dwell on the time when the theatres shut down, and now all parties join in opposing the Dutch. Nor are practical concerns allowed to intrude. All four participants in the dialogue were court poets, in fact, and wrote for the theatre; in 1664, the year before the conversation is supposed to have taken place, Sedley and Buckhurst ('Lisideius' and 'Eugenius') had both contributed to a translation of Corneille's *Pompey the Great*, and Dryden and Howard ('Crites') had already begun to quarrel about the use of rhyme. But the *Essay* puts them above the fray, not only by giving them classical names but also by detaching them from the wars of the London stage. Dryden fashions a theatre of the mind, where players and plebeians have no place. When the *Essay* was written, the major achievements of Restoration drama still lay in the future; *The Indian Queen*, on which Dryden and Howard collaborated in 1663, had won more praise for its spectacle than for any poetic merit. Yet Neander boldly claims that the playwrights of his own day 'have far surpass'd all the Ancients, and the Modern Writers of other Countreys'.[9] Dryden anticipates the theatrical triumphs that he and his companions hope to win, and declares a victory while the battle has only begun.

The main triumph of the *Essay*, however, belongs to the critical spirit itself. Practically speaking, the English critics and playwrights of Dryden's time had plenty of reasons to feel defensive. The Civil Wars had left the nation weak and divided; the king and his supporters returned from France with a sense of cultural and intellectual inferiority that would persist for decades if not

---

8 *The Works of John Dryden*, ed. H. T. Swedenberg et al., 20 vols. (Berkeley and Los Angeles: University of California Press, 1956–2002), vol. xvii, p. 15.
9 *Ibid.*, vol. xvii, p. 64.

for generations; English literary theory had been negligible compared to the confident and flourishing French critical establishment; new modes and styles of drama had passed England by. All this is largely absent from the surface of the *Essay*. Although Lisideius makes a case for the superior decorum of French theatre, Neander cleverly turns the tables by attributing the recent accomplishments of Molière and others to their knack of 'imitating afar off the quick turns and graces of the *English* Stage'.[10] Nor does the dialogue admit the superiority of French critical standards. The cultivated and well-informed English patriots command respect and pass judgement without hesitation. Dryden associates himself with an aristocracy of taste; as a professional writer, he does not bow to the noblemen with whom he converses.

Yet the fraternal critical conversation manufactured by Dryden, high-minded and public-spirited, remained an ideal with little relation to practice. Within a year of the *Essay*'s publication, Howard and Dryden rancorously attacked each other's principles, and in his preface to *Secret Love* (1668) Dryden confessed that his effort to write by the rules 'is a commendation which many of our Poets now despise, and a beauty which our common Audiences do not easily discern'.[11] The aristocratic and loyalist bias of the *Essay* could hardly sway critics outside its charmed circle. To some extent English national pride depended on the rough freedom and independence of citizens who spoke their minds. When Margaret Cavendish, soon to be Duchess of Newcastle, defended Shakespeare in her *CCXI Sociable Letters* (1664), she scorned those critics who would censure a play because it expressed 'a Clown's, or Fool's Humour, Expressions, Phrases, Garbs, Manners, Actions, Words, and Course of Life'; Shakespeare was great precisely because he had the 'Wit, to Express to the Life all Sorts of Persons, of what Quality, Profession, Degree, Breeding, or Birth soever'. From this point of view, the attempt to codify the rules of dramatic poetry, and to restrict the stage to 'persons of quality', might snuff the vital flame of English art.

The challenge to Dryden's imaginary ideal of a nation took many forms. In criticism, perhaps the most effective rejoinder came from Thomas Rymer in *The Tragedies of the Last Age Considered* (1677) and *A Short View of Tragedy* (1692). Rymer began his critical career by translating René Rapin's *Reflections on Aristotle's Treatise of Poesie, Containing the Necessary, Rational, and Universal Rules for Epick, Dramatick, and the Other Sorts of Poetry* (1674), and his later work combines a French zeal for universal rules with an English appeal to

---

10 *Ibid.*, vol. XVII, p. 45.
11 *Ibid.*, vol. IX, p. 115.

plain common sense and 'Poetical Justice' (a phrase he invented). Stylistically, his colloquial and truculent prose clashes with Dryden's politeness. But more important, his harsh views of English tragedy deny the national heritage celebrated by Dryden. Not only Jonson and Fletcher but Shakespeare himself are ridiculed for plots that 'delude our senses, disorder our thoughts, addle our brain, pervert our affections, hair our imaginations, corrupt our appetite, and fill our head with vanity, confusion, Tintamarre, and Jingle-jangle'.[12] In Dryden's Essay Lisideius had singled out Rollo (The Bloody Brother, 1639) as 'one Tragedy of ours, whose Plot has that uniformity and unity of design in it which I have commended in the French'.[13] Tragedies of the Last Age spends many pages deriding the grossness of Rollo, its failure 'either to move pitty or terror, either to delight or instruct'.[14] Dryden's first, informal response, written in his copy of Rymer's book, is characteristically conciliatory; he declares that 'the Model of Tragedy he has here given, is Excellent, and extream Correct; but that it is not the only Model of all Tragedy'.[15] Pity and terror, Dryden argues, do not exhaust the possibilities of tragedy; had Aristotle seen the variety of natural passions expressed by Shakespeare, he might well have changed his mind. A few years later, in 'The Grounds of Criticism in Tragedy' (1679), Dryden conceded still more to Rymer: contemporary English playwrights had imitated Shakespeare's bombast, not his universal mind: 'we who Ape his sounding words, have nothing of his thought, but are all outside; there is not so much as a dwarf within our Giants cloaths'.[16]

Rymer was not propitiated. A Short View of Tragedy mocks Dryden as well as his heroes and scorches the earth of English tragedy. By 1692 the loyalist's dream of a nation unified under the Stuarts had ended. After the flight of James II, Dryden's enemy Thomas Shadwell succeeded him as poet laureate and historiographer royal, and when Shadwell died in 1692 another enemy, Rymer himself, became the new historiographer. A Short View is most notorious for its disparagement of Othello as 'a Bloody Farce, without salt or savour'.[17] But Dryden believed that the thrust was really directed at him. In a preface to Examen poeticum (1693), he associates Rymer with 'Those who manifestly aim at the destruction of our Poetical Church and State: Who allow nothing to their Country-Men, either of this or of the former Age. These attack the Living

---

12 The Critical Works of Thomas Rymer, ed. Curt A. Zimansky (New Haven, CT: Yale University Press, 1956), p. 164.
13 The Works of John Dryden, vol. XVII, p. 37.
14 The Critical Works of Thomas Rymer, p. 24.
15 The Works of John Dryden, vol. XVII, p. 192.
16 Ibid., vol. XIII, p. 247.
17 The Critical Works of Thomas Rymer, p. 164.

by raking up the Ashes of the Dead: Well knowing that if they can subvert their Original Title to the Stage, we who claim under them, must fall of course'.[18] Here the dismantling of England's proud poetic traditions is explicitly linked to the overthrow of the Stuarts, a revolution that rewrites history in order to break any line of succession. Dryden had fostered the critical myth of an age of Augustus in which the great texts of the past, whether ancient or English, would be born again in new improved forms (as in his own *All for Love*). But another myth, the 'Whig interpretation of literary history', now began to take shape, and in this version the arts became truly refined only in the aftermath of the Glorious Revolution. From that perspective, Dryden's ideal nation had been a false start.

The opposition of these critical and historical views of the nation would be played out often in years to come. As its title announces, Jeremy Collier's *A Short View of the Immorality and Profaneness of the English Stage* (1698) derives from Rymer, and its swipes at Dryden and William Congreve, whom Dryden had proclaimed his poetic heir, recapitulate Rymer's appeals to common sense, the ancients and the rules. History was clearly on Collier's side. The aura of aristocratic privilege that marks Dryden's *Essay* had long since faded, and even the writers under attack were unwilling to defend the lewd language and behaviour exposed in their work. Dryden conceded his offences against 'good manners', and Congreve took refuge in disowning the vicious words he had put in his characters' mouths. But Collier insisted that such faults were not incidental but bred in the blood of the Restoration stage. His cleverest argument accuses the playwrights of vulgarising and defiling the supposedly noble men and women at whom the spectators gape: 'I hope the *Poets* don't intend to revive the old Project of Levelling, and *Vote* down the House of Peers'.[19] Dryden and other camp followers of 'quality', this implies, are in fact the worst enemies of the court; they publicly dishonour their former patrons. As a nonjuring clergyman who would not swear an oath to King William, Collier could hardly be considered a Whig, but *A Short View* did please the king. Repudiating the theatre, the critic had also condemned the old regime. Restoration critical values were in retreat; preachers and playgoers called for a reformation in art.

Yet Dryden's vision of literary history did not lack defenders. The leading critic of the next generation, John Dennis, entered the lists against both *Short Views*, championing not only the virtues of poetic drama but also the

---

18 *The Works of John Dryden*, vol. IV, p. 366.

19 Jeremy Collier, *A Short View of the Immorality and Profaneness of the English Stage* (London, 1698), p. 176.

national honour. *The Impartial Critick* (1693) responds to Rymer by vindicating English poets, particularly Shakespeare, that 'great Genius', and Dryden, whose 'Heroick Verse' (iambic pentameter) is said to be so perfect that 'he will never be exceeded by any Man, unless length of Time makes some strange Alteration in the Tongue'.[20] *The Usefulness of the Stage* (1698) responds to Collier by arguing that the stage is instrumental to the happiness of Englishmen, the welfare of the government and the advancement of religion. Dennis sets out to carry Dryden's work forward. As a literary historian, he tries to balance the claims of the ancients and moderns and thus to prepare the way for an English national school in which the examples of Homer and Virgil, spliced on the native stock of Shakespeare and Milton, will foster still greater glories to come. As a critic, he tries to formulate eternal rules for writing and judging poems. And above all he follows Dryden in the importance he attaches to the mission of the poet and critic, who bring a divine spark home to the people of England. Indeed, for Dennis England is the last best hope of mankind, for there alone poetry still clings to life.

During the first decade of the eighteenth century Dennis was known as 'the Critick', and he took his responsibility seriously. *The Advancement and Reformation of Modern Poetry* (1701) is one of a series of works that raise the stakes of criticism by charging it with the task of uniting poetry and religion. The ancient poets excelled the moderns, he argues, because they understood that the greatest poetry is always religious; but future English poets ought to excel the ancients, since Christianity far surpasses ancient religions. Hence critics must encourage poets to soar to the highest reaches of art, the true sublime of enthusiasm and passion. In *The Grounds of Criticism in Poetry* (1704) Dennis went still further, proposing a magnum opus that would define the nature of poetry and the rules of each poetic genre, enforced by a full review of the works of the best English poets. With heroic immodesty, he claims that his design 'is perhaps the greatest in this kind of Writing, that has been conceiv'd by the Moderns; for 'tis no less than an Attempt to restore and re-establish the noblest Art in every Branch of it'.[21] Dennis associates his critical quest with the sacred role of artists themselves. Since 'the great Design of Arts is to restore the Decays that happen'd to human Nature by the Fall, by restoring Order',[22] the critic who brings back the principles of that order will join in the work of salvation.

---

20 *The Critical Works of John Dennis*, ed. E. N. Hooker, 2 vols. (Baltimore, MD: Johns Hopkins University Press, 1939–43), vol. 1, p. 14.
21 *Ibid.*, vol. 1, p. 334.
22 *Ibid.*, vol. 1, p. 336.

The English public failed to requite this vision. Only seventy-seven sub-scribers were willing to pay a guinea for Dennis' opus, and he never carried it through. Perhaps his ambitions mounted too high to flourish in the temperate English air, where critics were supposed to know their place. Enthusiasm, Locke had said, rises 'from the Conceits of a warmed and over-weening Brain',[23] and a critic who not only recommended enthusiastic passions but obviously felt them himself was bound to be regarded with suspicion. As the new century progressed, good taste became the quality most appreciated in a critic. Dennis too made much of good taste, though he believed that it had been degenerating since the days of Charles II, when a circle of aristocratic and educated men had been able to guide the public. Nowadays 'the Vulgar', more interested in politics than poetry, had taken over the arts, and they were incapable of recognising the sublime or entering its spirit. At any rate, the new audience for criticism was not in tune with Dennis or his tastes. His strong opinions came to seem impolite, and the rules he defined seemed rigid. Most readers thought that their own tastes and those of the nation had been improving, not declining, and they preferred critics more ready to bend with the times.

Two complex and interrelated issues help to explain why Dennis' ambitions were doomed to be thwarted. The first was the struggle to rewrite English his-tory in order to accommodate present concerns. William Camden's *Britannia* (1586; English translation, 1610) had spurred antiquarian interest in local tra-ditions and annals, and after the Restoration a remarkable group of medieval scholars foraged for precedents to support their own views of church and state. Many of these scholars rebelled against any version of literary history that found its pattern of perfection in the Stuart court. It is no accident that both Rymer and Collier followed their criticism of Restoration drama with important antiquarian research that put a rich and diversified past in place of Dryden's emerging nation. In 1700 attacks on William III as a 'foreigner' outside the pure native strain provoked Defoe's poem *The True-Born English-man* (1701), which mocks the ancestor-worship of Jacobites and celebrates the 'Mongrel, half-bred Race' – Pict, Britain, Scot, Norwegian, Danish, Anglo-Saxon, Norman-French – that mixed into 'That Het'rogeneous Thing, *An Englishman*' (lines 340, 335). From this point of view it was not blue-blooded Augustus but Romulus and Remus, of obscure pedigree, who stood for the modern English breed. Six years later the Act of Union, yoking Scotland to

---

23 John Locke, *An Essay concerning Human Understanding*, ed. Peter H. Nidditch (Oxford: Clarendon Press, 1975), p. 699.

England and Wales, created a kingdom, Great Britain, that would inevitably require new myths of origin to justify its existence.

The British audience for literature was also increasingly heterogeneous. At the turn of the century, the London stage that Dennis found so degenerate was dominated by female playwrights, and the taste of playgoers, he grumbled, had sunk to that of 'a Green-sickness Girl' or 'an Hysterick Woman, who is cherish'd by a Stink, and sickens at a Perfume'.[24] Now anyone, even a woman, could pass for a critic. This bitter complaint responds to a fast-growing, confident public that hardly feels the want of a classical education, as well as to the writers and critics who flatter that public. Addison's famous praise for the 'old Song of *Chevy-Chase*' in *Spectators* 70 and 74 (1711) especially bothered Dennis. The essays take patriotic pride in pointing out the beauties of 'the favourite Ballad of the common People of *England*',[25] a song that has appealed to cognoscenti like Sidney and Jonson as well as to the rabble. Addison compares 'Chevy Chase' to the epics of Homer and Virgil, whose 'majestick Simplicity' is matched by the native bard's natural genius. A union of high and low inspires the critic's applause: the ballad describes the blood feuds of English and Scottish barons in order 'to deter Men from such unnatural Contentions' and bring about peace, and the critic describes the ballad in order to demonstrate that 'the same Paintings of Nature which recommend it to the most ordinary Reader, will appear Beautiful to the most refined'.[26] But Dennis was scandalised. No man of good sense could believe that the rabble were suited to judge the 'Human Nature exalted' of great poetry, or that the 'vile and trivial' doggerel of 'Chevy Chase' could possibly rival the sublime language of Virgil and Milton.[27] If Addison was not jesting, Dennis surmised, he must be pandering to the crowd.

Furthermore, such deference to the opinions of common people threatened the dignity of the nation. If literary history were no more than a chronicle of popular taste, in which vulgar and hearty Englishness counted more than the most discriminating classical judgement, then the decay of Britain could not be repaired. In the new, inclusive republic of readers, only one person would never be welcome: the critic himself. Dennis' fears were not groundless. Richard Steele had once been his friend, but throughout *The Tatler* and *Spectator* Steele enjoys baiting those who uphold the rules: 'of all Mortals a Critick is the silliest; for by inuring himself to examine all Things, whether they are

---

24 *The Critical Works of John Dennis*, vol. II, p. 167.
25 *The Spectator*, ed. Donald F. Bond, 5 vols. (Oxford: Clarendon Press, 1965), vol. I, p. 298.
26 *Ibid.*, vol. I, pp. 298, 299.
27 *The Critical Works of John Dennis*, vol. II, p. 37.

of Consequence or not, he never looks upon any Thing but with a Design of passing Sentence upon it; by which Means, he is never a Companion, but always a Censor'.[28] In *Tatler* 165 (1710) Addison contrasts sensible people with pedants: 'Of this shallow Species there is not a more importunate, empty, and conceited Animal than that which is generally known by the Name of a Critick.' An anecdote clinches the point, when Sir Timothy Tattle's pedantic opinions are comically punctured by a young lady he tries to impress, who 'had that natural Sense which makes her a better Judge than a Thousand Criticks'.[29] Versions of this tribute to common sense abound in the eighteenth century, as when Richardson's heroine Harriet Byron, in *Sir Charles Grandison* (1753–4), uses her home-bred eloquence to vanquish Mr Walden, a university pedant, in literary debate. Her taste has been formed by readings that grow on native soil: the Bible, good English books or classics in English translations, and Addison's essays; she needs no more.

A second issue, the war between Ancients and Moderns, also encouraged a preference for taste over rules. In its widest ramifications this debate might be viewed as a reorganisation of all human knowledge, as the overthrow of dead traditions by scientific methods, or as an argument between universal and relativistic moral values. In the narrower context of English criticism, however, the quarrel tended to focus on matters of education and taste. Paradoxically, the leading 'Moderns' were classical scholars like William Wotton and Richard Bentley, whose learning equipped them to analyse ancient texts, while the leading 'Ancients' were amateurs like Sir William Temple and Jonathan Swift, who cherished the spirit but not the letter of a few favourite works. When Temple pronounced that the Greek *Epistles of Phalaris* 'have more Race, more Spirit, more Force of Wit and Genius, than any others I have ever seen, either ancient or modern' ('An Essay upon the Ancient and Modern Learning', 1690), it was easy for Bentley to prove that those *Epistles* were late, crude forgeries ('A Dissertation upon the Epistles of Phalaris', 1697). But scholarly evidence scarcely affected Temple's main point, the usefulness of the *Epistles* in teaching readers what tyrants feel and how they behave – insights into human nature that had aided Temple's own distinguished diplomatic career, and that would remain valid whether or not the text that imparted them was authentic. A man of the world did not need to stoop to details. Hence the battle of the books was fought at cross-purposes. For the Moderns truth itself was at stake and history recorded what actually happened. For the Ancients history offered models of

---

28 *The Tatler*, ed. Donald F. Bond, 3 vols. (Oxford: Clarendon Press, 1987), No. 1, pp. 219–20.
29 *Ibid.*, vol. 2, pp. 415–17.

conduct and proved its worth by forming someone like Temple, a gentleman, not a scholar. No matter how much Greek Bentley had studied, his very being expressed the rage of a Modern.

This way of parcelling the critical world resulted in strange bedfellows. Swift's satirical 'Digression concerning Criticks,' in *A Tale of a Tub* (1704), charts a genealogy of 'True Criticks' descending from Momus and culminating with '*B–t—ly*, and *Rym—r*, and *W—tt—n*, and *Perrault*, and *Dennis*, who begat *Etcaetera* the Younger'.[30] By any fair standard Dennis belongs in another set, those Ancients who 'drew up Rules' by which 'a careful Reader' might 'form his Taste to a true Relish of the *Sublime* and the *Admirable*'.[31] But Dennis lacked the social skills to qualify for that honour. Instead he suited the role of an angry pedant, better equipped to hunt out faults than find occasions for praise. When Alexander Pope drew a portrait of a critic as '*fierce Tyrant*', in *An Essay on Criticism* (1711), Dennis naturally served as the model: '*Appius* reddens at each Word you speak, / And *stares, Tremendous*! With a *threatning Eye*' (lines 585–6; a reference to Dennis' bombastic tragedy *Appius and Virginia*); and this inevitably provoked a ferocious reply: *Reflections Critical and Satyrical, upon a Late Rhapsody, Call'd, An Essay upon Criticism* (1711). Dennis had many reasons to be offended. He had been reduced to a stereotype by a young wit who dared to contest the grounds where the old critic held sway, and where both men assumed the right to be Dryden's true heir. He was outraged by the insinuation 'that they alone are fit to be Criticks who have shewn themselves great Poets' (1: 398) (was that true of Aristotle, or of Dennis himself?). He was sure he discerned the pernicious politics of a Catholic Jacobite who secretly was 'setting up for Poet-Laureat against the coming over of the Pretender'[32] (Pope was sufficiently disturbed by the charge to revise some passages in later editions of the *Essay*). But most of all he resented Pope for posing as a high Ancient or 'Bully of *Parnassus*' (1: 414), slavishly downgrading all Moderns in order to raise himself.

Despite Pope's deference to the Ancients, however, his *Essay* pursues a modern line of thought by referring the fundamental questions of art to the mind of the reader. Even the title reverses old expectations. *An Essay on Criticism* follows the genre of Horace's *Art of Poetry*, brought up to date in versions by Vida and Boileau. But unlike those poets, Pope inventively yields pride of place to the *critic*; he teaches the art of reading, not writing, and glorifies 'true

---

30 Jonathan Swift, *A Tale of a Tub*, ed., A. C. Guthkelch and D. Nichol Smith (Oxford: Clarendon Press, 1958), p. 94.
31 *Ibid.*, p. 92.
32 *The Critical Works of John Dennis*, vol. 1, p. 415.

Taste' along with 'true *Genius*'. In one respect the *Essay* might be thought a deterrent to criticism, since it constantly warns us of the immense difficulty of good critical judgement: 'Ten Censure wrong for one who Writes amiss' (line 6). Yet it also stresses the moral and psychological virtue of criticism, which can bring us in tune with 'Nature' and thus train us to be not only better judges of poetry but also better human beings. The *Essay* systematically integrates the powers of the poet and the critic, or *Wit* and *Judgment*. It would be easy to misread the most famous passage, the exhortation to 'First follow NATURE', as advice to a poet; Vida, Boileau and Dryden had all written similar lines. But just as Pope's epitaph to Newton would make the great scientist no passive spectator of 'NATURE and Nature's Laws' but rather an active bearer of light, so the *Essay* refuses to distinguish creators from beholders. 'At once the *Source*, and *End*, and *Test* of *Art*', Nature inspires the critic as well as the poet (lines 68–73). Dennis accused Pope of not having made clear that to follow Nature was 'to consult that innate Original, and that universal Idea, which the Creator has fix'd in the minds of ev'ry reasonable Creature',[33] but Pope explicitly connects his reverence for the light of Nature to the '*glimm'ring Light*' or candle of reason that shines in every uncorrupted mind. Similarly, the oft-quoted definition of '*True Wit*' moves from the dress of thought to something 'That gives us back the Image of our Mind' (line 300). Great critics, like great poets, succeed by consulting the Nature that all the while dwells within them.

An Essay on Criticism represents a high-water mark for the critical claims of the Ancients. A young poet who introduced himself as a master critic had to be extraordinarily bold, and Pope accepted the challenge by finding a harmony not only between the poet and critic but also between ancient wisdom and modern English taste. These reconciliations depended on slippery terms. The *Essay* is notorious for the multiple and sometimes contradictory meanings it draws from key words such as nature, judgement and wit, and its favourite rhetorical figure, an amalgam of antonomasia and zeugma[34] that identifies an author with his subject – '*Nature* and *Homer* were, he found, the *same*', or Longinus '*Is himself* that great *Sublime* he draws' – magically fuses theory and practice together. Dennis was not the only reader who thought that such flourishes often blurred useful distinctions. Moreover, Pope's attempt to resolve potential conflicts through an appeal to one all-powerful synthetic Nature could not

---

33 *Ibid.*, vol. I, p. 418.
34 Antonomasia: Substituting a descriptive phrase for a proper name, or substituting a proper name for a quality associated with it.
  Zeugma: one part of speech (most often the main verb, but sometimes a noun) governs two or more other parts of a sentence (often in a series).

disarm hostile parties. In the short run, the illusion of Augustan uniformity that the *Essay* so brilliantly crafted did charm many readers, and readers today still imagine it speaks for its age. In the long run, however, the modern riptide was rising, and not even Pope could avoid being disillusioned when swamped by the nation he actually lived in – the nation of hack writers and South Sea Bubbles and upwardly striving commercial classes and dunces in power.

That nation adopted Addison as its critic. The world of *The Spectator* seems so closely linked to the daily life and coffee-house conversations of early eighteenth-century Britain, where fluent circulation of goods and ideas began to replace a fixed economy and traditional values, that Addison might be regarded not merely as a reflection of the English public sphere but as its creator. In his essays in criticism, what he offered the public above all was pleasure. As the growth of empire won over people at home by doling out creature comforts like sugar, coffee and tea, the growing print culture persuaded people that literature could sweeten their lives. No previous critic had been so entertaining. Addison's commendation of a fine taste as 'the utmost Perfection of an accomplished man'[35] resembles contemporary writings by Shaftesbury and Pope, who eulogise taste as an inner harmony that mirrors the harmony of Nature; and a later Anglo-Scots school would extend that line of thought in such works as Alexander Gerard's *An Essay on Taste* (1759) and Archibald Alison's *Essays on the Nature and Principles of Taste* (1790). But Addison stresses the warmth and coldness of tasteful responses, as if he were describing physical sensations. Hence he defines 'a fine Taste in Writing' in terms of an involuntary *'Faculty of the Soul, which discerns the Beauties of an Author with Pleasure, and the Imperfections with Dislike'*.[36] This definition introduces the most ambitious series of *The Spectator*, eleven essays on the pleasures of the imagination (nos. 411–21) which propose that the appreciation of beauty supports good health, since 'Delightful Scenes . . . have a kindly Influence on the Body' and 'set the Animal Spirits in pleasing and agreeable Motions'.[37] The effort of understanding can strain the mind, but envisioning great, uncommon or beautiful objects brings inward, healing joy. A friend and guide, the critic enables us to savour those pleasures.

He also offers the pleasure of feeling refined. Unlike such critics as Dennis and Pope, whose efforts to rectify English tastes in the arts are always haunted by fears that the nation has fallen on evil days, Addison Whiggishly promises constant improvement. It is true, he admits, that the French as well as the

---

35 *The Spectator* No. 409; vol. III, p. 528.
36 *Ibid.*
37 *Ibid.*, vol. III, p. 539.

ancients have been more elegant than English poets and readers, whose taste inclines toward the *'Gothick'*. But the Spectator intends to set things right. 'As the great and only End of these my Speculations is to banish Vice and Ignorance out of the Territories of *Great Britain*, I shall endeavour as much as possible to establish among us a Taste of polite Writing'.[38] The gentle self-mockery of such a sentence – Swiftian in its fanatical turn but not at all savage – does not blot out its ambitions. Instead it invites the reader to join in its project and relish politeness. Addison's distinctions among true, false and mixed wit adapt Locke's philosophy of mind to practical criticism, thus demonstrating that the most advanced thought can make the reader more keenly attentive to tiny and subtle pleasures. Similar intimations of progress provide a running thread in the essays, which convert the teeming marketplace, the unsettling new science, and the crazy quilt of the city into sources of delight. The spell of *The Spectator* gathers all the nation into a club of readers, both town and country, united by their common stake in getting the hang of good manners. Civilisation, the essays imply, is a Briton's pleasure and duty.

Nevertheless, some readers resisted the spell. Despite the breadth of the circle that Addison drew, Tories were not alone in feeling left out. The smoothness of critical judgement, which could soften the awe of *Paradise Lost* to an appreciation of beauties and fine poetical strokes, might capture the public but failed to impress more severe or scholarly critics. Perhaps it was all too easy. Pope's brilliant portrait of 'Atticus' as a timorous miser of praise whose arts are always calculated to extort applause for himself may be unfair, but it does catch the flaw of a critic who wants too much to be liked. There was something coercive, moreover, about Addison's masterful strategies of ingratiation. When the Spectator speaks to women, for instance, his good-natured chiding affects an avuncular care for curing their follies and purifying their tastes; but women who followed his advice would soon be strapped in silken chains that hardly allowed them to move – a tyranny of common sense and good manners. Eliza Haywood's *Female Spectator* (1744–46) is less ingratiating. Although modelled on Addison and Steele, it gradually adopts a grave, even sanctimonious tone, as if to warn women that the perils they face are not merely those of style. Great Britain was not so civilised, in fact. Left to their own devices, readers pursued and often favoured kinds of writing condemned as Gothic or worse by the critic who championed politeness. In the least convincing passage of his essay 'Of the Standard of Taste' (1757), Hume asserts in the name of common sense that any critic who preferred Bunyan to Addison would be pronounced

38 *Ibid.*, vol. 1, p. 245.

'absurd and ridiculous'.[39] Yet Bunyan's fervour also represented the heart of the nation. *The Spectator* might rule the world of politeness, but in the larger world of Britain readers liked to mix the rough with the smooth.

Addison's critical interests cast a long shadow, however. The 'Essay on the Pleasures of the Imagination', which the author himself declared an 'intirely new' undertaking, pioneered a major field of studies that eventually came to be called 'aesthetics'. Thus *An Inquiry into the Original of Our Ideas of Beauty and Virtue* (1725) by the Scottish philosopher Francis Hutcheson explicitly sets out to improve and dignify Addison's theory by arguing that 'the most moving Beautys bear a Relation to our *moral Sense*'.[40] Other theorists would extend the inquiry through a systematic analysis of all the senses involved in perceptions of art, as in Lord Kames' very influential *Elements of Criticism* (1762), or through an investigation of the physical or physiological causes of artistic effects, as in Burke's *A Philosophical Enquiry into the Origin of Our Ideas of the Sublime and Beautiful* (1757). Few of those theorists paid much attention to pleasure, in Addison's fashion; and when they did, it was the paradox of painful pleasures, called up by tragedy or the sublime, that tended to absorb them. From a philosophical point of view, a taste for politeness was likely to seem superficial. Yet prolonged fascination with aesthetic effects resulted in new kinds of practical criticism, more detailed and intense than ever before. Once Addison had admired the description of Dover Cliff in *King Lear*, for example – 'whoever can read it without growing giddy, must have a good Head, or a very bad one'[41] – a series of critics probed it more and more deeply, striving to find the precise connexion between Shakespeare's words and the workings of the minds through which they passed. Apparently these investigations had practical value; they led not only to better philosophical understanding but also to a better grasp of literary texts. By the end of the eighteenth century, an improvement in critical principles was taken for granted. Reading itself might be a progressive art.

Aesthetics also helped bring the nation together. Although the new field had English origins, with Locke's philosophy of mind as its inspiration and Shaftesbury and Addison as its first authors, Scottish thinkers soon took command: Hutcheson, Hume, Gerard, Kames, Hugh Blair, Adam Smith, Thomas Reid, Alison and Dugald Stewart, to mention only a few. A strong traditional emphasis on logic and rhetoric in Scottish universities supported these studies, and

---

39 Hume, 'Of the Standard of Taste', p. 231.
40 Francis Hutcheson, *An Inquiry into the Original of Our Ideas of Beauty and Virtue* (London, 1725), p. 240.
41 *The Tatler*, 117; vol. II, p. 199.

literary criticism provided a way of testing theories of rhetoric through the practical analysis of texts. Moreover, the search for universal principles of human nature accorded with the cosmopolitan ambitions of the Scottish Enlightenment, its determination to surmount any narrow parochial interest and to prove that old prejudices did not hamper Scotland (whatever the English might think). Scottish critics were disposed to take the long view. Thus *An Enquiry into the Life and Writings of Homer* (1735) by Thomas Blackwell, an Aberdeen professor of Greek, regards Homer less as a 'singular Phenomenon' than as the product of a time and culture that fell between the 'Barbarity' of earlier ages and the 'common Order, and established Discipline' of a well-ordered state.[42] At such fortunate moments of balance, when manners had not yet progressed too far, an epic poet could still draw directly on '*Marvellous* and *Wonderful*' subjects and on a poetical language alive with natural metaphors. Blackwell's notion that each work of literature reflects a stage in civilisation would stimulate research into the social, historical and biographical contexts of the arts. It also contributed to a growing interest in primitive societies and unspoiled poetic genius. James Macpherson, who 'transcribed' the poems of Ossian, was one of Blackwell's students.

Meanwhile critics began to look for the roots of English poetry in the past. Antiquarianism had already recovered many texts in Old and Middle English, and increased attention to the long background of British history supplied an ideological buttress against contemporary threats from abroad. But literary history proved especially useful for poets. According to Owen Ruffhead, Pope 'once had a purpose to pen a discourse on the rise and progress of English poetry, as it came from the Provincial poets, and had classed the English poets, according to their several schools and successions';[43] and the brief sketch Pope made was later studied by many scholars and poets. It concentrates on the evolution of styles, presumably culminating in the refinement or 'correctness' of present times. As a poet, Pope aimed to perfect the best work of the past by refurbishing it with his own polished versification; therefore he combs antique or outmoded texts for fine strokes that might be made better. The next generation of poets, however, viewed history differently – not least because they feared that Pope's art had brought history to a stop. 'To attempt any further improvement of versification will be dangerous', Samuel Johnson concluded.[44] Hence fledgling poets would have to dig out other forms and styles. When Thomas Gray sketched a history of English poetry, he searched for rhythms

---

42 London, 1735, p. 35.
43 Owen Ruffhead, *The Life of Alexander Pope, Esq.* (London, 1769), p. 328.
44 Johnson, *Lives of the English Poets*, vol. III, p. 251.

and images he could use in poems. He never wrote that history, but his studies bore fruit in two Pindaric odes, 'The Progress of Poesy' and 'The Bard,' which strive for a primordial sublimity and vehemence of expression, as well as in imitations of Norse and Welsh fragments. Other poets drew on Spenser and Milton, on ballads, or on a *'Fairy Way of Writing'* (giving voice to supernatural beings) that Dryden and Addison had associated with Shakespeare. The first wave of this revisionary poetics was rounded off by two works by the Warton brothers: Thomas Warton's *Observations on the Faerie Queene of Spenser* (1754), which places Spenser within 'the customs and genius of his age', and Joseph Warton's *Essay on the Writings and Genius of Pope* (vol. 1, 1756), which argues that Pope was a man of wit and a man of sense but not 'a TRUE POET'.

The British public cared less about such adventures in style, however, than about past achievements that covered the nation in glory. In the 1730s the patriot opposition to Robert Walpole's government found a hero in Shakespeare, representative of a golden age that rebuked the venality of the present day. Cobham's Temple of British Worthies at Stowe (1735) implicitly shames the current regime with emblems of historic national virtue. Great English authors could also be used to chastise the French. During the 1730s no critic was more influential in Britain than Voltaire, whose exile in England from 1726 to 1729 made him an advocate – if sometimes a patronising one – of British culture and its spirit of freedom. His *Letters on England* (1733), banned in France, confirmed the pride of Britons in matching their ancient, supercilious rival. Yet in the arts the British were still defensive, and here Voltaire's remarks could be wounding. Shakespeare, he wrote, 'considered the English Corneille', had a natural genius 'without the slightest spark of good taste or the least knowledge of the rules', and his so-called tragedies were actually 'monstrous farces'.[45] Aspersions like these impugned not only the national poet but also the national honour. In retaliation a critical industry set out to show that the French could neither understand nor measure up to Shakespeare. Elizabeth Montagu's full-length response to Voltaire, *An Essay on the Writings and Genius of Shakespear* (1769), convinced David Garrick (who did not need much convincing) 'that *England* may justly boast the honour of producing the greatest dramatic poet in the world' ('Advertisement', *An Ode . . . to Shakespeare*, London, 1769). In order to justify such claims, new principles of literary history would need to be formulated, subordinating ideas of progress to a reverence for the genius that had once sprung from English soil.

45 Voltaire (François-Marie Arouet), *Letters on England* (1733), trans. Leonard Tancock (Harmondsworth: Penguin, 1980), p. 92.

Preserving the national poet required better editions and annotations as well. Since the Restoration, Shakespeare's plays had been 'improved' by rewriting, as in Dryden's *Tempest* (1667) and *All for Love* (1677), or by editing that corrected apparent or imagined faults, as in the texts superintended by Nicholas Rowe (1709) and Pope (1725). These publishing ventures each teamed Shakespeare with a famous modern author, producing a composite work both old and new. But later editors set out to rescue the Bard from those who wanted to mend him. Lewis Theobald took pains to restore the original texts and explicate whatever seemed obscure (1733), and William Warburton tried to lay down canons of criticism to resolve disputed points (1747); each aimed to reconstruct an authentic Shakespeare. Retrospectively such editions, like Garrick's 'authentic' productions, seem period pieces that paste an eighteenth-century face on the Bard. Yet they did establish the principle that a text can be properly understood only when placed in the context of its own times. In 1765 Johnson summed up the lesson: 'Every man's performances, to be rightly estimated, must be compared with the state of the age in which he lived, and with his own particular opportunities'.[46] A good critic of Shakespeare would have to be a learned historian; to know England's playwright, one had to know England's past.

Moreover, a great English critic would have to take Shakespeare's measure. By the time that Johnson edited the plays, he was already a respected critic as well as a famous lexicographer; *A Dictionary of the English Language* (1755) had equipped him to gloss Shakespeare's words. Yet more than nine years passed between his proposals (1756) and the finished *Plays of William Shakespeare*. Perhaps he felt uncomfortable about what the nation expected. During the Seven Years' War, when patriotic adulation for the Bard was mobilised against the French and a production of *Henry V* was mounted every year, Johnson's aversion to the war turned him away from vainglorious nationalism. The notes he eventually wrote for *Henry V* are quite dry; he remarks that King Henry's rousing speech on St Crispin's Day, 'like many others of the declamatory kind, is too long', and of Henry's vaunt that 'we happy few' shall be remembered to the ending of the world, 'it may be observed that we are apt to promise to ourselves a more lasting memory than the changing state of human things admits'.[47] Such deflations express Johnson's reluctance to lead cheers for Shakespeare and England. Instead he separates virtues from vices and graces from faults,

---

46 *Johnson on Shakespeare*, vols. VII and VIII of The Yale Edition of the Works of Samuel Johnson, ed. Arthur Sherbo, 2 vols. (London and New Haven, CT: Yale University Press, 1968), vol. I, p. 81.
47 *Ibid.*, vol. II, p. 557.

as in the memorable set piece on Shakespeare's weakness for puns: 'A quibble was to him the fatal Cleopatra for which he lost the world, and was content to lose it.'[48] As a critic, Johnson sets himself against imaginative excess, the tendency of readers as well as writers to lose themselves in self-indulgent dreams. Shakespeare's plays, at their best, can cure this malady by offering pictures of life as it is, and the critic's task is not to glorify the national poet but rather to see him clearly and make the truth known.

Above all Johnson attends to the mind of the reader. The 'Preface to Shakespeare' does not compete with other testimonials to the poet, who already can 'claim the privilege of established fame and prescriptive veneration'. Taking that fame for granted, Johnson begins by asking *why* Shakespeare still is loved, and answers that question by scrutinising the audience as well as the writer and his works. 'Nothing can please many, and please long, but just representations of general nature.'[49] This formulation brings together the mind and what it observes. Since 'nature' principally means 'human nature', an honest and accurate imitation of the nature everyone shares will be familiar to all who look within. Hence the appeal of a work of art reminds the individual members of the audience that they are not alone, and the pleasure of recognising nature is reinforced by the pleasure of self-recognition. As Johnson goes on to say, Shakespeare's 'persons act and speak by the influence of those general passions and principles by which all minds are agitated, and the whole system of life is continued in motion'.[50] In this respect the plays are timeless and placeless, not merely Elizabethan and English, and they ought to endure as long as the system of life continues. Johnson founds his analysis on the homing instinct of the mind, which wanders in quest of novelty, like the errant foot of Donne's compasses, but in the end 'can only repose on the stability of truth'.

Thus Shakespeare too must be held to the norms of truth. By putting the mental health of the reader first, Johnson requires the plays to furnish 'domestick wisdom' and even to warn against their own extreme marvels and passions. The enchantment of theatrical sorcery will hardly excuse any playwright who caters to superstition. Though critics like Richard Hurd had already begun to idolise Shakespeare's *'rough magic'* and to maintain that 'he is greater when he uses Gothic manners and machinery, than when he employs classical',[51] Johnson attributes that witchcraft to an era when the English nation 'was yet struggling to emerge from barbarity' and 'the publick was gross and

---

48 *Ibid.*, vol. 1, p. 74.
49 *Ibid.*, vol. 1, p. 61.
50 *Ibid.*, vol. 1, p. 62.
51 Richard Hurd, *Letters on Chivalry and Romance* (London, 1762), pp. 50, 60.

dark'.[52] Once more the emphasis falls on what is best for the reader. Since phantoms prey upon impressionable minds – as Johnson's own blood had been chilled by the ghost in *Hamlet* – and since 'it is always a writer's duty to make the world better', a playwright should not kindle illusions but help to dispel them. Hence Johnson tends to shrink from heroes who want to be more than a human being can be. His favourite passage in Shakespeare, the death of Katherine in *Henry VIII*, exalts a heroine whom any reader might take as a pattern: 'This scene is above any other part of Shakespeare's tragedies, and perhaps above any scene of any other poet, tender and pathetick, without gods, or furies, or poisons, or precipices, without the help of romantick circumstances, without improbable sallies of poetical lamentation, and without any throes of tumultuous misery.'[53] The list of everything the scene excludes may remind us of other Shakespearean scenes, tumultuous and romantic. Johnson can hardly bear the deaths of Cordelia and Desdemona or the agonies of Lear and Othello. Taking the point of view of the common reader, the critic yearns for decency and justice.

Such common readers populate Johnson's nation and make it their own. Through all his later works they furnish a standard the critic must follow. The first edition of the *Prefaces to the English Poets* concluded with Gray: 'In the character of his *Elegy* I rejoice to concur with the common reader; for by the common sense of readers uncorrupted with literary prejudices, after all the refinements of subtilty and the dogmatism of learning, must be finally decided all claim to poetical honours.'[54] Resigning his authority at last, Johnson joyfully merges himself with the British public. To be sure, one might suspect this of being a trick – ventriloquism if not camouflage. The common reader to whom the critic defers is constructed according to Johnson's specifications, and perhaps in his image. The 'rabble', for instance, are barred, along with subtle and learned readers like Gray himself. One aim of Johnson's *Dictionary* had been to preserve a stock of words used by the best English authors, omitting the jargon and 'fugitive cant' of tradesmen and merchants as well as the fashionable neologisms recommended by Lord Chesterfield. In this way the history of England might live on in current usage, and the divisions of an increasingly specialised and compartmentalised nation might be verbally mended. Yet of course no dictionary could hold back the rising tide of language.

Similarly, no critical survey of English poets could ever satisfy all members of a heterogeneous public. The limited collection of poets, beginning with

---

52 *Johnson on Shakespeare*, vol. I, pp. 81–2.
53 *Ibid.*, vol. II, p. 653.
54 Johnson, *Lives of the English Poets*, vol. III, p. 441.

Cowley, that the publishers selected for Johnson to introduce, had no room for any woman, let alone for earlier, less saleable writers. Although a few poets straddled the Civil Wars, the edition suggests that the Restoration ushered in new harmonies of verse. The retrospective look at metaphysical poets in Johnson's preface to Cowley seems intended to distinguish an age when poets mainly endeavoured to show their learning and wit from an age when poets set out to copy nature and give pleasure to readers. Johnson charts a history in which progressive refinement characterises not only writers of verse but also the British public. Even his praise for Milton, a poet whose greatness magnifies 'the honour of our country', is qualified by disapproval of outworn poetic conventions: a weakness for allegory and pastoral, blank verse supported by a prejudice against rhyme, and the mingling of pagan and Christian gods. These faults should be obvious to any modern reader, Johnson assumes, thanks to advances in criticism and versification. The line of poetic progress culminates in a ringing rejoinder to Joseph Warton's demotion of Pope: 'If Pope be not a poet, where is poetry to be found?'[55] After this flourish, the rest of the Prefaces tend to be anticlimactic, assessing writers like Ambrose Philips who 'has added nothing to English poetry'.[56] Moreover, Johnson's faith in the sense of the English common reader may sometimes have wavered. While the Prefaces were still appearing, in June 1780, the Gordon riots broke out in London; as Johnson remarked, a mob that demolished a house in Grub Street 'could be no friend to the Muses!'[57] New tastes for the Gothic or for such primitive verse as Macpherson's also worked against any hope that the taste of readers was constantly getting better. From this point of view, Johnson's final impassioned tribute to the common reader might serve less as a description of current conditions than as a desperate wish for the future.

Meanwhile rival versions of English literary history were gaining ascendancy. Like Johnson, Thomas Warton subscribes to a theory of progress. At the end of the second volume of The History of English Poetry (3 vols, 1774–81), which has just reached the reign of Henry VIII, Warton chronicles the passing of 'ignorance and superstition, so opposite to the real interests of human society', as well as 'the savage pomp and the capricious heroism of the baronial manners'. Subsequently, 'literature, and a better sense of things, not only banished these barbarities, but superseded the mode of composition which was formed upon them. Romantic poetry gave way to the force of reason

---

55 Ibid., vol. III, p. 251.
56 Ibid., vol. III, p. 325.
57 Diaries and Letters of Madame d'Arblay, ed. Charlotte Barrett, 7 vols. (London, 1842), vol. I, p. 412.

and inquiry; as its own inchanted palaces and gardens instantaneously vanished, when the Christian champion displayed the shield of truth.' By studying Greek and Roman classics, the humanists would soon establish patterns of excellence and rules of criticism. Yet Warton regards these refinements as a poetic disaster. 'The lover of true poetry will ask, what have we gained by this revolution? It may be answered, much good sense, good taste, and good criticism. But, in the mean time, we have lost a set of manners, and a system of machinery, more suitable to the purposes of poetry, than those which have been adopted in their place. We have parted with extravagancies that are above propriety, with incredibilities that are more acceptable than truth, and with fictions that are more valuable than reality.'[58] Nostalgia for lost sources of poetry and an enchanted feudal nation dominates this history (or historical myth). The sharp distinction between imagination and truth, or feeling and reason, is not Warton's last word; volume three of the *History* moves tentatively toward a reconciliation of fancy and judgement in the Elizabethan age. Yet Warton's failure to bring the story beyond the early seventeenth century (he left just eighty-eight pages of a fourth volume) suggests an impasse in his historical scheme. The *History* anticipates Thomas Love Peacock's mischievous charge that 'A poet in our times is a semi-barbarian in a civilized community. He lives in the days that are past.'[59]

Dialectical swings between 'progressive' and 'romantic' views provide the impetus for much of eighteenth-century literary history and criticism. Discussions of prose fiction, in particular, endlessly circle around the difference between older 'romances' and up-to-date 'histories' or 'novels'. Warton's *History* begins with a long dissertation 'On the Origin of Romantic Fiction in Europe', which he derives, like William Warburton, from Arabian tales brought home by the Crusaders. Other critics focus more narrowly on the shift from seventeenth-century French romances to fictions that touch modern lives and times. As early as 1692, in his preface to *Incognita*, William Congreve contrasts the 'lofty language, miraculous contingencies, and impossible performances' of romances with his own kind of work, 'of a more familiar nature', which he calls a novel. Ordinarily such contrasts reinforce the idea of a sustained advance toward more involving and plausible fictional modes, as in the heading supplied for Johnson's influential *Rambler* 4 (1750): 'The modern form of romances preferable to the ancient. The necessity of characters

58 Thomas Warton, *The History of English Poetry*, 3 vols. (London, 1774–81), vol. II, pp. 462–3.
59 Thomas Love Peacock, *The Four Ages of Poetry* (1820), with Shelley's *Defence of Poetry* and Browning's *Essay on Shelley*, ed. H. F. B. Brett-Smith (Oxford: Blackwell, 1921), p. 16.

morally good.' At mid century the enormous popularity of works by Richardson, Fielding and Smollett, well publicised then and later as 'the rise of the novel', seemed to confirm that the new forms had triumphed.

Yet the terms of comparison always allowed a sudden critical and historical shift, as in Warton's bent for extravagant fables. The first English book on fiction, *The Progress of Romance* (1785) by Clara Reeve, distinguishes old and new forms in a way that seems slanted toward 'progress': 'The Romance in lofty and elevated language, describes what never happened nor is likely to happen. – The Novel gives a familiar relation of such things, as pass every day before our eyes, such as may happen to our friend, or to ourselves . . . until we are affected by the joys or distresses, of the persons in the story, as if they were our own.'[60] But Reeve's best-known work of fiction, *The Old English Baron* (1778), is a self-proclaimed 'Gothic Story', the offspring of Horace Walpole's *Castle of Otranto* (1764), which she tries to surpass in uniting 'the most attractive and interesting circumstances of the ancient Romance and modern Novel'.[61] In one important respect the romance might even do more good than the novel, according to Reeve, since these stories attract and interest women more than men, and a chivalric tale of courtly love and female power can help to raise women above the sad realities of life in a nation where men are despots (an oriental fable about a strong woman, *The History of Charoba, Queen of Ægypt*, accompanied *The Progress of Romance*). Stories of progress may well have prompted a backlash in late eighteenth-century Britain. The medieval revival that swept the country resulted not only in sophisticated tastes for barbarism, Gothicism and primitivism but also in better research and better texts, such as Thomas Tyrwhitt's pioneering edition of *The Canterbury Tales* (1775–8). At the same time, a growing appreciation of rugged landscapes led readers as well as travellers to wild, uncivilised scenes that had once been called 'romantic' and were cherished now as sublime or 'picturesque' – a term popularised by William Gilpin's *Three Essays* (1792) and put to use in Ann Radcliffe's Gothic tales.

These developments also reflect the rise of an empire. After the triumph of the Seven Years' War, Great Britain became accustomed to its new role as a world power, as well as to the challenges and anxieties that entailed. Henceforth a proper history of the nation, or of its literature, would have to take on a more sweeping perspective, one that included times long past and faraway

---

60 Clara Reeve, *The Progress of Romance*, ed. Esther M. McGill (New York: Facsimile Text Society, 1930), p. 111.
61 Clara Reeve, *The Old English Baron: A Gothic Story*, ed. James Trainer (London: Oxford University Press, 1967), p. 3.

places. William Robertson began his career with a *History of Scotland* (1759), then moved on to a *History of the Reign of the Emperor Charles V* (1769) that went back to the Roman Empire, and next to *The History of America* (1777). Literary critics and historians widened their range in similar ways. Thomas Gray's research included Erse, Norse and Welsh, and Thomas Warton expanded his plan so far, including the *Gesta Romanorum*, that eventually it unravelled. Hugh Blair's *Critical Dissertation on the Poems of Ossian* (1763) dips into the Eddas and Lapland songs, as well as Homer, in search of analogous bards. Thomas Percy gathered old ballads and took an interest in Chinese literature. Sir William Jones learned Sanskrit and studied the poetry of India and Persia. On a different front, Robert Lowth's *Lectures on the Sacred Poetry of the Hebrews* (1753; English translation, 1787) found an alternative to classical sources in biblical verse, whose parallel structures and sublime and passionate style suggested new principles for composing and analysing poetry in English. A world of poetry – or poetries – was opening to British critics and scholars. Moreover, the inner divisions of the nation, and of its reading public, were also increasingly clear. Class conflicts augmented the old religious and political quarrels, and many new forms of writing addressed a specific, narrowly defined audience – children, for instance. No single set of critical principles could encompass such diverse groups and interests.

Nevertheless, the power of critics continued to grow. 'Nation' and 'literature', two terms whose meanings were shifting, combined to produce 'English literature', a compelling new phrase. In Johnson's *Dictionary* (1755) 'nation' refers to 'a people', not a political state ('nationality' and 'nationalism' are absent), and 'literature' is defined as 'learning; skill in letters'. But readers of Johnson's *Prefaces* and Warton's *History* could take pride in a collective achievement or artistic supremacy that bound Britons together. The restriction of 'literature' to certain kinds of writing, supposed to have permanent worth, would soon require authoritative 'literary critics' – experts to sift enduring works of art from the chaff. This was a weighty responsibility, with implications for education: since English literature belonged to all Britons and constituted the best of their heritage, all good Britons ought to treasure it. Johnson had furthered that process, and when he died, in 1784, much of the nation acknowledged that its greatest living author had been a literary critic. Subsequently many other critics took up the challenge, reading works into and out of the English canon, and sometimes making room in literature for recent forms. When Anna Laetitia Barbauld collected *The British Novelists* in fifty volumes (1810), she concluded her introductory essay by identifying fiction with the spirit of Britain. 'It was said by Fletcher of Saltoun, "Let me make the ballads of a nation, and I care not who makes the laws." Might it not be said with as much propriety, Let me make the novels of a country, and let who will make the systems?'[62]

This insistence on the power of critics as well as authors survived an era of revolutions, just as Johnson's ideal of the poet as 'the legislator of mankind' (*Rasselas*, 1759) lived on in Shelley's declaration that 'Poets are the unacknowledged legislators of the World' (*A Defence of Poetry*, 1821). Even the hostility aimed at strong critics paid tribute to their widening influence. Johnson's *Prefaces* attracted a swarm of stinging replies, and Warton's *History* was countered with a full-length attack by Joseph Ritson (1782). Once the category of English literature had been invented, its guardians and revisionists both felt they spoke for the nation. Such heightened attention raised the stakes of criticism and accelerated the rate of critical change. As Addison's emphasis on polite good taste had been patronised by Johnson in the name of truth and the common reader, so Johnson's didactic emphasis was soon patronised by Coleridge in the name of imagination. By the end of the century, critics referred less often to rules and more often to genius. Yet critical judgements still followed the lines set down in the age when the British reading public came into its own. In 1795 Isaac D'Israeli called his own era an 'Age of Criticism', and many poets and critics were quick to agree. Henceforth those who defined the traditions of English literature would play a major role in defining the nation.

62 Anna Laetitia Barbauld, ed., *The British Novelists*, 50 vols. (London, 1810), vol. 1, p. 62.

Augustan England and British America

WILLIAM C. DOWLING

In Boswell's *Life of Johnson*, under the year 1778, a reader comes across one of those Johnsonian outbursts that caused Boswell to compare his hero's temper to a warm West Indian climate. The context is entirely benign. Johnson has been discussing with the Quaker Mrs Knowles the nature of Christian friendship. Then, without warning, comes the explosion. 'From this pleasing subject,' reports Boswell, 'he, I know not how or why, made a sudden transition to one upon which he was a violent aggressor; for he said, "I am willing to love all mankind, *except an American:*" and his inflammable corruption bursting into horrid fire, he "breathed out threatenings and slaughter;" calling them, "Rascals – Robbers – Pirates;" and exclaiming he'd "burn and destroy them."' When another lady present, Anna Seward, gently reproves his vehemence, the result is another explosion: 'He was irritated still more by this delicate and keen reproach; and roared out another tremendous volley, which one might fancy could be heard across the Atlantick.'[1]

Yet to anyone who had read Johnson's *Taxation No Tyranny*, the most searching analysis of American claims produced by anyone writing on the side of George III and his ministers, the explosion would have come as no surprise. For by 1778 Johnson had honestly concluded that the American colonists were simply Englishmen long permitted by mere geographical accident to escape their normal civic responsibilities. They were now, in his view, hypocrites who were trying to make that advantage permanent by mobilising an exploded vocabulary of Whig principles left over from the previous reign. English settlers in America, Johnson reminds readers of *Taxation No Tyranny*, are 'governed by English laws, entitled to English dignities, regulated by English counsels, and protected by English arms'. Indeed, the colonists' own most radical claim is that they are 'entitled to all the rights of Englishmen'. Since the British system

---

1 *Boswell's Life of Johnson*, ed. George Birkbeck Hill, rev. L. F. Powell, 6 vols. (Oxford: Clarendon Press, 1934–64), vol. III, p. 290. Subsequent parenthetical references are to this edition.

of parliamentary representation has always involved English subjects being bound by laws for which many do not vote – as even in modern democracies those who have not satisfied certain residence or other requirements may not vote – it is impossible to see why the American colonists should now imagine that they are not 'subject to English government, and chargeable by English taxation'.[2]

As historians like Bernard Bailyn and Gordon Wood have taught us to see,[3] Johnson was right to hear in American claims a Whig rhetoric associated with an earlier period of Hanoverian rule, and specifically with the Country opposition to Sir Robert Walpole, which would ultimately embrace everything from the radical 'commonwealthman' tradition of *Cato's Letters*[4] to the Tory opposition mounted from 1726 onwards by Bolingbroke's periodical *The Craftsman*. The language of Country opposition was that vocabulary of Corruption and Luxury associated with Machiavelli and James Harrington (author of *Oceana* [1656], which describes a fictional political utopia) and classical republican theory generally: the myth of a simple and virtuous republic now being undermined, like the Roman republic in the days of its decline, by a growing tendency to act out of selfish egoism rather than regard for the community as a whole. Augustan critics of Walpole's England usually traced this tendency back to the Glorious Revolution of 1688, when William of Orange and his Dutch advisors were thought to have imported into Britain a new money or market society based on credit and speculation. For the opposition to Walpole's 'Robinocracy,' in short, the classical republican world of luxury and corruption was in its latest guise the new world of the Bank of England, the South Sea Bubble and the National Debt.

The reason that Country ideology is crucial to an understanding of transatlantic literary relations is that, as demonstrated in such groundbreaking works as Isaac Kramnick's *Bolingbroke and his Circle* and Maynard Mack's *The Garden and the City*, the Augustan satire so widely read in both eighteenth-century England and the American colonies dwelt within the universe of classical republican thought. In Pope's Horatian poems or Gay's *Beggar's Opera* or Swift's *Gulliver's Travels*, the new money or market society symbolised by

---

2 Samuel Johnson, *Political Writings*, ed. Donald J. Greene (New Haven, CT: Yale University Press, 1977), 425. Subsequent parenthetical references in the text to are to this edition.

3 Bernard Bailyn, *The Ideological Origins of the American Revolution* (Cambridge, MA: Harvard University Press, 1967), Gordon Wood, *The Creation of the American Republic, 1776–1787* (Chapel Hill, NC: University of North Carolina Press, 1969).

4 *Cato's Letters*: published anonymously by John Trenchard and Thomas Gordon in *The London Journal* from 1720 to 1723, the 144 letters argued for freedom of conscience and freedom of speech.

Walpole appears as a system of Luxury and Corruption driven by what James Thomson in *The Seasons* calls 'unreal wants'. The speculative wealth that is silently working to dissolve the values of an older organic or traditional society thus represents what Yeats would later call the 'filthy modern tide': the blind or impersonal forces of historical transformation as the Augustans hoped they might be resisted by satire as a mode of symbolic action.[5] This is the world as well of such works as Thomson's *Liberty* and Richard Glover's *Leonidas* (1737), both of which were read with eager interest in the American colonies.

As Edmund Burke shrewdly saw, the vehemence of Johnson's antipathy to the American colonists originated in a deep personal embarrassment going back to Johnson's own early public appearances as an Augustan satirist. For as an author starting out in London, Johnson had demonstrated in such works as *Marmor Norfolienses* and the Swiftian *Complete Vindication of the Licensers of the Stage* a superb mastery of anti-Walpole satire. Only belatedly would he come to realise that the satiric mode he had taken up, the purely literary conventions absorbed almost unconsciously by aspiring writers in the milieu dominated by Swift and Pope and Gay, necessarily committed anyone who adopted it to a narrow and intransigent view of English politics and history. The entire story of Johnson's later politics is, in a sense, the story of an unending attempt to repudiate what his own relentlessly self-critical intelligence would come to regard as this embarrassing early lapse. This is why Burke, recorded by Boswell at a dinner party two years after Johnson's death, is so 'violent against Dr Johnson's political writings', by which he had in mind, in addition to *Taxation No Tyranny*, Johnson's pamphlets on the conflict with Spain over owner-ship of the Falkland Islands (*Thoughts on the late transactions respecting Falkland's Islands* 1771) and *The patriot: Addressed to the electors of Great Britain* (1774), in which he defended the House of Commons' attempts to nullify the election of the radical John Wilkes to parliament. In each case, Burke would maintain, the underlying reason that Johnson was driven to vituperation in denouncing any post-Walpole parliamentary Opposition was simply that Johnson always 'imputed to them the wickedness of his own opposition to Walpole'.[6]

---

5 In a poem called 'Statues' from Yeats' *Last Poems* (1939):

> We Irish, born into that ancient sect
> But thrown upon this filthy modern tide
> And by its formless, spawning, fury wrecked,
> Climb to our proper dark, that we may trace
> The lineaments of a plummet-measured face.
> (lines 28–32)

6 Boswell, *The English Experiment: 1785–1789*, eds. I. S. Lustig and F. A. Pottle (New York: McGraw-Hill, 1986), pp. 98–9.

To Johnson, the moment that had permanently discredited the Country vision of an England sinking irretrievably into luxury and corruption was that of the Seven Years' War and the accession to the English throne of George III, raised as a young man on principles very like those enunciated in Bolingbroke's *The Idea of a Patriot King*. Thus, for instance, in *The False Alarm*, Johnson reproves his fellow Tories because their long opposition to a Court party has led them reflexively to support John Wilkes. What they have failed to see, says Johnson, is 'that they have at last a king who knows not the name of party, and who wishes to be the common father of all his people' (*Political Writings*, p. 344). Within a few years, many other thoughtful English writers would have reached a similar conclusion. So, for instance, Joseph Warton in the second volume of his *Essay on Pope* – published some twenty years after the first volume – as he looks back on the Augustan frenzy of anti-Walpole opposition in the 1730s: 'Our country is represented as totally ruined, and overwhelmed with dissipation, depravity, and corruption. Yet this very country . . . in about twenty years afterwards, carried its triumphs over all its enemies . . . and astonished the most distant nations with a display of uncommon efforts, abilities, and virtues. So vain are the prognostications of poets, as well as politicians.'[7]

In *The Lives of the Poets*, Johnson's impatience with Country ideology most often shows up as a sense that other writers of his own generation should have been more self-critical about using a literary idiom taken over wholesale from the older Augustan writers. Typical, for example, is Johnson's peremptory dismissal of Thomson's poem *Liberty*: 'at this time a long course of opposition to Sir Robert Walpole had filled the nation with clamours for liberty, of which no man felt the want, and with care for liberty, which was not in danger'.[8] In any such comment, we glimpse the purely literary origins of Johnson's later politics, his effort unequivocally to disown his youthful embrace of Augustan conventions in a Walpolean England in which moral and political expression had been widely, and as he now thinks falsely, assumed to be inseparable. The wrath of Johnson's *Taxation No Tyranny* is directed not only against the American colonists, but against Englishmen still foolish enough to imagine that the Augustan writers, in their tireless denunciations of Walpole, had been turning out not simply brilliant satire but sound political theory.

As Bailyn's *Ideological Origins of the American Revolution* demonstrates, *Taxation No Tyranny* gets things essentially right. The American colonists really

---

7 Joseph Warton, *Essay on the Genius and Writings of Pope*, 2 vols. (London, 1782), vol. II, p. 426.
8 Samuel Johnson, *Lives of the English Poets*, ed. George Birkbeck Hill, 3 vols. (Oxford: Clarendon Press, 1905), vol. III, p. 289.

did imagine that the country to which they gazed across the Atlantic was in some sense still Walpole's England, that the machinery of Court corruption was as powerful in the age of George III and Lord Bute as in the earlier age of Pope and Swift and Thomson's *Liberty*. To explain literary and intellectual relations between England and America in the eighteenth century is thus to trace a process through which, beginning from an identical set of Augustan writings – in which category should be included Trenchard and Gordon's *Cato's Letters* along with Addison's *Cato*, Bolingbroke's *Craftsman* along with a more obviously 'literary' periodical like *The Spectator* – England and America would arrive at opposite conclusions about the nature of political rights in an age of empire.

The Excise Crisis of 1733, Sir Robert Walpole's attempt to raise revenue by passing new taxes on imported goods, would be Walpole's single greatest political setback until his fall nearly ten years later. The Excise Crisis united the landed gentry and the London traders, permitting Bolingbroke's *Craftsman* to proclaim that the terms 'Whig' and 'Tory' had become obsolete, that there had at long last emerged in England a single unified Country opposition to Walpole and a political system based on rampant corruption. This was not mere rhetoric. By 1733 many Tories and opposition Whigs did feel themselves to share a set of basic principles. The specific importance of the Excise Crisis was that Walpole's excise scheme seemed to all parties to Country ideology the very symbol of a new money or market society illegitimately trying to extend its power through taxes and imposts. The revenue brought in this way, Sir William Wyndham would say in an Opposition speech in the Commons in 1734, was nothing more than 'the plunder of the nation', to be used by Walpole to transform parliament from a representative body of Englishmen into 'a corrupt majority of his creatures, whom he retains in daily pay, or engages in his particular interest, by granting them those posts and places which ought never to be given to any but for the good of the public'.[9]

As a broad synthesis of Tory and Opposition Whig principles, Country ideology was sustained by a deep anxiety about the fate of traditional society, based either on land or on commerce directly connected to land-based prosperity, in a new world of unreal wealth. Partly, as with the South Sea Bubble, the unreality was that of speculative wealth, joint-stock investors grown obscenely rich overnight by the manipulation of paper, with nothing of genuine value having been produced. At a deeper level, however, the demonic

9 Quoted in W. A. Speck, *Stability and Strife: England 1714–1760* (London: Edward Arnold, 1984), p. 213.

visage of Walpole's system revealed itself more threateningly in the mysterious workings of credit, symbolising the impersonal forces of a money or market society operating outside human control to unfathomable ends. Even a writer like Defoe, normally a tireless promoter of the new financial order brought in by the Glorious Revolution, could be made uneasy by this new spectre of credit: 'Like the soul in the body it acts as all substance, yet it is itself immaterial; it gives motion, yet it cannot be said to exist . . . If I should say it is the essential shadow of something that is not, should I not puzzle the thing rather than explain it, and leave you and myself more in the dark than we were before?'[10]

For the Augustan writers, the same mysterious phenomenon was the metaphysical basis of the new order of corruption symbolised by Walpole. In an older world of what Marx called use value – which in Augustan writing is always the ideal of the landed estate where lord and tenants are bound together in an immemorial relation of mutual rights and obligations – corruption of the modern sort had been impossible. This is the point, for instance, of that brilliant and hilarious moment in the *Epistle to Bathurst* where Pope imagines a modern Walpole-like minister in a world where corruption remains in full force, but the invisible forces of money and credit have unaccountably vanished: 'A Statesman's slumbers how this speech would spoil! / "Sir, Spain has sent a thousand jars of oil; / Huge bales of British cloth blockade the door; / A hundred oxen at your levee roar."'[11] In reality, however, they have not vanished, and the world excoriated in Augustan satire remains one in which what Pope calls 'blest paper-credit' goes on silently dissolving the bonds of organic or traditional society:

> Blest paper-credit! last and best supply!
> That lends Corruption lighter wings to fly!
> Gold imp'd by thee, can compass hardest things,
> Can pocket states, can fetch or carry Kings;
> A single leaf shall waft an Army o'er,
> Or ship off Senates to a distant Shore;
> A leaf, like Sibyl's, scatter to and fro
> Our fates and fortunes, as the winds shall blow:
> Pregnant with thousands flits the Scrap unseen,
> And silent sells a King, or buys a Queen.
>
> (lines 69–78)

10 Quoted in Isaac Kramnick, *Bolingbroke and his Circle* (Cambridge, MA: Harvard University Press, 1968), p. 40.

11 *Epistle to Bathurst*, lines 43–6. All citations from Pope are from the one-volume Twickenham edition: *The Poems of Alexander Pope*, ed. John Butt (New Haven, CT: Yale University Press, 1963).

At the same time, no Augustan writer ever went the length of identifying the new world of 'blest paper-credit' with trade or commerce as such. To the contrary, a certain vision of English commerce is always celebrated in Augustan writing precisely in symbolic opposition to the unreal wealth of joint-stock manipulation and speculative trading. Moreover, such commerce is always viewed as an innocent alternative to the grisly realities of war, a new mode of benign competition through which each nation increases the prosperity of every other by exporting its own superfluous production in return for necessities and comforts that it cannot itself produce. A closely related vision of commerce as a harmonising influence is found in what scholars have called Whig panegyric, as, for instance, in Addison's famous paean to the Royal Exchange in *The Spectator*, or in Defoe's lyrical description in *A Plan of the English Commerce*: 'Trade is the wealth of the world; trade makes the difference as to rich or poor, between one nation and another; trade nourishes industry, and industry begets trade; trade disperses the national wealth of the world, and trade raises a new species of wealth, which nature knew nothing of.'[12]

The essence of this notion of trade, as Richard Feingold has argued in *Nature and Society*,[13] is that it is based on a Georgic vision positing real wealth as something deriving either from the land or useful labour. This explains, for instance, the constant moral emphasis on agriculture in Augustan writing – what I would call the Hesiodic miracle that, given sunlight and water, produces grain or fruit where literally nothing existed before – and accounts as well for such eighteenth-century poems as Dyer's *The Fleece*, which celebrates England's wool trade as the basis both of its prosperity and its civic virtue. The marked Georgic element even in so pronouncedly modern a work as Adam Smith's *Wealth of Nations* must be understood in this context. In the literature of British America, as we shall see, a poem like Grainger's *Sugar Cane* may be read primarily as an attempt to imagine England's colonial enterprise within the same context of Georgic values. For the Georgic idea, as David Shields has shown in *Oracles of Empire*, was shared by early eighteenth-century Englishmen and American colonists alike, underwriting an idealising vision in which England and her colonies represent subordinate parts of a system of international commerce through which nations grow in mutual amity while increasing in internal prosperity.[14]

---

12 Daniel Defoe, *A Plan of the English Commerce* (London, 1728), p. 68.
13 Richard Feingold, *Nature and Society: Later Eighteenth-Century Uses of the Georgic* (New Brunswick, NJ: Rutgers University Press, 1978).
14 David S. Shields, *Oracles of Empire: Poetry, Politics, and Commerce in British America, 1690–1750* (Chicago: University of Chicago Press, 1990), pp. 16–29.

The Country celebration of trade assumes a certain essential relation between commerce and liberty: only in a polity where the citizens enjoy fundamental rights will commerce truly flourish. Within the synthesis of Country ideology there are what might be called Whig and Tory versions of this idea. In the Tory version, more central to Augustan writing as such, Georgic commerce is always made possible by liberty conceived purely in classical republican terms, the harmony of a productive society in which all work at once for themselves and the community, with the monarch – Bolingbroke's ideal was always Queen Elizabeth – as the symbol of national unity and harmony: 'peace and prosperity on the happy land, joy sitting in every face, content in every heart; a people unoppressed, undisturbed, unalarmed . . . fleets covering the ocean, bringing home wealth by the returns of industry'.[15] The sheer attractiveness of this vision had moved a younger Alexander Pope, at the end of *Windsor-Forest*, to imagine a time when even the primitive peoples of the New World will be drawn into the harmonising system of international commerce. The prophetic speaker in Pope's concluding allegory is the Genius of the Thames:

> The Time shall come, when free as Seas or Wind,
> Unbounded *Thames* shall flow for all Mankind,
> Whole Nations enter with each swelling Tyde,
> And Seas but join the Regions they divide;
> Earth's distant Ends our Glory shall behold,
> And the New World launch forth to seek the Old.
> Then Ships of uncouth Form shall stem the Tyde,
> And Feather'd people crowd my wealthy Side,
> And naked Youths and painted Chiefs admire
> Our Speech, our Colour, and our strange Attire!
> Oh stretch thy Reign, fair *Peace!* From Shore to Shore,
> Till Conquest cease, and Slav'ry be no more.
>
> (lines 397–408)

This is Georgic commerce as the outward expression of civic virtue, an ideal that would eventually take on momentous significance in relations between England and her American colonies. For as David Lovejoy has shown, one great consequence of the Glorious Revolution in America was that it would persuade the colonists, in a way that would remain essentially constant for the next hundred years, that issues touching the regulation of commerce must

---

15 Bolingbroke, Lord [Henry St John] *The Works of Lord Bolingbroke*, 4 vols. (London, 1879, rpt. New York, AMS Press, 1966), vol. II, p. 429.

inevitably be constitutional issues involving the basic rights of Englishmen.[16] In England, on the other hand, an assumed relation between Georgic commerce and civic virtue would dominate politics only during the relatively brief period of the Excise Crisis, when Bolingbroke's *Craftsman* and other spokesmen for Country ideology were able to convince the nation that Walpole's scheme was an assault upon English liberties, an attempt to divert the resources produced by a virtuous commerce to the ends of a new order of political corruption sustained by unreal or speculative wealth. In the American colonies, in a society imagining itself as dwelling in a permanent state of Georgic or agrarian simplicity, the language of *The Craftsman* and Pope's Horatian poems and Thomson's *Liberty* would remain persuasive right up to the moment of the Declaration of Independence.

This is why, as readers of Bailyn's *Ideological Origins of the American Revolution* will recall, the Country polemic against Walpole and his Robinocracy retained so remarkable an urgency in the colonies long after Walpole's fall, and even his death (1745), in England. In Dr Alexander Hamilton's *Itinerarium* (1744), for instance, we find Hamilton on the road outside Newcastle, Pennsylvania, in 1744, falling into a company that includes a blusterer named Morison, who 'damned the late Sir Robert Walpole for a rascal. We asked him his reasons for cursing Sir Robert, but he would give us no other but this, that he was certainly informed by some very good gentlemen, who understood the thing right well, that the said Sir Robert was a damned rogue.'[17] Ten years later, in 1754, as Bailyn reports, Massachusetts opponents of a recent excise act will be freely borrowing the earlier arguments of Bolingbroke's *Craftsman* against Walpole's excise proposal of 1733.[18] Twelve years further on, in 1766, a Rhode Island writer will unhesitatingly identify the source of English oppression as a 'monied interest' immediately recognisable as the Robinocracy as Americans imagine it to have survived unaltered into the reign of George III, extending its sway 'by levying of taxes, by a host of tax gatherers, and a long train of dependents of the crown'.[19] And in 1775, writing from London to an American correspondent on the very eve of the Revolution, we may still hear Benjamin Franklin describing in the pure idiom of Country polemic an England where 'needless places, enormous salaries, pensions, perquisites, bribes . . . devour all revenue and produce continual necessity in the midst of natural plenty'.[20]

---

16 David Lovejoy, *The Glorious Revolution in America*. (New York: Harper and Row, 1972).
17 Carl Bridgenbaugh, ed., *Gentleman's Progress: The Itinerarium of Dr Alexander Hamilton* (Pittsburgh, PA: University of Pittsburgh Press, 1948), p. 14.
18 Bailyn, *Ideological Origins*, p. 53.
19 Quoted in *ibid.*, pp. 123–4.
20 Quoted in *ibid.*, p. 136.

In England, meanwhile, a momentous series of events was bringing about an alteration of consciousness so radical as to constitute the sort of break or rupture that the French theorist, Gaston Bachelard, called a *coupure épistémologique* (a sudden break in modes of consciousness or awareness). The major event was, of course, the Seven Years' War, the 'great war for empire' which, under Pitt's brilliant leadership, taught Englishmen to see themselves as situated at the centre of a global network of political and economic relations stretching out to North America and the East and West Indies and even, as it involved slavery in the southern colonies and the Caribbean, to the western coast of Africa. We have heard Warton's response to this new reality: the England thought by the Augustans to be sunk in luxury and corruption has, in twenty years, carried its triumphs over all its enemies and established dominion throughout the world. The other notable event was, as we have also seen, the accession of George III as patriot king, what Johnson has in mind in *The False Alarm* when he castigates the Wilkes agitators for attempting 'to alienate the affections of the people from the only king, who, for almost a century, has much appeared to desire, or much endeavoured to deserve them' (*Political Writings*, p. 342). In such utterance may be heard the general sense of the nation that, with the ascent of George III to the throne, the Hanoverian monarchy has at last become a truly English institution.

At a deeper level, however, the break or rupture associated with Pitt's victorious war or the accession of George III had to do not with foreign relations or the monarchy at home, but with a new way of thinking about money or credit. For the National Debt, a deep anxiety about which had lain at the very heart of Country ideology, had increased immensely during the Seven Years' War – as John Brewer shows in *The Sinews of Power*, the underlying social revolution of the early eighteenth century was as much economic as political or constitutional – and yet England had emerged prosperous at home and enormously powerful abroad.[21] Though a very few economic theorists (notably Isaac de Pinto) were moved by this to argue that the Debt was a good thing, most non-economists of all ideological persuasions would continue to imagine it in terms of a debt owed by one person to another, and therefore to think that the National Debt must, as soon as it was convenient, be paid off. The *coupure épistémologique* in this situation thus lies not in the idea

---

21 'The greatest eulogies to public credit came in the aftermath of the unprecedented expense and extraordinary victories of the Seven Years' War. Thomas Mortimer, the translator of Isaac de Pinto . . . as well as author of the best selling *Every Man His Own Broker*, praised public credit as "a national good".' John Brewer, *The Sinews of Power: War, Money, and The English State, 1688–1783* (London: Unwin Hyman, 1989), p. 210.

of indebtedness as such, but in the less conspicuous fact that the National Debt, as much for Tories like Johnson and Hume as for 'pragmatic' Whigs in the Walpole tradition, was at a certain point at mid century suddenly and unaccountably relieved of its terror.[22]

No better key to this submerged or hidden alteration in national consciousness could be found, perhaps, than Soame Jenyns' 'Thoughts on the National Debt', a fugitive essay by a minor writer better known to literary history as Johnson's unfortunate antagonist in a controversy about the origin of good and evil. The point of Jenyns' essay is that the National Debt, far from being a curse or a matter of doom and ruin, has become a new kind of national property on the basis of which both commerce and liberty might flourish, a kind of wealth-based-on-credit that is neither speculative nor unreal but, seen for what it is, entirely consistent with an expanded set of classical republican principles. 'Our houses are filled with the richest furniture', says Jenyns '. . . and our sideboards are covered with plate . . . All these infallible marks of riches have commenced and progressively increased with our debt.' Some of this wealth, he acknowledges, has 'flowed in from the East and West Indies', but even this ought 'also to be placed to the same account; because, without the aid of this fictitious wealth, we could never have so far extended our commerce or our conquests'.[23] A few years later, in the new United States of America, Alexander Hamilton would invoke a similar logic to justify his new banking system, confident all the while that he was operating within a context of sound classical republican values.

The key to Jenyns' analysis is to be found in his positive or untroubled use of the term 'fictitious wealth', which for writers like Swift and Bolingbroke had summed up in a phrase the horror and corruption of the Walpole regime. Jenyns's 'Thoughts on the National Debt' is in its way a brilliant bit of economic theory, the glimpsing of a new world of money and credit – grown so familiar to us now as to seem unextraordinary, but in the mid eighteenth century still so strange as barely to be conceivable – that represents, at its farthest reach of implication, a transformation of the historical order. The central point of Jenyns' analysis is that 'the circulation of money is money', a point given full

---

22 Hume, notes J. G. A. Pocock, 'was on friendly terms with Isaac de Pinto, the only political economist of the age to argue that the national debt was a thoroughly healthy phenomenon, but he retained a vivid image of a society destroying itself by heaping up the public indebtedness to the point where trade and agriculture were both brought to ruin'. 'David Hume and the American Revolution', in *Virtue, Commerce, and History* (Cambridge: Cambridge University Press, 1985), pp. 132–3.

23 *The Works of Soame Jenyns, Esq*, 2nd edn, 4 vols. (London, 1793), vol. II, p. 292. Subsequent parenthetical references are to this edition.

emphasis only when one mentally italicises the word *circulation*. Imagine, says Jenyns, what would happen in an isolated rural village if someone were, for purposes of demonstration, to distribute several thousand pounds among the villagers:

> A few thousand pounds diffused through the various occupations and profes-
> sions of a small town will maintain all the families of which it is composed
> better than the same sum would support one family if it remained unem-
> ployed in the hands of a single person. The butcher and the baker feed the
> tailor and the draper, who clothes them in return; the farmer employs the
> carpenter, the bricklayer, and the labourer, and they assist him by consuming
> part of his crop . . . They are all paid in their turns by the perpetual rotation
> of the same money. If, then, the circulating a small sum within such narrow
> limits can do all this, what will not the circulation of so many millions be able
> to effect in the hands of a great and powerful nation?   (p. 284)

The point of Jenyns' parable is that the Augustan writers, not due to ill-will but simply because they had unwittingly been imprisoned in an outmoded conceptual scheme, had been compelled to picture the National Debt in much the same terms as Franklin's Poor Richard, in the simpler society of British America, would continue to ask his listeners to picture personal debt, as a species of bondage created by lavishness and waste. ('Think what you do when you run in Debt', urges Poor Richard, '*You give to another Power over your Liberty.*') This is why Walpole's England always appears in Augustan writing as the national equivalent of the wastrel heir so often met with in eighteenth-century satire and fiction, squandering the family fortune while receiving nothing in return, his preferred means of self-destruction being, no doubt because of the analogy to stockjobbing and speculation as 'sterile' forms of economic exchange, midnight gambling for ruinous sums. The vista opened up by Jenyns' parable of the village, on the other hand, is one in which prudent investors are given a reliable source of property-in-the-nation while the nation as a whole grows steadily more prosperous. Consider, says Jenyns, what actually happens when the government borrows a million pounds to expand the navy, as happened when Pitt led the nation in the Seven Years' War:

> A loan is now opened for this sum at the rate of five per cent. And parliament
> proposes taxes to defray the annual interest of fifty thousand pounds. This is
> immediately filled, and the whole money paid into the Treasury, from whence
> it is soon issued out to pay the sailors, and the various tradesmen and artificers
> who are employed in the undertaking, the shipwright, the carpenter, the
> blacksmiths, the sail-makers, the painters, the caulkers, and the rope makers,

> to which must be added the brewers, the bakers, the farmer, and the grazier, with all those by whom provisions are produced or prepared . . . and thus the whole million quickly returns back to the public, that is, to the individuals who compose it. ('Thoughts on the National Debt', p. 281)

England is its own village, in short, and the National Debt is the means by which money is distributed among its various ranks and occupations. There is nothing in the least paradoxical in seeing that this 'village' has, through precisely the means Jenyns is analysing, so grown in consequence that its power now extends to the farthest ends of the globe. In particular, the principle that 'the circulation of money is money' permanently removes the terror that unreal or 'fictitious' wealth had had for the Augustans: 'All these millions in funds and loans, in principle and interest, in Bank, South Sea, and India Stock, in Bank Notes, Exchequer Bills, in Long and Short Annuities . . . so long as they are kept alive and in motion, are as good to all intents and purposes as gold and silver' (p. 303). Jenyns's 'Thoughts on the National Debt' in some ways resembles Bernard Mandeville's *Fable of the Bees* (1705). He knows he is arguing, in terms of what might be called current economic morality, the starkest of paradoxes, and is sometimes willing to be heard as virtually a satiric voice. Yet one suspects that Jenyns' readers settled finally on much the same response that Samuel Johnson remembered from his own youthful reading of Mandeville: 'He did not puzzle me; he opened my views into real life very much' (*Life*, vol. III, p. 292).

Jenyns' analysis serves to explain why a benign or positive view of English commerce would come so generally to command assent after the Seven Years' War, for that view is essentially what the Georgic ideal of Pope or Bolingbroke's Tory commerce looks like when the fear of Walpole's Robinocracy – that is, an opposing order of unreal or speculative wealth – has been removed. This is the ideal that sustains, for instance, William Julius Mickle's accomplished and widely read translation of the Portuguese poet Camoës' *Lusiad*, which Mickle presents as the 'epic poem of Commerce', and surrounds with an apparatus – historical notes, lengthy preface and introductory essays – that amount to a celebration of a Spirit of Commerce that, having come to birth in the Portugal of Henry the Navigator, has now transmigrated to eighteenth-century Britain. For Prince Henry is meant to serve, in Mickle's portrayal, as a ghostly counsellor to contemporary English statesmen: 'The wealth and power of ancient Tyre and Carthage showed him what a maritime nation might hope, and the flourishing colonies of the Greeks were the frequent topic of his conversation. Where the Grecian commerce, confined as it was, extended its influence, the deserts became cultivated fields, cities rose, and men were drawn from the woods and caverns to unite in society.'[24]

This view of commerce would become the basis of Englishmen's conception of themselves as a polite and commercial people. It is at the heart of those radical transformations in eighteenth-century ideology explored by J. G. A. Pocock in *Virtue, Commerce, and History*, where politeness emerges as the name of a sustainable moral equilibrium between 'virtue' and 'commerce'. As important, it had the crucial effect of subtracting commerce, which had played so long and controversial a role in the Augustan critique of Walpole's England, from the domain of politics. Thus it is, for instance, that the Samuel Johnson who always remains a Tory and an orthodox Christian in his deep commitment to an Augustinian view of human moral nature – the idea of a moral nature perpetually prone to weakness and error, no matter what gains or improvements occur at the level of material progress – will also and unparadoxically be the Johnson who cheerfully agrees to write a preface for Richard Rolt's *Dictionary of Trade and Commerce*, or who delights in the metropolitan bustle of a London existence, or who always hates, as he once says, to hear ancient times praised at the expense of modern times (*Boswell's Life of Johnson*, vol. IV, p. 217).

The context of Johnson's outburst against the Americans, then, shocking as it no doubt was to Mrs Knowles and others in the company, is a climate of opinion in which Englishmen generally had learned to think of commerce as an inevitably benign or civilising influence, and the American colonies, whose relation to the mother country was rooted in commerce, as among its primary beneficiaries. Thus, for instance, the conclusion of Mickle's lyrical account, in the introduction to his *Lusiad* translation, of the British empire in America: 'To have given a savage continent an image of the British constitution is indeed the greatest glory of the British crown.' From the genius of Prince Henry of Portugal, that visionary promoter of navigation and commerce, declares Mickle, 'did the British American empire arise, an empire which . . . will in a few centuries, perhaps, be the glory of the world' (p. x). The grim intrusion of history is registered only in the second edition, published in 1778: 'This was written ere the commencement of the unhappy civil war in America' (p. x). Mickle's crestfallen footnote marks the moment when Englishmen would learn that, as Samuel Johnson had been trying to tell them, England and her American colonies had for some time been speaking separate political languages.

24 William Julius Mickle, *The Lusiad: or, the Discovery of India*, 2nd edn (Oxford, 1778), pp. xxx–xxxi.

In eighteenth-century literary relations between England and America, transatlantic discourse may be taken as that focussing on the problem of imperium in the Roman or classical sense. This is a term very badly translated by our term 'empire', which, bearing as it does the traces of Lenin's twentieth-century attempt to work out a Marxist theory of imperialism, inevitably bears as well the political commitments of modern anti-colonial ideology.[25] The Roman imperium was originally nothing more than the power given to a general to command the legions assigned to him. Later it became the state of martial law imposed by a victorious general or *imperator* on a newly conquered province, and then only subsequently the custodial relation assumed by Rome – one normally leaving local customs, laws and forms of government intact, reserving to Rome the power of taxation and military rule – to any province included within the *pax Romana*. For Samuel Johnson composing *Taxation No Tyranny*, as for Edmund Burke delivering his great speech *On Conciliation with the American Colonies* in the House of Commons or John Adams writing as 'Novanglus' in distant Massachusetts, 'empire' was always a term to be translated by imperium in this older sense.[26]

Eighteenth-century writing having no reference to this notion of imperium is, even when produced in the American colonies, not transatlantic in any

25 For an exemplary instance of the distortions that inevitably result from the attempt to impose a modern or twentieth-century notion of 'empire' on eighteenth-century texts, see Suvir Kaul's account of 'the ideological project' of Thomas Gray's 'Ode on the Death of a Favorite Cat, Drowned in a Tub of Goldfishes'. Given his own understanding of 'empire', Kaul finds himself able to redescribe Gray's entire poem as 'one of the deliberate and consistent mystifications of the imperial process' that he imagines to be common in eighteenth-century writing, which for him consists in its entirety of 'repeated and varied enactments of certain cultural, political, and economic themes so that they are assimilated and consolidated as the hegemonic outlook of the nation state'. Suvir Kaul, 'Why Selima Drowns: Thomas Gray and the Domestication of the Imperial Ideal', *PMLA* 105.2 (March 1990), 223–32; these references pp. 233, 224. For more recent works written from a similar perspective, see, for instance, Laura Brown, *Ends of Empire: Women and Ideology in Early Eighteenth-Century English Literature* (Ithaca, NY and London: Cornell University Press, 1993), Erin Mackie, *Market à la Mode: Fashion, Commodity and Gender in 'The Tatler' and 'The Spectator'* (Baltimore, MD and London: Johns Hopkins University Press, 1997), and Kaul's own *Thomas Gray and Literary Authority* (Stanford, CA: Stanford University Press, 1992).

26 See P. J. Marshall's excellent discussion of this notion of imperium in relation to Burke's vision of empire as being 'like the empire of the Roman Republic . . . an empire of protection over a diverse collection of allies and provinces'. Marshall usefully quotes as one of Burke's sources Cicero's description of the Roman imperium in *De Officiis*:

> as long as the empire of the Roman People maintained itself by acts of service, not of oppression, wars were waged in the interests of our allies or to safeguard our supremacy; the end of our wars was marked by acts of clemency or by only a necessary degree of severity. The Senate was a haven of refuge for kings, tribes and nations, and the highest ambition of our magistrates and generals was to defend our provinces and allies with justice and honour. And so our government could be called more accurately a protectorate of the world than a dominion.

meaningful sense. For such writing tends simply to project a generalised world of English-speaking readers for whom distinctions of locality carry no special importance. Thus it is, for instance, that Jonathan Edwards, who looms so large in American intellectual histories as a distinctively American voice, the impassioned Northampton preacher of *Sinners in the Hands of an Angry God* and inspirer of the Great Awakening, is normally heard in eighteenth-century London simply as a theologian or thinker, attended to on much the same terms as one might attend to arguments advanced in Shaftesbury's *Characteristics* or Butler's *Analogy* or Hume's *Enquiry Concerning Human Understanding*. 'DR. MAYO. (to Dr. Johnson) "Pray, Sir, have you read Edwards, of New England, on Grace?" JOHNSON. "No, Sir." BOSWELL. "It puzzled me so much as to the freedom of the human will, by stating, with wonderful acute ingenuity, our being actuated by a series of motives which we cannot resist, that the only relief I had was to forget it" . . . JOHNSON. "All theory is against the freedom of the will; all experience for it"' (*Life*, vol. III, pp. 290–1).

At the same time, eighteenth-century writing that wholly presupposes the Roman model of imperium also tends to demote questions of locality to relative unimportance, and to do so, paradoxically enough, even when its geographical setting is transatlantic. Thus, for instance, the William Byrd of the early *London Diary* moves about the crowded streets of the metropolis simply as an Augustan gentleman, a theatregoer and coffee-house wit keeping company with such notable acquaintances as Congreve and Wycherley. But the William Byrd of the later *Secret Diary*, kept after he has returned from England to his Virginia plantation at Westover, is recognisably this same Augustan gentleman transported to another setting. '[19 June 1712.] I rose about 6 o'clock and read two chapters in Hebrew and some Greek in Lucian . . . The weather was very hot and sultry. I wrote a letter to England and then wrote a public account. Then I read some Latin in Sallust till dinner and then I ate some bacon and sallet. In the afternoon I made some punch and put it into bottles and then I wrote another account and afterwards read more Latin in Sallust. In the evening I took a walk about the plantation.'[27]

The solution to the paradox is that Byrd in either London or Virginia is, as his daily Greek and Latin reading suggests, someone moving primarily in the medium of an imagined classical antiquity. Thus Byrd walking about his

P. J. Marshall, 'Burke and Empire', in Stephen Taylor, Richard Connors and Clyve Jones, eds. *Hanoverian Britain and Empire*. (Woodbridge, Suffolk: Boydell Press, 1998), pp. 288–97 (pp. 291–2).

27 *The Secret Diary of William Byrd of Westover, 1709–1712*, eds. Louis B. Wright and Marion Tinling (Richmond, VA: The Dietz Press, 1941).

plantation at Westover is the Roman paterfamilias, in the extended Roman sense of 'family' that included *servi* or slaves as well as spouse and children, a conception that serves to explain Byrd's total absence of guilt about owning slaves. In the same way, Byrd voyaging from London to Virginia is, like Cicero on the way from Rome to Tusculum or Pliny to his northern villa, simply a traveller within an imperium understood in classical terms, as a homogenous cultural space projected onto a vast and diverse geographical territory. Nor is this unproblematic sense of imperium restricted to classically educated souls. The young Ben Franklin of the *Autobiography*, travelling to England with his friend James Ralph and taking up work in a London printing house, is moving within essentially the same cultural space. Transatlantic discourse as such thus emerges only when the notion of imperium is felt to have become problematic, leaving a writer unsure about how relations between England and her American colonies are to be grasped in terms of the Roman model.

The model most often breaks down when a writer is made to feel the urgency of some older myth that, in the manner of the pagan Golden Age or biblical Garden of Eden, identifies a more primitive social stage with a state of moral innocence. For the great problem of the imperium model would turn out to be that it disallowed any appeal from the corruptions of the present to a simpler or more virtuous past. In projecting a homogeneous cultural space, as in Cicero's *Ad Familiares* or Byrd's diaries, the notion of imperium inevitably projects as well an idea of time, a vast world frozen, as it were, within the political present of Rome or England. This is the restriction Robert Beverley is reacting against, for instance, when in *The History and Present State of Virginia* he deliberately summons those echoes of the Golden Age that had once been a feature of Elizabethan travel narrative. Thus the Indians encountered by Sir Walter Raleigh and his companions are duly recalled in Beverley's narrative as a people living in 'primitive innocence', the early explorers' landscape is seen as retaining 'the virgin purity and plenty of the first creation' and the countryside as 'so delightful, and desirable; so pleasant, and plentiful . . . the woods, and soil so charming, and fruitful, and all other things so agreeable, that Paradise itself seemed to be there, in its first native lustre'.[28]

Yet Beverley's *History and State of Virginia* always acknowledges its distance from Elizabethan travel narrative. It was published in England in 1705, when readers had long since come to understand that works like John Smith's *True Relation* or Hakluyt's *Principal Navigations* were quasi-mythological narratives

---

28 Robert Beverley, *The History and Present State of Virginia*, ed. Louis B. Wright (Chapel Hill, NC: University of North Carolina Press, 1947), p. 262.

consisting as much of European fantasies about the New World as sober records of navigation and exploration. We take the point of Beverley's invocations of the Golden Age only when we recall the dark and troubled political background against which *The History and Present State of Virginia* is being written – in particular, the turmoil of Bacon's Rebellion – in which relations between England and her American colonies had suddenly become a matter of violent contention.[29] This is a context in which any invocation of a simpler, more innocent past represents a deliberate break with the imperium model, an insistence in symbolic terms that America should be seen as the solution to some moral problem – degeneration, decline, civic corruption – for which the collective name is normally England, or Europe, or, more generally, the Old World. This is a pattern that will persist right up to the moment of the American Revolution, producing such works as Crèvecoeur's *Letters from an American Farmer* or, in a somewhat different register, the *Travels* of the American naturalist John Bartram.

In the earlier part of the eighteenth century, especially as events carry Augustan writing towards the moment of cultural crisis marked by Boling-broke's *Craftsman* and Pope's Horatian satires, the normal appeal against the monstrous corruption of Walpole's Robinocracy is to the idealised vision of the early Roman republic associated with Machiavelli's theory of *ritorno ai principii*, that return to moral origins or founding principles that alone can save from ruin a society otherwise rapidly sinking into luxury and corruption. It is the same sense of cultural crisis that would, a few years later, give John Brown's *Estimate of the Manners and Principles of the Times* so enormous an impact – 'We are,' said Brown in a phrase endlessly echoed in both Britain and the American colonies, 'rolling to the brink of a precipice that must destroy us' – and its solution in Augustan writing is always seen as a return to the state of virtuous simplicity symbolised by early Roman society, as here in Dyer's *The Ruins of Rome*:

> As yet they stood,
> Simple of life; as yet seducing wealth
> Was unexplor'd, and shame of poverty
> Yet unimagin'd – Shine not all the fields
> With various fruitage? murmur not the brooks
> Along the flowery valleys? They, content,

29 For a concise estimate of the effect of Bacon's Rebellion – the uprising led by Nathaniel Bacon, a Virginia planter who rallied the colonists against the tyrannical rule of Sir William Berkeley, the colonial governor – on transatlantic political relations, see Alison Gilbert Olson, *Anglo-American Politics 1660–1775* (Oxford: Oxford University Press, 1975.)

Feasted at Nature's hand, indelicate,
Blithe, in their easy taste; and only sought
To know their duties; that their only strife,
Their generous strife, and greatly to perform.
They through all shapes of peril and of pain,
Intent on honor, dar'd in thickest death
To snatch the glorious deed.[30]

In America this image of early Rome would produce something very like a shock of collective self-recognition, as though a mirror had been unexpectedly held up to the settlers of Virginia and Maryland and Massachusetts in the moment that they had their attention directed to the simplicity and virtue of the young Roman republic. The effect, as we have seen, was powerful and long-lasting, leading to a transatlantic debate that on the American side would be conducted largely in the language of Country ideology – that Whiggish cant that so infuriated Johnson – and an idea of republican simplicity that would die out in America only with the generation of Washington and Adams and Jefferson. In England, on the other hand, the same myth of Roman virtue would be accommodated in an altogether a different way, through an appeal to the notion of *translatio imperii* – the notion of liberty or freedom, and therefore of historical greatness, as migrating from older to younger civilizations – that would portray the virtue and simplicity of life in England's American colonies as simply a natural territorial extension of English civic virtue.

The myth of *translatio imperii* made its earliest appearance in Augustan writing as a story needed to make intelligible the Machiavellian theory of a return to former principles. For the civic mythology that gave heroic status to the tiny Greek city-states as they had been able miraculously to defeat the vast mercenary armies of Asiatic despotism – the subject, in Augustan England, of works like Glover's *Leonidas* – or to Cato as he had chosen to commit suicide rather than live in a Roman state that had collapsed into tyranny – the subject of Addison's *Cato*, so inspiring to Americans that Washington would have it performed for his troops at Valley Forge – also took upon itself the burden of explaining why states like Athens and Rome had subsequently fallen into decline. Part of the answer is that the *virtus* that carries a civilization upwards to greatness then also inevitably brings about, through luxury, its degeneration into a mere aggregation of self-interested individuals. To rise in

---

30 Parenthetical citations of Dyer, Glover and Grainger are to David French's reprint edition of Alexander Chalmers' *English Poets: Minor English Poets, 1660–1780: A Selection from Alexander Chalmers' The English Poets*, compiled by David P. French, 10 vols. (New York: Benjamin Blom, 1967). Further citations in the text to this edition are marked CF.

history is inevitably to gain power and wealth, but power and wealth then fatally undermine the *virtus* or disinterestedness – what Dyer means by saying that the early Romans sought only 'to know their duties' – that had previously led citizens to put the interest of the community as a whole before their own.

The myth of *translatio imperii* is also the story of how the liberty or freedom that led to the rise of Greece and Rome has been, through the course of human history, on a long migratory passage north and west, from the old and decaying civilisations of the Mediterranean to the young and vital states of northern Europe, the Dutch republic as it threw off the despotism of Catholic Spain in the seventeenth century, the English nation as it has been steadily rising in power and glory since the days of Elizabeth and the Armada. The *translatio imperii* theme is the great subject of Thomson's four-book blank verse poem *Liberty*, and the indispensable background to a poem like John Dyer's *The Fleece*, in which England's American colonies make their appearance as outposts of English liberty in the New World. Dyer's theme is Georgic commerce, that species of trade which, as deriving directly from the land and rural labour, at once preserves the *virtus* of the nation and permits it to spread to regions subject to its imperium, as English liberty has now spread to America:

> No land gives more employment to the loom,
> Or kindlier feeds the indigent; no land
> With more variety of wealth rewards
> The hand of labour: thither from the wrongs
> Of lawless rule, the free-born spirit flies;
> Thither Affliction, thither Poverty,
> And arts and sciences: thrice happy clime,
> Which Britain makes th'asylum of mankind.
>
> (Book IV)

In the American colonies, the idea of *translatio imperii*, and specifically the idea of America as what Dyer calls the asylum of mankind, would eventually provide a powerful impetus to American independence, which is why one hears so direct an echo of Dyer's language in, for instance, the famous ending of Tom Paine's *Common Sense*: 'Every spot of the old world is overrun with oppression. Freedom hath been hunted round the globe. Asia and Africa have long expelled her. Europe regards her like a stranger, and England hath given her warning to depart. O! receive the fugitive, and prepare in time an asylum for mankind.'[31] Yet this involves a transmutation of the *translatio imperii* theme never foreseen by poets like Dyer, for Paine's whole point is that England has

---

31 Thomas Paine, *Common Sense* (Mount Vernon, NY: A. Colish, 1976), 60.

herself been swallowed up, or is on the very brink of being swallowed up, by the same noisome tide of luxury and corruption that earlier inundated Greece and Rome. Only in America, separated by three thousand miles of ocean from the despotisms of the Old World, does liberty survive. The question is why, given the seemingly inexorable narrative logic of the *translatio imperii* story – Bishop George Berkeley's 'Westward the course of empire takes its way' – the conclusion that seemed so self-evident to the American colonists was never glimpsed as a possibility by the Augustan writers.

The answer is related to the notion of Georgic commerce celebrated in Dyer's *The Fleece*, and earlier given expression, as we have seen, in works like Pope's *Windsor-Forest* and Bolingbroke's *Idea of a Patriot King*. For the idea of a commerce rooted in Georgic values would very soon come to imply, within the larger structure of Augustan civic mythology, that liberty has historically always been the precondition of a thriving commerce. This is the essential idea, for instance, of Richard Glover's *London: or, the Progress of Commerce*, in which Glover retells the story of *translatio imperii* as the story of commerce, born together with liberty in the ancient state of Tyre, carried by Greek trading vessels around the shores of the Mediterranean, making its way northward – as in the standard *translatio imperii* story – to the Dutch republic in the seventeenth century, and now triumphantly visible in the ships of all nations crowding the wharves of eighteenth-century London. The seriousness with which Glover takes the notion that commercial prosperity follows in the wake of liberty may be felt in his treatment of the Dutch rebellion against Spain – that 'disgrace of Europe', looter of the New World and oppressor of the Old – and of its hero William of Orange. For their reward is the Dutch Golden Age, when 'favouring Commerce' had made the Dutch Republic into a world power, raising William's countrymen higher and higher

> . . . till, rever'd
> Among the mightiest, on the brightest roll
> Of fame they shone, by splendid wealth and power
> Grac'd and supported; thus a genial soil
> Diffusing vigour through the infant oak,
> Affords it strength to flourish, till at last
> Its lofty head, in verdant honours clad,
> It rears amidst the proudest of the grove.
>
> (CF, vol. VII, p. 20)

At any such moment, *The Progress of Commerce* moves very close to what Pocock and others have taught us to understand as a later eighteenth-century discourse of politeness, that theory of moral equilibrium that will generate such works as Adam Ferguson's *Essay on Civil Society* and Adam Smith's *The Wealth of Nations*. And in fact something very like the notion of polite civilisation is explicitly proclaimed elsewhere in Glover's poem, as when he imagines Commerce as a creative power in human societies, a goddess who by the wave of her sceptre is able to create smiling fields and vineyards in barren deserts, summon into being populous cities or with the invention of writing introduce the possibility of literature and philosophy and science, 'laws, learning, wisdom, Nature's works reveal'd / By godlike sages.' This is Commerce, in short, as 'a new-born power' working independently of human will or design to create civilisation as such, as a prophetic voice in Glover's poem proclaims while the gods observe her birth on the shores of ancient Tyre: 'She in lonely sands / Shall bid the tower-encircled city rise, / The barren sea shall people, and the wilds / Of dreary Nature shall with plenty clothe' (CF, vol. VII, p. 18).

By the end of *London: or, the Progress of Commerce*, the English imperium has been reimagined in terms that make liberty and commerce virtually interchangeable – 'Ye mariners of Britain,' cries Glover in the closing lines, apostrophising British sailors as the 'chosen train of Liberty and Commerce' – and in such a way as immediately to explain why the claims of the American colonists would, a few years later, seem so incomprehensible to English ears. As Eliga Gould has shown in *The Persistence of Empire*, the English people at the time of the Townshend Acts and the early years of the North ministry tended overwhelmingly to support their government's uncompromising attitude towards the colonies. The explanation, it is reasonable to suppose, is that the vision of imperium that emerged from Augustan writing was widely taken by readers of poems like *The Progress of Commerce* and *The Fleece* to guarantee that the American colonies, whose relations with England were rooted in commerce, must on that very account already be enjoying English liberty: *ubi imperium, ibi libertas*. The language of corruption and tyranny still being spoken in mid-century Philadelphia and Boston, in short, and spoken only a few years earlier in the drawing rooms and coffee houses of London, had become unintelligible to English ears.

The American Revolution may be taken, on this view, as an attempt to assert even to the point of armed resistance that the whole notion of imperium sustaining England's new vision of itself as a polite and commercial nation was nothing more than a grandiose self-deception, that the discourse of liberty and commerce could be seen to have an unresolved contradiction at its centre. The same sense of latent contradiction would come ominously to haunt transatlantic literary relations in the period immediately preceding the Revolution, as may be seen in James Grainger's *The Sugar Cane*, perhaps the most remarkable work to emerge from the long meditation on imperium that had begun with Pope's *Windsor-Forest*. For *The Sugar Cane*, a long poem on British sugar cultivation in the West Indies, is like Dyer's *The Fleece* a celebration of Georgic commerce, a work that, in the manner of Virgil's *Georgics* in ancient Rome or Hesiod's *Works and Days* in ancient Greece, is meant to remind a highly-developed civilisation that its roots are in the life of field and vineyard, and in the timeless world of rural toil that, in scenes far remote from the bustle of the agora or the forum, sustains the life of the shopkeeper and the statesman in every age.

In the normal manner of Georgic poetry, *The Sugar Cane* devotes a great deal of time to the most prosaic details of agricultural life, giving abundant advice about soil, weather, fertiliser, methods of irrigation, the care of farm animals, the best times for sowing and harvesting the crop. As with Virgil's *Georgics*, the great prototype of all such poems, the point is gradually to draw the reader – always, in the Georgic mode, a city-dweller – imaginatively into the deep unchanging rhythms of the agricultural year, to provide a moral vantage point from which civilisation may be perceived as what it after all is, a transitory show. In the same way, since British sugar cultivation in the West Indies uses Negro labour, Grainger gives much practical advice about buying African slaves: beware the Moco tribe, who tend to commit suicide in captivity. Do not be put off by the seeming stubbornness of the Minnah, who are hard workers when trained to agricultural tasks. Seek especially Negroes from western Africa, who are used to toilsome labour: 'Such are the children of the Golden Coast; / Such the Papaws, of Negroes far the best: / And such the num'rous tribes, that skirt the shore, / From rapid Volta to the distant Rey' (CF, vol. v, p. 284).

Given *The Sugar Cane*'s Georgic model, there is nothing contradictory in this, the world of classical antiquity having been one in which it was wholly consistent to rejoice in one's own status as a freeborn Greek or Roman while owning slaves. Virgil had written the *Georgics*, after all, against a background in which the Roman slaves working the fields surrounding the typical *villa rustica* were as numerous as those on any West Indian plantation. Yet *The Sugar Cane* is not simply a Georgic poem but a poem of Georgic commerce, a celebration of that new imperium through which British liberty is also imagined to have been spread through a network of commercial relations to England's North American colonies and possessions in the West Indies. Thus it is that Grainger's dissertation on the buying and care and maintenance of Negro slaves begins to falter under an intolerable strain of moral contradiction, moving fitfully from topic to topic, glancing sidelong at the dismaying possibility that Negro slaves, too, may be regarded as human beings, until at last there comes an impassioned outburst that negates everything that has gone before. Had his poetic Muse the power, cries Grainger,

> 'T would be the fond ambition of her soul
> To quell tyrannic sway; knock off the chains
> Of heart-debasing slavery; give to man,
> Of every colour and of every clime,
> Freedom, which stamps him image of his God.
> Then laws, Oppression's scourge, fair Virtue's prop,
> Offspring of Wisdom! Should impartial reign,
> To knit the whole in well-accorded strife;
> Servants, not slaves; of choice, and not compell'd;
> The Blacks should cultivate the cane-land isles.
>
> (CF, vol. VII, p. 286)

The sense of internal contradiction that produces this local and temporary collapse in *The Sugar Cane* brings us very close to that larger collapse in political discourse that would shortly bring about the American Revolution. Yet it may be noted in passing that the vision of imperium that had imagined liberty as spreading along with British commerce would have a curious afterlife, in a way that Grainger's outburst seems uncannily to anticipate, in later eighteenth-century abolitionist literature. Thus, for instance, the *Interesting Narrative* of Olaudah Equiano, perhaps the most remarkable contribution to that literature produced during the period, will end not with an appeal to religious conscience, or to social justice, but with a utopian fantasy in which slavery is abolished as Africa becomes a vast new market within the system of British commerce. The 'hidden treasures' of African agriculture and mineral wealth, declares Equiano, 'will be brought to light and into circulation': 'Industry, enterprize, and mining, will have their full scope, proportionably as they civilize. In a word, it lays open an endless field of commerce to the British manufacturers and merchant adventurers. The manufacturing interest and the general interests are synonymous. The abolition of slavery would be in reality an universal good.'[32]

---

32 Olaudah Equiano, *The Interesting Narrative of the Life of Olaudah Equiano, or Gustavus Vassa, the African. Written by Himself*, ed. Vincent Carretta (London: Penguin, 1955), p. 234.

In more immediate terms, the demand that Britain live up to its own assumptions concerning liberty and commerce, and specifically to the idea of imperium as the extension of English freedom through trade, would lead inexorably to the outbreak of hostilities in America. This is very clearly grasped in Burke's speech *On Conciliation with the Colonies*, his great attempt to intervene at the last possible moment to restore peace. The way the colonists have learned that they are freeborn Englishmen, Burke reminds his fellow members of parliament, is through a century and more of commercial relations with their mother country. This is the real point of the long disquisition on commerce that occupies the first part of Burke's address, that otherwise puzzling comparison of trade balances between England and North America, accompanied in its printed version by statistical tables comparing Britain's export trade in 1704 to her colonial trade in 1772. It is the idea that liberty and commerce are inseparable, Burke is trying to show, that is now needed to explain why the colonists understand such measures as the Stamp Act to be "contrary to the true principle of commerce," and therefore to their rights and liberties as Englishmen.[33]

The effect of the American Revolution on transatlantic discourse in England was abrupt and dramatic, conjuring away its vision of imperium as Prospero's airy vision is made to vanish in the play. The idealising images of America found in *Windsor Forest* or *The Fleece* vanish as well. The idea of America that begins to emerge resembles something very like the allegory of Glover's *London, or the Progress of Commerce* played in reverse, with the populous cities and crowded harbours summoned by the civilising power of commerce dissolving back into nothingness to reveal what we heard the prophetic speaker in Glover's poem portray as the original 'wilds of dreary nature'. The possibility of an American landscape thus stripped bare of idealising fantasy had long before occurred to Samuel Johnson, always impatient with the claims of the colonists. Why, he had asked in the *Literary Magazine* in 1756, would any sane Englishman wish to emigrate to America, 'why should any number of our inhabitants be banished from their trades and their homes to a trackless desert, where life is to begin anew'? (*Political Writings*, p. 211). But the lasting image of America as it would look when the vision of imperium had dissolved comes at the end of Goldsmith's *The Deserted Village*, when the forlorn English villagers gather on the strand to take ship to a New World suddenly revealed for what it really is:

---

33 *The Writings and Speeches of Edmund Burke*, eds. W. M. Elofson and John A. Woods, 9 vols. (Oxford: Clarendon Press, 1981–96), *Speech on Conciliation*, vol. III, pp. 105–68.

Far different there from all that charm'd before,
The various terrors of that horrid shore . . .
Those poisonous fields with rank luxuriance crowned
Where the dark scorpion gathers death around;
Where at each step the stranger fears to wake
The rattling terrors of the vengeful snake;
Where crouching tigers wait their hapless prey,
And savage men more murderous still than they.

Here ends transatlantic discourse in eighteenth-century English writing, on a note of abrupt disillusionment that summons into view an American landscape that will appear in essentially the same terms to nineteenth-century British travellers, the American south of Fanny Kemble's *Journal*, the horrifying squalor of backwoods life in Frances Trollope's *Domestic Manners of the Americans* or, in Illinois, the 'Eden' – that 'hideous swamp, choked with slime and matted growth' – purchased by the unwary hero of Dickens' *Martin Chuzzlewit*. When the discourse is taken up again, it will be on the other side of the Atlantic, by authors – Joseph Dennie and the *Port Folio* writers in Philadelphia, Washington Irving and the *Salmagundi* circle in New York – as appalled as Mrs Trollope or Dickens by the brutality and rawness of life in the New World, and turning back to eighteenth-century English literature, the world of Addison's Sir Roger de Coverley and Sterne's Uncle Toby and Goldsmith's Vicar of Wakefield, to seek for what has been lost. It is in such nineteenth-century works as Irving's *Bracebridge Hall*, imagining an older English society in terms perhaps only possible to an American writer, that the forlorn villagers of Goldsmith's deserted Auburn will make their way home again.

PART IV

*

LITERATURE AND SOCIAL
AND INSTITUTIONAL
CHANGE

The eighteenth-century periodical essay

ROBERT DeMARIA, JR

Despite deep roots in literary tradition and a far-reaching influence, the periodical essay is a genre that flourished only in a fifty-year period between 1709 and 1759. The rise of the genre begins with John Dunton's *Athenian Gazette* on 17 March 1691; its maturity arrives part way through Addison and Steele's *Tatler* (1709–11); and its decline is advanced when the last number of Goldsmith's short-lived *Bee* is published on 24 November 1759. In between the genre reaches its full flowering in Addison and Steele's daily *Spectator* (1711–12) and its most transcendent and durable form in Johnson's *Rambler* (1750–2).

More than most literary genres, the periodical essay belongs to a specific time period because of its tight connection to specific, datable changes in politics, in law and in publishing practices. The periodical essay is proper to a certain phase of periodical publication, which got its start in England during the Civil War but was not fully established until 1702, when the first true daily, the *Daily Courant*, began. In the early years, government control of the press had a powerful effect on periodical publication, which flourished most when there were disruptions in the government itself. *A Census of British Newspapers and Periodicals 1620–1800* contains a chronological list of periodicals in print in Britain. A correlation of this list with political events and relevant legal changes would show that periodical publication always rises at times of national crisis and always falls when licensing laws are enforced. The numbers rise and fall a good deal before 1688, when they rise, never again to fall off very considerably.[1] The official abandonment of licensing in 1695 is crucial to the establishment of various kinds of periodicals, including the single-essay periodical. Periodical publication continued to rise after 1760, but by then a trend was well under way that demoted and subsumed the periodical essay. Essays that formerly comprised the whole of a particular publication appeared more and more

---

1 R. S. Crane and F. B. Kaye (eds.), *A Census of British Newspapers and Periodicals 1620–1800* (Chapel Hill, NC: University of North Carolina Press, 1927), pp. 179–201.

frequently in magazines made up of heterogeneous material. A crucial example is Johnson's *Idler*, which appeared weekly as part of the *Universal Chronicle* from 1758 to 1760. As parts of magazines and other publications periodical essays survived in great numbers throughout the century and still survive. However, despite the obvious influence of their eighteenth-century antecedents, there are fundamental differences of production and reception between the true periodical essay and its generic progeny, feature articles in magazines, editorials and syndicated columns.[2]

In the periodical essay proper several characteristics come together more or less in concert: regular and frequent appearance (daily, ideally); presentation of a particular point of view, often 'spoken' by a literary persona or a related group of personae; correspondence with readers (either fictional or real); domination of the periodical by the essay and, ideally, complete identification of the two. All of these features, which combine perfectly in *The Spectator* (and perhaps in the six-day a week *Spectator* only), are tied to political movements. However, the periodical essay par excellence is not bound as much by partisan politics as by a less tendentious involvement with the public sphere of private individuals. The periodical essay, like all serial publication, is part of the evolution of the professional writer from his or her role as a creature of the court or parliament to his or her reliance on publishers and, through them, on the reading public. The audience for the periodical essay is educated, but not as learned as the audience for periodical writing in many of the 'Reviews', 'Works of the Learned', journals of societies (*Transactions of the Royal Society*, for example) and even book catalogues (such as the *Term Catalogues*). The ideal readers of the periodical essay may value learning and even have some, but the world is too much with them to permit settled habits of study. Youngish, often female, and nearly always middle-class, these readers are the same ones who embrace the rising new novel. In fact, many of the best periodical writers also composed fiction and early forms of the novel.

Although the periodical essays of the eighteenth century are stylistically diverse, as a group, they champion the 'improvement' and 'correction' of English. It is telling that several of the principal essayists of the century were also involved in plans to reform English by means of a national dictionary. Addison, Ambrose Philips, Swift and Pope all proposed dictionaries, and Johnson finished the job in 1755, three years after completing *The Rambler*.

2 My overview is indebted to Walter Graham, *English Literary Periodicals* (New York: Thomas Nelson and Sons, 1930), pp. 13–144.

From the *Athenian Mercury* to the *Tatler*

In 1691 the innovative and adventuresome John Dunton, just back from a commercial visit to Massachusetts, started *The Athenian Mercury*. His idea was to use the anonymity of print to create a dialogue between readers and a group of 'experts' who could answer their candid questions. In addition to Dunton, the Athenians were comprised of Richard Sault, a mathematician; John Norris, the author of *Miscellanies* (1689), a popular work of practical divinity; and Samuel Wesley, a recent Oxford graduate who would become well known as a writer of popular religious songs and as the father of John Wesley. The Athenian Society is an important precursor of the Scandal Club in Defoe's *Review*, the Bickerstaff family in *The Tatler* and the Spectator Club. Later on such fictional social groups were often replaced by singular personae, such as Mr Rambler, but the presence of personae is a crucial ingredient in the genre of the periodical essay.

The Athenian Mercury was dependent upon two growing social institutions: the coffee house and the post office. The first question in the second issue was, 'Whether the Author is not in League with the General Penny-Post Office?' This is a small joke, since Dunton solicited letters from his readers, and they would have been sent via the Penny-Post. From an economic standpoint, the periodical essay is linked generically to the letter, which had not yet become a very private sort of communication clearly distinct from the newsletter.[3] But the coffee house was even more important. So successful was Dunton in pervading the public sphere that after the first thirty numbers, he dares coffee-house owners not to subscribe: customers will leave if they don't find it; new customers will come if it is there.[4] Twenty-two years later, Addison claimed that each number of his *Spectator* attracted twenty readers in coffee houses and other places of public, middle-class resort. With 3,000 copies of each number in print, Addison claimed a daily readership of 60,000.[5] The mechanism of this amazing popularity was tooled up by *The Athenian Mercury*.

Like so many of the essay periodicals that followed it, *The Athenian Mercury* was printed on a folio half sheet, one leaf, double column on both sides. The

---

3 On the use of personal letters as newsletters, see Richard D. Brown, *Knowledge is Power: the Diffusion of Information in Early America, 1700–1865* (Oxford: Oxford University Press, 1991).

4 *The Athenian Gazette or Casuistical Mercury, Resolving all the most Nice and Curious Questions Proposed by the Ingenious*, 16 vols. (London, 1691–5), vol. II, no. 4. (The title was changed after the first number to *The Athenian Mercury*.)

5 *The Spectator*, ed. Donald F. Bond, 5 vols. (Oxford: Clarendon Press, 1965), vol. I, p. 44.

printing was tight and the format very inexpensive. It looked like a newspaper; it was read in the same venue as a newspaper; but its content concerned matters of interest to private individuals rather than to citizens or the state. Although they excluded politics, the questions were still quite various: 'Whether the Torments of the damn'd are visible to the Saints in Heaven? & vice versa?' 'Whether the Soul is Eternal, or pre-existent from the Creation, or contemporary with its Embrio?'[6] 'Whether Negroes shall rise so at the last Day?'[7] 'Why the Sea is salt?'[8] 'Whence proceeds weeping and laughing for the same cause?'[9] 'Whether is happier a Married or an Unmarried State?'[10] 'Whether most Persons do not Marry too young?'[11] 'Whether it be proper for Women to be *Learned?*'[12]

Like most of the essay periodicals of the eighteenth century, *The Athenian Mercury* courted a female readership (as political and review periodicals did not). Not long after beginning publication, Dunton declared that the first Tuesday in every month would be devoted to questions from women or about women, marriage, or love. He started this practice on 2 June 1691, and executed it very faithfully. The Athenians, unlike their namesakes, take women's issues very much to heart. For example, on 14 July 1691 *The Athenian Mercury* prints a prayer for women facing the prospect of marriage:

> From a profane Libertine, from one affectedly Pious, from a profuse Almoneer, from an Uncharitable Wretch; from a wavering Religioso, and an Injudicious Zealot — Deliver me!
>
> From one of a starch'd Gravity, or of a ridiculous Levity . . . From an extacy'd Poet, from a Modern Wit . . . From a *Venus* Darling, from a *Bacchus* Proselyte, from a Travelling Half, from a Domestick Animal; from all Masculine Plagues not yet recounted ———— Deliver me.[13]

Not surprisingly, Dunton's next project was a journal completely devoted to women's issues, and he hired a woman, the poet, Elizabeth Singer (later, Mrs Rowe), to handle the correspondence.

When he was in the employ of William Temple, a correspondent of the Athenians, the young Jonathan Swift wrote an unusually unironic ode on the Society. Although they were miraculously safe from Swift himself, Dunton

---

6 *Athenian Gazette*, vol. i, no. i.
7 *Ibid.*, vol. iii, no. 29.
8 *Ibid.*, vol. i, no. 2.
9 *Ibid.*, vol. i, no. 3.
10 *Ibid.*, vol. i, no. 4.
11 *Ibid.*, vol. i, no. 13.
12 *Ibid.*, vol. i, no. 18.
13 *Ibid.*, vol. ii, no. 15.

and his friends did not escape Swiftian excoriation for some of their attitudes. Readers submitted mock questions concerning scientific minutiae or excrement, and some smart critics of the Athenians set up their own journals with a wry take on Dunton's work. *The Jovial Mercury*, which lasted a few weeks in 1693, asked questions, such as 'Whether at the skip of a flea the earth moves out of its center?'[14] The infamous Tom Brown got into the act with *The London Mercury* (later called *The Lacedemonian Mercury*), a four-month wonder with scurrilous and humorous information. These works were ephemeral, however, while Dunton's continued over seven years and gave rise to many collateral publications.

The most important publication between *The Athenian Mercury* and *The Tatler* was Daniel Defoe's *Review* (1704–13). This remarkable work was a one-man propaganda machine for the ruling government.[15] It was originally titled *A Weekly Review of the Affairs of France: Purg'd from the Errors and Partiality of Newswriters and Petty-Statesmen, of all Sides*. France was at this juncture, as it so often was, England's enemy, and Defoe depicts it as 'a Martial Terrible Nation', despite its history as the home of 'a Contemptible Effeminate People'.[16] In the midst of his political work, however, Defoe also published what he called 'a little Diversion, as any thing occurs to make the World Merry; and whether Friend or Foe, one Party or another, if any thing happens so scandalous, as to require an open Reproof, the World may meet with it there'.[17] This section was called *Mercure Scandale: or Advice from the Scandal Club, translated out of French* and began appearing in the second number of the *Review*. Soon Defoe dropped the phrase 'translated out of French' and added, *A Weekly History of Nonsense, Impertinence, Vice and Debauchery*.

Advice from the Scandal Club uses the question-and-answer format of *The Athenian Mercury*, but it also includes 'debates' among the club members. One of the longest debates concerns the qualifications of a gentleman, and deals with the issue of duelling, which later became Steele's signature topic in *The Tatler*. Characteristically, Defoe is more sarcastic than Steele in his treatment of the subject. Whereas Steele takes the high road of civility and politeness in his arguments against duelling, Defoe prefers to go into the bedroom and show how a proper man handles the unpleasant discovery of his wife *in flagrante delicto*. The noble gentleman throws his wife out along with the man, but does

---

14 Graham, *English Literary Periodicals*, p. 37.
15 I draw heavily in this paragraph on Arthur Wellesley Secord's introduction to *Defoe's Review, Reproduced from the Original Editions*, 22 vols. (New York: Columbia University Press, 1938).
16 *Defoe's Review*, vol. I, no. I (19 February 1704), p. 6 (Secord, vol. I).
17 *Ibid.*, p. 4.

not demand 'satisfaction', unless the man wants to offer *his* wife's favours in recompense.[18] Around this time Defoe also expanded the list of standard products advertised in periodical journals to include remedies for venereal disease (ads in *The Athenian Mercury* are almost all for books). In his essays as well as in his ads, Defoe was implicitly critical of the Athenians' stuffiness; he was also less polite, less concerned with propriety and less earnest than the essayists who followed him in the next decade.

In September 1704 Defoe began giving the Scandal Club more scope by issuing a monthly supplement for it alone. In the introduction to the first such supplement, Mr Review acknowledges that the speaker's status as a 'club' is fictional, and he describes himself as less arrogant about his learning than his competitors: 'the hand that operates in this work, being *allegorically* rather than *significantly* call'd a *Society*; may be for sundry Reasons uncapable of Performance in so vast a Variety as is like to come before him . . . here is not, as was pretended in the *Athenian Mercury*, a Professor in all the Heads, which the Inquisitive World can propose . . .' He arrogates to himself the irony, but also the grandeur, of Socrates when he declares, 'if to know his own Ignorance be a Part of Wisdom, he hopes he may be put in for a share'.[19] Such a persona is well on the way to the philosophical speakers in Addison and Johnson who retain hints of Defoe's jauntily modest arrogance.

The independence of the Scandal Club essays from the rest of the *Review* progressed further in Defoe's creation of the *Little Review*, which was published twice a week on Wednesdays and Fridays beginning on 6 June 1705. In this form, Defoe's Scandal Club very much resembles *The Tatler*. In later years when Defoe contemplated reviving the short-lived *Little Review*, he said he was satisfied that *The Tatler* had continued his work. According to Defoe's introduction, the function of the *Little Review* was 'to make due Inquisition after the Improvement the Devil makes in the Manufacture of Vice, and to discover him as far as possible, in all his Agents, and their Meanders, Windings and Turnings in the Propagation of Crime'. The economic and political terms cast a sarcastic shadow of doubt on the seriousness of the mission, which is further undermined by Defoe's generally tart style. In number 6, for example, a man asks which of two attractive, prospective wives he should take; Defoe answers: 'Here's a Gentleman running Post for a Wife, and he has two considerable offers, according to his Description; one is a Pious Fool, the other a Housewifly Fool, and he wants to know which of these two Fools he should take.' Since the

18 *Defoe's Review*, vol. 1, no. 16 (29 April 1704), p. 79 (Secord, vol. 1).
19 *A Supplementary Journal to the Advice from the Scandal Club, Defoe's Review* (September 1704), p. 3 (Secord, vol. iii).

gentleman had described one woman as 'good-natured', Defoe feels compelled to answer, 'As to this Gentleman's Term (Good Natur'd), as in its literal Sence, it is Nonsense and Contradiction; Nature being in its Constitution Corrupt, we are bound to flee to its receiv'd vulgar Sence . . . Fool or W—re . . .'[20] But Defoe shows he can take satire as well as dish it out when he prints a hostile letter, to which he offers no answer:

> Stupid John,
> Arn't you a stupid Dog to receive all these Letters, and to uphold such a pack of Scandalous Rascals that breed Factions, and encourage Parties among the People? And trouble the World with a damn'd pack of Nonsense, about Murder, and I don't know what my self, and pretend to do all this for the good of the Publick, Peace of the Nation, Unity of the People, Concord of Christianity, and the Lord knows what . . . Therefore let the Stupid, Idle Society resolve me this Question among others, When they design to have done Writing – And that will be a great deal more acceptable to Public Ears, than to chat about a Fellow's Marriage, and consult his Abilities, and my A–se in a Bandbox – and be so very smart upon my Stupid Ass.[21]

The Stamp Act of 1712 forced Defoe to trim the *Review* to a single quarter of a folio sheet. Soon afterward (11 June 1713) he announced the end of the *Review* with a valediction that mixes satire and sentiment. The *Review* has been his addiction (or 'whore'), as some readers have had Swift's *Examiner* or Steele's *Guardian* for theirs. Although Defoe must give over his 'whore', he does so with difficulty and regret.

The Athenian Mercury, the *Little Review*, and before them Peter Motteux's *Gentleman's Journal*, which was itself inspired by *Le Mercure gallant* (1672–1710), may all have contributed to the development of *The Tatler*. Nevertheless, Donald F. Bond is justified in calling *The Tatler*'s principal editor the 'virtual founder of a new genre – the periodical essay'.[22] Although both Jonathan Swift and Joseph Addison played important roles in developing *The Tatler*, the less learned and intellectually less subtle Richard Steele was its true creator.

The genre of the periodical essay proper is not visible in the early numbers of *The Tatler*, but it gradually emerges. Like most periodicals, *The Tatler* is built on the material framework of the newspaper. This is hardly surprising because Steele was also the editor of the government-sponsored newspaper, *The London Gazette*. Moreover, at its inception *The Tatler* spent a good deal of space in the single half folio on the news. The news was published under the

---

20 *Little Review* (22 June 1705), pp. 21–2 (Secord, vol. v).
21 *Little Review* (22 June 1705), p. 23 (Secord, vol. v).
22 *The Tatler*, ed. Donald F. Bond, 3 vols. (Oxford: Clarendon Press, 1987), vol. i, p. xxix.

heading of St James' Coffee-house near Parliament. Other articles were marked as emanating from other places: literary criticism from Will's Coffee-house, where John Dryden had held the throne for many years; learned reports and reviews from the Grecian; gossip concerning 'Gallantry, Pleasure, and Entertainment' from White's Chocolate-house; and the personal reflections of the speaker from 'My own Apartment'. The speaker's name is Isaac Bickerstaff, a persona whom Swift had already made famous as an astrologer in *Predictions for the Year 1708*. Bickerstaff's humorous prediction that a crackpot almanack astrologer named Partridge would die within the year, set off a burst of imitations, counter-attacks and lampoons. As *The Tatler* progresses, Bickerstaff's fictional biography is revealed, several of his relatives are introduced and his apartment becomes the dominant dateline in the journal.

Signs that news will be replaced by fictional prose begin appearing as early as number 6, where Steele, perhaps at Swift's prompting, writes a journalistic version of the *Iliad*. As if he were an aggrieved MP, '*Achilles* assembles the Council, and encourages *Calchas* to speak for the Surrender of *Chryseis* to appease *Apollo*.'[23] The counterpart to this generic scrambling occurs in number 8, where Steele provides an epic version of the news concerning the death of Prince George and the arrival home of Marlborough (Steele's constant hero). In number 12 Steele declines to print news at all, preferring instead to quote Dryden on the subject of news. The literary, in a very modern sense of the word, seems to be winning out over the strictly journalistic. The news shrinks steadily from here on out and eventually, with many regressions to form, disappears altogether. Meanwhile the essays 'From My own Apartment' grow, reaching a milestone in number 48, the first issue to be comprised entirely of one continuous essay.

Swift's withdrawal from *The Tatler* and his replacement by Addison marks another important turning point in the history of *The Tatler* and of the periodical essay as a genre. When Steele began *The Tatler*, Swift was in many ways his guiding light. Swift probably negotiated with the publisher John Nutt, who had brought out *A Tale of a Tub* in 1704, and he contributed importantly to the content of early issues. For example, Swift's poem 'A Description of the Morning', first appeared in *Tatler* 9. The material circumstances of the poem's publication in a 'daily' sheet illuminates its own significance as a 'modern', tawdry, but richly experienced aubade. The poem captures a sense of the daily, elevating it, and thus epitomising an aspect of the periodical essay. Although it is impossible to prove who wrote what in *The Tatler*, Swift's influence is

23 *Ibid.*, vol. I, p. 57.

apparent for about the first six months. Number 51 contains a very Swiftian sieve for straining literary works of useless material, and in 59 the personage of Obadiah Greenhat begins his letter with Swiftian pompous naiveté: 'Having a peculiar Humour of desiring to be somewhat the better or wiser for what I read, I am always uneasy when, in any profound Writer, (for I read no others) I happen to meet with what I can't understand.' Despite its importance at the inception of *The Tatler*, however, the Swiftian tone is shed as the periodical essay approaches literary maturity.

In *Tatler* 18 Addison makes a brief appearance, but his first full number is 81. Perhaps as early as 41 he began supplying the various Latin epigrams that appear with greater frequency as the numbers roll on. The default epigram, mostly present in the early numbers is 'Quicquid agunt Homines Nostri Farrago Libelli', from Juvenal's first satire, meaning, roughly, whatever mankind does is grist for our mill. The switch to using a variety of epigrams is representative of the way Addison infuses *The Tatler* with his classical learning. Steele's quintessential concerns are offences against politeness and decorum. His Bickerstaff is a gallant defender of the ladies who believes the fair sex should be protected and kept safe at home: 'The Fair Sex, who are made of Man and not of Earth have a more delicate Humanity than we have . . .'[24] Steele's men are correspondingly tough: 'The highest Act of the Mind of Man is to possess it self with Tranquility in imminent Danger . . .'[25] While Steele tried to define the roles of men and women in society, Addison looks more deeply into human nature. His first full essay begins, 'There are two kinds of Immortality; that which the Soul really enjoys after this Life, and that imaginary Existence by which Men live in their Fame and Reputation.' Addison goes on from here to write a version of the Temple of Fame, an allegory that appears in Ovid's *Metamorphoses*, xII.39–63. Concerned with permanent human nature, the good and the just, Addison translates the periodical essay to a philosophical sphere while never losing touch with its roots in the quotidian world of polite society. But for all Addison's importance in *The Tatler*, he appeared relatively infrequently; it was in the sequel that he shone most brightly.

From *The Spectator* to *The Rambler*

More than most genres the periodical essay was subject to all sorts of unscrupulous competition: imitation, piracy, forgery and plagiarism. Dunton complained about his competitors, but also praised them in his 'Secret History

24 *Ibid.*, vol. 1, p. 472.
25 *Ibid.*, vol. 1, p. 310.

of the Periodical Writers'. He treated the authors of the eight best journals, including Defoe, and called them 'Weekly Writers, to distinguish them from "The Moderator", "Wandering Spy", "Rehearsal", "London Post", Interloping "Whipster", and that rabble of scandalous Hackneys . . .'[26] Although Dunton praises Defoe, he also complains that he ruined his monthly version of the 'Question-Project' in a 'sneaking injustice of interloping',[27] and printed some copy already given to *The Athenian Mercury*. Addison and Steele had still more to worry about along these lines than Dunton. First of all, not long after the inception of *The Tatler*, they faced imitators. The most successful of these was *The Female Tatler, by Mrs Crackenthorpe, a Lady that knows everything*. Delarivier Manley was the lead voice behind Mrs Crackenthorpe for numbers 1–51, but she seems to have yielded to others in numbers 52–115, including Susan Centlivre and Bernard Mandeville. The first issue hit the coffee houses on 8 July 1709, four months after *The Tatler* began. (There was also a spurious *Female Tatler*, edited by Thomas Baker, which began publishing with 'no. 19' for 19 August 1709.) To provide just one example, *The Female Tatler* (no. 56 (14 November 1709)) contained a racy story in which two cousins fight over the moral to be attached to stories they have heard about pre-marital sex and pregnancy. The ads in *The Female Tatler* were also somewhat racy and also aimed at women: one ad claimed, 'Head snuff cures dangerous distempers of the head such as apoplexies, Epilepsies, Lethargies, Vishegoes, Megrims . . . vapours . . . etc.' The sheet was vying for a place in the lady's dressing room and in the prurient interests of men. *The Tatler* advertised coffee and tea as well as books, and it expanded into the women's department (including snuff), especially under the influence of Charles Lillie, a 'perfumer' who sold 'toys', all kinds of fancy items for the dressing table. But *The Female Tatler* outdid *The Tatler* in its concentration on women both in articles and advertising.

Addison and Steele faced an even more dangerous challenge when an unidentified publisher brought out a book containing the first 100 *Tatlers*. Isaac Bickerstaff responded sharply in number 101:

> This Iniquity is committed by a most impregnable Set of Mortals, Men who are Rogues within the Law . . . These miscreants are a Set of Wretches we Authors call Pirates, who print any Book, Poem, or Sermon, as soon as it appears in the World, in a smaller Volume and sell it (as all other Thieves do stolen Goods) at a cheaper Rate.[28]

---

26 'The Secret History of the *Weekly* Writers', in *The Life and Errors of John Dunton, Citizen of London*, 2 vols. (London, 1818), vol. ii, p. 423.
27 *Ibid.*, vol. ii, p. 424.
28 *Tatler*, vol. ii, pp. 119–21.

Because the Licensing Act had lapsed in 1695 'piracy' was technically legal, and the original authors' and publishers' best course was to publish a better edition. This is just what Addison and Steele did, and thereby they set a standard for the publication of periodical essays that deeply influenced the genre. In future all successful journals looked towards the publication of volumes, and this affected the design of both the content and the format. Many essays, including Johnson's *Idler*, pre-determined their length of publication by figuring out what number best suited the subsequent, more lucrative packaging of them. In book form stripped of ads, usually reduced in size from folio to octavo (or smaller), bound, often with mottoes added or translated, with controversial numbers sometimes removed, read in a library or drawing room instead of a coffee house, the genre of the periodical essay was drastically changed.

On 2 January 1711, *The Tatler* ceased publication with number 271 in which Steele speaks *in propria persona* and, like an actor in a theatrical epilogue, throws himself on the mercy of his audience. On 6 January 1711 a spurious *Tatler* leaped into the breach, claiming that his 'very good friend Isaac Bickerstaff' had 'to visit friends in the country' and left him in charge of correcting the morals of the town. The themes are right, but the style is wooden. The twentieth fake (17 February 1711), numbered 291, begins 'it is certain that most of our Errors, whether in Conversation or Conduct, are owing to want of Reflection, and a right Way of thinking'. To sweep the decks of such plagiaristic imitators, less than three months later, 1 March 1711, Addison and Steele began *The Spectator*, the most successful series of periodical essays ever published.

Unlike *The Tatler*, *The Spectator* was conceived as a single unified essay, though there are many numbers (a high percentage by Steele) comprised of letters with commentary. England's first true daily newspaper, the *Daily Courant*, provided the publisher and the format, but *The Spectator* contained no political news. The eidolon or principal persona, Mr Spectator, provides auto-biographical notes in the first issue: he was a serious baby, a sullen youth and an excellent, quiet student; he has read everything and travelled everywhere, including Cairo, the ancient seat of human knowledge; he listens everywhere he goes but speaks only in his own club. Now, at the end of his life, he has decided 'to print my self out before I die'.

Isaac Bickerstaff was elderly and wise, but Mr Spectator is older, deeper, wiser, more removed from the world and a more developed 'I' than Isaac. To help him with issues of the day he has the six members of the Spectator Club. Two of these – Roger de Coverley and Will Honeycomb – speak so frequently that they become the focal points of periodicals within the periodical. The de Coverley papers, in fact, can boast a richer re-publication history than

The Spectator as a whole or any other part of it. Samuel Johnson compared Addison's creation of Sir Roger to Cervantes' creation of Don Quixote,[29] and both have frequently been named as progenitors of the characters typically encountered in novels. Like almost everything in the genre of the periodical essay, however, Addison's Sir Roger is not completely original: he may owe his inspiration to John Tutchin, who introduces a Roger of Coverly as an interlocutor in his *Observator* for 25 March 1704.[30] Addison's Roger is a knighted, old-fashioned bachelor, fifty-six years of age – 'cheerful, gay, and hearty, keeps a good House both in Town and Country; a great Lover of Mankind; but there is such a mirthful Cast in his Behaviour, that he is rather beloved than esteemed . . .'[31] More flamboyant is Will Honeycomb, a superannuated but charming gallant, a survivor of the court of Charles II who speaks of the past like Rochester's maimed debauchee and of the present like Alexander Pope's Sir Plume. From Dunton's Athenians to Addison's Spectators and Johnson's Mr Rambler, age and wisdom are essential ingredients of periodical personae in the eighteenth century.

Of the original 555 *Spectators*, 251 have been attributed to Addison and an equal number to Steele. However, Addison wrote 202 independent essays to 89 for Steele, who often relied on correspondents to fill his pages.[32] Among Addison's most famous contributions are the twelve papers on the 'Pleasures of the Imagination', which were immediately published separately; the eighteen Saturday papers on Milton's *Paradise Lost*, published separately in 1719; a series of three papers on broadsides and ballads, especially *Chevy Chase*; the sequence on English tragedy; and a group devoted to distinguishing true and false forms of wit and humour.

In his critical essays Addison consistently brings to bear standards derived from Aristotle, Horace, Cicero or Longinus, and he often adduces lines from classical poets. He tutors his readers, refines and disambiguates critical terms and instils principles of good taste as well as fine judgement. The essays are philosophical and highly literate, but they are also well-bred. It is not only unreasonable to like puns, in Addison's view, it is also coarse. A man with good taste is a gentleman who mixes learning with fine sensibility. Since he was writing for the tea table as much as the coffee house, it is not surprising that

---

29 Samuel Johnson, *Lives of the Poets*, ed. G. B. Hill, 3 vols. (Oxford: Clarendon Press, 1905), vol. II, p. 96.
30 *Spectator*, vol. I, p. 7n.
31 *Ibid.*, vol. I, p. 8.
32 Eustace Budgell wrote twenty-nine numbers; John Hughes six, and eighteen are unattributed: see *Spectator*, vol. I, p. xlv.

Addison describes his ideal reader as a tea aficionado who can distinguish all the varieties blindfold: 'A Man of a fine Taste in Writing will discern after the same manner, not only the general Beauties and Imperfections of an Author, but discover the several Ways of thinking and expressing himself, which diversify him from all other Authors, with the several Foreign Infusions of Thought and Language, and the particular Authors from whom they were borrowed.'[33]

As Addison gave depth to *The Spectator*, Steele maintained the journal's roots in modern, local experience. He wrote more often on phenomena of daily life in London, including the coffee house, the city tradesmen and a gang of London toughs called the Mohocks.[34] Steele could write criticism, but not with the thoughtfulness of Addison; Addison could write on the London streets, but not with as much compassion as Steele. When Addison writes on the cries of the London streets and on the signs and banners displayed there, he wants to reform them.[35] Steele's more convivial approach to the city is epitomised in number 454 in which he chronicles a twenty-four-hour span roving the streets of London. Nothing remarkable happens, but he watches the changes of the social landscape with pleasure: hackney-coachmen, fruit-wenches, beggars, ballad singers, silk-worms (compulsive shoppers), gamesters and poets all delight him. Steele's number 454 is a pattern for John Gay's *Trivia*, which in turn seems a forerunner of James Joyce's modern epic of city life *Ulysses*. Steele concludes with a comic epiphany that may have been beyond the reach of Addison's more critical intelligence:

> When I came to my Chamber I writ down these Minutes; but was at a Loss what Instruction I should propose to my Reader from the Enumeration of so many insignificant Matters and Occurrences; and I thought it of great Use, if they could learn with me to keep their Minds open to Gratification, and ready to receive it from any thing it meets with.[36]

Steele also made his essays echo daily life by including more new or ephemeral words than Addison. *The Tatler* is rich in first recorded usages, such as: 'quid nunc'; 'Free thinkers'; 'to vowell' (to pay a creditor with an IOU); 'to bite' (to catch with a trick); 'hack' (hackney coach).[37] A few words of lower street talk are alluded to, such as 'condom' and 'bitch', but the politeness

---

33 *Ibid.*, vol. III, p. 528.
34 *Ibid.*, respectively, vol. I, pp. 208–11; vol. IV, p. 479; vol. III, 186–8.
35 *Ibid.*, vol. I, pp. 115–18 and 251.
36 *Ibid.*, vol. IV, p. 103.
37 *Ibid.*, vol. I, pp. 89, 104, 105, 106, and 128 respectively.

of the journal forbids their use.[38] In *The Spectator* Steele is less adventuresome still (despite 'silkworm' in 454 and 'quearity' 17). Addison's newish words are more proper than Steele's and often philosophical, like the figurative use of 'chromatic' in a discussion of music in *Spectator* 29.[39] Swift and Defoe were both defenders of plain language in their journalistic writings, but Addison represents a different kind of conservatism, preferring, as Samuel Johnson would, a more latinate language purged of common cant.

Steele spearheads *The Spectator*'s efforts to make the world more polite to women. For example, Steele's fable of Inkle and Yarico in *Spectator* 11 is a more sensuous and pathetic statement of male European oppression than Addison's similarly intended fable of Maraton and Yatilda in 56. Addison seems quicker to ridicule coquettish women, their childish, 'French' behaviour (45) or their reading (37). Steele likes women more and is less quick to articulate the dismissive principle that 'Women were formed to temper Mankind, and soothe them into Tenderness and Compassion.'[40] It is dangerous to generalise about the differences between Addison and Steele in *The Spectator*; they could reverse roles at times, but in general Steele did more to maintain the immediacy and dailiness of a form that Addison was making more philosophical and remote.

Numerous publications were spun off *The Tatler* and *The Spectator*, many of them created by contributors: Steele himself continued to bring out new periodicals, including the important *Guardian*, its sequel *The Englishman*, and the less important but interesting *Lover*, *Reader* and *Tea-Table*; Ambrose Philips edited the second incarnation of *The Free Thinker*; Eustace Budgell did *The Bee*. These periodicals naturally followed in the tracks of *The Tatler* and *Spectator*. Other important periodical writers of the next couple of decades include Aaron Hill, whose *Plain Dealer* and *Prompter* were both successful; the Earl of Chesterfield, whose highly politicised *Common Sense* (1737–43) preceded his more literary contributions to *The World*; and Eliza Haywood, who edited the monthly *Female Spectator* from 1744–6. Of paramount importance too was Henry Fielding. He wrote mostly literary essays and co-edited *The Champion: or British Mercury* (1739–41) until his partner's partisan (anti-Walpole) politics drove him out of the editorial office. He then worked on two more politically oriented journals, *The True Patriot* (1745–6) and *The Jacobite's Journal* (1747–8), before he began the primarily moral and literary essays of *The Covent Garden Journal* (1752). Despite the high morality of some of Fielding's essays and the imposing moral sage he used as a persona (Alexander Drawcansir), *The Covent*

---

38 *Ibid.*, vol. i, pp. 130 and 470 respectively.
39 *Spectator*, vol. i, p. 123.
40 *Ibid.*, vol. i, p. 242.

Garden Journal was steeped in daily events and often drew on cases that had come before Fielding in his role as a criminal court judge. In his mixture of high morals with a knowledge of the street, however, Fielding was still following in the footsteps of *The Tatler*.

Before Fielding began work on his last periodical publication, Samuel Johnson was writing *The Rambler*, a work inspired not by *The Tatler* but by the most philosophical aspects of Addison's *Spectator*. From his earliest paid work, essays (now lost) in *The Birmingham Journal*, Johnson's whole career as a professional writer was wrapped up in periodical writing. He made his way into the literary world by writing ceaselessly for *The Gentleman's Magazine*, but *The Rambler* is certainly his most important periodical publication. The second periodical to be so called, *The Rambler* ran from 20 March 1750 to 14 March 1752, appearing every Tuesday and Saturday for a total of 204 numbers. Although extensive collaboration was the norm in essay periodicals, Johnson wrote all but seven *Ramblers* himself, and he collaborated on three of those. Johnson virtually did without the help of collaborators, and he entirely eschewed correspondence. *The Rambler* regularly invites letters to the editor, but there is no evidence that any were ever printed or even received. Sixty whole *Ramblers* and parts of many others are signed by correspondents, but all except seven of these appear to be Johnson's own creations.

Creating for himself a comfortable first-person singular persona was one of Johnson's greatest achievements in *The Rambler*, but his success owes much to the periodical essay tradition. As 'Mr Review', for example, Defoe was comfortable enough with his persona to announce in mid-sentence, 'the Author from hence speaks in the first Person'.[41] Johnson's Mr Rambler possesses more intangible aesthetic life than Defoe's Reviewer and therefore is less assimilable to his author. Addison's Mr Spectator is the most important precursor, but Addison divided his 'I' among other characters whom he found equally congenial. Johnson nearly becomes Mr Rambler, although he has trouble fitting on the mask at the start. *Rambler* 1, for example, discusses 'the difficulty of the first address on any occasion', and compares the writer's dilemma to that of the lover's. Johnson is not speaking *in propria persona*; he was a very seasoned writer by this time, although he was only forty years old. Mr Rambler is an older and graver man, but he is the sort of character Johnson would become. With his philosophical language, his mastery of classical literature and his concern with a kind of moral science, Mr Rambler cannot be fully disentangled from the later Johnson.

---

41 *Defoe's Review*, vol. I, no. 8 (1 April 1704), p. 46 (Secord, vol. 1).

Mr Rambler speaks on a wide variety of subjects, but a distinctive feature of the whole series of essays is its frequent use of a hackneyed moral statement as a springboard into a more complex consideration of an enduring question. There is a sense of age, almost of tiredness, about the old formulations, which Johnson articulates with architectural grandeur, even as early as number 2:

> That the mind of man is never satisfied with the objects immediately before it, but is always breaking away from the present moment, and losing itself in schemes of future felicity; that we forget the proper use of the time now in our power, to provide for the enjoyment of that which, perhaps, may never be granted us, has been frequently remarked; and as this practice is a commodious subject of raillery to the gay, and of declamation to the serious, it has been ridiculed with all the pleasantry of wit, and exaggerated with all the amplifications of rhetoric. Every instance, by which its absurdity might appear most flagrant, has been studiously collected; it has been marked with every epithet of contempt, and all the tropes and figures have been called forth against it.[42]

This way of using commonplaces can be seen as an extension of the allegory of authorship enacted in the creation of the eidolon: the topics are as old as the philosopher reciting them, but both are worth listening to again. Moreover, the most valuable writing finds not new truths but a new way of expressing them. *The Rambler* represents the full height of Johnson's philosophical prose, his attempt to establish a kind of reformed, scientific brand of English that would be more enduring than the shifting language of the coffee house and the exchange. Johnson therefore works against the grain of periodical writers, like Swift and Defoe, who wanted to reform English by simplifying it, and those, like Addison, Philips and Chesterfield, who wanted to make it more polite. Unlike these predecessors, of course, Johnson not only planned but also wrote a dictionary meant to stabilise the English language. But, like the style of *The Rambler*, the *Dictionary* too was more philosophical and less restrictive and polite than his predecessors would have liked.

The Rambler is not the most perfect periodical essay because it has less of the flavour of daily life than *The Tatler* or *The Spectator* or many other periodicals. *The Rambler* was not written for the coffee house; it had a relatively small circulation; and it was less often read in half-folio sheets than in magazines or in bound volumes. *The Rambler* is, however, the most profound essay periodical, and it best ties a genre founded on ephemerality to a permanent literary

---

42 *The Rambler*, ed. Walter J. Bate and Albrecht Strauss, The Yale Edition of the Works of Samuel Johnson, vols. III–V (New Haven, CT: Yale University Press, 1969), vol. III, p. 9.

tradition. Indeed, Johnson's *Rambler* is as closely connected to the essays of Bacon and Seneca as it is to its generic predecessors in the daily press. Nevertheless, Johnson does not ignore daily life. As James F. Woodruff has shown, many *Ramblers* derive their inspiration from immediate sources, such as the opening of a new lottery, the coming of spring or the arrival of a solemn day in the Christian calendar.[43] Other *Ramblers* may stem from events in Johnson's private life: a pair of essays critical of Milton's prosody, for example, seem to be daring responses to those who accused him of political bias in his support of William Lauder's trumped-up charges of plagiarism against Milton. In the code of literary analysis, he is making a public announcement that he will not be cowed into blind admiration of anyone.

True to the periodical tradition, Johnson takes up women's issues in *The Rambler*, even though he does not use the sort of cant that he branded as 'women's words' in the *Dictionary*. The female personae he assumes as putative writers to the *Rambler* usually have names made from classical roots, such as Rhodoclia, Tetrica, Mitissa, Misothea and Melania. They speak in philosophic language, but Johnson is as compassionate to the sufferings of women and as censorious of their foibles as any earlier periodical writers. The sorrowful prostitute Melissa says with real pathos, 'In this abject state I have now passed four years, the drudge of extortion and the sport of drunkenness; sometimes the property of one man, and sometimes the common prey of accidental lewdness . . .'[44] Johnson's women in *The Rambler* are a far cry from the brocaded coquettes of *The Tatler* and *Spectator*; Johnson is less interested in women's dress and language than Addison and Steele, but he is more sensitive to their particular problems and plights. Richard Steele's gallantry could never lead him to as profound a sympathy for women as Johnson expresses in *Rambler* 39:

> The condition of the female sex has been frequently the subject of compassion to medical writers, because their constitution of body is such, that every state of life brings its peculiar diseases: they are placed, according to the proverb, between Scylla and Charybdis, with no other choice than of dangers equally formidable; and whether they embrace marriage, or determine upon a single life, are exposed, in consequence of their choice, to sickness, misery, and death.[45]

43 James F. Woodruff, 'Johnson's Rambler and its Contemporary Context', *Bulletin of Research in the Humanities* 85 (1982), 27–64.
44 *The Rambler*, vol. v, p. 144.
45 *Ibid.*, vol. iii, p. 211.

In his second most important periodical, *The Idler*, Johnson wrote in an easier style and more often addressed quotidian subjects, such as advertisements, news writers and the Seven Years' War. Even in *The Idler*, however, Johnson never achieved the contact with daily London events registered in *The Tatler* and *Spectator*. These were models Johnson could not surpass in his attempts to mix the philosophical with the daily.

The end of the genre

In the years immediately following publication of the last *Rambler*, Johnson contributed twenty-nine essays to *The Adventurer*. Johnson's long-time associate and occasional imitator, John Hawkesworth, was the editor and principal essayist, but he was assisted by Thomas and Joseph Warton and by Bonnell Thornton, a figure involved in numerous periodical publications in mid century. A typographical twin of *The Rambler*, *The Adventurer* was also much more widely distributed in octavo book form than in the original folio leaves. In Johnson's lifetime there were thirteen re-publications of *The Adventurer* in book form and fifteen of *The Rambler*.[46] This pattern of publication contributed to the breakdown of the genre of the periodical essay, but of even greater importance was the gradual disappearance of the essay periodical. More and more in the second half of the century, essays were placed in the larger, more heterogeneous and less frequently published magazines.

Despite the growing power of the magazines, some old-fashioned imitators of *The Spectator* remained. Among the best of them was *The World*, which ran bi-weekly from 1753–5. When it was republished in book form, it boasted a list of contributors that included Horace Walpole, John Boyle, fifth Earl of Cork and Sir David Dalrymple. The most notable contributor of all was Lord Chesterfield, but he kept his identity out of the published index. The editor, Edward Moore, used the assumed name of Adam Fitzadam, a somewhat pompous and sarcastic but loveable philosopher who, much like Roger de Coverley, suddenly dies when the periodical ends. With this collection of aristocrats on his staff, Moore's journal was naturally concerned with politeness in manners, in dress and in language. A characteristic number (by Moore himself) begins, 'Of all the improvements in polite conversation, I know of nothing that is half so entertaining as the *double entendre*. It is a figure in rhetoric, which owes its birth,

---

46 For complete publication information on *The Rambler* and *Adventurer*, see J. D. Fleeman, *A Bibliography of the Works of Samuel Johnson: Treating his Published Works from the Beginnings to 1984*, 2 vols. (Oxford: Clarendon Press, 2000), vol. I, pp. 192–316 and 334–96.

as well as its name, to our inventive neighbours the French'.[47] Moore pursues the irony for several pages, before dispersing it in a final blast against false modesty, a sin encouraged by the double entendre. *The World* is also famous for its inclusion of two numbers by Lord Chesterfield (numbers 101–2) that concern the forthcoming publication of Johnson's *Dictionary*. Chesterfield's linguistic politics are nearer to Addison and Steele's than Johnson's, however, especially in 102 where he suggests infusing the *Dictionary* with more politeness and damping down its erudition.

Oliver Goldsmith's short-lived *Bee* well represents the transition of periodical publication dominance from the single-essay journals to the magazines. *The Bee* looked like a magazine, being printed on two octavo sheets yielding thirty-two small pages, but it was a weekly. It contains a few letters from real people; they are not correspondents, however, but famous men like Voltaire. *The Bee* also contains translations, poems and plagiarisms. In the midst of all this Goldsmith inserts several fine essays in his distinctive voice. He is to a degree an imitator of *The Rambler*, but he is often more ironic and paradoxical than Johnson. In number 3, for example, he propounds the cynical position that the 'true use of speech is not so much to express our wants as to conceal them'.[48] In *Bee* 4 Goldsmith treats the pains of authorship: he begins straightforwardly enough, 'Were I to measure the merit of my present undertaking by its success, or the rapidity of its sale, I might be led to form conclusions by no means favourable to the pride of an author.' But, the sarcasm that often infiltrates his tone arrives in the next two sentences: 'Should I estimate my fame by its extent, every News-Paper and every Magazine would leave me far behind. Their fame is diffused in a very wide circle, that of some as far as Islington (a few blocks away), and some yet farther still . . .'[49] Interestingly, Goldsmith contemplates giving up *The Bee*, but decides to write on, declaring, 'If the present generation will not hear my voice, hearken O posterity to you I call'.[50] This is the direction in which essayists were more and more looking at this time, but their rejection of ephemeral notoriety spells the end of the periodical-essay genre.

Further signs that the genre is ending appear in Goldsmith's many comments on other periodicals. He looks back wistfully on the success of 'the Spectator, and many succeeding essayists . . . the numerous compliments paid

---

47 *The World*, No. 201 (4 November 1756), rpt. vol. IV, New Edition (London, 1767), p. 277.
48 *Collected Works of Oliver Goldsmith*, ed. Arthur Friedman, 5 vols. (Oxford: Clarendon Press, 1966), vol. I, p. 394.
49 *Ibid.*, vol. I, p. 415.
50 *Ibid.*, vol. I, p. 416.

them in the course of their lucubrations . . . the frequent encouragements they met to inspire them with ardour and increase their eagerness to please. I have received *my letters* as well as they; but alas! not congratulatory ones . . .'[51] In 'A Reservie', part of number 5, Goldsmith reflects further on the death of the genre. His allegory of the Temple of Fame repeats Addison's theme in his first full essay for *The Tatler* (number 81), but Goldsmith's version is ironic and elegiac. Goldsmith imagines a coach on its way to the Temple with a dictatorial Charon in the driver's seat accepting or rejecting candidates for admission. Aaron Hill and Arthur Murphy, miscellaneous writers, are both rejected; Samuel Johnson is rejected when he presents his *Dictionary*, but his *Rambler* earns him immediate entry because the driver knows that at the court of Apollo some ladies like it even better than *The Spectator*.[52] Hume then presents his essays, but he is rejected for impiety. The only other author to gain a seat is Smollett, not for his journalism in *The Critical Review* or for his historical works, but for his 'romance' (meaning one of his novels, *Roderick Random*, perhaps). The allegory suggests that the great age of periodical writing is over and that it has yielded pride of place to the new genre of the novel. The seventh and last issue of *The Bee* was published on 17 November 1759.

Apart from *The Bee* and *The Busy Body*, another short-lived periodical, the journals to which Goldsmith contributed his many essays were mainly magazines containing a variety of other materials: *The Weekly Magazine*, *The Royal Magazine*, *The British Magazine*, *The Westminster Magazine*, *Lloyd's Weekly Post* and *The Public Ledger; or, Daily Register of Commerce and Intelligence*, among others. For *The Public Ledger* Goldsmith wrote a series of 119 Chinese letters, later published in book form, with many changes, as *The Citizen of the World* (1762). Goldsmith assumes the persona of a visitor to England from China; Lien Chi Altengi is a self-described 'philosophic wanderer', much like a correspondent to *The Bee* who said he was a 'philosophic vagabond'.[53] Goldsmith's itinerant philosophers resemble Johnson's Mr Rambler (*il vagabondo* in Italian translations) both in name and in their mutual commitment to stoical principles of life, which Goldsmith expresses in terms of Confucianism. However, the lucubrations of the Chinese visitor are also related to older periodical writings, Ned Ward's *London Spy*, for example, and *Spectator* 50, in which Addison writes an account of St Paul's supposedly by the four Iroquois sachems who visited London in 1710. These earlier works also use the invented foreign perspective to satirise London and have a laugh at foreigners' naiveté. They also all

51 *Ibid.*, vol. 1, p. 419.
52 *Ibid.*, vol. 1, p. 448.
53 *Ibid.*, vol. 11, p. 17 and n. 2.

represent a way of imposing fictional content on the newspaper format, one of the most characteristic moves in the genesis of the genre.

If Goldsmith's method is conventional in the genre of the essay periodical, his topics are even more so. Like earlier periodical writers, Lien says a good deal about women. London beauties, he reports,

> like to have the face of various colours, as among the Tartars of Koreki, frequently sticking on with spittle little black patches on every part of it, except on the tip of the nose, which I have never seen with a patch. You'll have a better idea of their manner of placing these spots, when I have finish'd a map of an English face patch'd up to the fashion, which shall shortly be sent to encrease your curious collection of paintings, medals and monsters.[54]

In another letter Lien encounters a prostitute, whom he takes at first for a remarkably generous person, especially when she offers to take his watch in for repair. Goldsmith, unlike Johnson, does not evince much sympathy for prostitutes, or for women in general, but he does use the episode to launch into a sermon against bigamy and sexual assault.

The style of *The Citizen of the World* is no more likely to infiltrate conversation than the style of *The Rambler*, and it also displays the weariness with common topics that Johnson expressed. Letter 100, for example, begins in typical *Rambler* fashion:

> Few virtues have been more praised by moralists, than generosity; every practical treatise of Ethics tends to encrease our sensibility of the distresses of others, and to relax the grasp of frugality. Philosophers that are poor praise it because they are gainers by its effects, and the opulent Seneca himself has written a treatise on benefits, though he was known to give nothing away.[55]

The style is not as grand as Johnson's and the antithesis more predictably positioned, but it is equally remote from the converse of daily life. Goldsmith was influenced by Johnson, but there is another reason for his non-conversational style: changes in the economics of publishing had moved the site of reading the periodical essay from the coffee house and the street to the drawing room and the library. In those confines conversation is more polite or even non-existent; hence it makes sense for the periodical to assume a more cerebral style, one meant to develop meaning through silent reading, rereading and contemplation, rather than through immediate, vocal response.

After 1760 the bulk of English periodical essays are published within the confines of venues like *The Royal Magazine*, *The Library*, *The Universal Museum*,

54 *Ibid.*, vol. II, pp. 25–6.
55 *Ibid.*, vol. II, p. 396.

The Complete Magazine, The Gazetteer, Town and Country Magazine and *The Lady's Magazine*. The titles suggest that the essay became something suitable for storage, part of an archive rather than a lively, diurnal announcement. There are exceptions, especially among political periodicals, such as John Wilkes' notorious *North Briton* (1762–3), but the literary economy of writer, format and reading public changed in such a way that the true periodical essay did not survive.

Public opinion and the political pamphlet

J. A. DOWNIE

The people of England, it is generally observed, are, of all nations in the world, the most addicted to Politics. The fact is certain, and the reason of it evident.[1]

Jürgen Habermas' influential model of the rise of public opinion as a force in the state argues that '[a] public sphere that functioned in the political realm arose first in Great Britain at the turn of the eighteenth century' when, with the end of censorship, 'a press devoted to the debate of political issues developed out of the pamphlet'. The principle of universal access is central to Habermas' thesis about the emergence (as opposed to the structural transformation) of the bourgeois public sphere. 'A public sphere from which specific groups would be *eo ipso* excluded was less than merely incomplete', he explains, 'it was not a public sphere at all.' As it consists of 'private persons come together as a public', the public sphere, in its appeal to reason as a governing principle, is in a crucial sense disinterested.[2]

The period from the later seventeenth to the middle of the eighteenth centuries has been described, quite rightly, as 'the first age of party'. This inevitably presents problems for a thesis in which 'rational-critical' debate is posited as being somehow free from party-political (or any other) considerations. On the contrary, it is clear that politicians immediately appreciated the possibilities presented by the existence of a free press for influencing parliamentary as well as public opinion. While Edmund Burke was drafting *Thoughts on the Cause of the Present Discontents* (1770), he received a letter from the Marquis of Rockingham:

---

1 Quoted from an advertisement for *The Political Register* printed at the end of [John Wilkes,] *A Letter to his Grace the Duke of Grafton* (London, 1767).
2 Jürgen Habermas, *The Structural Transformation of the Public Sphere: An Inquiry into a Category of Bourgeois Society*, trans. Thomas Burger (Cambridge, MA: Polity Press, 1989), pp. 57, 92, 85.

I wish it may be read by all the members of Parliament – and by all the politicians in town and country prior to the meeting of Parliament. I think it would take universally, and tend to form and to unite a party upon real and well founded principles – which would in the end prevail and re-establish order and Government in this country.[3]

Rockingham was by no means the first to grasp that, in an era in which political parties were not organisations that one joined as a card-carrying member, the press (in the broadest sense) was an unrivalled medium of communication. There was no other practicable means of informing back-bench MPs of the party line on any given issue, much less rank and file supporters outside Parliament. Thus Swift's *The Conduct of the Allies* (1711), for example, was carefully prepared as a statement of ministerial policy for government supporters in anticipation of the revelation, in the Queen's Speech which opened parliament in December 1711, that secret peace negotiations with France were underway. 'The house of commons have this day made many severe votes about our being abused by our allies', Swift wrote after the debate on the peace negotiations had taken place. 'Those who spoke, drew all their arguments from my book . . . all agree it was my book that spirited them to these resolutions.' As ministers were eager to influence national as well as parliamentary opinion, however, the fifth edition was printed 'in small' for 'great men', who 'subscrib[ed] for hundreds', to distribute throughout the country.[4]

Such tactics were apparent as soon as pre-printing censorship ended in 1695 consequent on the expiry of the Printing or Licensing Act (as it is more commonly known). Operating in the belief that political argument can influence the way people think, and therefore the way they act, the political pamphlet, like other forms of propaganda, attempts to manipulate its readers' political perceptions. The same applies to contributions to political journals. Written to inform and influence opinion, such writings do not always aim to convert opponents by force of argument alone. Although competent propagandists attempt to persuade, they do not necessarily seek to proselytise. Skilful political writers clearly have in mind some notion of a 'target reader' whose consciousness they wish to confirm or to alter. They define an aim or polemical objective which their writing is intended to accomplish, and they adopt a polemical strategy

---

3 *The Correspondence of Edmund Burke*, ed. Lucy S. Sutherland, 10 vols. (Cambridge: Cambridge University Press, 1960), vol. II, p. 43.
4 *The Prose Works of Jonathan Swift*, ed. Herbert Davis *et al*. 16 vols. (Oxford: Basil Blackwell, 1939–75), vol. XVI, pp. 480, 441.

to achieve this end, which is simply the complex of ploys and pitches assumed to manipulate the reader.

Political writing requires its own categories for analysis. In order to reach any conclusion, however tentative, about what constitutes a good political pamphlet, an assessment of polemical objective is needed. Only then can the pamphleteer's polemical strategy be appreciated. This, in turn, brings into prominence the significance of an awareness of context to criticism of political literature. Not only is it crucial to have an understanding of a pamphlet's historical background, the unspoken assumptions of the target reader should be included in any attempt at critical analysis. The reader's response is vital to successful propaganda, and pamphleteers should always take the sentiments if not the prejudices of their audience into consideration, as it is immensely difficult to go against the grain. Indeed, psychological research has suggested that readers will subconsciously (mis)interpret arguments so that they reaffirm existing prejudices. It is for this reason that attention should be paid not only to what an argument *is*, but what it does.[5]

The most successful pamphleteers use their knowledge of the prejudices of their target readers to attain their polemical objective. Perhaps the best eighteenth-century example of this is Swift's *The Conduct of the Allies*. Samuel Johnson, who failed to interpret Swift's polemical strategy correctly because he did not grasp his intention, was forced nevertheless to refer sardonically to 'this wonder-working pamphlet'. 'The purpose', he wrote in the *Life of Swift*, 'was to persuade the nation to a peace; and never had any writer more success.'[6] Clearly Johnson, himself a skilful political writer, appreciated the concept of polemical objective. Unfortunately, he failed to identify what Swift was up to in *The Conduct of the Allies*. Swift was not attempting to proselytise. His target reader was not an unsympathetic Whig utterly opposed to peace, but a Tory who wanted to be told that the nation had been exploited by the allies and the previous ministry, and Swift's conspiracy thesis pandered to the prejudices of this target reader.

Burke's *Reflections on the Revolution in France* (1790) operated in a similar way. Its primary aim was not to convert those who admired the initial achievements of the revolutionaries, but to give shape to the hitherto shapeless anxieties of the anti-Gallicans. Burke, in other words, was seeking to articulate arguments which could be used by those who were alarmed by what was happening in

5 On this point, see John Brewer, *Party Ideology and Popular Politics at the Accession of George III* (Cambridge: Cambridge University Press, 1976), pp. 33–4.
6 Samuel Johnson, *Lives of the Poets*, ed. E. B. Hill (Oxford: Clarendon Press, 1905), p. 19.

France. Most were men of property, and it was with this class, and not the 'swinish multitude', that Burke sought a broad solidarity. Playing on the fears of these target readers, Burke insinuates, over and over again, that while the British political system 'is placed in a just correspondence and symmetry with the order of the world', what is happening in France 'seems out of nature'. In this way, conservative ideology is presented not as an ideology at all, but as simply 'inevitable' or 'necessary' or 'planted in the nature of things'.[7] Little wonder, then, that the publication of Burke's 'pamphlet' was enthusiastically welcomed by the loyalists.

Awareness of context and appreciation of the way in which polemical writing is slanted to appeal to a preconceived audience assists the modern reader to recuperate what a political pamphlet is trying to do. As political writing cannot avoid being topical, however, the problem of bringing the details of a forgotten dispute to life remains. 'Who now reads Bolingbroke?', asked Burke, echoing William Arnall, who during Walpole's long tenure of office had dismissed the writers of the golden age of Anne's reign in identical manner: 'Who now reads, or even knows Lestrange's *Observator*, or Defoe's *Review*, or Leslie's *Rehearsals*, or the *Examiners*, with Shoals of other Writings, all of much Noise and some Esteem in their Day? I dare say that many of the present Generation never heard of their Names.'[8] Judging by the sheer amount of notice taken of them, pamphlets such as Perceval's *Faction Detected* (1743) or Mauduit's *Considerations on the Present German War* (1760) were of considerable importance to contemporaries although they are rarely read today. The most effective polemic is not necessarily the best written, and criticism of political literature always has to bear in mind that the aesthetic and the pragmatic can pull in opposite directions. The political writers of the past who continue to appeal to us do so because of the way in which they articulate their arguments, rather than on account of the arguments themselves.

Finally, it should be acknowledged that, although it is tempting to write of a pamphlet's 'influence', assessing the efficacy of a particular polemic is singularly problematic. Although propagandists, from the unknown author of the Martin Marprelate tracts onwards, evinced confidence about the possibility of influencing public opinion through the medium of print, it is rarely possible to document the definable alteration in political consciousness resulting from the publication of a particular pamphlet. As I have suggested, the most successful propagandists of the period preached to the converted, using their rhetoric to

7 Edmund Burke, *Reflections on the Revolution in France*, ed. Conor Cruise O'Brien (Harmondsworth: Penguin, 1969), pp. 173, 120, 92, 131.

8 [William Arnall], *Opposition No Proof of Patriotism* (London, 1735), p. 27.

rally sympathisers rather than to win over opponents. In addition, entrenched interest groups, in an unrepresentative and thoroughly undemocratic political system, were virtually fireproof. Walpole emerged almost entirely unscathed from the extended assault on his competence and integrity conducted by the most gifted writers of their generation. Similarly, the unprecedented stir created by Thomas Paine's *Rights of Man* failed to win the battle for the nation's political consciousness, and by the end of the century the radical pamphleteers had been all but silenced by the conservative reaction to events in France.

The rage of party

'Since the Act for Printing expired', the Secretary of State, Sir William Trumbull, observed in the summer of 1695, 'London swarmes with seditious Pamphletts.'[9] The expiry of the Licensing Act occurred during the same session of Parliament as the passing of the Triennial Act. As Daniel Defoe observed: 'The Certainty of a new Election in three Years is an unhappy Occasion of keeping alive the Divisions and Party-Strife among the People.'[10] Contemporaries were quick to make the connection between political activity and an increase in the numbers of newspapers and pamphlets. There were ten general elections between 1695 and 1715, and the heated political atmosphere of the 'first age of party' was stoked by the outpouring of the party presses.

The first Tories were monarchists who believed in indefeasible hereditary succession, passive obedience and non-resistance, and upheld the constitution in church and state. The Whigs, on the other hand, believed that sovereignty rested in the 'people' as represented in parliament, assumed that government was by the consent of the governed, and that the subject retained the right to resist any monarch who no longer commanded that consent. These rival versions of the constitution were tested by the Revolution of 1688–9, when James II was replaced on the throne by William and Mary. The Revolution Settlement had to be defended by force of arms, and two long, expensive continental wars raised new party-political issues. Supplementary to the fundamental question of how the military machine might be financed, the questions of how the War of the Spanish Succession should be waged and, ultimately, how and when it should be ended, gradually assumed burning significance.

9 Quoted in Raymond Astbury, 'The Renewal of the Licensing Act in 1693 and its Lapse in 1695', *The Library*, 5th series, 33 (1978), 317.
10 *Defoe's Review*, vol. v, p. 142, quoted in J. A. Downie, *Robert Harley and the Press: Propaganda and Public Opinion in the Age of Swift and Defoe* (Cambridge: Cambridge University Press, 1979).

For twenty years, the constitutional issues were debated by the most talented pamphleteers of their day, the most prolific of whom was Daniel Defoe. As a Whig who had twice taken up arms against James II, Defoe first came to prominence by writing in defence of his hero, William III. In addition to his best-selling verse satire on English xenophobia, *The True-Born Englishman*, Defoe sought to force a reluctant House of Commons to acknowledge the seriousness of the international situation. Typically, he chose an audacious way to achieve his objective. Couched in the form of a letter addressed to the Speaker, who was 'Commanded by Two Hundred Thousand *English-men*' – the approximate size of the electorate at the time – 'to Deliver it to the H[ous]e of C[ommon]s, and to inform them that it is no Banter, but Serious Truth', *Legion's Memorial* demanded that the people's representatives in parliament recognise 'the growing Power of *France*'. It was a bold stroke, surpassed only by the chutzpah of Defoe's conclusion: '*Englishmen* are no more to be Slaves to Parliaments, than to a King. *Our Name is Legion, and we are Many.*'[11]

Defoe's willingness to take personal as well as rhetorical risks in support of his beliefs often got him into trouble. *Legion's Memorial* had purported to be 'no Banter, but Serious Truth'. The following year, after the death of William III, he responded to what he perceived to be the growing threat to religious freedom with *The Shortest-Way with the Dissenters* (1702). Although critics are unable to agree about the pamphlet's polemical strategy – largely because there is no consensus about its polemical objective – it is indisputable that, on some level, it was intended as a hoax. The persona adopted by Defoe represented himself as a committed high-churchman offering 'Proposals for the Establishment of the Church', including hanging Dissenting preachers, and banishing their congregations. Only some time after the pamphlet's publication, apparently, did it emerge that these were not the genuine proposals of an Anglican bigot, but a satire of the extremism of high-church writers such as Henry Sacheverell, Charles Leslie and Philip Stubbs. The explanation that 'it seems Impossible to imagine it should pass for any thing other than a Banter on the High-flying Church-Men'[12] cut no ice with an outraged government. The damage had been done, and Defoe's punishment for writing and publishing a seditious libel was severe. He was made to stand in the pillory three times, fined £135 and put on a form of probation for seven years.

Defoe learned that irony was a dangerous weapon the hard way, but it did not prevent him from publishing *Reasons against the Succession of the House of*

---

11 *Political and Economic Writings of Daniel Defoe*, ed. W. R. Owens and P. N. Furbank, 8 vols. (London: Pickering & Chatto, 2000), vol. II, pp. 41–6.
12 *Ibid.* vol. III, p. 113.

Hanover; And What if the Pretender Should Come?; and *An Answer to a Question That No Body Thinks of, viz. But What if the Queen Should Die?* in 1713. Not only were the titles of these pamphlets dangerously controversial, the first two were risky exercises in irony, while each paragraph of the third ended with the refrain: *'But what if the Queen should die?'* Although all three pamphlets were patently written *in support of* the Hanoverian Succession, Defoe was again arrested and imprisoned as his opponents sought his silence. One anonymous adversary even took the opportunity presented by the three pamphlets to defame him as 'An *Animal* who shifts his Shape oftner than *Proteus*, and goes backwards and forwards like a Hunted *Hare*; a thorough-pac'd, true-bred *Hypocrite*, an *High-Church Man* one Day, and a *Rank Whig* the next'.[13]

As a back-handed compliment, this is of significance. Although his tactics occasionally failed to pay off, Defoe's genius as a pamphleteer consisted in his ability to manipulate his target reader. Often the same issues of authenticity with which we are familiar from narratives such as *Robinson Crusoe* and *Moll Flanders* were deliberately raised by Defoe himself with a rhetorical end in mind. That readers could apparently be taken in by pamphlets like the *Shortest Way* and *Reasons against the Succession of the House of Hanover* is evidence of Defoe's mastery of the persona. Articulating his views in a series of distinctive voices speaking in individually inflected accents, he was able to slant his texts convincingly towards a particular target reader. Thus *The Review*, the seminal essay paper Defoe carried on single-handedly between 1704 and 1713 to 'state facts right', first sought to influence moderate Tory opinion to convince them of the overriding importance of a land war waged on the Continent, and then, after the Ministerial Revolution of 1710, attempted the supremely difficult task of reconciling the Whigs to the new Tory-dominated government.[14]

After his incarceration for writing and publishing the *Shortest Way*, Defoe was recruited as a government propagandist by Robert Harley. He remained on the ministerial payroll for the rest of the reign of Queen Anne. Acutely aware of the importance of public as well as parliamentary opinion, Harley, later Earl of Oxford, painstakingly assembled a team of government writers, including the other great innovative pamphleteer of the age, Jonathan Swift. Recruited in 1710 to edit *The Examiner*, Swift is often described as a Tory because of his writings on behalf of the Oxford ministry. In his own statement of political

---

13 *Judas Discuvr'd, and Catch'd at last: Or, Daniel de Foe in Lobs Pound* (London, 1713), p. 3.
14 On this point, see J. A. Downie, 'Stating Facts Right About Defoe's *Review*', in J. A. Downie and Thomas N. Corns (eds.), *Telling People What to Think: Early Eighteenth-Century Periodicals from 'The Review' to 'The Rambler'* (London and Portland, OR: Frank Cass, 1993), pp. 8–22.

beliefs, *The Sentiments of a Church-of-England Man, with Respect to Religion and Government*, however, he made it plain that, despite holding high-church views, he regarded arbitrary power 'as a greater Evil than *Anarchy* it self'.[15] Indeed, he represented himself as an upholder of 'the old Whig principles, without the modern articles and refinements'.[16]

The best way to appreciate the range of Swift's extravagant polemical talent is to read through the series of essays he published in *The Examiner* between 2 November 1710 and 14 June 1711. The agenda had been set by Bolingbroke's *A Letter to the Examiner*, which advised the author to paint 'the present State of the War Abroad', and to 'Collect some few of the Indignities which have been this Year offer'd to Her MAJESTY, and of those Unnatural Struggles, which have betray'd the Weakness of a shatter'd Constitution'.[17] Swift's main objective, therefore, was to defend the policies of the new ministry, and one way of doing this was to denounce the previous ministers. His most famous *Examiner* essays – 'A Bill of British Ingratitude', the 'Letter to Crassus' and the indictment of Wharton as Verres, the Roman governor of Sicily – censure individuals. The personal attack was only one of his strategies, however. By insinuating a broad solidarity with the respectable members of the proper-tied elite, particularly the nobility and gentry, in contradistinction to 'those, who by their Birth, Education and Merit, could pretend no higher than to wear our liveries',[18] Swift attempted to drive a wedge between 'the present Body of *Whigs*' – 'a very odd Mixture of Mankind' – and 'those who call themselves the *Old Whigs*'. He professed not to be able to find 'any material Difference' between the old Whigs and 'a great Majority of the present *Tories*'.[19]

This was also the basic thrust of *The Conduct of the Allies*. Because he is pre-eminently acclaimed as a satirist, it is not sufficiently appreciated that Swift made use of other strategies. Although *The Conduct of the Allies* ostensibly set out to 'prove', 'by plain Matters of Fact', the thesis that 'no Nation was ever so long or so scandalously abused by the Folly, the Temerity, the Corruption, the Ambition of its domestick Enemies; or treated with so much Insolence, Injustice and Ingratitude by its foreign Friends',[20] this was merely a blind. Thus when Johnson remarked that 'it operates by the mere weight of facts, with very

15 Swift, *Prose Works*, vol. II, p. 15.
16 *The Correspondence of Jonathan Swift*, ed. Harold Williams, 5 vols. (Oxford: Clarendon Press, 1963–5), vol. IV, p. 100.
17 Swift, *Prose Works*, vol. III, p. 222.
18 *Ibid.*, vol. III, p. 12.
19 *Ibid.*, vol. III, p. 111.
20 *Ibid.*, vol. VI, p. 15.

little assistance from the hand that produced them',[21] he was actually indicating the extent to which he had been taken in by Swift's polemical strategy. The facts Swift employed were carefully selected with the prejudices of his target reader in mind, and he used his intimate knowledge of those prejudices to construct an elaborate but fictitious conspiracy thesis embracing the allies, the late ministry, the Marlboroughs, the Whigs, and the stockjobbers because, as he scathingly observed, '[i]t is the Folly of too many, to mistake the Eccho of a *London* Coffee-house for the Voice of the Kingdom'.[22]

The Whigs tried to neutralise Swift's rhetoric, but without conspicuous success. Even before Swift had taken over the authorship of *The Examiner*, Joseph Addison had begun to answer it in *The Whig-Examiner*. Largely on account of his contributions to *The Tatler* and *The Spectator*, Addison's skill as a political essayist is often overlooked. One has only to read the elaborate political allegory published as the third *Spectator* paper (written to influence the imminent elections for the Directors of the Bank of England) or the series of essays which made up *The Freeholder*, especially his brilliant caricature of the Tory country gentleman as the Foxhunter (who maintained 'that there had been no good Weather since the Revolution')[23] to recognise that a talented polemicist is at work. Addison was not prepared to reply to *The Examiner* point by point over an extended period, however. That task devolved upon John Oldmixon in *The Medley*, working under the supervision of Arthur Maynwaring. Maynwaring's importance as organiser of Whig propaganda and his skill as a controversialist has only recently come to light, documentary evidence demonstrating that he was responsible for pamphlets formerly attributed to Defoe.[24] After Maynwaring's death in 1712, Richard Steele began to spearhead the Whig propaganda initiative which, culminating in the publication of *The Crisis* early in 1714, aimed at destabilising the Oxford ministry by insinuating that the Protestant Succession was in danger.

Swift was given the job of undermining Whig propaganda. One of his strengths was his thorough understanding of the propagandist's milieu. His ability to identify and therefore to counter the thrust of his opponents' arguments was almost uncanny. What Swift did was to attack the Whig writers' credibility, especially Steele's, by drawing attention to 'that peculiar Manner of expressing himself, which the Poverty of our Language forceth me to call their

21 Johnson, *Lives of the Poets*, p. 19.
22 Swift, *Prose Works*, vol. VI, p. 53.
23 Joseph Addison, *The Freeholder*, ed. James Leheny (Oxford: Clarendon Press, 1979), p. 131.
24 For Maynwaring, see in particular, Henry L. Snyder, 'Arthur Maynwaring and the Whig Press, 1710–1712', in Rudolf Haas, Heinz-Joachim Müllenbrock and Claus Uhlig (eds.), *Literatur als Kritik des Lebens* (Heidelberg: Quelle & Meyer, 1977), pp. 120–36.

Style'.[25] One of his best political pamphlets, *The Publick Spirit of the Whigs: Set Forth in their Generous Encouragement of the Author of the Crisis: with some Observations on the Seasonableness, Candor, Erudition, and Style of that Treatise* (it is important to give the title in full) was essentially an exercise in literary criticism in which Swift first belittled Steele, and then simply revealed the purpose behind his pamphlet: 'Thus the Whigs among us give about the Cry, A *Pamphlet!* A *Pamphlet!* The *Crisis!* The *Crisis!* Not with a View of convincing their Adversaries, but to raise the Spirits of their Friends, recal their Stragglers, and unite their Numbers by Sound and Impudence; as Bees assemble and cling together by the Noise of Brass.'[26]

Swift's reputation is founded on his skill as a satirist, and the essence of the satirist's art lies in the painstaking manipulation of the reader. This is perhaps seen most clearly in Swift's Irish pamphlets. In *The Drapier's Letters* he headed up a campaign to encourage his countrymen to boycott William Wood's half-pence, copper coins to be circulated in Ireland and minted by Wood for a substantial profit under a licence from the English government. Assuming the character of a draper in order to address 'the vulgar' in the first two pamphlets, he subsequently brought into play the colonial character of the relationship between Britain and Ireland. The brilliant sustained irony of *A Modest Proposal* is informed by this issue also. Modulating between litotes and hyperbole (understatement and exaggeration) throughout the pamphlet, at certain points Swift contrives to give the impression that the narrator, who has started out as both calm and dispassionate, is able to control his feelings no longer. These instances – 'this Food will be somewhat dear, and therefore very *proper for Landlords*; who, as they have already devoured most of the Parents, seem to have the best Title to the Children'; 'this Kind of Commodity will not bear Exportation; the Flesh being of too tender a Consistence, to admit a long Continuance in Salt; *although, perhaps, I could name a Country, which would be glad to eat up our whole Nation without it*'[27] – still have the power to shock. They also reveal the basic strategy of *A Modest Proposal*, which is to confound the literal and the figurative. The landlords have not literally devoured the parents of the unfortunate beggar children; nor has England actually eaten up Ireland with or without salt. By removing the metaphor, as he does in suggesting that the solution to Ireland's ills is the eating of beggars' babies when they are a year old, however, Swift manipulates the reader to expose the actual consequences to Ireland of England's colonial policies.

25 Swift, *Prose Works*, vol. IV, p. 57.
26 *Ibid.*, vol. VIII, p. 34.
27 *Ibid.*, vol. XII, pp. 112, 117.

The opposition to Walpole

John, Lord Hervey – Pope's Lord Fanny – asserted in his memoirs that English letters had never been 'at a higher pitch, either for learning, strength of diction, or elegance of style', than in the reign of George II. 'All the good writing, too', he went on, 'was confined to political topics, either of civil, military, or ecclesiastical government, and all the tracts on these subjects printed in pamphlets. It might very properly be called the Augustan age of England for this kind of writing.'[28] While the most interesting writing actually appeared as contributions to periodicals rather than pamphlets as such, there can be little doubt that the administration of Sir Robert Walpole provoked a tremendous outburst of indignation at what Swift described as 'the worst times and Peoples, and Oppressions that History can shew'.[29] A literary opposition comprising, among others, Pope, Gay and Swift himself, Fielding, Thomson and the young Samuel Johnson subjected Walpole to a withering assault from the publication of *Gulliver's Travels* in 1726 right through to the four-book *Dunciad* of 1743 and beyond.

The sense of outrage at Walpole and all he stood for gathered a sizeable head of steam during the reign of George I. In a series of letters published in the *London Journal* signed 'Cato', John Trenchard and Thomas Gordon denounced the Directors of the South Sea Company and 'a conspiracy of stock-jobbers, who were, with merciless and unclean hands, rifling the publick itself, engrossing all its wealth, and destroying at once all publick and private faith'.[30] Rhetorically straightforward, *Cato's Letters* are essentially an anachronistic jeremiad which, in bemoaning the shift in power from the landed to the monied interest, appears to have followed the lead of Swift and Bolingbroke:

> What Briton, blessed with any sense of virtue, or with common sense; what Englishman, animated with a publick spirit, or with any spirit, but must burn with rage and shame, to behold the nobles and gentry of a great kingdom; men of magnanimity; men of breeding; men of understanding, and of letters; to see such men bowing down, like Joseph's sheaves, before the face of a dirty *stock-jobber*, and receiving laws from men bred behind counters, and the decision of their fortunes from hands still dirty with sweeping shops![31]

28 John, Lord Hervey, *Some Materials towards Memoirs of the Reign of King George II*, ed. Romney Sedgwick (London: Eyre & Spottiswoode, 1931), pp. 260–1.
29 Swift, *Correspondence*, vol. IV, p. 504.
30 John Trenchard and Thomas Gordon, *Cato's Letters*, ed. Ronald Hamowy, 2 vols. (Indianapolis IN: Liberty Fund, 1995), vol. I, p. 53.
31 *Ibid.*, vol. I, pp. 80–1.

The flagrant class terminology – not noticeably characteristic of a bourgeois public sphere accessible to all – sets the aristocracy (the nobility and gentry, the 'Men of Breeding') against the upstarts who have made their fortunes at the expense of the 'natural' leaders of society.

Trenchard and Gordon's indictment of the court Whigs' abandonment of Revolution principles reflects the changing political landscape. The peaceful accession of George I in 1714 ushered in a period of Whig dominance which endured until the accession of his great-grandson in 1760. Partly this was due to the repeal of the Triennial Act and the passing of the Septennial Act, and partly to the Whig ministers' successful efforts to proscribe the Tories en masse as a Jacobite party. *Cato's Letters'* explanation of the reasons behind the ministry's desire to perpetuate the party divisions of the previous reign constitutes the most convincing early attempt to counter Whig black propaganda of this type, as Trenchard and Gordon sought to keep alive the radical Whig agenda of an earlier era. Interestingly, after Trenchard's death in 1723, Gordon was bought off by Walpole and recruited as a ministerial apologist.

A little over a month after the publication of *Gulliver's Travels* in 1726, however, a new essay paper devoted to the exposure of 'the dark secrets of *political Craft*' made its appearance. *The Craftsman*, edited by the fictitious Caleb D'Anvers of Gray's-Inn, Esq., quickly became the leading opposition organ of propaganda in the struggle with Walpole. Most of the issues which had so exercised Cato – the South Sea Company, the depredations of stockjobbers and the threat posed to liberty by an encroaching executive – were taken up by *The Craftsman* as it endeavoured to construct a platform strong enough to accommodate a coalition of disaffected Whigs and Tories. 'All the best writers against the Court were concerned in the *Craftsman*', Hervey acknowledged, 'which made it a much better paper than any of that sort that were published on the side of the Court.'[32]

Chief among these was Bolingbroke. All his major political writings, including *Remarks on the History of England* and *A Dissertation upon Parties*, first published in *The Craftsman*, originally appeared in the form of letters. Bolingbroke's objective was, quite simply, the overthrow of Walpole, whom he blamed for the nation's assorted ills, and the various strategies he used to attack the Great Man and the '*general Corruption*' he was accused of promoting soon became very familiar to readers. Bolingbroke's first contributions to *The Craftsman* were transparent allegorical satires reminiscent of Addison's third *Spectator* paper. *Remarks on the History of England* works in a similar way, as English history is

---

32 Hervey, *Some Materials*, p. 263.

portrayed as a perpetual struggle between the spirit of faction and the spirit of liberty. 'A *Spirit of Liberty* will be always and wholly concern'd about *national Interests*, and very indifferent about *personal* and *private Interests*', Bolingbroke maintained. 'On the contrary, a *Spirit of Faction* will be always and wholly concern'd about *These*, and very indifferent about the *others*.'[33] *A Dissertation upon Parties* – the most frequently reprinted of Bolingbroke's writings – was also designed 'to expose the Artifice, and to point out the Series of Misfortunes, by which We were divided formerly into *Parties*, whose Contests brought even the fundamental Principles of our *Constitution* into Question, and whose Excesses brought *Liberty* to the very Brink of Ruin'. 'They are design'd to give true Ideas of *this Constitution*', Bolingbroke explained, 'and to revive in the Minds of Men the true Spirit of it.'[34]

Despite a scare during the Excise Crisis of 1733, Walpole remained in office. In 1735, Bolingbroke threw in the towel and left for France, leaving the field clear for a new kind of Whig opposition. From 1737 onwards, the 'Patriots' had their own essay paper, *Common Sense*, edited by the Jacobite, Charles Molloy, but with contributions from a formidable team, the most important of whom were George Lyttelton and Lord Chesterfield. As the notorious dream allegory entitled the 'Vision of the Golden Rump' which represented George II as a golden idol, shitting on his votaries with Queen Caroline and Walpole in attendance, graphically illustrates, Walpole continued to be the target although, because 'Common Sense must be free from all Prejudice, and Party Sense is observed to be rarely so', *Common Sense* claimed not to be a party-paper.[35] Instead, in its employment of wit and humour to ridicule ministerial propaganda, *Common Sense* recalls Swift's debunking of Whig propaganda in Anne's reign. 'In all former Reigns, the Wits were of the Side of the Ministers', it pointed out. 'I challenge the Ministerial Advocates to produce one Line of *Sense*, or *English*, written on their side of the Question for these last Seven Years.'[36]

Henry Fielding was an occasional contributor to *Common Sense* after the theatrical Licensing Act of 1737 put an end to his career as a dramatist. He was also deeply involved in *The Champion*, another periodical written in opposition to the Great Man. However, Fielding came to an accommodation with Walpole shortly before publishing *The Opposition: A Vision* in December 1741, in which

33 *Remarks on the History of England* (London, 1743), p. 28.
34 *A Dissertation upon Parties* (London, 1735), p. iv.
35 *Common Sense* (London, 1738), p. 171. The 'Vision of the Golden Rump' is reprinted in J. A. Downie, *To Settle the Succession of the State: Literature and Politics, 1678–1750* (London: Macmillan, 1994), pp. 133–5.
36 *Common Sense*, p. 248.

he satirised the motives of those who claimed that Walpole posed a threat to the nation's well-being.[37] Thus not only did the 'vast Trunk' containing the opposition's grievances turn out to be virtually empty, the 'huge Box' labelled 'PUBLIC SPIRIT' was 'cramm'd with *Ambition, Malice, Envy, Avarice, Disaffection, Disappointment, Pride, Revenge,* and many other heavy Commodities'.[38] Fielding continued to write in support of the ministry after Walpole's fall, his *A Serious Address to the People of Great Britain*, published while the Jacobite army was still in Edinburgh, enjoying the widest circulation as well as being the most notable of the pamphlets published during the 'Forty-Five' rebellion.

That little political writing of any note was provoked by the Forty-Five is indicative of a general trend. The Jacobite threat itself brought to an end the spirited anti-Hanoverian press campaign which characterised the years immediately following Walpole's fall. Henry Pelham appears to have been reluctant to spend money on the press. 'Those who have the Honour to know him', a disappointed Fielding observed in *The True Patriot*, 'assure me he hath the utmost Indifference for all Writers, and the greatest Contempt for any Good or Harm which they can do him.'[39] If the government was not prepared to fund propaganda, the opposition appears to have been equally uninterested. 'By the 1740s writers were giving politics far less attention', Robert Harris explains, so that 'the sharp retraction of public involvement in politics that undoubtedly occurred in the course of the decade . . . became very apparent after 1746'[40] and the end of the Jacobite threat at Culloden Moor.

Wilkes and liberty

The stability of the political order which had gradually been established since 1714 was severely tested during the 1760s. The accession of George III, the first Hanoverian monarch to have been born in Britain, offered an opportunity to cement national unity by abolishing the divisions in society perpetuated by the previous era of party conflict. The new king departed radically from his predecessors by welcoming with open arms the Tory nobility and gentry both at court and, as magistrates, in the localities. Less popular and ultimately

---

37 See Frederick G. Ribble, 'Fielding's Rapprochement with Walpole in late 1741', *Philological Quarterly* 80 (2001), 71–81.
38 Henry Fielding, *The Opposition: A Vision* (London, 1741), p. 16.
39 Henry Fielding, *The True Patriot and Related Writings*, ed. W. B. Coley (Oxford: Clarendon Press, 1987), p. 209.
40 Robert Harris, *A Patriot Press: National Politics and the London Press in the 1740s* (Oxford: Clarendon Press, 1993), p. 7.

divisive, however, was his indulgence of his Scottish favourite, the Earl of Bute, who gradually became the mark at which most opposition barbs were levelled.

George III had succeeded his grandfather while Britain was at war with France. The Seven Years' War (1756–63) was being waged on two separate fronts: on the Continent to protect allied – particularly Hanoverian – interests; and in the colonies, with conspicuous success given General Wolfe's capture of Quebec in 1759. Israel Mauduit's *Considerations on the Present German War* (1760) raised doubts about the wisdom of Britain's involvement on the Continent. Comparisons between the *Considerations* and Swift's *Conduct of the Allies* are readily apparent. Both pamphlets insinuated that British money was being spent in the interests of its allies, rather than in its own. Edition after edition appeared, while Mauduit's arguments were employed to attack William Pitt's war policy. It was not Pitt but Bute, however, who was blamed for negotiating what the opposition insisted was a disastrous peace. When Smollett, in *The Briton*, challenged opposition journalists to substantiate their criticisms of 'the Favourite', John Wilkes, the MP for Aylesbury, launched *The North Briton* with the specific purpose of discrediting Bute.

Written by Wilkes in collaboration with Charles Churchill, *The North Briton* played on English distrust of Scottish influence at court to confirm fears that what was designed was nothing less than 'the intire possession of the revenues of the whole country'.[41] Wilkes' strengths as a polemicist lay not in originality of thought or rhetorical skill, so much as in his exploitation of the range of resources available to the propagandist, among which was his painstaking construction of a public persona. This can best be illustrated by his response to the prosecution of *North Briton* no. 45 which, notoriously, had the temerity to reflect upon the king himself. George III was so infuriated that the Secretary of State, Lord Halifax, had little choice but to sign a general warrant for the arrest of the 'authors, printers and publishers' of the offending paper.

The absence of any named suspects gave Wilkes his cue. Throughout the rest of the decade he railed against 'the two great questions of GENERAL WARRANTS, and the SEIZURE OF PAPERS' – issues he portentously described as the 'cursed remains of the court of Star-Chamber'.[42] Wilkes' achievement was to succeed in making his own cause a kind of synecdoche for the rights and privileges of '*every* Englishman, in the person of Mr Wilkes'. The popular cry of 'Wilkes and Liberty' was appropriate because, on this reading, 'the North

---

41 *North Briton*, no. 6, quoted in Christopher Reid, *Edmund Burke and the Practice of Political Writing* (Dublin and New York: Gill and Macmillan, and St Martin's Press, 1985), p. 145.
42 [Wilkes,] *Letter to Grafton*, p. 15.

Briton was seized, for asserting the rights of every free-born Englishman'.[43] For all his self-promoting skill, however, Wilkes was unable to prevent the Commons resolving on 15 November 1763 that *North Briton* no. 45 was 'a false, scandalous and seditious libel, containing Expressions of the most unexampled Insolence and Contumely towards his Majesty'.[44] On the same day, Wilkes was named in the Lords as the author of the obscene *Essay on Woman*. Worse was to follow. Badly wounded in a duel the next day, Wilkes fled to Paris. In his absence, the Commons resolved that he was guilty of writing and publishing *North Briton* no. 45, and he was expelled from the House.

That was not the end of it, however. On his return from France, Wilkes was elected for the county of Middlesex in the general election of 1768. Understandably, the ministry did not want him to take his seat. Wilkes was duly tried, convicted and imprisoned for seditious and obscene libel on account of *North Briton* no. 45 and the *Essay on Woman*. Attention turned to the debate in parliament. On 21 November, a new figure entered the lists. 'Junius' drew attention to the Wilkes affair in the first of his letters to *The Public Advertiser*. 'In the present Instance the Duke of Grafton may possibly find that he has played a foolish Game', the letter prophetically concluded. 'He rose by Mr Wilkes's Popularity, and it is not impossible he may fall by it.'[45] During the months that followed, as he sought to bring about Grafton's downfall, Junius represented his scathing attacks on the administration as spirited attempts to protect the constitution.

By the late 1760s, anonymous letters to newspapers formed a significant element of day-to-day comment on politics. The identity of Junius remains unknown. Although his adversaries, including Johnson, derided his anonymity, it makes no essential difference to the appreciation of his vituperative skill. Junius had a genius for invective, and Grafton bore the brunt of a barrage of criticism directed at the ministry: 'THE finances of a nation, sinking under its debts and expences, are committed to a young nobleman already ruined by play ... As for business, the world yet knows nothing of his talents or resolution; unless a wayward, wavering inconsistency be a mark of genius and caprice a demonstration of spirit.'[46] Although he was an able political analyst, Junius' writings (like Wilkes') are notable not for their political insight – tellingly, Coleridge refers to him 'deviat[ing] into originality of thought' – but rather for their manner of attack. The predominantly abstract language in which

43 [John Wilkes,] *A Letter to the Right Hon. George Granville*, 3rd edn. (London, 1763), pp. 9, 7.
44 *Journals of the House of Commons*, vol. 29, p. 668.
45 'Junius', *The Letters of Junius*, ed. John Cannon (Oxford: Clarendon Press, 1978), p. 456.
46 *Ibid.*, p. 27.

they are written is in stark contrast to the highly personal nature of the vituperation which is Junius' trademark. (He preferred to call it 'personal satire'.)
Junius' readers undoubtedly expected him to be audacious. The method he
pursued was insolence masquerading as irony. Those who question Junius'
skill as a polemicist do so because they confound rational argument with
rhetorical effect. He grasped the significance of the persona he had invented,
and appreciated that the character of Junius had to be 'kept up with credit'.[47]
His high-handedness was a crucial element in the formula, and it is in this
respect that Coleridge is right when he remarks that the letters 'are suited to
their purpose, and perfect in their kind'.[48]

Although letters continued to appear above his name for a further two
years, the climax of Junius' campaign was his letter to the king of 19 December
1769, described by Horace Walpole as 'the most daring insult ever offered to
a prince but in times of open rebellion'.[49] 'When the complaints of a brave
and powerful people are observed to encrease in proportion to the wrongs
they have suffered', Junius opened, 'when, instead of sinking into submis-
sion, they are roused to resistance, the time will soon arrive at which every
inferior consideration must yield to the security of the Sovereign, and to the
general safety of the state.' Supposing that moment to have arrived, Junius
speculated 'in what terms . . . an honest man' would address 'a gracious, well-
intentioned prince, made sensible at last of the great duty he owed to his
people, and of his own disgraceful situation'.[50] In this letter, Junius, like Wilkes,
came dangerously close to exploding the polite fiction that the king could do
no wrong. If, however, the ultimate objective of the letters of Junius was
the overthrow of Grafton, then this goal was attained with his resignation in
January 1770.

Widely suspected of being the author of the letters of Junius, Edmund
Burke made his own contribution to the press campaign directed against the
administration in *Thoughts on the Cause of the Present Discontents*, although it
was too late to contribute to Grafton's fall. 'I will not believe, what no other
man living believes', Burke observed, 'that Mr Wilkes was punished for the
indecency of his publications, or the impiety of his ransacked closet.'[51] Yet
Burke had comparatively little to say about Wilkes or the Middlesex election.

47 *Ibid.*, p. 352.
48 T. M. Raysor (ed.), *Coleridge's Miscellaneous Criticism* (London: Constable & Co., 1936),
   p. 314.
49 Quoted in *Letters of Junius*, p. 159.
50 *Ibid.*
51 *The Writings and Speeches of Edmund Burke*, ed. Paul Langford, 8 vols. (Oxford: Oxford
   University Press, 1981), vol. II, p. 297.

Instead, as its title indicates, *Thoughts* proposed to deal with the underlying problems which the events of the 1760s had brought to the surface. This, in turn, highlights some of the issues raised by political writings. Certainly the pamphlet sold well and, for two principal reasons, it continues to be read today. Contemporaries remarked upon its 'fine turned and polished periods',[52] and it is indeed well written. In addition, Burke's articulated defence of party means that *Thoughts* can be read as political theory as much as a pamphlet written to meet a particular set of political circumstances. In this sense, the Middlesex election was simply an excuse. As Burke's purpose was much less specific, 'identifying and quantifying its impact is less easy'. 'Judged by the yardstick of his own aims', Paul Langford concludes, 'Burke's work was a limited success.'[53]

Meanwhile the Wilkes affair rumbled on. Despite his conviction, he was re-elected unopposed by the electors of Middlesex in February and March 1769. In April, however, Henry Lawes Luttrell stood against him and was declared elected by the Commons despite polling 296 votes to Wilkes' 1143. In this way, a major constitutional issue was raised by the Middlesex election – that of whether the House of Commons could dictate who would represent a constituency in parliament. An authoritative response was required, and Samuel Johnson was persuaded to write it.

From its opening periods onwards, *The False Alarm* is characteristically Johnsonian in style, method and manner:

> One of the chief advantages derived by the present generation from the improvement and diffusion of philosophy, is deliverance from unnecessary terrors, and exemption from false alarms. The unusual appearances, whether regular or accidental, which once spread consternation over ages of ignorance, are now the recreations of inquisitive security. The sun is no more lamented when it is eclipsed, than when it sets; and meteors play their coruscations without prognostic or prediction.[54]

As Johnson's purpose was to dispel any suggestion of irregularity, much less constitutional crisis, the impression of balanced thought was supplied by the employment of thesis followed by antithesis. *The False Alarm* is the finest of Johnson's political pamphlets not because of the strength of its argument, but because of what its argument accomplishes – the effective defusing of

---

52 Catherine Macaulay, *Observations on a Pamphlet* (London, 1770), p. 6.
53 In Burke, *Writings and Speeches*, vol. II, p. 248.
54 Samuel Johnson, *Political Writings*, ed. Donald J. Greene (New Haven, CT: Yale University Press, 1977), pp. 317–18.

the political situation. 'Nothing, therefore, is necessary, at this *alarming crisis'*, Johnson concluded, 'but to consider the alarm as false.'[55]

That Johnson refused to become engaged with the personal issues surrounding the Middlesex election, preferring instead to restrict his argument to matters of general principle, was part of his polemical strategy. Thus he did not even mention Wilkes by name until he had made his case. 'Lampoon itself would disdain to speak ill of him of whom no man speaks well', Johnson argued. 'It is sufficient that he is expelled the House of Commons, and confined in jail as being legally convicted of sedition and impiety.'[56] As a convicted felon, Johnson maintained, Wilkes was incapable of being a Member of Parliament. Wilkes responded to the 'Orator of Polysyllables' in typical style, combining abuse with heavy-handed innuendo. 'A certain protuberancy of diction may be very edifying to the maids of honour', he suggested; 'and the inflation of your periods cannot fail to find a passage into that quarter where the ERSE is said to have been *the reigning dialect'*.[57]

Despite their forceful arguments, Johnson's remaining political pamphlets are less striking as examples of successful polemic. *Thoughts on the late Transactions respecting Falkland's Islands* (1771) is mostly of interest for what Johnson has to say about the 'unusual phænomenon' of Junius, while *The Patriot* (1774) is a short pamphlet 'Addressed to the Electors of Great Britain' consequent on the snap general election of 1774. Johnson's final pamphlet, *Taxation no Tyranny* (1775), was a 'quasi-official' response to the Declaration of Rights issued by the American Constitutional Congress. Offering typically trenchant opinions on the American crisis without effectually extinguishing 'the delirious dream of republican fanaticism', Johnson convincingly argues the case for taxation. In addition, almost as an aside, he draws attention to the paradox at the heart of the colonists' complaint: 'If slavery be thus fatally contagious, how is it that we hear the loudest yelps for liberty among the drivers of negroes?'[58]

Reflections on the Revolution

Burke's *Reflections on the Revolution in France, and on the Proceedings in Certain Societies in London Relative to that Event*, at once 'the founding text of modern conservatism',[59] and the opening salvo of the loyalists in the pamphlet war

---

55 *Ibid.*, p. 345.
56 *Ibid.*, p. 319.
57 John Wilkes, *A Letter to Samuel Johnson, L.L.D.* (London, 1770), pp. 7–8.
58 Johnson, *Political Writings*, p. 454.
59 Gregory Claeys (ed.), *Political Writings of the 1790s*, 6 vols. (London: Pickering and Chatto, 1995), vol. I, p. xviii.

sparked off by the events of 1789, was really concerned with developments at home. Although it purported to be a letter to one of Burke's real-life French correspondents, it was actually a pamphlet of unprecedented length which sought to defend 'that *antient* constitution of government which is our only security for law and liberty'[60] against the threat posed not only by 'the late proceedings in France', but by the proceedings of the Society for Constitutional Information and the Revolution Society.

In a sermon delivered to the latter of these on 4 November 1789 and subsequently published, Dr Richard Price had argued that the Revolution of 1688 had been based on the principles of liberty of conscience, the right to resist arbitrary power and, above all, the 'right to chuse our own governors; to cashier them for misconduct; and to frame a government for ourselves'.[61] Burke focussed on the third of these principles, insisting that it 'affect[ed] our constitution in its vital parts'.[62] For Burke, the Revolution, in restoring the liberties of the subject, simply restated old rights. It did not fundamentally alter the constitution, much less give the people the right to choose their own form of government.

Replies to Burke's *Reflections* concentrated on his figurative use of language because, as Coleridge put it, Burke seemed to be able 'to reason *in* metaphors'.[63] Burke's opponents also observed that the *Reflections* was crucially different from his earlier pamphlets which, following carefully constructed arguments, had appealed to the reason rather than the emotions of his readers. Significantly, Burke made extensive use not merely of figurative language in the *Reflections*, but the language of sentiment. Thus the famous 'apostrophe' to Marie Antoinette – the emotive account of the 'unnatural' treatment she was forced to endure – is central, literally and figuratively, to Burke's purpose. Apologising for having 'dwelt too long on the atrocious spectacle of the sixth of October 1789', Burke explained that it was because 'the most important of all revolutions' could be 'dated from that day' – 'a revolution in sentiments, manners, and moral opinions'.[64]

An understanding of Burke's purpose in writing the *Reflections* allows us to appreciate his polemical strategy. His target reader was a conservative fearful of what was taking place in France, not an admirer of the achievements of the

---

60 Burke, *Reflections*, p. 117.
61 Richard Price, *A Discourse on the Love of our Country* (London, 1789), p. 34.
62 Burke, *Reflections*, p. 96.
63 *The Collected Works of Samuel Taylor Coleridge*, ed. Lewis Patton, 16 vols. (Princeton, NJ: Princeton University Press, 1970), vol. II, p. 31.
64 Burke, *Reflections*, p. 175.

revolutionaries. Burke grasped that once the ideological underpinnings of the British state were removed, then the position of the traditional leaders of society would be eroded also. These were the fears upon which he played. 'Some decent regulated pre-eminence, some preference (not exclusive appropriation) given to birth', he insisted, 'is neither unnatural, nor unjust, nor impolitic.' Why? The answer was straightforward in its appeal to vested interest. 'The power of perpetuating our property in our families is one of the most valuable and interesting circumstances belonging to it, and that which tends the most to the perpetuation of society itself.'[65]

It is for this reason that, throughout the *Reflections*, the social status of the revolutionaries is given prominence. Although Burke's reference to the 'swinish multitude' is the most famous instance of his preoccupation with rank, his opening gambit offers a clear indication of the direction the pamphlet will take: 'After I had read over the list of the persons and descriptions elected into the *Tiers Etat* nothing which they afterwards did could appear astonishing.'[66] The political implications to which Burke was drawing attention were stark. What was at risk was nothing less than order, hierarchy and stability, and the dominance of the landed elite itself, because '[t]he whole of the power obtained by this revolution will settle in the towns among the burghers, and the monied directors who lead them'.[67]

Although Raymond Williams has observed that 'the confutation of Burke on the French Revolution is now a one-finger exercise in politics and history',[68] as far as the pamphlet's polemical impact is concerned this is beside the point. By appealing to the emotions of his target readers, Burke's discourse became, in an important sense, unanswerable. This is not to say that answers were not published. Over seventy of them were, including Thomas Paine's *Rights of Man*, which considerably outsold the *Reflections*. Paine appreciated, however, that Burke's rhetoric needed to be deconstructed as much as answered. Like Swift's *The Publick Spirit of the Whigs*, Paine's pamphlet is partly straightforward literary criticism. 'I cannot consider Mr Burke's book in any other light than a dramatic performance', Paine remarked; 'and he must, I think, have considered it in the same light himself, by the poetical liberties he has taken of omitting some

---

65 *Ibid.*, pp. 141, 140.
66 *Ibid.*, p. 128.
67 *Ibid.*, p. 311.
68 Quoted in James T. Boulton, *The Language of Politics in the Age of Wilkes and Burke* (London and Toronto: Routledge & Kegan Paul and University of Toronto Press, 1963), p. 97.

facts, distorting others, and making the whole machinery bend to produce a stage effect.'[69]

Ridiculing Burke's suggestion that the Revolution of 1688 bound the English nation 'for themselves, and for *all their posterity for ever*', Paine represented the 'vanity and presumption of governing beyond the grave' as 'the most ridiculous and insolent of all tyrannies'.[70] Central to Paine's argument was that each generation had the right to choose its own laws and forms of government. In one sense, this did little more than restate the conclusion of Locke's *Two Treatises of Government*. Paine's championing of the concept of the sovereignty of the people was part of a much more radical agenda, however. In proposing to 'place another system of principles in opposition to' Burke's,[71] Paine made it clear not only that all men were born with rights, but that these rights were shared equally. As a consequence, every man (but *not* woman) had a voice in the decision-making process. The democratic thrust of Paine's polemic was alarming to the propertied. Its principles were described as 'not a jot better than those of highwaymen and housebreakers; for the object of both is EQUALIZING PROPERTY'.[72]

Paine's irreverent style was suited to his appeal to egalitarian principles. Opponents maintained that it was 'written in a kind of specious jargon, well enough calculated to impose upon the vulgar',[73] but identification with the ordinary working man was crucial to the polemical success of *Rights of Man*. Published in numerous cheap editions in order to reach the widest possible readership, Paine's pamphlet broke circulation records and provoked an unprecedented response. Paine's arguments were equally straightforward. The second part of *Rights of Man* even contained a package of social and economic reforms, including a tax on landed estates, aimed at remedying the distresses of the poor. It offered a challenge to the establishment which terrified the political elite, and which resulted in its proscription in December 1792.

Therefore if *Rights of Man* were to be judged by the harshest criterion of all – whether it achieved its polemical objective – it would be difficult not to conclude that it was at best a qualified success. While it appealed to the lower orders of society, it frightened the propertied, including those in positions of authority, to such an extent that political debate was virtually silenced for a time. Yet Paine was by no means the most radical pamphleteer of the

69 Thomas Paine, *Rights of Man*, ed. Henry Collins (Harmondsworth: Penguin, 1969), p. 81.
70 *Ibid.*, pp. 81, 63–4.
71 *Ibid.*, p. 63.
72 Quoted in Claeys, *Political Writings*, vol. I, p. xl.
73 Quoted in Boulton, *The Language of Politics*, p. 137.

1790s. Mary Wollstonecraft's campaign for women's rights ventured where not even Paine had been prepared to go, although even she stopped short of advocating female suffrage – presumably because she realised advocating such an extreme programme would not be worth the candle. William Godwin's *An Enquiry Concerning Social Justice*, on the other hand, veered towards anarchism in its belief that any form of government was, at best, a necessary evil. That the polemic of the radical pamphleteers came to nothing in the 1790s was less to do with any rhetorical shortcomings than with the forces of repression, as a thoroughly frightened political elite sought to silence public debate by all possible means.

Sentimental fiction: ethics, social critique and philanthropy

THOMAS KEYMER

It is among the paradoxes of the lachrymose fiction that bedewed the eyes of novel readers in the later eighteenth century that the foremost exponents of the sentimental mode were also its most cogent detractors. The prime example is Henry Mackenzie, whose much-reprinted *The Man of Feeling* (1771), with its successors *The Man of the World* (1773) and *Julia de Roubigné* (1777), made him the most fashionable novelist of his day. With its trembling alertness to the minutiae of suffering and sympathy, and the plaintive silences of its fractured narrative form, *The Man of Feeling* is the exemplary sentimental text. Yet Mackenzie was to retire from novel writing in his early thirties, and in an essay of 1785 he gave systematic development to anxieties about sentimental fiction and its ethical basis that had already quietly haunted his three novels. Surveying the emergent subgenres of fiction, he detects in 'that species called the *Sentimental*' a dangerous subversion of its central claim: that by engaging readers' sympathies with misfortune, it could activate, as well as merely represent, 'the most exalted benevolence'. Feeling had become an end in itself, narcissistically attentive to nothing more than its own exquisiteness. Deploring the inertia of 'refined sentimentalists . . . who open their minds to impressions which never have any effect upon their conduct', Mackenzie attributes to sentimental fiction a 'separation of conscience from feeling' which is, he adds, 'a depravity of the most pernicious sort'. Even in its foremost examples, it cultivates nothing better than self-admiration, and disengages the will from forms of practical action that only less modish virtues – duty, principle – have the power to impel.[1]

In staging his dour critique of the sentimental mode, no less than in producing its classic instance in the previous decade, Mackenzie was in tune with the

---

1 *Lounger* 20 (18 June 1785), in Ioan Williams (ed.), *Novel and Romance, 1700–1800: A Documentary Record* (London: Routledge, 1970), pp. 328–31 (at pp. 329–30).

times. As John Mullan observes, the category of 'sentimental novel' is not the invention of literary historians but a designation that was regularly flaunted on title pages in the wake of Sterne's *A Sentimental Journey* (1768)[2] – the earliest novel, after William Guthrie's obscure *The Friends: A Sentimental History* (1754), to make titular use of this voguish term. The number of self-declared 'sentimental novels' was never large – ten had appeared in London or Dublin by the date of Mackenzie's essay, including two by the soft-pornographer Treyssac de Vergy – but it is greatly swollen by the addition of 'sentimental romances', 'sentimental tales' and the like, and augmented further by the original serial fiction of the *Sentimental Magazine* (1773–77), which neatly summarised the defining claim of the whole subgenre when promising among its standing features 'a sentimental History, which, at the same Time that it forces the Tears of Sensibility from the Eye, shall inspire the Heart with the Love of Virtue'.[3] Here, and in such variations on the theme as *The Sentimental Spy: A Novel* (1773) or *The Delicate Objection; or, Sentimental Scruple* (1775), a badge of allegiance is worn that seems to have been the marketing pitch of choice in Mackenzie's creative heyday. Tearfulness was all, a point satirically made in Thomas Bridges' *The Adventures of a Bank-Note* (1770–1), where a library proprietor's declaration that his most lucrative commodity is 'a crying volume' prompts the fictional author to attempt the mode himself. His efforts reach their irriguous climax when the hero, tremulous but hitherto dry-eyed, at last vents 'convulsive emotions, which else must certainly have been fatal; tears coursed each other down his manly cheeks, and form'd a rapid current o'er his garments'.[4]

Yet in retrospect the 1770s can be seen to mark the peak for sentimental fiction. 'Six shillings-worth of sensibility' (the phrase is from Helen Maria Williams)[5] remained a viable product for decades, but as time went on even the most vacuous examples began to look uneasy with their own assumptions. In the 1780s there emerges a further line of novels which, even as they continue to rehearse the standard tropes of sentimental fiction, also advertise a critical detachment. With *The Sentimental Deceiver* (1784) and *The Curse of*

2 John Mullan 'Sentimental Novels', in John Richetti (ed.), *The Cambridge Companion to the Eighteenth-Century Novel* (Cambridge': Cambridge University Press, 1996), pp. 236–54 (at p. 236).

3 *Sentimental Magazine* I (March 1773), 3. I define 'sentimental fiction' as a subgenre in which the affective and didactic strategies expressed in this quotation predominate. 'Sensibility' is the state of emotional and moral responsiveness prized in sentimental fiction; 'sentimentalism' is the ideology enshrining this state as the most admirable and beneficial virtue.

4 Thomas Bridges, *The Adventures of a Bank-Note*, 4 vols. (London, 1770–1), vol. III, pp. 5, 86.

5 Helen Maria Williams, *Julia*, 2 vols. (London, 1790), vol. II, p. 49.

Sentiment (1787), *Excessive Sensibility* (1787) and *The Errors of Sensibility* (1793), the talismanic language of sentiment takes on a jaded or monitory edge; while in *Arulia; or, The Victim of Sensibility* (1790) and *Infidelity; or, The Victims of Sentiment* (Philadelphia, 1797) the cherished virtue of refined feeling, far from alleviating distress, becomes its primary cause. It was business as usual for other practitioners of the mode well into the nineteenth century, and their output was a live target not only for Austen but also for her lesser-known rivals: Eaton Stannard Barrett's *The Heroine* (1813), for example, repudiates sentimental fiction as making its readers 'admire ideal scenes of transport and distraction; and feel disgusted with the vulgarities of living misery'.[6] The main outlines of criticism had been drawn in the 1780s, however, and were to find their most strident expression in the aftermath of the French Revolution, when conservatives and radicals competed to associate sentimentalism with revolutionary or reactionary excess. Responding to Burke, Mary Wollstonecraft excoriated a rhetoric that elicited tears for affronted royalty while ignoring the oppression of millions, and in *A Vindication of the Rights of Woman* (1792) she turned her fire specifically on the sentimental novel. Her later novel *The Wrongs of Woman; or Maria* (1798) dramatises her view of the mode as luring female readers into a state of 'intoxicated sensibility', and as foisting on them a debilitating image of themselves as 'only born to feel'.[7] At the other end of the spectrum, a collaborative satire orchestrated in the *Anti-Jacobin* by George Canning, the future Prime Minister, implicates among the sanguinary forces of revolution a sentimental philanthropy that is energised in theory by 'the general love of all mankind', but anaesthetised in practice by a preference for suffering beetles over suffering kings. *A Sentimental Journey* swims into view when, audaciously associating the cult of feeling with revolutionary genocide, Canning excoriates readers who 'O'er a dead Jack-Ass pour the pearly show'r: – / But hear, unmov'd, of *Loire's* ensanguin'd flood, / Choak'd up with slain; – of Lyons drench'd in blood'.[8]

Though colourful allegations like these have been to the fore in recent accounts of the backlash against sensibility, perhaps the most telling critique emanated from Evangelical reformers who, by virtue of their strenuous humanitarian campaigning, were unusually well qualified to evaluate the philanthropic claims of sentimental fiction. In Hannah More, who wept at

6 Eaton Stannard Barrett, *The Heroine*, 2nd edn, 3 vols. (London, 1813), vol. III, p. 253.
7 Mary Wollstonecraft, *Mary and The Wrongs of Woman*, ed. Gary Kelly (Oxford: Oxford University Press, 1976), pp. 82, 98.
8 George Canning, *The Anti-Jacobin*, 2 vols. (Hildesheim: George Olms, 1970), vol. II, pp. 623–40 (no. 36, 9 July 1798), lines 94, 143–4. Canning refers to the Vendée and Lyon massacres of 1793–4.

Mackenzie's fiction and corresponded with him 'about the *pleasure* of the *pains* of sensibility',[9] the Evangelical critique gains added interest from her residual attraction to the mode. Her poem *Sensibility* (drafted in 1775 and published in 1782) is still sometimes read as uncritically celebrating 'the feeling heart' and 'Sympathy Divine' as agents of practical benevolence. Even in its original version, however, key passages are highly sceptical of sentimental ethics, lamenting the subordination of traditional notions of justice, faith and virtue to mere feeling, and finding in the picturesque misfortunes of sentimental writing a decoy that leaves real injustice ignored, or at best acknowledged 'cheaply with a tear'. Better one charitable act, More adds, 'Than all the periods Feeling e'er can turn, / Than all thy soothing pages, polish'd Sterne'.[10] More's later revision of this passage to read 'perverted Sterne' typifies her hardening attitude to 'the modish page' of sentimental literature, which displaces 'the sterner virtues' and solicits tears for merely fictional distresses, 'While real mis'ry unreliev'd retires'.[11] Elsewhere More deplores the self-indulgent torpor of sentimental readers, while dutiful Christians 'of less natural sympathy . . . have been quietly furnishing a regular provision for miseries';[12] and in both early and late versions the impulse of *Sensibility* is clearly to reassert traditional piety, as opposed to the caprice of feeling, as the only reliable source of benevolent action. It is significant that when More praises Richardson (as she does again in her didactic novel *Coelebs in Search of a Wife*) she does so with reference to the religious severity of his fiction, and not to the sentimental pleasures it seemed to offer: "'Tis not because the ready eye o'erflows / At *Clementina*'s, or *Clarissa*'s woes.'[13] The pattern returns in More's fellow-abolitionist, William Wilberforce, who praises the austere piety of Richardson's characters while castigating novel readers who make 'imaginary exertions on behalf of ideal misery, and yet shrink from the labours of active benevolence'. For Wilberforce, there could be little real connection between the chimeras of sentimental fiction and fixed philanthropic commitment: 'never was delicate sensibility proved to be more distinct from plain practical benevolence', as he wrote of Sterne.[14]

---

9 Mackenzie to More, 12 October 1778, in William Roberts, *Memoirs of the Life and Correspondence of Mrs Hannah More*, 2 vols. (London, 1834), vol. I, p. 134.
10 Hannah More, *Sensibility*, in *Sacred Dramas* (London, 1782), pp. 267–90 (at pp. 276, 281, 284, 285).
11 Hannah More, *Sensibility*, in *Poems* (1816), intro. Caroline Franklin (London: Routledge, 1996), pp. 167–87 (at pp. 182, 179, 180).
12 Hannah More, *Strictures on Female Education*, 2 vols. (London, 1799), vol. II, p. 111.
13 More, *Sacred Dramas*, p. 283.
14 William Wilberforce, *A Practical View of the Prevailing Religious System of Professed Christians* (London, 1797), pp. 283–4.

Sympathy and moral sense

Sentimental fiction would probably have aroused less vocal enmity had it been quieter in its moral claims. The underlying principle was simple enough: by concentrating its resources on evoking distress, and on engaging the emotions with fictional suffering, it would constitute a training-ground for the sympathies from which readers would emerge newly equipped to put them benignly into practice. The strength of the claim was not always proportionate to the quality of the accompanying text. As Charles Dodd predicted of his woeful *Curse of Sentiment*, 'the feeling mind must be instructed and interested – and the human heart greatly improved and regulated: it must influence to acts of benevolence and forbearance, and cannot fail to benefit in all the various connections between man and man, between society and individuals'.[15]

Prose fiction had been jerking sympathetic tears, of course, for a century or more. Historians of sensibility have taken their cue from *Tristram Shandy*, where Sterne whimsically urges his readers 'to study the pure and sentimental parts of the best *French* Romances'.[16] Maximillian E. Novak and Anne Mellor point to the experience of Dorothy Osborne in 1653, who wept for a heroine in Mme de Scudéry 'though shee were an imaginary person'; R. F. Brissenden detects 'the beginnings of literary sentimentalism' in *La Princesse de Clèves* and *Lettres portugaises* (both translated in the 1670s); George Starr finds significant anticipations in home-grown sources such as Behn's *Oroonoko* (1688) and Defoe's *Colonel Jack* (1722).[17] What was new after Richardson was the primacy of feeling in general, and tears in particular, and the perception of their moral value. This development had already been heralded by Prévost and others in France, where a concentrated mode of sentimental fiction was flourishing in the 1730s – and it is worth remembering that several British novelists began their careers by translating this kind of material, notably Mary Collyer with *The Virtuous Orphan* (1742) and Frances Brooke with *Letters from Lady Juliet Catesby* (1759).[18]

15 Charles Dodd, *The Curse of Sentiment*, 2 vols. (London, 1787), vol. I, pp. xviii–xix.
16 Laurence Sterne, *Tristram Shandy*, ed. Melvyn New *et al.*, 3 vols. (Gainesville, FL: University Presses of Florida, 1978–84), 1.18.57. Further parenthetical references are to this edition, cited by book/chapter/page.
17 Maximillian E. Novak and Anne Mellor (eds.), *Passionate Encounters in a Time of Sensibility* (Newark, DE: University of Delaware Press, 2000), p. 11; R. F. Brissenden, *Virtue in Distress: Studies in the Novel of Sentiment from Richardson to Sade* (London: Macmillan, 1974), p. 107; George Starr, 'Aphra Behn and the Genealogy of the Man of Feeling', *Modern Philology* 87 (1990), 362–72, and 'Only a Boy: Notes on Sentimental Novels', *Genre* 10 (1977), 501–27.
18 From, respectively, Marivaux, *La Vie de Marianne* (1731–42), and Riccoboni, *Lettres de milady Juliette Catesby* (1759).

Modern literary history has paid more attention to non-fictional traditions, however, and elaborate native genealogies have been constructed for the sentimental novel. In an essay which dominated the field for decades, R. S. Crane traced the underlying principles to Restoration and early eighteenth-century divinity. Developed in consoling response to the ideologies and experiences of the Civil Wars ('our Divines maintain against *Hobbs*', as Tindal writes in 1730, that man is 'a social creature, who naturally loves his own species, and is full of pity, tenderness & benevolence'), the doctrine involves several strands: the definition of virtue in terms of 'universal benevolence', a formulation frequently used in sermons to describe sympathetic fellow-feeling and the philanthropic attitude it was held to promote; the anti-Hobbesian assumption that such impulses are innate, inherently the possession of a species predisposed towards mutual affection and sociable good nature; the anti-stoical assumption that the tender passions are to be cultivated rather than repressed, and generate not only virtuous conduct but also pleasurable self-approval.[19] Aspects of Crane's thesis were later refuted, specifically his presentation of this doctrine as exclusive to latitudinarianism (though its most articulate proponents, like Benjamin Whichcote, were indeed latitudinarians), and as purely celebratory in tone. Rather than articulating a theologically untenable moral optimism, many of the divines turn out on inspection to be far from immune to Hobbesian fear: when John Norris of Bemerton warns that 'the condition of Man in this World is such, as makes it as *necessary* for him to be pitiful, as to be a sociable Creature', for example, he is not celebrating the natural pre-eminence of sympathy but urging its cultivation against the brutal alternative.[20] That said, it remains clear that the discourse of Anglican benevolism is an important precursor of sentimentalism, especially in the guarded form represented by Cambridge Platonists such as Norris, whom Sterne extensively plundered in his sermons and fiction.

The greatest weakness of Crane's argument was his quiet recourse to secular sources to illustrate the characteristically sentimental slippage from sympathy to self-affirmation that he wished to attribute to the divines: for example, the philosopher David Fordyce's view of sympathetic sorrow as 'a sort of pleasing

---

19 R. S. Crane, 'Suggestions Toward a Genealogy of the "Man of Feeling"', *ELH* 1 (1934), 205–30; Crane quotes Tindal (from *Christianity as Old as the Creation*, octavo edition (London, 1731), p. 49) at p. 226.

20 *Christian Blessedness* (London, 1690), p. 140 (emphasis added), quoted by Tim Parnell, 'A Story Painted to the Heart? *Tristram Shandy* and Sentimentalism Reconsidered', *Shandean* 9 (1997), 122–35 (at p. 124).

Anguish, that sweetly melts the Mind, and terminates in a Self-approving Joy'.[21] Fordyce was writing in 1754, shortly before the culmination, in Adam Smith, of a tradition of 'moral sense' philosophy that looks back to Shaftesbury and finds its classic expression in the Scottish Enlightenment. It is this tradition that has been seen as constructing, more fully than any other, the distinctive ethics of sentimental fiction. The key texts differ subtly and sometimes profoundly, and their intricacies resist conflation; but the common thread of feeling runs through them all. In Shaftesbury's *Characteristics* (1711), a recurrent theme is the existence in human nature of a 'natural moral sense', accessible more by intuition and emotion than by pure reason, predisposed to recognise and favour virtue while shrinking from villainy, and leaning towards sociability and benevolence as a matter of impulse. From the cultivation of this state, happiness arises, for *'to have the natural affections, such as are founded in . . . a sympathy with the kind or species, is to have the chief means and power of self-enjoyment'*; and this happiness is nowhere more fully felt than in 'the exercise of benignity and goodness, where, together with the most delightful affection of the soul, there is joined a pleasing assent and approbation of the mind'.[22]

Though wilfully unsystematic in his arguments (the primacy over reason of affability and feeling being part of his point), Shaftesbury exerted huge influence, popularly through the intoxicating slogans he generated ('the beauty of virtue'; 'happiness in virtue'; 'the sentiment of morals'), and intellectually through the rigorous defence of his position undertaken by Francis Hutcheson in the 1720s. Contesting the caustic attacks of Bernard Mandeville in *The Fable of the Bees*, Hutcheson placed innate sympathy at the centre of his notion of virtue. Benevolence and compassion – public benefits rooted, for Mandeville, in the private vices of self-interest and pride – 'are *Determinations of our Nature, previous to our Choice from Interest'*.[23]

With Hume in the next generation, the elevation of sympathy and the location of morality in subjective feeling are carried further. 'Morality . . . is more properly felt than judg'd of', Hume memorably contends, while sympathy in the largest sense becomes 'the chief source of moral distinctions'.[24] It is

21 David Fordyce, *The Elements of Moral Philosophy* (London, 1754), p. 263, quoted by Crane, 'Suggestions', p. 205.

22 Earl of Shaftesbury, *Characteristics*, ed. Lawrence E. Klein (Cambridge: Cambridge University Press, 1999), pp. 180, 200, 203.

23 Francis Hutcheson, *An Essay on the Nature and Conduct of the Passions and Affections*, intro. Paul McReynolds (Gainesville, FL: Scholars' Facsimiles and Reprints, 1969), p. 92.

24 David Hume, *A Treatise of Human Nature*, ed. L. A. Selby-Bigge, rev. P. H. Nidditch (Oxford: Clarendon Press, 1978), pp. 470, 618.

as though, in the absence of transcendent objective certainties, a process of sentimental compensation is at work, instilling moral ideas not by argument or induction but 'by an immediate feeling and finer internal sense'. Accompanying this emphasis on a naturally intuitive sentiment of morality is Hume's insistence that, as well as being innate (there are 'a thousand . . . marks of a general benevolence in human nature'), sympathy is the most attractive and productive human virtue: 'No qualities are more intitled to the general good-will and approbation of mankind', he declares in *An Enquiry Concerning the Principles of Morals* (1751), 'than beneficence and humanity, friendship and gratitude, natural affection and public spirit, or whatever proceeds from a tender sympathy with others'.[25] In this later work there develops an increased emphasis on the delicacy of sympathetic feeling, as well as on its beneficial – indeed constitutive – role in human society. When Hume expatiates on the intertwined merits and pleasures of benevolence, moreover, we hear not only the valorisation of sensibility that would become standard in sentimental fiction, but something of the same rhetoric. 'The tear naturally starts in our eye on the apprehension of a warm sentiment of this nature', he writes: 'our breast heaves, our heart is agitated, and every humane tender principle of our frame is set in motion, and gives us the purest and most satisfactory enjoyment.'[26]

Conspicuously less sanguine is Adam Smith, in whose *The Theory of Moral Sentiments* (1759) the capacity to enter sympathetically into the position and feelings, and especially the sorrows, of others becomes basic to the formation of all moral attitudes. Here too the rhetoric of sentimental fiction is anticipated, and at an early stage in his argument Smith considers the moral resonances of what would become a standard scenario for the novel, in which victims of misfortune renew yet also relieve their distress by communicating with a sympathising witness:

> Their tears accordingly flow faster than before, and they are apt to abandon themselves to all the weakness of sorrow. They take pleasure, however, in all this, and, it is evident, are sensibly relieved by it; because the sweetness of his sympathy more than compensates the bitterness of that sorrow, which, in order to excite this sympathy, they had thus enlivened and renewed.

Yet there also lurks in Smith an anxiety of insufficiency, a fear that the emotional participation underlying this idealised model of sympathetic exchange might

---

25 David Hume, *Enquiries concerning Human Understanding and concerning the Principles of Morals*, ed. L. A. Selby-Bigge, rev. P. H. Nidditch (Oxford: Clarendon Press, 1975), pp. 170, 300, 178.
26 *Ibid.*, p. 257.

not be so easily natural. Here the mere sympathy of the witness is enough to relieve the confiding unfortunates, who 'seem to disburthen themselves of a part of their distress . . . as if he had derived a part of it to himself'. A later passage, however, represents sympathy as less ideally proportioned, and sets 'the languid emotions' of the witness in alarming contrast with the victim's choking passions. 'We may even inwardly reproach ourselves with our own want of sensibility', Smith writes, 'and perhaps, on that account, work ourselves up into an artificial sympathy, which . . . is always the slightest and most transitory imaginable.' For all the moral significance and practical efficacy of sympathy, it now arises not through spontaneous impulse but through dogged effort, 'and generally, as soon as we have left the room, vanishes, and is gone for ever'. Convinced of the importance of fellow-feeling yet fearful for its survival, Smith seems hortatory rather than merely descriptive in his account of sympathy, and instead of blandly celebrating its power he tends to regret its feeble and fugitive nature. It is because of our ordinarily 'dull sensibility to the distresses of others' that he devotes so much attention to the mechanisms that might render it more active, and even allots a place, in passing, to the potential of the novel to educate the affections. In view of his obviously anti-stoical bent, there may be a certain faintness in Smith's praise of Richardson, Marivaux and Riccoboni as 'much better instructors than Zeno, Chrysippus, or Epictetus'.[27] But it is worth noting that further attention to the capacity of novels to develop 'the tender emotions' is paid in his lectures on belles lettres as delivered in the 1760s, and by Smith's intellectual heirs in the Scottish universities, such as Hugh Blair, who commends La Nouvelle Héloïse 'for tenderness of sentiment'.[28]

For all the differences between the religious reading of human nature in terms of generous emotion and the more far-reaching attempts of philosophers to ground morality itself in such emotion, it would misrepresent the fluidity of theological and philosophical discourses to divide them absolutely. They intertwine from the start, when Shaftesbury draws on Benjamin Whichcote ('the Preacher of Good-Nature', he calls him)[29] for his confidence in natural sociability, sympathy and benevolence. Both traditions, moreover, inform the novel, and the eclecticism of a writer like Sterne, who could rework Smith in

27 Adam Smith, The Theory of Moral Sentiments, ed. D. D. Raphael and A. L. Macfie (Oxford: Oxford University Press, 1976), pp. 15, 47, 143.

28 Adam Smith, Lectures on Rhetoric and Belles Lettres, ed. J. C. Bryce (Oxford: Oxford University Press, 1983), p. 111; Hugh Blair, Lectures on Rhetoric and Belles Lettres, 2 vols. (Carbondale, IL: Southern Illinois University Press, 1965), vol. II, p. 309.

29 In Shaftesbury's preface to Whichcote, Select Sermons (London, 1698), A8.

one passage and Norris in the next, should remind us that sentimental fiction absorbs a cluster of overlapping discourses and traditions, and is never wholly supervised by one. Further contributions to the brew come in the shape of medical writing, with its attempt to provide a strictly physiological account of human sensibility, and in literary traditions, notably the well-established strain of sentimental drama that reaches back to the beginning of the century. Typified in tragedy by Rowe (whose *Jane Shore* is linked with *Werther*, in Hannah More's *Sensibility*, as a similarly beguiling distraction from real suffering) and in comedy by Cibber and Steele, it includes among its more recent products the only play to be exempted from Richardson's diatribe against the London theatre of the 1730s, George Lillo's *The London Merchant*.[30]

Where moral-sense philosophy stands out is in the directness with which its vocabulary and propositions entered the novel. Unsurprisingly, Scots were in the forefront of the trend, whether in the sceptical vein of Tobias Smollett, or in the more accommodating manner of Henry Mackenzie (in youth an acolyte of Hume and Smith). Smollett typically disparages 'the moral sense so warmly contended for by . . . ideal philosophers', and populates his novels with villains in whom tokens of sympathy coexist pointedly with actual malevolence, as in the startling case of Peregrine Pickle, who attempts a rape with 'tears gushing from his eyes'.[31] The sympathetic encounters of Mackenzie's men of feeling involve a friendlier exploration of the same ethics, and the associated jargon is liberally used by English precursors of Mackenzie such as Frances Brooke, whose characters rhapsodise on 'that moral sense which heaven has imprinted on our souls', 'the sweet intercourse of warm beneficence' and the like.[32] The most intelligent exponents of the sentimental mode, however, are rather more measured. A pointed example comes in *The Cry* (1754), an experimental dialogue-novel by Sarah Fielding and the satirist Jane Collier, in which Cylinda is lured into the moral dangers of indiscipline and self-satisfaction by her uncritical enthusiasm for Shaftesbury. Parroting 'a great many of my author's favourite expressions, such as SOCIAL AFFECTIONS, PHILANTHROPY', she lapses into worship of her own understanding and merit:

30 Samuel Richardson, *The Apprentice's Vade Mecum* (London, 1734), 16.
31 Tobias Smollett, *Ferdinand Count Fathom*, ed. Damian Grant (Oxford: Oxford University Press, 1978), p. 263; Tobias Smollett, *Peregrine Pickle*, ed. James L. Clifford, rev. Paul-Gabriel Boucé (Oxford: Oxford University Press, 1983), p. 407.
32 Frances Brooke, *The History of Emily Montague*, ed. Mary Jane Edwards (Ottawa: Carleton University Press, 1985), p. 354; Frances Brooke, *Lady Julia Mandeville*, 2 vols. (London, 1763), vol. I, p. 133.

An altar was due to the former for its judicious distinctions of right from wrong, with its direction of my affections; and to the latter in that I was possessed of such natural good affections to need no directions. Voluntary UNCOMMANDED VIRTUES ... were the only ones I could bear to be possessed of, as they alone seemed to be the produce of my own determinations.

In *The Cry* as a whole, Cylinda's recantation of these excesses leaves pride of place to the more guarded sentimental ethics of Portia, whose recognition 'that the seeds of good-nature, benevolence, and every amiable quality are in almost every human breast' is tempered by her recognition that these virtues are 'choked and smothered by the rank weeds, which men ... take pains to cultivate'.[33]

Samuel Richardson

Samuel Richardson was even more wary than this, and his instinctive hostility to the ethics of moral sense is a good measure of the gulf that separates his writing from the tradition that sprang up around it. Hume he considered (insofar as he considered him at all) a 'very mischievous writer'.[34] In the 1751 edition of *Clarissa*, a disparaging reference to 'sentimental Unbelievers' points clearly at Shaftesburian deism, and one early critic saw the religious grounding of morality in *Sir Charles Grandison* (1753–4) as a pointed riposte to Shaftesbury's 'Notion of the *Beauty of Virtue* ... being a sufficient *Rule* and *Motive*'.[35] If Richardson thought of his own work as sentimental in any way, he did so in a sense radically unlike that of the imitators in whose usage (as Sir John Hawkins wrote) 'the words *sentiment* and *sentimentality* became ... the cant of his school'.[36] The earliest recorded occurrence of the word 'sentimental' comes in a letter of 1749, in which Richardson's friend and reader Lady Bradshaigh playfully asks him the meaning of a term 'so much in vogue amongst the polite'. It seems to comprehend 'every thing clever and agreeable', she adds, but previous answers had informed her only that 'it is – it is – *sentimental*'.[37] Richardson's immediate response does not survive, but he made

33 Sarah Fieldings and Jane Collier, *The Cry*, 3 vols. (London, 1754), vol. II, pp. 286, 280, 217.
34 *The Correspondence of Samuel Richardson*, ed. Anna Laetitia Barbauld, 6 vols. (London, 1804), vol. 5, p. 109.
35 Samuel Richardson, *Clarissa*, intro. Florian Stuber, 8 vols. (New York: AMS Press, 1990), vol. VIII, p. 292; Francis Plummer, *A Candid Examination of ... Sir Charles Grandison* (London, 1755), p. 9.
36 Sir John Hawkins, *The Life of Samuel Johnson*, 2nd edn (London, 1787), p. 384.
37 *Correspondence of Richardson*, vol. IV, pp. 282–3. A Sterne letter of 1739–40, mentioning 'sentimental repasts', is almost certainly a fake.

it public by inserting in his index to *Grandison*, under the heading 'Sentimental, what', a reference to a passage in which Charlotte, having delivered a series of moral maxims, rebukes herself as 'too *sentimental*'. Readers cannot bear sentiments, she adds: 'Story, story, story, is what they hunt after.'[38] The passage looks forward to Johnson's remark that one must 'read [Richardson] for the sentiment, and consider the story as only giving occasion to the sentiment',[39] and this remark in turn was delivered in light of the *Collection of the Moral and Instructive Sentiments* (1755) which Richardson compiled as a digest of his novels' wisdom. Fairly consistently, in Richardsonian usage, a sentiment is a statement of opinion or truth, which, though coloured at times by feeling, stems primarily from reason or faith. To be sentimental is to be sententious, and when compiling the table of maxims appended to *Grandison* he was, he writes, 'involved in sentimentizing'.[40] This was the primary sense of 'sentimental' and its cognates before about 1760, and Sterne may well have been instrumental in the later semantic shift. When protesting in 1762 that a Diderot play 'has too much sentiment in it . . . the speeches too long, and savour too much of *preaching*', he uses the older, Richardsonian meaning, and it has been suggested that the new signification popularised by *A Sentimental Journey* is, in effect, a sense-loan imported by Sterne from France in his last years.[41]

The difference of usage points to a fundamental mismatch between Richardson's own priorities and the trends his fiction impelled. For all their innovative qualities, his novels draw on commitments which (as he never tired of pointing out) were long outmoded by the time of writing, and if any one tradition can be said to permeate a fiction characterised above all by competing perspectives, it lies not with the fashionable theology of Crane's latitudinarians but with the austere practical divinity of an earlier generation, the generation of Joseph Hall and Jeremy Taylor. *Pamela* and *Clarissa* are shot through with notions of natural depravity and original sin, as displayed not only in the outward perils of each heroine but also in her inward recesses. As such, these novels could hardly be more inimical to the idea of locating virtue in unregulated effusions from the heart. Conscience, not feeling, is what matters, and in a fictional world where moral meanings remain vexed and obscure, and

38 Samuel Richardson, *Sir Charles Grandison*, ed. Jocelyn Harris, 3 vols. (Oxford: Oxford University Press, 1972), vol. III, p. 228).
39 James Boswell, *Life of Johnson*, ed. R. W. Chapman, rev. J. D. Fleeman, intro. Pat Rogers (Oxford: Oxford University Press, 1980), p. 480.
40 *Correspondence of Richardson*, vol. II, p. 286.
41 *Letters of Laurence Sterne*, ed. Lewis Perry Curtis (Oxford: Clarendon Press, 1935), p. 162; Erik Erämetsä, *A Study of the Word 'Sentimental' and of Other Linguistic Characteristics of Eighteenth-Century Sentimentalism* (Helsinki: Liikekirjapaino Oy, 1951), p. 54.

human perceptions flawed, nothing less than the dutiful piety of Pamela or the rigorous casuistry of Clarissa is an adequate guide. Feeling might have a role, as Richardson's writing increasingly recognises, but it must be disciplined by the spiritual and practical commitments of Christian virtue, and is admirable only insofar as it moves beyond the self. 'Greatness of mind', as he warned one sentimental reader, 'excludes not feeling . . . if the feeling be carried to the utmost of our power into deeds; into good deeds.'[42]

Yet for all Richardson's resistance to sentimental ethics, and for all the gulf between the testing complexities of his fiction and the cardboard characters and moral simplicities of its imitators, he also played a key role in developing the emphases on tearfulness, sympathy and benevolence that were to prevail after his death. The process is most marked in *Grandison*, but even *Pamela* anticipates sentimentalism in important ways. While drafting the novel in 1739, Richardson was already thinking of fiction in terms of the characteristically sentimental goal of promoting 'universal benevolence', a phrase he uses on the title page of *Aesop's Fables* and again in the preface he probably contributed to an edition of Penelope Aubin's novels. *Pamela* would do the same, above all through the sympathetic involvement with distress that was fostered among readers by letter-narration. The work would 'engage the Passions of every sensible Reader' and 'excite Compassion', thereby stimulating a capacity to feel for the misfortunes of others, which, though not in itself equivalent to virtue, might nevertheless become an agent of moral improvement. The process is dramatised when Mr B reads Pamela's letters. She warns that if he can read them 'with Tranquillity, and not be mov'd, it is a Sign of a very cruel and determin'd Heart', but in the event they serve, of course, to reform him. They do so as much through their piety as through their emotive power, but in the process of sentimental exaggeration that typifies the early reception of Richardson's fiction, feeling is what was stressed. In his contribution to the second edition, Aaron Hill holds up the example of a boy whose eyes 'were quite lost, in his *Tears*: which running down from his Cheeks in free Currents, had form'd two sincere little Fountains'.[43]

The same process is writ large in *Clarissa*, where the incidentally sentimental potential of the text came to dominate its reception. Though not in itself a sentimental novel, there is a sense in which *Clarissa* contains one. In its final phase, a prototypically sentimental narrator comes to the fore in the shape of Belford, the reforming libertine, and it is through his perspective that

42 *Correspondence of Richardson*, vol. II, p. 252.
43 Samuel Richardson, *Pamela*, ed. Thomas Keymer and Alice Wakely (Oxford: Oxford University Press, 2001), pp. 3, 239, 515.

Clarissa's lingering death is conveyed. Ludicrously incapable of her religious frame of reference (though he proposes 'one time or other . . . to give the whole Bible a perusal'), Belford experiences morality through the powerful but precarious agency of feeling alone. He offers, accordingly, the classic rationale of sentimental narration: 'it is my design', he tells Lovelace, 'to make thee *feel*'.[44] Richardson's own design went rather further, and he writes, by contrast, of enlisting sensibility not as an end in itself, but with a markedly different ulterior aim: 'my Story is designed to strengthen the tender Mind', he told Lady Bradshaigh, and to prepare readers 'by remote Instances, to support ourselves under real Affliction'.[45] It was Belford, however, who prevailed. Though Richardson clearly intended *Clarissa* to work more like *Holy Dying* than *The Man of Feeling*, the response of its readers was incorrigibly sentimental, and there is little evidence that they were able to progress from debilitating grief to the spiritual therapy he envisaged. Lady Bradshaigh 'shed a pint of tears' and was unable to sleep; the Highmore household was scattered in mourning, 'and in separate Apartments wept'; Sarah Fielding wrote that 'my only vent is tears; and unless tears could mark my thoughts as legibly as ink, I cannot speak half I feel'.[46] Variously disabled by their grief, Clarissa's weeping readers could at least find in it a proof of their own benevolence; and it is at this point in the history of the novel, very precisely, that it becomes commonplace to locate virtue in tears bestowed on purely fictional distress. Sarah Fielding feared for the moral condition of anyone who could read 'without being overwhelmed in Tears'; for Thomas Edwards, the closing volumes were 'a Touchstone, by which I shall judge who of my acquaintance have hearts'.[47]

Many instances survive from this extraordinary episode of *Clarissa*'s resistance to sentimental appropriation. When Colley Cibber refused to read the ending, declaring 'that he should no longer believe . . . Goodness governed the world, if merit, innocence, and beauty were to be so destroyed',[48] he could hardly have defined more perfectly *Clarissa*'s refusal to adopt the sentimental model of his own plays, in which good nature and feeling are panaceas. The same response gains fuller expression in an alternative ending written by Lady Bradshaigh's sister, Lady Echlin, who found the original 'so horribly shocking

---

44 Richardson, *Clarissa*, vol. VI, p. 393; vol. VIII, p. 33.
45 *Selected Letters of Samuel Richardson*, ed. John Carroll (Oxford: Oxford University Press, 1964), pp. 116, 111.
46 *Correspondence of Richardson*, vol. IV, p. 240; Victoria and Albert Museum, Forster MSS, XV, 2, fo. 12; *Correspondence of Richardson*, vol. II, pp. 60–1.
47 Sarah Fielding, *Remarks on Clarissa* (London, 1749), p. 42; Thomas Edwards, Bodleian Library, MS 1011, p. 95.
48 *Correspondence of Richardson*, vol. II, p. 128.

to humanity' that she felt compelled to reaffirm her faith in innate virtue by having Lovelace reform.[49] Yet for all the wrong-headedness of such readers, their influence over Richardson was now increasing. The subject of his last novel was urged on him by Lady Bradshaigh and others, and it was only after long persuasion that he undertook it. Conceived and composed within a circle of readers that had been brought together by their shared tears for Clarissa, *Grandison* reflects the tastes and priorities of this circle as much as it does Richardson's own. With its emphases on benign sentimental fellowship, and on social harmony grounded in shared feeling, it exactly reflects the community in which it was written. More disturbing aspects of the novel – notably the self-destructive sensibility of Clementina – imply at least some lingering reservations on Richardson's part about the primacy of feeling, and older notions of piety and duty remain strongly marked. Within its thematic limits, *Grandison* remains a truly Richardsonian novel of moral perplexity, conflict and debate. The sentimental consensus now dominates, however. 'A feeling heart . . . is a moral security of innocence', as the heroine of the novel, Harriet Byron, puts it: 'since the heart that is able to partake of the distress of another, cannot wilfully give it.' Compassion and benevolence are the resulting virtues, enshrined above all in the 'general *Philanthropist*' Sir Charles, 'whose whole delight is in doing good' and 'cultivating his innate good principles'. Social harmony results to a degree unthinkable in *Clarissa*, for 'there is a kind of magnetism in goodness . . . while trust, confidence, love, sympathy, and a reciprocation of beneficent actions, twist a cord which ties good men to good men'.[50]

Fictions of benevolence

Some of the most important sentimental novels after *Grandison* were written by members of Richardson's circle (notably Frances Sheridan's *Sidney Bidulph* (1761), which was dedicated to him), while Sophia Briscoe's *Miss Melmoth: or, The New Clarissa* (1771) typifies the way in which later novelists queued up to associate their writing with his. Yet most of this imitation went on in blind indifference to Richardson's complexity, to the point where one critic, contesting his reputation as 'what is vulgarly called a *sentimentalist*', could write that 'the inundation of froth and sentiment' now filling the libraries 'has

49 Lady Echlin, *An Alternative Ending to Richardson's Clarissa*, ed. Dimiter Daphinoff (Bern: Francke Verlag, 1982), p. 173.
50 Richardson, *Grandison*, vol. II, pp. 258, 61, 45.

taken place in direct contempt and defiance of the precept and example of Richardson'.[51] Drawing on *Clarissa* for their formulaic plots of beleaguered virtue and predatory vice, and on *Grandison* for their exaggerated models of masculine perfection and hysterical femininity, novels like these rapidly reduced their prototypes to moral melodrama, overwrought emotionalism and sensationalist excess. Here the traditional distinction of literary history between a rigorous and demanding 'novel of sentiment' in the mid century, and an increasingly conventionalised 'novel of sensibility' in which weeping, trembling and self-regarding delicacy of feeling gain precedence from about 1770, remains of use. Even in the 1760s the collapse into melodramatic extravagance and affective overkill was well advanced. By the end of the decade, it was no longer enough for fictional tears to trickle, flow or be shed, and the rhetoric of lachrymosity entered an inflationary spiral which finds its climax in the febrile pages of Henry Brooke's *The Fool of Quality* (1766–70). In this protracted exercise in sentimental hyperbole, 'the Tears of sympathising Humanity' pour forth in plenteous showers and violent torrents, passionate gushes and secret deluges, and the flood reaches its height when one character smugly reports how 'all the Sluices of my Soul . . . were laid open'. Brooke sometimes extends the variety by throwing in a mawkish single tear – 'a Tear of still Compassion' – but normally it is fluency of throughput that counts.[52] It is hard to think of another novel in which bodily fluids spurt so copiously, with the possible exception of *Memoirs of a Woman of Pleasure*. The comparison is not quite unjust. In contrast to the scenes of sympathetic exchange imagined by Adam Smith (which work, however feebly, to the sufferer's advantage), it is as though the objects of sympathy encountered by Brooke's quivering hero are there simply to serve him like Cleland's Fanny Hill, giving sentimental relief.

The accusation that sentimentalism is nothing more than sensual self-gratification was most famously levelled by Leslie Stephen, who defined it as 'the mood in which we make a luxury of grief'.[53] Implicit here is a denial of all the moral claims associated with the mode, and the allegation that, far from impelling its readers into outward action, sentimental fiction appropriates and trivialises suffering as merely a source of inward pleasure. What is striking about the novels themselves is the directness with which so many embrace

---

51 *Port Folio* (Philadelphia, 1802), vol. II, p. 185, quoted by Brissenden, *Virtue in Distress*, p. 104.
52 Henry Brooke, *The Fool of Quality*, 5 vols. (London, 1766–70), vol. v, p. 8; vol. III, p. 70; vol. II, p. 15.
53 Leslie Stephen, *History of English Thought in the Eighteenth Century*, 2nd edn, 2 vols. (London: Smith, Elder & Co., 1881), vol. II, p. 436.

this charge. The surviving characters in Frances Brooke's *Lady Julia Mandeville* end up resolved 'to indulge in all the voluptuousness of sorrow', and the anonymous *The Assignation: A Sentimental Novel* (1774) has barely begun when the hero vows to 'indulge this luxury of grief'. In Mackenzie's *Man of the World* (1773) the villain is contrasted with 'a more exquisite voluptuary', an idealised figure of benevolence who 'weeps with [the heroine]; – and the luxury of his tears! – baffles description', while in *Julia de Roubigné* (1777) the heroine dwells on 'the anguish of our sufferings, till there was a sort of luxury in feeling them'. Nor does the luxury end here. The characters' wallowing responses to the misfortunes they encounter are held up for emulation, thereby enabling the weeping reader to feel gratifyingly joined in a larger community of shared refinements. Central to this gratification is the thrill of self-approval, for to shed tears of sympathetic sorrow is to feel conscious – to feel, indeed, a briny proof – of one's own compassionate virtue. Henry Brooke makes all this a system: 'There is . . . a Species of Pleasure in Grief, a Kind of soothing and deep Delight that arises with the Tears which are pushed from the Fountain of Good in the Soul, from the Charities and Sensibilities of the human Heart divine.'[54]

Yet what if such fiction, while working on the eyes like an onion, fail to move the will? Brooke's language typifies the pervading problem of sentimental fiction, not so much in its flatulent rhetoric of human benevolence (a rhetoric Blake would shortly puncture) as in its evasiveness about practical action. The eager celebration of charity and sensibility goes hand in hand with a marked reticence about what real effect these sources of good will achieve, as though the bittersweet tears of sentimental fiction might not so much activate the sympathies as merely assuage or sate them. Nor is the problem here only that, by focussing compassion on fictional distress, sentimental narration can easily become a displacement activity, misdirecting or dissipating feelings that less frivolous texts might channel into action. By concentrating its resources on the tribulations of the elite, the sentimental novel leaves doubly obscured the condition and needs of the period's real victims: the casualties of social processes such as enclosure, industrialisation and the slave-trade, who might otherwise have seemed good candidates for sentimental evocation, but on whose exploitation the comforts of the novel-reading classes too closely depended. Coleridge memorably evokes the bad faith involved when

54 Frances Brooke, *Lady Julia Mandeville*, vol. II, p. 202; anon., *The Assignation: A Sentimental Novel*, 2 vols. (London, 1774), vol. I, p. 3; Henry Mackenzie, *The Man of the World*, 2 vols. (London, 1773), vol. I, p. 190; Henry Mackenzie, *Julia de Roubigné*, ed. Susan Manning (East Linton: Tuckwell, 1999), p. 81; Henry Brooke, *The Fool of Quality*, vol. III, p. 72.

denouncing an imaginary consumer of saccharine sentimentalism and sugared tea: 'She sips a beverage sweetened with human blood, even while she is weeping over the refined sorrows of Werter or of Clementina. Sensibility is not Benevolence.'[55]

Some novels were engagingly open about their priorities. Published with a socially prestigious subscriber-list, and probably written by the future Duchess of Devonshire, Georgiana Spencer, *Emma: or, The Unfortunate Attachment. A Sentimental Novel* (1773) is a conventional tale of decorous virtue in distress. Its most interesting moment comes when the heroine touches on the vexed relationship between inward feeling and outward virtue, and on the underlying principle that the capacity to sympathise tearfully with others is the source of moral awareness and benevolent action. Describing her treasured ability to 'feel . . . for the distressed', Emma wonders what her sentimental vocation might in practice involve. 'The demands on our purses are very trifling', she briskly concludes:

> the common objects of charity are relieved at a very small expence; the *scraps* and leavings of the most oeconomical table suffice to feed numbers of those. – To the *unfortunates* of an higher class a tear dropt in sympathy is a more acceptable donation than an handful of gold; and it is for these I have always suffered most.[56]

Which part of Emma's comfortable effusion, one might wonder, struck its readers as most congenial? The idea that the proper response to distress need not entail addressing the underlying structures that made it endemic, nor even require institutionalised philanthropy of a costly kind, but might creditably be dispensed at random, and in small change? Or was it the idea that the proper medium of sympathetic exchange was not the coin at all but the tear, whose liquid currency might best be spent on sufferers whose social standing could leave the whole delicious transaction uncontaminated by cash?

To ask these questions is not to make the supercilious assumption that eighteenth-century writers and readers are to be arraigned for failing to entertain or act on ideologies of social justice that were not yet in being. The campaign against slavery was only one of several philanthropic movements of the period, and the foundation and ongoing endowment of institutions such as the Foundling Hospital and the Magdalen House depended not just

---

55 Samuel Taylor Coleridge, *The Watchman*, ed. Lewis Patton (London: Routledge, 1970), p. 139 (no. 4, 25 March 1796).
56 Georgiana Spencer (?), *Emma; or, The Unfortunate Attachment*, 3 vols. (London, 1773), vol. i, pp. 106–7.

on the munificence of wealthy individuals but on a broad base of middle-class subscription. 'Charity is in fact the very Characteristic of this Nation at this Time', as Fielding wrote,[57] and plentiful outlets existed for the humanitarian exertions of anyone who cared to make them. When one considers the best-known philanthropists of the age, however, religious duty and Mandevillean self-assertion are the motives that spring to mind, and a direct relationship between sentimental writing and humanitarian action should not be assumed. It was with a view to harnessing the impulses of novel readers that one of the period's most energetic reformers, Jonas Hanway, entitled one of his polemics *A Sentimental History of Chimney Sweepers* (1785). Yet for all Hanway's efforts to target readers who prided themselves 'on *sympathy* in the sufferings of others', and to convince them that his subject does 'indeed constitute a Sentimental History, equal to any of the miseries which human nature seems capable of supporting', he rapidly discovers that practical humanitarian commitment requires a different mode of writing.[58] With its rigorous statistical analyses and grotesque corporeal specifications – the miseries Hanway details extend from inflamed sores and twisted limbs to cancerous diseases of the scrotum and inflamed urinary tracts – *A Sentimental History of Chimney Sweepers* is a world away from the picturesque distresses of Georgiana Spencer's *Emma*. If novels like hers were indeed a stimulus to practical virtue, rather than a mechanism for restricting sympathy to imagination alone, the process remains very unclear.

A minority of novels did adopt a socially reformatory posture, and urged a direct path from novel reading to moral action. Probably the best examples are a cluster of works written in support of the Magdalen House, an institution established in 1758 (with the prominent involvement of both Hanway and Richardson) to rehabilitate repentant prostitutes. In *Memoirs of a Magdalen* (1766), Hugh Kelly adapts the *Clarissa* plot – his ruined heroine is even reading *Clarissa* as the rake breaks in to abduct her – in order to promote 'that admirable institution called the Magdalen'.[59] Some years earlier, Richardson subsidised and printed *The Histories of Some of the Penitents in the Magdalen-House* (1759), an anonymous novel which some readers attributed to Sarah Fielding, though a more likely candidate is Sarah Scott's companion Lady Barbara Montagu. At a time when the Magdalen House remained a target of strait-laced censure, the author hopes to melt 'the contemptuous frown' of hostile readers 'into

---

57 Henry Fielding, *The Covent-Garden Journal*, ed. Bertrand A. Goldgar (Oxford: Clarendon Press, 1988), p. 247 (no. 44, 2 June 1752).
58 Jonas Hanway, *A Sentimental History of Chimney Sweepers* (London, 1785), pp. ii, xxix.
59 Hugh Kelly, *Memoirs of a Magdalen*, 2 vols. (London, 1766), vol. I, p. 172.

tears of pity', and even to make them donate (as several demonstrably did).[60] A further attempt to enlist fiction as a fundraising tool was made in the 1770s when – drawing on the techniques that enabled him, in his modishly philanthropic sermons, to move whole congregations to tears – the sentimentalist and swindler William Dodd appended short narratives in the same vein to his *Account of the Rise, Progress, and Present State of the Magdalen Hospital.*[61]

In their overt solicitude for particular categories of social outcast, their skilfully orchestrated calls to sympathy and the precise models they offer for ameliorative action, novels of this kind might seem to support Thomas Laqueur's view of sentimental narrative as a genuinely productive agent of social reform.[62] For all its good intentions, however, even *The Histories of Some of the Penitents in the Magdalen-House* remains open to question. By idealising its main heroine as a paragon of piety and decorum, it severely circumscribes the proper scope of sympathetic effort, and casts out the fallen mass who fail to fit. By dramatising the institution's capacity to restore its inmates 'to industry and order, [and] render them useful members of society',[63] moreover, it entwines sympathy with the rather more regulatory motive of rendering its objects of compassion tractable and productive. Above all, by focussing on individual circumstances and accidents, it forfeits the explanatory power so forcefully achieved, in contrast, by Jonas Hanway. In weeping at the plight of a fictional fallen woman, it highlights a symptom or consequence of social, economic and gender inequality, but effaces the underlying causes. Arguably, it even reinforces these causes by offering polite society the opportunity to congratulate itself on its compassionate posture towards evils of its own creation.

Beneath the ameliorative gestures of sentimentalism, recent criticism has sought to expose a fundamental social conservatism in the mode, or even an inbuilt complicity with exploitation. George Starr reads sentimental fiction as a more or less frivolous mode of pastoral for leisured readers, representing distress in such stylised and universalised forms as to be 'a cathartic reinforcement of the existing scheme of things rather than a challenge to it'. For John Richetti, 'by cultivating private sympathy and self-indulgent emotional responses to misery and injustice', it sets 'a controlling evasion or consoling

---

60 Anon., *The Histories of Some of the Penitents in the Magdalen-House*, 2 vols. (London, 1759), vol. i, p. v.

61 See Markman Ellis, *The Politics of Sensibility: Race, Gender and Commerce in the Sentimental Novel* (Cambridge: Cambridge University Press, 1996), pp. 177–8.

62 Thomas Laqueur, 'Bodies, Details, and the Humanitarian Narrative', in Lynn Hunt (ed.), *The New Cultural History* (Berkeley and Los Angeles: University of California Press, 1989), pp. 176–204.

63 *Histories of . . . Penitents*, vol. i, p. xix.

moral gesture . . . in place of analytical understanding or systemic criticism'.[64] Even the best sentimental novels look vulnerable to these lines of attack. In its scenes of affliction and histories of dispossession, Sarah Fielding's *David Simple* (1744–53) grimly satirizes the depredations of a distinctively modern world. Its compensatory models of virtue and community, however, suggest the paradox simultaneously articulated by the man of the hill in her brother's *Tom Jones* (1749), for whom 'great Philanthropy chiefly inclines us to avoid and detest Mankind'. Benevolence turns out to be scarce, indeed all but extinct, in the novel's world, and the idealised 'Man of Goodness and Virtue' for whom the hero searches proves an unattainable grail. Recoiling from a society so permeated by vice as to seem irredeemable, the novel represents sensibility as able to thrive only in utopian retreat, a 'little Society' which, in its sheer embattled remoteness, affirms nothing so much as the impossibility of larger change.[65]

Other novelists found it easier to propose models of transformative virtue, though all are transparently flawed. In *Lady Julia Mandeville*, Frances Brooke inserts an eloquent denunciation of enclosure and engrossment in her portrait of Lord T—, who has incurred 'the curse of thousands, and made his estate a scene of desolation'. Yet she sees no contradiction in placing her trust, even so, in a tradition of rural paternalism that was manifestly breaking down. Her exemplar is Lord Belmont, whose generosity works not 'by relieving so much as by preventing want', and drives him to 'go beyond the limits of his own estate to find objects of real distress'.[66] Even more implausible than this Tory solution is the Whiggish alternative floated in *The Fool of Quality*. Here virtuous sensibility is located with the new entrepreneurial energies of industry and commerce (forces which may have seemed less purely benign to their many victims, among whom one might relevantly number the eight miners killed in Lady Bradshaigh's Wigan coalfield a few years before she wept for Clarissa). In Henry Brooke's vision, it is the man of trade who 'knits into one Family and weaves into one Web the Affinity and Brotherhood of all Mankind', while the fabulous profits of emergent capitalism – 'Half a Million in the *Dutch* Funds'; 'near a Million of Money' – underwrite his hero's largesse.[67]

64 George Starr, 'Sentimental Novels of the Later Eighteenth Century', in John Richetti (ed.), *The Columbia History of the British Novel* (New York: Columbia University Press, 1994), pp. 181–98 (at p. 194); John Richetti, *The English Novel in History, 1700–1780* (London: Routledge, 1999), p. 244.

65 Henry Fielding, *Tom Jones*, ed. Martin C. Battestin and Fredson Bowers, 2 vols. (Oxford: Oxford University Press, 1975), p. 450; Sarah Fielding, *David Simple*, ed. Peter Sabor (Lexington, KY: University Press of Kentucky, 1998), pp. 76, 237.

66 Frances Brooke, *Lady Julia Mandeville*, vol. I, pp. 222, 58–9.

67 Henry Brooke, *The Fool of Quality*, vol. I, p. 99; vol. III, pp. 55, 87.

Although *David Simple, Lady Julia Mandeville* and *The Fool of Quality* may all be read as responding to, and even partly representing, the social dislocations involved in commercial modernity, all are finally evasive of the problems they depict, if not indeed collusive with their real agents. All promise remedies for the evils they bemoan, whether by retreating into nostalgic visions of harmonious fellowship or patrician care, or by constructing fantasies in which redemption springs miraculously from the new order. Such resolutions, however, are never more than flimsy; and this failure to progress beyond tears is characteristic of the mode. The sentimental representation of slavery is the most revealing case, not least because of the point of contrast offered by the uncompromising activism of Evangelical and other reformers who approached the issue from principle, not feeling. In Sarah Scott's *Sir George Ellison* (1766), the hero rebukes his wife (through whom he owns a sugar plantation) for weeping over a lapdog while 'hardened against the sufferings even of her fellow creatures'. His humanity is shared by Mackenzie's Savillon, in *Julia de Roubigné*, for whom 'the many thousands of my fellow-creatures groaning under servitude and misery' are a spur to sympathetic action. In both cases, however, sentimental and economic imperatives prove impossible to disentangle. By compassionately 'mitigating the sufferings' of the slaves on whom his affluence defends – Ellison abolishes the whip, improves diet and lodging and establishes a school to 'rectify their dispositions' – he not only reinforces their captivity through a process of sentimental abjection (Mrs Ellison would have wept too, he tells her, had she watched 'when they threw themselves at my feet, embraced my knees, and lift[ed] up their streaming eyes to heaven'), he also boosts productivity and profits to the point where 'he might have diminished their number; if compassion had not prevented him'.

Mackenzie is warier than Scott, but celebrates a similar process. Benignly convinced that even savages 'had principles of gratitude, which a good master might improve to his advantage', Savillon offers a notional liberty to his slaves, who may choose whether or not to work, though with the reminder that 'they must work, else we shall have no sugars to buy them meat and clothing'. Their leader responds in the statutory way – 'Yambu stood silent, and I saw a tear on his cheek' – and the sentimental experiment rapidly doubles production.[68] 'Although the particular arguments examined by these novels may appear naïve, under-developed or reactionary', writes Markman Ellis,

---

68 Sarah Scott, *The History of Sir George Ellison*, ed. Betty Rizzo (Lexington, KY: University Press of Kentucky, 1996), pp.13–17; Mackenzie *Julia de Roubigné*, pp. 97–101.

'at the time of their articulation they were not only innovative and forceful, but also brave and even radical.'[69] Unlike the fundamental critiques of slavery that were increasingly heard in the 1770s, however, the gradualist remedies of sentimental fiction not only leave in place the underlying injustice, but also find ways of rendering it more stable, efficient and rewarding. Even the cautious dramatisations of Behn's *Oroonoko* that were undertaken by John Hawkesworth and Francis Gentleman in 1759–60 look more trenchant. While reimagining and reinforcing the residually exploitative relationship between planter and slave, the novels suffuse it with a rosy glow of mutual affection that is sentimental in the nastiest sense: escapist and self-deluding.

Laurence Sterne

Sterne's sentimental turn has often been seen as opportunist, and it is clear that the origins of *Tristram Shandy* (1759–67) lie as much with Scriblerian or Rabelaisian satire as with recent trends in the novel. As a partly improvised exercise in serialisation, however, *Tristram Shandy* was always potentially responsive to market conditions, which, with characteristic self-consciousness, it inscribes within itself. In volumes VII and VIII (1765), Tristram confesses that he has 'ten cart-loads' of his previous instalment still unsold, and is at his wit's end how to revive sales (8.6.663). Sales had indeed passed their peak, and at the same time readers were urging Sterne to shift, in terms of both rhetoric and theme, into the new sentimental idiom. The somewhat anomalous Le Fever episode of volume VI had been praised for its pathos in the *Monthly Review*, and in 1765 the founder-editor of the journal, Ralph Griffiths, reiterated this praise while urging Sterne to suspend *Tristram Shandy* for a different project, in which he would 'awake our affections, engage our hearts'.[70] The following year a former slave, Ignatius Sancho, had specific ideas about the purposes to be served by a sentimental turn of this kind. Praising the general principles of philanthropy embodied in Uncle Toby, and a specific reference to slavery in one of Sterne's published sermons, Sancho adds that of all his favourite writers 'not one . . . has had a tear to spar[e] for the distresses of my poor moorish brethren, Yourself, and the truely humane author of Sr George Ellison excepted'. By resuming the topic, Sterne 'would ease the Yoke of many' and assist the cause of reform: 'think in me, you behold the uplifted hands of Millions of my moorish brethren – Grief (you pathetically observe) is eloquent – figure to

69 Ellis, *Politics of Sensibility*, p. 87.
70 Alan B. Howes (ed.), *Sterne: The Critical Heritage* (London: Routledge, 1974), p. 168.

yourselves their attitudes – hear their supplicatory address – humanity must comply[.]'[71]

There are good grounds for seeing Sterne's suspension of *Tristram Shandy* in 1767, and the transfer of his energies to a fashionably sentimental new work, as a response to the recommendations typified by Griffiths and Sancho, and indeed to their specific comments. His response was no more straightforward, however, than the glimpses of philanthropic sentimentalism that Griffiths and Sancho had already found in *Tristram Shandy*. The Le Fever episode, though in itself a tour de force of emotionally disrupted syntax and ennobling fellow-feeling, begins to bore Tristram after several chapters, and peters out in perfunctory summary. Far from being carried beyond himself in sympathetic response, Tristram longs to resume his own story. And though Uncle Toby is still widely seen as exemplifying the ethics of feeling, his vaunted good nature is oddly selective, at best. Tristram draws a 'lesson of universal good-will' – a lesson to which he owes 'one half of my philanthropy' – from the famous scene in which Toby releases a house-fly (2.12.131); yet in caring for insects while plea-surably re-enacting one bloody war and deploring the end of another, Toby may equally be read as embodying a satire on false sensibility. The sermons offer greater mileage to readers anxious to place Sterne, without complication, in the tradition of sentimental divinity, and the third ('Philanthropy recom-mended') is a case in point. Its sentimental reading of the Samaritan's motives celebrates an innate 'generosity and tenderness of nature which disposes us for compassion, abstracted from all considerations of self', and in which, 'without any observable act of the will, we suffer with the unfortunate'.[72] The reference to enslavement in another sermon, however, does little to develop this ethical position into a case for reformative action, and in context looks more like a piece of anti-Catholic polemic than a serious allusion to modern Caribbean slavery. Perhaps Sancho saw as much, and a measure of rebuke was implied by the wording of his approach to Sterne as an 'Epicurean in Charity' who, having made this glancing allusion, should now 'give half an hours attention to slavery (as it is this day undergone in the West Indies)'.[73]

There can be no question that in his last years Sterne enthusiastically refash-ioned himself as a sentimentalist, nor that the self-fashioning was widely taken at face value. 'The world has imagined, because I wrote Tristram Shandy, that I

---

71 Lawrence Sterne, *Letters*, ed. Lewis Perry Curtis (Oxford: Clarendon Press, 1935), pp. 282–3.
72 Lawrence Sterne, *Sermons*, ed. Melvyn New, 2 vols. (Gainesville, FL: University Press of Florida, 1996), vol. 1, p. 23.
73 *Letters of Sterne*, pp. 282–3.

was myself more Shandean than I really ever was', he told one reader in 1767: he had 'long been a sentimental being'. He also represented *A Sentimental Journey* according to the classic theory of sentimental didacticism – the purpose was 'to teach us to love the world and our fellow creatures better than we do – so it runs most upon those gentler passions and affections, which aid so much to it' – and gave much the same words to Yorick in the text itself.[74] These terms of reference came to dominate the novel's reception, yet great selective blindness was inevitably involved. In practice, the novel fails, or refuses, to sustain any clear distinction between sentimental sincerity and Shandean satire. Yorick's effusive sympathies border too often sickly concupiscence; his words and deeds are too often undermined by ironic innuendo; he is too epicurean (as Sancho might have put it), too self-absorbed, too much enraptured by distress not to seem, at times, a satirical butt. The popular compilation entitled *The Beauties of Sterne . . . Selected for the Heart of Sensibility* (1782) displays not only the desire of many readers to consume Sterne's writing as exclusively sentimental, but also its resistance as a whole to this desire. In his preface, the compiler deplores the contamination of the sentimental highlights he selects by the impurity of their original contexts, and he often has to crop aggressively to keep complicating ironies at bay.[75] A revealing case is his treatment of the celebrated Maria vignette from *Tristram Shandy*, which Sterne inserted in his closing volume as a trailer for *A Sentimental Journey*. At one level, Tristram's response to Maria's becoming woe is a classic instance of tender fellow-feeling; at another, it ironically identifies his sentimental voyeurism (which makes Maria look pointedly 'at her goat – and then at me – and then at her goat again' (9.24.783)) as lecherously exploitative of the distress on which it lingers. For Ralph Griffiths, the insouciant final line of the episode (in which, with the words 'What an excellent inn at Moulins!' (9.24.784), Tristram abruptly forgets Maria's plight for other pleasures) was 'an ill-tim'd stroke of levity; like a ludicrous epilogue . . . unnaturally tagged to the end of a deep tragedy'. Griffiths was right about the effect, of course, but failed to recognise its studious irony. In *The Beauties of Sterne*, the off-key exclamation – so damaging, as Griffiths adds, to 'every elevated, generous, or tender sentiment' of the previous lines – is simply cut.[76]

---

74 *Ibid.*, pp. 402–3, 401; see Sterne, *A Sentimental Journey*, ed. Melvyn New and W. G. Day (Gainesville, FL: University Press of Florida, 2002), p. 111. Further parenthetical references are to this edition.

75 See John Mullan, *Sentiment and Sociability: The Language of Feeling in the Eighteenth Century* (Oxford: Clarendon Press, 1988), p. 155.

76 Howes (ed.), *Sterne: The Critical Heritage*, p. 182.

A Sentimental Journey builds towards an extended reprise of this episode, and one need only remember Sterne's haunting rendering of the old French proverb – '*God tempers the wind*, said Maria, to the shorn lamb' (p. 152) – to see with what artistry he could cater to sentimental tastes. Yet he also contrives the disruptive survival of Shandean elements, allowing sentiment and satire to coexist and compete throughout the text, and allowing readers to consume it according to either rubric. The second Maria episode is the perfect example, shot through as it is with subversive hints which render ludicrous the object of Yorick's sympathy, while implicitly mocking his response as mere drooling affectation. The scene is rendered as an ironic debasement of pastoral elegy, in which, having been humiliatingly jilted by one oddly bucolic *surrogatus amantis* ('Her goat had been as faithless as her lover'), Maria glumly addresses the second, a lapdog named Sylvio, in the incongruous manner of a Marvell nymph. In the passage that follows, a suggestively eroticised exchange of bodily fluids gives way to a conclusion in which sentimental sympathy dwindles, to the exclusion of its object, into callous egotism. Steeping his handkerchief in his own tears, 'and then in hers – and then in mine – and then I wip'd hers again', Yorick reaches a pitch of sentimental rapture that is worlds away from Sterne's picture, in 'Philanthropy recommended', of a sympathy that rises above the self. As he smugly concludes, 'I am positive I have a soul' (pp. 150–1).

No less damaging to the standard claims of sentimentalism is another of Yorick's best-known exercises in sentimental objectification, 'The Captive', in which Sterne responds in characteristically ironic style to Sancho's invitation. Here the sentimental claim to express and impel active philanthropy is deftly punctured. Rather than have his sentimental tourist shed tears for Sancho's brethren, or elicit them from his readers, Sterne wryly identifies the subject as wholly beyond his hero's sympathetic reach. Only the threat of his own imprisonment brings Yorick to consider 'the miseries of confinement', and the exercise rapidly collapses in futile, picturesque abstraction. Failing to bring adequately to mind 'the millions of my fellow creatures born to no inheritance but slavery', he embarks instead on an idealised, imaginary 'portrait' of a man in a dungeon, and develops the picture with a connoisseurly relish that leaves practical philanthropy far behind (pp. 97–8). The solemnity with which this passage was later rendered on the canvas by several fashionable artists bears witness to its availability for purely sentimental consumption; but, as with the Maria episode, too much is in excess or contravention of the sentimental reading, and studiously so, for such a reading to seem secure. Always alert to the diversity of readerships and the multiplicity of meanings, Sterne offers his audience a text in which sentimental tastes are simultaneously fed and mocked. When he writes to his bookseller that *A Sentimental Journey* was 'likely to take in all Kinds of Readers', the more local ambiguity of 'take in' catches the effect to perfection: accommodating all readers, and probably fooling most, it provides the devotees of sentiment and the aficionados of satire with a text that can simultaneously be read in contrary ways. Or, as he more succinctly tells one sentimental reader, 'my Journey . . . shall make you cry as much as ever it made me laugh'.[77]

The failure of feeling

It is clear enough that Mackenzie's inheritance, even as he began writing *The Man of Feeling* before *A Sentimental Journey* appeared, was far from straightforward. Drawing on Sterne for his formal structure (a collage of episodes in which occasions and moments of vivid feeling take precedence over linear narrative), Mackenzie describes the novel as 'introducing a Man of Sensibility into different Scenes where his Feelings might be seen in their Effects'.[78] Exploratory more than didactic, it communicates its admiration for Harley's moral sense in wistful tones, and the vulnerability of his ideals, though never satirised with anything like Sterne's clarity, is repeatedly implied. Far from staging a bland celebration of the healing powers of benevolence, indeed, *The Man of Feeling* contains within itself, on several counts, a gloomy counter-argument to its apparent thesis. Its very form attests to the precariousness of sensibility in the modern world. The man of feeling is dead, and only the manuscript trace of his feeling survives. But this manuscript, torn to wad the shotgun of a wildfowling curate, has already contributed more to recreational slaughter than to sympathetic benevolence, and it reaches the reader in fragmentary form – a whimsically Ossianic gesture through which Mackenzie indicates, like Macpherson before him, the irrecoverableness of the virtue he enshrines.

In what survives, as much is said to contest the pretensions of sensibility as to uphold them. One cynical voice denounces sentimentalists who claim 'that the sensations of an honest heart, of a mind universally benevolent, make up the quiet bliss which they enjoy'. The pleasures such people celebrate depend not on sympathy at all, he goes on, but on a doubly culpable posture towards misfortune. When they hear the howling wind, their sense of comfort derives 'from the secret reflection of what houseless wretches feel from it'. When

77 Sterne, *Letters*, pp. 393, 401.
78 Henry Mackenzie, *Letters to Elizabeth Rose of Kilravock*, ed. Horst W. Drescher (Edinburgh: Oliver and Boyd, 1967), p. 16.

they offer charity, their benevolence, which they 'deduce immediately from the natural impulse of the heart, squints to [vanity] for its reward'.[79]

In its remaining fragments, *The Man of Feeling* documents Harley's sentimental encounters with a range of victims, some crushed by a universalised 'malevolence of fortune' (p. 126), others by forces teasingly associated by Mackenzie with the modern state: a speculator in government annuities and bonds, ruined by 'an unlucky fluctuation of stock' (p. 31); a father forced into naval service when a press-gang seizes his son. In the face of all this distress, however, little sign survives that Harley can alleviate the sufferings he witnesses, or even draw much personal sustenance from his own compassion. Where sentimental ethics in its most optimistic form had posited the uplifting power of sympathy on all sides, the victims for whom Harley weeps find little solace in a pity that leaves their losses unrestored, while Harley sinks under the burden of their grief. Again, where sentimental ethics had attributed innate benevolence to humane nature, Harley suffers a growing awareness that his own benevolence is unique, or at best that only 'a few friends . . . redeem my opinion of mankind' (p. 128). Finally, where sentimentalism had held out at least the possibility of social critique or action, Harley fails to accompany his one foray into analysis – an incongruously trenchant denunciation of British rule in India – with any comparable application to the evils directly to hand. (In a wry footnote, Mackenzie quietly acknowledges his novel's inability to weave its satirical perceptions about modern commerce and human depravity into connected analysis: 'there seems to have been, by some accident, a gap in the manuscript, from the words, "Expectation of a jointure," to these, "In short, man is an animal" ' (p. 41).)

Feeling falls short of healing, then, and becomes a kind of failing. Fugitive, fruitless and personally debilitating, sensibility issues only in death, and leaves only fragments of text. The closing words of the novel – 'as to the world – I pity the men of it' (p. 133) – place worldly rapacity in awkward balance with individual sensibility, but in this context the title of Mackenzie's follow-up novel of 1773 is gloomily pointed: *The Man of Feeling* gives way to *The Man of the World*, the frail and fleeting virtue of Harley to the thriving vice of Sindall.

The lingering anxieties of Mackenzie's text were seized on by others, often by analogy with Sterne. Several satirical prints by Thomas Rowlandson borrowed the title of *The Man of Feeling*, but wittily redefined the sentimental objectification in which it had specialised in such a way as to mock its

---

79 Henry Mackenzie, *The Man of Feeling*, ed. Brian Vickers (Oxford: Oxford University Press, 1967), p. 42. Further parenthetical references are to this edition.

Fig. 22.1 *A Man of Feeling* by Thomas Rowlandson (1811)

self-indulgence. Greedily groping the buttock of a simpering wench, Rowland-son's version of Yorick/Harley is a concupiscent parson for whom 'feeling' is simply a matter of fleshly self-gratification. Rather more subtle is an anony-mous novel of 1789, *The Man of Failing*. The natural son of a clergyman and wit 'who has gained much mistaken praise for the supposed benevolence or philanthropy of his heart' (reviewers instantly recognised Sterne), the man of failing is also depicted in ways that exaggerate the fragile and unavailing sensibility of Mackenzie's hero. Unable to persevere in sympathy or convert it to action ('want of exertion, and a natural indolence, generally hindered him from putting his good intentions towards any one in practice'), he wanders ineffectually through the novel as the exemplary sentimentalist, a character forever superficially touched, yet never truly moved.[80]

Nowhere is the impasse of feeling more brilliantly specified, however, than in Smollett's *Humphry Clinker*, a novel published within months of Mackenzie's triumph. Here Smollett involves his travelling protagonists in a telling scene of intertwined disasters. An iron on the travellers' coach has snapped, and in the nearest village 'the black-smith had been dead some days; and his wife, who had been lately delivered, was deprived of her senses'. Oblivious to the larger calamity, Humphry sets to work repairing the smaller, but the familiar ring of the anvil summons the distracted widow to the forge, 'where, throwing her arms about Clinker's neck, 'Ah, Jacob! (cried she) how could you leave me in such a condition?' It is the perfect sentimental vignette, all the more poignant for its teetering closeness to farce; yet this is also a vignette that beautifully symbolises the futility of its own mode. Crying for the misfortune of another while rectifying only his own – 'he hammered the iron and wept at the same time' – Humphry experiences, in stark form, the separation between ineffectual sympathy and purposeful action that had vexed sentimentalism all along.[81] If Carlyle was right to assert that 'nothing by Dante or any one else surpasses in pathos the scene where . . . Humphry's tears fall down and bubble on the hot iron',[82] it is because Humphry's pity for the widow's loss also dramatises a much larger lack: the paltry evanescence of the sentimentalist's tear, vaporised to nothing.

80 Anon., *The Man of Failing*, 2 vols. (London 1789), vol. i, pp. 145, 8.
81 Tobias Smollett, *Humphry Clinker*, ed. Lewis M. Knapp, rev. Paul-Gabriel Boucé (Oxford: Oxford University Press, 1984), pp. 185–6.
82 Lionel Kelly (ed.), *Tobias Smollett: The Critical Heritage* (London: Routledge, 1987), p. 343.

Folklore, antiquarianism, scholarship and high literary culture

ROBERT FOLKENFLIK

Andrew Fletcher of Saltoun claimed that 'if a man were permitted to make all the ballads, he need not care who should make the laws of a nation'.[1] At the beginning of the eighteenth century, then, at least one shrewd political observer recognised a relationship between nation, power and a particular literary kind associated with popular, anonymous production. National consciousness demands not only literary history, but also literary production. This story of scholars and antiquaries, translators and editors, and writers who ambiguously filled the roles required by what the age demanded will begin with the shaping notions of poets and move to the most controversial poet, who billed himself as a translator.

Although the term 'Folk-Lore' was not coined until 1846 by the antiquary William J. Thoms as a Saxon replacement for 'Popular Antiquities', the antiquities not of classical Greece and Rome but of the British Isles, the project itself can be seen as part of or related to a number of literary developments in the eighteenth century, including what René Wellek dubbed 'The Rise of English Literary History': the editing of early English literature, the revision of the canon, the concern for the oxymoronic 'British classics', as a title of 1796 put it. This activity was in turn part of larger interests in the past complexly forwarded by a range of developments at mid century including primitivism, the end of Jacobite threats, the awareness of a long and rich vernacular literary tradition.

William Collins wrote 'Ode on the Popular Superstitions of the Highlands of Scotland, Considered as the Subject of Poetry', around 1750 and addressed it to John Home, who would later encourage James Macpherson's *Fragments of Ancient Poetry* (1760) and his Highland collections. Collins' poem displays

---

1 Andrew Fletcher, 'An Account of A Conversation concerning a Right Regulation of Governments' (1704), in John Robertson (ed.), *Political Works* (Cambridge: Cambridge University Press, 1997), p. 179. He attributed the notion to a 'very wise man' he knew, but no one has doubted who that man was.

the cultural logic that prepared the way for Macpherson: it stages a poetic difference between Scotland ('whose ev'ry Vale / Shall prompt the Poet, and his Song demand') and England.[2] Home's 'genial Land' is not just pleasant and friendly, but a land filled with *genii loci*, a land of genius (line 17). Collins calls upon Home to tell these stories: 'The Native legends of thy Land rehearse' (p. 172, line 186). The poet's task is no longer imitation, but rehearsal or re-creation. Such 'false Themes' are imaginatively true ('to Nature true'), and they were believed by great poets in the past, Shakespeare and Tasso – the latter's reputation rose in England in tandem with Spenser's (lines 172, 189). Collins recaptures their glory by his own retelling, as he celebrates Fairfax for his translation of Tasso, another version of rehearsal. Collins' syntax registers the relation of the translator to the original. 'Prevailing Poet' is praise of Tasso, but the placement of the phrase after 'Fairfax' causes him to share it: "How have I sate ... / To hear His harp by British Fairfax strung. / Prevailing poet ..." (lines 196–8).

Such primitivism remained a constant for a number of poets in the later eighteenth century. Cowper's *The Task* (1785) plaintively praises a bygone innocence and simplicity: 'Would I had fall'n upon those happier days / That poets celebrate'.[3] He recognises that 'those days were never. Airy dreams / Sat for the picture' (*The Task*, Book IV, 'The Winter Evening', lines 525–6), yet he nevertheless 'still must envy them an age / That favour'd such a dream; in days like these / Impossible' (lines 529–31). To the extent that it is composed without a manuscript or oral basis, James Macpherson's Ossianic poetry is the fulfilment of the late eighteenth-century desire to be fooled by the imagination expressed in Collins and Cowper. Indeed, the same year as *Fingal* was published (1762), Richard Hurd drew on ancient wisdom to recommend such 'creditable deceits': '*they, who deceive, are honester than they who do not deceive; and they, who are deceived, wiser than they who are not deceived*'.[4]

Biding the question of the extent to which the Ossian poems are derived from oral or written tradition, one should recognise Macpherson's literary achievements: the development of significant new genres (fragment, prose poem), the fulfilment of the age's theoretical requirements for poetic excellence, the reconciling of ancient and modern literary tradition. (Sir Walter Scott's characterisation of Fingal as a combination of Achilles and Sir Charles

2 William Collins, *Poetical Works*, ed. Roger Lonsdale (Oxford: Oxford University Press, 1977), pp. 168, lines 13–14. Further parenthetical references are to this edition.
3 'The Task', *The Poems of William Cowper*, ed. John D. Baird and Charles Ryskamp (Clarendon Press: Oxford, 1995), p. 200, book 4, lines 513–14.
4 Richard Hurd, *Letters on Chivalry and Romance* (London, 1762), p. 103. Further parenthetical references are to this edition.

Grandison was not meant satirically.) Although eighteenth-century primitivism derived from many sources, the most important for Macpherson
was Thomas Blackwell's *An Enquiry into the Life and Writings of Homer* (1735).
Blackwell was Professor and Principal at Marischal College of the University of
Aberdeen when Macpherson studied there. Blackwell's notion that 'a Peoples
[*sic*] Felicity clips the Wings of their Verse' would have resonated with Macpherson in ways that went beyond its primitivism.[5] Indeed, a number of Blackwell's
poetic criteria and ideas about Homer, especially simplicity and sublimity, have
parallels in Macpherson's justifications of his Ossianic poetry and translation
of the *Iliad*. But by 1760 these were widely recognised as desiderata.

Macpherson, like Joyce's Stephen Dedalus, wished to 'forge the uncreated
conscience of his race', however we interpret the verb. One could argue that if
Ossian did not exist, he would have to be invented. In fact many have argued
in effect that this is precisely what Macpherson did in such poems as *Fingal*
(1762) and *Temora* (1763), though Oisein (spelled variously as Oisean, Ossain and
occasionally Ossian) was certainly a hero and bard of early Irish and Scottish
Gaelic poetry. If Macpherson has suddenly gained an increased importance
with the 'devolution' of English literature and a new spurt of Scottish nationalism at the end of the twentieth century which continues into this one, the
new apologists for Macpherson who insist upon his authenticity and stress the
quality of his achievement and influence have not gone uncontested.[6] William
Gillies, Professor of Celtic at the University of Edinburgh, refers in passing to
'the bogus productions of "Ossian" Macpherson', as does on occasion Derick
S. Thomson, the author of what remains the best account of Macpherson's
genuine debt to Gaelic poetry in his Ossian poems.[7] The relation of Macpherson and his Ossian poems to English and England is complex. His earliest
poetry is Jacobite in sympathy, but *The Highlander* is ultimately in favour of
accommodation to the English establishment. The *Scots Magazine*, in which

5 Thomas Blackwell, *An Enquiry into the Life and Writings of Homer* (London, 1735), p. 28.
   Further parenthetical references are to this edition.
6 Howard Gaskill, ' "Ossian" Macpherson: Towards a Rehabilitation', *Comparative Criticism*
   8 (1986), 113–46; Fiona Stafford, *The Sublime Savage: A Study of James Macpherson and the
   Poems of Ossian* (Edinburgh: Edinburgh University Press, 1988); Murray G. H. Pittock,
   Inventing and Resisting Britain: Cultural Identities in Britain and Ireland, 1685–1789 (London:
   Routledge, 1997), with a short chapter on Macpherson, and other books.
7 William Gillies, 'A Century of Gaelic Scholarship', in William Gillies (ed.), *Gaelic and
   Scotland: Alba agus à Ghaidhlig* (Edinburgh: Edinburgh University Press, 1989), p. 15. Derick
   S. Thomson, *The Gaelic Sources of Macpherson's 'Ossian'* (Edinburgh: Oliver and Boyd, 1952).
   See also Thomson's 'Macpherson's Ossian: Ballads to Epics,' in Bo Almqvist, Séamas Ó
   Catháin and Pádraig Ó Héalaí (eds.), *The Heroic Process: Form, Function and Fantasy in Folk
   Epic* (Dublin: The Glendale Press, 1987), pp. 243–64.

Jerome Stone published the first translation of the Gaelic ballads and Macpherson published some of his early poetry, was an anglicising journal. Hugh Blair, Macpherson's foremost champion, was an angliciser.

Macpherson's Ossian could have it both ways: at once a primitive genius exempt from Aristotle's rules (as Tobias Smollett claimed in an early review) and at the same time one who fulfilled them in his six-book epic beginning *in medias res*. Voltaire captured in a phrase spoken to Boswell what Macpherson had constructed: 'The Scottish Homer'. Thomas Sheridan confessed to Boswell that he preferred Ossian to either Homer or Virgil. Ossian was doubly primitive. Not only did he sing in the third century, but, as Collins argued, Scotland remained primitive while England was refined. Macpherson himself would later assert that 'the taste, which defines genius, by the points of the compass, is a subject fit for mirth', but he certainly benefited from it, as he recognised in adding that 'it is often a serious matter in the sale of the work'.[8] He justifies his poetic prose as an escape from 'fetters, which cramp the thought' (*Poems of Ossian*, p. 410), a phrase that links him to both Milton before and Blake after in rejecting the rhymed couplets in which he wrote his earlier poetry. Macpherson's use of prose for his translations has been linked to the Ossian stories' appearance in both poetic and prosaic form in the Gaelic tradition.[9] A stronger influence upon him, however, was the praise of poetic prose to be found in Robert Lowth's *De sacra poesi Hebraeorum: Praelectiones academicae* (*On the Sacred Poetry of the Hebrews*) [1753; English translation, 1787], and perhaps the critical tradition deriving from Aristotle and found in Sidney, Bacon and others in early modern England which insisted that poetry was not limited to verse. But what was most important about his poetic form was its total break with the still dominant rhymed couplet.

Although Macpherson represented his poems as actual translations of the poetry of Ossian, and probably believed his claim in part, *Fingal* may be taken as an 'imitation' in a liberalised version of the sense that Dryden gave it, a free translation 'where the translator (if now he has not lost that name) assumes the liberty not only to vary from the words and sense, but to forsake them both as he sees occasion . . . taking only some general hints from the original'.[10]

8 James Macpherson, 'Preface' (1773) to *The Poems of Ossian and Related Works*, ed. Howard Gaskill (Edinburgh: Edinburgh University Press, 1996), p. 409. Further references to *The Poems of Ossian* will be to this edition.
9 Donald E. Meek, 'The Gaelic Ballads of Scotland: Creativity and Adaptation', in Howard Gaskill (ed.), *Ossian Revisited* (Edinburgh: Edinburgh University Press, 1991), p. 25.
10 'Preface to *Ovid*', in *John Dryden*, ed. Keith Walker (Oxford: Oxford University Press, 1987), p. 160.

One could also argue that Macpherson gave Home and the Edinburgh literati just such a 'rehearsal' as Collins urged upon Macpherson's patron-to-be, one that imitates and translates.

It is difficult to credit the notion that Macpherson, encouraged by the Edinburgh literati, originally believed that the fragments he translated were part of the epic for which he received backing because only two of the original fifteen were based on actual ballads.[11] In fact, according to Thomson, Macpherson only drew upon sixteen or seventeen ballads in all his Ossian poems.[12] Even 'The Death of Oscur', his showpiece 'fragment' presented to Home, differs greatly from traditional ballads. If he had traditional ballads in Gaelic by heart, as he claimed, they were few in number. In *Fingal* he created the epic he did not find, and in *Temora* he achieved whole-cloth fabrication after Book One. Thomson refers to *Temora* as 'fraudulent'. A reading of Macpherson's notes for this poem suggests that he knew fully that he was deceiving his readers. The appearance of some lines of his own early poetry suggest that he enjoyed doing so.[13]

One may believe that C. K. Scott Moncrieff's translation of Proust's title *A la recherche du temps perdu* as the Shakespearian *A Remembrance of Things Past* has lost something, but it would be wrong to conclude Moncrieff was not translating Proust properly. Macpherson extends the standard eighteenth-century notion that poetry is good only if it survives translation (as opposed to modern ideas like Robert Frost's 'Poetry is what is lost in translation') to play with the metaphor of counterfeiting and make a claim for his own originality: 'Genuine poetry, like gold, loses little, when properly transfused; but when a composition cannot bear the test of a literal version, it is a counterfeit, which ought not to pass current. The operation must, however, be performed with skilful hands. A Translator, who cannot equal his original, is incapable of expressing its beauties' (*Poems of Ossian*, p. 412). Or, to put it another way, Macpherson the translator is equal to that original genius Ossian. The question became acute at this time because the notion of genius in its developed eighteenth-century form may be regarded as possessive individualism in the realm of the arts. 'Genius' became the supreme tribute in a century that invented copyright for intellectual 'property'.

11 Stafford, *The Sublime Savage*, p. 85.
12 Thomson, 'Macpherson's Ossian', p. 10. Thomson had only claimed fifteen or sixteen in his *The Gaelic Sources of Macpherson's 'Ossian'*.
13 In his edition of *The Poems of Ossian* (Edinburgh: Archibald Constable and Co., 1805) Malcolm Laing, for example, compares Macpherson's 'Blood forms a lake around' (*The Highlander*, Canto ii, line 115, 2:539) to *Fingal*'s 'Blood bursts and smokes around' (Book 1, 1: 35).

For nearly two hundred years we have had a very good idea of how Macpherson worked. Since 1952 we have had Derick Thomson's dispassionate close comparison of Macpherson's written sources with his Ossianic poetry, which has gone uncontested by those on either side of the division over authenticity. Thomson notes the way Macpherson reworked the passages in fragments into the longer poems and details Macpherson's inaccuracies when he did not understand a word or passage. Although Macpherson was not a very good Gaelic scholar, he was explicitly aware of employing Gaelic syntax: 'The arrangement of the words in the original is imitated, and the inversions of the style observed.'[14] Much of Macpherson's practice is within the range of expectations from a translator, but what we do not expect are the constant changes of the names of characters and locations to turn various ballads into a single narrative and the shift to Scottish history of stories that were properly Irish. He went on to make insupportable claims for the priority of Scottish language and culture in his *History of Great Britain* (1775). Scholars of Irish Gaelic have been Macpherson's harshest critics, and indeed Macpherson's *Fingal* was an undeclared cultural war against the Irish, and a demonstration of cultural power to the English. This amalgamation of Irish ballads in a Scottish epic is a new twist on Fletcher of Saltoun's observation.

Defenders have argued that Macpherson may have been unaware of this distortion, for oral tradition frequently substituted Scottish names and places for Irish ones, but Macpherson himself made changes in texts of this sort that we know he used in producing his own 'translation'. A second line of defence points out the analogy of the kinds of changes Macpherson made to the practice of the oral singers of ballads. But he certainly presents himself as an eighteenth-century scholar-translator rather than as the last of the Ossianic bards. More to the point, his notes again and again suggest that his procedures were not those that he claimed to follow. Macpherson's knowledge of written Gaelic was limited. His transcriptions have never been found, though he wrote of intending to put them in a major library. Although he unquestionably used the *Book of the Dean of Lismore* and some other manuscript material, he left nothing behind him of Gaelic transcriptions – that is, not third-century manuscripts but his own collections – that should have been guarded like the Holy Grail. At least one of Macpherson's informants busied himself translating Macpherson's English back into Gaelic to serve as putative manuscripts.

---

14 James Macpherson, 'A Dissertation concerning the Antiquity, &c. of the Poems of Ossian the Son of Fingal', in *Fingal* (London, 1762), p. xvi. Further parenthetical references are to this edition. Robert P. Fitzgerald calls attention to Macpherson's following the style of Gaelic ballads in 'The Style of Ossian', *Studies in Romanticism* 6 (1966): 22–33.

One scholar, noting Macpherson's intention 'to reduce the broken members of the piece into the order in which they now appear' (*Poems of Ossian*, p. 215), claims that 'the imagery is of surgery, a restorative resetting of fractured limbs', but I suspect that behind such language and that of Blair ('in some of the longer works, he may have combined and brought together some pieces which he found scattered and broken') and Adam Ferguson ('I was inclined to think some pains must have been bestowed, and even liberties taken, in piecing together what was found in separate or broken fragments, with defects attending all such traditionary strains') in years to come lies a suggestion that the Horatian 'disiecta membra poetae', the scattered limbs of the poet (Ossian for Orpheus), would be gathered into epic wholes.[15] Robert Lowth quoted this Horatian phrase in discussing the way the poetry of the Hebrew Bible maintained itself when translated into English prose, a highly relevant analogy.[16] Both Blair and Macpherson would also have known Blackwell's linkage of the '*Fragments of Orpheus* so called' to *Homer's Verses*' (*Enquiry*, p. 72), a possible model for turning fragments into epic, and Ferguson compares Macpherson's procedure to 'the scattered rhapsodies of Homer himself'.[17] Both Macpherson's defenders and opponents were largely unaware of how oral epics came about, knowledge attendant upon Robert Wood and F. A. Wolf later in the eighteenth century and Milman Parry in the twentieth.[18]

Whatever their origins, the Ossian poems were immensely popular and influential. Macpherson's poetry is incantatory, plangent, elegaic. Full of mist, wind, and water, nearly all of it, from its cadences to its actions, has a dying fall. Its nostalgia and melancholy snugly fit an age of sensibility. As with the cult of Mary Queen of Scots in the eighteenth century, 'Ossian' could be embraced even by many of the English because he was no threat. Macpherson can be defended, as Chatterton was defended after his exposure, on the grounds of

---

15 Thomas Keymer, 'Narrratives of Loss: *The Poems of Ossian* and *Tristram Shandy*' in Fiona Stafford and Howard Gaskill (eds.), *From Gaelic to Romantic: Ossianic Translations* (Amsterdam: Rodopi, 1998), p. 89; Blair and Ferguson's letters in Henry Mackenzie (ed.), *Report of the Committee of the Highland Society of Scotland . . . into the Nature of and Authenticity of the Poems of Ossian . . . with copious appendix* (Edinburgh: A. Constable, 1805), pp. 61, 64. *Horace, Satires, Epistles, Ars Poetica*, trans. H. Rushton Fairclough, Loeb Classical Library (Cambridge, MA: Harvard University Press, 1966) *Satires* 1.4.62, p. 52.

16 Robert Lowth, *Lectures on the Sacred Poetry of the Hebrews* (1753), trans. G. Gregory, 2 vols. (1787), vol. I, p. 71.

17 Thomas Blackwell, *An Enquiry into the Life and Writing of Homer* (London, 1735), p. 72.

18 For an even-handed account of what was known of oral poetry in the eighteenth-century, see Nicholas Hudson, '"Oral Tradition": The Evolution of an Eighteenth-Century Concept', in Alvaro Ribeiro and James E. Basker (eds.), *Tradition in Transition: Women Writers, Marginal Texts, and the Eighteenth-century Canon* (Oxford: Clarendon Press, 1996), pp. 161–76.

the poetry's excellence, regardless of the authenticity of the putative poet. In fact he was so defended by Gray and others who suspected a hoax but nevertheless responded to the poetry. At times the poetry must have been startling. Pope's famous couplet 'Now Shield with Shield, with Helmet Helmet clos'd, / To Armour Armour, Lance to Lance oppos'd', evokes ballet more than battle (*Iliad*, Book 4, lines 508–9). Macpherson's poetic prose, even with its debt to Pope, better represents martial violence: 'Swords sound on helmets, sound on shields; brass clashes, clatters, rings' (*Poems of Ossian*, p. 27). Macpherson was wildly appreciated throughout Europe by many who knew neither Gaelic nor English and read 'Ossian' in French, German, Spanish, Swedish or Italian. His 'translated' poetry achieved even greater fame in translation from English. Napoleon's favourite poet was Ossian, and he commissioned two huge canvases on Ossianic subjects for his château at Malmaison.

Macpherson published poetry and had poetic ambitions before the Ossianic fragments and poems brought him fame. Although he was encouraged to find and publish Gaelic poetry by Home, Adam Ferguson and Hugh Blair, and David Hume (before his apostasy), it is not difficult to discover the poet of 'On the Death of Marshall Keith' in the translator of Ossian. One would not have to squint hard to make out a Jacobite allegory of the restoration of the rightful ruler by Highland Scots in *Fingal*. The Jacobite pathos of poems that celebrate heroes and deeds of a time that is past even at the ostensible moment of the telling is manifest, and recent scholarship has been devoted to picking up nuances of contemporary history and debate, including an argument for a Scottish militia, in this poetry.[19]

What has received less attention is that the primitivism present in the poetic desires of Cowper and others required a great poet to be a poet who lived long ago. One can see this matter-of-fact assumption in a writer who figures in many of the developments discussed here, though he often is inimical to them. Samuel Johnson's poet/critic, Imlac, in *Rasselas* (1759) says: 'in almost all countries, the most ancient poets are considered as the best . . . Whatever be the reason, it is commonly observed that the early writers are in possession of nature, and their followers of art: that the first excel in strength and invention, and the latter in elegance and refinement.'[20] He might have instanced Blackwell among the observers. Imlac also asserts that 'No man was ever great

---

19 Richard B. Sher, *Church and University in the Scottish Enlightenment: The Moderate Literati of Edinburgh* (Edinburgh: Edinburgh University Press, 1985), pp. 257–61.
20 Samuel Johnson, *Rasselas and Other Tales*, ed. Gwin J. Kolb, The Yale Edition of the Works of Samuel Johnson, 16 vols. (New Haven, CT: Yale University Press, 1990), vol. XVI, pp. 39–40.

by imitation', a *sententia* opposed to centuries of literary theory that finds parallels elsewhere in Johnson's own work as well as in Young's *Conjectures on Original Composition* (also 1759), and the Warton brothers. The unuttered corollary of these dicta is that to rank among the 'best' writers, one needed to be an early writer. Such thinking would have a great impact upon a range of genres, upon the very concept of genre itself, but perhaps on none so much as the genre of the imitation. The difference between an imitation and a forgery, like the difference between a copy and a forgery in art, may be a matter of the claims made for the work. Ballad imitations continued to be written, but, like Percy's 'Hermit of Warwick', which Johnson parodied, they were now suspect. The notion (derided by Johnson) that it was, in Milton's phrase, 'an age too late' for poetry was widespread and led Macpherson, Chatterton and others to create ancient and medieval poets as figures who could circle behind the presumed impasse and become their mouthpieces.[21]

Macpherson's own Preface to *Fingal* points to the problems contemporary writers faced in relation to dead writers: 'Poetry, like virtue, receives its reward after death. The fame which men pursued in vain, when living, is often bestowed upon them when they are not sensible of it.' An explanation of why living authors do not receive proper credit for their poetry is an odd way to begin an account of an ancient author, and it becomes odder yet. He attributes this situation to the fact that 'It often happens, that the man who writes differs greatly from the same man in common life. His foibles, however, are obliterated by death, and his better part, his writings, remain: his character is formed from them, and he that was no extraordinary man in his own time, becomes the wonder of succeeding ages.' This observation becomes the prologue to claims for the authenticity of the poems, but to reach that point he first notes that 'This consideration might induce a man, diffident of his abilities, to ascribe his own compositions to a person, whose remote antiquity and whose situation, when alive, might well answer for faults which would be inexcusable in a writer of this age.' This consideration reverses the burden of the past and heaps the modern disadvantages on the shoulders of the ancient, who will be forgiven them. He attributes this position to an unnamed gentleman of his acquaintance who had not yet read the poems, but was convinced of their authenticity when he did. Finally, in a formula carefully enough worded to smack of equivocation, Macpherson adds 'it would be a

---

21 For an account of the role of literary theory of the time in shaping Macpherson and Chatterton's poetry, see Robert Folkenflik, 'Macpherson, Chatterton, Blake and the Great Age of Literary Forgery', *Centennial Review* 18 (1974), 378–91, on which I have drawn.

very uncommon instance of self-denial in me to disown them, were they really of my composition' (Preface to *Fingal*, pp. A3^{r-v}).

Macpherson's Preface hints at an *apologia pro vita sua*. In 1785 John Pinkerton went well beyond Macpherson's position. The year before Pinkerton owned his authorship of the second part of the ballad *Hardyknute*, itself of dubious heritage,[22] he audaciously defended literary forgery under the pseudonym Robert Heron: 'Perhaps in fact nothing can be more heroic and generous in literary affairs than a writer's ascribing to antiquity his own production; and thus sacrificing his own fame to give a higher satisfaction to the public.' He goes on to portray 'those of deeper minds' among his audience as 'not deceived by the fiction, as to their judgement; yet their fancy admits the deceit, and receives higher pleasure from it, than it possibly could were no deceit used'. He claims that calling 'such forgery criminal' is blasphemy, for Christ's parables were similar fictions.[23] Even without the over-the-top analogy to Christ, Pinkerton takes the poetic sympathy of Collins and Cowper for 'false themes' to 'Nature true' some steps farther.

Macpherson's notes to *Fingal* set the stage for Ossian's acceptance into the canon. Having billed the poem as an epic in its title, he compares it to Homer, Virgil, Milton and the Bible throughout the notes. The Appendix to Blair's *Critical Dissertation* which prefaced the poetry addressed the question of the poem's authenticity. In the wake of Macpherson William Duff's *Essay on Original Genius* (1767) argues in a section heading that 'Original Poetic Genius will in general be displayed in its utmost Vigour in the early and uncultivated Periods of Society, Which are peculiarly favourable to it; and that it will seldom appear in a very high Degree in Cultivated Life'.[24] He instances Ossian and Homer. Ossian was original in ways that Macpherson, that any modern poet, could not be, and 'originality' had replaced 'imitation' as a primary criterion of great poetry.

Adam Ferguson proved to be Macpherson's most incisive and eloquent defender, though what he said has received almost no attention. His comments centre on Gaelic, which he spoke. He notes that he is 'not surprised' that there remains little evidence of what Macpherson found:

> It was a language spoken in the cottage, but not in the parlour, or at the table of any gentlemen. Its greatest elegancies were to be learned from herdsmen

---

22 For the best account, see Ross Roy 'Hardyknute – Lady Wardlaw's Ballad?' in H. W. Matalene (ed.), *Romanticism and Culture* (Columbia, SC: Camden House, 1984), pp. 133–46.
23 Robert Heron, *Letters of Literature* (London, 1785), pp. 384–5.
24 William Duff, *Essay on Original Genius* (London, 1767), p. 260.

or deer-stealers. It was connected with disaffection, and proscribed by government. Schools were erected to supplant it, by teaching a different language. There were no books in it, but the manuals of religion, and these in so aukward and clumsy a spelling that few could read them. The fashionable world in the neighbourhood, as usual, derided the tone and accent of the Highlanders, believing their own to be models of elegance and harmony. It was more genteel to be ignorant than knowing of what such a language contained; and it required all the genius, learning, and courage of James Macpherson, to perceive and affirm that the ancient strains of Gaelic poetry might compare with those of other nations more celebrated.   (*Appendix to the Report*, p. 65)

One may believe that Macpherson was far more accommodationist and cynical than Ferguson's portrayal, and yet recognise the heroic persistence of the Gaelic language despite the political and class opposition it faced.

Macpherson recast Gaelic ballads as Ossianic epic in *Fingal*. Ironically, shortly after, Hurd's *Letters on Chivalry and Romance* and Percy's *Reliques* (1765) made the case both for ballads and for alternatives to the rules derived from Aristotle. An investigation of the ballad revival and of Chatterton, who drew on both the examples of Macpherson – a ballad collector among other things – and Percy for his forgeries, which characteristically took the form of ballads, will show some of the permutations of the themes at work in the period.

Addison's *Spectator* essays on the old English ballads (1711) were highly influential. Comparing 'Chevy Chase' to the *Aeneid* (Nos. 70, 74), and even finding the 'The Children in the Wood' Virgilian (No. 85), he praised the poems' 'simplicity' and 'beauties of nature'. Although clearly broadening the range of acceptable literature for the 'man of polite taste', Addison remained largely within the ambit of neoclassicism. In the years following Addison's praise of ballads, *A Collection of Old Ballads* (1723–25), edited anonymously, sold very well. The Scots alone produced a significant number of ballad collections. Allan Ramsay's *The Evergreen: A Collection of Scots Poems, Wrote by the Ingenious before 1600* (1724) was based on the Bannatyne MS. (1568). Both the dedication and the preface stress nationalistic reasons for valuing it at the same time that they remain within the protocols of mimesis: 'When these good old bards wrote, we had not yet made Use of imported trimming upon our Cloaths, nor of foreign Embroidery in our Writings.'[25] Although Ramsay quickly opposes Scottish pastoral to those of Greece and Rome, his book is an early salvo in the culture wars between England and Scotland. The revival of interest in the ballads has usually been taken as a product of high culture, of

25 Allan Ramsay, *The Evergreen: A Collection of Scots Poems, Wrote by the Ingenious before 1600*, 2 vols. (Edinburgh, 1724), vol. I, p. vii.

antiquarianism and scholarship,[26] but ballads continued to be written and hawked in the streets, and indeed these contemporary new broadsides and rewritings of traditional ballads were those that Fletcher of Saltoun had in mind. Additionally, a popular audience for the older ballads existed along with a broadside culture.

Thomas Percy's *Reliques of Ancient English Poetry* (1765) was both a watershed in the ballad revival and the most influential collection of its kind. The subtitle permits a great deal of leeway: *Consisting of Old Heroic Ballads, Songs, and other Pieces of our earlier Poets (Chiefly of the Lyric kind.) Together with some few of later Date.* 'English Poetry' in the title refers to the language, for it comes from the British Isles as well as British possessions. Percy even envisions his project in a letter to William Shenstone as a mock-imperial quest for booty from Wales, Ireland and the West Indies, as well as the 'Wilds of Staffordshire and Derbyshire': 'thus shall we ransack the whole British Empire'.[27] This claim need not be taken very seriously, but it falls into place as an English version of cultural nationalism.

Alhough Percy does not define the beginning of the 'later Date' of poetry, the ballads in *Reliques* range from the medieval and popular to such seventeenth-century poems as Sir John Suckling's 'Why so pale' and Sir Richard Lovelace's 'To Lucasta, on going to the Wars', and modern pastiches by Shenstone and James Grainger.[28] The spoils from his West Indian correspondence consisted of Grainger's imitation 'Bryan and Pereene, A West Indian Ballad', which tells the tale of an English sailor who swims back towards his Indian love only to be bitten in half by a shark. Percy never intended to include all the ballads of which he had copies, even when he judged them authentic, though he allowed for the possibility of subsequent volumes if the publication were successful, and he certainly added more poems in his revised editions. He includes one and only one of the Robin Hood ballads on the grounds that it was both unpublished and appeared to him to be more ancient. He also includes 'Hardyknute', which he believes was written in the form he prints in the early eighteenth century by Lady Elizabeth Wardlaw (Percy, *Reliques*, vol. II, pp. 87–8). Sometimes Percy's scholarship fails egregiously: his headnote to 'You meaner beautyes' asserts that '*The author and date of this little sonnet are unknown.*

26 Albert B. Friedman, *The Ballad Revival: Studies in the Influence of Popular on Sophisticated Poetry* (Chicago: University of Chicago Press, 1961).

27 Thomas Percy, *The Correspondence of Thomas Percy and William Shenstone*, eds. Cleanth Brooks and A. F. Falconer, *The Percy Letters* (New Haven, CT: Yale University Press, 1977), 7: 109–10. Further parenthetical references are to this edition.

28 Thomas Percy, *Reliques of Ancient English Poetry*, 3 vols. (London, 1765), vol. III, pp. 246, 259, 27. Further parenthetical references are to this edition.

Tis printed from a written copy, which had all the marks of great antiquity' (Percy, *Reliques*, vol. I, pp. 280–1). But not, one assumes, the watermarks: the poem is by Sir Henry Wotton and dates from the early seventeenth century. He includes poems by royalty: Queen Elizabeth, James I (the spurious selection in the first edition was replaced with two authentic sonnets in the second), Charles I, Charles II, as well as mad songs and ballads from Shakespeare's plays.

Percy also printed ancient and modern versions of several ballads, such as 'Chevy Chase' and 'The Boy and the Mantle', the first poem of the third volume. A diegetic hand points here to the boldface warning that 'Such Readers, as have no relish for pure antiquity, will find a more modern copy of this Ballad at the end of the volume' (Percy, *Reliques*, vol. III, p. 2). Percy appears to be aware of a bifurcated audience for ballads, one predicated by Addison in *Spectator* No. 70. If one wonders what such a reader is doing reading this far, it should be remembered that Percy switched the first and third volumes' ordering when the Countess of Northumberland became his patron. Had he published the third volume as first, as he originally planned, the epigraph would have come from Addison's *Spectator* No. 70 on the ballads. The double audience may also be a hidden nod to William Dicey (see Lance Bertelsen, chapter three in this volume), whose family was the most prolific printer of ballads recent and older. Percy corresponded with him and bought many of his ballads, but did not acknowledge his help.

Percy's procedures in relation to the ballads he printed may have been influenced by this double audience. Although the fragment had an honourable status among classicists, who published the fragmentary remains of the Greek and Roman writers, and an aesthetics of the fragmentary was on the rise in literature and art in the later eighteenth century (Macpherson, Sterne, the sketch), Percy typically not only emended poems but finished those in a fragmentary state. Ironically, he may have taken to heart the pointed lesson that Shenstone drew from Macpherson's first Ossianics, the *Fragments*: 'Let the Liberties taken by the Translator of the Erse-Fragments be a Precedent for *You*. Many old pieces *without* some alteration, will do nothing; and, *with your* amendments, will be striking' (*Percy Letters*, vol. VII, p. 118).

Percy's decision to lead with 'The Ballad of Chevy Chase' only followed his choice of the Countess of Northumberland as the dedicatee, though it appears both inspired and overdetermined. Sir Philip Sidney's praise of the poem ('I never heard the old song of [*Chevy Chase*] that I found not my heart moved more than with a trumpet') appears as an epigraph. Addison, who quotes Sidney, is mentioned in the headnote. The poem's hero is Percy, Earl of Northumberland. So this choice enables him to flatter a noble patron, link his name to hers and the poem's hero, set himself in a line of highly regarded critics of Elizabethan times and his own century, and display the fruits of his scholarship in opposition to misguided ignorance. Not bad for an afterthought, and the firmest stepping stone on his path to a bishopric.

This was a period in which shifting literary criteria had distinct implications for editors and literary scholars more generally. The time was ripe for Macpherson's *Fragments* as fragments, though, as Percy's correspondence and publication decisions concerning his *Reliques* demonstrate, the question of whether to present fragments as completed wholes was much mooted. Percy did. His scourge Joseph Ritson did not and was criticised by a reviewer when he followed the path late in the century that would win him the praise of modern medievalists: 'The great fault is that the editor has given his ballads almost literally as he found them.'[29] Both Shenstone and Percy used analogies from art to justify their practice. Shenstone recommended silently alternating '*a word or two*', but italicising 'a whole *Line* or More': 'It will have the appearance of a modern *Toe* or *Finger*, which is allowably added to the old Statues' (*Percy Letters*, vol. VII, pp. 72–3). One could argue that at times, as in *Temora*, Macpherson's practice was to provide a head, torso and extremities where he had perhaps hands and feet. Shenstone represents himself (duplicitously, for one cannot gather this from his letters to Percy) as 'less sanguine' about the success of Percy's *Reliques* 'than I should have been, had he shortened his notes, admitted more improvements, and rejected all such ballads as had no Plea but their *Antiquity*'.[30] Percy writing to Evan Evans (15 October 1761) of Macpherson's success at obtaining subscribers for *Fingal* adds that 'hardly one reader in ten believes the specimens already produced to be genuine'. He contrasts this situation with his own intentions: 'How much greater the attention would be due to an editor, who rescues the original itself from oblivion, and fixes it's [*sic*] meaning by an accurate version.'[31] Yet Percy's practice has left it to later scholars to determine just how sophisticated (in several senses of the word) his versions were. Bertrand Bronson's demolition of the much admired 'Edward, Edward' (which might better be called 'Davie, Davie' – the former name was not used in Scotland; the latter appears in oral versions) notes how many features of the poem do not accord with authentic oral versions.

---

29 Quoted by Bertrand H. Bronson, *Joseph Ritson: Scholar-at Arms*, 2 vols. (Berkeley: University of California Press, 1938), vol. I, p. 222.
30 Letter to Robert Dodsley (20 November 1762) in *The Correspondence of Robert Dodsley 1733–1764*, ed. James E. Tierney (Cambridge: Cambridge University Press, 1988), p. 466.
31 Thomas Percy, *The Correspondence of Thomas Percy and Evan Evans*, ed. A. Lewis, *The Percy Letters*, 9 vols. (New Haven, CT: Yale University Press, 1977), vol. V, p. 19.

In effect, despite the importance of his editorial work, Percy occupies territory shared by Macpherson and Chatterton. It is no wonder that Joseph Ritson believed Percy's manuscript did not exist. Ritson was the textual scholar's worst nightmare: someone who would impugn one's scholarship and motives in vituperative language and often be correct. For him Percy was a forger along with Macpherson and Chatterton.

When Blair asked Samuel Johnson if he thought 'any man of a modern age' could have written the Ossianic poems, Johnson answered memorably 'Yes, Sir, many men, many women, and many children'.[32] This famous rejoinder overstated the case, but it is tempting to answer, 'Perhaps not, but Thomas Chatterton could.' Before the decade of the 1760s was out, Chatterton was putting to use what he had learned from both Macpherson and Percy. Although he wrote seven 'British' Ossianic pieces and parodied Ossian in a letter, one of his closest approaches to Macpherson, 'The Hirlas II', derives from Evan Evans' Welsh translations, but catches the Ossianic rhythms as Evans only does infrequently. It begins 'Ere the sun was seen on the brow of the mountain, the clanging shields were heard in the valley'. His Manx poem 'Godred Crovan' gets the rhythms right: 'the son of Syrric sleeps upon the mountain, under the mossy rock'; 'The lions of the plain, Morvor and Essyr, will swell thy army, as the falling rain swells the silver brook'.[33] In his characteristic voices Chatterton is more uneven than Macpherson, whose work is largely of a piece, not to say monotone. Chatterton probably took heart from the reception of Macpherson, but, as he bitterly wished to remind Horace Walpole, who spurned the role of patron that Chatterton had hoped he would fill: 'Thou mayest call me cheat – / Say didst thou neer indulge in such deceit?/ Who wrote Otranto'? (p. 341). A number of writers paraded their own fictions as early literature. It is worth noticing that the framework of Walpole's Gothic novel divides the putative audience of the story into early readers who believed what they read and modern readers who read it as entertainment, a split that may remind us of Collins.

Chatterton's career displays the fate of an excellent imitator and parodist in an age that made originality the highest criterion of poetic greatness. Whereas Macpherson was unwilling to make his manuscripts available, Chatterton

---

32 James Boswell, *Life of Johnson*, ed. George Birkbeck Hill and L. F. Powell (Oxford: Clarendon Press, 1934–64), vol. 1, p. 396.

33 Thomas Chatterton, *The Complete Works of Thomas Chatterton*, ed. Donald S. Taylor and Benjamin B. Hoover, 2 vols. (Oxford: Clarendon Press, 1971), vol. 1, pp. 428, 345. Further parenthetical references are to this edition.

produced them, one might say, on demand. His Rowley poems depend on antiquarianism for their existence; he was himself a pseudo-antiquarian in producing them (with wills and other documents); and it was antiquarians (often satirised as gullible) who exposed him. Like Macpherson, Percy and Gray before him, he published fragments so nominated. Chatterton has been characterised as thinking that being medieval consisted of licence to spell however he wanted, but Percy anticipated him on extravagant spelling, as did the orthography of the very exact and scholarly Joseph Ritson, who gives us such monstrosities as: *Ancient Engleish Metrical Romanceës*.

Chatterton's imagined community centres on St Mary Redcliffe near Bristol. Chatterton's local attachments were entirely in keeping with a medieval scholarship that arose from the provinces (Percy, Ritson, Richard Gough) and insisted on the importance of the local for the national, a note that the Oxford-based Thomas Warton also struck: 'what is local is often national'.[34]

Chatterton is rightly best known for his putatively fifteenth-century poems, supposedly written by Thomas Rowley (spelled variously), a contemporary and newly discovered competitor of the very real John Lydgate. *Ælla* displays the impressive use to which he could put his reading of Percy's *Reliques*, and *An Excelente Balade of Charitie* joins Chaucer's diction and Spenserian stanza. With a mixture drawn from Macpherson's 'third-century' Ossian to the Renaissance Shakespeare, Chatterton parades the early canon before his reader, channelling it through his poet-mouthpieces. His nostalgic version of English nationalism portrays poet and patron linked in generous communal harmony. Those so inclined may detect traces of 'A tedious brief scene of young Pyramus and his love Thisbe' in his work, but at his best Chatterton justifies some of the extraordinary praise he received later from Keats and Dante Gabriel Rossetti.

Thomas Warton devoted the twenty-five page section VIII of the second volume of his *History of English Poetry* (1778) to the poems of Thomas Rowlie, pronouncing them modern, as did Percy. Chatterton had committed suicide in 1770, and his book only appeared in 1777. Given the claims of his Preface to the complete three-volume *History* (1774–81), Warton might have entitled his major work, echoing a form familiar in the century, *The Rise and Progress of English Poetry*. Near mid century Warton and his brother Joseph influentially shook up eighteenth-century conceptions of the canon by insisting upon bringing 'back Poetry into its right channel', as Joseph put it in the 'Advertisement' to his *Odes on Various Subjects* (1746), which was to be seen as an 'attempt'

---

34 Thomas Warton, *Specimen of a History of Oxfordshire* (London, 1783), p. iii.

to achieve that goal.[35] Thomas Warton's *History of English Poetry* (1774–81) may be regarded as another such attempt, though one with a difference. 'Invention and Imagination' were Joseph Warton's watchwords, not 'didactic Poetry . . . and Essays on moral Subjects'. He desired a return to Spenser, Shakespeare and Milton with a concomitant downgrading of Dryden and Pope (Joseph Warton, *Odes*, p. A2^r). This re-evaluation shifted the criteria for poetic excellence from refinement, which led Atterbury and Goldsmith to talk of parts of the period from 1660 to the early eighteenth century as an English 'Augustan Age', to the criteria that lay behind the poetry of 'Rowley' and 'Ossian'. Yet Thomas Warton's history promises, and to a large extent delivers, a teleological account of the 'improvement' of English literature: 'In an age advanced to the highest degree of refinement, that species of curiosity commences, which is busied in contemplating the progress of social life, in displaying the gradations of science, and in tracing the transitions from barbarism to civility.'[36] The concept of literature in this period is bound closely to ideals of language usage, of English literature to English. 'Correctness', a major criterion for Pope, is one of Warton's constant terms of praise. How far this is from the Wartons' role at mid century will be immediately apparent, and Thomas Warton's contradictory claims in his *History* help to show the conflict that obtained towards the end of the century.

The famous peroration at the conclusion of Thomas Warton's second volume, which contradicts the progressive narrative set up in the Preface and fitfully followed, sets out historical claims totally consonant with his brother's manifesto-like 'Advertisement' to his *Odes on Various Subjects* (1746):

> The customs, institutions, traditions, and religion, of the middle ages, were favorable to poetry. Their pageaunts, processions, spectacles, and ceremonies, were friendly to imagery, to personification and allegory. Ignorance and superstition, so opposite to the real interests of human society, are the parents of imagination. The very devotion of the Gothic times was romantic . . .
>
> Setting aside the consideration of the more solid advantages [from 'a better sense of things' produced by reason and inquiry], which are obvious . . . the lover of true poetry will ask, what have we gained by this revolution? It may be answered, much good sense, good taste, and good criticism. But, in the mean time, we have lost a set of manners, and a system of machinery, more suitable to the purposes of poetry, than those which have been adopted in their place. We have parted with extravagancies that are above propriety, with

---

35 Joseph Warton, *Odes on Various Subjects* (London, 1746), p. A2^r.
36 Thomas Warton, *The History of English Poetry*, 3 vols. (London, 1774–81), vol. 1, p. i. Further parenthetical references are to this edition.

incredibilities that are more acceptable than truth, and with fictions that are more valuable than reality.

(Thomas Warton, *The History of English Poetry*, vol. II, pp. 462–3)

Warton's text, however, offers little support for such firmly held beliefs in the judgements he makes about individual works in these volumes. Warton bemoans a loss that comes prior to the poets he most admires, indeed before Spenser, who occupies the place of honour in Warton's *Observations on the Faerie Queen* (1754).

Warton's rhetorical question above echoes his friend Richard Hurd's even better known formulation in *Letters on Chivalry and Romance* (1762): 'What we have gotten by this revolution, you will say, is a great deal of good sense. What we have lost, is a world of fine fabling' (p. 120). One may approve Warton's decision not to follow Hurd's commitment to system, but his own work threatens to dissipate through its miscellaneousness. What he offered instead of 'system' was, as his Preface puts it, 'free exertion of research'. In practice this meant that he would often go where his erudition led him. René Wellek recognises, not without a wince, Warton's penchant for bringing to bear parallels in literatures from many languages on English poetry as an anticipation of the discipline of Comparative Literature. Whereas Wellek thought that Warton's eighteenth-century historicism kept him from looking at the literature as literature, our more historical new millennium may value Warton's eye for the literary implications of those rituals he praises ('pageaunts, processions'), as in his account of the Elizabethan period, which he terms with some damage to his logic 'the most poetical age of these annals' (*The History of English Poetry*, vol. III, p. 490). To the extent that Warton succeeds, he does so as folklorist and antiquarian:

> When the queen paraded through a country-town, almost every pageant was a pantheon. When she paid a visit at the house of any of her nobility, at entering the hall she was saluted by the Penates, and conducted to her privy-chamber by Mercury. Even the pastry-cooks were expert mythologists. At dinner, select transformations of Ovid's metamorphoses were exhibited in confectionary: and the splendid iceing of an immense historic plumb-cake, was embossed with a delicious basso-relievo of the destruction of Troy . . . '
>
> (vol. III, p. 493)

The account of Anne Boleyn's coronation displays a similar sort of erudition and wit. Still, the most recent judgement of Middle English scholarship on Warton's achievement is severe: 'If the compendious *History of English Poetry* has any value today, it is principally as narrative, as literature itself, not as scholarship'.[37] In its time, however, it introduced its audience to much early literature and occupied a unique position as the pioneering literary history of England. Percy's four essays in the *Reliques*, gathered in a single volume in 1767, were the largest examination of Middle English literature prior to Warton.

Warton's unfinished history, starting after some throat-clearing with the eleventh century (no Anglo-Saxon), covers literature from the thirteenth through the sixteenth centuries, roughly from Chaucer to the Elizabethan period. The third volume concludes with Marlowe, Chapman, Barnaby Googe and prose writers, but not Shakespeare. It is a literary history, and though Warton denies at times that it is an anthology, it is that too. In fact one can find twenty-odd consecutive pages that consist of quotation of a poem with nothing but a bit of plot summary as stage setting in the text and a number of notes by Warton, as in his treatment of 'Gawain and Ywaine' (vol. III, pp. 109–34). He is capable of a tart comparative judgement. Of John Heywood, whom Queen Mary favoured, he says: 'What the FAIRY QUEEN could not procure for Spenser from the penurious Elisabeth and her precise ministers, Heywood gained by puns and conceits'(vol. III, p. 87). Perhaps his 'Exertion of research' ultimately failed him. When Warton died in 1790 he left only eighty-eight pages of the volume meant to cover the seventeenth and eighteenth centuries, though during his latter years he edited Milton's minor poems.

The poetry of Macpherson and Chatterton, while claimed as historical, was part of the making of national myth. Myth, which seemed rejected and exploded for much of the century, and was actually lurking not too far beneath the surface, would make a comeback. Blackwell anticipated this development in his *Letters concerning Mythology* (1748), but a range of seventeenth and eighteenth-century inquiries involving historians, chronologists (who attempted to reconcile biblical and historical accounts of the world's events), linguists, folklorists and others, both Deists and Christians, contributed to mythological syncretism, the attempt to find in a number of different cultures or national traditions similar mythic master narratives at work. Shelley's 'Adonais' with its melding of Hebrew Adonai and Greek Adonis is a one-word outcome of this scholarship.

Although such developments reach their apogee with the Romantics, the work of a poet born at mid-century may be a fitting place to end. William

---

37 David Matthews, *The Making of Middle English, 1765–1910* (Minneapolis, MN: University of Minnesota Press, 1999), p. xvi. For a favourable judgement, see Joseph M. Levine, 'Eighteenth-Century Historicism and the First Gothic Revival', *Humanism and History: Origins of Modern English Historiography* (Ithaca, NY: Cornell University Press, 1987), pp. 198–9.

Blake (b. 1757), whose allegiance was to imaginative truth rather than to Bacon, Newton and Locke, was one version of the reader sought throughout the later century by Collins, Cowper and others. From the perspective focussed upon here, Blake's carrying myth-making well beyond any other poet in the century is part of a logical development, one that in some sense Blake himself may have been recognising when he said 'I Believe both Macpherson & Chatterton, that what they say is Ancient, Is so . . . I own myself an admirer of Ossian equally with any other Poet whatever Rowley & Chatterton also.'[38] He believed them and learned from them. Although significant selections of older British poetry and northern poetry more generally appeared earlier, the 1760s saw an explosion of publications of such material. In addition to the *Reliques* Percy published *Five Pieces of Runic Poetry translated from the Islandic* (1763), as well as translations from Chinese and Hebrew. The bard of Gray, the poetic prose and giant figures of Macpherson, the lyricism of Chatterton, and antiquarian studies of Scandinavian literature, Druidism and even Hinduism all went into the making of Blake's poetry, as well as his religion. His artist figure Los is part of a mythology that does away with the 'silly Greek & Latin slaves of the sword' (Preface to *Milton*, p. 94) along with those heavenly bodies Mars and Saturn, who doubled as gods. Reversed, like the letters that appeared on Blake's copper plates, Los is Sol, the Sun, and a number of figures from a range of national mythologies and Blake's imagination take the place of the Greek and Roman gods and the cosmology that accompanies them. Blake's mythology is the poetic flowering of mythological syncretism.[39] It opposes an international and cosmic order to the narrow British nationalisms represented here. Los' 'I must Create a System, or be enslav'd by another Mans' (*Jerusalem*, p. 151) may be taken as Blake's recognition of the implications of Fletcher of Saltoun's aphorism with which this chapter began.

38 William Blake, 'Annotations to Wordsworth's *Poems*', *The Poetry and Prose of William Blake*, ed. David V. Erdman (Garden City, NY: Doubleday and Company, 1970), p. 655. Further parenthetical references are to this edition.
39 Burton Feldman and Robert Richardson's anthology with extensive introductions and bibliography, *The Rise of Modern Mythology 1680–1860* (Bloomington, IN: Indiana University Press, 1972), is the broadest account of this development.

PART V

*

LITERARY GENRES:
TRANSFORMATION AND NEW
FORMS OF EXPRESSIVENESS

24

Personal letters

PATRICIA MEYER SPACKS

Alexander Pope secretly arranged the publication of his own heavily manipulated letters in 1735. Lord Chesterfield employed letters to provide advice to his illegitimate son, advice that, in published form, supplied a conduct book for succeeding generations. Lady Mary Wortley Montagu gained posthumous fame by evoking life in Turkey through a series of letters published immediately after her death; James Boswell acquired early notoriety for his frivolous epistolary exchanges with another young man, published shortly after they were written. Thomas Gray's letters and William Cowper's were published, at least in part, for wide readerships soon after they died, and a selection of Horace Walpole's correspondence, chosen by him, appeared the year after his death. The familiar letters of travellers, literary celebrities and public wits attracted increasing audiences as the eighteenth century progressed in Britain. Well-codified generic rules often shaped their production. Letter-writing manuals had proliferated for several centuries, establishing public conventions for personal utterance. Yet, reading eighteenth-century correspondences from a chronological distance of more than two centuries, one can note diversity rather than conformity, feel the vigour of individual personality and marvel at the range of self-representation.

Liminalities and paradoxes mark personal letters in published form. Such letters poise between the public and the private: emanations of a solitary self, yet incomplete without an external reader; expressing the thoughts and feelings of an individual, yet couched partly in conventional terms; written for one particular other, but read by numerous originally unimaginable others; declaring authenticity but marked by artifice. Eighteenth-century interest in such paradoxes of private and public may be suggested by the proliferation of ostensible letters serving ostensibly public purposes. Political commentary, literary criticism, moral advice: a great range of substance could be discussed in the guise of published letters. Many eighteenth-century novels, of course, also assumed epistolary shape. By using the forms of personal correspondence, authors constructed a fiction of immediacy, a personal link at the foundation of their literary enterprise. They in effect invited their readers into the position of voyeurs, peering into a private exchange. The form suggested that even matters of public interest could best be discussed as the substance of intimate relationship. Personal epistolary exchange, convention had it, guaranteed authenticity. Lovelace, in Samuel Richardson's *Clarissa*, that most ambitious of epistolary novels, offers a significant false etymology for 'correspondence', declaring the word derived from the Latin word for 'heart'. His explanation calls attention to the period's dominant association of letter writing with revelation of the writer's true nature and feelings.

If the form of personal correspondence tacitly claimed directness and authenticity for public utterance, it also might stimulate awareness of acts of writing. Genuine letters as well as all other texts, in an era before the typewriter, existed as products of pens dipped in ink. The printed novels, manuals and treatises that adopted letter form by such a strategy reminded the literate of their own experiences of writing, of a person, a pen, a process preceding the published work. In this way, too, they claimed the personal as the ground of the public.

Actual personal letters written in eighteenth-century England, then, entered a textual world that abounded in printed simulacra of letters discussing diverse subjects in diverse rhetorical modes. This fact did not imply letter-writers' rush to publish their own private exchanges, although later readers might suspect that some glimpsed posterity looking over their shoulders. But awareness of the multifarious uses to which letters might be put encouraged the generic flexibility and the varying structures of artifice that mark the century's greatest letters. Literal personal letters, like their fictional imitations, offer narrative, moralising, political reflection, social data, religious meditation and literary criticism, as well as records of private emotion. Corresponding tonal shifts call attention to the rhetorical expertise letter writers employ. They often reveal self-consciousness about the act of writing and awareness of established expectation for letters as a literary mode. Asserting spontaneity and sincerity, they manifestly employ artifice. As acts of intimate communication, letters are shaped by consciousness of the receiver as well as the self. They demonstrate the intricate shifts and patternings of a form with a peculiarly complex relation both to audience and to literary convention.

No selection of eighteenth-century letters can fully convey the genre's diversities, but a small group spanning the century may indicate a representative range of subject and technique. Even a glance at letters across the period suggests marked changes between the beginning and the end of the century.[1] Pope's early letters openly reveal their performative aspects; Cowper's letters, at the century's end, declare themselves largely a record of his inner life. The difference derives from different modes of self-revelation, not from utterly opposed notions of a letter's proper functions, but it may register on the reader as a complete difference of kind.

Among many possibilities, then, this chapter will contemplate the correspondences of Alexander Pope, Lady Mary Wortley Montagu, Philip Dormer Stanhope, fourth Earl of Chesterfield, Horace Walpole, Hester Thrale Piozzi and William Cowper, most of whom demonstrated their literary skills in other genres as well. In Pope, chronologically the first of these, we find a striking concern with audience, manifest in his letters' history as well as their nature. A bizarre publication sequence, not entirely disentangled after almost three centuries, calls sharp attention to the ambiguities of letters as private exchange. Even a short version of events will suggest the difficulty of interpretation. By an elaborate series of subterfuges, Pope supplied the disreputable publisher Edmund Curll with a carefully edited selection of his letters. Curll, unaware that Pope was himself the source for the manuscript, published it in 1735 and was promptly denounced by the poet, who caused the publisher to be arraigned before parliament and made the 'unauthorised' publication the pretext for issuing another selection of his letters as 'correct'. To call the letters 'carefully edited' understates the actualities. Pope not only rewrote letters he had long ago sent; he assigned existing letters new recipients; and he may have constructed new letters for the volumes.

Critical consensus has assigned plausible reasons for Pope's behaviour. Under constant virulent attack because of his satiric writing, he had faced vituperation of his moral character as well as his literary skill. His correspondence with great men – noblemen like Lord Burlington, literary figures like

1 In 1582 Pope Gregory XIII (hence the name Gregorian Calendar) ordered ten days to be dropped from October to make up for the errors that had crept into the so-called Julian Calendar instituted by Julius Caesar, which made the year too long and added a day every one hundred and twenty-eight years. European countries adopted this calendar, which began the new year on January 1, but England and the American colonies retained the old Julian calendar, with its eleven-day difference (one added by a disagreement about a leap year) and its commencement of the year in March rather than in January until September 1752, when the extra days were added. So until then, some people in England and America used slash dates, for example 20 February 1714/15, which meant that it was already 1715 everywhere but in England and America. O.S. refers to the older Julian dating system; N.S. to the newer Gregorian calendar, which after 1752 was the standard in England and America as well.

Jonathan Swift – and his demonstration of warm friendship with such persons might help defend him against the charge of malignity. In his letters he professed more care for private virtue than for public accomplishment; such professions could also help his case. The published letters contributed to the careful construction of a powerful persona.

Even so rigid a moralist as Samuel Johnson considered Pope's manipulation of his letters a venial sin, although he conveys a certain uneasiness about the poet's epistolary artifice. Johnson observes that few collections of letters had been published before Pope's; consequently, his 'epistolary excellence had an open field'. Like many readers after him, Johnson suspected that Pope 'might have originally had publication in his mind, and have written with care, or have afterwards selected those [letters] which he had most happily conceived, or most diligently laboured'. 'Pope may be said to write always with his reputation in his head', Johnson concludes.[2] Quite apart from the question of his manoeuvres with Curll, Pope's writing as well as his editing indeed allows one to wonder whether his communications are directed towards a private recipient or to a larger collection of readers.

Such wondering could occur even to a contemporary, even, indeed, to a correspondent. Swift teases Pope as one who has 'been a writer of Letters almost from your infancy, and by your own confession had Schemes even then of Epistolary fame'.[3] Pope denies the charge, but a few months earlier he had betrayed just the kind of self-consciousness of which Swift accuses him:

> Now as I love you better than most I have met with in the world, and esteem you too the more the longer I have compar'd you with the rest of the world; so inevitably I write to you more negligently, that is more openly, and what all but such as love another will call writing worse. I smile to think how Curl would be bit, were our Epistles to fall into his hands, and how gloriously they would fall short of ev'ry ingenious reader's expectations?
>
> (28 November 1729)

The claims of negligence, and of such carelessness as a sign of love, repeat themselves in subsequent correspondence and in the writings of other voluminous letter writers. But Pope's reference to Curll, and to the possibility of tricking him, more than five years before he arranged the actual deception, indicates his constant awareness of possible publication for those epistles he

---

2 Samuel Johnson, *Lives of the English Poets*, ed. George Birkbeck Hill, 3 vols. (Oxford: Clarendon Press, 1905), vol. III, pp. 159, 160.
3 Alexander Pope, *Correspondence of Alexander Pope*, ed. George Sherburn, 5 vols. (Oxford: Clarendon Press, 1956), 26 February 1729/30. All further parenthetical references in the text are to this edition.

asserts to be the product of negligence and of love. One need not altogether doubt his assertions: he loves Swift and probably writes more spontaneously to him than to other correspondents. But a double consciousness manifests itself. Pope thinks of his letter's immediate recipient: the letters, not only to Swift but to his other correspondents, reveal complex tonalities of affection. He thinks also, though – the texts themselves reveal this fact – of every letter as above all an act of writing, therefore of shaping artifice. Compositions designed for immediate expressiveness, the letters also display immense literary skill.

In this respect, Pope's letters resemble those of other correspondents from his period (the first half of the eighteenth century) whose production has survived to our own time. Typically, these writers perform their literary power as well as fulfil the purposes of immediate communication. The kind of self-consciousness revealed in the claim of negligence is not only duplicated repeatedly by Pope, who obsessively observes the lack of 'wit' in his own 'spontaneous' writing, but also by writers like Lady Mary Wortley Montagu and Horace Walpole. A careful enactment of spontaneity manifests itself in many of the period's letters. Such artifice should not be mistaken for hypocrisy. It testifies, rather, to the literary significance accorded letters, in the eighteenth century, even in their first writing. In an era of e-mail, it may be difficult to recapture an earlier period's sense of the momentousness of words set down on paper. Although eighteenth-century epistolary convention dictated frequent claims, by their writers, of letters' worthlessness, recipients valued those letters. Recipients, indeed, in most instances paid the postage – and letters often note their happiness to do so. Writers' assertions of their own carelessness function as a token of intimacy: correspondents announce their willingness to make themselves vulnerable to literary criticism for the sake of their commitment to friendship, thus simultaneously alluding to the literary value of letters in general and disclaiming their own merits.

Pope, it goes without saying, filled an important place in eighteenth-century literary society. His friends bore names still familiar to us; his social life took him to numerous great houses. Yet his letters are often strikingly devoid of incident. The relative importance of narrative in the personal correspondence of later periods may testify to lives more obsessively filled with occupation than those of our predecessors. If the generic variety of eighteenth-century familiar letters derives partly from a relative paucity of narrative material, however, it also suggests the higher value placed on reflection and exploration, playful or serious, of ideas. Pope's letters, then, resemble those of his contemporaries and immediate successors in their emphasis on elements other than narrative.

He may briefly report events in his life – often trivial events. Thus, to his friend John Caryll:

> I'm now building a portico, in which I hope you will sit like Nestor on a stone at the gate, and converse delightfully with us, one of these days. Poetry has given place for the present, as it always does with me, to the beauties of nature and the pleasures of the spring advancing every day. I do not sing with birds; I love better to hear them. (8 March 1732/3)

The account of his building activities occupies only a few words; the letter writer emphasises, rather, his feeling for his friend. If he speaks of the pleasures of spring, he offers no detail; his elaboration focusses instead on his claim that poetry matters less to him, at least at the moment, than vague 'beauties of nature'. The assumption that his friend cares most about the writer's psychological state controls the letter's rhetoric.

Accounts of psychological states, however, remain reticent by twenty-first-century standards. Sometimes they too appear governed by convention. 'God deliver you from Law, me from Rhime!' Pope writes to William Fortescue, a lawyer friend, 'and give us leisure to attend what is more important' (23 August 1735). More elaborately (to a less close friend, Aaron Hill), 'I am very sensible, that my *Poetical* Talent is all that may make me *remember'd*: But it is my *Morality* only that must make me *Beloved*, or *Happy*' (5 February 1730/1). The claim that morality ('what is more important') matters more to him than poetry belongs to a repertoire of conventional attitudes that Pope frequently draws on – in his poetry as well as his letters. But he can also strike an utterly convincing personal note, as in this letter to Swift:

> I have every day wish'd to write to you, to say a thousand things; and yet I think I should not have writ to you now, if I was not sick of writing any thing, sick of myself, and (what is worse) sick of my friends too. The world is become too busy for me, everybody so concern'd for the publick, that all private enjoyments are lost, or disrelish'd. I write more to show you I am tired of this life, than to tell you any thing relating to it. I live as I did, I think as I did, I love you as I did: but all these are to no purpose: the world will not live, think, or love, as I do. (1 September 1733)

A sense of life's futility may also be a commonplace attitude, but Pope's formulation has an immediacy that carries conviction. His writing's force and directness contrast with the playful or elegant elaboration marking some of his other utterances in the correspondence. The broad rhetorical range that Pope displays itself supplies a substantial part of his epistolary self-construction. Style as well as substance makes the man.

If even a life as busy as Pope's supplied relatively little narrative material for letters, the lives of most eighteenth-century women yet more obviously provided scant opportunity for accounts of varied experience. Largely confined to their homes, cut off from public activity, typically limited to a repetitive round of occupations, they could hardly be expected to tell compelling stories about themselves. Yet women were, much contemporaneous evidence testifies, prolific letter writers; as Henry Tilney in Jane Austen's *Northanger Abbey* (written c. 1798, published 1818) would ironically observe, some thought them the best letter writers.

Experiments in secular autobiography remained largely tentative in eighteenth-century England. Earlier autobiographies had characteristically narrated conversion experiences, providing accounts of the spiritual life. Few women during the period ventured to try the secular form. Some kept diaries – Frances Burney's remain well known. But her diaries, like those of her contemporaries, often shaded into letters: the published version includes and draws on many letters to her sister. At this historical juncture, letter writing supplied the best opportunity for verbal self-discovery and self-invention, most especially for women. Some whose letters remain accessible, like Mary Granville Delany, conspicuously made something out of nothing, conducting for decades voluminous correspondences that created entertaining narrative out of the minutiae of ordinary daily life. Some, like the Bluestocking Elizabeth Carter, wrote letters of moral reflection, clearly intended for public view, thus declaring the importance of a female mind. Some offered accounts of their travels. All reveal ways of imagining themselves that extend well beyond what one might anticipate for women of confined lives.

Among the century's woman correspondents, Lady Mary Wortley Montagu probably was most famous. Unlike Hester Piozzi (discussed below), she did not make large public claims for herself. Unlike Elizabeth Carter, she did not assert troubling intellectual pretensions. The Turkish letters, accounts of her exotic experience during her husband's ambassadorship, offered both entertainment and information. Only this portion of Lady Mary's extensive correspondence reached publication during the eighteenth century, but we can now read much more. Absorbing though the Turkish material is, the other letters reveal more about their writer's gift for unexpected self-imagining. For much of her adult life, Lady Mary lived in Italy, in self-imposed exile from her country and her husband (only after his death did she return to England). She led a quiet existence, seeing few people of her own social class, immersing herself in such domestic pursuits as raising chickens. Through it all she wrote brilliant letters (especially to her daughter), using them to reflect on her own situation and the female situation in general and demonstrating a value system based on other criteria than public accomplishment.

Even Lady Mary's earlier letters, though, written before she left England and before she focussed on a reflective mode, reveal the kind of mental agility so attractive in Pope's correspondence – but mental agility with a female inflection. She wrote often to her depressed sister, Lady Mar, who eventually sank into incurable mental illness. Trying to entertain, she spun narrative out of the minutiae of social life and even out of her own lack of activity. 'Here, what between the Things one can't do and the Things one must not do, the Time but dully lingers on, thô I make as good a shift as any of my Neighbors.' This claim of ennui precedes a paragraph of delightful gossip, which, even while maintaining that 'There is no such thing as Love or Pleasure' in the immediate environment, mentions the various love affairs currently taking place in high life.[4]

Centuries after the names of participants in those love affairs can have meaning for most readers, the allusions to current scandal retain literary vitality by virtue of the energetic consciousness that originates them. Although Lady Mary rarely sounds moralistic or even explicitly judgemental, she constantly assesses herself and her milieu for interest and for value. The 'value' that proves relevant involves morality less often than entertainment: more specifically, the perceived needs and desires of a letter's recipient. More consistently even than Pope, Lady Mary writes always in manifest awareness of the person who will read what she produces. That fact is nowhere more apparent than in the flirtatious correspondence with Pope himself, her exact contemporary, during her time in Turkey, when the two constructed elaborate personae (Lady Mary's mainly cynical, Pope's extravagantly romantic) and engaged in mutually entertaining persiflage. Pope perhaps had more at stake in their exchanges, but both demonstrate extraordinary skill at imagining versions of themselves for the purpose of responsiveness. The personalities at work in these letters do not appear elsewhere in the correspondence of either participant.

Artifice once more, of course – but artifice in the service of communication. The unadorned self, these writers assume, is of no interest to anyone but itself. To make the effort to invent versions of selfhood that will answer the desires of a correspondent amounts to nothing less than genuine concern for another. Paradoxically, this kind of artifice exists for the sake of sincerity. It provides the disguise that makes communication possible.

---

4 *The Complete Letters of Lady Mary Wortley Montagu*, ed. Robert Halsband, 3 vols. (Oxford: Clarendon Press, 1965), October 1723. Further parenthetical references are to this edition.

To trace a single person's letters over a period of many years allows one to see how disguises change over time, and how various masks serve various purposes. The appeal of collections of letters lies partly here; the excellent twentieth-century editions of most of the letters that have been mentioned facilitate chronological reading. Although stylistic idiosyncrasies may persist through an entire series of correspondences, shifting stances are also manifest. Lady Mary's letters begin in her girlhood, before her marriage, and extend almost to her death. They include letters to her husband and to her ne'er-do-well son, as well as to her sister and her daughter. They incorporate the record of her romance with Edward Wortley Montagu, which led to her elopement and her unhappy marriage, and of an unsatisfactory later romance with a much younger Italian man, which preceded her move to Italy. In short, they tell the story of her life. More important: they tell the story of the defences she adopted in order to live that life.

An example from her early correspondence paired with one from her later years will illustrate a dramatic change in her epistolary persona. The early instance – she was twenty years old at the time – comes from her correspondence with Ann Wortley, her future husband's sister, during the period of uneasy courtship, throughout which Lady Mary sounds perpetually unsure about whether or not Wortley likes her. The letter at issue, though, concerns not Wortley's feelings but her own, and how she represents them.

> My dear, people never write calmly, but when they write indifferently. That I should ever do so to you, I take to be entirely impossible; I must be always very much pleased or in very great affliction: as you tell me of your friendship, or unkindly doubt mine. I can never allow even prudence and sincerity to have any thing to do with one another. At least I have always found it so in myself, who being devoted to the one, had never the least tincture of the other. What I am now doing, is a very good proof of what I say, 'tis a plain undesigning truth – your friendship is the only happiness of my life; and whenever I lose it, I have nothing to do but to take one of my garters and search for a convenient beam . . . Prudence is at the very time saying to me, are you mad; you won't send this dull, tedious, insipid, long letter to Mrs Wortley, will you? 'tis the direct way to tire out her patience. (21 August 1709)

Although it is not difficult to discern the authentic feeling in these lines, Lady Mary never openly acknowledges the nature of that feeling: the painful uncertainty in which she exists. She professes, and no doubt experiences, affection for her correspondent, but she obviously exaggerates the degree of affection, claiming it as her only happiness and announcing suicide as her only recourse if the relationship ruptures. Shifting poses protect her against the ravages of self-doubt, as she insists that she operates on the basis of sincerity rather than prudence, only to announce that prudence makes her question whether to send the letter. She claims the 'plain undesigning truth' of what she says, but moves immediately to the highly rhetorical invocation of beam and garter. The variable persona itself declares the unsureness that dominates the letter.

A twenty-first-century reader may find it most compelling to seek psychological revelation here, but the shifting tones and modes hold interest in themselves, illustrating the range of rhetorical resources available to even an inexperienced writer. The years of voluminous letter writing – which were also, of course, years of experience in life – brought Lady Mary greater sureness, or more control. In writing to her daughter, she adopts the consistent and effective voice of a woman of wisdom reflecting on the basis of long knowledge of life. Sometimes the voice sounds especially world-weary, but always it proclaims a certain distance from immediate happening. The power and appeal of the letters to Lady Bute (Lady Mary's daughter, married to John Stuart, 3rd Earl of Bute, the Prime Minister of Britain) comes from the combination of great energy (the same energy of observation notable in the much earlier letters to her sister) with the slightly remote tone of wisdom. An extended quotation will be necessary to demonstrate:

> I pity Lady M[ary] Cooke extreamly. You will be surpriz'd at this Sentiment when she is the present Envy of her Sex, in the possession of Youth, Health, Wealth, Wit, Beauty and Liberty. [Lady Mary Cooke's husband had recently died.] All these seeming Advantages will prove Snares to her. She appears to me walking blindfold upon Stilts, amid precipices. She is at a dangerous time of Life, when the passions are in full vigour, and we are apt to flatter our selves the understanding arriv'd at Maturity. People are never so near playing the Fool as when they think themselves wise. They lay aside that distrust which is the surest Guard against Indiscretion, and venture on many steps they would have tremble'd at, at fiveteen, and like children are never so much expos'd to falling as when they first leave off leading-strings. (1 March 1754)

The letter goes on to suggest that Lady Mary Cooke has one valuable resource at her disposal: her 'great Turn to Oeconomy', which the letter writer had long ago noticed. That, the letter continues, 'is an admirable shield against the most fatal weaknesses'.

The reflections on the young widow epitomise the shrewd judgement and energetic expression that mark Lady Mary Wortley Montagu's late letters. Her figure of walking blindfold on stilts among precipices lends startling concreteness to her concerns about an unprotected young woman. The nature of her concern corroborates her many letters about the upbringing of her grandchildren, in which she worries particularly about the girls, who will, she knows, live restricted lives despite their rank and privilege. Education, she writes, is the only help. Women who cultivate their minds will have resources to protect them, resources equivalent to Lady Mary Cooke's 'Turn to Oeconomy', also a mental capacity. Any young woman who runs away with a man, like Richardson's Clarissa, is a fool, this observer maintains. She writes from experience: she herself eloped, disastrously. The aura of clear-headed, faintly cynical practicality that envelops her comments on a vulnerable young woman persists through many of the letters, which never lapse into sentimentality and strikingly avoid self-pity.

Like other correspondences that have survived from the eighteenth century, Lady Mary's letters provide abstracts and brief chronicles of the time, as well as of individual lives; countless historians have mined them for data. By reading Lady Mary's communications, we learn not only of her rather eccentric personal life but of lives that take place around her, of customs that control those lives and of assumptions she and others bring to their daily exchanges. In addition to providing social data, letters also supply abundant psychological material: the stuff of novels, whether or not the letter writer acknowledges the fact. *Pamela*, Samuel Richardson's first, wildly popular epistolary novel, originated in a model letter he wrote for his handbook on letter writing. That was an imagined rather than an actual letter, but many genuine interchanges carry the same kind of plot potential. And, as the examples already cited indicate, not only the substance of what is said but the elegance, energy and originality of *how* creates these letters' appeal.

In some instances, such qualities as elegance and energy of style convey the substance of letters' communication. Lord Chesterfield's notorious instructions to his awkward illegitimate son, conveyed in a long correspondence, come to mind. The father's fundamental message is 'grace', which his letters embody. Lord Chesterfield's letters clarify the high value his period placed on social performance as an index of moral quality. Behaviour in society can exemplify an individual's attitude towards responsibility towards others and towards the self. The letters themselves, in Chesterfield's case, constitute social performance. Although intended for a single person (and despite the letters' high polish, there is no indication that their writer thought of publication), these verbal constructions demonstrate the force of an integrated set of values put into practice as interpersonal behaviour. Lord Chesterfield practises what he preaches: carefully controlled self-presentation and self-representation, always calculated in relation to its witnesses. The fact that his intensive efforts to shape his son in his own model ultimately failed perhaps suggests the system's limitation: no amount of calculation can finally control another person.

For readers long after the letters were written, Lord Chesterfield's performance manifests charm and wisdom, as well as a sometimes chilling sense of expediency. The father preaches hard work and constant attentiveness:

> I hope you employ your whole time, which few people do; and that you put every moment to profit of some kind or other. I call company, walking, riding, etc., employing one's time, and, upon proper occasions, very usefully; but what I cannot forgive in anybody is sauntering, and doing nothing at all, with a thing so precious as time, and so irrecoverable when lost.[5]

Thus even recreation becomes useful occupation. Chesterfield's tacit vision of progress depends, in the case of his son, on the possibility of transmitting effectively the lessons of his own life. So he criticises his past self unsparingly: for wasting time, for engaging in dissipation, for pursuing false notions of what will make him admired as a social being. If only his son can start life at the point of wisdom his father has painfully attained, the youth will be marked for success. Lord Chesterfield's fantasies recur: Stanhope will succeed him in parliament, or as Secretary of State; his son may even excel him. In the role of Pygmalion, he wishes to shape the being of a single man, to mould his male Galatea into that glimmering ideal, the man of the world.

The implications of that hackneyed phrase are for Chesterfield far-reaching. Contemplation of his correspondence reveals a set of hopeful cultural assumptions powerful in the eighteenth century. The theme of using time effectively, which reverberates through many of the letters, implies the peculiar optimism that marked much eighteenth-century thought – frequently in combination with equally conspicuous pessimism. Chesterfield appears to believe in almost infinite perfectibility. He acknowledges that no man is perfect – even as he articulates his desire that his son be exactly that. If only the boy will use every minute for self-improvement, he can attain almost unimaginable heights. The father tells a story of a man who buys a 'common edition' of Horace and every day tears out three or four pages to take with him to the 'necessary house'. While he performs his acts of excretion, he simultaneously refreshes his knowledge of the Latin poet. Finally he uses the sheets as toilet paper. Lord Chesterfield recommends the same course of intellectual and

---

5 *Letters of Philip Dormer Stanhope, Earl of Chesterfield*, ed. John Bradshaw, 3 vols. (London: George Allen & Unwin, 1892), 9 December O.S. 1746. Further parenthetical references are to this edition.

physical economy to his son, with no apparent sense of comedy. It partakes of the ideal, the vision of no moment unused, of the mind continually enriching itself.

The mind is much at issue here. The ordinary connotations of 'man of the world' emphasise the practice of social ritual rather than the development of personal virtue. For Chesterfield, though, ritual and virtue go hand in hand. He emphasises in the letters the importance of 'pleasing', of finding ways to ingratiate oneself with others so that those others might be willing to do a favour at some crucial time. But his definition of pleasing suggests the high seriousness of the matter: 'Do as you would be done by, is the surest method that I know of pleasing' (16 October O.S. 1747). That Lord Chesterfield recommends the Golden Rule will come as a surprise to readers who expect of him the morals of a whore, to recall Johnson's famous characterisation of the letters. To be sure, he recommends the Golden Rule as a matter of expediency. To read the letters as a whole, however, raises the possibility that expediency is a mask. At any rate, one must feel the tension between the nobleman's professed concern with surfaces and his almost obsessive insistence on the importance of getting to the bottom of things. 'Whatever you do, do it to the purpose; do it thoroughly, not superficially. *Approfondissez*: go to the bottom of things. Any thing half done or half known, is, in my mind, neither done nor known at all' (18 February O.S. 1748). He wants his son to seek out good company. But 'good company' means not only aristocrats (although Chesterfield shows lively appreciation of the usefulness of keeping company with those of rank and power), but also men of intellectual substance: he himself, he claims, values his association with Mr Pope and Mr Addison more than his connections with the aristocracy. The perfect man he imagines possesses the kind of social grace that will attract people of moral and intellectual weight and declare the high development of his mind and soul.

The alleged tension between concern with surfaces and with depths is perhaps a twenty-first-century imposition. Certainly Lord Chesterfield himself, far from acknowledging potential conflict between the two focusses of attention, deliberately brings them into conjunction over and over again, precisely to insist that no conflict exists. The tactic emphasises the momentousness of the writer's concern with social conduct. He takes this matter seriously because he assumes that relations among human beings entail their highest earthly obligations, their responsibilities to community and ultimately to society. Hence the Golden Rule as principle of pleasing. Manners reflect morals: an assumption still current as late as Jane Austen, and crucial to the period's understanding of itself.

Chesterfield's explicit reference to moral implication decreases, however. Like other collections of letters, Chesterfield's imply a narrative: in this case a narrative of his hopes for his son. At the beginning, when young Stanhope is fifteen years old, his father's hopes and expectations appear boundless. The early letters vibrate with intellectual as well as social aspiration. But Lord Chesterfield appears to have a network of spies throughout Europe. He receives frequent reports about his son – reports that emphasise, with striking consistency, the young man's social awkwardness. Despite his father's ceaseless injunctions ('the Graces, the Graces, the Graces'), the youth seems clumsy in company. He may, observers hint, be overweight. He enunciates badly and talks too fast. His father offers detailed prescriptions, but the negative reports continue. Stanhope turns sixteen, seventeen, eighteen; still observers note – with what degree of tact we can only surmise – his social ineptitude. Presumably as a result, Lord Chesterfield begins to write that he feels complete confidence in his son's intellectual and moral development and to stress ever more frantically the importance of allegedly superficial kinds of excellence. The impression a man makes on others will determine his opportunities in life. Style has determinative force. 'If you write epistles as well as Cicero, but in a very bad hand, and very ill-spelled, whoever receives will laugh at them; and if you had the figure of Adonis, with an awkward air and motions, it will disgust instead of pleasing. Study manner, therefore, in everything, if you would be anything' (19 November O.S. 1750). Lord Chesterfield never acknowledges his fear, but the increasing desperation of his recommendations about 'manner' and his warnings that he has observers everywhere, suggest the dawning realisation that all his care may come to nothing.

Whether one reads this as a tragic tale may depend on one's interpretation of Lord Chesterfield's 'manner'. The letters make it apparent that he consciously strives to embody in his prose the values he recommends. The suavity, authority and ease of the letters represent the aristocratic stance that he wishes his son to attain. One function of that stance is concealment: the gentleman, Chesterfield insists, protects his personal feelings and reveals them to no one. Suavity, authority and ease conceal, one may surmise, disappointment and finally, perhaps, discouragement. The ideal of using one's time fully, of perceiving sharply and consciously and making full use of one's perceptions (most people, Lord Chesterfield points out, don't see what they see or hear what they hear), of approaching perfection by disciplined thought, feeling and action – this impossibly ambitious ideal cannot be fulfilled. The father must finally use his manner to conceal the pain of his failure.

In the spectrum of eighteenth-century personal letters, this correspondence represents a formal extreme, exemplifying the high polish of a fully developed literary style infused with conviction of the intimate relation between style and substance. Chesterfield's intense awareness of his own practice appears less explicitly in the letters of men quite different from him, men, unlike him, not at all concerned with the didactic. Chesterfield virtually eschews narrative in letters to his son; his aristocratic contemporary, Horace Walpole, makes narrative his primary epistolary currency. Like Chesterfield, he reveals little directly about his psychic life; like Chesterfield and his other contemporaries, he suggests far more than he says. His voluminous correspondences (the letters have been collected in a forty-nine-volume modern edition), directed to friends of different sorts in different places, consciously and openly expose a great deal about the cultural life of his time, at least in the upper reaches of society. They also delineate new possibilities for how letters might draw upon other generic models.

Sometimes Walpole writes about politics; sometimes he engages in gossip; sometimes he details his activities on his beloved estate, Strawberry Hill, reporting on building and gardening; sometimes he tells of public events. Always his delight in narrative infuses his prose. He writes with a vividness that seems utterly unselfconscious, and writes as one who sees what he sees and hears what he hears to the fullest possible extent. Here he is on the funeral of George II:

> When we came to the chapel of Henry VII all solemnity and decorum ceased – no order was observed, people sat or stood where they could or would, the yeomen of the guard were crying out for help, oppressed by the immense weight of the coffin, the Bishop read sadly, and blundered in the prayers, the fine chapter, *Man that is born of a woman*, was chanted not read, and the anthem, besides being unmeasurably tedious, would have served as well for a nuptial . . . [Walpole then describes, with considerable sympathy, the Duke of Cumberland, a seriously ill son of the dead man.] This grave scene was fully contrasted by the burlesque Duke of Newcastle – he fell into a fit of crying the moment he came into the chapel and flung himself back in a stall, the Archbishop hovering over him with a smelling bottle – but in two minutes his curiosity got the better of his hypocrisy and he ran about the chapel with his glass to spy who was or was not there, spying with one hand and mopping his eyes with t'other.[6]

6 Horace Walpole, Selected Letters, ed. W. S. Lewis (New Haven, CT: Yale University Press, 1973), To George Montagu, 13 November 1760. Further parenthetical references are to this edition.

The brilliant perception of detail creates much of the sequence's energy, but one may also note the fine sense of action that informs, for example, the long succession of clauses strung together with commas in the first sentence, which comically duplicates in its syntax the disorder that it narrates. Walpole also reveals his intense interest in character, and in the tiny clues to character that any scene provides. And he shows a sharply judgemental mind combined with an eye for the comic. The burlesque Duke of Newcastle stands out brilliantly, and the writer leaves us in no doubt about what he thinks of the man. Yet his capacity for sympathy also emerges, in his account of the other duke, 'his face bloated and distorted with his late paralytic stroke', standing at the edge of a crypt that he may soon expect to inhabit himself.

The dramatic energy, focus and style that such a passage displays might figure equally well in a novel, and indeed one feels everywhere in Walpole's letters a novelistic delight in the interplay of character and in the nuances of scene. When he travels to France, he interests himself particularly in the characters of the women he meets, and in how the development of those characters is affected by their cultural context. Awareness of human suffering tempers his wicked pen; consciousness of common humanity modifies his aristocratic arrogance. Whether or not the events of his life hold obvious interest for others, he can make of them a story absorbing not only to himself but presumptively to his audience.

That audience, the original audience, is diverse: men and women, aristocrats and commoners, old friends and relatively new ones. Walpole's awareness of who will receive his letter manifestly shapes both his choice of subject – politics or landscaping or poetry or social event – and of style. Although always triumphantly artful, the writer varies his register from rollicking to melancholy. The melancholy note seems a particular sign of intimacy: with old friends like John Chute he allows himself to meditate on his own feelings at, for instance, Thomas Gray's death. Gray had been an intimate friend of his youth, but the two men were alienated for a time after a trip they took together to the Continent. Walpole reads of Gray's death in the newspaper and feels overwhelmed. His account of his own reactions is moving:

> As self lies so rooted in self, no doubt the nearness of our ages made the stroke recoil to my own breast; and having so little expected his death, it is plain how little I expect my own. Yet to you, who of all men living are the most forgiving, I need not excuse the concern I feel. I fear most men ought to apologize for their want of feeling, instead of palliating that sensation when they have it. I thought that what I had seen of the world had hardened my heart; but I find

that it had formed my language, not extinguished my tenderness. In short, I am really shocked – nay, I am hurt at my own weakness, as I perceive that when I love anybody, it is for my life; and I have had too much reason not to wish that such a disposition may very seldom be put to the trial. You, at least, are the only person to whom I would venture to make such a confession.

(5 August 1771)

Although there is a certain amount of self-aggrandisement in this outpouring (the claim that Walpole himself, unlike most men, suffers from excess rather than deficiency of feeling; the assertion that he loves for life), the real shock that the writer claims emerges sharply from his reflections. His compliments to Chute, the most forgiving of men, the only person to whom the mourner can confess his feelings, testify to how intensely Walpole now wishes to hold on to the friends remaining. He conveys grief, confusion, affection, self-congratulation – and characteristic awareness of his own egotism, self thinking always of self, even as he mourns.

The contrast between the passage on the king's burial and that on Walpole's reaction to Gray's death marks the polarities of this vast collection of letters. The writer's range derives partly from his sense of audience, partly from his fine self-awareness, partly from the breadth of his experience and the intensity of his attention to it. But the reader may also feel conscious of Walpole's unusual commitment to the full scope of his own feelings. In the account of the burial, emotion emerges only indirectly, yet distinctly; in the contemplation of a friend's loss, emotion makes the primary subject. Cool amusement, a spectator's delight in detail, sympathetic and apprehensive awareness of human mortality: such feelings work in the narrative of public ceremony. They contrast with the immediate sense of loss, confusion and clinging (holding on to himself and to his living friend) that mark the paragraph about Gray. One of Walpole's great gifts as a correspondent is his capacity to recognise and to render both emotional webs.

The letters prove as rich in ideas as in feelings. Walpole was intellectually playful, and his correspondence shows him jokingly trying to puzzle out what time sequences might be like on a newly discovered planet or thinking about how a world dominated by balloon travel would operate. He holds firm and often iconoclastic literary opinions: epic is an over-rated genre, belonging to antiquity and not to be imitated in modern times; the *Aeneid* lacks invention, good sense, variety and power over the passions; Dr Johnson displays 'teeth-breaking diction' (To William Mason, 3 April 1775); Boswell is ridiculous; Chatterton and Macpherson are frauds. He has vigorous political opinions, which he repeatedly elaborates, particularly about the war with the American colonies. (His sympathies are with the Americans.) He thinks about the nature of family responsibility, of friendship, of social life. Although he shows himself altogether capable of abstract thought, his ideas ring with special force because he draws on concrete details in expounding them. The letters, then, reveal the psychic operations of a man who both thinks and feels powerfully.

To emphasise Walpole's great range of subject and of approach calls attention to his sharp difference from Chesterfield, whose concentration on a single set of issues shapes the letters to his son, and whose letters are intended for a single recipient. Yet Walpole himself implicitly notes a crucial affinity to Chesterfield. In an important letter to John Pinkerton, author of a critical book entitled *Letters of Literature*, Walpole discusses reasons for the popularity of some writers of whom Pinkerton disapproves. He explicitly disclaims a role as disciple of Lord Chesterfield, but the quality he finds in all these writers – Virgil, Waller, Addison, Horace and others – is *grace*, which Walpole considers a quality of 'manner', and something more than style. Although he gives many examples, he never defines his term. Perhaps he comes closest to suggesting its nature when he notes his admiration of Addison's phrase, 'that Virgil tossed about his dung with an air of majesty' (26 June 1785).

For Chesterfield, 'grace' unites social, moral and aesthetic implication. Walpole makes less momentous claims, but his notion of 'manner' as greater than style suggests belief in the urgency of conveying personality through language. Grace of manner indeed characterises his letters: an elegance that communicates both vitality and polish and that creates the conviction that these are qualities of the man himself.

The 'grace' of Walpole's letters makes them seem highly meditated performances, but he is at pains to disclaim meditation. In 1778, at the age of sixty, he wrote Lady Ossory, complaining that she praises his letters excessively and reads them too carefully. 'It is impossible', he writes, 'to be quite easy and simple, while one thinks one's letters will be read more deliberately than they are written' (27 September 1778). He doesn't want to have 'Posterity' in mind when he writes. He tries only to be humble and natural. If such protestations sound disingenuous for a man who asked his friends to save his letters, a man with his eye clearly on posterity, one may also understand that the only way he could in practice write his charming, witty letters was to forget for the moment that they would have other readers than the ones immediately intended. Walpole always objects vigorously when he learns that someone is showing his communications to others. Six weeks before his death (at the age of seventy-nine), he begins a letter to Lady Ossory, 'You distress me infinitely by showing my idle notes, which I cannot conceive can amuse anybody' (15 January 1797). By this time such remarks are more than perfunctory: as many of the letters show, Walpole worries that his life has become so devoid of event that he no longer has material for entertainment. To the end, though, he struggles to convert even the most minimal happening into substance that might enlighten, amuse or enliven others. His standards of grace were very high indeed.

Some version of 'grace', an expressive mode deftly combining spontaneity with artifice, characterises all the writers discussed so far: Pope and Lady Mary as well as Walpole and Chesterfield. But not every well-known and readable correspondent of the period attempts the same kind of polish. Hester Thrale Piozzi exemplifies an epistolary virtue remote from Chesterfield's: that of gusto. For an elegant manner she substitutes an impression of energy barely under control. The bursting enthusiasm with which she records her thoughts, intuitions and speculations, as well as her experience, asserts a feminine sensibility sharply different from Lady Mary's, as also from more philosophical contemporaries like Elizabeth Carter, but meaningful even in its apparent incoherence.

Piozzi during her lifetime published her own correspondence with Dr Johnson, winning considerable mockery as a result (for her vanity in publishing and for the foolishness she sometimes displays in her exchanges with the great man). Her voluminous mass of other letters appeared only posthumously; not all the letters have yet been published. Like her personal journals (published as *Thraliana*), the letters proclaim a kind of artlessness that often endangers lucidity. Their insistent gaiety sometimes sounds a bit desperate, but Piozzi takes seriously a writer's obligation to be entertaining.

A typical example of her style and substance comes from a letter to her eldest daughter, Hester Maria Thrale ('Queeney'). Written on her European honeymoon with Gabriel Piozzi, an Italian musician whom she had married against the intense opposition of friends and children, the letter, like others from the period, suggests her determination to show that she is happy. But it also reveals something more, as Piozzi comments on the difference between London and Paris:

> A Town so very full of People and all so apparently *idle*, is no unobservable Contrast to our London, where even the Maid Servant who sits by a Soldier's Side in St James's Park – pretending to buy Milk for her Master the Linen drapers little Boy – looks hurried as she listens to the rough Courtship of her Sweetheart; and wipes her Face, & wishes to be at home; & wipes her Face again, but can't get the Anxiety off of it. *Here* nobody seems to be *expected* to

be busy; all sit, & chat, and call for Ice to cool them, tho' no appearance of Heat or Haste is discernible in their Countenances or Manner: The Servant lifts himself and his rich Laced Coat leisurely up the Derriere of his tranquil Lady's Equipage, and taking out his Snuffbox looks as if he would never cease to wonder at the Fatigue supported by our dapper Footmen . . . [7]

Piozzi here displays not only her sharp powers of observation but her imaginative energy. The vignette of the London servant girl, in a gratuitous but vivid touch assigned a linen draper as employer, reports on nothing the writer has specifically seen. It gives brilliant specificity to a type figure conceived in order to make the point about Paris. Piozzi expresses her culture shock by speculating about human consciousness. She invents the psyches that interest her, richly interpreting appearances in order to accord them immediate human significance as well as sociological meaning. She conveys an intricate mix of nostalgia for the sharply remembered ways of London and slightly wistful wonder at the different ways of Paris, where anxiety seems less widely diffused.

One can feel the strain in the careful paragraph, even without the biographical information that accounts for it. Mother and daughter had recently engaged in cruel acrimony; Queeney's contempt for Gabriel Piozzi appalled and saddened the woman who had committed herself to this Italian Catholic of dubious social standing. The specific strain resulting from the family situation expresses itself in literary terms, as a felt obligation to be entertaining. Piozzi creates and meets her own literary challenge, denying psychic distress (which might be thought to reflect on her marital choice) and transforming trivia into cause for reflection and delight.

The cost of the determination to entertain, which imbues even letters concerned with difficulty, illness or death, sometimes registers in a certain incoherence. War, politics, adultery and friendship (with Hannah More) tumble after one another in a paragraph from a later letter to Queeney:

Poor Lady Nelson whom last Week we looked upon as the happiest of our present Race of human Beings, some of us now regard with Compassion – since it has been said that her brave Husband tho' warm and tender in Defence of Italy, is not however wholly *disinterested:* a lovely Neapolitan holds the Victor in *her* Chains I'm told – let us see if Lord St Vincent succouring Lisbon will be caught in a like Snare, and renew the Old Ballad of the Spanish Lady. He will

7 *The Piozzi Letters: Correspondence of Hester Lynch Piozzi, 1784–1821*, eds. Edward A. Bloom and Lillian D. Bloom. 5 vols. (Newark, DE: University of Delaware Press, 1989), 14 September 1784). Further parenthetical references are to this edition.

I trust have *his* Ship freighted soon with the old crazy Queen of Portugal –
Things do go on ripening apace – Yet Hannah More says, notwithstanding all
She sees, and hears, and understands; that Affairs will take a *Crane-neck Turn,*
(that's her Expression:) and strike us all with Wonder, Joy, and Gratitude.

(12 February 1799)

Notes to the recent edition of Piozzi's letters elucidate the references, but
they hardly matter to the effect. The colliding interests of a vigorous consciousness dramatise themselves vividly in shifts of direction, obvious pleasure in
language, delight in trivial mental activity, the claim to know everything that's
going on. All Piozzi's letters manifest the same vigorous commitment to the
personal movements of consciousness. She seems willing to write about anything. The same letter to Queeney continues, four paragraphs later, 'The Idea
of the World being created by seven Angels seems to have originated from the
Seven Golden Candlesticks expressive of the *Seven* Spirits which Stand before
God's Throne' – and off she goes, speculating about the tradition of divination
and the relation between theology and trickery. One wonders what Queeney
made of it all.

In the course of his reflections on Pope's letters, Dr Johnson takes up the
question of 'hypocrisy' in personal correspondence. He points out the fallacy
of believing that 'the true characters of men may be found in their letters',
suggesting, on the contrary, that there is 'no transaction which offers stronger
temptations to fallacy and sophistication than epistolary intercourse'.[8]
Conversation encourages unpremeditated utterance; letters, written in leisure,
are calculated performances. Moreover, one has special incentive to present
himself attractively to a friend, whose good opinion one presumably values.
But this fact should not, Johnson says, be considered to imply the hypocrisy
of personal letters. People may represent themselves in letters as better
than they are, but they deceive themselves as well as their friends in the
process.

This characteristically hard-headed commentary in effect warns readers
against seeking authentic personality in private correspondence. Yet the pleasure of reading collections of letters, particularly at a chronological distance,
includes the possibility of glimpsing – or imagining – that one has found exactly
that. The letters of the eighteenth century, collected in multi-volume editions,
allow us to witness developments of rhetoric and attitudes over many years.
Piozzi's letters, like Pope's and Walpole's, often adjust the same material for

8 Johnson, *Lives of the English Poets*, vol. III, pp. 206, 207.

different recipients, relaying anecdotes and opinions a second time, or even a third or fourth, in slightly different form. Such minute and innocent modifications illustrate the processes of calculation, showing a writer devising subtly different versions of him- or herself according to the perceived needs, desires or expectations of a particular reader. One could hardly call this process 'fallacy and sophistication' – it entails no falsehood – but it dramatises the distance of letter writing from the unpremeditated.

Yet premeditation hardly implies inauthenticity. Like all self-representations, those in letters are multiply mediated. To read Piozzi's letters, for example, over an extended period allows the belated reader a prolonged encounter with a personality in action. Such letters recreate the vitality of individual character, reminding us on what small substance life's little dramas depend and how vividly character differentiates itself by response to minor happening. Piozzi's letters, tumbling all over themselves, communicate the delight of experience's sheer multiplicity; Pope's elegantly controlled utterances transmit his sense of a saving decorum that regulates emotional as well as economic exchange. Both correspondents, however, as well as many others whose letters have survived, speak to a period alien to their own of the private underpinnings of public events. Even Walpole, privy to matters of national interest, reporting on courts and politics, creates more interest in his personal responses than in large happenings.

The finest letter writer of the century's late years, William Cowper, provides evidence in his correspondence of how greatly epistolary ideals had changed since the early century. The elegance of his prose, unlike Pope's, conceals itself. Less eccentric than Piozzi in his verbal associations, he resembles her in the insistence (quiet, but no less powerful for that) with which he asserts his personality. Piozzi travels; the great cities of the Continent provide substance for her letters. Cowper goes nowhere. Subject to crippling depression, in the grip of what many would call religious delusion, he occupies himself with small routines and intimate pleasures. He reports his cat's antics and his rabbit's, the change of seasons, the health of his companion, Mary Unwin; he tells of gardening and assumes the urgency and ubiquity of prayer. His letters contain momentous material only inasmuch as they report the vagaries of his mental state and the progress of his poetry. Yet they retain the power to delight.

In a sense, the implicit ideal for a 'good letter' remains identical to that Pope assumed: the direct transmission of personality. But the concept of personality has changed. The late-century letter writer does not construct for communication a version of a proto-civic ideal. His implicit ideal appears to be private and personal. He exists for himself and for God; he enables his friends to see how he appears to himself rather than how he would wish to appear to a dispassionate judge. Such, at any rate, is the impression created by his letters, which offer glimpses of life apparently without decoration or disguise. We may imagine that 'fallacy and sophistication' devised those glimpses, but no *impression* of fallacy and sophistication remains.

When Cowper writes about his own poetry, he sometimes falls into brief self-congratulation. Characteristically, his recovery is charming:

> Running over what I have written, I feel that I should blush to send it to any but thyself. Another would charge me with being impelled by a vanity from which my conscience sets me clear, to speak so much of myself and my verses as I do. But I thus speak to none but thee, nor to thee do I thus speak from any such motives. I egotize in my letters to thee, not because I am of much importance to myself, but because to thee, both *Ego* and all that *Ego* does, is interesting. God doth know that when I labour most to excel as a poet, I do it under such mortifying impressions of the vanity of all human fame and glory, however acquired, that I wonder I can write at all.[9]

This sequence comes from a letter to his cousin, Lady Hesketh, with whom the poet has had a long, affectionate relationship. Cowper converts a moment of apparent self-absorption into a compliment. Instead of apologising, he insists that things are not as they seem: he does not value his writing when he thinks of matters eternal, as he frequently does – the body of the correspondence demonstrates this fact. His correspondent values him more highly than he values himself, the letter suggests; in the freedom of intimate relationship, he can allow himself both egotism and its explanation.

He can also allow himself playfulness. Two more instances from letters to Lady Hesketh suggest the kind of tone and subject that makes his letters delightful:

> My little dog was on the point of killing a most beautiful pheasant . . . but fortunately the Gardener caught him in his arms time enough to prevent it. Beau, the handsomest creature in the world were it not for the extreme brevity of his tail, observing the pheasant's felicity in that respect whose tail was of a length unexampled, conceived envy at the sight and wood [sic] have slain him. Foolish creature, could he by killing him have made that tail his own, who would not have laughed at a dog's rump adorned with a pheasant's tail! So little do we sometimes understand our own true advantage.

(12 May 1788)

---

9 *The Letters and Prose Writings of William Cowper*, eds. James King and Charles Ryskamp. 5 vols. (Oxford: Clarendon Press, 1979–81), 6 June 1789. Further parenthetical references are to this edition.

The moralising reflection, like the interpretation of Beau's action, partakes of playfulness, and both make an utterly trivial episode (nothing happens, after all: the dog might have, perhaps would have, killed a pheasant, but he did not) entertaining and even provide a brief illusion of substance.

A final instance:

> I have made in the Orchard the best Winter walk in all the parish, shelter'd from the East and from the North East, and open to the Sun, except at his rising, all the day. Then we will have Homer and Don Quixote, and then we will have saunter and Chat, and one Laugh more before we die. Our Orchard is alive with creatures of all kinds, poultry of ev'ry denomination swarms in it, and pigs the drollest in the world. By that time indeed they will have ceased to be pigs and will probably be converted into pork or bacon, but we have also a most fruitful sow from whom we expect a continual and endless succession of pigs similar to these.   (27 June 1788)

The passage mingles present and anticipated future. The winter walk, the poultry and the pigs exist in the present, given meaning by the writer's lively evocation; in the proximate future, the two correspondents may imagine reading, sauntering, chatting and laughing; the future also holds the death of writers and of pigs – though the sow's fertility promises constant rejuvenation of the pig supply. Cowper's idiosyncratic arrangement of detail almost allegorises his consistent self-representation in the letters: a poignant combination of despair (the unavoidable reality of death) and delight in the daily. Like many others during his century, he demonstrates how personal letters can function not only to communicate but to create a style and thus a version of self.

Diary and autobiography

STUART SHERMAN

In 1656 Margaret Cavendish, Duchess of Newcastle, published a short piece she named 'A True Relation of My Birth, Breeding, and Life'. Near the end, she rather anxiously invoked some ancient autobiographical precedents: 'I hope my Readers will not think me vain for writing my life, since there have been many that have done the like, as *Caesar*, *Ovid*, and many more, both men and women, and I know no reason I may not do it as well as they.'[1] There were, as she suggests, conspicuous antecedents for autobiography: mostly male, formidably famous, and widely scattered across space and time. But Cavendish's pronouncement works better as forecast than as retrospect. In England over the ensuing century and a half, 'many more' writers than ever before, 'both men and women', diverse in origin and status, working in both diary and autobiography, manuscript and print, found ample reason that they too, 'as well as' the more renowned practitioners of the past, could and should press their own lives onto the page. Some hundred years after Cavendish's assertion, such convictions received another imprimatur. '[T]here has rarely passed a life', Samuel Johnson declared in one essay, 'of which a judicious and faithful narrative would not be useful.'[2] In another, he concluded that the most useful such narrative is not biography but autobiography: 'Those relations are commonly of most value in which the writer tells his own story.'[3] The practice that Cavendish rather anxiously defended, Johnson confidently affirmed. In the years between, the stimuli towards self-inscription had become more varied, the models and precedents more promiscuous, the means and justifications

---

1 Margaret Cavendish, 'A True Relation of My Birth, Breeding, and Life', in *Paper Bodies: A Margaret Cavendish Reader*, eds. Sylvia Bowerbank and Sara Mendelson (Peterborough, Ontario: Broadview Press, 2000), p. 63. Subsequent page references are to this edition.

2 Samuel Johnson, *Ramber* No. 60, in *The Rambler*, eds. W. J. Bate and Albrecht B. Strauss, The Yale Edition of the Works of Samuel Johnson, vols. III–V (New Haven, CT: Yale University Press, 1969), vol. III, p. 320.

3 Samuel Johnson, *Idler* No. 84, in *The Idler*, ed. W. J. Bate, The Yale Edition of the Works of Samuel Johnson, vol. II (New Haven, CT: Yale University Press, 1963), p. 262.

more widely available. At no time in the past had self-writing attained so wide a sway over different genres, practitioners and audiences. Conscious of her own temerity, Cavendish appears in retrospect as early harbinger of a new burgeoning.

In all periods, of course, the full corpus of self-writing is intrinsically unknowable. Numberless documents disappear, through destruction or sequestration, casual or calculated. The long eighteenth century is striking partly for the abundance and variety of the self-writing that emerged at the time, and for the plenitude, at first kept secret, that has surfaced since. Amid the welter it has seemed most useful, by way of survey, to take up a few key texts under a sequence of compound rubrics whose pairings, often oppositional (Modesties and Vanities, Solitudes and Sociabilities), are meant to suggest the dialectic of modes, the complexity and the heterogeneity with which these burgeoning genres acquired new prominence and took new forms.

Origins and trajectories

The quintessential autobiography of the long eighteenth century is strictly speaking no autobiography at all, but a long, wildly successful lie: *The Life and Strange Surprizing Adventures of Robinson Crusoe* (1719). Within the narrative, Crusoe's prose self-record unfolds in three distinct, increasingly intricate stages of development. Shortly after washing up on the island, Crusoe draws up a two-column chart in which he reckons the 'Evil' and 'Good' in his situation; a little while later he begins 'a journal of every day's employment', which he sustains for a year until his ink runs out; decades later, after he has left the island, he writes his *Life*, transcribing into its early pages both his bi-columnar chart and a 'copy' (revised, abridged) of his island journal.[4] The resulting palimpsest amounts to a condensed history of self-writing. Though Defoe is making the whole thing up, he distils into it everything he knows or guesses about the origins and the trajectories of English autobiographical writing during the late seventeenth century. Good at guessing, he even gets key dates right. Crusoe washes up on his island in November 1659, and begins his journal before year's end. Two pivotal real-life writers shortly followed suit. On Sunday, 1 January 1660, back in London, at the start of a new week, month, year, and decade, Samuel Pepys commenced the journal of every day's employment that he would sustain, day by day, over the next nine years; in its copiousness

---

4 Daniel Defoe, *Robinson Crusoe*, ed. John Richetti (London: Penguin, 2001), pp. 54, 56. Subsequent page references are to this edition.

and consistency, it is unmatched by any English predecessor. Within a few months, John Evelyn commenced his *Kalendarium*, a detailed life-narrative initially written up in retrospect from notes compiled over the preceding decades. Both Pepys and Evelyn begin abruptly, plunging into particulars with no preliminary explanation as to what they're doing or why. Crusoe, by contrast, narrating in retrospect not only his experience but also his ways of writing it up, supplies at least provisional answers to the two central, elusive questions that hover around the sudden spate of self-writing in the seventeenth and eighteenth centuries: why this? why now?

One answer involves money. Looking back upon his two-column chart of Evil and Good, Crusoe proudly asserts that he wrote up his plight 'very impartially, like debtor and creditor' (p. 54). Construing his columns as a form of situational bookkeeping, he makes explicit one of the most significant templates for seventeenth-century self-depictions: the accountant's ledger. The methods that abetted new capitalism also begot new genres. Early diarists often absorbed their sense of both form and purpose from the techniques and goals of bookkeeping, bringing them to bear on questions other than – but still including – cash. Writers began to track self, health, soul, salvation, as though these too were questions of debt and credit.

English Calvinists developed the practice, and its underlying analogy, with particular zeal. In their relentless search for signs of their own salvation, of their fore-ordained membership among God's elect, they were widely urged to deploy diaries as both an instrument of reckoning and a source of solace on the quest. The meshed imperatives of careful bookkeeping and assiduous self-reckoning pervade seventeenth-century Puritan doctrine and practice, but appear nowhere more explicitly than in the first guidebook to diary-keeping, John Beadle's *The Journal or Diary of a Thankful Christian* (1656). In the book's preface, Beadle's fellow minister John Fuller spells out the core analogy: 'Tradesmen keep their shop books. Merchants their Accompt books . . . Some wary husbands [i.e., householders] have kept a Diary of dayly disbursements . . . A Christian that would be exact hath more need, and may reap much more good by such a Journall as this.'[5] But the template of the account book, better suited to numbers than to prose, proved susceptible to intriguing modulations. In Beadle's handbook, the fiscal metaphor gradually melds into a larger spiritual argument. Since faith is the chief sign of grace, Beadle argues,

---

5 John Beadle, *The Journal or Diary of a Thankful Christian* (London: Thomas Parkhurst, 1656), p. bɪv.

who would not . . . make it good [i.e., convincing] to their own souls, that they have obtained this precious grace of Faith? . . . And what better means can be used for the advancement of faith in the growth and strength of it, then a rich treasure of experience; every experiment of Gods favour to us, being a good prop for our faith for the future . . . Now doubtless such as will be well stored with such a treasure of experiments, had need keep a constant Diary by them of all Gods gracious dealings with them.[6]

Here the diarist is still tracking a stock of 'treasure', but the model is no longer money; it is 'experience' or, in Beadle's immediate and expressive rewording, 'experiment'. Both words derive from the Latin *experiri*: to try, prove, test. Much of seventeenth- and eighteenth-century self-writing originates in the conviction that, in every item recorded, from the broadest self-assessment to the most minute particulars, something is being tested, something is being proven, about the self and the world it moves in.

Pepys and Evelyn might recognise in Beadle's fudging of 'experience' with 'experiment' an alternative paradigm for their own endeavours. Both men were Fellows (and eventual officers) of the Royal Society for the Improving of Natural Knowledge, chartered by the new-crowned Charles II in 1662. That 'Improving', as Thomas Sprat made clear in his *History* of the Society published only five years later, was to be achieved by means of an indiscriminate and unceasing experimentation, and a copious cumulative record. The Society, Sprat writes,

has reduc'd its principal observations into one *common-stock*; and laid them up in publique *Registers*, to be nakedly transmitted to the next Generation of Men; and so from them, to their successors. And as their purpose was to heap up a mixt mass of *Experiments* . . . whatever they have recorded, they have done it, not as compleat Schemes of opinions, but as bare, unfinish'd Histories.[7]

The Society's innovations inhere not only in its method of experiment, but in its mode of record: a deliberately indiscriminate content, couched in a plain style ('a close, naked, natural way of speaking', in Sprat's famous phrase (p. 113)) and in an open-ended form. Pepys and Evelyn attended Society meetings enthusiastically, and often wrote up the experiments (in varying proportions of ardour and bemusement) along with their day's other data, in manuscripts that operated in accordance with Sprat's edicts. They produced, in plain prose, histories purportedly 'bare' (though actually crafted), incremental and

---

6 *Ibid.*, 'The Epistle Dedicatory' (unpaged).
7 Thomas Sprat, *History of the Royal Society*. eds. Jackson I. Cope and Harold Whitmore Jones (London: Routledge and Kegan Paul, 1959), pp. 114–15.

'unfinish'd', in which they set down, for transmission to the 'next Generation' and beyond, a record of experience that might well be described as 'a mixt mass of *Experiments*' testing and assessing the self's viability (social, sexual, political, economic, familial) in the wider world.

For these private registers, another rhythm of report provided a forceful precedent, both as model and as impetus. Weekly news-pamphlets first appeared in England during the 1620s, but attained new prominence and profitability during the Civil Wars when, with censorship suspended and factions flourishing, several hundred new periodicals came and went. Coming of age in the 1640s, Pepys and Evelyn (and for that matter Crusoe too) belonged to the first generation to consume its own current history in a form at once bare, unfinished and copiously reported, closely tracked at regular, rapid intervals, in news-books appearing once a week. In this new print context, diary-keeping functions partly as a private mode of news writing. In the diaries as in the news-books, the day's miscellany of report is couched in chronology, governed by the calendar.[8] Half a century later, with the advent of the periodical essay, the vectors of influence were partly reversed, as newsprint began to absorb elements of the autobiographical. In the pages of the thrice-weekly *Tatler* (1709–11) and the daily *Spectator* (1711–13), Addison and Steele reported abundantly on the private experience of their papers' fictive narrators. In *The Tatler*, Isaac Bickerstaff delivered frequent and lengthy 'Lucubrations' from the confines of 'my own Apartment'; Mr Spectator makes clear soon after his debut that 'the working of my own Mind, is the general Entertainment of my Life' – and that he means to make it a source of entertainment for his reader too.[9] *The Tatler* and *The Spectator* resembled newspapers in both their physical format and their periodical timing; but they often read like entries in a diary or episodes of autobiography – instalments in the cumulative self-portrait of a fictional narrator.

The new plenitude and polymorphousness of self-inscription during the seventeenth and eighteenth centuries imparts a peculiar twist to questions about genre, tradition and influence which can be posed more readily about more public modes of writing (plays, novels, poems, essays), where each new practitioner works from and against antecedents in the same kind, widely

8 See Daniel Woolf, 'News, History and the Construction of the Present in Early Modern England', in Brendan Dooley and Sabrina A. Baron (eds.), *The Politics of Information in Early Modern Europe* (London: Routledge, 2001), pp. 80–118; and Stuart Sherman, *Telling Time: Clocks, Diaries, and English Diurnal Form, 1660–1795* (Chicago: University of Chicago Press, 1996), pp. 109–34.

9 *Spectator* No. 4, in Joseph Addison and Richard Steele, *The Spectator*, ed. Donald Bond, 5 vols. (Oxford: Clarendon Press, 1965), vol. I, p. 21.

available. Two of the sharpest theorists of self-chronicling, Jerome Bruner and Elizabeth Bruss, construe the term 'autobiography 'as naming not a genre but a set of practices perpetually in flux because they are deeply and variously in debt to more public forms and fashions. One of the few constants about the practice, they suggest, is its absorptiveness. Those engaged in the 'autobiographical process', argues Bruner, draw on 'canonical forms' of narrative already available in the culture – particularly in the current forms of fiction.[10] Of course, the influence can work the other way too, as *Robinson Crusoe* readily demonstrates. There, emerging methods of self-writing determine and suffuse the book's entire texture. Beginning with *Crusoe*, the novel insistently presents itself as a branch of autobiography, each text's title proclaiming the name of its sole or principal narrator, who will unfold a long life story in the first person: Moll Flanders, Colonel Jack, Pamela, Clarissa, Tristram Shandy, Evelina. In seventeenth- and eighteenth-century writing, the story of the self operates everywhere – in diaries, autobiographies, memoirs, confessions, letters, essays, travel books, fiction – and the paths of influence are strikingly serpentine and self-reversing, winding from manuscript to print, from established public genres to emergent private practices, and then back again. 'Autobiography', asserts Bruss, 'is an act rather than a form.'[11] The act can assume or appropriate many forms, and it is the distinction of the long eighteenth century to have devised or developed more new ones than any period hitherto.

Time now to look closer at two of the most abiding.

Diary and autobiography

Diary and autobiography are often reckoned as representing opposite ends of the self-writing spectrum, as acts fundamentally distinguished by their operation over time. The diarist, in this opposition, deals in small, serial durations, and works more or less (in Samuel Richardson's famous phrase) 'to the moment', writing up recent events in regular or irregular instalments, one of whose chief characteristics is an ignorance of the instalments that will ensue. The autobiographer works with less ignorance and larger retrospect, recording his or her life perhaps from the moment of its inception to the present moment of composition, when the life is presumably full enough

---

10 Jerome Bruner, 'The Autobiographical Process', in Robert Folkenflik (ed.), *The Culture of Autobiography* (Stanford, CA: Stanford University Press, 1993), p. 49.

11 Elizabeth W. Bruss, *Autobiographical Acts* (Baltimore, MD: Johns Hopkins University Press, 1976), p. 19.

(of attainment, of discovery) to warrant the act of autobiography. Casual contrast tends also to construe the genres as differently embodied and directed: the diary as a manuscript composed by the self *for* the self; the autobiography, by contrast, as something written with the intent of prompt publication, as first and finally embodied in a book. By such a reckoning, diarists display marked kinship with the tortoise in Zeno's ancient paradox, making their way in tiny increments towards an endpoint that is by the logic of the proceedings personally unattainable: death (which no diarist can record in retrospect), and perhaps posthumous publication (which no diarist can witness). The autobiographer, by contrast, is Archimedean, working from a single vantage and seeking sufficient leverage to lift a whole life on to the printed page.

This familiar opposition tells part of the truth but is worth questioning too. Though the forms differ deeply, they fuse frequently. It may be worth tracking both the distinctions and the fusions, as they manifest themselves in two important early instances: Pepys' *Diary* (1660–9), and John Bunyan's *Grace Abounding to the Chief of Sinners* (1666). And since, in the conventional opposition between diary and autobiography, time is of the essence, it will be worthwhile to attend to the diarist and the autobiographer as they write up a momentary sensation: the sound of bells.

Pepys records that sound at the end of an entry just sixteen days into his diary.

> . . . and thence home, where I found my wife and maid a-washing. I sat up till the bell-man came by with his bell, just under my window as I was writing of this very line, and cried, 'Past one of the clock, and a cold, frosty, windy morning.' I then went to bed and left my wife and the maid a-washing still.[12]

Here, the very sentence that most assiduously preserves the moment also stays alert to its evanescence. The past tense in the verbs ('sat' up, 'came' by, 'was' writing) insists that the conjunctive moment of ringing and writing is (like the bellman) already past, despite the striving for simultaneity in 'this very line'; that the act of recording must always lag behind the action recorded, which is over by the time it is set down. (The bellman himself colludes in this design, announcing not 'one o'clock' exactly but some later instant when one o'clock is 'past'.) Pepys compasses the doubly transitory moment of the bellman's passing and his own recording within a prose enclosure, framing it on either side within the two nearly identical phrases about 'my wife and maid

---

12 Samuel Pepys, *The Diary of Samuel Pepys*, ed. Robert Latham and William Matthews, 11 vols. (Berkeley, CA: University of California Press, 1970–83), vol. 1, p. 19. Subsequent page references are to this edition.

a-washing.' But enclosure does not wholly clinch completion. The bellman has passed but the women are still washing; their verb, with its pleonastic prefix (a-) emphasising process, identifies a task in progress but as yet unfinished.

Pepys' diary too is such a task. 'Writing' is, aptly enough, the passage's other progressive verb, for it is by his way of writing that Pepys manages to mingle the motion of the life recorded with the fixity for which the record strives. The entry's last word, then, proves expressively poised. That final 'still', the only variant in the mirrored frame-phrases, both perpetuates the sense of process('still' clearly means 'yet', and can mean 'always') and imparts to it a sense of stasis, of coming to at least a provisional standstill, that accords well with its position as the entry's endpoint. The entry is over, the diary is ongoing; another entry will appear under tomorrow's date. The diarist contrives to possess the moment not by the mere act of inscription but by its particular tactics: by tiny prose strategies of motion and enclosure, he fulfils the potentiality of 'still' in both of its opposed senses.

Enclosure governs Pepys' diary as an insistent element of form. Nearly every entry begins with the word 'Up', ends with some variant of 'and so home and to bed', and thus undertakes implicitly to track the course of waking life that transpires between the two.

The diary's mechanisms of motion are subtler and more pervasive still; they inhere in the superabundance of connectives that knit the prose. A sample from the sentence preceding the bellman's appearance will suggest how they work: 'After that, Sheply, Harrison and myself, we went towards Westminster on foot, and at the Golden Lion, near Charing-cross, we went in and drank a pint of wine and so parted; and thence home, where I found my wife and maid a-washing' (p. 19). 'And', the most open of conjunctions because it asserts connection without specifying its nature, here controls the whole passage, appearing everywhere it *can* appear, whether it needs to or not. 'And so', Pepys' favourite variant, combines, in shifting proportions, simple temporal sequence ('and then'), causal connection ('and therefore'), and adverbial context ('and in that manner'), with several other shadings. Such locutions inculcate, in almost every sentence of the diary, its central temporal proposition, of the day as fluent continuum, full and flowing between the twin embankments of wake and sleep.

Bells work differently in Bunyan – and so do key conjunctions. In *Grace Abounding*'s third edition (1672), published six years after the first, he added this early anecdote concerning his love when young of 'ringing the changes': that recreational activity, at once musical, mathematical and athletic, in which a group of ringers sound the set of churchbells in a predetermined sequence of elaborately shifting patterns.

> Now you must know, that before this, I had taken much delight in ringing, but my Conscience beginning to be tender: I thought that such a practice was but vain, and therefore forced my self to leave it, yet my mind hanckered, wherefore I should go to the steeple house [i.e., the church's belltower, a few yards away from the church itself] and look on. But I thought this did not become Religion neither, yet I forced my self and would look on still; but quickly after, I began to think how if one of the Bells should fall . . . So after this, I would yet go to see them ring, but would not go further than the Steeple door, but then it came into my head, how if the Steeple it self should fall, and this thought . . . would . . . continually so shake my mind, that I durst not stand at the Steeple door any longer, but was forced to fly for fear it should fall upon my head.[13]

In Pepys's narrative, the bellman becomes a small element in a tacit but pervasive patterning, a temporal flow of outward fact framed by symmetries of his own devising and linked by 'ands'. In Bunyan's, the bells prompt an ever-deepening inward crisis, centred on his own depravity and death, its gradations meted out by a relentless sequence of alternating 'buts': 'but my Conscience . . . But I thought . . . but then it came into my head . . . but [I] was forced to fly for fear . . .'

Crisis is the book's key mode, and 'but' is that mode's key term. Like most seventeenth-century religious self-writing, *Grace Abounding* works from the Calvinist conviction that the 'elect' have already been chosen, and that it is their task to seek, find and then live in accordance with the truth of their election. Bunyan's narrative, like many by his sectarian contemporaries, deals not in a single moment of affirmative epiphany but in a relentless wavering between glad conviction and deep despair. Bunyan devotes a third of his text to a protracted crisis brought on by a moment's blasphemous thought. Haunted by the memory of that moment, Bunyan deems himself irreversibly fallen, until by a series of counsels, scriptures, signs and solaces, punctuated by episodes of backsliding and despair, all minutely analysed, he attains a firmer but still provisional conviction of his own status as the recipient of grace abounding.

In many respects, Pepys and Bunyan fulfil familiar expectations about their differing enterprises, secular diary and spiritual autobiography. Pepys tracks

---

13 John Bunyan, *Grace Abounding, with Other Spiritual Autobiographies,* ed. John Stachniewski and Anita Pacheco (Oxford: Oxford University Press, 1998), pp. 13–14. Subsequent page references are to this edition.

local ephemera (bells, laundry) over successive days; Bunyan deals in larger themes (salvation, grace) over compacted years. Pepys deals abundantly in the particulars that fill his days; Bunyan deals selectively in details that will illuminate his themes (Pepys' wife appears twice in the short bellman extract; Bunyan's only twice in the whole autobiography). Even the key conjunctions might serve as epitomes of contrasted form. 'And', after all, would seem to mark the diary's intrinsic, incremental, cumulative metier, each day, each detail, added to the one before. 'But', by contrast, would seem essentially the privilege of the autobiographer, who reckons in retrospect the principal turns that shaped the life. Bunyan's energetic self-revision (five editions in fourteen years) in effect extends the privilege, as reconsideration repeatedly remakes the text.

Yet diary and autobiography are so closely braided that points of difference become points of contact. The oscillation between grace and fall that Bunyan makes the central motion of his autobiography operates also, in cycles even more rapid and intense, in innumerable religious diaries, where the Calvinist directive to sift each thought for signs of salvation, coupled with the diarist's Beadle-esque imperative to record many such thoughts a day, can produce a phenomenally detailed fretfulness. Secular diarists worry too. Pepys first manifests his own propensity for oscillatory self-reckoning at the bottom of his diary's first page; here, as at hundreds of moments throughout his manuscript, the question he takes up so waveringly concerns not spiritual grace but material prosperity: 'My own private condition very handsome; and esteemed rich, but endeed very poor, besides my goods of my house and my office [i.e., employment], which at present is somewhat uncertain' (p. 2). For Pepys as for Bunyan, the habit of reconsideration informed the very making of the text. He revised plentifully, putting his entries through as many as five drafts; he finished his lapidary account of London's Great Fire three months after the fact, working from copious notes dashed off during the crisis. Again and again, in the juxtaposition of diary and autobiography, seeming antithesis gives way to fusion and synthesis. At many junctures, each genre aspires to the condition of the other.

Singularities and multiplicities

Self-writing may be inherently self-multiplying. The 'I' who writes is almost ineluctably different from the 'I' who performed whatever action the writing reports. The distance between them is self-evident in autobiography (the Bunyan who remembers the bells differs in important ways from the boy who feared them) but obtains also in diaries, as Pepys makes clear by his use of the past tense in the bellman episode. Diary and autobiography both flourished in large part as a means of tracking, and juxtaposing, variations in the self (rising status, increasing wealth) over the course of days, years or a lifetime, at an economically and socially motile moment when large changes were newly possible.

At the same time, diarists and autobiographers make manifest a driving desire to declare their own uniqueness. 'The writer's urge to establish his singularity', writes the theorist of autobiography John Sturrock, 'is an inaugural topos of the genre. It may be expressed very robustly, as it is by Nietzsche at the start of the preface to *Ecce Homo*: *"Listen! for I am such and such a person. For Heaven's sake do not confound me with anyone else."*'[14] Or the impulse may be expressed more intricately, not as a simple 'urge' but as a compelling crossplay between singularity – the uniqueness of the self portrayed – and multiplicity – the variety of the writer's selves displayed and tracked within the document. During the inaugural epoch in English self-writing, this dialectic gives energy to much of the prose. Its operations are particularly striking in two texts published at opposite ends of the long eighteenth century: Margaret Cavendish's 'A True Relation of My Birth, Breeding, and Life' (1656), and Olaudah Equiano's *The Interesting Narrative of the Life of Olaudah Equiano, or Gustavus Vassa, the African, Written by Himself* (1789). Cavendish and Equiano write from opposite ends of several other spectrums too – of gender, race, class – and from very different points along the differing vectors of their own life stories. Cavendish was a gentleman's daughter and a duke's wife. An ardent royalist, she was at the time of writing dispossessed of wealth and status by the exigencies of the Civil Wars: '[N]ot only the Family I am link't to is ruin'd, but the Family from which I sprung, by these unhappy Wars' ('A True Relation', p. 48). Equiano, by contrast, born in Africa and sold young into slavery, wrote near the end of a long ascent from subjugation into freedom and prosperity: '[W]hen I compare my lot with that of most of my countrymen [i.e., fellow Africans]', he declares on his first page, 'I regard myself as a *particular favourite of Heaven*, and acknowledge the mercies of Providence in every occurrence of my life.'[15] Despite obvious differences, though, the two autobiographies hold key elements in common. In both cases, the very act of producing an autobiography provided sufficient evidence of singularity: in 1656 few women, and in 1789 few former slaves, had composed such narratives, and fewer still had published. Within their texts, too, both Cavendish and Equiano lay strong, idiosyncratic

14 John Sturrock, 'Theory vs. Autobiography', in Folkenflik, *Culture of Autobiography*, p. 26.
15 Olaudah Equiano, *The Interesting Narrative of the Life*, ed. Vincent Caretta (London: Penguin, 1995), p. 31. Subsequent page references are to this edition.

STUART SHERMAN

claim to their own singularity. Each autobiographer grounds that claim in the unique mix of experience and experiment – the multiplicity and variety of selves and stations – compassed by her and his single, singular life.

Cavendish's autobiography deals extensively in Sturrockian self-proclamation, even at one point anticipating its key term. Discussing her famously eccentric taste in clothes, Cavendish explains that 'I did dislike any should follow my Fashions, for I always took delight in a *singularity*, even in acoutrements of habits' ('A True Relation', p. 60; emphasis added). Throughout her account, Cavendish's delight in singularity finds its fullest expression in the reckoning up of her idiosyncratic multiplicities, as in this explanation of her illegible handwriting:

> but my letters seem rather as a ragged rout, than a well armed body, for the brain being quicker in creating than the hand in writing, or the memory in retaining, many fancies are lost, by reason they ofttimes out-run the pen, where I, to keep speed in the Race, write so fast as I stay not so long as to write my letters plain, insomuch as some have taken my handwriting for some strange character . . . (p. 56)

'Strange character', of course, means something like code or cipher. Over the course of the sentence, Cavendish's wayward script becomes an emblem for the proudly strange human character of the autobiographer herself, determined to be read in the very act of proclaiming her indecipherability, and rendering in run-on syntax her innately elusive superabundance, where cherished 'fancies' proliferate so plentifully that they are often lost before transcription can render them at once both legible and obscure.

Near the end of 'A True Relation', Cavendish performs multiplicity another way, as a runaway wish list, a concatenation of self-applied superlatives: 'for I think it no crime to wish my self the exactest of Natures works, my thred of life the longest, my Chaine of Destinie the strongest, my minde the peaceablest; my life the pleasantest, my death the easiest, and the greatest Saint in Heaven . . .' (p. 61). Here again, Cavendish deploys plenitude to attest uniqueness. Her singularity, so she implies, consists not in the conviction that she can lay claim to all these superlatives (she admits that she cannot) but in the audacity – proclaimed in print, defiant of conventional gendered subordinations – with which she fancies them.

For Equiano, too, singularity inheres in multiplicity, a condition he encapsulates in the compound self-namings of his autobiography's title: *The . . . Life of Olaudah Equiano, or, Gustavus Vassa, the African . . .* The two proper names sketch the chronology of a bifurcated life. The first was given the author by his African forebears, the second imposed upon him by his British owner, with perhaps deliberate irony: Gustavus Vassa (1496–1550), who became King of Sweden after freeing his country from the Danes' dominion, had become in England a figure for liberation too, thanks to an anti-Walpolean play entitled *Gustavus Vassa, the Deliverer of his Country* (1738). Equiano, in his title, supplies for the hero's name a more extraordinary appositive: 'the African', which here strikingly attaches itself to the author's European rather than his natal name. By simple sequencing, the title limns an ineluctably doubled identity, whose components operate concurrently but shift place rapidly, quick to toggle at the pivot-point of a comma, or an 'or'.

'Or' is for Equiano what 'and' is for Pepys and 'but' for Bunyan: a key to the workings of the mind and text. Like Bunyan, whose book he deliberately echoes and emulates, Equiano tells the story of his own conversion, prompted in part by his encounter with a group of the faithful who 'seemed to be altogether certain of their calling and election of God' (p. 184). Once converted, though, Equiano quickly and definitively partakes of their confidence. He narrates no Bunyanesque failures of faith, no tormentingly unstable, relentlessly see-sawing convictions of damnation and grace (such agonised self-interrogation had disappeared from spiritual autobiography over the intervening century, thanks in part to the advent of the exuberant Methodism that Equiano himself espouses). In Equiano's *Interesting Life* oscillation inheres not in tribulation of the spirit but in the intricacy of his experience as a slave who has secured his own freedom, in the doubleness of witness embodied in the 'or' of his text's title. That word forecasts the frequency and rapidity with which, over the course of his *Narrative*, Equiano's entwined identities will shift, split or meld, at the hands of others or in the author's own self-reckonings. Even after he has bought his freedom, for example, Equiano is several times mistaken and re-recruited as a slave by mercenary whites. Within his own prose he will often shift perspectives, reporting a single experience from the vantage of both slave and free man, African and European, as in this account of what he observed upon his arrival in the Americas, at the slave market in Barbados:

> I remember in the vessel in which I was brought over, in the men's apartment, there were several brothers, who, in the sale, were sold in different lots; and it was very moving on this occasion to see and hear their cries at parting. O, ye nominal Christians! might not an African ask you, learned you this from your God? who says unto you, Do unto all men as you would men should do unto you? (p. 61)

Equiano writes now as an energetically Evangelical (not merely 'nominal') Christian, but he insists on interrogating his fellow Christians as 'an African' (and in the context of this narrative moment, an African not yet converted), as brother to those 'several brothers' dispersed by sale. From this complex pairing, within the autobiographer's 'I', of Christian brother and African other, arises the *Narrative*'s argument for abolition. For Cavendish, a singularity grounded in multiplicity (of fashions, of fancies) furnishes 'delight'; for Equiano it supplies a tool of advocacy. Where 'but' allows Bunyan to trace the oscillation of a change within himself, 'or' enables Equiano to pursue an aim more palpably ambitious: a change in the traffics and the cruelties of the globe.

Modesties and vanities

'I believe it is difficult', writes Equiano in his autobiography's opening sentence, 'for those who publish their own memoirs to escape the imputation of vanity' (*Interesting Narrative*, p. 31). Wary of the imputation, most autobiographers of the period sought to ward off the suspicion of self-conceit by insisting instead, at the start of the text, on their own anxious humility. Equiano, for example, promptly insists that 'I offer here the history of neither a saint' nor 'a hero' (p. 31).

Amid the welter of eighteenth-century self-writers, two stood out even to their contemporaries as pioneer performers in the intricate deployment of autobiographical vanity: Colley Cibber, and his daughter Charlotte Charke. Both were well-equipped for such innovation, having spent their entire lives in the theatre, Cibber as playwright-actor-manager in London, Charke more variously and precariously as London performer and strolling player. Part of the novelty of both the father's *Apology for the Life of Colley Cibber* (1740) and the daughter's *Narrative of the Life of Mrs Charlotte Charke* (1755) consisted in the temerity of their deeming their lives worthy of such sustained public narration. Such careers had hitherto been generally regarded as beneath documentation. Until now, published autobiographies had dealt primarily in the lives of eminent divines and statesmen, and no actor had seen fit to print so detailed an account of his or her endeavours. The audacity that impelled both Cibber's and Charke's narratives also shapes them, in ways that render them distinct from any antecedent, and deeply different from each other.

In the opening pages of his *Apology*, Cibber handles the problem of vanity two ways. He first shrugs it off, then takes it on. 'But why make my Follies publick?' he asks the friend to whom the book is ostensibly addressed, and promptly answers his own question with another: 'Why not?'[16] A little later, though, this negative turns positive. Cibber begins to explain why he *should* expose himself this way. He proposes to present

> as true a Picture of myself as natural Vanity will permit me to draw: For, to promise you that I shall never be vain, were a Promise that, like a Looking-glass too large, might break itself in the making: Nor am I sure I ought wholly to avoid that Imputation, because if Vanity be one of my natural Features, the Portrait wou'd not be like me without it. (p. 7)

By this logic, vanity will work cheerfully both for and against itself. It both prompts Cibber's self-display, and will be one of the chief elements exposed. As a 'natural Feature' of his character, it forms an indispensable part of 'the simple Truth' (p. 8) he proposes to tell. To the bemusement of his contemproraries, Cibber dealt with autobiographical vanity by declaring rather than denying it.

Fifteen years later, his daughter took his tactic several steps farther. In a deliberately outrageous prefatory letter, she dedicates the *Narrative* not (as did Cibber) to a typical, munificent patron, but to herself, promising as author 'to illustrate those WONDERFUL QUALIFICATIONS by which you have so EMINENTLY DISTINGUISH'D YOURSELF . . . [and which give] you a just Claim to the Title of a NON-PAREIL OF THE AGE'.[17] Hyperbolic irony here provides protective cover, as will become clear later in the letter, when Charke, mimicking numberless other dedications, solicits the addressee's (that is, her own) potentially lucrative endorsement: 'If, by your Approbation, the World may be perswaded into a tolerable Opinion of my Labours, I shall, for the Novelty-sake, venture for once to call you, FRIEND; a Name, I own, I never *as yet have known you by*' (p. 6). From the outset of her *Narrative*, Charke casts such relations between her 'selves' as contentious, disappointing and unstable. Her comic vanity, unlike her father's, makes room for ruefulness.

One of the ways Charke's *Narrative* lays just claim to the title of non-pareil is by its structure. As autobiography, it is *sui generis*. It came out not in bound volumes but in eight periodical instalments, small pamphlets, published on successive Saturdays. The *Narrative*'s jagged periodic structure sorts well with its substance, the account of a life lived improvisationally, from week to week and even from day to day, with few sustained stretches of stability. Whenever

---

16 Colley Cibber, *An Apology for the Life of Colley Cibber*, ed. B. R. S. Fone (Mineola, NY: Dover Publications, 2000), p. 5. Subsequent page references are to this edition.

17 Charlotte Charke, *A Narrative of the Life of Mrs Charlotte Charke*, ed. Robert Rehder (London: Pickering and Chatto, 1999), p. 5. Subsequent page references are to this edition.

Charke cannot find theatrical work in London, she resorts to playing in the provinces; when that work fails too, she takes on other jobs and other guises; at several points, for layered reasons (desire, security, safety from pursuit and prosecution), she dresses and passes as a man. Charke concludes her text with an expansive seven-item list, a quick retrospective recapitulation of her life and *Narrative*, ticking off at high speed the prodigious number of things she's done, the variety of identities she's assumed. The last item begins this way: '*7thly*, My being Gentleman[-servant] to a certain Peer; After my Dismission, becoming *only an Occasional Player*, while I was playing at *Bo-peep* [i.e., hide-and-seek] *with the World*. My turning Pork-Merchant; broke, through the inhuman Appetite of a hungry Dog [which ate her stock] . . . My settling in *Wales*, and turning Pastry-Cook and Farmer . . .' (pp. 141–2). This rapid-fire retrospective, and the *Narrative* that has elaborated it so audaciously, set Charke firmly apart from her biological and autobiographic forebear. For Cibber, the theatre was more or less monolithic: it happened in London, in one of two major playhouses. For Charke it happens everywhere, on the street, in a barn, in a prison (where she spends a night and, at the request of a fellow actor and inmate, performs Macheath's prison songs from *The Beggar's Opera*). For her as for her father, theatrical roles are jobs; but she makes clear that all her jobs are roles also, in the running act of impersonation that constitutes ineluctably her *Narrative* and her life.

Solitudes and sociabilities

Performance presumes an audience. Does writing presume a reader?

Writing tends to require solitude, and self-writing tends to compound it, cloistered within the imperatives, variably combined, of reflection, retrospection, privacy and secrecy. A core equivocation runs through much self-writing and often shapes it. Without the security of sequestration, many secrets might not get written down. But without the prospect of at least an imaginary readership, why commit the secrets to the page at all? In Sturrock's theory of autobiography, the 'inaugural topos of the genre' – the self-portrayer's assertion of singularity – is only the opening gambit in a 'double game' first solitary, then social, proceeding inexorably from the private to the public. The very act of writing, however solitary at the start, nonetheless signals 'the writer's wish to be reunited with those [i.e., a world of possible readers] from whom he has singled himself out'.[18]

18 Sturrock, 'Theory vs. Autobiography', pp. 26, 35.

The long eighteenth century abounded with new tactics of reunion. Two of their most intriguing practitioners, James Boswell (1740–95) and Frances Burney (1752–1840), began as enthusiastic young diarists and ended as eminent authors, plentifully published and widely read. Both secured for their copious private prose an emphatically public destiny. Their methods for doing so differ drastically, in ways that map their culture's gendered expectations concerning the practices of private writing and public self-portraiture. For Boswell, the whole purpose of self-writing is performance. For Burney, as for other women writers (notably her friend and mentor Hester Thrale), even the most private acts of autobiography are fraught with pressures and perils, with equivocations absorbed or abjured.

'I have discovered', Boswell announces on the seventh day of his first full journal, 'that we may be in some degree whatever character we choose.'[19] The sentence is in part an actor's credo, voiced by a lifelong addict of the theatre who is already cultivating friendships with the celebrated players Thomas Sheridan and David Garrick and who will shortly find brief bliss in a liaison with the actress he calls 'Louisa', who, as he likes to remind himself, has 'played many a fine lady's part' (*Journal*, p. 149). By the time he writes the sentence, Boswell has already contrived to make his journal a medium of performance, a kind of prose proscenium. Every week, he dispatched a fresh cluster of his daily entries in a postal packet addressed to his lifelong friend John Johnston back in Scotland. Each packet contained a cover letter, but within the pages of the journal itself Johnston occupies an elusive position, never directly addressed in the second person but repeatedly mentioned in the third, as in this entry where Boswell deliberates, characteristically, about what kind of character he should choose to be:

> I remember my friend Johnston told me one day . . . that I had turned out different from what he imagined, that he thought I would resemble Mr Addison . . . I felt strong dispositions to be a Mr Addison . . . Mr Addison's character in sentiment, mixed with a little of the gaiety of Sir Richard Steele, and the manners of Mr Digges, were the ideas which I aimed to realize.
>
> (p. 62)

These deliberations are meant to pose for Johnston implicit questions: have I disappointed you? What do you think of my current resolve? Boswell's triumvirate of role-models is suggestive. Addison was famously reticent (he thought up the silent Mr Spectator), Steele famously gregarious (he created

---

19 James Boswell, *Boswell's London Journal, 1762–1763*, ed. Frederick A. Pottle (New York: McGraw-Hill, 1950), p. 47. Subsequent page references are to this edition.

the loquacious *Tatler*). West Digges was a celebrated actor whose performances had first enthralled Boswell as a boy. Boswell here presents himself as choosing and combining three possible 'characters', and as poised among three modes of being: solitary (absorbed in his own thoughts), sociable (anxious for Johnston's response) and performative: soliloquising elaborately and calculatedly for a carefully chosen audience of one.

Boswell's thirty-year career as author was driven in part by his desire to find an ever wider audience for his first-person diurnal prose. He pursued this ambition more audaciously with each successive book: *An Account of Corsica: The Journal of a Tour to that Island, and Memoirs of Pascal Paoli* (1769; Paoli was the island's liberator); *The Journal of a Tour to the Hebrides with Samuel Johnson, LL D.* (1785); and *The Life of Samuel Johnson* (1791). In the *Life of Johnson* the transmutations from diary to biography become utterly pervasive and extraordinarily deft. The earliest chronological instance will serve as sample of this alchemy. In the published *Life*, Boswell recasts his first meeting with Johnson, at the bookshop of their mutual friend Tom Davies, as a stirring episode from a well-known play:

> Johnson unexpectedly came into the shop; and Mr Davies having perceived him through the glass-door in the room in which we were sitting, advancing towards us – he announced his aweful approach to me, somewhat in the manner of an actor in the part of Horatio, when he addresses Hamlet on the appearance of his father's ghost, 'Look, my Lord, it comes.'[20]

In his diary account of this same moment, Boswell makes no mention of *Hamlet*. In print he deploys the play as conduit through which he can transmit his layered private experience – awe then at Johnson's approach, loss now after Johnson's death – to a readership for whom Shakespeare's ghost-scene has long encoded such emotions. In a bookshop that is also suddenly Elsinore, Boswell contrives that Johnson effectually advances 'towards us', too; that subject, biographer and audience will converge on *Hamlet*'s common but near-mythic ground. Making new use of the theatrical impulses that have suffused his journals from the start, Boswell takes care that diurnal form will function brilliantly, not merely as public medium but as public monument.

For women writers, both the practice of the form and the envisioning of the monument proved more problematic. For thirty-two years, Johnson's friend Hester Thrale wrote up her private experiences in a series of elegantly bound

20 James Boswell, *The Life of Samuel Johnson*, ed. R. W. Chapman (Oxford: Oxford World Classics, 1980), p. 277.

manuscript volumes she had received as a gift from her husband, each one embossed, as she self-mockingly remarks on her first page, with 'the pompous Title of Thraliana'.[21] She elaborates on her misgivings later in the manuscript, while musing on one of Pope's rough drafts for his translation of the *Iliad*: '[S]trange that a man should keep such Things! – stranger still that a Woman should write such a Book as this; put down every Occurrence of her Life, every Emotion of her Heart, & call it a *Thraliana* forsooth – but then I mean to destroy it' (*Thraliana*, vol. I, p. 464). That intent accords well with a precept Johnson had often urged: that you can keep a detailed diary provided you plan to burn it. In Thrale's case, though, the scheme, never realised, amounts to an enabling fiction. It makes room for revelations, by affirming that no reader other than the writer will ever receive them. 'Equivocation will undo us', Hamlet suggests, but equivocation actually sustains Thrale, freeing her to write down every occurrence and emotion she chooses.

Burney, equivocal also, devised for her diary a different enabling fiction, more transparent and self-conscious than Thrale's, centred not on intent but on audience. Where Boswell, at twenty-two, dispatches his preening entries to his friend in Scotland, Burney, at sixteen, decides on the first page of her journal that she must address her revelations to a reader more elusive, of her own invention:

> But a thing of th[is] kind ought to be addressed to somebody . . . To whom, then, *must* I dedicate my wonderful, surprising & interesting adventures? – to *whom* da[re] I reveal my private opinions of my nearest Relations? the secret thoughts of my dearest friends? my own hopes, fears, reflections & dislikes? – Nobody!
>
> To Nobody, then, will I write my Journal! Since To Nobody can I be wholly unreserved – to Nobody can I reveal every thought, every wish of my Heart, with the most unlimited confidence, the most unremitting sincerity to the end of my Life![22]

Like Thrale, Burney pursues the grail of a daring comprehensiveness: 'every thought, every wish', in her words; 'every Occurrence . . . every Emotion', in Thrale's. Imagining a reader named Nobody, Burney manages to conflate the Boswellian appetite for an audience with the Thralian apprehension of

21 Hester Lynch Thrale, *Thraliana*, ed. Katherine C. Balderston, 2nd edn, 2 vols. (Oxford: Clarendon Press, 1951), vol. I, p. I. Subsequent page references are to this edition.
22 Frances Burney, *The Early Journals and Letters of Fanny Burney*, eds. Lars E. Troide *et al.*, 4 vols. (Kingston, Montreal: McGill-Queen's University Press, 1988–2003), vol. I, pp. I–2. Subsequent page references are to this edition.

exposure ('but then I mean to destroy it') and of eccentricity ('that a Woman should write such a Book as this'). Boswell indulges himself from the first in an actual audience; Thrale and Burney cannot afford the luxury. 'But why', Burney asks a few lines into her diary, '. . . must a *female* be made Nobody?' (*Early Journals*, vol. i, p. 2). The answer, as Thrale's text implies, is that a journal so comprehensive may body forth the woman writer's interior life (thought, wish, emotion) too palpably, and too particularly, to be acceptable to any eyes beyond the diarist's.

Burney's longer-term strategy, though, reversed her opening tactic. She contrived to supplant Nobody (who gradually disappears) with various alternate, actual audiences. Her long literary career, as both diarist and novelist, consists in working out ways, some of them quite convoluted, for securing readers without wholly sacrificing her sequestration. As Nobody ebbs from her journals, the narrative continues in the form not of clandestine manuscript but of journal *letters*, copious accounts of daily doings, most of them addressed, over a period of three decades, to Burney's favourite sister and confidante Susanna. Five years after commencing her diary to Nobody, Burney dispatched her first packet of journal letters from the seaside resort of Teignmouth; here the dated entries run in a closer series, with fewer interruptions, than in any narrative of the self that Burney had produced before. For women writers, journal letters, wherein 'every thought, every wish' might be vetted and assessed by an audience of family and friends, received broad cultural endorsement, because they seemed to replace dangerous diaristic secrecy with safe epistolary communality. This distinction replicates a wider division in the history of self-writing. For Crusoe, Pepys, Evelyn and subsequent male diarists, the continuity and comprehensiveness of the account go hand in hand with its privacy, and with the writer's leisure; the more securely private the narrative, the more thorough it tends to be. Crusoe on his island has all the time in the world; and even the busier Pepys can compose his detailed bellman entry, for example, partly because his wife and maid are busy elsewhere in the house, 'a-washing still'. In Burney's self-narrative, by contrast, copiousness is almost always a function of sociability, of the journal letter rather than the journal. The less private her writing, the more comprehensively she can write her time – and the more comfortably she can spend her time in writing.

The social and familial conditions that sustained Burney's journal letters also fostered her novel writing; at first, the one modulated into the other. She managed to create her first published novel, *Evelina* (1778) in a kind of open secrecy, sitting and writing in plain view of her family, by pretending to her father (who knew nothing of the project) that she was composing journal letters to Susanna instead. In one respect, she was telling the truth: she contructs the book primarily in the form of journal letters, addressed by the seventeen-year-old Evelina to her surrogate father. In her subsequent three novels she discarded the epistolary-journal mode, as had many of her contemporaries, in favour of sustained third-person narration. In the last decades of her long life, though, as the popularity of her fiction faded, Burney discovered within her own journals fresh possibilities for publication. By this time, diary manuscripts had begun making their way plentifully into print, expanding the available range and repertoire of 'stories of the self written by the self' as never before. The publication of Evelyn's diary, heavily abridged, in 1818, and of Pepys', energetically bowdlerised, in 1825, opened the floodgates, as scholars and publishers vied to get their hands on newly recovered manuscripts of self-chroniclers long dead. During this same period, Burney edited her own papers for posterity, subjecting the texts both to intermittent augmentations (clarifications, annotations and new explanatory interpolations) and to more drastic diminutions. She obliterated passages by pen, by scissors and by fire, and often took pains to conceal the fact of excision. At her death in 1840, she left her mass of private manuscripts to her niece Charlotte Barrett, without stipulating the decision her family had long begged of her, 'your own *positive* direction – that they *may* be published – or *never* be published –'.[23] She had remained equivocal to the last in adjudicating the rival claims of privacy and print, occlusion and audience, solitude and sociability. The publication of her *Diary and Letters*, in six volumes edited by Barrett, partly settled the question. Despite truncation, hers was the first woman's diary in Britain to be published on so grand a scale, and the first work by any diarist to be printed up so copiously so soon after the writer's death (Evelyn's, Pepys' and Boswell's manuscripts each dawdled more than a century before seeing print). In this respect, and despite equivocation, Burney ultimately outpaced her more confident male competition.

Lives and deaths

Nearly two centuries earlier, Margaret Cavendish had made a more blatant bid for immortality. 'Very ambitious', as she declares herself, to attain the pinnacle of fame, 'which is to live by remembrance in after-ages' ('A True Relation', pp. 61–2), she nonetheless makes clear in the 'True Relation's' closing sentence just how precarious that climb can be:

23 Frances Burney, *The Journals and Letters of Fanny Burney*, eds. Joyce Hemlow *et al.*, 12 vols. (Oxford: Clarendon Press, 1973), vol. 1, p. xii.

I intend this piece . . . not to please the fancy, but to tell the truth, lest after-Ages should mistake, in not knowing I was daughter to one Master *Lucas* of St *Johns* neer *Colchester*, in *Essex*, second wife to the Lord Marquis of *Newcastle*; for my Lord having had two Wives, I might easily have been mistaken, especially if I should dye, and my Lord Marry again. (p. 63)

The second Duchess of Newcastle fears posthumous confusion with the first or third, and that, she declares, is why she wrote 'this piece'. After-ages, it would seem, are prone to such 'mistake', to an annihilatory 'not knowing' that consigns to oblivion even the plainest data – name, address – of the concluded life. Death, the common fate, so threatens human singularity as to become self-writing's sharpest spur.

Nowhere is its pressure more palpable and precise than in the tiny, lapidary account of 'My Own Life' composed by the dying philosopher and historian David Hume. 'In spring 1775', he remarks at the start of his penultimate paragraph, 'I was struck with a disorder in my bowels, which at first gave me no alarm, but has since, as I apprehend it, become mortal and incurable.'[24] Noting with some satisfaction that 'it is difficult to be more detached from life than I am at present', Hume decided 'to conclude' his life-narrative 'historically with my own character' – with a summation of his salient traits.

I am, or rather was (for that is the style I must now use in speaking of myself, which emboldens me the more to speak my sentiments); I was, I say, a man of mild dispositions, of command of temper, of an open, social, and cheerful humour, capable of attachment, but little susceptible of enmity, and of great moderation in all my passions. (p. 10)

This astonishing sentence works an expressively subdued variation on the noisy Nietzchean autobiographical battle-cry, 'Listen! I am such and such a man . . .' Hume, writing 'historically', opts instead for the past tense, or more precisely for a push of past against present: 'I was, I say, a man . . .' This double play of the tenses enables him, as he remarks with quiet amusement in his closing sentence, to make 'a funeral oration of myself' (p. 11), and thereby to finesse the Zenonian paradox that besets all self-writing by occupying in imagination both sides of life's finish line without yet actually having to traverse it. In prose that cheerfully performs (and verifies) his professed detachment, Hume manages to delimit death's dominion.

24 David Hume, 'My Own Life', in *An Enquiry Concerning Human Understanding*, ed. Antony Flew (La Salle, IL: Open Court, 1988), p. 10. Subsequent page references are to this edition.

Edward Gibbon, historian of Rome as Hume had been of Britain, mastered detachment of another kind. The century's supreme ironist after Swift, he had devoted most of his writing life to anatomising the decline and fall of an empire that had deemed itself immortal. That work done, he turned his historian's energies upon himself, composing and revising a cluster of memoirs during the five last years of his life. There, he subjects certain pieties concerning both death and immortality to the same steady, sceptical scrutiny. After reckoning up, for example, the costs arising from his filial devotion to a spendthrift father – the dwindling of his patrimony, the suspension of his scholarly pursuits, the renunciation of the woman he adored ('I sighed like a lover; I obeyed like a son') – Gibbon adroitly debunks the conventional wisdom touching the deaths of forebears: 'The tears of a son are seldom lasting . . . Few, perhaps, are the children who, after the expiration of some months or years, would sincerely rejoice in the resurrection of their parents . . .'[25] Yet as Gibbon notes at a later moment of valediction, the human appetite for resurrection runs strong in other channels, however narrowed by the sobriety of years or the unlikelihood of prospect: 'In old age, the consolation of hope is reserved for the tenderness of parents, who commence a new life in their children; the faith of enthusiasts [i.e., religious fanatics] who sing hallelujahs above the clouds; and the vanity of authors who presume the immortality of their name and writings' (*Memoirs*, p. 176). Gibbon makes himself his own punchline. Authorial presumption is as suffused with 'hope' (and hence, implicitly, as open to delusion) as the precariousnesses of parenthood or the promise of celestial afterlife. Yet, as is often true in Gibbon, irony is not identical with annihilation; he mocks the presumption of immortality, but does not cancel the possibility. The pronouncement is further ironised, and the valedictory prolonged, by the writing-process that produced it, for this is the closing sentence not of the autobiography per se, but of its penultimate draft: the fifth of six manuscript versions that Gibbon composed, before his sudden death at fifty-six ended the process of vision and revision altogether. In each successive version, Gibbon recast his narrative in ways that registered the political and psychological pressures at work in him at the moment of writing; and he never resolved what was for him the vexing question whether to have the book published during his lifetime, or after death.[26] By a combination of accident

---

25 Edward Gibbon, *Memoirs of My Life*, ed. Betty Radice (London: Penguin, 1984), p. 154. Subsequent page references are to this edition.

26 For a detailed and subtle analysis of Gibbon's self-revisions, see David Womersley, *Gibbon and the 'Watchmen of the Holy City': The Historian and His Reputation, 1776–1815* (Oxford: Clarendon Press, 2002), pp. 207–332.

and temperament, Gibbon's memoirs come closer than perhaps any other autobiography of the period to the conditions that govern that other structure of self-writing, the diary: incremental, contingent, indefinite in duration and design. Prose postponements are one way to make the writing of the life – if not the life itself – last longer.

Even ending can entail postponement. Pepys, for example, wrapped up his diary rather in the manner of the autobiographer; he chose his endpoint, and supplied its rationale. He believed, incorrectly, that he was going blind, and that his work on the diary – tiny ciphers, inscribed by limited light – had helped destroy his eyesight. On 31 May 1669, 3,071 days after he had begun the document, he appended a coda to the day's entry in which he announced the end of the enterprise. 'And so', he writes for the last time, in the coda's closing sentence, 'I betake myself to that course which [is] almost as much as to see myself go into my grave – for which, and all the discomforts that will accompany my being blind, the good God prepare me' (*Diary*, vol. IX p. 565). But this cessation is itself equivocal, even procrastinatory. 'To see myself go into my grave' is to imagine himself both sighted and blind, living and dead, all at the same time. By these doublenesses, the diarist is able to construe even irreversible states of being – blindness, death – as though they were each a 'course' – of action, choice, endeavour. His phrasing encompasses much of the counterpoint, and much of the equivocation, between movement and fixity, among the claims of past, present and posterity, that animate all the abundant narratives of self that the ensuing decades would produce. In his diary's last sentence, as in that instance near its beginning when the passing bellman briefly tolled for him, Pepys sets down exigencies of the moment in an expressive mix of tenses and temporal vantages: the self who is, writing about the self who was, in ways which keep that self still moving and, moving, still.

The Gothic novel

TERRY CASTLE

Like literature itself, literary criticism has its fashions – its fads and caprices and strange gleamings – all of which can shed an instructive light on intellectual history and indeed life itself. Surely no literary-historical phenomenon has undergone a more sweeping critical re-evaluation over the past one hundred years than the late eighteenth-century vogue for the 'Gothic' – that exorbitant hankering after horror, gloom and supernatural grotesquerie so palpable in Britain in the literature and art of the 1790s especially. Long disparaged as one of the more regrettable, even absurd episodes in English literary history, the so-called 'Gothic Revival' of the later eighteenth century has in recent decades come to be seen as one of the signal aesthetic manifestations of the age – as a phenomenon both fascinating in its own right and crucial to a proper understanding of eighteenth-century art and culture more generally

Literary critics of the early decades of the twentieth century, contriving to establish the moral and intellectual gravity of their enterprise, had little patience with Gothic whimsy and extravagance. The Gothic craze has always been easy to satirize, of course: Jane Austen's delightfully irreverent *Northanger Abbey*, composed in the mid 1790s, when the vogue for the emotionally super-charged 'tale of terror' was at its height, provided the pattern for a host of later comic spoofs and burlesques. Most early twentieth-century scholars, eager to enter the lists against vulgarity (past and present) and the excesses of popular taste, took the great novelist's cue more or less reflexively. If Gothic fiction was to be discussed at all, it was hardly something to be taken very seriously. Thus Sir Leslie Stephen's animadversions in *English Literature and Society in the Eighteenth Century* (1907) on Horace Walpole's *The Castle of Otranto*, the first English novel to advertise itself (on its title page) as 'a Gothic Story.' Even as Sir Leslie confirmed, somewhat unwillingly, *Otranto*'s convulsive effect on contemporary readers – thanks to a sensational plot, exotic fake-medieval setting and welter of supernatural devices, the book had undoubtedly helped to establish an influential 'literary school' – it was nonetheless a mere 'squib' or 'plaything', and Walpole himself an 'indifferent dilettante, caring little for any principles and mainly desirous of amusement'.[1] On the Walpolean 'school' itself Stephen wasted no time at all: the names of Ann Radcliffe, Matthew Lewis, Clara Reeve, Sophia Lee, William Beckford, James Hogg, William Godwin, Regina Maria Roche, Charlotte Dacre, W. H. Ireland, Charles Maturin and other exponents of the post-*Otranto* Gothic mode are strikingly absent from his pages.

The pattern of disparagement continued into the teens and twenties. In *The Peace of the Augustans: A Survey of Eighteenth Century Literature as Place of Rest and Refreshment*, the otherwise exhaustive history of eighteenth-century prose and poetry he published in 1916, the great Edwardian critic George Saintsbury devoted only a few (characteristically risible) sentences to the Gothic and its admirers. Regarding Walpole's self-congratulatory claim in the preface to the second edition of *Otranto* to have reintroduced 'imagination' and 'romance' into the desiccated purlieus of English fiction ('invention has not been wanting; but the great resources of fancy have been dammed up, by a strict adherence to common life') Saintsbury was both arch and dismissive. As he drolly noted, not only was little 'Horace' a literary innovator, the self-appointed resuscitator of 'ancient romance', but a book collector, antiquarian and architectural taste-maker too. Besides producing the eighteenth century's first Gothic novel, he also created its first neo-Gothic private house: the elaborately turreted, much-imitated, pseudo-medieval fantasia known as Strawberry Hill. Using part of a vast fortune inherited from his father, the former Whig prime minister Sir Robert Walpole, Walpole had erected this fanciful 'little Gothic castle' in the countryside near Twickenham in gradual stages between 1752 and the mid 1770s.

He subsequently commemorated its design and lavish accoutrements in a privately published folio volume, *A Description of the Villa of Horace Walpole, Youngest Son of Sir Robert Walpole Earl of Orford, at Strawberry Hill near Twickenham. With an Inventory of the Furniture, Pictures, Curiosities, etc.* (1784). Yet despite these pretensions to connoisseurship, concluded Saintsbury, Walpole was nothing more than a frivolous *pasticheur*:

> [He] had no real love for things mediaeval in general, and no real understanding of romance in particular. His fad *was* a fad pure and simple and might have dated and directed itself in any other way and time where he could attain the credit of singularity and originality. There is hardly a a single genuine and unguarded expression of taste, throughout his immense body of writing,

---

1 Sir Leslie Stephen, *English Literature and Society in the Eighteenth Century* (New York and London: G. P. Putnam's Sons, 1907), p. 160.

which is sincerely Romantic when he is not 'speaking in character' – 'talking Strawberry'.[2]

No surprise, perhaps, that the bizarre episode he initiated in popular taste – a sort of mass devolution into 'talking Strawberry' – should have been 'irremediably ridiculed in Miss Austen's *Northanger Abbey*'.

In *The Architecture of Humanism: A Study in the History of Taste* (1914) the poet, art historian and (later) Boswell editor Geoffrey Scott was yet more scathing – if not outright apocalyptic. Scott's focus, as his title suggests, was architectural: his book is primarily a vindication of the Renaissance style of building – tempered, classical and reposeful – over the romantic would-be-medievalism perpetrated first by eighteenth-century Gothic revivalists such as Walpole, Batty Langley, James Wyatt and William Beckford, and later, by Victorian enthusiasts such as Ruskin, Pugin and Morris. Yet Scott's excoriation of what he called the 'Romantic Fallacy' of the past two centuries was as much an attack on a certain kind of literary sensibility as on neo-Gothic building itself. The late eighteenth-century 'catastrophe for style,' he argued – by which he meant the supplanting of the abstract, classically derived and 'purely sensuous' forms of Renaissance art and architecture by the stagily emblematic devices of Gothic – had likewise been a 'catastrophe for thought'.

> Romanticism may be said to consist in a high development of poetic sensibility towards the remote, as such. It idealises the distant, both of time and place; it identifies beauty with strangeness. In the curious and the extreme, which are disdained by a classical taste, and in the obscure detail which that taste is too abstract to include, it finds fresh sources of inspiration. It is most often retrospective, turning away from the present, however valuable, as being familiar. It is always idealistic, casting on the screen of an imaginary past the projection of its unfulfilled desires. Its most typical form is the cult of the extinct. In its essence, romanticism is not favourable to plastic form. It is too much concerned with the vague and the remembered to find its natural expression in the wholly concrete. Romanticism is not plastic; neither is it practical, nor philosophical, nor scientific. Romanticism is poetical.[3]

To be 'poetical' – or in love with the 'extinct' – was for Scott the worst kind of regressive fantasy and incompatible with the creation of a viable human world. The Gothic forms might be a 'romantic material, rich with the charm of history,' but they could never be reconciled, he insisted, with a 'living style,'

---

2 George Saintsbury, *The Peace of the Augustans* (Oxford: Oxford University Press, 1946), p. 169.
3 Geoffrey Scott, *The Architecture of Humanism: A Study in the History of Taste* (1914; rpt. New York: W. W. Norton, 1974), p. 41.

---

or result in anything other than 'a wholly false aesthetic'.[4] William Beckford's absurdly grandiose Fonthill Abbey (1796–1812) – a huge mock-monastery featuring a soaring 300-foot Gothic spire which subsequently collapsed in 1825, taking most of the surrounding buildings with it – was for Scott the perfect symbol of the fatal spuriousness of the Gothic mode. Beckford, like Walpole, was the author of a lurid supernatural tale – the notorious 'Oriental' fable *Vathek* (1786). Among various *diableries*, the hero-villain of the work, a depraved Arabian caliph named Vathek, erects a monstrous tower – subsequently destroyed by fire – in which he imprisons and torments various luckless members of his court. At Fonthill, wrote Scott, 'impressive galleries of flimsy Gothic delighted their master with vague suggestions of the Hall of Eblis, and a tower, three hundred feet in height, rose above them to recall the orgies of the wicked Caliph'. But as on a stage set, all was composed of veneer and hollow timber and the shoddiest of plasterwork: 'And the author of *Vathek*, contemplating in the torchlight his now crumpled, but once cloud-capped pinnacles, may stand for the romantic failure of his time – for the failure of the poetic fancy, unassisted, to achieve material style.'[5]

One might multiply indefinitely, perhaps, examples of anti-Gothic sentiment from the early part of the twentieth century. True, a few writers, if not exactly sympathetic, were somewhat less judgemental – including, interestingly enough, a number of women critics of the day. Virginia Woolf – or so some of her *TLS* reviews from the 1920s would suggest – took both a historical and a technical interest in Gothic experimentation, and even acknowledged finding 'considerable power' in the novels of Ann Radcliffe (1764–1823), the leading English proponent of the 'terror fiction' school of the 1790s.[6] At least two female critics of the period aimed at a more ambitious kind of rehabilitation. Both Edith Birkhead in *The Tale of Terror* (1921) and J. M. S. Tompkins in *The Popular Novel in England, 1770–1800* (1932) sought to explain the late eighteenth-century vogue for the supernatural tale in light of certain complex changes – social, psychic and philosophical – in eighteenth-century British culture itself.[7] Yet even these rather more dispassionate commentators could not always keep from indulging in the self-protective facetiousness that the

4 *Ibid.*, p. 43.
5 *Ibid.*, p. 41.
6 Virginia Woolf, 'Gothic Romance', *Times Literary Supplement*, 5 May 1921; rpt. in Andrew McNeillie (ed.), *The Essays of Virginia Woolf*, 4 vols. (London: The Hogarth Press, 1988), vol. III, p. 305.
7 See Edith Birkhead, *The Tale of Terror: A Study of the Gothic Romance* (London: Constable & Co., 1921) and J. M. S. Tompkins, *The Popular Novel in England 1770–1800* (1932; rpt. Lincoln, NE: University of Nebraska Press, 1961).

Gothic mode so often seemed to provoke. Confronting Joseph Fox's ludicrous advertisement to the reader in the preface to his *Santa-Maria; or the Mysterious Pregnancy* (1797) – 'Things MAY come out to chill – to make the sensitive soul thrill with horror – to make the very hair stand perched on its native habitual roost, where so long it had lain recumbent' – even the donnish Joyce Tompkins could not resist the comic opening: 'And [thus] the sensitive reader, tired of recumbent hair, bought the book, and indulged in "the strange luxury of artificial fear".'[8]

Since the twenties and thirties, the aims and methods of literary study have altered, of course, as critics in England and America have moved away from the primarily aesthetic and evaluative type of commentary favoured by writers like Saintsbury and Scott towards an intellectual approach at once (supposedly) more objective, historically inflected and sociological in emphasis. Over the last half century literary scholars have come to concern themselves less with traditional matters of judgement and taste – with determining whether, say, *The Castle of Otranto* is a good or bad or foolish work of art – and more with the intellectual, social and political contexts in which literary works (good *and* bad) have been produced. Our understanding of the Gothic has undoubtedly benefited from this 'postmodern' turn in critical method. Seen in retrospect, the anti-Gothicism of the first decades of the twentieth century was clearly powerfully aligned with other important intellectual tendencies of the time – notably literary modernism itself. Geoffrey Scott's brisk dismissal of the Gothic style of building – that it was excessively concerned with picturesque 'detail', too caught up in the 'poetical' evocation of distant times and places and not expressive enough of 'those more general values of Mass, Space, Line, and Coherence with which architecture properly deals' – echoed the anti-romantic principles of modernist writer-aestheticians from T. E. Hulme to T. S. Eliot, Ezra Pound and Wyndham Lewis.[9] Indeed, Scott's cool preference for form over content ('a combination of plastic forms has a sensuous value apart from anything we may *know* about them') seems from one angle but another version of modernism's own predilection for abstraction over symbolism, reason over sentiment and classical (or 'universal') forms over romantic and particularising ones.[10]

The anti-romantic point of view held sway for a long time – approaching a kind of zenith with the New Criticism of the 1940s and 1950s. (It is safe to say that there has never been a 'New Critical' examination of a Gothic novel.)

8 Tompkins, *Popular Novel*, p. 222.
9 See Scott, *Architecture of Humanism*, p. 53.
10 *Ibid.*, p. 51.

The pendulum has swung back again, of course, with a vengeance. We are now in love with historical detail, with the palpable *strangeness* of the past, and with recovering and rehabilitating once-derided, supposedly suspect or merely 'popular' literary modes. The classical interest in *form*, in how well a literary work is put together, has been superseded by an interest in *mentalité* – in what a work tells us (or what we presume it to be telling us) about the lost human world from which it emanates. The change, paradoxically, has been at once extraordinarily informative and in its own way curiously limiting. I shall return to the evaluative question – what good is Gothic? – towards the end of this chapter. It is not entirely clear that in seeking to overturn the anti-Gothic prejudices of early modernism through an appeal to history (to the notion that the Gothic can instruct us about late eighteenth-century social, political and cultural 'realities') recent critics have taken full account of – let alone neutralised – some of the more disturbing moral and psychological aspects of the Gothic mode. Yet for now it is enough to make a simpler point. The Gothic was itself in a manner of speaking the first 'postmodern' experiment in English literary history: the first full-blown effort to reanimate, artificially, an extinct historical style for the purposes of mass entertainment. It sought in the anachronistic resurrection of 'romance' an uncanny intensification of everyday emotional life. It should not surprise us that in our own age – in which demonic images from the past haunt us sleeping and waking – we should find in the Gothic resurgence of the late eighteenth century such a powerful reflection of our own aspirations and fears.

What have we learned about the Gothic of late? One might begin with the derivation of the word itself, and in particular its architectural application. (It is difficult – one quickly realises – to keep the architectural and the literary aspects of the Gothic phenomenon apart, even for the purposes of semantic clarification. As in Gothic fiction, where physical space and psychological space are routinely confounded, the one kind of Gothic 'infestation' was intellectually implicated in the other from the outset.) The words 'Goth' and 'Gothic' were originally ethnographic terms – used in England since the Middle Ages to refer to those warlike Germanic tribesmen, traditionally thought to have emanated from the Baltic island of Gotland, who between the third and fifth centuries AD invaded western and central Europe from the north and east, drove out the occupying Roman legions and helped precipitate the collapse of the Roman Empire in the west in 476 AD (The Goths overran the British Isles earlier in the fifth century, forcing the withdrawal of Roman troops there in 426 or 427.) The marauding Gothic tribes were described in two well-known

Latin texts of late antiquity: Julius Caesar's *De Bello Gallico*, or *Commentaries on the Gallic War* (c. 52 BC) and Tacitus' *Germania* (c. 98 AD), an influential translation of which, entitled *A Treatise on the Situation, Manners, and Inhabitants of Germany*, was published in England in 1777.

Not surprisingly, during the Italian Renaissance, with a rebirth of interest in classical antiquity, the term 'Gothic' became a byword for savagery and destructiveness. Humanist poets and philosophers regularly deprecated the Goths as crude barbarians who by obliterating the brilliant legacy of Greco-Roman culture had plunged Europe into centuries of moral and intellectual darkness. The spread of Christianity had alleviated the gloom somewhat, but much in the way of 'civilisation' had been lost. True, once established and diversified into the modern nations, the various fair-haired peoples descended from the Goths (the English, French, German, Dutch and Scandinavians) had developed their own artistic and architectural traditions: the great medieval cathedrals of northern Europe – so different in style from the ancient light-filled temples of the Mediterranean – were their most obvious and lasting monument. Yet 'Gothic' retained its negative associations, even as it developed new aesthetic meanings. It was in Italy, during the High Renaissance, that the term first took on its now-standard architectural sense – coming to signify any northern, non-classical or 'Germanic' style of building. The highly rationalised architecture of Greece and Rome had been founded on the so-called system of 'orders,' codified by Vitruvius in his *De Architectura* in the first century BC. Balance, symmetry and a strict mathematical adherence to decorum were the defining features of the classical style. Yet the 'rude' Gothic builders of the Middle Ages had wilfully ignored the orders and evolved instead their own 'free' and 'irregular' motifs: the pointed arch, the rib vault, the flying buttress, long galleries, clerestory windows and a type of arcaded wall-passage (still seen in surviving medieval English churches) known as a triforium.[11] In its various phases this 'Gothic' style had persisted in parts of Europe through the late fifteenth century. Today we revere the astounding visual intelligence and

11 For a general survey of the development of Gothic architecture in Europe see Paul Frankl, *Gothic Architecture*, trans. Dieter Pevsner (Baltimore, MD: Penguin Books, 1962). On the English Gothic style see Francis Bond, *Gothic Architecture in England: An Analysis of the Origin and Development of English Church Architecture from the Norman Conquest to the Dissolution of the Monasteries* (London: B. T. Batsford, 1905); Jean Bony, *The English Decorated Style: Gothic Architecture Transformed, 1250–1350* (Ithaca, NY: Cornell University Press, 1979); Peter Hampson Ditchfield, *English Gothic Architecture* (London: J. M. Dent, 1920); Samuel Gardner, *A Guide to English Gothic Architecture* (Cambridge: Cambridge University Press, 1922); and Nikolaus Pevsner, *The Englishness of English Art* (London: Architectural Press, 1956).

uncanny engineering skills exemplified in magnificent Gothic cathedrals, say, at Chartres, Salisbury or Winchester. By the time the Renaissance architect Alberti came to publish his *De re aedificatoria* in 1482, however, a polemical brief on behalf of the ancient Vitruvian system of orders, Gothic building had come to seem grotesque and bizarre, evocative indeed of the uncouth hordes among whom it had supposedly originated.

In England, the anti-Gothicism of the Renaissance survived in certain quarters well into the late seventeenth and early eighteenth century. For many classically educated men and women the terms 'Goth' and 'Gothic' would remain for some time loose catchwords for any kind of primitivism or offence to reason. Ancient Rome – or so wrote the poet John Dryden in his 'To Sir Godfrey Kneller' (1694) – had preserved the great artistic legacy of Greece, 'Till *Goths* and *Vandals*, a rude *Northern* Race, / Did all the matchless Monuments deface'.[12] Assailing an intellectual opponent in his *Characteristics* of 1733, the Earl of Shaftesbury complained that 'hardly a Tartar or a Goth would . . . reason so absurdly'.[13] 'O more than *Gothic* Ignorance!' exclaims Mrs Western of her loutish brother, Squire Western, in Henry Fielding's *Tom Jones* (1749).[14] And in *The Dunciad* (1743), his apocalyptic satire on the decay of wit and culture in the modern 'Age of Lead', Alexander Pope lamented the gloomy depredations of 'bold Ostrogoths' and 'fierce Visigoths' – whose mindless assaults on ancient learning foreshadowed the 'Hyperborean' ignorance of the present day.

Yet as early as the 1720s strong intellectual counterforces began to make themselves felt – first in architecture, then in the world of letters. In the wake of the Protestant revolution of 1688 and the (relatively) peaceful Hanoverian succession of 1714, Britain had entered on a period of both general political stability and enormous economic growth. Its commercial empire was expanding; its navy dominated the seas; and thanks to the institution of a national credit-based economy and accelerating developments in technology and manufacturing, it was modernising faster than any other country in Europe. National pride demanded new patriotic myths to underwrite Britain's growing power and prominence around the globe. One of the first intellectual by-products of this new cultural self-consciousness was a renewed interest in 'ancient' British history and the Goths in particular – who gradually came to be seen, through a

---

12 John Dryden, 'To Sir Godfrey Kneller', lines 47–8; in *The Poems and Fables of John Dryden*, ed. James Kinsley (London and Oxford: Oxford University Press, 1978), p. 497.
13 Anthony Ashley Cooper, Earl of Shaftesbury, *Characteristics of Men, Manners, Opinions, and Times* (1711; rpt., London, 1733), I, ii, 86.
14 Henry Fielding, *Tom Jones* (1749), vol. VII, p. iii.

complex process of ideological transvaluation, not as the illiterate marauders of old, but as primordial embodiments of a distinctively 'British' genius and cultural energy.[15] Tacitus' fleeting description in *Germania* of the old tribal councils of the Goths was both salient and exciting here: early eighteenth-century jurists and political commentators claimed to find in them not only the noble origins of the celebrated Anglo-Saxon *Witangemot*, or parliament, but the genesis of those age-old 'liberties' (the rights of assembly, habeas corpus, freedom of speech) guaranteed by the British constitution itself. Thus the poet James Thomson's paean in 'Liberty' (1734–6) to those inspired 'northern nations . . . fierce with freedom' who had thrown off the tyrannical Roman yoke in the person of Julius Caesar himself:

> Witness, Rome,
> Who saw'st thy Caesar from the naked land,
> Whose only fort was British hearts, repelled,
> To seek Pharsalian wreaths.[16]

Other writers eulogised the Goths' valour and magnanimity in battle, their innate love of fairness – they were thought to have devised the jury system – and their supposedly chivalrous treatment of women.[17]

One of the signal accomplishments of late twentieth-century scholarship has been to call attention to precisely this ideological and 'myth-making' aspect of the Gothic revival – especially in its early, mainly architectural, phase. The first half of the eighteenth century saw a veritable flurry of neo-Gothic construction in Britain, as various powerful Whig landowners, in league with nostalgically inclined architects and antiquarians, sought ways to celebrate in stone and

15 On eighteenth-century views of the ancient Goths and their contribution to British cultural and poetic tradition, see E. J. Clery and Robert Miles, eds., *Gothic Documents: A Sourcebook 1700–1820* (Manchester and New York: Manchester University Press, 2000), pp. 48–98; Paul Frankl, *The Gothic: Literary Sources and Interpretations through Eight Centuries* (Princeton, NJ: Princeton University Press, 1960); Samuel Kliger, *The Goths in England: A Study in Seventeenth and Eighteenth-Century Thought* (Cambridge, MA: Harvard University Press, 1952); Mark Madoff, 'The Useful Myth of Gothic Ancestry', *Studies in Eighteenth-Century Culture* 8 (1979), 337–50; R. J. Smith, *The Gothic Bequest: Medieval Institutions in British Thought, 1688–1863* (Cambridge: Cambridge University Press, 1987); Katie Trumpener, *Bardic Nationalism: The Romantic Novel and the British Empire* (Princeton, NJ: Princeton University Press, 1997); and Howard D. Weinbrot, *Britannia's Issue: The Rise of British Literature from Dryden to Ossian* (Cambridge and New York: Cambridge University Press, 1993).

16 James Thomson, *Liberty* (1734–6), in *Poetical Works of James Thomson*, ed. J. Logie Robertson (London: Oxford University Press, 1908), vol. II, pp. 640–3.

17 A discussion of the Goths' 'refined gallantry' with regard to women is to be found, for example, in letter III of Richard Hurd's *Letters on Chivalry and Romance* (1762), in *The Works of Richard Hurd, D. D.*, 8 vols. (London: Cadell and Davies, 1811). See also Clery and Miles, *Gothic Documents*, pp. 67–77.

plasterwork the growth and consolidation of the ancient 'British' constitution and the recently secured Protestant dispensation. It was a paradoxical process indeed: via the enabling myth of the ancient Goths, the architectural styles of the Middle Ages – in actuality a legacy of Britain's Catholic and feudal past – came to symbolise instead a new self-consciously Protestant (and specifically Whiggish) conception of evolving British political freedoms. Detached – at least in theory – from any lingering ecclesiastical meanings, Gothic became 'a repertoire of formal elements – pinnacles, tracery, pointed arches – that could be endlessly recontextualised, never wholly losing their evocative reference to the past, but capable of semantic adventure' and 'of assuming a new range of identities for the present'.[18]

Over the century hundreds of neo-Gothic structures were erected around the British Isles, typically on the grounds of the great aristocratic country seats. As the fashion for Gothic spread, every important landowner, it seemed, demanded a little mock-medieval tower or picturesque monastic 'ruin' somewhere on his property. Some of these whimsical creations were inspired pieces of architectural fantasia: Roger Morris' 'Gothic Tower' at Whitton Park (1734–5); William Kent's 'Merlin's Cave' at Richmond (1733); James Gibbs' 'Temple of Liberty' in the garden at Stowe (1741); Daniel Garrett's 'Culloden Tower' in Yorkshire (erected in 1746 to celebrate the Protestant rout of Bonny Prince Charlie and his supporters at Culloden the previous year); Robert Adam's Brizlee Tower at Alnwick Castle (1781); Michael 'Angelo' Rooker's Gatehouse at Battle Abbey, Sussex (1792). Others, like Beckford's Fonthill, verged, rather more unpleasantly, on monstrosity and kitsch. Yet informing every new 'Gothic' elevation was the nostalgic urge to connect – however oddly and artificially – with an imagined (romantic and heroic) national past. 'The result,' writes the architectural historian Chris Brooks, 'was a new class of landscape structure which as the poet and landscape gardener William Shenstone remarked, could "turn every bank and hillock . . . into historical ground".'[19] Individual connoisseurs might experiment with different components of the style: Walpole at Strawberry Hill – infatuated with the decorative caprices of late medieval church interiors – contrived a method for imitating fan-vaulting and filigreed tracery in papier mâché. But by the second half of the century most 'Persons of Refinement' were agreed – to build in Gothic was not only a way 'to say something about being British', but a potent means of asserting a deeper (if sometimes wishful) link between past and present.[20]

18 Chris Brooks, *The Gothic Revival* (London: Phaidon Press, 1999), p. 52.
19 *Ibid.*, p. 62.
20 *Ibid.*, p. 56.

Over the decades the same kind of transvaluation took place in the realm of letters – and, from one angle at least, for similarly chauvinistic reasons. As early as 1712, in a meditation on the 'Fairy Way of Writing' in *Spectator* No. 419, Joseph Addison had playfully lamented that while admirable in other respects, the cherished literary productions of classical antiquity lacked a certain 'Poetry': the sort that came of introducing into one's writing 'Persons who are not to be found in Being' – notably 'Fairies, Witches, Magicians, Demons, and departed Spirits.'

> Our Forefathers looked upon Nature with more Reverence and Horrour, before the World was enlightened by Learning and Philosophy, and loved to astonish themselves with the Apprehensions of Witchcraft, Prodigies, Charms and Enchantments. There was not a Village in *England* that had not a Ghost in it, the Churchyards were all haunted, every large Common had a Circle of Fairies belonging to it, and there was scarce a Shepherd to be met with who had not seen a Spirit.[21]

The dearth of 'Spirits' in ancient literature was to be regretted, the essayist averred, because tales of the supernatural inevitably 'raise a pleasing kind of Horrour in the Mind of the Reader, and amuse his Imagination with the Strangeness and Novelty of the Persons who are represented in them'.[22] Luckily, however, such pleasing horror was yet to be found – and close to home indeed. Precisely because of their dark and ghost-ridden past – not to mention a distinctly morbid national temperament – 'the *English*' had always excelled in the creation of baleful fancies.

> Among all the Poets of this Kind our *English* are much the best, by what I have yet seen, whether it be that we abound with more Stories of this Nature, or that the Genius of our Country is fitter for this sort of Poetry. For the *English* are naturally Fanciful, and very often disposed by that Gloominess and Melancholly of Temper, which is so frequent in our Nation, to many wild Notions and Visions, to which others are not so liable.[23]

The greatest example of this 'wild' native genius was indisputably the poet Shakespeare. Even when flouting the laws of nature outright, Shakespeare had an unmatched ability to make the reader believe in the vivacity of his visionary creations:

21 Joseph Addison, *The Spectator*, No. 419 (1712), in *The Spectator*, ed. Donald F. Bond, 5 vols. (Oxford: Oxford University Press, 1965), vol. III, p. 512.
22 *Ibid.*, vol. III, p. 572.
23 *Ibid.*, vol. III, p. 571.

There is something so wild and yet so solemn in the Speeches of his Ghosts, Fairies, Witches, and the like Imaginary Persons, that we cannot forbear thinking them natural, tho' we have no Rule by which to judge of them, and must confess, if there are such Beings in the World, it looks highly probable they should talk and act as he has represented them.[24]

Still other English masters had a similar 'Talent in Representations of this Kind': Milton when he depicted the frightful apparitions of Sin and Death in *Paradise Lost*, Spenser when he evoked 'a whole Creation of . . . shadowy Persons' – weird and arabesque – in his romance of *The Faerie Queene*.[25]

It was not long before critics were correlating the English poetic genius – and kindred fondness for the supernatural – with both the Goths and the Middle Ages. As in architecture, a pronounced taste for non-classical aesthetic models had begun to infiltrate the world of British letters by mid century. As poets, playwrights and novelists – like their counterparts in the visual and plastic arts – came increasingly to derogate classical tradition they turned once again to an imaginary English past to underwrite new and dizzyingly romantic creative imperatives. The Goths – now imagined as *ur*-poets, intoning 'sacred fables' in Britain's primordial forests – became the human symbols of a supposedly indigenous 'bardic' tradition: one untrammelled by the rules of decorum and the oppressive regularities of Greek and Latin aesthetics. English authors were at their strongest and most sublime – or so patriotically minded commentators came to insist – when they returned to their native 'Gothic' roots. Thus Spenser, Bishop Hurd asserted in his *Letters on Chivalry and Romance* (1762), was one of the noblest of English poets precisely because he revitalised those 'Gothic fictions and manners' first allegorised in the works of Chaucer and Malory.[26] Living in the 'dark shades of Gothic barbarism', wrote Elizabeth Montagu, 'before philosophy had . . . mitigated the austerity of ignorant devotion, or tamed the fierce spirit of enthusiasm,' the 'wondrous' Shakespeare 'had no resources but in the very phantoms that walked the night of ignorance and superstition'. Yet the very credulity of his 'Gothic' age was a priceless boon – for all these 'ghosts, fairies, goblins, elves, were as assistant to Shakespear, and gave as much of the sublime, and of the marvellous, to his fictions, as nymphs, satyrs, fawns, and even the triple Geryon, to the works of ancient bards'.[27] Contemporary poets and fabulists soon came to identify powerfully with the

24 *Ibid.*, vol. III, p. 572.
25 *Ibid.*, vol. III, pp. 572–3.
26 See Hurd, *Letters on Chivalry and Romance*, Letter VII.
27 Elizabeth Montagu, *An Essay on the Writings and Genius of Shakespear, Compared with the Greek and French Dramatic Poets, with Some Remarks upon the Misrepresentations of Mons. de Voltaire* (London, 1769), pp. 119,

bardic model of old. Greek poetry was all very well – Coleridge would declaim a few decades later – 'but if I wish my feelings to be affected, if I wish my heart to be touched, if I wish to melt into sentiment and tenderness, I must turn to the heroic songs of the Goths, to the poetry of the middle ages'.[28]

The wave of recent critical interest in the 'Britishness' of Gothic – in its not-so secret role in animating certain useful collective fantasies about the English political and cultural past – has been illuminating indeed. More acutely than ever we now apprehend the intellectual consanguinity between the Gothic phenomenon and the increasingly nationalistic preoccupations of eighteenth-century criticism: the effort to define a specifically 'English' literary canon, the rise of the cult of original genius, the celebration of Shakespeare as national poet, the revival of interest in local folk culture, 'popular antiquities' and vernacular literary genres such as the ballad and oral epic. We have likewise been helped – if at times a bit doggedly – to understand the often comical xenophobia of Gothic fiction itself. Even while revelling in murky exotic locales and romantic ages past – Walpole's *Castle of Otranto* is set in thirteenth-century Italy, Ann Radcliffe's *Mysteries of Udolpho* (1794) in sixteenth-century France and Italy during the wars of religion and Matthew Lewis' *The Monk* (1796) in Madrid during the Inquisition – English Gothic novelists regularly expatiated on the vice and superstition to be found in Catholic countries and on the natural predisposition of certain non-Anglo-Saxon (usually Mediterranean) racial types towards credulity, hypocrisy, physical cruelty and sexual depravity. Thus Radcliffe's sinister references to 'Italian revenge' and 'the delirium of Italian love' in *Udolpho*, or Matthew Lewis' ultra-lurid depiction of secret convent excesses in *The Monk*. In one of the numerous anti-Catholic vignettes in the Anglo-Irish writer Charles Maturin's *Melmoth the Wanderer* (1820) a character is held against his will in a 'convent of Ex-Jesuits' in Madrid, where he witnesses an especially phantasmagoric episode of monkish abuse:

> A naked human being, covered with blood, and uttering screams of rage and torture, flashed by me; four monks pursued him – they had lights. I had shut the door at the end of the gallery – I felt they must return and pass me – I was still on my knees, and trembling from head to foot. The victim reached the door, found it shut, and rallied. I turned, and saw a groupe [*sic*] worthy of Murillo. A more perfect human form never existed than that of this unfortunate youth. He stood in an atmosphere of despair – he was streaming with blood. The monks, with their lights, their scourges, and their dark habits, seemed like a

---

28 Samuel Taylor Coleridge, 'General Character of the Gothic Literature and Art' (1818), in *Coleridge's Miscellaneous Criticism*, ed. Thomas Middleton Raysor (London: Constable, 1936), p. 12.

groupe of demons who had made prey of a wandering angel, – the groupe resembled the infernal furies pursuing a mad Orestes. And, indeed, no ancient sculptor ever designed a figure more exquisite and perfect than that they had so barbarously mangled. Debilitated as my mind was by the long slumber of its powers, this spectacle of horror and cruelty woke them in a moment. I rushed forward in his defence – I struggled with the monks – I uttered some expressions which, though I was hardly conscious of, they remembered and exaggerated with all the accuracy of malice.[29]

The sado-homoerotic element here – at once voyeuristic and repellent – is typical of both Maturin's fiction and the Gothic genre in general. Like eighteenth-century pornographers (with whom they had more than little in common) Gothic novelists almost reflexively associated the monastic or conventual setting with the purportedly foreign 'abomination' of same-sex desire. It is peculiar, once again, that British fantasists should seek to restore a lost 'romance' to English literature by demonising the imagined erotic habits of Catholic monks and nuns, but there it is: the medievalised settings of the Gothic mode, conjoining with nationalistic imperatives, combined to produce – as if by socio-chemical reaction – precisely such dire yet titillating references to the 'pollutions' to be found in benighted nations across the Channel.

Yet at the same time it might be argued that, despite their many virtues, recent 'ideological' treatments of the Gothic have not entirely reversed the early twentieth-century prejudice against Gothic writing – nor indeed gone very far towards assessing the deeper cultural and psychological significance of characteristic Gothic themes and motifs. To the basic generic problem – why tales of horror and the supernatural should have proliferated so wildly in the British Isles during the second half of the eighteenth century – the responses typically proffered by modern-day scholars remain partial, muted, even oddly dissociated. To affirm, with Addison, that there is something distinctively 'British' about the Gothic mode is undoubtedly true, but it is hardly the whole story. Such bland generalisation does not begin to explain why the tale-of-terror craze spread so quickly to other countries and climes (notably Germany and the United States) or how we should understand the genre's strange kinetic shifts in mood and manner – from the epicene, campy, highly theatrical medievalism of Horace Walpole, through the dreamy, feminised, vision-weaving of Radcliffe, to the febrile sensation-mongering of Lewis, Hogg, Maturin, Bram Stoker and Poe. The emotional 'common denominator' linking such ill-assorted phenomena remains, it must be said, somewhat elusive.

29 Charles Robert Maturin, *Melmoth the Wanderer*, ed. Victor Sage (London: Penguin Books, 2000), p. 120.

In seeking a broader explanation for the popularity of Gothic, one could do worse than begin with a view much promulgated in the eighteenth century itself: that the appetite for Gothic story arose out of an encroaching sense of boredom and loss. Certainly by the 1760s, when Walpole galvanised the literary world with *The Castle of Otranto*, certain kinds of imaginative writing once popular in Britain had come to seem stale and over-familiar. 'The books that formed part of the ordinary library in the year 1764', Virginia Woolf reminds us, in her review of Edith Birkhead's *Tale of Terror* from 1921,

> were, presumably, Johnson's *Vanity of Human Wishes*, Gray's Poems, Richardson's *Clarissa*, Addison's *Cato*, Pope's *Essay on Man*. No one could wish for a more distinguished company. At the same time, as literary critics are too little aware, a love of literature is often roused and for the first years nourished not by the good books, but by the bad . . . In the eighteenth century there must have been a very large public which found no delight in the peculiar literary merits of the age; and if we reflect how long the days were and how empty of distraction, we need not be surprised to find a school of writers grown up in flat defiance of the prevailing masters. Horace Walpole, Clara Reeve and Mrs Radcliffe all turned their backs on their time and plunged into the delightful obscurity of the Middle Ages, which were so much richer than the eighteenth century in castles, barons, moats, and murders.[30]

Woolf's characteristic diffidence notwithstanding, the novelist touches here on a mid-century mood still insufficiently anatomised by historians of eighteenth-century taste. What seems to have taken hold in the world of English letters by the 1760s was in fact a kind of collective readerly malaise – a growing sense of vacuity, disappointment and anomie. Something mysterious and exciting had *gone*, both from literature and the world, and human emotional life was impoverished by its absence. In identifying the lost thing as 'poetry' and connecting it with the 'Reverence and Horrour' of the supernatural, Addison – to judge by the approbation of his contemporaries – moved on just the right track. A deep sense of imaginative deprivation pervades the works of mid-century commentators. Thus the wistful, almost erotic languor in Bishop Hurd's *Letters on Chivalry and Romance*. Exquisite 'Tales of Faery' had once predominated in English literature, he opined, until cruel 'Reason . . . drove them off the scene, and would endure these *lying wonders*, neither in their own proper shape, nor as masked in figures.' After '[wantoning] it so long in the world of fiction', lovely 'Fancy' had been 'constrained, against her will, to ally herself with strict truth, if she would gain admittance into reasonable

---

30 Woolf, 'Gothic Romance', p. 305.

company'. Hurd grieved at her fettering. 'What we have gotten by this revolution, you will say, is a great deal of sense. What we have lost, is a world of fine fabling; the illusion of which is so grateful to the *charmed Spirit*.'[31]

In his *History of English Poetry* (1778) the poet and critic Thomas Warton was equally disconsolate. He blamed the cold, 'scientific' and rationalising spirit of the sixteenth and seventeenth centuries for suppressing those wondrous 'incredibilities' more precious to the soul of man than truth itself.

> The fashion of treating every thing scientifically, applied speculation and theory to the arts of writing. Judgment was advanced above imagination, and rules of criticism were established. The brave eccentricities of original genius, and the daring hardiness of native thought, were intimidated by metaphysical sentiments of perfection and refinement . . . [The] lover of true poetry will ask what have we gained by this revolution? It may be answered, much good sense, good taste, and good criticism. But, in the mean time, we have lost a set of manners, and system of machinery, more suitable to the purposes of poetry than those which have been adopted in their place.[32]

What seemed, above all, to have vanished was the experience of *belief* itself. Try as one might to regain it, the state of credulous 'awe' produced by the ancient tales of miracles and witchcraft, ghosts and enchantments, seemed impossible to recover: humanity itself had been cruelly awakened from some long, dream-ridden, yet deeply enthralling slumber. Like the 'chimeras' of chivalry, the metaphysical visions of the past had evaporated 'as snow melts before the sun'.[33] Contemplating this process of spiritual disillusionment writers like Hurd and Warton found a sad, strange kinship with Cervantes' Don Quixote. He was both soul-mate and culture-hero, a mournful companion in loss. Just as the would-be knight had been jarred out of his fantasies by his crass friends, shaken from his chivalric daydreams and brought back to a world without magic – the dreariness of the merely *real* – so they felt themselves exiled in the ordinary, cut off from passionate feeling, estranged from some deeper and more intense mode of being. They deplored the heartlessness of his creator. In that Cervantes had wilfully embraced the role of sceptic and comic debunker, wrote John Pinkerton in his *Dissertation on the Origin and Progress of the Scythians or Goths* (1787), he was surely to be 'execrated'. Had Cervantes

---

31 Hurd, *Works*, vol. IV, p. 350.

32 Thomas Warton, *The History of English Poetry from the Close of the Eleventh to the Commencement of the Eighteenth Century*, 2 vols. (London: J. Dodsley, 1778), vol. II, p. 463.

33 James Beattie, 'On Fable and Romance', in *Dissertations Moral and Critical*, vol. II of *The Philosophical and Critical Works of James Beattie* (London: W. Strahan and T. Cadell, 1783), p. 563.

written three centuries sooner – depriving later ages of even more in the way of beautiful fable-making – 'we must have branded him as the greatest enemy of society that ever wrote'.[34]

For those less demoralised by Quixotean pathos, the question was how to restore – or at least approximate through art – a lost world of numinous sensation. The ruined architectural spaces of the medieval past once again provided a crucial hint. Something about the looming, claustral grandeur of the Gothic cathedrals had a power, it seemed, of reawakening exactly that 'sacred awe' – a sense of vast, encompassing and imponderable spiritual forces – elsewhere absent from the world. 'The contemplation of the works of antique art', Coleridge would subsequently argue, 'excites a feeling of elevated beauty, and exalted notions of the human self; but the Gothic architecture impresses the beholder with a sense of self-annihilation; he becomes, as it were, a part of the work contemplated.'[35] Might it not be possible to devise a kind of literature with the same soul-shaking effect? In the 1797 novel *Family Secrets*, the orator and bookseller Courtney Melmoth (Samuel Jackson Pratt) called explicitly for a mode of imaginative writing which would reproduce the primitive *étonnement* experienced in Gothic cathedrals.[36] It should hardly surprise us that the dank yet magnificent spaces of real-world Gothic – castles, crypts, cloisters and the like – figure so prominently within Gothic fiction. The late eighteenth century ineluctably regarded the Gothic edifice as a kind of sensation-machine: a sort of fantastic psychic compression-chamber in which one might recreate, atavistically, the thrilling sense of being overwhelmed by something bigger and more potent than oneself. In the absence of a real building a literary fabrication might serve just as well. In Gothic fiction's relentlessly 'architectural' obsessions – witnessed in titles such as *The Castle of Otranto*, *The Mysteries of Udolpho*, *The Castles of Athlyn and Dunbane*, *The Recess*, *The Old English Manor House*, *The Abbey of Clugny*, *The Priory of St Clair*, *Emmeline, or, The Orphan of the Castle*, *The Midnight Groan, or, The Spectre of the Chapel*, *The Children of the Abbey*, *The Church of St Siffrid*, *The Castle of Wolfenbach*, *The Castle of Hardayne* or *The Castle of St Vallery* (not to mention 'The Fall of the House of Usher', *The Tenant of Wildfell Hall* or *Wuthering Heights*) – we not only see the inevitable (punning) Gothic linkage between buildings and stories but the genre's presiding fantasies of self-enclaustration, physical debilitation and psychic surrender

---

34 John Pinkerton, *A Dissertation on the Origin and Progress of the Scythians or Goths, Being an Introduction to the Ancient and Modern History of Europe* (London: John Nichols, 1787), p. 138.
35 Coleridge, 'General Character of the Gothic Mind in the Middle Ages', in *Miscellaneous Criticism*, p. 7.
36 See Tompkins, *Popular Novel*, p. 221.

writ large. In order to replicate the 'sense of self-annihilation' associated with Gothic buildings, a novel – it was argued – had to arouse in its readers nothing less than metaphysical dread: some version – however fleeting or artificial – of that 'universal apprehension of superior agency' commonly associated with the supernatural.[37] Here Gothic aestheticians drew fruitfully on contemporary psychological theory – notably John Locke's famous notion that feelings and emotions derived from the association of ideas. (Men were afraid of the dark, Locke argued in his *Essay concerning Human Understanding*, because as children they been taught by 'nursemaids' or old women to connect 'the ideas of ghosts and goblins with that of darkness'. The association once made, 'night ever after becomes painful and horrible to the imagination').[38] Of all the human passions, wrote the critic John Dennis in 1704, none was 'more capable of giving a great spirit to poetry' than 'terror'. Terror was precisely that 'disturbance of mind proceeding from an apprehension of an approaching evil, threatening destruction or very great trouble to us or ours'. It made sense, therefore, that the greatest 'enthusiastic terror' should derive from 'religious ideas'. For what indeed, he concluded, 'can produce a greater terror than the idea of an angry god?'[39]

In calling for this spiritually fraught 'literature of terror' promoters of the Gothic usually invoked, in turn, the concept of the sublime – that rampant, radiant, yet also problematic master-trope of eighteenth-century psychology and aesthetics. The theory of the sublime seemed to authorise precisely those extreme themes and techniques necessary for the re-engagement of jaded readers. The concept itself had its origins in late antiquity. In *Peri Hupsous* (or *On the Sublime*) the first- or second-century Greco-Christian rhetorician Longinus had defined the sublime as any phenomenon that provoked 'astonishment' in a viewer and prompted him to contemplate the infinite majesty of God. Magnificent or threatening objects in nature (mighty torrents of water, erupting volcanoes, dizzying precipices) were sublime, but so too was any sort of poetry characterised by 'greatness' or 'grandeur' of expression. Confronting the dazzling verbal flights of Homer, Pindar, Sappho or the anonymous author of Scripture, Longinus suggested, the reader was drawn out of himself, lifted up and 'transported' into a state of religious ecstasy.

---

37 Nathan Drake, 'On Gothic Superstition', in *Literary Hours, or Sketches Critical and Narrative* (London, 1800), vol. II, p. 137.

38 See John Locke, *An Essay Concerning Human Understanding* (London, 1690), vol. II, ch. 3.

39 John Dennis, 'The Grounds of Criticism in Poetry' (1704) in Scott Elledge (ed.), *Eighteenth-Century Critical Essays*, 2 vols. (Ithaca, NY: Cornell University Press, 1961), vol. II, pp. 121–2.

In his 1757 *Philosophical Enquiry into the Origin of Our Ideas of the Sublime and the Beautiful*, Edmund Burke updated Longinus' concept of sublimity by relating it, once again, to the Lockean theory of mind. A sublime object, according to Burke, was anything that evoked an 'idea' of pain and terror, yet did not pose any real danger to the observer. When contemplated from a safe distance, objects ordinarily frightening in the extreme (typically anything dark, vast, powerful, obscure, gloomy, towering or 'irregular' in shape) became sources of deep, if perverse, excitement and pleasure. They stimulated the instinct of 'self-preservation', resulting in 'certain violent emotions of the nerves', but since they did no actual harm, the viewer was left with a paradoxical feeling of 'delight' and self-expansion.[40] Burke agreed with Longinus that poetry could induce the same sublime emotions inspired by real-world phenomena. Thanks to his magnificent yet sometimes 'obscure' trains of imagery – as in the description in *Paradise Lost* of 'the travels of the fallen angels through their dismal habitation' in Hell –

> – O'er many a dark and dreary vale
> They pass'd, and many a region dolorous;
> O'er many a frozen, many a fiery Alp;
> Rocks, caves, lakes, fens, bogs, dens and shades of death,
> A universe of death.

– Milton, for example, was able to produce in his readers the same gratifying state of 'fearful delight' associated with sublime objects in nature.[41] 'The sublime is an idea belonging to self-preservation', wrote Burke; 'it is therefore one of the most affecting we have'.[42]

Like antiquarianism and the craze for things medieval, the cult of the sublime provided Gothic novelists with a certain (dubious) intellectual respectability – not to mention a handy quasi-ethical justification for the somewhat distasteful psychic shock tactics they now began to unleash on more or less eager readers. Granted, certain aspects of the cult were benign enough. In the novels of Ann Radcliffe the new taste for sublimity expressed itself mainly in lady-like passages of nature description – albeit of an unusually protracted, engorged and stupendous sort. Radcliffe inevitably emphasised the sublime's uplifting effect on the mind and soul of the observer. Confronted by gleaming mountain crag, crashing torrent or bottomless chasm, even her most abused and downtrodden heroines find themselves exhilarated by such 'fearsome' evidences of

---

40 Edmund Burke, *A Philosophical Enquiry into the Origin of Our Ideas of the Sublime and Beautiful* (1757), ed. J. T. Boulton (London: Routledge & Kegan Paul, 1958), pp. 38–40.
41 *Ibid.*, pp. 174–5.
42 *Ibid.*, p. 86.

God's omnipotence. Thus the somewhat incongruous fit of spiritual transport felt by Emily St Aubert, heroine of *Udolpho*, when she is dragged through the Alps by her villainous brigand-kidnapper, Count Montoni –

> Emily, often as she travelled among the clouds, watched in silent awe their billowy surges rolling below; sometimes, wholly closing upon the scene, they appeared like a world of chaos, and, at others, spreading thinly, they opened and admitted partial catches of the landscape – the torrent, whose astounding roar had never failed, tumbling down the rocky chasm, huge cliffs white with snow, or the dark summits of the pine forests, that stretched mid-way down the mountains. But who may describe her rapture, when, having passed through a sea of vapour, she caught a first view of Italy; when, from the ridge of one of those tremendous precipices that hang upon Mount Cenis and guard the entrance of that enchanting country, she looked down through the lower clouds, and, as they floated away, saw the grassy vales of Piedmont at her feet, and, beyond, the plains of Lombardy extending to the farthest distance, at which appeared, on the faint horizon, the doubtful towers of Turin?[43]

Often enough, however, objects and scenes once deemed far too macabre, horrific or sexually perverse for polite literature came now to be valued for exactly those qualities: for their kinky-delightful effect on readers' nerves. Classical aesthetics held that some subjects were simply too shocking for a dramatist to represent directly: 'you will not let Medea slay her boys before the audience, or Atreus cook his horrid banquet of human flesh', wrote Horace in his *Ars Poetica*; 'anything that you thus thrust upon my sight I discredit and revolt at'.[44] Yet under the sway of the sublime, nothing – no matter how ghastly or repugnant – seemed too outré to enlist as a subject, so long as it provoked in readers some thrilled or 'affrighted' response. Thus Lewis in *The Monk* could depict the evisceration of an evil nun – she is mauled by a mob of 'Rioters' until 'no more than a mass of flesh, unsightly, shapeless, and disgusting' – without regard for decorum or good taste: the 'strong' sensations elicited by such a description – of fright, nausea, repulsion, *schadenfreude*, relief – merely set the seal on the sublimity of the work and its devices.[45] The decaying corpse, the carious skeleton, the blood-soaked apparition: such were

43 Ann Radcliffe, *The Mysteries of Udolpho*, ed. Bonamy Dobrée (Oxford and New York: Oxford University Press, 1998), p. 165.
44 Horace, *The Art of Poetry*, in E. C. Wickham, *Horace for English Readers: Being a Translation of the Poems of Quintus Horatius Flaccus into English Prose* (Oxford: Clarendon Press, 1903), p. 350.
45 Matthew Lewis, *The Monk*, ed. Howard Anderson (Oxford and New York: Oxford University Press), p. 356.

the Boschean dramatis personae of the new 'Satanic School' of British fiction. Literary *fashionistas* revelled in the gore. Even in 'the present polished period of society', Nathan Drake asserted, 'there are thousands who are yet alive to all the horrors of witchcraft, to all the solemn and terrible graces of the appalling spectre'. Artfully conducted, even the most grisly spectacle might result in the 'grateful astonishment' of readers and a 'welcome' (if regressive) sensation of fear.[46]

We do well to take seriously the extraordinary malaise – physical and metaphysical – that prompted this hunger for stimulation. The Gothic obsession with things dire and obscene sheds light not only on the evolution of taste but on certain troubled (and troubling) aspects of modernity itself. The reiterated complaint about the withdrawal of the numinous – the abrupt departure of 'wonder' from the world – should first of all be deeply heeded; for seen in broadest terms, the collective craving after Gothic was a kind of *symptom* – of the emotional void left by that complex and momentous historical transformation known as secularisation. It is no accident that the Gothic craze arose precisely at a time when age-old folk beliefs regarding apparitions, witchcraft, demonic possession, miracles, omens and the like had been largely supplanted – at least superficially – by new sceptical attitudes. Thanks to accelerating developments in science and technology, the waning of religious controversy and the subsequent rationalisation of countless aspects of everyday life, educated English men and women were now far less inclined than in past centuries to resort to supernatural explanations for bizarre or unsettling events. Official culture registered the change: parliament made witchcraft accusations illegal in Britain in 1736; and by mid century necromancy, astrology and other forms of occult belief had been similarly discredited.[47] A raft of phenomena once held to be supernatural in origin were reinterpreted in new and strictly materialistic terms. Ghosts and spectres, for example, traditionally seen as marvellous emissaries from an invisible spirit-world, came increasingly to be regarded as mental entities: hallucinatory figments arising from the diseased brain or 'sensorium' of the person who claimed to see them. By the 1790s – the break-out decade of Gothic experimentation – this 'scientific' theory of

---

46 Nathan Drake, 'On Gothic Superstition', in *Literary Hours, or Sketches Critical and Narrative*, 2 vols. (London, 1800; rpt. New York: Earland, 1970), vol. II, p. 137.
47 On the waning of supernatural belief in England see W. E. H. Lecky's magisterial nineteenth-century study, *The History of the Rise and Influence of the Spirit of Rationalism in Europe* (1865; rpt. New York: D. Appleton, 1919). For a brilliant and authoritative modern treatment of the phenomenon, see Keith Thomas, *Religion and the Decline of Magic* (New York: Charles Scribner's Sons, 1971).

apparitions was widely accepted, as popular medical treatises such as Alexander Crichton's *Nature and Origin of Mental Derangement* (1798) and Christoph Friedrich Nicolai's *Memoir on the Appearance of Spectres or Phantoms Occasioned by Disease* (1799) attested.[48]

Some Gothic novelists, paradoxically, sought to present themselves as propagandists for the new enlightened dispensation. Ann Radcliffe always played a famous double game. Her novels are crammed full of apparently supernatural events – strange knockings, unearthly music, subtly moving shrouds under which corpses seem to stir – all meant to keep the reader (like the heroine) in a state of 'terrific' mental unease. Yet by the end of the Radcliffean narrative, some all-too mundane explanation is inevitably forthcoming for every mystifying incident – usually accompanied by pedantic editorial asides on the follies of credulity and superstition. Radcliffe was much criticised for this banalising technique, and most of the terror writers who followed in her stead wholeheartedly rejected the clumsy 'explained supernatural' device. The gloomy fiends of Lewis and Maturin prowl the human world at will, unmolested by authorial temporising.

Yet even Radcliffe's ambiguous commitments do not undermine the larger point: that by the end of the eighteenth century, 'ghosts,' as J. M. S. Tompkins puts it, 'were a felt want'.[49] For all of its self-conscious archaism the Gothic is painfully modern in this aspect: its ineluctably god-deprived outlook. To be 'Gothic' in tendency is to hanker nostagically for some – *any* – spiritual manifestation: whether of deity, devil or something in between. (Figures such as Maturin's immortal Melmoth, living painfully on through the centuries, seem to inhabit an eerie realm between the human and the demonic.) But the missing *pneumaton* never materialises. The pathos – or bathos – of the Gothic mode lies precisely in the fact that no matter how dotingly invoked, the 'Invisible World' of old cannot be artificially reanimated. Reciting some gloomy passage from *The Monk* or *Udolpho* will never bring grim-faced Mephisto – or even a reeking minion – to one's darkened chamber at midnight. Critics often complain about the artistic ineptitude of Gothic fiction: that the things meant to boggle make us laugh. Yet at the deepest level such complaints register ontological as well as aesthetic disappointment. Even while celebrating the new imperatives of the Enlightenment, the eighteenth century also mourned – as we do – a lost world of supernatural beings. In the pale, magic-lantern-like illusionism of Gothic it

48 See Terry Castle, 'Spectral Politics: Apparition Belief and the Romantic Imagination', in *The Female Thermometer: Eighteenth-Century Culture and the Invention of the Uncanny* (Oxford and New York: Oxford University Press, 1995), pp. 168–89.

49 Tompkins, *Popular Novel*, p. 219.

learned to make do with cheap simulacra. Today, despite all the 'spectralising' marvels of photography, film, computer animation and virtual reality, we have no doubt learned to do the same.

Granted, even as the Gothic failed at the larger task – the reintegration of human and spirit worlds – it indubitably succeeded at a lesser: the intense arousal of readers. By eighteenth-century standards the novels of Walpole, Radcliffe and Lewis were extravagantly popular, spawning hundreds of imitations and knock-offs over the decades. (As Byron's touching tribute to her in *Childe Harold* attests, Radcliffe's vogue was particularly enduring, lasting well into the nineteenth century.) If Gothic necromancers inevitably failed to raise up real ghosts, their literary 'phantomising' exerted, over a generation, a kind of convulsive, contagious mass appeal. 'When a family was numerous', wrote Sir Walter Scott of *Udolpho*,

> the volumes always flew, and were sometimes torn, from hand to hand, and the complaints of those whose studies were thus interrupted, were a general tribute to the genius of the author. Another might be found of a different and higher description, in the dwelling of the lonely invalid, or unregarded votary of celibacy, who was bewitched away from a sense of solitude, of indisposition, of the neglect of the world, or of secret sorrow, by the potent charm of this mighty enchantress.[50]

Something about the form managed to gratify – the bathos of its spiritual ambitions notwithstanding.

This appeal was not at bottom, one suspects, primarily an intellectual one. Which isn't to say that Gothic fiction lacked a cognitive or epistemological dimension. At least since the 1960s critics have argued, if sometimes inchoately, for a certain 'heuristic' efficacy in the tale of terror: that it allowed for the expression of ideas and themes too difficult, taboo or transgressive to articulate in any other form. In a now-classic study, *The Fantastic: A Structural Approach to a Literary Genre* (1970), Tzvetan Todorov suggested, for example, that supernatural tales flourished when they did because, in an age of repressive decorums, they provided an imaginative format in which forbidden psychosexual themes – 'incest, homosexuality, love for several persons at once, necrophilia [and] excessive sensuality' – might be broached with relative impunity. According to Todorov the supernatural itself licensed this exploration of 'unspeakable' topics. 'The penalization of certain acts by society', he writes, 'provokes a penalization invoked in and by the individual himself, forbidding him to approach

---

50 Sir Walter Scott, *Lives of Eminent Novelists and Dramatists*, rev. edn (London and New York: Frederick Warne and Co., 1887), p. 555.

certain themes. More than a simple pretext, the fantastic is a means of combat against this kind of censorship as well as the other: *sexual excesses will be more readily accepted by any censor if they are attributed to the devil.*'[51] A good example of the 'blame it on the devil' phenomenon occurs in the opening sequence of Lewis' *The Monk*, when the proud yet susceptible cleric of the title, Ambrosio, appears to fall in love – scandalously enough – with a pretty boy-novice in his convent. Quasi-catamitical caresses ensue, but just as Ambrosio seems intent on consummating his unlawful passion, the 'boy' is revealed as a she-devil in disguise. Lewis is thus able to have it both ways: the taboo subject is foregrounded – homosexuality – only to be quickly neutralised by the supernatural (yet erotically normalising) explanation. Such teasing play with conceptual categories, Todorov argues, played a historic role in the creation of modern consciousness. By bringing subjects such as homosexuality at least partly into view, the Gothic fantasists of the late eighteenth century in fact prepared the intellectual ground, Todorov concludes, for pioneering new cognitive regimens – such as psychoanalysis – in which such themes might be confronted with greater directness, clarity and intellectual dispassion.[52]

Other critics find other kinds of 'ideas' in Gothic fiction. Feminist critics argue that by virtue of its melodramatic plots and exotic settings, the genre allowed for the covert expression of unorthodox opinions on gender and the moral, social and political status of women in late eighteenth-century British society. This 'subversive' articulation, the feminist argument usually goes, was allegorical in nature – a matter of hidden metaphors and symbolic topographies. Thus the grim Gothic castle might stand for the oppressive rulings of masculine law; the terrorisation of the heroine by the Gothic villain for the abusive nature of male–female relations under patriarchy; the penetration of crypt-like spaces for the threat (real or imagined) of female sexuality. An ideological contrast is sometimes drawn between Gothic novels written by men and those written by women – the former usually being seen, in the feminist view, as more complacent, if not reactionary, in their handling of sexual politics than the latter. A number of recent scholars have gone so far as to find in the fiction of Radcliffe, Reeve, Lee and the other female Gothicists a major critique of contemporary gender relations – one hauntingly akin, despite the fantastic displacement, to that put forward in Mary Wollstonecraft's *Vindication of the Rights of Woman* (1792) and other polemical feminist works of the period.

---

51 Tzvetan Todorov, *The Fantastic: A Structural Approach to a Literary Genre*, trans. Richard Howard (Ithaca, NY: Cornell University Press, 1975), p. 159.
52 See *ibid.*, pp. 160–2.

Yet for all of its interest and value, such theorising still seems to miss out on something: the essentially crude, even somatic exigencies of the genre. (Feminist critics in particular tend to over-intellectualise the form – with sometimes pedantic and repetitive results.) For a clue to the 'deep' pleasure of Gothic, we might ponder for a moment the intensely corporeal, even kinesiological language of its admirers. Enthusiasts like Sir Walter Scott and Nathan Drake wrote vividly of the 'thrilling' physical responses a truly terrifying Gothic tale could induce: gasping and breathlessness, chills, prickling hair on the neck, a sensation of immobilisation and panic, the convulsive tensing of 'nervous fibres', followed (usually) by exquisite feelings of relaxation and relief. Such responses were inevitably modelled within Gothic texts: Gothic heroines, for example, experience such kinetic arousal constantly – indeed, often appear incapable of experiencing anything but such arousal. (The primary function of the Gothic protagonist, one is tempted to suggest, may in fact be to serve on the reader's behalf as a kind of primitive 'sensing device' within the fictional world – as a sort of surrogate 'stimulus-receptor', whose reported reactions are meant to 'cue up' the same reactions in the reader. Self-analysis, moral problem-solving, the intellectual examination of one's surroundings – all of the other quasi-cognitive activities traditionally attributed to literary characters – seem here subordinated, if not overridden completely, by this single Pavlovian, even robotic, textual function.) Thus in *Udolpho*, when Emily St Aubert comes abruptly upon a mangled body being borne through a tunnel in Montoni's castle, her 'strength' immediately fails her and she has to grasp at a wall for support: 'A damp chillness came over her; her sight became confused; she knew not what had passed, or where she was, yet the groans of the wounded person still vibrated on her heart.' As always, Radcliffe notates the process of kinesiological normalisation too, for 'in a few moments,' once the cortège has passed, 'the tide of life seemed again to flow; [Emily] began to breathe more freely, and her senses revived'.[53] If the emotional self-reporting of Radcliffe's contemporaries is to be believed, such a passage might in fact serve as a trigger-point for similar responses in a susceptible reader.

Why might readers have enjoyed the vicarious activation of such responses? Perhaps, to put it baldly, because physical life itself had come to seem too safe, predictable and banal. Consider for a moment the nature of that 'present polished state of society' described by commentators like Nathan Drake. Though undoubtedly harsh by modern standards, late eighteenth-century bourgeois British culture represented, in phenomenological terms, the most comfortable,

---

53 Radcliffe, *Mysteries of Udolpho*, p. 318.

sedating, existentially 'buffered' society the Western world had yet seen. Scientific improvements, social and political reforms, the gradual 'refinement' of manners, the rise of new, cultivated pleasures – all had brought about, in the privileged classes especially, a growing faith in the perfectibility of human life. 'It is an age so full of light', wrote Sterne in *A Sentimental Journey* (1768) 'that there is scarce a country or corner of Europe whose beams are not crossed and interchanged with others.'[54] Once-dire threats to human security had been lessened or even abrogated – in some cases fairly recently. (Not least among these was the age-old menace posed by animal predators.) To be a prosperous denizen of a late eighteenth-century English city or town was to experience, increasingly, a generalised sense, above all, of being safe from attack: a kind of psychosomatic well-being – and concomitant moral optimism – unimaginable to previous generations.

But such complacency had its negative side too: sensual life had come to seem diminished, even deadened. A good deal of the psychic malaise of the mid to late eighteenth century may have been due, simply enough, to what might be called 'kinesiological ennui'. Spontaneous responses seemed to have been dulled; the instinctive life of the body routinised and overregulated. Polite society was no doubt tranquil – 'barbaric customs' had been banished – but it was also increasingly tedious. In the absence of strong sensation, more and more individuals seemed prone to psychosomatic disorders – such as that 'languor, listlessness, or want of resolution' described so painfully by James Boswell (a lifelong sufferer) as 'Hypochondria' or the spleen. Some artificial shock or stimulus was required: something to re-open, as it were, the blocked channels of feeling. The Gothic novel worked like caffeine in this respect, being first and foremost a stimulant, a kind of auto-intensifier, a way of feeling one's own body.

Yet we might take the hypothesis further. One is struck by a resemblance between the symptoms of 'Gothic arousal' and that atavistic physiological reflex – present in all living creatures including human beings – colloquially known as the 'fight or flight response'. Chills, involuntary tensing, racing heart, shortness of breath: such indeed are the stereotypical symptoms of the mammalian 'stress response' – that dramatic biochemical and hormonal reaction set in motion by the sympathetic nervous system whenever an organism confronts a threat to its survival. Such changes – in the view of evolutionary biology – serve a crucial adaptive function. By reallocating physiological

---

54 Laurence Sterne, *A Sentimental Journey Through France and Italy*, ed. Graham Petrie (Harmondsworth: Penguin Books, 1968), p. 36.

resources in the most efficient way, the 'fight or flight' mechanism allows an organism to respond quickly to a perceived danger, either by attacking it or running away.

According to Elias Canetti, the deepest, most ancient human fear is that of becoming *prey*. It expresses itself, even in the midst of civilised life, in lingering anxieties about being touched, grasped or seized, especially from behind.

> There is nothing that man fears more than the touch of the unknown. He wants to *see* what is reaching towards him, and to be able to recognise or at least classify it. Man always tends to avoid physical contact with anything strange. In the dark, the fear of an unexpected touch can mount to panic. Even clothes give insufficient security: it is easy to tear them and pierce through to the naked, smooth, defenceless flesh of the victim . . .
>
> The repugnance to being touched remains with us when we go about among people; the way we move in a busy street, in restaurants, trains or buses, is governed by it . . . The promptness with which apology is offered for an unintentional contact, the tension with which it is awaited, our violent and sometimes even physical reaction when it is not forthcoming, the antipathy and hatred we feel for the offender, even when we cannot be certain who it is – the whole knot of shifting and intensely sensitive reactions to an alien touch – proves that we are dealing here with a human propensity as deep-seated as it is alert and insidious; something which never leaves a man when he has once established the boundaries of his personality. [55]

With such observations in mind, one might float a theory: that through its charged symbolic play with the imagery of predation in particular – *of being seized and incorporated by something larger and more powerful than oneself* – the Gothic novel stimulated certain primitive affective mechanisms that had begun to atrophy as a result of the extraordinarily rapid civilisation – and banalisation – of contemporary life. The point was precisely to feel afraid, like a trapped or cornered animal. Such a theory would accord neatly with the ethnographic and symbolic meanings of '*Gothic*' noted earlier in this chapter. Though not, as we have seen, without their romantic admirers, the ancient Goths inevitably held sway in the eighteenth-century popular imagination as being among the great predators of human history – fabled marauders who had brought down Rome with the grim rapacity of wild beasts. It makes powerful metaphoric sense that a literary genre designed to arouse in the reader the visceral sensation of becoming prey should take on a name evoking the reputedly most fearsome and aggressive men and women of Western antiquity.

55 Elias Canetti, *Crowds and Power*, trans. Carol Stewart (1962; rpt. New York: Continuum Press, 1978), p. 15.

No reader of Gothic fiction can fail to notice how relentlessly it foregrounds the fight-or-flight scenario – sometimes again and again in the same work. Gothic fabulists delight in creating worlds in which assault is repeatedly threatened and escape nightmarishly difficult. The labyrinthine spaces of Gothic architecture, so emblematic of the form, seem designed precisely to intensify the vicarious sensation *that one is about to be seized*. With its bewildering irrationalisation of space – the mysterious portals and stairways, tunnels that seem to go nowhere, clanging trap-doors, blacked-out dungeons and crypts – the Gothic castle or convent, we realise, provides an exquisitely sinister mise-en-scène for fantasies of entrapment and immobilisation. One can't move in a straight line in Gothic space: everywhere one turns, it seems, there is something to impede one's movement or obscure the way, even as one senses a predator coming closer and closer.[56] The panic-filled 'trap and release' scenes so endlessly played out in classic Gothic narrative – Isabella's hysterical flight from Manfred through the maze-like basements of Otranto, Emily St Aubert's grim nocturnal escape from the fortress of Udolpho, Raymond's squirming, scrambling, frantic efforts to evade homicidal bandits in the 'German' section of *The Monk* – all evoke the syndrome in different ways: one *must get away*, but the way is potentially blocked or barred. The door is padlocked, the passageway sealed, one's screams muffled or smothered. One is literally on the verge of becoming *prey* – ensnared and consumed – as the churning, bestial imagery of Gothic pursuers and victims incessantly emphasises.

Such moments of threatened seizure, one may speculate, function as kinesio-logical arousal-points. When carried off artfully, they can exact from a reader, quite literally, a kind of mediated 'fight or flight' response: an artificial nervous excitement, or psychosomatic consternation, profoundly linked – however distantly – to what Burke called the 'instincts of self-preservation'. We cannot help but identify with the potential victim. Nor, perhaps, can we help sharing in the relief when the Gothic protagonist (inevitably) makes his or her way to safety. (All three of the breathless flights mentioned above turn out to be successful.) If it is intoxicating to imagine oneself a prey-animal, it is even more delightful to imagine oneself eluding capture: the fox disappearing into the undergrowth.

---

56 Compare Geoffrey Scott on the feeling of psychokinetic freedom – a sense that one can move about in swift and unimpeded ways – intimated by the regular forms of classical architecture. Renaissance buildings please us over those of the Gothic, he maintains, because with their open interior spaces and long, 'readable' perspectives, they represent 'the translation into architectural language of our pleasure in rapid, joyous, and even humorous physical movements'. Scott, *Architecture of Humanism*, p. 44.

It is my suspicion that such identification ultimately overrode gender roles: that the I-am-being-menaced fantasy gratified male and female readers alike. It is true that most Gothic victims are female; most Gothic predators male. Yet it is not the case, I think, that male readers necessarily identified with the predator-figure. (The passing comments of contemporary enthusiasts such as Scott and Drake would indeed suggest the opposite.) No one would wish to discount the appalling sociological truth regularly encrypted in Gothic fiction: that in real life, women are more frequently victims of male violence than vice versa. And though I referred earlier to the increasingly 'buffered' nature of late eighteenth-century bourgeois culture – and even postulated that a new sense of *being safe from attack* had begun to insinuate itself among the privileged classes – I am aware how much such speculation would need to be qualified along sexual lines. Even among women of the highest class, the sense of increasing physical security was surely never as great as it was among male contemporaries.

But fantasies of being chased, assailed, broken in upon – cruelly seized – seem to have carried a powerful cross-sex appeal. Aspects of narrative technique were no doubt partly responsible: just as makers of horror and suspense films do today, Gothic novelists typically presented their predation scenes from the victim's point of view – i.e., the 'prey' position – thus intensifying the reader's own sense of of vulnerability and isolation. A passage like the following, from *Otranto*, shows just how much the grippingly subjective camera-work of a film-maker like Hitchcock owes to Gothic narrative devices:

> Words cannot paint the horror of the princess's situation. Alone in so dismal a place [an underground passageway], her mind imprinted with all the terrible events of the day, hopeless of escaping, expecting every moment the arrival of Manfred, and far from tranquil on knowing she was within reach of somebody, she knew not whom, who for some cause seem concealed thereabouts, all these thoughts crowded on her distracted mind, and she was ready to sink under her apprehensions.[57]

Yet at the same time we should not underestimate the universal potency of certain reflexive impulses. In a recent study of contemporary Hollywood slasher films, a prominent feminist film scholar discovered that, contrary to her expectations, a majority of teenage boys who habitually attended such films reported identifying, not with the films' ravening stalkers and serial killers, but

57 Horace Walpole, *The Castle of Otranto*, ed. E. J. Clery (Oxford: Oxford University Press, 1996), pp. 28–9.

with their set-upon female victims.[58] Just so, one suspects – eighteenth-century men too became invested in the Gothic's masochistic psychic structures. Men as well as women have anxiety dreams, after all – and the same surfeiting relief when such dreams comes to an end.

One might take such conjectures further – into the still-mysterious realms of evolutionary psychology and neural biochemistry. If it is indeed the case that the 'civilising' tendencies in late eighteenth-century culture had somehow deadened age-old affective responses – might not Gothic fiction have had a useful adaptive function? To keep in train, so to speak, the physiological 'alert systems', once so necessary to the survival of the human organism? And what of the 'exquisite delight' associated with the Gothic's trap-and-release narrative rhythms? The prey animal possesses yet another adaptive reflex: when it is attacked, its sympathetic nervous system releases a massive stream of pain-killing endorphins – presumably, zoologists speculate, to block the agony of being torn apart and consumed. Might it not be bruited that the raising and calming of fictional terrors prompted a similar, if fleeting, sensation of chemically induced euphoria?

Such questions will no doubt strike some as deeply fanciful.[59] We have no scientific mechanisms for measuring the biochemical aspects of literary response – nor despite startling developments in neuroscience are we likely to have one any time soon. We have no way of knowing whether reading Gothic fiction delivers, say, an intoxicating rush of l-dopamine to the central nervous system, or a pleasing series of jolts to the readerly hypothalamus. Nonetheless, the notion that the Gothic tale, like the modern-day horror film, functioned primarily as a sensation-trigger is an extraordinarily clarifying one. It helps to explain, among other things, why eighteenth-century readers were so ready to tolerate the palpable absurdities of the genre. Gothic novels are notoriously full of solecisms: dropped plot lines, disappearing characters, historical anachronisms, strange authorial non sequiturs. (Often one has the

---

58 For a persuasive psychoanalytic account of the 'male viewer's stake in horror spectator-ship', see Carol J. Clover, *Men, Women, and Chainsaws: Gender in the Modern Horror Film* (Princeton, NJ: Princeton University Press, 1992).

59 This said, it should be noted that at time of writing (2001) neurologists have already succeeded in locating some of the chemical changes taking place in the brain during unusual emotional states – as, for example, when individuals have 'near-death' experi-ences or describe feelings of overwhelming spiritual ecstasy. See Sharon Begley, 'Religion and the Brain,' *Newsweek*, 7 May 2001, pp. 50–5. A growing body of scientific evidence suggests that not only is there 'a neural basis for religious experience' but that strong biochemical reactions in the brain may be at work in other powerful subjective states as well, including those associated with aesthetic experience.

unsettling feeling reading Radcliffe, for example, that one knows more about the fictional world than she does.) But few contemporary readers seemed to mind the sloppiness. If a story produced the obligatory 'chills' it had accomplished its task. In this brazen instrumentality the Gothic might again be compared to pornography – the other eighteenth-century 'master-genre' preeminently devoted to the physical arousal of readers. In fact, if the hypothesis regarding the somatic ennui of the late eighteenth century is correct, it is no surprise that both sorts of 'arousal-writing' should have proliferated so spectacularly in the period. In neither mode – Gothic or pornographic – was authorial success necessarily dependent on intellectual content, felicity of style, or philosophical consistency. Even in Sade, the most cerebral of pornographers and a great admirer of Gothic, the 'shudder' was still the first thing, whether the blissful convulsion of orgasm or the involuntary spasm of mortal terror.

Yet to mention Sade and pornography is to circle back to the larger question of value raised in the opening pages of this chapter. Indeed, one still wants to ask: what *good* is Gothic? The critics of the early twentieth century no doubt disparaged the Gothic mode as vehemently as they did partly on account of its flagrant instrumentality. As with pornography, the Gothic's crassly 'kinesthetic' designs on the reader were glaring, monotonous and ultimately degrading. Could a literary genre really be valuable, after all, whose principal goal seemed merely to induce a kind of reflexive nervous agitation in its readers? What of art's grander imperatives – to speak the truth? to register beauty? to clarify human consciousness? to help us live our lives?

I suggested at the outset that modern-day Gothic scholars had yet to take account of some of the more disturbing moral and psychological aspects of the Gothic mode. But some version of the point stands: despite recent critical attempts to amplify the socio-cultural importance of Gothic fiction, it is still possible to feel a fairly profound dissatisfaction with it – and on exactly such old-fashioned grounds. Mere chills are not enough, one often feels, to compensate for deeper emotional vacancies. Indeed, for all its advertised 'horrors', Gothic fiction may still strike an honest reader as inherently escapist and trivialising – and as a kind of 'wrong turn' in English literary history – despite the army of ideological claims now sometimes made for it. The jocose dismissals of Gothic in the first half of the century, granted, were often blithely reductive and ahistorical, but contemporary scholars have nonetheless been too quick to accept, perhaps, the wishful self-justifications offered by Gothic authors themselves. A more sceptical and expansive reconsideration of the place of

Gothic fiction in the history of the novel would seem now to be especially desirable.

With such possibilities in mind, I shall conclude by throwing down the polemical gauntlet. Horace Walpole, we recall, published *The Castle of Otranto* in 1764, a mere decade and a half after the appearance of surely the eighteenth century's greatest novel – in any language – Samuel Richardson's *Clarissa* (1748–9). In the preface to *Otranto*'s second edition (1765), Walpole complained that too strict an adherence to 'common life' on the part of his fellow novelists had 'cramped' imagination and dammed up 'the great resources of fancy'. In launching this squib he undoubtedly had Richardsonian realism in mind. By 'leaving the powers of fancy at liberty to expatiate through the boundless realms of invention', he hinted, his own novelistic procedures had allowed for 'more interesting situations' and the reanimation of 'romance'.[60]

Yet place *Otranto* next to *Clarissa*. Which is in fact the more 'interesting' work? The more unflinching? The more majestic? The more terrifying? *Otranto*'s most recent editor argues – in defence of Walpole – that his 'Gothic story' is really an important 'social allegory' in disguise: in the tale of Manfred, the usurper-prince of Otranto, who seeks to marry off his hapless daughter Matilda to a kinsman of the man he has dethroned in order to secure further his unlawful hold on power, we have a paradigm of civic and paternal authority monstrously abused. That Manfred should end up murdering Matilda – ostensibly by accident, in a farcically melodramatic scene in the novel's final pages – merely sets the seal on his exemplarity. He is the brutal embodiment of patriarchal greed and psycho-political violence. 'Although at one level,' she writes,

> *Otranto* could be read as an attempt to exorcize political demons by reworking and containing them within an amusing and fantastical story, there is another level at which the representation of power remains troublingly open and unresolved. Once we get beyond spotting Gothic conventions, the central logic of the story becomes apparent: the control of property over people . . . Far from being a problem restricted to the feudal past, or to the pages of romance, this was a live issue, bearing on the conflict between aristocratic and bourgeois ideals of social being.'[61]

But can we really 'get beyond' Gothic conventions? The conventions are the *Ding an sich*. From one angle *Otranto* is simply a rewrite of *Clarissa* – without

---

60 Walpole, *Castle of Otranto*, p. 9.
61 See E. J. Clery, Introduction, *ibid.*, pp. xxv and xxx–xxxi.

the emotional insight, wealth of psychological detail or intransigent artistic force. *Clarissa* too, of course, features a heroine cruelly persecuted by a father bent on enriching the family patrimony by marrying her off to the suitor of his choice. Yet in no way does Walpole imbue his puny version of the Richard-sonian 'family romance' with the dire psychic potency of the earlier novel. On the contrary: the very displacements that define Walpolean Gothic – the shift back to the medieval past, the leap across space to an exotic Italian 'clime,' the often ludicrous evocation of supernatural forces – drain away any real psychic energy (not to mention authentic dread) from the supposed allegory. They work, at times perniciously, to distract us from the real emotional issue. Thus in *Otranto*'s opening paragraph, when the narrator tells us that Manfred 'never showed any symptoms of affection to Matilda', we confront, as in *Clarissa*, the tragic gist of the situation: a father holds an inexplicable, dehumanising contempt for his daughter. But this passing, primal observation – surely the novel's only truly frightening sentence – is never allowed to sink in. Instead, Walpole immediately sets in motion a clamorous welter of Gothic 'business': colossal falling helmets, ancient prophecies, dour troops of knights who mate-rialise out of nowhere, clacking skeletons, gesticulating servants and all the rest of it.

An argument could be made that, far from liberating the novelistic imagin-ation, the Gothic craze of the later eighteenth century was in fact a repressive cultural phenomenon – an ornate, often puerile attempt to defend against the truly devastating moral information brought by the eighteenth-century realist novel: that ordinary human beings were capable of behaving satanically; that men could drive women to despair (*and* vice versa); that parents could be so wicked as to hound their own children to death. For sheer moral horror, there is nothing in Walpole, Radcliffe, Lewis or the other major Gothic writers to match certain passages in Defoe, Richardson, Fielding, Marivaux, Diderot, Laclos, Burney, Rousseau, Godwin, Inchbald or even Wollstonecraft. (Lest the presence of his name here surprise, it should be remembered that Fielding's view of familial relationships is often hardly less bleak than Defoe's or Richard-son's.) Yet what do Gothic writers do when confronted with the prospect of such local and inalienable horror? As if to erect an emotional screen, they hurry us along elsewhere – to a place of convents, potions, trapdoors, spectres and other flimsy decorative fakery – all designed to keep us from thinking too hard about what is really wrong with our lives.

In the sceptical reading I outline here, the spatio-temporal displacements of Gothic are precisely the problem: they invite us *not* to connect the abuses of the Gothic world with those of our own.[62] Infernal wickedness embodied in a literary character who supposedly 'lived' long ago, in a strange and faraway place, is undoubtedly easier to deal with than infernal wickedness embodied, say, in one's own father, mother, lover or child. Exotic evils can serve, ably enough, to draw attention away from the evil that lives at home. It would take the English novel some time, one might argue, to recover from the Gothic's Big Lie. Only when writers began setting their novels once again in 'real' time and space – in 'our' world, or some reasonable approximation of it – would contemporary fiction start to get its nerve back. Austen was crucial here, of course, but so too were figures like Mary Shelley and the Brontës. With them, horror came home again, to take up residence again with us – in the uncanny purlieus of the everyday.

62 The point cannot be stressed enough – that classic Gothic fiction is defined not only by its supernaturalist leanings but by the spatio-temporal displacement of its main action. Though often described as Gothic in inspiration, a work such as Mary Shelley's *Frankenstein* (1818) would not be a 'true' Gothic novel according to this definition, precisely because it is set in the near-present and in 'realistic' geographical spaces easily discoverable on a map (the Arctic Circle, Geneva, London, Scotland). Shelley, of course, makes no reference to supernatural forces – preferring to present the main events of her novel as the tragic repercussions of a scientific experiment gone awry.

Eighteenth-century travel literature

CAROLE FABRICANT

In *A Sentimental Journey* (1768), Laurence Sterne reflects upon 'how many a foul step the Inquisitive Traveller has measured to see sights and look into discoveries; all which, as Sancho Panza said to Don Quixote, they might have seen dry-shod at home' and pointedly asks, 'Where then, my dear country-men, are you going?'[1] 'To all corners of the globe,' a contemporary might well have replied; and indeed, by 1768 there were few distant climes that had not been sighted, explored, traded with, taken possession of, catalogued or writ-ten about by British travellers, who seemed to have little interest in remaining 'dry-shod at home' when they could experience first-hand both the pleasures and the 'travails' (a word closely linked to, and often interchangeable with, 'travel' during this period) of journeying abroad. The chief European destina-tions were France and Italy, countries that (despite their negative political and religious associations) possessed a particular cultural cachet for the affluent on the Grand Tour – the best known of the many (including increasingly middle-class) forms of European travel at the time. It is thus a fitting irony that Sterne's admonishments against foreign travel occur while he himself is preparing for a trip to Europe, and that what follows is an account of his journey through France.

That the term 'tourist' gained currency in the latter part of the century is, then, hardly coincidental. The word appears several times, for example, in the diaries of John Byng, its usage typified by his insistence on 'drag[ging] forth' a fatigued travelling companion because, as he wryly notes, 'we must move about as tourists'.[2] The self-consciousness reflected in this remark, of being a clearly identifiable figure defined by the act of touring and expected to behave

---

1 Laurence Sterne, *'A Sentimental Journey' and 'The Journal to Eliza'* (New York and London: Dutton/Everyman, 1975), p. 13; hereafter cited as *SJ* in the text.
2 John Byng, *The Torrington Diaries, Containing the Tours Through England and Wales of the Honorable John Byng (later Fifth Viscount Torrington) Between the Years 1781 and 1794*, 4 vols., ed. C. Bruyn Andrews (London: Eyre and Spottiswoode, 1934), vol. II, p. 380. The comment is from Bing's 1791 tour of Lincolnshire. Interestingly, the first *OED* citation is from 1800.

in particular ways as a result of this adopted role, pervades much of eighteenth-century travel literature, assuming an especially risible form in Arthur Young's remark, in his famous tour of France (1787–9), on the traveller's tendency to be 'upon the full silly gape' in the 'search for novelty, even in circumstances in which it is ridiculous to look for it' – as if Parisians, 'not being English, would be walking on their heads'.[3] Wandering through foreign lands 'upon the full silly gape' produced abundant material for contemporary satirists, but it also produced a memorable body of literature that worked to combat Britons' insularity and ignorance of the world around them.

The new preoccupation during this period with the figure of the traveller is reflected in Sterne's extended classification of different kinds of travellers, from the 'Lying' and 'Splenetic' ones to the 'The Sentimental Traveller', as exemplified by the author himself (*SJ*, pp. 11–12). This taxonomy presents travel as primarily an individual activity, rooted in differences of character and temperament. At the same time, it suggests travel's quasi-metaphorical status as a journey of the heart, mind or soul – underscored with particular dramatic (as well as comic) effect in Tristram's flight from death across France in Sterne's earlier novel, *Tristram Shandy* (1760–67). Missing here are the concrete historical mediations that tie any given journey, no matter how personal or paradigmatic in nature, to the social and material conditions enabling its existence, making travel a collective and (broadly speaking) political activity. Travellers journeyed abroad for an array of private reasons while at the same time bringing with them a consciousness of being citizens of a nation whose unique values and attributes set it apart from the countries they chose to visit.

The novelist Henry Fielding's journal of his voyage to Portugal in 1754, undertaken in the vain hope of recovering his severely impaired health, is by its very nature a highly personal account, filled with the trials and tribulations of a semi-invalid at sea forced to endure a scarcity of provisions, a tyrannical sea captain who claimed 'absolute dominion in his little wooden world' and petty bureaucrats who prevented the exhausted traveller from disembarking on foreign soil.[4] Yet even this constant preoccupation with bodily discomfort and material deprivation does not erase larger, more impersonal reflections on Britain's superiority to other nations. As his boat passes the English ports of Deptford and Woolwich, Fielding calls the ships in their yards 'noble sights'

---

3 Arthur Young, *Travels During the Years 1787, 1788, and 1789, Undertaken more particularly with a View of ascertaining the Cultivation, Wealth, Resources, and National Prosperity, of the Kingdom of France*, 2 vols. (Dublin, 1793), vol. 1, p. 17; hereafter cited as *France* in the text.
4 Henry Fielding, *The Journal of a Voyage to Lisbon* (London, 1755), p. 83; hereafter cited in the text.

that 'give us a just idea of the great perfection to which we are arrived in building those floating castles, and the figure which we may always make in Europe among the other maritime powers' (*Journal*, p. 59). Later, he notes that the sight of the rocky Portuguese coast is certain to 'make an Englishman proud of . . . his own country, which in verdure excels, I believe, every other country' (p. 211).

The Scottish novelist Tobias Smollett was also in part motivated by health problems when he set off for Europe almost a decade later. His *Travels through France and Italy* (1766) consists of a series of letters addressed mainly to physician friends and marked by a preoccupation with the filthy, disease-inducing conditions he encountered on his journey – e.g., a lodging house in Siena that 'stunk like a privy' and a grimy Genoese inn with a floor that 'had not been swept for half a century' – which made him a ripe target for Sterne's caricature of him as 'the learned SMELFUNGUS' writing about 'nothing but . . . his miserable feelings' (*SJ*, p. 30).[5] What this satirical portrait ignores are the work's many expressions of praise – for the architectural treasures and antiquities of Rome, for the beauties of the landscape around Nice, for the attributes making Florence 'a noble city' (Smollett, *Travels*, p. 227). At the same time, recurring passages remind us in no uncertain terms that its author is a Briton who regularly measured his surroundings against conditions back home and often found them wanting, typified by his claim that the Tyber 'is, in comparison with the Thames, no more than an inconsiderable stream' (p. 247). An even more pointed contrast governs his opposition between England as a country 'smiling with cultivation; the grounds exhibiting all the perfection of agriculture', with peasants 'well fed, well lodged, well cloathed', and France, whose common people display 'signs of poverty, misery, and dirt . . . their farmhouses mean, their furniture wretched, their apparel beggarly' (p. 310). That the stubbornly anti-romantic Smollett should draw such an idealised picture of England underscores the centrality to the traveller's consciousness, and to travel literature's very structure, of patriotic assumptions about Britain's role as a model for the world.

These examples underscore the larger ideological dimensions of eighteenth-century travel, whose diverse practitioners included merchants, adventurers, pirates, colonial settlers, country-house tourists in the British Isles, picturesque travellers, participants in the Grand Tour of the Continent and those involved in voyages of scientific exploration. All of these revealed the crucial ways in

---

5 Tobias Smollett, *Travels through France and Italy*, ed. Frank Felsenstein (Oxford: Oxford University Press, 1979), pp. 242, 21, 207; hereafter cited in the text.

which individual travels enacted a body of values and perspectives that (in different ways and degrees) helped promote British national interests both at home and abroad. Thus the intense competition throughout the century to discover the longitude was spurred on by a spirit of scientific inquiry and a genuine desire for knowledge while at the same time fuelled by a combination of very specific political, economic and military needs which culminated in the Longitude Act of 1714, whereby parliament offered a huge bounty to anyone who could unlock the mystery of the longitude and thus help ensure the safety and progress of British vessels on the high seas. This chapter will examine the multiple, interrelated dimensions of eighteenth-century travel through a discussion divided into four (at times overlapping) areas: European travel; women travellers on the Continent; domestic travel within Britain and Ireland; and global travel.

European travel

Consider Joseph Addison's *Remarks on Several Parts of Italy, in the Years 1701, 1702, 1703* – probably the single most popular and quoted piece of travel literature in the period, having gone through over a dozen editions by the end of the century. Its Preface paints Italy as an incomparable source of sensual gratification and enlightenment:

> There is certainly no Place in the World where a Man may Travel with greater Pleasure and Advantage than in *Italy*. One finds something more particular in the Face of the Country, and more astonishing in the Works of Nature, than can be met with in any other Part of *Europe*. It is the great School of Music and Painting, and contains in it all the noblest Productions of Statuary and Architecture both Ancient and Modern.[6]

By delineating his theme in these terms, Addison confers upon it a special importance at the same time that he elevates his own status as its commentator. His anxiety over the belatedness of his enterprise – rooted in his acute consciousness of the many tourists who have already traversed this terrain and 'often describ'd' its 'Rarities' – induces assurances to the reader that he has 'mention'd but few Things in common with others, that are not either set in a new Light, or accompany'd with different Reflections' (*Remarks*, p. 36; n.p.). He also makes a point of refuting the claims of other travel writers – e.g., that

---

6 Joseph Addison, *Remarks on Several Parts of Italy, In the Years 1701, 1702, 1703* (London, 1705), n.p.; hereafter cited in the text. The preface to this edition is unpaginated; the body of the work is numbered.

Venice is in danger of 'being left, within an Age or two, on the *Terra Firma*' – by invoking his own eye-witness testimony and the judgement of authorities he personally consulted (p. 82).

While downplaying the accounts of earlier seventeenth-century travellers, Addison repeatedly quotes from the descriptions of classical writers. He thus reinforces his persona as the educated, well-read traveller who has prepared mentally for his journey by taking measures 'to refresh [his] Memory among the *Classic* Authors, and to make such Collections out of 'em as [he] might afterwards have Occasion for' (n.p.). Thus fortified, he marks his arrival at Lake Benacus near Verona by noting that 'It was so rough with Tempests . . . that it brought into [his] Mind *Virgil's* Noble Description of it', and he proceeds to cite a passage from the *Georgics*; similarly, he quotes from the *Aeneid* to enhance the picture he draws of the River Velino (pp. 53–4; 161). In both cases, the cited passage is presented both in the original Latin and in the translation by John Dryden – one method by which Addison combines empirical perception with book learning to produce what we might think of as cultural capital: a body of values conferring a special authority on his own text while at the same time vindicating the unique claims to authority made by the *English* traveller, who is best qualified to follow in the path of '*Horace's* Voyage to *Brundisi*' and record 'the Changes that have been made in the Face of this Country since his Time' (p. 186), just as the English poet Dryden was the most qualified to adapt the ancients to a modern sensibility.

Addison used the lessons his travels taught him in *The Spectator* (1711–12), where, in a key series of essays, he extols sight as that 'most perfect' sense which 'brings into our reach some of the most remote Parts of the Universe' and takes his readers on a historical and geographical tour of the world that spans the globe from Europe to 'the Eastern Nations of the World', and that includes the architecture of ancient and modern times, from the Pyramids in Egypt and the Great Wall of China to the Pantheon at Rome (vol. III, p. 538; p. 553).[7] These essays contribute to a broadly cosmopolitan strain running throughout the periodical, expressly reflected in Richard Steele's assertion that the true end of foreign travel is 'to unlearn some odd Peculiarities in our Manners . . . as may possibly have been contracted from constantly associating with one Nation of Men, by a more free, general, and mixed Conversation' (vol. III, p. 368). Alongside this breadth of vision, there exists an opposite, even more pronounced tendency: to affirm England as the centre and sum total

---

7 Joseph Addison and Richard Steele, *The Spectator*, ed. Donald F. Bond, 5 vols. (Oxford: Clarendon Press, 1965), vol. III, p. 536; hereafter cited in the text.

of the universe, attracting a seemingly infinite diversity of cultures but at the same time subordinating them to Britain's commercial power. As a symbol of this power, London's Royal Exchange receives effusive treatment by Addison: 'It . . . gratifies my Vanity, as I am an *Englishman*, to see so rich an Assembly of Country-men and Foreigners consulting together upon the private Business of Mankind, and making this Metropolis a kind of *Emporium* for the whole Earth' (vol. 1, pp. 292–3). The Exchange allows Addison to mix with traders from around the world: 'I am a *Dane, Swede*, or *French-Man* at different times, or rather fancy my self like the old Philosopher, who upon being asked what Country-man he was, replied, That he was a Citizen of the World' (vol. 1, pp. 293–4). This striking expression of a deterritorialised identity coexists with an identity that is staunchly English, rooted in Addison's belief that only in London could such an ennobling spectacle of global diversity be staged, and that the only *true* 'Citizen of the World' is an Englishman.

Addison's writings prepared Britons to journey abroad both as sophisticated cosmopolites and as proud patriots eager to find in their foreign experiences confirmation of England's superiority. Both 'old' wealth and the nouveaux riches looked upon the expanding world as a repository for riches to be appropriated as the symbolic capital of a polite education or the material profits of a growing commercial empire. With Edward Gibbon it was the former of these ends that gave purpose and meaning to his travels on the Continent, providing him with the inspiration to produce *The Decline and Fall of the Roman Empire* (1776–88), its precise moment of conception recorded with a consciousness of its historic importance as Gibbon 'sat musing in the Church of Zoccolanti or Franciscan fryars, while they were singing Vespers in the Temple of Jupiter on the ruins of the Capitol' (15 October 1764).[8] Gibbon's visit to Rome was part of a Grand Tour motivated, as he explains in his memoirs, by an understanding that 'foreign travel compleats the education of an English Gentleman', allowing him to experience Europe 'in such a manner as was most agreeable to [his] taste and judgement' (*Memoirs*, p. 124). These concepts were crucial to Gibbon's course of 'instruction' abroad, linking the expansion of his personal horizons with the articulation of a body of values deemed essential for the cultured Englishman. Thus, Gibbon set out on his journey 'armed' with a commonplace book containing materials culled from both classical and modern works – not least, Addison's writings on Italy (p. 132). Crucial to his education abroad was the viewing of tourist attractions which alone could confer

---

8 Edward Gibbon, *Memoirs of My Life*, ed. Georges A. Bonnard (London: Thomas Nelson, 1966), p. 136; hereafter cited in the text.

sanction upon a traveller's itinerary – e.g., the 'churches, and palaces, conspicuous by their architecture' and 'treasures of art, [and] of learning' (pp. 124–5). When he singles out Rome as 'the great object of our pilgrimage', his wording underscores the extent to which tourism had already become a secularised form of religious ritual, a reverent journey made to famed cultural shrines (p. 133).[9]

Deeply invested in the role of broad-minded 'philosopher', hence critical of the stance of 'patriot' as narrowly identified with 'the exclusive interest and glory of his native country', Gibbon could look upon Europe as 'one great republic' whose inhabitants embody a high level of 'politeness and cultivation'.[10] Yet nationalistic assumptions continue to pervade his outlook, so that in the midst of praising the attributes of Paris, he notes that the city's opulence 'arises from the defects of its government and Religion' and declares, 'we [English] should be astonished at our own riches, if the labours of architecture, the spoils of Italy and Greece, which are now scattered from Inverary to Wilton were accumulated in a few streets between Marybone [sic] and Westminster' (Memoirs, p. 125). He also exults in the timing of his trip, when 'the British name' was particularly esteemed in Europe (p. 126). What Gibbon thus encounters in the world beyond England is a confirmation of England's global influence and envied status abroad.

Although Gibbon was determined that 'the narrative of [his] life must not degenerate into a book of travels' (p. 125), the account of his Grand Tour shows how central European travel was to the making of a 'polite' English gentleman, a great British historian, and a renowned honorary European whose final years were spent among the gentry in Lausanne, Switzerland. His travels had helped transform him into a celebrated author gratified equally by his domestic fame – reflected in 'the personal compliment which [Thomas Sheridan, speaking in Westminster Hall] paid me in the presence of the British nation' – and his worldwide recognition, whereby 'the conquests of our language and literature are not confined to Europe alone; and the writer who succeeds in London is speedily read on the banks of the Delaware and the Ganges' (pp. 181, 183).

The use of the Grand Tour to record the growth into manhood and the self-fashioning of a writer is even more overt in James Boswell's journals. In Italy, he proclaims, 'Nine months in this delicious country have done more for me than all the sage lessons which books, or men formed by books, could have

9 See Dean MacCannell's discussion of 'Sightseeing as Modern Ritual' in *The Tourist: A New Theory of the Leisure Class* (1976; New York: Schocken, 1989), pp. 42–8.
10 Edward Gibbon, *The History of the Decline and Fall of the Roman Empire*, 6 vols. (London, 1776–88), vol. III, pp. 633–4.

taught me. It was my imagination that needed correction, and nothing but travel could have produced this effect.'[11] Rejecting the 'ridiculous' figure he cut before he left Britain, he insists, 'Now I am a very different man. I have got a character which I am proud of.'[12] The goal of personal improvement merges in his journals with a lust for fame – one realised in part when he attained celebrity as 'Corsica Boswell' after becoming the first Briton to travel through that island and publish an account of it (1768). In seeking out meetings with great European thinkers such as Rousseau and Voltaire, Boswell defers to such father figures even as he uses these occasions to establish his own identity and authority. Coveting an interview with Rousseau, he notes: 'I wrote him a letter in which I told him all my worth, and claimed his regard as what I had a title to. "Open your door, then, Sir, to a man who dares to tell you that he deserves to enter it." Such was my bold and manly style.' Boswell's brashness is vindicated when he is ushered in to see Rousseau, even though the French philosopher was 'very ill' (Germany, p. 291). Throughout his journal, the British traveller in quest of enlightenment at the feet of the great becomes himself the object of admiration, thus underscoring the ideological contradictions of travel as a phenomenon at once other-directed and self-confirming. Boswell's regard for authority figures manifests itself on another level when he tells us, 'I had Addison's Travels with me. I shall compare his Remarks with every place which I visit' (Germany, p. 209). While touring Switzerland (site of the concluding section of Addison's Remarks), he visits Soleure and admits to feeling 'a kind of classical pleasure when I thought the Spectator has been here' (Germany, p. 209). Just as Addison had recreated Horace's voyage to Brundisi, Boswell was now following the route taken by Addison, who in the Scottish journal writer's hands sheds his proudly English identity and becomes the exemplar of the fully British traveller.

Women travellers on the Continent

Boswell's European journals point up the emphatically masculine character not only of the Grand Tour but of eighteenth-century travel as a whole. It is no coincidence that the great majority of travellers were male, with women

---

11 James Boswell, *Boswell on the Grand Tour: Italy, Corsica, and France, 1765–1766*, eds. Frank Brady and Frederick A. Pottle (New York: McGraw-Hill, 1955), p. 3.

12 James Boswell, *Boswell on the Grand Tour: Germany and Switzerland, 1764*, ed. Frederick A. Pottle (New York: McGraw-Hill, 1953), pp. 294–5; hereafter cited as *Germany* in the text.

finding it difficult to journey abroad because of the social constraints limiting their sphere of action and because of their economic dependence on men, who generally showed little interest in financing their kinswomen's pursuit of an education – much less adventures – abroad. This gender imbalance was reinforced by the conventional image of the traveller as a male penetrating a feminised landscape or exploring 'virgin' terrain, exemplified by John Bush's travels in Ireland, 'sailing from one beauty to another, from variety to variety', like a Turk 'amidst a seraglio of surrounding beauties', who individually are capable of giving him 'exquisite joy and satisfaction'.[13] Nevertheless, a small but significant number of eighteenth-century women not only managed to undertake foreign travel but also contributed in important ways to the literature of travel.

Lady Mary Wortley Montagu first went abroad in the summer of 1716 with her husband, Sir Edward Wortley Montagu, newly appointed as Ambassador to Turkey. Thus began a life of travels – and copious travel writing through letters – which spanned the better part of five decades, first as a diplomat's wife and later, as a single expatriate after her separation from Sir Edward. Montagu's best-known travel writings are her Turkish letters, but the letters from her other European travels are no less engaging and informative.[14] A collection containing both was published later in the century, with a 'Preface, by a Lady' that foregrounds gender as an issue central to both travel and travel writing:

> I confess, I am malicious enough to desire, that the world should see, to how much better purpose the LADIES travel than their LORDS; and that, whilst it is surfeited with *Male travels*, all in the same tone, and stuffed with the same trifles; a lady has the skill to strike out a new path, and to embellish a worn-out subject with variety of fresh and elegant entertainment.[15]

Here, the traditional exclusion of females from travel is invoked as an *empowering* circumstance, one that enables the enterprising woman to bring a new perspective to a subject rendered stale by generations of male writers.

13 John Bush, *Hibernia Curiosa* (London, 1768), pp. 95–6.
14 Recent studies of Montagu's Turkish letters include Billie Melman, *Women's Orients: English Women and the Middle East, 1718–1918* (Ann Arbor, MI: University of Michigan Press, 1992); Felicity A. Nussbaum, *Torrid Zones: Maternity, Sexuality, and Empire in Eighteenth-Century English Narratives* (Baltimore, MD and London: Johns Hopkins University Press, 1995), esp. pp. 137–49; and Srinivas Aravamudan, *Tropicopolitans: Colonialism and Agency, 1688–1804* (Durham, NC and London: Duke University Press, 1999), pp. 159–83.
15 *Letters of the Right Honourable Lady M — y W—y M—e: Written during her Travels in Europe, Asia, and Africa, To Persons of Distinction* (Berlin, 1781), p. v.

Bearing out the Preface writer's claims, Montagu presents vivid details generally lacking in the accounts of her male counterparts, including detailed scenes of daily life and domesticity. Writing from Rotterdam (1716) to her sister, for example, Montagu relates:

> All the streets are pav'd with broad stones, and before many of the meanest artificers' doors, seats of various colour'd marbles, and so neatly kept that I'll assure you I walked allmost all over the Town Yesterday, incognito, in my slippers without receiving one spot of Dirt, and you may see the Dutch maids washing the Pavement of the street with more aplication [sic] than ours do our bed chambers.[16]

Walking through town 'incognito' – a word often recurring in these letters – acquires particular significance because as a woman Montagu had to be warier than a man in wandering the streets of a foreign country alone and to show greater inventiveness in devising strategies of disguise to facilitate her rambles abroad. Montagu's close attention to dress highlights her gift for satire, evident in her relation of the 'monstrous' fashions she observed on her first visit to the Viennese court, in which she derides the women's elaborate yard-high headdresses called *bourlés* as being 'exactly of the same shape and kind, but about 4 times as big, as those rolls our prudent milk maids make use of to fix their Pails upon' (*Complete Letters*, vol. 1, p. 265). Montagu's satiric propensities produce a critical insight into the absurd forms of emulation motivated by status-seeking among the society women of Prague:

> They are dress'd after the Fashions [of Vienna], as people at Exeter imitate those of London. That is, their Imitation is more excessive than the Original, and 'tis not easy to describe what extrodinary [sic] figures they make. The person is so much lost between Head dress and Petticoat, they have as much occassion to write upon their backs, This is a Woman, for the information of Travellers, as ever sign post painter had to write, This is a bear.
>
> (vol. 1, pp. 280–1)

The semiotic confusion suggested by this remark assumes a special significance once Montagu arrives in Turkey, a country where clothes can easily give rise to cultural misunderstandings. When Montagu goes to the bagnio, or Turkish baths, she wears a travelling habit she realises must have 'appear'd very extrodinary' to the other women, all of whom she finds 'stark naked, without any Beauty or deffect conceal'd' (vol. 1, p. 313). After she describes

---

16 *The Complete Letters of Lady Mary Wortley Montagu*, 3 vols., ed. Robert Halsband (Oxford: Clarendon Press, 1965–7), vol. 1, p. 249; hereafter cited in the text.

their shapes and postures in some detail, it is the Turkish women's turn to examine Montagu and weigh the meaning of *her* appearance. They press her to undress so earnestly that 'I was at last forc'd to open my skirt and shew them my stays . . . for I saw they beleiv'd I was so lock'd up in that machine that it was not in my own power to open it, which contrivance they attributed to my Husband' (vol. I, p. 314). The conventional contrast between British liberty and Eastern despotism is here subverted by the image of the Turkish women's freedom and joyful nakedness set against the constrained, seemingly oppressed figure of the Englishwoman.

The Turkish women's equation of Montagu's clothes with a kind of chastity belt symbolically underscores what Montagu saw as British society's misogynistic treatment of women. As she observes to her sister, 'there is no part of the World where our Sex is treated with so much contempt as in England,' as shown by the fact that 'We are educated in the grossest ignorance' (vol. III, p. 40). A very different situation prevails in Italy, where 'the character of a learned Woman is far from being ridiculous . . . the greatest Familys being proud of having produc'd female Writers' (vol. III, p. 39). Montagu's feminist perspective is further apparent in her recurring depictions of female community, which counter the conventional portrayal of women as a sex given over to jealousy and back-biting. She finds an example of such community in the Turkish bagnio, which she concludes is the equivalent of a 'Women's coffée house' (vol. I, p. 314) – a comment particularly revealing in that London coffee houses were the exclusive domain of men. The caring relationship Montagu establishes with her female correspondents represents another form of female community and symbolises its durability in the face of both absence and distance.

Montagu's conviction that 'a very long stay, a diligent Enquiry, and a nice Observation are requisite even to a moderate degree of knowing a Foreign Country' made her highly critical of the Grand Tour, whose practitioners returned from abroad 'no more instructed than they might have been at home by the help of a Map' (vol. II, p. 494). She gained a deeper knowledge of other countries not only by her proficiency in several European languages but also by her study of both Arabic and Turkish – what she terms her 'Oriental Learning' – which enabled her to transcribe several stanzas written by a noted contemporary Turkish poet, Ibrahim Pasha, in a letter to Pope (vol. I, p. 337). Montagu's 'diligent' study of other cultures allowed her to speak with authority about a wide range of travel-related subjects, so that in writing to her daughter she had no need to invoke the authority of any male 'expert' to assert her confident judgement that 'When [Samuel Richardson, in *Sir Charles Grandison*] talks of Italy, it is plain he is no better acquainted with it than he is with the Kingdom of Mancomugi' (vol. III, p. 91).[17]

Hester (Thrale) Piozzi, the widow of a wealthy brewer, married an Italian musician in 1784 and embarked on a series of European travels which she recorded in copious letters and journals. Her prefatory remarks to a published volume of these travels, which express the hope that she has not been 'too daring' in placing her observations before the public, convey the tentativeness and anxiety of a female interloper on male terrain.[18] Yet Piozzi at the same time boldly feminises the publishing process by declaring that 'the labours of the press resemble those of the toilette, both should be attended to, and finished with care; but once complete, should take up no more of our attention; unless we are disposed at evening to destroy all effect of our morning's study' (*Observations*, p. 2). Nor was Piozzi reluctant to invoke a feminine sensibility as the basis for her critical judgements. In Calais, for example, she notes that the sight of women 'spinning at their door' is 'particularly consolatory to a British eye' since 'industry without bustle, and some appearance of gain without fraud, comfort one's heart; while all the profits of commerce scarcely can be said to make immediate compensation to a delicate mind, for the noise and brutality observed in an English port' (pp. 4–5). Piozzi's appropriation here of the 'British eye' allows her to assume a representative role in her travels abroad and helps underwrite a criticism of English 'commerce'.

Less erudite than Montagu's letters, Piozzi's journals share the latter's lively style and close attention to detail, which produce vivid descriptions of the customs and landscapes of the places she visits. Though lacking her predecessor's satirical bent, Piozzi too has a particular eye for dress, details of which go beyond literal description to suffuse the language of her journal. Hence in drawing a contrast between French and Italian character traits, she notes the Italians' 'delight in bringing forward the eminent qualities of every other nation; never insolently vaunting . . . their own' and opposes this quality to 'the national spirit and confined ideas of perfection inherent in a Gallic mind, whose sole politeness is an *appliqué* stuck upon their coat, but never *embroidered into it*' (p. 91). Such generalisations about innate national characteristics were a

---

17 Halsband's note suggests that this name is 'Possibly from Manco, crowned emperor of the Incas in 1534'. However, Isobel Grundy, editor of *Lady Mary Wortley Montagu: Selected Letters* (London: Penguin, 1997), speculates that Montagu's reference here is to Monoemugì, in south-east Africa, citing as her source Herman Moll's *Atlas Geographus* of 1714 (p. 416, n. 2).

18 Hester Lynch Piozzi, *Observations and Reflections Made in the Course of a Journey through France, Italy, and Germany*, ed. Herbert Barrows (Ann Arbor, MI: University of Michigan Press, 1967), p. 1; hereafter cited in the text.

commonplace at the time, but Piozzi is careful to support hers with empirical observations. For example, she describes a meeting in Venice with a Parisian woman who denigrates the ' "dismal palaces the Venetians are so fond of" ', insisting they are eclipsed by the splendors of the fair at St Ovid's in Paris (p. 91). But she observes that this was 'a very sensible and accomplished woman' who 'spoke with great acuteness and judgment' in other respects, further distancing herself from mere stereotypes. Moreover, Piozzi avoids a mindless chauvinism that assumes the superiority of all things British – she notes that the 'general [stock of] knowledge' for everyday conversation is more evident in France than in England, and she concedes that even the worst theatre in Venice is 'infinitely superior to ours' (pp. 92, 98).

Less overtly feminist than Montagu, Piozzi nevertheless contributed in her own way to the feminisation of travel literature – e.g., by acknowledging the influence of other women writers on her own work, like Boswell paying tribute to Addison. Reflecting on the coffee houses and casinos in Venice, Piozzi observes that 'They breathe the true spirit of our luxurious Lady Mary,' illustrating her point by quoting a 'famous stanza' from Montagu's poem, 'Lover: A Ballad' (p. 82). Her references to other prominent European women writers and artists – e.g., the painter Angelica Kauffman, held up as proof of the Romans' 'taste for living merit' (p. 91) – show that by this time cultural capital was no longer an exclusively male domain but also a potentially important component in the establishment of *female* authority. Moreover, Piozzi casts a quasi-feminist perspective on man's relationship to nature, reflecting that the Appenine Mountains 'lift their proud heads in vain' since 'Man renders them subservient to his imperial will'. But she ends abruptly: 'This is however no moment and no place to begin a panegyric upon the power of man, and of his skill to subjugate the works of nature, where the people are trembling at its past, and dreading its future effects' (p. 299). Despite the ambiguity here, it is difficult to ignore the critical tone (and loaded word choice) conveyed in the recognition that the frightful sublimity of nature has been eclipsed by the even more terrifying sublimity of man's 'imperial will' to assert control over his environs.

Later women travellers, building upon the examples of their predecessors, contributed in new ways to both the feminisation and the democratisation of the genre. Mary Wollstonecraft, for example, in the epistolary account of her 1795 journey through Scandinavia accompanied by her infant daughter, established an authoritative voice based in part on her maternal role, which allowed her to comment knowledgeably (at times critically) on the child-rearing practices in places such as Copenhagen and Tonsberg, Norway, where mothers 'injured their children by keeping them too warm' and spoiled them through a 'false tenderness'.[19] Identifying with the lower classes, Wollstonecraft replaces Montagu's ideal of upper-class female community with a notion of community that spurns 'the tyranny of wealth' for a model based on the cooperative relationship she observed between Norwegian farmers and their tenants (*Letters*, p. 62). As the century came to an end, the emergence of the romantic traveller, solitary in her wanderings and musings, produced the image of the 'female Robinson Crusoe, as unaided and unprotected, though in the midst of the world, as that imaginary hero in his uninhabited island', who depends for her survival on 'such resources as she could find, independently, in herself'.[20] Whether as upholder of community or lone wanderer, female writers redefined the role of traveller so that women could register both the ideals and the anxieties that animated their journeys.

Travels through the British Isles and Ireland

The growing popularity of European travel, far from siphoning off interest in travel within Britain itself, actually stimulated the latter since, as John Brome put it, 'it is very incongruous [for English travellers] to pretend to be acquainted with other Countries, and to be Strangers to their Own, which is an Epitome of all other[s]'.[21] Several factors contributed to the sharp rise in domestic travel. The increase in trade throughout the country created a network of new roads facilitating the movement of goods and people from one part of the country to another. The great country houses throughout Britain were opened up for a growing trade in tourists hungry to see how the rich and fashionable lived, and eager to outdo one another in providing detailed accounts of what they observed on their itineraries.[22] The appetites of these new tourists were stimulated by, and in turn gave rise to, an outpouring of published guidebooks and regional maps.

19 Mary Wollstonecraft, *Letters Written during a Short Residence in Sweden, Norway, and Denmark*, ed. Carol H. Poston (Lincoln, NE and London: University of Nebraska Press, 1976), pp. 81, 152; hereafter cited in the text.
20 See Frances Burney, *The Wanderer; or, Female Difficulties*, eds. Margaret Anne Doody, Robert L. Mack and Peter Sabor (Oxford and New York: Oxford University Press (World Classics), 1991), p. 873. This novel was begun in the 1790s although not published until 1814.
21 James Brome, *Travels Over England, Scotland, and Wales* (London, 1707), n.p.
22 See Esther Moir, *The Discovery of Britain: The English Tourists, 1540–1840* (London: Routledge & Kegan Paul, 1964); and Carole Fabricant, 'The Literature of Domestic Tourism and the Public Consumption of Private Property', in Felicity A. Nussbaum and Laura Brown (eds.), *The New Eighteenth Century: Theory, Politics, English Literature* (New York and London: Methuen, 1987), pp. 254–75.

One of the first and most important of these tourist materials was *Britannia* (1675), a splendidly illustrated road atlas of England and Wales in folio form, produced by John Ogilby as part of a multi-volumed world atlas. Given Ogilby's official position as 'His Majesty's Cosmographer and Geographic Printer', the highly patriotic tone of the work's dedicatory material – which portrays the project as a means of 'Raising up the Splendor of *Great Britains* Monarchy' – is hardly surprising. Along with recording and illustrating all of England's highways 'from *Shore* to *Shore*', the atlas claims to greatly advance the 'science' of geography through its use of '*ACTUAL DIMENSURATION*' – i.e., accurate measurements.[23] Although Ogilby's volume was not the first published atlas of Britain, it represented a new conception, its 100 coloured plates containing not only a general survey of the different parts of the country but also strip maps – detachable from the book for convenient personal use – charting minutely-detailed local itineraries. *Britannia's* function as a practical tour guide was enhanced in later eighteenth-century versions, which reduced the sumptuous but cumbersome folio to pocket-size road books that could easily be carried by travellers on foot.

One of the first tourists to make use of such a work was Celia Fiennes, who began keeping a journal in her early twenties, recording a series of journeys most of which she undertook riding side-saddle, accompanied only by two servants. Her journeys fall into four distinct parts: the early journeys in the south, from Newton Toney (her place of birth) to Salisbury, including excursions to Bath, London, and the Isle of Wight (*c.* 1682–4); the northern journey and the tour of Kent (1697); her 'Great Journey to Newcastle and to Cornwall' in 1698, the most extensive portion of her travels; and her final journeys (*c.* 1701–*c.* 1703), largely confined to London and its environs. Begun 'to regain [her health]' by variety and change of aire and exercise', these four journeys cover every county in England, and even include brief forays into Wales and Scotland.[24] Not published until the nineteenth century, the journals provided a large amount of practical tourist information that strongly suggests they were meant to be read by a contemporary audience. Showing little concern for grammar or punctuation, the journals make up for their somewhat slap-dash quality by their sense of immediacy and spontaneity; as Fiennes readily admits, 'as most I converse with knows both the freedom and easyness I speak

23 John Ogilby, *Britannia, Volume the First: Or, An Illustration of the Kingdom of England and Dominion of Wales: By a Geographical and Historical Description of the Principal Roads thereof* (London, 1675), these quotations are from the unpaginated Preface.
24 Celia Fiennes, *The Illustrated Journeys of Celia Fiennes 1685–c.1712*, ed. Christopher Morris (London and Sydney: MacDonald & Co., 1982), p. 32; hereafter cited in the text.

and write as well as my deffect [*sic*] in all, so they will not expect exactness or politeness in this book' (*Illustrated Journeys*, p. 32). She views domestic travel as a source of both useful knowledge and patriotic pride since it can 'add much to [England's] Glory and Esteem in our minds' and prevent the English from 'being strangers to themselves' (p. 32). In gender terms, travel offers women a cure for 'epidemick diseases of vapours' while it provides men in public service an opportunity to learn more about their own country so as to be able 'to promote and improve Manufacture and Trade' (p. 32).

Much of the journals is quintessential tourist literature, providing detailed accounts of major resorts and 'spaws' (i.e., spas), and anticipating the later spate of country-house guides by taking readers step-by-step through the country's most famous estates. Fiennes makes a point of providing the kind of information that would help future tourists make decisions about where to go. For example, those considering a visit to Buxton's baths would perhaps have thought twice about going if they had read Fienne's account of the poor but overpriced food and the lodgings often 'so crowded that three must lye in a bed' (p. 108). By contrast, Tunbridge Wells offers the visitor high-quality but inexpensive lodgings, along with many amenities designed to give the tourist her money's worth (pp. 126–7). Fiennes's observations on Bath are especially detailed. She carefully distinguishes among the five individual baths, offering practical information for the visitor; the Cross Bath, for example, 'has seates round it for the Gentlemen to sitt and round the walls are arches with seates for the Ladyes' (p. 44). Fiennes is not oblivious to the health hazards of mineral springs, warning of 'a white scum on the bath' that makes bathers 'breake out into heate and pimples', but she also attests to the waters' medicinal benefits, noting that a quart each morning is 'a good sort of Purge' (p. 46).

But Fiennes does not limit her account to standard tourist fare, showing an interest in more utilitarian concerns such as regional industries: e.g., cotton in Kendal (p. 165); pottery in Newcastle (p. 156); brick and tile in Nottingham (p. 88); dye-making in Exeter (p. 197); and shipbuilding in Plymouth (p. 201). She also records the types of soil in different parts of the country, such as the 'deep clay ground' of Rotherham and the 'good hard gravelly' roads along the River Tyne (pp. 103, 175), and comments at length on the country's mineral deposits, giving us a close look at the coal miners at work in Derbyshire, and differentiating the 'very finely pollish'd' cannel coal in Wigan from the 'Sea-coale' that gives Newcastle its reputation (pp. 161, 176). She further directs our attention to the making of 'Salt-Cakes' at Lymington and rock salt in Norwich, on the estate (not identified here) in which she owned a financial interest (pp. 69–70, 184–5). Fiennes' journals thus provide a wealth of information not only for the tourist but also for the businessman wanting to learn about England as a rapidly developing centre of commerce.

A similar combination of interests characterises the most famous piece of eighteenth-century domestic travel literature, Defoe's *A Tour Thro' the whole Island of Great Britain*, which went through nine editions during the half-century following its initial publication (1724–7). Over the course of this period, it was transformed into a popular guidebook which increasingly replaced Defoe's sections on economic geography with more typical tourist fare. In his Preface Defoe stresses his *Tour*'s focus on the present since 'the Face of Things so often alters, and the Situation of Affairs in this *Great British* Empire gives such new Turns . . . that there is Matter of new Observation every Day presented to the Traveller's Eye'.[25] These ongoing changes mean that 'no Description of *Great Britain* can be, what we call a finished Account, as no Cloaths can be made to fit a growing Child' (*Tour*, vol. i, p. 4) – a fact that justifies Defoe's work as a much-needed updating of earlier tours even as it attests to its own built-in obsolescence. The optimistic view conveyed of Britain, as a country that in 'every Age will find an Encrease of Glory', was rooted in Defoe's mercantile capitalist ideology and his vision of the continued commercial expansion of the British Empire (vol. i, p. 4). Invoking patriotism as a major *raison d'être* for the *Tour*, Defoe promises to counter the slanderous accounts of England written by envious foreigners and anticipates the day when '*Great Britain* as much exceeds the finest Country in *Europe*, as that Country now fancies they exceed her' (vol. i, p. 4).

Defoe establishes his authority as travel writer by stressing his reliance on eye-witness testimony, which makes him 'very little in Debt to other Mens Labours' and ensures 'a full Account of Things' (vol. i, pp. 3, 5). Countering the often random and shapeless nature of earlier travel guides, Defoe organises his book into thirteen letters that document 'A Tour, in Circuits' – i.e., a series of circular journeys covering different regions of the country, in which 'I began my Travels, where I Purpose to End them, *viz*. At the City of *London*' (vol. i, p. 5). Although this pattern is broken with Defoe's journey to Scotland, the focal role London plays as both starting point and destination for his other tours underscores its status as the commercial and demographic centre of Britain. His description of London contains a wealth of detail about almost every aspect of the city, including its streets, squares, public buildings, churches, hospitals, markets and prisons. Defoe stresses the difficulty of defining its

---

25 Daniel Defoe, *A Tour Thro' the whole Island of Great Britain, Divided into Circuits or Journies*, 2 vols., intro. G. D. H. Cole ((first edition, 1724–27), London: Peter Davies, 1927), vol. i, p. 3; hereafter cited in the text.

exact boundaries given the city's rapid expansion, to the point where 'We see several Villages, formerly standing, as it were, in the Country, and at a great Distance, now joyn'd to the Streets by continued Buildings' (vol. I, p. 317). A sign of the nation's prosperity, the city's spectacular growth is not without its negative side, most obvious in the unregulated development that has created the appearance of a 'monstrous City' spreading 'in a most straggling, confus'd Manner' (vol. I, pp. 318, 316–17). Yet these reservations about London's growth do not alter Defoe's assessment of London as 'the greatest City in the World', boasting incomparable treasures such as St Paul's Cathedral, which is (St Peter's excepted) 'beyond all the Modern Works of its Kind in *Europe*', and the Royal Exchange, 'the greatest and finest of the Kind in the World' (vol. I, pp. 173, 337, 333). Above all, London is extolled as a port 'made famous by the Opulence of its Merchants', with the wharfs along the Thames bringing in revenue 'said to amount to a prodigious Sum' (vol. I, pp. 173, 344). The *Tour* thus affirms the same middle-class values Defoe articulated in the *Review*, where he exalts the merchant as a 'universal scholar' who 'raises not families only, but towns, cities, provinces, and kingdoms'.[26]

Outside of London, Defoe directs his attention to more standard tourist fare such as 'the fine Seats of the Gentlemen' and the 'fine Palaces of the Nobility' near Newmarket (*Tour*, vol. I, pp. 88, 76). Yet even in these instances he does not stray very far from his favourite theme of middle-class enterprise. Thus he takes special note of ancient country seats that have fallen into the hands of businessmen through intermarriage or the extinction of a noble line, and pays tribute to the more recent creations of the nouveaux riches, such as villas in Surrey 'which are built with such a Profusion of Expence, that they look rather like Seats of the Nobility, than the Country Houses of Citizens and Merchants' (vol. I, p. 159). Defoe celebrates the new degree of social mobility that has undermined traditional ranks in society; for 'the present encrease of Wealth in the City of *London*, spreads it self into the Country, and plants Families and Fortunes, who in another Age will equal the Families of the antient Gentry' (vol. I, p. 15).

Defoe insists that even 'the wildest Part of the Country is full of Variety, [and] the most mountainous Places have their Rarities to oblige the Curious' (vol. II, p. 539) – an outlook that enables him not only to 'open up' remote regions in the north of England but also to devote a lengthy appendix to his travels through then largely ignored Scotland (including the rarely visited Highlands).

26 *The Best of Defoe's 'Review': An Anthology*, ed. William L. Payne (New York: Columbia University Press, 1951), pp. 124–5.

He explains that he intends to make neither a 'Paradise' nor a 'Wilderness' of Scotland but instead to show 'what it really is, what it might be' – and, in a politically pointed comment, 'what, perhaps, it would much sooner have been' had England not reneged on its pre-Union promises to the Scottish people (vol. II, p. 691). Duly critical of its problems, he yet finds much to praise about the country, judging Glasgow 'the cleanest and beautifullest, and best built City in *Britain, London* excepted' (vol. II, p. 744) and expressing admiration for the Scottish gentry, than whom 'none in *Europe* . . . better deserve the name of *Gentlemen*' (vol. II, p. 695). In according so much space and attention to England's northern neighbour, Defoe in effect raises its stature while at the same time vindicating his claim to having produced a truly comprehensive account of 'the Whole Island of Great Britain'.

Defoe's *Tour* prepared the way for subsequent travel writers to turn their attention to Scotland. After years of unheeded urgings, Samuel Johnson decided to accompany Boswell on a journey to Scotland in 1773, despite his abiding attachment to London and his generally unfavourable view of the Scottish, which Boswell ascribed to the fact that his friend was 'at bottom much of a *John Bull*; much of a blunt *true-born Englishman*'.[27] But despite what would seem a recipe for disaster, the tour not only proved surprisingly successful, it also produced a noteworthy travel account in Johnson's *A Journey to the Western Islands of Scotland* (1775), which tempers his anti-Scottish bias with an appreciation of what the country has to offer. There are, to be sure, complaints about the 'uniform nakedness' of the treeless landscape, and criticisms of the 'mediocrity of knowledge' in the universities.[28] Yet Johnson also notes that Scotland's educational system is 'not inadequate to the purposes of common life' – a key concession given his belief that 'the true state of every nation is the state of common life' (*Journey*, p. 22). Even further, he freely acknowledges that Scottish universities foster 'a [vigorous] spirit of enterprise' that enables students 'to find, or to make their way to employment, riches, and distinction' (pp. 160–1).

Johnson has a more unreservedly positive opinion about the country's hospitality towards strangers and its adherence to tradition – what he described to Boswell as 'the patriarchal life' (*Hebrides*, p. 167) – which he sees on his visits to country houses such as the Duke of Argyle's 'splendid seat' in Inverary'

27 James Boswell, *The Journal of a Tour to the Hebrides, with Samuel Johnson*, in *Boswell's Life of Johnson*, ed. George Birkbeck Hill, rev. L. F. Powell, 6 vols. (Oxford: Clarendon Press, 1934–64), vol. v, p. 20; hereafter cited as *Hebrides* in the text.
28 Samuel Johnson, *A Journey to the Western Islands of Scotland*, ed. Mary Lascelles (New Haven, CT and London: Yale University Press, 1971), pp. 8, 22; hereafter cited in the text.

(*Journey*, p. 158). Arriving at Boswell's father's estate, he finds that Lord Auchinleck has built a 'very stately' house and is quite taken with 'the sullen dignity of the old castle', recording how he eagerly 'clambered with Mr Boswell among the ruins, which afford striking images of ancient life' (p. 161). Johnson's encounter with the Scottish terrain made him uncharacteristically sensitive to the attractions of nature, so that he is clearly moved by the sublime scene visible from Slanes Castle – which feeds the eye with 'all the terrifick grandeur of the tempestuous ocean' – and on viewing the monastic ruins at Aberbrothick declares, 'I should scarcely have regretted my journey, had it afforded nothing more than [this] sight' (pp. 19, 11).

True, Johnson's growing appreciation of Scotland could express itself even at the end in rather back-handed compliments, as when he commends the conversation of the Scots for becoming 'every day less unpleasing to the English; their peculiarities wear[ing] fast away' (p. 162). Englishness remained for Johnson the ultimate standard of culture and social intercourse. Still, Boswell's assertion that Johnson returned from Scotland 'in great good humour, with his prejudices much lessened' deserves to be taken seriously (*Hebrides*, p. 20). The reflections of the final paragraph of the *Journey* in effect argue for the necessity of travel for a broad knowledge of life: 'Having passed my time almost wholly in cities, I may have been surprised by modes of life and appearances of nature, that are familiar to men of wider survey and more varied conversation . . . I cannot but be conscious that my thoughts on national manners, are the thoughts of one who has seen but little' (p. 164).

Compared to the growing tourist population in the British Isles, travellers to Ireland were few and far between. Viewed through the stereotype of '*The Barbarous Island*' and inhabited by what Edmund Spenser described as a 'savage nation', Ireland projected an image that did little to encourage visitors from abroad (at least beyond the English Pale centred in Dublin), gaining the interest of most Englishmen only for its exploitable resources and the income derived from absentee land ownership.[29] The relatively scant tourist trade contributed to the widespread ignorance about the country noted by Jonathan Swift (1724): 'As to *Ireland*, [the People of *England*] know little more than they do of *Mexico*; further than that it is a Country subject to the King of *England*, full of Boggs, [and] inhabited by wild *Irish Papists*.'[30] One of the few who attempted to

---

29 For '*The Barbarous Island*' see Sir Richard Cox, 'An Apparatus: Or Introductory Discourse to the History of Ireland', in *Hibernia Anglicana: or, The History of Ireland from the Conquest to this Present Time*, Part 1 (London, 1689), n.p. For Edmund Spenser, see *A View of the Present State of Ireland*, ed. W. L. Renwick (Oxford: Clarendon Press, 1970), p. 1.

30 Jonathan Swift, *The Prose Works of Jonathan Swift*, 14 vols., ed. Herbert Davis (Oxford: Basil Blackwell, 1939–68), vol. x, p. 103.

remedy this situation was Mary Granville, who first visited Dublin in 1731, later marrying Swift's friend, the Reverend Patrick Delany. With her aristocratic ties and connections at court, Granville viewed Ireland through the perspective of the country's Protestant elite, as is evident from the letters she sent to friends and family back in England, many illustrated with her own drawings. Her descriptions of the houses of the gentry – e.g., Bellamont Forest, the Palladian villa built for Thomas Coote by Sir Edward Lovett Pearce – show that the principles of English landscape design were being consciously imported into Ireland, and her praise of Eyrecourt, in Galway, for its 'great many fine woods and improvements that looked very English' underscores the extent to which England functions in her letters as an essential point of reference and as the standard for aesthetic value.[31]

In the spring of 1732, Granville travelled to the west of Ireland with the family of Robert Clayton, Bishop of Killala and Achonry. In her letters, she fleetingly acknowledges 'the poverty of the people' but devotes almost all of her attention to scenic attractions and the social activities of the well-to-do in Galway and Mayo (*Autobiography*, vol. I, p. 353). She is much taken with the rituals of entertaining among the Anglo-Irish gentry, noting that she has 'not seen less than fourteen dishes of meat for dinner, and seven for supper, during [her] peregrination' and concluding that 'no people *can be more hospitable or obliging*' (vol. I, p. 351). The Catholic natives are viewed at best as 'poor naked wretches' in need of charity from their superiors or as amusing oddities, like the 'wonderful little man' begging at her door, who was 'not more than *three feet* high . . . could only speak Irish and was very much deformed' (vol. II, p. 362; vol. III, p. 595). Granville's letters successfully counter the contemporary stereotype of Ireland as a menacing Other, a 'barbarous island' filled with bogs and 'wild Irish', presenting it instead as in many ways not unlike its neighbor across the channel and thus a fitting destination for the 'civilised' traveller. But they accomplish this end by rendering most of Ireland – including the overwhelming majority of its population and a substantial portion of its landscape – invisible.

Arthur Young's *A Tour in Ireland* (1780) serves as a counterbalance to Granville's travel accounts by recognising that the state of the poor 'ought to be one of the first objects of a traveller's attention, since from their ease or oppression, a multitude of conclusions may be drawn relative to government, wealth,

---

31 Mary Granville, *The Autobiography and Correspondence of Mary Granville, Mrs. Delany*, first series, 3 vols., ed. Lady Llanover (1861; London: AMS, 1974), vol. I, p. 385; hereafter cited in the text.

and national prosperity'.[32] Young's acute awareness of social inequity – epitomised in his perception that the British monarch's life of opulence depends on the labour of 'the most oppressed, the most unhappy peasant, in the remotest corner of Ireland' (*Tour*, vol. I, p. vi) – leads him to condemn the penal laws against the Catholics as the signs of an 'illiberal barbarism' and to reject 'that baleful monopolizing spirit of commerce' that governs nations to the detriment of their farming and landed interests (vol. I, pp. 66, xiv). A farmer in his own right, later editor of the popular *Annals of Agriculture*, Young had already garnered a sizeable reputation with his agricultural tours through England and Wales a dozen years earlier. Here, he travels through Ireland with an eye peeled for practices of husbandry as well as for forms of social life.

The *Tour* does include more typical tourist material. Thus Young lingers at Castletown, the famous Palladian mansion 'to which all travellers resort', pronouncing it 'the finest house in Ireland', and he records the 'magnificent' and 'sublime' scenery on the way to the renowned gardens at Powerscourt (vol. I, pp. 22, 132). Yet his greatest enthusiasm seems to be reserved for sights such as that of 'two large compost dunghills turning over and mixing', which he admits 'pleased [him] more than the sight of a palace would have done' (vol. I, p. 131). Descriptions of picturesque landscape invariably veer off into extended reflections on the amount of milk yielded by different breeds of cows or the best way to plant turnips. Moreover, Young's praise of a house or landscape is at times more a political than an aesthetic comment, as when his tribute to the 'magnificence' of Slaine Castle turns into a scathing rebuke to the absentee landlords who 'drain the kingdom of every shilling they can' (vol. I, pp. 40–1). The *Tour in Ireland* proved to be the least popular and lucrative of Young's prolific travel writings, perhaps because it remained in many ways resistant to the conventions of travel literature. But though a failure in commercial terms, the *Tour* made an important contribution to travel literature by demonstrating the genre's capacity for combining aesthetic and socio-economic perspectives, and by bearing out Young's claim that his account will correct 'the many erroneous ideas' in previous books about Ireland (vol. I, p. xxi).

Global travel

The rapid growth of travel beyond the bounds of Europe into remote areas of Africa, the Near and Far East, the South Pacific and the Americas provided

32 Arthur Young, *A Tour in Ireland*, 2 vols. (Dublin, 1780), vol. I, p. x; hereafter cited in the text.

impetus for a wide range of topographical and scientific studies even as it created new opportunities for commercial and colonial expansion. The immense popularity of the new literature of global travel was well exemplified by George Anson's *A Voyage round the World*, published in 1748 under the names of Richard Walter, the chaplain of Anson's flagship *The Centurion*, and Benjamin Robins, Engineer-General to the East India Company. Boasting of more than 1,800 advance subscribers, the volume was an immediate best-seller, spawning over a dozen new editions in rapid succession and making Anson into a celebrity. The Introduction acknowledges the amusement value of travel accounts but insists that 'the more intelligent part of mankind have always agreed, that from these relations . . . the more important purposes of navigation, commerce, and national interest may be greatly promoted'.[33] It also claims that no previous voyage ever furnished such an abundance of material 'for the improvement of geography and navigation' (*Voyage*, pp. 9–10). Yet the *Voyage* does not ignore the need to entertain its readers, offering vivid accounts of the heroic adventures of Anson and his crew on the high seas as part of a privateering venture, aided by a fleet of five gunner ships besides *The Centurion*, which included attacks along the Pacific coastline of Spanish America from Chile to Panama, the fomenting of rebellion in Peru and the capture of the great galleon from Manila off Acapulco.

Works like Anson's *Voyage* broadened the imaginative horizons of even those Britons who rarely left home. References to China were common at the time, with interest in the country stimulated by the importation of Chinese commodities and artefacts that fuelled the craze for *chinoiserie*. The irregular forms of Chinese landscape design, which Sir William Temple had earlier termed *sharawadgi*, were celebrated by Sir William Chambers in his *Dissertation on Oriental Gardening* (1772), a work that denigrates both European and English styles in favour of the highly complex spatial perspectives employed by the Chinese to create scenes viewable 'from as many points, and in as many directions as possible' to ensure 'an extensive, rich and variegated prospect'.[34] As Royal Architect, Chambers put his aesthetic ideals into practice by incorporating a precisely modelled Chinese pagoda into his redesign of Kew Gardens.

---

33 Richard Walter and Benjamin Robins, *A Voyage round the World in the Years* MDCCXL, I, II, III, IV, ed. Glyndwr Williams (London: Oxford University Press, 1974), p. 9; hereafter cited in the text.

34 Sir William Chambers, *Dissertation on Oriental Gardening* (London, 1772; rpt. Farnborough: Gregg International Publishers, 1972), p. 20. For Temple's discussion of *sharawadgi*, see 'Upon the Gardens of Epicurus; or, Of Gardening, in the Year 1685', in *Five Miscellaneous Essays by Sir William Temple*, ed. Samuel Holt Monk (Ann Arbor, MI: University of Michigan Press, 1963), pp. 29–30.

Chambers acquired his fascination with the Eastern aesthetic during his travels to Canton in 1744 as a supercargo for the Swedish East India Company. Other enthusiasts of *chinoiserie* who had never been anywhere near China created a fantasy world of 'Oriental' beauty in the midst of England. Lord Cobham, for example, built a Chinese house on the 'Elysian Fields' of his famous residence, Stowe (1738), paying tribute to the Eastern aesthetic while at the same time integrating it into a landscape that exalted the principles of British patriotism.[35]

Defoe was one of the first to recognise the enormous power of imaginative and vicarious forms of travel. While promoting his model of 'The Compleat English Gentleman', he assures his reader that even if he was unable to travel in his youth 'he may make the tour of the world in books . . . He may go round the globe with Dampier and Rogers, and kno' a thousand times more in doing it than all those illiterate sailors . . . [H]e discovers America with Columbus, conquers it with the great Cortez, and replunders it with Sir Francis Drake.'[36] Defoe's words point to the importance of the reading public in shaping the field of travel writing and show how readers, transformed into armchair travellers, could be made complicit in the great imperial project Britain was then undertaking. Defoe was himself the perfect exemplar of vicarious global travel, having written not only the travel fictions with which we are most familiar but also volumes such as *A New Voyage Round the World* (1725) and *A General History of Discoveries and Improvements* (1726). He also wrote the central sections on economic geography for a massive compendium, *Atlas Maritimus & Commercialis* (1728), subtitled 'A General View of the World, So far as relates to Trade and Navigation: Describing all the Coasts, Ports, Harbours, and Noted Rivers, according to the Latest Discoveries and most Exact Observations'.[37] This work reflected the new interest in map-making promoted by the British Admiralty with its 'Sett of Sea Charts' based on 'a New Globular Projection, Adapted for measuring *Distances* (as near as possible) by Scale and Compass'. Along with its claims to be serving the cause of scientific knowledge, the *Atlas* reveals strongly nationalistic aims, portraying Britain as 'the Center of the World's Commerce' and 'the most important [Island] in *Europe*, and perhaps in the World, with respect to its Strength' (*Atlas*, pp. iii, 1).

35 In this connection see Robert Batchelor, 'Concealing the Bounds: Imagining the British Nation through China', in Felicity A. Nussbaum (ed.), *The Global Eighteenth Century* (Baltimore, MD: Johns Hopkins University Press, 2003), pp. 84–91.
36 Daniel Defoe, *The Compleat English Gentleman*, ed. Karl D. Bülbring (London: David Nutt, 1890), pp. 225, 226.
37 *Atlas Maritimus & Commercialis* (London, 1728); hereafter cited in the text.

Various regions of the globe are in effect claimed for England by virtue of that nation's unrivalled enterprise and navigational skills, reflected in the superiority of its published atlases, where one can find, for example, 'the most authentick Account' of the Mississippi River, in contrast to the French maps, which are dismissed as 'fabulous and imaginary' (p. 298). The *Atlas'* account of the 'furious and barbarous' natives encountered by a group of Spanish missionaries outside of Buenos Aires along the Rio de Paraguay, who 'return'd with Horror' after witnessing the 'Savages' devour the Spaniards they had killed, reinforced British stereotypes about the character of the American Indians (p. 315).

Dampier and Rogers, those 'illiterate sailors' mentioned by Defoe, were two of the most popular travel writers during his lifetime. William Dampier's *A New Voyage round the World* (1697) spawned numerous imitations (and several 'continuations' of his own) and influenced subsequent fictional as well as factual travels – most notably, *Gulliver's Travels*. Interestingly, Dampier had begun his career on the high seas as a buccaneer; later, his writings and map-making skills won him a commission from the English Admiralty. This circumstance points to the equivocal relationship that existed between piracy and legitimate exploration, between private plunder and national conquest – one mordantly commented upon at the end of *Gulliver's Travels*. In the Preface to *A New Voyage round the World*, Dampier tells his reader 'to expect many things wholly new to him' since his travels include 'long Tracts of the Remoter Parts, both of the East and West Indies, some of which very seldom visited by English-men, and others as rarely by any Europeans'.[38] This was no idle boast – his visits to the western coast of Australia produced the first recorded description by an Englishman of the Aborigines, whom he deemed 'the miserablest People in the world', 'differ[ing] but little from Brutes', with 'great Bottle Noses, pretty full Lips, and wide Mouths' and with skins 'coal black, like that of the Negroes of Guinea' (*New Voyage*, vol. I, p. 453).

Dampier's description of the Australian Aborigines exemplifies the racial stereotypes that informed European views of foreign natives, whose bodily features and skin colour were emphasised by writers of the period. Rogers, for example, noted that the California natives 'had large Limbs' and 'a much blacker Complexion than any other People that [he] had seen in the South Seas' and asserted that the Hottentots of the Cape of Good Hope 'scarce

---

38 William Dampier, *A New Voyage round the World*, vol. I (6th edn; London, 1717), in *Dampier's Voyages*, 2 vols., ed. John Masefield (London: E. Grant Richards, 1906), vol. I, p. 19; hereafter cited in the text.

deserve to be reckon'd of the Human Kind, they are such ill look'd stinking nasty People'.[39] Such comments reflected a growing interest in what might be called racial anthropology, based on a scale extending from the most civilised and rational ethnic groups at the top to the most primitive and bestial at the bottom. Decades later, Edmund Burke demonstrated the pervasiveness of these views in describing 'the great Map of Mankind': '[T]here is no state or Gradation of barbarism, and no mode of refinement which we have not at the same instant under our View. The very different Civility of Europe and of China; The barbarism of Persia and Abyssinia. The erratick manners of Tartary, and of arabia. The Savage State of North America, and of New Zealand.'[40]

These kinds of racial views assume an especially blatant form in Edward Long's *History of Jamaica* (1774), which nevertheless contains a wealth of information about virtually every aspect of Jamaica, including exhaustive descriptions of the island's flora and fauna and a detailed account of the economics of Caribbean slavery with regard to major crops such as coffee and cotton. In addition, the work levels an incisive critique at the 'consummate tyranny and injustice' of the colonial administration, arguing that 'Men, entrusted with public offices so far from the Mother-state, require a chain, instead of a thread, to hold them within bounds.'[41] But despite Long's intention 'to display an impartial character of [Jamaica's] inhabitants of all complexions' (*History of Jamaica*, vol. I, p. 2), there is nothing at all 'impartial' in his reflections about Negroes: 'Their barbarity to their children debases their nature even below that of brutes. They have no moral sensations; no taste but for women; gormondizing, and drinking to excess; no wish but to be idle' (vol. II, p. 353). Long's relatively tolerant view of other groups (e.g., Mexicans, Northern Indians, Jews) highlights the blind bigotry of his attitude toward blacks. Though conceding they can be 'civilised' to some degree if caught young enough, he sees little improvement in the vast majority of slaves in America, who are 'marked with the same bestial manners . . . which debase their brethren [in Africa]' (vol. II, p. 354). Long's racial typology is most blatant in his insistence on a 'most intimate connexion and consanguinity' between the Negro and the orang-utang, who (he conjectures) engage in frequent 'amorous intercourse'

39 Woodes Rogers, *A Cruising Voyage round the World*, ed. G. E. Manwaring (New York: Longmans, Green & Co., 1928), pp. 229, 308.
40 Edmund Burke, *The Correspondence of Edmund Burke*, ed. George H. Guttridge, 10 vols. (Cambridge: Cambridge University Press, 1958–78), vol. III, p. 351.
41 Edward Long, *The History of Jamaica*, 3 vols. (London, 1774), vol. I, p. 3; hereafter cited in the text.

(vol. II, p. 370). His reference to the French naturalist Buffon, whose multi-volumed *Historie Naturelle* began appearing in 1749, underscores the degree to which scientific theories became part of the period's racial (and implicitly political) discourse. That David Hume expressed similar sentiments about Negroes' 'natural' inferiority to whites in his essay, 'Of National Characters', points to the collusion of philosophy as well as science in the legitimation of racial taxonomies.[42]

In the same year that Long's *History of Jamaica* was published, Janet Schaw, a young woman from an established Scottish family, accompanied her brother to the West Indies and North Carolina. The journal she kept of her sojourn on the American continent (1774–75) presents a lively account of life in Antigua, St Christopher, and the Carolinian area of Cape Fear. Schaw's social standing gave her access to the best families on the islands, whose style of living she records in detail, taking obvious delight in describing their sumptuous meals; on one occasion this included six different kinds of fish, 'vast varieties' of meats, 'fricassees of different kinds intermixed with the finest Vegetables in the world', and a rich array of exquisite tarts, pastries, puddings, cheesecakes and thirty-two varieties of fruit.[43] As if to preclude criticism of such conspicuous consumption, Schaw declares, 'Why should we blame these people for their luxury? since nature holds out her lap, filled with every thing that is in her power to bestow, it were sinful in them not to be luxurious' (*Journal*, p. 95). Justifying the imperative to embrace God's plenitude by fully indulging one's appetites, Schaw indirectly affirms the colonial imperative behind the British takeover of Caribbean lands and the righteousness of their exploitation of the land's natural riches.

With the eye of a landscape enthusiast, Schaw tours 'almost from one end of [Antigua] to the other', finding herself 'more and more pleased with its beauties, as every excursion affords new objects worthy of notice' (p. 100). A friend's plantation is portrayed in near-edenic terms, with an ideal climate and features that 'mock the poor imitation . . . produced by art' (p. 90). The slaves are presented as indigenous parts of the landscape – when Schaw first lands in

---

42 David Hume, *Essays: Moral, Political, and Literary*, ed. Eugene F. Miller (Indianapolis, IN: Liberty Fund, 1985), p. 208. For more on the scientific dimensions of eighteenth-century racialist typologies and their connection to the 'natural histories' of Buffon and Linnaeus, see Mary Louise Pratt, *Imperial Eyes: Travel Writing and Transculturation* (London and New York: Routledge, 1992), pp. 15–37.

43 [Janet Schaw], *Journal of a Lady of Quality; Being the Narrative of a Journey from Scotland to the West Indies, North Carolina, and Portugal, in the years 1774 to 1776*, ed. Evangeline Walker Andrews in collaboration with Charles McLean Andrews (New Haven, CT: Yale University Press, 1921; 1922), pp. 95–9; hereafter cited in the text. This work remained unpublished until the twentieth century.

Antigua, she sees 'a parcel of monkeys' coming down the lane and only later realises that 'what [she] took for monkeys were negro children, naked as they were born' (p. 78). The slaves contribute to the scene's aesthetic appeal, as when Schaw notes that her hostess at one of the plantations 'had standing by her a little Mulatto girl not above five years old, whom she retains as a pet. This brown beauty was dressed out like an infant Sultana, and is a fine contrast to the delicate complexion of her Lady' – a comment that supports what one critic terms Schaw's 'aesthetic argument for slavery'.[44] This argument is bolstered by Schaw's belief in Africans' innate suitability for slavery, since 'those from one coast [of Africa] are mere brutes and fit only for the labour of the field' (*Journal*, p. 128). Although repulsed by the evidence of whip lashes on the slaves' backs, she hastens to point out that 'When one comes to be better acquainted with the nature of the Negroes, the horrour of [the whippings] must wear off' since their 'Natures seems made to bear it' (p. 127). Schaw's writing demonstrates that delicate 'feminine' sensibilities were no bar to defending the most brutal of European practices.

There were other travel accounts that presented a very different view of Negroes and their plight. Alexander Falconbridge's *An Account of the Slave Trade on the Coast of Africa* (1788) contains an impassioned indictment of the cruelties suffered by slaves on the Middle Passage and calls for an end to this inhumane institution. A ship's surgeon sent to oversee the abolitionist settlement of 'Free Town' off the coast of Sierra Leone in 1791, Falconbridge was accompanied to Africa by his wife, Anna Maria Falconbridge, who also produced an account of her lengthy stay on the continent, one conveying its own denunciation of the cruel treatment of the 'wretched victims' of slavery, 'chained and parcelled out in circles, just satisfying the cravings of nature from a trough of rice placed in the centre of each circle.'[45] Yet following the death of her husband and her growing contempt for the 'hypocritical puritans' of the Sierra Leone Company, Falconbridge repudiates her prior abolitionist sentiments and declares that she 'cannot think the Slave Trade inconsistent with any moral, or religious law' as long as 'ignorance, superstition, and savageness, overspread Africa' – though she retains her belief in the Africans' capacity for 'improvement and cultivation' (*Narrative*, pp. 235–6, 238–9). Maria Falconbridge's account throws into sharp relief the ideological contradictions

44 Elizabeth A. Bohls, *Women Travel Writers and the Language of Aesthetics, 1716–1818*, Cambridge Studies in Romanticism 13 (Cambridge: Cambridge University Press, 1995), p. 49.
45 A. M. Falconbridge, *Narrative of Two Voyages to the River Sierra Leon, during the Years 1791–1793*, 2nd edn (London, 1802), Cass Library of African Studies (London: Frank Cass & Co., 1967), p. 32; hereafter cited in the text.

inherent in the experience of foreign travel, with its simultaneous ability to foster sympathy for other cultures and to provide validation for institutions that enslave and brutalise the latter.

But travel literature also provided a format in which (former) slaves could appropriate agency and become the active subjects rather than passive objects of voyage narratives. A case in point is *The Interesting Narrative of the Life of Olaudah Equiano, or Gustavus Vassa, the African. Written by Himself*, an enormously popular work that remained in print for a half-century after its initial London publication in 1789. The text deftly combines several genres – slave narrative, polemical tract, spiritual autobiography, providence literature and picaresque adventure – to present a vivid picture of a slave turned freed-man who becomes a celebrated writer, orator and Christian convert. Underpinning these different thematic and rhetorical threads are the conventions of travel narrative.[46] The memoir begins with a description of Equiano's childhood in the African village of Essaka – thought to be an area of modern Nigeria, home to today's Ibo people. In sharp contrast to the 'barbaric' Africa of most eighteenth-century travel accounts, Equiano's birthplace is 'a charming fruitful vale' inhabited by a highly civilised society living a rather edenic existence – one that comes to an abrupt end for Equiano when he is kidnapped and put on a slave ship headed for Virginia.[47] The ensuing hardships of the Middle Passage help fuel Equiano's impassioned jeremiads against the 'nominal Christians' who flagrantly violate God's commandment, 'Do unto all men as you would men should do unto you' (*Interesting Narrative*, p. 61). On another level, the Middle Passage launches Equiano's lifelong career as a traveller – one that begins with coerced voyages but concludes with a series of freely chosen journeys.

Equiano's years in captivity introduce him to various parts of the world, including England and America. Under his master, a merchant who transports goods and slaves from the islands of the Caribbean to the American colonies, Equiano develops navigational skills and hones his powers of observation. He becomes an entrepreneur in his own right, buying tumblers in St Eustatia to sell for a profit in Montserrat, and eventually expanding his trade – along

---

46 See Geraldine Murphy, 'Olaudah Equiano, Accidental Tourist', *Eighteenth-Century Studies* 27 (1994), 551–68.

47 Olaudah Equiano, '*The Interesting Narrative*' *and Other Writings*, ed. Vincent Carretta (New York and London: Penguin, 1995), p. 32; hereafter cited in the text. Carretta has recently raised questions about the accuracy of this version of Equiano's African childhood, suggesting that Equiano may instead have been a native of South Carolina; see 'Questioning the Identity of Olaudah Equiano, or Gustavus Vassa, the African', in Nussbaum (ed.), *The Global Eighteenth Century*, pp. 226–35.

with his geographical horizons – to include the French islands and American colonies. After finally purchasing his freedom, he returns to England, 'where [his] heart had always been', and begins a new life as an apprentice hairdresser (p. 147). But his 'roving disposition' produces a new series of travels – this time, expeditions of pleasure and instruction that at times sound like the typical Grand Tour (p. 171). Equiano is much taken with the 'rich and magnificent churches' of Genoa (though repulsed by the 'truly piteous and wretched' state of the galley-slaves there), and highly impressed with Naples, 'a charming city' where he is regaled with grand operas and 'a perfect view' of Mount Vesuvius erupting (p. 169). A later voyage to Malaga gives him an opportunity to admire 'one of the finest cathedrals [he] had ever seen' (p. 199). He spends six months in Turkey and finds much to recommend, including the Turks' 'great civility' and the 'richest and largest' fruit he ever ate (p. 167). When he returns to the Caribbean, it is not only as a trader but also as one interested to record the survival of 'native customs', including burial rituals and dances, among the Africans in Kingston, Jamaica (p. 172).

In the final episode of his memoir Equiano, 'roused by the sound of fame to seek new adventures', joins the expedition led by Constantine John Phipps (1773) seeking a passage to India via the North Pole (p. 172). Despite the failure of the four-month voyage, Equiano expresses pride in the fact that the crew had gone 'much farther [towards the North Pole], by all accounts, than any navigator had ever ventured before' (p. 177). By the end of the *Interesting Narrative* he has emerged as a celebrated personage whose book has brought him both fame and riches. The authority of his authorial voice derives from many sources: the piety of the Christian convert, the moral indignation of the abolitionist, the heroism of the adventurer on the high seas – and, not least, the independent, self-assured eye of the traveller.

Many other regions of the world were being opened up to the scrutiny of scientists, antiquarians and explorers, among them the Middle East and north-east Africa, earlier the object of scholarly investigation under the aegis of Arabic Studies at Oxford University. Richard Pococke's *A Description of the East* (1743–5), which records its author's five-year journey through Egypt and nearby regions (including Palestine, Syria, Mesopotamia and Cyprus), contains the earliest-known drawings of the Valley of the Kings and the Colossi of Memnon as well as striking descriptions of the sepulchres of the Kings of Thebes, with painted figures 'as fresh as if they were just finish'd, tho' they must be above two thousand years old'.[48] The work is now best known for Pococke's visit to

48 Richard Pococke, *A Description of the East, and Some other Countries*, 2 vols. (London, 1743–5), vol. I, p. 98; hereafter cited in the text.

Luxerein and his reference to statues there (no longer in evidence) mentioned by Diodorus, including a vast colossus with the inscription, 'I am the King of Kings, Osymanduas: If any would know how great I am, and where I lie, let him exceed the works that I have done': a passage thought to have been the inspiration for Shelley's great poem, 'Ozymandias' (Pococke, *Description*, vol. I, p. 108). James Bruce's *Travels to Discover the Source of the Nile* (1790) is the action-filled narrative of a brash adventurer with a keen interest in Moorish culture acquired while a British Consul-General in Tangiers, whose boasted study of Arabic books, including the Koran, 'had made [him] a very tolerable Arab'.[49] His lengthy sojourn at the Abyssinian Court in Gondar allowed him to record intimate details of a way of life little known to the outside world because of Abyssinia's centuries-old isolation. Although the relation of his adventures to a London audience was met with scepticism upon his return from the East (1772), Bruce's travels contain a wealth of information that both expands upon and corrects earlier Jesuit accounts of the region (especially the best-known one by Father Jerome Lobo, translated by Dr Johnson). That Londoners were far readier to accept the word of Johnson, author of a wholly idealised Abyssinia in his fable, *Rasselas* (1759), over Bruce's eye-witness testimony, underscores (among other things) the difficulty of distinguishing truth from fiction in eighteenth-century travel writing.

From a modern-day point of view, no doubt the most famous eighteenth-century traveller was James Cook, commander of three highly publicised and minutely recorded expeditions to the South Seas between the years 1768 and 1779. Though a self-described seaman from youth who 'has not the advantage of Education, acquired, nor Natural abilities for writing', he kept detailed journals of all that occurred in the course of the voyages and scrupulously revised them for publication, determined to personally shepherd them into print after the record of his first voyage fell into the hands of John Hawkesworth, who put out an edition of them (1773) that took considerable freedoms with Cook's text.[50] Although there had been earlier expeditions to the Pacific dating back to Magellan, Cook's was unique in the prominence it gave to a specifically scientific mission – i.e., to observe the transit of Venus across the sun on 3 June 1769 from St George's Island (Tahiti) – undertaken at the behest of the

49 James Bruce, *Travels to Discover the Source of the Nile, In the Years 1768, 1769, 1770, 1771, and 1772*, 5 vols. (Edinburgh and London, 1790; rpt. London: Gregg International Publishers, 1972 (1984)), vol. I, p. xiii.
50 James Cook, *The Journals of Captain James Cook on his Voyages of Discovery*, 4 vols., ed. J. C. Beaglehole (Hakluyt Society; Cambridge: Cambridge University Press, 1955–68), vol. II, p. (2); hereafter cited in the text. For a useful abridgement of this work, see *The Journals of Captain Cook*, ed. Philip Edwards (London: Penguin, 1999).

Royal Society and furthered by the presence on board of several botanists and astronomers. At the same time, Cook's commission from the British Admiralty included instructions to search for the 'southern continent' and 'with the Consent of the Natives to take possession of Convenient Situations in the Country in the Name of the King of Great Britain' or, if he found the Country uninhabited, to take possession 'as first discoverers and possessors' (*Journals*, vol. I, p. cclxxxiii). Thus Cook's first voyage exemplifies the extent to which the disinterested aims of scientific advancement and the eminently self-interested goal of colonial expansion had become intertwined.

On his first ship, the *Endeavour*, Cook steered a course around Cape Horn, arriving in Tahiti on 12 April 1769. Once there, he promulgated a set of rules for his crew to follow, the first being '*To endeavor by every fair means to cultivate a friendship with the Natives and to treat them with all imaginable humanity*' (vol. I, p. 75). This rule was made easier to carry out by the sociability of the natives, who flocked around the seafarers 'in great Numbers and in as friendly a Manner as [the crew] could wish' – though it was difficult 'to keep them from Stealing' (vol. I, pp. 78, 77). When one of the natives snatches a musket from the hands of a sentinel and is shot to death by him, Cook has the seaman whipped and uses 'every means in [his] power' to make amends for the incident, so that the next day the natives 'seem'd as friendly as ever' (vol. I, pp. 80, 81). After another sentry later commits a similar act, Cook declares that he 'was astonished beyond Measure at the inhumanity of the act' and orders the sentry to be flogged, relenting only after protestations from crew members who believed the shooting was justifiable self-defence against 'particularly Insolent' natives (vol. II, pp. 498, 500n). Incidents such as these reveal the potential for tragic misunderstandings inherent in intercultural encounters even as they illuminate the reasons behind Cook's reputation as one of the most humane of England's naval commanders. This reputation deserves to be taken seriously but with the caveat that although 'it was peaceful coexistence [with the natives] that he wanted . . . it *was* coexistence. His presence had to be accepted' – i.e., rejection of the Westerners as unwanted intruders was not an option.[51]

Eager to refute or counterbalance the often denigrating accounts of earlier travellers, Cook portrays a group of Australian Aboriginals by noting that their hair was 'neither wooly nor frizled nor did they want any of their fore teeth, as Dampier has mentioned those did he saw', and he emphasises that the

51 *The Journals of Captain Cook*, ed. Edwards, p. 612. For Cook's stellar reputation see Anna Neill, 'South Seas Trade and the Character of Captains', in Nussbaum (ed.), *The Global Eighteenth Century*, pp. 297–303.

eastern coastline of New Zealand is 'not that barren and Miserable Country that *Dampier* and others have discribed the western side to be' (vol. I, pp. 358, 397). In depicting the Aboriginals of New Zealand, Cook makes a point of noting that 'Their features are far from being disagreeable and their Voices are soft and tunable' (vol. I, p. 395); however, he also records their darker aspects. While docked in Queen Charlotte Sound, for example, he sees evidence of cannibalism first hand: 'I now saw the mangled head or rather the remains of it . . . . a peice of the flesh had been broiled and eat by one of the Natives in the presince of most of the officers' (vol. II, p. 293). But though his immediate reaction is one of horror, his curiosity and desire to be 'an eye wittness to a fact which many people had their doubts about' overcome his disgust and prompt him to order a piece of the flesh 'to be broiled and brought on the quarter deck where one of the Canibals eat it with a seeming food relish before the whole ships Company' (vol. II, p. 293). This rather shocking act of complicity is complemented by Cook's refusal to see this practice as an inevitable marker of barbarism – he insists that 'the New Zealanders are certainly in a state of civilization' since they have mastered various arts and their behaviour to the crew has been 'Manly and Mild' (vol. II, p. 294).

But it is of course Cook's depictions of Tahiti on which his enduring fame as a travel writer rests. His first voyage in particular is notable for its wealth of details on almost every aspect of Tahitian life, including the natives' eating habits, clothing (or relative lack of it) and practice of tattooing their bodies, as well as their music, wrestling and religious observances, based on their belief in one supreme being from whom 'sprung a number of inferior Deities *Eatuas* as they call them' (vol. I, p. 134). A number of passages record the Tahitians' lack of sexual inhibitions. While he is censorious of 'a very indecent dance' performed by young girls, Cook more typically remains non-judgemental about such practices, at times even going out of his way to stress their 'innocence' – as when he relates how a young native woman 'with as much Innocency as one could possibly conceve, expose'd herself intirely naked from the waist downwards' in an apparent fertility rite (vol. I, pp. 127, 93). The most famous episode in this regard is the so-called 'Point Venus scene' in which 'a young fellow above 6 feet high lay with a little Girl about 10 or 12 years of age publickly before several of our people and a number of the Natives' (vol. I, pp. 93–4). Noting that 'there were several women present' who seemed to be 'instruct[ing] the girl how she should act her part', Cook states that the whole scene 'appear'd to be done more from Custom than Lewdness' (vol. I, p. 94). Yet his language suggests an uncertainty about the event, underscored by the comment that the girl 'young as she was, did not seem to want it' – the latter pronoun referring either to the act of copulation or to the women's instruction, and the word 'want' signifying either 'desire' or 'lack'.[52]

That Cook does not attempt to resolve the ambiguity reflects his general refusal to assume the role of an authority on native customs. Thus in describing the Tahitians' religion, he notes it is a subject 'I have learnt so little of that I hardly dare touch upon it, and should have pass'd it over in silence' were it not that his readers will expect to see some account of it (vol. I, p. 134). He also 'candidly confessed' to Boswell that because his crew's 'knowledge of the language was so imperfect', they 'could not be certain of any information they got, or supposed they got' about the Pacific Islanders beyond strictly sensory perception.[53] In this regard Cook resists the model of the 'Orientalist' who utilises the nexus of knowledge and power to assert his authority over native others who are (in more ways than one) his subjects.[54] He further departs from this model by drawing a decidedly mixed picture of Western influence on indigenous tribes, who are 'far more happier than we Europeans' thanks to their intimate ties to nature and their lack of materialism, which means they are 'not disturb'd by the Inequality of Condition' (vol. I, p. 399). On a return trip to Queen Charlotte Sound he is dismayed to find that although in the past the Maoris there had seemed sexually modest, the males now regularly prostituted their own wives and daughters. Cook attributes this change chiefly to 'a commerce with Europeans' and offers a blistering condemnation of what results from these cultural encounters:

> [W]e debauch their Morals already too prone to vice and we interduce among them wants and perhaps diseases which they never before knew and which serves only to disturb that happy tranquillity they and their fore Fathers had injoy'd. If any one denies the truth of this assertion let him tell me what the Natives of the whole extent of America have gained by the commerce they have had with Europeans. (vol. II, p. 175)

Although Cook continued his expeditionary projects in spite of this insight, his bold words have reverberated over the ages as a continuing challenge to those who would claim to bring the 'blessings' of Western commerce and technology to 'primitive' nations.

52 This ambiguity of interpretation is emphasised by Neil Rennie in 'The Point Venus "Scene," Tahiti, 14 May 1769', in Nussbaum (ed.), *The Global Eighteenth Century*, pp. 249–50.

53 James Boswell, *Boswell: The Ominous Years 1774–1776*, eds. C. Ryskamp and F. A. Pottle (New York: McGraw-Hill, 1963), p. 341.

54 In this connection see Edward W. Said, *Orientalism* (1978; New York: Vintage Books, 1979), which posits that 'the essence of Orientalism is the ineradicable distinction between Western superiority and Oriental inferiority' (p. 42).

Cook's final voyage brings out the darker side both of the Polynesian 'paradises' and of the men who came halfway around the world to explore them. It is in this voyage that we see an often petulant Cook who treats both natives and crewmen with a harshness not seen before. And it is here, in the expedition's arrival in Hawaii during a ceremony revolving around fertility and kingship, that the clash of cultures turns violent and claims the life of Cook himself. But it is the earlier accounts of Tahiti that have come to define Cook's voyage in the minds of readers both then and now, fuelling fantasies of a sexual paradise that have influenced a host of artistic and literary representations, and testifying to the richly ambiguous nature of travel literature in its simultaneous claims upon the intellect and the imagination.

The complex interplay of factual travel accounts with the world of the imagination had a profound effect on the development of the eighteenth-century novel, the geographical spaces of an ever-expanding globe becoming part of the very conception of novelistic space, with readers along with characters embarked on journeys at once linear and circular, end-directed but digressive. This interplay produced a variety of literary hybrids, 'factual fictions' that combined realistic description with exploitation of the exotic and flights of often wild fancy.[55] Thus the setting of Aphra Behn's novella, *Oroonoko: Or, The Royal Slave* (1688) – Surinam, in the West Indies, where the author herself spent some time – unites detailed catalogues of Surinam's flora and fauna ('*Paraketoes*, great *Parrots*, *Muckaws*, and a thousand other Birds and Beasts') with an idealised landscape marked by 'eternal Spring', whose natives represent 'an absolute *Idea* of the first State of Innocence, before *Man* knew how to sin'.[56] The work incorporates many of the major motifs of travel narrative, including the conflict between civilisation and barbarism (here with an ironic twist in that the edenic innocence of the Surinam natives serves as a foil for the brutality and treachery of the Europeans) and a system of racial classification that elevates the Caucasian-looking African prince Oroonoko above others of his tribe, his finely-shaped mouth 'far from those great turn'd Lips, which are so natural to the rest of the Negroes' (*Oroonoko*, p. 8). The genre of travel

---

55 Critical studies on this subject include Percy G. Adams, *Travelers and Travel Liars, 1660–1800* (Berkeley and Los Angeles: University of California Press, 1962) and *Travel Literature and the Evolution of the Novel* (Lexington, KY: University Press of Kentucky, 1983); and Charles Batten, *Pleasurable Instruction: Form and Convention in Eighteenth-Century Travel Literature* (Berkeley and Los Angeles: University of California Press, 1978). Lennard Davis uses the term 'factual fiction' to describe the early English novel in *Factual Fictions: The Origins of the English Novel* (New York: Columbia University Press, 1983), but his focus is on the novel's relationship to journalism, not travel literature.

56 Aphra Behn, *Oroonoko: Or, The Royal Slave. A True History*, ed. Lore Metzger (New York: Norton, 1973), pp. 2, 43, 3; hereafter cited in the text.

literature provided Behn with materials enabling her to expand the boundaries of her slender fiction by setting its main action on 'a Continent whose vast Extent was never yet known . . . for, they say, it reaches from East to West one way as far as *China*, and another to *Peru*' (p. 48).

Defoe's first novel, *Robinson Crusoe* (1719), is likewise defined by a mixture of fact and fiction derived from the conventions of travel narrative. Based loosely on the story of Alexander Selkirk, marooned on the island of Juan Fernández for over four years, the novel features a protagonist cast away on a Caribbean island located near the mouth of the Orinoco River – not coincidentally, the site of its author's proposed establishment of a British colony.[57] A defining feature of Crusoe's activity is the charting out of unknown territory – perhaps not unlike Defoe's own mapping out of new literary terrain in his attempt to inhabit novelistic space. Although Crusoe's story is usually equated with his island confinement, the latter does not actually begin until he has had a number of other experiences, including several voyages to the coast of Africa, a two-year period of enslavement in the Moroccan seaport of Sallee, and a four-year sojourn in Brazil, where he becomes a prosperous trader and plantation owner. These early chapters, in the words of one critic, 'recapitulate the European "history of discovery" ' as it moved from the West African coast to the crossing of the Atlantic and the colonisation of the Caribbean.[58] By the time Crusoe leaves his island after twenty-eight years, it has become his undisputed 'Dominion', peopled with obedient 'Subjects' epitomised by the savage Friday, who kneels down and sets Crusoe's foot on his head, apparently 'in token of swearing to be [his] Slave for ever'.[59] On his return to England, Crusoe marries and settles down, but this stage of his life is quickly dispensed with in one brief paragraph, after which his 'Inclination to go Abroad' once again prevails, resulting in 'some very surprising Incidents' that he promises to give 'a farther Account' of (*Robinson Crusoe*, p. 305). This conclusion underscores the extent to which Crusoe operates within a framework defined by the conventions of travel literature, with its built-in imperative to keep moving – and

57 The location of Crusoe's island is indicated by the full title of the first edition, which states that Crusoe 'lived Eight and Twenty Years, all alone in an un-inhabited Island on the Coast of America, near the Mouth of the Great River of Oroonoque'. Defoe's scheme for a colony at the mouth of the Orinoco appeared in the *Weekly Journal* of 7 February 1719; see Maximillian Novak, *Realism, Myth, and History in Defoe's Fiction* (Lincoln, NE and London: University of Nebraska Press, 1983), p. 26.

58 Peter Hulme, *Colonial Encounters: Europe and the Native Caribbean, 1492–1797* (1986; London and New York: Routledge, 1992), p. 185.

59 Daniel Defoe, *Robinson Crusoe*, ed. J. Donald Crowley (Oxford: Oxford University Press (World Classics), 1990), pp. 241, 204; hereafter cited in the text.

narrating – in a world of seemingly endless opportunities for adventure and exploration.

As a consciously constructed 'factual fiction', Jonathan Swift's *Travels into Several Remote Nations of the World* (1726), better known as *Gulliver's Travels*, testifies to its author's extensive reading in both historical and fictional travel literature, which made up a large portion of his personal library.[60] The work parodies actual travel journals with lengthy passages about conditions at sea and maps charting the routes of Gulliver's voyages, and contains assurances by the narrator that he is 'a Writer who relates only plain Facts', thus differing from the common run of travel writers, who 'impose the grossest Falsities on the unwary Reader'.[61] The work's clever play with the conventions of non-fictional travel literature allowed Swift to cast his satiric net wide enough to take in many of his own readers, as Dr Arbuthnot indicates in his report to Swift: 'Gulliver is in every body's Hands[.] Lord Scarborow who is no inventor of Storys told me that he fell in company with a Master of a ship, who told him that he was very well acquainted with Gulliver, but that the printer had Mistaken, that he livd in Wapping, & not in Rotherhith.'[62] Arbuthnot's relation, however tongue-in-cheek, underscores the very real confusion created by the outpouring of books about travels that were sometimes true but in other instances made-up. Swift, fascinated by both types of accounts, was intrigued above all by the epistemological ambiguity that made it difficult to distinguish between the two.

For Defoe's Protestant capitalist hero, bent on providentially sanctioned empire building, Swift gives us a protagonist whose encounters with other cultures provide a critical perspective on the attitudes and practices that sustain empire. Gulliver is at times the bluff and hearty John Bull, epitome of the smug Englishman abroad, but he is more often the insecure Anglo-Irishman, conflicted about his identity and trying to find his bearings in an unfamiliar, often hostile world – circumstances calling to mind Swift's self-portrayal as 'a stranger in a strange land' (*Corr.*, vol. III, p. 341). He participates in the colonial enterprise – sailing on trading vessels to the Indies and bringing back native rarities from his travels – even as he adopts an anti-colonial stance by embracing the values of alien cultures and refusing to claim their lands

---

60 See Harold Williams, *Dean Swift's Library* (Cambridge: Cambridge University Press, 1932).

61 Jonathan Swift, *Gulliver's Travels*, ed. Paul Turner (Oxford: Oxford University Press (World Classics), 1998), pp. 285, 283; hereafter cited in the text.

62 *The Correspondence of Jonathan Swift*, 5 vols., ed. Harold Williams (Oxford: Clarendon Press, 1963–5), vol. III, p. 180; hereafter cited as *Corr.* in the text.

for the British crown. Moreover, he concludes his travels with a shockingly demystifying portrayal of colonisers as practitioners of genocide:

> Ships are sent with the first Opportunity; the Natives driven out or destroyed, their Princes tortured to discover their Gold; a free Licence given to all Acts of Inhumanity and Lust; the Earth reeking with the Blood of its Inhabitants: And this execrable Crew of Butchers employed in so pious an Expedition, is a *modern Colony* sent to convert and civilize an idolatrous and barbarous People.
>
> (p. 286)

The contradictions of Gulliver's role force readers to reflect on the ambiguities of their own position vis-à-vis this system of brutal conquest imposed in their name.

Gulliver's Travels is in many ways the quintessential travel book, alternately reproducing and parodying the conventions of the genre, and forcefully demonstrating both its capabilities and its limitations as an instrument for disseminating knowledge. In the process it suggests both the vast potential and the paralysing limitations of travel itself. If Gulliver's horizons are broadened by his contact with other societies, they ultimately contract to the four walls of his barn. The clarity of vision he gains into the moral shortcomings of British society supports the truism that travel is an enlightening experience, but his final stance as part-madman, part-fool, expressing revulsion at the smell of his wife and preferring to spend hours talking to his horses, offers us a bracing reminder that there is a darker side to enlightenment, and that travel can unhinge as well as edify the mind. What we thus see in this work are the combined comedic and tragic dimensions of travel, which promises an escape into otherness but too often results in a return to sameness – or even worse, (as in the case of the colonial 'Butchers' described by Gulliver) in a violence that destroys the other in the name of the same. The *Travels* is Swift's playful love song to his favourite genre, but also a dirge to its failure to 'deliver the goods' – to fulfil its tacit promise to 'mend the world' and bring about meaningful changes in the way that we think and live. All eighteenth-century travellers after Gulliver would be forced to confront the same contradictory mixture of hope and disenchantment, revelation and delusion, in their endeavours to recreate the 'great map of the world' not only in their own image but in the image of others as well.

Women novelists 1740s–1780s

FELICITY A. NUSSBAUM

In Jane Austen's *Northanger Abbey* Catherine Morland and her friend Isabella share a mutual passion for reading novels in spite of the fact that 'no species of composition has been so much decried'. When caught reading a novel, a typical young lady of the period, we are told, might blurt out in embarrassment, 'Oh! It is only a novel!' quickly putting it aside: 'It is only *Cecilia*, or *Camilla*, or *Belinda*.' Yet in defence of the genre, Austen's narrator remarks that a novel is 'only some work in which the greatest powers of the mind are displayed, in which the most thorough knowledge of human nature, the happiest delineation of its varieties, the liveliest effusions of wit and humour are conveyed to the world in the best-chosen language'.[1] Until recently literary scholars, rather than assenting to Austen's ironic appreciation of Frances Burney and Maria Edgeworth, have sometimes shared the young woman's attitude of 'affected indifference, or momentary shame' in taking pleasure in novel reading. In spite of critical reticence, recent attention to eighteenth-century women authors and readers has transformed the understanding of the English novel in the mid and late eighteenth century. Widely read by their contemporaries, these women and others like them had largely been lost to the literary history of the first half of the twentieth century. In fact, women novelists, except for Burney and Austen, were omitted from consideration in the previous edition of *The Cambridge History of English Literature*.[2]

A strong revisionist interest in women's writing, begun in the pioneering work of J. M. S. Tompkins, Joyce M. Horner and B. G. MacCarthy, and later sparked by the fresh wave of the feminist movement during the 1960s and 1970s, has considerably altered the history of the English novel.[3] The genre emerged

---

1 Jane Austen, *Northanger Abbey*, ed. Marilyn Butler (London: Penguin, 1995), p. 34. Though written in 1798–9, the novel was published posthumously in 1818.
2 'The Age of Johnson', in Sir A. W. Ward and A. R. Wallter (eds.), *The Cambridge History of English Literature* vol. x (Cambridge: Cambridge University Press, 1913).
3 See Janet Todd, preface to B. G. MacCarthy, *The Female Pen: Women Writers and Novelists 1621–1818* (New York: New York University Press, 1994, first published 1946–7), pp. xi–xxi.

as a distinctive form during the middle decades of the eighteenth century with Samuel Richardson's *Pamela* and *Clarissa*, Henry Fielding's *Tom Jones*, Laurence Sterne's *Tristram Shandy*, and Tobias Smollett's *Humphry Clinker*. The women who wrote novels that promulgated moral ideologies requisite to a decorous femininity often seemed to be mere imitators and borrowers from these literary greats. Women writers are now increasingly perceived as rivalling the male giants in creating satiric, picaresque, utopian, epistolary and Gothic fictions. The most significant novelists of this period, including Sarah Fielding, Eliza Haywood, Charlotte Lennox, Sarah Scott, Frances Sheridan, Frances Brooke and Frances Burney, are also heirs and antagonists to the amatory fiction of the Restoration and early eighteenth century by Aphra Behn, Delariviere Manley and Eliza Haywood. In addition, they alter and extend early invocations of morality from the early novelists Jane Barker and Elizabeth Rowe to combine elements from both traditions.

In some quarters women's writing has been freshly recognised only to diminish its achievement. Though sometimes figured as didactic novelists who simply modified the plots and conventions invented by men, Behn, Manley and Haywood inspired the British realist novels written by men.[4] Some critics have suggested that Eliza Haywood's parodic repetition of the characters, plots and language of the major male novelists actually highlighted women's ability to create innovative plots that circumvented the regnant double standard.[5] In fact, it would seem that a reciprocal relationship between the writers of both sexes prevailed. Both sexes invented new modes of writing, though women led the way in publishing epistolary novels in the late seventeenth century and in imagining new genres. Sarah Fielding's *The Governess; or Little Female Academy* (1749), for example, pioneered the first collected stories expressly written for children, and *David Simple* is very likely the first fictional man of feeling. Aphra Behn (*Oroonoko*) and Sarah Scott (*The History of Sir George Ellison*) were among the first to evoke sympathy against the cruelty to African slaves. Frances Brooke's *The History of Emily Montague* (1769) is reputed to be the inaugural Canadian novel. Charlotte Lennox experiments with Indian captivity narrative, and the New World setting for *Harriot Stuart* (1750 or 1751)

---

4 William B. Warner, *Licensing Entertainment: The Elevation of Novel Reading in Britain, 1684–1750* (Berkeley and Los Angeles: University of California Press, 1998).

5 Andrea Austin, 'Shooting Blanks: Potency, Parody, and Eliza Haywood's *The History of Miss Betsy Thoughtless*', in Kirsten T. Saxton and Rebecca P. Bocchicchio (eds.), *The Passionate Fictions of Eliza Haywood: Essays on Her Life and Work* (Lexington, KY: University of Kentucky Press, 2000), pp. 259–82; and Kristina Straub, 'Frances Burney and the Rise of the Woman Novelist', in John Richetti (ed.), *The Columbia History of the British Novel* (New York: Columbia University Press, 1994), pp. 199–219.

and *Euphemia* (1790) make her a candidate for America's first novelist. Near the century's end English women's exotic tales of mercenary flirts seeking husbands abroad launched the novel about India. There is further innovation in women's treatment of courtship and marriage plots: a female utopia in Sarah Scott's *Millenium Hall*, a divorce in Fielding's *The Countess of Dellwyn*, a woman who seeks a husband who will adopt her surname in order to retain her inheritance in Frances Burney's *Cecilia* and a heroine who proposes in *The Wanderer*. Yet to examine women's novels outside the context of other eighteenth-century genres is to offer a slightly skewed perspective; travel literature and didactic essays, for example, were more popular for both sexes than novels. Women writers also contributed significantly to translation (especially from the French), essay writing, periodical literature, poetry, memoirs, letters and eventually history. Though it is arguable that the expansion of merchant capital contributed to the rise of the novel at mid century, and that the development of mobile wealth enabled the rise to power of the middle class, the eighteenth-century novel did not possess the centrality it has today for readers and for literary historians.[6]

The period under consideration here falls between two feminist vindications, the translations of Poulain de la Barre by 'Sophia'(a still unidentified author of the 1740s), and Mary Wollstonecraft's polemical *Vindication of the Rights of Woman* (1792). Some critics have contended that the cult of domesticity mutes women's voices during these later decades of the eighteenth century, yet women novelists from the 1740s to the 1780s did not so much abandon feminism for reform, as assert the compatibility of reason and virtue. Didactic novels parallel educational treatises such as Sarah Fielding's children's stories in *The Governess*, Sarah Trimmer's *Fabulous Histories* (1786) and Mary Wollstonecraft's *Thoughts on the Education of Daughters* (1787).[7] The novels of this period share with misogynist satires of the Restoration and early eighteenth century a disdain for frivolous women but other thinkers such as Wollstonecraft seek to redeem women through education. The novels ridicule women while advancing their status, and they satirise domestic ideology while attempting to wrest female empowerment from unsympathetic circumstances.

---

6 Ian Watt, *The Rise of the Novel: Studies in Defoe, Richardson and Fielding* (London: Chatto and Windus, 1957).
7 Mitzi Myers, 'Impeccable Governesses, Rational Dames, and Moral Mothers: Mary Wollstonecraft and the Female Tradition in Georgian Children's Books', *Annual of the Modern Language Association Division on Children's Literature and the Children's Literature Association* 14 (New Haven, CT: Yale University Press, 1986), pp. 31–59.

Women of the middling class gained moral ascendancy as sexual difference began to assume its modern dimensions.[8] Women writers produced
fictions of intelligence, sensitivity and authority which instructed their sex
not just in appropriate behaviour, but in negotiating the dangerous terrain
to be crossed in entering 'the world' and in extracting some agency from
it. Their novels offer considerable insight into 'female difficulties', the subtitle of Frances Burney's *The Wanderer*: 'How utterly dependant [is a female]
upon situation – connexions – circumstances! How nameless, how for ever
fresh springing are her DIFFICULTIES, when she would owe her existence to
her own exertions! Her conduct is criticised, not scrutinized; her character is
censured, not examined; her labours are unhonoured, and her qualifications
are but lures to ill-will!'[9] Frances Brooke is typical in believing women especially qualified to compose moral writing because of their 'quick sensibility,
native delicacy of mind, facility of expression, and a style at once animated
and natural'.[10] Women possessed moral authority *because* of their exquisitely
tuned sensibilities which could all too easily be reduced to the capacity to
suffer, yet these suffering heroines also proved to be the prototype for *men* of
feeling. For in novels by Brooke, Sarah Fielding, Elizabeth Griffith and others,
there is a correspondent feminisation of the hero. This broad feminisation of
culture meant that both men and women who possessed sympathy, vulnerability and high emotion were regarded as properly sensible, while excessive
displays of these qualities categorised men as foppish, effeminate and a disgrace to their country. It is not too great a claim to make that women's writing,
though often treated as marginal, was central to eighteenth-century English
culture in fostering the prevailing moral ideology and weaving the fabric of the
nation.[11]

Most historians of the period agree that after the late seventeenth century,
women at both ends of the economic scale lost considerable economic power.
The mid eighteenth century also marks a radical displacement of daughters
in inheritance schemes as marriage ties steadily gain precedence over blood

8 Thomas Laqueur, *Making Sex: Body and Gender from the Greeks to Freud* (Cambridge,
   MA: Harvard University Press, 1990) argues that sexual difference assumes its modern
   meanings in the eighteenth century.
9 Frances Burney, *The Wanderer; or Female Difficulties*, eds. Margaret Doody, Robert L. Mack
   and Peter Sabor (Oxford: Oxford University Press, 1991).
10 Frances Brooke, *The Excursion*, eds. Paula Backscheider and Hope D. Cotton (Lexington,
   KY: University of Kentucky Press, 1997), p. 2.
11 Nancy Armstrong, *Desire and Domestic Fiction: A Political History of the Novel* (New York:
   Oxford University Press, 1987), focussing on women readers rather than writers, argues
   that conduct books helped shape modern subjectivity.

bonds.[12] Women of the middling rank sought ways to support themselves if they were single or to supplement their income if they were married. Besides being house servants or governesses, others became small tradeswomen and artisans vending linen, groceries, flowers or books. Many writing women were also actresses, playwrights or intimately connected with actors or theatre managers. Especially in the second half of the century women writers advanced into the public sphere in exchange for seeming to be a proper lady.[13] Women at once exemplified moral superiority and embodied economic value even as the split between domestic and commercial activity intensified. Encouraged to be shoppers and spenders while being reviled for their attraction to luxury, women of a certain class were also ciphers for money, tokens of economic exchange and fashion dolls who modelled the jewels and feathers of an increasingly visible empire. Especially after the 1740s, women writers wished to distance themselves from a degraded femininity which reflected the societal corruption endemic to an expanding market economy, while at the same time many benefited precisely from that commercial growth.[14]

For women without sufficient means, the prohibitive cost of a novel, usually a shilling or a bit more, could be circumvented through the newly improvised system for borrowing books. Circulating libraries, expanding after 1740 to more than a hundred in London and to several hundred in the provinces, broadly extended the audience for novels, many of whom were women:[15] 'Now a novel to sell shou'd please women because women are the chief readers of novels & perhaps the best judges', advised Frances Brooke.[16] The increased access to books encouraged imagined communities of readers to develop a shared body of values and knowledge, and to cohere into a middling class. In the area of education, women's literacy rate was most often a function

---

12 Ruth Perry, 'Women in Families: The Great Disinheritance', in Vivien Jones (ed.), *Women and Literature in Britain 1700–1800* (Cambridge: Cambridge University Press, 2000), pp. 111–31.

13 See Jürgen Habermas, *The Structural Transformation of the Public Sphere: an Inquiry into a Category of Bourgeois Society*, trans. Thomas Burger (Cambridge MA: M. I. T. Press, 1989); and Mary Poovey, *The Proper Lady and the Woman Writer: Ideology as Style in the Works of Mary Wollstonecraft, Mary Shelley, and Jane Austen* (Chicago: University of Chicago Press, 1984).

14 Kathryn Sutherland, 'Writings on Education and Conduct: Arguments for Female Improvement', and Harriet Guest, 'Eighteenth-Century Femininity: "A Supposed Sexual Character"' in Jones (ed.), *Women and Literature*, pp. 25–45 and pp. 46–68.

15 Cheryl Turner, *Living by the Pen: Women Writers in the Eighteenth Century* (London: Routledge, 1994), p. 133.

16 BL. ADD. 29, 747, f.68, ALS, Frances Brooke to James Dodsley 29 August [1770], cited in Frances Brooke, *The History of Emily Montague*, ed. Mary Jane Edwards (Ontario: Carleton University Press, 1985), p. xlvii. Subsequent references will be to this text.

of the economic status of their parents. Their tutoring by fathers or brothers sometimes spurred young eighteenth-century women to literary aspirations, and Elizabeth Carter's self-inflicted torture (awakening herself with an alarm of cold water) to discipline herself to learn the classical languages is legendary. There were also increased opportunities for formal learning because of the growth of ladies' academies. The fact that many women became governesses or teachers may have spurred to write instructional treatises to share with their charges. The burgeoning appetite for moral writing sparked by works such as Richardson's *Clarissa* and Johnson's *Rambler* nourished women's opportunities to publish, and new venues for publication included periodicals and reviews.

Though aristocratic patronage of fledgling writers gave way during this period to subscription or to selling a manuscript directly to a bookseller, authors such as Samuel Johnson, Samuel Richardson, Henry Fielding and Jonathan Swift encouraged women writers. Providing a dedication for Charlotte Lennox's *The Female Quixote* (1752), Johnson marked the publication of *Harriot Stuart* (1751) with a celebratory dinner when he reputedly crowned the author with a laurel wreath. Richardson printed Lennox's books, as well as those by Fielding, Haywood and Rowe. Henry Fielding's preface to the second edition of his sister Sarah's *The Adventures of David Simple* (1744) praised its 'beauties'. He also published her historical fiction, *Lives of Cleopatra and Octavia* (1757). Women too provided mutual sustenance for each other. A loosely affiliated group of intellectual women termed 'Bluestockings' (including Elizabeth Montagu, Elizabeth Vesey, Elizabeth Carter, Hester Chapone, Clara Reeve, Anna Seward, Catherine Talbot and others) eschewed card playing for intellectual exchange and formed informal communities to assist impoverished fellow writers.

Women wrote to survive or to supplement an independent income, though many expressed longings for fame in spite of turning necessity into a virtue. These women sometimes made the economic aspects of writing an alibi through diffident protests that justified their entering the public sphere. Sarah Scott seemed to encourage women to attend to aesthetic values in the midst of need: 'Now that the generality of Authors write for bread, or for butter to their bread . . . I think some who are not hurried by necessity should write for the hour of the age.'[17] Of the novelists in these decades, the unmarried Sarah Fielding wrote to supplement a small independent income, as did Eliza

17 Sarah Scott to E. Montagu, 2 August 1761, Montagu collection, Henry E. Huntington Library, San Marino, CA. Published by permission of the Huntington Library.

Haywood and Sarah Scott after the break-up of their respective marriages. Addressing the reader, Sarah Fielding modestly demurs: 'Perhaps the best Excuse that can be made for a Woman's venturing to write at all, is that which really produced this Book; Distress in her Circumstances: which she could not so well remove by another means in her power.'[18] Elizabeth Griffith, like the newly married Frances Burney D'Arblay, attempted to support herself and her husband through publishing an unusual two-volume set of which each had authored one novel, *The Delicate Distress* and *The Gordian Knot* (1769). Successful authors such as Elizabeth Inchbald and Charlotte Smith could only infrequently survive on the income from their books. Frances Burney was paid a mere twenty pounds sterling for *Evelina* (though her later fame brought an increase to 250 pounds sterling for *Cecilia*), and Charlotte Lennox struggled to support herself in the later years of her life. Though writing gained increasing respectability for women toward the end of the century, it seems unlikely that publishing even one novel per year could produce a living wage.[19]

Given the need to sell books, one might suspect that women novelists gained respect and achieved literary authority after mid century only through compromise and self-abnegation.[20] Certainly there were elements of silent self-censorship among writing women. Yet three novels written during the middle decades may be interpreted as women writers' subtle negotiation between assertion and restraint in the literary marketplace, between refusing to be restricted by cultural assumptions about women's nature and displaying the moral authority which derives from finely tuned sensibilities. This cluster includes Sarah Fielding's *David Simple* (1744), Eliza Haywood's *Betsy Thoughtless* (1751) and Charlotte Lennox's *The Female Quixote* (1752). *David Simple* is the first significant novel published after Samuel Richardson's very successful *Pamela* (1741), and readers felt his influence in it. An epistolary novel of a servant girl's resistance to her employer Mr B and their eventual marriage, *Pamela* opened a market for sentimental writing. Richardson, like Defoe before him, reproduced in 'writing to the moment' an intimate psychological portrait of a feminine subjectivity in its encounter with a steady, brutal challenge to virtue. Although we might interpret the novel as 'a struggle in which

---

18 'Advertisement to the Reader', Sarah Fielding, *The Adventures of David Simple*, ed. Linda Bree (London: Penguin Books, 2002), p. 2. All subsequent references to this edition are cited in the text.
19 Turner, *Living by the Pen*, pp. 102–26.
20 Jane Spencer, 'Women Writers and the Eighteenth-Century Novel', in John Richetti (ed.), *The Cambridge Companion to the Eighteenth-Century Novel* (Cambridge: Cambridge University Press, 1996), pp. 212–35.

[a woman's fiction] captures and translates the other into its terms',[21] unlike women's novels Pamela's version of events is always a male author's imagined impersonation of the sex.

All three mid century novelists use satire to counter claims that undesirable characteristics naturally adhere to women. Exploring domesticity, sentimentality and romance while railing against them, these novels at once reveal the evils that men perpetrate on women and satirise those who wilt under pressure. The psychomachic debates in the novels and the conduct books exemplify the contest for the soul and pen of the woman writer. The heroines of these novels learn to deal as diplomatically with flighty women as with rakish men in order to be worthy of the Trueworths and Glanvilles who reward them them with love, and incidentally with a coach and six. Replete with fraught friendships between morally suspect women and sanctimonious prigs, the novels suggest that virtuous beings are misled and misunderstood by an unbending society ruled by patriarchal structures which oppress 'the weaker sex'. Satire is one of the strategies which mediates this treacherous territory. Even reformation and its attendant rewards, while apparently heartfelt, may be risible events, and a strongly sexual and violent undercurrent often complicates the apparent efficacy of moral lessons.

The first two volumes of *David Simple* appeared in 1744 and a sequel, the tragic *Volume the Last*, was published nearly a decade later in 1753. In the preface written to puff the work, Henry Fielding remarks on his sister Sarah's want of learning while pointing out her skill in depicting the interior workings of the mind:

> For as the Merit of this Work consists in a vast Penetration into human Nature, a deep and profound Discernment of all the Mazes, Windings and Labyrinths, which perplex the Heart of Man to such a degree, that he is himself often incapable of seeing through them; and as this is the greatest, noblest, and rarest of all the Talents which constitute a Genius; so a much larger Share of this Talent is necessary, even to recognize these Discoveries, when they are laid before us, than falls to the share of a common Reader.   (p. 462)

Though the novel is not overtly feminist, it exposes the inadequacy of marital and familial structures to sustain social relations, and it celebrates the pleasures of forming a community of friends who pool their resources. David, his beloved Camilla, the wit Cynthia and her brother Valentine unite in friendship. David and Camilla's marriage evolves into an ideal companionate marriage, but the non-sexual friendship between the outspoken heroine Cynthia, whose

21 Armstrong, *Desire and Domestic Fiction*, 119.

wit leads to her disinheritance, and the gentle hero who possesses feminine virtues, is at the novel's core. In his search for a true friend David exhibits a maudlin sentimentality. Ruled by his passions, he 'had more of what *Shakespear* calls the *Milk of Human Kind* . . . for his Sensations were too strong, to leave him the free Use of his Reason' (p. 117). David is at once a model of sentiment and a parody of it. Cynthia, the bluestocking of the fiction, acts as the moral arbiter and guide for the small circle of friends and assumes the novel's satiric voice; yet unlike Burney's Mrs Selwyn in *Evelina* or Maria Edgeworth's Harriet Freke in *Belinda*, she escapes mockery in spite of her strong opinions. If David's untempered sentimentality is excessive and impractical, Cynthia's cleverness is unconventional. Satire, the very form that had been employed so powerfully against women writers in the Restoration and early eighteenth century, is by their pens turned to new purpose at mid century.

Like David Simple, Arabella, Lennox's imaginative heroine in *The Female Quixote* (who of course resembles Cervantes' Don Quixote), encounters an unfeeling and unsentimental world which challenges and ultimately defeats her romantic vision. Romance, according to some accounts, is repudiated by the 1750s,[22] though others would place the shift towards the novel and its heightened sense of realism much earlier in the century. Charlotte Lennox and Eliza Haywood both delight in creating rogue characters who espouse untenable parallels between romance fictions and reality. Lennox published half a dozen novels (most notably *The Life of Harriot Stuart*, 1750, and *Henrietta* 1758), as well as translations of historical memoirs from the French. Lennox's heroine, Arabella, had fully absorbed the French romances bequeathed to her after her mother's untimely death: 'Heroism, romantick Heroism, was deeply rooted in her Heart; it was her Habit of thinking, a Principle imbib'd from Education. She could not separate her Ideas of Glory, Virtue, Courage, Gen-erosity, and Honour, from the false Representations of them in the actions of *Oroondates, Juba, Artaxerxes*, and the rest of the Imaginary Heroes' (*The Female Quixote*, p. 329). Arabella defends their 'rules of Heroick Virtue', the very rules which she steadfastly refuses to accept as applicable to men rather than women. At last the Countess tries to persuade her to an historicist view of vice and virtue: 'Custom . . . changes the very Nature of Things, and what was honourable a thousand Years ago, may probably be look'd upon as infamous now' (p. 328). But it is her physician and moral guide, the Doctor, who cures Arabella of the romantic fever which threatens her life and her

---

22 Margaret Doody, 'Introduction', Charlotte Lennox, *The Female Quixote; or, The Adventures of Arabella*, ed. Margaret Dalziel (Oxford: Oxford University Press, 1989), p. xvii. All subsequent references to this edition are cited in the text.

future happiness with an encomium on the violence it inspires. He judges romances to be 'contemptible Volumes, with which Children are sometimes injudiciously suffer'd to amuse their Imaginations' (p. 374); absurd and criminal, they are 'empty Fictions . . . told with the solemn Air of historical Truth.' (p. 377). Romances, the avuncular counsellor enjoins, are French fictions written about events which transpired two thousand years earlier, and they are quite irrelevant to eighteenth-century England.

'A wild, extravagant, fabulous Story' according to Clara Reeve's critical work, *The Progress of Romance*, the romance allegedly provoked 'that respectful complaisance of the fair sex' to imagine resistance and capture.[23] Reeve does not suggest what Lennox implies: that romance, while confusing fact with fiction, is also a narrative of female power.[24] Arabella reveals another element in romance's appeal: 'Ladies of the highest Rank and sublimest Virtue, were often expos'd to a Variety of cruel Adventures which they imparted in Confidence to each other, when Chance brought them together' (p. 327). Romance then draws women together to confront the threat of ravishment, oppression or brute force. According to the Countess, both modernity and Christianity require that women abandon their addiction to an outdated form of romantic heroism. And yet, significantly, the Countess shows that women of intelligence and wit can read these romances without succumbing to 'false Representations'. Though the Doctor brings resolution to the book, the Countess like Cynthia might be imagined as the grave but forceful voice of the feminine.

In short, these three satiric novels navigate between the Scylla of foisting contempt on the sex, and the Charbydis of idealising them by provoking double-edged laughter. Their parodic thrust ridicules those who would denigrate women and confine them to particular ways of life on behalf of a supposed moral superiority. To describe these mid century novels as 'didactic fiction' or 'courtship novels' is incomplete at best. The central irony of *The Female Quixote* comes when Arabella recognises the hazard that a confused reality poses to her life, and her story abruptly ends. In fact, marriage often results from women's willingly duping themselves into romantic beliefs. According to these novels, marriage to the right man is deeply desirable in spite of the legal and economic realities which interrupt their *petites histoires* (a term to describe women's lives that another Arabella employs

---

23 Clara Reeve, *The Progress of Romance* in Gary Kelly (ed.), *Bluestocking Feminism: Writings of the Bluestocking Circle, 1738–1785*, vol. VI (London: Pickering and Chatto, 1999).
24 Jane Spencer, *The Rise of the Woman Novelist: From Aphra Behn to Jane Austen* (Oxford: Basil Blackwell, 1986), p. 184.

in Brooke's *History of Emily Montague*) on their wedding day.[25] As Arabella painfully discovers, to live within the bounds of realism means to relinquish her imagined authority. She abandons the passionately romantic views which would have been more appropriate to the scandalous fictions of the 1720s, and marriage brings a sentimentally satisfying, but profoundly oppressive, end.

By mid century the figure of the woman writer as the sentimental virtuous victim begins to supplant the image of woman writer as seduced maiden, lascivious aggressor or prostitute. Eliza Haywood, the most prolific of eighteenth-century women writers, plays a pivotal role in the critical narratives woven in the history of women's writing during this period. Seeming to develop a reformed attitude after her amatory fiction, Haywood offered more didactic novels in *Fortunate Foundlings* (1744), *Betsy Thoughtless* (1751) and *History of Jemmy and Jenny Jessamy* (1753).[26] Just why the notorious Haywood turned the tide towards moral fiction in the 1740s remains an object of conjecture. Perhaps she was mortally wounded by Alexander Pope's caricature of her in *The Dunciad* as the grotesque booby prize 'with cow-like udders, and with ox-like eyes', for whom two publishers vied in a pissing contest during the goddess Dulness' 'Olympic' games. Perhaps she cunningly responded to market changes, or her conscience pricked her, or maybe she simply found the seduction and betrayal plots had been exhausted. Curiously, her name (which had been proudly touted in her earlier amatory fiction) is dropped from the title pages of the later novels in favour of pseudonymity and anonymity.[27]

Like Lennox's Female Quixote, Haywood's central character in *Betsy Thoughtless* embodies a parody of the novel's conventions to suggest that romance is at once a woman's pornography and her life sustenance.[28] Betsy typifies the frivolity and silliness – the 'feminalities' as 'Queen of the Bluestockings' Elizabeth Montagu had called women's weaknesses – that substituted for women's education and reason. Orphaned at a young age like many eighteenth-century heroines, Betsy is much besieged by suitors Mr Saving and

25 Brooke, *The History of Emily Montague*, p. 126.
26 John Richetti, 'Histories by Eliza Haywood and Henry Fielding: Imitation and Adaptation', in Saxton and Bocchicchio (eds.), *The Passionate Fictions of Eliza Haywood*, p. 243.
27 Joyce M. Horner, *The English Women Novelists and their Connection with the Feminist Movement (1688–1797)*, (Northampton, MA: Smith College Studies in Modern Language 11, 1929–30), p. 21.
28 Eliza Haywood, *The History of Miss Betsy Thoughtless*, ed. Beth Fowkes Tobin (Oxford: Oxford University Press, 1997). All subsequent references will be to this text. On parody in Lennox, see Catherine Gallagher, *Nobody's Story: the Vanishing Acts of Women Writers in the Marketplace, 1670–1820* (Berkeley and Los Angeles: University of California Press, 1994).

Mr Gayland, and she also comes under the influence of the unscrupulous Lady Mellasin. Betsy's half-sister Mellasin (whose household allowance was misused to pay off a bribe), defies 'all the rules of virtue, modesty, and even common decency, for the gratification of her wild desires' (p. 321) and, like her misguided school friend Miss Forward, who actually bears an illegitimate child, is meant to be a negative example. Embodying within her the conflicts usually represented in two opposing character types, Betsy is both a giddy flirt and a reasonable woman: 'Thus did the dictates of a truly reasonable woman, and the idle humour of a vain coquette, prevail by turns over her fluctuating mind' (p. 237). In fact, Mr Goodman smilingly tells Betsy Thoughtless that the diplomatic skills required for her intrigues would serve her well as a minister of state (p. 110). She amusedly assesses the cost of lovers, exposing the extent to which an affair is a business deal, and sets them to competing for her hand while keeping her own sexual desire secret (p. 120). Betsy thus exemplifies within herself the irreconcilable conflicts confronting mid century eighteenth-century women.

Betsy's forestalling Mr Trueworth, the heroine's ideal lover, is the only hope to establish any control over her life, but readers of the novel also begin to understand that marriage would enslave Betsy and leave her without a story to tell. She 'resolved not to enter into a condition, which demanded some share of [settled behaviour], at least for a long time; that is, when she should be grown weary of the admiration, flatteries, and addresses of the men, and no longer found any pleasure in seeing herself preferred before all the women of her acquaintance' (p. 71). The novel, the narrator asserts, is written to dissuade its readers from a similar vanity which would encourage casually collecting marriage proposals before making a measured choice.

While the novelists' sympathies cannot always be accurately gauged from their fictions, the strong-minded Miss Mabel in *Betsy Thoughtless* vindicates the heroine and, like the Countess in *Female Quixote*, appears to be at the moral centre. Unlike Arabella, who worries very little about reputation, Betsy Thoughtless sometimes finds herself paralysed by the fear of scandal and public display. The loss of reputation brought serious economic repercussions even to women of the middling ranks. For example, Betsy compromises her name when she visits unattended the unprincipled Frederick Feneer. Left with little choice after this fatal error, Betsy settles for the mundane Mr Munden in the unhappiest of marriages. She gradually relinquishes financial independence in their disputes over pin money, her allowance for household expenses. Lady Trusty advises Betsy to focus on domestic concerns, among them 'the prices of beef and mutton' in the market, to economise sufficiently to compensate for Munden's extravagances by foregoing luxury items like chocolate and tea, to honour his authority and to submit to him sexually as a wifely duty. This advice is mediated by the reader's knowledge that her husband is a cad. Betsy laments that her necessary dependence limits her value to the economic: 'Is not all I am the property of Mr Munden[?]' (p. 495).

In short, these mid century novels oscillate between satiric fury at the restrictions placed on women and acquiescence to a double standard which propels the heroines through courtship and marriage. The progress of women writers in the eighteenth-century century from the licentious cohort of Behn, Manley and the early Haywood to the later more didactic novelists is an intricate path with many byways. Though Clara Reeve believed that Haywood had reformed her writing at mid century, *Betsy Thoughtless* teems with sexual intrigue and is sometimes reminiscent of racy Restoration comedy. Betsy is in possession of 'secrets', as if to assert (while winking at a reader who would search them out) that the topics of Haywood's earlier novels of seduction and betrayal lie just below the surface of her later novel. Flora, the traitorous daughter of Mr Goodman, malevolently broadcasts the lie that Betsy has borne a natural child. But among Betsy's secrets, including everything from barely disguised sexual desire to suppressed glee when Mrs Trueworth dies, is the socially unacceptable fact that she decidedly prefers the single to the married state: 'I have at present rather an aversion, than an inclination to a weded [*sic*] state' (p. 178). Her unwillingness to make an exception for Trueworth until her coquettish days are exhausted indicates her inability properly to assess *value*. Even as a reformed heroine she is, albeit unintentionally, seductive. In a scene distinctly suggestive of Haywood's earlier amatory fiction, Trueworth observes Betsy from a distance: 'He had a full view of every thing she did: – though she was in the most negligent night-dress that could be, she seemed as lovely to him as ever' (p. 543) as she in turn gazes upon the miniature likeness of him that she has earlier stolen. Unrestrained, he 'thrust himself as far as he was able between the branches of which the arbour was composed' (p. 543), confesses his love to her and throws his arms about her. The moment that 'had betrayed the secret of her heart to him, had also discovered it to herself' (p. 547). Betsy resists Trueworth until her husband actually expires, but the titillating scene differs only from Haywood's earlier fiction in the reformed heroine's resolution to remain true to her despised husband. (When she decides that marriage should be for love, not money or ambition, she is rewarded with a coach and livery.) In short, rather than thinking of Haywood, Fielding and Lennox as taking a radical turn into moralistic writing, we can see that these novels at mid century instead merely shift the focus from seduction to courtship, and from betrayal to indelicacy. The opposing elements remain a persistent, if subdued, presence in the novels. Eventually Betsy wins a second chance to marry Mr Trueworth after the deaths of their respective spouses, and she recognises how very dangerous had been her unwillingness to give up her independent state. When Trueworth believes that Betsy had given birth to an illegitimate child, he is the forerunner of many heroes in courtship novels, including Brooke's *The Excursion*, Burney's *Evelina* and *Camilla*, and Austen's *Mansfield Park*, in which the principal action is to rectify misapprehensions about the unthinking heroine's reputation in order to reinstate her as worthy of a proper marriage to the hero.

To a greater degree than *Betsy Thoughtless*, Haywood's *The History of Jemmy and Jenny Jessamy* (1753) furnishes a standard conduct book format in its cautionary tales against early marriage, excessive passion, gambling and infidelity; but in the process the novel entertains the reader with sexy and potentially murderous tales. As in *David Simple*, the novel depicts a perfect friendship between two innocents, the 'son of a gentleman of competent estate' and the 'sole daughter and heiress of a wealthy merchant'. Conventional plot contrivances – a forged letter, a false rumour and old flame – also pose threats to the potential marriage of hero and heroine as they roam the world to educate themselves. Jenny, a feisty but sensible heroine with a sermonising tendency, worries about Jemmy's fickleness since 'men, conscious of that superiority which custom and the matrimonial covenant has given them, never fail to exert it, and opposition on our side is struggling against the stream, and but serves to shew our weakness the more in the vain attempt'.[29] The private domestic sphere is writ large as Jenny seeks knowledge of men's inconstancy only to be reined in when she marries.

Yet Haywood represents the temptation to stray as equally powerful in women. In the protracted courtship, Jemmy learns that Jenny's unflagging virtue reassuringly contrasts to Liberia the gambler, Sophia the flirt and Celia the gold-digger, his former flame who offers real temptation. Celia details the pleasures of her exquisite clothing:

> rolls of various colour'd silks, – a great deal of lace and dresden work, with some pieces of holland of an extraordinary fineness; – and in the portmanteau was also a small ivory casket, containing a gold repeating watch and equipage, – a set of diamond buckles for my stays – a large pearl necklace with a solitaire, and several other trinkets of a considerable value. (vol. II, p. 253)

29 Eliza Haywood, *The History of Jemmy and Jenny Jessamy*, London 1753 (rpt New York: Garland Publishing Inc., 1974), 3 vols. vol. I, pp. 1, 77. All subsequent references will be to this text.

Like many other novels of this period, it warns that being dazzled by superficial display is indicative of moral decay, and Jenny rejoins, 'it is the mind which ought to be the chief object of our attention; it is there alone we are either beautiful or deform'd; and the pains we take to ornament and embellish that nobler part of us will not be thrown away' (vol. II, p. 18). Women novelists could not simply imitate male patterns of authorship and narration because of their decidedly different positions within economic and social structures. Women figured as avid consumers, as objects of circulation and exchange, who eschewed the middle-class values of thrift and moderation in the new economy but whose extravagant buying habits were, of course, crucial to its success. They attempt either to emulate manly virtues (thus laying themselves open to charges of being Amazons or harridans) or to value traditional femininity (thus seeming to underscore their perceived weakness). Satire and parody are cunning responses to this dilemma. As constructors of narrative, eighteenth-century women novelists experimented with ways to master the craft and their own subjectivities through the invention of new plots, the manipulation of genres and the inclusion of innovative subject matter.

Courtship plots in the novels of the mid and late eighteenth century often serve as an extraordinarily resilient and versatile backdrop, and sometimes as a diversion that allows authors to explore unconventional topics. Some of the novels in fact describe excruciatingly unhappy marriages, separation or divorce while drawing parallels between marriage and slavery or prostitution. Charlotte Smith's *Emmeline* (1788) dares to break an engagement with Frederic Delamere, and Sarah Scott's *Millenium Hall* (1762) – drawing upon a tradition of tracts which sought to improve women's education (especially Mary Astell's *A Serious Proposal to the Ladies* (1694–7) – imagines a utopian female community as an alternative to wedlock. Scott, the sister of Elizabeth Montagu, is among those who penned novels of sentiment saturated with extreme feeling as especially characteristic of women and worthy of emulation in the most of desirable men. The fictions constructed a private yet rigorously active code of conduct while shaping a new public realm in which critical reasoned opinion was formulated. Thus women were perhaps for the first time able to imagine female communities which could be sustained through moral exemplarity.

Constructed of sequential narratives that recount six women's loss of inheritance, seduction and betrayal, parental coercion and their own misguided actions, *Millenium Hall* offers a pattern of righteous living and moral reform within a convent-like Protestant community. Together these histories of female distress demonstrate a need for refuge and the wish to oppose tyranny in its many forms. These women occupy themselves with fostering a benevolent haven for the less fortunate, educating and caring for them, setting up linen and rug manufacturing and teaching the pious self-discipline characteristic of conduct book literature. Their behaviour makes a convert of the libertine Lamont, a male observer of the community who is slow to respect the capacities of women who govern themselves. Pooling their common property and economic resources, the ladies transform the refuge into an intellectual, social and spiritual society modelled on a combination of republican Rome and a Christian millennial vision.

More sentimental than satiric, Scott's later writing broadens its topics. Among her histories, translations and novels is *The History of Sir George Ellison* (1766), later revised and condensed as *The Man of Sensibility* (1774). Sir George Ellison, a sensitive hero in the tradition of Richardson's Sir Charles Grandison and Sarah Fielding's David Simple, develops a reputation for providing the most equitable treatment of 'a numerous race of slaves' (p. 10) he gains when he marries a wealthy widow in Jamaica. Upon returning to England, under the tutelage of Mrs Maynard (also a character in *Millenium Hall*), he imitates the ladies' model of economy with charitable projects for prisoners, the poor and the disabled. Scott and her lifelong companion, Barbara Montagu (Lady 'Bab') engaged in similar endeavours to assuage the conditions of the needy. Though the novel has been interpreted as abolitionist, its promotion of kind treatment to the slaves and teaching them literacy is more accurately described as ameliorist since Ellison's reforms rely upon the spoils of slavery for funding. Ellison's commercial ventures are justified by his emulation of the feminine traits of sensibility and moral reflection even as he awards his son 'a proper sum of ready money to purchase new slaves' (p. 138). Ellison evidences a gentle manliness in the New World while still protecting his vested interests, and he returns to England to solidify his integration of feminine virtue into the new economic man. In short, both men and women can exemplify a morality appropriate to the nation's interests.

Among other significant authors of novels of sentiment and virtue is Frances Sheridan (1724–66), born in Dublin though she lived in London for two periods after 1754. Educated by her brothers (just as the character Sir George tutors Sidney Bidulph), she married actor and theatre manager Thomas Sheridan. To alleviate his debt after the failure of Smock Alley theatre, she wrote plays as well as the novels *Memoirs of Miss Sidney Bidulph* (1761), *Conclusion of the Memoirs of Miss Sidney Bidulph* (2 vols. 1767) and a popular oriental novel, *The History of Nourjahad* (1767). Sheridan was among the many women writers of this time who were offered patronage (but without financial support) by Samuel Johnson, David Garrick, Richardson and other literati.

Sidney Bidulph is exemplary of the didactic novel, for even as it promulgates notions of passivity and reserve, it recounts the frustrations and complexities of female fragility. The innocent and virtuous Sidney falls deeply in love with the dashingly handsome and romantic Orlando Faulkland, who had fathered an illegitimate child with the passionate and adulterous Miss Burchell, a disreputably public woman, in spite of his apparent innate goodness. Discouraged by her mother from marrying such a man, she hastily weds Mr Arnold, whose drinking and public pleasures lead her to wish for a 'calm domestic life' (p. 108), and she determines gently to check his excesses and infidelity with the help of Miss Burchell's aunt, Mrs Gerrarde. Instead, Arnold accuses her of duplicity and turns her away with a separate maintenance and without her children. The very rules of social constraint lead to further misery and embarrassment.[30]

Throughout the intricate plot, virtue is rewarded principally with suffering rather than justice, a narrative effect that Sheridan's reviewers judged to be excessively cruel to the heroine. The journal method allows Sidney to reveal her desperate unhappiness exacerbated by serious financial difficulties: 'My days are spent in a painful constraint, to conceal the anguish of my own heart, that I may not aggravate that of my poor mother' (p. 157). In spite of her unfailing virtue, in the passionate ill-fated romance of Sidney and Faulkland each marries another who is unfaithful. When Sidney is eventually widowed, she painfully turns her finely calibrated sense of moral responsibility against her own desires and dutifully urges Faulkland finally to marry Miss Burchell, the woman with whom he shares a child. In this extremely sentimental novel, Sidney, suffering deeply but properly, denies herself the consummation of romance to oppose the idea that virtue is rewarded in this life. Recalling Pamela's palpitating desire for Mr B in Richardson's novel, the passion of the book is undeniable in spite of Sidney's nearly cheerful misery, and the sexual energy of the couple threatens to contradict or even to cancel the moral impulse of this novel in which pathos substitutes for romance.

The courtship novel reaches its pinnacle in Frances Burney's anonymously published epistolary novel, *Evelina or the History of a Young Lady's Entrance into the World* (1778). The book lightens its sentiment with raucous satire, unlike the novels of Scott and Sheridan, or its epistolary models, Richardson's *Pamela*

---

30 Jean Coates Cleary, 'Introduction', Frances Sheridan, *Memoirs of Miss Sidney Bidulph*, eds. Patricia Köster and Jean Coates Cleary (Oxford: Oxford University Press, 1995). All further references in the text are to this edition.

and *Clarissa*. Following in the path of her female predecessors, Burney creates exemplary women without the dignity and resilience of Austen's Elizabeth or Emma, 'at once ideal and unheroic'.[31] The naive Evelina is among the loveable and fallible heroines ultimately worthy of emulation. Raised by the Reverend Mr Villars, the innocent young Evelina debuts in London, Bristol Hotwells and Clifton in a sometimes painful, sometimes exhilarating, education in manners. Evelina finds herself 'terribly dirtied' both by a sudden rain shower and by the libertines who address her familiarly after her reputation is unjustly sullied in being taken for a prostitute.[32] Her series of social faux pas provide an opportunity for her well-meaning if unsophisticated adoptive father to guide her through moral education. Villars encourages her 'not only to *judge* but to *act*' for herself, but he accompanies the advice with a chilling caution about the precariousness of other's perceptions of her: 'Nothing is so delicate as the reputation of a woman: it is, at once, the most beautiful and most brittle of all human things' (p. 164). It is precisely this twin message of action and restraint which limits Evelina's exploration of her interiority. As she becomes increasingly sophisticated through attending plays, operas and ridottos in dance halls and public rooms, she also acclimates to her function as a public – though not too public – fashionable spectacle.

Like the heroes in the novels of Smollett and Fielding, Evelina seeks her familial identity in order to escape being 'a certain Miss Nobody,' as Burney calls herself in her own early diary. Discovering a lost father and a half-brother (a melancholy Scotch poet whom she prevents from suicide in a bold move justified by its charity), the story unfolds to reveal switched babies and mistaken motives. When a forged letter calls her judgement of suitor Lord Orville into question, Evelina's plight is revealed to be no fault of her own. The world of women is beset with such trickery, the reader is led to believe. Yet a woman's self-knowledge is exempt from the self-scrutiny which might produce too fixed a subjectivity, or too intimate a knowledge of her hidden desires. The advice that the Reverend Mr Tyrold offers his daughter in Burney's later novel *Camilla*, 'Struggle then against yourself as you would struggle against an enemy', is relevant here as well as in many courtship novels of this period. This new-found awareness, which the heroine does not dare to understand until her lover proclaims it, is central to the novels of Haywood, Lennox, Burney, Radcliffe, Edgeworth and Austen.

31 Horner, *The English Women Novelists*, p. 134.
32 Frances Burney, *Evelina, or the History of a Young Lady's Entrance into the World*, eds. Edward A. Bloom and Lillian Bloom (Oxford: Oxford University Press, 1982), p. 327. All subsequent references are to this text.

Though the comic plot in *Evelina* of vulgar cousins, broken coaches, attempted robberies, and near abduction by a libertine, is happily resolved, a strong and surprising violence perpetrated against women undergirds this novel of manners. Upon her introduction into the world, Evelina notices that many women endure abuse. The rough-and-tumble, grossly nationalist Captain Mirvan engages in brutish cruelty to her enraged French grandmother, Madame Duval, a termagant who embodies the worst of foreign influences. The men's antagonism toward bluestocking Mrs Selwyn, the crude Madame Duval and the octogenarian women forced to race to settle a bet also warns Evelina of the dangerous consequences resulting from social missteps. The outspoken 'masculine' Mrs Selwyn effects Evelina's reunion with her lost father, but the Amazon's wit and intelligence are in turn held up to ridicule. 'The best of men' (p. 406), Lord Orville, on the other hand, is valued for 'so *feminine* [a] delicacy' (p. 261), for gendered characteristics migrate (as they did in *Sir George Ellison*) from one sex to the other.[33] Evelina's virtue is rewarded when she is finally restored to fortune and rank, a condition which enables but also requires marriage in the terms of the novel. Recovering her identity allows her to lose it in marriage. The situation reverses itself in *Cecilia* when the heroine forfeits her fortune to marry her beloved. In short, Frances Burney, resembling her sister novelists Sarah Fielding, Haywood, Lennox, Scott and Sheridan, speaks in the language of traditional femininity while calling attention to its restrictions, absurdities and impossibilities.

The historical rise of domesticity at mid century coincides with England's loss of the American colonies, and the beginnings of a second empire in the Indian subcontinent and the Pacific, to produce an imaginative literature of the romantic past and the exotic present, sometimes intermingled together in the Gothic or the Oriental novel. These fictions link two distinct meanings of the domestic, one's personal abode and the home territory of the nation. The domain of the nation represents the familiar ground upon which empire is built, and both kinds of domesticity share an interest in the moral ascendancy of virtues defined as peculiarly feminine. Generating narratives of the foreign against which the nation can be represented as home *and* homeland helps to protect the domestic space from the corrupting influence of the unknown and the strange.

The novels of the 1760s and 1770s engage in a ritual of national purification in order to identify true patriots. The fascination with medieval history, especially

---

33 See Claudia Johnson, *Equivocal Beings: Politics, Gender, and Sentimentality in the 1790s: Wollstonecraft, Radcliffe, Burney, Austen* (Chicago: University of Chicago Press, 1995).

when set in Roman Catholic Italy or France, was most fully exhibited in Gothic novels to unite the classical past with the Other. First popularised by Horace Walpole's *Castle of Otranto*, the Gothic novel reached its fruition in the 1790s in the novels of Anne Radcliffe, *The Romance of the Forest* (1791), *Mysteries of Udolpho* (1794) and *The Italian* (1797). The ancient castles or mansions of Gothic tales are supremely undomestic and inhospitable, and they are haunted by the past and the foreign. Former occupants are displaced from their inheritances or imprisoned in secret rooms. Convents, no longer available in Protestant England, provide troubling resolution for independent or sexually precocious women, while priests and confessionals are juxtaposed with the illicit thrill of incest or other irregular familial relations. Tyrannical fathers, anthropomorphic objects and spectral remnants of violence conjure up a sublime terror tacitly associated with the threat of revolution at home and abroad.

In spite of the relative absence of explicit references to empire in women's fiction, spatial metaphors for the 'softer empire' pervade women's novels, and the feminine precepts which the whole nation wishes to possess make them worthy of promulgating the values of civilisation on the world at large.[34] The female figures of Britannia, of virtuous Roman matrons or of the nine muses come to represent a collective national identity, yet any *particular* identity, distinct from the generalised moral paradigm that dictates female conduct, amounts to a departure from acceptable standards of femininity.[35] Sarah Fielding's *Lives of Cleopatra and Octavia* (1757), for example, offers a national morality tale through the idealisation of Octavia, the true Roman spirit who sacrificed private pleasure to public good. In this dialogue of the dead, the emphasis is on history and biography in contrast to the romance between the lovers. Cleopatra's story, twice the length of Octavia's, recounts the life of an ambitious and exotic queen who employs love as an elaborate ruse to realise her ruling ambition. As in Arabella's fascinated emulation of Cleopatra in *The Female Quixote*, the Oriental elements adhere to her as a licentious woman obsessed with power and luxury. Anthony's misogyny and duplicity afford an example of sentimentality gone wrong and of the 'dastard Spirit of Effeminacy' which has 'destroyed the national Spirit of Defence', according to John Brown's popular and much reprinted *Estimate of the Manners and Principles of the Times* (1757), which laments the blurring of sexual boundaries during the

---

34 See Felicity Nussbaum, *Torrid Zones: Maternity, Sexuality, and Empire in Eighteenth-Century English Narratives* (Baltimore, MD: Johns Hopkins University Press, 1995).
35 Harriet Guest, *Small Change: Women, Learning, Patriotism, 1750–1810* (Chicago: University of Chicago Press, 2000).

Seven Years' War. Women writers speak for the nation and purify its moral stance as they evoke a domesticity which has further reaches.

Charlotte Smith's innovative *Emmeline, the Orphan of the Castle* (1788) contains sinister Gothic elements, and it is the likely target of Jane Austen's satire in *Northanger Abbey*. Sophia Lee's *The Recess* (1783–5) is a historical fiction loosely bound to facts in which the twin daughters of Mary, Queen of Scots, and the Duke of Norfolk, suffer imprisonment and misery. But the earliest Gothic novel written by an eighteenth-century woman is Clara Reeve's *The Old English Baron*, published in 1778 and first issued as *The Champion of Virtue: A Gothic Story* a year earlier. Reeve alleged that she united in an original way the 'ancient Romance and modern Novel at the same time it assumes a character and manner of its own, that differs from both'.[36] Reeve combined the marvellous, the probable and the pathetic to heighten sentimental appeal. This short popular novel saw thirteen editions by the end of the nineteenth century. Translated into French and German, and adapted for the stage, it attempted to ameliorate Horace Walpole's more violent extremes in *The Castle of Otranto*.[37] Clara Reeve's conventional apology in the preface to the second edition affects to withdraw into gendered retreat: 'I have also been prevailed upon, though with extreme reluctance, to suffer my name to appear in the title-page; and I do now, with the utmost respect and diffidence, submit the whole to the candour of the Public' (p. 6). Yet the tale relies upon bold women such as Lady Emma, who eventually wins the hero in spite of her outspoken nature. Reeve laid claim to both male influence and female originality. Set in fifteenth-century England (rather than the more common Italian setting), the novel focusses on the peasant Edmund Twyford whom Sir Philip Harclay befriends after his father's mysterious disappearance. Harclay restores his inheritance through Christian virtue. This tale emphasises the Englishness of the chivalric code, of manly honour and of natural claims to status, and it urges the purging of hidden criminal elements from the nation. As the courtship novel repeatedly demonstrates, the strength of the English nation depends on careful regulation of the private and the domestic.

The West and East Indies, as well as America, figure in novels as places where husbands, lovers and more distant relatives can be lost, found, banished, make or lose fortunes. The foreign domains offer new-found wealth to English cousins, or serve as the geographical origin of questionable characters. Though the decade of the 1770s fosters national doubts with the loss of the American

---

36 Clara Reeve, *The Old English Baron: A Gothic Story*, ed. James Trainer (London: Oxford University Press, 1967), p. 30. All subsequent references are to this edition.

37 James Trainer, 'Introduction', *ibid.*, pp. vii–viii.

colonies, the Battle of Plassey between the Nawab of Bengal and the East India Company brought imperial victory to England on 23 June 1757. Sheridan's *History of Nourjahad* (1767) and Reeve's *History of Charoba, Queen of Aegypt* (1785), along with Phoebe Gibbes' *Hartly House, Calcutta* (1789) give some sense of the range of women's Oriental adaptations, first popularised in England after the translation of Antoine Galland's *Arabian Nights' Entertainment*. Tales of the empire, of Eastern or Oriental tales, for example, are sometimes described as exerting a force as addictive as gambling or drinking spirits. The moral force of didactic fiction serves as an antidote to draw a nation together against external enemies both real and imagined, and to sanction the nation as 'home'.

When the French and Indian (or the Seven Years') War finally draws to a conclusion in 1763, Britain's most successful military venture newly incorporates Canada, the West Indies, the Philippines and India, to give birth to a more enduring empire. With England's greatly expanding naval and military power, national identity increasingly intertwines with issues of femininity. Colonial territory, the source for many luxury items which enhance women's marketability, comes to symbolise a lax morality since it offers potentially greater social and sexual freedom for Englishwomen. In the Americas, for example, the heroine of Brooke's *The History of Emily Montague* writes, 'There is no place where women are of such importance: not one of the sex, who has the least share of attractions, is without a levee of beaux interceding for the honour of attending her on some party, of which every day produces three or four' (p. 147).

Emily Montagu provides a fictionalised account of the author's sojourn in Quebec where her husband, co-manager of the Haymarket opera house, was a Protestant military chaplain during the Seven Years' War. This first Canadian novel is an epistolary exchange directed against Roman Catholic missionaries and French colonialist policies. The characters (including Arabella Fermor, a fortune-seeking coquette who shares the name of the heroine in Pope's *Rape of the Lock*) discuss the outcome of the war which is ending England's military rule in Canada, though Arabella insists there is 'no politics worth attending to but those of the little commonwealth of woman' (p. 98), by which she means the empire of love. In the person of Arabella's brother, William Fermor, Brooke is able to voice political opinions on monarchy, distribution of property, the commercial aspects of colonialism and the future of Canada. The wildly beautiful Gothic landscape attracts the spirited and virtuous Emily Montague to wish to settle amongst the Huron Indians. In its cultural observations (comparing Indians to Tartars and the Chinese, remarking on skin colour and customs, admiring the Huron), the novel resembles natural histories in which Englishwomen become a measure of civilisation to whom the 'savage' women are negatively compared. The sexually free Indian women are reputed to become strident and manly after marriage and capable of feeding their children the blood of Englishmen; but their independence appeals to the Englishwomen, and Emily prefers to remain in Canada where Rivers can better afford to marry her since fortune is valued differently in the colonies. Though the novel provides new twists to the courtship novel, once the female characters return to England, they declare their contentment with the nation, their private sphere and their softer empire.

In sum, the period from 1740 to the 1780s, before the flood of more explicitly political writing following the French Revolution in the 1790s, develops and extends the tradition of women's writing which will spark the extraordinary fictions of Jane Austen and the Brontë sisters. Influenced by conduct manuals and theories of female education, eighteenth-century women write domestic novels of courtship, marriage and manners which promulgate a moral authority complicated by complex strategies that intercede in the conflicting messages of action and restraint, decorum and passion, and sense and sensibility. They employ the very tools of misogynist Tory satirists in their own defence and claim the sentimental as their own. They invent complicated characters who harbour secret desires and engage in intrigue. Even while they attempt to avoid a degenerate femininity, women writers invigorate familiar forms and invent new ones to find distinctive voices. Virtue and morality, rather than being uniformly conveyed, are complicated by women's descriptions of a domesticity remarkably enlivened by sexuality and suspense, and profoundly intermingled with the public sphere and with the 'foreign', so as to transform their fiction into something we can no longer easily or finally describe as 'didactic' or 'courtship' novels. It is, then, no longer embarrassing to be discovered reading them.

Burke and the uses of eloquence: political prose in the 1770s and 1780s

FRANS DE BRUYN

The accession of George III to the throne of Great Britain in 1760 inaugurated a tumultuous new era in the country's politics. A succession of political crises agitated the nation, from the Wilkite disturbances of the 1760s and the American War of Independence to the impeachment of Warren Hastings and the ideological challenge of the French Revolution. The Wilkite controversy was sparked by the government's attempts to prosecute and silence John Wilkes, a radical member of parliament who had dared, in his newspaper *The North Briton*, to criticise the king directly in print. The political campaign against Hastings was motivated by allegations that, as head of the East India Company, he had grossly abused his position of power, enriching himself and his underlings at the expense of the people of India.

These political struggles inspired a formidable literature of political controversy. In the press, such eminent writers as Samuel Johnson, the pseudonymous Junius, Thomas Paine, Mary Wollstonecraft and William Godwin (among many others) placed their literary talents in the service of political polemic. In parliament the issues of the day elicited from members of both Houses speeches of such distinction that the latter part of the eighteenth century has come to be called the golden age of British parliamentary and forensic oratory. Opposition members, in particular, acquired a reputation for oratorical brilliance, most notably Edmund Burke, Charles James Fox and Richard Brinsley Sheridan. But in his mastery of contemporary political eloquence, Burke was widely conceded to be *primus inter pares*. No one else dominated quite like him all the available avenues and modes of political discourse, both in the press and in parliament.

This chapter will assess the grounds, the underlying premises, for the traditional consensus of literary history that confers upon Burke and his contemporaries the palm for oratorical distinction. A necessary preliminary to such an inquiry is an overview of the conditions and rationale for eloquence in the eighteenth century. Why was the study of rhetoric and public speaking deemed an essential part of a young gentleman's education in the period? How appropriate is it to speak of 'eloquence' in an age when ideas were communicated largely by means of the printed word? The latter question prompts reflections on several related issues: the connection between eloquence (or oratory) and literature, and the pertinence of a chapter on oratory in a volume devoted to *literary* history. These general considerations will furnish a context within which to appraise in more detail the literary and rhetorical means of political persuasion exploited by Burke and his contemporaries. What are the primary forms or genres of eloquence they employ; what elements of neighbouring literary genres and modes do they draw upon; and what are the characteristic idioms, discourses and modes of figuration they incorporate into their speeches? These are some of the key features to be inventoried in considering the rhetorical power of such classic political utterances as Burke's *Speech on Conciliation with the [American] Colonies* (1775) or his *Reflections on the Revolution in France* (1790).

The conditions of eighteenth-century eloquence

Eloquence in eighteenth-century Britain drew its inspiration from the classical era, especially democratic Athens in the age of Demosthenes and republican Rome in the time of Cicero. In *Tom Jones*, Henry Fielding affirms that William Pitt (the Elder) could never 'have produced those Orations that have made the Senate of England . . . a Rival in Eloquence to *Greece* and *Rome*, if he had not been so well read in the Writings of *Demosthenes* and *Cicero* as to have transfused their whole Spirit into his Speeches'.[1] From the ancients, eighteenth-century students of rhetoric had inherited the belief, amounting to a truism, that eloquence could flourish only in conditions of political freedom. Cicero gave lofty expression to this ideal in *De Oratore* [*The Making of an Orator*]. In this dialogue Cicero's spokesman, Crassus, extols the orator's capacity to govern the impulses of the crowd, the senate and the judiciary, and his power to oppose corruption, oppression and wickedness. Human civilisation itself, he argues, has been achieved only through the force of eloquence. 'What other power', Cicero writes, 'could have been strong enough either to gather scattered humanity into one place, or to lead it out of its brutish existence in the wilderness up to our present condition of civilisation as men and as

---

1 Henry Fielding, *The History of Tom Jones, a Foundling*, eds. Martin C. Battestin and Fredson Bowers (Middletown, CT: Wesleyan University Press, 1975), p. 740 (book xiv, ch. 1).

citizens?'[2] The Ciceronian orator characteristically identifies himself and his virtue with the political causes he espouses in his speeches. His authority as a speaker depends on his ability to project his *ethos*, his distinguishing character and moral disposition, to his listeners. His oratorical effectiveness is deemed, moreover, a function of his intellectual powers. An orator of true merit must have a knowledge of all important subjects and all liberal arts.

Burke's education in the classics at Trinity College, Dublin, and his participation there in an extra-curricular club devoted to the practice of public speaking and debate, introduced him to these classical ideals of eloquence and honed his rhetorical skills. Such skills were considered essential for any young gentleman who contemplated a respectable career in parliament, in the pulpit, or at the bar. Towards the end of his life, in his last great speech in the impeachment of Warren Hastings, Burke recalled the ideals his training in eloquence had inculcated:

> We have all, in our early education, read the Verrine Orations [of Cicero]. We may read them, not merely to instruct us, as they will do, in the principles of eloquence . . . but we may read them from a much higher motive . . . [as] a monument, by which it might be seen what course a great public accuser, in a great public cause, ought to pursue.[3]

Indeed, Burke's speeches in the impeachment of Warren Hastings, who was accused of systematic corruption during his tenure as governor-general of India, were consciously patterned after Cicero's prosecution (in 70 BC) of Verres, governor of Sicily, on similar charges of oppression and malfeasance. Adopting a stance that Burke must have found very attractive, Cicero had presented his prosecution of Verres as an 'act of defence': 'I am defending the entire province of Sicily; and therefore, in prosecuting only one single man, I feel . . . that I am not wholly abandoning my mission as rescuer and helper.'[4] Cicero and Burke both style themselves defenders of the helpless, and they invoke in their speeches a common ground of community and human order that unites geographically distant places or culturally disparate societies, whether Rome and Sicily, or Britain and India. (Burke's identification with Cicero was profoundly personal, as well as professional. Like the great

---

2 Marcus Tullius Cicero, *De Oratore*, trans. E. W. Sutton and H. Rackham, Loeb Classical Library, 2 vols. (London: Heinemann, and Cambridge, MA: Harvard University Press, 1942), vol. I, p. 25.

3 Edmund Burke, *Speech in Reply to the Defence of Warren Hastings* (Ninth Day of Reply, 16 June 1794), in *The Works of the Right Honourable Edmund Burke*, 8 vols. (London: Henry G. Bohn, 1857–89), vol. VIII, p. 407.

4 Marcus Tullius Cicero, *The Verrine Orations*, trans. L. H. G. Greenwood, Loeb Classical Library, 2 vols. (London: Heinemann, 1928), vol. I, p. 7.

Roman orator, Burke was a *novus homo* or new man, an ambitious intellectual and political climber without a distinguished family pedigree, whose relations with the aristocratic leadership of his country were uneasy and complicated.)

Like Cicero (or like Demosthenes, who recalls his fellow Athenians to a sense of their shared history and civic values with his stirring oratorical apostrophe, 'I swear it by those ancestors of yours who faced the dangers at Marathon'[5]), Burke attempts in his greatest speeches and polemics to reproduce the classical oratorical moment that conjures community into being. This strain of eloquence often coalesces with a newly imagined discourse of British nationhood. Burke represents the British polity as 'the image of a relation in blood; binding up the constitution of our country with our dearest domestic ties'.[6] Whether it is his reminder in his speeches on America of the ties that bind the British and the Americans – their affiliated past and common love of liberty – or his insistence in the *Reflections* that society is 'a partnership . . . between those who are living, those who are dead, and those who are to be born', Burke seeks to revivify the incantatory power attributed to ancient eloquence.[7] In so doing, he opposes the political rationalism of such thinkers as John Locke, whose 'liberal contractualism denies that eloquence has any place in the convocation or proper conduct of civil society'.[8]

Contrary to the judgement of posterity, however, many in eighteenth-century Britain lamented the absence of eloquence in their time. Hugh Blair expressed great surprise,

> that Great Britain should not have made a more conspicuous figure in Eloquence than it has hitherto attained; when we consider the enlightened, and . . . the free and bold genius of the country, which seems not a little to favour Oratory; and when we consider that, of all the polite nations, it alone possesses a popular government, or admits into the legislature, such numerous assemblies as can be supposed to lie under the dominion of Eloquence.[9]

5 Demosthenes, *Greek Orators–v: Demosthenes On the Crown*, trans. Stephen Usher (Warminster: Aris and Phillips, 1993), p. 123.
6 Edmund Burke, *Reflections on the Revolution in France*, in *The Writings and Speeches of Edmund Burke*, gen. ed. Paul Langford (Oxford: Clarendon Press, 1981–), vol. VIII, p. 84.
7 *Ibid.*, p. 147.
8 Adam Potkay, *The Fate of Eloquence in the Age of Hume* (Ithaca, NY and London: Cornell University Press, 1994), p. 4.
9 Hugh Blair, *Lectures on Rhetoric and Belles Lettres*, 2 vols. (London, 1783), vol. II, p. 38.

Blair published these remarks in 1783, by which time many of the great figures of eighteenth-century oratory, including Fox, Burke and the elder William Pitt, had made their mark on the political scene. His failure to perceive in the statesmen of his time any notable gift for eloquence is instructive, for it serves as a reminder that the circumstances of a 'polite', commercial and increasingly complex society were thought to be in many ways inimical to traditional conceptions of eloquence.

Blair's judgement echoes the opinion of the philosopher David Hume, who argues in his essay 'Of Eloquence' that the polite manners and rationality of an enlightened age are not to be seduced by the fiery sublimity characteristic of ancient oratory. Hume contrasts the modern courtroom, in which the merits of lawsuits are argued on the basis of precedents and statutes (requiring of pleaders at the bar a reasoned, logical discourse), with the ancient scene of justice, where Roman judges or Athenian juries, not confined to the letter of the law, could be swayed by the bravura performance of a skilful speaker. Similarly, modern legislators and educated audiences are governed by rules of polite decorum and by the inculcation of a 'correct turn of thinking' that should put them on their guard against deceptive 'flowers of Elocution': 'Our Public Speakers are obliged to be more reserved than the antients, in their attempts to elevate the imagination, and warm the passions; and, by the influence of prevailing taste, their own genius is sobered and chastened.'[10] In the view of Blair and Hume the ancient ideal of eloquence has been supplanted by an ideal of polite style, marked by rationality, plainness and simplicity, that eschews the 'primitive' appeal of rhetorical tropes and figures.

Burke and his contemporaries were masters, when it suited them, of this cool, perspicuous style. When Burke published his celebrated *Speech on Conciliation with the [American] Colonies*, the Duke of Richmond heaped praise on the propriety of his expression. 'It is so calm, so quiet, so reasonable, so just[,] so proper, that one cannot refuse conviction to every Part . . . You appear in this speech, not that lively astonishing orator that some other of Your works shew you to be, but the most wise, dispassionate, and calm Statesman.'[11] Yet, the passages of eloquence Burke is best remembered for today are precisely those that transgress comprehensively against these canons of polite taste. Whereas Hume maintains that it would be 'absurd . . . in our temperate and calm

10 *Ibid.*, vol. II, pp. 41–2.
11 Edmund Burke, *The Correspondence of Edmund Burke*, ed. Thomas W. Copeland, *et al.*, 10 vols. (Cambridge: Cambridge University Press, 1958–78), vol. III, p. 171.

speakers, to make use of an *Apostrophe*, like that noble one of Demosthenes'[12] (cited above), Burke defiantly places this rhetorical figure, in the form of an impassioned apostrophe to the Queen of France 'glittering like the morning-star, full of life, and splendor, and joy',[13] at the very centre of his *Reflections on the Revolution in France*. His fervid readiness to ignore the rules of polite style helps to explain why his greatest triumphs of eloquence so often aroused a marked uneasiness in his colleagues and outrage among his political oppo-nents. His friend Philip Francis warned him prophetically that his account of Marie Antoinette and of the death of chivalry would be derided as 'pure foppery', and so, in the event, it proved to be.[14] No other passage in the *Reflec-tions* provoked a reaction comparable to the sustained ridicule Burke's critics reserved for this apostrophe, yet the enthusiasm it aroused in his admirers was equally remarkable.

The intensity of this public response exposes to full view the ambivalence that displays of vehement eloquence provoked in eighteenth-century Britain. Had Burke prostituted his rhetorical talents to the service of demagoguery, or was his eloquence the handmaid of truth? Part of the problem in answering this question is that contemporaries perceived political eloquence to be chiefly a weapon of opposition, and in an era when the idea of an institutionalised 'loyal' opposition was as yet unknown, opposing voices were often stigmatised with the taint of party, factionalism and disloyalty. And insofar as such voices consciously appealed to popular feeling (as strong rhetorical tropes, including apostrophe, were thought to do), they were suspected of encouraging desta-bilising forces of democracy and mob rule. '[T]he less enlightened a nation is', observes George Campbell in his *Philosophy of Rhetoric* (1776), 'their language will of necessity the more abound in tropes.'[15] Yet, in his *Philosophical Enquiry* (1757), a youthful study of the sublime and the beautiful or the relationship between powerful feelings and the forms of art and nature, Burke had found the human response to objects of sublimity, including sublime or impassioned figurative language, to be rooted in universal psychological impulses. Accord-ingly, the use of such language represents, in his view, not a regression to a more primitive stage of human or social development, but a legitimate appeal to deep-seated 'natural feelings' from which 'we learn great lessons'. In the

12 David Hume, 'Of Eloquence', in *Of the Standard of Taste and Other Essays*, ed. John W. Lenz, The Library of Liberal Arts (Indianapolis, IN: Bobbs-Merrill, 1965), p. 62.
13 Burke, *Reflections*, p. 126.
14 Burke, *Correspondence*, vol. VI, p. 86.
15 George Campbell, *The Philosophy of Rhetoric*, 2 vols. (London, 1776), vol. II, p. 188.

Reflections, therefore, the pathos of Marie Antoinette's plight at the hands of the French revolutionaries must be emphasised as forcefully as possible, 'because in events like these our passions instruct our reason'.[16]

The vehemence of Burke's writings and speeches upon such occasions as the French Revolution or the impeachment of Warren Hastings can also be understood, paradoxically, as an outgrowth of a political scene in which the conditions of eloquence were imperfectly realised. If, as Longinus records in the dialogue that concludes his classical literary treatise, *On the Sublime*, 'Liberty' is the 'copious and fertile Source of all that is beautiful and ... great',[17] then one must suppose the 'managed' stage of eighteenth-century parliamentary politics, where patronage and influence (rather than rhetorical persuasion) secured votes, to have been an uninspiring theatre of eloquence. In his inaugural lecture as professor of rhetoric and oratory at Harvard University, John Quincy Adams diagnosed the problem astutely:

> The assemblies of . . . Athens and Rome, were held for the purpose of real deliberation. The fate of measures was not decided before they were proposed. Eloquence produced a powerful effect, not only upon the minds of the hearers, but upon the issue of the deliberation. In the only countries of modern Europe, where the semblance of deliberative assemblies has been preserved, corruption, here in the form of executive influence, there in the guise of party spirit, by introducing a more compendious mode of securing decisions, has crippled the sublimest efforts of oratory, and the votes upon questions of magnitude to the interest of nations are all told, long before the questions themselves are submitted to discussion.[18]

The point Adams makes here – that eloquence will not be found in assemblies where votes are counted before measures are introduced – had been put to Burke, some years earlier, by a friend who wondered why he 'took so much pains' with his speeches when he knew 'with certainty . . . that not one vote would be gained by it'.[19] Burke's response reveals a considerably more subtle and practical understanding of his political audience, both inside and outside the House of Commons, than the rhetorical models of republican theory could furnish.

16 Burke, *Reflections*, p. 131.
17 *Dionysius Longinus on the Sublime*, trans. W. Smith (London, 1739), section xliv, pp. 103–4
18 John Quincey Adams, *Lectures on Rhetoric and Oratory*, 2 vols. (Cambridge, MA: Hilliard and Metcalf, 1810), vol. I, pp. 22–3.
19 James Boswell, *Life of Johnson. Together with Boswell's Journal of a Tour to the Hebrides and Johnson's Diary of a Journey into North Wales*, eds. George Birkbeck Hill and L. F. Powell, 6 vols. (Oxford: Oxford University Press, 1934–50), vol. III, p. 233.

[I]f a man speaks well, he gradually establishes a certain reputation and consequence in the general opinion, which sooner or later will have its political
reward. Besides, though not one vote is gained a good speech has its effect.
Though an act which has been ably opposed passes into a law, yet in its progress
it is modelled, it is softened in such a manner, that we see plainly the Minister
has been told . . . it must be altered.

And the House of Commons, if not a pure deliberative body in the republican
mould, was not altogether corrupt either: 'There are many members who
generally go with the Minister, who will not go all lengths. There are many
honest well-meaning country gentlemen who are in parliament only to keep
up the consequence of their families. Upon most of these a good speech will
have influence.'[20]

These remarks reveal a great deal about Burke's sense of his audience, which
in turn furnishes much of the rationale for the forms, rhetoric and style of his
political utterances. First, he argues that there is, in fact, an occasional opening
for deliberation in the House. One group of members, those he designates
'well-meaning country gentlemen', enjoyed sufficient independence that their
votes could sometimes be secured by a persuasive speech. Second, the shape
of legislation and policy could be influenced by an ably conducted campaign
of opposition, in which skill in debate and extemporaneous speaking was
crucial. Third, and perhaps most importantly, Burke recognises that speaking
well gains him a wider audience 'without doors' (outside Parliament) and
establishes him in the 'general opinion'. His words are reported in newspapers
and read in pamphlets by the general public, thus playing an important role in
shaping public opinion, a force of growing significance in eighteenth-century
Britain. Burke himself estimated the class of 'political citizens' in the country
to consist of some 400,000 men, far too large a number to be addressed in
a public speech. To reach such an audience, he had to rely on the printed
word. Finally, though he omits to mention them, Burke is acutely aware that
he addresses a special audience, his associates and patrons in the aristocratic
Rockingham Whig party, whose favourable 'opinion' brings its own 'political
rewards'. As an Irishman without conspicuous social rank or landed property,
Burke depended on the patronage of men like Lord Rockingham and the Duke
of Portland to gain him access to political power. He was valuable to them
precisely because of his superior talents as a professional writer and speaker.
Throughout his career, Burke celebrated his connection with prominent Whig
landed families. His pioneering justification of political 'party' as a legitimate

20 *Ibid.*, vol. III, pp. 233–4.

expression of political will is premised on his party association with a club of like-minded gentlemen, whose wealth, titles and family connections give them a 'natural and fixed influence' in their country's affairs and, in theory at least, a permanent stake in their country's well-being.

Burke's sense of his primary audience evolved over the varied span of his political career, bringing to prominence different forms of political address in successive phases of his political life. The pamphlet predominated in the first years of his association with the Rockingham Whigs. His use of the pamphlet as his literary vehicle in these early years answered the need of the Rockingham Whigs to define themselves as a political grouping, not only to the public at large but also to themselves, to the party faithful. Thus, Burke called his *Thoughts on the Cause of the Present Discontents* (1770) his party's 'Creed', but he also conceived the pamphlet as 'holding out a Banner', in the Duke of Portland's phrase, to 'young men of property, & independent people in both Houses', whose support would be essential if Rockingham were ever to form a government.[21] These pamphlets employed, typically, genres of rational investigation, such as the 'enquiry' or the 'state of the nation' form.

During the period of Burke's peak prominence as a parliamentarian (in the years 1775 to 1790), the parliamentary speech succeeded as his favoured mode of discourse. This was the phase in his career when oratory, properly speaking, predominated, a circumstance reflected in the fact that most of his political publications in these years reproduce the oratorical form, complete with its elaborate rhetorical mode of organisation, on the printed page. Assessing this period of his output poses a special challenge to the literary historian, for no reliable system existed in Burke's day to record verbatim the debates and proceedings of parliament, and the records of speeches that have come down to us, in newspapers and in private letters and diaries, are limited in their completeness and accuracy. In a parliamentary diary that survives as one of the best of these records, Sir Henry Cavendish laments the fragmentariness of his transcription: 'Several speeches of the most able members are very imperfect; many *sublime and beautiful* passages, are lost, lost I fear, for ever.'[22] In singling out the loss of '*sublime and beautiful* passages' (a phrase associated with Burke, as author of the *Philosophical Enquiry*), Cavendish may well be alluding specifically

21 George Thomas Keppel, Earl of Albemarle, *Memoirs of the Marquis of Rockingham and His Contemporaries: with Original Letters and Documents Now First Printed*, 2 vols. (London: Richard Bentley, 1852), vol. II, p. 147.
22 Sir Henry Cavendish, *Sir Henry Cavendish's Debates of the Houses of Commons, During the Thirteenth Parliament of Great Britain, Commonly Called the Unreported Parliament*, ed. J. Wright, 2 vols. (London, 1841), vol. I, p. iv.

to him. Burke's rapidity of speech and pronounced Irish accent were widely considered to impede the effectiveness of his public speaking, and they must have complicated considerably Cavendish's task as a transcriber.

Because of the proscriptions on verbatim reporting, parliamentary addresses from this period that have made their way into print tend to be those delivered in circumstances which allowed more elaborate preparation than usual, thereby easing greatly a transition to the printed page. This was especially the case with speeches introducing formal motions or resolutions to the House. Burke's published speeches on *Conciliation* (1775), on *Economical Reform* (1780) and on the *Nabob of Arcot's Debts* (1785) all originated on such occasions. Unlike interventions in the midst of a debate, a speech introducing a motion permitted a reasoned exposition of the views espoused by Burke's party and could be prepared in large measure ahead of time. Such a speech would make a more suitable basis for a publication intended to sway the general public. Occasionally, however, as with the *Speech on American Taxation* (1774), public demand for a printed version of an address not initially designed for publication was such that Burke scrambled to reconstruct a text. 'The means of gratifying the public curiosity', he remarks in a prefatory note to the taxation speech, 'were obligingly furnished from the notes of some Gentlemen, Members of the last Parliament.'[23] The very fact that parliament so jealously guarded access to its deliberations was itself a powerful motive to publish. In *Thoughts on the Cause of the Present Discontents* (1770), Burke lamented the methods used by the government to stifle opposition voices: 'if he speaks [in the House], the doors are locked: a body of loquacious placemen go out to tell the world, that all he aims at is to get into office'. Thus, as the editor of Cavendish's *Debates* notes, 'there can be little doubt that [Burke] was induced to give [his *Thoughts on the Present Discontents*] to the world, because the public, from the constant exclusion of strangers, were kept in ignorance of what their representatives were doing in the House of Commons'.[24]

In the final decade of Burke's life, as he became increasingly estranged from his erstwhile political colleagues, he turned almost exclusively to the printed letter, a form he made his own and honed to an unparalleled sophistication and complexity. At this point in his career, his primary concern was to mobilise public opinion on the question of the French Revolution and thereby to influence government policy, but his use of the letter form as the literary means to this end harks back to the period when his political power lay in his private

23 Burke, *Speech on American Taxation*, in *Writings and Speeches*, vol. II, p. 408.
24 Burke, *Thoughts on the Causes of the Present Discontents*, in *Writings and Speeches*, vol. II, p. 299; Cavendish, *Debates*, vol. I, p. v.

relationship and personal correspondence with the Whig aristocracy. The published letters of his final years have an air of paradox about them, generically speaking. They employ an intimate, private form of writing that is pressed, at times awkwardly, into public service. Their mode of address acknowledges the continued concentration of power in the hands of a largely aristocratic oligarchy, whose representatives Burke singles out as his addressees. The fact of publication, however, recognises the increasingly influential voice of a much larger body of the public, whose combined opinion could sway government policy.

Burke's sometimes implausible use of the letter form in his last years reflects his embarrassment at the breach of political decorum he is committing. In a deferential political system, Andrew W. Robertson notes, the people are 'called upon not for deliberation but for decision'.[25] Deliberative rhetoric, that mode of argument designed to determine what is to be done, should remain confined to the precincts of the legislature, where an educated elite will decide on matters of policy. The interests of the people should be consulted, but they must never be 'called into council' to deliberate about *the real cause* or the *appropriate remedy*' for their grievances.[26] For Burke, the people are 'a sort of children that must be soothed and managed'.[27] This view of the people contrasts dramatically with that expressed by William Gladstone a century later:

> This is a self-governing country. Let us bring home to the minds of the people the state of the facts they have to deal with, and in Heaven's name let them determine whether or not this is the way they like to be governed . . . If it is acceptable, if it is liked by the people – they are the masters – it is for them to have it.[28]

For Gladstone, the people have become part of the deliberative process: they are to be consulted on the issues and given the final say on any question. Burke's writings on the French Revolution stand upon the brink of this sea change. As published works, they urge questions of political policy upon a readership of thousands, many of whom, in the radical camp, took on eagerly the role being handed them. But, as if to forestall the radical implications of debating deliberative matters out in the open, Burke encloses his words

25 Andrew W. Robertson, *The Language of Democracy: Political Rhetoric in the United States and Britain, 1790–1900* (Ithaca, NY and London: Cornell University Press, 1995), p. 5.
26 Burke, *Letter to Sir Hercules Langrishe*, in *Writings and Speeches*, vol. IX, p. 621.
27 Burke, *Speech at Bristol Previous to the Election: 6 September 1780*, in *Writings and Speeches*, vol. III, p. 662.
28 Quoted in Robertson, *Language of Democracy*, p. 4.

within the generic boundaries of the personal letter – letters whose ostensible recipients ('a gentleman in Paris', 'a member of the present Parliament', 'a noble lord') remain securely part of a patrician deliberative elite.

Eloquence and oratory: writing versus speaking

The idea of a scene of eloquence, a place where passionate and well-chosen words delivered to ardent listeners might alter the fate of nations or expose tyranny and injustice, was deeply attractive to the eighteenth-century imagination, but the reach of print culture in the period was such that eloquence was often experienced in a mediated form, via the printed word. In 1838 Henry Lord Brougham described the revolution the press had wrought upon the imagined scene of eloquence: 'Another engine has been invented for working upon the popular mind, whether to instruct, to persuade, or to please – an engine, too, of which the powers are not limited in time or in space.' The advent of the press had splintered the oratorical scene, that imagined primal moment when the 'orator of old' had played the roles of the 'Parliamentary debater, the speaker at public meetings, the preacher, the newspaper, the published sermon, the pamphlet, the volume, all in one'.[29]

For us, moreover, any direct encounter with an eighteenth-century oratorical performance, more than two centuries after the fact, is clearly an impossibility. These circumstances necessarily bring to the fore modes of literary and textual analysis as the primary means of appraising the political eloquence of the 1770s and 1780s, though the value of indirect historical evidence, such as eyewitness accounts of great speeches, is not to be overlooked. For eighteenth-century readers, accepting political texts as literary performances was not especially problematic, since, as George Campbell explains in *The Philosophy of Rhetoric* (1776), poetry and oratory were regarded as sister arts:

> Poetry indeed is properly no other than a particular mode or form of certain branches of oratory . . . [T]he direct end of the former, whether to delight the fancy as in epic, or to move the passions as in tragedy, is avowedly in part the aim, and sometimes the immediate and proposed aim, of the orator. The same medium language is made use of, the same general rules of composition, in narration, description, argumentation, are observed; and the same tropes and figures, either for beautifying or invigorating the diction, are employed by both.[30]

---

29 Henry Peter Brougham, Baron Brougham and Vaux, 'Dissertation on the Eloquence of the Ancients', in *Speeches of Henry Lord Brougham*, 4 vols. (Edinburgh, 1838), vol. IV, p. 380.
30 Campbell, *Philosophy of Rhetoric*, vol. I, pp. 14–15.

Poetry and oratory were viewed simply as two adjoining provinces of an extensive republic of letters, in which such writers as Swift, Johnson, Gibbon, Priestley or Burke could range unselfconsciously over a variety of forms and disciplines, from philosophy, history, science and economics, to what we today define as literature – essays, poems and plays.

A scant fifty years after Campbell, the connection between poetry and eloquence had been severed, seemingly irrevocably. In 'What Is Poetry?' (1833), John Stuart Mill proclaimed the grounds for divorce: 'eloquence is *heard*, poetry is *over*heard. Eloquence supposes an audience; the peculiarity of poetry appears to us to lie in the poet's utter unconsciousness of a listener.' The distinction between the two turns on the motivation of the speaker. If the 'act of utterance is not itself the end, but a means to an end', such as the 'desire of making an impression upon another mind', then the speaker has passed from the realm of poetry into the domain of eloquence.[31] Between the views of Campbell and those voiced by Mill a fundamental shift has taken place, from a didactic, rhetorical, genre-based conception of literature to one that values self-expression, subjectivity, the inner truth of one's feelings. Disinterestedness is a fundamental hallmark of Mill's account of poetry: he goes so far as to voice doubts about the poetic status of verse written for monetary profit or for publication.

Literary criticism in our own day no longer subscribes to such an immaculate conception of literary production. We recognise the pressures of circumstance, material conditions, institutional constraints and ideological commitment that shape the writer and the literary work. But even in such an atmosphere of heightened, politicised critical awareness, the rhetorical overtness of political eloquence, the immediate, practical, palpable designs it has on its audience, tends to set it apart, in degree if not in kind, from other forms of literary production. Burke's works were frequently captive to the demands of party and political office; his texts were often written in collaboration; and circumstances sometimes required him to employ pragmatic modes – memoranda, motions, resolutions, committee reports and articles of charge – far removed from the normal hierarchy of literary genres. As a result, studies of Burke have tended to read his writings as a continuous text, glossing over difficult questions of form, occasion and textual authority.

A further critical reflection on the propriety of submitting political texts, especially orations, to literary analysis is supplied by William Hazlitt in his

---

31 John Stuart Mill, 'What Is Poetry?' in *Essays on Poetry*, ed. F. Parvin Sharpless (Columbia, SC: University of South Carolina Press, 1976), pp. 12–13.

essay, 'On the Difference between Writing and Speaking'. His basic point is a simple one: writing well and speaking well are very different, even opposed, talents. 'The most dashing orator I ever heard is the flattest writer I ever read. In speaking, he was like a volcano vomiting out *lava*; in writing he is like a volcano burnt out.'[32] Hazlitt appears to be referring here to the radical polemicist John Thelwall, but his remark can also be applied with fair aptness to such speakers as Sheridan, whose oratorical performances garnered astonished (and astonishing) accolades but appear rather less sensational on the printed page. Hazlitt identifies two problems in translating oratorical prowess into print. The first is that printed words cannot convey the orator's performance. Gesture, voice, 'the speaking eye, the conscious attitude, the inexplicable dumb shew and noise' – all of these are irretrievably lost. The second and more intractable problem is that 'an orator can hardly get beyond *common-places*: if he does he gets beyond his hearers'.[33] Great thinkers and fine writers do not make the most successful speakers: they are – and this was precisely Burke's difficulty, in Hazlitt's view – 'too recondite' for their hearers. Oliver Goldsmith captured the paradox of his friend's eloquence: 'too deep for his hearers, [Burke] went on refining, / And thought of convincing, while they thought of dining'.[34]

To be immediately effective, Hazlitt argues, an oration must employ facts, maxims and arguments readily accessible to the audience. 'A common-place does not leave the mind "sceptical, puzzled, and undecided in the moment of action" . . . It operates mechanically, and opens an instantaneous and infallible communication between the hearer and speaker.' But rather than to appeal to the prejudices of his listeners, Burke 'endeavoured to *account for them*', and in so doing he introduced an unwonted degree of critical reflection into his speeches. He then compounded this transgression by clothing his originality in 'flowers of poetical fiction' and strewing 'the most dazzling colours of language over the Standing Orders of the House'. As a result, Hazlitt dryly notes, his performances were a 'double offence' to the House of Commons – 'an aggravation of the encroachments of his genius'.[35] The more profound and complex his observations, the less immediate their impact on the corporate sense of the House. New ideas require time and application to be properly

---

32 William Hazlitt, 'On the Difference between Writing and Speaking', in *The Plain Speaker*, in *The Complete Works of William Hazlitt*, ed. P. P. Howe, 21 vols. (London and Toronto: J. M. Dent and Sons, 1931), vol. XII, p. 264.

33 *Ibid.*, p. 265.

34 Oliver Goldsmith, *Retaliation*, in *The Collected Works of Oliver Goldsmith*, ed. Arthur Friedman, 5 vols. (Oxford University Press, 1966), vol. IV, p. 354.

35 Hazlitt, 'Writing and Speaking', p. 266.

considered, but the oratorical moment is transitory, and legislators are often compelled to decide issues upon the instant. 'In reading', by contrast, 'we may go over the page again, whenever any thing new or questionable "gives us pause".'[36]

Hazlitt uses the distinction between writing and speaking as an evaluative criterion. The nearer political eloquence approaches the condition of fine writing and poetry, the more canonical and permanent it is. Such evaluative judgements have their limitations, however, for they privilege literary value and intellectual originality over rhetorical or political effectiveness. In Sheridan's case, some of the most stirring passages in his speeches employ time-worn, even hackneyed, political commonplaces. A chief instance is his habitual reliance on the language of patriotism, a favourite political discourse of eighteenth-century Britain, employed frequently by political figures on all sides, including Burke. The 'patriotic' speaker, usually an opposition supporter, would denounce the government's encroachment on the ancient constitution and liberties of the country and would represent himself as restoring the constitution to its original purity. The constitution was threatened by corruption (bribery, patronage) and by arbitrary measures, evils generally ascribed to self-serving court politicians eager to maintain their grip on power.

During the French revolutionary period, Sheridan used the language of patriotism to great effect, defending the *Habeas Corpus* Act, which the Pitt administration sought to suspend, as a 'chief bulwark of the rights and liberties of Englishmen'[37] and denouncing the war with France as a pretext for the corrupt friends of government to line their own pockets. 'Oh! shame! shame! is this a time for selfish intrigues, and the little dirty traffic for lucre and emolument? . . . Is there nothing that whispers to that right honourable gentleman that the crisis is too big, that the times are too gigantic, to be ruled by the little hackneyed and every-day means of ordinary corruption?'[38] Defending the City of London's ancient right to control its own militia, which another member of the House had dismissed as a 'Gothic' privilege, he declares, 'Our ancestors had many such Gothic prejudices. They had a Gothic prejudice against a standing army; they had a Gothic prejudice against the erection of baracks [*sic*] . . . and, in short, they had so many Gothic notions about freedom and independence, that they had no doubt their memory was odious to the men of the present day.' The proposal to replace the old City militia with two

---

36 *Ibid.*, p. 267.
37 Richard Brinsley Sheridan, *Speeches of the Late Right Honourable Richard Brinsley Sheridan*, 5 vols. (London, 1816), vol. IV, p. 20.
38 *Ibid.*, vol. III, pp. 214–15.

professional army regiments is, in Sheridan's words, the joint contrivance of 'the craft of despotism and the laziness of commercial luxury, assisted by the vanity and corruption of individuals'.[39] A purer expression of the discourse of republican virtue could scarcely be found.

The effectiveness of such language, its power to communicate if not to persuade, was a direct function of its wide diffusion in the press, in parliament and on the hustings. We encounter it in the writings of Junius and Mary Wollstonecraft, as well as in Sheridan and Burke. Because it was well known and widely understood, it was easily accessible and commanded broad assent. A similar point can be made about the rhetorical ornamentation of Sheridan's speeches, which rely heavily on repetitive sentence structures or rhetorical schemes (as the reiteration of 'Gothic' in the passage above illustrates), rather than on the tropes or verbal transformations that Aristotle exalted as a sign of genius and the acme of rhetorical art. The rhythmical repetitions of schemes gave readier access to the ears of listeners. Lord Erskine urged this view in a prefatory letter to an edition of Fox's speeches (1815): 'Eloquence . . . consists more in the dextrous structure of periods, and in the powers and harmony of delivery, than in the extraordinary vigour of the understanding.'[40]

On this score, it is instructive to compare Sheridan's characterisation of Warren Hastings, in a celebrated speech delivered on 7 February 1787, with Burke's assessment a year later in his address opening the impeachment of Hastings. Sheridan drives home Hastings' misconduct with drumbeat insistence, accusing him 'of criminality of the blackest dye, – of tyranny the most vile and premeditated, – of corruption the most open and shameless, – of oppression the most severe and grinding, – of cruelty the most hard and unparalleled'.[41] By contrast, Burke presents Hastings as a 'captain-general of iniquity' (an ironic echo of his erstwhile title, governor-general of India). He relies on tropes, chiefly metaphor and personification, to introduce a complex point about the premeditated, organised, systematic character of corruption under Hastings' tutelage. 'We have brought before you the chief of the tribe, the head of the whole body of eastern offenders; a captain-general of iniquity, under whom all the fraud, all the peculation, all the tyranny, in India, are embodied, disciplined, arrayed, and paid . . . You strike at the whole corps, if you strike at the head.'[42]

39 *Ibid.*, vol. IV, p. 71.
40 Charles James Fox, *The Speeches of the Right Honourable Charles James Fox, in the House of Commons*, 6 vols. (London, 1815), vol. I, xi.
41 Sheridan, *Speeches*, vol. I, p. 277.
42 Burke, *Speech on the Impeachment of Warren Hastings* (15 February 1788), in *Works*, vol. VII, p. 15.

The success of Sheridan's speech is a matter of record. Sir Gilbert Elliot voiced the general opinion in a letter to his wife: 'It was by many degrees the most excellent and astonishing performance I ever heard, and surpasses all I ever imagined possible in eloquence . . . [H]e surpassed Pitt, Fox, and even Burke, in his finest and most brilliant orations.'[43] In light of this rapturous reception, Sheridan's refusal to publish his speeches, leaving behind only imperfect records of his orations, is significant. It would appear, as Sheridan's biographer James Morwood suggests, that his disinclination stemmed from 'his shrewd awareness of how much in his case the power of the words owed to the manner of their delivery'.[44] If Sheridan and Burke, two Irish writers whose careers held much in common, illustrate with peculiar aptness Hazlitt's thesis about the difference between spoken and written eloquence, the difference in the regard posterity has paid to their political utterances, which remains inevitably a function of the available textual evidence, should also caution us about the limitations in our perspective on eighteenth-century eloquence. Clearly, our present-day view is coloured by the fact that Burke left behind an extensively revised and published record of his political statements, while his partners and rivals in eloquence – Pitt (both elder and younger), Fox and Sheridan – did not.

We are also reminded that eloquence appears in many different, often incommensurate, guises. In the very period when Burke's political fame was at its peak, Thomas Paine penned two of the most widely read political pamphlets of all time, *Common Sense* (1776) and *Rights of Man* (1791). His mastery of a vigorous, colloquial, demotic style secured him a broad, unlettered audience. His writing enacts his conviction that the common people have a legitimate voice in debates about fundamental political issues. In *Rights of Man*, which Paine wrote in response to Burke's *Reflections*, this conviction manifests itself in a conscious opposition of literary styles. With calculated impudence Paine presents himself as a translator of Burke's ornate, involuted prose: 'As the wondering audience, whom Burke supposes himself talking to, may not understand all this learned jargon, I will undertake to be its interpreter.'[45] Mary Wollstonecraft also sought to deflect Burke's torrent of eloquence in the *Reflections*, responding to his text in a matter of weeks with her pamphlet

---

43 Gilbert Elliot, first Earl of Minto, *Life and Letters of Sir Gilbert Elliot*, 3 vols. (London: Longman, Green and Co., 1874), vol. I, pp. 123–4.
44 James Morwood, *The Life and Works of Richard Brinsley Sheridan* (Edinburgh: Scottish Academic Press, 1985), p. 125.
45 Thomas Paine, *Rights of Man*, in *The Complete Writings of Thomas Paine*, ed. Philip S. Foner, 2 vols. (New York: Citadel Press, 1945), vol. I, p. 319.

Vindication of the Rights of Men (1790). But rather than opposing a popular style to his learned one, as Paine does, she appropriates important elements of his educated, aristocratic medium into her own text, re-inflecting his elite discourse in a voice that is female, middle-class and radical. Yet, in attacking the rhetorical means of Burke's eloquence (along with his ideas), Paine and Wollstonecraft both pay involuntary tribute to his extraordinary talents as a writer and acknowledge the continuing power of his political idiom. It may well be, as Christopher Reid argues, that the failure of British radicalism in the 1790s to find 'a spokesman with quite Burke's rhetorical talents and sense of history . . . was to prove a serious, perhaps even a decisive weakness'.[46]

Eloquence and literary expression

Given the powerful reach of print culture in the eighteenth century, the very fact that Burke's eloquence was so closely allied to his literary abilities, which shone to greatest advantage in print, gave him a decided edge over his political rivals. When we inquire into the distinctive nature of that literary eloquence, what impresses time and again is his ability to use literary forms and conventions with a keen sense of their historical roots, political implications and ideological power. A prime example of this is his repeated presentation of the French Revolution as a great tragic drama. In *Reflections on the Revolution in France* he explains why he has been moved to represent Louis XVI and Marie Antoinette as tragic protagonists:

> when kings are hurl'd from their thrones by the Supreme Director of this great drama, and become the objects of insult to the base, and of pity to the good, we behold such disasters in the moral, as we should behold a miracle in the physical order of things. We are alarmed into reflexion; our minds (as it has long since been observed) are purified by terror and pity; our weak unthinking pride is humbled, under the dispensations of a mysterious wisdom.[47]

With a nod to Aristotle's *Poetics*, Burke places literary criticism in the service of political theory. Tragic performances, he argues, teach profound lessons about the importance of social hierarchy and political stability. He emphasises this point even more forcefully in his *Speech in Reply to the Defence of Warren Hastings* (11 June 1794).

46 Christopher Reid, *Edmund Burke and the Practice of Political Writing* (Dublin: Gill and Macmillan; New York: St Martin's, 1985), p. 2.
47 Burke, *Reflections*, pp. 131–2.

It is wisely provided in the constitution of our heart that we should interest ourselves in the fate of great personages. They are, therefore, made everywhere the objects of tragedy, which addresses itself directly to our passions and our feelings. And why? Because men of great place, men of great rank, men of great hereditary authority, cannot fall without a horrible crash upon all about them. Such towers cannot tumble without ruining their dependent cottages.[48]

For Burke tragedy is a political genre, as well as a literary one. Such a view was by no means unusual in a century that habitually read political, moral and didactic inferences into literary texts. But the conservative ideological spin he gives to the cathartic lessons inculcated by tragedy raises his interpretation above the ordinary run of literary criticism to a level of generalisation that qualifies it as an intervention in political philosophy. The debate becomes one about the enabling conditions of social and political order, with Burke insisting on the benefits of hierarchy and on the value of preserving existing political structures. Tragedy dramatises, in a safely distanced form, the dire consequences that follow from a dissolution of time-honoured political institutions, such as hereditary monarchy. By reminding individuals of the benefits of civil security, tragedy serves for Burke as a symbolic re-enactment of the original social contract, when the individual gave up the right 'to assert his own cause'.[49]

In the *Reflections*, Burke fuses form and idea so successfully that his critics felt compelled to respond to his views in the same terms, refuting his political arguments by questioning the tragic shape he gave to events in France and by attacking the premises of his theory of tragedy. Thus, Paine declares that Burke's book can scarcely be read as anything other than a 'dramatic performance' in which 'poetical liberties' are taken with the facts so as to make 'the machinery bend to produce a stage effect'.[50] He recognises that the *Reflections* is, despite its complexity, a supremely eloquent text. Its effectiveness stems from Burke's ability to construct an affecting and compelling narrative out of the confusion of events reported from Paris – a narrative with gripping scenes of Gothic horror, sentimental distress and tragic grandeur. Readers acquainted with the literary precedents for these scenes would feel their emotional allegiances solicited along familiar lines and might not stop to ascertain the veracity of Burke's account. Wollstonecraft presses farther than

48 Burke, *Speech in Reply* (Third Day, 3 June 1794), in *Works*, vol. VIII, p. 471.
49 Burke, *Reflections*, p. 110.
50 Paine, *Rights of Man*, p. 268.

Paine, exposing to view in her critique the assumptions about hierarchy and subordination that underwrite Burke's tragic enactment:

> your tears are reserved . . . for the declamation of the theatre, or for the downfall of queens, whose rank alters the nature of folly, and throws a graceful veil over vices that degrade humanity; whilst the distress of many industrious mothers, whose *helpmates* have been torn from them, and the hungry cry of helpless babes, were vulgar sorrows that could not move your commiseration.[51]

Another important instance of Burke's blending of literary and political forms is his habitual use of what may be termed the 'prospect view' or 'survey' as a mode of economic and political exposition. These are passages that inventory the external features of a country's landscape: its topography, state of cultivation, manufactures, architecture, towns and cities – all the visible evidence, in short, of productive human activity harnessing nature to the needs of society. One of the most extended of these surveys is the opening section of Burke's *Speech on Conciliation*. He reviews the population of the American colonies, the value of their commerce, their trade with Britain, their agriculture and their fisheries; and he concludes with a review of the American '*Temper and Character*'. His *Speech on Mr Fox's East India Bill* (1784) begins with a similar survey of the East India Company's possessions in India. Such empirical surveys of a country's wealth and power, based on the best available evidence (which was mostly ocular), appeared regularly in the period and were called 'states of the nation'. An early example is Guy Miège's *The New State of England* (1691). They are forerunners of the modern science of statistics.

Burke's surveys are no mere recitals of dry facts. He invariably enlivens his analyses with vivid, highly visual descriptions that make concrete the economic or political point he is making – verbal illustrations that enable his listeners to *see* the issue in question. Thus, to underscore the intrepidity and resourcefulness of American enterprise (and, by implication, America's inestimable value to the mother country), he conjures up in his mind's eye the whalers of New England plying their fishery.

> Whilst we follow them among the tumbling mountains of ice, and behold them penetrating into the deepest frozen recesses of Hudson's Bay and Davis's Streights, whilst we are looking for them beneath the Arctic circle, we hear that they have pierced into the opposite region of polar cold, that they are at the Antipodes, and engaged under the frozen serpent of the south . . . Nor is

51 Mary Wollstonecraft, *A Vindication of the Rights of Men* (London, 1790), p. 27.

the equinoctial heat more discouraging to them, than the accumulated winter of both the poles. We know that whilst some of them draw the line and strike the harpoon on the coast of Africa, others run the longitude, and pursue their gigantic game along the coast of Brazil. No sea but what is vexed by their fisheries. No climate that is not witness to their toils.[52]

This passage, which takes in a breathtaking bird's-eye view of the globe, owes a great deal to the descriptive technique of James Thomson's *The Seasons* (1730–46). Thomson's poem, in a manner characteristic of eighteenth-century Georgic-descriptive or topographical poetry, is punctuated by passages of visual assessment, in which the poetic speaker catalogues the landscape before him and draws a political conclusion from what he sees. In 'Summer', for example, Thomson pauses to 'sweep / The boundless Landskip' and deduces from the 'goodly prospect' spread out before him the political moral that 'Happy BRITANNIA' is a divinely blessed, well-ordered and wisely governed polity.[53]

The fact that Burke's political descriptions so closely resemble the loco-descriptive poetry of his contemporaries is no accident. The metaphors of sight and observation that characterise the poetry of Thomson or Pope are equally present in the 'state of the nation' form. Such shared features of the period's poetic and political genres reflect an underlying epistemological consensus: the unquestioned premises of an empirical, Lockean age that understands sensation and reflection to be the foundations of all knowledge. They reflect also the aristocratic Whig ethos of the period, which esteemed the landed gentleman – a man of cultivated, comprehensive, disinterested understanding – as the consummate observer and, by extension, as the ideal political leader. Burke's visual surveys embody both these assumptions. In the *Reflections*, for example, his prospect view of the kingdom of France underscores his contention that the state of France, economic and otherwise, was anything but parlous before the Revolution, and it supports his claim that he himself qualifies as one of those gentlemen whose encyclopedic comprehension mark them as the natural trustees of their country. His survey is punctuated by verbs of sight and reflection: 'when I consider', 'turn my eyes', 'bring before my view', 'recollect', 'contemplate', 'reckon', 'behold'.[54] Once again, literary form and ideological premise are seamlessly united. To adapt the conclusion of Alexander Pope's prospect view of the Thames valley in *Windsor Forest* (1713), Burke argues, in effect, 'And Peace and Plenty tell, a BOURBON reigns'.

52 Burke, *Conciliation*, in *Writings and Speeches*, vol. VIII, pp. 117–18.
53 James Thomson, *The Seasons*, ed. James Sambrook (Oxford: Oxford University Press. 1981), pp. 124–5 ('Summer', lines 1408–9, 1438, 1442).
54 Burke, *Reflections*, pp. 179–80.

Burke's interpolations of literary genres into his political polemics and speeches merit more detailed exploration than is possible here. His late writings on the French Revolution, especially *A Letter to a Noble Lord* (1796) and *Letters on a Regicide Peace* (1796–1812), are impassioned mixtures of elegy, satire, epic, apologia and prophetic jeremiad; and his great speeches on India are carefully constructed narratives that draw on the conventions of ancient chivalric romances, along with their modern counterparts, Gothic fiction and novels of sensibility. Like the questing hero of romance, Burke represents himself as the champion of virtue in distress:

> To give up all the repose and pleasures of life, to pass sleepless nights and laborious days, and, what is ten times more irksome to an ingenuous mind, to offer oneself to calumny and all its herd of hissing tongues and poisoned fangs, in order to free the world from fraudulent prevaricators, from cruel oppressors, from robbers and tyrants, has, I say, the test of heroic virtue, and well deserves such a distinction.[55]

He personifies India as a helpless damsel exposed to the pitiless rapacity of Warren Hastings and his henchmen, and he imagines himself as a knight errant beset by hissing, fanged serpents and dragons. Burke's political opponents were alert to this narrative strategy, and they sought to blunt its effectiveness by dismissing him as a deranged Don Quixote. 'In the rhapsody of his imagination', remarks Thomas Paine, 'he has discovered a world of wind mills, and his sorrows are that there are no Quixotes to attack them.'[56]

Burke's habitual borrowing of salient features and structures of illustrious literary forms (epic, tragedy, Georgic) can be understood also as an extension of the practice of allusion in eighteenth-century parliamentary discourse. By citing or alluding to culturally prestigious texts, speakers in parliament signalled their social and intellectual right of membership in an privileged political club, from which the vast majority of their countrymen were excluded. The act of quotation constituted 'an appeal to textual precedent and an assertion of cultural authority' on behalf of one's cause.[57] Speakers were, in fact, appraised for the aptness and inventiveness of their allusions. Nathaniel Wraxall, a member of parliament in the 1780s, reports that during the debate on the East India Bill in 1783, 'History, ancient and modern, poetry, even Scripture, all

---

55 Burke, *Speech in Reply* (First Day, 28 May 1794), in *Works*, vol. VIII, p. 471.
56 Paine, *Rights of Man*, p. 259.
57 Christopher Reid, 'Foiling the Rival: Argument and Identity in Sheridan's Speeches', in *Sheridan Studies*, ed. James Morwood and David Crane (Cambridge: Cambridge University Press, 1995), p. 119.

were successively pressed into the service . . . of the contending parties.'[58] Sheridan, in particular, excelled in this kind of debate, showing a ready ability to cap his rivals' quotations or to counter and contest them by seizing his opponents' allusions for his own purposes. In the East India debate, according to the account in Sheridan's *Speeches*, he 'took up the several quotations from Shakespeare, Milton, and the book of Revelations [*sic*]; of Mr Wilberforce, Mr Arden, and Mr Scott, foiling them each with their own weapons, and citing, with the most happy ease and correctness, passages from almost the same pages that controverted their quotations, and told strongly for the bill'.[59]

Wraxall's *Posthumous Memoirs*, in which the cultural capital of prominent members of parliament is assessed as minutely as their family antecedents, demonstrates how a member's cultural formation contributed to his standing in the House and, by extension, facilitated his access to power. Yet, as important as such knowledge was in furthering political ambition, it had to be worn lightly. P. G. D. Thomas, a historian of the eighteenth-century House of Commons, cautions us against overestimating the literary tone of debate: 'Speakers who wanted to win support paid more attention to legal and constitutional precedents than to classical quotations.'[60] Wraxall points out that Pitt quoted classical authors very sparingly, in the awareness that a large part of his audience, especially country members, 'were little conversant in the writings of the Augustan age or familiar with Horace'. By contrast, 'Burke's enthusiasm, his exhaustless memory, and luxuriant imagination, more frequently carried him away into the times of Virgil and Cicero', but, argues Wraxall, this load of intellectual treasure in his speeches told against his effectiveness as a speaker.[61] In this regard Lord Rockingham, who advised Burke in 1773 that the 'general rate of understanding in the House of Commons is not very acute', measured the intellectual temperature of the House more accurately than his protégé.[62] One senses a certain insecurity in the way Burke loaded up his addresses with literary quotations and allusions – a need to demonstrate his political qualifications, his acceptability, to colleagues more confident in their social station than he was.

As a mode of eloquence, Burke's copiousness of allusion shines more brightly on the printed page than in the heat of debate. In his publications his

---

58 Nathaniel Wraxall, *The Historical and the Posthumous Memoirs of Sir Nathaniel William Wraxall 1772–1784*, 5 vols. (London: Bickers and Son, 1884), vol. III, p. 169.
59 Sheridan, *Speeches*, vol. I, p. 72.
60 P. G. D. Thomas, *The House of Commons in the Eighteenth Century* (Oxford: Clarendon Press, 1971), p. 8.
61 Wraxall, *Memoirs*, vol. III, p. 12.
62 Burke, *Correspondence*, vol. II, p. 402.

allusions serve an expanded thematic role, beyond the game of one-upmanship played out on the floor of the House – though interesting parallels can be drawn, if one thinks in terms of cultural practices, between the function of allusion and 'imitation' in print, and their function in oral debate or conversation. Just as Alexander Pope's skill in poetic imitation (of Horace, for example) was judged by the aptness of the parallels he established between Horace's Rome and eighteenth-century England, so too a speaker could make his point more telling if the original context of a quotation corresponded strikingly to the subject at hand.[63] In print, however, patterns of allusion could resonate with much fuller implication. The rich texture of Burke's references to past writers, traditions and historical figures bespeaks his respect for the past. Through allusion, his writings themselves embody or enact his deepest political conviction, that political reform must be as much as possible an act of preservation: 'the useful parts of an old establishment are kept, and what is superadded is to be fitted to what is retained'.[64] In his later writings, especially on the French Revolution, his allusions come to function as a mode of cultural criticism, as 'a self-conscious expression of anxiety about cultural uprootedness and discontinuity in a dangerous new world'.[65] This anxiety manifests itself in an deliberate juxtaposition, patterned on the Scriblerian satire of Pope and Swift, between the literary monuments of antiquity, representing truth and permanence, and the degenerate culture of modern times – a farcical parade of atheists, enthusiasts, projectors, masqueraders, harlequins, freaks and monstrosities.

The ease with which Burke manipulates the symbolic counters of Scriblerian satire points to another important dimension of his political eloquence: the endless and effortless stream of images, metaphors and figures of speech that runs through all his writings. The range of his figurative inventiveness is too great to be illustrated here with any adequacy: there is a kind of Shakespearean luxuriance about it. Samuel Johnson defined the distinctive quality of Burke's style as 'Copiousness and fertility of allusion; a power of diversifying his matter, by placing it in various relations'.[66] To put the point another way, one might say that Burke was in the habit of thinking and arguing in images. Beginning, characteristically, with a simple image, such as the idea that the nation is like a family, he will proceed to tease out the implications of the image at great

63 See Reid, 'Foiling the Rival', p. 119.
64 Burke, *Reflections*, p. 216.
65 Gerald W. Chapman, *Edmund Burke: The Practical Imagination* (Cambridge, MA: Harvard University Press, 1967), p. 238.
66 Boswell, *Journal of a Tour to the Hebrides*, in *Life of Johnson*, vol. v, p. 213.

length. In the process the image expands into an elaborate analogy. In the *Reflections* Burke characterises this mode of argument as reasoning in 'the spirit of philosophic analogy'. In the case of his conception of the nation as a family or an 'image of a relation in blood', Burke imagines this family as the possessor of an ancestral estate. Part of the family patrimony is the English constitution, which he describes as an entailed inheritance: 'we receive, we hold, we transmit our government and our privileges, in the same manner in which we enjoy and transmit our property and our lives'.[67] Entailment was a widespread legal practice in eighteenth-century England, a means of passing on the family property to one's heirs with conditions attached spelling out the use and further transmission of that property. In many instances, heirs of family estates were not free to do with their property whatever they wished. Thus, Burke uses a social and legal practice familiar to his readers to make concrete an abstract idea about the historical continuity, stability and evolution of the body politic.

It is worth pausing briefly over Burke's procedure of 'analogy'. As a mode of philosophical argument analogy is most often encountered in theology, as in Joseph Butler's *The Analogy of Religion Natural and Revealed to the Constitution and the Course of Nature* (1736). It assumes that because one object resembles another in one or more respects, they may also resemble each other in another point or particular. Analogy, as Butler and Burke use it, is a mode of inductive and probabilistic reasoning that advances from what we know to what we cannot observe directly, but in the conviction that what we do not see directly conforms to the laws that govern our daily experience. As such, analogy is for them a procedure very much in the epistemological spirit of Lockean empiricism that dominated the age. In that same spirit, John Aikin warns about the limitations of analogy, citing the example of 'men of the world and politicians [who] have sometimes suffered themselves to be misled by analogical reasonings in opposition to the dictates of plain sense and experience'. Aikin sets out strict rules for evaluating the validity of analogical argument: 'It ought never to be forgotten that analogy, though frequently the sole applicable mode of argumentation, is always much short of real proof, and never carries the weight of experiment and observation. Very often indeed, it is no more than the sport of a lively imagination led away by a happy simile or a slight conformity . . .'[68] Aikin's strictures underscore an enduring paradox of Burke's eloquence, especially problematic for those who seek to interpret his words

---

67 Burke, *Reflections*, pp. 83–4.
68 John Aikin, 'On Reasoning from Analogy', in *Essays Literary and Miscellaneous* (London, 1811), pp. 432, 440.

and works rigorously as philosophical texts. For the philosopher and political theorist, the power of Burke's eloquence complicates the task of evaluating his arguments and his assumptions.

Romantic writers were soon to make much more sweeping claims for 'poetic analogy', as Ralph Waldo Emerson calls it: an idealist, Platonic view that the language of analogy is true because there is an underlying divine world of correspondences that makes it true. In Emerson's phrase, 'All thinking is analogizing, and 'tis the use of life to learn metonymy.'[69] This more exalted view of analogy contributes to the Romantic and nineteenth-century revaluation of Burke, his canonisation as the father of modern-day conservatism. Yet for Burke, analogy and the whole panoply of figurative language and imagery always remain pledged to the service of practical ends. His strength is in using such language to link the abstract and the concrete, the intellectual and the emotional, making his ideas relevant to the tangible concerns of his auditors and readers. His thought remains, as he himself said, that of a 'philosopher in action'.[70]

An adequate understanding of political eloquence in Britain during the 1770s and 1780s demands that we approach the subject from several points of view simultaneously. One approach is to ascertain what eloquence meant in its original historical context, how it functioned as a set of cultural practices shaped by the political institutions, social realities and power relations of the period. This kind of study establishes the norms of eloquence, the assumptions that governed the intelligibility of eloquent utterances in the late eighteenth century. Yet, it also makes us aware to what extent great writers and speakers such as Burke, Paine and Sheridan exceeded and transformed the context of eloquence in which they found themselves. To understand the greatness of their eloquence, we must strive to grasp in all its historical particularity the setting from which it emerged. Only then is it possible to evaluate the degree to which, in Burke's case, his utterances achieved a level of historical authority and philosophical generality rarely equalled in the career of a practising politician.

69 Ralph Waldo Emerson, *Poetry and Imagination*, in *Ralph Waldo Emerson*, The Oxford Authors, ed. Richard Poirier (Oxford: Oxford University Press, 1990), p. 445.
70 Burke, *Thoughts*, vol. II, p. 317.

PART VI

*

CONCLUSION

30

More is different: literary change in the mid and late eighteenth century

CLIFFORD SISKIN

> Because something is happening here
> But you don't know what it is
> Do you, Mr Jones?   Bob Dylan[1]

Something happened

Between 1700 and 1800 the body of writing we now call 'Literature' changed.[2] Whatever the exact placement of the bookends or the particular labels, all of our literary histories of the eighteenth century tell tales of difference. Even proponents of the 'long' eighteenth century extend the time frame not because they presume continuity but because they want the discontinuities *within* their area of expertise. While there is considerable disagreement about the date and nature of those changes, our anthologies enshrine the overall effect: what began as Neoclassical or Augustan ended as Romantic. We know something happened during the eighteenth century but we are not quite sure what it was.

The task is complicated from the start – that is, from our failure to agree on when the 'eighteenth century' starts. Although some of our anthologies and literary histories observe the double zeroes, most bundle it into a larger

I wish to thank my research assistant at the University of Glasgow, Thomas Mole, for his invaluable help in exploring earlier literary histories and in thinking about new ones.

1 Bob Dylan, 'Ballad of a Thin Man' in *Writings and Drawings* (New York: Alfred. A. Knopf, 1973), p. 190.
2 To signal the sacralization of texts, I am suggesting a typographical shorthand: 'literature' with a lower-case 'l' refers to the inclusive category of all kinds of writing; the upper-case version, 'Literature,' refers to the modern, disciplinary category. See my discussion of the consensus regarding the historicity of the term later in this chapter (pp. 810–11). For my contribution to the consensus, see Clifford Siskin, *The Work of Writing: Literature and Social Change in Britain 1700–1830* (Baltimore, MD: Johns Hopkins University Press, 1998), pp. 5–7.

package that starts decades earlier than 1700.[3] Paired with the Restoration, as in this volume, the eighteenth century becomes part of a period (1660–1780) that is fully one-third in the seventeenth century. Blackwell raises that percentage to 40 by pushing the start date back to an even earlier political event; their 1996 anthology runs from the English Civil War (1640) to the French Revolution (1789). 'Both events', notes the editor, 'influenced literature.'[4]

Whatever the wisdom of turning to such events, or the difficulty of measuring their influence, that practice has complicated all efforts to identify literary change *during* the chronological eighteenth century. Conditioned by the notion that the political causes or marks shifts in the literary, we are not sure what to do about change that appears to occur in the absence of such links. Despite an almost constant state of war throughout the century, both at home and abroad,[5] we have not found a political event on which to hang a new label or help explain the origins of an existing one. Was there only minor variation in literature before the Bastille? And was Romanticism thus a revolutionary revelation? Or, can we look beyond the assumptions that frame our volumes and find other means of sighting and explaining significant difference?

Almost all of the historical scholarship on the mid and late eighteenth century arises from attempts to answer one or both of the first two questions. On the one hand are claims of significant variation under a range of rubrics (e.g., 'Sensibility') and dates; on the other, are theoretically- and archivally-driven efforts to explain Romanticism's connection to the writing that preceded it. My purpose in this chapter is to bring both enterprises to bear upon the third question. Aided by new notions of change generated in other disciplines, as well as our own efforts to treat 'Literature' itself as a changing category, I want to make sense of the feeling that haunts all of our earlier labours: that something important *did* happen back then.

A survey of recent literary histories and anthologies does yield some usual suspects, in regard to both the dates and rubrics of change:

3 The eighteenth century is grouped with the Restoration in both the Oxford and Norton anthologies of English Literature. See Harold Bloom, Lionel Trilling, Martin Price, J. B. Trapp, Frank Kermode and John Hollander (eds.), *The Oxford Anthology of English Literature*, 2 vols. (Oxford: Oxford University Press, 1973), and M. H. Abrams and Stephen Greenblatt, (eds.), *The Norton anthology of English Literature*, 7th edn., 2 vols. (New York, London: Norton, 2000).

4 Robert DeMaria Jr. (ed.), *British Literature 1640–1789: An Anthology* (Oxford: Blackwell, 1996), p. xxiii. The editor's choice of boundary dates is, of course, subject to the demands of the publisher and the market.

5 Recent studies of Jacobitism have emphasised the ongoing violence in eighteenth–century Britain. See, for example, Eveline Cruickshanks and Jeremy Black (eds.), *The Jacobite Challenge* (Edinburgh: John Donald Publishers, 1988).

Dates – The one specific date that repeatedly surfaces in these accounts is 1740. Although some critics have gestured towards linking it to the political – the end of Walpole's ministerial reign – it is, as we shall see, most commonly addressed as a shift in authorial generations and/or styles and kinds. Whatever began there is seen always as yielding to Romanticism, but the moment of transition depends on the particular rubric at issue; the possibilities extend over three full decades, from the 1770s to 1800, with 1789 the familiar favourite.

The more general chronological pointers are, of course, the terms 'mid' and 'late'. The former gets a whole volume of the *Oxford History of English Literature*, its lack of specificity a seemingly innocuous acknowledgement of the difficulty of periodisation. However, the *Mid–Eighteenth Century* is, in fact, followed in that series by a volume that pins itself down precisely to *1789–1815*,[6] highlighting the difficulty specific to the eighteenth century: the absence of Bastilles and Waterloos. 'Mid' is not the solution for the Modern Language Association, however, which drops that range entirely, opting for dividing the eighteenth century into 'early' and 'late'. Where, then, do the 1740s belong? This is no trivial matter for Quintana and Whitley, whose anthology of English poetry specifies both the *Mid and Late Eighteenth Century*, arguing that '1740 to 1800 constitutes what is properly to be regarded as a definite era'. Only three sentences later, however, the 'definite' softens into the less determinate norm of eighteenth-century studies as the editors more tentatively restate the range as the 'art and culture of these five *or* six decades' (emphasis mine).[7]

Rubrics – Perhaps in part *because* it is such a chronologically indeterminate period, the number of attempts to pin at least parts of the eighteenth century down with labels is astonishing. We have smothered it with claims regarding periods and ages defined in terms of authors, genres, philosophical concepts and – most strangely and powerfully – even other periods. After the opening-decades alternatives of Neoclassical versus Augustan, the tagging goes into high gear. 1740 is, variously, the start

---

6 John Butt, *The Mid-Eighteenth Century*, in John Buxton and Norman Davis (eds.), *The Oxford History of English Literature*, 13 vols., vol. VIII (Oxford: Clarendon Press, 1979); W. L. Renwick, *English Literature 1789–1815*, in F. P. Wilson and Bonamy Dobree (eds.), *The Oxford History of English Literature*, 12 vols., vol. IX (Oxford: Clarendon Press, 1963).

7 Ricardo Quintana and Alvin Whitley (eds.), *English Poetry of the Mid and Late Eighteenth Century: An Historical Anthology* (New York: Knopf, 1963), p. 3. All further references in the text are to this edition.

of The Age of Johnson, The Aesthetic School of Poetry, The Elevation of the Novel, The Age of Prose, The Rise of the Periodical, Sensibility, Sentiment, Literary Loneliness, The Graveyard School, The Literature of Process, The Literature of Insubstantiality, The Mid Eighteenth Century and The Mid and Late Eighteenth Century. Perhaps out of guilt, after celebrating the first few decades, 1700–1745, *as* 'Eighteenth-Century Literature', the *Norton Anthology* lavishes a title of monarchical length on 1740–1785: 'The Emergence of New Literary Themes and Modes'.[8]

There is, of course, no lack of labels for the themes and modes that emerged in the latter decades of that span, 'Gothic' the most prominent among them. Hovering over all of these suspects and often obscuring their individual features, however, is the shadow cast by the period to come: the spectre – certainly horrific to those who see it as dismissive of the texts it describes – of 'preromanticism'.

The principle of convenience

The problem in pulling any of these suspects out of the line-up – or opting for preromantic – is not just not knowing what significant change looks like, but not knowing *how* to find out. In the absence of shared procedures and criteria, earlier efforts at identifying change are, as a group, strikingly haphazard – sometimes disarmingly so: 'All divisions of time in literary history are artificial and arbitrary', begins John Butt's mid-eighteenth century volume of *The Oxford History of English Literature*, 'but 1740 is as *convenient* a year to choose as any for the beginning of a new period' (p. 1, emphasis mine). Our histories are certainly 'artificial' in the sense of being made by us. Whether they are or need be entirely 'arbitrary', however, is another matter, particularly when that claim paves the way for 'convenience' as a first principle of organisation.

That turn to convenience sounds like laziness, but in this case it is more the product of exhaustion. Butt works hard to identify reasons for his periodisation, turning to the primary markers I identified earlier: authors and political events. By 1740, Butt notes, echoing the others who have sought significance in that date, Swift and Pope 'had each made his private retreat'. After sorting his way through a large sampling of dates generated by authorial lives and careers, he suggests that 'it is possible to detect enough evidence of changes in the making, with old careers ending and new careers beginning, to justify the convenience of opening a new volume at 1740' (p. 5).

8 Abrams, *Norton Anthology*, vol. 1, pp. 2060, 2063.

One might expect this justification to suffice, but only if the volume that followed traced those careers. Butt, however, is headed towards a different organisation, and so he explores other rationales. Offering a parallel argument to the reigns of authors, he gestures towards the event I noted earlier, observing that 'in 1740 a different kind of reign was coming to an end. Sir Robert Walpole had been in power with only a brief interval since 1721', retaining office 'until 1742' (p. 2). Following another run of dates that veers back from the political into the literary, Butt offers up yet another 'possible' mode of organisation: 'The interest of the literary scene in the 1740s might even suggest the propriety of organising this volume by surveys of each decade' (p. 5). That option, however, quickly sours. Within a few sentences, Butt finds himself stressing 'the peculiar character of the 1760s', thus implicitly calling into question the singling out of the 1740s as a distinctive moment to start the volume.

The literary historical principle of 'convenience', then, turns out not to be as simple as it sounds. In settling upon a date as simply a matter of convenience, the link between that date and the kind of history that follows is left unresolved. This is obviously the case if the rationale for convenience is left unexplained. However, even if the claim of convenience is elaborated – even if it is shown to be overdetermined, as with Butt – the problem may persist: the rationales may conflict with each other or point to other dates.

I dwell on 'convenience' for it is an astonishingly persistent principle in recent attempts to periodise the eighteenth century. It plays a crucial role, for example, in configuring both ends of the *Norton Anthology*'s effort. Readers of its 'Introduction to the Restoration and the Eighteenth Century' may even feel tempted to thank the 'literature of the period between 1660 and 1785' for co-operating so fully with our classificatory desires: it 'divides *conveniently*', we are informed, 'into three lesser periods of about forty years each' (emphasis mine, vol. i, p. 2053). Here, 'convenience' does sound almost like 'luck', but when the principle returns in volume ii to introduce the next major period, its specialised role in the anthology's process of periodisation is more clearly revealed.

That process closely follows the hermeneutic logic of taxonomising described by David Perkins. 'Literary histories are made out of literary histories', claims Perkins; 'not only their classifications but also their plots are derived from previous histories of the same field.'[9] The *Norton* declares its debt early in the Introduction: 'Following a widespread practice of historians

---

9 David Perkins, *Is Literary History Possible?* (Baltimore, MD: Johns Hopkins University Press, 1992), p. 73.

of English literature, we denote by the "Romantic period" the span between the year 1785, the midpoint of the decade in which Samuel Johnson died and Blake and Burns published their first poems, and 1830, by which time the major writers of the preceding century were either dead or no longer productive' (vol. II, p. 2). With the prior classification in mind, observes Perkins, 'reasoning goes from the concept to the canon, from the canon to the concept', confirming 'the validity of the classification . . . itself every time the texts are read' (*Is Literary History Possible?*, p. 72).

The *Norton* hops aboard that merry-go-round, but in a way that reveals how the most astute literary historians – because they *are* astute – can fall off. What if they have more than one 'prior classification' in mind, particularly one pertaining to a prior period? That is precisely what happens to the *Norton* editors as they try to move from the inherited concept of Romanticism to the canon that will validate it. Their thoughts continue to be shaped not only by that concept but also by their own prior conception of 1740–85 as the 'Emergence' of the 'New': 'especially in the 1740s and later there had emerged many of the critical concepts, as well as a number of the poetic subjects and forms, that were later exploited by Wordsworth and his contemporaries' (*Norton*, vol. I, pp. 6–7). How, then, can the Romantic represent a major new period when it merely 'exploited' the creations of a 'lesser period'? Can the *Norton* keep the circle going (concept>text>concept) by reasserting that 'Wordsworth's Preface *nevertheless* deserves its reputation as a turning point in English literature' (emphasis mine, vol. II, p. 7)?

The answer turns out to be, yet again, a matter of convenience. Thanks to Wordsworth, who 'gathered up isolated ideas, organized them . . . and made them the rationale for his own achievements', 'we can *conveniently*', the *Norton* assures us, 'use the concepts in this influential essay as points of departure for a survey of distinctive elements that are widespread in the theory and poetry of the Romantic period' (emphasis mine, vol. II, p. 7). Notice the repetitive diction – the 'widespread' 'elements' of the 'Romantic period' echoing the earlier intention of following the 'widespread practice' of denoting the 'Romantic period'. With Wordsworth providing convenience rather than originality, the *Norton* can reinscribe that standard practice, passing it on intact to its readers. Here, then, is another literary-historical function of 'convenience', not just as a lucky break that turns the previous 120 years into three easy pieces, but as the grease that keeps the hermeneutic circle smoothly turning.

For the mid and late eighteenth century, convenience-driven hermeneutics has meant ongoing marginalisation: 249 pages for 1740–85 in the seventh edition of the Norton versus 1,042 pages for the next forty-five years – the

Romantic ones.[10] The circularity appears to undermine our ability to change our understanding of change. We know that something important happened back then, but we conveniently fail to make that something important *to* our literary histories. The inertia envelopes consumers as well as producers. 'To the extent that readers already know the traditional taxonomies', points out Perkins, 'they expect them in literary histories. A literary historian who proposes different taxonomies must make an argument' (*Is Literary History Possible?*, p. 73).

From convenience to the click (the persistence of preromanticism)

No argument about the mid and late eighteenth century has been more powerful and more persistent than 'preromanticism'. And no single argument has been deployed in such drastically different ways. Originally formulated as a developmental tale in which Romanticism qualitatively culminates all that has gone before, preromanticism has been a mode of aesthetic subordination, at best, and of derisive dismissal, at worst. Either way, writing that may have seemed new, and potentially unsettling, became secondary and reassuring when put in its supposedly proper place as prelude to what came later. Preromanticism told us, that is, that we were right all along: the (Romantic) literature that we already valued was revalorised as a product of progress.

That story was first told, of course, by the Romantics themselves. From Wordsworth's denigration of Gray to Keats' 'grand march of intellect',[11] they cast the past as pointing to them. Before the nineteenth century was out, the critics followed. In 1893, William Lyons Phelps sought *The Beginnings of the English Romantic Movement* in a book subtitled *A Study in Eighteenth-Century Literature*. A few decades later, Eric Partridge claimed to have found more than just beginnings, identifying specific examples of

---

10 Since the *Norton Anthology* entries for 1740–1785 are not marked off from the rest of 'The Restoration and the Eighteenth Century' – and the divisions have a five-year overlap (1700–45 / 1740–85) – the count is a bit more complicated than the clearly delimited 'Romantic Period.' Since Pope is treated by the *Norton* as a writer of 'Eighteenth-Century Literature' (1700–45), I have not included works that spill over into the 1740s. I have, however, included in the count works published in the 1740s by Lady Mary Wortley Montagu and Mary Leapor.

11 See the Preface to *Lyrical Ballads* in William Wordsworth, *The Prose Works of William Wordsworth*, eds. W. J. B. Owen and Jane Worthington Smyser, 3 vols. (Oxford: Clarendon Press, 1974), vol. I, p. 132, and John Keats *Letters of John Keats*, ed. Robert Gittings (Oxford: Oxford University Press, 1970), p. 96.

what he called *Eighteenth-Century English Romantic Poetry*.[12] Processed by pre-romanticism, mid and late eighteenth-century texts became either preliminary or precocious, undeveloped versions of what was to come or the earliest, isolated examples of it.

Historically and conceptually, then, that process has been – yet again – a matter of convenience: once the Romantics set themselves up at the head of a developmental literary history, preromanticism has been the classificatory path of least resistance. Critics, that is, have found it easier to follow Romanticism's self-description than to come up with an alternative. Even those who recognise the consequences seem to find it hard to diverge very far from the beaten track. Worrying that mid and late eighteenth-century writing gets no 'identity of its own', Quintana and Whitley reject preromanticism in order to grant 'some importance' to understanding the age 'for its own sake'. But then they insist that 'it is equally important that we do so in order to clarify our understanding both of neoclassicism and romanticism' (*Historical Authology*, p. 3). Thomas Woodman similarly blames preromanticism for our judging the age 'solely and mainly' in terms of 'anticipation of what is to come', but then, echoing Partridge, decisively *re*-centres the 'what' in his volume's title: *Early Romantics*.[13]

If removing the label 'preromanticism' fails to free our literary histories of Romanticentrism, then why not try the counterintuitive move and keep it, but *as* a decentring device? In a brash and brilliant assertion of convenience, Marshall Brown stopped scraping away at this very sticky label and simply allowed it to do its work of highlighting the problem of periodisation. Rejecting both the preliminary and precocious variations of preromanticism, Brown invokes the term as a marker of difference. On the one hand, 'it does not designate a preliminary state of romanticism or a predisposition'; on the other, 'eighteenth-century writers either are romantics or they are not . . . they cannot

---

12 William Lyon Phelps, *The Beginnings of the English Romantic Movement; A Study in Eighteenth-Century Literature* (Boston: Ginn and Co., 1893). Eric Partridge, *Eighteenth-Century English Romantic Poetry (Up Till the Publication of the 'Lyrical Ballads', 1798)* (Paris, 1924; rpt. London: Norwood Editions, 1979). See also J. R. Watson (ed.), *Pre-Romanticism in English Poetry of the Eighteenth Century: The Poetic Art and Significance of Thomas Gray, Collins, Goldsmith, Cowper, Crabbe: A Casebook* (London: Macmillan, 1989).

13 From all of the writing of the age he is trying to highlight, Woodman, citing one of his contributors (David Fairer) fixes on Thomas Warton's use of the term 'romantic' in 1745. 'What, specifically,' he asks, 'is the relationship between this body of poetry and the later Romanticism as it is more commonly understood?' This is, of course, a legitimate and fascinating question – as are many asked and addressed in his volume, but it does perpetuate the Romantic fixation of preromanticism. See Thomas Woodman (ed.), *Early Romantics: Perspectives in British Poetry from Pope to Wordsworth* (New York and London: Macmillan/St Martin's Press, 1998), p. 2.

be both of their age and of a later one.' Teleology is thus not a problem for Brown but a solution. To be 'teleological enough' is to insist that the telos is a 'goal' that is 'not yet there when a teleological process is under way'. Brown's preromanticism is '*not yet* Romantic', and for that reason can be studied in its own terms.[14]

This use of the label does allow for sustained attention to mid and late eighteenth-century texts, but it leaves open the crucial theoretical and historical question of when and how writing shifts from the not-Romantic to the Romantic. Brown cites as 'closest' to his 'approach' Virgil Nemoianu's argument that 'the core of a high-Romantic alternative model was constituted when, say, around 1790, these autonomous modifications connected with an almost audible click'. There is something reassuring, almost comforting, about this notion of change: if we add enough features to the mix, at some point, somehow, everything will fall conveniently into place. In fact, if we think of 'convenience' as a matter more of 'fitness' and 'congruity'[15] than of 'chance' and 'luck', then the click, too, joins our list of convenience-based literary histories.

Brown is clearly wary of the apparent simplicity of such an explanation, arguing that the 'click' mechanism must be theoretically retrofitted to stand up under the burden of literary-historical inquiry. Nemoianu's description of the 'historical process', he argues, should be more 'dialectical': 'the Romantic 'click' comes only in part from adding together dispersed preromantic initiatives; it comes far more from resolving problems that the preromantic authors imaginatively projected' (*Preromanticism*, p. 386). In its dependence on authorial imaginations, the solution Brown engineers is aesthetic and highly normative: organising his book around 'masterpieces', he argues that 'the greatest authors in their greatest moments engaged in rigorously controlled struggles toward new modes of expression' (p. 3).

The issue here is the respective roles of the quantitative and the qualitative in our explanations of literary change. For Brown, the emphasis is on the qualitative. Unlike the standard deployments of preromanticism, his version does find masterpieces and greatness *in* the mid and late eighteenth century. Locating them is important to his kind of history, for he sees them as valuable both in themselves and as the engine of change, projecting problems that are

14 Marshall Brown, *Preromanticism* (Stanford, CA: Stanford University Press, 1991), pp. 2–6 and his example of the use of the terms in the Notes (1–4) p. 385. Woodman cites Brown's effort as 'bold' but does not differentiate it from earlier deployments of the term.
15 See the first three meanings in the *OED*. Etymologically, 'convenience' is from Latin 'convenientia, meeting together, agreement, accord, harmony, conformity'.

resolved by something new. Yet in his descriptions of that resolution – the click – a quantitative principle still seems at work: 'when new resources were found – and it happened with astonishing suddenness for Wordsworth, for Kant . . . the floodgates opened' (pp. 2–3). Whether the gates unlocked with a click of genius or gave way to a thunderous overflow of new resources, Brown's use of 'preromanticism' as a marker of difference makes a difference. It tests the limits of convenience, highlighting the tasks facing any new history of eighteenth-century literature. I am not suggesting that any intellectual strategy can or should avoid convenience, only that we be both wary of depending on it and aware of its effects. Literary history must, on the one hand, engage and explain change without recycling the developmental narratives already told by the texts being examined. On the other, it cannot shy away from the specific questions of quantity and quality posed by the 'click' – of whether and how things can add up to something else.

The new eighteenth century: quantity and quality

If new resources make for a click, then two centuries after the Romantic one, modern critics of the eighteenth century may have experienced their own. In the 1970s and 1980s, starting with the pioneering work of women scholars – including Janet Todd, Betty Rizzo, Germaine Greer and Gina Luria – the corpus of eighteenth-century writing began to take on a new look – one distinctly different from its existing canon of major and even minor writers. The mid 1980s was the watershed, with the publication in quick succession of Todd's *Dictionary of British and American Women Writers 1660–1800* in 1985, Dale Spender's *Mothers of the Novel* the next year, and Roger Lonsdale's *Eighteenth-Century Women Poets* a short time later (1989).[16] Suddenly, the profession at large had access to and knowledge about an extraordinarily broad range of texts and writers it had forgotten or ignored.

The shock was amplified by the publication at that same moment of Lonsdale's *New Oxford Book of Eighteenth-Century Verse* (1984). Over 800 pages long, it recovered works by males and females alike; perhaps more significantly, given the high proportion of such texts – over 60 per cent of all poetry books in the

---

16 Janet Todd (ed.), *Dictionary of British and American Women Writers 1660–1800* (London and Totowa, NJ: Methuen/Rowman and Allanheld, 1984), Dale Spender, *Mothers of the Novel: 100 Good Women Writers before Jane Austen* (London: Pandora, 1986), Roger Lonsdale (ed.), *The New Oxford Book of Eighteenth Century Verse* (Oxford: Oxford University Press, 1984).

1770s[17] – it featured those published anonymously as well. Subsequently and repeatedly acknowledged as 'pioneering',[18] this volume in conjunction with the others reconstituted the raw material of eighteenth-century studies, particularly the canonically threadbare middle. Scholarly production has certainly been affected, as have syllabi, and new anthologies have followed. However, the impact has not yet been felt at the level of periodisation – both dates and labels – and of arguments about literary-historical change.[19] In those areas of inquiry, more has strangely meant the same.

Even more strangely, Lonsdale himself seems to have anticipated the inertia. 'The history and the nature of eighteenth-century poetry may well appear disappointingly uncontentious topics', he observes in the Introduction; 'the general reader seems to know all too well what to expect from the age of Good Taste and Common Sense.' The next paragraph rehearses what he calls the 'readjustments' in the consensus, including generally minor shifts in authorial reputations, Northrop Frye's effort to highlight an 'age of sensibility' between 'reptilian Classicism' and 'mammalian Romanticism' and the recognition of a 'variety of interesting individual voices' in mid century. The ensuing summary of the literary history into which all of this has settled paints a familiar picture of those decades: 'between 1740 and 1760, the poets began retreating dispiritedly into a twilit, rural landscape to brood on Fancy and Melancholy . . . turning their backs on public experience, and losing any capacity or desire to observe the actualities of contemporary life with any precision or immediacy, let alone to transform them imaginatively' (*Eighteenth-Century Verse*, pp. xxxiii–xxxv). The diction is so precise and the delivery so sure-handed, that one might easily assume the opinions to be the author's own.

Perhaps this initial sense of authoritative familiarity is why the Introduction has been largely ignored by those trying to absorb the volume's content.

---

17 Lee Erickson, '"Unboastful Bard": Originally Anonymous English Romantic Poetry Book Publication, 1770–1835', *New Literary History* 33 (2002), 247. This article forms part of a special issue of *NLH* on anonymity.

18 See, for example, David Fairer and Christine Gerrard (eds.), *Eighteenth-Century Poetry: An Annotated Anthology* (Oxford: Blackwell, 1999), p. ixx.

19 The issue here is not whether these recovery efforts in general, and Lonsdale's anthology in particular, have inspired new readings of individual texts or even larger-scale reassessments of entire genres – they have. New histories of the novel, particularly ones featuring women novelists abound, and the poetry has also been reassessed. See, for example, Suvir Kaul, *Poems of Nation, Anthems of Empire: English Verse in the Long Eighteenth Century* (Charlottesville, VA: University Press of Virginia, 2000). Whether the new texts and authors and these studies of them will combine to reshape our literary histories is another matter. To take that step, I am arguing, we will need new conceptions of literary change.

Readers who persevere into the second section, however, will discover an essay that is as innovative as the selections it frames. It begins with a challenge to the orthodoxy that has just been rehearsed: 'Since the landscape of eighteenth-century poetry is now apparently so well mapped and likely to afford so few unexpected perspectives . . . it will seem outrageous to suggest that we still know very little about the subject' (p. xxxv). What issues would prompt Lonsdale to risk outrage? They turn out to be precisely the ones that motivate Brown's adventure with preromanticism – but in the opposite order of importance. The overriding message of Lonsdale's anthology is not claims of neglected quality, but, first and foremost, 'the sheer quantity of verse published in the century'. At this point in the Introduction, the bland rehearsal of literary-historical truisms gives way to the quantitative sublime: 'the thousands of substantial, separately published poems, the hundreds of volumes of collected poems by individual authors, the innumerable miscellanies by several hands, all the verse in the poetry sections of hundreds of magazines and newspapers' (pp. xxxv–xxxvi). In the face of these numbers, our limited literary histories stand accused of embodying an extraordinary intellectual arrogance. How can we be satisfied knowing so little in the face of so much?

It is not that the qualitative is not a central concern for Lonsdale. In fact, he addresses it head on, albeit in a somewhat mischievous manner: 'Yet the problem, *if it is allowed to be a problem*, of what is "literary" and what is "non-literary" may well confront some readers at various points in this anthology' (p. xxxviii). The qualification I have emphasised confirms Lonsdale's priorities: the point of the anthology is the shock of quantity in all of its variety – a wake-up call that should not be blunted by undue concern with its literariness. To achieve that end, he is even willing to dabble in some (perverse) pre-romanticism, putting Wordsworth's Preface to work valorising the verse that *Lyrical Ballads* is usually seen as superseding. 'In these and some other cases' of 'naivety or even clumsiness', suggests Londsdale regarding some of his less familiar authors, 'the reader may well "look round for poetry, and . . . be induced to enquire by what species of courtesy these attempts can be permitted to assume the title". If so, I am content to let these and many other poets anticipate the supposedly revolutionary challenge to polite taste which Wordsworth would introduce with these words in 1798' (p. xxxviii). The 'supposedly' was as close as Lonsdale came to a direct challenge to the standard shape of our literary histories. To have taken the next step and actually have formulated an alternative might have detracted from the revolutionary nature of the volume itself; its content alone was controversial enough in 1985. To keep readers focussed on the texts themselves, Lonsdale insisted on maintaining scholarly decorum, reassuring readers that his 'aim is less to subvert traditional accounts of the nature and development of eighteenth-century poetry than to supplement them' (p. xxxvii).

If those accounts had been – in the interim – productively supplemented, providing a more coherent and consistent history of change, then it might still be prudent to share Lonsdale's prudence. The ongoing confusion I have described, however – the cacophony of dates, labels and explications, especially for the mid and late century – suggests that it may now be time for change in our own practice. The traditional accounts, that is, have subverted themselves, and prudence suggests that we should re-aim our efforts. Now that the initial shock has worn off, the newly expanded eighteenth century can receive more than a brief Introduction. I would like to extend Lonsdale's advertisement for his anthology into a more systematic preface by picking up where he and Brown left off: the roles of quality and quantity in literary history. The issue is not what they (and others) did not do but what has happened since. Discussions of both issues were transformed at the end of the twentieth century – recast in ways that can, I will argue, cast new light on what *did* happen in the mid and late eighteenth century.

Quality and the historicity of literature

As long as the distinction between the literary and the non-literary is seen as a matter of 'absolute value' (Quintana and Whitley, *Historical Anthology*, p. 3), writing from those decades prompts two typical reactions. The most common is embarrassment. 'It seems scarcely necessary to point out', confess Quintana and Whitley, who do so anyway, 'that the poetry of these years is not the greatest in the language'(p. 3). Even Marshall Brown's more sympathetic view is carefully hedged: 'Masterpieces are few, and no major author of the period produced with anything like the ease of a Pope or a Wordsworth' (*Preromanticism*, 2).

The other standard response is the silver-lining defence. 'When such verse appears artless, unsubtle or inelegant', writes Lonsdale, 'I hope that qualities of individuality and freshness will compensate' (*Eighteenth-Century Verse*, p. xxxviii). Although usually understood to be a positive quality, 'individuality' has a more chequered history when applied to mid and late eighteenth-century authors. From Smart to Cowper and even Johnson, their distinctive features are often read as signs of individuality gone astray into eccentricity, self-absorption and madness. Compounding the problem, the formal features of their works are then marshalled as textual evidence of those maladies, and of an overall achievement that is reaffirmed as not quite 'like' – to use Brown's word – Pope's or Wordsworth's. Thus the compensatory qualities that Lonsdale attributes to mid and late eighteenth-century writing only exacerbate the 'problem' of its relationship to the qualitative.

Perhaps, then, we should take our cue not from those qualities but from the mischievous qualification that precedes them: '*if* it is allowed to be a problem' (emphasis mine Lonsdale, *Eighteenth-Century Verse*, p. xxxviii). Can there be a good reason, in the specific case of the mid and late eighteenth century, to avoid the problem of literariness? In 1984, Lonsdale most likely had in mind a simple holding action – a willing suspension of judgement for the sake of experiencing his quantitative sublime. But what if that experience of new resources changes our understanding not just of literary history, but of the history of the literary itself? We might then discover that the problem lies not just with the writing of that time – an assumption of the embarrassment and silver-lining scenarios – but in the way that writing and our criteria intersect.

That realisation is just now emerging from our encounter with the new eighteenth century. During the 1990s, historians of literature turned fully on their own object of inquiry, arriving at what even its critics now call a 'consensus'[20] regarding the historicity of 'literature' itself. This self-reflexive project put the field's fundamental qualitative distinction – literary versus non-literary – on to a new footing. The historical and theoretical foundations for doing so were laid in the 1970s and 1980s as critics recovered and then contemplated the full breadth of writing's past. 'Among all the narratives', asked Foucault, 'why is it that a number of them are sacralized, made to function as "literature"?'[21] The explanation, of course, is complex, but the nature and timing of the change turned out to be straightforward; it is captured quite clearly in the lexicographic record. The word that referred through most of the eighteenth century to all kinds of writing – *Britannica* still defined 'literature' in the 1770s as simply 'learning or skill in letters' – came, in the space of a few decades, to refer more narrowly to only certain texts within certain genres.[22] It came to define, that is, the specialised subject matter of a discipline.

The current consensus on our own historicity is thus a twofold proposition:

20 For an overview of the debate see *Eighteenth-Century Life* 21. 1 (1997).
21 Michel Foucault, 'The Functions of Literature' (dialogue with Roger-Pol Droit), trans. Alan Sheridan, in Michel Foucault, *Politics, Philosophy, Culture: Interviews and Other Writings, 1977–1984* (New York and London: Routledge, 1988), p. 308.
22 *Encyclopaedia Britannica*, 2nd edn, ed. James Tytler, 10 vols. (Edinburgh, 1777–84) and see Raymond Williams, *Keywords: A Vocabulary of Culture and Society* (New York: Oxford University Press, 1983), pp. 183–8.

First, that the category of 'literature' is historically variable; and

Second, that the modern variation – the subset of writing we now study as 'Literature' – emerged from the eighteenth century.

That scenario leaves the mid and late part of the century in a very awkward position. Might our pathologising of so many of its authors and texts, as well as the apparent laziness and confusion of our convenience-based histories, be at least in part the products of an anachronism – of a historical mismatch between categories and material? Let me be precise about the unique nature of that mismatch. If it was simply a matter of the material being written *before* the categories were formed, the situation would be problematic, but not any more than it would be for sixteenth- or seventeenth-century writing. The mid and late eighteenth century has been such a distinctive literary historical trouble spot – so many labels, yet so conspicuously absent from the anthologies – because it was the moment *in which* the categories were formed.

Think of Lonsdale's 'problem' of 'what is 'literary' and what is 'non-literary' in this light. The difficulty *peculiar* to a mid and late eighteenth-century text is not determining whether it is literary or what 'literary' itself is, but grasping the way in which the text is trapped between the two: its historical role in establishing the latter shapes the answer to the former. Wordsworth's 'problem' with Gray's sonnet, for example, is that he determines that only six of its lines are 'of any value' (*Prose Works*, pp. 132, 134). The other eight, he asserts, are 'curiously elaborate' in their 'poetic diction', and are thus of no use in a 'good poem'. For Gray, however, those are exactly the lines that do serve a specific qualitative purpose: he heightens their diction in order to secure poetry's special place in an expanding – more genres and more texts – literary field. In other words, both writers share the same goal of establishing literariness for poetry, but Wordsworth dismisses Gray for precisely the features that Gray employs to make that distinction.[23]

Just as we have felt compelled to divide up and label the eighteenth century again and again, so Wordsworth cannot judge Gray's poem as whole but must slice and dice, preserving a few bits but throwing out most. He experiences it as a mix: some parts from the past and some that speak to the present. Like us, he claims to be somewhat puzzled by this hybridity: it is 'curiously elaborate'. But Gray's decision to elaborate is, historically, anything but puzzling; given his position in literary history, it is both sensible and predictable. Poetic diction was already a hierarchical marker and was thus an obvious choice for elaboration as

---

23 The historical irony, then, is that the very features Gray employs to help set standards of literariness turn out to be the means by which his own literariness is (partially) denied.

the pressure on that hierarchy grew. By emphasising and enacting the inherited notion that 'the language of the age is never the language of poetry',[24] Gray was taking the practical step of using an available tool to tackle the suddenly more pressing task of lifting certain kinds of writing out of the growing mass of print. This tactic only *seems* like curious excess when the pressure is being handled in another manner. Whereas Gray tried to hierarchise by stressing difference through the elaboration of inherited features, Wordsworth hit upon the now conventional method of collapsing distinctions of kind in order to assert a new hierarchy of what we would now call aesthetic degree: poetry is just like prose but more pleasurable.[25]

The fact that we now apply the term 'aesthetic' to mid-century writers – Quintana and Whitley refer to 'the aesthetic school, the Wartons, the later Young, Gray, and Collins' (*Historical Anthology*, p. 5) – highlights the historical twist at work here. It was not, of course, their term, for the word was probably first used in Britain by William Taylor in the *Monthly Review* in 1798, the year so closely associated with Romanticism. However, it does date back in Germany to mid century. Taylor references Kant (1781), who critiques a duality of usage that he traces back to Baumgarten (1750–8): on the one hand, 'aesthetic' was linked etymologically to the study of the 'senses'; on the other, it performed the qualitative function that Coleridge reluctantly employs in 1821: 'I wish I could find a more familiar word than aesthetic, for works of taste and criticism.'[26]

Coleridge's usage became not only familiar but dominant by the mid nine-teenth century,[27] so its earlier connection to sense perception may now strike

---

24 Thomas Gray, *The Correspondence of Thomas Gray*, eds. Paget Toynbee and Leonard Whibley 3 vols. (Oxford: Clarendon Press, 1935), vol. I, p. 192.

25 See my explanation of the kind/degree strategy in Clifford Siskin, *The Historicity of Romantic Discourse* (New York: Oxford University Press, 1988), pp. 46–56, 107–8.

26 [William Taylor], review of *Observations sur le Sentiment du Beau et du Sublime* by Immanuel Kant, trans. Hercules Peyer-Imhoff (Paris, 1796), *The Monthly Review* 25 (1798), 584–5. Immanuel Kant, *Critique of Pure Reason*, trans. Paul Guyer and Allen W. Wood (Cambridge: Cambridge University Press, 1998), pp. 156, 173. Alexander Gottlieb Baumgarten, *Aesthetica* (Frankfurt-an-der-Oder: John Christian Kleyb, 1750–58). Samuel Taylor Coleridge, *Shorter Works and Fragments*, eds. H. J. Jackson and J. R. de J. Jackson, *The Collected Works of Samuel Taylor Coleridge*, 11 vols., Bollingen Series LXXV (Princeton, NJ: Princeton University Press, 1995), vol. II, p. 938.

27 See Sir William Hamilton, *Lectures on Metaphysics and Logic*, ed. H. L. Mansel and J. Veitch. LL.D. 4 vols. (Edinburgh, 1859–60), vol. I, Lecture vii, p. 124:

It is nearly a century since Baumgarten . . . first applied the term Æsthetic to the doctrine which we vaguely and periphrastically denominate the Philosophy of Taste, the theory of the Fine Arts, the Science of the Beautiful, etc., and this term is now in general acceptation, not only in Germany, but throughout the other countries of Europe. The term Apolaustic would have been a more appropriate designation.

us as curious. For the mid and late eighteenth century, however, they went together: the primary strategy for establishing a hierarchy of literary taste was, in fact, writing to the senses. This was the agenda explicitly theorised in 1757 by Edmund Burke. Operating from a view of knowledge that is sensationalistic and experiential, Burke's tract on *The Sublime and Beautiful* elaborates an entire system of human nature and experience through the extension of an absolute distinction between primary categories of pain and pleasure. The detailed descriptions that extend the argument are so saturated with sense that they strike us now as veering beyond the curious into the strange:

> for a single globe, (though somewhat pleasant to the feeling) yet by the regu-
> larity of its form, and the somewhat too sudden deviation of its parts from a
> right line, it is nothing near so pleasant to the touch as several globes, where
> the hand gently rises to one and falls to another; and this pleasure is greatly
> increased if the globes are in motion, and sliding over one another; for this soft
> variety prevents that weariness, which the uniform disposition of the several
> globes would otherwise produce.[28]

In its exquisite attention to the senses – and in its attempt to stimulate and evoke them – this is 'aesthetic' in the etymological sense. The purpose of the whole tract, however, is *also* aesthetic in our modern sense: the *Enquiry* concludes with an entire section on 'Words' that is qualitative and hierarchical. Burke puts the analytic weight of his entire system into an effort to sacralise the literary, raising it above all other form of expression – words work in a way that makes them even more powerful, he claims, than the 'things they represent' (*Enquiry*, p. 177).

The poetry that worries Wordsworth carries the same assumptions and is designed to work in the same fashion. By the 1740s, observe Quintana and Whitley, citing the influence of Hobbes, Locke and Addison, 'the individual was seen as responding to the messages conveyed to him by his senses from the outside world; the artist embodied this sense data in the imagery of the work of art; the reader of the poem or the view of the painting or sculpture experienced the work sensationalistically as he would any other object outside himself' 'This emphasis on effect', they conclude, 'is the outstanding characteristic of the aesthetic school flourishing in the middle decades: how the poet can produce effects with his verbal images, how the reader responds to them' (*Historical Anthology*, p. 8).

28 Edmund Burke, *A Philosophical Enquiry into the Origin of our Ideas of the Sublime and Beautiful*, ed. James T. Boulton (Notre Dame, IN, and London: University of Notre Dame Press, 1958), pp. 152–3.

Writing in the 1960s, before the critical 'click' of the new eighteenth century, Quintana and Whitley's examples are all male. But the case is now far stronger, and its implications clearer, with our current access to more writers, in general, and to women writers in particular. Mary Leapor's 'An Epistle to a Lady' is a template for the time, elaborating the key features of effect-based verse. Her opening effort to secure reader response is to us a curious mix of the conversational, the classical and the highly conventional:

> In vain, dear Madam, yes in vain you strive;
> Alas! to make your luckless Mira thrive.
> For Tycho and Copernicus agree,
> No golden Planet bent its Rays on me.
>
> 'Tis twenty Winters, if it is no more;
> To speak the Truth it may be Twenty four.
>
> (lines 1–6)

The mundane numerology of these last two lines would not seem far out of place in Wordsworth's 'Thorn':

> There is a thorn; it looks so old,
> In truth you'd find it hard to say
>   . . .
> I've measured it from side to side:
> 'Tis three feet long, and two feet wide.[29]

The epistle's other lines, however, would fare as poorly in Wordsworth's Preface as the eight in Gray's sonnet, their fate sealed by their elaborated syntax and conventional figures. For Leapor, those features had a distinct purpose – to lift poetry over prose – but they became liabilities under the different kind of lifting – lifting by degree – that became the singular norm for 'Literature'.

Leapor's mixed 'aesthetic' also prescribes a distinctly different narrative path for her poem. The initial heightening is characteristically followed by the embodiment of sense data in verbal images – a task that often enters the poetry thematically in the form of ekphrastic (that is to say, intensely and expressively visual) fantasies:

---

29 Lines 1–2 and 32–3. These last two lines are as published from 1798 through 1815. In 1820, they were replaced by 'Though but of compass small, and bare / To thirsty suns and parching air.' See *The Poetical Works of William Wordsworth*, ed. Ernest de Selincourt, 5 vols. (Oxford: Clarendon Press, 1941–9), vol. II, p. 241.

> Yet Mira dreams, as slumbring Poets may,
> And rolls in Treasures till the breaking Day:
> While Books and Pictures in bright Order rise,
> And painted Parlours swim before her Eyes:
> Till the shrill Clock impertinently rings,
> And the soft Visions move their shining Wings:
> Then Mira wakes, – her Pictures are no more,
> And through her Fingers slides the vanish'd Ore.
> Convinc'd too soon, her Eye unwilling falls
> On the blue Curtains and the dusty Walls:
> She wakes, alas! to Business and to Woes,
> To sweep her Kitchen, and to mend her Clothes.
>
> (lines 22–33)

Once again, both the diction and the content settle back into a Wordsworthian mundane of prose-like verse and rustic simplicity. For Leapor that becomes possible and desirable *because* it is mixed with the kind of lines that Wordsworth would excise. As a mid-century writer, she saw those lines as not undermining but valorising the text, making it 'aesthetic' in the qualitative sense by imbuing it with the aesthetic in the etymological sense – which was, as we saw in Burke, an emphatic turn to sense itself.

The personifications that Wordsworth abhors are centred and elaborated for just that purpose: by bringing abstract ideas and objects alive, they can become sources of heightened sensation – in this case, auditory as well as visual: we can hear the 'Clock' that paces this passage 'impertinently ring'. The more such figures, then, the better. They populate every poetic venue as active agents[30] that activate our senses. Thus the dense population of personifications roaming the pastoral fields of Gray's 'Eton College' ode – 'black Misfortune's baleful train!' – and the grand abstractions of 'Ambition', 'Grandeur', 'Honour', and 'Knowledge' that haunt the rustic simplicity of his 'Country Churchyard'.

Every mid and late eighteenth-century genre featured these figures, as all forms of writing competed for space in an increasingly crowded literary field. By labelling the language he deplores the 'common inheritance of poets' (*Prose Works*, p. 132), Wordsworth misses both the scope and historical specificity of this competition. He sees only the traditional usage within a single genre – 'expressions' that are 'foolishly repeated by bad poets' – rather than a strategic deployment across writing of all kinds. In prose, for example, even works that appear particularly congenial to Wordsworth's Romantic norm still centre

---

30 See my argument in Siskin, *Historicity*, pp. 68–78.

personifications of abstract ideas as agents to heighten and extend the narrative. Thus Edward Young's *Conjectures on Original Composition* (1759) turns to 'Admiration', rather than a Romantic 'I', to do its 'mischief', and personifies 'Genius' as 'a dear friend' to explore its original take on originality: whether 'men may be strangers to their own abilities'.[31]

The prose of the mid-century novel is equally saturated with such friends – friends in high places – in both conception and execution. Both Henry Fielding and Sarah Fielding conceive of their novels as generic mixes, a key ingredient always being features from established dominant forms. As a 'comic epic-poem in prose', *Joseph Andrews* (1741) seeks to raise the novel's literary profile by 'curiously' elaborating the already elaborate similes of epic. *The Cry*, subtitled *A New Dramatic Fable* (1754), tries to lift itself by lifting from the fable an allegorical design – a design that, as in Gray's poetry, reads the action as the moralistic escapades of personifications: Falsehood is the loser as Affectation and Fallacy battle Truth and Simplicity. From the drama comes another strange elaboration: the dividing of the action into scenes played before an 'audience' of 'allegorical phantoms'.[32]

Sterne was a master of such elaboration, and thus to critics who do not recognise it as a *shared* strategy of the time, he has seemed *sui generis*. But the more curious he appears within our 'aesthetic' norm, the more clearly representative he is of this mid and late eighteenth-century effort at elevation under pressure. Novels like *A Sentimental Journey* are paced, like the poetry, by personifications. At every point that we expect the individual 'I' to take over, they surface to raise the stakes, taking the action to what was then considered literary high ground: a universal human nature. Scene after scene in Sterne's novels, as in contemporary poetry and non-fiction prose, leaves us face-to-face with 'Liberty', 'Nature' and even Sensibility itself as the 'great, great SENSORIUM of the world'.[33]

As increasing competition required greater gradation, these genres also shared the task of framing a narrative *about* that process. Personifications proved particularly useful here as well. Writing began to turn upon itself, telling tales of its own pedigree in poems such as Gray's 'Progress of Poesy' (1754) and Collins' 'Ode on the Poetical Character'(1747). Read in isolation, and with

31 Edward Young, *Conjectures on Original Composition* (1759), A Scolar Press Facsimile (Menston: The Scolar Press, 1966), p. 51.
32 See Siskin, *Historicity*, pp. 132–3 and 86–7.
33 Laurence Sterne, *A Sentimental Journey Through France and Italy*, ed. Graham Petrie (Harmondsworth: Penguin, 1967), pp. 97, 133, 141.

their self-reflexiveness emerging strangely from a personified self, those texts have been taken as preromantic in Brown's weak sense – a flickering of what shone brighter later – rather than as the undertaking that *belongs* peculiarly to the mid and late eighteenth-century: the elaboration of literariness.

With the advent of the new eighteenth century, however, the breadth and persistence of that undertaking have become clear. Not only does it appears across genres, in prose such as Hurd's *Letters on Chivalry and Romance* (1762) and Warton's *History of English Poetry* (1774, 1781, 1785), but across genders as well: the many and mixed forms of women writers have turned out to provide telling testimony to the historicity of Literature. They range from the constituting of a 'Poetical Chronicle' of 'this Island' in Elizabeth Cooper's *The Muse's Library* (1737) to the sacralisation of Shakespeare in Charlotte Lennox's *Shakespear Illustrated* (1753–54), Elizabeth Montagu's *Essay* (1769) and Elizabeth Griffith's examination of his 'morality' (1775).[34]

To recover all of those works now is to recover recovery itself as a characteristic procedure of the mid and late eighteenth century. Percy's *Reliques* and Macpherson's *Ossian*, in league with the efforts mentioned above, spun a thread of literariness out of the tangled history of writing. The forgery controversies that helped to power that effort are as curious to us now as Gray's poetical diction was to Wordsworth – curious because we view them from the shelter of authenticity that we call 'Literature'.[35] As we recover *its* historicity, we can begin to grasp what was at stake back then – the elaboration of literariness on two planes: the vertical distancing of the literary from the everyday, effected by such figures as personification, and the horizontal linking of past to present into a chronicle that valorised that literariness as historical fact.

The resulting formation is *not* ours – the 'aesthetics' are of a different kind – but because we share a goal (differentiating the field of writing) we have had trouble acknowledging the difference. To respect it is to find a new reason – a historical one – for sharing Lonsdale's reluctance to turn the qualitative into a problem for this period. Instead, we can address the problem that *it* poses for us – the problem that Lonsdale and the other agents of the new eighteenth century have made newly visible: the role of the quantitative in literary change.

---

34 For selections from the works of these women, see, *Women Critics 1660–1820 An Anthology* ed. Folger Collective (Bloomington, IN: Indiana University Press, 1995).
35 Because that label does not quite fit mid-and late-century writing, we often find ourselves teaching it under different, mixed rubrics such as 'Poetry and Ideas from Johnson to Blake'.

Quantity and change: more is different

If literature as a category emerges from the quantitative sublime of the eighteenth century – a narrowing in the face of a proliferation – then we need to pin down what proliferated and when. Since the narrowing was both to certain genres and to certain texts in those genres, we may be looking for a two-part increase, one paced, perhaps, by the dates that dominate our standard literary histories: 1740 and 1780. John Butt's ruminations on the former do, in fact, settle, after the exhaustive search I have described, on genre: 'It is within the "kinds", then, that the achievements of the age are to be considered and assessed' (*Mid-Eighteenth Century*, p. 7).

What strikes Butt about the kinds of that time is their growing number and extraordinary variety – an observation that has been echoed in history after history. In *The Routledge History of Literature in English*, for example, the list of 'trends' in 'literary production' through the middle years of the eighteenth century is decidedly generic, emphasising the novel, magazines, criticism, drama and poetry.[36] Lonsdale's exploration of that poetry finds more and more kinds within kinds, a growing diversity after Pope in the 1740s. The Folger Collective is similarly struck by the multiplicity and heterogeneity of form in the criticism by women that they anthologise. Brown's preromanticism argument turns out to be an argument *about* this proliferation of form, with the new variety of 'vessels' crafted in the mid and late eighteenth century later being 'filled' by Romantic ideas (*Preromanticism*, p. 7).

This consensus – a remarkable one given the array of assumptions and procedures brought to bear on the period – suggests that the 'convenience' of 1740 as a date of change may actually be an effect not of the usual suspects – political events, authors, generations – but of numbers. Back then, the effect was preparatory: the proliferation of genres at mid century set the stage for an even more startling take-off in overall print production in the 1780s, our other standard date of change for the century. Publication of new novels, for example, reached, in James Raven's words, 'unprecedented levels in the late 1780s'.[37] Although the genre did experience in the 1740s the variation of kinds within kinds I have just described – most visibly in the epistolary and epic efforts of Richardson and Fielding – growth through most of the century had been slow and erratic. From an annual rate of only about four to twenty new

---

36 Ronald Carter and John McRae, *The Routledge History of Literature in English: Britain and Ireland* (London and New York: Routledge, 1997).
37 James Raven, *Judging New Wealth: Popular Publishing and Responses to Commerce in England, 1750–1800* (Oxford: Clarendon Press, 1992), pp. 31–41.

titles through the first four decades, and remaining – despite the popularity of *Pamela / Shamela* – within a range of roughly twenty to forty for the next three, new novel production peaked briefly near sixty in 1770 before a steep decline to well below forty during the latter half of that decade. Within the next seven years, however, the output jumped – more than doubled – to close to ninety, and continued to increase sharply into the next century. That rise of the novel – the real rise – was not against the grain; as James Raven has shown, those figures parallel the dramatic rise in the overall *ESTC* publication totals (Diagram 1).

To say that the narrowed category of Literature emerged from this two-stage proliferation is to put explanatory pressure on the term 'emerge'. But here we now have help from other disciplines, where 'emergence' has itself emerged as a powerful tool for analysing and articulating change. Contemporary systems theory offers it as an alternative to standard causal explanations; for literary historians and theorists, it can help us shake off our Romantic assumptions about change – assumptions that veer between two apparent opposites: the gradual development of 'Tintern Abbey' 's 'five long winters' on the one hand, and the apocalyptic revelation of *The Prelude*'s Simplon Pass, on the other.

As an alternative to the continuity of development, on the one hand, and the discontinuity of revelation, on the other, emergence theorises the relationship between the two by arguing that 'more is different'. As Kevin Kelly puts it, just as a flock is more than the sum of the birds, so the behaviour of a hive cannot be inferred from the actions of individual bees; based on the latter, one could never predict the former. One grain of sand cannot avalanche and a single molecule does not really have a temperature. 'Higher-level complexities', to put this more formally, 'cannot be inferred by lower-level existences.'[38] At a certain scale, a 'more' that can seem gradual and developmental leads suddenly to newly 'emergent behaviours', a change so abrupt that it can easily be experienced as revelation – the truth that was always already there, just waiting to be revealed.

When the production of print accelerates in the eighteenth century – in kind and in quantity – the inclusive body of writing that was then called

---

38 Kevin Kelly, *Out of Control: The Rise of Neo-Biological Civilization* (Reading, MA: Addison-Wesley, 1994), p. 13. See also Steven Johnson, *Emergence: The Connected Lives of Ants, Brains, Cities and Software* (London: Penguin, 2002), Malcolm Gladwell, *The Tipping Point: How Little Things Can Make a Big Difference* (London: Abacus, 2002), Harold J. Morowitz, *The Emergence of Everything: How the World Became Complex* (Oxford: Oxford University Press, 2002) and John H. Holland, *Emergence: From Chaos to Order* (Oxford: Oxford University Press, 2000).

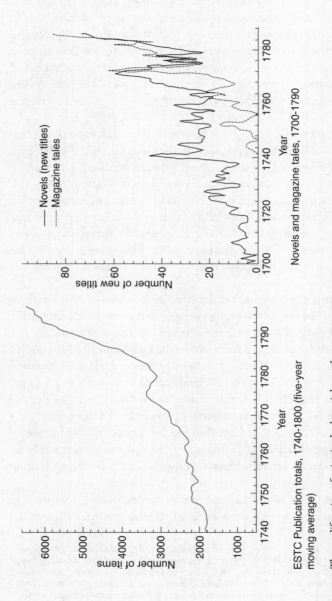

Diagram 1 The proliferation of print in the late eighteenth century

These figures are juxtaposed and discussed in James Raven, *Judging New Wealth* (Oxford: Oxford University Press, 1992), pp. 32–5. The data for the novel are from James Raven, *British Fiction 1750–1770: A Chronological Check-List of Prose Fiction Printed in Britain and Ireland* (Newark: University of Delaware Press, 1987). Raven makes use of Robert D. Mayo, *English Novel in the Magazines, 1740–1815* (Evanston: Northwestern University Press, 1962), and Edward W. Pitcher, 'Robert Mayo's *The English Novel in the Magazines, 1740–1815*; New Facts', *Library* 5th ser. 31.1 (Mar. 1976), 20–30. Reproduced by permission of Oxford University Press and James Raven.

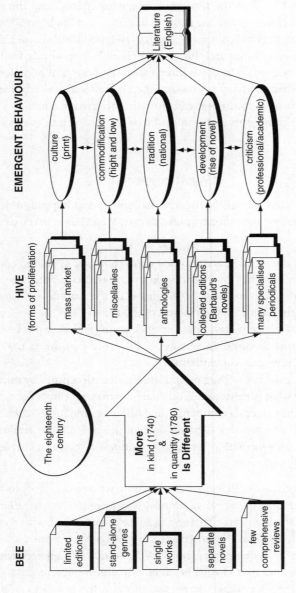

Diagram 2 The role of the quantitative in literary change

EMERGENT BEHAVIOUR

- culture (print)
- commodification (hight and low)
- tradition (national)
- development (rise of novel)
- criticism (professional/academic)

Literature (English)

HIVE
(forms of proliferation)

- mass market
- miscellanies
- anthologies
- collected editions (Barbauld's novels)
- many specialised periodicals

The eighteenth century

More
in kind (1740)
&
in quantity (1780)
Is Different

BEE

- limited editions
- stand-alone genres
- single works
- separate novels
- few comprehensive reviews

'literature' began to exhibit the emergent behaviours that we now experience under the rubric of 'Literature'. As illustrated in Diagram 2, the expansion of print in general leads to the formation of a mass market and the emergent behaviour of 'culture', including commodification into 'high' and 'low' forms. Increases in specific kinds of writing, such as the rise in anthologies, the popularity of collected editions and the spread of literary periodicals, lead to other emergent phenomena – in these three cases, the notion of a 'national tradition', the apotheosis of key genres and the professional and academic enterprise of 'criticism'. A commodified culture in the form of a national tradition highlighted by rising genres and valorised by the institutions of criticism gave us Literature.

What happened

'Convenience' and the 'click' suggest that something happened during the eighteenth century; the numbers and emergence can begin to tell us what and how.

First, they help us make sense of the dates that have appeared convenient. Whatever else they may correspond to, both are quantitative markers: the proliferation of print that begins with the variation of kinds in the 1740s culminates with the take-off of the 1780s.

Second, emergence materialises the click as an *effect* of that take-off. More of 'literature' became 'Literature', a difference that marks the advent of what we now call Romanticism.

Third, telling the tale of the mid and late eighteenth century by the numbers provides what no amount of qualitative worrying can: a rubric that can contain the currently competing, and often incompatible, labels surveyed earlier. These decades – the decades of the quantitative sublime – saw Britain's transformation into a *print culture* – a society saturated by the technology of print.

For that rubric to be useful in our periodisation, we need to clarify its historical specificity. The printing press, of course, was invented much earlier and its products had already been appearing in some quantity and with some force. But the key determinant of when a society becomes a print culture is the connection between quantity and effect – the moment of emergence: at what point does a quantitative change produce a qualitative difference?

In print culture we think and behave through the practices of print, our saturation in that technology governed by the paradox of access. On the one hand, saturation means that more people have more access to the technology; on the other, it signals that, strangely enough, direct access *is not* required – that even those lacking or refusing access are transformed by the ubiquitous presence of the technology. This is the tale now being retold by the early twenty-first-century advent of the electronic and digital. Whether individuals have the technology or try to avoid it, everyone now has the sense that there is nowhere to hide; in fact, the desire to hide is itself an index to saturation and confirmation of change.

For those who do engage the technology, the challenge of saturation is to transform the technology even as it transforms them. During the advent of print culture in eighteenth-century Britain, attempts at transformation took the form in writing of elaborations of standard practice that quickly became dated – 'curious' – as new norms took hold. The elaborators themselves were marginalised as the culture stabilised into its canonical forms. That is what happened *to* the mid and late eighteenth century in our literary histories, and that is why it has been so difficult to recover what actually happened *during* it.

Chronology

1660	Restoration of the Stuart monarchy: Charles II returns from exile in France
	Daniel Defoe born in London
1661	Robert Boyle's *The Sceptical Chymist* challenges the classical notion of the four elements
	Nicholas Hawksmoor, architect, born in Nottinghamshire
1662	Act of Uniformity passed, requiring office holders to be members of the Church of England
	Chartering of the Royal Society
1663	Drury Lane Theatre in London reopens
1664	Matthew Prior born in Dorsetshire
	The Conventicle Act outlaws nonconformist worship in gatherings of more than five people
	Second Anglo-Dutch War (to 1667): Dutch ships sail up the Thames and destroy much of the English fleet
1665–6	The Great Plague (kills over 70,000 people in London) and the Great Fire of London (destroys most of the old wooden city)
1667	John Milton, *Paradise Lost*
	Jonathan Swift born in Dublin
1668	John Dryden made Poet Laureate
1670	William Congreve born near Leeds
	John Milton, *Paradise Regained* and *Samson Agonistes*
1672	Joseph Addison born in Wiltshire
	Richard Steele born in Dublin
1674	Isaac Watts born in Southampton
	John Milton dies
1675	Greenwich Observatory established by Charles II
1678	John Bunyan, *Pilgrim's Progress*
	'Exclusion Crisis' as the Earl of Shaftesbury leads a movement to exclude James, Charles II's brother, from the succession to the throne
	Andrew Marvell dies
1681	John Dryden, *Absalom and Achitophel*
1683	Rye House Plot to kill King Charles II and the future King James II
1685	Death of Charles II – succeeded by his brother, the Catholic James II
	Louis XIV revokes the Edict of Nantes, ending religious toleration in France
	John Gay born in Devon

	Duke of Monmouth lands at Lyme Regis and leads Monmouth's Rebellion, but defeated this year at the Battle of Sedgemoor
1687	Isaac Newton, *Principia Mathematica*
1688	'Glorious Revolution': James II forced to abdicate (or to vacate the throne) and Prince William of Orange in the Netherlands invited to reign as William III of England, with James' daughter, Mary, as his queen
	Alexander Pope born in London
1689	Accession of William III and Mary II
	The Bill of Rights limits the powers of the monarchy over parliament and ratifies the 'Glorious Revolution'
	Aphra Behn dies
	Samuel Richardson born in Derbyshire
	Toleration Act reintroduces a level of toleration of nonconformists (excluding Catholics and Unitarians)
1690	John Locke, *An Essay concerning Human Understanding*
	William III defeats James II at the Battle of the Boyne in Ireland
1694	Founding of the Bank of England
1695	Licensing of the Press Act expires and is not renewed
1697	William Hogarth born in London
	Death of Queen Mary
1700	William Congreve, *The Way of the World*
	John Dryden, *Fables Ancient and Modern*
	John Pomfret, *The Choice*
	John Dryden dies
	James Thomson born in Scotland
1701	James II dies in exile
	Act of Settlement establishes Hanover succession
	Jethro Tull invents the seed drill
1702	Death of William III, accession of Queen Anne, James II's daughter
	England declares war against France and Spain: War of the Spanish Succession
	John Churchill, Duke of Marlborough, named Captain-General of the English army
1703	Samuel Pepys dies
	John Wesley born in Lincolnshire
	Daniel Defoe pilloried and jailed for his political pamphlet, *The Shortest Way with the Dissenters* (1702)
1704	English capture Gibraltar; Duke of Marlborough defeats the French at Blenheim
	Daniel Defoe begins *The Review* (through 1712)
	Jonathan Swift, *A Tale of a Tub* and *The Battle of the Books*
	Isaac Newton, *Optics*
	John Locke dies
1705	Bernard Mandeville, *The Grumbling Hive, or Knaves Turned Honest*

1706	The Battle of Ramillies, in the Low Countries, where Marlborough defeats the French and gains control of the Spanish Netherlands
	Sarah Fye Egerton, *Poems on Several Occasions*
	Isaac Watts, *Horae Lyricae*
1707	Union of England and Scotland ratified
	Henry Fielding born in Glastonbury, Somerset
1709	Samuel Johnson born in Lichfield
	George Berkeley, *A New Theory of Vision*
	Delarivier Manley, *The New Atalantis*
	Richard Steele, *The Tatler* (until 1711)
1710	Tories gain control of parliament under leadership of Robert Harley (later Earl of Oxford) and Henry St John (later Viscount Bolingbroke)
	Statute of Queen Anne passed by parliament, limiting copyright to twenty-eight years and recognising authors' rights
	Trial of Dr Henry Sacheverell for seditious libel
	George Berkeley, *The Principles of Human Knowledge*
1711	Addison and Steele's *The Spectator* begins publishing
	Founding of the South Sea Company
	George Frideric Handel's first English production, *Rinaldo*, with libretto by Aaron Hill, is produced at the King's Theatre
	David Hume born in Edinburgh
	Shaftesbury, *Characteristicks*
1712	Alexander Pope, *The Rape of the Lock* (two-canto version)
1713	Treaty of Utrecht, ending War of the Spanish Succession
	Laurence Sterne born in Clonmel, Ireland
	Jonathan Swift made Dean of St Patrick's Cathedral, Dublin
	Joseph Addison, *Cato*
	Alexander Pope, *Windsor-Forest*
1714	Death of Queen Anne
	Accession of George I, the Elector of Hanover
	Bernard Mandeville, *The Fable of the Bees*
	Alexander Pope, *The Rape of the Lock* (five-canto version)
	Nicholas Rowe, *The Tragedy of Jane Shore*
	Scriblerus Club meets regularly in Dr John Arbuthnot's quarters at St James' Palace
1715	Jacobite Rebellion in support of James II's son, 'James III', the 'Old Pretender'
	Death of Louis XIV of France
	Robert Harley (Earl of Oxford) and Henry St John (Viscount Bolingbroke) are impeached of high treason. Bolingbroke flees to France
	Nicholas Rowe appointed Poet Laureate
	Alexander Pope's translation of *The Iliad of Homer*
1716	Septennial Act passed, requiring general elections every seven years, not every three
	John Gay, *Trivia, or The Art of Walking the Streets of London*
	Lady Mary Wortley Montagu, *Town Eclogues, Court Poems*

1732	10 Downing Street, London presented by King George II to Sir Robert Walpole as residence for the First Lord of the Treasury (Prime Minister)
	William Hogarth, *A Harlot's Progress*
1733	Alexander Pope, *An Essay on Man*
	Flying shuttle loom invented by John Kay
1734	Alexander Pope, *An Epistle to Cobham*
1735	William Hogarth, *A Rake's Progress*
	Alexander Pope, *An Epistle to Dr Arbuthnot, An Epistle to a Lady*
	Carolus Linnaeus (Carl Linné) of Sweden, *Systema Naturae*
1736	George Frideric Handel, *Alexander's Feast*, with text by Dryden
1737	Theatrical Licensing Act passed, giving the Lord Chamberlain the power to license plays
	Edward Gibbon born in London
1738	Henry St John, Viscount Bolingbroke, *Letters on the spirit of patriotism: on the idea of a patriot king: and on the state of parties, at the accession of King George the First*
	Samuel Johnson, *London*
1739	'War of Jenkins' Ear' with Spain in South America and the West Indies
	David Hume, *Treatise of Human Nature*
	Jonathan Swift, *Verses on the Death of Dr Swift*
1740	Samuel Richardson, *Pamela*
	Colley Cibber, *An Apology for the Life of Colley Cibber*
	James Boswell born in Scotland
1741	Britain involved in the War of the Austrian Succession with Empress Maria Theresa of Austria against France, Spain, Bavaria, Prussia and Saxony
1742	Robert Walpole resigns, succeeded by Henry Pelham, who with his brother the Duke of Newcastle holds ministerial power until 1754
	George Frideric Handel, *Messiah*
	Henry Fielding, *Joseph Andrews*
	Alexander Pope, *The New Dunciad* (Book IV)
	Edward Young, *The Complaint, or Night Thoughts on Life, Death and Immortality* (to 1745)
1743	George II leads the British army in defeat of the French at the Battle of Dettingen in the War of the Austrian Succession
	Alexander Pope, *The Dunciad in Four Books*
1744	Alexander Pope dies
	Mark Akenside, *The Pleasures of the Imagination*
	Sarah Fielding, *The Adventures of David Simple*
	Eliza Haywood, *The Female Spectator* (to 1746)
	Joseph Warton, *The Enthusiast, or The Lover of Nature*
1745	Charles Edward Stuart ('Bonnie Prince Charlie' or the 'Young Pretender', James II's grandson) lands in Scotland and leads the Jacobite uprising
	Jonathan Swift dies
	Robert Walpole dies
	William Hogarth, *Marriage à la Mode*

1746	Battle of Culloden in Scotland and defeat of the 'Pretender' ('Bonnie Prince Charlie') and his allies
	William Pitt the elder made Paymaster General
	William Collins, *Odes on Several Descriptive and Allegorical Subjects*
	Joseph Warton, *Odes on Various Subjects*
1747	Samuel Richardson, *Clarissa* (to 1748)
	Thomas Gray, *Ode on a Distant Prospect of Eton College*
	Thomas Warton, *The Pleasures of Melancholy*
1748	John Cleland, *Memoirs of a Woman of Pleasure* (*Fanny Hill*)
	Treaty of Aix-la-Chapelle ending the War of the Austrian Succession
	David Hume, *An Enquiry concerning Human Understanding*
	Isaac Watts dies
	Tobias Smollett, *Roderick Random*
	Mary Leapor, *Poems Upon Several Occasions*
	James Thomson dies
1749	Henry Fielding, *Tom Jones*
	Charlotte Smith born in London
	Samuel Johnson, *The Vanity of Human Wishes*
1750	Samuel Johnson begins publishing *The Rambler* (runs until 1752)
1751	Death of Frederick, Prince of Wales, son of George II
	Eliza Haywood, *The History of Miss Betsy Thoughtless*
	Thomas Gray, *Elegy Written in a Country Churchyard*
	David Hume, *An Enquiry concerning the Principles of Morals*
	Tobias Smollett, *The Adventures of Peregrine Pickle*
1752	Frances Burney born in London
	Charlotte Lennox, *The Female Quixote*
	Christopher Smart, *Poems on Several Occasions*
1753	Founding of the British Museum
	Robert Lowth, *De Sacra Poesi Hebraeorum* (trans. as *Lectures on the Sacred Poetry of the Hebrews*, 1787)
1754	Henry Fielding dies in Lisbon
	David Hume, *The History of Great Britain* (through 1763)
	The French take Fort Duquesne as the Anglo-French War (also known as the French and Indian War) begins in North America
1755	Samuel Johnson, *A Dictionary of the English Language*
	A major earthquake strikes Lisbon
1756	The Seven Years' War between England and France begins
	Eliza Haywood dies
	Joseph Warton, *Essay on the Genius and Writings of Pope*, vol. 1
1757	Clive defeats Bengalis at Battle of Plassey – start of Empire in India
	The Nawab of Bengal is defeated in his attempt to expel the British from India
	Edmund Burke, *Philosophical Enquiry in the Origin of our Ideas on the Sublime and the Beautiful*
	William Blake born in London
	Colley Cibber dies

William Whitehead appointed Poet Laureate

Thomas Gray, *The Progress of Poesy, The Bard*

John Dyer, *The Fleece*

Benjamin Franklin arrives in England representing the interests of Pennsylvania, Georgia, New Jersey and Massachusetts (until 1765)

1758 Samuel Johnson, *The Idler* (runs until 1760)

1759 First two volumes of Laurence Sterne, *Tristram Shandy* (seven more volumes published, the last in 1767)

General Wolfe defeats the French under Montcalm at Quebec

Samuel Johnson, *Rasselas*

Robert Burns born in Scotland

George Frideric Handel dies

Adam Smith, *The Theory of Moral Sentiments*

1760 Death of George II

Accession of George III, first of the Hanoverians born in England

Josiah Wedgewood opens pottery works in Staffordshire

James Macpherson, *Fragments of Ancient Poetry Collected in the Highlands of Scotland*

1761 Samuel Richardson dies

Charles Churchill, *The Rosciad*

1762 James Macpherson, *Fingal, an Ancient Epic Poem*

Mary Collier, *Poems on Several Occasions*

Richard Hurd, *Letters on Chivalry and Romance*

Henry Home, Lord Kames, *Elements of Criticism*

Earl of Bute becomes Prime Minister

Samuel Johnson receives a pension of £300 from the government

1763 Peace of Paris ends the Seven Years' War with France

James Boswell meets Samuel Johnson

1764 Horace Walpole, *The Castle of Otranto*

Oliver Goldsmith, *The Traveller, or A Prospect of Society*

James Grainger, *The Sugar Cane*

William Shenstone, *The Works in Verse and Prose*

James Hargreaves invents the spinning jenny

1765 The Marquess of Rockingham becomes Prime Minister

Thomas Percy, *Reliques of Ancient English Poetry*

William Blackstone, *Commentaries on the Laws of England* (through 1769)

Samuel Johnson, *The Works of Shakespeare*

1766 William Pitt becomes Prime Minister and Earl of Chatham

Oliver Goldsmith, *The Vicar of Wakefield*

Christopher Anstey, *New Bath Guide*

1767 Adam Ferguson, *History of Civil Society*

1768 Laurence Sterne dies

Captain Cook's first voyage to Australia and New Zealand

Royal Academy of Art founded by Joshua Reynolds; other founding members include Paul Sandby, Benjamin West and Richard Wilson

Arthur Young, *Six Weeks' Tour through the Southern Counties*

1769	John Wilkes is expelled by the House of Commons, and is thrice re-elected by Middlesex, but the House again rejects him
	Joshua Reynolds delivers first of fifteen *Discourses on Art* at the Royal Academy
1770	William Wordsworth born in Cumbria
	Lord North becomes Prime Minister, and remains in the post until 1782
1771	Tobias Smollett dies
	Thomas Gray dies
	The first edition of the *Encyclopaedia Britannica*
	Lloyd's founded as Marine Insurance Company
	James Beattie, *The Minstrel*
	Henry Mackenzie, *The Man of Feeling*
	Tobias Smollett, *The Expedition of Humphry Clinker*
1772	Joseph Priestley and Daniel Rutgerford discover nitrogen independently
	Slavery declared illegal in Britain
	Sir William Jones, *Poems, Consisting Chiefly of Translations from the Asiatic Languages*
1773	Oliver Goldsmith, *She Stoops to Conquer*
	Anna Laetitia Barbauld, *Poems*
	Robert Fergusson, *Poems*
1774	Donaldson v. Beckett, law case in the House of Lords, establishes the financial rights of authors to the first publication of their work
	Joseph Priestley and Karl Scheele independently discover oxygen
	Warren Hastings becomes the first Governor General of India
	Thomas Warton, *History of English Poetry*, vol. 1
1775	Jane Austen born
	Samuel Johnson, *Journey to the Western Islands of Scotland*
	Richard Brinsley Sheridan, *The Rivals*
	Mary Robinson, *Poems*
	American Revolution begins with the battles of Lexington and Concord
1776	American Declaration of Independence
	Edward Gibbon, *Decline and Fall of the Roman Empire*, vol. 1
	Adam Smith, *An Inquiry into the Nature and Causes of the Wealth of Nations*
1777	Richard Brinsley Sheridan, *The School for Scandal*
	Thomas Chatterton, *Poems*
1778	Frances Burney, *Evelina*
1779	Samuel Johnson begins publishing *The Lives of the Poets (Prefaces, Biographical and Critical, to the Works of the English Poets)*
	Hume, *Dialogues concerning Natural Religion*
	William Cowper, *Olney Hymns*
	David Garrick dies
	Captain James Cook dies
1780	Gordon Riots: violent anti-Catholic riots in London as Lord Gordon presents a petition to Parliament requesting the repeal of the Catholic Relief Act of 1778 and a return to Catholic repression

1781	General Lord Cornwallis surrenders to Washington at Yorktown, Virginia to end the American Revolution
	Immanuel Kant, *Critique of Pure Reason*
1782	Invention of modern steam engine by James Watt
	Marquess of Rockingham Prime Minister, but dies that same year, succeeded by Lord Shelburne
	William Cowper, *Poems*
	Joseph Warton, *Essay on the Genius and Writings of Pope,* vol. 2
1783	Treaties of Paris and Versailles end the War of American Independence
	William Pitt, the Younger becomes Prime Minister at twenty-four
	Hugh Blair, *Lectures on Rhetoric and Belles Lettres*
	George Crabbe, *The Village*
1784	Samuel Johnson dies
	Charlotte Smith, *Elegiac Sonnets*
1785	Edward Cartwright patents his power loom
	James Boswell, *Journal of a Tour to the Hebrides* with Samuel Johnson
	William Cowper, *The Task*
	Thomas Reid, *Essays on the Intellectual Powers of Man*
1786	Robert Burns, *Poems, Chiefly in the Scottish Dialect.*
1787	US Constitution signed in Philadelphia
	James Madison and Alexander Hamilton, *The Federalist Papers* begin
	Trial of Warren Hastings begins
	Mary Wollstonecraft, *Thoughts on the Education of Daughters*
1789	French Revolution begins; fall of the Bastille in Paris
	William Blake, *Songs of Innocence*
1790	Edmund Burke, *Reflections on the Revolution in France*
	Mary Wollstonecraft, *A Vindication of the Rights of Man*
1791	James Boswell, *The Life of Samuel Johnson*
	Thomas Paine, *The Rights of Man*
1792	Joshua Reynolds dies
	Arthur Young, *Travels*
	Mary Wollstonecraft, *A Vindication of the Rights of Woman*
1793	Execution of Louis XVI of France
	France declares war against England

Bibliographies

CHAPTER I BIBLIOGRAPHY

The English Short Title Catalogue, London: British Library, in progress.

The House of Longman, 1794–1914, microfilm edn, Cambridge: Chadwyck Healey, 1978.

Alston, Robin, *Library History Database*. http://www.r-alston.co.uk/contents.html, 1998–.
   Order and Connexion: Studies in Bibliography and Book History, Woodbridge: Boydell and Brewer, 1997.

Altick, Richard D., *The English Common Reader: A Social History of the Mass Reading Public 1800–1900*, Chicago and London: University of Chicago Press, 1957.

Aspinall, A., 'Statistical Accounts of the London Newspapers in the Eighteenth Century,' *English Historical Review* 63 (1948), 201–32.

Baines Reed, Talbot, *A History of the Development of Old English Letter Foundries*. rev. edn, A. F. Johnson, London: Faber and Faber, 1952.

Ball, Johnson, *William Caslon, 1693–1766: The Ancestry, Life and Connections of England's Foremost Letter-Engraver and Type-Founder*, Kineton: Roundwood Press, 1973.

Barnard, John, and D. F. Mckenzie (eds.), *The History of the Book in Britain*: Volume IV *1557–1695*, Cambridge: Cambridge University Press, 2002.

Belanger, Terry, 'A Directory of the London Book Trade, 1766', *Publishing History* 1 (1977), 7–48.
   'Booksellers' Sales of Copyright: Aspects of the London Book Trades, 1718–1768', unpublished PhD dissertation, Columbia University, 1970.
   'Booksellers' Trade Sales 1718–1768', *The Library* 5th ser., 30 (1975), 281–302.
   'Publishers and Writers in Eighteenth-Century England,' in Rivers, Isabel (ed.), *Books and their Readers in Eighteenth-Century England*, Leicester: Leicester University Press, 1982, pp. 5–25.

Besterman, Theodore (ed.), *The Publishing Firm of Cadell and Davies: Select Correspondence and Accounts, 1783–1836*, Oxford: Oxford University Press, 1938.

Birkbeck Hill, George, and L. F. Powell (eds.), *Boswell's Life of Johnson*, 2nd edn, 6 vols., Oxford: Clarendon Press, 1964.

Blagden, Cyprian, 'Booksellers' Trade Sales 1718–1768', *The Library* 5th ser., 5 (1951), 243–57.

Blakey, Dorothy, *The Minerva Press 1790–1820*, London: Printed for the Bibliographical society at the University Press, Oxford, 1939.

Blayney, Peter W. M, *The Bookshops in Paul's Cross Churchyard*. Occasional Papers of the Bibliographical Society, no. 5, London, 1990.

Borsay, Peter, and Angus McInnes, 'Debate: Leisure Town or Urban Renaissance?', *Past and Present* 126 (Feb. 1990), 189–202.

Borsay, Peter, 'The English Urban Renaissance: The Development of a Provincial Urban Culture *c.* 1680 – c. 1760', *Social History* 2 (1977), 581–603.

Boyce, George, James Curran and Pauline Wingate (eds.), *Newspaper History from the Seventeenth Century to the Present Day*, London and Beverly Hills, CA: Constable and Sage, 1978.

Brack, O. M. Jr. (ed.), *Writers, Books, and Trade: An Eighteenth-Century English Miscellany for William B. Todd*, New York: AMS Press, 1994.

Bruntjen, Sven H. A., *John Boydell, 1719–1804: A Study of Art Patronage and Publishing in Georgian London*, New York and London: Garland Press, 1985.

Clayton, Timothy, *The English Print 1688–1802*, New Haven, CT and London: Yale University Press, 1997.

Coleman, D. C., *The British Paper Industry, 1495–1860*, Oxford: Clarendon Press, 1958.

Collier, J., *The Parents and Guardians Directory*, London, 1761.

Collins, A. S., *Authorship in the Days of Johnson: Being a Study of the Relation Between Author, Patron, Publisher, and Public, 1726–1780*, London: R. Holden and Co., 1927.

The Profession of Letters: A Study of the Relation of Author to Patron, Publisher, and Public, 1780–1832, New York: Dutton, 1929.

Corfield, P. J., *The Impact of English Towns, 1700–1800*, Oxford: Oxford University Press, 1982.

Cranfield, G. A., *The Development of the Provincial Newspaper, 1700–1760*, Oxford: Oxford University Press, 1962.

Crump, Michael, and Michael Harris (eds.), *Searching the Eighteenth Century*, London: British Library, 1983.

Dibdin, Thomas Frognall, *Bibliomania; or Book Madness: A Bibliographical Romance*, London, 1811.

Dowell, Stephen, *A History of Taxation and Taxes in England*, 3 vols., 3rd edn., London: Frank Cass, 1965.

Ferdinand, C. Y., *Benjamin Collins and the Provincial Newspaper Trade in the Eighteenth Century*, Oxford: Clarendon Press, 1997.

Fergus, Jan, and Janice Farrar Thaddeus, 'Women, Publishers, and Money, 1790–1820', *Studies in Eighteenth-Century Culture* 17 (1988), 191–207.

Fontaine, Laurence, *et al.* (eds.), *Des Personnes aux institutions: réseaux et culture du crédit du XVIe au XXe siècle en Europe*, Louvain-la-Neuve: Bruylant-Academia, 1997.

Foxon, David, and James McLaverty, *Pope and the Early Eighteenth-Century Book Trade*, Oxford: Clarendon Press, 1991.

Grosley, Pierre Jean, *A Tour to London: or, New Observations on England and its Inhabitants*, trans. Thomas Nugent, 2 vols., London, 1772.

Harris, Michael, *London Newspapers in the Age of Walpole: A Study of the Origins of the Modern English Press*, London and Toronto: Associated University Press, 1987.

Hunt, Arnold, Giles Mandelbrote and Alison Shell (eds.), *The Book Trade and its Customers 1450–1900*, Winchester and New Castle, DE: St Paul's Bibliographies and Oak Knoll Press, 1997.

Hutt, Allen, *Fournier: The Compleat Typographer*, London: Muller, 1972.

Innes, Joanna, 'Jonathan Clark, Social History and England's "Ancien Regime"', *Past and Present* 115 (May 1987), 165–200.

Isaac, Peter, and Barry McKay, *Images and Texts: Their Production and Distribution in the 18th and 19th Centuries*, Winchester and New Castle, DE: St Paul's Bibliographies and Oak Knoll Press, 1997.

Lippincott, Louise, *Selling Art in Georgian London: The Rise of Arthur Pond*, New Haven, CT and London: Yale University Press, 1983.

Love, Harold, *Scribal Publication in Seventeenth-Century England*, Oxford: Clarendon Press, 1993.

McDowell, Paula, *The Women of Grub Street: Press Politics and Gender in the London Literary Marketplace 1678–1730*, Oxford: Clarendon Press, 1998.

McInnes, Angus, 'The Emergence of a Leisure Town: Shrewsbury, 1660–1760', *Past and Present* 120 (Aug. 1988), 53–87.

McKitterick, David, *Set in Print: The Fortunes of an Idea, 1450–1800: The Lyell Lectures, 2000*, Oxford: Oxford University Press, 2001.

Mann, Phyllis G., 'Death of a London Bookseller', *Keats–Shelley Memorial Bulletin* 15 (1964), 11.

Marston, E., *Sketches of Booksellers of Other Days*, New York: Scribner, 1901.

Maslen, K. I. D., and John Lancaster, *The Bowyer Ledgers: The Printing Accounts of William Bowyer, Father and Son*, London and New York: Bibliographical Society and Bibliographical Society of America, 1991.

Maxted, Ian, *The London Book Trades 1775–1800*, Folkestone: J. Maxted, 1977.

Mumby, Frank Arthur, *Publishing and Bookselling*, London: Jonathan Cape, 1934.

Myers, Robin, and Michael Harris (eds.), *Author–Publisher Relations in the Eighteenth and Nineteenth Centuries*, Oxford: Oxford Polytechnic Press, 1983.

Economics of the British Booktrade, 1605–1939, Cambridge: Chadwyck Healey, 1986.

Sale and Distribution of Books from 1700, Oxford: Oxford Polytechnic Press, 1982.

Serials and their Readers, 1620–1914, Winchester and New Castle, DE: St Paul's Bibliographies and Oak Knoll Press, 1993.

Spreading the Word: The Distribution Networks of Print, 1550–1850, Winchester and New Castle, DE: St Paul's Bibliographies and Oak Knoll Press, 1990.

The Stationers' Company and the Book Trade 1550–1990, Winchester and New Castle, DE: St Paul's Bibliographies and Oak Knoll Press, 1997.

Myers, Robin, *The Stationers' Company Archive, 1551–1984*, Winchester and Detroit: St Paul's Bibliographies, 1990.

Nettel, Reginald, ed., *Journeys of a German* [Carl Philip Moritz] *in England in 1782*, London: Jonathan Cape, 1965.

Nichols, John, *Literary Anecdotes of the Eighteenth Century*, 9 vols. London, 1812–15, rpt. edn, New York: AMS Press, 1966.

Pardoe, F. E., *John Baskerville of Birmingham: Letter-Founder and Printer*, London: F. Muller, 1975.

Pollard, H. G., and A. Ehrman, *The Distribution of Books by Catalogue*, Cambridge: Roxburghe Club, 1965.

Pollard, M., *Dublin's Trade in Books 1550–1800*, Oxford: Clarendon Press, 1989.

Raven, James, and Antonia Forster, *The English Novel 1770–1799: A Bibliographical Survey of Prose Fiction Published in the British Isles, Volume 1*, Oxford University Press, 2000.

Raven, James, Helen Small and Naomi Tadmor (eds.), *The Practice and Representation of Reading in England*, Cambridge Cambridge University Press, 1996.

Raven, James, Nigel Hall, *et al.*, *Mapping the Print Culture of Eighteenth-Century London* (http://www.members.tripod.co.uk/bookhistory/. 1999–.

Raven, James, 'The Book Trades', in Isabel Rivers (ed.), *Books and Their Readers in Eighteenth-Century England: New Essay*, London and New York: Continuum and Leicester University Press, 2001.

    Judging New Wealth: Popular Publishing and Responses to Commerce in England, 1750–1800, Oxford: Clarendon Press, 1992.

    'New Reading Histories, Print Culture, and the Identification of Change: The Case of Eighteenth-Century England', *Social History* 23 (1998), 268–87.

    'The Noble Brothers and Popular Publishing', *The Library* 6th ser., 12 (1990), 293–345.

Rees, Thomas, and John Britton, *Reminiscences of Literary London from 1779 to 1853*, London, 1896.

Rose, Mark, *Authors and Owners: The Invention of Copyright*, Cambridge, MA and London: Harvard University Press, 1993.

Shorter, Alfred H., *Water Paper Mills in England,* London: Society for the Protection of Ancient Buildings, 1966.

Solomon, Harry M., *The Rise of Robert Dodsley: Creating the New Age of Print,* Carbondale and Edwardsville: Southern Illinois University Press, 1996.

Sutherland, James, *The Restoration Newspaper and its Development*, Cambridge: Cambridge University Press, 1986.

Sweet, Rosemary, *The English Town 1680–1840: Government, Society and Culture*, London: Longman, 1999.

Thomson, Alistair G., *The Paper Industry in Scotland, 1590–1861*, Edinburgh and London: Scottish Academic Press, 1974.

Tierney, James E. (ed.), *The Correspondence of Robert Dodsley 1733–1764*, Cambridge: Cambridge University Press, 1988.

Timperley, C. H., *Encyclopaedia of Literary and Typographical Anecdote*, London, 1842.

Treadwell, Michael, 'London Trade Publishers, 1675–1750', *The Library* 6th ser. 4 (1982), 99–134.

Updike, Daniel Berkeley, *Printing Types: Their History, Forms and Use: A Study in Survivals*, 2 vols., Cambridge, MA: Belknap Press, 1962.

Walker, R. B., 'Advertising in London Newspapers, 1650–1750', *Business History* 15 (1973), 112–30.

Wallis, Philip, *At the Sign of the Ship: Notes on the House of Longman, 1724–1974*, London, private edn, 1974.

Walters, Gwyn, 'The Booksellers in 1759 and 1774: The Battle for Literary Property,' *The Library* 5th ser., 29 (1974), 287–311.

West, William, *Fifty Years' Recollections of an Old Bookseller*, London, 1837.

Wiles, R. M., *Serial Publication in England before 1750*, Cambridge: Cambridge University Press, 1957.

Williams, Clare (ed.), *Sophie in London, 1786 Being the Diary of Sophie von la Roche*, London: Batsford, 1933.

Zachs, William, *The First John Murray and the Late Eighteenth-Century Book Trade*, London: British Academy and Oxford University Press, 1998.

CHAPTER 2 BIBLIOGRAPHY
Primary works

Addison, Joseph, and Richard Steele, *The Spectator*, 5 vols., ed. D. F. Bond, Oxford: Clarendon Press, 1965.

Astell, Mary, *A Serious Proposal to the Ladies*, ed. Patricia Springborg, London, 1997.

Chudleigh, Mary, Lady, *The Poems and Prose of Mary, Lady Chudleigh*, ed. Margaret Ezell, Oxford: Oxford University Press, 1993.

Dryden, John, *Works*, ed. H. T. Swedenberg *et al.*, 20 vols., Berkeley and Los Angeles: University of California Press, 1956–2002.

Finch, Anne, Countess of Winchelsea, *The Anne Finch Wellesley Manuscript Poems*, ed. Barbara McGovern and Charles H. Hinnant, Athens, GA: University of Georgia Press, 1998.

Johnson, Samuel, *Lives of the Poets*, ed. G. B. Hill, 3 vols., Oxford: Oxford University Press, 1905.

Kerby-Miller, Charles (ed.), *The Memoirs of the Extraordinary Life, Works, and Discoveries of Martinus Scriblerus*, New Haven, CT: Yale University Press, 1950.

Montagu, Lady Mary Wortley, *Complete Letters*, ed. Robert Halsband, 3 vols., Oxford: Oxford University Press, 1965–67.

Philips, John, *Poems*, ed. M. Lloyd-Thomas, London, 1927.

Philips, Katherine, *Collected Works*, ed. Patrick Thomas, 3 vols., Stump Cross, Essex: Stump Cross Books, 1990.

Poems on Affairs of State: Augustan Satirical Verse, 1660–1714, ed. George Lord *et al.*, 7 vols., New Haven, CT: Yale University Press, 1963–74.

Pope, Alexander, *Poems*, ed. John Butt *et al.*, 11 vols., New Haven, CT: Yale University Press, 1938–68.

Works, ed. Whitwell Elwin and J. W. Courthope, 10 vols., London: J. Murray, 1871–9.

Spence, Joseph, *Observations, Anecdotes, and Characters of Books and Men*, ed. James Osborn, 2 vols., Oxford: Oxford University Press, 1966.

Swift, Jonathan, *Complete Poems*, ed. Pat Rogers, London: Penguin, 1983.

Correspondence, ed. Harold Williams, 5 vols., Oxford: Oxford University Press, 1963–5.

Wilmot, John, Earl of Rochester, *Letters*, ed. Jeremy Treglown, Chicago: University of Chicago Press, 1980.

Wilmot, John, *Poems*, ed. Keith Walker, Oxford: Oxford University Press, 1984.

Secondary works

Allen, Robert J., *The Clubs of Augustan London*, Cambridge, MA: Harvard University Press, 1933.

Barash, Carol, *English Women's Poetry, 1649–1714: Politics, Community, and Linguistic Authority*, Oxford: Oxford University Press, 1996.

Beal, Peter, *In Praise of Scribes: Manuscripts and Their Makers in Seventeenth-Century England*, Oxford: Oxford University Press, 1998.

Beljame, Alexander, *Men of Letters and the English Public in the Eighteenth Century, 1660–1744, Dryden, Addison, Pope,* trans. E. O. Lorimer, London: Kegan Paul, 1948.

Brewer, John, *The Pleasures of the Imagination: English Culture in the Eighteenth Century,* New York: Ferrar Straus Giraux, 1997.

Bronson, Bertrand, *Facets of the Enlightenment: Studies in English Literature and its Contexts,* Berkeley: University of California Press, 1968.

Bruckmann, Patricia, *A Manner of Correspondence: A Study of the Scriblerus Club,* Montreal: McGill-Queen's University Press, 1997.

Collins, A. S., *Authorship in the Days of Johnson,* New York: McGill-Queen's University Press, 1927.

Ezell, Margaret, 'The *Gentleman's Journal* and the Commercialization of Restoration Coterie Literary Practices', *Modern Philology* 89 (1991–2), 323–40.

  Social Authorship and the Advent of Print, Baltimore, MD: Johns Hopkins University Press, 1999.

Geduld, Harry M., *Prince of Publishers: A Study of the Work and Career of Jacob Tonson,* Bloomington: University of Indiana Press, 1969.

Griffin, Dustin, 'Augustan Collaboration', *Essays in Criticism* 37 (1987), 1–10.

  'Fictions of Eighteenth-Century Authorship', *Essays in Criticism* 43 (1993), 181–94.

  Literary Patronage in England, 1650–1800, Cambridge: Cambridge University Press, 1996.

Habermas, Jürgen, *The Structural Transformation of the Public Sphere: An Inquiry into a Category of Bourgeois Society,* trans. Thomas Burger, Cambridge, MA: M.I.T. Press, 1989.

Harris, Brice, 'Captain Robert Julian, Secretary to the Muses', *ELH* 10 (1943), 294–309.

Kernan, Alvin, *Printing Technology, Letters, & Samuel Johnson,* Princeton, NJ: Princeton University Press, 1987, republished as *Samuel Johnson and the Impact of Print.*

King, Kathryn, 'Jane Barker, *Poetical Recreations,* and the Sociable Text', *ELH* 61 (1994), 551–70.

Klein, Lawrence, 'Coffeehouse Civility, 1660–1714: An Aspect of Post-Courtly Culture in England', *Huntington Library Quarterly* 59 (1997), 31–51.

Levine, Joseph M., *The Battle of the Books: History and Literature in the Augustan Age,* Ithaca, NY: Cornell University Press, 1991.

Lillywhite, Bryant, *London Coffee Houses: A Reference Book of Coffee Houses of the Seventeenth and Eighteenth and Nineteenth Centuries,* London: Allen & Unwin, 1963.

Love, Harold, *Scribal Publication in Seventeenth-Century England,* Oxford: Oxford University Press, 1993.

Lynch, Kathleen, *Jacob Tonson, Kit-Cat Publisher,* Knoxville: University of Tennessee Press, 1971.

Macaulay, Thomas Babington, *History of England,* vol. 1, London, 1849.

McDowell, Paula, *The Women of Grub Street: Press, Politics, and Gender in the London Literary Marketplace,* Oxford: Oxford University Press, 1998.

McGovern, Barbara, *Anne Finch and her Poetry: A Critical Biography,* Athens, GA: University of Georgia Press, 1998.

Rochester: The Critical Heritage, ed. David Farley-Hills, London: Routledge & Kegan Paul, 1972.

Saunders, James, *The Profession of English Letters,* London: Routledge & Kegan Paul, 1964.

Stallybrass, Peter, and Allon White, *The Politics and Poetics of Transgression,* Ithaca, NY: Cornell University Press, 1986.

Vieth, David M., *Attribution in Restoration Poetry: A Study of Rochester's Poems of 1680*, New Haven, CT: Yale University Press, 1963.

Wheatley, Henry B., *London, Past and Present: Its History, Associations, and Traditions*, 3 vols., London: J. Murray, 1891.

Wilson, J. H., *The Court Wits of the Restoration*, Princeton, NJ: Princeton University Press, 1948.

Winn, James, *John Dryden and his World*, New Haven, CT: Yale University Press, 1987.

CHAPTER 3 BIBLIOGRAPHY

Primary works

Addison, Joseph, and Richard Steele, *The Spectator*, ed. Donald Bond, 5 vols., Oxford: Clarendon Press, 1965.

Blake, William, *For Children: The Gates of Paradise*, London, 1793.

Boswell, James, *Boswell's London Journal 1762–1763*, ed. Frederick Pottle, New York: McGraw-Hill, 1950.

Brown, Tom, *Amusements Serious and Comical*, ed. Arthur L. Hayward, London: Routledge & Sons, Ltd., 1927.

Defoe, Daniel, *The Family Instructor*, London, 1715.

Farquhar, George, *The Stage-Coach*, London, 1704.

Fielding, Henry, *The Author's Farce*, ed. Charles B. Woods, Lincoln: University of Nebraska Press, 1966.

   The Mock Doctor, London, 1732.

Garrick, David, *Harlequin's Invasion*, London, 1759.

Gay, John, *The Beggar's Opera*, ed. Edgar V. Roberts, Lincoln: University of Nebraska Press, 1969.

   The What D'ye Call It, London, 1715.

Hill, John, *The Young Secretary's Guide*, London, 1687.

Hogarth, William, 'Autobiographical Notes', in Joseph Burke (ed.), *The Analysis of Beauty*, Oxford: Clarendon Press, 1955.

James, Elinor, *Elinor James's Advice to the King and Parliament*, London, 1715.

Joe Miller's Jests, London, 1739.

Johnson, Charles, *The Force of Friendship*, London, 1710.

Johnson, Samuel, *The Idler and The Adventurer*, eds. W. J. Bate, John M. Bullitt, L. F. Powell, New Haven, CT: Yale University Press, 1963.

[More, Hannah], 'Patient Joe: Or, the Newcastle Collier', *Cheap Repository Shorter Tracts*, London, 1798.

Moore, Francis, *Vox Stellarum*, London, 1700.

A Narrative of All the Robberies, Escapes, &c of John Sheppard, London, 1724.

Newbery, John, *A Little Pretty Pocket-Book*, ed. M. F. Thwaite, New York: Harcourt, Brace & World, 1967.

Partridge, John, *Merlinus Liberatus*, London, 1680.

Pope, Alexander, *The Poems of Alexander Pope*, ed. John Butt, New Haven, CT: Yale University Press, 1963.

The Prison-Breaker; or, the Adventures of John Sheppard, London, 1725.

Rich, John, *Apollo and Daphne: or, Harlequin Mercury*, London, 1725.

   Harlequin a Sorcerer: With the Loves of Pluto and Proserpine, London, 1725.

   Letters Written to and for Particular Friends, on the Most Important Occasions, London, 1741.

   Perseus and Andromeda, London, 1730.

Richardson, Samuel, *The Apprentice's 'Vade Mecum': or, Young Man's Pocket-Companion*, London, 1734.

Settle, Elkanah, *The Siege of Troy*, London, 1703.

Sheridan, Richard Brinsley, *The Critic*, ed. Cecil Price, 2 vols., Oxford: Clarendon Press, 1973.

Smart, Christopher, *The Midwife; or the Old Woman's Magazine*, 3 vols., London, 1751–3.

   Parables of Our Lord and Saviour Jesus Christ. Done into familiar verse, with occasional applications, for the use an improvement of younger minds, London, 1768.

Spence, Joseph, *Observations, Anecdotes, and Characters of Books and Men, Collected from Conversation*, ed. James M. Osborn, 2 vols., Oxford: Clarendon Press, 1966.

Swift, Jonathan, *The Poems of Jonathan Swift*, ed. Harold Williams, 3 vols., 2nd edn, Oxford: Clarendon Press, 1958.

   The Prose Works of Jonathan Swift, ed. Herbert J. Davis *et al.*, 16 vols., Oxford: Blackwell, 1939–74.

Thurmond, John, *Harlequin Shepard*, London, 1724.

Walker, Thomas, *The Quaker's Opera; or, The Escapes of Jack Sheppard*, London, 1728.

Watts, Isaac, *Divine Songs Attempted in easy Language, for the Use of Children*, 13th edn, London, 1735.

The Whole Duty of Man, laid down in a Plain and Familiar Way for the Use of All, but especially the Meanest Reader, London, 1653.

Wolley, Hannah, *The Compleat Servant-Maid; or, The Young Maiden's Tutor*, 4th edn, London, 1685.

   The Gentlewoman's Companion: or, A Guide to the Female Sex Containing Directions of Behaviour, in All Places, Companies, relations and Conditions, from their Childhood Down to Old Age, London, 1675.

Wilkes' Jest Book; or the Merry Patriot, London, 1770.

Secondary works

Altick, Richard D., *The Shows of London*, Cambridge, MA: Harvard University Press, 1978.

Armstrong, Nancy, *Desire and Domestic Fiction: A Political History of the Novel*, Oxford: Oxford University Press, 1987.

Avery, Emmett L. (ed.), *The London Stage 1660–1800, Part 2: 1700–1729*, Carbondale: Southern Illinois University Press, 1960.

Backscheider, Paula, *Spectacular Politics: Theatrical Power and Mass Culture in Early Modern England*, Baltimore, MD: Johns Hopkins University Press, 1993.

Bertelsen, Lance, *Henry Fielding at Work: Magistrate, Businessman, Writer*, New York: Palgrave, 2000.

   The Nonsense Club: Literature and Popular Culture 1749–1764, Oxford: Clarendon Press, 1986.

Capp, Bernard, *English Almanacs 1500–1800: Astrology and the Popular Press*, Ithaca, NY: Cornell University Press, 1979.

Colley, Linda, *Britons: Forging the Nation 1707–1837*, New Haven, CT: Yale University Press, 1992.

Darton, F. J. Harvey, *Children's Books in England,* Cambridge: Cambridge University Press, 1932.

Dugaw, Dianne, *Warrior Women and Popular Balladry, 1650–1850,* Cambridge: Cambridge University Press, 1989.

Glen, Heather, *Vision and Disenchantment: Blake's 'Songs' and Wordsworth's 'Lyrical Ballads',* Cambridge: Cambridge University Press, 1983.

George, M. D., *London Life in the Eighteenth Century,* London, 1925, rpt. Chicago: Academy Chicago Publishers, 1984.

Harris, Tim (ed.), *Popular Culture in England, c. 1500–1800,* London: Macmillan, 1995.

Hornbeck, Katherine, 'Richardson's *Familiar Letters* and the Domestic Conduct Books', *Smith College Studies in Modern Languages* 19. 2 (January 1938), 1–29.

Hughes, Leo, *A Century of English Farce,* Princeton, NJ: Princeton University Press, 1956.

Hume, Robert D., *Henry Fielding and the London Theatre 1728–1737,* Oxford: Clarendon Press, 1988.

Hunter, J. Paul, *Before Novels: The Cultural Contexts of Eighteenth-Century Fiction,* New York: W. W. Norton, 1990.

Linebaugh, Peter, *The London Hanged: Crime and Civil Society in the Eighteenth Century,* Cambridge: Cambridge University Press, 1992.

McDowell, Paula, *The Women of Grub Street: Press, Politics, and Gender in the London Literary Marketplace 1678–1730,* Oxford: Clarendon Press, 1998.

McKendrick, Neil, John Brewer and J. H. Plumb (eds.), *The Birth of a Consumer Society,* Bloomington: Indiana University Press, 1982.

Midgley, Graham, *The Life of Orator Henley,* Oxford: Clarendon Press, 1973.

Mullan, John and Christopher Reid (eds.), *Eighteenth-Century Popular Culture: A Selection,* Oxford: Oxford University Press, 2000.

Neuburg, Victor E., *The Penny Histories,* London: Oxford University Press, 1968.

O'Brien, John, 'Eighteenth-Century Pantomime and the Cultural Location of Entertainment(s)', *Theatre Journal* 50.4 (1998), 489–510.

Pedersen, Susan, 'Hannah More Meets Simple Simon: Tracts, Chapbooks, and Popular Culture in Late Eighteenth-Century England', *Journal of British Studies* 25 (1986), 84–113.

Paulson, Ronald, *Hogarth,* rev. edn, 3 vols., New Brunswick, NJ: Rutgers University Press, 1993.

  Popular and Polite Art in the Age of Hogarth and Fielding, Notre Dame, IN: University of Notre Dame Press, 1979.

Reay, Barry, *Popular Cultures in England 1550–1750,* New York: Longman, 1998.

Rogers, Pat, *Grub Street: Studies in a Subculture,* London: Methuen, 1972.

  Literature and Popular Culture in Eighteenth-Century England, Brighton, Sussex: The Harvester Press, 1986.

Sechelski, Denise S., 'Garrick's Body and the Labor of Art in Eighteenth-Century Theater', *Eighteenth-Century Studies* 29 (1996), 377–8.

Shepard, Leslie, *The History of Street Literature,* Newton Abbot: David & Charles, 1973.

Simons John (ed.), *Guy of Warwick and Other Chapbook Romances,* Exeter: University of Exeter Press, 1998.

Spufford, Margaret, *Small Books and Pleasant Histories,* London: Methuen & Co, 1981.

Stallybrass, Peter and White, Allon, *The Politics and Poetics of Transgression*, London: Methuen, 1986.

Thompson, E. P., *Customs in Common: Studies in Traditional Popular Culture*, New York: The New Press, 1993.

The Making of the English Working Class, New York: Vintage, 1966.

Thwaite, M. F., *From Primer to Pleasure*, London: The Library Association, 1963.

Todd, Dennis, *Imagining Monsters: Miscreations of the Self in Eighteenth-Century England*, Chicago: University of Chicago Press, 1995.

Winton, Calhoun, *John Gay and the London Theatre*, Lexington: University Press of Kentucky, 1993.

CHAPTER 4 BIBLIOGRAPHY

Primary works

Aubin, Penelope, *A collection of entertaining histories and novels: designed to promote the cause of virtue and honour, principally founded on facts and interspersed with a variety of beautiful and instructive incidents*, London, 1739.

Behn, Aphra, *Love Letters Between a Nobleman and His Sister*, vol. II of *The Works of Aphra Behn*, ed. Janet Todd, Oxford: Oxford University Press, 1993.

Fielding, Henry, *The History of Tom Jones, A Foundling*, intro. and commentary, Martin C. Battestin, ed. Fredson Bowers, Oxford: Oxford University Press, 1974.

Haywood, Eliza, *Love in Excess; or The Fatal Enquiry*, ed. David Oakleaf, Peterborough, Ontario: Broadview Press, 1994.

Manley, Delariviere, *The New Atalantis*, ed. Rosalind Ballaster, London: Penguin, 1991.

Reeve, Clara, *The Progress of Romance*, 2 vols. Colchester, 1785.

Secondary works

Ballaster, Ros, *Seductive Forms: Women's Amatory Fiction from 1684 to 1740*, Oxford: Oxford University Press, 1992.

Benjamin, Walter, *The Origins of German Tragic Drama*, intro. George Steiner, trans. George Osborne, London: Verso New Left Books, 1985.

Bowers, Toni O'Shaughnnesy, 'Sex, Lies and Invisibility: Amatory Fiction from the Restoration to Mid-Century', in John Richetti (ed.), *The Columbia History of the English Novel*, New York: Columbia University Press, 1994, pp. 50–72.

Brown, Laura, *Ends of Empire: Women and Ideology in Early Eighteenth-Century English Literature*, Ithaca, NY: Cornell University Press, 1993.

De Certeau, Michel de, *Practice of Everyday Life*, trans. Steven F. Rendall, Berkeley and Los Angeles: University of California Press, 1984.

DeJean, Joan, *Tender Geographies: Women and the Origins of the Novel in France*, New York: Columbia University Press, 1991.

Eaves, T. C. Duncan, and Ben D. Kimpel, *Samuel Richardson: A Biography*, Oxford: Oxford University Press, 1971.

Gardiner, Judith Kegan, ' "The First English Novel": Aphra Behn's *Love Letters*, The Canon, and Women's Taste', *Tulsa Studies in Women's Literature* 8 (1989), 201–22.

Habermas, Jürgen, *The Structural Transformation of the Public Sphere*, trans. Thomas Burger, Cambridge, MA: M.I.T. Press, 1989.

Keymer, Thomas and Peter Sabor, eds., *The Pamela Controversy: Criticisms and Adaptations of Samuel Richardson's Pamela, 1740–1750*, 6 vols., London: Pickering & Chatto, 2001.

Modleski, Tania, *Loving with a Vengeance*, New York: Methuen, 1984.

Radway, Jancie A., *Reading the Romance: Women, Patriarchy, and Popular Literature*, Chapel Hill: University of North Carolina Press, 1984.

Reeve, Clara. *The Progress of Romance*, Colchester, 1785.

Richetti, John, *Popular Fiction Before Richardson: Narrative Patterns: 1700–1739*, Oxford: Clarendon Press, 1969; rpt. 1992.

Saxton, Kirsten T. and Rebecca P. Bocchicchio (eds.), *The Passionate Fictions of Eliza Haywood: Essays on Her Life and Work*, Lexington: University Press of Kentucky, 2000.

Schofield, Mary Anne (ed.), *Masquerade Novels of Eliza Haywood*, Delmar, NY: Scholars Facsimiles and Reprints, 1986.

Spencer, Jane, *The Rise of the Woman Novelist: from Aphra Behn to Jane Austen*, Oxford: Basil Blackwell, 1986.

Todd, Janet, *The Sign of Angelica: Women, Writing, and Fiction, 1660–1800*, New York: Columbia University Press, 1989.

Turner, Cheryl, *Living by the Pen: Women Writers in the Eighteenth Century*, London: Routledge, 1992.

Warner, William B., *Licensing Entertainment: the Elevation of Novel Reading in Britain, 1684–1750*, Berkeley: University of California Press, 1998.

Watt, Ian, *The Rise of the Novel: Studies in Defoe, Richardson, and Fielding*, Berkeley and Los Angeles: University of California Press, 1957.

CHAPTER 5 BIBLIOGRAPHY

Primary works

Behn, Aphra, *The Works of Aphra Behn*, ed. Janet Todd, 7 vols., London: Pickering and Chatto, 1992–6.

Boyle, Roger, *The Dramatic Works, of Roger Boyle, Earl of Orrery*, ed. W. S. Clark, 2 vols., Cambridge, MA: Harvard University Press, 1937.

Burnaby, William, *The Dramatic Works of William Burnaby*, ed. F. E. Budd, London: Eric Partridge, 1931.

Cavendish, Margaret, Duchess of Newcastle, *Plays Never before Printed*, London, 1668.

Centlivre, Susannah, *The Dramatic Works*, 3 vols., London: Pearson, 1872.

Cibber, Colley, *The Dramatic Works of Colley Cibber*, 4 vols., London, 1760.

Congreve, William, *The Complete Plays of William Congreve*, ed. Herbert Davis, Chicago: University of Chicago Press, 1967.

Crowne, John, *The Comedies of John Crowne: a Critical Edition*, ed. B. J. McMullin, New York: Garland, 1984.

The Dramatic Works of John Crowne, ed. James Maidment and W. H. Logan, 4 vols., Edinburgh: Patterson, 1872–4.

Danchin, Pierre, ed., *The Prologues and Epilogues of the Restoration 1660–1700*, 7 vols., Nancy: Presses universitaires de Nancy, 1981–8.

Dryden, John, *The Works of John Dryden*, gen. eds. Edward Niles Hooker, H. T. Swedenberg Jr and Alan Roper, 20 vols., Berkeley and Los Angeles: University of California Press, 1956–2002.

Etherege, Sir George, *The Dramatic Works of Sir George Etherege*, ed. H. F. B. Brett-Smith, 2 vols., Oxford: Blackwell, 1927.

Farquhar, George, *The Works of George Farquhar*, ed. Shirley Strum Kenny, Oxford: Clarendon Press, 1988.

Gay, John, *Dramatic Works*, ed. John Fuller, 2 vols., Oxford: Clarendon Press, 1983.

Lee, Nathaniel, *The Works of Nathaniel Lee*, ed. Thomas B. Stroup and Arthur L. Cooke, 2 vols., New Brunswick, NJ: Scarecrow Press, 1954–5.

Otway, Thomas, *The Works of Thomas Otway*, ed. J. C. Ghosh, 2 vols., Oxford: Clarendon Press, 1932.

Pepys, Samuel, *The Diary of Samuel Pepys*, ed. Robert Latham and William Matthews, 11 vols., London: G. Bell & Sons, 1970–83.

Sedley, Sir Charles, *The Poetical and Dramatic Works of Sir Charles Sedley*, ed. V. de Sola Pinto, 2 vols., London: Constable, 1928.

Shadwell, Thomas, *The Complete Works of Thomas Shadwell*, ed. Montague Summers, 5 vols., London: The Fortune Press, 1927.

Southerne, Thomas, *The Works of Thomas Southerne*, ed. Robert Jordan and Harold Love, 2 vols., Oxford: Oxford University Press, 1989.

Steele, Sir Richard, *The Plays of Sir Richard Steele*, ed. Shirley Strum Kenny, Oxford: Clarendon Press, 1971.

Vanbrugh, Sir John, *The Complete Works of Sir John Vanbrugh*, ed. Bonamy Dobrée and Geoffrey Webb, 4 vols., London: Nonesuch Press, 1927.

Wilmot, John, second Earl of Rochester, *The Works of John Wilmot, Earl of Rochester*, ed. Harold Love, Oxford: Oxford University Press, 1999.

Wycherley, William, *The Plays of William Wycherley*, ed. Arthur Friedman, Oxford: Clarendon Press, 1979.

Secondary works

Canfield, J. Douglas, *Nicholas Rowe and Christian Tragedy*, Gainsville: University of Florida Press, 1977.

  Tricksters and Estates: On the Ideology of Restoration Comedy, Lexington: University Press of Kentucky, 1997.

Danchin, Pierre, *The Prologues and Epilogues of the Restoration 1660–1700*, 7 vols., Nancy: Publications de l'université de Nancy II, 1981–8.

Dobrée, Bonamy, *Restoration Comedy 1660–1720*, London: Oxford University Press, 1921.

Fisk, Deborah Payne, *The Cambridge Companion to Restoration Drama*, Cambridge: Cambridge University Press, 2000.

Fujimura, Thomas H., *The Restoration Comedy of Wit*, Princeton, NJ: Princeton University Press, 1952.

Holland, Norman N., *The First Modern Comedies: the Significance of Etherege, Wycherley and Congreve*, Cambridge, MA: Harvard University Press, 1959.

Holland, Peter, *The Ornament of Action: Text and Performance in Restoration Comedy*, Cambridge: Cambridge University Press, 1979.

Hughes, Derek, *English Drama 1660–1700*, Oxford: Oxford University Press, 1996.

Hughes, Leo, *A Century of English Farce*, Princeton, NJ: Princeton University Press, 1956.

Hume, Robert D., *English Drama in the Later Seventeenth Century*, Oxford: Oxford University Press 1976.

  Henry Fielding and the London Theatre, 1728–1737, Oxford: Oxford University Press, 1988.

Jordan, Robert J., *The Convict Theatres of Early Australia: 1788–1840*, Sydney: Currency Press, 2002.

Kewes, Paulina, *Authorship and Appropriation: Writing for the Stage in England, 1660–1710*, Oxford: Oxford University Press, 1998.

Knights, L. C., 'Restoration Comedy: the Reality and the Myth', in *Explorations: Essays in Criticism, Mainly on the Literature of the Seventeenth Century*, London: Chatto and Windus, 1946, pp. 131–49.

Loftis, John, *The Politics of Drama in Augustan England*, Oxford: Oxford University Press, 1963.

The London Stage, 1660–1800, Part 1: 1660–1700, ed. William Van Lennep; Part 2: 1700–1729, ed. Emmett L. Avery, 2 vols., and Part 3: 1729–1747, ed. Arthur H. Scouten, 2 vols., Carbondale: Southern Illinois University Press, 1960–5.

Love, Harold, *Congreve*, Oxford: Blackwell, 1974.

  'Constructing Classicism: Dryden and Purcell', in Paul Hammond and David Hopkins (eds.), *John Dryden: Tercentenary Essays*, Oxford: Oxford University Press, 2000, pp. 92–112.

  'Dryden, Rochester and the invention of the "Town"', in *John Dryden (1631–1700): His Politics, his Plays, and his Poets*, Newark, DE: University of Delaware Press, 2004, pp. 36–51.

Luckett, Richard, 'Exotick but rational entertainments', in Marie Axton and Raymond Williams (eds.), *English Drama: Forms and Development. Essays in Honour of Muriel Clara Bradbrook*, Cambridge: Cambridge University Press, 1977, pp. 123–41.

Lynch, Kathleen M., *The Social Mode of Restoration Comedy*, New York: Macmillan, 1926.

Maguire, Nancy Klein, *Regicide and Restoration: English Tragicomedy 1660–1671*, Cambridge: Cambridge University Press, 1992.

Manley, Lawrence, *Literature and Culture in Early Modern London*, Cambridge: Cambridge University Press, 1995.

Markley, Robert, *Two-edg'd Weapons: Style and Ideology in the Comedies of Etherege, Wycherley, and Congreve*, Oxford: Oxford University Press, 1988.

Marshall, Geoffrey, *Restoration Serious Drama*, Norman: University of Oklahoma Press, 1975.

McCarthy, B. Eugene, *William Wycherley: a Biography*, Athens, OH: Ohio University Press, 1980.

Milhous, Judith and Hume, Robert D., 'The Multimedia Spectacular on the Restoration Stage', in Shirley Strum Kenny (ed.), *British Theatre and the Other Arts, 1660–1800*, Washington: Folger Books, 1984, pp. 41–66.

  Producible Interpretations: Eight English Plays, 1675–1707, Carbondale: Southern Illinois University Press, 1985.

  A Register of English Theatrical Documents 1660–1737, 2 vols., Carbondale: Southern Illinois University Press, 1991.

Thomas Betterton and the Management of Lincoln's Inn Fields, 1695–1708, Carbondale: Southern Illinois University Press, 1979.

Nicoll, Allardyce, *A History of English Drama 1660–1900*, 6 vols., Cambridge: Cambridge University Press, 1959.

Owen, Susan J., *Restoration Theatre in Crisis*, Oxford: Oxford University Press, 1996.

Owen, Susan J. (ed.), *A Companion to Restoration Drama*, Oxford: Blackwell, 2001.

Palmer, John, *Comedy of Manners*, London: Bell, 1913.

Pearson, Jacqueline, *The Prostituted Muse*, Hemel Hempstead: Harvester Wheatsheaf, 1988.

Roberts, David, *The Ladies: Female Patronage of Restoration Drama 1660–1700*, Oxford: Oxford University Press, 1989.

Powell, Jocelyn, *Restoration Theatre Production*, London: Routledge, 1984.

Price, Curtis, *Henry Purcell and the London Stage*, Cambridge: Cambridge University Press, 1984.

Music in the Restoration Theatre, Ann Arbor, MI: UMI Research Press, 1979.

Rivero, Albert J., *The Plays of Henry Fielding: A Critical Study of His Dramatic Career*, Charlottesville: University Press of Virginia, 1989.

Rothstein, Eric, *Restoration Tragedy: Form and the Process of Change*, Madison: University of Wisconsin Press, 1967.

Slagle, Judith (ed.), *Thomas Shadwell Reconsider'd*, published as *Restoration* 20 (1996).

Smith, Dane, *Plays about the Theatre in England*, London: Oxford University Press, 1936.

Smith, John Harrington, *The Gay Couple in Restoration Comedy*, Cambridge, MA: Harvard University Press, 1948.

Styan, J. L., *Restoration Comedy in Performance*, Cambridge: Cambridge University Press, 1986.

Turner, James G., 'The Libertine Sublime: Love and Death in Restoration England', *Studies in Eighteenth-century Culture* 19 (1989), 99–115.

Underwood, Dale, *Etherege and the Seventeenth-century Comedy of Manners*, New Haven, CT Yale University Press, 1957.

Whyman, Susan E., *Sociability and Power in Late-Stuart England: the Cultural Worlds of the Verneys 1660–1700*, Oxford: Oxford University Press, 1999.

Winn, James A., 'Theatrical Culture 2: Theatre and Music', in Stephen N. Zwicker (ed.), *The Cambridge Companion to English Literature 1650–1740*, Cambridge: Cambridge University Press, 1998, pp. 104–19.

CHAPTER 6 BIBLIOGRAPHY

Primary works (editions of Dryden)

The Critical and Miscellaneous Prose Works of John Dryden, ed. Edmond Malone, 3 vols., London, 1800.

The Essays of John Dryden, ed. W. P. Ker, Oxford: Oxford University Press, 1900.

John Dryden: Selected Poems, ed. Steven N. Zwicker and David Bywaters, Harmondsworth: Penguin, 2001.

The Letters of John Dryden, ed. Charles E. Ward, Durham, NC: University of North Carolina Press, 1942.

Of Dramatic Poesy and Other Critical Essays, ed. George Watson, 2 vols., London: Everyman Dutton, 1962.

The Poems of John Dryden, ed. James Kinsley, 4 vols., Oxford: Oxford University Press, 1958.

The Works of John Dryden, eds., E. N. Hooker and H. T. Swedenberg, Jr., *et al.* 20 vols., Berkeley and Los Angeles: University of California Press, 1956–2002.

The Works of John Dryden, ed. Walter Scott, 18 vols., Edinburgh, 1808, rev. George Saintsbury, Edinburgh, 1882–93.

Primary works (bibliography)

Arthur E. Case, *A Bibliography of English Poetical Miscellanies, 1521–1750*, Oxford: Oxford University Press, 1935.

James and Helen Kinsley (eds.), Dryden: *The Critical Heritage*, London: Routledge and Kegan Paul, 1972.

David J. Latt, and Samuel Holt Monk, *John Dryden: A Survey and Bibliography of Critical Studies, 1895–1974*, Minneapolis: University of Minnesota Press, 1976.

Hugh Macdonald, *John Dryden: A Bibliography of Early Editions and of Drydeniana*, Oxford: Oxford University Press, 1939.

Primary works (biography)

Johnson, Samuel, 'Life of Dryden', *Lives of the English Poets*, London, 1779–81.

Osborn, James M., *John Dryden: Some Biographical Facts and Problems,* New York: Columbia University Press 1940; rev. edn, 1965.

Scott, Sir Walter, *The Life of John Dryden*, in volume I of *The Works*, ed. Scott.

Ward, Charles E., *The Life of John Dryden*, Chapel Hill, NC: University of North Carolina Press, 1961.

Winn, James A., *John Dryden and his World*, New Haven, CT: Yale University Press, 1987.

Secondary works (history)

Harris, Tim, *Politics Under the Later Stuarts: Party Conflict in a Divided Society, 1660–1715*, New York: Longman, 1993.

Hutton, Ronald, *The Restoration: A Political and Religious History of England and Wales, 1658–1667*, Oxford: Oxford University Press, 1985.

Hutton, Ronald, *Charles the Second: King of England, Scotland, and Ireland,* Oxford: Oxford University Press, 1989.

Jones, J. R., *Country and Court: England, 1658–1714*, Cambridge, MA: Harvard University Press, 1978.

Miller, John, *Popery and Politics in England, 1660–1688*, Cambridge: Cambridge University Press, 1973.

Seaward, Paul, *The Restoration 1660–1688*, New York: St Martin's Press, 1991.

Smuts, R. Malcolm (ed.), *The Stuart Court and Europe: Essays in Politics and Political Culture*, Cambridge: Cambridge University Press, 1996.

Spurr, John, *The Restoration Church of England, 1649–1689*, New Haven, CT: Yale University Press, 1991.

Secondary works (criticism)

Brown, Laura, *English Dramatic Form, 1660–1740*, New Haven, CT: Yale University Press, 1981.

Brower, Reuben, *Alexander Pope: Poetry of Allusion,* Oxford: Oxford University Press, 1959.

Bywaters, David, *Dryden in Revolutionary England*, Berkeley and Los Angeles, University of California Press, 1991.

Caldwell, Tayna, *Time to Begin Anew: Dryden's Georgics and Aeneis*, Lewisburg, PA: Bucknell University Press, 2000.

Eliot, T. S., *Homage to John Dryden*, London: The Hogarth Press, 1924.

Erskine-Hill, Howard, *Poetry and the Realm of Politics: Shakespeare to Dryden,* Oxford: Oxford University Press, 1996.

Gelber, Michael, *The Just and the Lively: The Literary Criticism of John Dryden*, Manchester: Manchester University Press, 1999.

Green Susan, and Steven N. Zwicker (eds.), *John Dryden, A Tercentenary Miscellany*, San Marino, CA: Huntington Library, 2001.

Griffin, Dustin, *Literary Patronage in England, 1650–1740*, Cambridge: Cambridge University Press, 1996.

Hammond, Paul, and David Hopkins (eds.), *John Dryden, Tercentenary Essays*, Oxford: Oxford University Press, 2000.

Hammond, Paul, *Dryden and the Traces of Classical Rome*, Oxford: Oxford University Press, 1999.

Harth, Phillip, *Pen for a Party: Dryden's Tory Propaganda in Its Contexts*, Princeton, NJ: Princeton University Press, 1993.

Hill, Geoffrey, *The Enemy's Country*, Stanford, CA: Stanford University Press, 1991.

Hopkins, David, *John Dryden*, Cambridge: Cambridge University Press, 1986.

Hoxby, Blair, *Literature and Economics in the Age of Milton*, New Haven, CT: Yale University Press, 2002.

Hughes, Derek, *Dryden's Heroic Plays*, London: Macmillan, 1981.

Hume, Robert D., *Dryden's Criticism*, Ithaca, NJ: Cornell University Press, 1970.

Kewes, Paulina, *Authorship and Appropriation: Writing for the Stage in England, 1660–1710*, Oxford: Oxford University Press, 1998.

Kirsch, Arthur C., *Dryden's Heroic Drama*, Princeton, NJ: Princeton University Press, 1965.

Kramer, David Bruce, *The Imperial Dryden: The Poetics of Appropriation in Seventeenth-Century England*, Athens, GA: University of Georgia Press, 1994.

Kroll, Richard, *The Material Word: Literate Culture in the Restoration and Early Eighteenth Century*, Baltimore, MD: Johns Hopkins University Press, 1991.

Levine, Joseph, *Between the Ancients and the Moderns: Baroque Culture in Restoration England*, New Haven, CT: Yale University Press, 1999.

Love, Harold, *Scribal Publication in Seventeenth-Century England*, Oxford: Oxford University Press, 1993.

MacFadden, George, *Dryden the Public Writer: 1660–1685*, Princeton, NJ: Princeton University Press, 1978.

MacLean, Gerald (ed.), *Culture and Society in the Stuart Restoration*, Cambridge: Cambridge University Press, 1995.

Maguire, Nancy Klein, *Regicide and Restoration: English Tragicomedy 1660–1671*, Cambridge: Cambridge University Press, 1992.

McKeon, Michael, *Politics and Poetry in Restoration England: The Case of Dryden's Annus Mirabilis*, Cambridge, MA: Harvard University Press, 1975.

Miner, Earl, *Dryden's Poetry*, Bloomington: University of Indiana Press, 1967.

Owen, Susan, *Restoration Theater and Crisis*, Oxford: Oxford University Press, 1996.

Orr, Bridget, *Empire on the English Stage: 1660–1714*, Cambridge: Cambridge University Press, 2001.

Paulson, Ronald, *The Fictions of Satire*, Baltimore, MD: Johns Hopkins University Press, 1967.

Ricks, Christopher, *Allusion to the Poets*, Oxford: Oxford University Press, 2002.

Roper, Alan, *Dryden's Poetic Kingdoms*, New York: Barnes & Noble, 1965.

Schilling, Bernard, *Dryden and the Conservative Myth: A Reading of 'Absalom and Achitophel'*, New Haven, CT: Yale University Press, 1961.

Van Doren, Mark, *The Poetry of John Dryden*, New York: Harcourt Brace, 1920.

Verrall, A. W., *Lectures on Dryden*, Cambridge: Cambridge University Press, 1914.

Weinbrot, Howard, *Augustus Caesar in 'Augustan' England*, Princeton, NJ: Princeton University Press, 1978.

Zwicker, Steven N., *Dryden's Political Poetry: The Arts of Disguise*, Princeton, NJ: Princeton University Press, 1983.

CHAPTER 7 BIBLIOGRAPHY

Primary works

A Collection of the Best English Poetry, by Several Hands . . . in Two Volumes, London: T. Warner, 1717.

Dryden, John, *The Poems of John Dryden*, ed. James Kinsley, 4 vols., Oxford: Oxford University Press, 1958.

Lonsdale, Roger (ed.), *Eighteenth-Century Women Poets: An Oxford Anthology*, Oxford: Oxford University Press, 1989.

   The New Oxford: Oxford Book of Eighteenth Century Verse, Oxford: Oxford University Press, 1984.

Pope, Alexander, *The Poems of Alexander Pope*, ed. John Butt *et al.*, New Haven, CT: Yale University Press, 1963.

Prior, Matthew, *The Literary Works of Matthew Prior*, ed. H. Bunker Wright and Monroe K. Spears, 2nd edn, Oxford: Clarendon Press, 1971.

Swift, Jonathan, *The Poems of Jonathan Swift*, ed. Harold Williams, 3 vols., Oxford: Clarendon Press, 1937.

   The Prose Works of Jonathan Swift, ed. Herbert Davis, 14 vols., Oxford: Basil Blackwell, 1957.

Trapp, Joseph, *Lectures on Poetry* (London, 1742), with a new introduction by John Vladimir Price, London: Routledge / Thoemmes Press, 1994.

Bibliographies

Secondary works

Adams, Percy G., *Graces of Harmony: Alliteration, Assonance, and Consonance in Eighteenth-Century British Poetry*, Athens, GA: University of Georgia Press, 1977.

Chapin, Chester, *Personification in Eighteenth-Century English Poetry*, New York: Columbia University Press, 1955.

Daiches, David, *A Critical History of English Literature*, London: Secker and Warburg, 1960.

Davie, Donald, *Articulate Energy: An Inquiry Into the Syntax of English Poetry*, London: Routledge and Kegan Paul, 1955.

Purity of Diction in English Verse, new edn, London: Chatto and Windus, 1967.

Doody, Margaret Anne, *The Daring Muse: Augustan Poetry Reconsidered*, Cambridge: Cambridge University Press, 1985.

Edwards, Thomas R., *Imagination and Power: A Study of Poetry on Public Themes*, New York: Oxford University Press, 1971.

Ehrenpreis, Irvin, *Acts of Implication: Suggestion and Covert Meaning in the Works of Dryden, Swift, Pope, and Austen*, Berkeley and Los Angeles: University of California Press, 1980.

Literary Meaning and Augustan Values, Charlottesville: University Press of Virginia, 1974.

Ezell, Margaret, *Social Authorship and the Advent of Print*, Baltimore, MD: Johns Hopkins University Press, 1999.

Fairer, David, *English Poetry of the Eighteenth Century, 1700–1789*, London and New York: Longman, 2003.

Fry, Paul H., *The Poet's Calling in the English Ode*, New Haven, CT: Yale University Press, 1980.

Fussell, Paul, *The Rhetorical World of Augustan Humanism: Ethics and Imagery From Swift to Burke*, Oxford: Clarendon Press, 1965.

Theory of Prosody in Eighteenth-Century England, New London: Connecticut College, 1954.

Griffin, Dustin, *Regaining Paradise: Milton and the Eighteenth Century*, Cambridge: Cambridge University Press, 1986.

Hunter, J. Paul, *Before Novels: The Cultural Contexts of Eighteenth-Century Fiction*, New York: W. W. Norton, 1990.

Jack, Ian, *Augustan Satire: Intention and Idiom in English Poetry, 1660–1750*, Oxford: Clarendon Press, 1952.

Love, Harold, *Scribal Publication in Seventeenth-Century England*, Oxford: Clarendon Press, 1993.

Marotti, Arthur F., *Manuscript, Print, and the English Renaissance Lyric*, Ithaca, NY: Cornell University Press, 1995.

Mell, Donald C., *English Poetry, 1660–1800: A Guide to Information Sources*, Detroit: Gale Research, 1982.

Morris, David B., *The Religious Sublime. Christian Poetry and Critical Tradition in 18th-Century England*, Lexington: University Press of Kentucky, 1972.

Nokes, David, and Janet Barron, *An Annotated Critical Bibliography of Augustan Poetry*, New York: St Martin's Press, 1989.

Piper, William Bowman, *The Heroic Couplet*, Cleveland, OH: Press of Case Western Reserve University, 1969.

Price, Martin, *To the Palace of Wisdom: Studies in Order and Energy From Dryden to Blake*, Garden City, NY: Doubleday, 1965.

Rawson, Claude J., *Order From Confusion Sprung: Studies in Eighteenth-Century Literature From Swift to Cowper*, Boston and London: Allen & Unwin, 1985.

Rogers, Pat, *The Augustan Vision*, London: Weidenfeld and Nicolson, 1974.

Rothstein, Eric, *Restoration and Eighteenth-Century Poetry, 1660–1780*, Boston: Routledge & Kegan Paul, 1981.

Sitter, John (ed.), *The Cambridge Companion to Eighteenth-Century Poetry*, Cambridge: Cambridge University Press, 2001.

Smith, David Nichol, *Some Observations on Eighteenth-Century Poetry*, 2nd edn, Toronto: University of Toronto Press, 1960.

Spacks, Patricia Meyer, *The Insistence of Horror: Aspects of the Supernatural in Eighteenth-Century Poetry*, Cambridge, MA: Harvard University Press, 1962.

The Poetry of Vision: Five Eighteenth-Century Poets, Cambridge, MA: Harvard University Press, 1967.

Sutherland, James, *English Literature of the Late Seventeenth Century*, New York: Oxford University Press, 1969.

A Preface to Eighteenth-Century Poetry, Oxford: Clarendon Press, 1948.

Trickett, Rachel, *The Honest Muse: A Study in Augustan Verse*, Oxford: Clarendon Press, 1967.

Watson, J. R., *The English Hymn: A Critical and Historical Study*, Oxford: Clarendon Press, 1997.

Weinbrot, Howard, *Alexander Pope and the Traditions of Formal Verse Satire*, Princeton, NJ: Princeton University Press, 1982.

Britannia's Issue: The Rise of British Literature from Dryden to Ossian, Cambridge: Cambridge University Press, 1995.

Eighteenth-Century Satire: Essays on Text and Context From Dryden to Peter Pindar, New York: Cambridge University Press, 1988.

The Formal Strain: Studies in Augustan Imitation and Satire, Chicago: University of Chicago Press, 1969.

Williams, Anne, *Prophetic Strain: The Greater Lyric in the Eighteenth Century*, Chicago: University of Chicago Press, 1984.

Zwicker, Steven N., *The Cambridge Companion to English Literature 1650–1740*, Cambridge: Cambridge University Press, 1998.

CHAPTER 8 BIBLIOGRAPHY

Primary works

Baillie, Joanna, *Poems: 1790*, New York: Woodstock, 1994.

Bannerman, Anne, *Poems by Anne Bannerman*, Edinburgh, 1800.

Barbauld, Anna Laetitia, *Poems*, London, 1773.

Barber, Mary, *Poems on Several Occasions*, London, 1734.

Brereton, Jane, *Merlin: A Poem. Humbly inscrib'd to Her Majesty. To which is added, the Royal Hermitage: a poem. Both by a lady*, London, 1735.

Poems on Several Occasions: By Mrs Jane Brereton. With Letters to her Friends, and an Account of her Life, London, 1744.

Carter, Elizabeth, *All the Works of Epictetus, which are Now Extant; Consisting of His Discourses, Preserved by Arrian, in Four Books, the Enchiridion, and Fragments. Translated from the Original Greek, by Elizabeth Carter. With an Introduction, and Notes, by the Translator*, London, 1758.

Poems on Several Occasions, 2d edn, London, 1766.

Cavendish, Margaret, 'To the Two Most Famous Universities in England', Preface to *Philosophical and Physical Opinions*, reprinted in Moira Ferguson (ed.), *First Feminists: British Women Writers, 1578–1799*, Bloomington: Indiana University Press, 1985.

Centlivre, Susanna, *An Epistle to the King of Sweden from a Lady of Great-Britain*, London, 1717.

Chapone, Hester, *The Works of Mrs Chapone, Containing Letters on the Improvement of the Mind, Addressed to a Young Lady. And Miscellanies in Prose and Verse*, 2 vols. Dublin, 1775.

Chudleigh, Mary, *The Ladies Defence: or, the Bride-Woman's Counsellor Answer'd: A Poem. In a Dialogue between Sir John Brute, Sir William Loveall, Melissa, and a Parson*, London, 1701.

The Poems and Prose of Mary, Lady Chudleigh, ed. Margaret Ezell, New York: Oxford University Press, 1993.

Clarke, [Adam], *The Georgian Era. Memoirs of the most eminent persons, who have flourished in Great Britain, from the accession of George the First to the demise of George the Fourth*, 4 vols., London, 1832–4.

Cockburn, Catherine Trotter, 'Verses, occasion'd by the Busts in the Queen's Hermitage, and Mr Duck being appointed Keeper of the Library in Merlin's Cave'. By the Authoress of a Treatise (not yet publish'd) in Vindication of Mr Lock, against the injurious charge of Dr Holdsworth,' *The Gentleman's Magazine* 7 (May 1737), 308.

Coleridge, Samuel T., *Poems: to which are now added Poems by Charles Lamb and Charles Lloyd*, London, 1797.

Colman, George (ed.), *Poems by Eminent Ladies*, 2 vols., London, 1755.

Colman, George, *Poems by the most eminent ladies of Great-Britain and Ireland. Particularly . . . Selected, with an Account of the Writers, by G. Colman and B. Thornton, Esqrs.*, 2 vols., London, 1773.

Poems by the Most Eminent Ladies of Great Britain and Ireland. Re-published from the Collection of G. Colman and B. Thornton, Esqrs. with Considerable Alterations, Additions, and Improvements, 2 vols., London, [1785].

Cowley, Abraham, *Poems: viz. I. Miscellanies. II. The mistress, or, love verses. III. Pindarique odes. And IV. Davideis, or a sacred poem of the troubles of David*, London, [1656].

Darwall, Mary, *Original Poems on Several Occasions*, London, 1764.

Poems on Several Occasions, 2 vols., Walsall, 1794.

Davys, Mary, *The Works of Mrs Davys: Consisting of, Plays, Novels, Poems, and Familiar Letters. Several of which never before publish'd*, 2 vols., London, 1725.

Dixon, Sarah, *Poems on Several Occasions*, Canterbury, 1740.

Dodsley, Robert (ed.), *A Collection of Poems in Six Volumes. By Several Hands*, 6 vols., London, 1737.

Dodsley, Robert, *A Collection of Poems in Three Volumes. By several hands*, 3 vols., London, 1748.

A Collection of Poems in Six Volumes. By Several Hands, 6 vols., London, 1755.

A Collection of Poems in Six Volumes. By Several Hands, 6 vols., London, 1758.

Dyce, Alexander (ed.), *Specimens of the British Poetesses; Selected and Chronologically Arranged by the Rev. Alexander Dyce*, London, 1825.

Edwards, Thomas, *The Canons of Criticism*, 7th edn, 1748; New York: Augustus M. Kelley Publishers, 1970.

Egerton, Sarah Fyge, *The Female Advocate: Or, An Answer to A Late Satyr Against the Pride, Lust and Inconstancy, &c. of Woman. Written by a Lady in Vindication of her Sex*, London, 1686. *Poems on Several Occasions, Together with a Pastoral*, London, [1703].

Eugenia, *The Female Advocate; or, A Plea for the Just Liberty of the Tender Sex, and Particularly of Married Women. Being Reflections on a Late Rude and Disingenuous Discourse, Delivered by Mr John Sprint, in a Sermon at a Wedding, May 11th, at Sherburn in Dorsetshire, 1699. By a Lady of Quality*, London, 1700.

Falconar, Maria and Harriet Falconar. *Poetic Laurels for Characters of Distinguished Merit . . . by Maria and Harriet Falconar*. London, 1791.

Finch, Anne, *The Anne Finch Wellesley Manuscript Poems*, eds. Barbara McGovern and Charles H. Hinnant, Athens, GA: University of Georgia Press, 1998.

The Poems of Anne Countess of Winchilsea from the Original Edition of 1713 and from Unpublished Manuscripts, ed. Myra Reynolds, Chicago: University of Chicago Press, 1903.

The Flower-Piece: A Collection of Miscellany Poems. By Several Hands, London, 1731.

Gay, John, *Fables*, London, 1727.

Gildon, Charles (ed.), *A New Miscellany of Original Poems, On Several Occasions*, London, 1701.

Gould, Robert, *Love given o're: or, A Satyr against the pride, lust, and inconstancy &c. of woman*, London, 1682.

Poems Chiefly Consisting of Satyrs and Satirical Epistles, London, [1689].

Gray, Thomas, *An Elegy Written in a Country Church Yard*, London, 1751.

Hands, Elizabeth, *The Death of Amnon. A Poem. With An Appendix: Containing Pastorals, and other Poetical Pieces*, Coventry, 1789; London: Routledge/Thoemmes Press, 1996.

Jones, Mary, *Miscellanies in Prose and Verse*, Oxford, 1750.

The Lady's Poetical Magazine, or Beauties of British Poetry, 3 vols., London, 1782.

Langhorne, John, 'Review of *Original Poems on Several Occasions*, by Mary Darwall', *Monthly Review* 30 (June 1764), 445–50.

Leapor, Mary, *Poems upon Several Occasions. By Mrs Leapor of Brackley in Northamptonshire*, London, 1748.

Poems upon Several Occasions. By the Late Mrs Leapor of Brackley in Northamptonshire. The Second and Last Volume, London, 1751.

Lennox, Charlotte, *Poems on Several Occasions. Written by a Young Lady*, London, 1747.

Loftt, Capel, *Laura: An Anthology*, 5 vols., London, 1813.

Madan, Judith, *The Progress of Poetry*, London, 1783.

Masters, Mary, *Familiar Letters and Poems on Several Occasions*, London, 1755.

Poems on Several Occasions. By a Young Gentleman, London, 1724.

Poems on Several Occasions, London, 1733.

Miller, Anna Riggs, Lady (ed.), *Poetical Amusements at a Villa near Bath*, 4 vols., London, 1776–81.

Monck, Mary, *Marinda. Poems and Translations upon Several Occasions*. London, 1716.

Montagu, Lady Mary Wortley, *Essays and Poems and Simplicity: A Comedy*, eds. Robert Halsband and Isobel Grundy, Oxford: Oxford University Press, 1977.

Letters of the Right Honourable Lady M—y W—y M—e: Written, During her Travels in Europe, Asia and Africa, to Persons of Distinction, Men of Letters, &c. in Different Parts of Europe. Which Contain, among other Curious Relations, Accounts of the Policy and Manners of the Turks, 3 vols., London, 1763.

The Poetical Works of the Right Honorable Lady M—y W—y M—e, London, 1768.

Six Town Eclogues. With Some other Poems, London, 1747.

Murry, Ann, *Mentoria: Or, the Young Ladies Instructor, in Familiar Conversations on Moral and Entertaining Subjects*, London, 1778.

Poems on Various Subjects, London, 1779.

Opie, Amelia, *Amelia Opie. Poems*, ed. Donald Reiman, New York: Garland Publishing, Inc., 1978.

Pearch, George (ed.), *A Collection of Poems in Two Volumes. By Several Hands*, 2 vols., London, 1768.

A Collection of Poems in Four Volumes. By Several Hands, 4 vols., London, 1770.

A Collection of Poems, in Four Volumes by Several Hands, 4 vols., London, 1775.

Pennington, Montagu, *Memoirs of the Life of Mrs Elizabeth Carter: with a New Edition of Her Poems: To Which Are Added, Some Miscellaneous Essays in Prose, Together with Her Notes on the bible, and Answers to Objections Concerning the Christian Religion*, London, 1807.

The Poetical Magazine; or, Temple of the Muses. Consisting Chiefly of Original Poems and Occasional Selections from Scarce and Valuable Publications. By a society of gentlemen, 2 vols., London, 1804.

The Poetical Register, and Repository of Fugitive Poetry, 8 vols., London, 1802.

Pope, Alexander, *Poems*, ed. John Butt, 11 vols., London: Methuen, 1951–69.

Prior, Matthew, *The Literary Works of Matthew Prior*, ed. H. Bunker Wright and Monroe K. Spears, 2 vols., 1959; Oxford: Oxford University Press, 1971.

Reeve, Clara, *Original Poems on Several Occasions*, London, 1769.

Rowe, Elizabeth Singer, *The Miscellaneous Works in Prose and Verse*, 2 vols., London, 1739.

Poems on Several Occasions, Written by Philomela, London, 1696.

Savage, Mary, *Poems on Various Subjects and Occasions; (From the Author's Manuscript, in the Hands of the Editor.)*, 2 vols., London, 1777.

Scott, Mary, *The Female Advocate; A Poem Occasioned by Reading Mr Duncombe's Feminead*, 1774; intro. Gae Holladay, The Augustan Reprint Society, publication number 24, Los Angeles: University of California Press, 1984.

Scott, Walter (ed.), *The Poetical Works of Anna Seward* (1810), 3 vols., New York: AMS, 1974.

Shiels, Robert (ed.), *The Lives of the Poets of Great Britain and Ireland, To the Time of Dean Swift. Compiled from ample Materials scattered in a Variety of Books, and especially from the MS. notes of the late ingenious, Mr Coxeter and others, collected for this Design by Mr Cibber*, 5 vols., London, 1753.

Smith, Charlotte, *The Emigrants, a poem, in two books*, London, 1793.

The Poems of Charlotte Smith, ed. Stuart Curran, New York: Oxford University Press, 1993.

Sprint, John, *The Bride-womans Counseller. Being a Sermon Preach'd at a Wedding, May the 11th, 1699, at Sherbourn, in Dorsetshire*, London, [1708].

Tate, Nahum (ed.), *Poems by Several Hands and on Several Occasions*, London, 1685.

Thomas, Ann, *Poems on Various Subjects, by Mrs Ann Thomas, of Millbrook, Cornwall, an officer's widow of the Royal Navy*, Plymouth, 1784.

Tollet, Elizabeth, *Poems on Several Occasions. With Anne Boleyn to King Henry VIII. An Epistle*, London, 1724.

Poems on Several Occasions. With Anne Boleyn to King Henry VIII. An Epistle, London, 1755.

Walpole, Horace. *The Yale Edition of Horace Walpole's Correspondence*, ed. Wilmarth S. Lewis, 48 vols., New Haven, CT: Yale University Press, 1937–83.

Williams, Helen Maria, *Julia: A Novel*, 2 vols., London, 1790; New York: Garland, 1974.

Poems, 2 vols., London, 1786.

Wordsworth, William (ed.), *Poems and Extracts Chosen by William Wordsworth for an Album Presented to Lady Mary Lowther Christmas, 1819*, London: Henry Frowde, 1905.

Yearsley, Ann, *The Rural Lyre; A Volume of Poems: Dedicated to the Right Honourable The Earl of Bristol, Lord Bishop of Derry*, 1796; London: Routledge / Thoemmes, 1996.

Secondary works

Barash, Carol, *English Women's Poetry, 1649–1714: Politics, Community, and Linguistic Authority*, Oxford: Clarendon Press, 1996.

Brooks, Stella, 'The Sonnets of Charlotte Smith', *Critical Survey* 4 (1992), 9–21.

Brower, Reuben, 'Lady Winchilsea and the Poetic Tradition of the Seventeenth Century', *SP* 42 (1945), 61–80.

Dobrée, Bonamy, *English Literature in the Early Eighteenth Century 1700–1740*, Oxford: Clarendon Press, 1959.

Doody, Margaret Anne, 'Swift Among the Women', *The Yearbook of English Studies* 18 (1988), 68–92.

Eves, Charles, *Matthew Prior: Poet and Diplomatist*, New York: Octagon Books, 1973.

Ezell, Margaret, *The Patriarch's Wife*, Chapel Hill: University of North Carolina Press, 1987.

Feldman, Paula R. and Daniel Robinson (eds.), *A Century of Sonnets*, New York: Oxford University Press, 1999.

Ferguson, Moira, *Subject to Others: British Women Writers and Colonial Slavery, 1670–1834*, New York: Routledge, 1992.

Fletcher, Loraine, *Charlotte Smith: A Critical Biography*, New York: St Martin's Press, 1998.

Fullard, Joyce (ed.), *British Women Poets 1660–1800: An Anthology*, Troy, NY: Whiston Publishing Company, 1990.

Gibson, Rebecca, '"My Want of Skill": Apologias of British Women Poets, 1660–1800', in Frederick Keener and Susan Lorsch (eds.), *Eighteenth-Century Women and the Arts*, New York: Greenwood Press, 1988, pp. 80–6.

Greer, Germaine, *Slip-shod Sibyls: Recognition, Rejection and the Woman Poet*, London: Viking Press, 1995.

Hinnant, Charles, *The Poetry of Anne Finch: An Essay in Interpretation*, Newark: University of Delaware Press, 1994.

King, Kathryn, 'Elizabeth Singer Rowe's Tactical Use of Print and Manuscript', in Nathan Tinker and George Justice (eds.), *Women's Writing and the Circulation of Ideas: Scribal Publication in England, 1550–1800*, Cambridge: Cambridge University Press, 2002.

Labbe, Jacqueline, 'Selling One's Sorrows: Charlotte Smith, Mary Robinson, and the Marketing of Poetry', *Wordsworth Circle* 25 (1994), 68–71.

Landry, Donna, *The Muses of Resistance: Laboring-Class Women's Poetry in Britain, 1739–1796*, Cambridge: Cambridge University Press, 1990.

Lonsdale, Roger (ed.), *Eighteenth-Century Women Poets*, Oxford: Oxford University Press, 1989.

Madan, Falconer, *The Madan Family and Maddens in Ireland and England: A Historical Account*, Oxford: printed for subscribers by John Johnson, 1933.

McGovern, Barbara, *Anne Finch and Her Poetry: A Critical Biography*, Athens: University of Georgia Press, 1992.

Mell, Donald C. (ed.), *Pope, Swift, and Women Writers*, Newark: University of Delaware Press, 1996.

Mergenthal, Sylvia, 'Charlotte Smith and the Romantic Sonnet Revival', in Susanne Fendler (ed.), *Feminist Contributions to the Literary Canon: Setting Standards of Taste*, Lewiston, ME: Edwin Mellor Press, 1997, pp. 65–79.

Messenger, Ann, *Woman and Poet in the Eighteenth Century: The Life of Mary Whateley Darwall (1738–1825)*, New York: AMS Press, 1999.

New Princeton Encyclopedia of Poetry and Poetics, eds. Alex Preminger and T. V. F. Brogan, Princeton, NJ: Princeton University Press, 1993.

Owen, W. J. B., and Jane W. Smyser (eds.), *The Prose Works of William Wordsworth*, 3 vols., Oxford: Clarendon Press, 1974.

Pitcher, E. W., 'Mary Whateley Darwall's Poem on "Female Friendship" (1776)', *Notes and Queries* 243 (1998), 469–472.

Robinson, Daniel, 'Reviving the Sonnet: Women Romantic Poets and the Sonnet Claim', *European Romantic Review*, 6 (1995), 98–127.

Rowton, Frederic, *The Female Poets of Great Britain Chronologically Arranged with Copious Selections and Critical Remarks by Frederic Rowton. A Facsimile of the 1853 edition with a Critical Introduction and bibliographical Appendices by Marilyn L. Williamson*, Detroit: Wayne State University Press, 1981.

Schlueter, Paul, and June Schlueter (eds.), *An Encyclopedia of British Women Writers*, New York and London: Garland Publishing, 1988.

Stanesa, Jamie, 'Anne Finch (1661–1720)', in *Dictionary of Literary Biography*, ed. John Sitter, vol. xcv, Detroit: Gale Research, Inc., 1990.

Stanton, Judith P., 'Charlotte Smith's "Literary Business": Income, Patronage, and Indigence', *The Age of Johnson*, 1 (1987), 393.

'Statistical Profile of Women Writing in English from 1660 to 1800', in Frederick Keener and Susan Lorsch (eds.), *Eighteenth-Century Women and the Arts*, New York: Greenwood Press, 1988, pp. 247–54.

Todd, Janet (ed.), *A Dictionary of British and American Women Writers, 1660–1800*, Totowa, NJ: Rowman & Allanheld, 1985.

Tucker, Bernard (ed.), *The Poetry of Laetitia Pilkington (1712–1750) and Constantia Grierson (1706–1733)*, Lewiston, ME: E. Mellen Press, 1996.

Weinbrot, Howard, *Augustus Caesar in 'Augustan' England*, Princeton, NJ: Princeton University Press, 1978.

Williamson, Marilyn L., *Raising Their Voices: British Women Writers, 1650–1750*, Detroit: Wayne State University Press, 1990.

CHAPTER 9 BIBLIOGRAPHY

Primary works

Swift, Jonathan, *Correspondence*, ed. Harold Williams, 5 vols., Oxford: Clarendon Press, 1963–5.
  Poems, ed. Harold Williams, 3 vols., Oxford: Clarendon Press: 2nd edn, 1958.
  Prose Works, ed. Herbert Davis *et al.*, 16 vols., Oxford: Blackwell, 1939–74.
  A Tale of A Tub, ed. A. C. Guthkelch and D. Nichol Smith, Oxford: Clarendon Press, 1958.

Secondary works

Boyle, Frank, *Swift as Nemesis: Modernity and its Satirist*, Palo Alto, CA: Stanford University Press, 2000.
Brady, Frank (ed.), *Twentieth-Century Interpretations of 'Gulliver's Travels'*, Englewood Cliffs, NJ: Prentice-Hall, 1968.
Bullitt, John M., *Jonathan Swift and the Anatomy of Satire: A Study of Satiric Technique*, Cambridge, MA: Harvard University Press, 1953.
Donoghue, Denis, *Jonathan Swift: A Critical Introduction*, Cambridge: Cambridge University Press, 1969.
Donoghue, Denis (ed.), *Jonathan Swift: A Critical Anthology*, Harmondsworth: Penguin, 1971.
Ehrenpreis, Irvin, *The Man, His Works, and the Age*, 3 vols., London: Methuen and Cambridge, MA: Harvard University Press, 1962–83.
Ewald, William Bragg, *The Masks of Jonathan Swift*, Cambridge, MA: Harvard University Press, 1954.
Goldgar, Bertrand A., *Walpole and the Wits: The Relation of Politics to Literature, 1722–1742*, Lincoln, NE: University of Nebraska Press, 1976.
Kelly, Ann Cline, *Jonathan Swift and Popular Culture: Myth, Media, and the Man*, New York: Palgrave, 2002.
Kramnick, Isaac, *Bolingbroke and his Circle: The Politics of Nostalgia in the Age of Walpole*, Cambridge, MA: Harvard University Press, 1969.
Lock, F. P., *The Politics of 'Gulliver's Travels'*, Oxford: Clarendon Press, 1980.
Nokes, David, *Jonathan Swift: A Hypocrite Reversed: A Critical Biography*, Oxford: Oxford University Press, 1985.
Paulson, Ronald, *Theme and Structure in Swift's Tale of a Tub*, New Haven, CT: Yale University Press, 1960.
Price, Martin, *Swift's Rhetorical Art: A Study in Structure and Meaning*, New Haven, CT: Yale University Press, 1953.
Rawson, Claude, ed., *The Character of Swift's Satire*, Newark: University of Delaware Press, 1983.
Rawson, Claude, *God, Gulliver, and Genocide: Barbarism and the European Imagination, 1492–1945*, Oxford: Oxford University Press, 2001.
Rogers, Pat, *Grub Street: Studies in a Subculture*, London: Methuen, 1972.
Rosenheim, Edward W., *Swift and the Satirist's Art*, Chicago: University of Chicago Press, 1963.

Traugott, John (ed.), *Discussions of Jonathan Swift*, Boston: D. C. Heath, 1962.

Tuveson, Ernest (ed.), *Swift, a Collection of Critical Essays*, Englewood Cliffs, NJ: Prentice-Hall, 1964.

Williams, Kathleen (ed.), *Swift: The Critical Heritage*, London: Routledge, 1970.

CHAPTER 10 BIBLIOGRAPHY

Primary works

Barrell, John, and John Bull (eds.), *A Book of English Pastoral Verse*, Oxford: Oxford University Press, 1975.

Denham, Sir John, *Expans'd Hieroglyphicks. A Critical Edition of Sir John Denham's Cooper's Hill*, ed. Brendan O Hehir, Berkeley and Los Angeles: University of California Press, 1969.

Diaper, William, *The Complete Works*, ed. Dorothy Broughton, London: Routledge and Kegan Paul, 1952.

Dodsley, Robert, *Public Virtue. A Poem in Three Books. I. Agriculture. II. Commerce. III. Arts*, London: Dodsley, 1753. (Only Book I was published.)

Dryden, John (trans.), *The Works of Virgil, Translated into English Verse*, 1697.

Fairer, David, and Gerrard, Christine (eds.), *Eighteenth-Century Poetry. An Annotated Anthology*, Oxford and Maldon, MA: Blackwell Publishers, 1999.

de Fontenelle, Bernard le Bovier, 'Discours sur la nature de l'églogue' (1688), trans. Peter Motteux, 'Of Pastorals', published with Bossu's *Treatise of the Epick Poem*, London, 1695.

Gay, John, *Poetry and Prose*, ed. Vinton A. Dearing and Charles E. Beckwith, 2 vols., Oxford: Clarendon Press, 1974.

Goldsmith, Oliver, *Collected Works*, ed. Arthur Friedman, 5 vols. Oxford: Clarendon Press, 1966.

Hesiod. *Works and Days*, ed. M. L. West, Oxford: Clarendon Press, 1978.

Hesiod. *Theogony and Works and Days*, trans. M. L. West, Oxford: Oxford University Press, 1988.

Lonsdale, Roger (ed.), *The Poems of Gray, Collins, and Goldsmith*, London and Harlow: Longmans, 1969.

Montagu, Lady Mary Wortley, *Essays and Poems and Simplicity, A Comedy*, ed. Robert Halsband and Isobel Grundy, Oxford: Clarendon Press, 1977.

Paine, Thomas, *Rights of Man*, ed. Henry Collins, Harmondsworth: Penguin, 1969.

Parnell, Thomas, *Collected Poems*, ed. Claude Rawson and F. P. Lock, Newark: University of Delaware Press; London and Toronto: Associated University Presses, 1989.

Philips, Ambrose, *Poems*, ed. M. E. Segar, Oxford: Basil Blackwell, 1937.

Philips, John, *Cyder. A Poem in Two Books*, ed. John Goodridge and J. C. Pellice, Cheltenham: The Cyder Press, 2001.

Pope, Alexander, *Pastoral Poetry and An Essay on Criticism*, ed. E. Audra and Aubrey Williams, New Haven, CT: Yale University Press; London: Methuen, 1961.

Purney, Thomas, *Works*, ed. H. O. White, Oxford: Basil Blackwell, 1933.

A Full Enquiry into the True Nature of Pastoral [1717]; Augustan Reprint Society, no. 11, 1948.

Rapin, René, *Dissertatio de Carmine Pastorali*, prefixed to his *Eclogae Sacrae* (1659), translated as 'A Treatise de Carmine Pastorali' in *Idylliums of Theocritus*, trans. Thomas Creech. Oxford, 1684.

Shenstone, William, *The Works in Verse and Prose, of William Shenstone, Esq.*, 2 vols., London, 1764.

Smart, Christopher, *Poetical Works IV. Miscellaneous Poems English and Latin*, ed. Karina Williamson, Oxford: Clarendon Press, 1987.

Stephens, John Calhoun (ed.), *The Guardian*, Lexington: University Press of Kentucky, 1982.

Swift, Jonathan, *The Complete Poems*, ed. Pat Rogers, Harmondsworth: Penguin, 1983.

Theocritus, *Idylls*, trans R. C. Trevelyan, Cambridge: Cambridge University Press, 1947.

Thomas, James, *The Seasons*, ed. James Sambrook Oxford: Clarendon Press, 1981.

Thompson, Isaac, *A Collection of Poems Occasionally Writ On Several Subjects*, Newcastle, 1731.

Tonson, Jacob (ed.), *Poetical Miscellanies: The Sixth Part*, London, 1709.

Virgil, *The Georgics*, trans. L. P. Wilkinson, Harmondsworth: Penguin, 1982.

[Warton, Thomas], *Five Pastoral Eclogues, The Scenes of which are Suppos'd to lie among the Shepherds, oppress'd by the War in Germany*, London: Dodsley, 1745

Secondary works

Alpers, Paul (ed.), *The Singer of the Eclogues. A Study of Virgilian Pastoral. With a New Translation of the Eclogues*, Berkeley, Los Angeles and London: University of California Press, 1979.

Bergstrom, Carson, 'Purney, Pastoral, and the Polymorphous Perverse', *British Journal for Eighteenth-Century Studies* 17 (1994), 149–63.

Bernard, John D., *Ceremonies of Innocence: Pastoralism in the Poetry of Edmund Spenser*, Cambridge: Cambridge University Press, 1989.

Chalker, John, *The English Georgic: A Study in the Development of a Form*, London: Routledge & Kegan Paul, 1969.

Congleton, J. E., *Theories of Pastoral in England, 1684–1798*, Gainesville: University of Florida Press, 1952.

Crawford, Rachel, 'English Georgic and British Nationhood', *ELH* 65 (1998), 123–58.
   Poetry, Enclosure, and the Vernacular Landscape, 1700–1830, Cambridge: Cambridge University Press, 2002.

Fairer, David, 'Organizing Verse: Burke's *Reflections* and Eighteenth-Century Poetry', *Romanticism* 3 (1997), 1–19.

Feingold, Richard, *Nature and Society: Later Eighteenth-Century Uses of the Pastoral and Georgic*, Hassocks: Harvester Press, 1978.

Gilmore, John, *The Poetics of Empire: A Study of James Grainger's The Sugar-Cane*, London and New Brunswick: Athlone Press, 2000.

Goodridge, John, *Rural Life in Eighteenth-Century Poetry*, Cambridge: Cambridge University Press, 1995.

Haber, Judith, *Pastoral and the Poetics of Self-Contradiction: Theocritus to Marvell*, Cambridge: Cambridge University Press, 1994.

Halperin, David M., *Before Pastoral: Theocritus and the Ancient Tradition of Bucolic Poetry*, New Haven, CT and London: Yale University Press, 1983.

Low, Anthony, *The Georgic Revolution*, Princeton: Princeton University Press, 1985.

McKeon, Michael, 'Surveying the Frontier of Culture: Pastoralism in Eighteenth-Century England', *Studies in Eighteenth-Century Culture* 26 (1998), 7–28.

Miles, Gary B., *Virgil's Georgics: A New Interpretation*, Berkeley, Los Angeles and London: University of California Press, 1980.

Mounsey, Chris, 'Christopher Smart's *The Hop-Garden* and John Philips's *Cyder*: a Battle of the Georgics? Mid-Eighteenth-Century Poetic Discussions of Authority, Science and Experience', *British Journal for Eighteenth-Century Studies* 22 (1999), 67–84.

Pellicer, J. C., 'The Georgic at Mid-Eighteenth Century and the Case of Dodsley's Agriculture', *Review of English Studies* 54 (2003), 67–93.

Rosenmeyer, Thomas G., *The Green Cabinet: Theocritus and the European Pastoral Lyric*, Berkeley and Los Angeles: University of California Press, 1969.

Sambrook, James, *English Pastoral Poetry*, Boston, MA: Twayne, 1983.

Segal, Charles, *Poetry and Myth in Ancient Pastoral: Essays on Theocritus and Virgil*, Princeton, NJ: Princeton University Press, 1981.

Sherburn, George, *The Early Career of Alexander Pope*, Oxford: Clarendon Press, 1934.

Wasserman, Earl R., *The Subtler Language: Critical Readings of Neoclassic and Romantic Poems*, Baltimore, MD: Johns Hopkins University Press, 1959.

CHAPTER II BIBLIOGRAPHY

Primary works

Akenside, Mark, *Poetical Works*, ed. Robin Dix, Cranbury, NJ, and London: Associated University Presses, 1996.

Barbauld, Anna Laetitia Aikin, *Poems*, ed. William McCarthy and Elizabeth Kraft, Athens: University of Georgia Press, 1994.

Churchill, Charles, Poetical Works, ed. Douglas Grant, Oxford: Clarendon Press, 1956.

Cowper, William, *Poems*, ed. John D. Baird and Charles Ryskamp, 3 vols., Oxford: Clarendon Press, 1980–95.

Crabbe, George, *The Complete Poetical Works*, ed. Norma Dalrymple-Champneys and Arthur Pollard, 3 vols., Oxford: Clarendon Press, 1988.

Fairer, David and Gerrard, Christine (eds.), *Eighteenth-Century Poetry: An Annotated Edition*, 2nd edn, Oxford: Blackwell Publishers, 2004.

Lonsdale, Roger (ed.), *Eighteenth-Century Women Poets: An Oxford Anthology*, Oxford: Oxford University Press, 1989.

The New Oxford Book of Eighteenth Century Verse, Oxford: Oxford University Press, 1984.

The Poems of Gray, Collins, and Goldsmith, London: Longmans, 1969.

Smart, Christopher, *Poetical Works*, ed. Karina Williamson and Marcus Walsh, 4 vols., Oxford: Clarendon Press, 1980–7.

Spence, Joseph, *Observations, Anecdotes, and Characters of Books and Men*, ed. James M. Osborn, Oxford: Clarendon Press, 1966.

Temple, William, 'Of Poetry' [1690], in *Five Miscellaneous Essays by Sir William Temple*, ed. Samuel Holt Monk, Ann Arbor: University of Michigan Press, 1963.

Warton, Joseph, *Odes on Various Subjects*, London: R. Dodsley, 1746.

Young, Edward, *Night Thoughts*, ed. Stephen Cornford, Cambridge: Cambridge University Press, 1989.

Secondary works

Armstrong, Isobel, and Virginia Blain (eds.), *Women's Poetry in the Enlightenment: The Making of a Canon, 1730–1820*, London and New York: Macmillan Press and St Martin's Press, 1999.

Bate, W. J., *The Burden of the Past and the English Poet*, Cambridge, MA: Harvard University Press, 1970.

Davie, Donald, *The Eighteenth-Century Hymn in England*, Cambridge: Cambridge University Press, 1993.

Doody, Margaret Anne, *The Daring Muse: Augustan Poetry Reconsidered*, Cambridge: Cambridge University Press, 1985.

Erskine-Hill, Howard, *Poetry of Opposition and Revolution: Dryden to Wordsworth*, Oxford: Clarendon Press, 1996.

Fairer, David, *English Poetry of the Eighteenth Century, 1700–1789*, London and New York: Longman, 2003.

Fulford, Tim, *Landscape, Liberty and Authority: Poetry, Criticism and Politics from Thomson to Wordsworth*, Cambridge: Cambridge University Press, 1996.

Gleckner, Robert F., *Gray Agonistes: Thomas Gray and Masculine Friendship*, Baltimore, MD: Johns Hopkins University Press, 1997.

Griffin, Dustin, *Patriotism and Poetry in Eighteenth-Century Britain*, Cambridge: Cambridge University Press, 2002.

　Regaining Paradise: Milton and the Eighteenth Century, Cambridge: Cambridge University Press, 1986.

Hutchings, W. B., and William Ruddick (eds.), *Thomas Gray: Contemporary Essays*, Liverpool: Liverpool University Press, 1993.

Kaul, Suvir, *Poems of Nation, Anthems of Empire: English Verse in the Long Eighteenth Century*, Charlottesville: University Press of Virginia, 2000.

Knapp, Steven, *Personification and the Sublime: Milton to Coleridge*, Cambridge, MA: Harvard University Press, 1985.

McCarthy, B. Eugene, *Thomas Gray: The Progress of a Poet*, Madison, NJ: Fairleigh Dickinson University Press, 1997.

Rothstein, Eric, *Restoration and Eighteenth-Century Poetry, 1660–1780*, Boston: Routledge & Kegan Paul, 1981.

Sitter, John (ed.), *The Cambridge Companion to Eighteenth Century Poetry*, Cambridge: Cambridge University Press, 2001.

　Literary Loneliness in Mid-Eighteenth-Century England, Ithaca, NY: Cornell University Press, 1982.

Tillotson, Geoffrey, *Augustan Poetic Diction*, London: Athlone Press, 1964.

Weinbrot, Howard, *Britannia's Issue: The Rise of British Literature from Dryden to Ossian*, Cambridge: Cambridge University Press, 1995.

Woodman, Thomas, *Early Romantics: Perspectives in British Poetry from Pope to Wordsworth*, Basingstoke: Macmillan Press, 1998.

CHAPTER 12 BIBLIOGRAPHY

Primary works

Coleman the elder, George, *Plays*, ed. Kalman A. Burnim, 6 vols., New York: Garland, 1983 (facsimile of eighteenth-century editions).

Coleman the younger, George, *Plays*, ed. Peter A. Tasch, 2 vols., New York: Garland, 1981 (facsimile of eighteenth-century editions).

Cowley, Hannah, *Plays* ed. Frederick M. Link, 2 vols., New York: Garland, 1979 (facsimile of eighteenth-century editions).

Cumberland, Richard, *Plays*, ed. Roberta F. S. Borkat, 6 vols., New York: Garland, 1982 (facsimile of eighteenth-century editions).

Cumberland, Richard, *Unpublished Plays*, ed. Richard J. Dircks, 2 vols., New York: AMS, 1991–2.

Foote, Samuel, *Plays*, ed. Paula R. Backscheider and Douglas Howard, 3 vols., New York: Garland, 1983 (facsimile of eighteenth-century editions).

Garrick, David, *Plays*, ed. Harry William Pedicord and Fredrick Louis Bergmann, 7 vols., Carbondale: Southern Illinois University Press, 1980–2.

Gay, John, *Dramatic Works*, ed. John Fuller, 2 vols., Oxford: Clarendon Press, 1983.

Goldsmith, Oliver, *Collected Works*, ed. Arthur Friedman, 5 vols., Oxford: Clarendon Press, 1966.

Inchbald, Elizabeth, *Plays*, ed. Paula R. Backscheider, 2 vols., New York: Garland, 1980 (facsimile of eighteenth-century editions).

Kelly, Hugh, *Plays*, ed. Larry Carver, New York: Garland, 1980 (facsimile of eighteenth-century editions).

Lillo, George, *Dramatic Works*, ed. James L. Steffensen, Oxford: Clarendon Press, 1993.

Macklin, Charles, *Four Comedies*, ed. J. O. Bartley, London: Sidgwick and Jackson, 1968.

Moore, Edward, *Plays*, ed. J. Paul Hunter, New York: Garland, 1979 (facsimile of eighteenth-century editions).

Murphy, Arthur, *Plays*, ed. Richard B. Schwartz, 4 vols., New York: Garland, 1979 (facsimile of eighteenth-century editions).

Sheridan, Richard Brinsley, *Dramatic Works*, ed. Cecil Price, 2 vols., Oxford: Clarendon Press, 1973.

Secondary works

Appleton, William W., *Charles Macklin: An Actor's Life*, Cambridge, MA: Harvard University Press, 1960.

Auburn, Mark S., *Sheridan's Comedies: Their Contexts and Achievements*, Lincoln: University of Nebraska Press, 1977.

Backscheider, Paula R., *Spectacular Politics: Theatrical Power and Mass Culture in Early Modern England*, Baltimore, MD: Johns Hopkins University Press, 1993.

Barnett, Dene, *The Art of Gesture: The Practices and Principles of 18th Century Acting*, Heidelberg: Carl Winter Universitätsverlag, 1987.

Bataille, Robert R., *The Writing Life of Hugh Kelly: Politics, Journalism, and Theater in Late-Eighteenth-Century London*, Carbondale: Southern Illinois University Press, 2000.

Bate, Jonathan, *Shakespearean Constitutions: Politics, Theatre, Criticism 1730–1830*, Oxford: Clarendon Press, 1989.

Bernbaum, Ernest, *The Drama of Sensibility*, Boston: Ginn, 1915.

Bevis, Richard W., *English Drama: Restoration and Eighteenth Century, 1660–1789*, London: Longman, 1988.

    The Laughing Tradition: Stage Comedy in Garrick's Day, Athens: University of Georgia Press, 1980.

Brown, Laura, *English Dramatic Form, 1660–1760*, New Haven, CT: Yale University Press, 1981.

Burling, William J., *Summer Theatre in London, 1661–1820, and the Rise of the Haymarket Theatre*, Madison, NJ: Fairleigh Dickinson University Press, 2000.

Burroughs, Catherine, ed., *Women in British Romantic Theatre: Drama, Performance, and Society, 1790–1840*, Cambridge: Cambridge University Press, 2000.

Conolly, L. W., *The Censorship of English Drama, 1737–1824*, San Marino, CA: Huntington Library, 1976.

Craik, T. W. (gen. ed.), *The Revels History of Drama in English*, vols. v and vi, London: Methuen, 1975–6.

Dircks, Phyllis T., *The Eighteenth-Century English Burletta*, ELS Monograph Series, University of Victoria Vancouver, 1999.

Donohue, Joseph W., Jr, *Dramatic Character in the English Romantic Age*, Princeton, NJ: Princeton University Press, 1970.

Ellis, Frank H., *Sentimental Comedy: Theory and Practice*, Cambridge: Cambridge University Press, 1991.

Fiske, Roger, *English Theatre Music in the Eighteenth Century*, 1973, 2nd edn, Oxford: Oxford University Press, 1986.

Freeman, Lisa, *Character's Theater: Genre and Identity on the Eighteenth-Century English Stage*, Philadelphia: University of Pennsylvania Press, 2002.

Gagey, Edmond McAdoo, *Ballad Opera*, New York: Columbia University Press, 1937.

Genest, John, *Some Account of the English Stage from the Restoration in 1660*, 10 vols., Bath: Carrington, 1832.

Girdham, Jane, *English Opera in Late Eighteenth-Century London: Stephen Storace at Drury Lane*, Oxford: Clarendon Press, 1997.

Gray, Charles Harold, *Theatrical Criticism in London to 1795*, New York: Columbia University Press, 1931.

Green, Clarence C., *The Neo-Classic Theory of Tragedy in England During the Eighteenth Century*, Cambridge, MA: Harvard University Press, 1934.

Highfill, Philip H., Jr, Kalman A. Burnim and Edward A. Langhans, *A Biographical Dictionary of Actors, Actresses, Musicians, Dancers, Managers, and Other Stage Personnel in London, 1660–1800*, 16 vols., Carbondale: Southern Illinois University Press, 1973–93.

Hughes, Leo, *The Drama's Patrons*, Austin: University of Texas Press, 1971.

Hume, Robert D. (ed.), *The London Theatre World, 1660–1800*, Carbondale: Southern Illinois University Press, 1980.

Hume, Robert D. 'Goldsmith and Sheridan and the Supposed Revolution of "Laughing" against "Sentimental" Comedy' (1972), rpt. in Hume, *The Rakish Stage*, pp. 312–55.

    Henry Fielding and the London Theatre, 1728–1737, Oxford: Clarendon Press, 1988.

'Henry Fielding and Politics at the Little Haymarket, 1728–1737', in John M. Wallace (ed.), *The Golden & the Brazen World: Papers in Literature and History, 1650–1800*, Berkeley: University of California Press, 1985, pp. 79–124.

'The Multifarious Forms of Eighteenth-Century Comedy' (1981), rpt. in Hume, *The Rakish Stage*, pp. 214–44.

The Rakish Stage, Carbondale: Southern Illinois University Press, 1983.

Jones, Chris, *Radical Sensibility: Literature and Ideas in the 1790s*, London: Routledge, 1993.

Kenny, Shirley Strum, 'Humane Comedy', *Modern Philology* 75 (1977), 29–43.

'Perennial Favorites: Congreve, Vanbrugh, Cibber, Farquhar, and Steele', *Modern Philology* 73 (1976), S4–S11.

Kewes, Paulina, ' "[A] Play, which I presume to call ORIGINAL": Appropriation, Creative Genius, and Eighteenth-Century Playwriting', *Studies in the Literary Imagination* 34 (2001), 17–47.

Kinservik, Matthew J., *Disciplining Satire: The Censorship of Satiric Comedy on the Eighteenth-Century London Stage*, Lewisburg, PA: Bucknell University Press, 2002.

Langhans, Edward A., 'The Theatres', ch. 2 of Hume, ed., *The London Theatre World, 1660–1800*, pp. 35–65.

Leacroft, Richard, *The Development of the English Playhouse*, London: Eyre Methuen, 1973.

Liesenfeld, Vincent J., *The Licensing Act of 1737*, Madison: University of Wisconsin Press, 1984.

Lynch, James J., *Box, Pit, and Gallery*, Berkeley: University of California Press, 1953.

MacMillan, Dougald, 'The Rise of Social Comedy in the Eighteenth Century', *Philological Quarterly* 41 (1962), 330–8.

McVeigh, Simon, *Concert Life in London from Mozart to Haydn*, Cambridge: Cambridge University Press, 1993.

Milhous, Judith, and Robert D. Hume , 'The London Theatre Cartel of the 1720s: British Library Additional Charters 9306 and 9308', *Theatre Survey* 26 (1985), 21–37.

'Playwrights' Remuneration in Eighteenth-Century London', *Harvard Library Bulletin*, n.s. 10 (1999), 3–91.

Moody, Jane, *Illegitimate Theatre in London, 1770–1840*, Cambridge: Cambridge University Press, 2000.

Nicoll, Allardyce, *A History of English Drama, 1660–1900*, 6 vols., Cambridge: Cambridge University Press, 1952–1959.

Nolte, Fred O., in *The Early Middle Class Drama (1696–1774)*, Lancaster, PA: privately published, 1935.

Pedicord, Harry William., *The Theatrical Public in the Time of Garrick*, New York: King's Crown Press, 1954.

Price, Curtis, and Robert D. Hume , 'Ballad Opera', in Stanley Sadie (ed.), *The New Grove Dictionary of Opera*, 4 vols., London: Macmillan, 1992, vol. 1, pp. 289–92.

Ranger, Paul, *'Terror and Pity reign in every Breast': Gothic Drama in the London Patent Theatres, 1750–1820*, London: Society for Theatre Research, 1991.

Rawson, Claude, 'Notes on "Delicacy"', *Order from Confusion Sprung: Studies in Eighteenth-Century Literature from Swift to Cowper*, London: Allen & Unwin, 1985, pp. 341–54.

Rosenfeld, Sybil, *Strolling Players and Drama in the Provinces, 1660–1765*, Cambridge: Cambridge University Press, 1939.

Sherbo, Arthur, *English Sentimental Drama*, East Lansing: Michigan State University Press, 1957.

Southern, Richard, *Changeable Scenery*, London: Faber and Faber, 1952.

Tasch, Peter A., *The Dramatic Cobbler: The Life and Works of Isaac Bickerstaff*, Lewisburg, PA: Bucknell University Press, 1971.

Tave, Stuart M., *The Amiable Humorist: A Study in the Comic Theory and Criticism of the Eighteenth and Early Nineteenth Centuries*, Chicago: University of Chicago Press, 1960.

Temperley, Nicholas, 'Burletta', in Sadie, ed. *New Grove Dictionary of Opera*, vol. 1, pp. 648–9.

Todd, Janet M., *Sensibility: An Introduction*, London: Methuen, 1986.

Van Lennep, William Emmett L. Avery, Arthur H. Scouten, George Winchester Stone, Jr, and Charles Beecher Hogan (eds)., *The London Stage, 1660–1800*, 5 parts in 11 vols., Carbondale: Southern Illinois University Press, 1960–8.

Visser, Colin, 'Scenery and Technical Design', in Hume, ed., *The London Theatre World*, pp. 66–118.

White, Eric Walter, *A History of English Opera*, London: Faber and Faber, 1983.

Wilson, John Harold, *A Preface to Restoration Drama*, 1965; rpt. Cambridge, MA: Harvard University Press, 1968.

CHAPTER 13 BIBLIOGRAPHY

Primary works

Addison, Joseph, *The Spectator*, ed. Donald F. Bond, 5 vols., Oxford: Clarendon Press, 1965.

Anderson, Robert, *Cumberland Ballads*, ed. T. Ellwood, Ulverston: W. Holmes, 1904.
Poems on Various Subjects, Carlisle, 1798.
The Poetical Works of Robert Anderson, Author of Cumberland Ballads, &c., 2 vols., Carlisle, 1820.

Baillie, Joanna, *Selected Poems 1762–1851*, ed. Jennifer Breen, Manchester: Manchester University Press, 1999.

Beattie, James, *The Minstrel, In Two Books: With some other Poems; A New Edition*, London, 1784.
Scoticisms, arranged in Alphabetical Order, designed to correct improprieties of speech and writing, Edinburgh and London, 1787.

Blair, Hugh, 'A Critical Dissertation on the Poems of Ossian' (1763), in James Macpherson, *The Poems of Ossian*, ed. Howard Gaskill, Edinburgh: Edinburgh University Press, 1996, pp. 343–99.
Lectures on Rhetoric and Belles Lettres, 2 vols., London and Edinburgh, 1783.

Burns, Robert, *Letters*, ed. J. De Lancey Ferguson, rev. 2nd edn, ed. G. Ross Roy, 2 vols., Oxford: Clarendon Press, 1985.
Poems, selected by Don Paterson, London: Faber, 2001.
Poems and Songs, ed. James Kinsley, 3 vols., Oxford: Clarendon Press, 1968.
Songs, ed. Donald A. Low, London: Routledge, 1993.

Carlyle, Thomas, 'The Life of Burns. By J. G. Lockhart', *Edinburgh Review* 48 (1828), 267–312.

Child, F. J. (ed.), *The English and Scottish Popular Ballads* (1882–1898), facsimile edition, 5 vols., New York: The Folklore Press, 1956.

Crawford, Thomas, David Hewitt, and Alexander Law, eds., *Longer Scottish Poems. Volume II. 165–1830*, Edinburgh: Scottish Academic Press, 1987.

Donn, Rob, *Songs and Poems in the Gaelic Language*, Inverness, 1829.

Duck, Stephen, *Poems on Several Occasions*, London, 1736.

Duff, William, *An Essay on Original Genius*, London, 1967.

Fergusson, Robert, *Poems*, ed. Matthew P. McDiarmid, 2 vols., Edinburgh and London: The Scottish Texts Society, 1954–6.

Forbes, William, *An Account of the Life and Writings of James Beattie*, 2 vols., Edinburgh, 1806.

Gerard, Alexander, *An Essay on Genius*, London, 1774.

Johnson, Samuel, *The Oxford Authors: Samuel Johnson*, ed. Donald Greene, Oxford: Oxford University Press, 1984.

Kerr, Robert, *Memoirs of the Life, Writings, and Correspondence of William Smellie* (1811), ed. Richard B. Sher, 2 vols., Bristol: Thoemmes, 1996.

MacDonald, Alexander, *Ais-Eiridh na Sean-Chanoin Albannaich*, Edinburgh, 1751.

  Poems, ed. A. MacDonald and A. MacDonald, Inverness: Northern Counties Newspaper and Printing Company, 1924.

Macintyre, Duncan Ban, *Songs*, ed. A. Macleod, Edinburgh: Scottish Texts Society, 1952.

Mackenzie, Henry, untitled review of Robert Burns' *Poems Chiefly in the Scottish Dialect*, *The Lounger* 97 (9 December 1786), 385–8.

Maclaine, Allan H., ed., *The Christis Kirk Tradition: Scots Poems of Folk Festivity*, Glasgow: The Association for Scottish Literary Studies, 1996.

Macpherson, James, *The Poems of Ossian*, ed. Howard Gaskill, Edinburgh: Edinburgh University Press, 1996.

Percy, Thomas, *Reliques of Ancient English Poetry*, 3 vols., London, 1765.

Pinkerton, John, *Scottish Poems*, 3 vols., Edinburgh, 1792.

Pope, Alexander, *The Twickenham Edition of the Works of Alexander Pope*, gen. ed. John Butt, 11 vols., London and New Haven, CT: Methuen and Yale University Press, 1938–68.

Ramsay, Allan, *The Ever Green*, 2 vols., Edinburgh, 1724.

  Poems by Allan Ramsay and Robert Fergusson, ed. A. M. Kinghorn and A. Law, Edinburgh and London, 1974.

  The Tea-Table Miscellany, 4 vols., Edinburgh, 1724–37.

  Works, ed. Burns Martin, John W. Oliver, Alexander Kinghorn and Alexander Law, 6 vols., Edinburgh and London: The Scottish Texts Society, 1951–74.

Relph, Josiah, *A Miscellany of Poems*, Wigton, 1747.

Scott, Walter, *Minstrelsy of the Scottish Border*, 2 vols., Kelso, 1802.

  Minstrelsy of the Scottish Border, 2nd edn, 3 vols., Edinburgh and London, 1803.

Sheridan, Thomas, *A Course of Lectures on Elocution*, London, 1762.

Thomson, James, *The Seasons*, ed. James Sambrook, Oxford: Clarendon Press, 1981.

Thomson, William, *Orpheus Caledonius*, London, 1725.

Watson, James, *James Watson's Choice Collection of Comic and Serious Scots Poems*, ed. Harriet Harvey Wood, 2 vols., Edinburgh and Aberdeen: The Scottish Texts Society, 1977, 1991.

Watson, Roderick, ed., *The Poetry of Scotland: Gaelic, Scots and English*, Edinburgh: Edinburgh University Press, 1995.

Watson, William, ed., *Bardachd Ghaidhlig: Gaelic Poetry 1550–1900*, 3rd edn, reprint, Inverness: An Commun Gaidhealach, 1976.

Young, Edward, *Conjectures on Original Composition* (1759), ed. Edith Morley, Manchester and London: Manchester University Press and Longman, 1918.

Secondary works

Anderson, Benedict, *Imagined Communities: Reflections on the Origin and Spread of Nationalism,* rev. edn, London: Verso, 1991.

Baron, Michael, *Language and Relationship in Wordsworth's Writing,* London and New York: Longman, 1995.

Basker, James, G. 'Scotticisms and the Problem of Cultural Identity in Eighteenth-Century Britain', in John Dwyer and Richard B. Sher (eds.), *Sociability and Society in Eighteenth-Century Scotland,* pp. 81–95.

Bhabha, Homi, *The Location of Culture,* London: Routledge, 1994.

Butt, John, 'The Revival of Scottish Vernacular Poetry in the Eighteenth Century', in F. W. Hilles and Harold Bloom (eds.), *From Sensibility to Romanticism: Essays Presented to Frederick A. Pottle,* New York: Oxford University Press, 1965.

Christmas, William J., *The Lab'ring Muses: Work, Writing, and the Social Order in English Plebeian Poetry, 1730–1830,* Newark, DE: University of Delaware Press, and London: Associated University Presses, 2001.

Colley, Linda, *Britons: Forging the Nation 1707–1837,* London: Yale University Press, 1992.

Craig, David, *Scottish Literature and the Scottish People 1680–1830,* London: Chatto and Windus, 1961.

Crawford, Robert (ed.), *Robert Burns and Cultural Authority,* Edinburgh: Edinburgh University Press, 1997.

The Scottish Invention of English Literature, Cambridge: Cambridge University Press, 1998.

Crawford, Robert, and Mick Imlah (eds.), *The New Penguin Book of Scottish Verse,* London: Penguin, 2000.

Crawford, Robert, *Devolving English Literature,* Oxford: Clarendon Press, 1992.

Crawford, Thomas, *Burns: A Study of the Poems and Songs,* Edinburgh and London: Oliver and Boyd, 1960.

Daiches, David, *The Paradox of Scottish Culture: The Eighteenth-Century Experience,* London: Oxford University Press, 1964.

Davis, Leith, *Acts of Union: Scotland and the Literary Negotiation of the British Nation 1707–1830,* Stanford, CA: Stanford University Press, 1999.

Dunn, David, '"A Very Scottish Kind of Dash": Burns's Native Metric', in Crawford (ed.), *Robert Burns and Cultural Authority,* pp. 58–85.

Dwyer, John and Sher, Richard B. (eds.), *Sociability and Society in Eighteenth-Century Scotland,* Edinburgh: Edinburgh University Press, 1993.

Fielding, Penny, *Writing and Orality: Nationality, Culture, and Nineteenth-Century Scottish Writing,* Oxford: Oxford University Press, 1996.

Heaney, Seamus, 'Burns's Art Speech', in Crawford (ed.), *Robert Burns and Cultural Authority,* pp. 216–33.

Jack, R. D. S., 'Burns as Sassenach Poet', in Simpson (ed.), *Burns Now,* pp.150–66.

Kidd, Colin, *British Identities Before Nationalism,* Cambridge: Cambridge University Press, 1999.

Subverting Scotland's Past: Scottish Whig Historians and the Creation of an Anglo-British Identity, 1689–c1830, Cambridge: Cambridge University Press, 1993.

Landry, Donna, *The Muses of Resistance: Laboring-class Women's Poetry in Britain, 1739–1796,* Cambridge: Cambridge University Press, 1990.

Low, Donald A, (ed.), *Critical Essays on Robert Burns*, London: Routledge, 1975.
  (ed.), *Robert Burns: The Critical Heritage*, London and Boston: Routledge, 1974.
MacCue, Kirsteen, 'Burns, Women and Song', in Crawford (ed.), *Robert Burns and Cultural Authority*, pp. 40–57.
McCalman, Iain (ed.), *An Oxford Companion to the Romantic Age: British Culture 1776–1832*, Oxford: Oxford University Press, 1999.
McClure, J. Derrick (ed.), *Scotland and the Lowland Tongue*, Aberdeen: Aberdeen University Press, 1983).
McGuirk, Carol, *Robert Burns and the Sentimental Era*, Athens: University of Georgia Press, 1985.
McIntyre, Ian, *Dirt and Deity: A Life of Robert Burns*, London: Harper Collins, 1995.
Mugglestone, Lynda, *'Talking Proper'*, Oxford: Clarendon Press, 1995.
Murison, David, 'The Language of Burns', in Low (ed.), *Critical Essays on Robert Burns*, pp. 54–69.
Pittock, Murray G. H., *Poetry and Jacobite Politics in Eighteenth-Century Britain and Ireland*, Cambridge: Cambridge University Press, 1994.
Sher, Richard B., *Church and University in the Scottish Enlightenment*, Edinburgh: Edinburgh University Press, 1985.
Simpson, Kenneth (ed.), *Burns Now*, Edinburgh: Canongate, 1994.
Simpson, Kenneth, *The Protean Scot: The Crisis of Identity in Eighteenth-Century Scottish Literature*, Aberdeen: Aberdeen University Press, 1988.
Smith, Olivia, *The Politics of Language 1791–1819*, Oxford: Oxford University Press, 1984.
Sutherland, Kathryn, 'The Native Poet: the Influence of Percy's Minstrel from Beattie to Wordsworth', *Review of English Studies* ns33 (1982), 414–33.
Trumpener, Katie, *Bardic Nationalism: The Romantic Novel and the British Empire*, Princeton, NJ: Princeton University Press, 1997.
Weinbrot, Howard, *Britannia's Issue: The Rise of British Literature from Dryden to Ossian*, Cambridge: Cambridge University Press, 1995.
Williams, Raymond, *The Country and the City*, Oxford: Oxford University Press, 1973, rpt. London: Hogarth Press, 1993.
Withers, Charles, *Gaelic in Scotland, 1698–1981*, Edinburgh: John Donald, 1984.

CHAPTER 14 BIBLIOGRAPHY

Primary works

Alexander, William, *A History of Women, from the Earliest Antiquity to the Present Time*, 2 vols., London, 1779.
Bolingbroke, Henry St John, Viscount, *Historical Writings*, ed. Isaac Kramnick, Chicago: University of Chicago Press, 1972.
Burnet, Gilbert, *The History of His Own Time*, 2 vols., London: 1723, 1734.
  The History of the Reformation of the Church of England, 3 vols., London, 1679–1715.
Chapone, Hester, *Letters on the Improvement of the Mind*, in *Bluestocking Feminism: Writings of the Bluestocking Circle, 1738–85*, 6 vols., London: Pickering and Chatto, 1999, vol. III, ed. Rhoda Zuk.

Bibliographies

Clarendon, Edward Hyde, Earl of, *The History of the Rebellion and Civil Wars in England*, ed. W. Dunn Macray, 6 vols., Oxford: Oxford University Press, 1888, rpt. 1992.

Ferguson, Adam, *An Essay on the History of Civil Society*, ed. Fania Oz-Salzberger, Cambridge: Cambridge University Press, 1995.

Gibbon, Edward, *The History of the Decline and Fall of the Roman Empire*, ed. David Womersley, 3 vols., Harmondsworth: Allen Lane, 1994.

Goldsmith, Oliver, *The History of England*, 4 vols., London, 1771.

The History of England, in a Series of Letters from a Nobleman to his Son, London, 1764.

Henry, Robert, *The History of Great Britain*, 6 vols., London, 1771–93.

Hobbes, Thomas, *Behemoth or the Long Parliament*, ed. M. M. Goldsmith, 2nd edn, London: Frank Cass, 1969.

Hume, David, *The History of England*, ed. William B. Todd, 7 vols., Indianapolis, IN: The Liberty Press, 1983.

Hurd, Richard, *Letters on Chivalry and Romance*, London, 1762.

Hutchinson, Lucy, *Memoirs of the Life of Colonel Hutchinson*, ed. N. H. Keeble, London: J. M. Dent, 1995.

Kames, Henry Home, Lord, *Sketches of the History of Man*, 2 vols., Edinburgh, 1774.

Macaulay, Catharine, *The History of England*, 8 vols., London, 1763–83.

The History of England from the Revolution to the Present Time, in a series of Letters, Bath, 1778.

Macpherson, James, *An Introduction to the History of Great Britain and Ireland*, London, 1771.

Millar, John, *The Origin of the Distinction of Ranks*, ed. J. V. Price, Bristol: Thoemmes Press, 1990.

Oldmixon, John, *A Critical History of England*, 2 vols., London, 1724–6.

Pinkerton, John, *A Dissertation on the Origin and Progress of the . . . Goths*, London, 1787.

Rapin de Thoyras, Paul, *The History of England*, trans. N. Tindal, 15 vols., London, 1725–31.

Reeve, Clara, *The Progress of Romance*, in *Bluestocking Feminism: Writings of the Bluestocking Circle, 1738–85*, 6 vols., London, Pickering and Chatto, 1999, vol. IV, ed. Gary Kelly.

Robertson, William, *An Historical Disquisition concerning the Knowledge which the Ancients had of India*, London, 1791.

The History of America, 2 vols., London, 1777.

The History of the Reign of the Emperor Charles V, 3 vols., London, 1769.

The History of Scotland, 2 vols., London, 1759.

Smollett, Tobias, *A Compleat History of England*, 4 vols., London, 1757–8.

A Continuation of the Complete History of England, 5 vols., London, 1760–5.

Strutt, Joseph, *A Complete View of the Manners, Customs, Arms, Habits etc. of the Inhabitants of England*, 3 vols., London, 1775–6.

Temple, William, *An Introduction to the History of England*, London, 1695.

Whitaker, John, *The Genuine History of the Britons Asserted*, London, 1772.

Secondary works

Braudy, Leo, *Narrative Form in History and Fiction: Hume, Fielding and Gibbon*, Princeton, NJ: Princeton University Press, 1970.

Brown, Steward J. (ed.), *William Robertson and the Expansion of Empire*, Cambridge: Cambridge University Press, 1997.

Burrow, J. W., *Gibbon,* Oxford: Oxford University Press, 1985.

Butterfield, Herbert, *The Whig Interpretation of History,* Harmondsworth: Penguin, rprt. 1973.

Carnochan, Bliss, *Gibbon's Solitude: The Inward World of the Historian,* Stanford, CA: Stanford University Press, 1987.

Damrosch, Leo, *Fictions of Reality in the Age of Hume and Johnson,* Madison: University of Wisconsin Press, 1989.

Forbes, Duncan, *Hume's Philosophical Politics,* Cambridge: Cambridge University Press, 1975.

Hicks, Philip, *Neoclassical History and English Culture: From Clarendon to Hume,* Basingstoke: Macmillan, 1996.

Hill, Bridget, *The Republican Virago: The Life and Times of Catharine Macaulay,* Oxford: Oxford University Press, 1992.

Kenyon, J. P., *The History Men: The Historical Profession in England since the Renaissance,* London: Weidenfeld and Nicholson, 1983.

Levine, Joseph M., *The Battle of the Books: History and Literature in the Augustan Age,* Ithaca, NY: Cornell University Press, 1991.

   Humanism and History: Origins of Modern Historiography, Ithaca, NY: Cornell University Press, 1987.

McGillivray, Royce, *Restoration Historians and the English Civil War,* The Hague: Martinus Nijhoff, 1974.

Mayer, Robert, *History and the Early English Novel: Matters of Fact from Bacon to Defoe,* Cambridge: Cambridge University Press, 1997.

O'Brien, Karen, 'The History Market', in Isabel Rivers (ed.), *Books and their Readers in Eighteenth-Century England: New Essays,* London: Continuum, 2001.

   Narratives of Enlightenment: Cosmopolitan History from Voltaire to Gibbon, Cambridge: Cambridge University Press, 1997.

Phillips, Mark Salber, *Society and Sentiment: Genres of Historical Writing in Britain, 1740–1820,* Princeton, NJ: Princeton University Press, 2000.

Phillipson, Nicholas, *Hume,* London: Weidenfeld and Nicholson, 1989.

Pocock, J. G. A., *The Enlightenments of Edward Gibbon, 1737–1764,* Cambridge: Cambridge University Press, 1999.

   Narratives of Civil Government: Barbarism and Religion, Cambridge: Cambridge University Press, 1999.

Porter, Roy, *Edward Gibbon: Making History,* London: Weidenfeld and Nicolson, 1988.

Preston Peardon, Thomas, *The Transition in English Historical Writing: 1760–1830,* New York: Columbia University Press, 1933.

Okie, Laird, *Augustan Historical Writing: Histories of England in the English Enlightenment,* Lanham, MD: University Press of America, 1991.

Sher, Richard B., *Church and University in the Scottish Enlightenment,* Princeton, NJ: Princeton University Press, 1985.

Spadafora, David, *The Idea of Progress in Eighteenth-Century Britain,* New Haven, CT: Yale University Press, 1990.

Sweet, Rosemary, *The Writing of Urban Histories in Eighteenth-Century England,* Oxford: Oxford University Press, 1997.

Watson Brownley, Martine, *Clarendon and the Rhetoric of Historical Form*, Philadelphia: University of Pennsylvania Press, 1985.

Wexler, Victor, *David Hume and the History of England*, Philadelphia: American Philosophical Society, 1979.

Womersley, David, *The Transformation of The Decline and Fall of the Roman Empire*, Cambridge: Cambridge University Press, 1988.

Woolf, D. R., 'A Feminine Past? Gender, Genre and Historical Knowledge in England, 1500–1800', *American Historical Review* 102 (1997), 645–79.

Reading History in Early Modern England, Cambridge: Cambridge University Press, 2001.

Wormald, B. H. G., *Clarendon: Politics, History and Religion*, Cambridge: Cambridge University Press, 1951, rpt. 1976.

Zimmerman, Everett, *The Boundaries of Fiction: History and the Eighteenth-Century British Novel*, Ithaca, NY: Cornell University Press, 1996.

CHAPTER 15 BIBLIOGRAPHY

Primary works

Addison, Joseph, and Richard Steele, *The Spectator*, ed. Donald F. Bond, 5 vols., Oxford: Clarendon Press, 1965.

Alison, Archibald, *Essays on the Nature and Principles of Taste*, Edinburgh, 1790.

Astell, Mary, *Reflections upon Marriage*, 3rd edn., London, 1706.

Bacon, Francis, *The Advancement of Learning and the New Atlantis*, ed. Arthur Johnston, Oxford: Clarendon Press, 1974.

Berkeley, George, *The Works of George Berkeley, Bishop of Cloyne*, eds. A. A. Luce and T. E. Jessup, 9 vols., London: Thomas Nelson and Sons Ltd., 1949.

Burke, Edmund, *A Philosophical Enquiry into the Origin of our Ideas of the Sublime and Beautiful*, ed. James T. Boulton, Notre Dame, IN, and London: University of Notre Dame Press, 1958.

Burnet, Thomas, *The Theory of the Earth*, 2nd edn, London, 1691.

Butler, Joseph, *The Analogy of Religion, Natural and Revealed*, London, 1736.

Carter, Elizabeth, *Sir Isaac Newton's Philosophy Explain'd for the Use of the Ladies. In Six Dialogues on Light and Colours*, London, 1739.

Campbell, George, *The Philosophy of Rhetoric*, ed. Lloyd F. Bitzer, Carbondale and Edwardsville: Southern Illinois University Press, 1963.

Descartes, René, *Discourse on Method and Meditations*, trans. Laurence J. Lafleur, Indianapolis, IN: Bobbs-Merrill, 1960.

Drake, Judith, *An Essay in Defence of the Female Sex*, London, 1696.

Fontenelle, M. de, *Fontenelle's Dialogues of the Dead*, trans. John Hughes, London, 1708.

Gerard, Alexander, *An Essay on Taste*, London, 1759.

Hartley, David, *Observations on Man, His Frame, his Duty, and his Expectations*, London, 1749.

Haywood, Eliza, *The Female Spectator*, ed. Kathryn R. King and Alexander Pettit, 4 vols., London: Pickering and Chatto, 2001.

Love in Excess: or The Fatal Enquiry, 2nd edn, ed. David Oakleaf, Peterborough, Ontario: Broadview Literary Texts, 2000.

The Mercenary Lover, or the Unfortunate Heiresses, London: N. Dobb, 1726; rprt. New York: Garland Press, 1973.

Selections from 'The Female Spectator', ed. Patricia Meyer Spacks Oxford: Oxford University Press, 1999.

Hume, David, *An Enquiry concerning Human Understanding,* in *Enquiries concerning Human Understanding, and concerning the Principles of Morals* ed. L. A. Selby-Bigge, 3rd edn, Oxford: Clarendon Press, 1975.

A Treatise of Human Nature: Being an Attempt to Introduce the Experimental Method of Reasoning into Moral Subjects, ed. L. A. Selby-Bigge, 2nd edn, Oxford: Clarendon Press, 1978.

Hutcheson, Francis, *An Inquiry into the Original of our Ideas of Beauty and Virtue; in Two Treatises,* 2nd edn, London, 1726; reprt. New York: Garland Press, 1971.

Kant, Immanuel, *Critique of Judgment,* trans. J. H. Bernard, New York: Hafner Press, 1951.

Leland, John, *A View of the Principal Deistical Writers that have appeared in England in the Last and Present Century,* London, 1754–5.

Locke, John, *An Essay concerning Human Understanding,* ed. Peter H. Nidditch, Oxford: Clarendon Press, 1975.

Monboddo, James Burnett, Lord, *Antient Metaphysics: or, the Science of Universals,* 6 vols., Edinburgh, 1779–99.

Ray, John, *The Wisdom of God Manifested in the Works of the Creation,* London, 1691.

Reid, Thomas, *Essays on the Intellectual Powers of Man,* Edinburgh, 1785.

Shaftesbury, Anthony Ashley Cooper, third Earl of, *Characteristicks of Men, Manners, Opinions, Times,* 6th edn, 3 vols., Indianapolis, IN: Liberty Fund, 2001.

Sterne, Laurence, *The Florida Edition of the Works of Laurence Sterne,* eds. Melvyn New and Joan New, 5 vols., Gainesville: University Presses of Florida, 1978.

Wilkins, John, *Of the Principles and Duties of Natural Religion: Two Books,* 4th edn, London, 1699.

Wollstonecraft, Mary, *A Vindication of the Rights of Woman,* ed. Carol H. Poston, New York: Norton, 1975.

Secondary works

Cavell, Stanley, *Disowning Knowledge in Six Plays of Shakespeare,* Cambridge: Cambridge University Press, 1987.

Christensen, Jerome, *Practicing Enlightenment: Hume and the Formation of a Literary Career,* Madison: University of Wisconsin Press, 1987.

Derrida, Jacques, *The Archeology of the Frivolous,* trans. John P. Leavey, Jr, Lincoln and London: University of Nebraska Press, 1980.

Kenshur, Oscar, *Dilemmas of Enlightenment: Studies in the Rhetoric and Logic of Ideology,* Berkeley: University of California Press, 1993.

Noggle, James, *The Skeptical Sublime: Aesthetic Ideology in Pope and the Tory Satirists,* Oxford: Oxford University Press, 2001.

Nussbaum, Martha C., *Love's Knowledge: Essays on Philosophy and Literature,* New York and Oxford: Oxford University Press, 1990.

Perry, Ruth, *The Celebrated Mary Astell: An Early English Feminist,* Chicago: University of Chicago Press, 1986.

Prince, Michael B., 'Mauvais Genres', *New Literary History* 34 (2003), 452–79.
    Philosophical Dialogue in the British Enlightenment: Theology, Aesthetics, and the Novel, Cambridge: Cambridge University Press, 1996.
Redwood, John, *Reason, Ridicule and Religion: the Age of Enlightenment in England, 1660–1750,* Cambridge, MA: Harvard University Press, 1976.
Richetti, John J. *Philosophical Writing: Locke, Berkeley, Hume,* Cambridge, MA: Harvard University Press, 1983.
Rorty, Richard, *Philosophy and the Mirror of Nature,* Princeton, NJ: Princeton University Press, 1979.
Tavor Bannet, Eve, *Scepticism, Society, and the Eighteenth-Century Novel,* London: Macmillan, 1987.
Watt, Ian, *The Rise of the Novel,* Berkeley: University of California Press, 1957.

CHAPTER 16 BIBLIOGRAPHY
Primary works

Addison, Joseph, and Richard Steele, *The Spectator,* ed. Donald F. Bond, 5 vols., Oxford: Clarendon Press, 1965.
Boswell, James, *Boswell On the Grand Tour. Germany and Switzerland, 1764,* ed. Frederick A. Pottle, New York: McGraw-Hill, 1953.
Dryden, John, *Of Dramatic Poesy and Other Critical Essays,* ed. George Watson, 2 vols., London: Dent Everyman's Library, 1962.
Elledge, Scott, and Donald Schier (eds.), *The Continental Model. Selected French Critical Essays of the Seventeenth Century, in English Translation,* rev. edn Ithaca, NY: Cornell University Press, 1970.
Spingarn, J. E. (ed.), *Critical Essays of the Seventeenth Century,* 3 vols. Bloomington: Indiana University Press, 1957.
Sprat, Thomas, *History of the Royal Society,* ed. Jackson I. Cope and Harold Whitmore Jones, St Louis: Washington University Studies, 1958.
Voltaire, *Candide and other Writings,* ed. Haskell Block, New York: Random House Modern Library, 1956.
    Correspondance, ed. Theodore Besterman, 13 vols., Paris: Gallimard, Bibiliotheque de la Pléiade, 1963ff.
    Letters concerning the English Nation, ed. Nicholas Cronk, Oxford: Oxford University Press, 1994, 1999.

Secondary works

Aldridge, A. Owen, *Voltaire and the Century of Light,* Princeton, NJ: Princeton University Press, 1975.
Ascoli, Georges, *La Grande Bretagne devant l'opinion française au xviie siècle,* Paris: Gamber, 1930.
Barnouw, Jeffrey, 'The Beginnings of "Aesthetics" and the Leibnizian Conception of Sensation', in Paul Mattick, Jr (ed.) *Eighteenth-Century Aesthetics and the Reconstruction of Art,* Cambridge: Cambridge University Press, 1993, pp. 52–95.

'The Contribution of English Language and Culture to Voltaire's Enlightenment', *Voltaire et ses combats*, 2 vols., Oxford: Voltaire Foundation, 1997, vol. I, pp. 77–88.

'Feeling in Enlightenment Aesthetics', in *Studies in Eighteenth-Century Culture*, vol. XVIII, East Lansing, MI: Colleagues Press, 1988, pp. 323–42.

'Hobbes's Psychology of Thought: Endeavors, Purpose and Curiosity', *History of European Ideas* 10. 5, (1989), 519–45.

'Johnson and Hume Considered as the Core of a New "Period Concept" of the Enlightenment', *Transactions of the Fifth International Congress on the Enlightenment*, I, *Studies in Voltaire and the Eighteenth Century*, vol. CXC, Oxford: Voltaire Foundation, 1980, 189–96.

'Learning from Experience, or Not: From Chrysippus to Rasselas', *Studies in Eighteenth-Century Culture*, vol. XXXIII, Baltimore, MD: Johns Hopkins University Press, 2004.

'The Morality of the Sublime: Kant and Schiller', *Studies in Romanticism* 19 (1980), 497–514.

'The Morality of the Sublime: To John Dennis', *Comparative Literature* 35 (1983), 21–42.

'Passion as "Confused" Perception or Thought: Descartes, Malebranche and Hutcheson', *Journal of the History of Ideas* 53 (1992), 397–424.

'Readings of *Rasselas*. "Its Most Obvious Moral" and the Moral Role of Literature', *Enlightenment Essays* 7 (1976), 17–39.

Bastide, Charles. *The Anglo-French Entente in the Seventeenth Century*, London: John Lane, 1914.

Beebee, Thomas O., *'Clarissa' on the Continent*, University Park: Pennsylvania State University Press, 1990.

Besterman, Theodore, *Voltaire*, Chicago: University of Chicago Press, 1976

Bonno, Gabriel, *La Culture et la civilisation britanniques devant l'opinion française de la Paix d'Utrecht aux 'Lettres philosophiques' (1713–1734)*, Philadelphia, PA: American Philosophical Society, 1948.

Fabian, Bernhard, 'English Books and Their Eighteenth-Century Readers', in Paul J. Korshin (ed.), *The Widening Circle. Essays on the Circulation of Literature in Eighteenth-Century Europe*, Philadelphia: The University of Pennsylvania Press, 1976.

Goldgar, Anne, *Impolite Learning. Conduct and Community in the Republic of Letters, 1680–1750*, New Haven, CT: Yale University Press, 1995.

Greene, Donald, 'Voltaire and Johnson', in Alfred J. Bingham and Virgil W. Topazio (eds.), *Enlightenment Studies in honour of Lester G. Crocker*, Oxford: The Voltaire Foundation, 1979, pp. 111–31.

Grieder, Josephine, *Anglomania in France, 1740–1789. Fact, Fiction, and Political Discourse*, Geneva: Droz, 1985.

Hogwood, Christopher, *Handel*, London: Thames and Hudson, 1984.

Hope, Quentin M., *Saint-Evremond and his Friends*, Geneva: Droz, 1999.

Saint-Evremond. The Honnête Homme as Critic, Bloomington: Indiana University Press, 1962.

Horsman, E. A., 'Dryden's French Borrowings', *Review of English Studies*, n.s. I (1950).

Legouis, Pierre, 'Corneille and Dryden as Dramatic Critics,' in J. Dover Wilson (ed.), *Seventeenth Century Studies Presented to Sir Herbert Grierson*, Oxford: Clarendon Press, 1938, pp. 269–91.

Levine, Joseph M., *The Battle of the Books. History and Literature in the Augustan Age*, Ithaca, NY: Cornell University Press, 1991.

Between the Ancients and the Moderns. Baroque Culture in Restoration England, New Haven, CT: Yale University Press, 1999.

Maurer, Michael, *Aufklärung und Anglophilie in Deutschland*, Göttingen: Vandenhoeck & Ruprecht, 1987.

McCracken, Charles J., *Malebranche and British Philosophy*, Oxford: Clarendon Press, 1983.

Miller, Stephen, *Three Deaths and Enlightenment Thought. Hume, Johnson, Marat*, Lewisburg, PA: Bucknell University Press, 2001.

Petit, Leon, *La Fontaine et Saint-Evremond, ou la tentation de l'Angleterre*, Toulouse: Privat, 1953.

Porter, Roy, *The Enlightenment* (Studies in European History), Atlantic Highlands, NJ: Humanities Press, 1990.

Enlightenment: Britain and the Creation of the Modern World, London: Allen Lane: the Penguin Press, 2000.

'The Enlightenment in England', in Roy Porter and Mikulas Teich (eds.), *The Enlightenment in National Context*, Cambridge: Cambridge University Press, 1981, pp. 1–18.

Potkay, Adam, *The Passion for Happiness. Samuel Johnson and David Hume*, Ithaca, NY: Cornell University Press, 2000.

Purver, Margery, *The Royal Society: Concept and Creation*, Cambridge, MA: M.I.T. Press, 1967.

Rousseau, André Michel, *L'Angleterre et Voltaire*, 3 vols., Oxford: Voltaire Foundation, Studies on Voltaire and the Eighteenth Century, 145–7, 1976.

Schoneveld, Corneilis W., *Intertraffic of the Mind. Studies in Seventeenth-Century Anglo-Dutch Translation with a Checklist of Books Translated from English into Dutch, 1600–1700*, Leiden: Brill, 1983.

Temmer, Mark J., *Samuel Johnson and Three Infidels: Rousseau, Voltaire, Diderot*, Athens: University of Georgia Press, 1988.

Texte, Joseph, *Jean-Jacques Rousseau and the Cosmopolitan Spirit in Literature: A Study of the Literary Relations between France and England during the Eighteenth Century*, London: Duckworth, 1899.

van Tieghem, Phillippe, *Les Influences étrangères sur la littérature française (1550–1880)*, 2nd edn, Paris: Presses Universitaires de France, 1967.

Wedgwood, C. V., *Seventeenth-Century English Literature*, Oxford: Oxford University Press, 1950.

Williamson, George, 'The Occasion of *An Essay of Dramatic Poesy*', *Seventeenth Century Contexts*, rev. edn, Chicago: University of Chicago Press, 1969, pp. 272–88.

Yolton, John W., *et al.* (ed.), *The Blackwell Companion to the Enlightenment*, Oxford: Blackwell, 1991.

CHAPTER 17 BIBLIOGRAPHY

Primary works

Alleine, Joseph, *An Alarme to Unconverted Sinners*, London, 1672.

[?Allestree, Richard], *The Practice of Christian Graces. Or The Whole Duty of Man*, London, 1658.

Arderne, James, *Directions concerning the Matter and Stile of Sermons*, ed. J. Mackay, Oxford: Basil Blackwell, 1952.

Baxter, Richard, *The Autobiography of Richard Baxter*, abridged J. M. Lloyd Thomas, ed. N. H. Keeble, London: Everyman, 1985 (much reduced from *Reliquiae Baxterianae*).

    A Call to the Unconverted, in *Practical Works of the Rev. Richard Baxter*, ed. W. Orme, 23 vols., London: James Duncan, 1830, vol. VII.

    A Christian Directory, in *Practical Works of the Rev. Richard Baxter*, ed. W. Orme, 23 vols., London: James Duncan, 1830, vols. II–VI.

    The Poor Man's Family Book, in *Practical Works of the Rev. Richard Baxter*, ed. W. Orme, 23 vols., London: James Duncan, 1830, vol. XIX.

    Reliquiae Baxterianae, London, 1696.

Richard Baxter and Margaret Charlton: A Puritan Love-Story, ed. J. T. Wilkinson, London: George Allen & Unwin, 1928 (contains *A Breviate of the Life of Margaret Baxter*, by Richard Baxter).

Birch, Thomas, *The Life of the Most Reverend Dr John Tillotson, Lord Archbishop of Canterbury*, 2nd edn, London, 1753.

Bunyan, John, *Grace Abounding to the Chief of Sinners*, ed. Roger Sharrock, Oxford: Clarendon Press, 1962.

    The Holy War, ed. Roger Sharrock and James F. Forrest, Oxford: Clarendon Press, 1980.

    The Life and Death of Mr Badman, ed. James F. Forrest and Roger Sharrock, Oxford: Clarendon Press, 1988.

    The Miscellaneous Works of John Bunyan, gen. ed. Roger Sharrock, 13 vols., Oxford: Clarendon Press, 1976–94.

    The Pilgrim's Progress, ed. J. B. Wharey, 2nd edn rev. Roger Sharrock, Oxford: Clarendon Press, 1960.

Butler, Joseph, *The Analogy of Religion Natural and Revealed to the Constitution and Course of Nature*, in *The Works of Bishop Butler*, ed. J. H. Bernard, 2 vols., London: Macmillan, 1900, vol. II.

Clarke, Samuel, *A Discourse Concerning the Unchangeable Obligations of Natural Religion, and the Truth and Certainty of the Christian Revelation*, London, 1706.

Cowper, William, *The Poems of William Cowper*, ed. John D. Baird and Charles Ryskamp, 3 vols., Oxford: Clarendon Press, 1980–95.

Dennis, John, *The Critical Works of John Dennis*, ed. Edward Niles Hooker, 2 vols., Baltimore: Johns Hopkins Press, 1939–43.

Doddridge, Philip, *Lectures on Preaching*, in *The Works of the Rev. Philip Doddridge, D. D.*, ed. E. Williams and E. Parsons, 10 vols., Leeds, 1802–5, vol. V.

    Some Remarkable Passages in the Life of the Honourable Col. James Gardiner, in *The Works of the Rev. Philip Doddridge, D. D.*, ed. E. Williams and E. Parsons, 10 vols., Leeds, 1802–5, vol. IV.

    The Rise and Progress of Religion in the Soul, in *The Works of the Rev. Philip Doddridge, D. D.*, ed. E. Williams and E. Parsons, 10 vols., Leeds, 1802–5, vol. I.

Ellwood, Thomas, *The History of the Life of Thomas Ellwood*, ed. C. G. Crump, London: Methuen, 1900.

Fox, George, *The Journal*, ed. Nigel Smith, Harmondsworth: Penguin, 1998.

Glanvill, Joseph, 'Anti-fanatical Religion, and Free Philosophy', in *Essays on Several Important Subjects in Philosophy and Religion*, London, 1676.

An Essay concerning Preaching, London, 1678.

Hervey, James, *Meditations and Contemplations*, 4th edn, 2 vols., London, 1748.

Theron and Aspasio, 3 vols., London, 1755.

Hutchinson, Lucy, *Memoirs of the Life of Colonel Hutchinson*, ed. N. H. Keeble, London: Everyman, 1995.

Jackson, Thomas (ed.), *The Lives of Early Methodist Preachers*, 3rd edn, 6 vols., London: Wesleyan Conference Office, 1865–6.

Law, William, *A Practical Treatise upon Christian Perfection*, London, 1726.

A Serious Call to a Devout and Holy Life, London, 1729.

The Works of the Reverend William Law, 9 vols., London, 1762.

Letsome, S. and J. Nicholl (eds.), *A Defence of Natural and Revealed Religion: Being a Collection of the Sermons Preached at the Lecture Founded by the Honourable Robert Boyle, Esq.*, 3 vols. London, 1739.

Locke, John, *An Essay Concerning Human Understanding*, ed. P. H. Nidditch, Oxford: Clarendon Press, 1975.

The Reasonableness of Christianity As delivered in the Scriptures, ed. John C. Higgins-Biddle, Oxford: Clarendon Press, 1999.

Lowth, Robert, *Lectures on the Sacred Poetry of the Hebrews*, trans. from the Latin by G. Gregory, London, 1787.

Milton, John, *Paradise Lost*, ed. Alastair Fowler, 2nd edn, London: Longman, 1998.

Newton, John, *An Authentic Narrative of Some Remarkable and Interesting Particulars in the Life of* ******, in *The Works of the Rev. John Newton*, 6 vols., London, 1808–9, vol. I.

Newton, John, and William Cowper, *Olney Hymns*, London, 1779.

Patrick, Simon, *A Friendly Debate betwixt Two Neighbours, The One a Conformist, The Other a Non-Conformist*, in *The Works of Symon Patrick, D. D.*, ed. A. Taylor, 9 vols., Oxford University Press, 1858, vol. V.

Scott, Thomas, *The Force of Truth: An Authentic Narrative*, London, 1779.

Smart, Christopher, *Jubilate Agno*, in *The Poetical Works of Christopher Smart*, ed. Karina Williamson and Marcus Walsh, 6 vols., Oxford: Clarendon Press, 1980–96, vol. I.

Religious Poetry 1763–1771, in *The Poetical Works of Christopher Smart*, ed. Karina Williamson and Marcus Walsh, 6 vols., Oxford: Clarendon Press, 1980–96, vol. II.

A Translation of the Psalms of David, in *The Poetical Works of Christopher Smart*, ed. Karina Williamson and Marcus Walsh, 6 vols., Oxford: Clarendon Press, 1980–96, vol. III.

The Spectator, ed. Donald F. Bond, 5 vols., Oxford: Clarendon Press, 1965.

Sterne, Laurence, *The Sermons of Laurence Sterne*, ed. Melvyn New, *The Florida Edition of the Works of Laurence Sterne*, vols. IV–V, Gainesville: University Press of Florida, 1996

Taylor, Jeremy, *Holy Living and Holy Dying*, ed. P. G. Stanwood, 2 vols., Oxford: Clarendon Press, 1989.

Thomson, James, *The Seasons*, ed. James Sambrook, Oxford: Clarendon Press, 1981.

Tillotson, John, *The Works of the Most Reverend Dr John Tillotson, Lord Archbishop of Canterbury*, ed. R. Barker, 12 vols., London, 1742–3.

Watts, Isaac, *The Psalms of David, Hymns and Spiritual Songs, Horae Lyricae*, in *The Works of the Rev. Isaac Watts D. D.*, ed. Edward Parsons, 7 vols., Leeds, 1800, vol. VII.

Wesley, John, *A Christian Library*, ed. Thomas Jackson, 2nd edn, 30 vols., London, 1819–27.

A Collection of Hymns for the Use of the People called Methodists, ed. Franz Hildebrandt and Oliver A. Beckerlegge, *The Works of John Wesley*, vol. VII, Nashville, TN: Abingdon Press, first pub. Oxford University Press, 1983.

Journal and Diaries, ed. W. Reginald Ward and Richard P. Heitzenrater, *The Works of John Wesley*, vols. XVIII–XXIV, Nashville: Abingdon Press, 1988–2003.

Whitefield, George, *The Two First Parts of his Life, with his Journals, Revised corrected, and abridged*, London, 1756.

Whitefield's Journals, To which is Prefixed his 'Short Account' and 'Further Account', ed. William Wale, facsimile with introduction by William V. Davis, Gainesville, FL: Scholars' Facsimiles and Reprints, 1969.

Wilkins, John, *Ecclesiastes, or, A Discourse concerning the Gift of Preaching* rev. edn, London, 1669 (1st pub. 1646).

Of the Principles and Duties of Natural Religion, ed. John Tillotson, 6th edn, London, 1710 (1st pub. 1675).

Young, Edward, *Night Thoughts*, ed. Stephen Cornford, Cambridge: Cambridge University Press, 1989.

Secondary works

Bebbington, D. W., *Evangelicalism in Modern Britain: A History from the 1730s to the 1980s*, London: Unwin Hyman, 1989.

Bolam, C. G., Jeremy Goring, H. L. Short, Roger Thomas, *The English Presbyterians: From Elizabethan Puritanism to Modern Unitarianism*, London: Allen & Unwin, 1968.

Bossy, John, *The English Catholic Community, 1570–1850*, London: Darton, Longman and Todd, 1975.

Brown, Raymond, *The English Baptists of the Eighteenth Century*, London: The Baptist Historical Society, 1986.

Davie, Donald, *The Eighteenth-Century Hymn in England*, Cambridge: Cambridge University Press, 1993.

A Gathered Church: The Literature of the English Dissenting Interest, 1700–1930, London: Routledge, 1978.

Davies, Horton, *Worship and Theology in England*, vol. II, *From Andrewes to Baxter and Fox 1603–1690*, Princeton, NJ: Princeton University Press, 1975; vol. III, *From Watts and Wesley to Maurice 1690–1850*, Princeton: Princeton University Press, 1961.

Davies, Rupert, and Gordon Rupp (eds.), *A History of the Methodist Church in Great Britain*, vol. I, London: Epworth Press, 1965.

Escott, Harry, *Isaac Watts Hymnographer: A Study of the Beginnings, Development, and Philosophy of the English Hymn*, London: Independent Press, 1962.

Every, George, *The High Church Party 1688–1718*, London: SPCK, 1956.

Fairchild, Hoxie Neale, *Religious Trends in English Poetry*, vol. I: *1700–1740: Protestantism and the Cult of Sentiment*, New York: Columbia University Press, 1939; vol. II: *1740–1780: Religious Sentimentalism in the Age of Johnson*, New York: Columbia University Press, 1942.

Green, Ian, *The Christian's ABC: Catechisms and Catechizing in England c. 1530–1740*, Oxford: Clarendon Press, 1996.

Print and Protestantism in Early Modern England, Oxford: Oxford University Press, 2000.

Green, Richard, *The Works of John and Charles Wesley: A Bibliography*, London: C. H. Kelly, 1896.

Griffin, Dustin, *Regaining Paradise: Milton and the Eighteenth Century*, Cambridge: Cambridge University Press, 1986.

Guest, Harriet, *A Form of Sound Words: The Religious Poetry of Christopher Smart*, Oxford: Clarendon Press, 1989.

Hindmarsh, D. Bruce, *John Newton and the English Evangelical Tradition between the Conversions of Wesley and Wilberforce*, Oxford: Clarendon Press, 1996.

Humphreys, A. R., *The Augustan World*, London: Methuen, 1964 (1st pub. 1954).

Keeble, N. H. (ed.), *John Bunyan: Conventicle and Parnassus*, Oxford: Clarendon Press, 1988.

Keeble, N. H., *The Literary Culture of Nonconformity in Later Seventeenth-Century England*, Leicester: Leicester University Press, 1987.

Richard Baxter: Puritan Man of Letters, Oxford: Clarendon Press, 1982.

Lessenich, Rolf P. *Elements of Pulpit Oratory in Eighteenth-Century England (1660–1800)*, Cologne: Böhlau Verlag, 1972.

McAdoo, H. R., *The Spirit of Anglicanism: A Survey of Anglican Theological Method in the Seventeenth Century*, London: Adam & Charles Black, 1965.

Morris, David B., *The Religious Sublime: Christian Poetry and Critical Tradition in Eighteenth-Century England*, Lexington: University Press of Kentucky, 1972.

Noll, Mark A., David W. Bebbington and George A. Rawlyk (eds.), *Evangelicalism: Comparative Studies of Popular Protestantism in North America, the British Isles, and Beyond, 1700–1990*, New York: Oxford University Press, 1994.

Nuttall, G. F., *Richard Baxter and Philip Doddridge: A Study in a Tradition*, London: Dr Williams's Library, 1951.

Overton, John Henry, *The Evangelical Revival in the Eighteenth Century*, 2nd edn, London: Longmans, Green, and Co., 1891.

Rack, Henry D., *Reasonable Enthusiast: John Wesley and the Rise of Methodism*, London: Epworth Press, 1989.

Reedy, Gerard, SJ, *The Bible and Reason*, Philadelphia: University of Pennsylvania Press, 1985.

Rivers, Isabel (ed.), *Books and their Readers in Eighteenth-Century England*, Leicester: Leicester University Press, 1982.

Books and their Readers in Eighteenth-Century England: New Essays, London: Leicester University Press, 2001.

Rivers, Isabel, *Reason, Grace, and Sentiment: A Study of the Language of Religion and Ethics in England, 1660–1780*, vol. I, *Whichcote to Wesley*, vol. II, *Shaftesbury to Hume*, Cambridge: Cambridge University Press, 1991–2000.

Sambrook, James, *The Eighteenth Century: The Intellectual and Cultural Context of English Literature, 1700–1789*, 2nd edn, London: Longman, 1993.

Simon, Irène, *Three Restoration Divines: Barrow, South, Tillotson*, 2 vols, Paris: Belles Lettres, 1967–76.

Smith, Ruth, *Handel's Oratorios and Eighteenth-Century Thought*, Cambridge: Cambridge University Press, 1995.

Sommerville, C. John, *Popular Religion in Restoration England*, Gainesville: University Presses of Florida, 1977.

Spurr, John, *The Restoration Church of England, 1646–1689*, New Haven,CT: Yale University Press, 1991.

Stephen, Leslie, *History of English Thought in the Eighteenth Century*, 2 vols., Harbinger edn, London: Rupert Hart-Davis, 1962 (lst pub. 1876).

Stranks, C. J., *Anglican Devotion: Studies in the Spiritual Life of the Church of England between the Reformation and the Oxford Movement*, London: SCM Press, 1961.

Suarez, Michael, and Michael Turner, eds. *The Cambridge History of the Book in Britain*, vol. v, 1695–1830, Cambridge University Press, forthcoming.

Sullivan, Robert E., *John Toland and the Deist Controversy*, Cambridge, MA: Harvard University Press, 1982.

Sykes, Norman, *From Sheldon to Secker: Aspects of English Church History 1660–1768*, Cambridge: Cambridge University Press, 1959.

Walsh, John, Colin Haydon and Stephen Taylor, *The Church of England c. 1689–1833: From Toleration to Tractarianism*, Cambridge: Cambridge University Press, 1993.

Watkins, Owen, *The Puritan Experience*, London: Routledge, 1972.

Watson, J. R., *The English Hymn: A Critical and Historical Study*, Oxford: Clarendon Press, 1997.

Watts, Michael R., *The Dissenters: From the Reformation to the French Revolution*, Oxford: Clarendon Press, 1985 (lst pub. 1978).

Young, B. W., *Religion and Enlightenment in Eighteenth-Century England: Theological Debate from Locke to Burke*, Oxford: Clarendon Press, 1998.

CHAPTER 18 BIBLIOGRAPHY

Primary works

Addison, Joseph, *et al.*, *The Spectator* (1711–14), ed. Donald F. Bond, 5 vols., Oxford: Clarendon Press, 1965.

Barbauld, Anna Laetitia (ed.), *The British Novelists*, 50 vols., London, 1810.

Behn, Aphra, *The Works of Aphra Behn*, ed. Janet Todd, 7 vols., London: Pickering & Chatto, 1992–6.

Blackwell, Thomas, *An Enquiry into the Life and Writings of Homer*, London, 1735.

Burke, Edmund, *A Philosophical Enquiry into the Origin of Our Ideas of the Sublime and Beautiful*, ed. James T. Boulton, South Bend, IN: University of Notre Dame Press, 1958.

Cavendish, Margaret, *ccxi Sociable Letters*, London, 1664.

Collier, Jeremy, *A Short View of the Immorality and Profaneness of the English Stage*, London, 1698.

Congreve, William, *Amendments of Mr Collier's False and Imperfect Citations*, London, 1698.
Incognita: or, Love and Duty reconcil'd. A Novel, ed. H. F. B. Brett-Smith, Oxford: Blackwell, 1922.

Defoe, Daniel, *The True-Born Englishman: A Satyr*, London, 1701.

Dennis, John, *The Critical Works of John Dennis*, ed. E. N. Hooker, 2 vols., Baltimore, MD: Johns Hopkins University Press, 1939–43.

D'Israeli, Isaac, *An Essay on the Manners and Genius of the Literary Character*, London, 1795.

Dryden, John, *The Works of John Dryden*, ed. H. T. Swedenberg *et al.*, 20 vols., Berkeley and Los Angeles: University of California Press, 1956–2002.

Fielding, Henry, *The History of Tom Jones: A Foundling*, ed. Fredson Bowers, Middleton, CT: Wesleyan University Press, 1975.

Joseph Andrews, ed. Martin C. Battestin, Middleton, CT: Wesleyan University Press, 1967.

Garrick, David, *An Ode upon Dedicating a Building, and Erecting a Statue, to Shakespeare, at Stratford upon Avon*, London, 1769.

Gilpin, William, *Three Essays: On Picturesque Beauty; On Picturesque Travel; and On Sketching Landscape*, London, 1792.

Haywood, Eliza, *The Female Spectator*, 7th edn, 4 vols., London, 1771.

Hume, David, *Essays, Moral, Political, and Literary* (1777), ed. Eugene F. Miller, Indianapolis, IN: Liberty Classics, 1987.

Hurd, Richard, *Letters on Chivalry and Romance*, London, 1762.

Hutcheson, Francis, *An Inquiry into the Original of Our Ideas of Beauty and Virtue*, London, 1725.

Johnson, Samuel, *Johnson on Shakespeare*, ed. Arthur Sherbo, 2 vols., London and New Haven, CT: Yale University Press, 1968.

Lives of the English Poets, ed. G. B. Hill, 3 vols., Oxford: Clarendon Press, 1905.

Kames, Henry Home, Lord, *The Elements of Criticism*, 2 vols., Edinburgh, 1762.

Locke, John, *An Essay concerning Human Understanding*, ed. Peter H. Nidditch, Oxford: Clarendon Press, 1975.

Manley, Delariviere, *The Secret History of Queen Zarah and the Zarazians*, London, 1705.

Montagu, Elizabeth, *An Essay on the Writings and Genius of Shakespear*, London, 1769.

Peacock, Thomas Love, *The Four Ages of Poetry* (1820), with Shelley's *Defence of Poetry* and Browning's *Essay on Shelley*, ed. H. F. B. Brett-Smith, Oxford: Blackwell, 1921.

Pope, Alexander, *Pastoral Poetry and An Essay on Criticism*, ed. E. Audra and Aubrey Williams, London and New Haven, CT: Yale University Press, 1961.

Reeve, Clara, *The Old English Baron: A Gothic Story*, ed. James Trainer, London: Oxford University Press, 1967.

The Progress of Romance, ed. Esther M. McGill, New York: Facsimile Text Society, 1930.

Richardson, Samuel, *The History of Sir Charles Grandison*, ed. Jocelyn Harris, 3 vols., Oxford: Oxford University Press, 1972.

Ritson, Joseph, *Observations on the Three First Volumes of the History of English Poetry*, London, 1782.

Ruffhead, Owen, *The Life of Alexander Pope, Esq.*, London, 1769.

Rymer, Thomas, *The Critical Works of Thomas Rymer*, ed. Curt A. Zimansky, New Haven, CT: Yale University Press, 1956.

Shaftesbury, Anthony Ashley Cooper, third Earl of, *Characteristics of Men, Manners, Opinions, Times* (1711), ed. Lawrence E. Klein, Cambridge: Cambridge University Press, 1999.

Steele, Richard, *et al.*, *The Tatler*, ed. Donald F. Bond, 3 vols., Oxford: Clarendon Press, 1987.

Swift, Jonathan, *A Tale of a Tub*, ed. A. C. Guthkelch and D. Nichol Smith, Oxford: Clarendon Press, 1958.

Temple, Sir William, *Five Miscellaneous Essays*, ed. Samuel H. Monk, Ann Arbor: University of Michigan Press, 1963.

Trapp, Joseph, *Lectures on Poetry*, trans. William Bowyer and William Clarke, London, 1742.

Voltaire (François-Marie Arouet), *Letters on England* (1733), trans. Leonard Tancock, Harmondsworth: Penguin, 1980.

Warton, Joseph, *Essay on the Genius and Writings of Pope*, 2 vols., London, 1762–82.

Warton, Thomas, *A History of English Poetry: An Unpublished Continuation*, ed. Rodney M. Baine, Los Angeles: William Andrews Clark Memorial Library, University of California, 1953.

    The History of English Poetry, 3 vols., London, 1774–81.

    Observations on the Fairie Queene of Spenser, London, 1754.

Young, Edward, *Conjectures on Original Composition* (1759), ed. Edith J. Morley, Manchester: Manchester University Press, 1918.

Secondary works

Abrams, M. H., *The Mirror and the Lamp: Romantic Theory and the Critical Tradition*, Oxford: Oxford University Press, 1953.

Atkins, J. W. H., *English Literary Criticism: 17th and 18th Centuries*, London: Methuen, 1951.

Barker-Benfield, G. J., *The Culture of Sensibility*, Chicago: University of Chicago Press, 1992.

Barrell, John, *English Literature in History 1730–80: An Equal, Wide Survey*, New York: St Martin's Press, 1983.

Basker, James G., *Tobias Smollett, Critic and Journalist*, Newark: University of Delaware Press, 1988.

Bate, W. J., *From Classic to Romantic: Premises of Taste in Eighteenth-Century England*, Cambridge, MA: Harvard University Press, 1946.

Chapman, Gerald W. (ed.), *Literary Criticism in England, 1660–1800*, New York: Knopf, 1966.

Colley, Linda, *Britons: Forging the Nation 1707–1837*, London and New Haven, CT: Yale University Press, 1992.

Crane, R. S., 'English Neoclassical Criticism: An Outline Sketch,' in R. S. Crane (ed.), *Critics and Criticism Ancient and Modern*, Chicago: University of Chicago Press, 1952.

    'On Writing the History of Criticism in England, 1650–1800,' in *The Idea of the Humanities*, 2 vols., Chicago: University of Chicago Press, 1967.

Dobson, Michael, *The Making of the National Poet: Shakespeare, Adaptation and Authorship, 1660–1769*, Oxford: Clarendon Press, 1992.

Douglas, David C., *English Scholars 1660–1730*, London: Eyre & Spottiswoode, 1951.

Eagleton, Terry, *The Ideology of the Aesthetic*, Oxford: Blackwell, 1990.

Elledge, Scott, ed., *Eighteenth-Century Critical Essays*, 2 vols., Ithaca, NY: Cornell University Press, 1961.

Engell, James, *Forming the Critical Mind: Dryden to Coleridge*, Cambridge, MA.: Harvard University Press, 1989.

Graham, Walter, *English Literary Periodicals*, New York: T. Nelson, 1930.

Griffin, Robert J., *Wordsworth's Pope: A Study in Literary Historiography*, Cambridge: Cambridge University Press, 1995.

Habermas, Jürgen, *The Structural Transformation of the Public Sphere* (1962), trans. Thomas Burger, Cambridge, MA: M.I.T. Press, 1989.

Hagstrum, Jean, *Samuel Johnson's Literary Criticism*, Minneapolis: University of Minnesota Press, 1952.

Hipple, Walter John, *The Beautiful, The Sublime, and the Picturesque in Eighteenth-Century British Aesthetic Theory*, Carbondale: Southern Illinois University Press, 1957.

Howell, Wilbur Samuel, *Eighteenth-Century British Logic and Rhetoric*, Princeton, NJ: Princeton University Press, 1971.

Kramnick, Jonathan Brody, *Making the English Canon: Print-Capitalism and the Cultural Past, 1700–1770*, Cambridge: Cambridge University Press, 1998.

Levine, Joseph M., *The Battle of the Books: History and Literature in the Augustan Age*, Ithaca, NY: Cornell University Press, 1991.

Lipking, Lawrence, *The Ordering of the Arts in Eighteenth-Century England*, Princeton, NJ: Princeton University Press, 1970.

Miller, Henry Knight, 'The Whig Interpretation of Literary History,' *Eighteenth-Century Studies* 6 (1972), 60–84.

Monk, Samuel H., *The Sublime: A Study of Critical Theories in xviii-Century England*, New York: Modern Language Association, 1935.

Morris, David B., *The Religious Sublime*, Lexington: University of Kentucky Press, 1972.

Newman, Gerald, *The Rise of English Nationalism: A Cultural History 1740–1830*, New York: St Martin's Press, 1987.

Nisbet, H. B., and Claude Rawson, *The Cambridge History of Literary Criticism*, vol. iv, *The Eighteenth Century*, Cambridge: Cambridge University Press, 1997.

Pittock, Joan, *The Ascendancy of Taste: The Achievement of Joseph and Thomas Warton*, London: Routledge and Kegan Paul, 1973.

Ross, Trevor, *The Making of the English Literary Canon*, Montreal: McGill University Press, 1998.

Spadafora, David, *The Idea of Progress in Eighteenth-Century Britain*, New Haven, CT: Yale University Press, 1990.

Spingarn, J. E. (ed.), *Critical Essays of the Seventeenth Century*, 3 vols., Oxford: Clarendon Press, 1908–9.

Sutton, John L., 'The Source of Mrs Manley's Preface to *Queen Zarah*', *Modern Philology* 82 (1984), 167–72.

Walsh, Marcus, *Shakespeare, Milton, and Eighteenth-Century Literary Editing*, Cambridge: Cambridge University Press, 1997.

Wellek, René, *A History of Modern Criticism: 1750–1950*, vol. i, *The Later Eighteenth Century*, New Haven, CT: Yale University Press, 1955.

The Rise of English Literary History, Chapel Hill: University of North Carolina Press, 1941.

Weinbrot, Howard D., *Britannia's Issue: The Rise of British Literature from Dryden to Ossian*, Cambridge: Cambridge University Press, 1993.

Williams, Raymond, *Keywords: A Vocabulary of Culture and Society*, London: Fontana, 1976.

Wimsatt, William K., and Brooks, Cleanth, *Literary Criticism: A Short History*, New York: Knopf, 1962.

Women Critics 1660–1820: An Anthology, ed. The Folger Collective on Early Women Critics, Bloomington: Indiana University Press, 1995.

Womersley, David (ed.), *Augustan Critical Writing*, London: Penguin, 1997.

CHAPTER 19 BIBLIOGRAPHY

Primary works

Beverley, Robert, *The History and Present State of Virginia*, ed. Louis B. Wright, Chapel Hill: University of North Carolina Press, 1947.

Bolingbroke [Henry St John, Viscount Bolingbroke]. *The Works of Lord Bolingbroke*, 4 vols., London, 1879, rpt. New York: AMS Press, 1966.

Boswell, James, *Boswell's Life of Johnson*, ed. George Birkbeck Hill, rev. L. F. Powell. 6 vols., Oxford: Clarendon Press, 1934–64.

Burke, Edmund, *The Writings and Speeches of Edmund Burke*, ed. W. M. Elofson and John A. Woods. 9 vols., Oxford: Clarendon Press, 1981–96.

Byrd, William, *The Secret Diary of William Byrd of Westover, 1709–1712*, ed. Louis B. Wright and Marion Tinling, Richmond, VA: The Dietz Press, 1941.

Defoe, Daniel, *A Plan of the English Commerce*, London, 1728.

Equiano, Olaudah, *The Interesting Narrative of the Life of Olaudah Equiano, or Gustavus Vassa, the African. Written by Himself*, ed. Vincent Carretta, London: Penguin, 1955.

French, David P., ed., *Minor English Poets, 1660–1780: A Selection from Alexander Chalmers' 'The English Poets'*, 10 vols., New York: Benjamin Blom, 1967.

Hamilton, Dr Alexander, *Gentleman's Progress: The Itinerarium of Dr Alexander Hamilton*, Pittsburgh: University of Pittsburgh Press, 1948.

Jenyns, Soame, *The Works of Soame Jenys, Esq.* 2nd edn, 4 vols., London, 1793.

Johnson, Samuel, *Political Writings*, ed. Donald J. Greene, New Haven, CT: Yale University Press, 1977.

Lustig, Irma, and Frederick A. Pottle (eds.), *Boswell: The English Experiment*, London: Heinemann, 1986.

Mickle, William Julius, *The Lusiad: or, the Discovery of India. Translated from the Original Portuguese of Luis de Camöens*, 2nd edn, Oxford, 1778.

Paine, Thomas, *Common Sense*, Mount Vernon, NY: A. Colish, 1976.

Pope, Alexander, *Poems*, ed. John Butt, New Haven, CT: Yale University Press, 1963.

Warton, Joseph, *Essay on the Genius and Writings of Pope*, 2 vols., London, 1782.

Secondary works

Bailyn, Bernard, *The Ideological Origins of the American Revolution*, Cambridge, MA: Harvard University Press, 1967.

Brewer, John, *The Sinews of Power: War, Money, and the English State, 1688–1783*, London: Unwin Hyman, 1989.

Brown, Laura, *Ends of Empire: Women and Ideology in Early Eighteenth-Century English Literature*, Ithaca, NY: Cornell University Press, 1993.

Dowling, William C., *The Epistolary Moment: The Poetics of the Eighteenth-Century Verse Epistle*, Princeton, NJ: Princeton University Press, 1991.

'Ideology and the Flight from History in Eighteenth-Century Poetry', in Leo Damrosch (ed.), *The Profession of English Literature*, Madison: University of Wisconsin Press, 1992.

Literary Federalism in the Age of Jefferson, Columbia: University of South Carolina Press, 1999.

Feingold, Richard, *Nature and Society: Later Eighteenth-Century Uses of Georgic*, New Brunswick, NJ: Rutgers University Press, 1978.

Fuller, Randall, 'Theaters of the American Revolution: The Valley Forge *Cato* and the Meschianza in their Transcultural Contexts', *Early American Literature* 34.2 (1999), 126–46.

Gould, Eliga H., *The Persistence of Empire: British Political Culture in the Age of the American Revolution*, Chapel Hill: University of North Carolina Press, 2000.

Kaul, Suvir, *Thomas Gray and Literary Authority*, Stanford, CA: Stanford University Press, 1992.

'Why Selima Drowns: Thomas Gray and the Domestication of the Imperial Ideal', PMLA 105.1 (1990), 223–32.

Kramnick, Isaac, *Bolingbroke and his Circle*, Cambridge, MA: Harvard University Press, 1968.

Lovejoy, David S., *The Glorious Revolution in America*, New York: Harper and Row, 1972.

Mackie, Erin, *Market à la Mode: Fashion, Commodity and Gender in The Tatler and The Spectator*, Baltimore, MD: Johns Hopkins University Press, 1997.

Marshall, P. J., 'Burke and Empire', in Stephen Taylor, Richard Connors and Clyve Jones (eds.), *Hanoverian Britain and Empire*, Woodbridge, Suffolk: Boydell Press, 1998.

Olson, Alison Gilbert, *Anglo-American Politics 1660–1775*, Oxford: Oxford University Press, 1975.

Pocock, J. G. A., *Virtue, Commerce, and History*, Cambridge: Cambridge University Press, 1985.

Shields, David S., *Oracles of Empire: Poetry, Politics, and Commerce in British America, 1690–1750*, Chicago: University of Chicago Press, 1990.

Speck, W. A., *Stability and Strife: England, 1714–1760*, London: Edward Arnold, 1984.

Wood, Gordon, *The Creation of the American Republic, 1776–1787*, Chapel Hill: University of North Carolina Press, 1969.

CHAPTER 20 BIBLIOGRAPHY

Primary works

Addison, Joseph, Richard Steele, *et al.*, *The Spectator* (1711–12), ed. Donald F. Bond, 5 vols., Oxford: Clarendon Press, 1965.

Addison, Joseph, Richard, Steele, *The Tatler* (1709–11), ed. Donald F. Bond, 3 vols., Oxford: Clarendon Press, 1987.

Manley, Delariviere, Susan Centlivre, *et al.*, *The Female Tatler* (1709–10), *by Mrs Crackenthorpe, a Lady that knows everything*; rpt. ed. Fidelis Morgan, London: Dent, 1992.

Defoe, Daniel, *Defoe's Review* (1704–13), *Reproduced from the Original Editions*, ed. Arthur Wellesley Secord, 22 vols., New York: Columbia University Press, 1938.

Dunton, John, *The Athenian Gazette or Casuistical Mercury, Resolving all the most Nice and Curious Questions Proposed by the Ingenious* (London: John Dunton, 1691–5), 16 vols.

Fielding, Henry, *The Champion: or British Mercury*, 1739–41.

The Covent Garden Journal (1752), ed. Gerard Edward Jensen, New Haven, CT: Yale University Press, 1915.

Goldsmith, Oliver, *The Bee* (1759) in *Collected Works of Oliver Goldsmith*, ed. Arthur Friedman, 5 vols., Oxford: Clarendon Press, 1966, vol. I, pp. 343–508.

The Citizen of the World (1762) in *The Public Ledger; or, Daily Register of Commerce and Intelligence*, in *Collected Works*, ed. Friedman, vol. II.

Haywood, Eliza (ed.), *The Female Spectator* (1744–46); rpt. ed. J. Firmager, London: Duckworth, 1993.

Johnson, Samuel, *The Idler* (1758–60) *and The Adventurer* (1753–54), ed. W. J. Bate, John M. Bullitt and L. F. Powell, *The Yale Edition of the Works of Samuel Johnson*, vol. II, New Haven, CT: Yale University Press, 1963.

The Rambler (1750–52), ed. Walter J. Bate and Albrecht Strauss, *The Yale Edition of the Works of Samuel Johnson*, vols. III—V, New Haven, CT: Yale University Press, 1969.

Moore, Edward (ed.), *The World* (1753–55); rpt. 4 vols., London: R. and J. Dodsley, 1755.

Steele, Richard *et al.*, *The Guardian* (1713).

Richard Steele's Periodical Journalism, ed. Rae Blanchard, Oxford: Clarendon Press, 1959.

Swift, Jonathan, *The Examiner* (1710–11); rpt. ed. Herbert Davis, Oxford: Blackwell, 1959.

Wilkes, John, Charles Churchill, *et al.*, *The North Briton* (1762–3).

Secondary works

Barker, Hannah, *Newspapers, Politics, and Public Opinion in Late Eighteenth-Century England*, Oxford: Clarendon Press, 1999.

Bateson, F. W. (ed.), *Cambridge Bibliography of English Literature*, Cambridge: Cambridge University Press, vol. II (1941), pp. 660–8.

Beljame, Alexandre, *Men of Letters and the English Public in the Eighteenth Century*, ed. Bonamy Dobrée, trans. E. O. Lorimer, London: Kegan Paul, 1948.

Bond, Richmond, *The Tatler: The Making of a Literary Journal*, Cambridge, MA: Harvard University Press, 1971.

Cox, Susan M., and Janice Budeit (eds.), *Early English Newspapers: Bibliography and Guide to the Microform Collection*, 1983; rpt. New York: Gale Group, n.d. (PDF file).

Crane, R. S. and F. B. Kaye (eds.), *A Census of British Newspapers and Periodicals 1620–1800*, Chapel Hill: University of North Carolina Press, 1927.

Dunton, John, 'The Secret History of the Periodical Writers', in *The Life and Errors of John Dunton, Citizen of London*, 2 vols., London: J. Nichols, son, and Bentley, 1818.

Graham, Walter, *English Literary Periodicals*, New York: Thomas Nelson and Sons, 1930.

Hammond, Brean, *Professional Imaginative Writing in England 1670–1740*, Oxford: Clarendon Press, 1997.

McIntosh, Carey, *The Evolution of English Prose, 1700–1800*, Cambridge: Cambridge University Press, 1998.

Milford, R. T., and D. M. Sutherland, *A Catalogue of English Newspapers and Periodicals in the Bodleian Library, 1620–1800*, Oxford Bibliographical Society Proceedings and Papers, vol. IV, pt. 2 (1935).

Moureau, François, *Le Mercure galant de Dufresny (1710–1714) ou le journalisme à la mode*, Oxford: Voltaire Foundation, 1982.

Schwartz, Richard M., 'Johnson's "Mr Rambler" and the Periodical Tradition', *Genre* 7 (1974), 196–204.

Siegert, Bernhard, *Relays: Literature as an Epoch of the Postal System*, trans. Kevin Repp, Stanford, CA: Stanford University Press, 1999.

Sullivan, Alvin, *British Literary Magazines: The Augustan Age and the Age of Johnson, 1698–1788*, New York: Greenwood Press, 1983.

Watson, George (ed.), *New Cambridge Bibliography of English Literature*, Cambridge: Cambridge University Press, vol. II (1971), cols. 1269–90.

Woodruff, James F., 'Johnson's Rambler and its Contemporary Context', *Bulletin of Research in the Humanities* 85 (1982), 27–64.

CHAPTER 21 BIBLIOGRAPHY

Primary works

Addison, Joseph, *The Freeholder*, ed. James Leheny, Oxford: Clarendon Press, 1979.

Burke, Edmund, *Reflections on the Revolution in France*, ed. Conor Cruise O'Brien, Harmondsworth: Penguin, 1969.

  The Writings and Speeches of Edmund Burke, 8 vols., ed. Paul Langford, Oxford: Oxford University Press, 1981.

Claeys, Gregory (ed.), *Political Writings of the 1790s*, 6 vols., London: Pickering and Chatto, 1995.

Defoe, Daniel, *Political and Economic Writings of Daniel Defoe*, ed. W. R. Owens and P. N. Furbank, 8 vols., London: Pickering & Chatto, 2000.

Ellis, Frank H., ed., *Swift vs. Mainwaring: 'The Examiner' and 'The Medley'*, Oxford: Clarendon Press, 1985.

Fielding, Henry, *The True Patriot and Related Writings*, ed. W. B. Coley, Oxford: Clarendon Press, 1987.

Johnson, Samuel, *Political Writings*, ed. Donald J. Greene, New Haven, CT: Yale University Press, 1977.

'Junius', *The Letters of Junius*, ed. John Cannon, Oxford: Clarendon Press, 1978.

Paine, Thomas, *Rights of Man*, ed. Henry Collins, Harmondsworth: Penguin, 1969.

Swift, Jonathan, *Prose Works*, ed. Herbert Davis *et al.*, 16 vols., Oxford: Basil Blackwell, 1939–75.

[St John, Henry, Viscount Bolingbroke,] *A Dissertation upon Parties*, London, 1735.

  Remarks on the History of England, London, 1743.

Trenchard, John, and Thomas Gordon, *Cato's Letters*, 2 vols., ed. Ronald Hamowy, Indianapolis, IN: Liberty Fund, 1995.

Secondary works

Boulton, James T., *The Language of Politics in the Age of Wilkes and Burke*, London and Toronto: Routledge & Kegan Paul and University of Toronto Press, 1963.

Brewer, John, *Party Ideology and Popular Politics at the Accession of George III*, Cambridge: Cambridge University Press, 1976.

Habermas, Jürgen, *The Structural Transformation of the Public Sphere: An Inquiry into a Category of Bourgeois Society*, trans. Thomas Burger, Cambridge, MA: Polity Press, 1989.

Dickinson, H. T., *Liberty and Property: Political Ideology in Eighteenth-Century Britain*, London: Weidenfeld and Nicolson, 1977.

Downie, J. A., *Robert Harley and the Press: Propaganda and Public Opinion in the Age of Swift and Defoe*, Cambridge: Cambridge University Press, 1979.

Downie, J. A., and Thomas N. Corns (eds.), *Telling People What to Think: Early Eighteenth-Century Periodicals from 'The Review' to 'The Rambler'*, London and Portland, Oregon: Frank Cass, 1993.

Goldgar, Bertrand A., *Walpole and the Wits: The Relation of Politics to Literature, 1722–1742*, Lincoln: University of Nebraska Press, 1976.

Harris, Robert, *A Patriot Press: National Politics and the London Press in the 1740s*, Oxford: Clarendon Press, 1993.

Rea, Robert R., *The English Press in Politics, 1760–1774*, Lincoln: University of Nebraska Press, 1963.

Reid, Christopher, *Edmund Burke and the Practice of Political Writing*, Dublin: Gill and Macmillan, 1985.

CHAPTER 22 BIBLIOGRAPHY

Primary works

Bridges, Thomas, *The Adventures of a Bank-Note*, 4 vols., London, 1770–1.

Briscoe, Sophia, *Miss Melmoth; or, The New Clarissa*, 3 vols., London, 1771.

Brooke, Frances, *The History of Emily Montague*, ed. Mary Jane Edwards, Ottawa: Carleton University Press, 1985.

 Lady Julia Mandeville, 2 vols., London, 1763.

Brooke, Henry, *The Fool of Quality*, 5 vols., London, 1766–70.

Echlin, Elizabeth, Lady, *An Alternative Ending to Richardson's Clarissa*, ed. Dimiter Daphinoff, Bern: Francke Verlag, 1982.

Fielding, Henry, *The History of Tom Jones, A Foundling*, ed. Martin C. Battestin and Fredson Bowers, 2 vols., Oxford: Oxford University Press, 1975.

Fielding, Sarah, *The Adventures of David Simple and Volume the Last*, ed. Peter Sabor, Lexington: University Press of Kentucky, 1998.

 Remarks on Clarissa, introd. Peter Sabor, Augustan Reprint Society Publ. Nos. 231–2, Los Angeles: William Andrews Clark Memorial Library, 1985.

Fielding, Sarah, and Jane Collier, *The Cry: A New Dramatic Fable*, 3 vols., London, 1754.

Goldsmith, Oliver, *The Vicar of Wakefield*, ed. A Friedman, Oxford: Oxford University Press, 1981.

Graves, Richard, *The Spiritual Quixote*, ed. Clarence Tracy, Oxford: Oxford University Press, 1967.

Guthrie, William, *The Friends: A Sentimental History*, 2 vols., London, 1754.

Hume, David, *Enquiries Concerning Human Understanding and Concerning the Principles of Morals*, ed. L. A. Selby-Bigge, rev. P. H. Nidditch, Oxford: Clarendon Press, 1975.

 A Treatise of Human Nature, ed. L. A. Selby-Bigge, rev. P. H. Nidditch, Oxford: Clarendon Press, 1978.

Hutcheson, Francis, *An Essay on the Nature and Conduct of the Passions and Affections*, introd. Paul McReynolds, Gainesville, FL: Scholars' Facsimiles and Reprints, 1969.

Kelly, Hugh, *Memoirs of a Magdalen*, 2 vols., London, 1766.

Mackenzie, Henry, *Julia de Roubigné*, ed. Susan Manning, East Linton: Tuckwell, 1999.

 The Man of Feeling, ed. Brian Vickers, Oxford: Oxford University Press, 1967.

 The Man of the World, 2 vols., London, 1773.

Montagu, Lady Barbara (?), *The Histories of Some of the Penitents in the Magdalen-House*, 2 vols., London, 1759.

Richardson, Samuel, *Clarissa; or, The History of a Young Lady*, introd. Florian Stuber, 8 vols., New York: AMS Press, 1990.

Correspondence, ed. Anna Laetitia Barbauld, 6 vols., London, 1804.

The History of Sir Charles Grandison, ed. Jocelyn Harris, 3 vols., Oxford: Oxford University Press, 1972.

Pamela; or, Virtue Rewarded, ed. Thomas Keymer and Alice Wakely, Oxford: Oxford University Press, 2001.

Scott, Sarah, *A Description of Millenium Hall*, ed. Gary Kelly, Peterborough, Ontario: Broadview, 1995.

The History of Sir George Ellison, ed. Betty Rizzo, Lexington: University Press of Kentucky, 1996.

Shaftesbury, Anthony Ashley Cooper, 3rd Earl of, *Characteristics of Men, Manners, Opinions, Times*, ed. Lawrence E. Klein, Cambridge: Cambridge University Press, 1999.

Sheridan, Frances, *Memoirs of Miss Sidney Bidulph*, ed. Patricia Köster and Jean Coates Cleary, Oxford: Oxford University Press, 1995.

Smith, Adam, *The Theory of Moral Sentiments*, ed. D. D. Raphael and A. L. Macfie, Oxford: Oxford University Press, 1976.

Smollett, Tobias, *The Adventures of Ferdinand Count Fathom*, ed. Damian Grant, Oxford: Oxford University Press, 1971.

The Adventures of Peregrine Pickle, ed. James L. Clifford, rev. Paul-Gabriel Boucé, Oxford: Oxford University Press, 1983.

The Expedition of Humphry Clinker, ed. Lewis M. Knapp, rev. Paul-Gabriel Boucé, Oxford: Oxford University Press, 1984.

Spencer, Georgiana (?), *Emma; or, The Unfortunate Attachment*, 3 vols., London, 1773.

Sterne, Laurence, *Letters*, ed. Lewis Perry Curtis, Oxford: Clarendon Press, 1935.

The Life and Opinions of Tristram Shandy, Gentleman, ed. Melvyn New *et al.*, 3 vols, Gainesville: University Presses of Florida, 1978–84.

A Sentimental Journey through France and Italy and Continuation of the Bramine's Journal, ed. Melvyn New and W. G. Day, Gainesville: University Press of Florida, 2002.

Sermons, ed. Melvyn New, 2 vols, Gainesville: University Press of Florida, 1996.

Secondary works

Barker, Gerard A., '*David Simple*: The Novel of Sensibility in Embryo', *Modern Language Studies* 12 (1982), 69–80.

Barker-Benfield, G. J., *The Culture of Sensibility: Sex and Society in Eighteenth-Century Britain*, Chicago: University of Chicago Press, 1992.

Benedict, Barbara M., *Framing Feeling: Sentiment and Style in English Prose Fiction, 1745–1800*, New York: AMS Press, 1994.

Braudy, Leo, 'The Form of the Sentimental Novel', *Novel* 7 (1973–4), 5–13.

Bredvold, Louis I., *The Natural History of Sensibility*, Detroit, MI: Wayne State University Press, 1962.

Brissenden, R. F., *Virtue in Distress: Studies in the Novel of Sentiment from Richardson to Sade*, London: Macmillan, 1974.

Brown, Marshall, *Preromanticism*, Stanford, CA: Stanford University Press, 1991.

Conger, Sydney McMillen (ed.), *Sensibility in Transformation: Creative Resistance to Sentiment from the Augustans to the Romantics*, Rutherford, NJ: Fairleigh Dickinson University Press, 1990.

Crane, R. S., 'Suggestions Toward a Genealogy of the "Man of Feeling"', *ELH* 1 (1934), 205–30.

De Bruyn, Frans, 'Latitudinarianism and Its Importance as a Precursor of Sensibility', *JEGP* 80 (1981), 349–60.

Ellis, Markman, *The Politics of Sensibility: Race, Gender and Commerce in the Sentimental Novel*, Cambridge: Cambridge University Press, 1996.

Erämetsä, Erik, *A Study of the Word 'Sentimental' and of Other Linguistic Characteristics of Eighteenth-Century Sentimentalism in England*, Helsinki: Liikekirjapaino Oy, 1951.

Fairer, David, 'Sentimental Translation in Mackenzie and Sterne', *Essays in Criticism* 49 (1999), 132–51.

Frye, Northrop, 'Towards Defining an Age of Sensibility', *ELH* 23 (1956), 144–52.

'Varieties of Eighteenth-Century Sensibility', *Eighteenth-Century Studies* 24 (1990–91), 157–72.

Greene, Donald, 'Latitudinarianism and Sensibility: The Genealogy of the "Man of Feeling" Reconsidered', *Modern Philology* 75 (1977), 159–83.

Harkin, Maureen, 'Mackenzie's *Man of Feeling*: Embalming Sensibility', *ELH* 61 (1994), 317–40.

Howes, Alan B. (ed.), *Sterne: The Critical Heritage*, London: Routledge, 1974.

Humphreys, A. R., 'The "Friend of Mankind" (1700–60) – An Aspect of Eighteenth-Century Sensibility', *RES* 24 (1948), 203–18.

Keymer, Tom, *Richardson's Clarissa and the Eighteenth-Century Reader*, Cambridge: Cambridge University Press, 1992.

Laqueur, Thomas W., 'Bodies, Details, and the Humanitarian Narrative', in Lynn Hunt (ed.), *The New Cultural History*, Berkeley and Los Angeles: University of California Press, 1989, pp. 176–204.

Lynch, Deidre, 'Personal Effects and Sentimental Fictions', *Eighteenth-Century Fiction* 12 (2000), 345–68.

Markley, Robert, 'Sentimentality as Performance: Shaftesbury, Sterne, and the Theatrics of Virtue', in Felicity Nussbaum and Laura Brown (eds.), *The New Eighteenth Century: Theory, Politics, English Literature*, London: Methuen, 1987, pp. 210–30.

Marshall, David, 'Adam Smith and the Theatricality of Moral Sentiments', *Critical Inquiry* 10 (1984), 592–613.

Mayo, Robert D., *The English Novel in the Magazines 1740–1815*, Evanston, IL: Northwestern University Press, 1962.

McGann, Jerome, *The Poetics of Sensibility: A Revolution in Literary Style*, Oxford: Clarendon Press, 1996.

Mullan, John, *Sentiment and Sociability: The Language of Feeling in the Eighteenth Century*, Oxford: Clarendon Press, 1988.

'Sentimental Novels', in John Richetti (ed.), *The Cambridge Companion to the Eighteenth-Century Novel*, Cambridge: Cambridge University Press, 1996, pp. 236–54.

Novak, Maximillian B., and Anne Mellor (eds.), *Passionate Encounters in a Time of Sensibility*, Newark: University of Delaware Press, 2000.

Parnell, J. T., 'A Story Painted to the Heart? *Tristram Shandy* and Sentimentalism Reconsidered', *Shandean* 9 (1997), 122–35.

Richetti, John, *The English Novel in History, 1700–1780*, London: Routledge, 1999.

Rivers, Isabel, *Reason, Grace, and Sentiment: A Study of the Language of Religion and Ethics in England, 1660–1780*, Cambridge: Cambridge University Press, 2 vols., 1991–2000.

Rodgers, James, 'Sensibility, Sympathy, Benevolence: Physiology and Moral Philosophy in *Tristram Shandy*', in L. J. Jordonova (ed.), *Languages of Nature: Critical Essays on Science and Literature*, London: Free Association Books, 1986, pp. 117–58.

Rousseau, G. S., 'Nerves, Spirits, and Fibres: Towards Defining the Origins of Sensibility', in R. F. Brissenden and J. C. Eade (eds.), *Studies in the Eighteenth Century III: Papers presented at the Third David Nichol Smith Memorial Seminar*, Toronto: University of Toronto Press, 1976, pp. 137–57.

Starr, G. A., 'Aphra Behn and the Genealogy of the Man of Feeling', *Modern Philology* 87 (1990), 362–72.

'Only a Boy: Notes on Sentimental Novels', *Genre* 10 (1977), 501–27.

'Sentimental De-education', in Douglas Lane Patey and Timothy Kegan (eds.), *Augustan Studies: Essays in Honor of Irvin Ehrenpreis*, Newark: University of Delaware Press, 1985, pp. 253–62.

'Sentimental Novels of the Later Eighteenth Century', in John Richetti (ed.), *The Columbia History of the British Novel*, New York: Columbia University Press, 1994, pp. 181–98.

Sheriff, John K., *The Good-Natured Man: The Evolution of a Moral Ideal, 1660–1800*, Tuscaloosa, AL: University of Alabama Press, 1982.

Skinner, Gillian, *Sensibility and Economics in the Novel, 1740–1800: The Price of a Tear*, Basingstoke: Macmillan, 1999.

Stephanson, Raymond, 'Richardson's "Nerves": The Physiology of Sensibility in *Clarissa*', *Journal of the History of Ideas* 49 (1988), 267–85.

Todd, Janet, *Sensibility: An Introduction*, London: Methuen, 1986.

van Sant, Ann Jessie, *Eighteenth-Century Sensibility and the Novel: The Senses in Social Context*, Cambridge: Cambridge University Press, 1993.

Williams, Carolyn D., '"The Luxury of Doing Good": Benevolence, Sensibility, and the Royal Humane Society', in Roy Porter and Marie Mulvey Roberts (eds.), *Pleasure in the Eighteenth Century*, New York: New York University Press, 1996, pp. 77–107.

CHAPTER 23 BIBLIOGRAPHY

Primary works

Blackwell, Thomas, *An Enquiry into the Life and Writings of Homer*, London, 1735.

Blair, Hugh, *A Critical Dissertation on the Poems of Ossian, the Son of Fingal*, London, 1762.

Blake, William, *The Poetry and Prose of William Blake*, ed. David V. Erdman, Garden City, NY: Doubleday and Company, 1970.

Boswell, James, *Life of Johnson*, ed. George Birkbeck Hill and L. F. Powell, Oxford: Clarendon Press, 1934–64.

Chatterton, Thomas, *The Complete Works of Thomas Chatterton*, ed. Donald S. Taylor and Benjamin B. Hoover, 2 vols., Oxford: Clarendon Press, 1971.

Collins, William, *Poetical Works*, ed. Roger Lonsdale, Oxford: Oxford University Press, 1977.

Cowper, William, 'The Task', *The Poems of William Cowper*, ed. John D. Baird and Charles Ryskamp, Oxford: Clarendon Press, 1995.

Dodsley, Robert, *The Correspondence of Robert Dodsley 1733–1764*, ed. James E. Tierney, Cambridge: Cambridge University Press, 1988.

Dryden, John, 'Preface to *Ovid*', *John Dryden*, ed. Keith Walker, Oxford: Oxford University Press, 1987.

Duff, William, *Essay on Original Genius*, London, 1767.

Fletcher, Andrew. 'An Account of A Conversation concerning a Right Regulation of Governments', *Political Works*, ed. John Robertson, Cambridge: Cambridge University Press, 1997.

Heron, Robert, *Letters of Literature*, London, 1785.

Horace, *Satires, Epistles, Ars Poetica*, trans. H. Rushton Fairclough, Loeb Classical Library, Cambridge, MA: Cambridge University Press, 1966.

Hurd, Richard, *Letters on Chivalry and Romance*, London, 1762.

Johnson, Samuel, *Rasselas* in *Rasselas and Other Tales*, ed. Gwin J. Kolb, The Yale Edition of the Works of Samuel Johnson, 16 vols. New Haven, CT: Yale University Press, 1990.

Laing, Malcolm (ed.), *The Poems of Ossian*, Edinburgh: Archibald Constable and Co., 1805.

Lowth, Robert, *Lectures on the Sacred Poetry of the Hebrews*, trans. G. Gregory, London, 1787.

Macpherson, James, *Fingal*, London, 1762.

    The Poems of Ossian and Related Works, ed. Howard Gaskill, Edinburgh: Edinburgh University Press, 1996.

Percy, Thomas, *The Correspondence of Thomas Percy and Evan Evans*, ed. A. Lewis, 9 vols., *The Percy Letters*, New Haven, CT: Yale University Press, 1977.

    The Correspondence of Thomas Percy and William Shenstone, ed. Cleanth Brooks and A. F. Falconer, *The Percy Letters*, New Haven, CT: Yale University Press, 1977.

    Reliques of Ancient English Poetry, 3 vols., London, 1765.

Ramsay, Allan (ed.), *The Ever Green: A Collection of Scots Poems, Wrote by the Ingenious before 1600*, 2 vols., Edinburgh, 1724.

Report of the Committee of the Highland Society of Scotland appointed to inquire into the nature and authenticity of the poems of Ossian, by Henry Mackenzie; with copious appendix containing some of the principal documents on which the report is founded, Edinburgh: A. Constable, 1805.

Sidney, Sir Philip, *An Apology for Poetry*, ed. Geoffrey Shepherd, Manchester: Manchester University Press, 1973.

Thomas Warton, *The History of English Poetry*, 3 vols., London, 1774–81.

    Specimen of a History of Oxfordshire, London, 1783.

Secondary works

Bronson, Bertrand H., *Joseph Ritson: Scholar-at Arms*, 2 vols., Berkeley: University of California Press, 1938.

Feldman, Burton, and Robert Richardson (eds.), *The Rise of Modern Mythology 1680–1860*, Bloomington: Indiana University Press, 1972.

Fitzgerald, Robert P., 'The Style of Ossian', *Studies in Romanticism* 6 (1966), 22–33.

Folkenflik, Robert, 'Macpherson, Chatterton, Blake and the Great Age of Literary Forgery', *Centennial Review*, 18 (1974), 378–91.

Friedman, Albert B., *The Ballad Revival: Studies in the Influence of Popular on Sophisticated Poetry*, Chicago: University of Chicago Press, 1961.

Gaskill, Howard, ' "Ossian" Macpherson: Towards a Rehabilitation', *Comparative Criticism* 8 (1986), 113–46.

Gillies, William, 'A Century of Gaelic Scholarship', in William Gillies (ed.), *Gaelic and Scotland: Alba agus a' Ghàidhlig*, Edinburgh: Edinburgh University Press, 1989.

Groom, Nick, *The Making of Percy's 'Reliques'*, Oxford: Clarendon Press, 1999.

Hudson, Nicholas, ' "Oral Tradition": The Evolution of an Eighteenth-Century Concept' in Alvaro Ribeiro and James G. Basker (eds.), *Tradition in Transition: Women Writers, Marginal Texts, and the Eighteenth-century Canon*, Oxford: Clarendon Press, 1996, pp. 161–76.

Keymer, Thomas, 'Narrratives of Loss: *The Poems of Ossian* and *Tristram Shandy*', in Fiona Stafford and Howard Gaskill (eds.), *From Gaelic to Romantic: Ossianic Translations*, Amsterdam: Rodopi, 1998.

Levine, Joseph M., *Humanism and History: Origins of Modern English Historiography*, Ithaca, NY: Cornell University Press, 1987.

Matthews, David, *The Making of Middle English, 1765–1910*, Minneapolis: University of Minnesota Press, 1999.

Meek, Donald E., 'The Gaelic Ballads of Scotland: Creativity and Adaptation', in Howard Gaskill (ed.), *Ossian Revisited*, Edinburgh: Edinburgh University Press, 1991, pp. 19–48.

Murphy, Peter T., *Poetry as an Occupation and an Art in Britain 1760–1830*, Cambridge: Cambridge University Press, 1993.

Pittock, Murray G. H., *Inventing and Resisting Britain: Cultural Identities in Britain and Ireland, 1685–1789*, London: Routledge, 1997.

Roy, Ross, '*Hardyknute* – Lady Wardlaw's Ballad?' in H. W. Matalene (ed.), *Romanticism and Culture*, Columbia, SC: Camden House, 1984, pp. 133–46.

Sher, Richard B., *Church and University in the Scottish Enlightenment: The Moderate Literati of Edinburgh*, Edinburgh: Edinburgh University Press, 1985.

Stafford, Fiona, *The Sublime Savage: A Study of James Macpherson and the Poems of Ossian*, Edinburgh: Edinburgh University Press, 1988.

Thomson, Derick S., *The Gaelic Sources of Macpherson's 'Ossian'*, Edinburgh: Oliver and Boyd, 1952.

'Macpherson's *Ossian*: Ballads to Epics', in Bo Almqvist, Séamas Ó Catháin, and Pádraig Ó Héalaí (eds.), *The Heroic Process: Form, Function and Fantasy in Folk Epic*, Dublin: The Glendale Press, 1987, pp. 243–64.

CHAPTER 24 BIBLIOGRAPHY

Primary works

Carter, Elizabeth, *Letters from Mrs Elizabeth Carter to Mrs Montagu Between the Years 1755 and 1800*, 3 vols., New York: AMS Press, 1973.

Chesterfield, Philip Dormer Stanhope, Earl of, *Letters of Philip Dormer Stanhope, Earl of Chesterfield*, ed. John Bradshaw, 3 vols., London: George Allen & Unwin, 1892.

Cowper, William, *Letters and Prose Writings*, ed. James King and Charles Ryskamp. 5 vols., Oxford: Clarendon, 1979–81.

Delany, Mary, *The Autobiography and Correspondence of Mrs Delaney*, ed. Sarah Chauncey Woolsey, 2 vols., Boston: Roberts Brothers, 1882.

Montagu, Mary Wortley, Lady, *Complete Letters*, ed. Robert Halsband, 3 vols., Oxford: Clarendon Press, 1965.

Piozzi, Hester Lynch, *The Piozzi Letters: Correspondence of Hester Lynch Piozzi, 1784–1821*, ed. Edward A. Bloom and Lillian D. Bloom, 5 vols., Newark: University of Delaware Press, 1989.

Pope, Alexander, *Correspondence*, ed. George Sherburn, 5 vols., Oxford: Clarendon Press, 1956.

A Series of Letters Between Mrs Elizabeth Carter and Miss Catherine Talbot, from the Year 1741 to 1770, 4 vols., New York: AMS Press, 1975.

Walpole, Horace, *Selected Letters*, ed. W. S. Lewis, New Haven, CT: Yale University Press, 1973.

Secondary works

Anderson, Howard, Philip B. Daghlian, and Irvin Ehrenpreis (eds.), *The Familiar Letter in the Eighteenth Century*, Lawrence: University of Kansas Press, 1968.

Earle, Rebecca (ed.), *Epistolary Selves: Letters and Letter-Writers, 1600–1945*, Aldershot: Ashgate, 1999.

Gilroy, Amanda, and W. M. Verhoeven (eds.), *Epistolary Histories: Letters, Fiction, Culture*, Charlottesville: University Press of Virginia, 2000.

Redford, Bruce, *The Converse of the Pen: Acts of Intimacy in the Eighteenth-Century Familiar Letter*, Chicago: University of Chicago Press, 1986.

Stewart, Keith. 'Towards Defining an Aesthetic for the Familiar Letter in Eighteenth-Century England', *Prose Studies* 5 (1982), 179–92.

Vickery, Amanda, *The Gentleman's Daughter: Women's Lives in Georgian England*, New Haven, CT and London: Yale University Press, 1998.

Wright, Susan, 'Private Language Made Public: The Language of Letters as Literature', *Poetics* 18 (1989), 549–78.

CHAPTER 25 BIBLIOGRAPHY

Primary works

Beadle, John, *The Journal or Diary of a Thankful Christian*, London, 1656.

Boswell, James, *Boswell's London Journal, 1762–1763*, ed. Frederick A. Pottle, New York: McGraw-Hill, 1950.

The Life of Samuel Johnson, ed. R. W. Chapman, Oxford: Oxford World Classics, 1980.

Bunyan, John, *Grace Abounding, with Other Spiritual Autobiographies*, ed. John Stachniewski with Anita Pacheco, Oxford: Oxford University Press, 1998.

Burney, Frances, *Early Journals and Letters*, ed. Lars E. Troide *et al.*, 4 vols., Kingston, Montreal: McGill-Queen's University Press, 1988–2003.

The Journals and Letters, ed. Joyce Hemlow *et al.*, 12 vols., Oxford: Clarendon Press, 1973–84.

Cavendish, Margaret, 'A True Relation of My Birth, Breeding, and Life', in Sylvia Bowerbank and Sara Mendelson (eds.), *Paper Bodies: A Margaret Cavendish Reader*, Peterborough, Ontario: Broadview Press, 2000.

Charke, Charlotte, *A Narrative of the Life of Mrs Charlotte Charke*, ed. Robert Rehder, London: Pickering & Chatto, 1999.

Cibber, Colley, *An Apology for the Life of Colley Cibber; With an Historical View of the Stage During His Own Time*, ed. B. R. S. Fone, Mineola, NY: Dover Publications, 2001.

Defoe, Daniel. *Robinson Crusoe*, ed. John Richetti, London: Penguin, 2001.

Equiano, Olaudah, *The Interesting Narrative of the Life*, ed. Vincent Carretta, London: Penguin, 1995.

Gibbon, Edward, *Memoirs of My Life*, ed. Betty Radice, London: Penguin, 1984.

Hume, David, 'My Own Life', in *An Enquiry Concerning Human Understanding*, ed. Antony Flew, La Salle, IL: Open Court, 1988.

Pepys, Samuel, *The Diary of Samuel Pepys*, ed. Robert Latham and William Matthews, 11 vols., Berkeley and Los Angeles: University of California Press, 1970–83.

Thrale, Hester Lynch, *Thraliana*, ed. Katherine C. Balderston, 2nd edn, 2 vols. Oxford: Clarendon Press, 1951.

Secondary works

Baruth, Philip E. (ed.), *Introducing Charlotte Charke*, Champaign, IL: University of Illinois Press, 1998.

Bruss, Elizabeth W., *Autobiographical Acts: The Changing Situation of a Literary Genre*, Baltimore, MD: Johns Hopkins University Press, 1976.

Coleman, Patrick, Jayne Lewis and Jill Kowalik (eds.), *Representations of the Self from the Renaissance to Romanticism*, Cambridge: Cambridge University Press, 2000.

Folkenflik, Robert (ed.), *The Culture of Autobiography*, Stanford, CA: Stanford University Press, 1993.

Mascuch, Michael, *Origins of the Individualist Self: Autobiography and Self-Identity in England, 1591–1791*, Stanford, CA: Stanford University Press, 1996.

Nussbaum, Felicity, *The Autobiographical Subject: Gender and Ideology in Eighteenth-Century England*, Baltimore, MD: Johns Hopkins University Press, 1989.

Porter, Roy (ed.), *Rewriting the Self: Histories from the Renaissance to the Present*, London: Routledge, 1997.

Spacks, Patricia Meyer, *Imagining a Self: Autobiography and Novel in Eighteenth-Century England*, Cambridge, MA: Harvard University Press, 1976.

Sherman, Stuart, *Telling Time: Clocks, Diaries, and English Diurnal Form, 1660–1795*, Chicago: University of Chicago Press, 1996.

John Sturrock, *The Language of Autobiography: Studies in the First Person Singular*, Cambridge: Cambridge University Press, 1993.

Womersley, David, *Gibbon and the 'Watchmen of the Holy City': The Historian and His Reputation, 1776–1815*, Oxford: Clarendon Press, 2002.

Woolf, Daniel, 'News, History and the Construction of the Present in Early Modern England', in Brendan Dooley and Sabrina A. Baron (eds.), *The Politics of Information in Early Modern Europe*, London: Routledge, 2001, pp. 80–118.

CHAPTER 26 BIBLIOGRAPHY

Primary works

Addison, Joseph, *The Spectator*, 5 vols., ed. Donald F. Bond, Oxford: Clarendon Press, 1965.

Burke, Edmund, *A Philosophical Enquiry into the Origin of Our Ideas of the Sublime and Beautiful*, ed. J. T. Boulton, London: Routledge & Kegan Paul, 1958.

Coleridge, Samuel Taylor, 'General Character of the Gothic Literature and Art', in *Coleridge's Miscellaneous Criticism*, ed. Thomas Middleton Raysor, London: Constable, 1936, pp. 11–17.

'General Character of the Gothic Mind in the Middle Ages', in Raysor, ed., *Coleridge's Miscellaneous Criticism*, pp. 6–10.

Dennis, John, 'The Grounds of Criticism in Poetry', in Scott Elledge (ed.), *Eighteenth-Century Critical Essays*, 2 vols., Ithaca, NY: Cornell University Press, 1961.

Drake, Nathan, 'On Gothic Superstition', in *Literary Hours, or Sketches Critical and Narrative*, 2 vols., London, 1800, rpt. New York: Garland, 1970.

Hurd, Richard, *Letters on Chivalry and Romance*, in *The Works of Richard Hurd, D. D.* 8 vols., London: Cadell and Davies, 1811.

Lewis, Matthew, *The Monk*, ed. Howard Anderson, Oxford and New York: Oxford University Press, 1973.

Maturin, Charles Robert, *Melmoth the Wanderer*, ed. Victor Sage, London: Penguin, 2000.

Montagu, Elizabeth, *An Essay on the Writings and Genius of Shakespear, Compared with the Greek and French Dramatic Poets, with Some Remarks upon the Misrepresentations of Mons. de Voltaire*, London, 1769.

Pinkerton, John, *A Dissertation on the Origin and Progress of the Scythians or Goths, Being an Introduction to the Ancient and Modern History of Europe*, London: John Nichols, 1787.

Radcliffe, Ann, *The Mysteries of Udolpho*, ed. Bonamy Dobrée, with an introduction by Terry Castle, Oxford and New York: Oxford University Press, 1998.

Scott, Sir Walter, *Lives of Eminent Novelists and Dramatists*, rev. edn, London and New York: Frederick Warne and Co., 1887.

Walpole, Horace, *The Castle of Otranto*, ed. E. J. Clery, Oxford: Oxford University Press, 1996.

Warton, Thomas, *The History of English Poetry from the Close of the Eleventh to the Commencement of the Eighteenth Century*, 2 vols., London: J. Dodsley, 1778.

Secondary works

Aguirre, Manuel, *The Closed Space: Horror Literature and Western Symbolism*, Manchester: Manchester University Press, 1990.

Aldrich, Megan, *Gothic Revival*, London: Phaidon Press, 1994.

Ashfield, Andrew, and Peter De Bolla (eds.), *The Sublime: A Reader in British Eighteenth-Century Aesthetic Theory*, Cambridge: Cambridge University Press, 1996.

Barker-Benfield, G. J., *The Culture of Sensibility: Sex and Society in Eighteenth-Century Britain*, Chicago: University of Chicago Press, 1992.

Birkhead, Edith, *The Tale of Terror: A Study of the Gothic Romance*, London: Constable & Co., 1921.

Bloom, Harold (ed.), *Classic Horror Writers*, New York and Philadelphia: Chelsea House, 1994.

Bond, Francis, *Gothic Architecture in England: An Analysis of the Origin and Development of English Church Architecture from the Norman Conquest to the Dissolution of the Monasteries*, London: B. T. Batsford, 1905.

Bony, Jean, *The English Decorated Style: Gothic Architecture Transformed, 1250–1350*, Ithaca, NY: Cornell University Press, 1979.

Braverman, Richard, ' "Dunce the Second Reigns Like Dunce the First": The Gothic Bequest in *The Dunciad*', *ELH: A Journal of English Literary History* 62 (1995), 863–82.

Brewer, John, *The Pleasures of the Imagination: English Culture in the Eighteenth Century*, New York: Farrar Straus & Giroux, 1997.

Brooks, Chris, *The Gothic Revival*, London: Phaidon Press, 1999.

Byron, Glennis, and David Punter (eds.), *Spectral Readings: Toward a Gothic Geography*, New York: St Martin's Press, 1999.

Calloway, Stephen, Michael Snodin, and Clive Wainwright, *Horace Walpole and Strawberry Hill*, London: London Borough of Richmond-on-Thames, 1980.

Canetti, Elias, *Crowds and Power*, trans. Carol Stewart, New York: Continuum Press, 1978.

Carter, Margaret L., *Specter or Delusion? The Supernatural in Gothic Fiction*, Ann Arbor: University of Michigan Press, 1987.

Castle, Terry, 'Spectral Politics: Apparition Belief and the Romantic Imagination', in *The Female Thermometer: Eighteenth-Century Culture and the Invention of the Uncanny*, Oxford and New York: Oxford University Press, 1995, pp. 168–89.

'The Spectralization of the Other in *The Mysteries of Udolpho*,' in Castle, *Female Thermometer*, pp. 120–39.

Clark, Sir Kenneth, *The Gothic Revival: An Essay in the History of Taste*, Harmondsworth, Middlesex: Penguin, 1964.

Clery, E. J., *The Rise of Supernatural Fiction, 1762–1800*, Cambridge: Cambridge University Press, 1995.

Clery, E. J., and Robert Miles (eds.), *Gothic Documents: A Sourcebook 1700–1820*. Manchester and New York: Manchester University Press, 2000.

Colley, Linda, *Britons: Forging the Nation 1707–1837*, New Haven, CT and London: Yale University Press, 1992.

Davenport-Hines, Richard, *Gothic: Four Hundred Years of Excess, Horror, Evil and Ruin*, New York: North Point Press, 1998.

Day, William Patrick, *In the Circles of Fear and Desire: A Study of Gothic Fantasy*, Chicago: University of Chicago Press, 1985.

De Bolla, Peter, *The Discourse of the Sublime: Readings in History, Aesthetics and the Subject*, Oxford: Oxford University Press, 1989.

Ditchfield, Peter Hampson, *English Gothic Architecture*, London: J. M. Dent, 1920.

Doody, Margaret Anne, 'Deserts, Ruins and Troubled Waters: Female Dreams in Fiction and the Development of the Gothic Novel', *Genre* 10 (1977), 529–72.

Eastlake, Charles L., *A History of the Gothic Revival*, London: Longman's, Green, 1872.

Edmundson, Mark, *Nightmare on Main Street: Angels, Sadomasochism, and the Culture of Gothic*, Cambridge, MA: Harvard University Press, 1997.

Elias, Norbert, *The Civilizing Process: Sociogenetic and Psychogenetic Investigations*, rev. edn, trans. Edmund Jephcott, ed. Eric Dunning, Johan Goudsblom and Stephen Mennell, Oxford: Blackwell, 2000.

Elias, Norbert, and Eric Dunning, *Quest for Excitement: Sport and Leisure in the Civilizing Process*, Oxford and New York: Basil Blackwell, 1986.

Ellis, Kate Ferguson, *The Contested Castle: Gothic Novels and the Subversion of Domestic Ideology*, Urbana: University of Illinois Press, 1989.

Ferguson, Frances, *Solitude and the Sublime*, London and New York: Routledge, 1992.

Fleenor, Juliann E. (ed.), *The Female Gothic*, Montreal and London: Eden Press, 1983.

Fotheringill, Brian, *Beckford of Fonthill*, London: Faber and Faber, 1979.

Frank, Frederick S. (ed.), *Guide to the Gothic II: An Annotated Bibliography of Criticism, 1983–1993*, Lanham, MD: Scarecrow Press, 1995.

Frank, Frederick S., *The First Gothics: A Critical Guide to the English Gothic Novel*, New York and London: Garland, 1987.

Frankl, Paul, *Gothic Architecture*, trans. Dieter Pevsner, Baltimore, MD: Penguin, 1962.
  The Gothic: Literary Sources and Interpretations through Eight Centuries, Princeton, NJ: Princeton University Press, 1960.

Gardner, Samuel, *A Guide to English Gothic Architecture*, Cambridge: Cambridge University Press, 1922.

Gelder, Ken, *The Horror Reader*, London and New York: Routledge, 2000.

Graham, Kenneth W. (ed.), *Gothic Fictions: Prohibition/Transgression*, New York: AMS Press, 1989.

Grunenberg, Christopher (ed.), *Gothic: Transmutations of Horror in Late Twentieth-Century Art*, London and Cambridge, MA: M.I.T. Press, 1997.

Haggerty, George, *Gothic Fiction/Gothic Form*, University Park: Pennsylvania State University Press, 1989.
  'Literature and Homosexuality in the Later Eighteenth Century: Walpole, Beckford and Lewis', *Studies in the Novel* 18 (1986), 341–52.
  Men in Love: Masculinity and Sexuality in the Eighteenth Century, New York: Columbia University Press, 1999.

Harwell, Thomas Meade (ed.), *The English Gothic Novel: A Miscellany in Four Volumes*, Salzburg: Salzburg Studies in English Literature, 1986.

Henn, T. R., *Longinus and English Criticism*, Cambridge: Cambridge University Press, 1934.

Honour, Hugh, *Horace Walpole*, London: Longmans, Green, 1957.

Howard, Jacqueline, *Reading Gothic Fiction: A Bakhtinian Approach*, Oxford: Clarendon Press, 1994.

Janowitz, Anne F., *England's Ruins: Poetic Purpose and the National Landscape*, Cambridge, MA: Blackwell, 1990.

Johnson, Claudia L., *Equivocal Beings: Politics, Gender and Sentimentality in the 1790s – Wollstonecraft, Radcliffe, Burney, Austen*, Chicago: University of Chicago Press, 1995.

Kiely, Robert, *The Romantic Novel in England*, Cambridge, MA: Harvard University Press, 1972.

Kilgour, Maggie, *The Rise of the Gothic Novel*, London: Routledge, 1995.

Kliger, Samuel, *The Goths in England: A Study in Seventeenth- and Eighteenth-Century Thought*, Cambridge, MA: Harvard University Press, 1952.

Kramnick, Jonathan Brody, *Making the English Canon: Print-Capitalism and the Cultural Past, 1700–1770*, Cambridge: Cambridge University Press, 1998.

Lecky, W. E. H., *The History of the Rise and Influence of the Spirit of Rationalism in Europe*, New York: D. Appleton, 1919.

Lewis, W. S., *Horace Walpole*, New York: Pantheon Books, 1961.

Lyndenberg, Robin, 'Gothic Architecture and Fiction: A Survey of Critical Responses', *The Centennial Review* 22 (1978), 95–109.

Macaulay, James, *The Gothic Revival 1745–1845*, Glasgow: Blackie, 1975.

Madoff, Mark, 'The Useful Myth of Gothic Ancestry', *Studies in Eighteenth-Century Culture* 8 (1979), 337–50.

McCarthy, Michael J., *The Origins of the Gothic Revival*, New Haven, CT and London: Yale University Press, 1987.

McKinney, David D., 'The Castle of My Ancestors: Walpole and Strawberry Hill', *British Journal of Eighteenth-Century Studies* 13 (1990), 199–214.

McNutt, Dan J., *The Eighteenth-Century Gothic Novel: An Annotated Bibliography of Criticism and Selected Texts*, New York: Garland, 1974.

Miles, Robert, *Ann Radcliffe: The Great Enchantress*, Manchester: Manchester University Press, 1995.

  Gothic Writing 1750–1820: A Genealogy, London and New York: Routledge, 1993.

Moers, Ellen, *Literary Women*, Garden City, NY: Anchor Press, 1977.

Monk, Samuel Holt, *The Sublime: A Study of Critical Theories in XVIII-Century England*, Ann Arbor: University of Michigan Press, 1960.

Morrissey, Lee, *From the Temple to the Castle: An Architectural History of British Literature*, Charlottesville: University Press of Virginia, 1999.

Mowl, Timothy, *Horace Walpole: The Great Outsider*, London: John Murray, 1996.

Mullan, John, *Sentiment and Sociability: The Language of Feeling in the Eighteenth Century*, Oxford: Oxford University Press, 1988.

Napier, Elizabeth, *The Failure of Gothic: Problems of Disjunction in an Eighteenth-Century Literary Form*, Oxford: Oxford University Press, 1987.

Nicolson, Marjorie Hope, *Mountain Gloom and Mountain Glory: The Development of the Aesthetics of the Infinite*, Ithaca, NY: Cornell University Press, 1959.

Ostergard, Derek E. (ed.), *William Beckford 1760–1844: An Eye for the Magnificent*, New Haven, CT and London: Yale University Press, 2001.

Pevsner, Nikolaus, *The Englishness of English Art*, London: Architectural Press, 1956.

Piggott, Stuart, *Ruins in a Landscape: Essays in Antiquarianism*, Edinburgh: Edinburgh University Press, 1976.

Poovey, Mary, 'Ideology in *The Mysteries of Udolpho*', *Criticism* 21 (1979), 307–30.

Porter, Roy, *Mind-Forg'd Manacles: A History of Madness in England from the Restoration to the Regency*, London: Athlone Press, 1987.

Praz, Mario, *The Romantic Agony*, trans. Angus Davidson, London: Oxford University Press, 1954.

Punter, David (ed.), *A Companion to the Gothic*, Oxford: Blackwell, 2000.

Punter, David, *Gothic Pathologies: The Text, the Body, and the Law*, New York: St Martin's Press, 1998.

    The Literature of Terror: A History of Gothic Fiction from 1765 to the Present Day, London: Longmans, 1980.

Railo, Eino, *The Haunted Castle: A Study of the Elements of English Romanticism*, New York: Gordon Press, 1974.

Richter, David H., 'Gothic Fantasia: The Monsters and the Myths: A Review Article', *The Eighteenth Century: Theory and Interpretation* 28 (1987), 149–170.

    The Progress of Romance: Literary Historiography and the Gothic Novel, Columbus: Ohio State University Press, 1996.

    'The Reception of the Gothic Novel in the 1790s', in Robert W. Uphaus (ed.), *The Idea of the Novel in the Eighteenth Century*, East Lansing, MI: Colleagues Press, 1988.

Rogers, Deborah D. (ed.), *The Critical Response to Ann Radcliffe*, Westport, CT: Greenwood Press, 1994.

Rogers, Deborah D., *Ann Radcliffe: A Bio-bibliography*, Westport, CT: Greenwood Press, 1996.

Sabor, Peter, *Horace Walpole: The Critical Heritage*, London: Routledge & Kegan Paul, 1987.

Sage, Victor (ed.), *The Gothick Novel: A Casebook*, London: Macmillan, 1990.

    Horror Fiction in the Protestant Tradition, London: Macmillan, 1988.

Sage, Victor, and Allan Lloyd Smith (eds.), *Gothick Origins and Innovations*, Amsterdam and Atlanta: Rodopi, 1994.

Saintsbury, George, *The Peace of the Augustans: A Survey of Eighteenth-Century Literature as a Place of Rest and Refreshment*, Oxford: Oxford University Press, 1946.

Scott, Geoffrey, *The Architecture of Humanism: A Study in the History of Taste*, New York: W. W. Norton, 1974.

Sedgwick, Eve Kosofsky, *Between Men: Male Homosocial Desire in English Literature*, New York: Columbia University Press, 1985.

    The Coherence of Gothic Conventions, New York: Arno Press, 1980.

Smith, R. J., *The Gothic Bequest: Medieval Institutions in British Thought, 1688–1863*, Cambridge: Cambridge University Press, 1987.

Spector, Robert Donald, *The English Gothic: A Bibliographic Guide to Writers from Horace Walpole to Mary Shelley*, Westport, CT: Greenwood Press, 1984.

Stephen, Sir Leslie, *English Literature and Society in the Eighteenth Century*, New York and London: G. P. Putnam's Sons, 1907.

Summers, Montague, *A Gothic Bibliography*, New York: Fortune Press, 1941.

    The Gothic Quest: A History of the Gothic Novel, London: Fortune Press, 1938.

Thomas, Keith, *Religion and the Decline of Magic*, New York: Charles Scribner's Sons, 1971.

Todorov, Tzvetan, *The Fantastic: A Structural Approach to a Literary Genre*, trans. Richard Howard, Ithaca, NY: Cornell University Press, 1975.

Tompkins, J. M. S., *The Popular Novel in England 1770–1800*, Lincoln: University of Nebraska Press, 1961.

Trumpener, Katie, *Bardic Nationalism: The Romantic Novel and the British Empire*, Princeton, NJ: Princeton University Press, 1997.

Varma, Devendra P., *The Gothic Flame*, New York: Russell and Russell, 1966.

Vidler, Anthony, *The Architectural Uncanny: Essays in the Modern Unhomely*, Cambridge, MA: M.I.T. Press, 1992.

Weinbrot, Howard D., *Britannia's Issue: The Rise of British Literature from Dryden to Ossian*, Cambridge: Cambridge University Press, 1993.

Woolf, Virginia, 'Gothic Romance', *Times Literary Supplement*, 5 May 1921, rpt. in Andrew McNeillie (ed.), *The Essays of Virginia Woolf*, 4 vols., London: The Hogarth Press, 1988, vol. III, pp. 304–7.

CHAPTER 27 BIBLIOGRAPHY

Primary works

Addison, Joseph *Remarks on Several Parts of Italy, In the Years 1701, 1702, 1703*, London, 1705.

Addison, Joseph, and Richard, Steele, *The Spectator*, 5 vols., ed. Donald F. Bond, Oxford: Clarendon Press, 1965.

Behn, Aphra, *Oroonoko: Or, The Royal Slave*, ed. Lore Metzger, New York: Norton, 1973.

Boswell, James, *Boswell on the Grand Tour: Germany and Switzerland, 1764*, ed. Frederick A. Pottle, New York: McGraw-Hill, 1953.

    Boswell on the Grand Tour: Italy, Corsica, and France, 1765–1766, ed. Frank Brady and Frederick A. Pottle, New York: McGraw-Hill, 1955.

Bruce, James, *Travels to Discover the Source of the Nile, in the Years 1768–1772*, 5 vols., Edinburgh and London, 1790.

Cook, James, *The Journals of Captain James Cook on his Voyages of Discovery*, 4 vols., ed. J. C. Beaglehole, Hakluyt Society, Cambridge: Cambridge University Press, 1955–1968.

Dampier, William, *A New Voyage round the World*, in *Dampier's Voyages*, 2 vols., ed. John Masefield, London: E. Grant Richards, 1906.

Defoe, Daniel, *Captain Singleton*, ed. Shiv K. Kumar, intro. Penelope Wilson, Oxford: Oxford University Press, 1990.

    Robinson Crusoe (1719), ed. J. Donald Crowley, Oxford: Oxford University Press, 1990.

    A Tour Thro' the whole Island of Great Britain, 3 vols., London, 1724–7; intro. G. D. H. Cole, 2 vols., London: Peter Davies, 1927.

Equiano, Olaudah, *'The Interesting Narrative' and Other Writings*, ed. Vincent Carretta, New York and London: Penguin, 1995.

Fielding, Henry, *The Journal of a Voyage to Lisbon*, London, 1755.

Fiennes, Celia, *The Illustrated Journeys of Celia Fiennes 1685-c.1712*, ed. Christopher Morris, London and Sydney: MacDonald & Co., 1982.

Gibbon, Edward, *Memoirs of My Life*, ed. Georges A. Bonnard, London: Thomas Nelson, 1966.

Johnson, Samuel, *The History of Rasselas, Prince of Abissinia*, ed. D. J. Enright, London: Penguin, 1985.

    A Journey to the Western Islands of Scotland, ed. Mary Lascelles, New Haven, CT: Yale University Press, 1971.

Long, Edward, *The History of Jamaica*, 3 vols., London, 1774.

Montagu, Lady Mary Wortley, *Complete Letters*, 3 vols., ed. Robert Halsband, Oxford: Clarendon Press, 1965–7.

Piozzi, Hester Lynch, *Observations and Reflections Made in the Course of a Journey through France, Italy, and Germany*, ed. Herbert Barrows, Ann Arbor: University of Michigan Press, 1967.

Pococke, Richard, *A Description of the East, and Some other Countries*, 2 vols., London, 1743–5.

Rogers, Woodes, *A Cruising Voyage round the World*, ed. G. E. Manwaring, London: Longmans, Green, & Co., 1928.

[Schaw, Janet], *Journal of a Lady of Quality; Being the Narrative of a Journey from Scotland to the West Indies, North Carolina, and Portugal, in the years 1774 to 1776*, ed. Evangeline Walker Andrews and Charles McLean Andrews, New Haven, CT: Yale University Press, 1921.

Smollett, Tobias, *The Adventures of Roderick Random*, ed. Paul-Gabriel Boucé, Oxford: Oxford University Press, 1979.

   The Expedition of Humphry Clinker, London: Penguin, 1985.

   Travels through France and Italy, ed. Frank Felsenstein, Oxford: Oxford University Press, 1979.

Sterne, Laurence, *A Sentimental Journey* (with *The Journal to Eliza*), intro. Daniel George, New York and London: Dutton/Everyman, 1975.

Swift, Jonathan, *Gulliver's Travels*, ed. Paul Turner, Oxford: Oxford University Press, 1998.

Walter, Richard and Benjamin Robins, *A Voyage round the World in the Years* MDCCXL, *I, II, III, IV*, ed. Glyndwr Williams, Oxford: Oxford University Press, 1974.

Wollstonecraft, Mary, *Letters Written during a Short Residence in Sweden, Norway, and Denmark*, ed. Carol H. Poston, Lincoln: and London University of Nebraska Press, 1976.

Young, Arthur, *A Tour in Ireland*, 2 vols., Dublin, 1780.

   Travels During the Years 1787, 1788, and 1789 . . . [through] the Kingdom of France, 2 vols., Dublin, 1793.

Secondary works

Adams, Percy G., *Travelers and Travel Liars, 1660–1800*, Berkeley and Los Angeles: University of California Press, 1962.

Aravamudan, Srinivas, *Tropicopolitans: Colonialism and Agency, 1688–1804*, Durham, NC and London: Duke University Press, 1999.

Batten, Charles, *Pleasurable Instruction: Form and Convention in Eighteenth-Century Travel Literature*, Berkeley and Los Angeles: University of California Press, 1978.

Black, Jeremy, *The British Abroad: The Grand Tour in the Eighteenth Century*, New York: St Martin's Press, 1992.

Bohls, Elizabeth A., *Women Travel Writers and the Language of Aesthetics, 1716–1818*, Cambridge Studies in Romanticism 13, Cambridge: Cambridge University Press, 1995.

Colley, Linda, *Captives: Britain, Empire and the World, 1600–1850*, London: Jonathan Cape, 2002.

Edwards, Philip, *The Story of the Voyage: Sea-narratives in Eighteenth-century England*, Cambridge: Cambridge University Press, 1994.

Grove, Richard H., *Green Imperialism: Colonial Expansion, Tropical Island Edens, and the Origins of Environmentalism, 1600–1800*, Cambridge: Cambridge University Press, 1995.

Hulme, Peter, *Colonial Encounters: Europe and the Native Caribbean, 1492–1797*, London and New York: Routledge, 1992.

Marshall, P. J., and Glyndwr Williams, *The Great Map of Mankind: British Perceptions of the World in the Age of Enlightenment*, London: J. M. Dent & Sons, 1982.

Matar, Nabil, *Turks, Moors, and Englishmen in the Age of Discovery*, New York: Columbia University Press, 1999.

Melman, Billie, *Women's Orients: English Women and the Middle East, 1718–1918*, Ann Arbor: University of Michigan Press, 1992.

Moir, Esther, *The Discovery of Britain: The English Tourists, 1540–1840*, London: Routledge & Kegan Paul, 1964.

Neill, Anna, *British Discovery Literature and the Rise of Global Commerce*, London: Palgrave, 2002.

Nussbaum, Felicity A. (ed.), *The Global Eighteenth Century*, Baltimore, MD: Johns Hopkins University Press, 2003.

Pratt, Mary Louise, *Imperial Eyes: Travel Writing and Transculturation*, London and New York: Routledge, 1992.

Rennie, Neil, *Far-Fetched Facts: The Literature of Travel and the Idea of the South Seas*, Oxford: Oxford University Press, 1995.

Said, Edward W., *Orientalism*, New York: Pantheon, 1978.

Stafford, Barbara Maria, *Voyage into Substance: Art, Science, Nature, and the Illustrated Travel Account, 1760–1840*, Cambridge, MA: M.I.T. Press, 1984.

Telscher, Kate, *India Inscribed: European and British Writing on India: 1600–1800*, Oxford: Oxford University Press, 1995.

Turner, Katherine, *British Travel Writers in Europe 1750–1800*, Burlington, VT: Ashgate, 2001.

CHAPTER 28 BIBLIOGRAPHY

Primary works

Austen, Jane, *Northanger Abbey*, ed. Marilyn Butler, London: Penguin, 1995.

Behn, Aphra, *Oroonoko, The Rover and Other Works*, ed. Janet Todd, London: Penguin, 1992.

Brooke, Frances, *The Excursion*, ed. Paula Backscheider and Hope D. Cotton, Lexington: The University Press of Kentucky, 1997.

The History of Emily Montague, ed. Mary Jane Edwards, Ontario: Carleton University Press, 1985.

Burney, Frances, *Camilla or A Picture of Youth*, ed. Edward A. Bloom and Lillian D. Bloom, Oxford: Oxford University Press, 1983.

Cecilia, or Memoirs of an Heiress, ed. Peter Sabor and Margaret Anne Doody, Oxford: Oxford University Press, 1988.

Evelina, or the History of a Young Lady's Entrance into the World, ed. Edward A. Bloom and Lillian D. Bloom, Oxford: Oxford University Press, 1982.

The Wanderer, ed. Margaret Doody, Robert L. Mack, and Peter Sabor, Oxford: Oxford University Press, 1991.

Edgeworth, Maria, *Belinda*, ed. Kathryn J. Kirkpatrick, Oxford: Oxford University Press, 1994.

Fielding, Sarah, *The Adventures of David Simple*, ed. Linda Bree, London: Penguin, 2002.

The Governess, or, The Little Female Academy, ed. Mary Cadogan, London: Pandora, 1987.

The History of the Countess of Dellwyn, in The Flowering of the Novel Series, New York: Garland, 1974.

The History of Ophelia, London, 1760.

The Lives of Cleopatra and Octavia, ed. Christopher D. Johnson, Lewisburg, PA: Bucknell University Press, 1994.

Gibbes, Phoebe. *Hartly House, Calcutta: A Novel of the Days of Warren Hastings*, rprt. from 1789 edn, Calcutta: Thacker, Spink, and Co., 1908; Calcutta: Bibash Gupta, 1984.

Griffith, Elizabeth, *The Delicate Distress*, ed. Cynthia Booth Ricciardi and Susan Staves, Lexington: University Press of Kentucky, 1997.

Haywood, Eliza, *The Fortunate Foundlings*, in The Flowering of the Novel Series, New York: Garland, 1974.

The History of Jemmy and Jenny Jessamy, in The Flowering of the Novel Series, New York: Garland, 1974.

The History of Miss Betsy Thoughtless, ed. Beth Fowkes Tobin, Oxford: Oxford University Press, 1997.

Life's Progress through the Passions, in The Flowering of the Novel Series, New York: Garland, 1974.

Lennox, Charlotte, *Euphemia*, Gainesville, FL: Scholars' Facsimiles and Reprints, 1989.

The Female Quixote; or, the Adventures of Arabella, ed. Margaret Dalziel, intro. Margaret Doody, Oxford: Oxford University Press, 1989.

Henrietta, London 1758.

The Life of Harriot Stuart, Written by Herself, ed. Susan Kubica Howard, Madison, NJ: Fairleigh Dickinson University Press, 1995.

Reeve, Clara, *The History of Charoba, Queen of Aegypt*, in *Oriental Tales*, ed. Robert L. Mack, Oxford: Oxford University Press, 1992.

The Old English Baron: A Gothic Story, ed. James Trainer, London: Oxford University Press, 1967.

The Progress of Romance, in *Bluestocking Feminism: Writings of the Bluestocking Circle, 1738–1785*, vol. VI, ed. Gary Kelly, London: Pickering and Chatto, 1999.

Scott, Sarah, *A Description of Millenium Hall*, ed. Gary Kelly, Peterborough, Ontario: Broadview Literary Texts, 1995.

The History of Sir George Ellison, ed. Betty Rizzo, Lexington: University of Kentucky Press, 1995.

Sheridan, Frances, *The History of Nourjahad*, in *Oriental Tales*, ed. Robert L. Mack, Oxford: Oxford University Press, 1992.

Memoirs of Miss Sidney Bidulph, ed. Patricia Köster and Jean Coates Cleary, Oxford: Oxford University Press, 1995.

Smith, Charlotte. *Emmeline, the Orphan of the Castle*, ed. Anne Henry Ehrenpreis, Oxford: Oxford University Press, 1971.

Secondary works

Armstrong, Nancy, *Desire and Domestic Fiction: A Political History of the Novel*, New York: Oxford University Press, 1987.

Austin, Andrea, 'Shooting Blanks: Potency, Parody, and Eliza Haywood's *The History of Miss Betsy Thoughtless*', in Kirsten T. Saxton and Rebecca P. Bocchicchio (eds.), *The Passionate Fictions of Eliza Haywood: Essays on Her Life and Work*, Lexington: University of Kentucky Press, 2000, pp. 259–82.

Barker, Hannah and Elaine Chalus (eds.), *Gender in Eighteenth-Century England: Roles, Representation and Responsibilities*, London: Longman, 1997.

Barker-Benfield, C. J., *The Culture of Sensibility: Sex and Society in Eighteenth-Century Britain*, Chicago: University of Chicago Press, 1992.

Brown, Laura, *The Ends of Empire: Women and Ideology in Early Eighteenth-Century English Literature*, Ithaca, NY: Cornell University Press, 1993.

Castle, Terry, *Masquerade and Civilization: The Carnivalesque in Eighteenth-Century English Culture and Civilization*, Stanford, CA: Stanford University Press, 1986.

Epstein, Julia, *The Iron Pen: Frances Burney and the Politics of Women's Writing*, Madison: University of Wisconsin Press, 1989.

Ferguson, Moira, *Subject to Others: British Women Writers and Colonial Slavery, 1670–1834*. London: Routledge, 1992.

Gallagher, Catherine, *Nobody's Story: the Vanishing Acts of Women Writers in the Marketplace, 1670–1820*, Berkeley and Los Angeles: University of California Press, 1994.

Guest, Harriet, 'Eighteenth-Century Femininity: "A Supposed Sexual Character"', in Vivien Jones (ed.), *Women in the Eighteenth Century, 1700–1800*, Cambridge: Cambridge University Press, 2000.

  Small Change: Women, Learning, Patriotism, 1750–1810, Chicago: University of Chicago Press, 2000.

Habermas, Jürgen, *The Structural Transformation of the Public Sphere: an Inquiry into a Category of Bourgeois Society*, trans. Thomas Burger, Cambridge, MA: M.I.T. Press, 1991.

Horner, Joyce M., *The English Women Novelists and their Connection with the Feminist Movement (1688–1797)*, Northampton, MA: Smith College Studies in Modern Language 11, 1929–30.

Johnson, Claudia, *Equivocal Beings: Politics, Gender, and Sentimentality in the 1790s: Wollstonecraft, Radcliffe, Burney, Austen,* Chicago: University of Chicago Press, 1995.

Jones, Vivien (ed.), *Women in the Eighteenth Century, 1700–1800*, Cambridge: Cambridge University Press, 2000.

Laqueur, Thomas, *Making Sex: Body and Gender from the Greeks to Freud*, Cambridge, MA: Harvard University Press, 1990.

MacCarthy, B. G., *The Female Pen: Women Writers and Novelists 1621–1818*, Preface by Janet Todd, New York: New York University Press, 1946–7; reissued 1994.

Mullan, John, *Sentiment and Sociability: The Language of Feeling in the Eighteenth Century*. Oxford: Clarendon Press, 1988.

Myers, Mitzi, 'Impeccable Governesses, Rational Dames, and Moral Mothers: Mary Wollstonecraft and the Female Tradition in Georgian Children's Books', *Annual of the Modern Language Association Division on Children's Literature and the Children's Literature Association*, 14, Yale University Press (1986), 31–59.

Nussbaum, Felicity, *Torrid Zones: Maternity, Sexuality, and Empire in Eighteenth-Century English Narratives*, Baltimore, MD: Johns Hopkins University Press, 1995.

Paulson, Ronald, *Satire and the Novel in Eighteenth-Century England*, New Haven, CT: Yale University Press, 1967.

Perry, Ruth. 'Women in Families: The Great Disinheritance', in Vivien Jones (ed.), *Women and Literature in Britain 1700–1800* Cambridge: Cambridge University Press, 2000, pp. 111–31.

Poovey, Mary, *The Proper Lady and the Woman Writer: Ideology as Style in the Works of Mary Wollstonecraft, Mary Shelley, and Jane Austen*, Chicago: University of Chicago Press, 1984.

Richetti, John (ed.), *The Cambridge Companion to the Eighteenth-Century Novel*, Cambridge: Cambridge University Press, 1996.

Richetti, John, *The English Novel in History 1700–1780*, London: Routledge, 1999.

'Histories by Eliza Haywood and Henry Fielding: Imitation and Adaptation', in Kirsten Saxton and Rebecca P. Bocchicchio (eds.), *The Passionate Fictions of Eliza Haywood*, Lexington: University Press of Kentucky, 2000, pp. 240–58.

Saxton, Kirsten T. and Rebecca P. Bocchicchio (eds.), *The Passionate Fictions of Eliza Haywood: Essays on Her Life and Work*, Lexington: University of Kentucky Press, 2000.

Schofield, Mary Anne, and Cecilia Macheski (eds.), *Fetter'd or Free? British Women Novelists, 1670–1815*, Athens: Ohio University Press, 1986.

Skinner, Gillian, *Sensibility and Economics in the Novel, 1740–1800: The Price of a Tear*, London: Macmillan, 1999.

Spacks, Patricia Meyer, *Desire and Truth: Functions of Plot in Eighteenth-Century English Novels*, Chicago: University of Chicago Press, 1989.

Spencer, Jane, *The Rise of the Woman Novelist: From Aphra Behn to Jane Austen*, Oxford: Basil Blackwell, 1986.

'Women Writers and the Eighteenth-Century Novel', in John Richetti (ed.), *The Cambridge Companion to the Eighteenth-Century Novel*, Cambridge: Cambridge University Press, 1996, pp. 212–35.

Staves, Susan, *Married Women's Separate Property in England: 1660–1833*, Cambridge, MA: Harvard University Press, 1990.

Straub, Kristina, 'Frances Burney and the Rise of the Woman Novelist', in John Richetti (ed.), *The Columbia History of the British Novel*, New York: Columbia University Press, 1994, pp. 199–219.

Sutherland, Kathryn, 'Writings on Education and Conduct: Arguments for Female Improvement', in Vivien Jones (ed.), *Women and Literature in Britain 1700–1800*, Cambridge: Cambridge University Press, 2000, pp. 25–45.

Todd, Janet (ed.), *A Dictionary of British and American Writers, 1660–1800*, Totawa, NJ: Rowman and Littlefield, 1986.

Todd, Janet, *The Sign of Angellica: Women, Writing, and Fiction, 1660–1800*, New York: Columbia University Press, 1989.

Tompkins, J. M. S., *The Popular Novel in England 1770–1800*, Lincoln: University of Nebraska Press, 1961.

Turner, Cheryl, *Living by the Pen: Women Writers in the Eighteenth Century*, London: Routledge, 1994.

Warner, William B., *Licensing Entertainment: The Elevation of Novel Reading in Britain, 1684–1750*, Berkeley and Los Angeles: University of California Press, 1998.

Watt, Ian. *The Rise of the Novel: Studies in Defoe, Richardson and Fielding*, London: Chatto and Windus, 1957.

CHAPTER 29 BIBLIOGRAPHY

Primary works

Aikin, John, 'On Reasoning from Analogy', in *Essays Literary and Miscellaneous*, London, 1811.

Anon, *The Art of Eloquence. A Didactic Poem*, London, 1785.

Anon, *The New Art of Speaking, or, a Complete Modern System of Rhetoric, Elocution, and Oratory . . . Inscribed to the Hon. C. Fox and E. Burke, Esq.*, London: Alex. Hogg, *c.* 1785.

Anon, *An Ode on the Powers of Eloquence*, London, 1755.

Anon, *Rhetoric; or the Principles of Oratory Delineated*, London, 1736.

Adams, John Quincy, *Lectures on Rhetoric and Oratory*, 2 vols., Cambridge: Hilliard and Metcalf, 1810.

Blair, Hugh, *Lectures on Rhetoric and Belles Lettres* (1783), 2 vols., ed. Harold F. Harding, Carbondale and Edwardsville: Southern Illinois University Press, 1965.

Brougham, Henry Peter, Baron Brougham and Vaux, 'Dissertation on the Eloquence of the Ancients', in *Speeches of Henry Lord Brougham*, 4 vols., Edinburgh, 1838, vol. IV, pp. 375–446.

Burke, Edmund, *The Correspondence of Edmund Burke*, ed. Thomas W. Copeland, *et al.*, 10 vols., Cambridge: Cambridge University Press and Chicago: University of Chicago Press, 1958–78.

   A Philosophical Enquiry into the Origin of Our Ideas of the Sublime and Beautiful, ed. James T. Boulton, London: University of Notre Dame Press, 1958.

   The Works of the Right Honourable Edmund Burke, Bohn's British Classics, 8 vols. London: Henry G. Bohn, 1854–89.

   The Writings and Speeches of Edmund Burke, ed. Paul Langford, *et al.*, Oxford: Oxford University Press, 1981–.

Campbell, George, *The Philosophy of Rhetoric*, 2 vols. London, 1776.

Cicero, Marcus Tullius, *De Oratore*, Loeb Classical Library, trans. E. W. Sutton and H. Rackham, 2 vols., London: Heinemann, and Cambridge, MA: Harvard University Press, 1942.

   M. T. Cicero de Oratore. Or His Three Dialogues upon the Character and Qualifications of an Orator, trans. William Guthrie, London, 1742. (Guthrie's 'Preface' (pp. iii–xxxiii) to this translation is a useful statement of the political rationale for eloquence in eighteenth-century Britain.)

   The Verrine Orations, Loeb Classical Library, trans. L. H. G. Greenwood, 2 vols., London: Heineman, and Cambridge, MA: Harvard University Press, 1928.

Cobbett, William (ed.), *The Parliamentary History of England from the Earliest Period to the Year 1803*, London, 1817.

Demosthenes, *Greek Orators – v: Demosthenes On the Crown*, trans. Stephen Usher, Warminster: Aris and Phillips, 1993.

Elliot, Gilbert, *Life and Letters of Sir Gilbert Elliot*, 3 vols., London: Longman, Green and Co., 1874.

Fox, Charles James, *The Speeches of the Right Honourable Charles James Fox, in the House of Commons*, 6 vols., London, 1815.

Hume, David, 'Of Eloquence', in *Of the Standard of Taste and Other Essays*, The Library of Liberal Arts, ed. John W. Lenz, Indianapolis, IN: Bobbs-Merrill, 1965.

Lawson, John, *Lectures Concerning Oratory*, Dublin, 1758; rpt., Carbondale and Edwardsville: Southern Illinois University Press, 1972.

Leland, Thomas, *Dissertation on the Principles of Human Eloquence*, 2nd edn, Dublin, 1765.

Paine, Thomas, *The Complete Writings of Thomas Paine*, ed. Philip S. Foner, 2 vols. New York: Citadel Press, 1945.

Priestley, Joseph, *Course of Lectures on Oratory and Criticism* (1777), ed. Vincent M. Bevilacqua and Richard Murphy, Carbondale: Southern Illinois University Press, 1965.

Quintilian, *M. Fabius Quinctilianus His Institutes of Eloquence: or, the Art of Speaking in Public*, trans. William Guthrie, 2 vols., London, 1756. Also available in a modern Loeb edition: *The Institutio Oratoria of Quintilian*, trans. Harold Edgeworth Butler, London: Heinemann, and Cambridge, MA: Harvard University Press, 1953.

Sheridan, Richard Brinsley, *Speeches of the Late Right Honourable Richard Brinsley Sheridan*, 5 vols., London, 1816.

Ward, John, *A System of Oratory*, London, 1759.

Wollstonecraft, Mary, *A Vindication of the Rights of Men*, London, 1790.

Wraxall, Nathaniel, *The Historical and the Posthumous Memoirs of Sir Nathaniel William Wraxall 1772–1784*, 5 vols., London: Bickers and Son, 1884.

Secondary works

Browne, Stephen H., *Edmund Burke and the Discourse of Virtue*, Tuscaloosa and London: University of Alabama Press.

Bryant, Donald C., *Rhetorical Dimensions in Criticism*, Baton Rouge: Louisiana State University Press, 1973.

Boulton, James T., *The Language of Politics in the Age of Wilkes and Burke*, London: Routledge and Kegan Paul; Toronto: University of Toronto Press, 1963; rpt. Westport, CT: Greenwood, 1975.

Chapman, Gerald W., *Edmund Burke: The Practical Imagination*, Cambridge, MA: Harvard University Press, 1967.

Claussen, E. Neal, and Karl R. Wallace, 'Editors' Introduction', John Lawson, *Lectures Concerning Oratory*, Carbondale and Edwardsville: Southern Illinois University Press, 1972.

De Bruyn, Frans, 'Edmund Burke's Gothic Romance: The Portrayal of Warren Hastings in his Writings and Speeches on India', *Criticism* 29 (1987), 415–438.

   The Literary Genres of Edmund Burke: The Political Uses of Literary Form, Oxford: Clarendon Press, 1996.

Dobson, J. F., *The Greek Orators*, London: Methuen, 1919.

Durant, Jack D., 'Sheridan and Language', in James Morwood and David Crane (eds.), *Sheridan Studies*, Cambridge: Cambridge University Press, 1995, pp. 96–113.

Hazlitt, William, 'On the Difference between Writing and Speaking', in *The Plain Speaker: Opinions on Books, Men and Things*, in *The Complete Works of William Hazlitt*, ed. P. P. Howe. 21 vols. London and Toronto: J. Dent and Sons, 1931, vol. XII, pp. 262–79.

Jebb, R. C., *The Attic Orators from Antiphon to Isaeos*, 2 vols., London: Macmillan, 1876. See especially Jebb's 'Introduction', vol. I, pp. lxiii-xxxvii.

Lessenich, Rolf P., *Elements of Pulpit Oratory in Eighteenth-Century England (1660–1800)*, Köln: Böhlau Verlag, 1972.

Lock, F. P., *Edmund Burke: Volume I, 1730–84*, Oxford: Clarendon Press, 1998.

Mahoney, John L., 'Classical Form and the Oratory of Edmund Burke', *Classical Folia* 24 (1970), 46–81.

'Edmund Burke and the East India Bill of Charles James Fox: The Classical Oration in the Service of Eighteenth-Century Politics', *Burke Newsletter* 4 (1963) , 210–19.

'Sheridan on Hastings: The Classical Oration and Eighteenth-Century Politics', *Burke Newsletter* 6 (1965), 414–22.

McLoughlin, T., 'Edmund Burke's Formal Training in Oratory', *English Studies in Africa* 11 (1968), 161–72.

Mill, John Stuart. 'What Is Poetry?' in *Essays on Poetry*, ed. F. Parvin Sharpless, Columbia: University of South Carolina Press, 1976, pp. 3–22.

Morwood, James, *The Life and Works of Richard Brinsley Sheridan*, Edinburgh: Scottish Academic Press, 1985.

Oliver, Robert T., *The Influence of Rhetoric in the Shaping of Great Britain: From the Roman Invasion to the Early Nineteenth Century*, Newark: University of Delaware Press; London and Toronto: Associated University Presses, 1986.

Potkay, Adam, *The Fate of Eloquence in the Age of Hume*, Ithaca, NY and London: Cornell University Press, 1994.

Reid, Christopher, *Edmund Burke and the Practice of Political Writing*, Dublin: Gill and Macmillan; New York: St Martin's, 1985.

'Foiling the Rival: Argument and Identity in Sheridan's Speeches', in James Morwood and David Crane (eds)., *Sheridan Studies*, Cambridge: Cambridge University Press, 1995, pp. 114–30.

'Patriotism and Rhetorical Contest in the 1790s: The Context of Sheridan's *Pizarro*', in James Morwood and David Crane (eds.), *Sheridan Studies*, Cambridge: Cambridge University Press, 1995, pp. 114–30.

'Whose Parliament? Political Oratory and Print Culture in the Later 18th Century', *Language & Literature: Journal of the Poetics & Linguistics Association* 9 (2000), 122–34.

Robertson, Andrew W., *The Language of Democracy: Political Rhetoric in the United States and Britain, 1790–1900*, Ithaca, NY and London: Cornell University Press, 1995.

Smith, Olivia, *The Politics of Language 1791–1819*, Oxford: Oxford University Press, 1984.

Thomas, P. G. D., *The House of Commons in the Eighteenth Century*, Oxford: Clarendon Press, 1971.

Usher, Stephen, *Greek Oratory: Tradition and Originality*, Oxford: Oxford University Press, 1999.

CHAPTER 30 BIBLIOGRAPHY

Primary works

Baumgarten, Alexander Gottlieb, *Aesthetica*, Frankfurt-an-der-Oder: John Christian Kleyb, 1750–8.

Burke, Edmund, *A Philosophical Enquiry into the Origin of our Ideas of the Sublime and Beautiful*, ed. James T. Boulton, Notre Dame, IN, and London: University of Notre Dame Press, 1958.

Coleridge, Samuel Taylor, *Shorter Works and Fragments* vol. II, ed. H. J. Jackson and J. R. de J. Jackson, Bollingen Series, ed. Kathleen Coburn, *The Collected Works of Samuel Taylor Coleridge*, vol. LXXV, Princeton, NJ: Princeton University Press, 1995.

Dylan, Bob, *Writings and Drawings*, New York: Alfred. A. Knopf, 1973.

Fielding, Henry, *Joseph Andrews: with Shamela and Related Writings*, ed. Homer Goldberg, New York: Norton, 1987.

Fielding, Sarah, *The Cry*, intro. Mary Anne Schofield, Delmar, NY: Scholars' Facsimiles & Reprints, 1986.

Gray, Thomas, *Correspondence*, ed. Paget Toynbee and Leonard Whibley, 3 vols., Oxford: Clarendon Press, 1935.

Hamilton, Sir William, *Lectures on Metaphysics and Logic*, ed. H. L. Mansel and J. Veitch LL.D., 4 vols., Edinburgh, 1859–60.

Kant, Immanuel, *Critique of Pure Reason*, trans. Paul Guyer and Allen W. Wood, Cambridge: Cambridge University Press, 1998.

Keats, John, *Letters of John Keats*, ed. Robert Gittings, Oxford: Oxford University Press, 1970.

Sterne, Laurence, *A Sentimental Journey Through France and Italy* ed. Graham Petrie, Harmondsworth: Penguin, 1967.

[Taylor, William], review of *Observations sur le Sentiment du Beau et du Sublime* by Immanuel Kant, trans. Hercules Peyer-Imhoff (Paris, 1796), *The Monthly Review* 25 (1798), 584–5.

Tytler, James (ed.), *Encyclopaedia Britannica,* 2nd edn, 10 vols., Edinburgh, 1777–84.

Wordsworth, William, *The Poetical Works of William Wordsworth*, ed. Ernest de Selincourt, 5 vols., Oxford: Clarendon Press, 1941–9.

The Prose Works of William Wordsworth, ed. W. J. B. Owen and Jane Worthington Smyser, 3 vols., Oxford: Clarendon Press, 1974.

Young, Edward, *Conjectures on Original Composition*, Scolar Press Facsimile, Menston: The Scolar Press, 1966.

Secondary works

Abrams, M. H., and Stephen Greenblatt (eds.), *The Norton Anthology of English Literature*, 7th edn, 2 vols., New York, London: Norton, 2000.

Bloom, Harold, Lionel Trilling, Martin Price, J. B. Trapp, Frank Kermode and John Hollander, (eds.), *The Oxford Anthology of English Literature*, 2 vols., Oxford: Oxford University Press, 1973.

Brown, Marshall, *Preromanticism,* Stanford: CA: Stanford University Press, 1991.

Butt, John, *The Mid-Eighteenth Century*, *The Oxford History of English Literature*, ed. John Buxton and Norman Davis, 13 vols., vol. VIII, Oxford: Clarendon Press, 1979.

Carter, Ronald, and John McRae, *The Routledge History of Literature in English: Britain and Ireland,* London and New York: Routledge, 1997.

Cruickshanks, Eveline, and Jeremy Black (eds.), *The Jacobite Challenge*, Edinburgh: John Donald Publishers, 1988.

DeMaria Jr, Robert (ed.), *British Literature 1640–1789: An Anthology*, Oxford: Blackwell, 1996.

Erickson, Lee, '"Unboastful Bard": Originally Anonymous English Romantic Poetry Book Publication, 1770–1835', *New Literary History* 33 (2002), 247–78.

Fairer, David, and Christine Gerrard (eds.), *Eighteenth-Century Poetry: An Annotated Anthology,* Oxford: Blackwell, 1999.

Folger Collective (ed.), *Women Critics 1660–1820: An Anthology*, Bloomington: Indiana University Press, 1995.

Foucault, Michel, 'The Functions of Literature' (dialogue with Roger-Pol Droit), trans. Alan Sheridan, in Michel Foucault, *Politics, Philosophy, Culture: Interviews and Other Writings, 1977–1984*, New York and London: Routledge, 1988, pp. 307–13.

Frye, Northrop, 'Towards Defining an Age of Sensibility', *ELH* 23.2 (1956), 144–52.

'Varieties of Eigtheenth-Century Sensibility', *Eighteenth-Century Studies* 24.2 (1990–1), 157–72.

Gladwell, Malcolm, *The Tipping Point: How Little Things Can Make a Big Difference*, London: Abacus, 2002.

Holland, John H., *Emergence: From Chaos to Order*, Oxford: Oxford University Press, 2000.

Johnson, Steven, *Emergence: The Connected Lives of Ants, Brains, Cities and Software*, London: Penguin, 2002.

Kaul, Suvir, *Poems of Nation, Anthems of Empire: English Verse in the Long Eighteenth Century*, Charlottesville: University Press of Virginia, 2000.

Kelly, Kevin, *Out of Control: The Rise of Neo-Biological Civilization*, Reading, MA: Addison-Wesley, 1994.

Lonsdale, Roger (ed.), *The New Oxford Book of Eighteenth Century Verse*, Oxford: Oxford University Press, 1984.

Miller, Thomas P., 'What is Literature?: A Response to Richard Terry', *Eighteenth-Century Life* 21.1 (1997), 102–3.

Morowitz, Harold J., *The Emergence of Everything: How the World Became Complex*, Oxford: Oxford University Press, 2002.

Nemoianu, Virgil, *A Theory of the Secondary*, Baltimore, MD: Johns Hopkins University Press, 1989.

Partridge, Eric, *Eighteenth Century English Romantic Poetry*, Paris, 1924; rpt. London: Norwood Editions, 1979.

Perkins, David, *Is Literary History Possible?* Baltimore, MD: Johns Hopkins University Press, 1992.

Phelps, William Lyon, *The Beginnings of the English Romantic Movement; A Study in Eighteenth-Century Literature*, Boston: Ginn and Co., 1893.

Quintana, Ricardo, and Whitley, Alvin (eds.), *English Poetry of the Mid and Late Eighteenth Century: An Historical Anthology*, New York: Knopf, 1963.

Raven, James, *Judging New Wealth: Popular Publishing and Responses to Commerce in England, 1750–1800*, Oxford: Clarendon Press, 1992.

Renwick, W. L., *English Literature 1789–1815*, in F. P. Wilson and Bonamy Dobree (eds.), *The Oxford History of English Literature* 12 vols., vol. ix Oxford: Clarendon Press, 1963.

Siskin, Clifford, 'A Response to Richard Terry's "Literature, Aesthetics, and Canonicity in the Eighteenth Century"', *Eighteenth-Century Life* 21.1 (1997), 104–7.

The Historicity of Romantic Discourse, New York: Oxford University Press, 1988.

The Work of Writing: Literature and Social Change in Britain 1700–1830, Baltimore, MD: Johns Hopkins University Press, 1998.

Spender, Dale, *Mothers of the Novel: 100 Good Women Writers before Jane Austen*, London: Pandora, 1986.

Terry, Richard, 'Literature, Aesthetics, and Canonicity in the Eighteenth Century', *Eighteenth-Century Life* 21.1 (1997), 80–101.

Todd, Janet (ed.), *Dictionary of British and American Women Writers 1660–1800*, London and Totowa, NJ: Methuen/Rowman and Allanheld, 1984.

Watson, J. R. (ed.), *Pre-Romanticism in English Poetry of the Eighteenth Century: The Poetic Art and Significance of Thomas Gray, Collins, Goldsmith, Cowper, Crabbe: A Casebook*, London: Macmillan, 1989.

Williams, Raymond, *Keywords: A Vocabulary of Culture and Society*, New York: Oxford University Press, 1983.

Woodman, Thomas (ed.), *Early Romantics: Perspectives in British Poetry from Pope to Wordsworth*, New York and London: Macmillan/St Martin's Press, 1998.

Index